WILEY CPA Examination Review

2004

Regulation

O. Ray Whittington, CPA, PhD

Patrick R. Delaney, CPA, PhD

WILEY

JOHN WILEY & SONS, INC.

CONTENTS

[1] *As explained in Chapter 1, this book is organized into 17 modules (manageable study units). The numbering of the modules commences with number 21 to correspond with the numbering system used in our two-volume set.*

PREFACE

Passing the CPA exam upon your first attempt is possible! The *Wiley CPA Examination Review* preparation materials provide you with the necessary materials (visit our website at www.wiley.com/cpa for more information). It's up to you to add the hard work and commitment. Together we can beat the first-time pass rate of less than 20%. All Wiley CPA products are continuously updated to provide you with the most comprehensive and complete knowledge base. Choose your products from the Wiley preparation materials and you can proceed confidently. You can select support materials that are exam-based and user-friendly. You can select products that will help you pass!

Remaining current is one of the keys to examination success. Here is a list of what's new in this edition of the *Wiley CPA Examination Review Regulation.*

Here is a list of what's new in this edition of the *Wiley CPA Examination Review Regulation* text:

- The new AICPA Content Specification Outline on Regulation for the Computerized CPA Examination
- Discussion and examples of the new simulation style questions
- Tax law changes for 2003 (tested on the 2004 examination)
- Coverage of latest business law legislation
- Coverage of the Sarbanes-Oxley Act of 2002, including

  - The Public Company Accounting Oversight Board
  - New Independence Rules
  - Regulation of CPA firms

The objective of this work is to provide you with the knowledge to pass Regulation portion of the Uniform Certified Public Accounting (CPA) Exam. The text is divided up into seventeen areas of study called modules. Each module contains written text with discussion, examples, and demonstrations of the key exam concepts. Following each text area, actual American Institute of Certified Public Accountants (AICPA) unofficial questions and answers are presented to test your knowledge. We are indebted to the AICPA for permission to reproduce and adapt examination materials from past examinations. Author constructed questions and simulations are provided for new areas or areas that require updating. All author constructed questions and simulations are modeled after AICPA question formats. The multiple-choice questions are grouped into topical areas, giving candidates a chance to assess their areas of strength and weakness. Selection and inclusion of topical content is based upon current AICPA Content Specification Outlines. Only testable topics are presented. If the CPA exam does not test it, this text does not present it.

The CPA exam is one of the toughest exams you will ever take. It will not be easy. But if you follow our guidelines and focus on your goal, you will be thrilled with what you can accomplish.

Ray Whittington
November 2003

**Don't forget to visit our website at www.wiley.com/cpa
for supplements and updates.**

ABOUT THE AUTHORS

Ray Whittington, PhD, CPA, CMA, CIA, is the Ledger & Quill Director of the School of Accountancy at DePaul University. Prior to joining the faculty at DePaul, Professor Whittington was the Director of Accountancy at San Diego State University. From 1989 through 1991, he was the Director of Auditing Research for the American Institute of Certified Public Accountants (AICPA), and he previously was on the audit staff of KPMG. He previously served as a member of the Auditing Standards Board of the AICPA and as a member of the Accounting and Review Services Committee and the Board of Regents of the Institute of Internal Auditors. Professor Whittington has published numerous textbooks, articles, monographs, and continuing education courses.

Patrick R. Delaney was the Arthur Andersen LLP Alumni Professor of Accountancy and Department Chair at Northern Illinois University. He received his PhD in Accountancy from the University of Illinois. He had public accounting experience with Arthur Andersen LLP and was coauthor of *GAAP: Interpretation and Application*, also published by John Wiley & Sons, Inc. He served as Vice President and a member of the Illinois CPA Society's Board of Directors, and was Chairman of its Accounting Principles Committee; was a past president of the Rockford Chapter, Institute of Management Accountants; and had served on numerous other professional committees. He was a member of the American Accounting Association, American Institute of Certified Public Accountants, and Institute of Management Accountants. Professor Delaney was published in *The Accounting Review* and was a recipient of the Illinois CPA Society's Outstanding Educator Award, NIU's Excellence in Teaching Award, and Lewis University's Distinguished Alumnus Award. He was involved in NIU's CPA Review Course as director and instructor.

ABOUT THE CONTRIBUTORS

Duane R. Lambert, JD, MBA, CPA, is a Professor of Business Administration at California State University, Hayward, where he teaches courses in Business Law and Accounting. He also has been, on different occasions, a Visiting Lecturer and Visiting Professor at the University of California, Berkeley. Professor Lambert has "Big Five" experience and also has several years experience teaching CPA review courses and helping examinees prepare successfully for the CPA examination. He wrote and revised the Business Law Modules. He also prepared answer explanations for the multiple-choice questions and other objective questions.

Edward C. Foth, PhD, CPA, is the KPMG Faculty Fellow and Administrator of the Master of Science in Taxation Program at DePaul University. Professor Foth is the author of CCH Incorporated's *Study Guide for Federal Tax Course, Study Guide for CCH Federal Taxation: Comprehensive Topics*, and coauthor of their *S Corporation Guide*. Professor Foth prepared the answer explanations to the multiple-choice and other objective questions in Income Taxes, wrote new questions, selected the mix of questions, and updated items to reflect revisions in the tax law.

Susan Smith, MA, CAS (English), CPA, Garvey International, Inc. Ms. Smith taught rhetoric and technical writing at Northern Illinois University. Ms. Smith prepared material for "Improving Your Writing" in Chapter 3.

1 BEGINNING YOUR CPA REVIEW PROGRAM

To maximize the efficiency of your review program, begin by studying (not merely reading) this chapter and the next three chapters of this volume. They have been carefully organized and written to provide you with important information to assist you in successfully completing the Regulation section of the CPA exam. Beyond providing a comprehensive outline to help you organize the material tested on the Regulation section, Chapter 1 will assist you in organizing a study program to prepare for the Regulation exam. Self-discipline throughout your study program is essential.

GENERAL COMMENTS ON THE EXAMINATION

The Uniform CPA Examination will be delivered in a computer-based format beginning April 5, 2004. The final paper-based version of the CPA exam was given in November 2003. While there are still a lot of unknowns about the new format, there is also good news. You may take the exam one section at a time. As a result, your studies can be focused on that one section, improving your chances for success. In addition, the exam is no longer offered twice a year. During eight months of every year, you may take the exam on your schedule, six days a week and in the morning or in the afternoon.

Successful completion of the Regulation section of the CPA Examination is an attainable goal. Keep this point foremost in your mind as you study the first four chapters in this volume and develop your study plan.

Purpose of the Examination[1]

The Uniform CPA Examination is designed to test the entry-level knowledge and skills necessary to protect the public interest. These knowledge and skills were identified through a Practice Analysis performed in 2000, which served as a basis for the development of the content specifications for the new exam. The skills identified as necessary for the protection of the public interest include

- Analysis—the ability to organize, process, and interpret data to develop options for decision making.
- Judgment—the ability to evaluate options for decision-making and provide an appropriate conclusion.
- Communication—the ability to effectively elicit and/or express information through written or oral means.
- Research—the ability to locate and extract relevant information from available resource materials.

---

[1] *More information may be obtained from the AICPA's **Information for Uniform CPA Examination Candidates,** which is usually sent to CPA candidates by their State Board of Accountancy as they apply to sit for the CPA examination. You can also find the publication on the AICPA's website at www.cpa-exam.org.*

- Understanding—the ability to recognize and comprehend the meaning and application of a particular matter.

For the Regulation section the Board of Examiners have provided the following matrix to illustrate the interaction of content and skills.

Content Specification Outline Areas	Skill Categories					Content Weights
	Communication	Research	Analysis	Judgment	Understanding	
I. Ethics and professional responsibility						15-20%
II. Business law						20-25%
III. Federal tax procedures and accounting issues						8-12%
IV. Federal taxation of property transactions						8-12%
V. Federal taxation—individuals						12-18%
VI. Federal taxation—entities						22-28%
Skills Weights	0-14%	9-19%	9-19%	8-18%	45-55%	

You should keep these skills foremost in your mind as your prepare and sit for the Uniform CPA exam.

The CPA examination is one of many screening devices to assure the competence of those licensed to perform the attest function and to render professional accounting services. Other screening devices include educational requirements, ethics examinations, and work experience.

The examination appears to test the material covered in accounting programs of the better business schools. It also appears to be based upon the body of knowledge essential for the practice of public accounting and the audit of a medium-sized client. Since the examination is primarily a textbook or academic examination, you should plan on taking it as soon as possible after completing your undergraduate accounting education.

Examination Content

Guidance concerning topical content of the new computer-based exam in Regulation can be found in a document prepared by the Board of Examiners of the AICPA entitled *Uniform CPA Examination— Examination Content Specifications*. We have included the content outline for Regulation at the beginning of Chapter 5. The outline should be used as an indication of the topics' relative emphasis on the exam.

The Board's objective in preparing this detailed listing of topics tested on the exam is to help "in assuring the continuing validity and reliability of the Uniform CPA Examination." These outlines are an excellent source of guidance concerning the areas and the emphasis to be given each area on future exams.

They are provided to each candidate in *Information for Uniform CPA Examination Candidates* along with the examination application, or may be downloaded at the AICPA's exam website, www.cpa-exam.org.

New accounting and auditing pronouncements, including those in the governmental and not-for-profit areas, are tested in the testing window starting six months after the pronouncement's *effective* date. If early application is permitted, a pronouncement is tested six months after the *issuance* date; candidates are responsible for the old pronouncement also until it is superseded. The exam covers the Internal Revenue Code and federal tax regulations in effect six months before the date of the exam. For the Regulation section, federal laws are tested six months following their *effective* date and for uniform acts one year after their adoption by a simple majority of jurisdictions. This section deals with federal and widely adopted uniform laws. If there is no federal or uniform law on a topic, the questions are intended to test knowledge of the law of the majority of jurisdictions. Professional ethics questions are based on the AICPA *Code of Professional Conduct* because it is national in its application, whereas codes of other organizations and jurisdictions may be limited in their application. The AICPA posts content changes regularly on its Internet site. The address is www.cpa-exam.org.

Nondisclosure and Computerization of Examination

Beginning May 1996, the Uniform CPA Examination became nondisclosed. For each exam section, candidates are required to sign a *Statement of Confidentiality*, which states that they will not divulge the nature and content of any exam question. In April of 2004, the CPA exam will become computer-based. After that date, candidates take the exam at Prometric sites in the 54 jurisdictions in which the CPA exam is offered. From April 5, 2004, going forward the CPA exam will be offered continually during the testing windows shown below.

Testing Window (Exam Available)	January through February	April through May	July through August	October through November
AICPA Review & Update (Exam Unavailable)	March	June	September	December

One or more exam sections may be taken during any exam window, and the sections may be taken in any desired order. **However, no candidate will be allowed to sit for the same section more than once during any given testing window.** In addition, a candidate must pass all four sections of the CPA exam within a "rolling" eighteen-month period, which begins on the date he or she passes a section. In other words, you must pass the other three sections of the exam within eighteen months of when you pass the first section. If you do not pass all sections within the eighteen-month period, credit for any section(s) passed outside the eighteen-month period will expire and the section(s) must be retaken.

The following table compares the sections of the prior pencil-and-paper exam with the new computer-based exam. If you have earned conditional credit on the pencil-and-paper exam, the table also shows the section of the computer-based exam for which you will be given credit.

Pencil-and-Paper Examination up to November 2003 (15.5 hours in 2 days)	*Computer-Based Examination commencing April 5, 2004 (14 hours over flexible period of time)*
Auditing (4.5 hours)	Auditing & Attestation (4.5 hours)
Financial Accounting & Reporting (4.5 hours)	Financial Accounting & Reporting (4 hours)
Accounting & Reporting (3.5 hours)	Regulation (3 hours)
Business Law & Professional Responsibilities (3 hours)	Business Environment & Concepts (2.5 hours)

Candidates should keep abreast of the latest developments regarding transition rules and requirements from their state boards of accountancy. We will post more detailed information as it becomes available on the CPA Examination Review Wiley website at www.wiley.com/cpa.

Types of Questions

The computer-based Uniform CPA Examination consists of two basic question formats.

1. Multiple-Choice—questions requiring the selection of one of four responses to a short scenario.
2. Simulations—case studies that are used to assess knowledge and skills in a context approximating that found on the job through the use of realistic scenarios and tasks, and access to normally available and familiar resources.

The multiple-choice questions are much like the ones that have constituted a majority of the CPA examination for years. **And the good news is that these types of questions constitute about 70% of the Regulation section.** The simulations are new and information about this type of question is somewhat limited. However, we have attempted in this manual to use the latest available information to design study materials that will make you successful in answering simulation problems. You should refer to the AICPA website (www.cpa-exam.org) for the latest information about the format and content of this new type of question.

State Boards of Accountancy

The right to practice public accounting as a CPA is governed by individual state statutes. While some rules regarding the practice of public accounting vary from state to state, all State Boards of Accountancy use the Uniform CPA Examination and AICPA advisory grading service as one of the requirements to practice public accounting. Every candidate should contact the applicable State Board of Accountancy to determine the requirements to sit for the exam (e.g., education, filing dates, references, and fees). For comparisons of requirements for various state boards and those policies that are uniform across jurisdictions you should refer to the website of the National Association of State Boards of Accountancy (NASBA) at www.nasba.org.

A frequent problem candidates encounter is failure to apply by the deadline. **Apply to sit for the examination early. Also, you should use extreme care in filling out the application and mailing required ma-**

terials to your State Board of Accountancy. If possible, have a friend review your completed application before mailing with check, photo, etc. Candidates may miss a particular CPA examination window simply because of minor technical details that were overlooked (check not signed, photo not enclosed, question not answered on application, etc.). **Because of the very high volume of applications received in the more populous states, the administrative staff does not have time to call or write to correct minor details and will simply reject your application.** This can be extremely disappointing, particularly after spending many hours preparing to sit for a particular exam.

The various state boards, their websites, and telephone numbers are listed on the following page. Be sure to inquire of your state board for specific and current requirements.

It is possible for candidates to sit for the examination in another state as an out-of-state candidate. Candidates desiring to do so should contact the State Board of Accountancy in their home state.

Exam Scheduling

Once you have been cleared to take the exam by the applicable state board, you will receive by mail a "Notice to Schedule" and may then schedule to sit for one or more sections of the exam. A Test Center Locator and Scheduler application is available on Prometric's website at www.prometric.com. This tool allows candidates to quickly determine the most convenient center and reserve a seat and time at the chosen center. Scheduling may also be accomplished by telephone or in-person at a test center. **To assure that you get your desired location and time period it is imperative that you schedule early. To get your first choice of dates, you are advised to schedule at least 45 days in advance. You will not be scheduled for an exam fewer than five days before testing.**

ATTRIBUTES OF EXAMINATION SUCCESS

Your primary objective in preparing for the Regulation section is to pass. Other objectives such as learning new and reviewing old material should be considered secondary. The six attributes of examination success discussed below are **essential**. You should study the attributes and work toward achieving/developing each of them **before** taking the examination.

1. **Knowledge of Material**

    Two points are relevant to "knowledge of material" as an attribute of examination success. **First,** there is a distinct difference between being familiar with material and knowing the material. Frequently candidates confuse familiarity with knowledge. Can you remember when you just could not answer an examination question or did poorly on an examination, but maintained to yourself or your instructor that you knew the material? You probably were only familiar with the material. On the CPA examination, familiarity is insufficient; you must know the material. Remember, the exam will test your ability to analyze data, make judgments, communicate, perform research, and demonstrate understanding of the material. Knowledgeable discussion of the material is required on the CPA examination. This text contains outlines of the topical areas in regulation. Return to the original material (e.g., your business law and tax textbooks, Code Sections, etc.) only if the outlines do not reinforce material you already know. **Second,** the Regulation exam tests a literally overwhelming amount of material at a rigorous level. **Furthermore,** as noted earlier, the CPA exam will test new material, sometimes as early as six months after issuance. In other words, you are not only responsible for material you learned in your business law and tax courses, but also for all new developments in business law and income tax.

2. **Commitment to Exam Preparation**

    Your preparation for the CPA exam should begin at least two months prior to the date you plan to schedule your seating for an exam section. If you plan to take more than one section, you should start earlier. Over the course of your preparation, you will experience many peaks and valleys. There will be days when you feel completely prepared and there will also be days when you feel totally overwhelmed. This is not unusual and, in fact, should be expected.

    The CPA exam is a very difficult and challenging exam. How many times in your college career did you study months for an exam? Probably not too many. Therefore, candidates need to remain focused on the objective—succeeding on the CPA exam.

    Develop a personal study plan so that you are reviewing material daily. Of course, you should schedule an occasional study break to help you relax, but don't schedule too many breaks. Candidates who dedicate themselves to studying have a much greater chance of going through this process one time. On the other hand, a lack of focus and piecemeal preparation will only extend the process over a number of exam sittings.

	STATE BOARD WEB ADDRESS	TELEPHONE #
AK	www.dced.state.ak.us/occ/pcpa.htm	(907) 465-3811
AL	www.asbpa.state.al.us	(334) 242-5700
AR	www.state.ar.us/asbpa	(501) 682-1520
AZ	www.accountancy.state.az.us	(602) 364-0900
CA	www.dca.ca.gov/cba	(916) 263-3680
CO	www.dora.state.co.us/accountants	(303) 894-7800
CT	www.sots.state.ct.us/sboa/sboaindex.html	(860) 509-6179
DC	dcra.dc.gov/information/build_pla/occupational/accountancy/index.shtm	(202) 442-4461
DE	www.professionallicensing.state.de.us	(302) 744-4500
FL	www.myflorida.com	(850) 487-1395
GA	www.sos.state.ga.us/plb/accountancy/	(478) 207-1400
GU	www.guam.net/gov/gba	(671) 477-1050
HI	www.state.hi.us/dcaa/pvl/areas_accountancy.html	(808) 586-2696
IA	www.state.ia.us/iacc	(515) 281-4126
ID	www.state.id.us/boa	(208) 334-2490
IL	www.illinois-cpa-exam.com or www.dpr.state.il.us	(217) 333-1565
IN	www.state.in.us/pla/bandc/accountancy/	(317) 232-5987
KS	www.ksboa.org	(785) 296-2162
KY	cpa.state.ky.us	(502) 595-3037
LA	www.cpaboard.state.la.us	(504) 566-1244
MA	www.state.ma.us/reg/boards/pa	(617) 727-1806
MD	www.dllr.state.md.us/license/occprof/account.html	(410) 230-6322
ME	www.maineprofessionalreg.org	(207) 624-8603
MI	www.michigan.gov/cis/0,1607,7-154-10557_12992_13878---,00.html	(517) 241-9249
MN	www.boa.state.mn.us	(651) 296-7938
MO	www.ecodev.state.mo.us/pr/account/	(573) 751-0012
MS	www.msbpa.state.ms.us	(601) 354-7320
MT	www.discoveringmontana.com/dli/pac	(406) 841-2389
NC	www.state.nc.us/cpabd	(919) 733-4222
ND	www.state.nd.us/ndsba	(800) 532-5904
NE	www.nol.org/home/bpa	(402) 471-3595
NH	www.state.nh.us/accountancy	(603) 271-3286
NJ	www.state.nj.us/lps/ca/nonmed.htm	(973) 504-6380
NM	www.rld.state.nm.us/b&c/accountancy/index.htm	(505) 841-9108
NV	www.cpa@nvaccountancy.com	(775) 786-0231
NY	www.op.nysed.gov/cpa.htm	(518) 474-3817
OH	www.state.oh.us/acc	(614) 466-4135
OK	www.oab.state.ok.us	(405) 521-2397
OR	www.boahost.com/index.lasso	(503) 378-4181
PA	www.dos.state.pa.us/bpoa/accbd/mainpage.htm	(717) 783-1404
PR	www.estado.gobierno.pr/contador.htm	(787) 722-4816
RI	www.dbr.state.ri.us	(401) 222-3185
SC	www.llr.state.sc.us/pol/accountancy/default.htm	(803) 896-4770
SD	www.state.sd.us/dol/acountancy	(605) 367-5770
TN	www.state.tn.us/commerce/boards/tnsba	(615) 741-2550
TX	www.tsbpa.state.tx.us	(512) 305-7800
UT	www.dopl.utah.gov	(801) 530-6396
VA	www.boa.state.va.us	(804) 367-8505
VI	www.dlca.gov.vi	(340) 773-4305
VT	vtprofessionals.org	(802) 828-2837
WA	www.cpaboard.wa.gov	(360) 753-2585
WI	www.drl.state.wi.us	(608) 266-5511
WV	www.state.wv.us/wvboa/	(304) 558-3557
WY	cpaboard.state.wy.us	(307) 777-7551

NOTE: The publisher does not assume responsibility for errors in the above information. You should request information concerning requirements in your state at least six months in advance of the exam dates.

3.   Solutions Approach

The solutions approach is a systematic approach to solving the questions and simulations found on the CPA examination. Many candidates know the material fairly well when they sit for the CPA exam, but they do not know how to take the examination. Candidates generally neither work nor answer questions efficiently in terms of time or grades. The solutions approach permits you to avoid drawing "blanks" on

CPA exam questions; using the solutions approach coupled with grading insights (see below) allows you to pick up a sizable number of points on test material with which you are not familiar. Chapter 3 outlines the solutions approach for multiple-choice questions and simulations.

4. **Grading Insights**

Your score on each section of the exam is determined by the sum of points assigned to individual questions and simulation parts. Thus, you must attempt to maximize your points on each individual item.

The number of points assigned to a multiple-choice question varies depending upon its difficulty level, easy, medium, or hard. **In other words, you will receive more points for correctly answering a hard question than correctly answering an easy question.** Multiple-choice questions are organized in 25-to-30-question testlets, and each testlet includes questions from all of the content areas of the Regulation section.

With respect to the multiple-choice testlets, the CPA exam uses a form of adaptive testing known as multistage testing. Using this technique the average difficulty of subsequent testlet(s) is determined by how the candidate has performed on the previous testlet(s). Therefore, if you get a testlet with a preponderance of very difficult questions, do not become discouraged. It may mean that you performed very well on the previous testlet(s). In addition, since the number of points assigned to hard or medium questions will be greater than the number of points for easy questions, you have an opportunity to accumulate a large number of total points on that testlet.

Simulations will include more extensive scenarios and a number of requirements. For example, the requirements may involve calculations, form completion, research, or written communication. The points assigned to the requirements will vary according to their difficulty. Most of the requirements will be graded by the computer. Only those that involve written communication will be graded manually. The simulations will make use of a number of commonly used tools such as spreadsheets and electronic research databases. Therefore, you need to become proficient in the use of these tools to maximize your score on the simulations.

5. **Examination Strategy**

Prior to sitting for the examination, it is important to develop an examination strategy (i.e., an approach to working efficiently throughout the exam). Your ability to cope successfully with 3 hours of examination can be improved by

a. Recognizing the importance and usefulness of an examination strategy
b. Using Chapter 4, Taking the Examination, and previous examination experience to develop a "personal strategy" for the exam
c. Testing your "personal strategy" on example examinations under conditions similar to those at the testing centers (using similar tools and databases and with a time limit)

6. **Examination Confidence**

You need confidence to endure the physical and mental demands of 3 hours of test-taking under tremendous pressure. Examination confidence results from proper preparation for the exam which includes mastering the first four attributes of examination success. Examination confidence is necessary to enable you to overcome the initial frustration with questions for which you may not be specifically prepared.

This study manual, when properly used, contributes to your examination confidence. Build confidence by completing the questions contained herein.

Common Candidate Mistakes

The CPA Exam is a formidable hurdle in your accounting career. With a first-time pass rate of about 30% on each section, the level of difficulty is obvious. The good news, though, is that about 75% of all candidates (first-time and re-exam) sitting for each examination eventually pass. The authors believe that the first-time pass rate could be higher if candidates would be more careful. Eight common mistakes that many candidates make are

1. Failure to understand the exam question requirements
2. Misunderstanding the supporting text of the problem
3. Lack of knowledge of material tested, especially recently issued pronouncements
4. Failure to develop proficiency with practice tools such as electronic research databases and spreadsheets
5. Inability to apply the solutions approach

6.   Lack of an exam strategy (e.g., allocation of time)
7.   Sloppiness and computational errors
8.   Failure to proofread and edit

These mistakes are not mutually exclusive. Candidates may commit one or more of the above items. Remind yourself that when you decrease the number of common mistakes, you increase your chances of successfully becoming a CPA. Take the time to read carefully the exam question requirements. Don't jump into a quick start, only to later find out that you didn't understand what information the examiners were asking for. Read slowly and carefully. Take time to recall your knowledge. Respond to the question asked. Apply an exam strategy such as allocating your time among all question formats. Do not spend too much time on the multiple-choice testlets, leaving no time to spend on preparing your simulation responses. Upon completion of any communication requirements, proofread and edit your answer. Answer questions quickly but precisely, avoid common mistakes, and increase your score.

PURPOSE AND ORGANIZATION OF THIS REVIEW TEXTBOOK

This book is designed to help you prepare adequately for the Regulation Examination. There is no easy way to prepare for the successful completion of the CPA Examination; however, through the use of this manual, your approach will be systematic and logical.

The objective of this book is to provide study materials supportive to CPA candidates. While no guarantees are made concerning the success of those using this text, this book promotes efficient preparation by

1.   Explaining how to **maximize your score** through analysis of examination grading and illustration of the solutions approach
2.   **Defining areas tested** through the use of the content specification outlines described. Note that predictions of future exams are not made. You should prepare yourself for all possible topics rather than gambling on the appearance of certain questions.
3.   **Organizing your study program** by comprehensively outlining all of the subject matter tested on the examination in 17 easy-to-use study modules. Each study module is a manageable task which facilitates your exam preparation. Turn to Chapter 5 and peruse the contents to get a feel for the organization of this book.
4.   **Providing CPA candidates with previous examination questions** organized by topic (e.g., contracts, commercial paper, etc.) Questions have also been developed for new areas and in simulation format.
5.   **Explaining the AICPA unofficial answers** to the examination questions included in this text. The AICPA publishes unofficial answers for all questions from exams administered prior to 1996 and for any released questions from exams administered on or after May 1996. However, no explanation is made of the approach that should have been applied to the examination questions to obtain these unofficial answers. Relatedly, the AICPA unofficial answers to multiple-choice questions provide no justification and/or explanation.

As you read the next few paragraphs which describe the contents of this book, flip through the chapters to gain a general familiarity with the book's organization and contents. Chapters 2, 3, and 4 are to help you "maximize your score."

Chapter 2   Examination Grading and Grader Orientation
Chapter 3   The Solutions Approach
Chapter 4   Taking the Examination

Chapters 2, 3, and 4 contain material that should be kept in mind throughout your study program. Refer back to them frequently. Reread them for a final time just before you sit for the exam.

Chapter 5 (Regulation Modules) contains

1.   AICPA Content Specification Outlines of material tested on the Regulation Examination
2.   Multiple-choice questions
3.   Essay problems (included because they develop many of the skills necessary to answer multiple-choice questions and simulations, e.g., writing skills)
4.   Simulation problems
5.   AICPA unofficial answers with the author's explanations for the multiple-choice questions
6.   AICPA unofficial answers prefaced by the author's answer outlines for the essay problems

7.   Author answers to simulation problems
8.   Example of complete simulations in Appendix A

Also included at the end of this text is a complete Sample Regulation Examination. The sample exam is included to enable candidates to gain experience in taking a "realistic" exam. While studying the modules, the candidate can become accustomed to concentrating on fairly narrow topics. By working through the sample examination near the end of their study programs, candidates will be better prepared for taking the actual examination. Because some simulations require the use of research materials, it is useful to have the appropriate electronic research database (Internal Revenue Code and Income Tax Regulations) or printed versions of the Internal Revenue Code and Income Tax Regulations to complete the sample examination. **Remember that this research material will not be available to answer the multiple-choice questions.**

Other Textbooks

This text is a comprehensive compilation of study guides and outlines; it should not be necessary to supplement them with accounting textbooks and other materials for most topics. You probably already have business law and tax textbooks. In such a case, you must make the decision whether to replace them and trade familiarity (including notes therein, etc.), with the cost and inconvenience of obtaining the newer texts containing a more updated presentation.

Before spending time and money acquiring a new book, begin your study program with *CPA EXAMINATION REVIEW: REGULATION* to determine your need for a supplemental text.

Ordering Other Textual Materials

If you want to order AICPA materials, locate an AICPA educator member to order your materials, since educator members are entitled to a 30% discount and may place website or telephone orders. The backlog at the order department is substantial; website or telephone orders decrease delivery time.

AICPA (CPA2Biz)   Address: Order Department
                                                               CPA2Biz
        Telephone: 888-777-7077   P.O. Box 2209
        Website: www.CPA2Biz.com   Jersey City, NJ 07303-2209

A variety of supplemental CPA products are available from John Wiley & Sons, Inc. By using a variety of learning techniques, such as software, computer-based learning, and audio CDs, the candidate is more likely to remain focused during the study process and to retain information for a longer period of time. Visit our website at **www.wiley.com/cpa** for other products, supplements, and updates.

Working CPA Questions

The AICPA content outlines, study outlines, etc., will be used to acquire and assimilate the knowledge tested on the examination. This, however, should be only **one-half** of your preparation program. The other half should be spent practicing how to work questions. Some candidates probably spend over 90% of their time reviewing material tested on the CPA exam. Much more time should be allocated to working previous examination questions **under exam conditions**. Working previous examination questions serves two functions. First, it helps you develop a solutions approach as well as solutions that will maximize your score. Second, it provides the best test of your knowledge of the material.

The multiple-choice questions and answer explanations can be used in many ways. First, they may be used as a diagnostic evaluation of your knowledge. For example, before beginning to review commercial paper you may wish to answer 10 to 15 multiple-choice questions to determine your ability to answer CPA examination questions on commercial paper. The apparent difficulty of the questions and the correctness of your answers will allow you to determine the necessary breadth and depth of your review. Additionally, exposure to examination questions prior to review and study of the material should provide motivation. You will develop a feel for your level of proficiency and an understanding of the scope and difficulty of past examination questions. Moreover, your review materials will explain concepts encountered in the diagnostic multiple-choice questions.

Second, the multiple-choice questions can be used as a poststudy or postreview evaluation. You should attempt to understand all concepts mentioned (even in incorrect answers) as you answer the questions. Refer to the explanation of the answer for discussion of the alternatives even though you selected the correct response. Thus, you should read the explanation of the unofficial answer unless you completely understand the question and all of the alternative answers.

Third, you may wish to use the multiple-choice questions as a primary study vehicle. This is probably the quickest but least thorough approach in preparing for the exam. Make a sincere effort to understand the question and to select the correct response before referring to the unofficial answer and explanation. In many cases, the explanations will appear inadequate because of your lack of familiarity with the topic. Always refer back to an appropriate study source, such as the outlines and text in this volume, your business law and tax textbooks, Code Sections, etc.

The multiple-choice questions outnumber the simulations by greater than 10 to 1 in this book. This is similar to the proposed content of the new computer-based examination. One problem with so many multiple-choice questions is that you may overemphasize them. Candidates generally prefer to work multiple-choice questions because they are

1. Shorter and less time-consuming
2. Solvable with less effort
3. Less frustrating than essay questions

Another problem with the large number of multiple-choice questions is that you may tend to become overly familiar with the questions. The result may be that you begin reading the facts and assumptions of previously studied questions into the questions on your examination. Guard against this potential problem by reading each multiple-choice question with **extra** care.

Beginning with the April 2004 computer-based examination, the AICPA began testing with simulations. Simulation problems prepared by the author and revised from prior CPA exam problems are incorporated in the modules to which they pertain. Also, Appendix A to the manual contains more complete simulations. (See the listing of question material at the beginning of Chapter 5.)

Even though they are no longer included on the CPA exam, essay problems from previous exams are also included in this manual. Essay problems require the ability to organize and compose a solution, as well as in-depth knowledge of the subject matter. They are useful in developing the skills necessary to answer simulations. The essay problems and unofficial answers may also be used for study purposes without preparation of answers. Before turning to the unofficial answers, study the problem and outline the solution (either mentally or in the margin of the book). Look at our answer outline preceding the unofficial answer for each problem and compare it to your own. Next, read the unofficial answer, underlining keywords and phrases. The underlining should reinforce your study of the answer's content and also assist you in learning how to structure your solutions. Answer outlines, representing the major concepts found in the unofficial answer, are provided for each Regulation essay problem. These will facilitate your study of essay problems.

The questions and solutions in this volume provide you with an opportunity to diagnose and correct any exam-taking weaknesses prior to sitting for the examination. Continually analyze your incorrect solutions to determine the cause of the error(s) during your preparation for the exam. Treat each incorrect solution as a mistake that will not be repeated (especially on the examination). Also attempt to generalize your weaknesses so that you may change, reinforce, or develop new approaches to exam preparation and exam taking.

After you have reviewed for the Regulation section of the exam, work the complete Regulation Sample Exam provided in Appendix B.

SELF-STUDY PROGRAM

CPA candidates generally find it difficult to organize and complete their own self-study programs. A major problem is determining **what** and **how** to study. Another major problem is developing the self-discipline to stick to a study program. Relatedly, it is often difficult for CPA candidates to determine how much to study (i.e., determining when they are sufficiently prepared.) The following suggestions will assist you in developing a **systematic**, **comprehensive**, and **successful** self-study program to help you complete the Regulation exam.

Remember that these are only suggestions. You should modify them to suit your personality, available study time, and other constraints. Some of the suggestions may appear trivial, but CPA candidates generally need all the assistance they can get to systemize their study programs.

Study Facilities and Available Time

Locate study facilities that will be conducive to concentrated study. Factors that you should consider include

1. Noise distraction
2. Interruptions

3. Lighting
4. Availability (e.g., a local library is not available at 5:00 A.M.)
5. Accessibility (e.g., your kitchen table vs. your local library)
6. Desk or table space

You will probably find different study facilities optimal for different times (e.g., your kitchen table during early morning hours and local libraries during early evening hours.)

Next review your personal and professional commitments from now until the exam to determine regularly available study time. Formalize a schedule to which you can reasonably commit yourself. At the end of this chapter, you will find a detailed approach to managing your time available for the exam preparation program.

Self-Evaluation

The *CPA EXAMINATION REVIEW: REGULATION* self-study program is partitioned into 17 topics or modules. Since each module is clearly defined and should be studied separately, you have the task of preparing for the CPA Regulation exam by tackling 17 manageable tasks. Partitioning the overall project into 17 modules makes preparation psychologically easier, since you sense yourself completing one small step at a time rather than seemingly never completing one or a few large steps.

By completing the following "Preliminary Estimate of Your Present Knowledge of Subject" inventory below, organized by the 17 modules in this program, you will tabulate your strong and weak areas at the beginning of your study program. This will help you budget your limited study time. Note that you should begin studying the material in each module by answering up to 1/4 of the total multiple-choice questions covering that module's topics (see instruction 4.A. in the next section). This "mini-exam" should constitute a diagnostic evaluation as to the amount of review and study you need.

PRELIMINARY ESTIMATE OF YOUR PRESENT KNOWLEDGE OF SUBJECT*

No.	Module	Proficient	Fairly Proficient	Generally Familiar	Not Familiar
	Regulation				
21	Professional Responsibilities				
22	Federal Securities Acts				
23	Contracts				
24	Sales				
25	Commercial Paper				
26	Secured Transactions				
27	Bankruptcy				
28	Debtor-Creditor Relationships				
29	Agency				
30	Regulation of Employment and Environment				
31	Property				
32	Insurance				
	Federal Taxation				
33	Individual				
34	Transactions in Property				
35	Partnership				
36	Corporate				
37	Gift and Estate				

* *NOTE: The numbering of modules in this text commences with number 21 to correspond with the numbering system used in our two-volume set.*

Time Allocation

The study program below entails an average of 68 hours (Step 5. below) of study time. The breakdown of total hours is indicated in the left margin.

[2 1/2 hrs.]   1. Study Chapters 2-4 in this volume. These chapters are essential to your efficient preparation program. (Time estimate includes candidate's review of the examples of the solutions approach in Chapters 2 and 3.)

[1/2 hr.]   2. Begin by studying the introductory material at the beginning of Chapter 5.

3. Study one module at a time. The modules are listed above in the self-evaluation section.

4. For each module

[6 hrs.]   A. Work 1/4 of the multiple-choice questions (e.g., if there are 40 multiple-choice questions in a module, you should work every 4th question). Score yourself.
This diagnostic routine will provide you with an index of your proficiency and familiarity with the type and difficulty of questions.
Time estimate: 3 minutes each, not to exceed 1 hour total.

[22 hrs.]   B. Study the outlines and illustrations. Where necessary, refer to your business law and tax textbooks and original authoritative pronouncements (e.g., code sections). (This will occur more frequently for topics in which you have a weak background.)
Time estimate: 1 hour minimum per module with more time devoted to topics less familiar to you.

[15 hrs.]   C. Work the remaining multiple-choice questions. Study the explanations of the multiple-choice questions you missed or had trouble answering.
Time estimate: 3 minutes to answer each question and 2 minutes to study the answer explanation of each question missed.

[3 hrs.]   D. Work the other essay problems.
Time estimate: 20 minutes for each essay problem and 10 minutes to study the answer explanations for each item missed.

[15 hrs.]   E. Under exam conditions, work at least one simulation problem per module and the simulations in Appendix A. Work additional problems as time permits.
Time estimate: 20 minutes for each essay question and 10 minutes to review the answer outline and unofficial answer for each question worked.

[4 hrs.]   F. Work through the sample CPA examination presented as Appendix B. Each exam should be taken in one sitting.
Take the examination under simulated exam conditions (i.e., in a strange place with other people present [your local municipal library or a computer lab]). Apply your solutions approach to each question and your exam strategy to the overall exam.
You should limit yourself to the time you will have when taking the actual CPA exam section (3 hours for the Regulation section). Spend time afterwards grading your work and reviewing your effort. It might be helpful to do this with other CPA candidates. Another person looking over your exam might be more objective and notice things such as clarity of written assignments, etc.
Time estimate: To take the exam and review it later, approximately 4 hours.

5. The total suggested time of 68 hours is only an average. Allocation of time will vary candidate by candidate. Time requirements vary due to the diverse backgrounds and abilities of CPA candidates. Allocate your time so you gain the most proficiency in the least time. Remember that while 68 hours will be required, you should break the overall project down into 17 more manageable tasks. Do not study more than one module during each study session.

Using Notecards

Below are one candidate's notecards on business law topics which illustrate how key definitions, lists, etc., can be summarized on index cards for quick review. Since candidates can take these anywhere they go, they are a very efficient review tool.

1) Consideration of _Land_ (i.e., mortgages, leases)
2) Agreements > _1 year_ (From "date" of agreement)
3). Answer for _Debt of another_
4) Consideration of _Marriage_
5) Sale of goods > $500
NOTE: a) Any form will do
b) Can be in more than one document
c) Writing need not occur at time of contract

Commercial Paper → _Requirement of Negotiability_
1) Must be in writing (written)
2) Must be signed by person who is ordering payment (signed)
3) Promise (note) or order (draft) to pay (promise or order)
4) Must be unconditional
5) State a specific amount of money (sum certain)
6) Contain no other promises or orders
7) Be payable on demand or at a definite time
8) Be payable "To Order" or "Bearer"

Prepared by Maureen McBeth, Northern Illinois University CPA Law Faculty member

Level of Proficiency Required

What level of proficiency must you develop with respect to each of the topics to pass the exam? You should work toward a minimum correct rate on the multiple-choice questions of 80%. Working toward a correct rate of 80% or higher will give you a margin.

Warning: Disproportional study time devoted to multiple-choice (relative to simulations) can be disastrous on the exam. You should work a substantial number of essay and simulation problems under exam conditions, even though multiple-choice questions are easier to work and are used to gauge your proficiency. The authors believe that practicing essay questions will also improve your proficiency on the multiple-choice questions.

Multiple-Choice Feedback

One of the benefits of working through previous exam questions is that it helps you to identify your weak areas. Once you have graded your answers, your strong areas and weak areas should be clearly evident. Yet, the important point here is that you should not stop at a simple percentage evaluation. The percentage only provides general feedback about your knowledge of the material contained within that particular module. The percentage **does not** give you any specific feedback regarding the concepts which were tested. In order to get this feedback, you should look at the questions missed on an individual basis because this will help you gain a better understanding of **why** you missed the question.

This feedback process has been facilitated by the fact that within each module where the multiple-choice answer key appears, two blank lines have been inserted next to the multiple-choice answers. As you grade the multiple-choice questions, mark those questions which you have missed. However, instead of just marking the questions right and wrong, you should now focus on marking the questions in a manner which identifies **why** you missed the question. As an example, a candidate could mark the questions in the following manner: ✓ for math mistakes, x for conceptual mistakes, and ? for areas which the candidate was unfamiliar with. The candidate should then correct these mistakes by reworking through the marked questions.

The objective of this marking technique is to help you identify your weak areas and thus, the concepts which you should be focusing on. While it is still important for you to get between 75% and 80% correct when working multiple-choice questions, it is more important for you to understand the concepts. This understanding applies to both the questions answered correctly and those answered incorrectly. Remember, questions on the CPA exam will be different from the questions in the book; however, the concepts will be the same. Therefore, your preparation should focus on understanding concepts, not just getting the correct answer.

Conditional Candidates

If you have received conditional status on the examination, you must concentrate on the remaining section(s). Unfortunately, many candidates do not study after conditioning the exam, relying on luck to get them through the remaining section(s). Conditional candidates will find that material contained in Chapters 1-4 and the information contained in the appropriate modules will benefit them in preparing for the remaining section(s) of the examination.

PLANNING FOR THE EXAMINATION

Overall Strategy

An overriding concern should be an orderly, systematic approach toward both your preparation program and your examination strategy. A major objective should be to avoid any surprises or anything else that would rattle you during the examination. In other words, you want to be in complete control as much as possible. Control is of paramount importance from both positive and negative viewpoints. The presence of control on your part will add to your confidence and your ability to prepare for and take the exam. Moreover, the presence of control will make your preparation program more enjoyable (or at least less distasteful). On the other hand, a lack of organization will result in inefficiency in preparing for and taking the examination, with a highly predictable outcome. Likewise, distractions during the examination (e.g., inadequate lodging, long drive) are generally disastrous.

In summary, establishing a systematic, orderly approach to taking the examination is of paramount importance.

1. Develop an overall strategy at the beginning of your preparation program (see below)
2. Supplement your overall strategy with outlines of material tested on the Regulation exam
3. Supplement your overall strategy with an explicitly stated set of question-amd problem solving-procedures—the solutions approach

4. Supplement your overall strategy with an explicitly stated approach to each examination session (See Chapter 4)
5. Evaluate your preparation progress on a regular basis and prepare lists of things "to do." (See Weekly Review of Preparation Program Progress on following page.)
6. RELAX: You can pass the exam. Over 20,000 candidates successfully complete the exam each year. You will be one of them if you complete an efficient preparation program and execute well (i.e., solutions approach and exam strategy) while writing the exam.

The following outline is designed to provide you with a general framework of the tasks before you. You should tailor the outline to your needs by adding specific items and comments.

A. Preparation Program (refer to Self-Study Program discussed previously)

1. Obtain and organize study materials
2. Locate facilities conducive for studying and block out study time
3. Develop your solutions approach (including solving simulations as well as multiple-choice questions)
4. Prepare an examination strategy
5. Study the material tested recently and prepare answers to actual exam questions on these topics under examination conditions
6. Periodically evaluate your progress

B. Physical Arrangements

1. Apply to and obtain acceptance from your State Board
2. Schedule your test location and time

C. Taking the Examination (covered in detail in Chapter 4)

1. Become familiar with location of the test center and procedures
2. Implement examination strategies and the solutions approach

Weekly Review of Preparation Program Progress

The following pages contain a hypothetical weekly review of program progress. You should prepare a similar progress chart. This procedure, taking only 5 minutes per week, will help you proceed through a more efficient, complete preparation program.

Make notes of materials and topics

1. That you have studied
2. That you have completed
3. That need additional study

Weeks to go	Comments on progress, "to do" items, etc.
8	1) Read RESP, FEDE → made notecards 2) Worked some MC Questions and Essay and Simulation Problems
7	1) Read CONT and SALES → made notecards 2) Worked some MC Questions and Essay and Simulation Problems in these areas
6	1) Read CPAP and SECU → made notecards 2) Worked some MC Questions and Essay and Simulation Problems in these areas 3) Reviewed remedies for breach
5	1) Read BANK, DBCR, AGEN → made notecards 2) Worked some MC Questions and Essay and Simulation Problems in these areas 3) Reviewed firm offer examples and battle of forms

4	1)	*Read EMEN, PROP, INSU → made notecards*
	2)	*Worked some MC Questions and Essay and Simulation Problems in these areas*
3	1)	*Read ITAX, PTAX → made notecards*
	2)	*Worked some MC Questions and Essay and Simulation Problems in these areas*
2	1)	*Read CTAX, GETX → made notecards*
	2)	*Worked some MC Questions and Essay and Simulation Problems in these areas*
1	1)	*Worked Complete Simulations in Appendix A*
	4)	*Reviewed weak modules*
0	1)	*Took sample exam in Regulation*
	2)	*Reviewed exam policies and procedures*
	3)	*Reviewed notecards*

Time Management of Your Preparation

As you begin your CPA exam preparation, you obviously realize that there is a large amount of material to cover over the course of the next 2 to 3 months. Therefore, it is very important for you to organize your calendar, and maybe even your daily routine, so that you can allocate sufficient time to studying. An organized approach to your preparation is much more effective than a last week cram session. An organized approach also builds up the confidence necessary to succeed on the CPA exam.

An approach which we have already suggested is to develop weekly "to do" lists. This technique helps you to establish intermediate objectives and goals as you progress through your study plan. You can then focus your efforts on small tasks and not feel overwhelmed by the entire process. And as you accomplish these tasks you will see yourself moving one step closer to realizing the overall goal, succeeding on the CPA exam.

Note, however, that the underlying assumption of this approach is that you have found the time during the week to study and thus accomplish the different tasks. Although this is an obvious step, it is still a very important step. Your exam preparation should be of a continuous nature and not one that jumps around the calendar. Therefore, you should strive to find available study time within your daily schedule, which can be utilized on a consistent basis. For example, everyone has certain hours of the day which are already committed for activities such as jobs, classes, and, of course, sleep. There is also going to be the time you spend relaxing because CPA candidates should try to maintain some balance in their lives. Sometimes too much studying can be counterproductive. But there will be some time available to you for studying and working through the questions. Block off this available time and use it only for exam prep. Use the time to accomplish your weekly tasks and to keep yourself committed to the process. After awhile your preparation will develop into a habit and the preparation will not seem as overwhelming as it once did.

**NOW IS THE TIME
TO MAKE YOUR COMMITMENT**

2 EXAMINATION GRADING

All State Boards of Accountancy use the AICPA advisory grading service. As your grade is to be determined by this process, it is very important that you understand the AICPA grading process and its **implications for your preparation program and for the solution techniques you will use during the examination.**

The AICPA has a full-time staff of CPA examination personnel under the supervision of the AICPA Board of Examiners, which has responsibility for the CPA examination.

This chapter contains a description of the AICPA grading process including a determination of the passing standard.

Setting the Passing Standard of the Uniform CPA Examination

As a part of the development of any licensing process, the passing score on the licensing examination must be established. This passing score must be set to distinguish candidates who are qualified to practice from those who are not. After conducting a number of studies of methods to determine passing scores, the Board of Examiners decided to use candidate-centered methods to set passing scores for the computer-based Uniform CPA Examination. In candidate-centered methods, the focus is on looking at actual candidate answers and making judgments about which sets of answers represent the answers of qualified entry-level CPAs. To make these determinations, the AICPA convened panels of CPAs during 2003 to examine candidate responses and set the passing scores for multiple-choice questions and simulations. The data from these panels provide the basis for the development of question and problem points (relative weightings). **As with the previous pencil-and-paper exam, a passing score on the computer-based examination is 75%.**

Grading the Examination

Most of the responses on the computer-based CPA examination are objective in nature. Obviously, this includes the responses to the multiple-choice questions. However, it also includes most of the responses to the requirements of simulations. Requirements of simulations include responses involving check boxes, entries into spreadsheets, form completion, graphical responses, drag and drop, and written communications. All of these responses, with the exception of written communications, are computer graded. Therefore, no consideration is given to any comments or explanations outside of the structured responses.

Graders are used to score the responses involving written communication, (e.g., a written memorandum). These responses are graded for both technical content and quality of the written communication. Similar to the process involved in grading the prior pencil-and-paper examination, a **second review** will be performed for all candidates that earn initial grades that are just below the 75-point cut-off.

Multiple-Choice Grading

Regulation exams contain three multiple-choice testlets of from 25 to 30 questions each. **Ten to fifteen percent of these questions will be pretest questions that will not be considered in the candidate's score.** Also, the possible score on a question and on a testlet will vary based on the difficulty of the questions. The makeup of the second testlet provided to a candidate will be determined based upon the candidate's performance on the first testlet, and the makeup of the third testlet will be determined by the candidate's performance on the first two testlets. Therefore, you should not be discouraged if you a get a difficult set of questions; it may merely mean that you performed very well on the previous testlet(s). Also, you will receive more raw points for hard and medium questions than for easy questions.

Your answers to the multiple-choice questions are graded by the computer. Your grade is based on the total number of correct answers weighted by their difficulty, and with no penalty for incorrect answers. As mentioned earlier, 10-15% of the multiple-choice questions are pretest items that are not included in the candidate's grade.

Simulation Grading

As indicated previously, a majority of the responses to the simulations will be computer graded. They will typically involve checking a box, selecting a response from a list, or dragging and dropping an answer. The responses involving written communications will be graded for both technical content and writing skills. These responses are scored based on the following criteria:

1. Coherent organization
2. Conciseness
3. Clarity
4. Use of standard English
5. Responsiveness to the requirements of the question
6. Appropriateness for the reader

As with the multiple-choice questions, a small percentage of the simulation requirements will be pretest items that will not be included in the candidate's grade.

Chapter 3 will provide detailed suggestions on ways that you may use the information about grading to maximize your score.

**NOW IS THE TIME
TO MAKE YOUR COMMITMENT**

---

3 THE SOLUTIONS APPROACH

The solutions approach is a systematic problem-solving methodology. The purpose is to assure efficient, complete solutions to CPA exam questions, some of which are complex and confusing relative to most undergraduate accounting problems. This is especially true with regard to the new simulation type problems. Unfortunately, there appears to be a widespread lack of emphasis on problem-solving techniques in accounting courses. Most accounting books and courses merely provide solutions to specific types of problems. Memorization of these solutions for examinations and preparation of homework problems from examples is "cookbooking." "Cookbooking" is perhaps a necessary step in the learning process, but it is certainly not sufficient training for the complexities of the business world. Professional accountants need to be adaptive to a rapidly changing complex environment. For example, CPAs have been called on to interpret and issue reports on new concepts such as price controls, energy allocations, and new taxes. These CPAs rely on their problem-solving expertise to understand these problems and to formulate solutions to them.

The steps outlined below are only one of many possible series of solution steps. Admittedly, the procedures suggested are **very** structured; thus, you should adapt the suggestions to your needs. You may find that some steps are occasionally unnecessary, or that certain additional procedures increase your own problem-solving efficiency. Whatever the case, substantial time should be allocated to developing an efficient solutions approach before taking the examination. You should develop your solutions approach by working previous CPA questions and problems.

Note that the steps below relate to any specific question or problem; overall examination or section strategies are discussed in Chapter 4.

Multiple-Choice Screen Layout

The following is a computer screenshot that illustrates the manner in which multiple-choice questions will be presented:

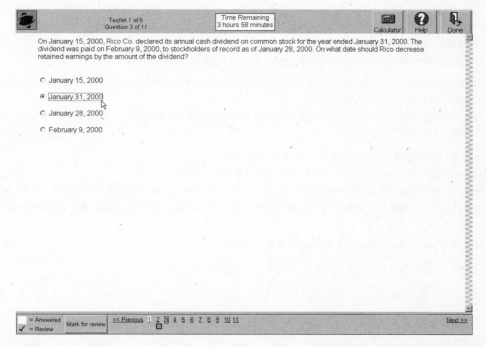

As indicated previously, multiple-choice questions will be presented in three individual testlets of 25 to 30 questions each. Characteristics of the computerized testlets of multiple-choice questions include the following:

1. You may move freely within a particular testlet from one question to the next or back to previous questions until you click the "Done" button. Once you have indicated that you have finished the testlet by clicking on the "Done" button, you can never return to that set of questions.
2. A button on the screen will allow you to mark a question for review if you wish to come back to it later.
3. A computer calculator is available as a tool.
4. The time remaining for the entire exam section is shown on the screen.
5. The number of the questions out of the total in the testlet is shown on the screen.
6. The "Help" button will provide you with help in navigating and completing the testlet.

The screenshot above was obtained from the AICPA's tutorial at www.cpa-exam.org. Candidates are urged to complete the tutorial and other example questions on the AICPA's website to obtain additional experience with the computer-based testing.

Multiple-Choice Question Solutions Approach Algorithm

1. **Work individual questions in order.**

   a. If a question appears lengthy or difficult, skip it until you can determine that extra time is available. Mark it for review to remind you to return to a question that you have skipped or need to review.

2. **Read the stem of the question without looking at the answers.**

   a. The answers are sometimes misleading and may cause you to misread or misinterpret the question.

3. **Read each question *carefully* to determine the topical area.**

   a. Study the requirements **first** so you know which data are important.
   b. Note keywords and important data.
   c. Identify pertinent information.
   d. Be especially careful to note when the requirement is an **exception** (e.g., "Which of the following is **not** an effective disclaimer of the implied warranty of merchantability?").
   e. If a set of data is the basis for two or more questions, read the requirements of each of the questions first before beginning to work the first question (sometimes it is more efficient to work the questions out of order).
   f. Be alert to read questions as they are, not as you would like them to be. You may encounter a familiar looking item; don't jump to the conclusion that you know what the answer is without reading the question completely.

4. **Anticipate the answer before looking at the alternative answers.**

   a. Recall the applicable principle (e.g., offer and acceptance, requisites of negotiability, etc.) and the respective applications thereof.
   b. If a question deals with a complex area, it may be very useful to set up a timeline or diagram using abbreviations.

5. **Read the answers and select the *best* alternative.**
6. **Click on the correct answer (or your educated guess).**
7. **After completing all of the questions including the ones marked for review click on the "Done" button to close out the testlet. Remember once you have closed out the testlet you can never return to it.**

Multiple-Choice Question Solutions Approach Example

A good example of the multiple-choice solutions approach follows.

Step 3:

Topical area? Contracts—Revocation and Attempted Acceptance

Step 4:

Principle? An offer may be revoked at any time prior to acceptance and is effective when received by offeree

Step 5:

a. Incorrect - Mason's acceptance was ineffective because the offer had been revoked prior to Mason's acceptance.

b. Incorrect - Same as a.

c. **Correct** - Peters' offer was effectively revoked when Mason learned that the lawn mower had been sold to Bronson.

d. Incorrect - Peters' was not obligated to keep the offer open because no consideration had been paid by Mason. Note that if consideration had been given, an option contract would have been formed and the offer would have been irrevocable before June 20.

13. On June 15, Peters orally offered to sell a used lawn mower to Mason for $125. Peters specified that Mason had until June 20 to accept the offer. On June 16, Peters received an offer to purchase the lawn mower for $150 from Bronson, Mason's neighbor. Peters accepted Bronson's offer. On June 17, Mason saw Bronson using the lawn mower and was told the mower had been sold to Bronson. Mason immediately wrote to Peters to accept the June 15 offer.

Which of the following statements is correct?

a. Mason's acceptance would be effective when received by Peters.

b. Mason's acceptance would be effective when mailed.

c. Peters' offer had been revoked and Mason's acceptance was ineffective.

d. Peters was obligated to keep the June 15 offer open until June 20.

Currently, all multiple-choice questions are scored based on the number correct, weighted by a difficulty rating (i.e., there is no penalty for guessing). The rationale is that a "good guess" indicates knowledge. Thus, you should answer all multiple-choice questions.

Simulations

Simulations are case-based multiple-part problems designed to

- Test integrated knowledge
- More closely replicate real-world problems
- Assess research, written communication, and other skills

Each simulation will be designed to take from 25 to 45 minutes.

The parts of simulations are separated by computer tabs. Typically they begin with directions and/or a situation and continue with various tabs requiring responses and possibly a resource tab. An example is shown below.

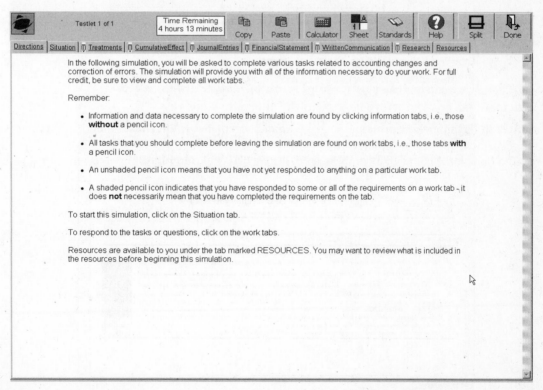

While the tabs without the pencils are informational in nature, the tabs with pencils require a response.

Any of the following types of responses might be required on simulation parts:

- Multiple selection
- Drop-down selection
- Numeric and monetary inputs
- Formula answers
- Check box response
- Enter spreadsheet formulas

The screenshot below illustrates a part that requires the candidate to complete a journal entry by selecting from a list of accounts and inputting amounts.

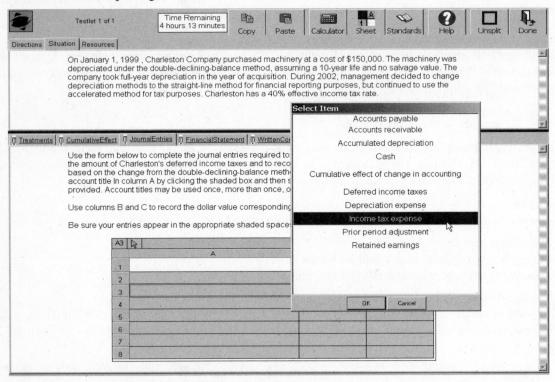

The screenshot below illustrates a requirement to complete a tax form.

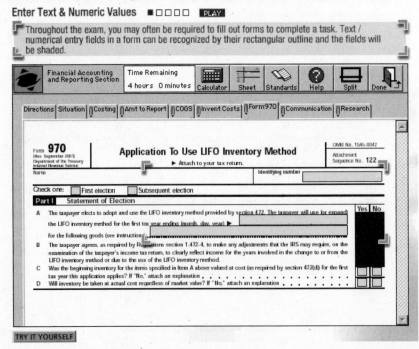

To complete the simulations, candidates are provided with a number of tools, including

- Calculator
- Scratch spreadsheet (The spreadsheet will likely have the wizard functions disabled which means that candidates will have to construct spreadsheet formulas without assistance.)
- The ability to split windows to show two tabs on the screen (e.g., you can examine the situation tab in one window and a particular requirement in a second window)
- Access to professional literature databases to answer research requirements
- Cut and paste functions
- A spellchecker to correct written communications

In addition, the resource tab provides other resources that may be needed to complete the problem. For example, a resource tab might contain a present value table for use in answering a lease problem.

A window on the screen shows the time remaining for the entire section and the "Help" button provides instructions for navigating the simulation and completing the requirements.

The screenshots above were obtained from the AICPA's tutorial at www.cpa-exam.org. You are urged to complete the tutorial and any other illustrative problems that are on the AICPA's website to obtain additional experience with the computer-based testing.

Simulations Solutions Approach Algorithm

The following solutions approach is suggested for answering simulations:

1. **Review the entire problem.** Tab through the problem in order to get a feel for the topical area and related concepts that are being tested. Even though the format of the question may vary, the exam continues to test your understanding of applicable principles or concepts. Relax, take a deep breath, and determine your strategy for conquering the simulation.
2. **Identify the requirements of the problem.** This step will help you focus in more quickly on the solution(s) without wasting time reading irrelevant material.
3. **Study the items to be answered.** As you do this and become familiar with the topical area being tested, you should review the concepts of that area. This will help you organize your thoughts so that you can relate logically the requirements of the simulation with the applicable concepts.
4. **Answer each tab requirement one at a time.** If the requirements don't build on one another, don't be afraid to answer the tab requirements out of order. Also, if the scenario is long or complex, you may wish to use the split screen function to enable you to view the simulation data while answering a requirement.
5. **Use the scratch paper (which will be provided) and the spreadsheet and calculator tools to assist you in answering the simulation. The box below provides some important review material for spreadsheet formulas.**

Spreadsheet Mathematical Operations

Symbol		Operation	Example
+	Plus sign	Addition	$345 + 633 = 978$
–	Minus sign	Subtraction	$72 - 22 = 50$
*	Asterisk	Multiplication	$12 * 4 = 48$
/	Backslash	Division	$60/12 = 5$
^	Caret	Exponentiation	$10\char94 2 = 100$

Order of computations in formula

1. Exponentiation
2. Multiplication and division
3. Addition and subtraction

Research Components of Simulations

All simulations will include a research component. Research components of simulations require candidates to search the professional literature in electronic format and interpret the results. In the Regulation section the professional literature database includes

- Internal Revenue Code and Income Tax Regulations

Shown below is a screenshot of the research page for the Regulation section of the CPA examination.

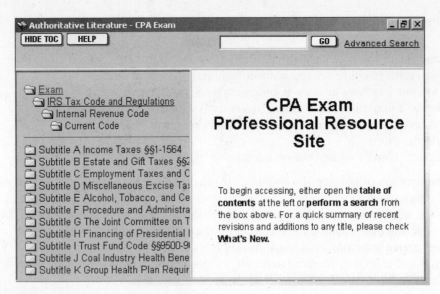

The code and regulations may be searched using the table of contents or a keyword search. Therefore, knowing important code sections may speed up your search.

If possible, it is important to get experience using electronic version of the Internal Revenue Code and Income Tax Regulations to sharpen your skills. If that is not available, you should use the printed copy of the professional standards to answer the simulation problems in the manual.

Chapter 5 of this manual contains guidance on how to perform research on the AICPA Professional Standards database.

Communication Requirements of Simulations

The communications requirements of simulations will involve some real-world writing assignment that a CPA might have to perform, such as a memorandum to a client explaining a tax issue, or a memorandum to the working papers addressing a tax issue. The following screenshot illustrates a screenshot of a part requiring the composition of a memorandum to a junior accountant.

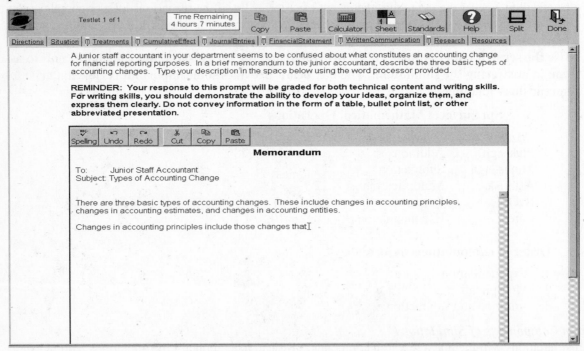

Candidates' writing skills will be graded according to the following characteristics:

1. **Coherent organization**

Candidates should organize their responses in a manner that is logical and easy to follow. Jumbled paragraphs and disorderly sentences will only confuse the grader and make his/her job more difficult. The following techniques will help improve written coherence.[2]

- Use short paragraphs composed of short sentences
- Indent paragraphs to set off lists, equations, key ideas, etc. when appropriate
- Maintain coherence **within** paragraphs

  - Use a topic sentence at the beginning of each paragraph
  - Develop and support this topic throughout the rest of the paragraph
  - Present old or given information before discussing new information
  - Discuss ideas in chronological order
  - Use parallel grammatical structure
  - Be consistent in person, verb tense, and number
  - Substitute pronouns or synonyms for previously used keywords
  - Use transitions (e.g., therefore, finally)

- Maintain coherence **between** paragraphs

  - Repeat keywords from previous paragraph
  - Use transitions

Candidates are strongly advised to keyword outline their responses **before** writing their communications. This technique helps the candidate to focus on the flow of ideas s/he wants to convey before starting the actual writing task.

2. **Conciseness**

Candidates should express themselves in as few words as possible. Complex, wordy sentences are hard to understand. Conciseness can be improved using the following guidelines.

- Write in short sentences
- Use a simple word instead of a long word if it serves the same purpose
- Avoid passive constructions (e.g., **was** evaluat**ed**)
- Use words instead of phrases
- Combine sentences, if possible
- Avoid empty fillers (e.g., **it is** apparent; **there seems to be**)
- Avoid multiple negatives (e.g., **no** reason for **not** using)

3. **Clarity**

Written responses should leave no doubt in the reader's mind as to the meaning intended. Clarity can be improved as follows:

- Do **not** use abbreviations
- Use correct terminology
- Use words with specific and precise meanings
- Write in short, well-constructed sentences
- Make sure subjects and verbs agree in number
- Make sure pronouns and their antecedents agree in number (e.g., the partnership must decide how **it** (not **they**) wants to split profits.)
- Avoid unclear reference to a pronoun's antecedent (e.g., A should inform B that **he** must perform on the contract by January 1.—Who does "he" refer to?)

4. **Use of standard English**

Spelling, punctuation, and word usage should follow the norm used in most books, newspapers, and magazines. Note the following common mistakes:

- Confusion of its/it's
  *The firm issued **its** stock.*
  ***It's** (it is) the stock of that firm.*

- Confusion of there/their/they're

---

[2] *Adapted from **Writing for Accountants** by Aletha S. Hendrickson (Cincinnati, OH: Southwestern Publishing Co., 1993) pp.128-209.*

> **There** *will be a contract.*
> **Their** *contract was signed last week.*
> **They're** *(they are) signing the contract.*

- Spelling errors
  Separate **not** *seperate*
  Receivable **not** *recievable*

The word processing software that you will use to write the communication on the exam will likely have a spell check function. Use it.

5. **Appropriateness for the reader**

Candidates will be asked to prepare a communication for a certain reader (e.g., a memorandum for a client). Writing that is appropriate for the reader will take into account the reader's background, knowledge of the subject, interests, and concerns. (When the intended reader is not specified, the candidate should write for a knowledgeable CPA.)

Intended readers may include those who are unfamiliar with most terms and concepts, and who seek financial information because of self-interest (i.e., clients, stockholders). Try the following techniques for these readers:

- Avoid jargon, if possible (i.e., HDC, etc.)
- Use parenthetical definitions

  - *limited partner (liable only to the extent of contributed capital)*
  - *marketable equity securities (short-term investments in stock)*

- Set off definitions as appositives

  A note, a two-party negotiable instrument, may become uncollectible.

- Incorporate a "you" attitude

The requirement of a question may also specify that the response should be directed to professionals who are knowledgeable of most terms and concepts. Employ the following techniques with these readers:

- Use jargon
- Refer to authoritative sources (i.e., Code section 543)
- Incorporate a "we" attitude

Again, preparing a keyword outline will assist you in meeting many of these requirements. You should also reread each written communication in its entirety. Writing errors are common during the exam, so take your time to proofread and edit your answers. Again, make use of the spell check function of the word processing software if it is available.

Methods for Improving Your Writing Skills

1. **Organization**

Logical organization is very important. Again, this is where the keyword outline helps.

2. **Syntax, grammar, and style**

By the time you sit for the CPA exam, you have at your disposal various grammatical constructs from which you may form sentences. Believe it or not, you know quite a bit of English grammar; if you did not, you would never have made it this far in your studies. So in terms of your grammar, relax! You already know it.

A frequent problem with writing occurs with the syntactic structure of sentences. Although the Board of Examiners does not expect the rhetoric of Cicero, it does expect to read and understand your answer. The way in which the graders will assess writing skills further indicates that they are looking more for writing skills at the micro level (sentence level) than at the macro level (organizational level).

a. Basic syntactic structure (transitive and intransitive action verbs)

Most English sentences are based on this simple dynamic: that someone or something (the subject) does some action (the predicate). These sentences involve action verbs and are grouped in the following categories:

(1)   Subject-Verb

   The TAXPAYER WAITED for 3 weeks to get a refund.

(2)   Subject-Verb-Direct Object (The object receives the action of the verb.)

The TAXPAYER SIGNED the CONTRACT.

(3)   Subject-Verb-Indirect Object-Direct Object (The direct object receives the action of the verb, but the indirect object is also affected by this action, though not in the same way as the direct object.)

The IRS GAVE US a DEFINITE DECISION well beyond our expectations.

b.   Syntactic structure (linking verbs)

Linking verbs are verbs which, rather than expressing action, say something about the subject's state of being. In sentences with linking verbs, the subject is linked to a work which describes it or renames it.

(1)   Subject-Linking Verb-Nominative (The nominative renames the subject.)

In the field of Accounting, the FASB IS the standard-setting BOARD.

(2)   Subject-Linking Verb-Adjective (The adjective describes the subject.)

Evidence of SCIENTER IS always HELPFUL in proving fraud.

c.   Subordinate clauses

(1)   Adverbial clauses (subordinating connector + sentence). These clauses modify the action of the main clause.

When amounts are not substantiated, a nondeductible expense is incurred.

(2)   Noun clauses (nominal connectors + sentence). These clauses function as nouns in the main sentence.

When a tax return is not signed, we know that the return is not filed.

(3)   Adjective clauses [relative pronoun + verb + (object/nominative/adjective)]. These clauses function as noun modifiers.

The court with the highest authority is the one that sets the precedent.

d.   The above are patterns which form basic clauses (both dependent and independent). In addition, numerous phrases may function as modifiers of the basic sentence elements.

(1)   Prepositional (a preposition + an object)

of the FASB
on the data
about a new type of depreciation

(2)   Verbal

(a)   Verb + ing + a modifier (noun, verb, adverb, prepositional phrase)

i]   Used as an adjective

the expense requiring substantiation
the alternative minimizing taxes

ii]   Used as a noun (gerund)

Performing all of the duties required by a contract is necessary to avoid breach.

(b)   Verb + ed + modifier (noun, adverb, prepositional phrase)

i]   Used as an adjective

The basis used when historical cost cannot be determined is estimated value.

(c)   Infinitive (to + verb + object)

i]   Used as a noun

The company needs to respond by filing an amended tax return.

4.   **Sentence clarity**

a.   When constructing your sentences, do not separate basic sentence elements with too many phrases.

The liability for partnership losses exceeding capital contributions is another characteristic of a general partnership.

Better: *One characteristic of a general partnership is the liability for partnership losses which exceed capital contributions..*

b. Refrain from lumping prepositional and infinitive phrases together.

The delegation of authority by a corporate director of day-to-day or routine matters to officers and agents of that corporation is a power and a duty of the director.

Better: *Delegating authority for routine matters to officers and agents is a power and a duty of corporations' directors.*

c. Make sure that your pronouns have a clear and obvious referent.

When an accountant contracts with a client for the primary benefit of a third party, they are in privity of contract.

Better: *When known to be a primary beneficiary of an accountant-client contract, a third party is in privity of contract with the accountant.*

d. Make sure that any adjectival verbal phrase clearly modifies a noun stated in the sentence.

To avoid incurring a penalty, each return was prepared exactly as required.

Better: *To avoid incurring a penalty, we prepared each return exactly as required.*

Time Requirements for the Solutions Approach

Many candidates bypass the solutions approach, because they feel it is too time-consuming. Actually, the solutions approach is a time-saver and, more importantly, it helps you prepare better solutions to all questions and simulations.

Without committing yourself to using the solutions approach, try it step-by-step on several questions and simulations. After you conscientiously go through the step-by-step routine a few times, you will begin to adopt and modify aspects of the technique which will benefit you. Subsequent usage will become subconscious and painless. The important point is that you must try the solutions approach several times to accrue any benefits.

In summary, the solutions approach may appear foreign and somewhat cumbersome. At the same time, if you have worked through the material in this chapter, you should have some appreciation for it. Develop the solutions approach by writing down the steps in the solutions approach algorithm at the beginning of this chapter, and keep them before you as you work CPA exam questions and problems. Remember that even though the suggested procedures appear **very structured** and **time-consuming,** integration of these procedures into your own style of problem solving will help improve **your** solutions approach. The next chapter discusses strategies for the overall examination.

**NOW IS THE TIME
TO MAKE YOUR COMMITMENT**

---

4 TAKING THE EXAMINATION

This chapter is concerned with developing an examination strategy (e.g., how to cope with the environment at the test center, time management, etc.).

EXAMINATION STRATEGIES

Your performance during the examination is final and not subject to revision. While you may sit for the examination again if you are unsuccessful, the majority of your preparation will have to be repeated, requiring substantial, additional amounts of time. Thus, examination strategies (discussed in this chapter) that maximize your exam-taking efficiency are very important.

Getting "Psyched Up"

The CPA exam is quite challenging and worthy of your best effort. Explicitly develop your own psychological strategy to get yourself "up" for the exam. Pace your study program such that you will be able to operate at peak performance when you are actually taking the exam. A significant advantage of the new computerized exam is that if you have scheduled early in a testing window and do not feel well, you can reschedule your sitting. However, once you start the exam, you cannot retake it in the same testing window, so don't leave the exam early. Do the best you can.

Lodging, Meals, Exercise

If you must travel to the test center, make advance reservations for comfortable lodging convenient to the test center. Do not stay with friends, relatives, etc. Both uninterrupted sleep and total concentration on the exam are a must. Consider the following in making your lodging plans:

1. Proximity to the test center
2. Availability of meals and snacks
3. Recreational facilities

Plan your meal schedule to provide maximum energy and alertness during the day and maximum rest at night. Do not experiment with new foods, drinks, etc., around your scheduled date. Within reasonable limits, observe your normal eating and drinking habits. Recognize that overconsumption of coffee during the exam could lead to a hyperactive state and disaster. Likewise, overindulgence in alcohol to overcome nervousness and to induce sleep the night before might contribute to other difficulties the following morning.

Tenseness should be expected before and during the examination. Rely on a regular exercise program to unwind at the end of the day. As you select your lodging for the examination, try to accommodate your exercise pleasure (e.g., running, swimming etc.).

To relieve tension or stress while studying, try breathing or stretching exercises. Use these exercises before and during the examination to start and to keep your adrenaline flowing. Remain determined not to have to sit for the section another time.

In summary, the examination is likely to be both rigorous and fatiguing. Expect it and prepare for it by getting in shape, planning methods of relaxation during the exam and in the evening before, and finally, building the confidence and competence to complete the exam (successfully).

Test Center and Procedures

Visit the test center before the examination to assure knowledge of the location. Remember: no surprises. Having a general familiarity with the facilities will lessen anxiety prior to the examination. Talking to a recent veteran of the examination will give you background for the general examination procedures.

Upon completion of check-in at the test location, the candidate

• Is seated at a designated workstation

- Begins the exam after proctor launches the session
- Is monitored by a Test Center Administrator
- Is videotaped

Upon completion of the examination, the candidate

- Signs out
- Collects his/her belongings
- Turns in scratch paper
- Is given a Post Exam Information sheet

If you have any remaining questions regarding examination procedure, call or write your state board or go to Prometric's website at www.prometric.com.

Allocation of Time

Budget your time. Time should be carefully allocated in an attempt to maximize points per minute. While you must develop your own strategy with respect to time allocation, some suggestions may be useful. Allocate 5 minutes to reading the instructions. When you begin the exam you will be given an inventory of the total number of testlets and simulations, including the suggested times. Budget your time based on this inventory.

Plan on spending 1 1/2 minutes working each of the individual multiple-choice questions. The time allocated to the simulations will vary. On the Regulation section you can expect shorter simulations with suggested times of about 30 minutes or less.

Techniques for Time Management

The Regulation exam has three testlets of multiple-choice questions with from 25 to 30 questions each. As you complete each testlet keep track of how you performed in relation to the AICPA suggested time. The Regulation section will also have two simulations. After you finish the multiple-choice testlets, budget your time for the simulations based on your remaining time and the AICPA suggested times. For example, if you have one hour remaining to complete two simulations that each have the same AICPA suggested time, budget ½ hour for each simulation. Remember that you alone control watching your progress towards successfully completing this exam.

Examination Rules

While complete information about the examination has not been released at the time of publication of this manual, here is the information that has been disseminated to date.

1. Prior to the start of the examination, you will be required to sign a *Statement of Confidentiality*.
2. You will not be allowed to take any materials with you. Lockers will be provided for your personal effects. Any reference during the examination to books or other materials or the exchange of information with other persons shall be considered misconduct sufficient to bar you from further participation in the examination.
3. Penalties will be imposed on any candidate who is caught cheating before, during, or after the examination. These penalties may include expulsion from the examination, denial of applications for future examinations, and civil or criminal penalties.
4. You may not leave the examination room with any notes about the examination.

Refer to the brochure *Information for Uniform CPA Examination Candidates* for other rules.

CPA EXAM CHECKLIST

One week before you are scheduled to sit

___ 1. Review law and taxation notecards, and other law and taxation notes for important terms, lists, and key phrases.

___ 2. If time permits, work through a few questions in your weakest areas so that the applicable principles and concepts are fresh in your mind.

___ 3. Assemble materials listed under 1. above into a "last review" notebook to be taken with you to the exam.

What to bring

___ 1. *Identification*—You should bring your government issued identification and any other required registration material.

___ 2. *Hotel confirmation*—(if you must travel).

___ 3. *Cash*—Payment for anything by personal check is rarely accepted.

___ 4. *Major credit card*—American Express, Master Card, Visa, etc.

___ 5. *Alarm clock*—This is too important an event to trust to a hotel wake-up call that might be overlooked.

___ 6. *Clothing*—Should be comfortable and layered to suit the possible temperature range in the testing room.

___ 7. *Earplugs*—Even though examinations are being given, there may be constant activity in the testing room (e.g., people walking around, rustling of paper, clicking of keyboards, people coughing, etc.). The use of earplugs may block out some of this distraction and help you concentrate better.

___ 8. *Other*—Any "last review" materials.

Evenings before exams

1. Reviewing the evening before the exam could earn you the extra points needed to pass a section. Just keep this last-minute effort in perspective and do **not** panic yourself into staying up all night trying to cover every possible point. This could lead to disaster by sapping your body of the endurance needed to attack questions creatively during the next day.

2. Reread key outlines or notecards for Regulation the evening before, reviewing important terms, key phrases, and lists (i.e., essential elements for a contract, requirements for a holder in due course, computation of taxable income, etc.).

3. Go over mnemonics and acronyms you have developed as study aids. Test yourself by writing out the letters on paper while verbally giving a brief explanation of what the letters stand for.

4. **Set your alarm and get a good night's rest!** Being well rested will permit you to meet each day's challenge with a fresh burst of creative energy.

Exam-taking strategy

1. Review the AICPA suggested times for the testlets and simulations to plan your time allocation during the exam.

2. The crucial technique to use for business law and tax simulation questions is to read through each fact situation **carefully,** underlining keywords such as "oral," "without disclosing," "qualified pension plan," etc. Then **read each choice** carefully before you start eliminating inappropriate answers. In business law and tax, often the first or second answer may **sound** correct, but a later answer may be **more correct**. Be discriminating! Reread the question and choose the right response.

3. If you are struggling with questions beyond your time limit, use the strategy of dividing simulation questions into two categories.

   a. Questions for which you **know** you lack knowledge to answer: Drawing from any resources you have, narrow answers down to as few as possible; then make an **educated guess**.

   b. Questions for which you feel you should be getting the correct answer: Mark the question for review. Your mental block may clear, or you may spot a simple error in logic that now can be corrected

4. Remember: **never** change a first impulse question answer later unless you are **absolutely certain** you are right. It is a proven fact that your subconscious often guides you to the correct answer.

5. Begin the simulations, carefully monitoring your time. Read all requirement tabs and organize your thoughts around the concepts, mnemonics, acronyms, and buzzwords that are responsive to the requirements.

6. Constantly compare your progress with the time remaining. **Never** spend excessive amounts of time on one testlet or simulation.

7. The cardinal rule is **never,** but **never,** leave an answer blank.

HAVE YOU MADE YOUR COMMITMENT?

5 REGULATION EXAM CONTENT

Preparing for the Regulation Exam

Regulation is a section of the exam that was added with the computerization of the exam in April 2004. Its content consists of most of the material that was previously in the Business Law and Professional Responsibilities combined with the Taxation topics that were included in the Accounting and Reporting section. **In preparing for the Regulation exam, you should take a systematic approach such as the one detailed in Chapter 1.**

First, in approaching your study, you should become acquainted with the nature of the Regulation exam itself. The content specification outlines are printed on the following page.

Relatedly, you should evaluate your competence by working 10 to 20 multiple-choice questions from each of the modules (21-37) in this volume. This diagnostic routine will acquaint you with the specific nature of the questions tested on each topic as well as indicate the amount of study required per topic. You should work toward an 80% correct response rate as a minimum on each topic.

Second, study the content of modules 21-37 emphasizing the concepts of each topic such as legal liability of accountants, elements of a contract, and taxable income. You may have to refer to your textbooks, etc., for topics to which you have had no previous exposure.

Third, work the multiple-choice and simulations under examination conditions.

AICPA Content Specification Outline

The AICPA Content Specification Outline of the coverage of Regulation appears below. This outline was issued by the AICPA, effective as of April 2004.

AICPA CONTENT SPECIFICATION OUTLINE: REGULATION

I.   Ethics and Professional and Legal Responsibilities **(15%-20%)**

   A. Code of Professional Conduct
   B. Proficiency, Independence, and Due Care
   C. Ethics and Responsibilities in Tax Practice
   D. Licensing and Disciplinary Systems Imposed by the Profession and State Regulatory Bodies
   E. Legal Responsibilities and Liabilities
      1. Common Law Liability to Clients and Third Parties
      2. Federal Statutory Liability
   F. Privileged Communications and Confidentiality

II. Business Law **(20%-25%)**

   A. Agency
      1. Formation and Termination
      2. Duties and Authority of Agents and Principals
      3. Liabilities and Authority of Agents and Principals
   B. Contracts
      1. Formation
      2. Performance
      3. Third-Party Assignments
      4. Discharge, Breach, and Remedies
   C. Debtor-Creditor Relationships
      1. Rights, Duties, and Liabilities of Debtors, Creditors, and Guarantors
      2. Bankruptcy

   D. Government Regulation of Business
      1. Federal Securities Acts
      2. Other Government Regulation (Antitrust, Pension, and Retirement Plans, Union and Employee Relations, and Legal Liability for Payroll and Social Security Taxes)
   E. Uniform Commercial Code
      1. Negotiable Instruments and Letters of Credit
      2. Sales
      3. Secured Transactions
      4. Documents of Title and Title Transfer
   F. Real Property, Including Insurance

III. Federal Tax Procedures and Accounting Issues **(8%-12%)**

   A. Federal Tax Procedures
   B. Accounting Periods
   C. Accounting Methods Including Cash, Accrual, Percentage-of-Completion, Completed-Contract, and Installment Sales
   D. Inventory Methods, Including Uniform Capitalization Rules

IV. Federal Taxation of Property Transactions **(8%-12%)**

   A. Types of Assets
   B. Basis of Assets
   C. Depreciation and Amortization
   D. Taxable and Nontaxable Sales and Exchanges

E. Income, Deductions, Capital Gains and Capital Losses, Including Sales and Exchanges of Business Property and Depreciation Recapture

V. Federal Taxation—Individuals (**12%-18%**)

A. Gross Income—Inclusions and Exclusions
B. Reporting of Items from Pass-Through Entities, Including Passive Activity Losses
C. Adjustments and Deductions to Arrive at Taxable Income
D. Filing Status and Exemptions
E. Tax Computations, Credits, and Penalties
F. Alternative Minimum Tax
G. Retirement Plans
H. Estate and Gift Taxation, Including Transfers Subject to the Gift Tax, Annual Exclusion, and Items Includible and Deductible from Gross Estate

VI. Federal Taxation—Entities (**22%-28%**)

A. Similarities and Distinctions in Tax Reporting Among Such Entities as Sole Proprietorships, General and Limited Partnerships, Subchapter C Corporations, Subchapter S Corporations, Limited Liability Companies, and Limited Liability Partnerships
B. Subchapter C Corporations

1. Determination of Taxable Income and Loss, and Reconciliation of Book Income to Taxable Income
2. Tax Computations, Credits, and Penalties, Including Alternative Minimum Tax
3. Net Operating Losses

4. Consolidated Returns
5. Entity/Owner Transactions, Including Contributions and Distributions

C. Subchapter S Corporations

1. Eligibility and Election
2. Determination of Ordinary Income, Separately Stated Items, and Reconciliation of Book Income to Taxable Income
3. Basis of Shareholder's Interest
4. Entity/Owner Transactions, Including Contributions and Liquidating and Nonliquidating Distributions
5. Built-In Gains Tax

D. Partnerships

1. Determination of Ordinary Income, Separately State Items, and Reconciliation of Book Income to Taxable Income
2. Basis of Partner's Interest and Basis of Assets Contributed to the Partnership
3. Partnership and Partner Elections
4. Partner Dealing with Own Partnership
5. Treatment of Partnership Liabilities
6. Distribution of Partnership Assets
7. Ownership Changes and Liquidation and Termination of Partnership

E. Trusts

1. Types of Trusts
2. Income and Deductions
3. Determination of Beneficiary's Share of Taxable Income

RESEARCHING INCOME TAX ISSUES[1]

Research components of Regulation section will involve a research database that includes the Internal Revenue Code, IRS Regulations, and IRS Publication 17.

The Internal Revenue Code

The Internal Revenue Code of 1986, as Amended (commonly called IRC, or simple the Code) is the most important source of federal income tax law. The IRC is actually Title 26 of the United States Code. The US Code is the complete set of laws passed by Congress. All laws dealing with one topic are consolidated under one title of the US Code. For example, Title 10 of the US Code contains all of the military laws of the United States.

Any changes when Congress passes a new tax law are integrated in the Code. The Code has been amended almost every year since it was reformed in 1986. Prior to that, the Code was reorganized in 1954, and from then until 1986, it was known as the Internal Revenue Code of 1954, as Amended. Before the IRC of 1954, the tax law was contained in the Internal Revenue Code of 1939, the first IRC. Before 1939, the tax law was an unorganized series of tax acts.

Code Organization

There are many different subdivision to the Code, each with a different purpose and name. The Code is divided into subtitles, chapters, parts, subparts, and sections. Some common subtitles of the Code are

Subtitle A	Income Taxes
Subtitle B	Estate and Gift Taxes
Subtitle C	Employment Taxes

---

[1] *This section was prepared by Gerald E. Whittenburg, Ph.D., CPA. For more information about tax research refer to West's Federal Tax Research, 6th Edition (Thomas South-Western)*

Subtitle D   Miscellaneous Excise Taxes
Subtitle E   Alcohol, Tobacco, and Certain Excise Taxes
Subtitle F   Procedures and Administration

Each Subtitle is divided into chapters. The chapters contained in Subtitle A are

Chapter 1   Normal and Surtaxes
Chapter 2   Tax on Self-Employment Income
Chapter 3   Withholding Tax and Nonresident Aliens and Foreign Corporations
Chapter 4   [Repealed]
Chapter 5   Tax on Transfers to Avoid Income Tax
Chapter 6   Consolidated Returns

The chapters are again subdivided into numerous subchapters. Some of the notable subchapters of Chapter 1 are

Subchapter A   Determination of Tax Liability
Subchapter B   Computation of Taxable Income
Subchapter C   Corporate Distributions and Adjustments
Subchapter E   Accounting Periods and Methods
Subchapter I   Natural Resources
Subchapter K   Partners and Partnerships
Subchapter N   International Taxation
Subchapter S   Tax Treatment of S Corporations

Each subchapter may be further divided into parts and subparts, as needed.

The smallest unique part of the Code is the section. The section is normally the basic reference when citing a provision of the Internal Revenue Code. In day-to-day tax practice, reference to larger divisions of the Code such as subtitles and chapters are generally disregarded. Currently, the sections in the Code are numbered from 1 to over 9,000, albeit many numbers are skipped to allow for future expansion of the tax law. Each Code section may be further subdivided into subsections, paragraphs, subparagraphs, and clauses. As an example, the following Code section reference is to the definition of the term medical for purposes of the medical care deduction:

Citation: Section 213(d)(1)(A), where

213 is the Section Number
(d) is the Subdivision
(1) is the Paragraph
(A) is the Subparagraph

The tax practitioner can be assured that there is only one Section 213 in the Code and that this is a specific tax reference that cannot be confused with any other provision of the Code.

The Regulations

A Treasury Regulation is the Government's official interpretation or explanation of a Code section. Regulations require an intensive review and a public comment process before they are issued in final form. Regulations are classified as interpretative or legislative. An Interpretative Regulation is issued under the general authority of Section 7805(a) of the Code. A Legislative Regulation is issued when Congress specifically delegates the authority to the Treasury to write regulations for a specific purpose. The passive loss Regulations under Section 469 are an example of Legislative Regulations. Of the two types of regulation, the Legislative Regulations have a higher level of authority than the Interpretative Regulations.

Regulations are first issued in proposed form by the Treasury in the Federal Register and Internal Revenue Bulletin. Interested parties are given a period of time to comment on the Proposed Regulation. The Treasury may hold public hearings on the Proposed Regulations if there is sufficient interest in the Purposed Regulation. After the comment period, the government may modify (or in some cases, withdraw) the Proposed Regulation. After the changes have been made, a Regulation will be published as a Treasury Decision (TD) and the Regulation will become a final Regulation and incorporated into the Code of Federal Regulations. Although a Proposed Regulation is not in effect, the tax researcher cannot ignore it, because Proposed Regulations have a high probability of becoming a final Regulation.

When there is a major change in the Code, the government often issues Temporary Regulations. These Regulations are issued without the normal comment period. However, Temporary Regulations are enforceable final Regulations and should not be confused with Proposed Regulations which are, in effect, an "Exposure Draft" of a Regulation.

The interpretation of a citation of a Regulation is as follows:

Citation: Reg. Sec. 1.121-2(b)(1), where

> 1 is the type of Regulation
> 121 is the Related Code Section
> 2 is the Regulation Number
> (b) is the Regulation Paragraph
> (1) is the Regulation Subparagraph

A Temporary Regulation would have a capital "T" after the Regulation number in its citation. A Proposed Regulation would have as an identifier "Prop. Reg." The Regulation type identifies the general topic area of the Regulation. The common types of Regulations are

Type 1	Income Taxes
Type 2	Estate Taxes
Type 25	Gift Taxes
Type 31	Employment Taxes
Type 301	Administrative and Procedural

IRS Publications

The Internal Revenue Service publishes more than one hundred Taxpayer Information Publications (TIPs) on many different topics. In the research database for Regulation, the only publication is

Publication 17, Your Federal Income Tax

While an Internal Revenue Service publication can contain much useful information, taxpayers must be careful when depending on them. IRS publications do not normally give primary citations (e.g., Code, Regulation, etc.) and do not normally give contrary authority. For example, if a court has ruled against an Internal Revenue Service position in a matter, the IRS publication will not mention the adverse ruling. Also, the Internal Revenue Service disclaims any damages suffered because a taxpayer relied on one of its publications. Thus, if a publication has an error on it, and a taxpayer relies on it, the taxpayer is still liable for any tax and interest caused by the error. However, the taxpayer will usually have any penalties waived that were incurred by relying on an Internal Revenue Service publication.

Database Searching

Searching a database consists of the following five steps:

1. Define the issue. What is the research question to be answered?
2. Select the database to search (e.g., the Statement on Auditing Standards and Interpretations).
3. Choose a keyword or table of contents search.
4. Execute the search. Enter the keyword(s) or click on the appropriate table of contents item and complete the search.
5. Evaluate the results. Evaluate the research to see if an answer has been found. If not, try a new search.

EXAMPLE: Bill and Betty support their 18-year old daughter and her husband who live with and are supported by them. Both the daughter and her husband are full-time students at a local community college and have no income. Bill and Betty would like to know if their daughter's husband qualifies as a dependent on their tax return. The research database search would be as follows:

> 1. *Define the issue. Does a daughter's husband qualify as a relative for dependant purposes?*
> 2. *Select the database to search. Internal Revenue Code.*
> 3. *Choose appropriate keywords. "Son-in-law," or "dependent"*
> 4. *Execute the search. A search should find Section 152(a)(8)*
> 5. *Evaluate the results. A son-in-law is a qualified relative.*

The research would then write a memo explaining his or her findings, including the citation to Code Section 152(a)(8).

Advanced Searches

When performing advanced searches it is useful to understand Boolean operators. Boolean operators allow you to make more precise queries of a database.

1. The Boolean "AND" narrows your search by retrieving only cites that contain every one of the keywords listed.

    EXAMPLE: *Dependent AND son-in-law*

    This query would only retrieve cites that include both dependent and son-in-law.

2. The Boolean "OR" actually expands your search by retrieving all cites that contain either or both of the keywords.

    EXAMPLE: *Real property OR tangible property*

    This query would retrieve cites that include either real property or tangible property, or both.

3. The Boolean "NOT" narrows your search by retrieving only cites that containing the first keyword but not the second.

    EXAMPLE: *Capital gains NOT short-term*

    This query would retrieve cites that include capital gains but not short-term.

6 PROFESSIONAL RESPONSIBILITIES AND BUSINESS LAW

Module 31/Property (PROP)

Module 32/Insurance (INSU)

Simulations

Sample Examination

PROFESSIONAL RESPONSIBILITIES AND BUSINESS LAW
ON THE REGULATION EXAMINATION

The professional responsibilities and business law portion of the Regulation exam tests the candidate's

1. Ability to recognize legal problems
2. Knowledge of legal principles with respect to the topics listed above
3. Ability to apply the legal principles to the problem situation in order to derive the textbook solution

According to the content specification outline for the Regulation exam, professional responsibilities and business law will constitute about 40% of the exam. Of the 40% about 18% will cover ethics and professional and legal responsibilities, and about 22% will cover business law topics. Refer to "Self-Study Program" in Chapter 1 for detailed suggestions on how to study these topics, outlines, and questions. The basic procedure for each of the twelve professional responsibilities and business law modules is

1. Work 1/4 of the multiple-choice questions to indicate your proficiency and familiarity with the type and difficulty of questions.
2. Study the outlines in this volume.
3. Work the remaining multiple-choice questions. Study the answer explanations of those you missed or had trouble with.
4. Work the essay questions (retained to help you prepare for multiple-choice questions).
5. Work the simulation problems.

It is important to note that it is very unlikely that the Regulation exam will have simulations on the topics of professional responsibilities and business law. The AICPA has indicated that all simulations will include a research component and the research database on the Regulation exam is a income tax database. Therefore, you should assume that the simulations will relate to taxation topics.

Sources of the Law

Law comes from both statutes and common law. Common law has evolved through court decisions. Decisions of higher courts are binding on lower courts in the same jurisdiction. Statutory law has priority over common law; therefore, common law applies when no statute covers the issue in question. Court cases can also be used to interpret the meaning of statutes.

Some of the law tested on the CPA exam comes from federal statutory law. Examples of this are the Security Act of 1933, the Securities Exchange Act of 1934, and the Sarbanes-Oxley Act of 2002. Other law affected heavily by federal statutes includes bankruptcy law, a good portion of employment law, and parts of accountants' legal liability as provided in the securities laws. The AICPA uses the guideline that federal laws are tested six months following their effective date.

Most of business law is regulated by the individual states and therefore may differ from state to state. However, several uniform laws have been adopted by many states. One example is the Uniform Commercial Code (UCC) which has been adopted by all states (sometimes with changes) except Louisiana, and also is the law in the District of Columbia. This uniform law and others are not federal laws but are laws that each jurisdiction may choose to adopt by statute. Often these uniform laws are amended. For example, the Uniform Commercial Code has been amended a few times. The AICPA has published the guideline that the "uniform acts [are tested] one year after their adoption by a simple majority of jurisdictions." This is also interpreted to mean that as these uniform laws are amended, the amended version is tested one year after a simple majority of jurisdictions have adopted it.

When the states have not adopted uniform laws, general rules of law can still be stated by examining how the majority of states settle an area of law either with their own common law or their own statutes. These are called the majority rule when it can be shown that a majority of jurisdictions have settled the legal issue the same way. The CPA exam generally tests the majority rules; however, it tests some minority rules that are considered very significant. For example, the CPA exam has tested in the accountants' legal liability area, both the majority rule and a minority rule known as the Ultramares decision, as discussed in Module 21. The AICPA has generally not published guidelines on when such minority rules are tested or when new majority rules would be tested.

PROFESSIONAL RESPONSIBILITIES

Overview

The Code of Professional Conduct consists of two sections

1. Principles—which provide the framework
2. Rules—which govern the performance of professional services

The first part of this module contains many rules and interpretations. These are covered over many pages in part A. of this module. Because this entire area is detailed and has typically been tested with just a few multiple-choice questions, less priority and weight should be given to this area in your study. The remainder of this module, however, should be studied well.

Accountants' legal liability is often tested on the CPA exam by use of essay questions that require the candidate to apply the legal principles contained in this module to hypothetical fact patterns. Multiple-choice questions are also used which require application as well as knowledge of this material.

Accountants' civil liability arises primarily from contract law, the law of negligence, fraud, the Securities Act of 1933, and the Securities Exchange Act of 1934. The first three are common law and largely judge-made law, whereas the latter two are federal statutory law.

The agreement between an accountant and his/her client is generally set out in a carefully drafted engagement letter. Additionally, the accountant has a duty to conduct his/her work with the same reasonable care as an average accountant. This duty defines the standard used in a negligence case. It is important to understand

1. When an accountant can be liable to his/her client.
2. When an accountant can be liable to third parties.
3. That an accountant is liable to the client and to all third parties that relied on the financial statements when the accountant committed fraud, constructive fraud, or was grossly negligent; furthermore in these cases, the accountant can be assessed punitive damages.
4. The extent of liability under the Securities Act of 1933 and the Securities Exchange Act of 1934 as well as how they differ from each other and from common law.

The CPA examination also tests the dual nature of the ownership of the accountant's working papers. Although the accountant owns the working papers and retains them as evidence of his/her work, confidentiality must be maintained. Therefore, the CPA cannot allow this information to reach another without the client's consent. In general, privileged communications between a CPA and the client are not sanctioned under federal statutory law or common law, but the privilege is in existence in states that have passed statutes granting such a right.

A. Code of Conduct and Other Responsibilities

1. Code of Professional Conduct

    a. The Code is applicable to all AICPA members, not merely those in public practice
    b. Compliance with the Code depends primarily on members' understanding and voluntary actions, and only secondarily on

        (1) Reinforcement by peers,
        (2) Public opinion, and
        (3) Disciplinary proceedings.

            (a) Possible disciplinary proceedings include from joint trial board panel **admonishment, suspension** (for up to two years), or **expulsion** from AICPA, or acquittal

    c. The Code provides **minimum** levels of acceptable conduct relating to all services performed by CPAs, unless wording of a standard specifically excludes some members

        (1) For example, some standards do not apply to CPAs not in public practice

    d. Overall structure of the Code goes from very generally worded standards to more specific and operational rules

        (1) Interpretations and rulings remaining from the prior Code are even more specific

    e. The Principles section consists of six Articles

        I. Responsibilities
        II. The Public Interest
        III. Integrity
        IV. Objectivity and Independence
        V. Due Care
        VI. Scope and Nature of Services

2. Code of Professional Conduct—Principles

   a. Outline of six Articles in Section 1 of the Code

      Article I—Responsibilities. In carrying out their responsibilities as professionals, members should exercise sensitive professional and moral judgments in all their activities.

      Article II—The Public Interest. Members should accept the obligation to act in a way that will serve the public interest, honor the public trust, and demonstrate commitment to professionalism.

      (1) A distinguishing mark of a professional is acceptance of responsibility to public.

         (a) The accounting profession's public consists of clients, credit grantors, governments, employers, investors, business and financial community, and others.

         (b) In resolving conflicting pressures among groups an accountant should consider the public interest (the collective well-being of the community).

      Article III—Integrity. To maintain and broaden public confidence, members should perform all professional responsibilities with the highest sense of integrity.

      (1) Integrity can accommodate the inadvertent error and honest difference of opinion, but it cannot accommodate deceit or subordination of principle.

      (2) Integrity

         (a) Is measured in terms of what is right and just

         (b) Requires a member to observe **principles of objectivity, independence, and due care**

      Article IV—Objectivity and Independence. A member should maintain objectivity and be free of conflicts of interest in discharging professional responsibilities. A member in public practice should be independent in fact and appearance when providing auditing and other attestation services.

      (1) Overall

         (a) Objectivity a state of mind

            1] Objectivity imposes obligation to be impartial, intellectually honest, and free of conflicts of interest.

            2] Independence precludes relationships that may appear to impair objectivity in rendering attestation services.

         (b) Regardless of the service performed, members should protect integrity of their work, maintain objectivity, and avoid any subordination of their judgment.

      (2) Members in public practice require maintenance of objectivity and independence (includes avoiding conflict of interest).

         (a) Attest services—require independence in fact and in appearance

      (3) Members **not in public practice**

         (a) Are unable to maintain appearance of independence, but must maintain objectivity

         (b) When employed by others to prepare financial statements, or to perform auditing, tax, or consulting services, must remain objective and candid in dealings with members in public practice

      Article V—Due Care. A member should observe the profession's technical and ethical standards, strive continually to improve competence and the quality of services, and discharge professional responsibility to the best of the member's ability.

      (1) Competence is derived from both education and experience.

      (2) Each member is responsible for assessing his or her own competence and for evaluating whether education, experience, and judgment are adequate for the responsibility taken.

Article VI—Scope and Nature of Services. A member in public practice should observe the Principles of the Code of Professional Conduct in determining the scope and nature of services to be provided.

(1) Members should

    (a) Have in place appropriate internal quality control procedures for services rendered

    (b) Determine whether scope and nature of other services provided to an audit client would create a conflict of interest in performance of audit

    (c) Assess whether activities are consistent with role as professionals

3. Code of Professional Conduct—Rules, Interpretations, and Rulings

    a. Combined outline of Section 2 of the code (rules) integrated with interpretation and rulings

Rule 101 Independence. A member in public practice shall be independent in the performance of professional services as required by standards promulgated by designated bodies.

Interpretation 101-1. Independence is impaired if

(1) During the period of the professional engagement a covered member

    (a) Had or was committed to acquire any direct or material indirect financial interest in the client.

    (b) Was a trustee of any trust or executor or administrator of any estate if such trust or estate had or was committed to acquire any direct or material indirect financial interest in the client.

    (c) Had a joint closely held investment that was material to the covered member.

    (d) Except as specifically permitted in interpretation 101-5, had any loan to or from the client, any officer or director of the client, or any individual owning 10% or more of the client's outstanding equity securities or other ownership interests.

(2) During the period of the professional engagement, a partner or professional employee of the firm, his or her immediate family, or any group of such persons acting together owned more than 5% of a client's outstanding equity securities or other ownership interests.

(3) During the period covered by the financial statements or during the period of the professional engagement, a partner or professional employee of the firm was simultaneously associated with the client as a

    (a) Director, officer, or employee, or in any capacity equivalent to that of a member of management;

    (b) Promoter, underwriter, or voting trustee; or

    (c) Trustee for any pension or profit-sharing trust of the client.

Application of the Independence Rules to a Covered Member's Immediate Family

(1) Except as stated in the following paragraph, a covered member's immediate family is subject to Rule 101 [ET Section 101.01], and its interpretations and rulings.

(2) The exceptions are that independence would not be considered to be impaired solely as a result of the following:

    (a) An individual in a covered member's immediate family was employed by the client in a position other than a key position.

    (b) In connection with his or her employment, an individual in the immediate family of one of the following covered members participated in a retirement, savings, compensation, or similar plan that is sponsored by a client or that invests in a client (provided such plan is normally offered to all employees in similar positions):

        1] A partner or manager who provides ten or more hours of nonattest services to the client; or

        2] Any partner in the office in which the lead attest engagement partner primarily practices in connection with the attest engagement.

(3) For purposes of determining materiality under Rule 101 [ET Section 101.01], the financial interests of the covered member and his or her immediate family should be aggregated.

Application of the Independence Rules to Close Relatives

(1) Independence would be considered to be impaired if

    (a) An individual participating on the attest engagement team has a close relative who had

        1] A key position with the client; or
        2] A financial interest in the client that

            a] Was material to the close relative and of which the individual has knowledge; or
            b] Enabled the close relative to exercise significant influence over the client.

    (b) An individual in a position to influence the attest engagement or any partner in the office in which the lead attest engagement partner primarily practices in connection with the attest engagement has a close relative who had

        1] A key position with the client; or
        2] A financial interest in the client that

            a] Was material to the close relative and of which the individual has knowledge; and
            b] Enabled the close relative to exercise significant influence over the client.

Important Definitions

(1) **Covered member.** A covered member is

    (a) An individual on the attest engagement team;
    (b) An individual in a position to influence the attest engagement;
    (c) A partner or manager who provides nonattest services to the attest client beginning once he or she provides ten hours of nonattest services to the client within any fiscal year and ending on the later of the date

        (1) The firm signs the report on the financial statements for the fiscal year during which those services were provided; or
        (2) He or she no longer expects to provide ten or more hours of nonattest services to the attest client on a recurring basis;

    (d) A partner in the office in which the lead attest engagement partner primarily practices in connection with the attest engagement;
    (e) The firm, including the firm's employee benefit plans; or
    (f) An entity whose operating, financial, or accounting policies can be controlled (as defined by generally accepted accounting principles [GAAP] for consolidation purposes) by any of the individuals or entities described in (a) through (e) or by two or more such individuals or entities if they act together.

(2) **Individual in a position to influence the attest engagement.** An individual in a position to influence the attest engagement is one who

    (a) Evaluates the performance or recommends the compensation of the attest engagement partner;
    (b) Directly supervises or manages the attest engagement partner, including all successively senior levels above that individual through the firm's chief executive;
    (c) Consults with the attest engagement team regarding technical or industry-related issues specific to the attest engagement; or
    (d) Participates in or oversees, at all successively senior levels, quality control activities, including internal monitoring, with respect to the specific attest engagement.

(3) **Period of the professional engagement.** The period of the professional engagement begins when a member either signs an initial engagement letter or other agreement to perform attest services or begins to perform an attest engagement for a client, whichever is earlier. The period lasts for the entire duration of the professional relationship (which could cover many pe-

riods) and ends with the formal or informal notification, either by the member or the client, of the termination of the professional relationship or by the issuance of a report, whichever is later. Accordingly, the period does not end with the issuance of a report and recommence with the beginning of the following year's attest engagement.

(4) **Key position.** A key position is a position in which an individual

(a) Has primary responsibility for significant accounting functions that support material components of the financial statements;

(b) Has primary responsibility for the preparation of the financial statements; or

(c) Has the ability to exercise influence over the contents of the financial statements, including when the individual is a member of the board of directors or similar governing body, chief executive officer, president, chief financial officer, chief operating officer, general counsel, chief accounting officer, controller, director of internal audit, director of financial reporting, treasurer, or any equivalent position.

(5) **Close relative.** A close relative is a parent, sibling, or nondependent child.

(6) **Immediate family.** Immediate family is a spouse, spousal equivalent, or dependent (whether or not related).

Interpretation 101-2. A former partner (shareholder, or equivalent) is not considered a member of the firm and does not affect firm independence when the former partner

(1) Has retirement benefits **fixed** as to amount and dates, although benefits may be adjusted for inflation

(2) Does not participate in firm business after a reasonable transition

(3) Does not **appear** to participate in the firm's business

(a) For example, the former partner's name should not be associated with the CPA firm in an office building directory, or in membership lists of business, professional, or civic organizations

(b) Simply providing an office to the former partner (including secretarial and telephone services) is acceptable

Interpretation 101-3. When a CPA performs nonattest services for an attest client it **may or may not** impair independence.

(1) Must meet following requirements to retain appearance that CPA is not employee of client

(a) Evaluate the effect of nonattest services on independence

(b) Must not perform management functions or make management decisions

(c) Responsibility for decisions must remain with client's board of directors and management

(d) Establish understanding with client regarding the services, preferable in an engagement letter

(e) Make sure that client understands its responsibility to

1] Designate a management-level individual(s) to oversee services

2] Evaluate the adequacy of the services and findings

3] Make management decisions, including accepting responsibility for the results

4] Establish and maintain internal controls

(2) The Sarbanes-Oxley Act of 2002 places traditional restrictions on nonattest services for audits of public companies (see Section F.)

Interpretation 101-4. CPA who is a director of a nonprofit organization where board is large and representative of community leadership is **not** lacking independence if

(1) Position purely honorary

(2) Position identified as honorary on external materials

(3) CPA participation restricted to use of name

(4) CPA does not vote or participate in management affairs

Interpretation 101-5. Loans from financial institution clients and related terminology.

(1) Independence is not impaired by certain "grandfathered" and other loans from financial institution clients

    (a) Grandfathered loans that are permitted (home mortgages, other secured loans, loans immaterial to CPA) that were obtained

        1] Prior to January 1, 1992, under standards then in effect

        2] From a financial institution for which independence was not required, and the financial institution subsequently became an attest client

        3] Obtained from a financial institution for which independence was not required, and the loan was sold to an attest client **or**

        4] Obtained by a CPA prior to becoming a member of CPA firm of which the financial institution is an attest client

    NOTE: All of the above must be kept current and not renegotiated after the above dates. Also, the collateral on other secured loans must equal or exceed the remaining loan balance.

    (b) Other permitted loans from a financial institution attest client

        1] Automobile loans and leases collateralized by automobile

        2] Loans of surrender value under an insurance policy

        3] Borrowings fully collateralized by cash deposits at same financial institution (e.g., "passbook loans")

        4] Credit cards and cash advances on checking accounts of $5,000 or less

(2) Terminology

    (a) Loan—Financial transactions that generally provide for repayment terms and a rate of interest

    (b) Financial institution—An entity that makes loans to the general public as part of its normal business operations

    (c) Normal lending procedures, terms, and requirements—Comparable to those received by other borrowers during period, when considering

        1] Amount of loan and collateral

        2] Repayment terms

        3] Interest rate, including "points"

        4] Closing costs

        5] General availability of such loans to public

Interpretation 101-6. Effect of threatened litigation

(1) Client-CPA actual or threatened litigation

    (a) Commenced by present management alleging audit deficiencies, impairs

    (b) Commenced by auditor against present management for fraud, deceit impairs

    (c) Expressed intention by present management alleging deficiencies in audit work impairs if auditor believes **strong possibility** of claim

    (d) Immaterial not related to audit **usually** does **not** impair (i.e., billing disputes)

(2) Litigation by client security holders or other third parties generally does not impair unless material client-CPA cross-claims develop.

(3) If independence is impaired, CPA should disassociate and/or disclaim an opinion for lack of independence.

Interpretation 101-7. (Deleted)

Interpretation 101-8. A CPA's financial interests in nonclients may impair independence when those nonclients have financial interests in the CPA's clients.

Interpretation 101-9. (Deleted) .

Interpretation 101-10. Describes members' duties for independence when auditing entities included in governmental financial statements

(1) Generally, auditor of a material fund type, fund account group, or component unit of entity that should be disclosed in notes of general-purpose financial statements, but is not auditing primary government, should be independent with respect to those financial statements and primary government

(2) Also should be independent if, although funds and accounts are separately immaterial, they are material in the aggregate

Interpretation 101-11. Modified application of Rule 101 for certain engagements to issue restricted-use reports under the Statements on Standards for Attestation Engagements

(1) Rule 101: Independence and its interpretations and rulings apply to all attest engagements. However, for purposes of performing engagements to issue reports under the Statements on Standards for Attestation Engagements (SSAE) that are restricted to identified parties, only the following covered members, and their immediate families, are required to be independent with respect to the responsible party[1] in accordance with Rule 101:

    (a) Individuals participating on the attest engagement team;

    (b) Individuals who directly supervise or manage the attest engagement partner; and

    (c) Individuals who consult with the attest engagement team regarding technical or industry-related issues specific to the attest engagement.

(2) In addition, independence would be considered to be impaired if the firm had a financial relationship covered by interpretation 101-1.A with the responsible party that was material to the firm.

(3) In cases where the firm provides non-attest services to the responsible party that are proscribed under interpretation 101-3 and that do not directly relate to the subject matter of the attest engagement, independence would not be considered to be impaired.

(4) In circumstances where the individual or entity that engages the firm is not the responsible party or associated with the responsible party, individuals on the attest engagement team need not be independent of the individual or entity, but should consider their responsibilities under interpretation 102-2 with regard to any relationships that may exist with the individual or entity that engages them to perform these services.

(5) This interpretation does not apply to an engagement performed under the Statement on Auditing Standards or Statement on Standards for Accounting and Review Services, or to an examination or review engagement performed under the Statements on Standards for Attestation Engagements.

Interpretation 101-12. Independence is impaired if during professional engagement or while expressing an opinion, member's firm had any material cooperative arrangement with client.

(1) Cooperative arrangement exists when member's firm and client participate jointly in business activity such as

    (a) Joint ventures to develop or market a product or service

    (b) Arrangements to provide services or products to a third party

    (c) Arrangements to combine services or products of the member's firm with those of client to market them with references to both parties

    (d) Arrangements under which member firm or client act as distributor of other's products or services

(2) Joint participation with client is not a cooperative arrangement and is thus allowed if all of the following three conditions are present.

    (a) Participation of the firm and client are governed by separate agreements

    (b) Neither firm nor client assumes any responsibility for the other

    (c) Neither party is an agent of the other

---

[1] *As defined in the SSAE.*

Interpretation 101-13.

(1) Member may be asked by client to perform extended audit services (i.e., member may assist client in internal audit activities or member may extend audit services beyond what GAAS requires). Member performing extended audit services does not impair independence if member does not act or appear to act as a manager or employee of client.

(2) Example that would impair independence includes performing ongoing monitoring or control activities (i.e., reviewing loan originations for client). Another example that would impair independence is if member determines which internal control recommendations should be used by client.

Rule 102 Integrity and Objectivity. In performance of **any** professional service, a member shall (a) maintain objectivity and integrity, (b) avoid conflicts of interest, and (c) not knowingly misrepresent facts or subordinate judgment.

(1) In tax matters, resolving doubt in favor of client does not, by itself, impair integrity or objectivity.

Interpretation 102-1. Knowingly making or permitting false and misleading entries in an entity's financial statements or records is a violation.

Interpretation 102-2. A conflict of interest may occur if a member performing a professional service has a **significant relationship** with another person, entity, product, or service that **could be viewed** as impairing the member's objectivity.

(1) If the member believes that the professional service can be performed with objectivity, and if the relationship is disclosed to and consent is obtained from the client, employer, or other appropriate parties, the rule does not prohibit performance of the professional service.

(2) Nothing in this interpretation overrides Rule 101 (on independence), its interpretations, and rulings.

Interpretation 102-3. When a member deals with his/her employer's external accountant, the member must be candid and not knowingly misrepresent facts or knowingly fail to disclose material facts.

Interpretation 102-4. If a member and his/her supervisor have a disagreement concerning the preparation of financial statements or the recording of transactions, the member should

(1) Allow the supervisor's position if that position is an acceptable alternative with authoritative support and/or does not result in a material misstatement.

(2) Report the problem to higher levels in firm if supervisor's position could cause material misstatements in records.

(3) Consider quitting firm if after reporting the problem to upper management, action is not taken. Consider reporting this to regulatory authorities and external accountant.

Interpretation 102-5. Those involved in educational services such as teaching full- or part-time at a university, teaching professional education courses, or engaged in research and scholarship are subject to Rule 102.

Interpretation 102-6. Sometimes members are asked by clients to act as advocates in support of clients' position on tax services, consulting services, accounting issues, or financial reporting issues. Member is still subject to Rule 102. Member is also still subject to Rules 201, 202, and 203. Member is also subject to Rule 101 for professional services requiring independence.

*NOTE: While CPA candidates should read the rulings to better understand the ethics rules and interpretations, it is **not** necessary to memorize them; consider them to be illustrations. Gaps in sequence are due to deleted sections.*

Rule 101, 102 Ethics Rulings

Independence and Integrity Ethics Rulings

1. If a member accepts more than a token gift from a client, independence may be impaired.

2. A member may join a trade association which is a client, without impairing independence, but may not serve in a capacity of management.

3. If a member is cosigner of a client's checks, independence is impaired.

4. Independence is impaired if a member prepares a client's payroll and conditions of Interpretation 101-3 are not met.

7. Independence is impaired if a member supervises client office personnel on a monthly basis.

8. Extensive accounting and consulting services, including interpretation of statements, forecasts, etc., do not impair independence.

9. Independence is impaired if the member cosigns checks or purchase orders or exercises general supervision over budgetary controls.

10. The independence of an elected legislator (a CPA) in a local government is impaired with respect to that governmental unit.

11. Mere designation as executor or trustee, without actual services in either capacity, does not impair independence, but actual service does.

12. If a member is a trustee of a foundation, independence is impaired.

14. Independence of a member serving as director or officer of a local United Way or similar organization is not impaired with respect to a charity receiving funds from that organization unless the organization exercises managerial control over that charity.

16. Independence is impaired if a member serves on the board of a nonprofit social club if the board has ultimate responsibility for the affairs of the club.

17. The acquisition of equity or debt securities as a condition for membership in a country club does not normally impair independence; serving on the club's governing board or taking part in its management does impair independence.

19. Independence is impaired if a member serves on a committee administering a client's deferred compensation program.

20. Membership on governmental advisory committees does not impair independence with respect to that governmental unit.

21. A member serving as director of an enterprise would not be independent with respect to the enterprise's profit sharing and retirement trust.

29. A member's independence is impaired when owning bonds in a municipal authority.

31. A member's ownership of an apartment in a co-op apartment building would impair the member's and the firm's independence.

33. A member impairs independence upon joining a client's employee benefit plan.

35. A member's ownership of shares in a mutual investment fund which owns stock in the CPA's clients normally would not impair independence.

36. A member who is a member of an investment club, holding stock in a client, lacks independence.

38. A member serving with a client bank in a cofiduciary capacity, with respect to a trust, does not impair independence with respect to the bank or trust department (if the estate's or trust's assets were not material).

39. A member who acts as a transfer agent and/or registrar is not independent with respect to the company.

41. Independence is not impaired when a member's retirement plan is invested and managed by an insurance company in a separate account, not a part of the general assets of the insurance company.

48. A university faculty member cannot be independent to a student senate fund because the student senate is a part of the university which is the member's employer.

51. A member who provides legal services to a client is not independent with respect to the client.

52. Independence is impaired when prior year fees for professional services, whether billed or unbilled, remain unpaid for more than one year prior to the date of the report.

54. A member's independence is not impaired by performing appraisal, valuation, or actuarial services for a client, if all significant judgments are determined or approved by the client and if the client is able to provide an informed judgment on the results of the services.

55. A member's independence is not impaired if the member is involved in hiring and instructing new personnel during a systems implementation. The client must make all significant management decisions and the member must restrict supervisory activities to initial instruction and training.

56. Independence is impaired by recruiting and hiring a controller and/or cost accountant for a client company. The member may, however, recommend position descriptions and candidate specifications as well as initially screen and recommend qualified candidates.

58. Independence is impaired when a member owns a building and leases space to a client.

60. If a member audits an employee benefit plan, independence is impaired with respect to employer if a partner or professional employee of the firm had significant influence over such employer, was in a key position with the employer, or was associated with the employer as a promoter, underwriter, or voting trustee.

61. Participation by a member's spouse in an employee stock ownership plan of a client does not impair independence until a right of possession of the stock exists.

64. Independence with respect to a fund-raising foundation is impaired if a member serves on the board of directors of the entity for whose benefit the foundation exists (unless position is purely honorary).

65. Member who is **not** in public practice may use CPA designation in connection with financial statements and correspondence of member's employer. May also use CPA designation on business cards if along with employment title. Member may **not** imply independence from employer. Member cannot state that transmittal is in conformity with GAAP.

66. Independence is impaired by a member's retirement or savings plan which includes a direct or material indirect financial interest in an attest client.

67. If a client financial institution merely services a member's loan, independence is not impaired.

68. A member may not hold a direct financial interest in an attestation client, even when held in a blind trust.

69. A member with a material limited partnership interest is not independent of other limited partnerships that have the same general partner.

70. Maintaining state or federally insured deposits (e.g., checking accounts, savings accounts, certificates of deposit) in a financial institution does not impair independence; uninsured deposits do not impair independence if the uninsured amounts are immaterial.

71. CPA Firm A is not independent of an entity audited by Firm B. CPA Firm B may only use Firm A personnel in a manner similar to internal auditors without impairing Firm B's independence.

72. A member (and the member's firm) are not independent if the member serves on the advisory board of a client unless the advisory board (1) is truly advisory, (2) has no authority to make or appear to make management decisions, and (3) membership is distinct with minimal, if any, common membership with management and the board of directors.

73. The "period of the professional engagement" during which independence is required starts when services requiring independence begin, and ends when there is notification of termination of the professional relationship.

74. A member must be independent to issue an audit opinion or a review report, but need not be independent to issue a compilation report (such lack of independence is disclosed).

75. Membership in a credit union does not impair audit independence if (1) the member qualifies as a credit union member on grounds other than by providing professional services, (2) the member does not exert significant influence over the credit union, (3) the member's loans (if any) from credit union are normal (see Interpretation 101-1), and (4) the conditions of ruling 70 have been met.

77. When a member is offered (or seeks) employment with a client, that member should remove himself/herself from the engagement until the employment offer is rejected or employment is no longer being considered; when a member becomes aware that an individual participated on the engagement in those circumstances, that member should consider the need to reperform work or other appropriate procedures.

79. A member's independence is impaired if s/he is a general partner in a partnership that invests in a client of the member's firm; if s/he is a limited partner, independence is impaired if the partnership invests in a material portion of the client.

81. A member's investment in a limited partnership impairs independence with respect to the limited partnership; when the investment is material, independence is impaired with respect to both the general partner of the limited partnership and any subsidiaries of the limited partnership.

82. When a member is the campaign treasurer for a mayoral candidate, independence is impaired with respect to the candidate's campaign organization, but independence is not impaired with respect to the candidate's political party or the municipality.

85. A member may serve as a bank director, but this is generally not desirable when s/he has clients that are bank customers; performing both services is allowed, however, if the relationship is disclosed and acceptable to all appropriate parties. Revealing confidential client information without client permission is a violation of the Code, even when the failure to disclose such information may breach the member's fiduciary responsibility as a director.

86. A partially secured, "grandfathered loan" will not impair independence if the portion of the loan that exceeds the value of the collateral is not material to the member's net worth.

87. The date a loan commitment was made may be used as the date of a transaction for purposes of determining whether a loan qualifies as "grandfathered."

88. A loan from a financial institution to a limited partnership in which CPAs have a combined interest exceeding 50% of the total limited partnership interest impairs independence unless the loan qualifies as "grandfathered."

89. A member's independence with respect to a financial institution is impaired if that member is a general partner in a partnership financed by the financial institution unless the loan qualifies as "grandfathered."

90. If a member has outstanding credit card loans to a financial institution of over $5,000, independence will not be impaired if that member reduces the outstanding balance to $5,000 or less on a current basis.

91. Independence is not impaired when a member has an "operating lease" from a client made under normal terms; independence is impaired by a "capital lease" from a client unless the "loan" related to the lease qualifies as "grandfathered."

92. A material joint investment in a vacation home with an officer, director, or principal stockholder of an attest client will impair independence.

93. When a member serves as a director or officer for the United Way or a similar organization and that organization provides funds to local charities that are the member's clients, a conflict of interest will not be considered to exist if the relationship is disclosed and consent is obtained from the appropriate parties.

94. Independence is not impaired if client in the engagement letter agrees to release, indemnify, defend, and hold harmless the member from any liability and costs from misrepresentations of management.

95. An agreement by the member and a client to use alternative dispute resolution techniques in lieu of litigation before a dispute arises does not impair independence.

96. A commencement of an alternative dispute resolution does not impair independence unless the member's and client's positions are materially adverse so that the proceedings are similar to litigation, such as binding arbitration.

97. If a member performs internal audit procedures for client, independence is impaired if the member performs a management function such as helping in client's approval of loans. Testing system of internal control does not impair independence.
98. A loan from a nonclient who is a subsidiary of a client does impair independence. Loan from a nonclient parent does not impair independence with respect to a client subsidiary if the subsidiary is not material to the parent.
99. If a member is asked by a company to provide personal financial planning or tax services for its executives and the member may give the executives recommendations adverse to the company, before accepting and while doing this work, the member should consider Rule 102 on Integrity and Objectiv-ity and Rule 301 on Confidential Client Information. The member can perform the work if s/he believes it can be done with objectivity.
100. A member who was independent when his/her report was issued, may resign the report or consent to its use at a later date when his/her independence is impaired, if no postaudit work is performed while impaired.
101. Member serving as expert witness does not serve as advocate but as one having specialized knowledge, training, and experience—should arrive at position objectively.
102. If a member indemnifies client for damages, losses or costs arising from lawsuits, claims, or settlements relating directly or indirectly to clients acts, this impairs independence.

Rule 201 General Standards. Member must comply with the following standards for all professional engagements:

(1) Only undertake professional services that one can reasonably expect to complete with professional competence
(2) Exercise due professional care

   (a) Member may need to consult with experts to exercise due care

(3) Adequately plan and supervise engagements
(4) Obtain sufficient relevant data to afford a reasonable basis for conclusions and recommendations

Interpretation 201-1. Competence to complete an engagement includes

(1) Technical qualifications of CPA and staff
(2) Ability to supervise and evaluate work
(3) Knowledge of technical subject matter
(4) Capability to exercise judgment in its application
(5) Ability to research subject matter and consult with others

Interpretations 201-2, 3, 4. (Deleted)

Rule 202 Compliance with Standards. A member who performs auditing, review, compilation, consulting services, tax or other services shall comply with standards promulgated by bodies designated by Council.

NOTE: The designated bodies are

(1) Financial Accounting Standards Board
(2) Governmental Accounting Standards Board
(3) AICPA designated bodies

   (a) Accounting and Review Services Committee
   (b) Auditing Standards Board
   (c) Management Advisory Services Executive Committee

Rule 203 Accounting Principles. Member cannot provide positive or negative assurance that financial statements are in conformity with GAAP if statements contain departures from GAAP having a material effect on statements taken as a whole except when unusual circumstances would make financial statements following GAAP misleading.

(1) When unusual circumstances require a departure from GAAP, CPA must disclose in report the departure, its effects (if practicable), and reasons why compliance would result in a misleading statement.

Interpretation 203-1. CPAs are to allow departure from SFAS only when results of SFAS will be misleading.

(1) Requires use of professional judgment
(2) Examples of possible circumstances justifying departure are

    (a) New legislation
    (b) New form of business transaction

Interpretation 203-2. FASB Interpretations are covered by Rule 203

(1) Also unsuperseded ARB and APB

Interpretation 203-3. (Deleted)

Interpretation 203-4. Rule 203 also applies to communications such as reports to regulatory authorities, creditors, and auditors.

Rule 201, 202, 203 Ethics Rulings

7. A CPA who is in partnership with non-CPAs may sign the report with the firm name, his own name, and indicate "certified public accountant."
8. A member selecting subcontractors for consulting services engagements is obligated to select subcontractors on the basis of professional qualifications, technical skills, etc.
9. A member should be in a position to supervise and evaluate work of a specialist in his employ.
10. If a member prepares financial statements as a stockholder, partner, director, or employee of an entity, any transmittal should indicate the member's relationship and should not imply independence. If transmittal indicates financial statements are in accordance with GAAP, Rule 203 must be met. If financial statements are on member's letterhead, member should disclose lack of independence.
11. Rule 203 applies to members performing litigation support services.

Rule 301 Confidential Client Information. Member in public practice shall not disclose confidential client information without client consent except for

(1) Compliance with Rule 202 and 203 obligations
(2) Compliance with enforceable subpoena or summons
(3) AICPA review of professional practice
(4) Initiating complaint or responding to inquiry made by a recognized investigative or disciplinary body

Interpretation 301-1. (Deleted)

Interpretation 301-2. (Deleted)

Interpretation 301-3. A member who is considering selling his/her practice, or merging with another CPA, may allow that CPA to review confidential client information without the specific consent of the client.

(1) The member should take appropriate precautions (e.g., obtain a written confidentiality agreement) so that the prospective purchaser does not disclose such information.

*NOTE: This exception only relates to a review in conjunction with a purchase or merger. It **does not** apply to the review of working papers **after** a CPA has purchased another's practice. AU 315, discussed in detail later in this module, requires that the successor who wishes to review predecessor auditor working papers should request the client to authorize the predecessor to make such working papers available.*

Rule 302 Contingent Fees.

(1) A member in public practice shall not

    (a) Perform for a contingent fee any professional services when the member or member's firm also performs any of the following services for that client

        1] Audits or reviews of financial statements
        2] Compilations when the member is independent and expects that a third party may use the financial statements
        3] Examinations of prospective financial information

    (b) Prepare an original or amended tax return or claims for a tax refund for a contingent fee for any client

(2) Solely for purposes of this rule, (a) fees fixed by courts or other public authorities, or (b) in tax matters, fees determined based on the results of a judicial proceeding or findings of governmental agency, are not regarded as contingent and are therefore permitted

Interpretation 302-1. Examples related to contingent fees

(1) A contingent fee **would be permitted** in various circumstances in which the amounts due are not clear; examples are

   (a) Representing a client in an examination by a revenue agent
   (b) Filing amended tax returns based on a tax issue that is the subject of a test case **involving a different taxpayer**

(2) A contingent fee **would not be permitted** for preparing an amended tax return for a client claiming a refund that is clearly due to the client because of an inadvertent omission

Rule 301, 302 Ethics Rulings

1. A member may utilize outside computer services to process tax returns as long as there is no release of confidential information.
2. With client permission, a member may provide P&L percentages to a trade association.
3. A CPA withdrawing from a tax engagement due to irregularities on the client's return should urge successor CPA to have client grant permission to reveal reasons for withdrawal.
5. A member may use a records retention agency to store client records as long as confidentiality is maintained.
6. A member may be engaged by a municipality to verify taxpayer's books and records for the purpose of assessing property tax. The member must maintain confidentiality.
7. Members may reveal the names of clients without client consent unless such disclosure releases confidential information.
14. A member has a responsibility to honor confidential relationships with nonclients. Accordingly, members may have to withdraw from consulting services engagements where the client will not permit the member to make recommendations without disclosing confidential information about other clients or nonclients.

15. If the member has conducted a similar consulting services study with a negative outcome, the member should advise potential clients of the previous problems providing that earlier confidential relationships are not disclosed. If the earlier confidential relationship may be disclosed (through client knowledge of other clients), the member should seek approval from the first client.
16. In divorce proceedings a member who has prepared joint tax returns for the couple should consider both individuals to be clients for purposes of requests for confidential information relating to prior tax returns. Under such circumstances the CPA should consider reviewing the legal implications of disclosure with an attorney.
17. A contingent fee or a commission is considered to be "received" when the performance of the related services is complete and the fee or commission is determined.
18. Identical to Ruling 85 under Rule 101.
19. A member's spouse may provide services to a member's attest client for a contingent fee and may refer products or services for a commission.
20. When a member learns of a potential claim against him/her, the member may release confidential client information to member's liability carrier used solely to defend against claim.
21. Identical to Ruling 99 under Rule 102.

Rule 501 Acts Discreditable. A member shall not commit an act discreditable to the profession.

Interpretation 501-1. Retention of client records after client has demanded them is discreditable.

(1) A CPA may keep analyses and schedules prepared by the client for the CPA and need not make them available to the client.
(2) A CPA may keep workpapers with information not reflected in the client's books (adjusting, closing, consolidating entries, etc.) until payment of fees due is received.

Interpretation 501-2. Discrimination on basis of race, color, religion, sex, age, or national origin is discreditable.

Interpretation 501-3. In audits of governmental grants, units, or other recipients of governmental monies, failure to follow appropriate governmental standards, procedures, etc. is discreditable.

Interpretation 501-4. Negligently making (or permitting or directing another to make) false or misleading journal entries is discreditable.

Interpretation 501-5. When a governmental body, commission, or other regulatory agency has requirements beyond those required by GAAS, members are required to follow them.

(1) Failure to follow these requirements is considered an act discreditable to the profession, unless the member discloses in the report that such requirements were not followed and the reasons therefor.

Interpretation 501-6. Member who solicits or discloses May 1996 or later Uniform CPA Examination question(s) and/or answer(s) without AICPA written authorization has committed an act discreditable to profession in violation of Rule 501.

Rule 502 *Advertising and Other Forms of Solicitation.* In public practice, shall not seek to obtain clients by false, misleading, deceptive advertising or other forms of solicitation.

Interpretation 502-1. (Deleted)

Interpretation 502-2. Advertising that is false, misleading or deceptive is prohibited, including advertising that

(1) Creates false or unjustified expectations
(2) Implies ability to influence a court, tribunal, regulatory agency or similar body or official
(3) Contains unrealistic estimates of future fees
(4) Would lead a reasonable person to misunderstand or be deceived

Interpretations 502-3, 4. (Deleted)

Interpretation 502-5. CPA may render services to clients of third parties as long as all promotion efforts are within Code.

Rule 503 *Commissions and Referral Fees.*

(1) A member in public practice may not accept a commission for recommending a product or service to a client when the member or member's firm also performs any of the following services for that client

   (a) Audits or reviews of financial statements
   (b) Compilations when the member is independent and expects that a third party may use the financial statements
   (c) Examinations of prospective financial information

(2) A member who receives a commission [not prohibited in (1) above] shall disclose that fact to the client
(3) A member who accepts a referral fee for recommending or referring any service of a CPA to any person or entity, or who pays a referral fee to obtain a client, must disclose such acceptance or payment to the client

Rule 504. (Deleted)

Rule 505 *Form of Practice and Name.* Member may practice public accounting in form of proprietorship, partnership, professional corporation, etc. and may not practice under a misleading name.

(1) May include past partners.
(2) An individual may practice in name of a former partnership for up to two years (applies when all other partners have died or withdrawn).
(3) A firm name may include a fictitious name or indicate specialization if name is not misleading.
(4) Firm may not designate itself as member of AICPA unless all partners or shareholders are members.
(5) Appendix B to Code of Professional Conduct allows non-CPA ownership of CPA firms under certain conditions.

(a) 66 2/3% (super majority) of ownership (both voting rights and financial interest) must belong to CPAs. Non-CPA owners must be involved in own principal occupation, not practice accounting, and not hold selves out as CPAs.

(b) CPAs must have ultimate responsibility in firm, not non-CPAs.

(c) Non-CPA owners must abide by AICPA Code of Professional Conduct, CPE requirements and hold a baccalaureate degree.

(d) Non-CPAs not eligible to be members of AICPA.

Interpretation 505-1. For a CPA in public practice, the allowable interest in an organization providing accounting services depends upon state law regarding practice in the corporate form.

(1) If the corporate form is permitted, the CPA may have an unlimited investment in any accounting organization.

(2) If the corporate form is not permitted, the member's relationship to the corporation must be solely as an investor, and the investment cannot allow the member significant influence over the corporation.

Interpretation 505-2. Applicability of rules to members who operate a separate business that provides accounting services.

(1) A member in public practice who participates in the operation of a separate business that performs accounting, tax, etc. services must observe all of the Rules of Conduct.

(2) A member not otherwise in the practice of public accounting must observe the Rules of Conduct if the member holds out as a CPA and performs for a client any professional services included in public accounting.

Rule 501, 502, 503, 505 Ethics Rulings and Other Responsibilities Ethics Rulings

Due to rescinding the advertising and solicitation prohibition, the majority of the ethics rulings have been suspended.

2. A member may permit a bank to collect notes issued by a client in payment of fees.

3. A CPA employed by a firm with non-CPA practitioners must comply with the rules of conduct. If a partner of such a firm is a CPA, the CPA is responsible for all persons associated with the firm to comply with the rules of conduct.

33. A member who is a course instructor has the responsibility to determine that the advertising materials promoting the course are within the bounds of Rule 502.

38. A member who is controller of a bank may place his CPA title on bank stationery and in paid advertisements listing the officers and directors of the bank.

78. CPAs who are also attorneys may so indicate on their letterhead.

82. A member may write a financial management newsletter (being advertised for sale) with his name featured prominently.

108. Members interviewed by the press should observe the Code of Professional Conduct and not provide the press with any information for publication that the member could not publish himself.

117. A member may be a director of a consumer credit company if he is not the auditor.

134. Members who share offices, employees, etc., may not indicate a partnership exists unless a partnership agreement **is** in effect.

135. CPA firms that are members of an association cannot use letterhead that indicates a partnership rather than an association.

136. Where a firm consisting of a CPA and a non-CPA is dissolved, and an audit is continued to be serviced by both, the audit opinion should be signed by both individuals, such that a partnership is not indicated.

137. The designation "nonproprietary partner" should not be used to describe personnel as it may be misleading.

138. A member may be a partner of a firm of public accountants when all other personnel are not certified, and at the same time practice separately as a CPA.

139. A member in practice with a non-CPA would have to conform to the Code of Conduct, and would not be permitted to represent itself as a partnership of CPAs.

140. A partnership practicing under the name of the managing partner who is seeking election to high office may continue to use the managing partner's name plus "and Company" if the managing partner is elected and withdraws from the partnership.

141. A CPA in partnership with a non-CPA is ethically responsible for all acts of the partnership and those of the non-CPA partner.

144. A CPA firm may use an established firm name in a different state even though there is a difference in the roster of partners.

145. Newly merged CPA firms may practice under a title that includes the name of a previously retired partner from one of the firms.

146. CPA firms may not designate themselves as Members of the American Institute of Certified Public Accountants unless all their partners or shareholders are members of the AICPA.

158. If a member who is in the practice of public accounting also participates in the operation of a separate business that provides data processing services to public, the member must comply with all rules of conduct in connection with this business.
176. A CPA firm's name, logo, etc., may be imprinted on newsletters and similar publications if the CPA has a reasonable basis to conclude that the information is not fake, misleading, or deceptive.
177. Performing centralized billing services for a doctor is a public accounting service and must be conducted in accordance with the Code.
179. CPA firms which are members of an association (for purposes of joint advertising, training, etc.) should practice in their own names, although they may indicate membership in the association.
182. A member need only return records originally provided to the member by the client for a terminated engagement (in this case preparation of a tax return).
183. A CPA firm may designate itself "Accredited Personal Financial Specialists" on its letterhead and in marketing materials if all partners or shareholders of the firm currently have the AICPA-awarded designation.
184. Identical to Ruling 18 under Rule 302.
185. A member may purchase a product from a supplier and resell it to a client at a profit without disclosing the profit to the client.
186. A member may contract for support services from a computer-hardware maintenance servicer and bill them to a client at a profit without disclosing the profit to the client.
187. Identical to Ruling 19 under Rule 302.
188. When a member refers products to clients through distributors and agents, the member may not perform for those clients the services described in Rule 503 [part (1) of the outline of Rule 503].
189. When individuals associated with a client entity have an internal dispute, and have separately asked a member for client records, the member need only supply them once, and to the individual who previously has been designated or held out as the client's representative.

4. Responsibilities in Consulting Services

   a. In January of 1991 a new series of pronouncements on consulting services, *Statements on Standards for Consulting Services* (SSCS), became effective. This series of pronouncements replaces the three *Statements on Standards for Management Advisory Services*. These standards apply to CPAs in public practice who provide consulting services.

   b. Outline of SSCS 1 Definitions and Standards

      (1) Comparison of consulting and attest services

         (a) **Attest services**—Practitioner expresses a conclusion about the reliability of a written assertion that is the responsibility of another party (the asserter)
         (b) **Consulting services**—Practitioner develops the findings, conclusions and recommendations presented, generally only for the use and benefit of the client; the nature of the work is determined solely by agreement between the practitioner and the client
         (c) Performance of consulting services **for an attest client** requires that the practitioner maintain independence and does not in and of itself impair independence

         NOTE: *While one must remain objective in performing consulting services, independence is not required unless the practitioner also performs attest (e.g., audit) services for that client.*

      (2) Definitions

         (a) **Consulting services practitioner**—A CPA holding out as a CPA (i.e., a CPA in public practice) while engaged in the performance of a consulting service for a client
         (b) **Consulting process**—Analytical approach and process applied in a consulting service

            1] This definition **excludes** services subject to other AICPA technical standards on auditing (SAS), other attest services (SSAE), compilations and reviews (SSARS), most tax engagements, and recommendations made during one of these engagements as a direct result of having performed these excluded services

         (c) **Consulting services**—Professional services that employ the practitioner's technical skills, education, observations, experiences, and knowledge of the consulting process

      (3) Types of consulting services

         (a) **Consultations**—Provide counsel in a short time frame, based mostly, if not entirely, on existing personal knowledge about the client

        1]   Examples: reviewing and commenting on a client business plan, suggesting software for further client investigation

    (b) **Advisory services**—Develop findings, conclusions and recommendations for client consideration and decision making

        1]   Examples: Operational review and improvement study, analysis of accounting system, strategic planning assistance, information system advice

    (c) **Implementation services**—Place an action plan into effect

        1]   Examples: Installing and supporting computer system, executing steps to improve productivity, assisting with mergers

    (d) **Transaction services**—Provide services related to a specific client transaction, generally with a third party

        1]   Examples: Insolvency services, valuation services, information related to financing, analysis of a possible merger or acquisition, litigation services

    (e) **Staff and other support services**—Provide appropriate staff and possibly other support to perform tasks specified by client

        1]   Examples: Data processing facilities management, computer programming, bankruptcy trusteeship, controllership activities

    (f) **Product services**—Provide client with a product and associated support services

        1]   Examples: Sale, delivery, installation, and implementation of training programs, computer software, and systems development

(4) Standards for Consulting Services

    (a) General Standards of Rule 201 of Code of Professional Conduct

        1]   Professional competence
        2]   Due professional care
        3]   Planning and supervision
        4]   Sufficient relevant data

    (b) Additional standards established for this area (under Rule 202 of Code of Professional Conduct)

        1]   Client interest—Must serve client interest while maintaining **integrity** and **objectivity**
        2]   Understanding with client—Establish either in **writing or orally**
        3]   Communication with client—Inform client of any conflicts of interest, significant reservations about engagement, significant engagement findings

    (c) Professional judgment must be used in applying SSCS

        1]   Example: Practitioner not required to decline or withdraw from a consulting engagement when there are mutually agreed upon limitations with respect to gathering relevant data

5. Responsibilities in Personal Financial Planning

    a. Definition, scope and standards of personal financial planning

        (1) Personal financial planning engagements are only those that involve developing strategies and making recommendations to assist a client in defining and achieving personal financial goals

        (2) Personal financial planning engagements involve all of following

            (a) Defining engagement objectives
            (b) Planning specific procedures appropriate to engagement
            (c) Developing basis for recommendations
            (d) Communicating recommendations to client

    (e) Identifying tasks for taking action on planning decisions

(3) Other engagements may also include

    (a) Assisting client to take action on planning decisions
    (b) Monitoring client's progress in achieving goals
    (c) Updating recommendations and helping client revise planning decisions

(4) Personal financial planning does not include services that are limited to, for example

    (a) Compiling personal financial statements
    (b) Projecting future taxes
    (c) Tax compliance, including, but not limited to, preparation of tax returns
    (d) Tax advice or consultations

(5) CPA should act in conformity with AICPA Code of Professional Conduct

    (a) Rule 102, Integrity and Objectivity

        1] A member shall maintain objectivity and integrity, be free of conflicts of interest, and not knowingly misrepresent facts or subordinate his/her judgment to others

    (b) Rule 201

        1] A member shall undertake only those professional services that member can reasonably expect to be completed with professional competence, shall exercise due professional care in the performance of professional services, shall adequately plan and supervise performance of professional services, and shall obtain sufficient relevant data to afford a reasonable basis for conclusions or recommendations

    (c) Rule 301, Confidential Client Information

        1] Member in public practice shall not disclose any confidential client information without specific consent of client

    (d) Rule 302, Contingent Fees

        1] Rules must be followed

(6) When a personal financial planning engagement includes providing assistance in preparation of personal financial statements or financial projections, the CPA should consider applicable provisions of AICPA pronouncements, including

    (a) Statements on Standards for Accounting and Review Services
    (b) Statement on Standards for Attestation Engagements Financial Forecasts and Projections
    (c) Audit and Accounting Guide for Prospective Financial Information
    (d) Personal Financial Statements Guide

(7) The CPA should document his/her understanding of scope and nature of services to be provided

    (a) Consider engagement letter

(8) Personal financial planning engagement should be adequately planned
(9) Engagement's objectives form basis for planning engagement

    (a) Procedures should reflect materiality and cost-benefit considerations

(10) Relevant information includes understanding of client's goals, financial position, and available resources for achieving goals

    (a) External factors (such as inflation, taxes, and investment markets) and nonfinancial factors (such as client attitudes, risk tolerance, spending habits, and investment preferences) are also relevant information
    (b) Relevant information also includes reasonable estimates furnished by client's advisors, or developed by CPA

   (11) Recommendations should ordinarily be in writing and include summary of client's goals and significant assumptions and description of any limitations on work performed

   (12) Unless otherwise agreed, CPA is not responsible for additional services, for example,

     (a) Assisting client to take action on planning decisions

     (b) Monitoring progress in achieving goals

     (c) Updating recommendations and revising planning decisions

  b. Working with other advisers

   (1) If CPA does not provide a service needed to complete an engagement, s/he should restrict scope of engagement and recommend that client engage another adviser

   (2) If client declines to engage another adviser, CPA and client may still agree to proceed with engagement

  c. Implementation engagement functions and responsibilities

   (1) Implementation engagements involve assisting client to take action on planning decisions developed during personal financial planning engagement

   (2) Implementation includes activities such as selecting investment advisers, restructuring debt, creating estate documents, establishing cash reserves, preparing budgets, and selecting and acquiring specific investments and insurance products

   (3) When undertaking implementation engagement, CPA should apply existing professional standards and published guidance

 6. Responsibilities in Business and Industry

  a. Internal auditing

   (1) Internal auditors are employed by company to perform audits on that company

     (a) Do financial, operational, and compliance audits

     (b) In financial auditing, evaluate effectiveness of internal control procedures

       1] Used to comply with, among other items, Foreign Corrupt Practices Act that requires companies to have effective internal control

   (2) Internal auditors do not need CPA license but instead may get Certified Internal Auditor (CIA) designation

     (a) Rely on Institute of Internal Auditors for professional guidance rather than AICPA

     (b) Guidelines for internal audits not as well developed as those for external audits

     (c) Some firms have CPA firm perform internal audit functions

       1] This outsourcing to CPAs is controversial

       2] AICPA considers it "extended audit services"

         a] Acceptable for CPAs if management understands it has ultimate responsibility for internal control

   (3) Standards for Professional Practice of Internal Auditing issued by Institute of Internal Auditing

     (a) Divided into five general sections

       1] Independence—Independent in sense that organization puts no restrictions on auditor's judgment

         a] Independence defined differently than AICPA; must be independent of **activities** they audit since they are employees of organization they are auditing

         b] Reporting is often directly to audit committee or board of directors

       2] Professional proficiency

       3] Scope of work

> > a] Not only accounting and financial controls but also internal control procedures and operational auditing
> > b] Evaluate compliance with company policies and goals
>
> > 4] Performance of audit work
>
> > a] Requires effective planning and communication of audit results
>
> > 5] Management of internal auditing department
>
> > a] Coordinate with external audit
> > b] Work of internal auditor supplements but does not substitute for work of outside auditors in financial statement audit
> > c] External auditors do not control internal auditors but often review work to avoid needless duplication

(4) Internal auditors responsible to management—external auditors responsible to users of financial statements

(a) Audit methods are similar
(b) Decisions about materiality or risk often different because internal auditors responsible to management
(c) Permitted for external auditors to use internal auditors to assist audit

1] May reduce audit fee

b. Operational auditing—looking at improving efficiency and performance in firm or government

(1) There are no generally accepted standards
(2) Reporting is to management
(3) Often about nonfinancial areas (i.e., personnel)
(4) Can be performed by internal, external, or government auditors

c. Compliance auditing—determination on how organization has complied with requirement of specified laws or regulations

(1) CPAs often hired to apply procedures to attest to management's assertion that company is complying with specified regulations—if so, CPA can issue unqualified opinion on compliance

7. Responsibilities in Governmental Auditing

a. Include audits of government organizations as well as those made by government audit agencies such as the GAO (Government Accounting Office)

(1) Audits may be accomplished by government auditors at local, state, or federal level or by CPA firms

b. Auditors must comply with all relevant AICPA and government auditing standards

(1) Must comply with government auditing standards (GAS) established by GAO

(a) These are published in "Yellow Book" and are known as "Yellow Book standards"—auditing standards in Yellow Book usually same as AICPA's GAAS with important exceptions

1] Threshold for materiality often lower because of sensitivity of government activities
2] Makes compliance auditing requirement for laws and regulations
3] Working papers standards are more detailed

(b) Government auditing standards include requirements for continuing education and training for governmental auditing

1] For auditors involved in government audits, twenty-four of eighty hours every two years for CPE must relate to governmental auditing

(c) GAS pronouncements require reporting on compliance with laws and regulations as well as internal control

(d) GAS pronouncements also cover financial statement audits

    1] Whether financial statements are presented fairly in accordance with GAAP

    2] Whether internal control procedures are in place

(e) GAS pronouncements also cover performance audits of governmental entities

    1] Economy and efficiency audits, including looking into whether entity has complied with laws and regulations on its economy and efficiency

    2] Includes program audits to see if entity has complied with laws and regulations governing program

(2) Must also comply with generally accepted auditing standards

(a) These include all relevant AICPA generally accepted auditing standards

(b) Members of AICPA violate AICPA Code of Professional Conduct if fail to follow GAS

c. Single Audit Act established use of single organization-wide government audits to reduce duplication

(1) State and local governments as well as other entities often get funding from several federal government sources—in past, this would require several audits to see that regulations for each source are complied with

(2) State and local governments receiving $300,000 or more in federal funds in a fiscal year are now audited under the Single Audit Act and OMB Circular A-133 (*Audits of States, Local Governments, and Nonprofit Organizations*)

(3) If they receive $300,000 or more in a year, they have the option of being audited under the Single Audit Act or under other federal requirements on each individual program

(4) Single Audit Act mandates two additional reports

(a) Report on compliance with laws and regulations

(b) Report on entity's internal control

(5) Single Audit Act also requires that auditors report on several other areas

(a) Schedule of federal financial assistance

(b) Compliance with requirements having material effect on federal financial assistance programs

    1] Auditors required to report on whether organization has met requirements of laws and regulations that may materially affect each major program

        a] Program is a major program if its expenditures meet threshold in relation to total expenditures of whole organization on all federal programs

        b] For example—If organization's total expenditures are less than or equal to $100 million for year, a major program is one that expends $300,000 or 3% of the total expenditures of the organization, whichever is larger

            i] For organizations over $100 million, rule to determine if it is major program is based on sliding scale in Single Audit Act

(c) Internal control procedures

(d) Compliance with general requirements of federal assistance programs that Congress mandates (many of these are for other than financial goals)

    1] Examples include requirements involving drug-free workplace, prohibitions against civil rights violations, prohibitions against use of federal funds for partisan political purposes

8. Disciplinary Systems of the Profession and State Regulatory Bodies

a. Joint trial board panel may discipline CPAs—possible results include

(1) Acquittal
(2) Admonishment
(3) Suspension for up to two years
(4) Expulsion from AICPA

    (a) May still practice public accounting using valid license issued by state

        1] Violation of state code, however, can result in revocation of CPA certificate and loss of ability to practice public accounting

    (b) Any member who departs from rulings or interpretations has burden justifying it in any disciplinary proceedings
    (c) **Automatic expulsion** from AICPA takes place when

        1] Member's CPA certificate is revoked by state board of accountancy or by some other authorized body
        2] Member convicted of felony
        3] Member files or helps to prepare fraudulent tax return for client or self
        4] Member intentionally fails to file tax return that was required

    (d) Professional Ethics Division may investigate ethics violations and may sanction those that are less serious using less severe remedies
    (e) In addition, court decisions have consistently held that even if an individual is not a member of AICPA, that individual is still expected to follow profession's Code of Professional Conduct
    (f) The individual state CPA board and societies monitor ethical matters

        1] Typically ethics complaints can be referred to state societies as well as to AICPA
        2] State boards license CPAs and can revoke or suspend licenses

  b. Securities Exchange Commission actions against accountant

    (1) After a hearing, SEC can revoke or suspend accountant from practicing before SEC if accountant willfully violated federal securities laws or regulations, or has acted unethically or unprofessionally
    (2) SEC can revoke or suspend accountant upon conviction of felony or misdemeanor in which moral turpitude was involved
    (3) SEC can prohibit accountant or accounting firm from doing work for SEC clients
    (4) SEC can penalize accountants with civil fines and mandates to pay profits gained from violations of securities laws and regulations

  c. Joint Ethics Enforcement Program

    (1) Most state societies have agreements with AICPA to allow referrals of ethics complaints to each other

B. Accountant's Legal Liabilities

1. Common Law Liability to Clients

  a. Liability to clients for breach of contract

    (1) Occurs if accountant fails to perform substantially as agreed under contract

      (a) Duties under contract may be

        1] Implied—accountant owes duty in contract to perform in nonnegligent manner
        2] Express—accountant owes duty to perform under terms of the contract

          a] This duty can extend liability beyond that which is standard under a normal audit
          b] Typically, terms are expressed in engagement letter that should specify clearly and in writing the following:

            i] Type and scope of engagement to avoid misunderstandings between CPA and client ii] Procedures and tests to be used

iii] That engagement will not necessarily uncover fraud, mistakes, defalcations, or illegal actions unless CPA agrees to greater responsibility

iv] Engagement letter should be signed by at least client (accountant will typically sign also) but oral contract for audit still enforceable without engagement letter

(b) Accountant (CPA) is said to be in privity of contract with client when contract exists between them

1] Reverse also true (i.e., client is in privity of contract with CPA)

(c) Accountant is not an insurer of financial statements and thus does not guarantee against losses from fraud

1] "Normal" audit is not intended to uncover fraud, shortages, or defalcations, in general but is meant to provide audit evidence needed to express opinion on fairness of financial statements

(d) Accountant is not normally liable for failure to detect fraud, etc. **unless**

1] "Normal" audit or review would have detected it, or

2] Accountant by agreement has undertaken greater responsibility such as defalcation audit, or

3] Wording of audit report indicates greater responsibility

EXAMPLE: A CPA has been hired by a client to perform an audit. A standard engagement letter is used. During the course of the audit, the CPA fails to uncover a clever embezzlement scheme by one of the client's employees. The CPA is not liable for the losses unless a typical, reasonable audit should have resulted in discovery of the scheme.

(e) In an audit or review of financial statements, accountant is under duty to investigate when s/he discovers or becomes aware of suspicious items

1] Investigation should extend beyond management's explanations

(2) Client should not interfere or prevent accountant from performing

EXAMPLE: A CPA firm issues its opinion a few days late because of its client's failure to supply needed information. The CPA firm is entitled to the full fee agreed upon under the contract (engagement).

(3) When breach of contract occurs

(a) Accountant is not entitled to compensation if breach is major

EXAMPLE: M failed to complete the audit by the agreed date. If time is of the essence so that the client receives no benefit from the audit, M is not entitled to compensation.

(b) Accountant is entitled to compensation if there are only minor errors but client may deduct from fees paid any damages caused by breach

(c) Client may recover any damages caused by breach even if accountant is not entitled to fee

(d) In general, punitive damages are not awarded for breach of contract

b. Liability to clients based on negligence

(1) Elements needed to prove negligence against accountant

(a) Accountant had duty to perform with same degree of skill and judgment possessed by average accountant

1] This is the standard used in cases involving ordinary negligence (or simply called negligence)

a] Different phrases are used for this standard, that is,

i] Duty to exercise due care

ii] Duty of skill of average, reasonable accountant (or CPA) iii]   Duty to act as average (or reasonable) accountant (or CPA) would under similar circumstances

iv]   Duty of judgment of ordinary, prudent accountant (or CPA)

2]   Standard for accountants is guided by

a]   State and federal statutes

b]   Court decisions

c]   Contract with client

d]   GAAS and GAAP (persuasive but not conclusive)

i]   Failure to follow GAAS virtually establishes lack of due care but reverse not true (i.e., following GAAS does not automatically preclude negligence but is strong evidence for presence of due care)

e]   Customs of the profession (persuasive but not conclusive)

EXAMPLE: W, a CPA, issued an unqualified opinion on the financial statements of X Company. Included in the assets was inventory stated at cost when the market was materially below cost. This violation of GAAP can be used to establish that W was negligent. Also, the client can sue under contract law because W has an implied duty in the contract to not be negligent.

EXAMPLE: A CPA, while performing the annual audit, detects material errors in the previously issued audit report. The CPA has a duty to correct these material errors.

EXAMPLE: A CPA failing to warn a client of known internal weakness is falling below this standard.

(b) Accountant breached duty owed of average reasonable accountant

(c) Damage or loss results

1]   Limited to actual losses that use of reasonable care would have avoided

2]   Punitive damages not normally allowed for ordinary negligence

3]   Contributory negligence may be a complete defense by CPA in many states if client's own negligence substantially contributed to accountant's failure to perform audit adequately

(d) Causal relationship must exist between fault of accountant and damages of plaintiff

1]   Also, cause should be proximate (i.e., foreseeable)

EXAMPLE: A CPA negligently fails to discover during an audit that several expensive watches are missing from the client's inventory. Subsequently, an employee is caught stealing some watches. He confesses to stealing several before the audit and more after the audit when he found out he did not get caught. Only 5 of the watches can be recovered from the employee, who is unable to pay for those stolen. The CPA may be liable for those losses sustained after the audit if discovery could have prevented them. However, the CPA normally would not be liable for the watches taken before the audit when the loss is not the proximate result of the negligent audit. But if there were watches that could have been recovered at time of audit but can't be now, the CPA could be liable for those watches even though they were taken before audit.

c.   Accountant's liability is not based solely on honest errors of judgment; liability requires at least negligence under common law

d.   Liability to client for fraud, gross negligence, or constructive fraud

(1) Common law fraud of accountant is established by following elements:

(a) Misrepresentation of material fact or accountant's expert opinion

(b) Scienter, shown by either

1]   Intent to mislead with accountant's knowledge of falsity, or

2]   Reckless disregard of the truth

(c) Reasonable or justifiable reliance by injured party

(d) Actual damages

(2) Called constructive fraud or gross negligence if when proving above four elements, reckless disregard of the truth is established instead of knowledge of falsity

EXAMPLE: During the course of an audit, a CPA fails to verify the existence of the company's investments which amount to a substantial portion of the assets. Many of these, it is subsequently found, were nonexistent. Even in the absence of intent to defraud, the CPA is liable for constructive fraud based on reckless disregard of the truth.

EXAMPLE: Care and Less Co., CPAs, uncover suspicious items during the course of their audit of Blue Co. Because their audit steps did not require the additional steps needed to check into these suspicious items, the CPAs failed to uncover material errors. Even if a typical audit would not have required these additional audit steps, the CPAs are liable for the damages that result because they have a duty to look into such circumstances when they come to their attention.

    (3) Contributory negligence of client is not a defense available for accountant in cases of fraud, constructive fraud, or gross negligence

    (4) Privity of contract is not required for plaintiff to prove fraud, constructive fraud, or gross negligence

    (5) Punitive damages may be added to actual damages for fraud, constructive fraud, or gross negligence

2. Common Law Liability to Third Parties (Nonclients)

  a. Client is in privity of contract with accountant based on contractual relationship

    (1) In typical accountant-client relationship, there usually is no privity of contract between the accountant and third parties

    (2) Traditionally, accountants could use defense of no privity against suing third parties in contract and negligence cases

      (a) Ultramares decision is leading case in which accountants held liable only to parties for whose primary benefit financial statements are intended

        1] This generally means only client or third-party beneficiaries since these were in privity of contract with accountant

        2] However, anyone (including third parties) who can prove fraud or constructive fraud may recover

      (b) This is a significant **minority** rule today

  b. More recently, many courts have expanded liability to some third parties. The following distinctions should be understood:

    (1) Foreseen party—third party who accountant knew would rely on financial statements, or member of limited class that accountant knew would rely on financial statements, for specified transaction

      (a) **Majority rule** is that accountant is liable to foreseen third parties for negligence

        1] Rationale for not allowing liability to more third parties is that accountants should not be exposed to liability in indeterminate amount to indeterminate class

EXAMPLE: A CPA agrees to perform an audit for ABC Client knowing that the financial statements will be used to obtain a loan from XYZ Bank. Relying on the financial statements, XYZ Bank loans ABC $100,000. ABC goes bankrupt. If XYZ can establish that the financial statements were not fairly stated, thus causing the bank to give the loan, and if negligence can be established, most courts will allow XYZ Bank to recover from the CPA.

EXAMPLE: Facts are the same as in the example above except that XYZ Bank was not specified. Since the CPA knew that some bank would rely on these financial statements, the actual bank is a foreseen party since it is a member of a limited class and most courts will allow for liability.

      (b) Accountant liable for fraud, constructive fraud, or gross negligence to all parties whether foreseen or not

    (2) Distinguish foreseen party and foreseeable party

      (a) Foreseeable party—any party that accountant could reasonably foresee would receive financial statements and use them

        1] **Majority rule** is that accountant **not** liable to mere foreseeable parties for negligence

EXAMPLE: A CPA is informed that financial statements after being audited will be used to obtain a loan from a bank. The audited financial statements are also shown to trade creditors and potential investors. The bank is a foreseen third party but these other third parties are not actually foreseen parties and generally cannot recover from the CPA for ordinary negligence. They may qualify as foreseeable third parties since creditors or investors are the types of parties whom an accountant should reasonably foresee as users of the audited financial statements.

3. Statutory Liability to Third Parties—Securities Act of 1933

    a. General information on the Securities Act of 1933

        (1) Covers regulation of sales of securities registered under 1933 Act

            (a) Requires registration of initial issuances of securities with SEC
            (b) Makes it unlawful for registration statement to contain untrue **material** fact or to omit **material** fact

                1] Material fact—one about which average prudent investor should be informed
                2] Most potential accountant liability occurs because registration statement (and prospectus) includes audited financial statements
                3] Accountant's legal liability arises for untrue material fact or omission of material fact in registration statement (or prospectus)
                4] 1933 Act does not include periodic reports to SEC or annual reports to stockholders (these are in the 1934 Act below)

    b. Parties that may sue

        (1) Any purchaser of registered securities

            (a) Plaintiff need not be initial purchaser of security
            (b) Purchaser generally must prove that specific security was offered for sale through registration statement

                1] Exchange and issuance of stock based on a merger counts as a sale

        (2) Third parties can sue without having privity of contract with accountant under Federal Securities Acts

    c. Liability under Section 11 of the 1933 Act

        (1) This imposes liability on auditors (and other experts) for misstatements or omissions of material fact in certified financial statements or other information provided in registration statements
        (2) Proof requirements

            (a) Plaintiff (purchaser) must prove damages were incurred
            (b) Plaintiff must prove there was material misstatement or omission in financial statements included in registration statement
            (c) If these two are proven, it is sufficient to win against the CPA and shifts burden of proof to accountant who may escape liability by proving one of the following defenses

                1] "Due diligence," that is, after reasonable investigation, accountant had reasonable grounds to believe that statements were true while there was no material misstatement

                NOTE: Although the basis of liability is not negligence, an accountant who was at least negligent will probably not be able to establish "due diligence."

                2] Plaintiff knew financial statements were incorrect when investment was made
                3] Lack of causation—loss was due to factors other than the misstatement or omission
                4] Following generally accepted auditing standards is generally valid as a defense for CPA

            (d) Plaintiff **need not** prove reliance on financial statements unless security was purchased at least twelve months after effective date of registration statement
            (e) Plaintiff **need not** prove negligence or fraud

d. Damages

   (1) Difference between amount paid and market value at time of suit

   (2) If sold, difference between amount paid and sale price

   (3) Damages cannot exceed price at which security was offered to public

   (4) Plaintiff cannot recover decrease in value after suit is brought

      (a) Accountant is given benefit of any increase in market value during suit

e. Statute of limitations

   (1) Action must be brought against accountant within one year from discovery (or when discovery should have been made) of false statement or omission

   (2) Or if earlier, action must be brought within three years after security offered to public

f. This liability can come from negligence in reviewing events subsequent to date of certified balance sheet

   (1) This is referred to as S-1 review when made for registration statement under securities regulations

> *EXAMPLE: An accountant performed an audit and later performed an S-1 review to review events subsequent to the balance sheet date. The accountant did not detect certain material events during this S-1 review even though there was sufficient evidence to make the accountant suspicious. Further investigation was required to avoid liability.*

> *NOTE: This example was based on the case of Escott v. BarChris Construction Corporation.*

4. Statutory Liability to Third Parties—Securities Exchange Act of 1934

a. General information on Securities Exchange Act of 1934

   (1) Regulates securities sold on national stock exchanges

      (a) Includes securities traded over-the-counter and other equity securities where the corporation has more than $10 million in total assets and the security is held by 500 or more persons at the end of a fiscal year

   (2) Requires each company to furnish to SEC an annual report (Form 10-K)

      (a) Includes financial statements (not necessarily the same as an annual report to shareholders) attested to by an accountant

      (b) Accountant civil liability comes from two sections—10 and 18

         1] Section 10 (including Rule 10b-5)—makes it unlawful to

            a] Employ any device, scheme, or artifice to defraud

            b] Make untrue statement of material fact or omit material fact

            c] Engage in act, practice, or course of business to commit fraud or deceit in connection with purchase or sale of security

         2] Section 18—makes it unlawful to make false or misleading statement with respect to a material statement unless done in "good faith"

b. Parties who may sue

   (1) Purchasers **and** sellers of registered securities

      (a) Note that under the 1933 Act, only purchasers may sue

      (b) Exchanges and issuances of stock based on merger included in 1934 Act

c. Proof requirements—Section 10, in general including Rule 10b-5

   (1) Plaintiff (purchaser or seller) must prove damages resulted in connection with purchase or sale of security in interstate commerce

   (2) Plaintiff must prove there was a material misstatement or omission in information released by firm

        (a) Information may, for example, be in form of audited financial statements in report to stockholders or in Form 10-K

    (3) Plaintiff must prove justifiable reliance on financial information
    (4) Plaintiff must prove existence of **scienter** (the intent to deceive, manipulate, or defraud)

        (a) Includes reckless disregard of truth or knowledge of falsity
        (b) Negligence alone will not subject accountant to liability under this section but lack of good faith will

    (5) Note that these proof requirements differ in very significant ways from proof requirements under the 1933 Act
    (6) Plaintiff cannot recover if s/he is reckless or fraudulent

  d. Proof requirements—Section 18

    (1) Plaintiff (purchaser or seller) must prove

        (a) S/he incurred damages
        (b) There was a material misstatement or omission on report (usually Form 10-K) filed with SEC
        (c) S/he read and relied on defective report

    (2) Then burden of proof is shifted to accountant who may escape liability by proving s/he acted in "good faith"

        (a) Although basis of liability here is not negligence, an accountant who has been grossly negligent typically will not be able to establish "good faith"
        (b) An accountant who has been only negligent will probably be able to establish "good faith"

  e. Damages

    (1) Generally, difference between amount paid and market value at time of suit
    (2) If sold, difference between amount paid and sale price

5. Summary of auditors' defenses under Securities Act of 1933 and Securities Exchange Act of 1934*

• **Defenses** available to auditors:		
	1934 Act	*1933 Act*
1. Audit was performed with **due care**	Yes	Yes
2. Misstatement was immaterial	Yes	Yes
3. Plaintiff had prior knowledge of misstatement	Yes	Yes
4. Plaintiff did not rely on information	Yes	No
5. Misstatement was not cause of loss	Yes	Yes

    • Due diligence is a defense for the 1933 Act **only** (Do not use for 1934)

    * *Prepared by Debra R. Hopkins, Northern Illinois University*

C. Legal Considerations Affecting the Accountant's Responsibility

1. Accountant's working papers

  a. Consist of notes, computations, etc. that accountant accumulates when doing professional work for client
  b. Owned by accountant unless there is agreement to the contrary
  c. Ownership is essentially custodial in nature (to serve dual purpose)

    (1) To preserve confidentiality

        (a) Absent client consent, cannot allow transmission of information in working papers to another

           1] However, accountant must produce, upon being given an enforceable subpoena, workpapers requested by court of law or government agency

              a] Subpoenas should be limited in scope and specific in purpose b] Accountant may challenge a subpoena as being too broad and unreasonably burdensome

     (2) Retention by accountant as evidence of nature and extent of work performed for legal or other reasons

2. Privileged communications between accountant and client

    a. Do not exist at common law so must be created by statute

      (1) Only a few states have privileged communications
      (2) Federal law does not recognize privileged communications
      (3) If accountant acting as agent for (hired by) one who has privileged communication such as an attorney, then accountant's communications are privileged

    b. To be considered privileged, accountant-client communication must

      (1) Be located in a jurisdiction where recognized
      (2) Have been intended to be confidential at time of communication
      (3) Not be waived by client

    c. If considered privileged, valid grounds exist for accountant to refuse to testify in court concerning these matters

      (1) This privilege is, in general, for benefit of client
      (2) Can be waived by client
      (3) If part of privileged communication is allowed, all of privilege is lost

    d. Code of Professional Conduct prohibits disclosure of confidential client data unless

      (1) Client consents

        (a) Note that if client is a partnership, each partner is actually a client and therefore each must give consent

      (2) To comply with GAAS and GAAP
      (3) To comply with enforceable subpoena (e.g., courts where privilege not recognized)
      (4) Quality review under AICPA authorization
      (5) Responding to AICPA or state trial board

    e. US Supreme Court has held that tax accrual files are not protected by accountant-client privilege

3. Illegal acts by clients

    a. Situations in which there may be a duty to notify parties outside the client

      (1) Form 8-K disclosures (change of auditors)
      (2) Disclosure to successor auditor (AU315)
      (3) Disclosure in response to subpoena
      (4) Disclosure to funding agency for entities receiving governmental financial assistance

4. CPA certificates are issued under state (not federal) jurisdiction
5. Acts of employees

    a. Accountant is liable for acts of employees in the course of employment

      EXAMPLE: XYZ, a partnership of CPAs, hires Y to help perform an audit. Y is negligent in the audit, causing the client damage. The partners cannot escape liability by showing they did not perform the negligent act.

    b. Insurance typically used to cover such losses

6. Duty to perform audit is not delegable because it is contract for personal services
7. Generally, basis of relationship of accountant to his/her client is that of independent contractor
8. Insurance

    a. Accountants' malpractice insurance covers their negligence
    b. Fidelity bond protects client from accountant's fraud

    c. Client's insurance company is subrogated to client's rights (i.e., has same rights of recovery of loss against accountant that client had)

  9. Reliance by auditor on other auditor's work

    a. Principal auditor still liable for all work unless audit report clearly indicates divided responsibility

    b. Cannot rely on unaudited data; must disclaim or qualify opinion

  10. Subsequent events and subsequent discovery

    a. Generally not liable on audit report for effect of events subsequent to last day of fieldwork

      (1) Unless report is dated as of the subsequent event

      (2) Liability extends to effective date of registration for reports filed with SEC

    b. Liable if subsequently discovered facts that existed at report date indicate statements were misleading **unless**

      (1) Immediate investigation is conducted, and

      (2) Prompt revision of statements is possible, or

      (3) SEC and persons known to be relying on statements are notified by client or CPA

    c. Accountant liable if s/he makes assurances that there are no material changes after fieldwork or report date when in fact there are material changes

      (1) Therefore accountant should perform sufficient audit procedures before giving this assurance

  11. Liability from preparation of unaudited financial statements

    a. Financial statements are unaudited if

      (1) No auditing procedures have been applied

      (2) Insufficient audit procedures have been applied to express an opinion

    b. Failure to mark each page, "unaudited"

    c. Failure to issue a disclaimer of opinion

    d. Failure to inform client of any discovery of something amiss

      (1) For example, circumstances indicating presence of fraud

D. Criminal Liability

  1. Sources of liability

    a. Securities Act of 1933 and Securities Exchange Act of 1934

      (1) Can be found guilty for **willful** illegal conduct

        (a) Misleading omission of material facts

        (b) Putting false information in registration statement

      (2) Subject to fine of up to $10,000 and/or up to five years prison

      (3) Examples of possible criminal actions

        (a) CPA aids management in a fraudulent scheme

        (b) CPA covers up prior year financial statement misstatements

    b. Criminal violations of Internal Revenue Code

      (1) For willfully preparing false return (perjury)

      (2) For willfully assisting others to evade taxes (tax evasion)

    c. Criminal liability under RICO (Racketeer Influenced and Corrupt Organizations)

      (1) Covers individuals affiliated with businesses or associations involved in a pattern of racketeering

        (a) Racketeering includes organized crime but also includes fraud under the federal securities laws as well as mail fraud

1] Accountants subject to criminal penalty through affiliation with accounting firm or business involved in racketeering

(b) Pattern of racketeering means at least two illegal acts of racketeering in previous ten years

(2) RICO has also been expanded to allow civil suit by private parties

(a) Treble damages allowed (to encourage private enforcement)
(b) Has been held to apply against accountants even without a criminal indictment or conviction

E. Responsibilities of Auditors under Private Securities Litigation Reform Act

1. Auditors who audit financial statements under Federal Securities Exchange Act of 1934 are required to establish procedures to

   a. Detect material illegal acts
   b. Identify material related-party transactions, and
   c. Evaluate ability of firm to continue as going concern

2. If auditor detects possible illegal activity, must inform audit committee or board of directors

   a. If senior management or board fails to take remedial action and if illegal activities are material so that departure from standard audit report or auditor resignation is indicated, auditor shall report this to board of directors

      (1) Board has one day to notify SEC of this report

         (a) If not done, auditor must furnish SEC with copy of auditor's report to board and/or resign from audit

3. Civil liability may be imposed by SEC for auditor's failures under Act

   a. Auditors are protected from private civil suits for these reports to SEC under this Act

4. Amends Federal Securities Act of 1933 and Federal Securities Exchange Act of 1934

   a. Law passed to reduce lawsuits against accounting firms and issuers of securities

      (1) SEC's enforcement of securities laws not affected by act because law governs private litigation

5. Creates "safe harbor" from legal liability for preparation of forward-looking statements

   a. Including projections of income, revenues, EPS, and company plans for products and services
   b. To fall within safe harbor, written or oral forward-looking statement should include cautions and identify assumptions and conditions that may cause projections to vary
   c. Purpose is to encourage company to give investors more meaningful information without fear of lawsuits

6. Discourages class action lawsuits for frivolous purposes

   a. Accomplished by

      (1) Providing for stringent pleading requirements for many private actions under Securities Exchange Act of 1934
      (2) Awards costs and attorneys' fees against parties failing to fulfill these pleading requirements

7. Changes rules on joint and several liability, so that liability of defendants is generally proportionate to their degree of fault

   a. This relieves accountants (and others) from being "deep pockets" except up to their proportional fault
   b. Exception—joint and several liability is imposed if defendant **knowingly** caused harm

   EXAMPLE: Plaintiffs suffered $2 million in damages from securities fraud of a company. The auditors of the company are found to be 15% at fault. If the auditors did not act knowingly, they can be held liable for the 15% or $300,000. If they acted knowingly, they can be held liable for up to the full $2 million based on joint and several liability.

    c. Accountants liable for the proportionate share of damages they actually (and unknowingly) caused plus an additional 50% where principal defendant is insolvent

F. New Responsibilities and Provisions under Sarbanes-Oxley Act

1. This act is predicted to generate not only provisions summarized here but also new laws and regulations for at least the next few years—new information for this module and selected changes in other modules will be available when relevant for your preparation for CPA exam

    a. Sarbanes-Oxley Act, also known as Public Company Accounting Reform and Investor Protection Act, is receiving much attention in accounting profession, Congress, and business community at large

    b. This Act already has and will continue to have further important impacts

    c. Act is most extensive change to federal securities laws since 1930s—formulates new design for federal regulation of corporate governance of public companies and reporting obligations

    d. Act changes some accountability standards for auditors, legal counsel, securities analysts, officers and directors

2. New federal crimes involving willful nonretention of audit and review workpapers

    a. Retention required for five years (in some cases seven years)

    b. Destroying or falsifying records to impede investigations

    c. Provides for fines or imprisonment up to twenty years or both

    d. Applies to accountant who audits issuer of securities

        (1) Now also applies to others such as attorneys, consultants, and company employees

    e. Act requires SEC to issue new rules and then periodically update its rules on details of retaining workpapers and other relevant records connected with audits or reviews

3. Creates new Public Company Accounting Oversight Board

    a. Board is nonprofit corporation not federal agency.

        (1) Violation of rules of this Board treated as violation of Securities Exchange Act of 1934 with its penalties

    b. Consists of five members

        (1) Two members must be or have been CPAs

        (2) Three members cannot be or cannot have been CPAs

        (3) None of Board members may receive pay or profits from CPA firms

    c. Board regulates firms that audit SEC registrants, not accounting firms of private companies

    d. Main functions of Board are to

        (1) Register and conduct inspections of public accounting firms

            (a) This replaces peer reviews

        (2) Set standards on auditing, quality control, independence, or preparation of audit reports

            (a) May adopt standards of existing professional groups or new groups

            (b) Accounting firm must have second partner review and approve each audit report

            (c) Accounting firm must report on examination of internal control structure along with description of material weaknesses

        (3) May regulate nonaudit services CPA firms perform for clients

        (4) Enforce compliance with professional standards, securities laws relating to accountants and audits

        (5) Perform investigations and disciplinary proceedings on registered public accounting firms

        (6) May perform any other duties needed to promote high professional standards and to improve auditing quality

4. Material services must receive preapproval by audit committee, and fees for those services must be disclosed to investors
5. Act lists several specific service categories that issuer's public accounting firm cannot legally do, even if approved by audit committee, such as

    a. Bookkeeping or other services relating to financial statements or accounting records
    b. Financial information systems design and/or implementation
    c. Appraisal services
    d. Internal audit outsourcing services
    e. Management functions
    f. Actuarial services
    g. Investment or broker-dealer services
    h. Board permitted to exempt (on case by case basis) services of audit firm for audit client
    i. Note that Act does **not** restrict auditor from performing these services to nonaudit clients or to private companies
    j. Act intended to restrict specified categories performed for public audit clients
    k. Act permits auditor as a registered public accounting firm to perform nonaudit services not specifically prohibited (e.g., tax services) when approved by issuer's audit committee

6. Act requires that both assigned audit partner having primary responsibility for a certain audit and audit partner who reviews audit can do the audit services for that issuer for only five consecutive years

    a. If public company has hired employee of an audit firm to be its CEO, CFO, or CAO within previous year, that audit firm may not audit that public company

7. Act requires increased disclosure of off-balance-sheet transactions
8. Act mandates that pro forma financial disclosures be reconciled with figures done under GAAP
9. Act creates new federal laws against destruction or tampering with audit workpapers or documents that are to be used in official proceedings
10. Act increases protection of whistleblowers by better protections from retaliation because of participation in proceedings against securities fraud

    a. Also, provides that employees may report securities fraud directly to audit committee to provide information anonymously and confidentially

11. Public Companies may not make or modify personal loans to officers or directors with few exceptions
12. Annual reports filed with SEC that contain financial statements need to incorporate all material corrections noted by CPA firms
13. Each company must disclose on current basis information on financial condition that SEC determines is useful to public
14. SEC authorized to discipline professionals practicing before SEC

    a. SEC may censure, temporarily bar or permanently bar him/her for

        (1) Lack of qualifications needed
        (2) Improper professional conduct
        (3) Willful violation of helping another violate securities laws or regulations

15. Public Company Accounting Oversight Board set up to register CPAs providing auditing services to public entities
16. Auditor reports to audit committee
17. Auditors to retain workpapers for five years

    a. Failure to do so is punishable by prison term of up to ten years

18. Sarbanes-Oxley Act directed SEC to perform various tasks including several studies to formulate regulations; some of these studies have deadlines in the future and are expected to be used to promulgate new important regulations—others have been completed, resulted in regulations by SEC and have force of law including the following

    a. Require disclosure of differences between pro forma financial results and GAAP
    b. Require that "critical" accounting policies be reported from auditors to audit committee

   c. SEC will tell NYSE and NASDAQ to prohibit any public company from being listed whose audit committee does not meet specified requirements on auditor appointment, oversight, and compensation

      (1) Only independent directors can serve on audit committee

   d. Companies required to disclose if they have adopted a code of ethics
   e. Names of "financial experts" required who serve on companies' audit committees
   f. Actions prohibited that fraudulently manipulate or mislead auditors
   g. New conflict of interest rules for analysts
   h. SEC may petition courts to freeze payments by companies that are extraordinary

19. CEOs and CFOs of most large companies listed on public stock exchanges are now required to certify financial statements filed with SEC

   a. This generally means that they certify that information "fairly represents in all material respects the financial conditions and results of operations" of those companies and that

      (1) Signing officer reviewed report
      (2) Company's report does not contain any untrue statements of material facts or does not omit any statements of material facts to the best of his/her knowledge
      (3) Officers have internal control system in place to allow honest certification of financial statements

         (a) Or if any deficiencies in internal control exist, they must be disclosed to auditors

20. Blackout periods established for issuers of certain security transaction types that limit companies' purchase, sale, or transfer of funds in individual accounts
21. Stiffer penalties for other white-collar crimes including federal law covering mail fraud and wire fraud

G. Additional statutory liability against accountants

  1. Auditors are required to use adequate procedures to uncover illegal activity of client
  2. Civil liability is proportional to degree of responsibility

   a. One type of responsibility is through auditors' own carelessness
   b. Another type of responsibility is based on auditor's assisting in improper activities that s/he is aware or should be aware of

MULTIPLE-CHOICE QUESTIONS (1-67)

1. Which of the following best describes what is meant by the term generally accepted auditing standards?
- a. Rules acknowledged by the accounting profession because of their universal application.
- b. Pronouncements issued by the Auditing Standards Board.
- c. Measures of the quality of the auditor's performance.
- d. Procedures to be used to gather evidence to support financial statements.

2. For which of the following can a member of the AICPA receive an automatic expulsion from the AICPA?

I. Member is convicted of a felony.
II. Member files his own fraudulent tax return.
III. Member files fraudulent tax return for a client knowing that it is fraudulent.

- a. I only.
- b. I and II only.
- c. I and III only.
- d. I, II, and III.

3. According to the standards of the profession, which of the following circumstances will prevent a CPA performing audit engagements from being independent?
- a. Obtaining a collateralized automobile loan from a financial institution client.
- b. Litigation with a client relating to billing for consulting services for which the amount is immaterial.
- c. Employment of the CPA's spouse as a client's director of internal audit.
- d. Acting as an honorary trustee for a not-for-profit organization client.

4. The profession's ethical standards most likely would be considered to have been violated when a CPA represents that specific consulting services will be performed for a stated fee and it is apparent at the time of the representation that the
- a. Actual fee would be substantially higher.
- b. Actual fee would be substantially lower than the fees charged by other CPAs for comparable services.
- c. CPA would **not** be independent.
- d. Fee was a competitive bid.

5. According to the ethical standards of the profession, which of the following acts is generally prohibited?
- a. Issuing a modified report explaining a failure to follow a governmental regulatory agency's standards when conducting an attest service for a client.
- b. Revealing confidential client information during a quality review of a professional practice by a team from the state CPA society.
- c. Accepting a contingent fee for representing a client in an examination of the client's federal tax return by an IRS agent.
- d. Retaining client records after an engagement is terminated prior to completion and the client has demanded their return.

6. According to the profession's ethical standards, which of the following events may justify a departure from a Statement of Financial Accounting Standards?

	New legislation	Evolution of a new form of business transaction
a.	No	Yes
b.	Yes	No
c.	Yes	Yes
d.	No	No

7. May a CPA hire for the CPA's public accounting firm a non-CPA systems analyst who specializes in developing computer systems?
- a. Yes, provided the CPA is qualified to perform each of the specialist's tasks.
- b. Yes, provided the CPA is able to supervise the specialist and evaluate the specialist's end product.
- c. No, because non-CPA professionals are **not** permitted to be associated with CPA firms in public practice.
- d. No, because developing computer systems is **not** recognized as a service performed by public accountants.

8. Stephanie Seals is a CPA who is working as a controller for Brentwood Corporation. She is not in public practice. Which statement is true?
- a. She may use the CPA designation on her business cards if she also puts her employment title on them.
- b. She may use the CPA designation on her business cards as long as she does not mention Brentwood Corporation or her title as controller.
- c. She may use the CPA designation on company transmittals but not on her business cards.
- d. She may not use the CPA designation because she is not in public practice.

9. According to the standards of the profession, which of the following activities would most likely **not** impair a CPA's independence?
- a. Providing advisory services for a client.
- b. Contracting with a client to supervise the client's office personnel.
- c. Signing a client's checks in emergency situations.
- d. Accepting a luxurious gift from a client.

10. Which of the following reports may be issued only by an accountant who is independent of a client?
- a. Standard report on an examination of a financial forecast.
- b. Report on consulting services.
- c. Compilation report on historical financial statements.
- d. Compilation report on a financial projection.

11. According to the standards of the profession, which of the following activities may be required in exercising due care?

	Consulting with experts	Obtaining specialty accreditation
a.	Yes	Yes
b.	Yes	No
c.	No	Yes
d.	No	No

12. Larry Sampson is a CPA and is serving as an expert witness in a trial concerning a corporation's financial statements. Which of the following is(are) true?

I. Sampson's status as an expert witness is based upon his specialized knowledge, experience, and training.
II. Sampson is required by AICPA ruling to present his position objectively.
III. Sampson may regard himself as acting as an advocate.

    a. I only.
    b. I and II only.
    c. I and III only.
    d. III only.

13. According to the ethical standards of the profession, which of the following acts is generally prohibited?
    a. Purchasing a product from a third party and reselling it to a client.
    b. Writing a financial management newsletter promoted and sold by a publishing company.
    c. Accepting a commission for recommending a product to an audit client.
    d. Accepting engagements obtained through the efforts of third parties.

14. To exercise due professional care an auditor should
    a. Critically review the judgment exercised by those assisting in the audit.
    b. Examine all available corroborating evidence supporting managements assertions.
    c. Design the audit to detect all instances of illegal acts.
    d. Attain the proper balance of professional experience and formal education.

15. Kar, CPA, is a staff auditor participating in the audit engagement of Fort, Inc. Which of the following circumstances impairs Kar's independence?
    a. During the period of the professional engagement, Fort gives Kar tickets to a football game worth $75.
    b. Kar owns stock in a corporation that Fort's 401(k) plan also invests in.
    c. Kar's friend, an employee of another local accounting firm, prepares Fort's tax returns.
    d. Kar's sibling is director of internal audit at Fort.

16. On June 1, 2000, a CPA obtained a $100,000 personal loan from a financial institution client for whom the CPA provided compilation services. The loan was fully secured and considered material to the CPA's net worth. The CPA paid the loan in full on December 31, 2001. On April 3, 2001, the client asked the CPA to audit the client's financial statements for the year ended December 31, 2001. Is the CPA considered independent with respect to the audit of the client's December 31, 2001 financial statements?
    a. Yes, because the loan was fully secured.
    b. Yes, because the CPA was **not** required to be independent at the time the loan was granted.
    c. No, because the CPA had a loan with the client during the period of a professional engagement.
    d. No, because the CPA had a loan with the client during the period covered by the financial statements.

17. Which of the following statements is(are) correct regarding a CPA employee of a CPA firm taking copies of information contained in client files when the CPA leaves the firm?

I. A CPA leaving a firm may take copies of information contained in client files to assist another firm in serving that client.
II. A CPA leaving a firm may take copies of information contained in client files as a method of gaining technical expertise.

    a. I only.
    b. II only.
    c. Both I and II.
    d. Neither I nor II.

18. Which of the following statements is correct regarding an accountant's working papers?
    a. The accountant owns the working papers and generally may disclose them as the accountant sees fit.
    b. The client owns the working papers but the accountant has custody of them until the accountant's bill is paid in full.
    c. The accountant owns the working papers but generally may **not** disclose them without the client's consent or a court order.
    d. The client owns the working papers but, in the absence of the accountant's consent, may **not** disclose them without a court order.

19. According to the profession's standards, which of the following would be considered consulting services?

	Advisory services	Implementation services	Product services
a.	Yes	Yes	Yes
b.	Yes	Yes	No
c.	Yes	No	Yes
d.	No	Yes	Yes

20. According to the standards of the profession, which of the following events would require a CPA performing a consulting services engagement for a nonaudit client to withdraw from the engagement?

I. The CPA has a conflict of interest that is disclosed to the client and the client consents to the CPA continuing the engagement.
II. The CPA fails to obtain a written understanding from the client concerning the scope of the engagement.

    a. I only.
    b. II only.
    c. Both I and II.
    d. Neither I nor II.

21. Which of the following services may a CPA perform in carrying out a consulting service for a client?

I. Analysis of the client's accounting system.
II. Review of the client's prepared business plan.
III. Preparation of information for obtaining financing.

    a. I and II only.
    b. I and III only.
    c. II and III only.
    d. I, II, and III.

22. Under the Statements on Standards for Consulting Services, which of the following statements best reflects a CPA's responsibility when undertaking a consulting services engagement? The CPA must

    a. Not seek to modify any agreement made with the client.

    b. Not perform any attest services for the client.

    c. Inform the client of significant reservations concerning the benefits of the engagement.

    d. Obtain a written understanding with the client concerning the time for completion of the engagement.

23. Which of the following services is a CPA generally required to perform when conducting a personal financial planning engagement?

    a. Assisting the client to identify tasks that are essential in order to act on planning decisions.

    b. Assisting the client to take action on planning decisions.

    c. Monitoring progress in achieving goals.

    d. Updating recommendations and revising planning decisions.

24. Which of the following is correct concerning internal auditing?

    a. The internal auditor often coordinates his/her work with that of the company's external auditors.

    b. The internal auditor must maintain independence in the sense of doing the audit completely independently from the external auditors.

    c. The internal auditor has no responsibility to maintain independence.

    d. The work of the internal auditors, if they are CPAs, substitutes for the work of external auditors.

25. Which of the following is(are) true concerning independent auditors involved in governmental accounting?

    I. They must meet requirements for continuing education that include some governmental auditing.

    II. Members of the AICPA violate the AICPA Code of Professional Conduct if they fail to follow generally accepted government auditing standards.

    a. I only.

    b. II only.

    c. Both I and II.

    d. Neither I nor II.

26. Which of the following is correct regarding the Single Audit Act?

    I. The Act mandates that local and state governments receiving $300,000 or more in federal funds in a fiscal year are to be audited under this Act.

    II. The purpose of this Act is to reduce duplication in organization-wide governmental audits.

    III. For government entities covered under this Act, only one audit every five years is required.

    a. I only.

    b. II only.

    c. I and II only.

    d. II and III only.

27. Cable Corp. orally engaged Drake & Co., CPAs, to audit its financial statements. Cable's management informed Drake that it suspected the accounts receivable were materially overstated. Though the financial statements Drake audited included a materially overstated accounts receivable balance, Drake issued an unqualified opinion. Cable used the financial statements to obtain a loan to expand its operations. Cable defaulted on the loan and incurred a substantial loss.

If Cable sues Drake for negligence in failing to discover the overstatement, Drake's best defense would be that Drake did **not**

    a. Have privity of contract with Cable.

    b. Sign an engagement letter.

    c. Perform the audit recklessly or with an intent to deceive.

    d. Violate generally accepted auditing standards in performing the audit.

28. Which of the following statements best describes whether a CPA has met the required standard of care in conducting an audit of a client's financial statements?

    a. The client's expectations with regard to the accuracy of audited financial statements.

    b. The accuracy of the financial statements and whether the statements conform to generally accepted accounting principles.

    c. Whether the CPA conducted the audit with the same skill and care expected of an ordinarily prudent CPA under the circumstances.

    d. Whether the audit was conducted to investigate and discover all acts of fraud.

29. Ford & Co., CPAs, issued an unqualified opinion on Owens Corp.'s financial statements. Relying on these financial statements, Century Bank lent Owens $750,000. Ford was unaware that Century would receive a copy of the financial statements or that Owens would use them to obtain a loan. Owens defaulted on the loan.

To succeed in a common law fraud action against Ford, Century must prove, in addition to other elements, that Century was

    a. Free from contributory negligence.

    b. In privity of contract with Ford.

    c. Justified in relying on the financial statements.

    d. In privity of contract with Owens.

30. When performing an audit, a CPA

    a. Must exercise the level of care, skill, and judgment expected of a reasonably prudent CPA under the circumstances.

    b. Must strictly adhere to generally accepted accounting principles.

    c. Is strictly liable for failing to discover client fraud.

    d. Is **not** liable unless the CPA commits gross negligence or intentionally disregards generally accepted auditing standards.

31. When performing an audit, a CPA will most likely be considered negligent when the CPA fails to

    a. Detect all of a client's fraudulent activities.

    b. Include a negligence disclaimer in the client engagement letter.

    c. Warn a client of known internal control weaknesses.

    d. Warn a client's customers of embezzlement by the client's employees.

32. A CPA's duty of due care to a client most likely will be breached when a CPA
   a. Gives a client an oral instead of written report.
   b. Gives a client incorrect advice based on an honest error of judgment.
   c. Fails to give tax advice that saves the client money.
   d. Fails to follow generally accepted auditing standards.

33. Which of the following elements, if present, would support a finding of constructive fraud on the part of a CPA?
   a. Gross negligence in applying generally accepted auditing standards.
   b. Ordinary negligence in applying generally accepted accounting principles.
   c. Identified third-party users.
   d. Scienter.

34. If a CPA recklessly departs from the standards of due care when conducting an audit, the CPA will be liable to third parties who are unknown to the CPA based on
   a. Negligence.
   b. Gross negligence.
   c. Strict liability.
   d. Criminal deceit.

35. In a common law action against an accountant, lack of privity is a viable defense if the plaintiff
   a. Is the client's creditor who sues the accountant for negligence.
   b. Can prove the presence of gross negligence that amounts to a reckless disregard for the truth.
   c. Is the accountant's client.
   d. Bases the action upon fraud.

36. A CPA audited the financial statements of Shelly Company. The CPA was negligent in the audit. Sanco, a supplier of Shelly, is upset because Sanco had extended Shelly a high credit limit based on the financial statements which were incorrect. Which of the following statements is the most correct?
   a. In most states, both Shelly and Sanco can recover from the CPA for damages due to the negligence.
   b. States that use the Ultramares decision will allow both Shelly and Sanco to recover.
   c. In most states, Sanco cannot recover as a mere foreseeable third party.
   d. Generally, Sanco can recover but Shelly cannot.

37. Under the Ultramares rule, to which of the following parties will an accountant be liable for negligence?

	Parties in privity	Foreseen parties
a.	Yes	Yes
b.	Yes	No
c.	No	Yes
d.	No	No

Items 38 and 39 are based on the following:

   While conducting an audit, Larson Associates, CPAs, failed to detect material misstatements included in its client's financial statements. Larson's unqualified opinion was included with the financial statements in a registration statement and prospectus for a public offering of securities made by the client. Larson knew that its opinion and the financial statements would be used for this purpose.

38. In a suit by a purchaser against Larson for common law negligence, Larson's best defense would be that the
   a. Audit was conducted in accordance with generally accepted auditing standards.
   b. Client was aware of the misstatements.
   c. Purchaser was **not** in privity of contract with Larson.
   d. Identity of the purchaser was **not** known to Larson at the time of the audit.

39. In a suit by a purchaser against Larson for common law fraud, Larson's best defense would be that
   a. Larson did **not** have actual or constructive knowledge of the misstatements.
   b. Larson's client knew or should have known of the misstatements.
   c. Larson did **not** have actual knowledge that the purchaser was an intended beneficiary of the audit.
   d. Larson was **not** in privity of contract with its client.

40. Quincy bought Teal Corp. common stock in an offering registered under the Securities Act of 1933. Worth & Co., CPAs, gave an unqualified opinion on Teal's financial statements that were included in the registration statement filed with the SEC. Quincy sued Worth under the provisions of the 1933 Act that deal with omission of facts required to be in the registration statement. Quincy must prove that
   a. There was fraudulent activity by Worth.
   b. There was a material misstatement in the financial statements.
   c. Quincy relied on Worth's opinion.
   d. Quincy was in privity with Worth.

41. Beckler & Associates, CPAs, audited and gave an unqualified opinion on the financial statements of Queen Co. The financial statements contained misstatements that resulted in a material overstatement of Queen's net worth. Queen provided the audited financial statements to Mac Bank in connection with a loan made by Mac to Queen. Beckler knew that the financial statements would be provided to Mac. Queen defaulted on the loan. Mac sued Beckler to recover for its losses associated with Queen's default. Which of the following must Mac prove in order to recover?

   I. Beckler was negligent in conducting the audit.
   II. Mac relied on the financial statements.

   a. I only.
   b. II only.
   c. Both I and II.
   d. Neither I nor II.

Items 42 and 43 are based on the following:

   Dart Corp. engaged Jay Associates, CPAs, to assist in a public stock offering. Jay audited Dart's financial statements and gave an unqualified opinion, despite knowing that the financial statements contained misstatements. Jay's opinion was included in Dart's registration statement. Larson purchased shares in the offering and suffered a loss when the stock declined in value after the misstatements became known.

42. In a suit against Jay and Dart under the Section 11 liability provisions of the Securities Act of 1933, Larson must prove that

a. Jay knew of the misstatements.
b. Jay was negligent.
c. The misstatements contained in Dart's financial statements were material.
d. The unqualified opinion contained in the registration statement was relied on by Larson.

43. If Larson succeeds in the Section 11 suit against Dart, Larson would be entitled to
a. Damages of three times the original public offering price.
b. Rescind the transaction.
c. Monetary damages only.
d. Damages, but only if the shares were resold before the suit was started.

Items 44 and 45 are based on the following:

Under the liability provisions of Section 11 of the Securities Act of 1933, a CPA may be liable to any purchaser of a security for certifying materially misstated financial statements that are included in the security's registration statement.

44. Under Section 11, a CPA usually will **not** be liable to the purchaser
a. If the purchaser is contributorily negligent.
b. If the CPA can prove due diligence.
c. Unless the purchaser can prove privity with the CPA.
d. Unless the purchaser can prove scienter on the part of the CPA.

45. Under Section 11, which of the following must be proven by a purchaser of the security?

	Reliance on the financial statements	Fraud by the CPA
a.	Yes	Yes
b.	Yes	No
c.	No	Yes
d.	No	No

46. Ocean and Associates, CPAs, audited the financial statements of Drain Corporation. As a result of Ocean's negligence in conducting the audit, the financial statements included material misstatements. Ocean was unaware of this fact. The financial statements and Ocean's unqualified opinion were included in a registration statement and prospectus for an original public offering of stock by Drain. Sharp purchased shares in the offering. Sharp received a copy of the prospectus prior to the purchase but did not read it. The shares declined in value as a result of the misstatements in Drain's financial statements becoming known. Under which of the following Acts is Sharp most likely to prevail in a lawsuit against Ocean?

	Securities Exchange Act of 1934, Section 10(b), Rule 10b-5	Securities Act of 1933, Section 11
a.	Yes	Yes
b.	Yes	No
c.	No	Yes
d.	No	No

47. Danvy, a CPA, performed an audit for Lank Corporation. Danvy also performed an S-1 review to review events subsequent to the balance sheet date. If Danvy fails to further investigate suspicious facts, under which of these can he be found negligent?
a. The audit but not the review.
b. The review but not the audit.
c. Neither the audit nor the review.
d. Both the audit and the review.

48. Dart Corp. engaged Jay Associates, CPAs, to assist in a public stock offering. Jay audited Dart's financial statements and gave an unqualified opinion, despite knowing that the financial statements contained misstatements. Jay's opinion was included in Dart's registration statement. Larson purchased shares in the offering and suffered a loss when the stock declined in value after the misstatements became known.

In a suit against Jay under the antifraud provisions of Section 10(b) and Rule 10b-5 of the Securities Exchange Act of 1934, Larson must prove all of the following **except**
a. Larson was an intended user of the false registration statement.
b. Larson relied on the false registration statement.
c. The transaction involved some form of interstate commerce.
d. Jay acted with intentional disregard of the truth.

49. Under the antifraud provisions of Section 10(b) of the Securities Exchange Act of 1934, a CPA may be liable if the CPA acted
a. Negligently.
b. With independence.
c. Without due diligence.
d. Without good faith.

50. Under Section 11 of the Securities Act of 1933, which of the following standards may a CPA use as a defense?

	Generally accepted accounting principles	Generally accepted fraud detection standards
a.	Yes	Yes
b.	Yes	No
c.	No	Yes
d.	No	No

51. Dart Corp. engaged Jay Associates, CPAs, to assist in a public stock offering. Jay audited Dart's financial statements and gave an unqualified opinion, despite knowing that the financial statements contained misstatements. Jay's opinion was included in Dart's registration statement. Larson purchased shares in the offering and suffered a loss when the stock declined in value after the misstatements became known.

If Larson succeeds in the Section 10(b) and Rule 10b-5 suit, Larson would be entitled to
a. Only recover the original public offering price.
b. Only rescind the transaction.
c. The amount of any loss caused by the fraud.
d. Punitive damages.

52. Which of the following statements is correct with respect to ownership, possession, or access to a CPA firm's audit working papers?
a. Working papers may **never** be obtained by third parties unless the client consents.
b. Working papers are **not** transferable to a purchaser of a CPA practice unless the client consents.

c. Working papers are subject to the privileged communication rule which, in most jurisdictions, prevents any third-party access to the working papers.

d. Working papers are the client's exclusive property.

53. Which of the following statements is correct regarding a CPA's working papers? The working papers must be

a. Transferred to another accountant purchasing the CPA's practice even if the client hasn't given permission.

b. Transferred permanently to the client if demanded.

c. Turned over to any government agency that requests them.

d. Turned over pursuant to a valid federal court subpoena.

54. To which of the following parties may a CPA partnership provide its working papers, without being lawfully subpoenaed or without the client's consent?

a. The IRS.

b. The FASB.

c. Any surviving partner(s) on the death of a partner.

d. A CPA before purchasing a partnership interest in the firm.

55. To which of the following parties may a CPA partnership orvide its working papers without either the client's consent or a lawful subpoena?

	The IRS	The FASB
a.	Yes	Yes
b.	Yes	No
c.	No	Yes
d.	No	No

56. A CPA is permitted to disclose confidential client information without the consent of the client to

I. Another CPA who has purchased the CPA's tax practice.

II. Another CPA firm if the information concerns suspected tax return irregularities.

III. A state CPA society voluntary quality control review board.

a. I and III only.

b. II and III only.

c. II only.

d. III only.

57. Thorp, CPA, was engaged to audit Ivor Co.'s financial statements. During the audit, Thorp discovered that Ivor's inventory contained stolen goods. Ivor was indicted and Thorp was subpoenaed to testify at the criminal trial. Ivor claimed accountant-client privilege to prevent Thorp from testifying. Which of the following statements is correct regarding Ivor's claim?

a. Ivor can claim an accountant-client privilege only in states that have enacted a statute creating such a privilege.

b. Ivor can claim an accountant-client privilege only in federal courts.

c. The accountant-client privilege can be claimed only in civil suits.

d. The accountant-client privilege can be claimed only to limit testimony to audit subject matter.

58. A violation of the profession's ethical standards most likely would have occurred when a CPA

a. Issued an unqualified opinion on the 2002 financial statements when fees for the 2001 audit were unpaid.

b. Recommended a controller's position description with candidate specifications to an audit client.

c. Purchased a CPA firm's practice of monthly write-ups for a percentage of fees to be received over a three-year period.

d. Made arrangements with a financial institution to collect notes issued by a client in payment of fees due for the current year's audit.

59. Which of the following statements concerning an accountant's disclosure of confidential client data is generally correct?

a. Disclosure may be made to any state agency without subpoena.

b. Disclosure may be made to any party on consent of the client.

c. Disclosure may be made to comply with an IRS audit request.

d. Disclosure may be made to comply with generally accepted accounting principles.

60. McGee is auditing Nevus Corporation and detects probable criminal activity by one of the employees. McGee believes this will have a material impact on the financial statements. The financial statements of Nevus Corporation are under the Securities Exchange Act of 1934. Which of the following is correct?

a. McGee should report this to the Securities Exchange Commission.

b. McGee should report this to the Justice Department.

c. McGee should report this to Nevus Corporation's audit committee or board of directors.

d. McGee will discharge his duty by requiring that a note of this be included in the financial statements.

61. Which of the following is an auditor not required to establish procedures for under the Private Securities Litigation Reform Act?

a. To develop a comprehensive internal control system.

b. To evaluate the ability of the firm to continue as a going concern.

c. To detect material illegal acts.

d. To identify material related-party transactions.

62. Which of the following is an auditor required to do under the Private Securities Litigation Reform Act concerning audits under the Federal Securities Exchange Act of 1934?

I. Establish procedures to detect material illegal acts of the client being audited.

II. Evaluate the ability of the firm being audited to continue as a going concern.

a. Neither I nor II.

b. I only.

c. II only.

d. Both I and II.

63. Lin, CPA, is auditing the financial statements of Exchange Corporation under the Federal Securities Exchange Act of 1934. He detects what he believes are probable material illegal acts. What is his duty under the Private Securities Litigation Reform Act?

     a.   He must inform the principal shareholders within ten days.

     b.   He must inform the audit committee or the board of directors.

     c.   He need not inform anyone, beyond requiring that the financial statements are presented fairly.

     d.   He should not inform anyone since he owes a duty of confidentiality to the client.

64. The Private Securities Litigation Reform Act

     a.   Applies only to securities not purchased from a stock exchange.

     b.   Does not apply to common stock of a publicly held corporation.

     c.   Amends the Federal Securities Act of 1933 and the Federal Securities Exchange Act of 1934.

     d.   Does not apply to preferred stock of a publicly held corporation.

65. Bran, CPA, audited Frank Corporation. The shareholders sued both Frank and Bran for securities fraud under the Federal Securities Exchange Act of 1934. The court determined that there was securities fraud and that Frank was 80% at fault and Bran was 20% at fault due to her negligence in the audit. Both Frank and Bran are solvent and the damages were determined to be $1 million. What is the maximum liability of Bran?

     a. $0

     b. $ 200,000

     c. $ 500,000

     d. $1,000,000

66. Which of the following nonattest services are auditors allowed to perform for a public company?

     a.   Bookkeeping services.

     b.   Appraisal services.

     c.   Tax services.

     d.   Internal audit services.

67. Which of the following Boards has the responsibility to regulate CPA firms that audit public companies?

     a.   Auditing Standards Board.

     b.   Public Oversight Board.

     c.   Public Company Accounting Oversight Board.

     d.   Accounting Standards Board.

PROBLEMS

NOTE: These types of problems are no longer included in the CPA Examination but they have been retained because they are useful in developing skills to complete simulations.

Problem 1   (15 to 20 minutes)

Dill Corp. was one of three major suppliers who sold raw materials to Fogg & Co. on credit. Dill became concerned over Fogg's ability to pay its debts. Payments had been consistently late and some checks had been returned, marked "insufficient funds." In addition, there were rumors concerning Fogg's solvency. Dill decided it would make no further sales to Fogg on credit unless it received a copy of Fogg's current, audited financial statements. It also required Fogg to assign its accounts receivable to Dill to provide security for the sales to Fogg on credit.

Clark & Wall, CPAs, was engaged by Fogg to perform an examination of Fogg's financial statements upon which they subsequently issued an unqualified opinion. Several months later, Fogg defaulted on its obligations to Dill. At this point Dill was owed $240,000 by Fogg. Subsequently, Dill discovered that only $60,000 of the accounts receivable that Fogg had assigned to Dill as collateral was collectible.

Dill has commenced a lawsuit against Clark & Wall. The complaint alleges that Dill has incurred a $180,000 loss as a result of negligent or fraudulent misrepresentations contained in the audited financial statements of Fogg. Specifically, it alleges negligence, gross negligence, and actual and/or constructive fraud on the part of Clark & Wall in the conduct of the audit and the issuance of an unqualified opinion.

State law applicable to this action follows the majority rule with respect to the accountant's liability to third parties for negligence. In addition, there is no applicable state statute which creates an accountant-client privilege. Dill demanded to be provided a copy of the Fogg workpapers from Clark & Wall who refused to comply with the request claiming that they are privileged documents. Clark & Wall has asserted that the entire action should be dismissed because Dill has no standing to sue the firm because of the absence of any contractual relationship with it (i.e., a lack of privity).

Required:

Answer the following, setting forth reasons for any conclusions stated.

a. Will Clark & Wall be able to avoid production of the Fogg workpapers based upon the assertion that they represent privileged communications?

b. What elements must be established by Dill to show negligence on the part of Clark & Wall?

c. What is the significance of compliance with GAAS in determining whether the audit was performed negligently?

d. What elements must be established by Dill to show actual or constructive fraud on the part of Clark & Wall?

Problem 2   (15 to 20 minutes)

Birk Corp. is interested in acquiring Apple & Co. Birk engaged Kaye & Co., CPAs, to audit the 2003 financial statements of Apple. Both Birk and Apple are engaged in the business of providing management consulting services.

While reviewing certain contracts entered into by Apple, Kaye became concerned with the proper reporting of the following matters:

• On December 5, 2003, Apple entered into an oral agreement with Cream Inc., to perform certain management advisory services for Cream for a fee of $150,000 per month. The services were to have commenced on February 15, 2004, and to have ended on December 20, 2004. Apple reported all of the revenues related to the contract on its 2003 financial statements. This constituted 30% of Apple's income for 2003.

• On February 8, 2003, Apple purchased the assets of Nestar & Co., a small management consulting firm. Apple and Nestar entered into a written agreement with regard to the transaction that required Apple to pay Nestar $80,000 a year for five years. The agreement required Nestar to transfer all of its assets and goodwill to Apple. Further, the agreement required Nestar not to compete with Apple or Apple's successors for a period of three years within the city where the majority of Nestar's clients were located. Nestar's office was also located in this city. Other Nestar clients were located throughout the state.

On February 1, 2004, Birk acquired all of Apple's outstanding stock. Birk's decision was based on the unqualified opinion issued by Kaye on Apple's 2003 financial statements. Within ten days after the merger, Cream decided not to honor the agreement with Apple and gave notice that it had selected another management consulting firm. This caused the market value of the Apple stock acquired by Birk to decrease drastically.

On May 2, 2003, Birk learned that Nestar opened a management consulting firm three blocks from where Nestar's office had been located on February 8, 2003.

Based on the foregoing, Birk has commenced an action against Kaye alleging negligence in performing the audit of Apple's financial statements.

Required:

Answer the following, setting forth reasons for any conclusions stated.

a. Discuss whether the December 5, 2003 agreement between Cream and Apple is enforceable.

b. Discuss whether the agreement of Nestar not to compete with Apple is enforceable against Nestar.

c. Discuss whether Birk will prevail in its action against Kaye & Co., CPAs.

SIMULATION PROBLEMS

Simulation Problem 1   (10 to 15 minutes)

Situation	
	Analysis

Under Section 11 of the Securities Act of 1933 and Section 10(b), Rule 10b-5, of the Securities Exchange Act of 1934, a CPA may be sued by a purchaser of registered securities.

	Analysis
Situation	

Items 1 through 6 relate to what a plaintiff who purchased securities must prove in a civil liability suit against a CPA. For each item determine whether the statement must be proven under Section 11 of the Securities Act of 1933, under Section 10(b), Rule 10b-5, of the Securities Exchange Act of 1934, both Acts, or neither Act.

	Only *Section 11* **(A)**	*Only* *Section 10(b)* **(B)**	*Both* **(C)**	*Neither* **(D)**
The plaintiff security purchaser must allege or prove				
1. Material misstatements were included in a filed document.	O	O	O	O
2. A monetary loss occurred.	O	O	O	O
3. Lack of due diligence by the CPA.	O	O	O	O
4. Privity with the CPA.	O	O	O	O
5. Reliance on the document.	O	O	O	O
6. The CPA had scienter.	O	O	O	O

Simulation Problem 2   (10 to 15 minutes)

Assume that you are analyzing relationships for your firm to identify independence problems.

Determine for each of the following numbered situations whether or not the auditor (a covered member of the firm) is considered to be independent. If the auditor's independence would **not** be impaired select No.   If the auditor's independence would be impaired select Yes.

		Yes	*No*
1.	The auditor is a cosigner of a client's checks.	○	○
2.	The auditor is a member of a country club which is a client.	○	○
3.	The auditor owns a large block of stock in a client but has placed it in a blind trust.	○	○
4.	The auditor placed her checking account in a bank which is her client. The account is fully insured by a federal agency.	○	○
5.	The client has not paid the auditor for services for the past two years.	○	○
6.	The auditor is leasing part of his building to a client.	○	○
7.	The auditor joins, as an ordinary member, a trade association which is also a client.	○	○
8.	The auditor has an immaterial, indirect financial interest in the client.	○	○

MULTIPLE-CHOICE ANSWERS*

1. c __ __	15. d __ __	29. c __ __	43. c __ __	57. a __ __
2. d __ __	16. b __ __	30. a __ __	44. b __ __	58. a __ __
3. c __ __	17. d __ __	31. c __ __	45. d __ __	59. b __ __
4. a __ __	18. c __ __	32. d __ __	46. c __ __	60. c __ __
5. d __ __	19. a __ __	33. a __ __	47. d __ __	61. a __ __
6. c __ __	20. d __ __	34. b __ __	48. a __ __	62. d __ __
7. b __ __	21. d __ __	35. a __ __	49. d __ __	63. b __ __
8. a __ __	22. c __ __	36. c __ __	50. b __ __	64. c __ __
9. a __ __	23. a __ __	37. b __ __	51. c __ __	65. b __ __
10. a __ __	24. a __ __	38. a __ __	52. b __ __	66. c __ __
11. b __ __	25. c __ __	39. a __ __	53. d __ __	67. c __ __
12. b __ __	26. c __ __	40. b __ __	54. c __ __	
13. c __ __	27. d __ __	41. c __ __	55. d __ __	1st: __/67 = __%
14. a __ __	28. c __ __	42. c __ __	56. d __ __	2nd: __/67 = __%

MULTIPLE-CHOICE ANSWER EXPLANATIONS

A.2. Code of Professional Conduct—Principles

1. (**c**) The requirement is to identify the statement that best describes the meaning of generally accepted auditing standards. Answer (c) is correct because generally accepted auditing standards deal with measures of the quality of the performance of audit procedures (AU 150). Answer (d) is incorrect because procedures relate to acts to be performed, not directly to the standards. Answer (b) is incorrect because generally accepted auditing standards have been issued by predecessor groups, as well as by the Auditing Standards Board. Answer (a) is incorrect because there may or may not be **universal** compliance with the standards.

2. (**d**) All of these can result in the automatic expulsion of the member from the AICPA. Answer (a) is incorrect because although the conviction of a felony can result in automatic expulsion, likewise can the other two. Answers (b) and (c) are incorrect because all three can result in automatic expulsion from the AICPA.

A.3. Code of Professional Conduct—Rules, Interpretations, and Rulings

3. (**c**) According to the Code of Professional Conduct, Rule 101 regarding independence, a spouse may be employed by a client if s/he does not exert significant influence over the contents of the client's financial statements. This is a key position as defined by the Interpretation of Rule 101.

4. (**a**) According to Rule 102 of the Code of Professional Conduct, in performing any professional service, a member shall maintain objectivity and integrity, avoid conflicts of interest, and not knowingly misrepresent facts. Answer (a) is correct as this would be knowingly misrepresenting the facts. Answers (b) and (d) are incorrect as these are not intentional misstatements. Answer (c) is incorrect because while one must remain objective while performing consulting services, independence is not required unless the CPA also performs attest services for that client.

5. (**d**) The requirement is to determine which act is generally prohibited. Answer (d) is correct because "If an engagement is terminated prior to completion, the member is required to return only client records" (ET 501). Answer (a) is incorrect because issuing a modified report explaining a

failure to follow a governmental regulatory agency's standards when conducting an attest service is not prohibited. Answer (c) is incorrect because accepting a contingent fee is allowable when representing a client in an examination by a revenue agent of the client's federal or state income tax return (ET 302). Answer (b) is incorrect because revealing confidential client information during a quality review of a professional practice by a team from the state CPA society is not prohibited (ET 301).

6. (**c**) According to Rule 203 of the Code of Professional Conduct, CPAs are allowed to depart from a Statement of Financial Accounting Standards only when results of the Statement of Financial Accounting Standards would be misleading. Examples of possible circumstances justifying departure are new legislation and a new form of business transaction.

7. (**b**) The requirement is to determine whether a CPA may hire a non-CPA systems analyst and, if so, under what conditions. Answer (b) is correct because ET 291 allows such a situation when the CPA is qualified to supervise and evaluate the work of the specialist. Answer (a) is incorrect because the CPA need not be qualified to perform the specialist's tasks. Answer (c) is incorrect because non-CPA professionals are permitted to be associated with CPA firms in public practice. Answer (d) is incorrect because nonprofessionals may be hired, and because developing computer systems is recognized as a service performed by public accountants.

8. (**a**) She may use the CPA designation on her business cards when she does not imply independence but shows her title and her employer. Therefore, answer (b) is incorrect. Answer (c) is incorrect because she may use the CPA designation on her business cards or company transmittals if she does not imply independence. Answer (d) is incorrect because under the above situations, she can use the CPA designation.

9. (**a**) The requirement is to determine the activity that would most likely **not** impair a CPA's independence. Accounting and consulting services do not normally impair independence because the member's role is advisory in nature (ET 191). Answers (b) and (c) are incorrect because

---

management functions are being performed (ET 191). Answer (d) is incorrect because accepting a luxurious gift impairs a CPA's independence (ET 191).

10. (a) The requirement is to identify the type of report that may be issued only by an independent accountant. Answer (a) is correct because AT 101 requires an accountant be independent for all attestation engagements. An attestation engagement is one in which the accountant expresses a conclusion about the reliability of assertions which are the responsibility of another party. A standard report on an examination of a financial forecast requires the auditor to express an opinion, which requires an accountant to be independent. Answer (b) is incorrect because CS 100 indicates that consulting services are fundamentally different from the attestation function, and therefore do not require independence of the accountant. Answers (c) and (d) are incorrect because AR 100 indicates that an accountant who is not independent is not precluded from issuing a report on a compilation of financial statements.

11. (b) Per ET 56, due care requires a member to discharge professional responsibilities with competence and diligence. Competence represents the attainment and maintenance of a level of understanding and knowledge that enables a member to render services with facility and acumen. It also establishes the limitations of a member's capabilities by dictating that consultation or referral may be required when a professional engagement exceeds the personal competence of a member or a member's firm. Accordingly, answer (b) is correct as it may be required to consult with experts in exercising due care. Due care does not require obtaining specialty accreditation.

12. (b) Under ruling 101 under Rule of Conduct 102, when a CPA is acting as an expert witness, s/he should **not** act as an advocate but should give his/her position based on objectivity. The expert witness does this based on specialized knowledge, training, and experience.

13. (c) The requirement is to determine which act is generally prohibited. Answer (c) is correct because "a member in public practice shall not for a commission recommend or refer to a client any product or service, or for a commission recommend or refer any product or service to be supplied by a client, or receive a commission when the member or the member's firm perform for that client: (1) an audit of a financial statement; or (2) a compilation of a financial statement when the member expects that a third party will use the financial statement and the member's compilation report does not disclose a lack of independence; or (3) an examination of prospective financial information." Answer (a) is incorrect because a member may purchase a product and resell it to a client. Any profit on sale would not constitute a commission (ET 591).

14. (a) The principle of due care requires the member to observe the profession's technical and ethical standards, strive continually to improve competence and the quality of services, and discharge responsibility to the best of the member's ability. Answer (b) is incorrect as the auditor is not required to examine **all** corroborating evidence supporting management's assertions, but rather to examine evidence on a scope basis based on his/her consideration of materiality and level of risk assessed. Answer (c) is incorrect as the auditor should be aware of the possibility of illegal acts, but

an audit provides no assurance that all or any illegal acts will be detected. Answer (d) is not the best answer because competence is derived from both education and experience. The principle of due care requires the member to strive to improve competence, however, attaining the proper balance of professional experience and formal education is not a criterion for exercising due care.

15. (d) The fact that a close relative of Kar works for Fort impairs Kar's independence. Answer (a) is incorrect because the gift is of a token amount which does not impair Kar's independence. Answer (b) is incorrect because a joint financial investment must be material to impair independence, and this would generally not occur with respect to a retirement plan. Answer (c) is incorrect because preparation of the client's tax return is not a service that impairs independence.

16. (b) Independence is not required for the performance of a compilation engagement. Answer (a) is incorrect because if the CPA is required to be independent, a mortgage loan would not be permitted even if it was fully secured. Answer (c) is incorrect because the CPA was not required to be independent of the client. Answer (d) is incorrect because the CPA was not required to be independent of the client.

17. (d) Both of the statements are incorrect; either would violate Rule 301 on confidential client information. Answer (a) is incorrect because statement I also is incorrect. Answer (b) is incorrect because statement II also is incorrect. Answer (c) is incorrect because statements I and II are both incorrect.

18. (c) Information in the CPA's working papers is confidential and may not be disclosed except with the client's consent or by court order. Answer (a) is incorrect because disclosure of the information would generally violate Rule 301 on confidential client information. Answers (b) and (d) are incorrect because the CPA owns the working papers.

A.4. Responsibilities in Consulting Services

19. (a) Types of consulting services include consultations, advisory services, implementation services, transaction services, staff and other support services, and product services.

20. (d) According to the Statements on Standards for Consulting Services, independence is not required for performance of consulting services unless the CPA also performs attest services for that client. However, the CPA must remain objective in performing the consulting services. Furthermore, the understanding with the client for performing the services can be established either in writing or orally.

21. (d) CS 100 indicates that the nature and scope of consulting services is determined solely by the practitioner and the client, typically in which the practitioner develops findings, conclusions, and recommendations for the client. All three services listed would fall under the definition of consulting services.

22. (c) The AICPA Statement on Standards for Consulting Services, Section 100, describes general standards for all consulting services, in addition to those established under the AICPA Code of Professional Conduct. Section 100 addresses the areas of client interest, understanding with the client, and communication with the client. Specifically, this section states that the accountant should inform the client of significant reservations concerning the scope or benefits of the engagement.

23. **(a)** Personal financial planning engagements are only those that involve developing strategies and making recommendations to assist a client in defining and achieving personal financial goals. Personal financial engagements involve all of the following:

1. Defining engagement objectives
2. Planning specific procedures appropriate to engagement
3. Developing basis for recommendations
4. Communicating recommendations to client
5. Identifying tasks for taking action on planning decisions.

Other engagements may also include, but generally are not **required** to perform, the following:

1. Assisting client to take action on planning decisions
2. Monitoring client's progress in achieving goals
3. Updating recommendations and helping client revise planning decisions.

A.6. Responsibilities in Business and Industry

24. **(a)** Internal auditors are employees of the organization they are auditing. The external auditors are allowed to use work performed by internal auditors to aid them in the audit. They still must perform an independent audit but can coordinate their work to avoid duplication of effort. Answer (b) is incorrect because independence for internal auditors means that they must be independent of the activities they audit within the firm. Answer (c) is incorrect because although internal auditors do not need to meet the same standards of independence as external auditors, they do need to be independent of the activities they are auditing. Answer (d) is incorrect because their work may supplement but not substitute for the work of the external auditors.

A.7. Responsibilities in Governmental Auditing

25. **(c)** Independent auditors who are involved in governmental auditing must complete continuing education requirements that include continuing education and training for governmental auditing. It is specified that all members of the AICPA involved in government audits must follow generally accepted government auditing standards or be in violation of the AICPA Code of Professional Conduct.

26. **(c)** The Single Audit Act was passed by Congress to reduce duplications of many governmental audits that were overlapping because entities often receive federal funds from multiple sources. This act applies to local governments or state governments that in a fiscal year receive $300,000 or more of federal funds. There is no specification that allows a governmental audit only once every five years.

B.1. Common Law Liability to Clients

27. **(d)** A CPA is not automatically liable for failure to discover a materially overstated account. The CPA can be liable if the failure to discover was due to the CPA's own negligence. Although performing an audit in accordance with GAAS does not guarantee that there is no negligence, it is normally a good defense against negligence. Answer (a) is incorrect because there was privity of contract with Cable. There was an oral agreement constituting a contractual relationship, therefore this would not be a good defense. Answer (b) is incorrect because an oral contract for an audit is still enforceable without a signed engagement letter. Answer (c) is incorrect because a CPA does not have to perform an audit recklessly or with an intent to deceive to be liable for negligence. Negligence simply means that a CPA failed to exercise due care owed of the average reasonable accountant in performing an audit.

28. **(c)** In order to meet the required standard of due care in conducting an audit of a client's financial statements, a CPA has the duty to perform with the same degree of skill and judgment expected of an ordinarily prudent CPA under the circumstances. Answer (a) is incorrect because the client's expectations do not guide the standard of due care. Rather, the standard of due care is guided by state and federal statute, court decisions, the contract with the client, GAAS and GAAP, and customs of the profession. Answer (b) is incorrect because it is generally the client's responsibility to prepare its financial statements in accordance with generally accepted accounting principles. Answer (d) is incorrect because a CPA is not normally liable for failure to detect fraud or irregularities unless (1) a "normal" audit would have detected it, (2) the accountant by agreement has undertaken greater responsibility, or (3) the wording of the audit report indicates greater responsibility.

29. **(c)** The following elements are needed to establish fraud against an accountant: (1) misrepresentation of the accountant's expert opinion, (2) scienter shown by either the accountant's knowledge of falsity or reckless disregard of the truth, (3) reasonable reliance by injured party, and (4) actual damages. Answer (a) is incorrect because contributory negligence of a third party is not a defense available for the accountant in cases of fraud. Answers (b) and (d) are incorrect because privity of contract is not a requirement for an accountant to be held liable for fraud.

30. **(a)** In the performance of an audit, a CPA has the duty to exercise the level of care, skill, and judgment expected of a reasonably prudent CPA under the circumstances. Answer (b) is incorrect because a CPA performing an audit must adhere to generally accepted **auditing** standards. It is the client's responsibility to prepare its financial statements in accordance with generally accepted accounting principles. Answer (c) is incorrect because an accountant is not liable for failure to detect fraud unless (1) a "normal" audit would have detected it, (2) the accountant by agreement has undertaken greater responsibility such as a defalcation audit, or (3) the wording of the audit report indicates greater responsibility for detecting fraud. Answer (d) is incorrect because a CPA **can** be liable for negligence, which is simply a failure to exercise due care in performing an audit. The CPA does not have to be grossly negligent or intentionally disregard generally accepted auditing standards to be held liable for negligence.

31. **(c)** A CPA will be liable for negligence when s/he fails to exercise due care. The standard for due care is guided by state and federal statutes, court decisions, contracts with clients, conformity with GAAS and GAAP, and the customs of the profession. Per the AICPA Professional Standards, AU 325, requires that if the auditor becomes aware of weaknesses in the design or operation of the internal control structure, these weaknesses, termed reportable conditions, be communicated to the audit committee of the client. Answer (a) is incorrect because a CPA is not normally liable for failure to detect fraud. Answer (b) is incorrect because including a negligence disclaimer in an engagement letter has no bearing on whether the CPA is negligent. Answer (d) is incorrect because generally a CPA is not required to inform a client's customers of embezzlements although knowledge of the embezzlements may adversely affect the CPA's audit opinion.

32.   (d)   A CPA's duty of due care is guided by the following standards: (1) state and federal statutes, (2) court decisions, (3) contract with the client, (4) GAAS and GAAP, and (5) customs of the profession. Therefore, failure to follow GAAS constitutes a breach of a CPA's duty of due care. Answer (a) is incorrect because issuance of an oral rather than written report does not necessarily constitute a failure to exercise due care. Answers (b) and (c) are incorrect because the standard of due care requires the CPA to exercise the skill and judgment of an ordinary, prudent accountant. An honest error of judgment or failure to provide money saving tax advice would not breach the duty of due care if the CPA acted in a reasonable manner.

33.   (a)   A CPA's liability for constructive fraud is established by the following elements: (1) misrepresentation of a material fact, (2) reckless disregard for the truth, (3) reasonable reliance by the injured party, and (4) actual damages. Gross negligence constitutes a reckless disregard for the truth. Answer (b) is incorrect because ordinary negligence is not sufficient to support a finding of constructive fraud. Answer (c) is incorrect because the liability for constructive fraud does not depend upon the identification of third-party users. Answer (d) is incorrect because the presence of the intent to deceive is needed to satisfy the scienter requirement for fraud. However, even in the absence of the intent to deceive, the CPA can be liable for constructive fraud based on reckless disregard of the truth.

B.2.   Common Law Liability to Third Parties (Nonclients)

34.   (b)   A foreseeable third party is someone not identified to the CPA, but who may be expected to receive the accountant's audit report and rely upon it. Even though this party is unknown to the CPA, the CPA is liable for gross negligence or fraud.

35.   (a)   Lack of privity can be a viable defense against third parties in a common law case of negligence or breach of contract. A client's creditor is not in privity of contract with the accountant. Answers (b) and (d) are incorrect because plaintiffs who are suing for fraud, constructive fraud, or gross negligence, which involves a reckless disregard for the truth, need not show privity of contract. Answer (c) is incorrect because the accountant's client is in privity of contract with the accountant due to their contractual agreement.

36.   (c)   Since Sanco was a foreseeable third party instead of an actually foreseen third party by the CPA, Sanco in most states cannot recover. Answer (a) is incorrect because most states do not extend liability to mere foreseeable third parties for simple negligence. Answer (b) is incorrect because the Ultramares decision limited liability to parties in privity of contract with the CPA. Answer (d) is incorrect because the client can recover for damages caused to it when negligence is established.

37.   (b)   Under the Ultramares rule, the accountant is held liable only to parties whose primary benefit the financial statements are intended. This generally means only the client or third-party beneficiaries who are in privity of contract with the accountant. Many courts have more recently departed from the Ultramares decision to allow foreseen third parties to recover from the accountant. However, those courts that adhere to the Ultramares rule do not expand liability to foreseen parties.

38.   (a)   In order to establish common law liability against an accountant based upon negligence, it must be proven that (1) the accountant had the duty to exercise due care, (2) the accountant breached the duty of due care, (3) damage or loss resulted, and (4) a causal relationship exists between the fault of the accountant and the resulting damages. The accountant may escape liability if due care can be established. The standard for due care is guided by state and federal statute, court decisions, contract with client, GAAS and GAAP, and customs of the profession. Although following GAAS does not automatically preclude negligence, it is strong evidence for the presence of due care. Answer (b) is incorrect because although the client may be aware of the misstatement, the auditor has the responsibility to detect the material misstatement if it is such that an average, reasonable accountant should have detected it. Answer (c) is incorrect because the client and Larson intended for the opinion and the financial statements to be used by purchasers. Therefore, a purchaser is considered a third-party beneficiary and is in privity of contract. Answer (d) is incorrect because the accountant need not know the specific identity of a third-party beneficiary to be held liable for negligence.

39.   (a)   To establish a CPA's liability for common law fraud, the following elements must be present: (1) misrepresentation of a material fact or the accountant's expert opinion, (2) scienter, shown by either an intent to mislead or reckless disregard for the truth, (3) reasonable or justifiable reliance by injured party, and (4) actual damages resulted. If Larson did not have actual or constructive knowledge of the misstatements, the scienter element would not be present and thus Larson would not be liable. Answers (b) and (d) are incorrect because neither contributory negligence of the client nor lack of privity of contract are defenses available to the accountant in cases of fraud. Answer (c) is incorrect because an accountant is generally liable to all parties defrauded. Therefore, the accountant need not have actual knowledge that the purchaser was an intended beneficiary.

B.3.   Statutory Liability to Third Parties—Securities Act of 1933

40.   (b)   The Securities Act of 1933 requires that a plaintiff need only prove that damages were incurred and that there was a material misstatement or omission in order to establish a prima facie case against a CPA. The Act does not require that the plaintiff prove that s/he relied on the financial information or that there was negligence or fraud present. The Securities Act of 1933 eliminates the necessity for privity of contract.

41. **(c)**   Mac is a third party that the accountant knew would rely on the financial statements. Queen's financial statements contained material misstatements. Mac can recover by showing that the accountant was negligent in the audit. Mac also needs to establish that it did rely on the financial statements in order to recover from the accountant for the losses on Queen.

42. **(c)**   Under the Securities Act of 1933, a CPA is liable to any third-party purchaser of registered securities for losses resulting from misstatements in the financial statements included in the registration statement. The plaintiff (purchaser) must establish that damages were incurred, and that the misstatements were material misstatements of facts. Answer (a) is incorrect because under the 1933 Act it is not necessary for the purchaser of securities to prove "scienter," or knowledge of material misstatement, on the part of the CPA. Answers (b) and (d) are incorrect because under the 1933 Act, the plaintiff need not prove negligence on the part of the CPA or that there was reliance by the plaintiff on the financial statements included in the registration statement.

43. **(c)**   In a Section 11 suit under the 1933 Act, the plaintiff may recover damages equal to the difference between the amount paid and the market value of the stock at the time of the suit. If the stock has been sold, then the damages are the difference between the amount paid and the sale price. Answer (a) is incorrect because damages of triple the original price are not provided for under this act. Answer (b) is incorrect because recission is not a remedy under this act. Answer (d) is incorrect because if the shares have not been sold before the suit, then the court uses the difference between the amount paid and the market value at the time of the suit.

44. **(b)**   Under Section 11 of the 1933 Act, if the plaintiff proves damages and the existence of a material misstatement or omission in the financial statements included in the registration statement, these are sufficient to win against the CPA unless the CPA can prove one of the applicable defenses. Due diligence is one of the defenses. Answer (a) is incorrect because contributory negligence is not a defense under Section 11. Answer (c) is incorrect because the purchaser need not prove privity with the CPA. Answer (d) is not correct because the purchaser needs to prove the above two elements but not scienter.

45. **(d)**   To impose liability under Section 11 of the Securities Act of 1933 for a misleading registration statement, the plaintiff must prove the following: (1) damages were incurred, and (2) a material misstatement or omission was present in financial statements included in the registration statement. The plaintiff generally is not required to prove the defendant's intent to deceive nor must the plaintiff prove reliance on the registration statement.

46. **(c)**   The proof requirements necessary to establish an accountant's liability under the Securities Act of 1933, Section 11 are as follows: (1) the plaintiff must prove damages were incurred, and (2) the plaintiff must prove there was a material misstatement or omission in financial statements included in the registration statement. To establish an accountant's liability under the Securities Exchange Act of 1934, Section 10(b), Rule 10b-5, the following elements must be proven: (1) damages resulted to the plaintiff in connection with the purchase or sale of a security in interstate commerce, (2) a material misstatement or omission existed in information released by the firm, (3) the plaintiff justifiably relied on the financial information, and (4) the existence of scienter. Because Sharp can prove that damages were incurred and that the statements contained material misstatements, Sharp is likely to prevail in a lawsuit under the Securities Act of 1933, Section 11. However, Sharp would be unable to prove justifiable reliance on the misstated information or the existence of scienter; thus, recovery under the Securities Exchange Act of 1934, Section 10(b), Rule 10b-5, is unlikely.

47. **(d)**   If an accountant is negligent, s/he may have liability not only for a negligently performed audit but also for a negligently performed review when there were facts that should require the accountant to investigate further because of their suspicious nature. This is true even though a review is not a full audit.

B.4.   Statutory Liability to Third Parties—Securities Exchange Act of 1934

48. **(a)**   In order to establish a case under the antifraud provisions of Section 10(b) and Rule 10b-5 of the 1934 Act, the plaintiff has to prove that the defendant either had knowledge of the falsity in the registration statement or acted with reckless disregard for the truth. In addition, the plaintiff must show that the transaction involved interstate commerce so that there is a constitutional basis for using this federal law. S/he also must prove justifiable reliance. The plaintiff need not prove that s/he was an intended user of the false registration statement.

49. **(d)**   Under Rule 10b-5 of Section 10(b) of the Securities Exchange Act of 1934, a CPA may be liable if s/he makes a false statement of a material fact or an omission of a material fact in connection with the purchase or sale of a security. Scienter is required which is shown by either knowledge of falsity or reckless disregard for the truth. Of the four answers given, lack of good faith best describes this scienter requirement. Answer (a) is incorrect because negligence is not enough under this rule. Answer (b) is incorrect because independence is not the issue under scienter. Answer (c) is incorrect because although due diligence can be a defense under Section 11 of the Securities Act of 1933, it is not the standard used under Section 10(b) of the Securities Exchange Act of 1934.

50. **(b)**   Under Section 11 of the Securities Act of 1933, the CPA may be liable for material misstatements or omissions in certified financial statements. The CPA may escape liability by showing due diligence. This can often be proven by the CPA showing that s/he followed Generally Accepted Accounting Principles. There are not generally accepted fraud detection standards that the CPA can use as a defense.

51. **(c)**   In a civil suit under Section 10(b) and Rule 10b-5, the damages are generally the difference between the amount paid and the market value at the time of suit, or the difference between the amount paid and the sales price if sold. Answer (a) is incorrect because recovery of the full original public offering price is not used as the damages. Answer (b) is incorrect because the above described monetary damages are used. Answer (d) is incorrect because punitive damages are not given under this rule.

C.1. Accountant's Working Papers

52. **(b)** In general, the accountant's workpapers are owned by the accountant. However, the CPA's ownership of the working papers is custodial in nature and the CPA is required to preserve confidentiality of the client's affairs. Normally, the CPA firm cannot allow transmission of information included in the working papers to third parties without the client's consent. This prevents a CPA firm from transferring workpapers to a purchaser of a CPA practice unless the client consents. Answer (c) is incorrect because the privileged communication rule does not exist at common law and has only been enacted by a few states. Additionally, the privileged communications rule only applies to communications which were intended to be privileged at the time of communication. Answer (a) is incorrect because working papers may be obtained by third parties without the client's consent when they appear to be relevant to issues raised in litigation (through a subpoena).

53. **(d)** The working papers are owned by the CPA, but the CPA must preserve confidentiality. They cannot be transmitted to another party unless the client consents or unless the CPA is required to under a valid court or governmental agency subpoena. Answers (a) and (c) are incorrect because these do not preserve the confidentiality. Answer (b) is incorrect because the CPA retains the working papers as evidence of the work done.

54. **(c)** Any of the partners of a CPA partnership can have access to the partnership's working papers. Third parties outside the firm need to have the client's consent or a legal subpoena.

C.2. Privileged Communications between Accountant and Client

55. **(d)** To preserve confidentiality, a CPA (including a CPA partnership) may not allow transmission of information in the working papers to other parties. Exceptions are consent of the client or the production of an enforceable subpoena. There are no exceptions for the IRS or the FASB, thus making answers (a), (b), and (c) incorrect.

56. **(d)** In a jurisdiction having an accountant-client privilege statute, the CPA generally may not turn over workpapers without the client's permission. It is allowable to do so, however, for use in a quality review under AICPA authorization or to be given to the state CPA society quality control panel. Answers (a), (b), and (c) are incorrect because the client would have to give permission for the CPA to turn over the confidential workpapers to the purchaser of the CPA practice, as well as to another CPA firm in regard to suspected tax return irregularities.

57. **(a)** Privileged communications between the accountant and client are recognized only in a few states. Therefore, if a state statute has been enacted creating such a privilege, Ivor will be able to prevent Thorp from testifying. Answer (b) is incorrect because federal law does not recognize accountant-client privileged communication. Answer (d) is incorrect because Ivor will not be able to prevent Thorp from testifying about the nature of the work performed in the audit unless a privileged communication statute has been enacted in that state. Answer (c) is incorrect because privileged communication does not exist at common law but must be created by state statute. Criminal law is

based on common law and varies by state. However, as a general rule, in states that recognize accountant-client privilege, it can be claimed in both civil and criminal suits.

58. **(a)** The requirement is to identify the situation in which it is most likely that a violation of the profession's ethical standards would have occurred. Answer (a) is correct because independence is impaired if fees remain unpaid for professional services of the preceding year when the report on the client's current year is issued. Accordingly, no report should have been issued on the 2002 financial statements when fees for the 2001 audit were unpaid. Answer (b) is incorrect because CPAs may recommend a position description (ET 191) without violating the profession's ethical standards. Answer (c) is incorrect because a practice may be purchased for a percentage of fees to be received. Answer (d) is incorrect because the Code of Professional Conduct does not prohibit arrangements with financial institutions to collect notes issued by a client in payment of professional fees.

59. **(b)** A CPA must not disclose confidential information of a client unless the client gives consent to disclose it to that third party. Answer (a) is incorrect because state agencies need a subpoena before the CPA must comply. Answer (c) is incorrect because the IRS does not have the right to force a CPA to turn over confidential information of a client without either the client's consent or an enforceable subpoena. Answer (d) is incorrect because although the CPA can use the client information to defend a lawsuit, the CPA is not normally requested to disclose confidential information to comply with Generally Accepted Accounting Principles.

E. Responsibilities of Auditors under Private Securities Litigation Reform Act

60. **(c)** Under the Private Securities Litigation Reform Act, the auditor should inform first the audit committee or the board of directors. Answer (a) is incorrect because the Securities Litigation Reform Act does not require that the SEC be informed unless after the audit committee or board of directors is informed, no remedial action is taken. Answer (b) is incorrect because the Justice Department need not be informed of this under the Private Securities Litigation Reform Act. Answer (d) is incorrect because inclusion of the problem in a note of the financial statements is not enough; the audit committee or the board of directors should be informed.

61. **(a)** The Private Securities Litigation Reform Act requires that auditors of firms covered under the Securities Exchange Act of 1934 establish procedures to do the items in (b), (c), and (d). Developing a comprehensive internal control system is not specifically mentioned, although part of this would be helpful in accomplishing the three stated items.

62. **(d)** Under the Private Securities Litigation Reform Act, an auditor who audits financial statements under the Federal Securities Exchange Act of 1934 is required to establish procedures to (1) detect illegal acts, (2) identify material related-party transactions, and (3) evaluate the ability of the firm to continue as a going concern.

63. **(b)** Under the Private Securities Litigation Reform Act, he is required to report this to the audit committee of the firm or the board of directors. Answer (a) is incorrect because he need not report this to the shareholders but to the audit committee or the board of directors. Answers (c) and (d) are incorrect because he is required under the Reform Act to inform the audit committee or the board of directors.

64. (c) The Private Securities Litigation Reform Act amends both the 1933 and 1934 Acts. Answer (a) is incorrect because it applies to the 1933 and 1934 Acts which apply to stocks sold on a stock exchange. Answers (b) and (d) are incorrect because this Reform Act applies to securities covered under the 1933 and 1934 Acts which may include both common and preferred stock of a publicly held corporation.

65. (b) Bran is liable under the Private Securities Litigation Reform Act for her proportionate fault of the liability since she acted unknowingly. Answer (a) is incorrect because Bran was determined to be 20% at fault. Answers (c) and (d) are incorrect because the Reform Act changes the joint and several liability for unknowing conduct and substitutes proportionate liability.

66. (c) The Sarbanes-Oxley Act of 2002 established a number of nonattest services that may not be performed by the auditor for a public company. Tax services may be performed but must be approved by the company's audit committee.

67. (c) The Sarbanes-Oxley Act established the Public Accounting Oversight Board to regulate CPA firms that audit public companies.

ANSWER OUTLINE

Problem 1   Accountant-Client Privilege; CPA's Negligence; CPA's Fraud

a.   No accountant-client privilege recognized at common law and no applicable state statute

Right to assert privilege rests with client not accountant

b.   Elements necessary to establish CPA's negligence

• Legal duty to protect plaintiff from unreasonable risk

• Failure of CPA to perform with due care or competence

• Failure to exercise due care caused plaintiff's loss

• Actual damage resulted from failure to exercise due care

• Plaintiff was within a known and intended class of third-party beneficiaries

c.   Significance of compliance with GAAS

• Primary standard against which CPA's conduct tested

• Considered "the custom of the industry"

• Failure to meet GAAS will result in finding of CPA's negligence

• Meeting GAAS not conclusive evidence of CPA's not being negligent

d.   Elements necessary to establish CPA's actual or constructive fraud

• False representation of fact by CPA

• Actual fraud requires knowledge by CPA that statement was false (scienter). Constructive fraud inferred from gross negligence or reckless disregard for truth

• Intention to have plaintiff rely on false statement

• Reasonable reliance on false statement

• Damage results from reliance

UNOFFICIAL ANSWER

Problem 1   Accountant-Client Privilege; CPA's Negligence; CPA's Fraud

a.   No. Since there is no accountant-client privilege recognized at common law and there is no applicable state statute which creates an accountant-client privilege, Clark & Wall will be required to produce its workpapers. Furthermore, the right to assert the accountant-client privilege generally rests with the client and not with the accountant.

b.   The elements necessary to establish a cause of action for negligence against Clark & Wall are

• A legal duty to protect the plaintiff (Dill) from unreasonable risk.

• A failure by the defendant (Clark & Wall) to perform or report on an engagement with the due care or competence expected of members of its profession.

• A causal relationship (i.e., that the failure to exercise due care resulted in the plaintiff's loss).

• Actual damage or loss resulting from the failure to exercise due care.

In addition to the foregoing, Dill must be able to establish that it is within a known and intended class of third-party beneficiaries in order to recover damages from Clark & Wall for negligence. This is necessary because Clark &

Wall has asserted that it is not in privity of contract with Dill.

c.   The primary standards against which the accountant's conduct will be tested are GAAS. Such standards are generally known as "the custom of the industry." Failure by Clark & Wall to meet the standards of the profession will undoubtedly result in a finding of negligence. However, meeting the standard of the profession will not be conclusive evidence that Clark & Wall was not negligent, although it is of significant evidentiary value.

d.   The requirements to establish actual or constructive fraud on the part of Clark & Wall are

1.   A false representation of fact by the defendant (Clark & Wall).

2.   For actual fraud, knowledge by the defendant (Clark & Wall) that the statement is false (scienter) or that the statement is made without belief that it is truthful. Constructive fraud may be inferred from gross negligence or a reckless disregard for the truth.

3.   An intention to have the plaintiff (Dill) rely upon the false statement.

4.   "Justifiable" reliance upon the false statement.

5.   Damage resulting from said reliance.

ANSWER OUTLINE

Problem 2   Statute of Frauds; Restraint of Trade; Accountant's Liability for Negligence

The agreement between Cream and Apple is unenforceable

Statute of Frauds requires an agreement that cannot possibly be performed within one year of its **creation** to be in writing

The agreement between Apple and Nestar is likely to be enforceable

An agreement not to compete will be enforceable if it protects legitimate property interests and is reasonable with respect to both time and geographic area

The agreement protects goodwill which a buyer of a business has a right to protect

Birk will prevail against Kaye

Kaye was required to perform the audit with due care

Kaye was negligent in issuing an unqualified opinion on financial statements that contained material misstatements

UNOFFICIAL ANSWER

Problem 2   Statute of Frauds; Restraint of Trade; Accountant's Liability for Negligence

a.   The December 5 oral agreement between Cream and Apple is unenforceable because the agreement failed to comply with the requirements of the Statute of Frauds. A contract that cannot possibly be performed within one year from the making of the contract falls within the provisions of the Statute of Frauds. As the facts clearly indicate, the December 5 oral agreement could not possibly be performed within one year of the making of the agreement (December 5, 2003) since the agreement required Apple to continue to perform until December 20, 2004. Therefore, the oral agreement is unenforceable.

b.   The agreement between Nestar and Apple restricting Nestar from competing with Apple for three years within the city where Nestar's office and the majority of Nestar's clients were located is likely to be enforceable. An agreement not to compete will be enforceable if there has been a sale of a business including goodwill and the purpose of the restraint is to protect a property interest of the purchaser; the restraint is reasonable as to the geographic area covered; and the restraint is reasonable as to the time period. Under the facts of this case, the agreement not to compete is likely to be enforceable. The transaction involves the sale of Nestar's management consulting business and goodwill. The purpose of the restraint is to protect the goodwill. The three-year time period is reasonable. The limitation on the geographic area covered by the restraint to only the city where Nestar's office and the majority of Nestar's clients are located appears to be reasonable.

c. Birk will prevail in its action against Kaye based on negligence. Kaye owed a duty to Birk to conduct the audit with due care. Kaye failed to conduct the audit with due care by issuing an unqualified opinion on Apples' 2003 financial statements when, in fact, Apple had made a material error by reporting all of the revenues related to the unenforceable December 5 agreement on its 2003 financial statements. Kaye's issuance of an unqualified opinion despite the material error caused Birk to suffer damages as evidenced by the drastic decrease in the market value of Apple stock.

SOLUTIONS TO SIMULATION PROBLEMS

Simulation Problem 1

1. **(C)** Section 11 of the Securities Act of 1933 imposes liability on auditors for misstatements or omissions of a material fact in certified financial statements or other information provided in registration statements. Similarly, under Section 10(b), Rule 10b-5 of the Securities Exchange Act of 1934, the plaintiff must prove there was a material misstatement or omission in information released by the firm such as audited financial statements. Actually, if the examiners wish to emphasize the phrase "filed document" in the question, then the answer would be (A). Under Section 10(b), the material misstatement may occur in information released by the firm rather than filed. Since the requirements state "...**must** allege or prove," technically the answer would be (D), since the plaintiff could allege or prove **omission** of material facts instead of material **misstatements** stated in the question. Therefore, this question depends upon how technical one decides to get on these points.

2. **(C)** Under both Section 11 of the 1933 Act and Section 10(b) of the 1934 Act, the plaintiff must allege or prove that s/he incurred monetary damages.

3. **(D)** Under Section 11 of the 1933 Act, the burden of proof is shifted to the defendant, accountant. The accountant may then defend him- or herself by establishing due diligence. The plaintiff does not have to show lack of due diligence by the CPA. Under Section 10(b), the plaintiff must prove scienter.

4. **(D)** The plaintiff does not have to prove that s/he was in privity with the CPA under either section.

5. **(B)** Under Section 10(b), the plaintiff must prove justifiable reliance on the financial information. This is not true under Section 11 in which the plaintiff need prove only the items in item **1.** and item **2.** discussed above.

6. **(B)** The plaintiff does have to prove that the CPA had scienter under Section 10(b) of the 1934 Act. Scienter is not needed under the 1933 Act, however.

Simulation Problem 2

1.   **(Y)** Since the auditor is a cosigner on a client's check, the auditor could become liable if the client defaults. This relationship impairs the auditor's independence.

2.   **(N)** Independence is not impaired because membership in the country club is essentially a social matter.

3.   **(Y)** An auditor may not hold a direct financial interest in a client. Putting it in a blind trust does not solve the impairment of independence.

4.   **(N)** If the auditor places his/her account in a client bank, this does not impair independence if the accounts are state or federally insured. If the accounts are not insured, independence is not impaired if the amounts are immaterial.

5.   **(Y)** The auditor's independence is impaired when prior years' fees for professional services remain unpaid for more than one year.

6.   **(Y)** The auditor's independence is impaired when s/he leases space out of a building s/he owns to a client.

7.   **(N)** When the auditor does not serve in management, s/he may join a trade association who is a client.

8.   **(N)** Independence is impaired for direct financial interests and material, indirect financial interests but not for immaterial, indirect financial interests.

FEDERAL SECURITIES ACTS AND ANTITTRUST LAW

Overview

The bulk of the material tested on the exam from this area comes from the Securities Act of 1933, as amended, and the Securities Exchange Act of 1934, as amended. Topics included under the scope of the 1933 Act are registration requirements, exempt securities, and exempt transactions. The purposes of the 1933 Act are to provide investors with full and fair disclosure of a security offering and to prevent fraud. The basic prohibition of the 1933 Act is that no sale of a security shall occur in interstate commerce without registration and without furnishing a prospectus to prospective purchasers unless the security or the transaction is exempt from registration.

The purpose of the 1934 Act is the establishment of the Securities Exchange Commission to assure fairness in the trading of securities subsequent to their original issuance. The basic scope of the 1934 Act is to require periodic reports of financial and other information concerning registered securities, and to prohibit manipulative and deceptive devices in both the sale and purchase of securities.

The exam often tests on the Federal Securities Acts; however, this is sometimes combined with accountant's liability or is included within questions concerning corporate or limited partnership law.

Candidates should also understand the important parts of the Sherman Act, the Clayton Act, the Robinson-Patman Act, and the Federal Trade Commission Act. These laws as amended form the basis for Antitrust Law which is now testable on the CPA exam.

A. Securities Act of 1933 (Generally applies to initial issuances [primary offerings] of securities)

1. Purposes of the Act are to provide potential investors with full and fair disclosure of all material information relating to issuance of securities (such that a prudent decision to invest or refrain from investing can be made) and to prevent fraud or misrepresentation

   a. Accomplished by

      (1) Requiring a registration statement to be filed with Securities Exchange Commission (SEC) before either a public sale or an offer to sell securities in interstate commerce

         (a) This is the fundamental thrust of the 1933 Act
         (b) SEC is a government agency comprised of commissioners and its staff that was created to administer and enforce the Federal Securities Laws. The Commission interprets the acts, conducts investigations, adjudicates violations, and performs a rule-making function to implement the acts.

            1] Can subpoena witnesses
            2] Can obtain injunction preventing sale of securities
            3] Cannot assess monetary penalties without court proceedings
            4] Cannot prosecute criminal acts

      (2) Requiring prospectuses to be provided to investors with, or before, the sale or delivery of the securities to provide public with information given to SEC in registration statement
      (3) Providing civil and criminal liabilities for failure to comply with these requirements and for misrepresentation or fraud in the sale of securities even if not required to be registered

   b. SEC does not evaluate the merits or value of securities

      (1) SEC can only compel full and fair disclosure
      (2) In theory, public can evaluate merit of security when provided with full and fair disclosure
      (3) SEC's function is not to detect fraud or to stop offerings where fraud or unethical conduct is suspected

   c. The major items you need to know are

      (1) That a registration statement and prospectus are usually required
      (2) Which transactions are exempt from registration
      (3) Which securities are exempt from registration
      (4) What the liability is for false or misleading registration statements

2. Definitions

   a. Security—any note, stock, bond certificate of interest, debenture, investment contract, etc., or any interest or instrument commonly known as a security

      (1) General idea is that investor intends to make a profit on the investment through the efforts of others rather than through his/her own efforts

> *EXAMPLE: W is a general partner of WDC partnership in Washington, D.C. Usually, W's interest would not be considered a security because a general partner's interest typically involves participation in the business rather than mere investment.*

   (a) Includes limited partnership interests

   (b) Includes rights and warrants to subscribe for the above

   (c) Includes treasury stock

   (d) Investment contract is a security when money is invested in a common enterprise with profits to be derived from the effort of others

> *EXAMPLE: Blue Corporation in Florida owns several acres of orange trees. Blue is planning on selling a large portion of the land with the orange trees to several individuals in various states on a row-by-row basis. Each purchaser gets a deed and is required to purchase a management contract whereby Blue Corporation maintains all the land and oranges and then remits the net profits to the various purchasers. Even though it may appear that each individual purchased separately the land with the oranges and a management contract, the law looks at the "big picture" here. Since in reality the individuals are investing their money, and the profits are derived from the efforts of others, the law treats the above fact pattern as involving securities. Therefore, the Securities Acts apply.*

b. Person—individual, corporation, partnership, unincorporated association, business trust, government

c. Controlling person—has power, direct/indirect, to influence the management and/or policies of an issuer, whether by stock ownership, contract, position, or otherwise

> *EXAMPLE: A 51% stockholder is a controlling person by virtue of a majority ownership.*

> *EXAMPLE: A director of a corporation also owns 10% of that same corporation. By virtue of the stock ownership and position on the board of directors, he has a strong voice in the management of the corporation. Therefore, he is a controlling person.*

d. Insiders—(applies to the Securities Exchange Act of 1934) include officers, directors, and owners of more than 10% of any class of issuer's equity securities

   (1) Note that debentures not included because not equity securities

   (2) For purposes of this law to avoid a "loophole," insiders include "beneficial owners" of more than 10% of the equity stock of issuer

      (a) To determine amount of "beneficial ownership," add to the individual's equity ownership, equity stock owned by

         1] Owner's spouse

         2] Owner's minor children

         3] Owner's relative in same house

         4] Owner's equity stock held in trust in which owner is beneficiary

> *EXAMPLE: X owns 6% of the common stock of ABC Company in Philadelphia. Her spouse owns 3% of ABC Company's common stock. Stock was also placed in the name of their two minor children, each owning 1% of ABC Company's common stock. X has beneficial ownership of 11% of the equity securities of ABC Company so she is an insider for the 1934 Act. Note that her husband also qualifies as an insider.*

> *EXAMPLE: Use the same facts as in the previous example except that all four individuals owned debentures of ABC Company. Since these are not equity securities, none qualifies as an insider.*

> *EXAMPLE: L is an officer who owns 4% of the common stock of XYZ Company in Washington, DC. Since L is an officer, s/he is an insider even though the ownership level is below 10%.*

e. Underwriter—any person who has purchased from issuer with a view to the public distribution of any security or participates in such undertaking

   (1) Includes any person who offers or sells for issuer in connection with the distribution of any security

   (2) Does not include person who sells or distributes on commission for underwriter (i.e., dealers)

f. Sales of securities are covered by these laws

   (1) Issuance of securities as part of business reorganization (e.g., merger or consolidation) constitutes a sale and must be registered with SEC unless the issue otherwise qualifies as an exemption from the registration requirements of 1933 Act

   (2) Issuance of stock warrants is considered a sale so that requirements of 1933 Act must be met

(3) Employee stock purchase plan is a sale and therefore must comply with the provisions of the 1933 Act

    (a) Company must also supply a prospectus to each employee to whom stock is offered

(4) Stock dividends or splits are not sales

g. Registration statement—the statement required to be filed with SEC before initial sale of securities in interstate commerce

  (1) Includes financial statements and all other relevant information about the registrant's property, business, directors, principal officers, together with prospectus

  (2) Also, includes any amendment, report, or document filed as part of the statement or incorporated therein by reference

  (3) It is against law to sell, offer to sell, or offer to purchase securities before filing registration statement

  (4) Registration statement and prospectus become public upon filing

    (a) Effective date of registration statement is 20th day after filing

    (b) Against law to sell securities until effective date but issuer may **offer** securities upon filing registration statement.

    (c) Such offers may be made

      1] Orally

      2] By tombstone ads that identify security, its price, and who will take orders

      3] By a "red-herring prospectus"

        a] Legend in red ink (thus, red-herring) is printed on this preliminary prospectus indicating that the prospectus is "preliminary" and that a registration statement has been filed but has not become effective.

h. Prospectus—any notice, circular, advertisement, letter, or communication offering any security for sale (or merger)

  (1) May be a written, radio, or television communication

    (a) SEC adopted new "plain English" rule for important sections of companies' prospectuses, including risk factor sections

  (2) After the effective date of registration statement, communication (written or oral) will not be considered a prospectus if

    (a) Prior to or at same time, a written prospectus was also sent, or

    (b) If it only states from whom written prospectus is available, identifies security, states price, and who will execute orders for it (i.e., tombstone ad)

3. Registration requirements

a. Registration is required under the Act if

  (1) The securities are to be offered, sold, or delivered in interstate commerce or through the mail

    (a) Interstate commerce means trade, commerce, transportation, or communication (e.g., telephone call) among more than one state or territory of US

      1] Interpreted very broadly to include trade, commerce, etc. that is within one state but affects interstate commerce

      EXAMPLE: A corporation issues securities to individuals living only in Philadelphia. It is further shown that this issuance affects trade in Delaware. Interstate commerce is affected because although Philadelphia is of course in one state, the effects on at least one other state allow the Federal Securities Acts to take effect under our Constitution. Therefore, registration of these securities is required under the Federal Law unless exemptions are found as discussed later.

  (2) Unless it is an exempted security or exempted transaction as discussed later

b. Issuer has primary duty of registration

(1) Any person who sells unregistered securities that should have been registered may be liable to a purchaser (unless transaction or security is exempt)

(2) Liability cannot be disclaimed in writing or orally by issuer

c. Information required, in general, in registration statements

(1) Financial statements audited by independent CPA

(2) Names of issuer, directors, officers, general partners, underwriters, large stockholders, counsel, etc.

(3) Risks associated with the securities

(4) Description of property, business, and capitalization of issuer

(5) Information about management of issuer

(6) Description of security to be sold and use to be made by issuer of proceeds

d. Prospectus is also filed as part of registration statement

(1) Generally must contain same information as registration statement, but it may be condensed or summarized

e. Registration statement and prospectus are examined by SEC

(1) Amendments are almost always required by SEC

(2) SEC may issue stop-order suspending effectiveness of registration if statement appears incomplete or misleading

(3) Otherwise registration becomes effective on 20th day after filing (or on 20th day after filing amendment)

(a) Twenty-day period is called the waiting period

(4) It is unlawful for company to sell the securities prior to approval (effective registration date)

(a) However, preliminary prospectuses are permitted once registration statement is filed

f. Applies to both corporate and noncorporate issuers

g. Registration covers a single distribution, so second distribution must also be registered

h. Shelf registration is exception to requirement that each new distribution of nonexempt securities requires a new filing

(1) Allows certain qualified issuers to register securities once and then offer and sell them on a delayed or continuous basis "off the shelf"

(2) Advantage is that issuer can respond better to changing market conditions affecting stock

i. Different registration forms are available

(1) Form S-1

(a) This is basic long-form registration statement

(2) Forms S-2 and S-3

(a) These forms adopted by SEC to ease much of burden of disclosures required under federal securities regulation

(b) Require less detailed disclosures than Form S-1

(c) Integrate information required under 1933 and 1934 Acts

1] Firms already on file with SEC under 1934 Act may incorporate much information by reference to avoid additional disclosure

(3) Forms SB-1 and SB-2

(a) These forms permitted for small businesses under Regulation S-B

1] Reduce amount of financial and nonfinancial information required when registering under 1933 Act and when reporting quarterly information under 1934 Act

2] Small business issuer is generally one that has revenues less than $25 million

4. Exempt securities (need not be registered but still subject to antifraud provisions under the Act)

    a.   Commercial paper (e.g., note, draft, check, etc.) with a maturity of nine months or less

        (1) Must be for commercial purpose and not investment

        EXAMPLE: OK Corporation in Washington, DC wishes to finance a short-term need for more cash for current operations. OK will do this by issuing some short-term notes which all have a maturity of nine months or less. These are exempt from the registration requirements.

    b.   Intrastate issues—securities offered and sold only within one state

        (1) Issuer must be resident of state and doing 80% of business in the state and must use at least 80% of sale proceeds in connection with business operations in the state

        (2) All offerees and purchasers must be residents of state

        (3) For nine months after last sale by issuer, resales can only be made to residents of state

        (4) All of particular issue must qualify under this rule or this exemption cannot be used for any sale of the issue

        EXAMPLE: A regional corporation in need of additional capital makes an offer to the residents of the state in which it is incorporated to purchase a new issue of its stock. The offer expressly restricts sales to only residents of the state and all purchasers are residents of the state.

    c.   Small issues (Regulation A)—issuances up to $5,000,000 by issuer in twelve-month period may be exempt if

        (1) There is a notice filed with SEC

        (2) An offering circular (containing financial information about the corporation and descriptive information about offered securities) must be provided to offeree. Financial statements in offering circular need not be audited.

        (3) Note that an offering circular (statement) is required under Regulation A instead of the more costly and time-consuming prospectus

        (4) Nonissuers can sell up to $1,500,000 in twelve-month period

    d.   Securities of governments, banks, quasi governmental authorities (e.g., local hospital authorities), savings and loan associations, farmers, co-ops, and common carriers regulated by ICC

        (1) Public utilities are not exempt

    e.   Security exchanged by issuer exclusively with its existing shareholders so long as

        (1) No commission is paid

        (2) Both sets of securities must have been issued by the same person

        EXAMPLE: A stock split is an exempt transaction under the 1933 Act and thus, the securities need not be registered at time of split.

    f.   Securities of nonprofit religious, educational, or charitable organizations

    g.   Certificates issued by receiver or trustee in bankruptcy

    h.   Insurance and annuity contracts

5. Exempt transactions or offerings (still subject, however, to antifraud provisions of the Act; may also be subject to reporting requirements of the 1934 Act)

    a.   Sale or offer to sell by any person **other than** an issuer, underwriter, or dealer

        (1) Generally covers sales by individual investors on their own account

        (2) May be transaction by broker on customer's order

            (a) Does not include solicitation of these orders

        (3) Exemption does not apply to sales by controlling persons because considered an underwriter or issuer

    b.   **Regulation D** establishes three important exemptions in Rules 504, 505, and 506 under the 1933 Act

        (1) Rule 504 exempts an issuance of securities up to $1,000,000 sold in twelve-month period to any number of investors (this is also known as seed capital exemption)

            (a) General offering and solicitations are permitted under Rule 504

(b) Issuer need not restrict purchasers' right to resell securities

(c) No specific disclosure is required

(d) Must send notice of offering to SEC within fifteen days of first sale of securities

(2) Rule 505 exempts issuance of up to $5,000,000 in twelve-month period

(a) No general offering or solicitation is permitted within twelve-month period

(b) Permits sales to thirty-five unaccredited (nonaccredited term sometimes used) investors and to unlimited number of accredited investors within twelve months

1] Accredited investors are, for example, banks, savings and loan associations, credit unions, insurance companies, broker dealers, certain trusts, partnerships and corporations, also natural persons having joint or individual net worth exceeding $1,000,000 or having joint or individual net income of $200,000 for two most recent years

2] SEC must be notified within fifteen days of first sale

(c) The issuer must restrict the purchasers' right to resell the securities; in general must be held for two years or else exemption is lost

(d) These securities typically state that they have not been registered and that they have resale restrictions

(e) Unlike under Rule 504, if nonaccredited investor purchases these securities, audited balance sheet must be supplied (i.e., disclosure is required) as well as other financial statements or information, if readily available

1] If purchased only by accredited investors, no disclosure required

(3) Rule 506 allows private placement of unlimited amount of securities

(a) In general, same rules apply here as outlined under Rule 505

(b) However, an additional requirement is that the unaccredited investors (up to thirty-five) must be sophisticated investors (individuals with knowledge and experience in financial matters) or be represented by individual with such knowledge and experience

> EXAMPLE: *A growing corporation is in need of additional capital and decides to make a new issuance of its stock. The stock is only offered to ten of the president's friends who regularly make financial investments of this sort. They are interested in purchasing the stock for an investment and each of them is provided with the type of information that is regularly included in a registration statement.*

(4) Disclosures for offerings under $2,000,000 have been simplified to be similar to disclosures under Regulation A

(5) A controlling person who sells restricted securities may be held to be an underwriter (and thus subject to the registration provisions) unless requirements of Rule 144 are met when controlling person is selling through a broker

(a) If the following are met, the security can be sold without registration

1] Broker performs no services beyond those of typical broker who executes orders and receives customary fee

2] Ownership (including beneficial ownership) for at least two years

3] Only limited amounts of stock may be sold—based on a specified formula

4] Public must have available adequate disclosure of issuer corporation

5] Notice of sale must be filed with SEC

c. Postregistration transactions by dealer (i.e., dealer is not required to deliver prospectus)

(1) If transaction is made at least forty days after first date security was offered to public, or

(2) After ninety days if it is issuer's first public issue

(3) Does not apply to sales of securities that are leftover part of an allotment from the public issue

6. Antifraud provisions

a. Apply even if securities are exempt or the transactions are exempt as long as interstate commerce is used (use of mail or telephone qualifies) to sell or offer to sell securities

b. Included are schemes to defraud purchaser or making sale by use of untrue statement of material fact or by omission of material fact

       (1) Proof of negligence is sometimes sufficient rather than proof of scienter

       (2) Protects purchaser, not seller

7. Civil liability (i.e., private actions brought by purchasers of securities)

   a. Purchaser may recover if can establish that

       (1) Was a purchase of a security issued under a registration statement containing a misleading statement or omission of a material fact, and

          (a) May also recover if issuer or any person sold unregistered securities for which there is no exemption

       (2) Suffered economic loss

       (3) Privity of contract is **not** necessary

> EXAMPLE: *Third parties who have never dealt with issuer but bought securities from another party have a right to recover when the above is established despite lack of privity.*

       (4) Need **not** prove that defendant intended to deceive

       (5) Purchaser need **not** rely on registration statement to recover

   b. Purchaser of securities may recover from

       (1) The issuer

       (2) Any directors, partners, or underwriters of issuer

       (3) Anyone who signed registration statement

       (4) Experts of authorized statements (e.g., attorneys, accountants, engineers, appraisers)

   c. Burden of proof is shifted to defendant in most cases; however, except for the issuer, defendant may use "due diligence" defense

       (1) Due diligence defense can be used successfully by defendant by proving that

          (a) As an expert, s/he had reasonable grounds after reasonable investigation to believe that his/her own statements were true and/or did not contain any omissions of material facts by the time the registration statement became effective

> EXAMPLE: *Whitewood, a CPA, performs a reasonable audit and discovers no irregularities.*

          (b) S/he relied on an expert for the part of the registration statement in question and did believe (and had reasonable grounds for such belief) that there were no misstatements or material omissions of fact

> EXAMPLE: *Greenwood, a CPA, relies on an attorney's work as a foundation for his own work on contingent liabilities.*

          (c) S/he did reasonably believe that after a reasonable investigation, statements not in the province of an expert were true or that material omissions did not exist

> EXAMPLE: *Lucky, an underwriter, made a reasonable investigation on the registration statement and did reasonably believe no impropriety existed even though misstatements and omissions of material facts existed. Note that the issuer is liable even if s/he exercised the same care and held the same reasonable belief because the issuer is liable without fault and cannot use the due diligence defense.*

   d. Seller of security is liable to purchaser

       (1) If interstate commerce or mail is used, and

       (2) If registration is not in effect and should be, or

       (3) If registration statement contains misstatements or omissions of material facts

       (4) For amount paid plus interest less any income received by purchaser

       (5) Even if seller no longer owns any of the securities

       (6) Buyer may ask for rescission instead of damages

   e. Statute of limitations is

       (1) Two years after discovery is made or after discovery should have reasonably been made of fraud

       (2) In any event no longer than five years after offering of securities

8. Criminal liability

    a. If person intentionally (willfully) makes an untrue statement or intentionally omits a material fact, or willfully violates SEC Act or regulation

        (1) Reckless disregard of the truth may also qualify
        (2) Tampering with documents to be used in official proceedings do qualify

    b. If person uses interstate commerce or mail to fraudulently sell any security
    c. Person is subject to fine or imprisonment up to twenty years or both

        (1) Injunctions are also available

    d. Criminal liability available even if securities are exempt or transactions are exempt

        (1) For example, criminal sanctions available if fraudulent means used to sell securities even though exemption available

9. Increased protection for whistleblowers of public companies

B. Securities Exchange Act of 1934 (Generally applies to subsequent trading of securities—must comply separately with 1933 Act if applicable, that is, initial issuances rather than subsequent trading)

1. Purposes of the Act

    a. To federally regulate securities exchanges and securities traded thereon
    b. To require periodic disclosure by issuers of equity securities
    c. To require adequate information be provided in various transactions
    d. To prevent unfair use of information by insiders
    e. To prevent fraud and deceptive practices

2. Following securities must be registered with SEC

    a. Over-the-counter and other equity securities traded in interstate commerce where corporation has assets of more than $10 million and 500 or more shareholders

        (1) Equity securities—stock, rights to subscribe to, or securities convertible into stock (not ordinary bonds)

    b. Securities that are traded on any national securities exchange must be registered

        (1) Securities exempted under 1933 Act may still be regulated under 1934 Act

    c. Securities offered by issuer who was required to register under 1933 Act

3. Required disclosures in registration include

    a. Names of officers and directors
    b. Nature of business
    c. Financial structure of firm
    d. Any bonus and profit-sharing provisions

4. Sanctions available to SEC under the 1934 Act

    a. Revocation or suspension of registration
    b. Denial of registration
    c. Permanent or temporary suspension of trading of securities (injunction)
    d. May order accounting and disgorgement of gains made illegally
    e. May sanction individuals violating foreign laws
    f. May require large traders to identify selves

5. Exempt securities

    a. Obligations of US government, guaranteed by, or in which US government has interest
    b. Obligations of state or political subdivision, or guaranteed thereby
    c. Securities of federally chartered bank or savings and loan institution
    d. Securities of common carrier regulated by ICC
    e. Industrial development bonds

6. Issuers of securities registered under the 1934 Act must file the following reports with SEC

   a. Annual reports (Form 10-K) must be certified by independent public accountant
   b. Quarterly reports (Form 10-Q) must be filed for each of first three fiscal quarters of each fiscal year of issuer

      (1) Not required to be certified by CPA

   c. Monthly reports (Form 8-K) when material events occur such as change in corporate control, significant change or revaluation of assets, or change in amount of issued securities

      (1) Filed within fifteen days after material event occurs

   d. Similar reports must be given to shareholders

      (1) However, annual report need not be given if issuer had to disclose under 1934 Act only because it made a registered offering under 1933 Act

7. Whether registered under 1934 Act or not, securities registered during previous year under 1933 Act must have periodic reports filed with SEC by issuers
8. Proxy solicitations

   a. Proxy—grant of authority by shareholder to someone else to vote his/her shares at meeting
   b. Proxy solicitation provisions apply to solicitation (by any means of interstate commerce or the mails) of holders of securities required to be registered under the 1934 Act—must be reported to SEC
   c. Proxy statement must be sent with proxy solicitation

      (1) Must contain disclosure of all material facts concerning matters to be voted upon

         (a) Either misstatements or omissions of material facts are violations of proxy rules
         (b) Material means that it would likely affect vote of average shareholder on proposed action

      (2) Purpose is for fairness in corporate action and election of directors

   d. Requirements of proxy itself

      (1) Shall indicate on whose behalf solicitation is made
      (2) Identify clearly and impartially each matter to be acted on

   e. Some of inclusions in proxy material

      (1) Proposals by shareholders that are a proper subject for shareholders to vote on
      (2) Financial statements for last two years, certified by independent accountant, if

         (a) Solicitation is on behalf of management, and
         (b) It is for annual meeting at which directors are to be elected

   f. Any person who owns at least 5% or has held stock for six months or more has right of access to lists of shareholders for lawful purpose
   g. The proxy statement, proxy itself, and any other soliciting material must be filed with SEC
   h. Brokers are required to forward proxies for customers' shares held by broker
   i. Incumbent management is required to mail proxy materials of insurgents to shareholders if requested and expenses are paid by the insurgents
   j. Remedies for violation of proxy solicitation rules

      (1) Civil action by aggrieved shareholder for damages caused by material misinformation or omissions of material facts
      (2) Or injunctions possible
      (3) Or court may set aside vote taken and require a new proxy solicitation with full and fair disclosure

9. Tender offers

   a. Tender offer is invitation by buyer (bidder) to shareholders of targeted company to tender shares they own for sale for price specified over a period of time

b.   Reporting and disclosure requirements apply to tender offers to provide shareholders full disclosure by both the bidder and targeted company

10.   Short-swing profits

a.   Corporation is entitled to recover profits from any insider who sells stock of company within six months of its purchase
b.   Profits that can be recovered are calculated by matching highest sale price with lowest purchase price found within six months
c.   Losses cannot be used to offset these profits

11.   Antifraud provisions—very broad scope

a.   Unlawful to manipulate process and create appearance of active trading (not good-faith transactions by brokers)
b.   Unlawful to use any manipulative or deceptive devices in purchase or sale of securities

(1)   Applies to all securities, whether registered or not (as long as either mail, interstate commerce, or a national stock exchange is used)—this is important
(2)   Includes any act, practice, or scheme which is deceptive or manipulative (against SEC rules and/or regulations)—most importantly, it is unlawful to make any false statement of a material fact or any omission of a material fact that is necessary to make statement(s) not misleading (in connection with purchase or sale of security, whether registered or not)

(a)   This is Rule 10b-5 promulgated by the SEC under Section 10(b) of the Act

1]   There are no exemptions under Rule 10b-5

(3)   Plaintiff must prove

(a)   Defendant made material false statement or omission of material fact in connection with purchase or sale of securities

1]   The basic test of materiality is whether a reasonable person would attach importance to the fact in determining his/her choice of action in the transaction
    EXAMPLE: A broker offers to sell a stock and omits to tell the purchaser that the corporation is about to make an unfavorable merger.

(b)   Defendant acted with scienter which is either

1]   Knowledge of falsity, or
2]   Reckless disregard for the truth
3]   Note that negligence is not sufficient
4]   Note that with antifraud provisions under the **1933** Act scienter need not necessarily be proven

(c)   Defendant must have relied upon false statements or omissions
(d)   Defendant who suffers damages may

1]   Sue for monetary damages, or
2]   Rescind transaction

(4)   Applies to brokers who intend to never deliver securities or who intend to misappropriate proceeds of sales

(a)   SEC by US Supreme Court ruling has power to sue brokers for fraud

(5)   Applies to any seller, buyer, or person who lends his/her name to statements used in the buying and selling of securities. Cross reference this to the 1933 Act that only applies to sellers or offerors of securities
(6)   Applies to insider who buys or sells on inside information until it is disseminated to public

(a)   Includes broad scope of insiders such as officers, directors, accountants, lawyers, employees at the various levels of firm, consultants, agents, representatives of firm, and any other persons owing a fiduciary duty to company

(7) Even if exempt from registration under 1934 Act, still subject to antifraud provisions

(8) Extensive potential liability for insiders

    (a) Must forego trading if one has such knowledge until public has information

        1] Includes insiders and anyone with knowledge (e.g., accountant, attorney, engineer)

        2] Illegal for person (tipper) to give inside information to another person (called tippee)

        3] Tippee is liable if acts on inside information until information is known by public

            a] Tipper is liable for illegal profits of tippee

12. Civil liability

    a. Any person who intentionally (willfully) manipulates a security may be liable to the buyer or seller of that security if the buyer or seller is damaged

      (1) Note that both buyers and sellers may recover under the 1934 Act

    b. Any person who makes a misleading (or of course false) statement about any material fact in any application, report, or document is liable to an injured purchaser or seller if s/he

      (1) Relied on the statement, and

      (2) Did not know it was false or misleading

      (3) Privity of contract is not necessary

      (4) However, the party sued can avoid liability if s/he can prove s/he

          (a) Acted in good faith, and

          (b) Had no knowledge that the statement(s) was (were) materially misleading or false

          (c) SEC may collect liability funds for victims of securities fraud

13. Criminal liability

    a. Has been increased due to Sarbanes-Oxley Act

      (1) Individuals in violation of Rule 10b-5 may be put in prison for up to twenty years and/or may be fined for up to five million dollars

          (a) May be put in prison for up to twenty-five years and/or fined for willful violation of 1934 Act

      (2) Corporations or partnerships are subject to fines of up to twenty-five million dollars

    b. Criminal liability can also be used for intentional false or misleading statements on material facts provided in applications, reports, or other documents under this Act

14. Both private parties and SEC now have civil remedies against violators of 1934 Act

    a. Private parties may recover from those who violate rule 10b-5 as well as from others sharing responsibility such as attorneys, accountants, corporations

      (1) Private parties may also rescind contracts to purchase contacts when violations hurt them

    b. SEC authorized to give awards to individuals that provide information leading to prosecution of insider-trading violators

15. Statute of limitations extended for securities fraud

16. Reporting requirements of insiders under 1934 Act

    a. Must file statement with SEC

      (1) Discloses amount of equity securities

      (2) Time of statement disclosure

          (a) When securities registered, or

          (b) When registration statement becomes effective, or

          (c) Within ten days of person attaining insider status

      (3) Insider must report any changes in ownership within ten days

17. Foreign Corrupt Practices Act

   a. Unlawful for any domestic company or its officers or employees or agents to offer or give to foreign officials or to political party or political officials something of value to influence decisions

      (1) Excluded are routine governmental actions that do not involve official's discretion such as processing applications or permits
      (2) Amendment includes attempt by supplier to obtain any improper advantage is unlawful

   b. Requires companies having registered securities to maintain system of internal control and to maintain accurate accounting and to protect integrity of independent audits
   c. Actions of foreign citizens or organizations committed within US also covered

18. Regulation Fair Disclosure (Reg FD) from SEC requires corporation to disseminate its data equally among investors and analysts to help avoid conflicts of interest by analysts

   a. If one mistakenly gives out inside information s/he must disclose it publicly as soon as is practicable and always within 24 hours or less
   b. Applies also to giving nonpublic information to shareholders who are likely to trade based upon it

C. Sarbanes-Oxley Act of 2002

1. New federal law that contains many reforms that affect this Module, Module 21, and other selected Modules

   a. Act also directs SEC to conduct several studies and to promulgate regulations for corporations, accounting profession, other professions, directors, officers that are expected to affect issues for CPA exam

      (1) New laws and new regulations are expected from this for at least the next few years—each new piece of information will be available when relevant for your preparation for CPA exam

2. Act covers all public companies
3. Section 906 certification provision of Act requires that each periodic report that contains financial reports of the issuer must be accompanied with written statement of CEO or CFO that certifies that reports comply fully with relevant securities laws and also fairly present the financial condition of company in all material aspects

   a. Any officer who makes certification while knowing it does not comply with SEC requirements can be fined up to $1,000,000 or imprisoned for up to ten years, or both

      (1) Officers can be fined for up to $5,000,000 or imprisoned for up to twenty years, or both, for willful violation of this certification requirement
      (2) SEC now permitted to freeze payments to officers and directors during investigation of wrongdoings
      (3) SEC may now prevent unfit individuals from serving as officers or directors of public companies

   b. CEO and CFO must give up any bonuses, incentive-based pay and profits on sales of stock that they received during 12-month time before financial statements are required to be restated because of omissions or misstatements of material facts.

4. Section 302 certification makes officers responsible for maintaining effective internal controls and requires principal executive and financial officers to disclose all significant internal control deficiencies to issuer's auditors and audit committee

   a. Also, requires that they report any fraud (whether material or not) involving management or employees with role in internal controls

5. Act amends Securities Exchange Act of 1934 to make it illegal for issuer to give various types of personal loans to or for any executive officer or director
6. CEO and CFO must give up any bonus, any compensation that is equity based or incentive based, or any profit from sale of corporation's securities during period when corporation was required to restate financial statements due to wrongdoings

    a. CEO and CFO must give up these bonuses and profits even if wrongdoings were not by them but also if they were by any other officer or employee

    b. Act now requires that any wrongdoing officer give up profits from stock sales or bonuses received due to stock being overpriced because of false information

       (1) Act allows not only that improper gains be recovered but also any remedy needed to protect investors

7. Attorneys required to report to chief legal counsel or CEO such things as material violations of securities laws or breach of fiduciary duties

    a. Attorneys must report this to audit committee (or another committee) or board of directors if counsel or CEO does not take action

8. Companies must disclose material off-balance-sheet liabilities and transactions

9. Pro forma information disclosed to public in financial reports, press releases, etc., must not contain any untrue statement of a material fact or omit any material fact

    a. Pro forma information must also be reconciled with financial statements prepared in accordance with GAAP

10. Accelerates deadline for insiders to report any trading of their own company's securities to two days

11. New rules require disclosures, both financial and nonfinancial, to aid public in assessing risk better pertaining to companies (e.g., disclosing off-balance-sheet financing)

    a. Also, aid in purpose of Act to produce reports under Securities Acts that are timely and reliable

D. Internet Securities Offering (ISO) (Direct Public Offerings [DPO])

1. ISO used primarily by small businesses to accumulate capital

2. SEC created electronic database of corporate information

    a. Allows access to much data formerly available only to big institutions

       (1) Thus tends to level playing field between small investors and large investors

       (2) Also, tends to level playing field between small and large businesses

    b. Allows electronic filing

    c. Companies may market securities faster and more cheaply by circumventing paperwork of investment bankers

    d. These securities are typically riskier because often avoid screening processes of various professionals

3. In general, securities laws and regulations apply to ISO

4. Prospectuses may be placed on-line

5. Secondary market for securities may also be accomplished on websites

E. Electronic Signatures and Electronic Records

1. Federal law specifies that no agreement, record, or signature required by federal securities laws or state laws can be denied legal effect because it is electronic record or contains electronic signature

    a. Also applies to electronic signatures between investment advisors, brokers, dealers, and customers

    b. SEC may specify manner of file retention but may not discriminate against any specific technology in effort to promote advances in technology

F. State "Blue-Sky" Laws

1. These are state statutes regulating the issuance and sale of securities

    a. They contain antifraud and registration provisions

2. Must be complied with **in addition** to federal laws

3. Exemptions from federal laws are not exemptions from state laws

G. Antitrust Law

1. The main purpose of federal antitrust laws is to promote the production and distribution of goods and services in the most economical and efficient manner by preserving free, competitive markets

   a. Also promotes fairness and gives consumer a wider choice

2. Regulation (for our concerns) is by federal law, so interstate commerce must be affected before the activity is regulated

   a. If there is a substantial economic effect on interstate commerce, then by court decisions federal law governs

      (1) Even if a business is only carried on within a state, it may substantially affect interstate commerce if it

         (a) Competes or deals with businesses that do business among several states, or
         (b) Purchases or sells a substantial amount of products that come from or wind up in interstate commerce

         EXAMPLE: *Wholesale dealers in a state agree to divide the state market among them. This agreement is intrastate but it reduces the chances for out-of-state dealers to enter the local market and therefore the agreement affects interstate commerce.*

3. If the contract in restraint of trade is illegal, it is unenforceable by the parties, in addition to possible criminal or civil penalties and injunctions

   a. Vertical restraints are agreements between parties from different levels of the distribution chain (i.e., between manufacturer and retailer)
   b. Horizontal restraints are agreements between parties of the same level of the distribution chain (i.e., between two restraints or two manufacturers)

4. Some contracts in restraint of trade **are** legal and enforceable

   a. Seller of a business agrees not to compete with the buyer

      (1) Only valid if for a reasonable time and a reasonable geographic area and if a proper business interest is sought to be protected

         (a) Reasonable time is what is fair under the circumstances to protect buyer (e.g., one year)
         (b) Reasonable area would be where the business is conducted (e.g., neighborhood). If business is statewide, then restriction can be for whole state

         EXAMPLE: *Seller of a bakery covenants not to compete in the immediate locality for one year. This is a reasonable area and also a reasonable length of time.*

   b. Similarly, partners and employees can covenant not to compete with partnership or employer while relationship lasts and for a reasonable time thereafter and within a reasonable area
   c. Buyer or lessee of property may covenant not to use it in competition with, or to the injury of, the seller or lessor

      (1) Same standards of reasonableness apply

5. Exceptions to the antitrust laws

   a. Labor unions unless they join with nonlabor group and act in violation
   b. Patents are a twenty-year monopoly; fourteen years for design patents
   c. Copyrights are a monopoly for the author's life plus seventy years

      (1) For publishers, 95 years after publication or 120 years after creation

   d. Trademarks are a monopoly with an indefinite number of renewals if still used
   e. Insurance business that is covered by state regulations
   f. US exporters may cooperate to compete with foreign entities
   g. State allowed to have quotas on oil marketed for interstate commerce

H. Sherman Act of 1890

1. Contracts, combinations, and conspiracies in restraint of trade are illegal

   a. Only unreasonable restraints are illegal (Rule of Reason)

      (1) Determined on a case-by-case basis

   b. Per Se violations

      (1) Per se violations are unreasonable as a matter of law; they do not have to be proven unreasonable

      (2) Not justifiable, nor defendable

   c. Generally applies to horizontal restraints (i.e., among competitors)

      (1) Price fixing (agreement) is a per se violation

         (a) Whether it actually affects prices or not
         (b) Whether the fixed price is fair or not (presumed unfair)
         (c) Dollar volume is unimportant; existence of any price fixing agreement is illegal
         (d) An actual agreement is not necessary if the parties have a tacit understanding and adhere to it
         (e) Includes quantity limitations and minimum, maximum, buying, and selling prices

      (2) Joint boycotts (i.e., group agreements not to deal with another) are per se violations

         (a) Does not include individual refusals to deal with someone as long as not part of an attempt to monopolize

      (3) Horizontal territorial limitations is a per se violation

         EXAMPLE: Two competitors agree not to sell in each other's section of the city.

   d. Vertical territorial limitations (e.g., franchising agreements) where franchisee receives an exclusive right to sell in a specific territory but is precluded from selling in any area are no longer per se violations but presently only illegal if unreasonable (Rule of Reason)

      EXAMPLE: A distributor requires dealer to sell only in X suburban area.

   e. Vertical resale price maintenance is illegal, i.e., seller sets a minimum or maximum price to which the buyer must adhere when s/he resells

      (1) This is a per se violation

2. Formation of, or the attempt to form a monopoly is illegal

   a. Monopoly is the power to exclude competition and/or to control prices

      (1) Percentage share of the market is a determining factor

         (a) Various cases now generally hold that 70% of market is monopolistic power
         (b) A much lower percentage will suffice if the charge is attempting to monopolize rather than holding monopoly power

      (2) The relevant market consists of the product market and the geographic market

         (a) Product market consists of commodities reasonably interchangeable by consumers

            EXAMPLE: In a case involving a cellophane wrapping manufacturer, the product market was flexible wrapping material.

         (b) Geographic market is the area in which the defendant and competitors sell the product

            EXAMPLE: A geographic market for a major beer brewer is national while for a taxi company it is very local.

   b. It must be an unreasonable monopolistic tendency

      (1) Therefore, the high percentages above are required to constitute a monopoly

    (2) If no intent, or monopoly is thrust on defendant then not illegal

        (a) Growth resulting from superior product, quality of management, or historical accident is not illegal

        (b) There must not be any predatory or coercive conduct

> EXAMPLE: *There are several hotels in a town. Business drops and all but one close. The remaining hotel has taken no action to get the others to close. Although the remaining hotel has a monopoly it was thrust upon the hotel and is therefore not illegal.*

3. Sanctions (not mutually exclusive, both civil and governmental prosecution available)

   a. Injunctions, forced divisions, forced divestiture (by individuals, corporations, or government)

      (1) Government may seize property shipped in interstate commerce and violating party forfeits it

   b. Criminal penalties (by government)
   c. Treble damages (by individuals and corporations)

      (1) That is, actual damages (e.g., loss of profits, multiplied by three)
      (2) Plus attorney fees and court costs
      (3) Instituted to encourage private parties to enforce the antitrust laws

I.   Clayton Act of 1914

1. Supplemented the Sherman Act to prohibit a corporation from acquiring the stock of a competing corporation (merger) where the effect **might** substantially lessen competition or tend to create a monopoly

   a. Acquisitions tending to create a monopoly are violations

      (1) No actual monopoly need be created
      (2) To cope with monopolistic trends in their incipiency
      (3) Applies where there is a reasonable likelihood the merger or acquisition will substantially lessen competition
      (4) As under the Sherman Act, use the percentage of market (product and geographic) test

   b. Amendment of 1950 added the prohibition of the acquisition of assets of another corporation where the effect might lessen competition

      (1) Thus both asset and stock acquisitions are covered
      (2) Includes vertical mergers (sellers-buyers) and conglomerate mergers (e.g., not in same industry) as well as horizontal mergers (competitors)

> EXAMPLE: *A shoe manufacturer buys out one of its retailers. This is a vertical merger.*
> EXAMPLE: *A shoe retailer buys out another shoe retailer. This is a horizontal merger.*
> EXAMPLE: *A pen manufacturer buys out a clothing retailer. This is a conglomerate merger.*

   c. Suit may be brought both before or after completion of the merger

      (1) For example, preliminary injunction to prevent violation
      (2) For example, forced divestiture anytime after completion of a merger if competitor threatened

   d. Under "failing company doctrine," a merger that is anticompetitive may be allowed if

      (1) The acquired company is failing, and
      (2) There is no other willing purchaser whose acquisition of the company would reduce competition less

2. Besides mergers, the Clayton Act prohibits the following arrangements if they substantially lessen competition

   a. Price discrimination between different purchasers

      (1) Allowed if seller saved actual costs by sale to that buyer
      (2) Allowed to temporarily meet competition

    b. Interlocking directorates

       (1) Applies to a director sitting on boards of two or more competing corporations that are "large"

          (a) Dollar threshold to be "large corporation" adjusted yearly by FTC

    c. Tying arrangements

       (1) Occurs where seller forces buyer to take one or more other products as a condition to acquiring the desired product

        EXAMPLE: A manufacturer of a very popular line of jeans requires its retailers to also stock the manufacturer's line of shirts in order to obtain the jeans.

       (2) Only applies to sales and leases, not consignments
       (3) Recently courts use Rule of Reason for tying agreements rather than per se violations

    d. Exclusive dealing arrangements

       (1) Occur where seller requires buyer to buy only seller's products (i.e., may not deal in the commodities of a competitor)

        EXAMPLE: A sporting goods manufacturer requires its retailers not to sell its competitor's goods.

       (2) A violation if a substantial dollar amount or substantial percentage of the market is involved

          (a) Then presumed to be anticompetitive (i.e., a per se violation)

3. Judicial standards for Clayton Act violations

    a. If competition is not lessened, it is not illegal
    b. Quantitative considerations

       (1) Sales volume of product, in dollars
       (2) Control of the market (e.g., percentage share)

    c. Qualitative considerations

       (1) Strength of competitors
       (2) Ease of entry into industry by newcomers

4. Sanctions

    a. Injunctions, forced divisions, forced divestitures (by individuals, corporations, or government)
    b. Treble damages (by individuals, corporations)

J. Federal Trade Commission Act of 1914

1. Created the Federal Trade Commission (FTC)

    a. FTC has authority to enforce most of the antitrust laws
    b. FTC has exclusive authority to enforce this Act's prohibitions (i.e., individuals may not enforce)
    c. FTC has authority to determine what practices are unfair or undesirable

2. Prohibits unfair methods of competition and deceptive practices involving advertising, telemarketing, electronic advertising.

    a. FTC has exclusive authority under this Act and can determine what is unfair
    b. FTC may stop unfair and deceptive practices in their incipiency (i.e., before an actual violation occurs) as well as after a violation occurs

      EXAMPLE: An oil company agreed with a tire company that the oil company would promote the sale of the tire company's accessories to the oil company's independent dealers. There was no tying or overt coercion in these promotions to the independent dealers, but the dominant position of the oil company over its dealers created strong potential for stifling competition. The agreement was therefore an unfair method of competition.

    c. Unfairness standards

       (1) Cause of substantial injury to competitors or consumers

        (2) Offends public policy

        (3) Oppressive or unscrupulous practices

  3. Sanctions

    a. Cease and desist orders

        (1) Civil penalty for each violation

        (2) Each day of continued violation is separate offense

        (3) FTC may also use cease and desist orders for the Sherman Act and Clayton Act

K. Robinson-Patman Act of 1936

  1. Amended the Clayton Act to expand control in the area of price discrimination

    a. Also makes buyers (in addition to sellers) liable for price discrimination

  2. Prohibits

    a. Discrimination as to price between purchasers of goods of like quality and grade

        (1) If the effect is to substantially lessen competition or tend to create a monopoly

        (2) Or if the effect is to injure or prevent competition by competitors or customer's competitors

        (3) Includes price discrimination between different geographical areas unless based on cost

    b. Special discounts, rebates, or commissions (e.g., brokerage fees, to customers)

        (1) Services (e.g., advertising) not allowed either unless on a proportionate basis to all customers

        (2) To prevent favoritism to purchasers of quantity

        (3) Illegal per se

    c. Buyers also are prohibited from knowingly inducing or receiving a discrimination in price or service

  3. Price (differential) discrimination is allowed if

    a. It can be directly related to lower costs caused by production and sales in quantity (i.e., functional)

        (1) This cost differential must be proven; reliance on the general assumption that larger quantities are cheaper is not accepted

    b. Price discrimination is to meet lawful competition

        (1) If a competitor has a low price, this may be met

        (2) Only to keep old customers, not to gain new ones

        (3) Competitor's price must be lawful (i.e., price discrimination cannot be met with price discrimination)

    c. There is no substantial lessening of competition nor injury of competition

  4. Sanctions

    a. Injunctions (by individual, corporations, government)

    b. Criminal penalties

    c. Treble damages (by individuals, corporations)

MULTIPLE-CHOICE QUESTIONS (1-44)

1. A preliminary prospectus, permitted under SEC Regulations, is known as the
  a. Unaudited prospectus.
  b. Qualified prospectus.
  c. "Blue-sky" prospectus.
  d. "Red-herring" prospectus.

2. Under the Securities Exchange Act of 1934, which of the following types of instruments is excluded from the definition of "securities"?
  a. Investment contracts.
  b. Convertible debentures.
  c. Nonconvertible debentures.
  d. Certificates of deposit.

3. A tombstone advertisement
  a. May be substituted for the prospectus under certain circumstances.
  b. May contain an offer to sell securities.
  c. Notifies prospective investors that a previously-offered security has been withdrawn from the market and is therefore effectively "dead."
  d. Makes known the availability of a prospectus.

4. Under the Securities Act of 1933, which of the following statements most accurately reflects how securities registration affects an investor?
  a. The investor is provided with information on the stockholders of the offering corporation.
  b. The investor is provided with information on the principal purposes for which the offering's proceeds will be used.
  c. The investor is guaranteed by the SEC that the facts contained in the registration statement are accurate.
  d. The investor is assured by the SEC against loss resulting from purchasing the security.

5. Which of the following statements concerning the prospectus required by the Securities Act of 1933 is correct?
  a. The prospectus is a part of the registration statement.
  b. The prospectus should enable the SEC to pass on the merits of the securities.
  c. The prospectus must be filed after an offer to sell.
  d. The prospectus is prohibited from being distributed to the public until the SEC approves the accuracy of the facts embodied therein.

Items 6 and 7 are based on the following facts:

Sandy Corporation is considering the following issuances:

  I. Notes with maturities of three months to be used for commercial purposes and having a total aggregate value of $500,000.
  II. Notes with maturities of two years to be used for investment purposes and having a total aggregate value of $300,000.
  III. Notes with maturities of two years to be used for commercial purposes and having a total aggregate value of $200,000.

6. Which of the above notes is(are) exempt securities and need not be registered under the Securities Act of 1933?

  a. I only.
  b. II only.
  c. I and III only.
  d. I, II, and III.

7. Which of the above notes is(are) subject to the antifraud provisions of the Securities Act of 1933?
  a. I only.
  b. II only.
  c. I and III only.
  d. I, II, and III.

8. Which of the following is **not** a security under the definition for the Securities Act of 1933?
  a. Any note.
  b. Bond certificate of interest.
  c. Debenture.
  d. All of the above are securities under the Act.

9. Which of the following requirements must be met by an issuer of securities who wants to make an offering by using shelf registration?

	Original registration statement must be kept updated	*The offer must be a first-time issuer of securities*
a.	Yes	Yes
b.	Yes	No
c.	No	Yes
d.	No	No

10. Which of the following securities would be regulated by the provisions of the Securities Act of 1933?
  a. Securities issued by not-for-profit, charitable organizations.
  b. Securities guaranteed by domestic governmental organizations.
  c. Securities issued by savings and loan associations.
  d. Securities issued by insurance companies.

11. Which of the following securities is exempt from registration under the Securities Act of 1933?
  a. Shares of nonvoting common stock, provided their par value is less than $1.00.
  b. A class of stock given in exchange for another class by the issuer to its existing stockholders without the issuer paying a commission.
  c. Limited partnership interests sold for the purpose of acquiring funds to invest in bonds issued by the United States.
  d. Corporate debentures that were previously subject to an effective registration statement, provided they are convertible into shares of common stock.

12. Universal Corp. intends to sell its common stock to the public in an interstate offering that will be registered under the Securities Act of 1933. Under the Act,
  a. Universal can make offers to sell its stock before filing a registration statement, provided that it does **not** actually issue stock certificates until after the registration is effective.
  b. Universal's registration statement becomes effective at the time it is filed, assuming the SEC does **not** object within twenty days thereafter.
  c. A prospectus must be delivered to each purchaser of Universal's common stock unless the purchaser qualifies as an accredited investor.

d. Universal's filing of a registration statement with the SEC does **not** automatically result in compliance with the "blue-sky" laws of the states in which the offering will be made.

13. If securities are exempt from the registration provisions of the Securities Act of 1933, any fraud committed in the course of selling such securities can be challenged by

	SEC	Person defrauded
a.	Yes	Yes
b.	Yes	No
c.	No	Yes
d.	No	No

14. Issuers of securities are normally required under the Securities Act of 1933 to file a registration statement with the Securities Exchange Commission before these securities are either offered or sold to the general public. Which of the following is a reason why the SEC adopted the registration statement forms called Form S-2 and Form S-3?
   a. To require more extensive reporting.
   b. To be filed along with Form S-1.
   c. To reduce the burden that issuers have under the securities laws.
   d. To reduce the burden of disclosure that issuers have for intrastate issues of securities.

15. Regulation D provides for important exemptions to registration of securities under the Securities Act of 1933. Which of the following would be exempt?

   I. Issuance of $500,000 of securities sold in a twelve-month period to forty investors.
   II. Issuance of $2,000,000 of securities sold in a twelve-month period to ten investors. The issuer restricts the right of the purchasers to resell for two years.

   a. I only.
   b. II only.
   c. Both I and II.
   d. Neither I nor II.

16. Pix Corp. is making a $6,000,000 stock offering. Pix wants the offering exempt from registration under the Securities Act of 1933. Which of the following provisions of the Act would Pix have to comply with for the offering to be exempt?
   a. Regulation A.
   b. Regulation D, Rule 504.
   c. Regulation D, Rule 505.
   d. Regulation D, Rule 506.

17. Eldridge Corporation is seeking to offer $7,000,000 of securities under Regulation D of the Securities Act of 1933. Which of the following is(are) true if Eldridge wants an exemption from registration under the Securities Act of 1933?

   I.   Eldridge must comply with Rule 506 of Regulation D.
   II. These securities could be debentures.
   III. These securities could be investment contracts.

   a. I only.
   b. I and II only.
   c. II and III only.
   d. I, II, and III.

18. An offering made under the provisions of Regulation A of the Securities Act of 1933 requires that the issuer
   a. File an offering circular with the SEC.
   b. Sell only to accredited investors.
   c. Provide investors with the prior four years' audited financial statements.
   d. Provide investors with a proxy registration statement.

19. Which of the following facts will result in an offering of securities being exempt from registration under the Securities Act of 1933?
   a. The securities are nonvoting preferred stock.
   b. The issuing corporation was closely held prior to the offering.
   c. The sale or offer to sell the securities is made by a person other than an issuer, underwriter, or dealer.
   d. The securities are AAA-rated debentures that are collateralized by first mortgages on property that has a market value of 200% of the offering price.

20. Regulation D of the Securities Act of 1933
   a. Restricts the number of purchasers of an offering to thirty-five.
   b. Permits an exempt offering to be sold to both accredited and nonaccredited investors.
   c. Is limited to offers and sales of common stock that do not exceed $1.5 million.
   d. Is exclusively available to small business corporations as defined by Regulation D.

21. Frey, Inc. intends to make a $2,000,000 common stock offering under Rule 505 of Regulation D of the Securities Act of 1933. Frey
   a. May sell the stock to an unlimited number of investors.
   b. May make the offering through a general advertising.
   c. Must notify the SEC within fifteen days after the first sale of the offering.
   d. Must provide all investors with a prospectus.

22. Under Regulation D of the Securities Act of 1933, which of the following conditions apply to private placement offerings? The securities
   a. Cannot be sold for longer than a six-month period.
   b. Cannot be the subject of an immediate unregistered reoffering to the public.
   c. Must be sold to accredited institutional investors.
   d. Must be sold to fewer than twenty nonaccredited investors.

23. Which of the following statements concerning an initial intrastate securities offering made by an issuer residing in and doing business in that state is correct?
   a. The offering would be exempt from the registration requirements of the Securities Act of 1933.
   b. The offering would be subject to the registration requirements of the Securities Exchange Act of 1934.
   c. The offering would be regulated by the SEC.
   d. The shares of the offering could **not** be resold to investors outside the state for at least one year.

24. Pix Corp. is making a $6,000,000 stock offering. Pix wants the offering exempt from registration under the

Securities Act of 1933. Which of the following requirements would Pix have to comply with when selling the securities?

   a.   No more than thirty-five investors.
   b.   No more than thirty-five nonaccredited investors.
   c.   Accredited investors only.
   d.   Nonaccredited investors only.

25. Which of the following transactions will be exempt from the full registration requirements of the Securities Act of 1933?

   a.   All intrastate offerings.
   b.   All offerings made under Regulation A.
   c.   Any resale of a security purchased under a Regulation D offering.
   d.   Any stockbroker transaction.

26. Under Rule 504 of Regulation D of the Securities Act of 1933, which of the following is(are) required?

   I.   No general offering or solicitation is permitted.
   II.   The issuer must restrict the purchasers' right to resell the securities.

   a.   I only.
   b.   II only.
   c.   Both I and II.
   d.   Neither I nor II.

27. Dean, Inc., a publicly traded corporation, paid a $10,000 bribe to a local zoning official. The bribe was recorded in Dean's financial statements as a consulting fee. Dean's unaudited financial statements were submitted to the SEC as part of a quarterly filing. Which of the following federal statutes did Dean violate?

   a.   Federal Trade Commission Act.
   b.   Securities Act of 1933.
   c.   Securities Exchange Act of 1934.
   d.   North American Free Trade Act.

28. The Securities Exchange Commission promulgated Rule 10b-5 under Section 10(b) of the Securities Exchange Act of 1934. Which of the following is(are) purpose(s) of the Act?

	To rate securities so investors can choose *more wisely*	To encourage disclosure of information *relevant to investors*	To deter fraud involving *securities*
a.	No	No	Yes
b.	No	Yes	Yes
c.	Yes	Yes	Yes
d.	Yes	Yes	No

29. Integral Corp. has assets in excess of $4 million, has 350 stockholders, and has issued common and preferred stock. Integral is subject to the reporting provisions of the Securities Exchange Act of 1934. For its 2001 fiscal year, Integral filed the following with the SEC: quarterly reports, an annual report, and a periodic report listing newly appointed officers of the corporation. Integral did not notify the SEC of stockholder "short swing" profits; did not report that a competitor made a tender offer to Integral's stockholders; and did not report changes in the price of its stock as sold on the New York Stock Exchange. Under SEC reporting requirements, which of the following was Integral required to do?

   a.   Report the tender offer to the SEC.
   b.   Notify the SEC of stockholder "short swing" profits.

   c.   File the periodic report listing newly appointed officers.
   d.   Report the changes in the market price of its stock.

30. Which of the following factors, by itself, requires a corporation to comply with the reporting requirements of the Securities Exchange Act of 1934?

   a.   Six hundred employees.
   b.   Shares listed on a national securities exchange.
   c.   Total assets of $2 million.
   d.   Four hundred holders of equity securities.

31. The registration provisions of the Securities Exchange Act of 1934 require disclosure of all of the following information **except** the

   a.   Names of owners of at least 5% of any class of nonexempt equity security.
   b.   Bonus and profit-sharing arrangements.
   c.   Financial structure and nature of the business.
   d.   Names of officers and directors.

32. Under the Securities Act of 1933, which of the following statements is correct concerning a public issuer of securities who has made a registered offering?

   a.   The issuer is required to distribute an annual report to its stockholders.
   b.   The issuer is subject to the proxy rules of the SEC.
   c.   The issuer must file an annual report (Form 10-K) with the SEC.
   d.   The issuer is **not** required to file a quarterly report (Form 10-Q) with the SEC, unless a material event occurs.

33. Which of the following persons is **not** an insider of a corporation subject to the Securities Exchange Act of 1934 registration and reporting requirements?

   a.   An attorney for the corporation.
   b.   An owner of 5% of the corporation's outstanding debentures.
   c.   A member of the board of directors.
   d.   A stockholder who owns 10% of the outstanding common stock.

34. The Securities Exchange Commission promulgated Rule 10b-5 from power it was given the Securities Exchange Act of 1934. Under this rule, it is unlawful for any person to use a scheme to defraud another in connection with the

	Purchase of any security	*Sale of any security*
a.	Yes	Yes
b.	Yes	No
c.	No	Yes
d.	No	No

35. The antifraud provisions of Rule 10b-5 of the Securities Exchange Act of 1934

   a.   Apply only if the securities involved were registered under either the Securities Act of 1933 or the Securities Exchange Act of 1934.
   b.   Require that the plaintiff show negligence on the part of the defendant in misstating facts.
   c.   Require that the wrongful act must be accomplished through the mail, any other use of interstate commerce, or through a national securities exchange.
   d.   Apply only if the defendant acted with intent to defraud.

Items 36 through 38 are based on the following:

Link Corp. is subject to the reporting provisions of the Securities Exchange Act of 1934.

36. Which of the following situations would require Link to be subject to the reporting provisions of the 1934 Act?

	Shares listed on a national securities exchange	More than one class of stock
a.	Yes	Yes
b.	Yes	No
c.	No	Yes
d.	No	No

37. Which of the following documents must Link file with the SEC?

	Quarterly reports (Form 10-Q)	Proxy Statements
a.	Yes	Yes
b.	Yes	No
c.	No	Yes
d.	No	No

38. Which of the following reports must also be submitted to the SEC?

	Report by any party making a tender offer to purchase Link's stock	Report of proxy solicitations by Link stockholders
a.	Yes	Yes
b.	Yes	No
c.	No	Yes
d.	No	No

39. Which of the following events must be reported to the SEC under the reporting provisions of the Securities Exchange Act of 1934?

	Tender offers	Insider trading	Soliciting proxies
a.	Yes	Yes	Yes
b.	Yes	Yes	No
c.	Yes	No	Yes
d.	No	Yes	Yes

40. Adler, Inc. is a reporting company under the Securities Exchange Act of 1934. The only security it has issued is voting common stock. Which of the following statements is correct?

a. Because Adler is a reporting company, it is **not** required to file a registration statement under the Securities Act of 1933 for any future offerings of its common stock.

b. Adler need **not** file its proxy statements with the SEC because it has only one class of stock outstanding.

c. Any person who owns more than 10% of Adler's common stock must file a report with the SEC.

d. It is unnecessary for the required annual report (Form 10-K) to include audited financial statements.

41. Which of the following is correct concerning annual reports (Form 10-K) and quarterly reports (Form 10-Q)?

a. Both Form 10-K and Form 10-Q must be certified by independent public accountants and both must be filed with the SEC.

b. Both Form 10-K and Form 10-Q must be certified by independent public accountants but neither need be filed with the SEC.

c. Although both Form 10-K and Form 10-Q must be filed with the SEC, only Form 10-K need be certified by independent public accountants.

d. Form 10-K must be certified by independent public accountants and must also be filed with the SEC; however, Form 10-Q need not be certified by independent public accountants nor filed with the SEC.

42. Burk Corporation has issued securities that must be registered with the Securities Exchange Commission under the Securities Exchange Act of 1934. A material event took place a week ago, that is, there was a change in the control of Burk Corporation. Which of the following statements is correct?

a. Because of this material event, Burk Corporation is required to file with the SEC, Forms 10-K and 10-Q.

b. Because of this material event, Burk Corporation is required to file Form 8-K.

c. Burk Corporation need not file any forms with the SEC concerning this material event if the relevant facts are fully disclosed in the audited financial statements.

d. Burk Corporation need not file any form concerning the material event if Burk Corporation has an exemption under Rules 504, 505, or 506 of Regulation D.

43. Loop Corp. has made a major breakthrough in the development of a micropencil. Loop has patented the product and is seeking to maximize the profit potential. In this effort, Loop can legally

a. Require its retailers to sell only Loop's products, including the micropencils, and **not** sell similar competing products.

b. Require its retailers to take stipulated quantities of its other products in addition to the micropencils.

c. Sell the product at whatever price the traffic will bear even though Loop has a monopoly.

d. Sell the product to its retailers upon condition that they do not sell the micropencils to the public for less than a stated price.

44. Robinson's pricing policies have come under attack by several of its retailers. In fact, one of those retailers, Patman, has instigated legal action against Robinson alleging that Robinson charges other favored retailers prices for its products which are lower than those charged to it. Patman's legal action against Robinson

a. Will fail unless Patman can show that there has been an injury to competition.

b. Will be sufficient if the complaint alleges that Robinson charged different prices to different customers and there is a reasonable possibility that competition may be adversely affected.

c. Is groundless since one has the legal right to sell at whatever price one wishes as long as the price is determined unilaterally.

d. Is to be tested under the Rule of Reason and if the different prices charged are found to be reasonable, the complaint will be dismissed.

PROBLEMS

NOTE: These types of problems are no longer included in the CPA Examination but they have been retained because they are useful in developing skills to complete simulations.

Problem 1   (15 to 20 minutes)

Various Enterprises Corporation is a medium sized conglomerate listed on the American Stock Exchange. It is constantly in the process of acquiring smaller corporations and is invariably in need of additional money. Among its diversified holdings is a citrus grove which it purchased eight years ago as an investment. The grove's current fair market value is in excess of $2 million. Various also owns 800,000 shares of Resistance Corporation which it acquired in the open market over a period of years. These shares represent a 17% minority interest in Resistance and are worth approximately $2 1/2 million. Various does its short-term financing with a consortium of banking institutions. Several of these loans are maturing; in addition to renewing these loans, it wishes to increase its short-term debt from $3 to $4 million.

In light of the above, Various is considering resorting to one or all of the following alternatives in order to raise additional working capital.

• An offering of 500 citrus grove units at $5,000 per unit. Each unit would give the purchaser a 0.2% ownership interest in the citrus grove development. Various would furnish management and operation services for a fee under a management contract and net proceeds would be paid to the unit purchasers. The offering would be confined almost exclusively to the state in which the groves are located or in the adjacent state in which Various is incorporated.

• An increase in the short-term borrowing by $1 million from the banking institution which currently provides short-term funds. The existing debt would be consolidated, extended, and increased to $4 million and would mature over a nine-month period. This would be evidenced by a short-term note.

• Sale of the 17% minority interest in Resistance Corporation in the open market through its brokers over a period of time and in such a way as to minimize decreasing the value of the stock. The stock is to be sold in an orderly manner in the ordinary course of the broker's business.

Required:

Answer the following, setting forth reasons for any conclusions stated.

In separate paragraphs discuss the impact of the registration requirements of the Securities Act of 1933 on each of the above proposed alternatives.

Problem 2   (15 to 25 minutes)

Perry, a staff accountant with Orlean Associates, CPAs, reviewed the following transactions engaged in by Orlean's two clients: World Corp. and Unity Corp.

WORLD CORP.

During 2003, World Corp. made a $4,000,000 offering of its stock. The offering was sold to fifty nonaccredited investors and 150 accredited investors. There was a general advertising of the offering. All purchasers were provided with material information concerning World Corp. The offering was completely sold by the end of 2003. The SEC was notified thirty days after the first sale of the offering.

World did not register the offering and contends that the offering and any subsequent resale of the securities are completely exempt from registration under Regulation D, Rule 505, of the Securities Act of 1933.

UNITY CORP.

Unity Corp. has 750 equity stockholders and assets in excess of $100,000,000. Unity's stock is traded on a national stock exchange. Unity contends that it is not a covered corporation and is not required to comply with the reporting provisions of the Securities Exchange Act of 1934.

Required:

a. 1.   State whether World is correct in its contention that the offering is exempt from registration under Regulation D, Rule 505, of the Securities Act of 1933. Give the reason(s) for your conclusion.

2.   State whether World is correct in its contention that on subsequent resale the securities are completely exempt from registration. Give the reason(s) for your conclusion.

b. 1.   State whether Unity is correct in its contention that it is not a covered corporation and is not required to comply with the reporting requirements of the Securities Exchange Act of 1934 and give the reason(s) for your conclusion.

2.   Identify and describe two principal reports a covered corporation must file with the SEC.

SIMULATION PROBLEMS

Simulation Problem 1   (10 to 15 minutes)

Situation			
	Rule 504	Rule 506	Rule 505

You will have 15 questions based on the following information:

Butler Manufacturing Corp. planned to raise capital for a plant expansion by borrowing from banks and making several stock offerings. Butler engaged Weaver, CPA, to audit its December 31, 2001 financial statements. Butler told Weaver that the financial statements would be given to certain named banks and included in the prospectuses for the stock offerings.

In performing the audit, Weaver did not confirm accounts receivable and, as a result, failed to discover a material overstatement of accounts receivable. Also, Weaver was aware of a pending class action product liability lawsuit that was not disclosed in Butler's financial statements. Despite being advised by Butler's legal counsel that Butler's potential liability under the lawsuit would result in material losses, Weaver issued an unqualified opinion on Butler's financial statements.

In May 2003, Union Bank, one of the named banks, relied on the financial statements and Weaver's opinion in giving Butler a $500,000 loan.

Butler raised an additional $16,450,000 through the following stock offerings, which were sold completely:

• June 2003—Butler made a $450,000 unregistered offering of Class B nonvoting common stock under Rule 504 of Regulation D of the Securities Act of 1933. This offering was sold over one year to thirty nonaccredited investors and twenty accredited investors by general solicitation. The SEC was notified eight days after the first sale of this offering.

• September 2003—Butler made a $10,000,000 unregistered offering of Class A voting common stock under Rule 506 of Regulation D of the Securities Act of 1933. This offering was sold over one year to 200 accredited investors and thirty nonaccredited investors through a private placement. The SEC was notified fourteen days after the first sale of this offering.

• November 2003—Butler made a $6,000,000 unregistered offering of preferred stock under Rule 505 of Regulation D of the Securities Act of 1933. This offering was sold during a one-year period to forty nonaccredited investors by private placement. The SEC was notified eighteen days after the first sale of this offering.

Shortly after obtaining the Union loan, Butler began experiencing financial problems but was able to stay in business because of the money raised by the offerings. Butler was found liable in the product liability suit. This resulted in a judgment Butler could not pay. Butler also defaulted on the Union loan and was involuntarily petitioned into bankruptcy. This caused Union to sustain a loss and Butler's stockholders to lose their investments. As a result

• The SEC claimed that all three of Butler's offerings were made improperly and were not exempt from registration.
• Union sued Weaver for

     • Negligence
     • Common Law Fraud

• The stockholders who purchased Butler's stock through the offerings sued Weaver, alleging fraud under Section 10(b) and Rule 10b-5 of the Securities Exchange Act of 1934.

These transactions took place in a jurisdiction providing for accountant's liability for negligence to known and intended users of financial statements.

	Rule 504		
Situation		Rule 506	Rule 505

Part a.

Items 1 through 5 are questions related to the June 2003 offering made under Rule 504 of Regulation D of the Securities Act of 1933. For each item, indicate your answer by choosing either Yes or No.

	Yes	*No*
1. Did the offering comply with the dollar limitation of Rule 504?	O	O
2. Did the offering comply with the method of sale restrictions?	O	O
3. Was the offering sold during the applicable time limit?	O	O
4. Was the SEC notified timely of the first sale of the securities?	O	O
5. Was the SEC correct in claiming that this offering was not exempt from registration?	O	O

		Rule 506		
Situation	Rule 504			Rule 505

Part b.

Items 6 through 10 are questions related to the September 2003 offering made under Rule 506 of Regulation D of the Securities Act of 1933. For each item, indicate your answer by choosing either Yes or No.

	Yes	*No*
6. Did the offering comply with the dollar limitation of Rule 506?	O	O
7. Did the offering comply with the method of sale restrictions?	O	O
8. Was the offering sold to the correct number of investors?	O	O
9. Was the SEC notified timely of the first sale of the securities?	O	O
10. Was the SEC correct in claiming that this offering was not exempt from registration?	O	O

			Rule 505
Situation	Rule 504	Rule 506	

Part c.

Items 11 through 15 are questions related to the November 2003 offering made under Rule 505 of Regulation D of the Securities Act of 1933. For each item, indicate your answer by choosing either Yes or No.

	Yes	*No*
11. Did the offering comply with the dollar limitation of Rule 505?	O	O
12. Was the offering sold during the applicable time limit?	O	O
13. Was the offering sold to the correct number of investors?	O	O
14. Was the SEC notified timely of the first sale of the securities?	O	O
15. Was the SEC correct in claiming that this offering was not exempt from registration?	O	O

Simulation Problem 2   (10 to 15 minutes)

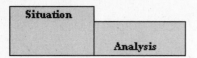

Coffee Corp., a publicly held corporation, wants to make an $8,000,000 exempt offering of its shares as a private placement offering under Regulation D, Rule 506, of the Securities Act of 1933. Coffee has more than 500 shareholders and assets in excess of $1 billion, and has its shares listed on a national securities exchange.

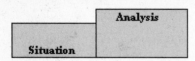

Items 1 through 5 relate to the application of the provisions of the Securities Act of 1933 and the Securities Exchange Act of 1934 to Coffee Corp. and the offering. For each item, select from List II whether only statement I is correct, whether only statement II is correct, whether both statements I and II are correct, or whether neither statement I nor II is correct.

List II
A. I only.
B. II only.
C. Both I and II.
D. Neither I nor II.

1. I.   Coffee Corp. may make the Regulation D, Rule 506, exempt offering.
    II. Coffee Corp., because it is required to report under the Securities Exchange Act of 1934, may **not** make an exempt offering.

2. I.   Shares sold under a Regulation D, Rule 506, exempt offering may only be purchased by accredited investors.
    II. Shares sold under a Regulation D, Rule 506, exempt offering may be purchased by any number of investors provided there are **no** more than thirty-five nonaccredited investors.

3. I.   An exempt offering under Regulation D, Rule 506, must **not** be for more than $10,000,000.
    II. An exempt offering under Regulation D, Rule 506, has **no** dollar limit.

4. I.   Regulation D, Rule 506, requires that all investors in the exempt offering be notified that for nine months after the last sale **no** resale may be made to a nonresident.
    II. Regulation D, Rule 506, requires that the issuer exercise reasonable care to assure that purchasers of the exempt offering are buying for investment and are **not** underwriters.

5. I.   The SEC must be notified by Coffee Corp. within five days of the first sale of the exempt offering securities.
    II. Coffee Corp. must include an SEC notification of the first sale of the exempt offering securities in Coffee's next filed Quarterly Report (Form 10-Q).

MULTIPLE-CHOICE ANSWERS

1.	d	__ __	11.	b	__ __	21.	c	__ __	31.	a	__ __	41.	c	__ __
2.	d	__ __	12.	d	__ __	22.	b	__ __	32.	c	__ __	42.	b	__ __
3.	d	__ __	13.	a	__ __	23.	a	__ __	33.	b	__ __	43.	c	__ __
4.	b	__ __	14.	c	__ __	24.	b	__ __	34.	a	__ __	44.	b	__ __
5.	a	__ __	15.	c	__ __	25.	b	__ __	35.	c	__ __			
6.	a	__ __	16.	d	__ __	26.	d	__ __	36.	b	__ __			
7.	d	__ __	17.	d	__ __	27.	c	__ __	37.	a	__ __			
8.	d	__ __	18.	a	__ __	28.	b	__ __	38.	a	__ __	1st:	__/44= __%
9.	b	__ __	19.	c	__ __	29.	c	__ __	39.	a	__ __	2nd:	__/44= __%
10.	d	__ __	20.	b	__ __	30.	b	__ __	40.	c	__ __			

MULTIPLE-CHOICE ANSWER EXPLANATIONS

A.   Securities Act of 1933

1.   (d)   A preliminary prospectus is usually called a "red-herring" prospectus. The preliminary prospectus indicates that a registration statement has been filed but has not become effective.

2.   (d)   Securities include debentures, stocks, bonds, some notes, and investment contracts. The main idea is that the investor intends to make a profit on the investment through the efforts of others. A certificate of deposit is a type of commercial paper, not a security.

3.   (d)   A tombstone advertisement is allowed to inform potential investors that a prospectus for the given company is available. It is not an offer to sell or the solicitation of an offer to buy the securities. Answer (a) is incorrect because the tombstone ad informs potential purchasers of the prospectus and cannot be used as a substitute for the prospectus. Answer (b) is incorrect because it informs of the availability of the prospectus and cannot be construed as an offer to sell securities. Answer (c) is incorrect because the tombstone ad notifies potential purchasers of the prospectus. It does not notify that the securities have been withdrawn from the market.

4.   (b)   The registration of securities under the Securities Act of 1933 has as its purpose to provide potential investors with full and fair disclosure of all material information relating to the issuance of securities, including such information as the principal purposes for which the offering's proceeds will be used. Answer (a) is incorrect because information on the stockholders of the offering corporation is not required to be reported. Answer (c) is incorrect because the SEC does not guarantee the accuracy of the registration statements. Answer (d) is incorrect because although the SEC does seek to compel full and fair disclosure, it does not evaluate the securities on merit or value, or give any assurances against loss.

5.   (a)   If no exemption is applicable under the Securities Act of 1933, public offerings must be registered with the SEC accompanied by a prospectus. Answer (b) is incorrect because the SEC does not pass on nor rate the securities. Answer (c) is incorrect because the prospectus is given to prospective purchasers of the securities. Answer (d) is incorrect because the SEC does not pass on the merits or accuracy of the prospectus.

6.   (a)   Notes are exempt securities under the Securities Act of 1933 if they have a maturity of nine months or less and if they are also used for commercial purposes rather than investments. The actual dollar amounts in the question are not a factor. The notes described in II are not exempt for two reasons; they have a maturity of two years and are used for investment purposes. The notes in III are not exempt because the maturity is two years even though they are for commercial purposes.

7.   (d)   Whether the securities are exempt from registration or not, they are still subject to the antifraud provisions of the Securities Act of 1933.

8.   (d)   The definition of a security is very broad under the Securities Act of 1933. The basic idea is that the investor intends to make a profit through the efforts of others rather than through his/her own efforts. Notes, bond certificates of interest, and debentures are all considered securities.

9.   (b)   If an issuer of securities wants to make an offering by using shelf registration, the actual issuance takes place over potentially a long period of time. Therefore, s/he must keep the original registration statement updated. There is no requirement that the offeror must be a first-time issuer of securities.

10.   (d)   Under the 1933 Act, certain securities are exempt. Although insurance and annuity contracts are exempt, securities issued by the insurance companies are not. Answer (a) is incorrect because securities of nonprofit organizations are exempt. Answer (b) is incorrect because securities issued by or guaranteed by domestic government organizations are exempt. Answer (c) is incorrect because securities issued by savings and loan associations are exempt.

11.   (b)   Securities exchanged for other securities by the issuer exclusively with its existing shareholders are exempt from registration under the 1933 Act as long as no commission is paid and both sets of securities are issued by the same issuer. Answer (a) is incorrect because nonvoting common stock is not exempted under the Act. The amount of the par value is irrelevant. Answer (c) is incorrect because although the securities of governments are themselves exempt, the limited partnership interests are not. Answer (d) is incorrect because no such exemption is allowed.

12.   (d)   Even though the issuer may comply with the Federal Securities Act of 1933, it must also comply with any applicable state "blue-sky" laws that regulate the securities at the state level. Answer (a) is incorrect because it is unlawful for the company to offer or sell the securities prior to the effective registration date. Answer (b) is incorrect because registration becomes effective on the twentieth day after filing unless the SEC issues a stop order. Answer (c) is incorrect because a prospectus is any notice, circular, advertisement, letter, or communication offering the security for sale. No general offering or solicitation is allowed under Rules 505 or 506 of Regulation D whether the purchaser is accredited or not.

13.   (a)   Even if the securities are exempt under the Securities Act of 1933, they are still subject to the antifraud provisions. Both the person defrauded and the SEC can challenge the fraud committed in the course of selling the securities.

14.   (c)   The SEC adopted the Forms S-2 and S-3 to decrease the work that issuers have in preparing registration statements by permitting them to give less detailed disclosure under certain conditions than Form S-1 which is the basic long form. Answer (a) is incorrect because these forms decrease, not increase, reporting required. Answer (b) is incorrect because when permitted, these forms are used instead of Form S-1 which is the standard long-form registration statement. Answer (d) is incorrect because the purpose of the forms was not directed at intrastate issues.

A.5.   Exempt Transactions or Offerings

15.   (c)   The issuance described in I is exempt because Rule 504 exempts an issuance of securities up to $1,000,000 sold in a twelve-month period to any number of investors. The issuer is not required to restrict the purchasers' resale. The issuance described in II is also exempt because Rule 505 exempts an issuance up to $5,000,000 sold in a twelve-month period. It permits sales to thirty-five unaccredited investors and to any number of accredited investors. Since there were only ten investors, this is met. The issuer also restricted the purchasers' right to resell for two years as required.

16.   (d)   Under Regulation D, Rule 504 exempts an issuance of securities up to $1,000,000 sold in a twelve-month period. Rule 505 exempts an issuance of up to $5,000,000 in a twelve-month period. So Rule 506 has to be resorted to for amounts over $5,000,000. Regulation A can be used only for issuances up to $1,500,000.

17.   (d)   When more than $5,000,000 in securities are being offered, an exemption from the registration requirements of the Securities Act of 1933 is available under Rule 506 of Regulation D. Securities under the Act include debentures and investment contracts.

18.   (a)   Under Regulation A of the 1933 Act, the issuer must file an offering circular with the SEC. Answer (b) is incorrect because the rules involving sales to unaccredited and accredited investors are in Regulation D, not Regulation A. Answer (c) is incorrect because although financial information about the corporation must be provided to offerees, the financial statements in the offering circular need not be audited. Answer (d) is incorrect because the issuer is not required to provide investors with a proxy registration statement under Regulation A.

19.   (c)   Sales or offers to sell by any person **other than** an issuer, underwriter, or dealer are exempt under the 1933 Act. Answer (a) is incorrect because the Act covers all types of securities including preferred stock. Answer (b) is incor-

rect because closely held corporations are not automatically exempt. Answer (d) is incorrect because debentures, as debt securities, are covered under the Act even if they are highly rated or backed by collateral.

20.   (b)   Regulation D of the Securities Act of 1933 establishes three important exemptions in Rules 504, 505, and 506. Although Rules 505 and 506 have some restrictions on sales to nonaccredited investors, all three rules under Regulation D allow sales to both nonaccredited and accredited investors with varying restrictions. Answer (a) is incorrect because although Rules 505 and 506 allow sales to up to thirty-five nonaccredited investors, all three rules allow sales to an unlimited number of accredited investors. Answer (c) is incorrect because Rule 506 has no dollar limitation. Rule 505 has a $5,000,000 limitation in a twelve-month period and Rule 504 has a $1,000,000 limitation in a twelve-month period. Answer (d) is incorrect because Regulation D is not restricted to only small corporations.

21.   (c)   Under Rule 505 of Regulation D, the issuer must notify the SEC of the offering within fifteen days after the first sale of the securities. Answer (a) is incorrect because under Rule 505, the issuer may sell to an unlimited number of **accredited** investors and to thirty-five unaccredited investors. Answer (b) is incorrect because no general offering or solicitation is permitted. Answer (d) is incorrect because the accredited investors need not receive any formal information. The unaccredited investors, however, must receive a formal registration statement that gives a description of the offering.

22.   (b)   The private placement exemption permits sales of an unlimited number of securities for any dollar amount when sold to accredited investors. This exemption also allows sales to up to thirty-five nonaccredited investors if they are also sophisticated investors under the Act. Resales of these securities are restricted for two years after the date that the issuer sells the last of the securities. Answer (a) is incorrect because there is no such restriction of sale. Answer (c) is incorrect because sales may be made to an unlimited number of accredited investors and up to thirty-five nonaccredited investors. Answer (d) is incorrect because sales can be made to up to thirty-five nonaccredited investors.

23.   (a)   When the issuer is a resident of that state, doing 80% of its business in that state, and only sells or offers the securities to residents of the same state, the offering qualifies for an exemption under the 1933 Act as an intrastate issue. Answer (b) is incorrect as the offering also qualifies for an exemption under the 1934 Act. Therefore, as the offering is exempted from both the 1933 and 1934 Acts, it would not be regulated by the SEC. Answer (d) is incorrect because resales can only be made to residents of that state nine months after the issuer's last sale.

24.   (b)   Rule 506 permits sales to thirty-five unaccredited investors and to an unlimited number of accredited investors. The unaccredited investors must also be sophisticated investors (i.e., individuals with knowledge and experience in financial matters).

25.   (b)   Under Regulation A, an offering statement is required instead of the more costly disclosure requirements of full registration under the Securities Act of 1933. Answer (a) is incorrect because not all intrastate offerings are exempt. They must meet specified requirements to be exempt. Answer (c) is incorrect because many securities sold under Regulation D cannot be resold for two years. Answer (d) is incorrect because there is no such exemption for stockbroker transactions.

26. (d) Under Rule 504 of Regulation D, general offerings and solicitations are permitted. Also, the issuer need not restrict the purchasers' right to resell. Note that both I and II are requirements of Rules 505 and 506 of Regulation D.

B. Securities Exchange Act of 1934

27. (c) Under the Securities Exchange Act of 1934, issuers of securities registered under this Act must file quarterly reports (Form 10-Q) for the first three quarters of each fiscal year. The financial data in these may be unaudited; however, material misinformation is a violation of the 1934 Act. Answer (a) is incorrect—the Federal Trade Commission Act does not apply to this action. Answer (b) is incorrect because the Securities Act of 1933 applies to the initial issuance of securities and not to the secondary market of publicly traded securities. Answer (d) is incorrect because NAFTA is an agreement designed to promote free trade between the US, Mexico, and Canada.

28. (b) Purposes of Section 10(b) of the Securities Exchange Act of 1934 include deterring fraud in the securities industry and encouraging disclosure of relevant information so investors can make better decisions. The SEC does not rate the securities.

29. (c) Under the Securities Exchange Act of 1934, issuers of securities registered under this Act must file annual and quarterly reports with the SEC. The company must also file current reports covering certain material events such as a change in the amount of issued securities, a change in corporate control, or a change in newly appointed officers. Answer (a) is incorrect because a competitor's making a tender offer need not be reported to the SEC. Answer (b) is incorrect because Integral Corp. need not notify the SEC of stockholder "short swing profits." Answer (d) is incorrect because the company need not report information on the market price of its stock to the SEC. This market price information is already public information because the stock is traded on the New York Stock Exchange.

30. (b) Securities must be registered with the SEC if they are traded on any national securities exchange. Securities must also be registered if they are traded in interstate commerce where the corporation has more than $10 million in assets **and** 500 or more shareholders.

31. (a) The Securities Exchange Act of 1934 has registration provisions that require specified disclosures including bonus and profit-sharing arrangements, the financial structure and nature of this business, and names of officers and directors.

32. (c) Under the Federal Securities Act of 1933, which incorporates the filing requirements of the Federal Securities Exchange Act of 1934, the issuer must file with the SEC an annual report on Form 10-K. Answer (a) is incorrect because the issuer must file the annual report with the SEC but is not required to distribute it to its stockholders. Answer (b) is incorrect because the solicitation of proxies trig-

gers certain proxy solicitation rules. Answer (d) is incorrect because it is the current report on Form 8-K that is filed when material events occur. The Form 10-Q is filed each of the first three quarters of each year and is known as the quarterly report.

33. (b) Under the 1934 Act, insiders include officers and directors of the corporation as well as owners of 10% or more of the stock of the corporation. Accountants, attorneys, and consultants can also be insiders subject to further regulation under the 1934 Act. Creditors, that is, owners of debentures are not considered to be insiders.

34. (a) Under Rule 10b-5, it is unlawful to use schemes to defraud in connection with the purchase **or** sale of any security. Note that this rule was made from powers given the SEC under the Securities Exchange Act of 1934, which applies to purchases in addition to sales of securities.

35. (c) For the Securities Exchange Act of 1934 to apply, including the antifraud provisions of Rule 10b-5, there must be shown a federal constitutional basis such as use of the mail, interstate commerce, or a national securities exchange. Answer (a) is incorrect because the antifraud provisions apply whether or not the securities had to be registered under either the 1933 Act or the 1934 Act. Answer (b) is incorrect because under Rule 10b-5, the plaintiff must prove more than negligence (i.e., either knowledge of falsity or reckless disregard for the truth in misstating facts). Answer (d) is incorrect because the plaintiff could recover if the defendant acted with reckless disregard for the truth.

36. (b) If the shares are listed on a national securities exchange, they are subject to the reporting provisions of the 1934 Act. There is no provision concerning a corporation owning more than one class of stock that by itself requires that it be subject to the reporting provisions of the 1934 Act.

37. (a) Under the 1934 Act, Link must file with the SEC annual reports (Form 10-K), quarterly reports (form 10-Q), current reports (Form 8-K) of certain material events, and proxy statements when proxy solicitations exist.

38. (a) When there is a proxy solicitation, Link must make a report of this to the SEC. Also, reports of tender offers to purchase securities need to be submitted to the SEC.

39. (a) A tender offer is a request to the shareholders of a given company to tender their shares for a stated price. If the tender offer was unsolicited, the corporation must report this to the SEC under the reporting provisions of the Securities Exchange Act of 1934. Also, trading by insiders such as officers, directors, or shareholders owning at least 10% of the stock of a corporation registered with the SEC must also be reported to the SEC under the 1934 Act. Likewise, solicitation of proxies must be reported to the SEC.

40. (c) Under the Securities Exchange Act of 1934 which applies if interstate commerce or the mail is used, any purchaser of more than 5% of a class of equity securities must file a report with the SEC. Answer (d) is incorrect because the required annual report (Form 10-K) must be certified by independent public accountants. Answer (a) is incorrect because each company must also comply with the filing requirements under the Securities Act of 1933. Answer (b) is incorrect because there is no exemption from filing proxy statements simply because the company has only one class of stock.

41.   (c)   Forms 10-K (annual reports) and 10-Q (quarterly reports) must be filed with the SEC. Forms 10-K containing financial statements must be certified by independent public accountants. However, this is not true of Forms 10-Q which cover the first three fiscal quarters of each fiscal year of the issuer.

42.   (b)   When certain material events take place, such as a change in corporate control, the corporation covered under the 1934 Act must file Form 8-K, a current report, with the SEC within fifteen days after the material event occurs. Answer (a) is incorrect because Burk Corporation must file Forms 10-K, annual reports, and Forms 10-Q, quarterly reports, whether or not a material event has taken place. Answer (c) is incorrect because there is no such exception provided. Answer (d) is incorrect because Rules 504, 505, and 506 under Regulation D apply to the initial issuance of securities under the Securities Act of 1933 and do not relieve Burk Corporation from the filing requirements with the SEC under the 1934 Act.

43.   (c)   Government creation of monopoly status through a patent is permissible under the antitrust law as long as no other anticompetitive conduct is involved. Loop Corporation is, therefore, entitled to sell the micropencil at a price determined by the normal competitive forces of supply and demand. A patent grants the holder a twenty-year exclusive right to market the product. The twenty years starts at the application date. For design patents, the period is fourteen years. Answer (a) is incorrect because prohibiting the retailers from selling competing products is an exclusive dealing agreement which is illegal where the effect is to substantially lessen competition in that market. Answer (b) is incorrect because tying agreements involving patented products are illegal per se if a substantial amount of business is involved. Answer (d) is incorrect because imposing a minimum resale price on the retailers is a vertical price fixing agreement which is also illegal per se.

44.   (b)   The Robinson-Patman Act prohibits price discrimination in interstate commerce of commodities of like grade and quality. A violation of the act exists if the effect of the price discrimination may be to substantially lessen competition or tend to create a monopoly. Therefore, all that Patman must do to maintain a sufficient legal action is to allege that due to Robinson's pricing activities there is a reasonable possibility that competition may be adversely affected. Answer (a) is incorrect because Patman does not have to show actual injury to competition; Patman must show that such discrimination may substantially lessen competition. Answer (c) is incorrect because Congress purposely adopted the Robinson-Patman Act to prevent unilateral price determination which has the resultant effect of lessening competition or tending to create a monopoly. Answer (d) is incorrect because the reasonableness of the prices charged is irrelevant. The issue is whether the price discrimination may substantially lessen competition or tend to create a monopoly.

ANSWER OUTLINE

Problem 1　Registration Requirements under 1933 Act

Since sale of interest in citrus groves meets definition of
security, must comply with registration requirement of
1933 Act
  Unless one of the three exemptions are present
    Small offering exemption
    Intrastate offering exemption
    Private offering exemption
  None met; therefore, Various must comply
Short-term note qualifies as exempt security under 1933 Act
  Since it is commercial paper with maturity of nine months
   or less
    And proceeds to be used for current operations
  Also qualifies as exempt transaction as private offering
Issue is whether Various is a controlling person of Resis-
tance Corporation
  If not controlling person, sale of these shares exempted
   from registration requirements
    Under casual sales exemption
  If controlling person, Various must meet registration re-
   quirements of 1933 Act
    Unless sale of shares meets requirements of Rule 144

UNOFFICIAL ANSWER

Problem 1　Registration Requirements under 1933 Act

    The sale of the ownership interests in the citrus groves
qualifies as a security under the 1933 Act. A security is the
sale of any interest in a scheme where a person invests
money in a common enterprise and is led to expect profits
solely from the endeavors of others. The purchasers of the
citrus grove units would be expecting profits from the operation and management of these units by Various. Consequently, unless an exemption can be found under the 1933
Act, Various must file a registration statement with the SEC,
and such statement must be approved before the issuance of
these interests. The only possible exemptions would be an
intrastate offering, a small offering and a private offering.
The sale of citrus grove interests would not constitute an
intrastate offering because interests are offered to persons
residing in more than one state. This offering would not
qualify as a small offering in that the aggregate value would
exceed $1,500,000. Also, it does not appear that it is a pri-
vate offering, since the offering is not limited to a small
number of sophisticated investors.

    The issuance of a short-term note by Various would not
require the filing of a registration statement with the SEC.
Commercial paper having a maturity date not exceeding nine
months is exempt from the registration requirements of the
1933 Act. This is only true if the proceeds gained from the
issuance of this paper have been or are to be used for current
operations. However, if the proceeds are to be used for
long-term capital investments, this exemption would not
apply. Since the problem states the instrument would be
used to finance current operations, it appears that the note
would qualify as an exemption to the 1933 Securities Act
requirement for filing. It appears that the requirements for a
private placement would be met in this situation. The offering is limited to one sophisticated investor, since institutional investors such as banks and insurance companies are
considered to be sophisticated in nature.

    Concerning Various' sale of the Resistance shares, the
important fact is to determine whether Various qualifies as a
controlling person of Resistance Corporation. If Various
does not qualify as a controlling person, the sale of these
shares would be exempted from the registration requirements of the 1933 Act under the casual sales exemption.
The casual sales exemption states that a transaction by any
person other than an issuer, underwriter, or dealer is exempt
from registration. A controlling person in a corporation has
been construed to mean anyone with direct or indirect power
to determine the policies of the business. Obviously, ownership of a majority share of existing stock in a company
would constitute control. However, in past court decisions,
as little as 10% ownership of outstanding shares has been
determined to constitute control when combined with such
other factors as being a member of the board of directors; an
officer of the corporation; or the fact that the remaining
shares are distributed over a large number of shareholders.
Thus, the fact that Various only owns 17% would not keep it
from being a controlling person. If held to be a controlling
person, Various' sale of shares would not fall within the
casual sales exemption of the 1933 Act. Since this exemption is not met, Various would have to file a registration
statement when selling these shares even though the sale is
accomplished through a broker. However, the SEC does
permit controlling persons to sell limited quantities of their
securities without registration of their security if their sale
complies with requirements of Rule 144. Rule 144 requires:
adequate information concerning the company be publicly
available; sale of no more than 1% of all outstanding shares
of that class during any three month period; that all sales
take place in broker's transactions, with the broker receiving
only the ordinary brokerage commission and the broker not
engaging in any solicitations of offers to buy from prospective purchasers. Thus, even if Various was considered to be
a controlling person, upon compliance with the above requirements, Various would still be able to sell a limited
number of its shares without registration.

ANSWER OUTLINE

Problem 2　Exemptions from Registration under Regulation D of the Securities Act of 1933; Reporting Requirements of the Securities Exchange Act of 1934

a. **1.**　World's first contention is incorrect because it
violated the following rules under Rule 505:

- Sales are limited to thirty-five nonaccredited
investors
- A general advertising is not permitted
- The SEC must be notified within fifteen days
of first sale

   2.　World's second contention is incorrect because securities originally sold under Regulation D are restricted securities
They must be registered prior to resale unless another exemption applies

b. **1.**　Unity's contention is incorrect for either of two
reasons:

- Unity has 500 or more stockholders and assets
in excess of $10,000,000
- Unity's securities are traded on a national security exchange

2. Covered corporations must file following with
SEC:

- Quarterly Reports (10-Qs)
- Annual Reports (10-Ks)
- Current Reports (8-Ks)

These reports should present a complete, current
picture of business operations and matters affecting the value of securities

UNOFFICIAL ANSWER

Problem 2　　Exemptions from Registration under Regulation D of the Securities Act of 1933; Reporting Requirements of the Securities Exchange Act of 1934

a.　1.　　World is incorrect in its first contention that the
offering is exempt from registration under Regulation D,
Rule 505, of the Securities Act of 1933. World did not
comply with the requirements of Rule 505 for the following
reasons: the offering was sold to more than thirty-five
nonaccredited investors; there was a general advertising of
the offering; and the SEC was notified more than fifteen
days after the first sale of the offering.

2.　　World is also incorrect in its second contention that
the resale of the securities would be completely exempt from
registration if the offering were exempt. Securities originally purchased under a Regulation D limited offering exemption are restricted securities. They must be registered
prior to resale unless sold subject to another exemption.

b.　1.　　Unity is incorrect in its contention that it is not
required to comply with the reporting requirements of the
Securities Exchange Act of 1934. Unity must comply because it has more than 500 stockholders and total assets in
excess of $10,000,000. Alternately, Unity must comply
because its shares are traded on a national securities exchange.

2.　　A covered corporation must file the following reports with the SEC: Quarterly Reports (10-Qs); Annual
Reports (10-Ks); and Current Reports (8-Ks). These reports
are intended to provide a complete, current statement of all
business operations and matters affecting the value of the
corporation's securities.

SOLUTIONS TO SIMULATION PROBLEMS

Simulation Problem 1

1.   **(Y)** Rule 504 exempts an issuance of securities up to $1,000,000 sold in a twelve-month period to any number of investors. Butler made the offering for $450,000.

2.   **(Y)** This offering involved a general solicitation which is now allowed under Rule 504.

3.   **(Y)** This offering was sold over the applicable twelve-month period in Rule 504.

4.   **(Y)** The SEC was sent notice of this offering eight days after the first sale. Under Rule 504, the SEC must be notified within fifteen days of the first sale of the securities.

5.   **(N)** Even though this stock was sold by general solicitation, this is allowed under Rule 504.

6.   **(Y)** Rule 506 allows private placement of an unlimited dollar amount of securities.

7.   **(Y)** These securities were sold through private placement which is appropriate under Rule 506.

8.   **(Y)** Rule 506 allows sales to up to thirty-five nonaccredited investors who are sophisticated investors with knowledge and experience in financial matters. It allows sales to an unlimited number of accredited investors.

9.   **(Y)** The SEC was notified fourteen days after the first sale of the offering which is within the fifteen-day rule.

10.   **(N)** Since this offering met the requirements discussed in 6. through 9. above, the SEC was incorrect.

11.   **(N)** Rule 505 exempts an issuance of securities up to $5,000,000. Butler made a $6,000,000 unregistered offering of preferred stock.

12.   **(Y)** The offering was sold during the applicable twelve-month period.

13.   **(N)** Rule 505 permits sales to thirty-five nonaccredited investors. Butler went over this limit by selling to forty nonaccredited investors.

14.   **(N)** The SEC was notified eighteen days after the first sale of this offering which is over the fifteen-day requirement.

15.   **(Y)** This offering was not exempt from registration because it went over the $5,000,000 limit and the stock was sold to more than thirty-five nonaccredited investors.

Simulation Problem 2

1. (**A**) Statement I is correct because under Regulation D, Rule 506, the corporation may make a private placement of an unlimited amount of securities if it meets certain requirements. Statement II is incorrect. Coffee Corp. may still make an exempt offering under the Securities Act of 1933 even if it will be subject to the requirements of the Securities Exchange Act of 1934.

2. (**B**) Statement I is incorrect because up to thirty-five non-accredited investors may purchase shares under Regulation D, Rule 506, if they are sophisticated investors. Statement II is correct because Rule 506 does allow sales to up to thirty-five nonaccredited investors **assuming they are also** sophisticated investors, that is, individuals with knowledge and experience in financial matters, or individuals represented by people with such knowledge and experience.

3. (**B**) Statement I is incorrect and Statement II is correct for the same reason. Regulation D, Rule 506, has no dollar limit on the placement of securities as long as other requirements are met.

4. (**B**) Statement I is incorrect because Regulation D has no requirements putting restrictions on resales to nonresidents. Statement II is correct because Regulation D requires that the issuer take reasonable steps to see that purchasers of the exempt offering are not underwriters and are buying for investment.

5. (**D**) Statement I is incorrect. Under Regulation D, the SEC must be notified within fifteen days of the first sale of the securities. Statement II is incorrect because the Quarterly Reports do not require SEC notification of the first sale of exempt securities.

CONTRACTS

Overview

The area of contracts is very heavily tested on the CPA examination. A large portion of the contract rules serves as a basis for many other law topics; consequently, a good understanding of the material in this module will aid you in comprehending the material in other modules.

It is important that you realize that there are two sets of contract rules to learn. The first is the group of common-law contract rules that, in general, apply to contracts that are not a sale of goods. Examples of contracts that come under common law are those that involve real estate, insurance, employment, and professional services. The second set is the contract rules contained in Article Two of the Uniform Commercial Code (UCC). The UCC governs transactions involving the sale of goods (i.e., tangible personal property). Hence, if the contract is for the sale or purchase of tangible personal property, the provisions of the UCC will apply, and not the common law. For every contract question, it is important that you determine which set of rules to apply. Fortunately many of the rules under the two sets are the same. The best way for you to master this area is to first study the common-law rules for a topic. Then review the rules that are different under the UCC. Since the common law and the UCC rules have much in common, you will be learning contract law in the most understandable and efficient manner.

Contract law is tested by both essay and multiple-choice questions. You need to know the essential elements of a contract because the CPA examination tests heavily on offer and acceptance. Also, understand that an option is an offer supported by consideration. Distinguish between an option and a firm offer and understand how these are affected by revocations and rejections. You need to comprehend what consideration is and that it must be bargained for to be valid. The exam also requires that you understand that "past consideration" and moral obligations are not really consideration at all. You should have a solid understanding of the Statute of Frauds.

Once a contract is formed, third parties can obtain rights in the contract. An assignment is one important way this can happen.

If a contract is not performed, one of the parties may be held in breach of contract. Note that the possible remedies include monetary damages, specific performance, liquidated damages, and anticipatory repudiation.

A. Essential Elements of a Contract

1. Offer
2. Acceptance

    a. When offer and acceptance have occurred, an agreement is said to have been made

3. Consideration
4. Legal capacity
5. Legality (legal purpose)
6. Reality of consent

    a. Technically not a true element, but important to consider because may be necessary for enforceability of contract

7. Statute of Frauds

    a. Not a true element, but each factual situation should be examined to determine whether it applies because certain contracts must be in writing as explained later

B. Types of Contracts

1. Express contract—terms are actually stated orally or in writing
2. Implied contract—terms of contract not specifically given but some or all of terms are inferred from conduct of parties and circumstances
3. Executed contract—one that has been fully performed
4. Executory contract—one that has not been fully performed by both parties
5. Quasi contract—not a real contract but public policy creates legal obligation in certain circumstances
6. Unilateral contract—one party gives promise for completion of requested act

    EXAMPLE: A promises to pay B $1,000 to cross the Golden Gate Bridge on foot within one week. This is a unilateral offer. Once B does the act it is a unilateral contract.

7. Bilateral contract—each party exchanges promises

    EXAMPLE: A promises to deliver 100 widgets to B for $1,000 and B promises to buy and pay for them.

8. Voidable contract—one that is enforceable unless party that has right pulls out of contract

C. Discussion of Essential Elements of a Contract

    1. Offer

        a. May be either written or oral (or sometimes by actions)

            EXAMPLE: Offeror takes can of soup to check out stand and pays for it without saying anything.

        b. Based on intent of offeror

           (1) Courts use objective test to determine intent

               (a) That is, would reasonable person think that offer had been intended

           (2) Subjective intent (what offeror actually intended or meant) is not considered

           (3) Promises made in apparent jest are not offers

               (a) Promises that objectively appear real are offers

                   EXAMPLE: S says, "I offer to sell to you, B, my car for $5,000." This is an offer, even though S may be actually joking, as long as given the way it was said, a reasonable person would think that S did intend to make the offer to sell his/her car.

           (4) Statements of opinion or of intent are not offers

               EXAMPLE: A doctor tells a patient that he will fully recover in a couple of days, but it actually takes two weeks. This is a statement of opinion, not an offer.

               EXAMPLE: "I am going to sell my car for $400." This is a statement of intent, not an offer.

           (5) Invitations to negotiate (preliminary negotiations) are not offers (e.g., price tags or lists, auctions, inquiries, general advertisements)

               EXAMPLE: A says: "What would you think your car is worth?" B says: "About $5,000." A says: "I accept your offer so I'll buy it for $5,000." B never gave an offer. However, when A said that he would accept, this is actually an offer that B may then accept if she wishes.

        c. Offer must be definite and certain as to what will be agreed upon in contract under common law

           (1) Courts allow some reasonable terms to be left open if customary to do so

               EXAMPLE: C calls P, a plumber, to come and fix a clogged drain. No price is mentioned. However, upon P's completion of the work, he has the right to collect customary fee from C.

           (2) Under UCC, output or requirements contracts are considered reasonably definite because output is based upon actual output that does occur in good faith and requirements are actual good-faith requirements

        d. Must be communicated to offeree by offeror or his/her agent

           (1) Offeree may learn of a public offer (e.g., reward) in any way; s/he merely needs knowledge of it

        e. Unilateral offer is one that expects acceptance by action rather than with promise

            EXAMPLE: M says he will pay J $5 if she will mow his lawn. M has made a unilateral offer that is accepted when J mows the lawn. If J never mows the lawn, there is no contract and therefore no breach of contract.

           (1) Unilateral contract contains one promise (offer by offeror) and acceptance by action

        f. Bilateral offer is one that expects acceptance by a promise from offeree

           (1) Bilateral contract is formed when offeree accepts with a promise

               EXAMPLE: R says to E, "Will you agree to work for me for three months at $5,000 per month?" This is a bilateral offer.

           (2) Bilateral contract contains two promises

        g. Mistakes in transmission of offer are deemed to be offeror's risk because s/he chose method of communication; therefore, offer is effective as transmitted

        h. Termination of offer

(1) Rejection by offeree

    (a) Must be communicated to offeror to be effective

    (b) Rejection is effective when received by offeror

(2) Revocation by offeror

    (a) Generally, offeror may revoke offer at any time prior to acceptance by offeree

        1] Revocation is effective when received by offeree

            EXAMPLE: X offers to sell his car to Y stating that the offer will remain open for ten days. However, on the fifth day Y receives a revocation of the offer from X. The offer would be terminated on the fifth day even though X stated that it would remain open for ten days.

    (b) If offeree learns by reliable means that offeror has already sold subject of offer, it is revoked

    (c) Public offers must be revoked by same amount of publicity used in making offer

        EXAMPLE: Offer of reward for apprehension of arsonist in a newspaper makes headlines. It cannot be revoked by a small notice in the back of the newspaper.

    (d) An **option** is an offer that is supported by consideration and cannot be revoked before stated time

        1] Option is actually a separate contract to keep offer open

            a] Also called an option contract

                EXAMPLE: O offers to sell her car to P and states that she will keep the offer open for ten days if P will pay her $50. P pays the $50 and six days later O attempts to revoke the offer. P then accepts the offer by the seventh day. An agreement has been formed because the offer was an option and could not be revoked before the ten days. Note that there were actually two contracts between O and P. The first one was the option to keep the offer open. The second was the actual sale of the car.

                EXAMPLE: Same example as above except that O asked P to promise to pay $50 within ten days to keep the offer open. The result is the same because a promise to pay money is also consideration.

        2] Also, rejection does not terminate option

        3] Note differences between option and firm offer by merchants concerning sale of goods under UCC as discussed later

(3) Counteroffer is a rejection coupled with offeree making new offer

    EXAMPLE: An offer is made to sell a car for $3,000 and a counteroffer is, "I'll give you $2,500."

    (a) Mere inquiry or request for additional or different terms is not a counteroffer and does not terminate offer

        EXAMPLE: An offer is made to sell a car for $3,000 and an inquiry is, "Will you sell for $2,500?"

(4) Lapse of time may terminate offer

    (a) Offeror may specify period of time (e.g., one week)

    (b) If no time is specified, after reasonable time

(5) Death or insanity of offeror terminates ordinary offers

(6) Illegality

    (a) Offer terminates if after making offer and before it is accepted, it becomes illegal

        EXAMPLE: X offers to rent to Y an upstairs floor for a cabaret. Before Y accepts, the city adopts a fire code making use of the premises illegal without substantial rebuilding.

(7) Bankruptcy or insolvency of either offeror or offeree terminates offer

(8) Impossibility

    (a) Offer terminates if after making offer and before it is accepted, performance becomes impossible

        EXAMPLE: X offers his car to Y for $500, but before Y agrees to the purchase, X's car is destroyed by fire.

      (9) Destruction of subject matter

2. Acceptance

  a. May be written or oral

  b. Offer may be accepted only by person to whom it was directed

     (1) Use objective test—to whom would a reasonable person believe it to be directed?

     (2) Rewards can usually be accepted by anyone who knows of them

  c. Offeree must have knowledge of offer in order to accept

EXAMPLE: D advertises a reward of $100 for the return of his pet dog. G, unaware of the offer, returns D's dog. G cannot require that D pay the $100 (if he later hears of the offer) because he was unaware of the offer when he returned the dog. He could not "accept" an offer he did not know existed.

  d. Intent to accept is required

     (1) Courts generally find click-on agreements legally enforceable when the offeree completes the contract on-line by clicking on a button that shows acceptance

       (a) Main issue is that offeree did clearly intend to accept offer by this action

  e. Acceptance must generally be in form specified by offer

  f. Acceptance must be unequivocal and unconditional (mirror image rule) under common law

     (1) An acceptance that attempts to change terms of offer is not acceptance, but is both a rejection and a counteroffer

EXAMPLE: O offers to sell some real estate for $100,000 cash. E says "I accept. I'll give you $50,000 now and $50,000 plus 13% interest one year from now."

       (a) Mere inquiry or request is not a counteroffer so offer remains in effect

EXAMPLE: O gives the same offer as above but this time E asks if O would accept $50,000 now and $50,000 plus 13% interest one year from now. The offer is neither accepted nor terminated.

     (2) A condition which does not change or add to terms of contract is not a counteroffer (i.e., a condition that is already part of contract because of law, even though not expressed in previous negotiations)

  g. Silence is not acceptance unless

     (1) Offer indicated silence would constitute acceptance (e.g., offer states "your silence is acceptance," and offeree intended his/her silence as acceptance)

       (a) If offeree does not intend to accept, such language has no effect

         1] Offeree is under no duty to reply

     (2) Offeree has taken benefit of services or goods and exercised control over them when s/he had opportunity to reject them

       (a) However, statutes usually override common law rule by providing that unsolicited merchandise may be treated as a gift

     (3) Through prior dealings, by agreement between parties, or when dictated by custom, silence can be acceptance

  h. Time of acceptance under common law

     (1) If acceptance is made by method specified in offer or by same method used by offeror to communicate the offer, acceptance is effective when sent (e.g., when placed in mail or when telegram is dispatched)

EXAMPLE: Offeror mails a written offer without stating the mode of acceptance. Offeree mails acceptance. Offeror, before receipt, calls offeree to revoke the offer. The contract exists because acceptance was effective when mailed and revocation of offer came too late.

(a) Exception: If offeree sends rejection and then acceptance, first received is effective even though offeree sent acceptance by same method used by offeror

(2) Other methods of acceptance are considered effective when actually received by offeror
(3) Late acceptance is not valid—it is a counteroffer and a valid contract is formed only if original offeror then accepts
(4) If acceptance is valid when sent, a lost or delayed acceptance does not destroy validity

> EXAMPLE: *R wires an offer to E asking her to accept by mail. The acceptance is correctly mailed but never arrives. There is a valid agreement.*

(5) Offeror can change above rules by stating other rule(s) in offer

> EXAMPLE: *Offeror mails a written offer to offeree stating that acceptance is valid only if **received** by the offeror within ten days. Offeree mails back the acceptance within ten days but it arrives late. Acceptance has not occurred even though the offeree used the same method.*

i. Once there is an offer and acceptance, an agreement is formed

(1) Details can be worked out later
(2) Formalization often occurs later
(3) Attempted revocations or rejections after agreement is formed are of no effect

j. Offers, revocations, rejections, and counteroffers are valid when received (under both common law and UCC)

(1) Compare with rules for acceptances which are sometimes valid when sent and other times are valid when received

> EXAMPLE: *S offers to sell his land to B for $20,000. The offer is mailed to B. Later that same day, S changes his mind and mails B a revocation of this offer. When B receives the offer, she mails her acceptance. B receives the revocation the day after she mailed the acceptance. S and B have a valid contract because the acceptance was valid when sent but the revocation would have been valid when B received it. Once the offer is accepted, any attempted revocation will not be valid.*

> EXAMPLE: *Use the same facts as above except that the offeree uses a different method than the mailed acceptance. If B receives the revocation before S receives the acceptance, there is no contract.*

k. **Uniform Commercial Code rules** (Important differences from common-law rules above for offers and acceptances)

(1) The UCC applies to sale of goods, for example, tangible personal property (not real property, services, or insurance contracts)
(2) A **written** and **signed** offer for sale of goods, **by a merchant** (i.e., one who regularly deals goods under contract), giving assurance that it will be held open for specified time is irrevocable for that period

(a) Called firm offer

> EXAMPLE: *Herb, an automobile dealer, offers to sell a car to Ike stating, "I promise to keep this offer open for forty-five days." Since the offer is not written and signed by Herb, the firm offer rule does not apply and Herb may revoke the offer at any time prior to Ike's acceptance.*

> EXAMPLE: *Same facts as above except that the offer is written and signed by Herb. In this case, the firm offer rule applies and Herb cannot revoke the offer for the stated period.*

(b) Unlike an option, no consideration needed
(c) Period of irrevocability may not exceed three months

> EXAMPLE: *A merchant in a signed, written offer agrees to keep the offer open for four months. The firm offer may be revoked or otherwise terminated once three months has passed.*

(d) If no time is specified, reasonable time is inferred, up to three months
(e) If assurance is given on form supplied by offeree, it must be separately signed by offeror
(f) Compare

1] Firm offer rule does not work under common law
2] Options are valid under UCC as well as common law and do not require a merchant seller

      3]   Options are not limited to three months

> *EXAMPLE: C (not a merchant) agrees to sell an automobile to B, with the offer to remain open for four months. This is not a firm offer so C may revoke this offer at any time by communicating the revocation to B.*

> *EXAMPLE: Same facts as above except that B pays C to keep the offer open for four months. C cannot revoke this offer for four months because although it is not a firm offer, it is an option.*

> *EXAMPLE: Same facts as the first example except that C is a merchant and engages in a signed written offer. This is a firm offer that C could not revoke during the first three months, but could revoke the offer during the last month.*

(3) Unless otherwise indicated, an offer for sale of goods shall be construed as inviting acceptance in any manner and by any medium reasonable under circumstances

(4) Time of acceptance under UCC

    (a) Acceptance valid when sent if reasonable method used

> *EXAMPLE: A offers to sell her stereo to B. The offer is sent via telegram. B mails back an acceptance. This acceptance is valid when B mails the acceptance even though B used a method different from that used for the offer because it was an offer to sell under the UCC.*

> *EXAMPLE: Same as above except that the offer was to sell land rather than a stereo. The acceptance is valid when received by A because the common law rules apply.*

> *EXAMPLE: A telegraphs an offer to B without specifying when acceptance is valid but does state the offer will remain open for five days. Within the five days, B mails back the acceptance which arrives after that five days. If the subject matter is a sale of goods, there is a contract because the acceptance was good when sent. Under common law, however, the acceptance takes effect under these facts when received, so no contract would result.*

    (b) Above rule does not apply if another rule is stated in offer

> *EXAMPLE: O faxes an offer to sell his car to B for $17,000. The offer states that O must receive the acceptance in three days. B mails back the acceptance in two days but the letter does not arrive until the fourth day. No contract is formed.*

(5) An offer to buy goods may be accepted either by seller's promise to ship the goods or by the actual shipment

    (a) Blurs distinction between unilateral and bilateral contracts

    (b) With respect to a unilateral offer, beginning of performance by offeree (i.e., part performance) will bind offeror if followed within a reasonable time by notice of acceptance

(6) Unequivocal acceptance of offer for sale of goods is not necessary under UCC (Battle of Forms)

    (a) An acceptance containing additional terms is valid acceptance (unless acceptance is expressly conditional upon offeror's agreement to additional terms)

        1]   Recall, under common law, this would be a rejection and counteroffer

    (b) Between nonmerchants, the additional terms are considered proposals to offeror for additions to contract, and unless offeror agrees to the additions, contract is formed on offeror's terms

    (c) Between merchants, these additional terms become part of contract and contract is formed on offeree's terms unless

        1]   Original offer precludes such additions
        2]   New terms materially alter original offer
        3]   The original offeror gives notice of his/her objection within a reasonable time

> *EXAMPLE: O offers to sell M a group of stereos under certain terms including a three-month warranty. Both parties are merchants. M faxes back that he accepts the offer but that he wants a one-year warranty. O and M have a contract. The three-month warranty is part of the contract because the one-year warranty is a material alteration.*

    (d) If at least one party is a nonmerchant, use nonmerchant rule

> *EXAMPLE: O, a merchant, offers by telegram to sell B, a nonmerchant, a truck for $20,000 that B had looked at earlier. B telegraphs back that he accepts the offer and adds an additional term that the seat be re-upholstered. O and B have a contract. The additional term is only a proposal to the contract.*

(7) Even if terms are left open, a contract for sale of goods will not fail for indefiniteness if there was intent to contract and a reasonable basis for establishing a remedy is available

    (a) Open price term—construed as reasonable price at time of delivery

        1] Or parties may agree to decide price at future date or can agree to allow third party to set price

> *EXAMPLE: B accepts an offer from S to buy 1,000 bushels of pears in one month. No mention is made of the price. The contract is valid and the price will be the market value of the pears at the time of delivery.*

> *EXAMPLE: Same as above except that B and S agree to let N decide what the price will be for the pears. This is a valid contract.*

> *EXAMPLE: Un D. Sided and Tube Issy agree on a contract for 1,000 bushels of avocados to be delivered in three months for a price that they will decide in one month. If they fail to agree on the price, the contract will be for the market value at delivery.*

    (b) Open place of delivery term—seller's place of business, if any

        1] Otherwise, seller's residence or if identified goods are elsewhere and their location is known to both parties at time of contracting, then at that location

    (c) Open time of shipment or delivery—becomes a reasonable time

    (d) Open time for payment—due at time and place of delivery of goods or at time and place of delivery of documents of title, if any

        1] If on credit, credit period begins running at time of shipment

(8) What is a reasonable price or reasonable time becomes a jury question to interpret contract if parties to contract already formed cannot agree on interpretation and therefore litigate meaning of contract

(9) Even if writings do not establish a contract, conduct by parties recognizing a contract will establish one

    (a) The terms will be those on which writings agree and those provided for in UCC where not agreed on (e.g., reasonable price, place of delivery)

    (b) Often occurs when merchants send preprinted forms to each other with conflicting terms and forms are not read for more than quantity and price

l. Auctions

    (1) Bid is offer

    (2) Bidder may retract bid until auctioneer announces sale completed

    (3) If auction is "with reserve," auctioneer may withdraw goods before s/he announces completion of sale

    (4) If auction "without reserve," goods may not be withdrawn unless no bid made within reasonable time

    (5) Auctions are "with reserve" unless specified otherwise

m. On-line auctions

    (1) Many individuals and businesses are conducting auctions on-line

        (a) Many businesses sell excess inventory or services this way

        (b) Becoming increasingly popular as buyers and sellers rely on fluidity of contract-making abilities

3. Consideration—an act, promise, or forbearance that is offered by one party and accepted by another as inducement to enter into agreement

a. A party binds him/herself to do (or actually does) something s/he is not legally obligated to do, or when s/he surrenders legal right

EXAMPLE: B pays S $500 for S's stereo that he hands over to B. B's consideration is the $500. S's consideration is the stereo.

EXAMPLE: S gives B a stereo today. B promises to pay S $500 in one week. The promise to pay $500, rather than the $500 itself, is the consideration. Thus, the element of consideration is met today.

EXAMPLE: A hits and injures P with his car. P agrees not to sue A when A agrees to settle out of court for $10,000. A's promise to pay the money is consideration. P's promise to refrain from bringing a lawsuit is consideration on his/her side.

EXAMPLE: Using the fact pattern above, further assume that it is not clear whether A is at fault. The settlement (contract) is still enforceable if made in good faith because of possible liability.

b. Legal detriment does not have to be economic (e.g., giving up drinking, smoking, and swearing)

   (1) If party agrees to have something accomplished but has someone else do it, this is consideration

c. Consideration must be bargained for (this is essential)
d. Preexisting legal duty is not sufficient as consideration because no new legal detriment is suffered by performing prior obligation

   (1) Agreement to accept from debtor a lesser sum than owed is unenforceable if the debt is a liquidated (undisputed) debt

   EXAMPLE: C agrees to accept $700 for a $900 debt that D owes C. The amount is not disputed. D still owes C the additional $200.

      (a) But if debtor incurs a detriment in addition to paying, creditor's promise to accept lesser sum will be binding

      EXAMPLE: X owes Y $1,000. Y agrees to accept $500 and X will also install Y's new furnace at no additional cost.

      (b) Note that agreement to accept a lesser sum is enforceable if amount of debt is unliquidated (disputed) because both parties give up right to more favorable sum

      EXAMPLE: C claims that D owes him $1,000. D claims that the amount owed is $600. If C and D agree to settle this for $700, the agreement is supported by consideration since C gave up right to attempt to collect more than $700 and D gave up right to attempt settlement for a lesser sum.

   (2) Promise to pay someone for refraining from doing something s/he has no right to do is unenforceable
   (3) Promise to pay someone to do something s/he is already obligated to do is not enforceable.

   EXAMPLE: Agreement to pay police officer $200 to recover stolen goods is unenforceable.

   EXAMPLE: X promises to pay Y, a jockey, $50 to ride as hard as he can in the race. Y already owes his employer, Z, that duty so there is no consideration to enforce the agreement.

      (a) Agreement to pay more to finish a job, such as building a house, is unenforceable unless unforeseen difficulties are encountered (e.g., underground stream or marshy land under a house)

e. Past consideration (consideration for a prior act, forbearance, or agreement) is not sufficient for new contract because it is not bargained for
f. Moral obligation except in a minority of states is not consideration

   (1) In majority of states these need no consideration

      (a) Promise to pay debt barred by statute of limitations.
      (b) Promise to pay debt barred by bankruptcy. Promise must adhere to strict rules stated in Bankruptcy Reform Act of 1978 concerning reaffirmations of dischargeable debts.

g. Consideration must be legally sufficient

   (1) This does not refer to amount of consideration but refers to validity of consideration

> EXAMPLE: *C does not have a CPA license. For $1,000 he promises not to hire himself out as a CPA. This promise is not supported by legally sufficient consideration because C has no right to hire himself out as a CPA.*

h. Adequacy of consideration—courts generally do not look into amount of exchange as long as it is legal consideration and **bargained for**

i. In majority of states, seals placed on contracts are not substitutes for consideration

j. Modifying existing contracts

   (1) Modification of contract needs new consideration on both sides to be legally binding

> EXAMPLE: *S agrees in a written contract to sell a piece of land to P for $40,000. S later changes his mind and demands $50,000 for the same piece of land. The original contract is enforceable (at $40,000) even if P agrees to the increased price because although P has agreed to give more consideration, S has not given any new consideration.*

   (2) Under UCC, a contract for sale of goods may be modified orally or in writing without consideration if in good faith

> EXAMPLE: *S agrees to sell P 300 pairs of socks for $1.00 each. Due to rapid price increases in S's costs, he asks P if he will modify the price to $1.20 each. P agrees. The contract as modified is enforceable because it is covered under the UCC and does not need new consideration on both sides.*

k. Requirements contracts

   (1) If one party agrees to supply what other party requires, agreement is supported by consideration

      (a) Reason: supplying party gives up right to sell to another; purchasing party gives up right to buy from another

      (b) Cannot be required to sell amounts unreasonably disproportionate to normal requirements

l. Output contract

   (1) If one party agrees to sell all his/her output to another, agreement is supported by consideration because s/he gives up right to sell that output to another

      (a) However, illusory contracts are not supported by consideration (e.g., party agrees to sell all s/he wishes)

m. Promissory estoppel acts as substitute for consideration and renders promise enforceable—promisor is estoppel from asserting lack of consideration

   (1) Elements

      (a) Detrimental reliance on promise

      (b) Reliance is reasonable and foreseeable

      (c) Damage results (injustice) if promise is not enforced

   (2) Usually applied to gratuitous promises but trend is to apply to commercial transactions. At least recovery of expenses is allowed.

> EXAMPLE: *A wealthy man in the community promises to pay for a new church if it is built. The church committee reasonably (and in good faith) relies on the promise and incurs the expenses.*

n. Mutuality of obligation—means both parties must be bound or neither is bound

   (1) Both parties must give consideration by paying or promising to pay for the act, promise, or forbearance of the other with something of legal value

o. Promise to donate to charity is enforceable based on public policy reasons

4. Legal Capacity

a. An agreement between parties in which one or both lack the capacity to contract is void or, in some cases, voidable

b. Minors (persons under age eighteen or twenty-one)

   (1) A minor may contract, but agreement is voidable by minor

        (a) Adult is held to contract unless minor disaffirms

    (2) If minor has purchased nonnecessaries, when minor disaffirms, s/he is required to give back any part s/he still has

        (a) Minor may recover all of consideration given
        (b) In most courts, minor need not pay for what s/he cannot return
        (c) A few courts require minor to pay for use or depreciation of equipment or machinery

    (3) Minor is liable for reasonable value of necessaries furnished to him/her

        (a) Minor may disaffirm contract if it is executory (i.e., not completed)
        (b) Necessaries include food, clothing, shelter, education, etc., considering his/her age and position in life

    (4) Minor may disaffirm contract at any time until a reasonable time after reaching majority age

        (a) Failure to disaffirm within reasonable time after reaching majority acts as ratification (e.g., one year is too long in the absence of very special circumstances such as being out of the country)

    (5) Minor may choose to ratify within a reasonable time after reaching age of majority

        (a) By words, either orally or in writing but must ratify all, or
        (b) By actions that indicate ratification
        (c) Ratification prior to majority is not effective

    (6) If minor misrepresents his/her age when making contract, courts are split on effect

        (a) Some courts allow minor to disaffirm contract anyway but allow other party to sue for fraud
        (b) Some allow minor to disaffirm if minor returns consideration in similar condition
        (c) Other courts will not allow minor to disaffirm especially if it was a business contract

    (7) A minor usually is liable for own torts (civil wrongs), but this may depend on his/her age (above 14 commonly liable)

        (a) Parents are not liable for torts of minors unless they direct or condone certain conduct or were negligent themselves

  c. Incompetent persons

    (1) Contract by person adjudicated insane is void

        (a) Insane person need not return consideration

    (2) If contract is made before adjudication of insanity, it may be voidable by incompetent person

        (a) Where courts hold such agreements voidable, restitution is condition precedent to disaffirmance

  d. Legal capacity of one intoxicated is determined by his/her ability to understand and by degree of intoxication

    (1) Contracts are enforceable, in general, unless extent of intoxication at time contract made was so great that intoxicated party did not understand terms or nature of contract—then contract voidable at option of one intoxicated if s/he returns items under contract

  e. Corporations contract through agents and are limited by their charters

5. Legality

  a. Agreement is unenforceable if it is illegal or violates public policy
  b. When both parties are guilty, neither will be aided by court (i.e., if one party had already given some consideration, s/he will not get it back)

    (1) But if one party repudiates prior to performance, s/he may recover his/her consideration

EXAMPLE: X contracts to buy stolen goods from Y. If X pays Y but then repents and refuses to accept the stolen goods, X may recover the money he paid Y.

c.   When one party is innocent, s/he will usually be given relief

   (1) A member of a class of people designed to be protected by statute is considered innocent (e.g., purchaser of stock issued in violation of blue-sky laws)

d.   Types of illegal contracts

   (1) Agreement to commit crime or tort

      (a) If agreement calls for intentional wrongful interference with a valid contractual relationship, it is an illegal agreement

         1] However, a sale of a business containing a covenant prohibiting seller from owning or operating similar business as well as the termination of an employee who has agreed not to compete are legal and enforceable provided the agreement

            a] Protects legitimate interests of buyer or employer without creating too large a burden on seller or employee (based on ability to find other work)
            b] Is reasonable as to length of time under the circumstances to protect those interests
            c] Is reasonable as to area to protect interests of same area
            d] Same whether employer or employee initiated termination

               EXAMPLE: Seller of a small bakery agrees not to compete in Washington, DC, for six months.

   (2) An agreement to not press criminal charges for consideration is illegal

      EXAMPLE: A has embezzled money from his employer. The employer agrees to not press charges if A pays back all of the money.

   (3) Services rendered without a license when statute requires a license

      (a) Two types of licensing statutes

         1] Regulatory licensing statute—one that seeks to protect public from incapable, unskilled, or dishonest persons

            a] Contract is unenforceable by either party
            b] Even if work done, other need not pay because not a contract

               EXAMPLE: X, falsely claiming to have a CPA license, performs an audit for ABC Company. Upon learning the true facts, ABC may legally refuse to pay X any fees or expenses.

         2] Revenue-seeking statute—purpose is to raise revenue for government

            a] Contract is enforceable

               EXAMPLE: Y, based on a contract, performed extensive yard work for M. M then finds out that Y failed to obtain a license required by the local government to raise revenue. M is obligated to pay Y the agreed-upon amount.

   (4) Usury (contract for greater than legal interest rate)
   (5) Contracts against public policy

      (a) Contracts in restraint of trade such as covenant not to compete after end of an employment contract

         1] Courts must balance need of former employer such as protection of trade secrets or customer base with need of employee to practice his/her line of work
         2] Typically, contract will restrict employee from competing in named areas for stated period of time
         3] Employer must show that covenant not to compete is needed to protect interests of employer and that restraints are reasonable as to geographical area and as to time period

(b) Upon sale of business, seller agrees to not compete with sold type of business in named areas for stated period of time

    1] Courts are less restrictive than in employment contract situation but will look at reasonableness as to geographical area, reasonableness as to time, and whether covenant is unduly restrictive for public's need

(c) Exculpatory clauses are clauses found in contracts in which one party tries to avoid liability for own negligence

    1] These are generally against public policy and not enforceable unless both parties have relatively equal bargaining power

    EXAMPLE: An automobile dealership agrees to fix the engine of a car brought in by a consumer for repair. A clause in the contract provides that the dealer will not be liable for any mistakes it may make during the repair.

6. Reality of Consent—If one of the following concepts is present, a contract may be void (i.e., no contract) or voidable (i.e., enforceable until party having right decides to pull out).

  a. Fraud—includes following elements

    (1) Misrepresentation of a material fact

      (a) Can be falsehood or concealment of defect
      (b) Silence is not misrepresentation unless there is duty to speak, for example,

        1] Fiduciary relationship between parties
        2] Seller of property knows there is a dangerous latent (hidden) defect

      (c) Must be statement of past or present fact

        1] Opinion (e.g., of value) is not fact

          a] Experts' opinion does constitute fraud

          EXAMPLE: An expert appraiser of jewelry appraises a diamond to be worth $500 when he knows it is actually worth $1,500. This fulfills the "misrepresentation of a material fact" element and also scienter element. If the remaining elements of fraud are met, then there is fraud.

        2] Opinions about what will happen in future (expert or not) do not satisfy fact requirement

        EXAMPLE: A real estate agent tells a prospective buyer that the income property she is considering purchasing will earn at least 50% more next year than last year.

        3] Puffing or sales talk is not fact

        EXAMPLE: A seller claims her necklace is worth $1,000. The buyer pays $1,000 and later finds out that he can buy a very similar necklace from another seller for $700. Even if the other elements of fraud are present, this opinion does not constitute fraud.

        4] Presently existing intention in mind of the speaker is fact

    (2) Intent to mislead—"scienter"

      (a) Need knowledge of falsity with intent to mislead, **or**
      (b) Reckless disregard for truth can be substituted

        1] If all elements (1) through (4) are present but reckless disregard is proven instead of actual knowledge of falsity, then it is called constructive fraud

    (3) Reasonable reliance by injured party

      (a) One who knows the truth or might have learned it by a reasonable inquiry may not recover
      (b) One cannot reasonably rely on opinions about future

    (4) Resulting in injury to others
    (5) Remedies for fraud

(a) Defrauded party may affirm agreement and sue for damages under tort of deceit, or if party is sued on contract, then s/he may set up fraud in reduction of damages, or

(b) Defrauded party may rescind contract and sue for damages that result from the fraud

(6) Fraud may occur

(a) In the inducement

1] The misrepresentation occurs during contract negotiations

2] Creates voidable contract at option of defrauded party

> EXAMPLE: *A represents to B that A's car has been driven 50,000 miles when in fact it has been driven for 150,000 miles. If B purchases A's car in reliance on this misrepresentation, fraud in the inducement is present, creating a voidable contract at B's option.*

(b) In the execution

1] Misrepresentation occurs in actual form of agreement

2] Creates void contract

> EXAMPLE: *Larry Lawyer represents to Danny that Danny is signing his will, when in fact he is signing a promissory note payable to Larry. This promissory note is void because fraud in the execution is present.*

(7) Fraud is also called intentional misrepresentation

b. Innocent misrepresentation

(1) An innocent misstatement made in good faith (i.e., no scienter)

(2) All other elements same as fraud

(3) Creates right of rescission (cancellation) in other party—to return both parties to their precontract positions to extent practicably possible

(a) All benefits returned by both parties as much as possible

(b) Does not allow aggrieved party to sue for damages

c. Mistake—an act done under an erroneous conviction

(1) Mutual mistake (i.e., by both parties) about material characteristics of subject matter in contract makes contract voidable by either party

> EXAMPLE: *S and B make a contract in which B agrees to buy a boat from S. Although neither party knew it at the time, this boat had been destroyed before this contract was made. This is a mutual mistake about the existence of the boat; therefore, either party may void this contract by law. Note that legally either party may pull out although usually only one party may wish to do so.*

(a) Also exists when both parties reasonably attach different meanings to word or phrase

(b) Also called bilateral mistake

(c) Mistake about value of subject matter is not grounds for voiding contract

(2) Unilateral mistake generally does not allow party to void contract

(a) Major exception for mistakes in computations for bids

1] Contract based on mistake is voidable by party making mistake if calculation is far enough off so that other party should have known that a mistake was made

d. Duress—a contract entered into because of duress can be voided because of invalid consent

(1) Any acts or threats of violence or extreme pressure against party or member of party's family, which in fact deprives party of free will and causes him/her to agree, is duress

> EXAMPLE: *X threatens to criminally prosecute Y unless he signs contract. This contract is made under duress.*

(a) May involve coercion that is social or economic that leaves him/her with no reasonable alternative

(2) Physical duress in which party agrees to contract under physical force

(3) Extreme duress causes agreement to be void

(4) Ordinary duress creates voidable agreement

e. Undue influence—unfair persuasion of one person over another which prevents understanding or voluntary action

(1) Usually occurs when very dominant person has extreme influence over weaker person

(a) Weakness can result from physical, mental, or emotional weakness or combinations of these

(2) Also occurs through abuse of fiduciary relationship (e.g., CPA, attorney, guardian, trustee, etc.)

(3) Normally causes agreement to be voidable

f. Unconscionable contract—an oppressive contract in which one party has taken severe, unfair advantage of the other, usually because of latter's absence of choice or poor education

(1) Under these circumstances court may void contract or reform terms so as to be fair to both parties

g. Changes in weather conditions, economic conditions, etc., that cause hardship to one party will not create voidable contracts when conditions are not so extreme that the parties could have contemplated them

EXAMPLE: B had a contract to purchase 50,000 gallons of heating oil from S at specified prices. B refuses to take more than 40,000 gallons because the weather was warmer than normal. B is obligated on all 50,000 gallons because the warmer weather could have been contemplated by the parties.

h. Infancy, incompetency, and noncompliance with Statute of Frauds may also create voidable contract

i. Adhesion contract—offeror is in position to say "take it or leave it" because of superior bargaining power

(1) Usually occurs when large business entity requires its customers to use their standard form contract without allowing modification

7. Conformity with the Statute of Frauds

a. Contracts required to be in writing and signed by party to be charged—these are said to be within the Statute

(1) An agreement to sell land or any interest in land

(a) Includes buildings, easements, and contracts to sell real estate

(b) Part performance typically satisfies Statute even though real estate contract was oral, but this requires

1] Possession of the land
2] Either part payment or making of improvements on real estate
3] Many courts require all three

(2) An agreement that cannot be performed within one year from the making of agreement

(a) Contract that can be performed in exactly one year or less may be oral

EXAMPLE: W agrees to hire X for ten months starting in four months. This contract must be in writing because it cannot be performed until fourteen months after the agreement is made.

(b) Any contract which can conceivably be completed in one year, irrespective of how long the task actually takes, may be oral

EXAMPLE: A agrees to paint B's portrait for $400. It actually is not completed until over a year later. This contract did not have to be in writing because it was possible to complete it within one year.

(c) If performance is contingent on something which could take place in less than one year, agreement may be oral

EXAMPLE: "I will employ you as long as you live." Party could possibly die in less than one year.

(d) But if its terms call for more than one year, it must be written even if there is possibility of taking place in less than one year

> *EXAMPLE: "I will employ you for five years." The employee's death could occur before the end of five years, but the terms call for the writing requirement under the Statute of Frauds.*

(e) Generally, if one side of performance is complete but other side cannot be performed within year, it is not within Statute (i.e., may be oral). Especially true if performance has been accepted and all that remains is the payment of money.

> *EXAMPLE: X agrees to pay E $6,000 salary per month and a bonus of $50,000 if he works for at least two years. After two years, X refuses to pay the bonus. The $50,000 is payable and the Statute of Frauds is no defense here.*

(3) An agreement to answer for debt or default of another (contract of guaranty)

(a) A secondary promise is within this section of the Statute of Frauds (i.e., must be in writing)

> *EXAMPLE: "If Jack doesn't pay, I will."*

(b) A primary promise is not within this section of the Statute of Frauds because it is in reality the promisor's own contract

> *EXAMPLE: "Let Jack have it, and I will pay."*

(c) Promise for benefit of promisor may be oral

> *EXAMPLE: Promisor agrees to answer for default of X, because X is promisor's supplier and he needs X to stay in business to keep himself in business.*

(d) Promise of indemnity (will pay based on another's fault, for example, insurance) is not within Statute

(e) Assignor's promise to assignee, guaranteeing obligor's performance is not within Statute

(4) Agreement for sale of goods for $500 or more is required to be in writing under UCC

> *EXAMPLE: Oral contract for the sale of fifty calculators for $10 each is not enforceable.*

> *EXAMPLE: Oral contract to perform management consulting services over the next six months for $100,000 is enforceable because the $500 rule does not apply to contracts that come under common law.*

> *EXAMPLE: Same as previous example except that the agreed time was for fourteen months. This one was required to be in writing to be enforceable because of the one-year rule.*

(a) Exceptions to writing requirement (these are important)

1] Oral contract involving specially manufactured goods (i.e., not saleable in ordinary course of business) if seller has made substantial start in their manufacture (or even made a contract for necessary raw materials) is enforceable

2] Oral contract is enforceable against party who admits it in court but not beyond quantity of goods admitted

3] Goods that have been paid for (if seller accepts payment) or goods which buyer has accepted are part of enforceable contract even if oral

> *EXAMPLE: B orally agrees to purchase 10,000 parts from S for $1 each. B later gives S $6,000 for a portion of the parts. S accepts the money. In absence of a written agreement, B may enforce a contract for 6,000 parts but not for the full 10,000 parts.*

(b) Modifications of written contracts involve two issues under UCC

1] New consideration on both sides is not required under UCC although it is required under common law

a] Under UCC, modification must be done in good faith

2] Modified contract must be in writing if contract, as modified, is within Statute of Frauds (i.e., sale of goods for $500 or more)

EXAMPLE: S agrees orally to sell B 100 widgets for $4.80 each. B later agrees, orally, to pay $5.00 for the 100 widgets due to changed business conditions. The modified contract is not enforceable because it must have been in writing. Therefore, the original contract is enforceable.

EXAMPLE: Same as above except that the modification is in writing. Now the modified contract is enforceable despite the fact that S is giving no new consideration.

EXAMPLE: X and Y have a written contract for the sale of goods for $530. They subsequently both agree orally to a price reduction of $40. The modified contract for $490 is enforceable.

    (c) Parties may exclude future oral agreements in a signed writing

  (5) Agreement for sale of intangibles over $5,000 must be in writing (e.g., patents, copyrights, or contract rights)

  (6) Sale of securities must be in writing

    (a) Must include price and quantity

b. When a writing is required and the UCC applies, it must

  (1) Indicate in writing that a contract for sale has been made
  (2) Be signed by party to be charged, and
  (3) Specify quantity of goods sold
  (4) However, note the following:

    (a) Any written form will do (e.g., letter, telegram, receipt, fax)
    (b) Need not be single document (e.g., two telegrams)
    (c) Need not be made at same time as contract

      1] Must be made before suit is brought
      2] Need not exist at time of suit (i.e., may have been destroyed)

    (d) Signature need not be at end nor be in a special form so long as intent to authenticate existed (e.g., initials, stamp, printed letterhead, etc., of party to be charged)

      1] Generally, signature sent by fax is enforceable

    (e) May omit material terms (e.g., price, delivery, time for performance) as long as quantity is stated. Reasonable terms will be inferred.
    (f) Exception to signature requirement exists under UCC when both parties are merchants— one party may send signed written confirmation stating terms (especially quantity) of oral agreement to other party within reasonable time, then nonsigning party must object within ten days or the contract is enforceable against him/her

EXAMPLE: B agreed on January 10 to purchase 100 widgets at $6 each from S. They agreed that delivery would take place on January 31. On January 14, B sent S a letter on B's letterhead that stated: "We no longer need the 100 widgets we ordered on January 10. Don't ship them."
*   This contract is enforceable against B even though the writing was later than the original oral agreement.*

EXAMPLE: Note that in the example above, if B and S are both merchants, not only is the contract enforceable against B, but it is also enforceable against S (the nonsigning party) unless S objects in ten days.

    (g) Only a few states allow a seal to substitute for signature when signature required

c. Noncompliance with Statute of Frauds (i.e., failure to make a writing) will make contract unenforceable

  (1) Promissory estoppel when aggrieved party has justifiably relied upon promise and when court rules justice demands it, may be used to defeat defense that contract was required to be in writing under Statute of Frauds

d. Other issues for signed writing

  (1) Parol evidence rule

    (a) Provides that any written agreement intended by parties to be final and complete contract (called an integration) may not be contradicted by previous or contemporaneous (written or oral) evidence

1] Applies to such written contracts whether Statute of Frauds required writing or not

2] Evidence of integration is often shown by a clause such as "This agreement is the complete agreement between the parties; no other representations have been made."

EXAMPLE: A and B enter into a home purchase agreement which is intended as a complete contract. B wishes to introduce oral evidence into court that the price of $150,000 that was in the home purchase agreement was put in to get a larger loan from a bank. B claims that they orally agreed the price would be $130,000. The oral evidence is not allowed to contradict the written contract under the parol evidence rule.

(b) Exceptions (party may present oral proof)

1] To show invalidity of contract between parties (e.g., fraud, forgery, duress, mistake, failure of consideration)

2] To show terms not inconsistent with writing that parties would not be expected to have included

EXAMPLE: Builder promises orally to use reasonable care not to damage nearby trees when building a house.

3] To explain intended meaning of an ambiguity (proof cannot contradict terms in contract but can explain them)

4] To show condition precedent—proof can be presented to show a fact or event must occur before agreement is valid

5] Under UCC, written terms may be supplemented or explained by course of dealing, usage of trade, or course of performance

(c) Does not apply to subsequent transactions (e.g., promises made after original agreement, or separate and distinct agreement made at same time as written contract)

EXAMPLE: M and N have a complete written employment contract. Later, M and N orally modify the contract with M agreeing to pay more and N agreeing to take on more duties. The oral evidence is allowed because it arose subsequent to the written contract.

8. Contracting using faxes

   a. Legal issues arise with use of faxes

   (1) Was an agreement really reached?

   (a) Courts examine faxes to see if "meeting of minds" actually took place under common law principles

   1] Businesses should retain all faxes concerning contract to preserve paper trail

   (2) Validity of signatures sent by faxes

   (a) Majority of courts that have examined this issue conclude that signatures sent by fax are valid

9. Contracting on-line

   a. When individuals make contracts over the Internet, basic rules of contract law still apply; however, this technology has created and will create more additional legal issues—only some of which have been settled

   b. E-SIGN Act—Federal law that makes electronic signatures valid like written ones, also makes electronic documents as valid as ones on paper

   (1) Electronic signature is valid only if parties in contract had agreed for it to be

   (2) Electronic document is valid only if it is in form that is retainable and is accurately reproduced

   (3) Some documents are exempt from E-SIGN Act such as wills, court papers, foreclosures

   (4) Act is considered important to promote use of technology

   (a) Does not provide uniform standard for authenticating e-signatures

   1] However, recommended methods to authenticate e-signatures include

   a] Use devices that recognize iris of user's eye or other portions of eye

   b] Use devices that recognize fingerprints

   c] Use secret passwords

d]   Use cards to identify persons such as "smart cards"

(b) Various states are adopting statutes that provide for procedures to determine validity of e-signatures

(c) Many companies enter into written contracts to accept electronic data and e-signatures between them

(d) Companies and individuals may use exceptions that exist under statute of frauds without need to resort to E-SIGN Act or state statutes

10. Computer shrink-wrap licenses and contracts generally enforceable

a.   Sale of shrink-wrap licenses is often conducted over Internet

b.   Individual or company often buys these without seeing or reviewing them first (thus the term shrink-wrap)

(1) Court cases have held these shrink-wrap licenses or goods purchased on-line to be enforceable especially if purchaser has time to examine them with right of return

D. Assignment and Delegation

1.   Assignment is the transfer of a right under a contract by one person to another

2.   Delegation is the transfer of duties under a contract

3.   Generally, a party's rights in a contract are assignable and duties are delegable

a.   No consideration is needed for valid assignment

(1) Gratuitous assignments are revocable

EXAMPLE: A owes B a debt for services B performed for A, but B has been unable to collect because A has been in financial difficulty. B may gratuitously assign this debt to X if X can collect it. If A's financial position improves, B may revoke the assignment to X and collect the debt himself or assign it to another for consideration.

b.   Rights may be assigned without delegating duties, or duties may be delegated without assigning rights

c.   Partial assignments may be made (e.g., only assign part of one's rights such as right to receive money)

d.   An assignment of a contract is generally taken to mean both assignment of rights and delegation of duties unless language or facts indicate otherwise

e.   Exceptions to ability to make assignments and delegations

(1) Contract involving personal services, trust, or confidence (e.g., an artist cannot delegate his/her duty to paint a portrait)

(a) With permission, these can be delegated

(b) Note that a contractor building a house according to a blueprint can delegate his/her duty to someone qualified

(2) Provision of contract or statute prohibits assignment or delegation

(a) Trend is to look with disfavor on prohibitions against assignments where only a right to money is concerned

(b) The UCC makes prohibition against assignment of monetary rights ineffective

(3) If assignment would materially change risk or burden of obligor

(a) For example, insurance contracts, requirement and output contracts, and contracts where personal credit is involved

f.   A delegation of duties is not an anticipatory breach

EXAMPLE: X Company contracted to deliver certain goods to Y. If X Company is low on these goods, it may delegate this duty to S Company, its subsidiary. It is not an anticipatory breach because X has not indicated that performance will not occur.

4.   An assignment generally extinguishes any rights of assignor but a delegation does not relieve delegant of his/her duties

   a. The assignee acquires assignor's rights against obligor and has exclusive right to performance
   b. If obligor has notice of assignment, s/he must pay assignee, not assignor

   (1) If obligor has no notice, s/he may pay assignor and assignee can only recover from assignor

   c. Unless there is a novation, delegating party is still liable if delegatee does not perform

   (1) Novation occurs when one of original parties to contract is released and new party is substituted in his/her place

   (a) Requires consent of all three parties

   EXAMPLE: A sells a car to B and accepts payments over time. B sells the car to C who agrees to take over the payments. No novation has occurred unless A agrees to accept C and release B.

5. Party taking an assignment generally steps into shoes of assignor—s/he gets no better rights than assignor had

   a. Assignee is subject to any defenses obligor could assert against assignor
   b. If assignee releases obligor, then assignor is also released

   EXAMPLE: A and B enter into a contract in which B agrees to pay A $300 for a stereo he received. A assigns his right to the $300 to C. C then releases B from the obligation of paying C the $300. This also releases A.

6. Assignor for value makes implied warranties to assignee that

   a. Assignor will do nothing to impair rights of assignee
   b. Assignor has no knowledge of any fact that would impair value of assignment

7. If assignor makes more than one assignment of same right, there are two rules to be applied depending upon the state

   a. First assignment prevails regardless of notices (majority rules)
   b. First assignee to give notice to obligor prevails (minority rules)

E. Third-Party Beneficiary Contracts

1. Contracting parties enter into agreement intended to benefit third party(ies)

   a. Creditor beneficiary—a debtor contracts with a second party to pay the debt owed to creditor (third-party beneficiary)

   EXAMPLE: X owes C $100. X contracts with Y to paint Y's house if Y will pay C $100. C is a creditor beneficiary.

   EXAMPLE: B buys some real estate from S and agrees to assume S's mortgage that is owed to XYZ bank. XYZ is a creditor beneficiary because B and S made a contract in which B agreed to pay XYZ. If B later defaults, XYZ may recover from either B or S. XYZ may recover from S based on the original contract. XYZ may recover from B because XYZ is a creditor beneficiary.

   EXAMPLE: Buyer purchases some property subject to a mortgage that the seller owes a Bank. The bank is not a third-party beneficiary because buyer did not agree to pay the mortgage. The seller is still the only debtor on the mortgage.

   b. Donee beneficiary—almost the same as creditor beneficiary except promisee's intent is to confer a gift upon third party through promisor's performance

   EXAMPLE: X contracts to buy Y's car if Y will deliver it to D, X's son. D is a donee beneficiary.

   c. Incidental beneficiary—third party who receives an unintended benefit from a contract. S/he obtains **no** rights under the contract

   EXAMPLE: X and Y contract to build an apartment building. A, a nearby store owner, would benefit from increased business and is an incidental beneficiary.

2. Only intended beneficiary (creditor or donee) can maintain an action against contracting parties for nonperformance

   a. Intent of the promisee controls
   b. Creditor beneficiary can proceed against either contracting party

   EXAMPLE: X owes C $100. X contracts with M to paint M's house if M will pay C $100. If X does not paint M's house, C may sue X because X still owes C $100. C may also sue M, because M now owes C $100 under the contract. C is a creditor beneficiary and can sue either party.

    c. Donee beneficiary can proceed against the promisor only

> *EXAMPLE: X contracts to buy Y's car if Y will deliver it to D. If Y does not deliver the car, D may sue Y. However, D may not sue X because it was a gift from X, not an obligation.*

   3. If the third-party beneficiary contract is executory, the parties may rescind and defeat the third party's rights

> *EXAMPLE: X owes C $100. X contracts with Y to paint Y's house if Y will pay C $100. X and Y may rescind the contract before Y pays C $100. Then there is no contract for C to enforce; however, C may still sue X for the $100 owed. Or in other words, C has no third-party rights on an executory contract.*

   4. The promisor can assert any defenses against third-party beneficiary that s/he has against promisee

F. Performance of Contract

   1. Duty to perform may depend upon a condition

    a. Condition precedent is condition that must occur before stated promise or duty in contract becomes due

> *EXAMPLE: B agrees to plant trees on specified land once C removes an old tennis court from the land.*

    b. Condition subsequent is condition that when it occurs it modifies or takes away a duty specified in contract.

> *EXAMPLE: M agrees to rent N a certain home until M finds a buyer.*

    c. Satisfaction as a condition—normally when a contract guarantees satisfaction, this means agreement is performed when a reasonable person would be satisfied. However, if agreement is expressly conditioned upon personal satisfaction of one of contracting parties, then performance does not occur until that party is actually satisfied.

   2. Tender of performance is an offer to perform (e.g., offer to pay debt)

> *EXAMPLE: X has contracted to buy goods from Y with delivery and payment to take place concurrently. X must offer the money to Y before Y has breached the contract for failure to deliver.*

   3. Under the **doctrine of substantial performance** (very important), performance is satisfied if

    a. There has been substantial performance (i.e., **deviations are minor**), and
    b. There has been **good-faith** effort to comply with contract
    c. Then damages for deviations are deducted from price if above are met
    d. This is often used in relation to construction contracts

   4. Payment of less than agreed-upon sum does not fulfill obligation unless both parties compromise based on a bona fide dispute as to amount owed
   5. Executory contract—has not yet been performed; only promises have been given
   6. Standards of interpretation of contracts

    a. For ordinary words, courts use normal meaning in dictionary
    b. For technical words, courts use technical meaning supplied by expert testimony if necessary
    c. Any ambiguity in contract is construed against party who drafted contract.
    d. Typed words prevail over preprinted words—handwritten words prevail over both preprinted and typed words
    e. When both parties are members of same profession or trade, words are given meaning in that profession or trade unless contact states otherwise.

G. Discharge of Contracts

   1. By agreement—new consideration is necessary, but often it is supplied by a promise for a promise (e.g., both parties agreeing to release other party of contractual obligation)

    a. Both parties may mutually agree to rescind contract
    b. Under UCC, no consideration is needed to modify a contract (for sale of goods) if in good faith
    c. A novation is an agreement by three parties whereby a previous agreement is discharged by creation of a new agreement

(1) May involve substitution of creditors, debtors, or of obligations

> *EXAMPLE: X has agreed to do some accounting work for Y for $2,000. Since X is very busy, X, Y, and Z all agree to let X out of the contract and insert Z in his place. This is a novation. X and Y no longer have any obligations to each other.*

> *EXAMPLE: A party purchases land and assumes a mortgage. The original mortgagor is still liable unless a novation has occurred.*

2. By performance becoming objectively impossible

   a. But mere fact of performance becoming more costly does not excuse performance

> *EXAMPLE: A agreed to sell a specified quantity of corn to B at specified prices. He had planned to sell his own corn until his crop was destroyed. Even though he may make less profit or even suffer a loss, he can still fulfill the contract by purchasing the corn from others to resell to B under his contract.*

3. By breach of contract
4. Anticipatory breach (repudiation) is renunciation before performance is due

   a. May sue at once, or
   b. Cancel contract, or
   c. Wait until time performance is due or for a reasonable time and then sue
   d. If other party has not changed position in reliance upon the repudiation, repudiating party can retract repudiation and perform at appointed time, thereby discharging his/her contractual obligation

> *EXAMPLE: X agrees to convey and Y agrees to pay for land on April 1. On February 1, Y learns that X has sold the land to Z. Y may sue before April 1, or he may wait and sue on April 1.*

> *EXAMPLE: M agrees to deliver 1,000 widgets to Q by December 1. Three months before that date, M says, he will be unable to deliver on December 1.*

H. Remedies

1. Monetary damages

   a. Purpose is to place injured party in as good a position as s/he would have occupied if contract had been performed
   b. Actual or compensatory damages are equal to amount caused by breach

   (1) This is the **most common remedy** under contract law
   (2) Damages must be foreseeable before being recoverable

   c. Punitive damages are generally not allowed in contract law
   d. Liquidated damage clause is a provision agreed to in a contract to set the amount of damages in advance if a breach occurs

   (1) These are used instead of awarding actual compensatory damages
   (2) Not enforceable if punitive; therefore, amount set in advance must be reasonably based on what actual damages are expected to be
   (3) For sales of goods, if contract has no provision for liquidated damages, seller may retain deposit of up to $500 when buyer defaults

   e. Party injured by breach must use reasonable care to minimize loss because s/he cannot recover costs that could have been avoided—called mitigation of damages

> *EXAMPLE: One who receives perishables which are not the goods bargained for must take reasonable steps to prevent loss from spoilage.*

> *EXAMPLE: X contracts to fix Y's car. After X begins work, Y breaches and says "Stop." X cannot continue to work and incur more costs (i.e., put in more parts and labor).*

2. Rescission—cancellation of contract whereby parties are placed in position they were in before contract was formed
3. Specific performance—compels performance promised

   a. Used only when money damages will not suffice (e.g., when subject matter is unique, or rare, as in contract for sale of land)
   b. Injured party may seek compensatory damages if s/he chooses

    c.   Not available to compel personal services

4. Restitution—return of consideration to injured party
5. Injunction—compels an act or restrains an act
6. Release—one party relieves other party of part of obligations in contract
7. Waiver—one party voluntarily gives up some right in contract either by express agreement or by consistently not enforcing such right in past
8. Arbitration—resolution of dispute, outside of judicial system, agreed to by disputing parties
9. Reformation—if parties have failed to express true intentions in contract, court may reform it to express true intentions of contract

    a.   Note—court needs clear proof

I. Statute of Limitations

1. Bars suit if not brought within statutory period

    a.   Periods vary for different types of cases
    b.   Periods vary from state to state

2. Statute begins to run from time cause of action accrues (e.g., breach)
3. Running of statute may be stopped when defendant is absent from jurisdiction

J. Jurisdiction over Defendant for On-Line Transactions

1. Courts generally grant plaintiffs personal jurisdiction over defendants in foreign state if plaintiff intentionally engaged in commercial activities for use outside of home state
2. Generally, websites or advertising by persons or entities seen by others in other jurisdictions do not create personal jurisdiction to allow lawsuits in those other jurisdictions

    a.   Minimum contacts such as actively selling products are needed to require defendant to defend self in other state

3. Parties to contracts made on-line may agree to use law of given jurisdiction just as in other contracts

    a.   Often, websites put forum selection clause at end of home page in case lawsuit is brought against on-line company

        (1) Some courts may not enforce these clauses since they are not negotiable and thus lead to adhesion contracts

            (a) Increasing trend is not to enforce these unless they are fair and reasonable because they are typically in small print at end of home page

MULTIPLE-CHOICE QUESTIONS (1-57)

1. Carson Corp., a retail chain, asked Alto Construction to fix a broken window at one of Carson's stores. Alto offered to make the repairs within three days at a price to be agreed on after the work was completed. A contract based on Alto's offer would fail because of indefiniteness as to the
   a. Price involved.
   b. Nature of the subject matter.
   c. Parties to the contract.
   d. Time for performance.

2. On September 10, Harris, Inc., a new car dealer, placed a newspaper advertisement stating that Harris would sell ten cars at its showroom for a special discount only on September 12, 13, and 14. On September 12, King called Harris and expressed an interest in buying one of the advertised cars. King was told that five of the cars had been sold and to come to the showroom as soon as possible. On September 13, Harris made a televised announcement that the sale would end at 10:00 PM that night. King went to Harris' showroom on September 14 and demanded the right to buy a car at the special discount. Harris had sold the ten cars and refused King's demand. King sued Harris for breach of contract. Harris' best defense to King's suit would be that Harris'
   a. Offer was unenforceable.
   b. Advertisement was **not** an offer.
   c. Television announcement revoked the offer.
   d. Offer had **not** been accepted.

3. On June 15, Peters orally offered to sell a used lawn mower to Mason for $125. Peters specified that Mason had until June 20 to accept the offer. On June 16, Peters received an offer to purchase the lawn mower for $150 from Bronson, Mason's neighbor. Peters accepted Bronson's offer. On June 17, Mason saw Bronson using the lawn mower and was told the mower had been sold to Bronson. Mason immediately wrote to Peters to accept the June 15 offer. Which of the following statements is correct?
   a. Mason's acceptance would be effective when received by Peters.
   b. Mason's acceptance would be effective when mailed.
   c. Peters' offer had been revoked and Mason's acceptance was ineffective.
   d. Peters was obligated to keep the June 15 offer open until June 20.

4. Calistoga offers to sell her home to Drake for $300,000. Drake asks her if she would accept $250,000. Which of the following is true?
   a. Drake's response is mere inquiry; therefore, the $300,000 offer by Calistoga is still in force.
   b. Drake's response is a counteroffer effectively terminating the $300,000 offer and instigating an offer for $250,000.
   c. Drake's response is a rejection of the $300,000 offer, and there is no offer for $250,000 because it is too indefinite to be an offer.
   d. Because of ambiguity, both offers are terminated by operation of law.

5. Opal offered, in writing, to sell Larkin a parcel of land for $300,000. If Opal dies, the offer will

   a. Terminate prior to Larkin's acceptance only if Larkin received notice of Opal's death.
   b. Remain open for a reasonable period of time after Opal's death.
   c. Automatically terminate despite Larkin's prior acceptance.
   d. Automatically terminate prior to Larkin's acceptance.

6. On April 1, Fine Corp. faxed Moss an offer to purchase Moss' warehouse for $500,000. The offer stated that it would remain open only until April 4 and that acceptance must be received to be effective. Moss sent an acceptance on April 4 by overnight mail and Fine received it on April 5. Which of the following statements is correct?
   a. No contract was formed because Moss sent the acceptance by an unauthorized method.
   b. No contract was formed because Fine received Moss' acceptance after April 4.
   c. A contract was formed when Moss sent the acceptance.
   d. A contract was formed when Fine received Moss' acceptance.

7. On February 12, Harris sent Fresno a written offer to purchase Fresno's land. The offer included the following provision: "Acceptance of this offer must be by registered or certified mail, received by Harris no later than February 18 by 5:00 p.m. CST." On February 18, Fresno sent Harris a letter accepting the offer by private overnight delivery service. Harris received the letter on February 19. Which of the following statements is correct?
   a. A contract was formed on February 19.
   b. Fresno's letter constituted a counteroffer.
   c. Fresno's use of the overnight delivery service was an effective form of acceptance.
   d. A contract was formed on February 18 regardless of when Harris actually received Fresno's letter.

8. Kay, an art collector, promised Hammer, an art student, that if Hammer could obtain certain rare artifacts within two weeks, Kay would pay for Hammer's postgraduate education. At considerable effort and expense, Hammer obtained the specified artifacts within the two-week period. When Hammer requested payment, Kay refused. Kay claimed that there was no consideration for the promise. Hammer would prevail against Kay based on
   a. Unilateral contract.
   b. Unjust enrichment.
   c. Public policy.
   d. Quasi contract.

9. On September 27, Summers sent Fox a letter offering to sell Fox a vacation home for $150,000. On October 2, Fox replied by mail agreeing to buy the home for $145,000. Summers did not reply to Fox. Do Fox and Summers have a binding contract?
   a. No, because Fox failed to sign and return Summers' letter.
   b. No, because Fox's letter was a counteroffer.
   c. Yes, because Summers' offer was validly accepted.
   d. Yes, because Summers' silence is an implied acceptance of Fox's letter.

10. Wick Company made a contract in writing to hire Zake for five years for $150,000 per year. After two years, Zake asked Wick for a raise of $20,000 per year. Wick at first refused but agreed after Zake put on some pressure. After the fifth year, Zake left and Wick sued to get back the extra $20,000 per year for the last three years. Who wins?

    a. Zake, because Wick agreed to the raise.

    b. Zake, if the raise was agreed to in writing.

    c. Wick, even though Wick agreed to the raise.

    d. Wick, because Zake had applied some pressure to get the raise.

11. Grove is seeking to avoid performing a promise to pay Brook $1,500. Grove is relying on lack of consideration on Brook's part. Grove will prevail if he can establish that

    a. Prior to Grove's promise, Brook had already performed the requested act.

    b. Brooks' only claim of consideration was the relinquishment of a legal right.

    c. Brook's asserted consideration is only worth $400.

    d. The consideration to be performed by Brook will be performed by a third party.

12. Dunne and Cook signed a contract requiring Cook to rebind 500 of Dunne's books at $0.80 per book. Later, Dunne requested, in good faith, that the price be reduced to $.70 per book. Cook agreed orally to reduce the price to $.70. Under the circumstances, the oral agreement is

    a. Enforceable, but proof of it is inadmissible into evidence.

    b. Enforceable, and proof of it is admissible into evidence.

    c. Unenforceable, because Dunne failed to give consideration, but proof of it is otherwise admissible into evidence.

    d. Unenforceable, due to the statute of frauds, and proof of it is inadmissible into evidence.

13. In which of the following situations does the first promise serve as valid consideration for the second promise?

    a. A police officer's promise to catch a thief for a victim's promise to pay a reward.

    b. A builder's promise to complete a contract for a purchaser's promise to extend the time for completion.

    c. A debtor's promise to pay $500 for a creditor's promise to forgive the balance of a $600 liquidated debt.

    d. A debtor's promise to pay $500 for a creditor's promise to forgive the balance of a $600 disputed debt.

14. Which of the following will be legally binding despite lack of consideration?

    a. An employer's promise to make a cash payment to a deceased employee's family in recognition of the employee's many years of service.

    b. A promise to donate money to a charity on which the charity relied in incurring large expenditures.

    c. A modification of a signed contract to purchase a parcel of land.

    d. A merchant's oral promise to keep an offer open for sixty days.

15. Rail, who was sixteen years old, purchased an $800 computer from Elco Electronics. Rail and Elco are located in a state where the age of majority is eighteen. On several occasions Rail returned the computer to Elco for repairs.

Rail was very unhappy with the computer. Two days after reaching the age of eighteen, Rail was still frustrated with the computer's reliability, and returned it to Elco, demanding an $800 refund. Elco refused, claiming that Rail no longer had a right to disaffirm the contract. Elco's refusal is

    a. Correct, because Rail's multiple requests for service acted as a ratification of the contract.

    b. Correct, because Rail could have transferred good title to a good-faith purchaser for value.

    c. Incorrect, because Rail disaffirmed the contract within a reasonable period of time after reaching the age of eighteen.

    d. Incorrect, because Rail could disaffirm the contract at any time.

16. Green was adjudicated incompetent by a court having proper jurisdiction. Which of the following statements is correct regarding contracts subsequently entered into by Green?

    a. All contracts are voidable.

    b. All contracts are valid.

    c. All contracts are void.

    d. All contracts are enforceable.

17. All of the following are effective methods of ratifying a contract entered into by a minor **except**

    a. Expressly ratifying the contract after reaching the age of majority.

    b. Failing to disaffirm the contract within a reasonable time after reaching the age of majority.

    c. Ratifying the contract before reaching the age of majority.

    d. Ratifying the contract by implication after reaching the age of majority.

18. Under a personal services contract, which of the following circumstances will cause the discharge of a party's duties?

    a. Death of the party who is to receive the services.

    b. Cost of performing the services has doubled.

    c. Bankruptcy of the party who is to receive the services.

    d. Illegality of the services to be performed.

19. Which of the following would be unenforceable because the subject matter is illegal?

    a. A contingent fee charged by an attorney to represent a plaintiff in a negligence action.

    b. An arbitration clause in a supply contract.

    c. A restrictive covenant in an employment contract prohibiting a former employee from using the employer's trade secrets.

    d. An employer's promise **not** to press embezzlement charges against an employee who agrees to make restitution.

20. Which of the following, if intentionally misstated by a seller to a buyer, would be considered a fraudulent inducement to make a contract?

    a. Nonexpert opinion.

    b. Appraised value.

    c. Prediction.

    d. Immaterial fact.

21. If a buyer accepts an offer containing an immaterial unilateral mistake, the resulting contract will be

    a. Void as a matter of law.

b. Void at the election of the buyer.

c. Valid as to both parties.

d. Voidable at the election of the seller.

22. If a person is induced to enter into a contract by another person because of the close relationship between the parties, the contract may be voidable under which of the following defenses?

a. Fraud in the inducement.

b. Unconscionability.

c. Undue influence.

d. Duress.

23. Long purchased a life insurance policy with Tempo Life Insurance Co. The policy named Long's daughter as beneficiary. Six months after the policy was issued, Long died of a heart attack. Long had failed to disclose on the insurance application a known preexisting heart condition that caused the heart attack. Tempo refused to pay the death benefit to Long's daughter. If Long's daughter sues, Tempo will

a. Win, because Long's daughter is an incidental beneficiary.

b. Win, because of Long's failure to disclose the pre-existing heart condition.

c. Lose, because Long's death was from natural causes.

d. Lose, because Long's daughter is a third-party donee beneficiary.

24. Petersen went to Jackson's home to buy a used car advertised in the newspaper. Jackson told Petersen that "it is a great car" and that "the engine had been overhauled a year ago." Shortly after he bought the car, Petersen began experiencing problems with the engine. When Jackson refused to refund his money, Petersen sued for fraud based on it was not a "great car" and also based on the fact, as learned later, the overhaul was done thirteen months ago, not a year. Will Petersen win his case?

a. Yes, Jackson's statement that "it is a great car" is actionable fraud.

b. Yes, Jackson's statement about the overhaul is actionable fraud.

c. Yes, both the statement that "it is a great car" and the statement about the overhaul are actionable fraud.

d. No.

25. A building subcontractor submitted a bid for construction of a portion of a high-rise office building. The bid contained material computational errors. The general contractor accepted the bid with knowledge of the errors. Which of the following statements best represents the subcontractor's liability?

a. Not liable because the contractor knew of the errors.

b. Not liable because the errors were a result of gross negligence.

c. Liable because the errors were unilateral.

d. Liable because the errors were material.

26. Maco, Inc. and Kent contracted for Kent to provide Maco certain consulting services at an hourly rate of $20. Kent's normal hourly rate was $90 per hour, the fair market value of the services. Kent agreed to the $20 rate because Kent was having serious financial problems. At the time the agreement was negotiated, Maco was aware of Kent's finan-

cial condition and refused to pay more than $20 per hour for Kent's services. Kent has now sued to rescind the contract with Maco, claiming duress by Maco during the negotiations. Under the circumstances, Kent will

a. Win, because Maco refused to pay the fair market value of Kent's services.

b. Win, because Maco was aware of Kent's serious financial problems.

c. Lose, because Maco's actions did **not** constitute duress.

d. Lose, because Maco **cannot** prove that Kent, at the time, had **no** other offers to provide consulting services.

27. To prevail in a common law action for fraud in the inducement, a plaintiff must prove that the

a. Defendant was an expert with regard to the misrepresentations.

b. Defendant made the misrepresentations with knowledge of their falsity and with an intention to deceive.

c. Misrepresentations were in writing.

d. Plaintiff was in a fiduciary relationship with the defendant.

28. Under the UCC Sales Article, a plaintiff who proves fraud in the formation of a contract may

a. Elect to rescind the contract and need **not** return the consideration received from the other party.

b. Be entitled to rescind the contract and sue for damages resulting from the fraud.

c. Be entitled to punitive damages provided physical injuries resulted from the fraud.

d. Rescind the contract even if there was **no** reliance on the fraudulent statement.

29. On June 1, 2001, Decker orally guaranteed the payment of a $5,000 note Decker's cousin owed Baker. Decker's agreement with Baker provided that Decker's guaranty would terminate in eighteen months. On June 3, 2001, Baker wrote Decker confirming Decker's guaranty. Decker did not object to the confirmation. On August 23, 2001, Decker's cousin defaulted on the note and Baker demanded that Decker honor the guaranty. Decker refused. Which of the following statements is correct?

a. Decker is liable under the oral guaranty because Decker did **not** object to Baker's June 3 letter.

b. Decker is **not** liable under the oral guaranty because it expired more than one year after June 1.

c. Decker is liable under the oral guaranty because Baker demanded payment within one year of the date the guaranty was given.

d. Decker is **not** liable under the oral guaranty because Decker's promise was **not** in writing.

30. Nolan agreed orally with Train to sell Train a house for $100,000. Train sent Nolan a signed agreement and a downpayment of $10,000. Nolan did not sign the agreement, but allowed Train to move into the house. Before closing, Nolan refused to go through with the sale. Train sued Nolan to compel specific performance. Under the provisions of the Statute of Frauds

a. Train will win because Train signed the agreement and Nolan did **not** object.

b. Train will win because Train made a downpayment and took possession.

   c.   Nolan will win because Nolan did **not** sign the agreement.

   d.   Nolan will win because the house was worth more than $500.

31. Cherry contracted orally to purchase Picks Company for $1,500,000 if it is profitable for one full year after the making of the oral contract. An auditor would be brought in at the end of the year to verify this. Even though the company turns out to be profitable during the upcoming year, Cherry refuses to go through with the contract, claiming that it was unenforceable because it was not in writing. Is Cherry correct?

   a.   Yes, because the contract could not be completed within one year.

   b.   Yes, because the contract was for $500 or more.

   c.   No, because the company was profitable as agreed for one year.

   d.   No, because Picks Company relied on Cherry's promise.

32. Which of the following statements is true with regard to the Statute of Frauds?

   a.   All contracts involving consideration of more than $500 must be in writing.

   b.   The written contract must be signed by all parties.

   c.   The Statute of Frauds applies to contracts that can be fully performed within one year from the date they are made.

   d.   The contract terms may be stated in more than 1 document.

33. Carson agreed orally to repair Ives' rare book for $450. Before the work was started, Ives asked Carson to perform additional repairs to the book and agreed to increase the contract price to $650. After Carson completed the work, Ives refused to pay and Carson sued. Ives' defense was based on the Statute of Frauds. What total amount will Carson recover?

   a. $0

   b. $200

   c. $450

   d. $650

34. Landry Company contracted orally with Newell to pay her $50,000 for the completion of an ethics audit of Landry Company. The report is to span a period of time of at least ten months and is due in fourteen months from now. Newell has agreed orally to perform the ethics audit and says that she will begin within three months, noting that even if she delays the full three months, she will have the report ready within the fourteen-month deadline. Does this contract fall under the Statute of Frauds?

   a.   Yes, because the contract is for $500 or more.

   b.   Yes, because the deadline for the contract is over one year.

   c.   No, despite the due date of fourteen months.

   d.   No, because both parties waived the Statute of Frauds by their oral agreement.

35. Rogers and Lennon entered into a written computer consulting agreement that required Lennon to provide certain weekly reports to Rogers. The agreement also stated that Lennon would provide the computer equipment necessary to perform the services, and that Rogers' computer would not be used. As the parties were executing the agreement, they orally agreed that Lennon could use Rogers' computer. After executing the agreement, Rogers and Lennon orally agreed that Lennon would report on a monthly, rather than weekly, basis. The parties now disagree on Lennon's right to use Rogers' computer and how often Lennon must report to Rogers. In the event of a lawsuit between the parties, the parol evidence rule will

   a.   Not apply to any of the parties' agreements because the consulting agreement did **not** have to be in writing.

   b.   Not prevent Lennon from proving the parties' oral agreement that Lennon could use Rogers' computer.

   c.   Not prevent the admission into evidence of testimony regarding Lennon's right to report on a monthly basis.

   d.   Not apply to the parties' agreement to allow Lennon to use Rogers' computer because it was contemporaneous with the written agreement.

36. Where the parties have entered into a written contract intended as the final expression of their agreement, which of the following agreements will be admitted into evidence because they are **not** prohibited by the parol evidence rule?

	Subsequent oral agreements	Prior written agreements
a.	Yes	Yes
b.	Yes	No
c.	No	Yes
d.	No	No

37. In negotiations with Andrews for the lease of Kemp's warehouse, Kemp orally agreed to pay one-half of the cost of the utilities. The written lease, later prepared by Kemp's attorney, provided that Andrews pay all of the utilities. Andrews failed to carefully read the lease and signed it. When Kemp demanded that Andrews pay all of the utilities, Andrews refused, claiming that the lease did not accurately reflect the oral agreement. Andrews also learned that Kemp intentionally misrepresented the condition of the structure of the warehouse during the negotiations between the parties. Andrews sued to rescind the lease and intends to introduce evidence of the parties' oral agreement about sharing the utilities and the fraudulent statements made by Kemp. The parol evidence rule will prevent the admission of evidence concerning the

	Oral agreement regarding who pays the utilities	Fraudulent statements by Kemp
a.	Yes	Yes
b.	No	Yes
c.	Yes	No
d.	No	No

38. Joan Silver had viewed some land that she wished to purchase. It was offered for sale by Daniel Tweney over the Internet for $200,000. Silver believes this to be a good deal for her and thus wishes to purchase it. Silver and Tweney have communicated on-line and wish to make a contract for the land over the Internet. Which of the following statements is(are) correct?

I. Because this contract is covered by the Statute of Frauds, this contract cannot be accomplished over the Internet.

II. Because of the parol evidence rule, this contract cannot be completed over the Internet.

III. Because this contract is covered by the Uniform Commerical Code, it may not be accomplished over the Internet.

    a. Only I is correct.
    b. I and II only are correct.
    c. I and III only are correct.
    d. Neither I, II, nor III is correct.

39. Generally, which of the following contract rights are assignable?

	Option contract rights	Malpractice insurance policy rights
a.	Yes	Yes
b.	Yes	No
c.	No	Yes
d.	No	No

40. One of the criteria for a valid assignment of a sales contract to a third party is that the assignment must

    a. Be supported by adequate consideration from the assignee.
    b. Be in writing and signed by the assignor.
    c. Not materially increase the other party's risk or duty.
    d. Not be revocable by the assignor.

Items 41 and 42 are based on the following:

Egan contracted with Barton to buy Barton's business. The contract provided that Egan would pay the business debts Barton owed Ness and that the balance of the purchase price would be paid to Barton over a ten-year period. The contract also required Egan to take out a decreasing term life insurance policy naming Barton and Ness as beneficiaries to ensure that the amounts owed Barton and Ness would be paid if Egan died.

41. Barton's contract rights were assigned to Vim, and Egan was notified of the assignment. Despite the assignment, Egan continued making payments to Barton. Egan died before completing payment and Vim sued Barton for the insurance proceeds and the other payments on the purchase price received by Barton after the assignment. To which of the following is Vim entitled?

	Payments on purchase price	Insurance proceeds
a.	No	Yes
b.	No	No
c.	Yes	Yes
d.	Yes	No

42. Which of the following would describe Ness' status under the contract and insurance policy?

	Contract	Insurance policy
a.	Donee beneficiary	Donee beneficiary
b.	Donee beneficiary	Creditor beneficiary
c.	Creditor beneficiary	Donee beneficiary
d.	Creditor beneficiary	Creditor beneficiary

43. Your client, Bugle, owns a parking lot near downtown San Francisco. One day Bugle is excited because he learns that Fargo, who owns a parking lot next door, has made a contract with ABC Company to sell her land. ABC Company can then construct a building that will contain several nice professional offices. Bugle figures that he will charge more for his parking. He later discovers that the contract fell through. He says that when he finds out who breached the contract, he will sue that party for lost profits that he would have earned. Which of the following is correct?

    a. If Fargo was the one who breached the contract, Bugle may sue her if ABC had already made some payments on the contract.
    b. If ABC was the party who breached, ABC is liable to Bugle.
    c. Bugle may sue either party, and the nonbreaching party may then recover from the breaching party.
    d. Bugle has no legal rights against either party.

44. Baxter, Inc. and Globe entered into a contract. After receiving valuable consideration from Clay, Baxter assigned its rights under the contract to Clay. In which of the following circumstances would Baxter **not** be liable to Clay?

    a. Clay released Globe.
    b. Globe paid Baxter.
    c. Baxter released Globe.
    d. Baxter breached the contract.

45. Mackay paid Manus $1,000 to deliver a painting to Mackay's friend Mann. When they met and signed the contract, Mackay said she wanted the painting delivered as soon as possible because it was a gift for Mann's birthday. Several months have passed without the delivery. Mann can maintain lawsuits against which parties to get the painting?

    a. Manus only.
    b. Mackay only.
    c. Manus, but only if he also brings suit against Mackay.
    d. Manus or Mackay at Mann's option.

46. Ferco, Inc. claims to be a creditor beneficiary of a contract between Bell and Allied Industries, Inc. Allied is indebted to Ferco. The contract between Bell and Allied provides that Bell is to purchase certain goods from Allied and pay the purchase price directly to Ferco until Allied's obligation is satisfied. Without justification, Bell failed to pay Ferco and Ferco sued Bell. Ferco will

    a. Not prevail, because Ferco lacked privity of contract with either Bell or Allied.
    b. Not prevail, because Ferco did **not** give any consideration to Bell.
    c. Prevail, because Ferco was an intended beneficiary of the contract between Allied and Bell.
    d. Prevail, provided Ferco was aware of the contract between Bell and Allied at the time the contract was entered into.

47. Parc hired Glaze to remodel and furnish an office suite. Glaze submitted plans that Parc approved. After completing all the necessary construction and painting, Glaze purchased minor accessories that Parc rejected because they did not conform to the plans. Parc refused to allow Glaze to complete the project and refused to pay Glaze any part of the contract price. Glaze sued for the value of the work performed. Which of the following statements is correct?

    a. Glaze will lose because Glaze breached the contract by **not** completing performance.
    b. Glaze will win because Glaze substantially performed and Parc prevented complete performance.
    c. Glaze will lose because Glaze materially breached the contract by buying the accessories.
    d. Glaze will win because Parc committed anticipatory breach.

48. Which of the following types of conditions affecting performance may validly be present in contracts?

	Conditions precedent	Conditions subsequent	Current conditions
a.	Yes	Yes	Yes
b.	Yes	Yes	No
c.	Yes	No	Yes
d.	No	Yes	Yes

49. Which of the following actions if taken by one party to a contract generally will discharge the performance required of the other party to the contract?
- a.   Material breach of the contract.
- b.   Delay in performance.
- c.   Tender.
- d.   Assignment of rights.

50. Which of the following actions will result in the discharge of a party to a contract?

	Prevention of performance	Accord and satisfaction
a.	Yes	Yes
b.	Yes	No
c.	No	Yes
d.	No	No

51. To cancel a contract and to restore the parties to their original positions before the contract, the parties should execute a
- a.   Novation
- b.   Release
- c.   Rescission
- d.   Revocation

52. Kaye contracted to sell Hodges a building for $310,000. The contract required Hodges to pay the entire amount at closing. Kaye refused to close the sale of the building. Hodges sued Kaye. To what relief is Hodges entitled?
- a.   Punitive damages and compensatory damages.
- b.   Specific performance and compensatory damages.
- c.   Consequential damages or punitive damages.
- d.   Compensatory damages or specific performance.

53. Ames Construction Co. contracted to build a warehouse for White Corp. The construction specifications required Ames to use Ace lighting fixtures. Inadvertently, Ames installed Perfection lighting fixtures which are of slightly lesser quality than Ace fixtures, but in all other respects meet White's needs. Which of the following statements is correct?
- a.   White's recovery will be limited to monetary damages because Ames' breach of the construction contract was **not** material.
- b.   White will **not** be able to recover any damages from Ames because the breach was inadvertent.
- c.   Ames did not breach the construction contract because the Perfection fixtures were substantially as good as the Ace fixtures.
- d.   Ames must install Ace fixtures or White will **not** be obligated to accept the warehouse.

54. Master Mfg., Inc. contracted with Accur Computer Repair Corp. to maintain Master's computer system. Master's manufacturing process depends on its computer system operating properly at all times. A liquidated damages clause in the contract provided that Accur pay $1,000 to Master for each day that Accur was late responding to a service request. On January 12, Accur was notified that Master's computer system failed. Accur did not respond to Master's service request until January 15. If Master sues Accur under the liquidated damage provision of the contract, Master will
- a.   Win, unless the liquidated damage provision is determined to be a penalty.
- b.   Win, because under all circumstances liquidated damage provisions are enforceable.
- c.   Lose, because Accur's breach was **not** material.
- d.   Lose, because liquidated damage provisions violate public policy.

55. Nagel and Fields entered into a contract in which Nagel was obligated to deliver certain goods to Fields by September 10. On September 3, Nagel told Fields that Nagel had no intention of delivering the goods required by the contract. Prior to September 10, Fields may successfully sue Nagel under the doctrine of
- a.   Promissory estoppel.
- b.   Accord and satisfaction.
- c.   Anticipatory repudiation.
- d.   Substantial performance.

56. Maco Corp. contracted to sell 1,500 bushels of potatoes to LBC Chips. The contract did not refer to any specific supply source for the potatoes. Maco intended to deliver potatoes grown on its farms. An insect infestation ruined Maco's crop but not the crops of other growers in the area. Maco failed to deliver the potatoes to LBC. LBC sued Maco for breach of contract. Under the circumstances, Maco will
- a.   Lose, because it could have purchased potatoes from other growers to deliver to LBC.
- b.   Lose, unless it can show that the purchase of substitute potatoes for delivery to LBC would make the contract unprofitable.
- c.   Win, because the infestation was an act of nature that could **not** have been anticipated by Maco.
- d.   Win, because both Maco and LBC are assumed to accept the risk of a crop failure.

57. Ordinarily, in an action for breach of a construction contract, the statute of limitations time period would be computed from the date the
- a.   Contract is negotiated.
- b.   Contract is breached.
- c.   Construction is begun.
- d.   Contract is signed.

PROBLEMS

NOTE: These types of problems are no longer included in the CPA Examination but they have been retained because they are useful in developing skills to complete simulations.

Problem 1   (15 to 25 minutes)

Victor Corp. engaged Bell & Co., CPAs, to audit Victor's financial statements for the year ended December 31, 2003. Victor is in the business of buying, selling, and servicing new and used construction equipment. While reviewing Victor's 2003 records, Bell became aware of the following disputed transactions:

•   On September 8, Victor sent Ambel Contractors, Inc. a signed purchase order for several pieces of used construction equipment. Victor's purchase order described twelve different pieces of equipment and indicated the price Victor was willing to pay for each item. As a result of a mathematical error in adding up the total of the various prices, the purchase price offered by Victor was $191,000 rather than the correct amount of $119,000. Ambel, on receipt of the purchase order, was surprised by Victor's high price and immediately sent Victor a written acceptance. Ambel was aware that the fair market value of the equipment was approximately $105,000 to $125,000. Victor discovered the mistake in the purchase order and refused to purchase the equipment from Ambel. Ambel claims that Victor is obligated to purchase the equipment at a price of $191,000, as set forth in the purchase order.

•   On October 8, a Victor salesperson orally contracted to service a piece of equipment owned by Clark Masons, Inc. The contract provided that for a period of thirty-six months, commencing November 2000, Victor would provide routine service for the equipment at a fixed price of $15,000, payable in three annual installments of $5,000 each. On October 29, Clark's president contacted Victor and stated that Clark did not intend to honor the service agreement because there was no written contract between Victor and Clark.

•   On November 3, Victor received by mail a signed offer from GYX Erectors, Inc. The offer provided that Victor would service certain specified equipment owned by GYX for a two-year period for a total price of $81,000. The offer also provided as follows:

> "We need to know soon whether you can agree to the terms of this proposal. You must accept by November 15, or we will assume you can't meet our terms."

On November 12, Victor mailed GYX a signed acceptance of GYX's offer. The acceptance was not received by GYX until November 17, and by then GYX had contracted with another party to provide service for its equipment. Victor has taken the position that GYX is obligated to honor its November 3 offer. GYX claims that no contract was formed because Victor's November 12 acceptance was not received timely by GYX.

•   On December 19, Victor contracted in writing with Wells Landscaping Corp. The contract required Victor to deliver certain specified new equipment to Wells by December 31. On December 23, Victor determined that it would not be able to deliver the equipment to Wells by December 31 because of an inventory shortage. Therefore, Victor made a written assignment of the contract to Master Equipment, Inc. When Master attempted to deliver the equipment on December 31, Wells refused to accept it, claiming that

Victor could not properly delegate its duties under the December 19 contract to another party without the consent of Wells. The contract is silent with regard to this issue.

Required:

State whether the claims of Ambel, Clark, GYX, and Wells are correct and give the reasons for your conclusions.

Problem 2   (15 to 20 minutes)

In a signed letter dated March 2, 2003, Stake offered to sell Packer a specific vacant parcel of land for $100,000. Stake had inherited the land, along with several apartment buildings in the immediate vicinity. Packer received the offer on March 4. The offer required acceptance by March 10 and required Packer to have the property surveyed by a licensed surveyor so the exact legal description of the property could be determined.

On March 6, Packer sent Stake a counteroffer of $75,000. All other terms and conditions of the offer were unchanged. Stake received Packer's counteroffer on March 8, and, on that day, telephoned Packer and accepted it. On learning that a survey of the vacant parcel would cost about $1,000, Packer telephoned Stake on March 11 requesting that they share the survey cost equally. During this conversation, Stake agreed to Packer's proposal.

During the course of the negotiations leading up to the March communications between Stake and Packer, Stake expressed concern to Packer that a buyer of the land might build apartment units that would compete with those owned by Stake in the immediate vicinity. Packer assured Stake that Packer intended to use the land for a small shopping center. Because of these assurances, Stake was willing to sell the land to Packer. Contrary to what Packer told Stake, Packer had already contracted conditionally with Rolf for Rolf to build a forty-eight-unit apartment development on the vacant land to be purchased from Stake.

During the last week of March, Stake learned that the land to be sold to Packer had a fair market value of $200,000. Also, Stake learned that Packer intended to build apartments on the land. Because of this information, Stake sued Packer to rescind the real estate contract, alleging that

•   Packer committed fraud in the formation of the contract, thereby entitling Stake to rescind the contract.

•   Stake's innocent mistake as to the fair market value of the land entitles Stake to rescind the contract.

•   The contract was not enforceable against Stake because Stake did not sign Packer's March 6 counteroffer.

Required:

State whether Stake's allegations are correct and give the reasons for your conclusions.

SIMULATION PROBLEMS

Simulation Problem 1   (5 to 10 minutes)

For each of the numbered statements or groups of statements select either A, B, or C.

<u>List</u>

A.   Both parties have given consideration legally sufficient to support a contract.
B.   One of the parties has **not** given consideration legally sufficient to support a contract. The promise, agreement, or transaction is generally **not** enforceable.
C.   One of the parties has **not** given consideration legally sufficient to support a contract. However, the promise, agreement, or transaction **is** generally enforceable.

	(A)	(B)	(C)
1. Party S feels a moral obligation because Party F let S stay in his place for free when S attended college. S now promises to pay F for the past kindness.	○	○	○
2. F agrees to deliver all of the sugar that Company S will need in her business for the following year. S agrees to purchase it at the market price.	○	○	○
3. F does not smoke for one year pursuant to S's agreement to pay F $200 if she does not smoke for one year.	○	○	○
4. F dies leaving a valid will which gives S $100,000.	○	○	○
5. F is an auditor of XYZ Company. S is a potential investor of XYZ and offers to pay F $1,000 if F performs a professional, quality audit of XYZ Company. The $1,000 is in addition to the fee F will get from XYZ. F does perform a professional, quality audit.	○	○	○
6. F had agreed, in writing, to work for S for five years for $100,000 per year. After two years, F asks for a 20% raise. S first agrees then later changes his mind. F, while not agreeing to additional duties or changing his position, wants to enforce the raise in salary.	○	○	○
7. S promised to pay F $1,000 if he crosses the Golden Gate Bridge on his hands and knees. F does so.	○	○	○
8. F promised to pay S $200 for a computer worth $2,000. S agreed to the deal.	○	○	○
9. F agreed to purchase all of the parts from S that S can produce in her business for the next six months. S also agreed.	○	○	○
10. S agreed to accept $1,000 from F for a $1,500 debt that is not disputed. S now wants the additional $500. Focus on the agreement to accept the lesser amount.	○	○	○
11. S agreed to accept $1,000 from F for a debt that S claims is $1,500 but F in good faith claims is $800. F agreed to the $1,000 initially, then decides he will pay only $800. Focus on the enforceability of the agreement for $1,000.	○	○	○
12. S agreed to donate $100 to F, a public charity.	○	○	○

Simulation Problem 2   (10 to 15 minutes)

Situation			
	Contractual Relationship	Assignment	Memo

On December 15, Blake Corp. telephoned Reach Consultants, Inc. and offered to hire Reach to design a security system for Blake's research department. The work would require two years to complete. Blake offered to pay a fee of $100,000 but stated that the offer must be accepted in writing, and the acceptance received by Blake no later than December 20.

On December 20, Reach faxed a written acceptance to Blake. Blake's offices were closed on December 20 and Reach's fax was not seen until December 21.

Reach's acceptance contained the following language:

"We accept your $1,000,000 offer. Weaver has been assigned $5,000 of the fee as payment for sums owed Weaver by Reach. Payment of this amount should be made directly to Weaver."

On December 22, Blake sent a signed memo to Reach rejecting Reach's December 20 fax but offering to hire Reach for a $75,000 fee. Reach telephoned Blake on December 23 and orally accepted Blake's December 22 offer.

	Contractual Relationship		
Situation		Assignment	Memo

Part a. **Items 1 through 7** relate to whether a contractual relationship exists between Blake and Reach. For each item, determine whether the statement is true or false.

		True	*False*
1.	Blake's December 15 offer had to be in writing to be a legitimate offer.	O	O
2.	Reach's December 20 fax was an improper method of acceptance.	O	O
3.	Reach's December 20 fax was effective when sent.	O	O
4.	Reach's acceptance was invalid because it was received after December 20.	O	O
5.	Blake's receipt of Reach's acceptance created a voidable contract.	O	O
6.	If Reach had rejected the original offer by telephone on December 17, he could not validly accept the offer later.	O	O
7.	Reach's December 20 fax was a counteroffer.	O	O

		Assignment	
Situation	Contractual Relationship		Memo

Part b. **Items 8 through 12** relate to the attempted assignment of part of the fee to Weaver. Assume that a valid contract exists between Blake and Reach. For each item, determine whether the statement is true or false.

		True	*False*
8.	Reach is prohibited from making an assignment of any contract right or duty.	O	O
9.	Reach may validly assign part of the fee to Weaver.	O	O
10.	Under the terms of Reach's acceptance, Weaver would be considered a third-party creditor beneficiary.	O	O
11.	In a breach of contract suit by Weaver, against Blake, Weaver would not collect any punitive damages.	O	O
12.	In a breach of contract suit by Weaver, against Reach, Weaver would be able to collect punitive damages.	O	O

			Memo
Situation	Contractual Relationship	Assignment	

Part c. **Items 13 through 15** relate to Blake's December 22 signed memo. For each item, determine whether the statement is True or False.

		True	*False*
13.	Reach's oral acceptance of Blake's December 22 memo may be enforced by Blake against Reach.	O	O
14.	Blake's memo is a valid offer even though it contains no date for acceptance.	O	O
15.	Blake's memo may be enforced against Blake by Reach.	O	O

MULTIPLE-CHOICE ANSWERS

1. a __ __	13. d __ __	25. a __ __	37. c __ __	49. a __ __
2. b __ __	14. b __ __	26. c __ __	38. d __ __	50. a __ __
3. c __ __	15. c __ __	27. b __ __	39. b __ __	51. c __ __
4. a __ __	16. c __ __	28. b __ __	40. c __ __	52. d __ __
5. d __ __	17. c __ __	29. d __ __	41. c __ __	53. a __ __
6. b __ __	18. d __ __	30. b __ __	42. d __ __	54. a __ __
7. b __ __	19. d __ __	31. a __ __	43. d __ __	55. c __ __
8. a __ __	20. b __ __	32. d __ __	44. a __ __	56. a __ __
9. b __ __	21. c __ __	33. d __ __	45. a __ __	57. b __ __
10. c __ __	22. c __ __	34. c __ __	46. c __ __	
11. a __ __	23. b __ __	35. c __ __	47. b __ __	1st: __/57 = __%
12. c __ __	24. d __ __	36. b __ __	48. a __ __	2nd: __/57 = __%

MULTIPLE-CHOICE ANSWER EXPLANATIONS

C.1. Offer

1.   **(a)**   Under common law, an offer must be definite and certain as to what will be agreed upon in the contract. Essential terms are the parties involved, the price, the time for performance, and the subject matter (quantity and type). The price element of the contract was not present.

2.   **(b)**   Advertisements in almost all cases are merely invitations for interested parties to make an offer. Thus, Harris has not made an offer, but is seeking offers through the use of the advertisement.

3.   **(c)**   Generally an offeror may revoke an offer at any time prior to acceptance by the offeree. Revocation is effective when it is received by the offeree. Revocation also occurs if the offeree learns by a reliable means that the offeror has already sold the subject of the offer. In this situation, Peters' offer was effectively revoked when Mason learned that the lawn mower had been sold to Bronson. Therefore, Mason's acceptance was ineffective. Answers (a) and (b) are incorrect because the offer had been revoked prior to Mason's acceptance. Answer (d) is incorrect because Peters was not obligated to keep the offer open. Note that if consideration had been paid by Mason to keep the offer open, an option contract would exist and the offer could not be revoked before the stated time.

4.   **(a)**   Drake did not intend to reject the $300,000 offer but is simply seeing if Calistoga might consider selling the home for less. Answer (b) is incorrect because a counteroffer takes place when the original offer is rejected and a new offer takes its place. Answer (c) is incorrect because Drake showed no intention of rejecting the offer by his mere inquiry. Answer (d) is incorrect because ambiguity is not one of the grounds to have an offer terminated by operation of law.

5.   **(d)**   An offer automatically terminates upon the occurrence of any of the following events: (1) the death or insanity of either the offeror or offeree, (2) bankruptcy or insolvency of either the offeror or offeree, or (3) the destruction of the specific, identified subject matter. Thus the offer automatically terminates at the date of Opal's death. It does not matter whether Larkin received notice of the death. If Larkin had accepted the offer prior to Opal's death, a valid contract would have been formed.

C.2. Acceptance

6.   **(b)**   Under the mailbox rule, an acceptance is ordinarily effective when sent if transmitted by the means authorized by the offeror, or by the same means used to transmit the offer if no means was authorized. However, the offeror may stipulate that acceptance is effective only when received by the offeror. In this situation, no contract was formed because Moss' acceptance was not received by the date specified in Fine's offer. Under common law, a method of acceptance other than the means specified in the offer or the method used to communicate the offer, is considered effective when received by the offeror.

7.   **(b)**   Fresno's acceptance by overnight delivery was made by a method other than the methods specified by Harris in the written offer. When acceptance is sent by a method other than the method specified in the offer or different than the method used to transmit the offer, acceptance is considered valid only when actually received by the offeror. Late acceptance is not valid, but instead constitutes a counteroffer. A valid contract would be formed only if the original offeror (Harris) then accepts.

8.   **(a)**   A unilateral offer exists when the offeror expects acceptance of an offer by action of the offeree. A unilateral contract is then formed when the offeree accepts the contract through performance of the offeror's required action. In this case, a valid contract is formed when Hammer accepts Kay's unilateral offer by obtaining the artifacts within a two-week period. Answers (b) and (d) are incorrect because a quasi contract is an implied-in-law rather than express agreement which results when one of the parties has been unjustly enriched at the expense of the other. The law creates such a contract when there is no binding agreement present to keep the unjust enrichment from occurring. Answer (c) is incorrect because public policy causes enforcement of promises despite lack of any other legal enforcement of the contract. For example, public policy would normally allow enforcement of a promise by a debtor to pay a debt barred by the statute of limitations.

9.   **(b)**   Common law applies to this contract because it involves real estate. In this situation, Fox's reply on October 2 is a counteroffer and terminates Summers' original offer made on September 27. The acceptance of an offer must conform exactly to the terms of the offer under common law. By agreeing to purchase the vacation home at a price different from the original offer, Fox is rejecting

Summers' offer and is making a counteroffer. Answer (a) is incorrect because the fact that Fox failed to return Summers' letter is irrelevant to the formation of a binding contract. Fox's reply constitutes a counteroffer as Fox did not intend to accept Summers' original offer. Answer (c) is incorrect because Summers' offer was rejected by Fox's counteroffer. Answer (d) is incorrect because with rare exceptions, silence does not constitute acceptance.

C.3. Consideration

10. (c) Both Zake and Wick had a contract that was binding for five years. For them to modify this contract, both of them must give new consideration under common law rules which apply to employment contracts such as this one. When Wick agreed to the raise, only Wick gave new consideration in the form of $20,000 additional each year. Zake did not give new consideration because he would perform in the last three years as originally agreed. Answers (a) and (b) are incorrect because Zake did not give new consideration whether or not the raise was in writing. Answer (d) is incorrect because duress needed to make a contract voidable or void requires more than "some pressure."

11. (a) Consideration is an act, promise, or forbearance which is offered by one party and accepted by another as inducement to enter into an agreement. A party must bind him/herself to do something s/he is not legally obligated to do. Furthermore, the consideration must be bargained for. Past consideration is not sufficient to serve as consideration for a new contract because it is not bargained for. Answer (b) is incorrect because relinquishment of a legal right constitutes consideration. Answer (c) is incorrect because even though the consideration must be adequate, courts generally do not look into the amount of exchange, as long as it is legal consideration and is bargained for. Answer (d) is incorrect as this performance by a third party is still deemed consideration.

12. (c) The rebinding of Dunne's books is considered a service and not a sale of goods, therefore, common law applies. Under common law, modification of an existing contract needs new consideration by both parties to be legally binding. Since Dunne has not given any new consideration for Cook's reduction in price, the contract is unenforceable. Additionally, the parol evidence rule prohibits the presentation of evidence of any prior or contemporaneous oral or written statements for the purpose of modifying or changing a written agreement intended by the payor to be the final and complete expression of their contract. However, it does not bar from evidence any oral or written agreements entered into by the parties subsequent to the written contract. Therefore, the agreement between Dunne and Cook is unenforceable, but evidence of the modification is admissible into evidence. Note that if the contract had been for the sale of goods (UCC), modification of the contract terms would have been enforceable. Under the UCC, a contract for the sale of goods may be modified orally or in writing without new consideration if such modification is done in good faith.

13. (d) A preexisting legal duty is not sufficient as consideration because no new legal detriment is suffered by performing the prior obligation. For example, when a creditor agrees to accept as full payment an amount less than the full amount of the undisputed (liquidated) debt, the agreement lacks valid consideration to be enforceable.

However, when the amount of an obligation is disputed, the creditor's promise to accept a lesser amount as full payment of the debt is enforceable. Preexisting legal duties are not valid as consideration.

14. (b) A promise to donate money to a charity which the charity relied upon in incurring large expenditures is a situation involving promissory estoppel. Promissory estoppel acts as a substitute for consideration and renders the promise enforceable. The elements necessary for promissory estoppel are (1) detrimental reliance on a promise, (2) reliance on the promise is reasonable and foreseeable, and (3) damage results (injustice) if the promise is not enforced. Answer (a) is incorrect because the failure to enforce an employer's promise to make a cash payment to a deceased employee's family will not result in damages, and therefore, promissory estoppel will not apply. Answer (c) is incorrect because the modification of a contract requires consideration, unless the contract involves the sale of goods under the UCC. Answer (d) is incorrect because an irrevocable oral promise by a merchant to keep an offer open for sixty days is an option contract that must be supported by consideration. A firm offer under the UCC requires an offer signed by the merchant.

C.4. Legal Capacity

15. (c) A minor may disaffirm a contract at any time during his minority and within a reasonable time after reaching the age of majority. When Rail disaffirmed the contract two days after reaching the age of eighteen, he did so within a reasonable time after reaching majority age. Answer (a) is incorrect because Rail could ratify the contract only after reaching the age of majority. Answer (b) is incorrect because although Rail could have transferred good title to a good-faith purchaser for value, Rail's title was still voidable and subject to disaffirmance. Answer (d) is incorrect because Rail could disaffirm the contract only for a reasonable time after reaching the age of majority. Failure to disaffirm within a reasonable time serves to act as ratification.

16. (c) When a person has previously been adjudicated by a court of law to be incompetent, all of the contracts that s/he makes are void. Answer (a) is incorrect because the contracts are only voidable at the option of Green if there was no formal, previous court determination of incompetence for Green. Answer (b) is incorrect because once the court determines that Green is incompetent, all of the contracts that s/he makes are not valid but are void. Answer (d) is incorrect because the contracts cannot be enforced by either Green or the other contracting party.

17. (c) Ratification of a contract prior to reaching majority age is not effective. A minor **may** ratify a contract expressly or by actions indicating ratification after reaching the age of majority. Failure to disaffirm within a reasonable time after reaching majority age **does** act as ratification.

C.5. Legality

18. (d) An agreement is unenforceable if it is illegal or violates public policy. Therefore, if the personal services of the contract are illegal, the party will not have to perform them. Answer (a) is incorrect because the death of the party who is to **receive** the benefits does not terminate the duties under the contract. His/her heirs can still receive and pay for the personal services. Answer (b) is incorrect because making less profit or losing money are not grounds for getting out of a contract. Answer (c) is incorrect because bankruptcy of the receiver does not discharge the performer from the contract, although it can allow for forgiveness of all or part of the payment.

19. (d)   An employer's promise not to press criminal charges against an employee-embezzler who agrees to return the embezzled money is not legally binding. The promise not to press charges is an illegal bargain, and, even if the employee returns the money, the employer is free to cooperate in prosecution of the criminal.

C.6. Reality of Consent

20. (b)   Fraud is the intentional misrepresentation of a material fact upon which a third party reasonably relies to his or her detriment. An intentionally misstated appraised value would be an example of a fraudulent inducement to make a contract. Answers (a) and (c) are incorrect because a third party cannot reasonably rely on a nonexpert opinion or a prediction. Answer (d) is incorrect because by definition, fraud applies to material facts.

21. (c)   An immaterial unilateral mistake generally does not allow either party to void the contract.

22. (c)   Undue influence is a defense that makes a contract voidable. Classic situations of this concept involve close relationships in which a dominant person has extreme influence over a weaker person. Answer (a) is incorrect because although fraud in the inducement can make a contract voidable, it typically does not occur between parties that have a close relationship. Answer (b) is incorrect because unconscionability involves an oppressive contract in which one party has taken severe, unfair advantage of another which is often based on the latter's absence of choice or poor education rather than the parties' close relationship. Answer (d) is incorrect because duress involves acts or threats of violence or pressure, which need not result from close relationships.

23. (b)   An insurance policy is voidable at the option of the insurer if the insured failed to inform the insurer at the time of application of a fact material to the insurer's risk (e.g., failure to disclose a preexisting heart condition on a life insurance application). The insured's concealment causes the policy to be voidable regardless of the type of beneficiary designated or the nature of the insured's death.

24. (d)   One of the elements needed to prove fraud is a misrepresentation of a material fact. That statement that "it is a great car" is sales talk or puffing and does not establish this element. The fact that the overhaul was done thirteen months earlier instead of the stated one year is not a misrepresentation of a **material** fact.

25. (a)   A mistake is an understanding that is not in agreement with a fact. A unilateral mistake (made by one party) generally does not allow the party to void the contract. However, a mistake unknown to the party making it becomes voidable if the other party recognizes it as a mistake. Particularly, this is the case in bid contract computations. The contract is voidable by the party making the mistake if the other party knew of the mistake or if the cal-culation was far enough off that the other party should have known that a mistake was made.

26. (c)   Duress is any wrongful threat or act of violence made toward a person (or his family) which forces a person to enter into a contract against his will. For duress to be present, a threat must be made and the threatened party must believe that the other party has the ability to carry out the threat. In this situation, Maco's actions did not constitute duress. Kent's safety and property were in no way threatened by Maco and Kent was able to validly consent to the contract. Answers (a) and (b) are incorrect because regardless of Kent's financial problems and the FMV of Kent's services, duress was not present in that Kent was able to enter into the contract at will. Answer (d) is incorrect because Maco does not need to prove that Kent had no other offers to provide financial services.

27. (b)   To establish a common law action for fraud, the following elements must be present: (1) misrepresentation of a material fact, (2) either knowledge of the falsity with intent to mislead or reckless disregard for the truth (scienter), (3) reasonable reliance by third party, and (4) injury resulted from misrepresentation. If the misrepresentation occurs during contract negotiations, fraud in the inducement is present resulting in a contract voidable at the option of the injured party. Answer (a) is incorrect because the defendant need not be an expert with regard to the misrepresentation to establish fraud in the inducement. Answer (c) is incorrect because the misrepresentation may be written or oral. Answer (d) is incorrect because the presence of fraud in the inducement does not require a fiduciary relationship between the parties.

28. (b)   There are two remedies for fraud under the UCC Sales Article: (1) the plaintiff may affirm the agreement and sue for damages under the tort of deceit, or (2) the plaintiff may rescind the contract and sue for damages resulting from the fraud. Answer (a) is incorrect because the plaintiff must return any consideration received from the other party when the contract is rescinded. Answer (c) is incorrect because although punitive damages are allowed in fraud actions because they are intentional torts, they do not require physical injuries. Answer (d) is incorrect because without reliance by the plaintiff on the misrepresentation, there is no fraud, and therefore, the plaintiff may not rescind the contract.

C.7. Conformity with the Statute of Frauds

29. (d)   The Statute of Frauds requires that a contract to answer the debt or default of another be in writing and signed by the party to be charged. The guarantee that Decker made was only oral. Answer (b) is incorrect, as the reason Decker is not liable for the oral guaranty is not because it expires more than one year after June 1, but because a contract of guaranty must be in writing. Decker is not liable regardless of Baker's confirmation letter; thus answer (a) is incorrect. Answer (c) is incorrect because Decker's oral guaranty is not enforceable. The time period between the date of the oral guaranty and the date payment is demanded has no bearing in this situation.

30. (b)   Any agreement to sell land or any interest in land falls under the requirements of the Statute of Frauds. Agreements within the Statute of Frauds require contracts to be in writing and signed by the party to be charged (the party being sued). An exception to the above rule is "part performance" by the purchaser. Part performance exists when the purchaser of property takes possession of the property with the landowner's consent. Some states also require either partial payment for the property or permanent improvement of the property by the purchaser. Answer (b) is correct because even though Nolan failed to sign a written agreement, the part performance exception has been satisfied. Answer (a) is incorrect because the fact that Nolan simply failed to object to the agreement does not make the contract valid under the Statute of Frauds. Answer (c) is incorrect because the part performance exception has been met and Train will therefore prevail. Answer (d) is incorrect because no such requirement exists to alleviate Nolan's liability. The part performance rule allows Train to prevail. Note that **all** sales of land are covered under the Statute of Frauds, and not just those greater than $500.

31. (a) Contracts that cannot be performed within one year must be in writing. In this case Cherry agreed to purchase Picks Company if an audit after one year shows that the company has been profitable. This would take longer than a year to perform. Answer (b) is incorrect because the $500 provision is in the Uniform Commercial Code for a sale of goods. Answer (c) is incorrect because despite the actual profitability, the contract could not be completed within one year of the making of the contract. Answer (d) is incorrect because although promissory estoppel may be used in the absence of a writing, there are not the facts sufficient to show promissory estoppel.

32. (d) Contracts which fall within the requirements of the Statute of Frauds are required to be in writing and signed by the party to be charged. It is not required that the contract terms be formalized in a single writing. Two or more documents may be combined to create a writing which satisfies the Statute of Frauds as long as one of the documents refers to the others. Answer (a) is incorrect because the Statute of Frauds requires that agreements for the sale of goods for $500 or more be in writing; however, contracts that come under common law are not included in this requirement. Answer (b) is incorrect because the Statute of Frauds requires that the written contract be signed by the party to be charged, not by all parties to the contract. Answer (c) is incorrect because the Statute of Frauds applies to contracts that **cannot** be performed within one year from the making of the agreement.

33. (d) The Statute of Frauds applies to the following types of contracts: (1) an agreement to sell land or any interest in land, (2) an agreement that cannot be performed within one year from the making of the agreement, (3) an agreement to answer for the debt or default of another, and (4) an agreement for the sale of goods for $500 or more. Since the agreement between Carson and Ives meets none of the above requirements, it is an enforceable oral contract under common law. Furthermore, under common law, modification of an existing contract needs new consideration by both parties to be legally binding. Since Ives received the benefit of additional repairs to his book, Carson's increase in the contract price is enforceable. Therefore, Carson will recover $650.

34. (c) Under The Statute of Frauds, agreements that can be performed within one year of their making can be oral. In this case the ethics audit need only span ten months

and the completion of the report will take less than one additional month for a total of less than one year. We know that the report can be done in less than a month because Newell points out that even if she delays start for three months, she will still complete the ten-month audit before the fourteen-month deadline. The fact that it might take longer than a year does not require it to be in writing since it **possibly could** be completed within one year. Answer (a) is incorrect because the $500 provision is for sales of goods not services. Answer (b) is incorrect because the contract can be completed within one year. Answer (d) is incorrect because there is no such provision involved here for the Statute of Frauds.

C.7.d.(1) Parol Evidence Rule

35. (c) The parol evidence rule provides that a written agreement intended by contracting parties to be a final and complete contract may not be contradicted by previous or contemporaneous oral evidence. The parol evidence rule does not apply to any subsequent oral promises made after the original agreement. Thus, the subsequent oral agreement between Rogers and Lennon regarding Lennon's right to report on a monthly basis will be allowed as evidence in a lawsuit between the parties. Answer (a) is incorrect because the parol evidence rule applies to all written contracts regardless of the applicability of the Statute of Frauds. Answer (b) is incorrect because the parol evidence rule will prevent the admission into evidence of the contemporaneous oral agreement that Lennon could use Rogers' computer. Answer (d) is incorrect because the parol evidence rule does apply to the contemporaneous oral agreement.

36. (b) The parol evidence rule provides that any written agreement intended by parties to be final and complete contract may not be contradicted by previous or contemporaneous evidence, written or oral. Thus, previous written agreements are prohibited by the rule. Exceptions to the parol evidence rule include proof to invalidate the contract between the parties, to show terms not inconsistent with writing that parties would not be expected to have included, to explain the intended meaning of an ambiguity, or to show a condition precedent. The parol evidence rule does not apply to subsequent transactions, such as oral promises made after the original agreement.

37. (c) The parol evidence rule prohibits the presentation as evidence of any prior or contemporaneous oral statements concerning a written agreement intended by the parties to be the final and complete expression of their contract. Therefore, the evidence related to the oral agreement regarding the payment of utilities would not be allowed. However, the parol evidence rule does **not** bar the admission of evidence which is presented to establish fraud.

C.9. Contracting On-line

38. (d) Even though this contract falls under the Statute of Frauds and, therefore, generally must be written and signed, most states have passed laws allowing contracts to be made over the Internet to facilitate commerce. The statutes encourage technology to overcome concerns over authenticity of such contracts. Therefore, answer (a) is incorrect. Answer (b) is incorrect because the parol evidence rule does not specify when a contract must be written and signed.

Answer (c) is incorrect because a sale of land is governed by common law rules and not the UCC.

D. Assignment and Delegation

39. (b)   Assignment is the transfer of a right under a contract by one person to another. Almost all contract rights are assignable as long as the parties agree to it, but there are some exceptions. Contracts involving personal services, trust or confidence are not assignable. If assignment would materially change the risk or burden of the obligor, it is not allowed. For example, a contract for insurance against certain risks are not assignable because they were made upon the character of the contracting party (the insured). Assigning the rights to another party would alter the risk. Therefore, malpractice insurance policy rights are not assignable. A further exception is that future rights are not assignable, with the exception under the UCC that future rights for the sale of goods are assignable, whether based on an existing or nonexisting contract. As the assignment of option contract rights does not fall under any exception, they would be assignable.

40. (c)   Assignment is the transfer of a right under a contract by one person to another. No consideration is needed for valid assignment. Normally an assignment is done in writing, but any act, oral or written, is sufficient if it gives clear intent of the assignment. Only situations included under the Statute of Frauds are required to be in writing. When consideration is given in exchange for an assignment, it is irrevocable. Also, as a general rule a gratuitous assignment is revocable unless it is evidenced by a writing signed by the assignor, effected by a delivery of a writing used as evidence of the right (i.e., bill of lading), and the assignment is executed. A contract right cannot be assigned if it would materially change the risk or burden of the obligor.

41. (c)   Assignment is the transfer of a right under a contract by one person to another. If the obligor has notice of the assignment, s/he must pay the assignee, not the assignor. The contract between Barton and Egan provided for both payments on the purchase price and the insurance policy in case of Egan's death. Because Barton assigned his contract rights to Vim, Vim was then entitled to payments on the purchase price and the insurance proceeds. Since Barton received payments on the purchase price and insurance proceeds after the assignment, Vim is entitled to sue Barton for these amounts.

E. Third-Party Beneficiary Contracts

42. (d)   When a debtor contracts with a second party to pay the debt owed to a creditor, the creditor becomes a creditor beneficiary. Barton contracted with Egan for Egan to pay Ness the business' debts. The contract also required Egan to provide a life insurance policy to pay Ness if Egan died. In both the contract and the insurance policy, Ness was a creditor beneficiary. Neither the contract nor the insurance policy were entered into to confer a gift to Ness, and therefore he was not a donee beneficiary.

43. (d)   Bugle would have received an unintended benefit under the contract between Fargo and ABC Company. Therefore, Bugle is an incidental beneficiary, not an intended beneficiary and, thus, has no legal rights against either Fargo or ABC. No matter who breached the contract, Bugle has no rights against either party.

44. (a)   In an assignment, the assignee (Clay) acquires the assignor's (Baxter) rights against the obligor (Globe) and has the right to performance. Baxter is still liable to the assignee if Globe does not perform. However, if Clay released Globe from the contract, Baxter would also be released and no longer liable to Clay. Answer (b) is incorrect because if the obligor has no notice of the assignment, s/he may pay the assignor, and the assignee must recover from the assignor. Thus, if Globe was unaware of the assignment and paid Baxter, Clay would have to collect from Baxter. Answers (c) and (d) are incorrect because even if Baxter released Globe or breached the contract, Baxter would still be liable to Clay.

45. (a)   Mann is a donee beneficiary and, thus, can bring suit against the promissor, Manus, only. He cannot maintain a suit against Mackay, who was just giving a gift. Mann cannot maintain any action against Mackay either alone or in combination with Manus.

46. (c)   When a debtor contracts with a second party to pay the debt owed to a creditor, the creditor becomes a creditor beneficiary. A creditor beneficiary has the right to enforce the contract which gives him the intended benefits and may commence an action for nonperformance against either of the contracting parties. For this reason, Ferco (creditor beneficiary) will prevail in a lawsuit against Bell because Ferco has an enforceable right to receive payment. Answer (a) is incorrect because Ferco, as a creditor beneficiary, has the right to recover from either Bell or Allied. Answer (b) is incorrect because the creditor beneficiary is not required to give consideration to have an enforceable right. Answer (d) is incorrect because having knowledge of the contract between Bell and Allied at the time the contract was made is not necessary to later enforce this legal action. Ferco must establish that he is a creditor beneficiary to maintain an action for nonperformance.

F. Performance of Contract

47. (b)   Under the doctrine of substantial performance, a contract obligation may be discharged even though the performance tendered was not in complete conformity with the terms of the agreement. Under this doctrine, if it can be shown that the defect in performance was only minor in nature, that a good-faith effort was made to conform completely with the terms of the agreement, and if the performing party is willing to accept a decrease in compensation equivalent to the amount of the minor defect in performance, the contractual obligation will be discharged. Since the defect in Glaze's performance was only minor in nature, and since Parc refused to allow Glaze to complete the project, Glaze will prevail in its action against Parc. Anticipatory breach applies only to executory bilateral contracts. An executory contract is a contract wherein both parties have yet to perform. In this instance, Glaze has substantially performed its part of the agreement.

48. (a)   The duty to perform a contract may depend upon a condition. Conditions that could be present include: condition precedent, which is one that must occur before there is duty to perform; condition subsequent, which is one that removes a preexisting duty to perform; or condition concurrent, which is mutually dependent upon performance at nearly the same time.

G. Discharge of Contracts

49. (a) Once one party materially breaches the contract, the other party is discharged from performing his or her obligations under the contract. Answer (b) is incorrect because a reasonable delay in the performance of the contract is not a breach unless time was of the essence. Answer (c) is incorrect because tender or offer to pay or perform obligates the other party to do what s/he promised. Answer (d) is incorrect because assignment of rights typically is allowed under contract law.

50. (a) The discharge of a contract can come about in several ways. The first is by agreement. Accord and satisfaction involves an agreed substitute for performance under the contract (accord) and the actual performance of that substitute (satisfaction). An agreement can also be entered into by three parties whereby the previous agreement is discharged by the creation of a new agreement (a novation). The second method of discharge is by release of the contract or parties from performance. Another method of discharging a contract is by performance of the specified action becoming impossible, such as destruction of the subject matter, or death of a party where personal service is necessary. Lastly, breach of the contract discharges the injured party.

51. (c) Rescission entails canceling a contract and placing the parties in the position they were in before the contract was formed. Answer (a) is incorrect as a novation is an agreement between three parties whereby a previous agreement is discharged by the creation of a new agreement. Answer (b) is incorrect because release is a means of discharging (abandoning) a contract but it does not place the parties in the same position as before the contract. Answer (d) is incorrect because revocation is used by an offeror to terminate an offer.

H. Remedies

52. (d) The remedy of specific performance is used when money damages will not sufficiently compensate the afflicted party due to the unique nature of the subject matter of the contract. In a contract for the sale of land, the buyer has the right to enforce the agreement by seeking the remedy of specific performance because real property is considered unique. Another remedy for this breach of contract would be for the buyer to seek compensatory damages. If the buyer desires, s/he may seek this remedy instead of specific performance. However, in this situation, Hodges could only sue for either specific performance or compensatory damages but would not be entitled to both remedies. An injured party is generally not allowed to seek punitive damages. Punitive damages are awarded only when the court is seeking to punish a party for their improper actions and are not usually granted in breach of contract actions.

53. (a) Under the doctrine of substantial performance, a contract obligation may be discharged even though the performance tendered was not in complete conformity with the terms of the agreement. If it can be shown that the defect in performance was only minor in nature, that a good-faith effort was made to conform completely with the terms of the agreement, and if the performing party is willing to accept a decrease in compensation equivalent to the amount of the minor defect in performance, the contractual obligation will be discharged. Because Ames' breach of contract was both inadvertent and not material, the doctrine of substantial performance applies and recovery will be limited to monetary damages. The installation of fixtures other than those specified in the contract constitutes a breach, although the breach is considered immaterial. The doctrine of substantial performance applies in this situation and the contractual obligation will be discharged.

54. (a) A liquidated damage clause is a contractual provision which states the amount of damages that will occur if a party breaches the contract. The liquidated damage clause is enforceable if the amount is reasonable in light of the anticipated or actual harm caused by the breach. Excessive liquidated damages will not be enforceable in court even if both parties have agreed in writing. A clause providing for excessive damages is a penalty and the courts will not enforce a penalty. Materiality does not impact the enforceability of liquidated damage provisions.

55. (c) The doctrine of anticipatory repudiation allows a party to either sue at once or wait until after performance is due when the other party indicates s/he will not perform. This doctrine is in effect because Nagel told Fields that Nagel had no intention of delivering the goods (i.e., repudiation of the contract) prior to the date of performance. Answer (a) is incorrect because promissory estoppel acts as a substitute for consideration which is an element in the forming of a contract but is not relevant in this fact situation. Answer (b) is incorrect because accord and satisfaction is an agreement wherein a party with an existing duty or performance under a contract promises to do something other than perform the duty originally promised in the contract. Answer (d) is incorrect because the doctrine of substantial performance would allow for a contract obligation to be discharged even though the performance tendered was not in complete conformity with the terms of the agreement. In this case, Fields is suing Nagel for breach of contract.

56. (a) Events occurring after a contract is entered into usually do not affect performance. Some exceptions to this rule include subsequent illegality of the performance, death of a party, or destruction of the subject matter, all of which constitute impossibility of performance. In this case, even though Maco's own potatoes were destroyed, it wasn't specified that Maco's own potato crop be used to fulfill the contract. It was not impossible, therefore, for Maco to perform, because he could have purchased potatoes from another grower to deliver to LBC. If there had been a worldwide infestation of the potato crop, Maco would have reason to not perform on the basis of impossibility.

I. Statute of Limitations

57. (b) The statute of limitations bars suit if it is not brought within the statutory period. The period varies for different types of cases and from state to state. The statute begins to run from the time the cause of action accrues (e.g., breach).

ANSWER OUTLINE

Problem 1   Unilateral Mistake; Statute of Frauds under Service Contract; Effectiveness of Acceptance; Assignment and Delegation

Ambel's claim is incorrect

   Victor will be granted relief

   Ambel knew the approximate FMV of equipment

   Had reason to know that a mathematical error had been made by Victor

   Therefore, the mistaken party will be granted relief from the offer

Clark's claim is correct

   Victor can't enforce the oral contract with Clark

   Statute of Frauds requires a written contract if terms cannot be performed within one year of its creation

   These terms span over one year

GYX's claim is incorrect

   Victor has a valid contract with GYX

   An acceptance of an offer is effective when dispatched, if an appropriate mode of communication is used.

   Since GYX's offer was by mail, Victor's communication of acceptance by mail is appropriate and effective on November 12, not when GYX received the acceptance on November 17.

   The acceptance was effective before the November 15 deadline

Wells is incorrect

   Victor is entitled to assign the contract.

   Unless assignment is prohibited in the contract, statute, or public policy, or the duties are personal in nature, a contract is assignable.

UNOFFICIAL ANSWER

Problem 1   Unilateral Mistake; Statute of Frauds under Service Contract; Effectiveness of Acceptance; Assignment and Delegation

Ambel is incorrect. The general rule is that when a party knows, or reasonably should know, that a mistake has been made in the making of an offer, the mistaken party will be granted relief from the offer. In this case, because Ambel was aware of the approximate fair market value of the equipment, it had reason to be aware of the mathematical error made by Victor and will not be allowed to take advantage of it.

Clark is correct. A contract that cannot by its terms be performed within one year from the date it is made must be evidenced by a writing that satisfies the requirements of the Statute of Frauds. The contract between Victor and Clark is not enforceable by Victor against Clark, because the contract was oral and provided for performance by the parties for longer than one year from the date the contract was entered into.

GYX is incorrect. An acceptance of an offer is effective when dispatched (in this case, when mailed), provided that the appropriate mode of communication is used. The general rule is that an offer shall be interpreted as inviting acceptance in any manner and by any medium reasonable in the circumstances. In this case, GYX made its offer by mail. An acceptance by mail, if properly addressed with adequate postage affixed, would be considered a reasonable manner and method of acceptance. Therefore, Victor's acceptance

was effective (and a contract was formed) when the acceptance was mailed on November 12 and not when received by GYX on November 17.

Wells is incorrect. As a general rule, most contracts are assignable and delegable unless: prohibited in the contract, the duties are personal in nature, or the assignment or delegation is prohibited by statute or public policy. Victor was entitled to assign the contract to Master, because none of these exceptions apply to the contract.

ANSWER OUTLINE

Problem 2   Fraud; Mistake under a Contract; Statute of Frauds under Real Estate Contract

First allegation is correct—Stake may rescind contract

   Packer committed fraud in formation of contract

   Elements of fraud

      False representation of material fact

      Intent to mislead (scienter)

      Reasonable reliance by injured party

Second allegation is incorrect

   Mistake involving adequacy of consideration generally does not allow aggrieved party to rescind contract

Third allegation is correct

   Counteroffer is unenforceable

   Real estate contract must satisfy Statute of Frauds

      Must be in writing

      Must be signed by party to be charged

UNOFFICIAL ANSWER

Problem 2   Fraud; Mistake under a Contract; Statute of Frauds under Real Estate Contract

Stake's first allegation, that Packer committed fraud in the formation of the contract, is correct and Stake may rescind the contract. Packer had assured Stake that the vacant parcel would be used for a shopping center when, in fact, Packer intended to use the land to construct apartment units that would be in direct competition with those owned by Stake. Stake would not have sold the land to Packer had Packer's real intentions been known. Therefore, the elements of fraud are present

  •   A false representation;

  •   Of a fact;

  •   That is material;

  •   Made with knowledge of its falsity and intention to deceive;

  •   That is justifiably relied on.

Stake's second allegation, that the mistake as to the fair market value of the land entitles Stake to rescind the contract, is incorrect. Generally, mistakes as to adequacy of consideration or fairness of a bargain are insufficient grounds to entitle the aggrieved party to rescind a contract.

Stake's third allegation, that the contract was not enforceable against Stake because Stake did not sign the counteroffer, is correct. The contract between Stake and Packer involves real estate and, therefore, the Statute of Frauds requirements must be satisfied. The Statute of Frauds requires that a writing be signed by the party against whom enforcement is sought. The counteroffer is unenforceable against Stake, because Stake did not sign it. As a result, Stake is not obligated to sell the land to Packer under the terms of the counteroffer.

SOLUTIONS TO SIMULATION PROBLEMS

Simulation Problem 1

1. **(B)** Party F gave S a gift in the past. S's promise to now pay for the usage is not enforceable because F's action is past consideration, and the contract needs consideration on both sides. Furthermore, S's feeling of a moral obligation does not create consideration.

2. **(A)** This is an example of a requirements contract. F has given consideration because s/he gave up the right to sell that sugar to someone else.

3. **(A)** F refrained from doing something which she had a right to do. This constitutes consideration.

4. **(C)** This is not enforceable under contract law because S does not give any consideration in return. It is enforceable, however, as a will which does not require the elements of a contract such as consideration, but does require other formalities.

5. **(B)** F already had a preexisting legal duty to do a professional, quality audit of XYZ Company.

6. **(B)** F had a contract to work for S for five years for $100,000 per year. F is not giving any new consideration for the raise since during that five years, he already is obligated to complete the contract.

7. **(A)** F did something which he did not have to do in exchange for the agreed $1,000. This is a unilateral contract.

8. **(A)** F agreed to pay $200 and in exchange S agreed to sell the computer. Both have given consideration that is **legally** sufficient. Legally sufficient refers to the validity of the consideration, not the amount. Consideration does not have to be of equal value as long as it is legal consideration and bargained for.

9. **(A)** Both parties have given consideration for this output contract. F gave up the right to buy these parts elsewhere and S gave up the right to sell her output to someone else.

10. **(B)** F has a preexisting legal duty to pay the full $1,500. When S agreed to accept less, F gave up nothing. F still owes the remaining $500.

11. **(A)** In this case, both parties gave consideration. S, in agreeing to accept the $1,000, gave up the right to collect more of the disputed amount. F gave up the right to pay less of the disputed amount.

12. **(C)** Although the charity gave no consideration in exchange for the promised donation, the promise to donate to a charity is generally enforceable based on public policy reasons.

Simulation Problem 2

Part a.

1.   **(F)** Although the final contract has to be in writing to be enforceable since performance of contract would take longer than a year, the offer itself can be oral.

2.   **(F)** The offer specified that the acceptance must be in writing. Since Reach put the acceptance in writing and faxed it to Blake, this was a proper method of acceptance.

3.   **(F)** Common law applies to this fact pattern since the contract does not involve a sale of goods. Reach's attempted acceptance stated $1,000,000 instead of $100,000 as contained in the offer. Reach's attempted acceptance thus was instead a counteroffer. Under both common law and the Uniform Commercial Code, offers, revocations, rejections and counteroffers are valid when received.

4.   **(F)** Blake's offer specified that the acceptance must be received no later than December 20. Reach's faxed acceptance was received in Blake's office on December 20 on the fax machine. Therefore, Blake did receive the fax on time even though it was not seen until the following day.

5.   **(F)** Reach's attempted acceptance stated $1,000,000 instead of $100,000 as contained in the offer. Since the terms did not match, no contract was formed, voidable or otherwise.

6.   **(T)** Since there is no firm offer or option contract, the rejection terminates the offer.

7.   **(T)** Since the December 20 fax terms did not match the original offer's terms, it serves as a counteroffer which rejects the original offer and creates a new offer.

Part b.

8.   **(F)** Parties may typically assign the contract right to receive money to another party.

9.   **(T)** When parties have a right to receive money, they may validly assign all or a portion of this right to a third party.

10.   **(T)** The terms of Reach's acceptance names Weaver as a third-party beneficiary to receive $5,000. Since the intent was to pay a debt owed by Reach to Weaver, this makes Weaver a creditor beneficiary.

11.   **(T)** Punitive damages are not awarded for mere breach of contract cases such as this suit by Weaver against Blake.

12.   **(F)** In a suit by Weaver against Reach, no punitive damages will be awarded since this would be only a breach of contract case.

Part c.

13.   **(F)** Since the work would require two years to complete, the contract cannot be performed within one year and, therefore, must be in writing to be enforceable. The party to be charged must have signed the contract and Reach did not do this.

14.   **(T)** An offer does not need to have a date for acceptance, in which case, the offer remains open for a reasonable time.

15.   **(T)** Blake's signed memo sets forth an offer which was later accepted orally by Reach. This can be construed as enough written evidence to satisfy the Statute of Frauds. Because Blake, the party to be charged, signed the memo, it is enforceable against Blake by Reach.

SALES

Overview

The law of sales governs contracts for the sale of goods. Since a sale of goods is involved, Article 2 of the Uniform Commercial Code (UCC) applies. A sale of goods under the UCC is the sale of tangible, moveable property.

One of the areas tested in sales is product liability. When studying this area, you should pay particular attention to the different legal theories under which an injured party may recover. Realize that an injured party may recover under the legal theories of breach of warranty, negligence, and strict liability. It is important that you know the circumstances under which these theories may be used. Other areas that are often tested are warranties; disclaimers; risk of loss; and remedies, rights, and duties of the buyer and seller.

You should understand that a binding contract may be present under the UCC if the parties had intended to be bound, even though certain elements of a contract may be missing. These open terms will be filled by specific provisions of the UCC. The parties to a sale need not be merchants for the UCC to apply; however, some rules vary if merchants are involved in the sales contract.

As you study this area, note that it builds on much of the material under contracts in the previous module. Therefore, as you study this area you should review the contract law rules, especially those in the previous module that apply to the UCC.

A. Contracts for Sale of Goods

1. Article 2 of the Uniform Commercial Code, in general, controls contracts for the sale of goods for any dollar amount

   a. "Goods" include tangible personal property (whether specially manufactured or not)

      (1) Do not include sales of investment securities, accounts receivable, contract rights, copyrights, or patents

      EXAMPLE: S sells B a stereo. The UCC applies.

      EXAMPLE: S sells a home to B. The common law rules rather than the UCC rules apply to this contract since it involves the sale of real property.

      EXAMPLE: F sells to M several bushels of wheat. The UCC applies to fungible goods also (i.e., goods in which one unit is considered the equivalent of the other units).

   b. In general, UCC applies to sales and leases of hardware as well as to sales and licensing of software.

      (1) However, if software is heavily customized based on services of consultant, common law applies.

   c. Article 2 of UCC has been passed into law by every state (except Louisiana which has adopted only portions of UCC)

      (1) Federal courts also use principles in Article 2 for sales of goods.

   d. UCC applies whether sale is between merchants or consumers but some rules change if merchant involved

      EXAMPLE: S sells his used refrigerator to B, a neighbor. The UCC applies to this transaction.

   e. Thrust of UCC is to find a contract in cases where it is the intent of the parties to do so, even though some technical element of contract may be missing

   f. Open terms (missing terms) will not cause a contract for sale of goods to fail for indefiniteness if there was intent to contract and a reasonable basis for establishing a remedy is available

      (1) Elements of sales contracts are generally same as common law contracts

2. General concepts

   a. Merchant—one who deals in the kind of goods being sold, or one who holds self out as having superior knowledge and skills as to the goods involved, or one who employs another who qualifies as a merchant

   b. Firm offer—a written, signed offer concerning the sale of goods, by a merchant, giving assurance that it will be held open for a specified time is irrevocable for that period, not to exceed three months

      (1) Note that only offeror need be a merchant under this rule

(2) If firm offer does not state specific time, it will remain open for reasonable time, not to exceed three months

(3) Written form may be supplied by either party as long as it is signed by merchant-offeror

> EXAMPLE: *M, a merchant, agrees in a letter signed by M to sell B 1,000 widgets, with the offer to remain open for five weeks. Even if M tries to revoke this offer before the five-week period, B may still accept.*

> EXAMPLE: *M, a merchant, agrees in signed writing to sell B 1,000 widgets, stating that the offer will remain open for 120 days. B accepts the offer on the 95th day. If nothing has occurred to terminate offer prior to acceptance, offer and acceptance are present. The irrevocable nature of this offer would end after ninety days, but the offer would not automatically terminate. The offer would remain in existence for the stated period (120 days) unless terminated by other means.*

> EXAMPLE: *Same facts as above except that B gives M $100 to keep the offer open for six months. This is an option supported by consideration, so the firm offer restrictions do not apply. That is, the offer remains open for the full six months. (This would be true even if M is not a merchant.)*

c. Battle of forms—between merchants, additional terms included in the acceptance become part of the contract unless

(1) Original offer precludes such, or

(2) New terms materially alter the original offer, or

(3) The original offeror gives notice of his/her objection within a reasonable time

> EXAMPLE: *P offers in writing to sell to Q 1,000 type xxx widgets for $10,000. Q replies, "I accept, but I will personally pick these up with my truck." Both P and Q are merchants. They have a contract with the stated delivery terms.*

d. Under the UCC, a contract may be modified without new consideration if done in good faith

> EXAMPLE: *B agrees in a contract to buy 300 electrical parts for $1.00 each from S. B later points out to S that he can get the same parts from D for $.90 each and asks for a price reduction. S reduces the price to $.90 each. This new contract is enforceable even though B gave no new consideration. Note that if S had required B to pay the $1.00 as originally agreed, B would be in breach of contract if he failed to go through with the original contract.*

(1) Common law requires new consideration on both sides for any modification

> EXAMPLE: *B agreed, in a written contract, to pay $10,000 to S for certain real estate. Later, B said he was having difficulty getting the $10,000 so S agreed to reduce the price to $9,000. S can still enforce the full $10,000 because B gave no new consideration for the modification.*

e. Recall that under UCC version of Statute of Frauds, contracts for sale of goods for $500 or more must be in writing with some exceptions

(1) Writing must contain quantity and signature of party to be charged

    (a) Need not contain all details required under common law version

(2) If contract is modified, must be in writing if after modification it is for $500 or more

> EXAMPLE: *B agrees in a contract to buy widgets from S for $500. Later, S agrees to a reduction in price to $490. The first contract must be in writing (absent any exceptions), but the modified contract may be oral.*

f. Consignment—arrangement in which agent (consignee) is appointed by consignor to sell goods if all the following conditions are met

(1) Consignor keeps title to goods,

(2) Consignee is not obligated to buy or pay for goods,

(3) Consignee receives a commission upon sale, and

(4) Consignor receives proceeds of sale

g. Document of title—any document that in the regular course of business is accepted as adequate evidence that the person in possession of the document is entitled to receive, hold, and dispose of the document and the goods it covers

h. Bill of lading—a document of title that is issued by a private or common carrier in exchange for goods delivered to it for shipment. It may be negotiable or nonnegotiable.

i. Warehouse receipt—a document of title issued by a person engaged in the business of storing goods (i.e., a warehouseman). It acknowledges receipt of the goods, describes the goods stored, and contains the terms of the storage contract. It may be negotiable or nonnegotiable.

B. Product Liability—a manufacturer or seller may be responsible when a product is defective and causes injury or damage to a person or property. There are three theories under which manufacturers and sellers may be held liable. (In each fact pattern, consider all three, although proof of any one creates liability.)

1.   Warranty Liability—purchaser of a product may sue based on the warranties made

a.   Warranty of title

(1) Seller warrants good title, rightful transfer and freedom from any security interest or lien of which the buyer has no knowledge

EXAMPLE: A seller of stolen goods would be liable to a buyer for damages.

(2) Merchant warrants goods to be free of rightful claim of infringement (e.g., patent or trademark), unless buyer furnished specifications to seller for manufacture of the goods

(3) Can only be disclaimed by specific language or circumstances that give buyer reason to know s/he is receiving less than full title

(a) Cannot be disclaimed by language such as "as is"

b.   Express warranties (may be written or oral)

(1) Any affirmation of fact or promise made by the seller to the buyer that relates to the goods and becomes part of the basis of the bargain creates an express warranty that the goods shall conform to the affirmation or promise

(a) Sales talk, puffing, or a statement purporting to be merely the seller's opinion does not create a warranty

(b) No reliance is necessary on part of buyer

(c) Must form part of the basis of bargain

1] Would include advertisements read by buyer
2] Normally would not include warranties given after the sale or contract was made

(d) No intent to create warranty is needed on the part of the seller

(e) Seller or buyer may be merchant or consumer

(2) Any description of the goods which is made part of the basis of the bargain creates an express warranty that the goods shall conform to the description

(3) Any sample or model that is made part of the basis of the bargain creates an express warranty that the goods shall conform to the sample or model

(4) It is not necessary to the creation of an express warranty that the seller use formal words such as "warranty" or "guarantee"

c.   Implied warranties

(1) Warranty of merchantability—goods are fit for ordinary purpose

(a) This warranty also guarantees that goods are properly packaged and labeled

(b) This warranty applies if

1] Seller is a merchant with respect to goods of the kind being sold, and
2] Warranty is not modified or excluded
3] Then if goods not fit for ordinary use, breach of this warranty occurs

(2) Warranty of fitness for a particular purpose

(a) Created when the seller knows of the particular use for which the goods are required and further knows that the buyer is relying on skill and judgment of seller to select and furnish suitable goods for this particular use

EXAMPLE: A buyer relies upon a paint salesperson to select a particular exterior house paint that will effectively cover existing siding.

(b) Buyer must actually rely on seller's skill and judgment

       (c) Product is then warranted for the particular expressed purpose and seller may be liable if the product fails to so perform

       (d) Applicable both to merchants and nonmerchants

  d. UCC, being consumer oriented, allows these warranties to extend to parties other than the purchaser even without privity of contract (contractual connection between parties)

    (1) Extends to a buyer's family and also to guests in the home who may reasonably be expected to use and/or be affected by the goods and who are injured

      EXAMPLE: A dinner guest breaks a tooth on a small piece of metal in the food. Note that in food, the substance causing injury normally must be foreign, not something customarily found in it (bone in fish).

  e. Disclaimers—warranty liability may be escaped or modified by disclaimers (also available at common law without rules defining limits of disclaimers)

    (1) A disclaimer of merchantability can be written or oral but must use the word "merchantability" unless all implied warranties are disclaimed as in (3) below

    (2) To disclaim the implied warranty of fitness for a particular purpose, the disclaimer must be in writing and conspicuous

    (3) Both the warranty of merchantability and fitness for a particular purpose can be disclaimed by oral or written language such as "as is" or "with all faults"

    (4) Written disclaimers must be clear and conspicuous

    (5) If the buyer has had ample opportunity to inspect the goods or sample, there is no implied warranty as to any defects which ought reasonably to have been discovered

    (6) Implied warranties may be excluded or modified by course of dealings, course of performance, or usage of trade

    (7) A disclaimer inconsistent with an express warranty is not effective (i.e., a description of a warranty in a contract cannot be disclaimed)

    (8) Limitations on consequential damages for personal injuries are presumed to be unconscionable if on consumer goods

2. Negligence

  a. Must prove the following elements

    (1) Duty of manufacturer to exercise reasonable (due) care

      (a) Consider likelihood of harm, seriousness of harm, and difficulty of correction

      (b) May be based on violation of statute but this is not necessary

      (c) If accident is type that would not normally happen without negligence, then presumption of negligence exists

    (2) Breach of duty of reasonable care

      (a) Insufficient instructions may cause breach of duty

    (3) Damages or injury

    (4) Cause in fact

      (a) In general, if injury would not have happened without defendant's conduct, there is cause in fact

    (5) Proximate cause

      (a) General standard here is whether the type of injury was foreseeable

  b. Privity of contract is not needed because suit not based on contract

    EXAMPLE: A car manufacturer is negligent in the manufacture and design of brakes and as a result, a driver is severely injured. The driver may sue the manufacturer even if he bought the car from a retailer.

    EXAMPLE: In the example above, even a pedestrian injured because of the brake problem may recover from the manufacturer.

   c. Often difficult to prove this type of negligence because facts are frequently controlled by defendant

   d. Defenses to negligence

     (1) Contributory negligence

       (a) That is, plaintiff helped cause accident

       (b) Complete bar to recovery

       (c) Some states instead use comparative negligence in which damages are allocated between plaintiff and defendant based on relative fault

     (2) Assumption of risk

3. Strict liability

   a. Manufacturers, sellers, and lessors who normally deal in this type of product are liable to users of products without proof of fault or lack of reasonable care if following other elements are proven

     (1) Product was defective when sold

       (a) Based on poor design, inadequate warnings, improper assembly, or unsafe materials

     (2) Defect is unreasonably dangerous to user

       (a) Based on normal expectations

     (3) Product reaches user without significant changes

     (4) Defect caused the injury

   b. Defense of contributory negligence, comparative negligence, disclaimer or lack of privity is unavailable

     (1) Assumption of risk and misuse are defenses

      EXAMPLE: Herb is injured while lifting up his power lawnmower to trim his hedges. Manufacturer would not be liable since product was not being used for intended purpose.

C. Transfer of Property Rights

1. If party having voidable title transfers goods to a good-faith purchaser for value, the latter obtains good title

   a. Examples in which there is voidable title

     (1) Goods paid for with a check subsequently dishonored

     (2) Goods obtained by fraud, mistake, duress, or undue influence

     (3) Goods obtained from minor

     (4) Thief does **not** have voidable title but void title

      EXAMPLE: B buys a stereo from S but the check bounces. P, a good-faith purchaser, pays B for the stereo. S cannot get the stereo from P but must recover money from B.

      EXAMPLE: Same as above except that B stole the stereo. P does not obtain title of the stereo.

2. If a person entrusts possession of goods to a merchant who deals in those goods, a good-faith purchaser for value obtains title to these goods, unless s/he knew that this merchant did not own the goods

   EXAMPLE: C leaves his watch at a shop for repairs. The shop mistakenly sells the watch to B who is unaware of C's interest. C cannot force B to turn over the watch because B now has title. Of course, C can recover monetary damages from the shop.

3. Passage of title

   a. Once goods are identified to the contract, the parties may agree as to when title passes

     (1) Sale cannot take place until goods exist and have been identified to the contract

       (a) Identification—occurs when the goods that are going to be used to perform the contract are shipped, marked or otherwise designated as such

       (b) Identification gives buyer

       1] An insurable interest in the goods once they are identified to contract

       2] Right to demand goods upon offering full contract price once other conditions are satisfied

  b. Otherwise, title generally passes when the seller completes his/her performance with respect to physical delivery

    (1) If a destination contract, title passes on tender at destination (i.e., buyer's place of business)

    (2) If a shipping (point) contract, title passes when seller puts goods in the possession of the carrier

  c. If seller has no duty to move the goods

    (1) Title passes upon delivery of documents of title

       EXAMPLE: Delivery of negotiable or nonnegotiable warehouse receipt passes title to buyer.

    (2) If no document of title exists, title passes at the time and place of contracting if the goods are identifiable

    (3) If goods not identified, there is only a contract to sell; no title passes

  d. Rejection (justified or not) of goods or a justified revocation of acceptance by buyer reverts title to seller

  e. Taking a security interest is irrelevant to passage of title

D. Risk of Loss and Title

1. Risk of loss is independent of title under UCC, but rules regarding the transfer of both are similar
2. General rules

  a. Parties may agree as to which party bears risk of loss or has title; otherwise UCC rules below apply

  b. Shipment terms

    (1) FOB destination point—seller retains risk of loss and title and bears costs of transportation until s/he tenders delivery of goods at point of destination

      (a) FOB means "free on board"

    (2) FOB shipping point—buyer obtains risk of loss and title and bears shipping costs once goods are delivered to carrier

      EXAMPLE: Seller is in San Francisco and buyer is in Chicago: FOB San Francisco.

      EXAMPLE: Under FOB shipping point contract, seller delivers perishable goods to a nonrefrigerated carrier. Seller still has risk of loss since carrier was not appropriate type.

    (3) CIF—shipping contract (shipping point contract) in which cost, insurance, and freight are included in price

      (a) Seller puts goods in hands of a carrier and obtains insurance in buyer's name, who then has risk of loss and title

    (4) C & F—shipping contract in which cost and freight are included in price

      (a) Seller need not buy insurance for buyer

      (b) Risk of loss and title pass to buyer upon delivery of goods to carrier

    (5) COD—Collect on delivery

      (a) Carrier not to deliver goods until paid for

      (b) Buyer cannot inspect goods first unless stated in contract

  c. In international sales shipment contracts under United Nations Convention for the International Sale of Goods, risk of loss passes to buyer upon delivery to first carrier for transmission to buyer.

    (1) This can be modified by agreement.

d. If no shipping terms are specified, then seller holds conforming goods for buyer and gives buyer notice to allow buyer to take possession of goods

e. Sale on approval—goods may be returned even if they conform to the contract

   (1) Not considered sold until buyer approves or accepts as sale
   (2) Goods bought for trial use
   (3) Seller retains title and risk of loss until buyer accepts goods
   (4) Creditors of buyer cannot reach goods until buyer accepts

f. Sale or return—goods may be returned even if they conform to the contract

   (1) Goods bought for use or resale
   (2) Sale is final if goods not returned during period specified
   (3) Buyer obtains risk of loss and title according to shipping terms in contract

     (a) Both risk of loss and title return to seller if and when goods are returned to seller
     (b) Return of goods is at buyer's expense
     (c) Buyer retains risk of loss during shipment back to seller if returns goods

   (4) Creditors of buyer can reach the goods while in buyer's possession, unless notice of seller's interest is posted or filed as required
   (5) Also termed sale and return

g. Often difficult to distinguish sale on approval vs. sale or return

   (1) Unless buyer and seller agree otherwise

     (a) Transaction is deemed to be sale on approval if goods for buyer's use
     (b) Transaction is presumed to be sale or return if goods are for buyer's resale

h. Effect of breach on risk of loss

   (1) If seller breaches

     (a) Risk of loss remains with seller until cure by seller or acceptance by buyer to extent of buyer's deficiency in insurance coverage
     (b) Title passes under original terms despite delivery of nonconforming goods

   (2) If buyer breaches

     (a) Risk of loss passes to buyer to extent of seller's deficiency in insurance for a commercially reasonable time

i. If goods are held in warehouse and seller has no right to move them, risk of loss passes to buyer

   (1) Upon proper negotiation of a negotiable document of title
   (2) Within a reasonable time after delivery of a nonnegotiable document of title
   (3) Once warehouseman acknowledges buyer's right to goods if no document of title

j. Voidable title

   (1) One who purchases in good faith from another who has voidable title takes good title

     (a) Good faith—purchaser unaware of facts that made previous title voidable
     (b) One may obtain voidable title by purchasing with a check that is later dishonored

       EXAMPLE: A purchases 1,000 widgets from B. B had purchased these from C but B's check had been dishonored by the bank before A purchased the widgets. A was unaware of these facts. B's title was voidable but A takes good title as a good-faith purchaser.

k. In situations not covered above, risk of loss passes to buyer on physical receipt of goods if seller is a merchant. Otherwise, risk passes on tender of delivery.

l. Risk of loss can be covered by insurance. In general, party has an insurable interest whenever s/he can suffer damage.

   (1) Buyer usually allowed an insurable interest when goods are identified to the contract
   (2) Seller usually has an insurable interest so long as s/he has title or a security interest

E. Performance and Remedies under Sales Law

1. In general, either party may, upon breach by other, cancel the contract and terminate executory obligations

    a. Unlike common law rescission, however, cancellation does not discharge a claim for damages

2. Seller's duty to perform under a contract for sale is excused if performance as agreed has been made impracticable by the occurrence of a contingency, the nonoccurrence of which was a basic assumption on which the contract was made

    a. May sometimes substitute performance if, for example, method of delivery specified in contract is not available so seller chooses another reasonable delivery method

3. Anticipatory breach (anticipatory repudiation) takes place when party indicates that s/he will not be performing contract and performance is not yet due

    a. Aggrieved party has options

        (1) Treat it as a **present** breach of contract and use remedies available for breach of contract

            (a) Sue for damages, or
            (b) Cancel contract

        (2) Aggrieved party may wait for performance for reasonable time hoping party will change his/her mind
        (3) Aggrieved party may demand assurance of performance and treat silence as breach of contract under UCC
        (4) Punitive damages are not allowed

    b. If aggrieved party is seller of uncompleted goods, then seller may

        (1) Complete goods and identify to contract,
        (2) Cease and sell for scrap, or
        (3) Proceed in other reasonable manner

    c. Any of the above must be done while exercising reasonable commercial judgment
    d. Buyer who breaches is then liable for damages measured by whatever course of action seller takes

4. Either party may demand adequate assurance of performance when reasonable grounds for insecurity arise with respect to performance of the other party

    a. For example, buyer falls behind in payments or seller delivers defective goods to other buyers
    b. Party may suspend performance while waiting for assurance
    c. Failure to provide assurance within a reasonable time, not to exceed thirty days, is repudiation of the contract
    d. Provision in contract, that seller may accelerate payment when s/he has a good-faith belief that makes him/her insecure, is valid

5. Seller's remedies

    a. Seller has right to cure nonconformity (i.e., tender conforming goods)

        (1) Within original time of contract, or
        (2) Within reasonable time if seller thought nonconforming tender would be acceptable
        (3) Seller must notify buyer of his intention to cure

    b. Seller may resell goods if buyer breaches before acceptance

        (1) May be public or private sale

            (a) If private, must give notice to buyer who breached; otherwise, losses cannot be recovered
            (b) If seller resells in a commercially reasonable manner, s/he may recover any loss on the sale from the buyer who breached, but s/he is not responsible to buyer who breached for profits made on resale
            (c) In any event, good-faith purchasers take free of original buyer's claims

c. If seller learns that buyer is insolvent and buyer does not have the document of title, seller may stop delivery of goods in carrier's possession unless buyer pays cash

d. Seller may recover goods received by an insolvent buyer if demand is made within ten days of receipt

   (1) However, if the buyer has made a written misrepresentation of solvency within three months before delivery, this ten-day limitation does not apply

   (2) If buyer is insolvent, seller may demand cash to make delivery

e. Seller may recover damages

   (1) If buyer repudiates agreement or refuses goods, seller may recover the difference between market price at time of tender and contract price, plus incidental damages, minus expenses saved due to buyer's breach

   (2) If the measure of damages stated above in (1) is inadequate to place the seller in as good a position as performance would have, then the seller can sue for the lost profits, plus incidental damages, less expenses saved due to the buyer's breach

      (a) Loss profits are consequential damages and as such are recoverable when foreseeable by breaching party

   (3) The seller can recover the full contract price when

      (a) The buyer has already accepted the goods
      (b) Conforming goods have been destroyed after the risk of loss had transferred to buyer
      (c) The seller is unable to resell the identified goods

f. Under Uniform Computer Information Transactions Act (UCITA), licensor of its software has special self-help remedies available to protect its software, the right to be paid for usage, or its trade secrets.

   (1) Licensor may use bugs, etc., that disable that software from further misuse if certain requirements are met

      (a) Licensee must have specifically agreed to that self-help remedy
      (b) Licensor must give licensee at least fifteen days notice before using that remedy as well as who licensee can contact about any questions
      (c) Licensor is not permitted to use this remedy if there is a significant risk of personal injury or public safety, or if there is a significant risk to information of other parties

6. Buyer's remedies

a. Buyer may reject nonconforming goods, either in entirety or any commercial unit (e.g., bale, carload, etc.)

   (1) Buyer has right to inspect goods before acceptance or payment

      (a) Must do so in reasonable time and give notice to seller (failure may operate as acceptance)
      (b) Buyer must have reasonable time to inspect

   (2) Buyer must care for goods until returned

   (3) If buyer is a merchant, s/he must follow reasonable instructions of seller (e.g., ship, sell)

      (a) Right to indemnity for costs

   (4) If goods are perishable or threatened with decline in value, buyer must make reasonable effort to sell

   (5) Buyer has a security interest in any goods in his/her possession to the extent of any payments made to seller and any expenses incurred

      (a) S/he may sell the goods to recover payments

b. Under Uniform Computer Information Transactions Act (UCITA), consumers who make electronic errors while ordering have special rights, if consumer, upon learning of error, does following

(1) Immediately notifies seller that s/he made error (as soon as s/he learns of error)
(2) Buyer does not use or benefit from information, software or products ordered
(3) Delivers all copies to seller or destroys them at seller's request
(4) Buyer in error pays all costs of processing and shipping to seller
(5) Note that nonconsumer buyer may not use these more favorable provisions of this Act

> EXAMPLE: Buyer intends to purchase one copy of a DVD from ABC Company. The buyer, who is purchasing this DVD for consumer use, mistakenly orders ten copies from ABC's website. The buyer is protected by following the steps given above.

c. Buyer may accept nonconforming goods

(1) Buyer must pay at contract price but may still recover damages (i.e., deduct damages from price if s/he gives seller notice)
(2) Buyer may revoke acceptance in a reasonable time if

(a) Accepted expecting nonconformity to be cured
(b) Accepted because of difficulty of discovering defect
(c) Accepted because seller assured conformity

d. Buyer may recover damages measured by the difference between the contract price and the market value of the goods at the time buyer learns of the breach, plus any incidental damages and consequential damages

(1) Consequential damages are damages resulting from buyer's needs that the seller was aware of at the time of contracting
(2) Consequential damages cannot be recovered if buyer could reasonably have prevented these (mitigation of damages)

e. Buyer has the right of cover

(1) Buyer can buy substitute goods from another seller—buyer will still have the right to damages after engaging in "cover"

(a) Damages are difference between cost of cover and contract price, plus incidental and consequential damages
(b) Failure to cover does not bar other remedies

f. Once goods to the contract have been identified, buyer obtains rights in those goods

(1) Identification occurs when goods under contract are

(a) Shipped
(b) Marked as part of the contract, or
(c) In some way designated as part of contract

(2) Buyer obtains

(a) Insurable interest in those goods, and
(b) Right to obtain goods, called replevin, upon offering contract price

1] Replevin is not allowed if buyer can cover

g. Buyer may obtain specific performance if goods are unique or in other proper circumstances even if goods are not identified to the contract

(1) Proper circumstances may exist when other remedies (such as monetary damages or remedy of cover) are inadequate

> EXAMPLE: S agrees to sell B an antique car of which only one exists. If S later refuses to go through with the contract, B may require S to sell him the unique car under the remedy of specific performance.

7. Statute of limitations for sale of goods is four years

a. An action for breach must be commenced within this period
b. Parties may agree to reduce to not less than one year but may not extend it
c. Statute of limitations begins running when the contract is breached

F. Leases under UCC

1. Law governing leases has been slow to develop and has been "tacked on" for various other areas of law such as property law and secured transactions
2. Now Article 2A of the UCC applies to any transaction creating a lease regardless of form
3. Article 2A is now law in majority of states
4. Article 2A is quite lengthy, but for purpose of CPA exam, note that its provisions are similar to Article 2 except that Article 2A applies to leases and Article 2 applies to sales of goods
5. Under Article 2A

   a. Lessor is person who transfers right to possess named goods and to use them in described ways by lessee

6. Note the following provisions where Article 2A is similar to Article 2:

   a. Statute of frauds except that stated minimum is $1,000 instead of $500 that applies to sales of goods

      (1) There are three exceptions to Statute of Frauds whereby leases need not be in writing even if for $1000 or more (note that these are similar to three exceptions to Statute of Frauds for sales of goods)

         (a) Specially manufactured goods when goods are not suitable for sale or lease in the ordinary course of lessor's business
         (b) Lessor or lessee admits to oral lease in court proceedings

            1] Only enforceable up to quantity admitted

         (c) Part acceptance in which lease is enforceable up to amount accepted by lessee

            EXAMPLE: E leases under an oral agreement 900 personal computers. A, the lessor, ships 400 of the personal computers to E. After accepting the 400, E decides she does not want to lease the other 500. E is liable for the lease of the 400 personal computers under the part acceptance exception even though the agreement was oral. She would be liable for the lease of the full 900 personal computers if the agreement had been for less than $1,000 which is not the case here.

   b. Rules on acceptance, revocation of acceptance, and rejection of goods
   c. Remedies are similar to sellers' and buyers' remedies including the important concept of cure
   d. Principles for performance include anticipatory repudiation or breach, (including use of adequate assurance to avoid a breach), and the concept of impracticability
   e. Leases may be assigned
   f. Use general principles of contract and sales law for these

      (1) Warranties
      (2) Parol evidence
      (3) Firm offers
      (4) Risk of loss rules
      (5) Concept of unconscionable agreements

   g. Provision for sublease by lessee
   h. Leased goods may become fixtures
   i. Lessor has right to take possession of leased property after default without requirement of court adjudication

7. Leases under Article 2A of UCC may be in any manner sufficient to show by words or conduct that lessor and lessee intended to form a lease of identified goods
8. Finance lease is three-party transaction in which lessor acquires title or right to possess goods from supplier

   a. Lessor does not manufacture or supply goods for lessee but third-party supplier does according to lease agreement

G. Contracts for the International Sales of Goods (CISG)

   1. Contracts for sales of goods between persons or companies of different countries follow the important rules of CISG

   2. Many provisions of CISG are similar to UCC provisions but differences are handled under CISG because USA has this treaty with many countries in South America, Central America, North America, and most countries in Europe

      a. By Constitutional Law, CISG has priority over UCC when it applies and when it conflicts with UCC

      b. The following are important areas where CISG and UCC are different

         (1) Price terms

            (a) May be left open under UCC, in which case UCC provides that price is reasonable price at time of delivery

               1] Other specified exceptions allowed under UCC

            (b) CISG requires that price term be included for there to be a contract

               1] CISG allows exception if method to determine price in future is clearly specified in contract

         (2) Time contract formed

            (a) Unlike UCC, CISG specifies that contract is formed only when acceptance is received by offeror

            (b) Also under CISG, acceptance happens at moment requested act is performed, not at the time notice is given of acceptance to offeror

         (3) Acceptances

            (a) CISG provides that there is no contract if terms in acceptance are different from terms in offer

               1] Acceptance is effective if differences are not material

                   a] However, almost ever term in contract under CISG is considered material

         (4) Irrevocable offers

            (a) UCC allows offers that are not supported by consideration to be irrevocable if they are written and also meet certain other criteria

            (b) CISG allows offeror to make offer irrevocable by orally stating so

         (5) Written contracts

            (a) UCC has $500 rule for sales of goods

            (b) CISG provides that sales contracts may be oral with no rule regarding amount of money

               1] Also provides that proof of contract can be by any reasonable means

         (6) Parties are encouraged to have choice-of-language and choice-of-law clauses in contracts to help settle any disputes

MULTIPLE-CHOICE QUESTIONS (1-47)

1. Under the Sales Article of the UCC, when a written offer has been made without specifying a means of acceptance but providing that the offer will only remain open for ten days, which of the following statements represent(s) a valid acceptance of the offer?

I. An acceptance sent by regular mail the day before the ten-day period expires that reaches the offeror on the eleventh day.

II. An acceptance faxed the day before the ten-day period expires that reaches the offeror on the eleventh day, due to a malfunction of the offeror's printer.

    a. I only.
    b. II only.
    c. Both I and II.
    d. Neither I nor II.

2. Under the Sales Article of the UCC, a firm offer will be created only if the
    a. Offer states the time period during which it will remain open.
    b. Offer is made by a merchant in a signed writing.
    c. Offeree gives some form of consideration.
    d. Offeree is a merchant.

3. On May 2, Mason orally contracted with Acme Appliances to buy for $480 a washer and dryer for household use. Mason and the Acme salesperson agreed that delivery would be made on July 2. On May 5, Mason telephoned Acme and requested that the delivery date be moved to June 2. The Acme salesperson agreed with this request. On June 2, Acme failed to deliver the washer and dryer to Mason because of an inventory shortage. Acme advised Mason that it would deliver the appliances on July 2 as originally agreed. Mason believes that Acme has breached its agreement with Mason. Acme contends that its agreement to deliver on June 2 was not binding. Acme's contention is
    a. Correct, because Mason is not a merchant and was buying the appliances for household use.
    b. Correct, because the agreement to change the delivery date was not in writing.
    c. Incorrect, because the agreement to change the delivery date was binding.
    d. Incorrect, because Acme's agreement to change the delivery date is a firm offer that cannot be withdrawn by Acme.

4. Under the Sales Article of the UCC, which of the following statements is correct?
    a. The obligations of the parties to the contract must be performed in good faith.
    b. Merchants and nonmerchants are treated alike.
    c. The contract must involve the sale of goods for a price of more than $500.
    d. None of the provisions of the UCC may be disclaimed by agreement.

5. Which of the following contracts is handled under common law rules rather than under Article 2 of the Uniform Commercial Code?
    a. Oral contract to have hair styled in which expensive products will be used on the hair.
    b. Oral contract to purchase a textbook for $100.
    c. Written contract to purchase an old handcrafted chair for $600 from a private party.
    d. Written contract to purchase a heater from a dealer to be installed by the buyer in her home.

6. Cookie Co. offered to sell Distrib Markets 20,000 pounds of cookies at $1.00 per pound, subject to certain specified terms for delivery. Distrib replied in writing as follows:

> We accept your offer for 20,000 pounds of cookies at $1.00 per pound, weighing scale to have valid city certificate.

Under the UCC
    a. A contract was formed between the parties.
    b. A contract will be formed only if Cookie agrees to the weighing scale requirement.
    c. No contract was formed because Distrib included the weighing scale requirement in its reply.
    d. No contract was formed because Distrib's reply was a counteroffer.

7. EG Door Co., a manufacturer of custom exterior doors, verbally contracted with Art Contractors to design and build a $2,000 custom door for a house that Art was restoring. After EG had completed substantial work on the door, Art advised EG that the house had been destroyed by fire and Art was canceling the contract. EG finished the door and shipped it to Art. Art refused to accept delivery. Art contends that the contract cannot be enforced because it violated the Statute of Frauds by not being in writing. Under the Sales Article of the UCC, is Art's contention correct?
    a. Yes, because the contract was not in writing.
    b. Yes, because the contract cannot be fully performed due to the fire.
    c. No, because the goods were specially manufactured for Art and cannot be resold in EG's regular course of business.
    d. No, because the cancellation of the contract was not made in writing.

8. On May 2, Handy Hardware sent Ram Industries a signed purchase order that stated, in part, as follows:

> Ship for May 8 delivery 300 Model A-X socket sets at current dealer price. Terms 2/10/net 30.

Ram received Handy's purchase order on May 4. On May 5, Ram discovered that it had only 200 Model A-X socket sets and 100 Model W-Z socket sets in stock. Ram shipped the Model A-X and Model W-Z sets to Handy without any explanation concerning the shipment. The socket sets were received by Handy on May 8.
Which of the following statements concerning the shipment is correct?
    a. Ram's shipment is an acceptance of Handy's offer.
    b. Ram's shipment is a counteroffer.
    c. Handy's order must be accepted by Ram in writing before Ram ships the socket sets.
    d. Handy's order can only be accepted by Ram shipping conforming goods.

9. Under the UCC Sales Article, which of the following conditions will prevent the formation of an enforceable sale of goods contract?
    a. Open price.
    b. Open delivery.
    c. Open quantity.
    d. Open acceptance.

10. Webstar Corp. orally agreed to sell Northco, Inc. a computer for $20,000. Northco sent a signed purchase order to Webstar confirming the agreement. Webstar received the purchase order and did not respond. Webstar refused to deliver the computer to Northco, claiming that the purchase order did not satisfy the UCC Statute of Frauds because it was not signed by Webstar. Northco sells computers to the general public and Webstar is a computer wholesaler. Under the UCC Sales Article, Webstar's position is

a. Incorrect because it failed to object to Northco's purchase order.
b. Incorrect because only the buyer in a sale-of-goods transaction must sign the contract.
c. Correct because it was the party against whom enforcement of the contract is being sought.
d. Correct because the purchase price of the computer exceeded $500.

11. Patch, a frequent shopper at Soon-Shop Stores, received a rain check for an advertised sale item after Soon-Shop's supply of the product ran out. The rain check was in writing and stated that the item would be offered to the customer at the advertised sale price for an unspecified period of time. A Soon-Shop employee signed the rain check. When Patch returned to the store one month later to purchase the item, the store refused to honor the rain check. Under the Sales Article of the UCC, will Patch win a suit to enforce the rain check?

a. No, because one month is too long a period of time for a rain check to be effective.
b. No, because the rain check did not state the effective time period necessary to keep the offer open.
c. Yes, because Soon-Shop is required to have sufficient supplies of the sale item to satisfy all customers.
d. Yes, because the rain check met the requirements of a merchant's firm offer even though no effective time period was stated.

12. A sheep rancher agreed in writing to sell all the wool shorn during the shearing season to a weaver. The contract failed to establish the price and a minimum quantity of wool. After the shearing season, the rancher refused to deliver the wool. The weaver sued the rancher for breach of contract. Under the Sales Article of the UCC, will the weaver win?

a. Yes, because this was an output contract.
b. Yes, because both price and quantity terms were omitted.
c. No, because quantity cannot be omitted for a contract to be enforceable.
d. No, because the omission of price and quantity terms prevents the formation of a contract.

13. Under the Sales Article of the UCC, the warranty of title

a. Provides that the seller cannot disclaim the warranty if the sale is made to a bona fide purchaser for value.
b. Provides that the seller deliver the goods free from any lien of which the buyer lacked knowledge when the contract was made.
c. Applies only if it is in writing and assigned by the seller.
d. Applies only if the seller is a merchant.

14. Under the Sales Article of the UCC, most goods sold by merchants are covered by certain warranties. An example of an express warranty would be a warranty of

a. Usage of trade.
b. Fitness for a particular purpose.
c. Merchantability.
d. Conformity of goods to sample.

15. Under the Sales Article of the UCC, which of the following statements is correct regarding the warranty of merchantability arising when there has been a sale of goods by a merchant seller?

a. The warranty must be in writing.
b. The warranty arises when the buyer relies on the seller's skill in selecting the goods purchased.
c. The warranty cannot be disclaimed.
d. The warranty arises as a matter of law when the seller ordinarily sells the goods purchased.

16. On May 2, Handy Hardware sent Ram Industries a signed purchase order that stated, in part, as follows:

Ship for May 8 delivery 300 Model A-X socket sets at current dealer price. Terms 2/10/net 30.

Ram received Handy's purchase order on May 4. On May 5, Ram discovered that it had only 200 Model A-X socket sets and 100 Model W-Z socket sets in stock. Ram shipped the Model A-X and Model W-Z sets to Handy without any explanation concerning the shipment. The socket sets were received by Handy on May 8.

Assuming a contract exists between Handy and Ram, which of the following implied warranties would result?

I. Implied warranty of merchantability.
II. Implied warranty of fitness for a particular purpose.
III. Implied warranty of title.

a. I only.
b. III only.
c. I and III only.
d. I, II, and III.

17. Under the UCC Sales Article, an action for breach of the implied warranty of merchantability by a party who sustains personal injuries may be successful against the seller of the product only when

a. The seller is a merchant of the product involved.
b. An action based on negligence can also be successfully maintained.
c. The injured party is in privity of contract with the seller.
d. An action based on strict liability in tort can also be successfully maintained.

18. Which of the following conditions must be met for an implied warranty of fitness for a particular purpose to arise in connection with a sale of goods?

I. The warranty must be in writing.
II. The seller must know that the buyer was relying on the seller in selecting the goods.

a. I only.
b. II only.
c. Both I and II.
d. Neither I nor II.

19. Under the UCC Sales Article, the implied warranty of merchantability

a. May be disclaimed by a seller's oral statement that mentions merchantability.

b. Arises only in contracts involving a merchant seller and a merchant buyer.

c. Is breached if the goods are **not** fit for all purposes for which the buyer intends to use the goods.

d. Must be part of the basis of the bargain to be binding on the seller.

20. Cook Company, a common carrier trucking company, made a contract to transport some video equipment for Jackson Company. Cook is trying to limit its liability in the contract. In which of the following situations can Cook **not avoid** liability?

I. In transit, the driver of Cook's truck damages the video equipment when the driver causes an accident.

II. An unknown thief steals the video equipment while in transit. Cook committed no negligence in this theft.

III. The video equipment is destroyed when a bridge under the truck collapses because of an earthquake.

a. I only.

b. I and II only.

c. I, II, and III.

d. I and III only.

21. High sues the manufacturer, wholesaler, and retailer for bodily injuries caused by a power saw High purchased. Which of the following statements is correct under strict liability theory?

a. Contributory negligence on High's part will always be a bar to recovery.

b. The manufacturer will avoid liability if it can show it followed the custom of the industry.

c. Privity will be a bar to recovery insofar as the wholesaler is concerned if the wholesaler did **not** have a reasonable opportunity to inspect.

d. High may recover even if he **cannot** show any negligence was involved.

22. To establish a cause of action based on strict liability in tort for personal injuries that result from the use of a defective product, one of the elements the injured party must prove is that the seller

a. Was aware of the defect in the product.

b. Sold the product to the injured party.

c. Failed to exercise due care.

d. Sold the product in a defective condition.

23. A common carrier bailee generally would avoid liability for loss of goods entrusted to its care if the goods are

a. Stolen by an unknown person.

b. Negligently destroyed by an employee.

c. Destroyed by the derailment of the train carrying them due to railroad employee negligence.

d. Improperly packed by the party shipping them.

24. McGraw purchased an antique rocking chair from Tillis by check. The check was dishonored by the bank due to insufficient funds. In the meantime, McGraw sold the rocking chair to Rio who had no knowledge that McGraw's check had been dishonored. Which of the following is correct?

a. Tillis may repossess the rocking chair from Rio.

b. Tillis may recover money damages from Rio.

c. Tillis may recover money damages from McGraw.

d. Tillis may recover damages from McGraw based on fraud.

25. Yancie took her bike in to Pete's Bike Sales and Repair to have it repaired. Pete said he would need to have her leave it for two days. The next day, one of Pete's employees sold Yancie's bike to Jake. Jake paid for the bike with a credit card, unaware that Pete did not own the bike. Which of the following is correct?

a. Yancie can repossess the bike from Jake if she pays Jake. Yancie then recovers the price from Pete.

b. Pete can repossess the bike from Jake and then return it to Yancie.

c. Yancie can sue Jake for monetary damages only.

d. Jake has title to the bike.

26. Under the Sales Article of the UCC, unless a contract provides otherwise, before title to goods can pass from a seller to a buyer, the goods must be

a. Tendered to the buyer.

b. Identified to the contract.

c. Accepted by the buyer.

d. Paid for.

27. Under the Sales Article of the UCC, in an FOB place of shipment contract, the risk of loss passes to the buyer when the goods

a. Are identified to the contract.

b. Are placed on the seller's loading dock.

c. Are delivered to the carrier.

d. Reach the buyer's loading dock.

28. On May 2, Lace Corp., an appliance wholesaler, offered to sell appliances worth $3,000 to Parco, Inc., a household appliances retailer. The offer was signed by Lace's president, and provided that it would not be withdrawn before June 1. It also included the shipping terms: "FOB Parco's warehouse." On May 29, Parco mailed an acceptance of Lace's offer. Lace received the acceptance June 2.

If Lace inadvertently ships the wrong appliances to Parco and Parco rejects them two days after receipt, title to the goods will

a. Pass to Parco when they are identified to the contract.

b. Pass to Parco when they are shipped.

c. Remain with Parco until the goods are returned to Lace.

d. Revert to Lace when they are rejected by Parco.

29. Under the Sales Article of the UCC and the United Nations Convention for the International Sale of Goods (CISG), absent specific terms in an international sales shipment contract, when will risk of loss pass to the buyer?

a. When the goods are delivered to the first carrier for transmission to the buyer.

b. When the goods are tendered to the buyer.

c. At the conclusion of the execution of the contract.

d. At the time the goods are identified to the contract.

30. Which of the following statements applies to a sale on approval under the UCC Sales Article?

a. Both the buyer and seller must be merchants.

b. The buyer must be purchasing the goods for resale.

c. Risk of loss for the goods passes to the buyer when the goods are accepted after the trial period.

d. Title to the goods passes to the buyer on delivery of the goods to the buyer.

31. Under the Sales Article of UCC, which of the following events will result in the risk of loss passing from a merchant seller to a buyer?

	Tender of the goods at the seller's place of business	Use of the seller's truck to deliver the goods
a.	Yes	Yes
b.	Yes	No
c.	No	Yes
d.	No	No

32. Cey Corp. entered into a contract to sell parts to Deck, Ltd. The contract provided that the goods would be shipped "FOB Cey's warehouse." Cey shipped parts different from those specified in the contract. Deck rejected the parts. A few hours after Deck informed Cey that the parts were rejected, they were destroyed by fire in Deck's warehouse. Cey believed that the parts were conforming to the contract. Which of the following statements is correct?

   a. Regardless of whether the parts were conforming, Deck will bear the loss because the contract was a shipment contract.
   b. If the parts were nonconforming, Deck had the right to reject them, but the risk of loss remains with Deck until Cey takes possession of the parts.
   c. If the parts were conforming, risk of loss does **not** pass to Deck until a reasonable period of time after they are delivered to Deck.
   d. If the parts were nonconforming, Cey will bear the risk of loss, even though the contract was a shipment contract.

33. Under the Sales Article of the UCC, which of the following factors is most important in determining who bears the risk of loss in a sale of goods contract?

   a. The method of shipping the goods.
   b. The contract's shipping terms.
   c. Title to the goods.
   d. How the goods were lost.

34. Bond purchased a painting from Wool, who is not in the business of selling art. Wool tendered delivery of the painting after receiving payment in full from Bond. Bond informed Wool that Bond would be unable to take possession of the painting until later that day. Thieves stole the painting before Bond returned. The risk of loss

   a. Passed to Bond at Wool's tender of delivery.
   b. Passed to Bond at the time the contract was formed and payment was made.
   c. Remained with Wool, because the parties agreed on a later time of delivery.
   d. Remained with Wool, because Bond had **not** yet received the painting.

35. Funston, a retailer, shipped goods worth $600 to a customer by using a common carrier. The contract used by the common carrier, and agreed to by Funston, limited liability to $100 unless a higher fee is paid. Funston did not pay the higher fee. The goods were shipped FOB destination point and were destroyed in transit due to a flash flood. Which of the following is correct?

   a. Funston will suffer a loss of $500.
   b. Funston will suffer a loss of $600.

   c. Funston's customer will suffer a loss of $500.
   d. Funston's customer will suffer a loss of $600.

36. Under the Sales Article of the UCC, which of the following statements regarding liquidated damages is(are) correct?

I. The injured party may collect any amount of liquidated damages provided for in the contract.
II. The seller may retain a deposit of up to $500 when a buyer defaults even if there is no liquidated damages provision in the contract.

   a. I only.
   b. II only.
   c. Both I and II.
   d. Neither I nor II.

37. Under the Sales Article of the UCC, and unless otherwise agreed to, the seller's obligation to the buyer is to

   a. Deliver the goods to the buyer's place of business.
   b. Hold conforming goods and give the buyer whatever notification is reasonably necessary to enable the buyer to take delivery.
   c. Deliver all goods called for in the contract to a common carrier.
   d. Set aside conforming goods for inspection by the buyer before delivery.

38. Under the Sales Article of the UCC, which of the following rights is(are) available to a seller when a buyer materially breaches a sales contract?

	Right to cancel the contract	Right to recover damages
a.	Yes	Yes
b.	Yes	No
c.	No	Yes
d.	No	No

39. Under the Sales Article of the UCC, the remedies available to a seller when a buyer breaches a contract for the sale of goods may include

	The right to resell goods identified to the contract	The right to stop a carrier from delivering the goods
a.	Yes	Yes
b.	Yes	No
c.	No	Yes
d.	No	No

40. Lazur Corp. entered into a contract with Baker Suppliers, Inc. to purchase a used word processor from Baker. Lazur is engaged in the business of selling new and used word processors to the general public. The contract required Baker to ship the goods to Lazur by common carrier pursuant to the following provision in the contract: "FOB Baker Suppliers, Inc. loading dock." Baker also represented in the contract that the word processor had been used for only ten hours by its previous owner. The contract included the provision that the word processor was being sold "as is" and this provision was in a larger and different type style than the remainder of the contract.

Assume that Lazur refused to accept the word processor even though it was in all respects conforming to the contract and that the contract is otherwise silent. Under the UCC Sales Article,

a. Baker can successfully sue for specific performance and make Lazur accept and pay for the word processor.
b. Baker may resell the word processor to another buyer.
c. Baker must sue for the difference between the market value of the word processor and the contract price plus its incidental damages.
d. Baker cannot successfully sue for consequential damages unless it attempts to resell the word processor.

41. On February 15, Mazur Corp. contracted to sell 1,000 bushels of wheat to Good Bread, Inc. at $6.00 per bushel with delivery to be made on June 23. On June 1, Good advised Mazur that it would not accept or pay for the wheat. On June 2, Mazur sold the wheat to another customer at the market price of $5.00 per bushel. Mazur had advised Good that it intended to resell the wheat. Which of the following statements is correct?
a. Mazur can successfully sue Good for the difference between the resale price and the contract price.
b. Mazur can resell the wheat only after June 23.
c. Good can retract its anticipatory breach at any time before June 23.
d. Good can successfully sue Mazur for specific performance.

42. Pickens agreed to sell Crocket 100 cases of napkins with the name of Crocket's restaurant on the napkins. In the enforceable contract, it was specified that delivery will take place on April 15, 2001, which is one month after Pickens and Crocket signed the contract. Crocket wanted the napkins by April 15 because the grand opening of the restaurant was scheduled for April 17. On April 11, Pickens tells Crocket that he has too many orders and will not be able to deliver the napkins. What options does Crocket have?

I. Treat it as a present breach of contract and cancel the contract.
II. Wait for a reasonable time to see if Pickens will deliver.

a. I only.
b. II only.
c. Either I or II.
d. Neither I nor II.

43. Under the Sales Article of the UCC, which of the following rights is(are) available to the buyer when a seller commits an anticipatory breach of contract?

	Demand assurance of performance	*Cancel the contract*	*Collect punitive damages*
a.	Yes	Yes	Yes
b	Yes	Yes	No
c.	Yes	No	Yes
d.	No	Yes	Yes

44. Larch Corp. manufactured and sold Oak a stove. The sale documents included a disclaimer of warranty for personal injury. The stove was defective. It exploded causing serious injuries to Oak's spouse. Larch was notified one week after the explosion. Under the UCC Sales Article, which of the following statements concerning Larch's liability for personal injury to Oak's spouse would be correct?
a. Larch **cannot** be liable because of a lack of privity with Oak's spouse.

b. Larch will **not** be liable because of a failure to give proper notice.
c. Larch will be liable because the disclaimer was **not** a disclaimer of all liability.
d. Larch will be liable because liability for personal injury **cannot** be disclaimed.

45. Under the Sales Article of the UCC, which of the following events will release the buyer from all its obligations under a sales contract?
a. Destruction of the goods after risk of loss passed to the buyer.
b. Impracticability of delivery under the terms of the contract.
c. Anticipatory repudiation by the buyer that is retracted before the seller cancels the contract.
d. Refusal of the seller to give written assurance of performance when reasonably demanded by the buyer.

46. Rowe Corp. purchased goods from Stair Co. that were shipped COD. Under the Sales Article of the UCC, which of the following rights does Rowe have?
a. The right to inspect the goods before paying.
b. The right to possession of the goods before paying.
c. The right to reject nonconforming goods.
d. The right to delay payment for a reasonable period of time.

47. Sklar, CPA, purchased from Wiz Corp. two computers. Sklar discovered material defects in the computers ten months after taking delivery. Three years after discovering the defects, Sklar commenced an action for breach of warranty against Wiz. Wiz has raised the statute of limitations as a defense. The original contract between Wiz and Sklar contained a conspicuous clause providing that the statute of limitations for breach of warranty actions would be limited to eighteen months. Under the circumstances, Sklar will
a. Win because the action was commenced within the four-year period as measured from the date of delivery.
b. Win because the action was commenced within the four-year period as measured from the time he discovered the breach or should have discovered the breach.
c. Lose because the clause providing that the statute of limitations would be limited to eighteen months is enforceable.
d. Lose because the statute of limitations is three years from the date of delivery with respect to written contracts.

PROBLEMS

NOTE: These types of problems are no longer included in the CPA Examination but they have been retained because they are useful in developing skills to complete simulations.

Problem 1   (15 to 25 minutes)

Debco Electronics, Inc. sells various brands of computer equipment to retail and business customers. An audit of Debco's 2003 financial statements has revealed the following transactions:

• On September 1, 2003, a Debco salesperson orally agreed to sell Rapid Computers, Inc. eight TMI computers for $11,000, to be delivered on October 15, 2003. Rapid sells computers to the general public. The Debco salesperson sent Rapid a signed confirmation of the sales agreement. Rapid received the confirmation on September 3, but did not respond to it. On October 15, 2003, Debco tendered delivery of the computers to Rapid. Rapid refused to accept delivery, claiming it had no obligation to buy the computers because it had not signed a contract with Debco.

• On October 12, 2003, Debco mailed TMI Computers, Inc. a signed purchase order for certain specified computers for delivery by November 30, 2003. The purchase order also stated the following:

> This purchase order will not be withdrawn on or before October 31, 2003. You must accept by that date or we will assume you cannot meet our terms. Ship FOB our loading dock.

TMI received the purchase order on October 15, 2003.

• On October 25, Debco mailed the following signed correspondence to TMI, which TMI received on October 29:

> Cancel our October 12, 2003 purchase order. We have found a better price on the computers.

• On October 31, 2003, TMI mailed the following signed correspondence to Debco, which Debco received on November 3:

> We have set aside the computers you ordered and turned down other offers for them. Therefore, we will ship the computers to you for delivery by November 30, 2003, FOB your loading dock with payment terms 2/10; net 30.

There were no further communications between TMI and Debco.

TMI shipped the computers on November 15, and Debco received them on November 29. Debco refused to accept delivery. In justifying its refusal to accept delivery, Debco claimed the following:

• Its October 25 correspondence prevented the formation of a contract between Debco and TMI;

• TMI's October 31 correspondence was not an effective acceptance because it was not received by Debco until November 3;

• TMI's October 31 correspondence was not an effective acceptance because it added payment terms to Debco's purchase order.

Debco, Rapid, and TMI are located in a jurisdiction that has adopted the UCC.

Required:

a. State whether Rapid's claim is correct and give the reasons for your conclusions.

b. State whether Debco's claims are correct with regard to the transaction involving TMI and give the reasons for your conclusions.

SIMULATION PROBLEMS

Simulation Problem 1   (10 to 15 minutes)

Situation	
	Analysis

Angler Corp., a food distributor, is involved in the following disputes:

•   On September 8, Angler shipped the wrong grade of tuna to Mason Restaurants, Inc. under a contract that stated as follows: "FOB Angler's loading dock." During shipment, the tuna was destroyed in an accident involving the common carrier's truck. Mason has refused to pay for the tuna, claiming the risk of loss belonged to Angler at the time of the accident.

•   On October 3, Angler shipped 100 bushels of peaches to Classic Foods, Inc., a retail grocer. Because of a delay in shipping, the peaches rotted. Classic elected to reject the peaches and notified Angler of this decision. Angler asked Classic to return the peaches at Angler's expense. Classic refused the request, claiming it had no obligation to do so.

•   On October 23, Angler orally contracted to sell Regal Fast-Food 1,500 pounds of hamburger meat for $1,500. Delivery was to be made on October 31. On October 29, after Angler had shipped the hamburger meat to Regal, Regal sent Angler the following signed correspondence:

"We are not going to need the 1,500 pounds of meat we ordered on October 23. Don't ship."

Regal rejected the shipment and claimed it is not obligated to purchase the hamburger meat because there is no written contract between Angler and Regal.

	Analysis
Situation	

Determine whether each of the numbered legal conclusions is Correct or Incorrect.

		Correct	*Incorrect*
1.	When the accident happened, the risk of loss belonged to Angler.	O	O
2.	If Angler had shipped the correct grade of tuna to Mason, the risk of loss would have been Angler's at time of the accident.	O	O
3.	The contract between Angler and Mason was an FOB destination point contract.	O	O
4.	Angler had title to the tuna at time of the accident since Angler shipped nonconforming goods.	O	O
5.	Classic is required to return the peaches at Angler's expense per Angler's instructions.	O	O
6.	Classic may throw the peaches away because they were rotted.	O	O
7.	Since Classic elected to reject the rotted peaches, Classic may not also sue for damages.	O	O
8.	Regal is not obligated to purchase the hamburger meat because there was no written contract between Angler and Regal.	O	O
9.	The Uniform Commercial Code applies to the contract between Angler and Regal.	O	O
10.	Regal's correspondence to Angler, dated October 29, satisfies the appropriate Statute of Frauds.	O	O
11.	Angler should keep the hamburger until Regal finally accepts it and sue Regal for $1,500.	O	O
12.	Assuming that all of the original facts are the same except that Regal never sent Angler the correspondence dated October 29, then Angler may hold Regal in breach of contract.	O	O
13.	Assuming that all of the original facts are the same except that the contract was for $450, then Angler may hold Regal in breach of contract.	O	O
14.	Assume that all of the original facts are the same except that Regal never sent Angler the correspondence and Angler shipped to Regal 800 pounds of the hamburger on October 29. Regal accepted the 800 pounds. Regal, then, on October 31 orally rejected the shipment for the remaining 700 pounds. Under these facts, the contract is enforceable against Regal for the 800 pounds but not the full 1,500 pounds.	O	O
15.	Under the same facts found in **14.** above, the contract is enforceable against Regal for the full 1,500 pounds.	O	O

Simulation Problem 2   (5 to 10 minutes)

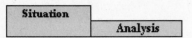

On February 1, Grand Corp., a manufacturer of custom cabinets, contracted in writing with Axle Co., a kitchen contractor, to sell Axle 100 unique, custom-designed, kitchen cabinets for $250,000. Axle had contracted to install the cabinets in a luxury condominium complex. The contract provided that the cabinets were to be ready for delivery by April 15 and were to be shipped FOB seller's loading dock. On April 15, Grand had eighty-five cabinets complete and delivered them, together with fifteen standard cabinets, to the trucking company for delivery to Axle. Grand faxed Axle a copy of the shipping invoice, listing the fifteen standard cabinets. On May 1, before reaching Axle, the truck was involved in a collision and all the cabinets were damaged beyond repair.

Items 1 through 5 refer to the above fact pattern. For each item, determine whether (A), (B), or (C) is correct.

1. ○ A. The contract between Grand and Axle was a shipment contract.
    ○ B. The contract between Grand and Axle was a destination contract.
    ○ C. The contract between Grand and Axle was a consignment contract.

2. ○ A. The risk of loss for the eighty-five custom cabinets passed to Axle on April 15.
    ○ B. The risk of loss for the 100 cabinets passed to Axle on April 15.
    ○ C. The risk of loss for the 100 cabinets remained with Grand.

3. ○ A. The contract between Grand and Axle was invalid because **no** delivery date was stated.
    ○ B. The contract between Grand and Axle was voidable because Grand shipped only eighty-five custom cabinets.
    ○ C. The contract between Grand and Axle was void because the goods were destroyed.

4. ○ A. Grand's shipment of the standard cabinets was a breach of the contract with Axle.
    ○ B. Grand would **not** be considered to have breached the contract until Axle rejected the standard cabinets.
    ○ C. Grand made a counteroffer by shipping the standard cabinets.

5. ○ A. Axle is entitled to specific performance from Grand because of the unique nature of the goods.
    ○ B. Axle is required to purchase substitute goods (cover) and is entitled to the difference in cost from Grand.
    ○ C. Axle is entitled to punitive damages because of Grand's intentional shipment of nonconforming goods.

1. c __ __	11. d __ __	21. d __ __	31. d __ __	41. a __ __
2. b __ __	12. a __ __	22. d __ __	32. d __ __	42. c __ __
3. c __ __	13. b __ __	23. d __ __	33. b __ __	43. b __ __
4. a __ __	14. d __ __	24. c __ __	34. a __ __	44. d __ __
5. a __ __	15. d __ __	25. d __ __	35. b __ __	45. d __ __
6. a __ __	16. c __ __	26. b __ __	36. b __ __	46. c __ __
7. c __ __	17. a __ __	27. c __ __	37. b __ __	47. c __ __
8. a __ __	18. b __ __	28. d __ __	38. a __ __	
9. d __ __	19. a __ __	29. a __ __	39. a __ __	1st: __/47 = __%
10. a __ __	20. b __ __	30. c __ __	40. b __ __	2nd: __/47 = __%

MULTIPLE-CHOICE ANSWER EXPLANATIONS

A. Contracts for Sale of Goods

1. **(c)** Under the Sales Article of the UCC, acceptance is valid when sent if a reasonable method is used; therefore answer (c) is correct as both acceptances were sent prior to the end of the ten-day period.

2. **(b)** A firm offer is a written, signed offer concerning the sale of goods, by a merchant, giving assurance that it will be held open for a specified time and is irrevocable for that period, not to exceed three months. Answer (a) is incorrect because if the firm offer does not state a period of time, it will remain open for a reasonable period of time, not to exceed three months. Answer (c) is incorrect as consideration is not required for a firm offer, but for an option contract. Answer (d) is incorrect because under the firm offer rule, only the offeror need be a merchant.

3. **(c)** Under the UCC, an oral modification of an existing contract for the sale of goods for a price less than $500 is considered binding. Since the washer and dryer Mason contracted to buy cost less than $500, Acme's oral agreement to change the date of delivery would be enforceable. The fact that Mason is not a merchant won't affect whether or not the oral modification is binding. In order to have a firm offer, the offer must be made by a merchant in a signed writing which gives assurance that the offer will be held open. In this situation, the modification of an offer already accepted is being discussed rather than a firm offer.

4. **(a)** Under the Sales Article of the UCC, both the seller and buyer are obligated to perform a contract in good faith. Answer (b) is incorrect because certain provisions, such as the battle of forms provision, only apply to merchants. Answer (c) is incorrect because the Sales Article of the UCC applies to the sale of goods without regard to the price of goods. Answer (d) is incorrect because certain provisions of the UCC may be disclaimed by written or oral agreement, such as warranty liability.

5. **(a)** Article 2 of the UCC applies to sales of goods. Common law generally applies to contracts for services and real estate. Even though goods are used in this service contract, the predominate feature of this contract is the service. Article 2 of the UCC governs this contract even though it is oral and for a small sum. Even though the chair at one time involved a lot of labor, it is still a sale of goods. Also, whether the parties are merchants or not is not an issue on whether Article 2 applies. The heater which is not yet installed in the home is a sale of goods. Once it is installed in the home, it becomes part of the real estate for any future

sale of the home. Common law rules would apply to any such future sale.

6. **(a)** Under common law, an acceptance must be unequivocal and unqualified in agreeing to the precise terms specified by the offer. However, the Uniform Commercial Code alters this general rule as far as the sales of goods is concerned. Under the UCC, an acceptance containing additional terms is a valid acceptance unless the acceptance is expressly conditional upon the offeror's agreement to the additional terms. In this situation, a valid contract has been formed between Cookie Co. and Distrib Markets. Distrib Markets' acceptance was not conditional upon Cookie's agreement to the additional term and, thus, a contract is formed regardless of Cookie's agreement or objection to the additional term. This contract was for the sale of goods and is governed by the UCC rather than by common law. Under common law, Distrib Markets' reply would have been a rejection and counteroffer; but under the UCC, a contract was formed.

7. **(c)** This exception for specially manufactured goods, even if the contract is for over $500, is one of the important exceptions found in the Statute of Fraud provisions of the Uniform Commercial Code. Answer (a) is incorrect because the exception for specially manufactured goods applies to this fact pattern and thus this contract need not be in writing. Answer (b) is incorrect because the fire did not prevent the custom door contract from being performed. Answer (d) is incorrect because the contract was fully enforceable and Art had no legal right to cancel the contract.

8. **(a)** Ram may accept the offer by shipping the goods. Under the UCC, shipping nonconforming goods constitutes an acceptance, also unless the seller notifies the buyer that the shipment is given only as an accommodation to the buyer. Answer (b) is incorrect because this shipment counts as an acceptance, not as a counteroffer. Answer (c) is incorrect because an order to buy goods for prompt shipment allows the seller to accept by either a prompt promise to ship or by the actual prompt shipment itself.

9. **(d)** In order to have a contract, there must be both an offer and an acceptance. Even though an acceptance can occur in different ways, by speech, by writing, or by action, the actual acceptance is a required element of a contract. Under the UCC Sales Article, a binding contract may be present if the parties had intended to form a contract even though certain elements of the contract are missing. These open terms will be filled by specific provisions of the UCC, including provisions for open price, open delivery, or open quantity. Note that in the case of quantity, output contracts, requirements contracts, and exclusive dealing's contracts are enforceable though the actual quantity may not be known in advance.

10. **(a)** The UCC provides that a confirmation satisfies the UCC Statute of Frauds, if an oral contract between merchants is confirmed in writing within a reasonable period of time, and the confirmation is signed by the party sending it and received by the other party. Both parties are bound unless the party receiving the confirmation submits a written objection within ten days of receipt. In this situation, a valid contract has been formed since Webstar did not object to Northco's purchase order. In a sale-of-goods transaction, the contract must be signed by the party to be charged to be enforceable. However, in the case of a written confirmation of an oral agreement between merchants, the confirmation need only be signed by the party sending the confirmation. The use of a signed purchase order satisfies the UCC Statute of Frauds.

11. **(d)** A firm offer is an offer for the sale of goods that is written and signed by a merchant (or employee of the merchant) that agrees to keep the offer open. This offer is valid without consideration for three months since no time was specified in the fact pattern. Patch will win in a suit to enforce the rain check because Patch tried to use it one month later. Answer (a) is incorrect because the UCC specifies a three-month period when no time is detailed in the firm offer. Answer (b) is incorrect because when no time is specified, the UCC gives Patch three months to accept the offer. Answer (c) is incorrect because there was no offer and acceptance when Patch first tried to purchase the advertised item.

12. **(a)** An output contract is enforceable under the UCC even though an actual quantity is not mentioned in the contract. The output contract is supported by consideration because the seller has agreed not to sell that output to any other party. Answer (b) is incorrect because when the price is omitted, the UCC construes it as the reasonable price at the time of delivery. The quantity is construed as the output of the sheep rancher. Answer (c) is incorrect because although quantity is an important term in the contract, the UCC allows the quantity term to be defined by output. Answer (d) is incorrect because the UCC allows price terms to be based on the reasonable price and quantity terms to be defined by output.

B.1.a.   Warranty of Title

13. **(b)** Under the warranty of title, the seller warrants good title, rightful transfer and freedom from any security interest or lien of which the buyer has no knowledge at the time of sale. Answer (a) is incorrect because the warranty of title can be disclaimed by specific language or circumstances which give the buyer reason to know s/he is receiving less than full title. Answer (c) is incorrect because the warranty does not have to be in writing. Answer (d) is incorrect because the seller does not have to be a merchant for the seller to give the warranty of title.

B.1.b.   Express Warranties

14. **(d)** In the Sales Article of the UCC, express warranties include warranties that the goods will conform to any description used or any sample or model shown. Answer (a)

is incorrect because although usage of trade can help interpret terms used in contracts, it is not a warranty. Answers (b) and (c) are incorrect because the warranty of fitness for a particular purpose and the warranty of merchantability are both implied warranties.

B.1.c.   Implied Warranties

15. **(d)** The implied warranty of merchantability, which guarantees that goods are fit for ordinary purposes, arises as a matter of law when the seller is a merchant who ordinarily sells the goods purchased. Answer (a) is incorrect because the warranty is implied, and therefore need not be in writing. Answer (c) is incorrect because the warranty applies unless specifically disclaimed by the merchant.

16. **(c)** The implied warranty of merchantability is always implied if the seller is a merchant with respect to the type of goods being sold. Since Ram is a merchant, this warranty would apply. Also, under the UCC, the seller warrants good title, rightful transfer, and freedom from any security interest or lien of which the buyer has no knowledge when the contract was made. This warranty of title applies unless the merchant specifically disclaims it. In this situation, both the implied warranty of merchantability and the implied warranty of title apply. The implied warranty of fitness for a particular purpose is created only when a seller has reason to know the buyer's particular purpose and knows the buyer is relying on the skill and judgment of the seller selecting the goods.

17. **(a)** The implied warranty of merchantability applies only when the seller is a merchant with respect to the type of goods being sold. The seller must be a merchant in order for the buyer to successfully sue under this warranty. Answer (b) is incorrect because the buyer does not have to prove negligence to be able to recover under this implied warranty. Answer (c) is incorrect because the implied warranty of merchantability extends to parties other than the purchaser even without privity of contract. Answer (d) is incorrect because an action for a breach based on the warranty of merchantability would not depend on the outcome of an action based on strict liability.

18. **(b)** The implied warranty of fitness for a particular purpose is created when a seller (merchant or nonmerchant) has reason to know the buyer's particular purpose and knows the buyer is relying on the skill and judgment of the seller selecting the goods. Since the warranty of fitness for a particular purpose is an implied warranty, there is no requirement that it be made in writing.

19. **(a)** The implied warranty of merchantability may be disclaimed by a seller's oral or written statement. This statement normally must contain some form of the word "merchantability" to be effective. However, goods sold "as is" or "with all faults" are an exception to that rule. Answer (b) is incorrect because the implied warranty of merchantability arises whenever the seller is a merchant with respect to the goods being sold. The status of the buyer is irrelevant. Answer (c) is incorrect because the implied warranty of merchantability guarantees that the goods are of an average fair quality and are fit for ordinary purposes. Under this warranty, the seller does not guarantee that the goods are fit for all purposes for which the buyer intends to use the goods. Answer (d) is incorrect because this warranty is always implied if the seller is a merchant. It does not have to be a part of the basis of the bargain to be binding on the seller.

B.3.   Strict Liability

20.   (b)   Common carriers' liability is based on strict liability. As such, the common carrier is liable for losses to property whether or not the common carrier was negligent. Common law exceptions to strict liability include natural disasters which are responsible for damages.

21.   (d)   Under the theory of strict liability, the plaintiff must establish the following: (1) the seller was engaged in the business of selling the product, (2) the product was defective, (3) the defect was unreasonably dangerous to the plaintiff, and (4) the defect caused injury to the plaintiff. If the plaintiff can prove these elements, then the seller will be liable regardless of whether the seller was negligent or at fault for the defect. Thus, High can recover even if he cannot show any negligence was involved. Answer (a) is incorrect because contributory negligence is not an available defense in a strict liability case. Answer (b) is incorrect because the manufacturer's only defenses are misuse and assumption of risk by the buyer. The fact that the manufacturer followed the custom of the industry is irrelevant under strict liability. Answer (c) is incorrect because privity of contract is not a defense under strict liability since the suit is not based on contract law.

22.   (d)   Under the theory of strict liability, the plaintiff must establish the following: (1) the seller was engaged in the business of selling the product, (2) the product was defective when sold, (3) the defect was unreasonably dangerous to the plaintiff, and (4) the defect caused injury to the plaintiff. If the plaintiff can prove these elements, then the seller will be liable regardless of whether the seller was negligent or at fault for the defect.

23.   (d)   The standard of care required for a common carrier bailee is based on strict liability rather than reasonable care. Common carrier bailees, however, are not liable for acts of God, acts of the shipper, or acts of a public enemy. In this case, the improper packing was done by the party doing the shipping. Answer (a) is incorrect because acts or theft by other parties make the common carrier liable. Answer (b) is incorrect because acts such as negligence, by others, still leave the common carrier liable. Answer (c) is incorrect because acts of a railroad employee cause the common carrier to be liable.

C.   Transfer of Property Rights

24.   (c)   Since Rio was a good-faith purchaser, Rio obtains good title to the rocking chair. Therefore, the remedy that Tillis has left is to sue McGraw for money damages. There are insufficient facts to show fraud.

25.   (d)   If a person entrusts possession of goods to a merchant who normally deals in that type of goods, a good-faith purchaser obtains title to those goods. Jake purchased the bike as he was unaware that Pete did not own the bike. As a good-faith purchaser, he obtains title to the bike. Answer (a) is incorrect because Yancie cannot repossess the bike from Jake because Jake obtained good title to the bike. Yancie can, however, get the value of the bike from Pete. Answer (b) is incorrect because Jake obtains title to the bike

and, thus, Pete cannot repossess it from him. Answer (c) is incorrect because Yancie can recover the value of the bike from Pete, not Jake.

26.   (b)   A requirement needed for the title of goods to pass to the buyer is that the goods must have been identified to the contract. Answers (a) and (c) are incorrect because the seller can keep possession of goods and identify them to the contract and still have title pass to the buyer. Answer (d) is incorrect because title passes to the buyer based upon the terms of the agreement. Payment can take place before or after.

D.   Risk of Loss and Title

27.   (c)   In an FOB place of shipment contract, the buyer obtains the risk of loss once the goods are delivered to the carrier.

28.   (d)   The title of goods generally passes to the buyer when the seller completes performance with respect to the physical delivery of the goods. Because the shipping terms of the contract are FOB Parco's warehouse, the title of goods passes to Parco on tender at the destination. This is true even if the goods are nonconforming. However, Parco's rejection of the appliances will revert the title of the goods back to Lace at the time of the rejection.

29.   (a)   Under the Sales Article of the Uniform Commercial Code and the United Nations Convention for the International Sale of Goods, generally the risk of loss of the goods sold will pass to the buyer when the seller delivers goods to the first carrier for transmission to the buyer. Answers (b), (c), and (d) are incorrect because these would result in risk of loss to the buyer only if the contract specifically stated so, thus changing the general rule.

30.   (c)   The purchase of goods on a sale on approval allows the buyer to return the goods even if they conform to the contract. Therefore, the seller retains the title and the risk of loss until the buyer accepts the goods.

31.   (d)   Risk of loss transfers from a merchant seller to a buyer upon the buyer's physical receipt of goods. Therefore, neither tender of the goods at the seller's place of business, nor use of the seller's truck to deliver the goods are events which transfer risk of loss to the buyer as the merchant seller still retains possession of the goods.

32.   (d)   The UCC places risk of loss on the breaching party. Since Cey shipped nonconforming goods, it breached the contract and would have risk of loss until the nonconforming goods were accepted by the buyer or until the goods were cured by Cey. Since Deck rejected the goods and Cey did not cure the goods, risk of loss remained with Cey. Shipping terms have no bearing on risk of loss in this situation because the goods did not conform to the contract. Answer (a) is incorrect because Deck would only bear risk of loss if the goods conformed to the contract. Answer (b) is incorrect because the risk of loss was never transferred to Deck since the goods were nonconforming. Answer (c) is incorrect because if the goods were conforming, risk of loss would pass to Deck at Cey's warehouse based on the shipping terms "FOB Cey's warehouse."

33. **(b)**   The parties to the contract may agree as to which party bears risk of loss. In the absence of this, under the UCC, the shipping terms determine who bears risk of loss.

34. **(a)**   In this situation, since Wool is not a merchant seller, the risk of loss passed to Bond on Wool's tender of delivery. If Wool had been a merchant seller, then the risk of loss would not have passed until the buyer received the goods. Answers (c) and (d) are incorrect because the risk of loss passed when the nonmerchant seller (Wool) tendered delivery of the painting. Answer (b) is incorrect because the risk of loss would not pass at the time the contract was formed since the seller still had possession of the painting and had not attempted to deliver it to the buyer.

35. **(b)**   Common carriers are not liable for losses due to causes deemed acts of God. Although a common carrier may limit its damages to a dollar amount specified in the contract, it is not liable at all in this case. Funston, not the customer, had the risk of loss due to the FOB terms.

E.5. Seller's Remedies

36. **(b)**   Statement I is incorrect because a liquidated damages provision is enforced if it is not punitive but amounts to a reasonable estimate of what the loss will be in the event of a breach of contract. If a reasonable estimate of the loss from a breach of contract cannot be estimated with a reasonable degree of certainty, the parties can agree on an amount, but still the amount cannot be punitive. Statement II is correct because a seller is allowed to retain a deposit of up to $500 when a buyer defaults even if the parties had not agreed to a liquidated damages clause.

37. **(b)**   The seller generally discharges his obligation to the buyer by placing conforming goods at the buyer's disposition and giving the buyer reasonable notice to enable the buyer to take delivery.

38. **(a)**   Under the Sales Article of the UCC, the seller has the following remedies against the buyer upon breach: withhold delivery of the goods; stop delivery of the carrier of the goods; resell the goods; recover compensatory and incidental damages; recover the goods from the buyer upon the buyer's insolvency; cancel the contract. Therefore, answer (a) is correct as the seller has the rights of contract cancellation and damage recovery available to him/her.

39. **(a)**   The UCC gives the seller a choice of many remedies when the buyer breaches the contract involving a sale of goods. These remedies include allowing the seller to resell the goods identified to the contract and to recover the amount that the seller receives that is less than the contract price. Also, once the buyer breaches, the seller may suspend his/her performance and may prevent the carrier from making the delivery of the goods.

40. **(b)**   A seller has the right to resell goods to another if the buyer refuses to accept the goods upon delivery. Answer (a) is incorrect because specific performance is not a remedy available to the seller. Baker cannot force Lazur to accept the word processor. Answer (c) is incorrect because Baker has a couple of additional remedies available. Baker can recover the full contract price plus incidental damages if he is unable to resell the identified goods. Alternatively, if the difference between the market value and contract price is inadequate to place Baker in as good a position as performance would have, then Baker can sue for lost profits plus incidental damages. Answer (d) is incorrect because Baker could sue for consequential damages that Lazur had reason to know Baker would incur as a result of Lazur's breach.

41. **(a)**   By advising Mazur on June 1 that it would not accept or pay for the wheat, Good has engaged in anticipatory repudiation. Anticipatory repudiation occurs when a party renounces the duty to perform the contract before the party's obligation to perform arises. Anticipatory repudiation discharges the nonrepudiating party (Mazur) from the contract and allows this party to sue for breach immediately. In this situation, Mazur could successfully sue Good for the difference between the resale price and the contract price on June 2. Answer (b) is incorrect because Mazur was discharged from the contract on June 1 and would not have to wait until after June 23 to resell the wheat. Answer (c) is incorrect because Good would only be allowed to retract its anticipatory breach if Mazur had ignored this breach and awaited performance at the appointed date. Answer (d) is incorrect because specific performance is only allowed for unique goods or for other situations in which monetary damages are not appropriate.

E.6. Buyer's Remedies

42. **(c)**   Pickens has committed an anticipatory breach of contract. Thus, Crocket, as the aggrieved party, has different options. Crocket may treat it as a present breach of contract with the remedies available for breach of contract. One of these remedies is that the aggrieved party (Crocket) may cancel the contract. Another option is that Crocket may wait for a reasonable time to see if Pickens will change his/her mind and still deliver.

43. **(b)**   The buyer has the following remedies against the seller: upon receipt of nonconforming goods, the buyer may reject the goods, accept the goods, or accept any unit and reject the remainder; the buyer has the right to cover (purchase goods elsewhere upon the seller's breach); the buyer may recover damages (not punitive) for nondelivery of goods or repudiation of the sales contract by the seller; the buyer may recover damages (not punitive) for breach in regard to accepted goods; the buyer may recover goods identified in the contract in possession of the seller upon the seller's insolvency; the buyer may sue for specific performance when the goods are unique; the buyer has the right of replevin (form of legal action to recover specific goods from the seller which are being withheld from the buyer wrongfully); the buyer can cancel the contract; the buyer has a security interest in the goods after the seller's breach; the buyer can recover liquidated damages.

44. **(d)**   UCC Section 2-719(3) states that a limitation of damages for personal injury **in the case of consumer goods** is considered to be unconscionable and thus not allowed. Although limitations of damages for personal injury in the case of nonconsumer goods can be allowed, answer (d) is correct since one limits "personal injury" to the stove which was apparently being used for consumer use in this fact pattern. Answer (a) is incorrect because under the UCC, the spouse, being a member of the household expecting to use the stove, may recover for damages. Answer (b) is incorrect because Larch was notified shortly after the explosion. This notice, however, was not required. Answer (c) is incorrect because even though the disclaimer did not disclaim all liability, it did attempt to disclaim personal injury. This disclaimer for personal injuries, however, is not allowed for the reasons mentioned above. Answer (d) is chosen as being more specific than answer (c).

45. **(d)** Either party in a sales contract under the Sales Article of the UCC may demand adequate assurance of performance when reasonable grounds for insecurity exist with respect to the performance of the other party. Refusal to give written assurance will release the other party from all obligations from the sales contract. Answer (a) is incorrect because the buyer has assumed the risk of loss. Answer (b) is incorrect because a seller may substitute another reasonable delivery method if the method of delivery specified in the contract has been made impracticable. A seller may recover damages based on a buyer's repudiation of the agreement, but here the repudiation has been retracted and the obligations of buyer and seller remain intact.

46. **(c)** The Sales Article of the UCC provides that a buyer has the right to reject goods which are not in conformity with the terms of contract between seller and buyer. The buyer also has the option to accept nonconforming goods and recover damages resulting from the nonconformity. The UCC allows the buyer to inspect the goods before payment except when they are shipped COD. When goods are shipped COD, the buyer's payment for the goods is required for delivery.

E.7. Statute of Limitations

47. **(c)** The statute of limitations for the sale of goods is generally four years; however, the parties may agree to reduce the statute to a period of not less than one year. Therefore, Sklar will lose because the clause providing that the statute of limitations would be limited to eighteen months is enforceable, and the action was not brought within the required time period. Answer (b) is incorrect because a breach of warranty occurs upon the tender of delivery, not upon the discovery of the defect, and the statute begins running at the time the breach occurs. Answer (d) is incorrect because the statute is eighteen months as outlined in the contract.

ANSWER OUTLINE

Problem 1   Statute of Frauds under UCC; Firm Offer;
                Acceptance with Different Terms

a.   Rapid's claim is incorrect
        An oral contract between merchants under the UCC
           is binding even if the party that receives the con-
           firmation fails to sign it
           Signature is only required of party that sends the
              confirmation
        Receiving party will not be bound if written objec-
           tion to confirmation made within ten days of re-
           ceipt
           Rapid did not make a written objection so will be
              bound to oral contract

b.   Debco's first claim is incorrect
        Debco's October 12 purchase order is a firm offer
           under the UCC because:
           • Debco is merchant
           • Purchase order is written and signed
           • Purchase order states it will not be withdrawn
              for time specified
        A firm offer cannot be revoked
           Debco's October 25 attempt will be ineffective
     Debco's second claim is incorrect
        Acceptance of an offer is effective when sent if us-
           ing a reasonable method
           TMI's acceptance was effective when mailed on
              October 31
     Debco's third claim is incorrect
        Acceptance is effective even if terms are different
           from offer if expression to accept is definite
           TMI's October 31 acceptance was effective de-
              spite additional payment terms

UNOFFICIAL ANSWER

Problem 1   Statute of Frauds under UCC; Firm Offer;
                Acceptance with Different Terms

a.   Rapid's claim is incorrect. Both Debco and Rapid are
merchants under the UCC because they both deal in the type
of goods involved in the transaction (computers).
     The UCC provides that a confirmation satisfies the
UCC Statute of Frauds, if an oral contract between merchants is

     •   Confirmed in writing within a reasonable period of
time, and
     •   The confirmation is signed by the party sending it
and received by the other party

     Both parties are bound even though the party receiving
the confirmation fails to sign it. This is correct unless the
party receiving the confirmation submits a written objection
within ten days of receipt. Rapid will be bound even though
it did not sign the confirmation because no written objection
was made.

b.   Debco's first claim, that its October 25 correspondence
prevented the formation of a contract, is incorrect. Debco's
October 12 purchase order will be regarded as a firm offer
under the UCC because:

     • Debco is a merchant.
     • The purchase order is in writing and signed.
     • The purchase order states that it will not be with-
       drawn for the time specified.

     Because Debco's October 12 purchase order is consid-
ered a firm offer, Debco cannot revoke it, and its October 25
attempt to do so is ineffective.
     Debco's second claim, that TMI's October 31 corre-
spondence is not an effective acceptance because it was not
received until November 3, is incorrect. An acceptance of
an offer is effective when dispatched (in this case, when
mailed), provided that an appropriate mode of communication is used. The UCC provides that an offer shall be construed as inviting acceptance in any manner and by any medium reasonable in the circumstances. In this case, Debco
made its offer by mail, which, if adequately addressed with
proper postage affixed, would be considered a reasonable
manner and medium for acceptance. As a result, TMI's
acceptance was effective when mailed on October 31.
     Debco's third claim, that TMI's acceptance is not ef-
fective because it added payment terms to Debco's offer, is
also incorrect. The UCC provides that a definite and timely
expression of acceptance of an offer will form a contract,
even if the terms of the acceptance are different from those
in the offer, unless acceptance is expressly made conditional
on accepting the different terms. Therefore, TMI's October 31 correspondence, which expressly stated that TMI
would ship the computers ordered by Debco, was an effective acceptance, and a contract was formed despite the fact
that TMI added payment terms.

SOLUTIONS TO SIMULATION PROBLEMS

Simulation Problem 1

1.   (C) Angler breached the contract by shipping nonconforming goods to Mason. Therefore, Angler retains the risk of loss until it cures or until Mason accepts the goods despite the nonconformity.

2.   (I) This was an FOB shipping point contract so that the risk of loss would have passed over to the buyer upon delivery to the carrier.

3.   (I) Because the terms were FOB the seller's loading dock, it was an FOB shipping point contract.

4.   (I) Title and risk of loss do not necessarily pass to a buyer at the same time. In this case, risk of loss remained with the seller because of the shipment of nonconforming goods. However, title passed under the original terms despite the breach of contract.

5.   (C) Classic is obligated to follow any reasonable instructions of the seller as a merchant who rejects goods, even nonconforming, under a contract.

6.   (I) Classic must follow the reasonable instructions given by Angler to return the peaches at Angler's expense.

7.   (I) Classic may also sue for any damages that were caused by the delay in shipping.

8.   (I) Although the contract must be evidenced by a writing because it involved a sale of goods for more than $500, the correspondence that Regal sent to Angler on October 29 satisfies the writing requirement under the UCC Statute of Frauds. It indicated that a contract had been made. It was signed by Regal, the party to be charged, and it stated the quantity. The price was not needed in the correspondence.

9.   (C) The Uniform Commercial Code applies because the contract was for a sale of goods (i.e., hamburger meat).

10.   (C) The correspondence satisfies the UCC Statute of Frauds which does not require that all terms be in writing.

11.   (I) Angler should resort to an appropriate remedy such as reselling the hamburger to someone else in a commercially reasonable fashion. If Angler gets less than the original contract price, it may recover the difference from Regal.

12.   (I) Since there was no writing to evidence the contract for $1,500, it is not enforceable.

13.   (C) The contract need not be in writing because it was for less than $500.

14.   (C) Since Angler shipped and Regal accepted a portion of the goods, the oral contract is enforceable up to the amount shipped and accepted. This is one of the exceptions in the UCC Statute of Frauds.

15.   (I) The exception in the UCC Statute of Frauds allows the oral contract to be enforced up to the amount delivered and accepted or paid for.

Simulation Problem 2

1. **(A)** The terms of the contract were "FOB seller's loading dock" which is a shipment contract. Answer (B) is incorrect because a destination contract would state terms meaning FOB buyer's location. Answer (C) is incorrect because a consignment is treated as a sale or return. That is, the owner of the goods delivers them to another party to attempt to sell them. If this other party, known as the consignee, does not sell the goods, they are returned. Such is not the case in this fact pattern.

2. **(C)** Risk of loss would normally pass to the buyer, Axle Co., under this shipment contract. However, since the seller, Grand, breached the contract, risk of loss remains with Grand. Since the cabinets are "custom designed, kitchen cabinets" for a luxury condominium complex, they would need to match. Therefore, the 100 units could be construed as a commercial unit and the risk of loss for the entire 100 cabinets remained with Grand. Answer (A) is incorrect because the 100 cabinets were a commercial unit and thus the risk of loss of the entire commercial unit remained with Grand. Answer (B) is incorrect because even though the terms were "FOB seller's loading dock," the risk of loss remained with the seller, Grand, because of Grand's breach of contract.

3. **(B)** The contract between Grand and Axle was voidable because Axle may at its option choose to accept or reject all or part of the cabinets. Answer (C) is incorrect because if the contract were void, neither party would have the option of remaining in the contract. Answer (A) is incorrect because under the UCC, if the delivery date is not stated, the time becomes within a reasonable time.

4. **(A)** Once Grand ships nonconforming goods, a breach of contract has occurred. Answer (B) is incorrect because the breach has occurred even without Axle needing to reject the shipment. Axle then has the right to accept all, part, or none of the shipment. Answer (C) is incorrect because the shipment of nonconforming goods acts as a breach rather than a counteroffer.

5. **(A)** Since the cabinets are unique and custom-designed, specific performance is allowed if Axle so chooses. Answer (B) is incorrect because Axle is not required to cover, especially because the cabinets are unique. Answer (C) is incorrect because punitive damages are generally not allowed for a breach of contract even if the breach is intentional.

COMMERCIAL PAPER

Overview

Commercial paper is heavily tested on the CPA exam. Coverage includes the types of negotiable instruments, the requirements of negotiability, negotiation, the holder in due course concept, defenses, and the rights of parties to a negotiable instrument. The functions of commercial paper are to provide a medium of exchange that is readily transferable like money and to provide an extension of credit. It is easier to transfer than contract rights and not subject to as many defenses as contracts are. To be negotiable, an instrument must

a. Be written
b. Be signed by the maker or drawer
c. Contain an unconditional promise or order to pay
d. State a fixed amount in money
e. Be payable on demand or at definite time
f. Be payable to order or bearer

These requirements must be present on the face of the instrument. Instruments that do not comply with these provisions are nonnegotiable and are transferable only by assignment. The assignee of a nonnegotiable instrument takes it subject to all defenses.

A central theme of exam questions on negotiable instruments is the liability of the primary parties and of the secondarily liable parties under various fact situations. Similar questions in different form emphasize the rights that a holder of a negotiable instrument has against primary and secondary parties. Your review of this area should emphasize the legal liability arising upon execution of negotiable commercial paper, the legal liability arising upon various types of endorsements, and the warranty liabilities of various parties upon transfer or presentment for payment. A solid understanding of the distinction between real and personal defenses is required. Also tested is the relationship between a bank and its customers.

A. General Concepts of Commercial Paper

1. Commercial paper has two important functions

    a. Used as a substitute for money

    EXAMPLE: *One often pays a bill with a check instead of using cash.*

    b. Used as extension of credit

    EXAMPLE: *X gives a promissory note to Y for $100 that is due one year later.*

2. To encourage commercial paper to be transferred more easily by making it easier to be collected, **negotiable** commercial paper was established

    a. If an instrument is negotiable, favorable laws of Article 3 of UCC apply as discussed in this module

    b. If an instrument is nonnegotiable, laws of ordinary contract law apply (i.e., assignment of contract rights)

       (1) Assignees of contract rights can get only the rights given by the assignor and therefore are burdened by any defenses between prior parties

       EXAMPLE: *C receives a nonnegotiable instrument from B. C now wishes to collect from A, the one who had issued the nonnegotiable note to B when he purchased some goods from B. Assume that A would have owed B only two-thirds of the amount stated on the instrument due to defects in the goods. Since C obtained only the rights that B had under an assignment under contract law, C can only collect two-thirds from A on this nonnegotiable instrument.*

3. It is helpful to get "the big picture" of negotiable instruments (negotiable commercial paper) before covering details

    a. Whether an instrument is negotiable or not is determined by looking at its form and content on the face of the instrument

       (1) This is so that individuals seeing an instrument can determine whether it is negotiable or not
       (2) If a person has a negotiable instrument and also is a holder in due course (discussed later), s/he may collect on instrument despite most defenses that may be raised such as contract defenses

B. Types of Commercial Paper

1. Article 3 of UCC describes two types of negotiable commercial paper

    a. A draft (also called bill of exchange)

(1) Has three parties in which one person or entity (drawer) orders another (drawee) to pay a third party (payee) a sum of money

EXAMPLE:

> *June 5, 2002*
>
> *On June 5, 2003, pay to the order of Bob Smith $1,000 plus 10% annual interest from June 5, 2002.*
>
> *To: ABC Corporation*
>
> *(Signed) Sue Van Deventer*

The above is a draft in which Sue Van Deventer is the drawer, ABC Corporation is the drawee, and Bob Smith is the payee

(a) A check

1] Is a special type of draft that is payable on demand (unless postdated) and drawee must be a bank

a] Definition of bank includes savings and loan associations, credit unions, and trust companies

2] One writing check is drawer (and customer of drawee bank)

b. A note (also called a promissory note)

(1) Unlike a draft or check, is a two-party instrument

(a) One party is called the maker—this party promises to pay a specified sum of money to another party called the payee

EXAMPLE:

> *July 10, 2002*
>
> *I promise to pay to the order of Becky Hoger $5,000 plus 10% annual interest on July 10, 2003.*
>
> *(Signed) Bill Jones*

The above is a note in which Bill Jones is the maker and Becky Hoger is the payee.

(2) May be payable on demand or at a definite time

(a) Certificate of deposit (CD)

1] Is an acknowledgment by a financial institution of receipt of money and promise to repay it

a] Most CDs are commercial paper so that they can be easily transferred

2] Is actually a special type of note in which financial institution is the maker

C. Requirements of Negotiability

1. All of the following requirements must be on face of instrument for it to be a negotiable instrument (be sure to know these)
2. To be negotiable, the instrument must

a. Be written
b. Be signed by maker or drawer
c. Contain an unconditional promise or order to pay
d. State a fixed amount in money
e. Be payable on demand or at a definite time
f. Be payable to order or to bearer, unless it is a check

3. Details of requirements of negotiability

a. **Must be in writing**

   (1) Satisfied by printing, typing, handwriting or any other reduction to physical form that is relatively permanent and portable

b. **Must be signed by maker (of a note or CD) or drawer (of a draft or check)**

   (1) Signature includes any symbol used with intent to authenticate instrument

      (a) Rubber stamp, initials, letterhead satisfy signing requirement
      (b) Assumed name or trade name operates as that party's signature
      (c) Signature may be anywhere on face of instrument

c. **Must contain an unconditional promise or order to pay**

   (1) If payment depends upon (is subject to) another agreement or event, then it is conditional and therefore destroys negotiability

   EXAMPLE: An instrument that is otherwise negotiable states that it is subject to a particular contract. This condition destroys the negotiability of this instrument.

   EXAMPLE: An instrument states: "I, Janice Jones, promise to pay to the order of Richard Riley, $1,000 if the stereo delivered to me is not defective." This instrument is not negotiable whether the stereo is defective or not because it contains a conditional promise.

      (a) However, the following are permitted and do not destroy negotiability

         1] Instrument may state its purpose

            EXAMPLE: On a check, the drawer writes "for purchase of textbooks."

         2] Instrument may refer to or state that it arises from another agreement
         3] Instrument is permitted to show that it is secured by a mortgage or by collateral
         4] Instrument is permitted to contain promise to provide extra collateral
         5] Instrument is permitted to limit payment out of particular fund

   (2) An IOU is not a promise or order to pay but an acknowledgement of debt, thus, an IOU is not negotiable

d. **Must state a fixed amount in money—called sum certain under former law**

   (1) Amount of principal but not interest must be determinable from instrument without need to refer to other sources

      (a) Stated interest rates are allowed because amount can be calculated

         EXAMPLE: A negotiable note states that $1,000 is due one year from October 1, 2001 at 14% interest.

         EXAMPLE: A note states that $1,000 is payable on demand and bears interest at 14%. This also is negotiable because once payment is demanded, the amount of interest can be calculated.

         1] Variable interest rates are allowed and do not now destroy negotiability even if formula for interest rate or amount requires reference to information outside of negotiable instrument

            EXAMPLE: The following do not destroy negotiability in an otherwise negotiable instrument: Interest rates tied to some published key interest rate, consumer index market rate, etc.

         2] If interest rate based on legal rate or judgment rate (fixed by statute), then negotiability not destroyed

      (b) Stated different rates of interest before and after default or specified dates are allowed
      (c) Stated discounts or additions if instrument paid before or after payment dates do not destroy negotiability
      (d) Clauses allowing collection costs and attorney's fees upon default are allowed because they reduce the risk of holding instruments and promote transferability
      (e) Must be payable only in money

        1]   Option to be payable in money or something else destroys negotiability because of possibility that payment will not be in money

           EXAMPLE: A note is payable in $1,000 or its equivalent in gold. This note is not negotiable.

        2]   Foreign currency is acceptable even though reference to exchange rates may be needed due to international trade realities

   e.   **Must be payable on demand or at a definite time**

      (1)   On demand includes

        (a)   Payable on sight
        (b)   Payable on presentation
        (c)   No time for payment stated

      (2)   It is a definite time if payable

        (a)   On a certain date, or
        (b)   A fixed period after sight, or
        (c)   Within a certain time, or
        (d)   On a certain date subject to acceleration

           1]   For example, when a payment is missed, total balance may become due at once

        (e)   On a certain date subject to an extension of time if

           1]   At option of holder, or
           2]   At option of maker or drawer only if extension is limited to a definite amount of time

      (3)   It is not definite if payable on an act or event that is not certain as to time of occurrence

           EXAMPLE: An instrument contains a clause stating that it is payable ten days after drawer obtains a bank loan. This destroys negotiability.

   f.   **Must be payable to order or to bearer unless it is a check (these are magic words of negotiability and are often a central issue on the CPA exam)**

      (1)   Instrument is payable to order if made payable to the order of

        (a)   Any person, including the maker, drawer, drawee, or payee
        (b)   Two persons together or alternatively
        (c)   Any entity

      (2)   Instrument is also payable to order if it is payable "to A or order"
      (3)   Instrument other than a check is not payable to order if it is only payable to a person (e.g., "Pay John Doe")

           EXAMPLE: A draft that is otherwise negotiable states: "Pay to XYZ Corporation." This statement destroys negotiability because the draft is not payable "to the order of" XYZ Corporation.

        (a)   It is not negotiable
        (b)   "Pay to the order of John Doe" would be negotiable

      (4)   If a **check** says "pay to A," it is negotiable order paper—this is not true of other instruments
      (5)   Instrument is payable to bearer if it is payable to

        (a)   "Bearer"
        (b)   "Cash"
        (c)   "A person or bearer" is bearer paper if "bearer" handwritten

           1]   However, "pay to John Doe, the bearer" is not negotiable because it is not payable to order or to bearer but to a person and simply refers to him as the bearer

        (d)   "Order of bearer" or "order of cash"
        (e)   Pay to the order of (payee left blank) is bearer paper unless holder inserts payee's name

(6) Instrument cannot be made payable to persons consecutively (i.e., maker cannot specify subsequent holders)

D. Interpretation of Ambiguities in Negotiable Instruments

1. Contradictory terms

   a. Words control over figures
   b. Handwritten terms control over typewritten and printed (typeset) terms
   c. Typewritten terms control over printed (typeset) terms

2. Omissions

   a. Omission of date does not destroy negotiability unless date necessary to determine when payable

   EXAMPLE: A check is not dated. It is still negotiable because a check is payable on demand.

   EXAMPLE: A draft states that it is payable thirty days after its date. If the date is left off, it is not payable at a definite time and, therefore, it is not negotiable.

   b. Omission of interest rate is allowed because the judgment rate of interest (rate used on a court judgment) is automatically used
   c. Statement of consideration or where instrument is drawn or payable not required

3. Other issues

   a. Instrument may be postdated or antedated and remain negotiable

   (1) Bank is not liable for damages to customer if it pays on postdated check before date on check unless individual notifies bank not to pay check earlier in a separate written document
   (2) Once customer does this, bank is liable for any damages caused by early payment

   b. Instrument may have a provision that by endorsing or cashing it, the payee acknowledges full satisfaction of debt and remain negotiable
   c. If an instrument is payable to order of more than one person

   (1) Either payee may negotiate or enforce it if payable to him/her in the alternative

   EXAMPLE: "Pay $100 to the order of X or Y." Either X or Y may endorse it.

   (2) All payees must negotiate or enforce it if **not** payable to them in the alternative

   d. If not clear whether instrument is draft or note, holder may treat it as either

E. Negotiation

1. There are two methods of transferring commercial paper

   a. By assignment

   (1) Assignment occurs when transfer does not meet all requirements of negotiation
   (2) Assignee can obtain only same rights that assignor had

   b. By negotiation

   (1) One receiving negotiable instrument by negotiation is called a holder
   (2) If holder further qualifies as a holder in due course (as discussed later) s/he can obtain **more rights** than what transferor had
   (3) There are two methods of negotiation

      (a) Negotiating order paper requires both endorsement by transferor and delivery of instrument

         1] Order paper includes negotiable instruments made payable to the order of X

      (b) Negotiating bearer paper may be accomplished by delivery alone (endorsement not necessary)

      EXAMPLE: A check is made payable to the order of cash.

1] Subsequent parties may require endorsements (even though UCC does not) for identification

2] Holder may, in any event, endorse it if s/he chooses to do so

(4) Endorsement (Indorsement) refers to signature of payee, drawee, accommodation endorser, or holder

2. Types of endorsements

a. Blank endorsement

(1) Does not specify any endorsee

EXAMPLE: *A check made to the order of M on the front can be endorsed in blank by M writing only his signature on the back.*

(2) Converts order paper into bearer paper

(3) Note that bearer paper may be negotiated by mere delivery

EXAMPLE: *B endorses a check in blank that had been made payable to his order. He lost it and C found it who delivered it to D. D is a valid holder since C's endorsement was not required.*

b. Special endorsement

(1) Indicates specific person to whom endorsee wishes to negotiate instrument

EXAMPLE: *On the back of a check payable to the order of M. Jordan he signs as follows: Pay to L. Smith, (signed) M. Jordan.*

(a) Note that words "pay to the order of" are not required on back as endorsements—instrument need be payable to order or to bearer on front only

(b) Also, note that if instrument is not payable to order or to bearer on its face, it **cannot** be turned into a negotiable instrument by using these words in an endorsement on the back

EXAMPLE: *A particular instrument would have been negotiable except that on the front it was payable to A. On the back, A signed it. "Pay to the order of B, (signed) A." This does not convert it into a negotiable instrument.*

(2) Bearer paper may be converted into order paper by use of special endorsement

EXAMPLE: *A check made out to cash is delivered to Carp. Carp writes on the back; Pay to Durn, (signed) Carp. It was bearer paper until this special endorsement.*

EXAMPLE: *Continuing the previous example, Durn simply endorses it in blank. The check is bearer paper again.*

(3) If last (or only) endorsement on instrument is a blank endorsement, any holder may convert that bearer paper into order paper by writing "Pay to X," etc., above that blank endorsement

c. Restrictive endorsement

(1) Requires endorsees to comply with certain conditions

EXAMPLE: *Endorsement reads "For deposit only, (signed) A. Bell."*

EXAMPLE: *Another endorsement reads "Pay to X only if X completes work to my satisfaction on my car within three days of the date on this check, (signed) A." Neither X nor any subsequent holder can enforce payment until this condition has been met.*

(2) Note that conditions in restrictive endorsements do not destroy negotiability even though conditions placed on front of instruments do destroy negotiability because they create conditional promises or orders to pay

(3) Endorsements cannot prohibit subsequent negotiation

EXAMPLE: *Above her endorsement, M wrote: "Pay to N only." This indicates that N is the new endorsee but does not stop further negotiation after N when N endorses.*

d. Qualified endorsement

(1) Normally, endorser, upon signing, promises automatically to pay holder or any subsequent endorser amount of instrument if it is later dishonored

(2) Qualified endorsement disclaims this liability

EXAMPLE: Ann Knolls endorses "Without recourse, (signed) Ann Knolls."

(3) Qualified endorsements, otherwise, have same effects as other endorsements

(4) Combinations of endorsements occur

(a) Special qualified endorsement

EXAMPLE: "Pay to Pete Bell without recourse, (signed) Tom Lack." Tom Lack has limited his liability and also Pete Bell's endorsement is needed to negotiate this instrument further.

(b) Blank qualified endorsement

EXAMPLE: "Without recourse, (signed) D. Hamilton."

(c) Endorsement that is restrictive, qualified, and blank

EXAMPLE: "For deposit only, without recourse, (signed) Bill Coffey."

(d) Endorsement that is restrictive, qualified, and special

EXAMPLE: "Pay to X if she completes work today, without recourse, (signed) D. Magee."

3. If payee's name misspelled, s/he may endorse in proper spelling or misspelling or both

a. But endorsee may require both

4. If an order instrument is transferred for value without endorsement, transferee may require endorsement from transferor

a. Upon obtaining endorsement, will become a holder

5. Federal law standardizes endorsements on checks—endorser should turn check over and sign in designated area

a. Purpose is to avoid interference with bank's endorsements
b. Endorsements placed outside this area do not destroy negotiability but may delay clearing process.

6. If check has statement that it is nonnegotiable, check is still negotiable

a. This is not true of other negotiable instruments whereby such statement destroys negotiability

F. Holder in Due Course

1. Concept of **holder in due course** (also called **HDC**) is very important for CPA exam purposes. A HDC is entitled to payment on negotiable instrument **despite most defenses** that maker or drawer of instrument may have

a. Recall that an assignee of contract rights receives only rights that assignor had (i.e., assignee takes subject to all defenses that could have been asserted against assignor)
b. Likewise, an ordinary holder of a negotiable instrument has same rights as assignee

2. To be holder in due course, a taker of instrument must

a. Be a **holder** of a properly negotiated negotiable instrument
b. Give **value** for instrument

(1) Holder gives value if s/he

(a) Pays or performs agreed consideration

1] An executory promise (promise to give value in the future) is not value until performed

(b) Takes as a satisfaction of a previous existing debt
(c) Gives another negotiable instrument
(d) Acquires a security interest in the instrument (e.g., the holder takes possession of the instrument as collateral for another debt)

(2) A bank takes for value to the extent that credit has been given for a deposit and withdrawn

(a) FIFO method is used to determine whether it has been withdrawn (money is considered to be withdrawn from an account in the order in which it was deposited)

(3) Value does not have to be for full amount of instrument;

(a) Purchase at a discount is value for full face amount of instrument provided HDC took in good faith (i.e., as long as not too large a discount)

EXAMPLE: Purchase of a $1,000 instrument in good faith for $950 is considered full value, but purchase of the same instrument for $500 is not considered full value when market conditions show that the discount is excessive.

EXAMPLE: Handy purchases a negotiable note that has a face value of $1,000. She gives $600 in cash now and agrees to pay $350 in one week. Handy has given value only to the extent of $600 and thus can qualify as a HDC for $600. Once she pays the remaining $350, she qualifies as a HDC for the full $1,000. Note that even though she paid only $950, she has HDC status for the entire $1,000 because it was a reasonable discount.

c. Take in **good faith**

(1) Good faith defined as honesty in fact and observance of reasonable commercial standards of fair dealing

d. Take **without notice** that it is overdue, has been dishonored, or that any person has a defense or claim to it

(1) Holder has notice when s/he knows or has reason to know (measured by objective "reasonable person" standard)
(2) Overdue

EXAMPLE: H acquires a note or draft that is three weeks past the due date on the instrument.

(a) Instrument not overdue if default is on payment of interest only
(b) Domestic check, although payable on demand, is overdue ninety days after its date

(3) Defense or claim

(a) Obvious signs of forgery or alteration so as to call into question its authenticity
(b) Incomplete or irregular
(c) If purchaser has notice of any party's claim or that all parties have been discharged

(4) There is no notice of a defense or claim if

(a) It is antedated or postdated
(b) S/he knows that there has been a default in payment of interest

(5) But if one acquires notice **after** becoming a holder and giving value, s/he may still be a HDC

(a) That is, once one is a HDC, acquiring notice does not end HDC status

3. Payee of a negotiable instrument may qualify as a HDC if meets all requirements

G. Rights of a Holder in Due Course (HDC)

1. The general rule is that a transfer of a negotiable instrument to a HDC cuts off all **personal defenses** against a HDC

a. Personal defenses are assertable against ordinary holders and assignees of contract rights to avoid payment

EXAMPLE: Art Dobbs negotiates a note to Mary Price in payment of a stereo. Mary negotiates this note to D. Finch who qualifies as a HDC. When Finch seeks payment, Dobbs points out that Price breached the contract by never delivering the stereo. Finch, as a HDC, still has the right to collect because breach of contract is a personal defense. Dobbs then has to seek recourse directly against Price.

b. EXCEPTION—HDC takes subject to all personal defenses of person with whom HDC directly dealt

2. Some defenses are assertable against any party including a HDC—these defenses are called **real (or universal) defenses**

3. Types of **personal defenses**

    a. Breach of contract

        (1) Includes breach of warranty

    b. Lack or failure of consideration

    c. Prior payment

EXAMPLE: Maker of a negotiable note pays on the note but does not keep or cancel the note. A subsequent party who qualifies as a HDC seeks to collect on this same note. Maker, having only a personal defense, must pay the HDC even though it was paid previously.

    d. Unauthorized completion

EXAMPLE: X signs a check leaving the amount blank. He tells Y to fill in the amount necessary to buy a typewriter. Y fills in $22,000 and negotiates the check to a HDC. The HDC may enforce the full amount of the check against X.

    e. Fraud in the inducement

        (1) Occurs when person signs a negotiable instrument and knows what s/he is signing; however, s/he was induced into doing so by intentional misrepresentation

    f. Nondelivery

        (1) Occurs when bearer instrument is lost or stolen

EXAMPLE: M issues a note that is bearer paper. It is stolen by T who sells it to a HDC. The HDC wins against M.

    g. Ordinary duress or undue influence

        (1) Most types of duress are considered a personal defense unless they become very extreme and thus are considered real defenses

EXAMPLE: Signing a check based on fear of losing a real estate deal constitutes a personal defense.

    h. Mental incapacity

        (1) Personal defense if state law makes transaction voidable

        (2) Real defense if state law makes transaction void

    i. Illegality

        (1) Personal defense if state law makes transaction voidable

        (2) If state law makes it void, then real defense

    j. Theft by holder or subsequent holder after theft

4. **Real Defenses**

    a. Forgery

        (1) Forgery of maker's or drawer's signature does not act as his/her signature

            (a) Does allow forger to be held liable

EXAMPLE: X forges M's name on a note and sells it to P. P cannot collect from M whether she is a HDC or not. Her recourse is against X.

    b. Bankruptcy

    c. Fraud in the execution

        (1) Occurs when a party is tricked into signing a negotiable instrument believing it to be something else

            (a) This defense will not apply if signer, based on his/her age, experience, etc., should have known what was happening

        (2) Recall that fraud in the inducement is a personal defense

    d. Minority (or infancy)

(1) When minor may disaffirm contract under state law, then is a real defense for a negotiable instrument

e. Mental incapacity, illegality, or extreme duress

   (1) Real defenses if transaction is void under state law

f. Material alteration of instrument

   (1) Is actually only partially a real defense

      (a) If dollar amount was altered, then HDC can collect according to original terms—a non-HDC collects nothing

      (b) If an instrument was incomplete originally and then completed without authorization, HDC can enforce it as completed—a non-HDC collects nothing

   (2) Material alteration exists when terms between any two parties are changed in any way including

      (a) Changes in amount, rate of interest, or days

         1] Considered "material" even if small change such as a penny

> *EXAMPLE: Janice Parks negotiates a $200 negotiable note to Jim Bivins. Bivins deftly changes the amount to $500 and transfers it to E. Melvin for $500 who qualifies as a HDC. The HDC can collect only the original $200 from Janice Parks.*

> *EXAMPLE: Same facts as before except that the material alteration is poorly done by Jim Bivins so that E. Melvin could not qualify as a holder in due course because the change was obvious. E. Melvin cannot collect even the original $200.*

      (b) Additions to writing or removal of part of instrument

      (c) Completion of instrument without authorization

      (d) But not material alteration if done to correct error on address or math computations, or to place marks on instrument for audit purposes

         1] Alterations that are not material are neither real nor personal defenses so all non-HDCs as well as HDCs can enforce the instrument

      (e) Not a real defense if maker's or drawer's negligence substantially contributed to the alteration—is a personal defense

5. Holder through a holder in due course

a. A party who does not qualify as a HDC but obtains a negotiable instrument from a HDC is called a holder through a holder in due course

b. Obtains all rights of a HDC

   (1) Based on fact that is an assignee who gets rights of previous party

   (2) Also called shelter provision

c. A HDC "washes" an instrument so that any holder thereafter can be a holder through a holder in due course

> *EXAMPLE: A HDC transfers a note to H.V. Shelter who knew that the maker of the note has a personal defense. Shelter does not qualify as a HDC but has the same rights because he is a holder through a holder in due course.*

> *EXAMPLE: Extending the example, H.V. Shelter gives the note to B. Evans. B. Evans does not qualify as a HDC (no value given) but is a holder through a holder in due course.*

d. Exceptions

   (1) If a party reacquires an instrument, his/her status remains what it originally was

> *EXAMPLE: P acquires a check from the payee. Neither qualifies in this case as a holder in due course. P delivers the check to Q who qualifies as a HDC. If the check is negotiated back to P, his rights remain those of a non-HDC.*

   (2) One who was involved in fraud or illegality affecting the instrument may not become a holder through a holder in due course

6. FTC holder in due course rule

   a. Applies when seller of consumer goods or services receives a note from a consumer or arranges a loan with a bank, etc., for that consumer

   b. Requires seller or lender to put a notice on these negotiable instruments that all holders take subject to any defenses which debtor could assert against seller

   c. Note that rule does not apply to any nonconsumer transactions and does not apply to any consumer noncredit transactions

   EXAMPLE: Connie Consumer purchases goods for consumer use and writes out a check. Subsequent holders are governed by ordinary HDC law.

H. Liability of Parties—there are two general types of warranties on negotiable instruments: contractual liability and warranty liability

1. Contractual liability

   a. Refers to liability of any party who signs negotiable instrument as a maker, drawer, drawee, or endorser

   b. Maker of a note has **primary liability** that means s/he has absolute liability to pay according to note's terms until it is paid or until statute of limitations (period to sue) has run

   c. No party of a draft (or check) initially has primary liability because drawee has only been ordered to pay by drawer

      (1) Drawee's obligation is to drawer to follow order but has not promised to holder of the draft to pay

      (2) Drawee obtains primary liability if s/he accepts (certifies) draft which means s/he promises to holder to pay it when due

         (a) Often, holder may simply present draft for payment without asking for acceptance

         (b) Some drafts require acceptance before they are paid

         (c) Even if draft does not require it, holder may request acceptance (especially on a time draft before due date)

   d. Drawer has **secondary liability** on draft—s/he is liable only if drawee fails to pay

   e. Endorsers of note or draft have secondary liability—holder can hold endorser liable if primary parties obligated to make payment fail to pay and if following conditions met

      (1) Holder must demand payment or acceptance in a timely manner

         (a) This demand is called presentment

         (b) Presentment for payment must be on or before due date or within reasonable time for demand instruments

            1] For domestic checks, holder must present check for payment within thirty days of its date in order to hold drawer secondarily liable

      (2) Holder must give endorsers timely notice of dishonor (i.e., that note or draft was refused payment or acceptance)

         (a) For domestic checks, holder must present check for payment within thirty days of endorsement to hold endorser secondarily liable

   f. Drawers and endorsers may avoid secondary liability by signing without recourse

   g. Upon certification of check, drawer and all previous endorsers are discharged from liability because bank has accepted check and agreed to pay it

2. Warranty liability—two types under which holder can seek payment from secondary parties are transfer warranties and presentment warranties

   a. Transfer warranties—transferor gives following transfer warranties whenever negotiable instrument is transferred for consideration

      (1) Transferor has good title

      (2) All signatures are genuine or authorized

(3) Instrument has not been materially altered

(4) No defense of any party is good against transferor

(5) Transferor has no notice of insolvency of maker, drawer, or acceptor

b. These warranties generally give loss to parties that dealt face to face with wrongdoer and thus were in best position to prevent or avoid forged, altered, or stolen instruments

(1) Party bearing loss must then seek payment if possible, from one who forged, altered, or stole instrument

c. Note that transferor, if s/he did not endorse, makes all five warranties only to immediate transferee but if transferor did endorse, makes them to all subsequent holders taking in good faith

d. Presentment warranties—holder presenting negotiable instrument for payment or acceptance makes only warranties of title, of no knowledge that drawer's signature is unauthorized, or of no material alteration

(1) HDC does not give these three warranties to bank

e. To recover under warranty liabilities (either transfer or presentment warranties), party does not have to meet conditions of proper presentment, dishonor, or timely notice of dishonor that are required under contractual liability against endorsers

3. Signatures by authorized agents

a. Agent may sign on behalf of another person (principal) and that principal is liable, not agent, if signature indicates the principal is liable

EXAMPLE: A negotiable instrument has the following signature, signed entirely by A. Underwood, the authorized agent: Mary Johnson, by A. Underwood, agent.

EXAMPLE: If A. Underwood had simply signed Mary Johnson as she had authorized, this would also bind Mary Johnson.

EXAMPLE: If A. Underwood had signed his name only, he is liable. The principal is not liable even if agent intended her to be because her name is not on the instrument.

4. Accommodation party is liable on the instrument in the capacity in which s/he has signed even if taker knows of his/her accommodation status

EXAMPLE: Accommodating maker is liable as a maker would be.

EXAMPLE: Accommodating endorser is liable as an endorser would be.

a. Accommodation party is one who signs to lend his/her name to other party

EXAMPLE: Father-in-law endorses a note for son-in-law so creditor will accept it.

(1) Notice of default need not be given to accommodation party

(2) The accommodation party has right of recourse against accommodated party if accommodation party is held liable

5. Holding parties liable

a. If there are multiple endorsers, each is liable in full to subsequent endorsers or holders

(1) That is, liability moves from bottom up

EXAMPLE: A negotiable note has the following endorsements on the back from top to bottom: A, B, C, D, and E. Suppose E has sought payment from the maker but was unsuccessful. E, therefore, can seek payment from any previous endorser. Assume he collects from C. C then seeks payment from B. (He may seek from B or A but not D.)

EXAMPLE: Note that in the previous example, if A eventually pays, he may try to collect from the maker. If unsuccessful, A may not try to collect from any endorser up the line from him.

6. Discharge of parties

a. Once primary party pays, all endorsers are discharged from liability

b. Cancellation of prior party's endorsement discharges that party from liability

(1) Oral renunciation or oral attempt to discharge a party is not effective

    c. Intentional destruction of instrument by holder discharges prior parties to instrument

7. Liability on instruments with forged signatures

    a. Person whose signature was forged on instrument is not liable on that instrument

       (1) Unless later ratifies it

    b. Forged signature operates as signature of forger

    c. Therefore, if signature of **maker or drawer** is forged, instrument can still be negotiated between parties and thus a holder can acquire good title

       (1) Recall that forgery is a real defense so that innocent maker or drawer cannot be required to pay even a HDC—forger can be required to pay if found

    d. However, a **forged endorsement** does **not** transfer title; thus, persons receiving it after forgery cannot collect on it

       (1) Three important exceptions to rule that forged endorsements cannot transfer title are imposter rule, fictitious payee rule, and negligence of maker or drawer—these cause maker or drawer to be liable

          (a) **Imposter rule** applies when maker or drawer issues a note or draft to an imposter thinking s/he actually is the real payee—when that imposter forges the real payee's name, this effectively negotiates this note or draft so that a subsequent holder (if not part of scheme) can collect from maker or drawer

             1] Note that this rule normally places loss on person who was in best position to avoid this scheme (i.e., maker or drawer)

                a] Of course, upon payment, maker or drawer may try to collect from imposter

                   EXAMPLE: J. Loux owes Larsen (whom she has not met) $2,000. Sawyer, claiming to be Larsen, gets Loux to issue him a check for $2,000. Sawyer forges Larsen's endorsement and transfers the check to P. Jenkins. Jenkins can collect from Loux because of the imposter rule exception.

                   EXAMPLE: If in the example above, J. Loux had given the check to the real Larsen and he lost it, the imposter rule would not apply even if someone found the check and forged Larsen's endorsement. No one after the forgery can collect on the check.

             2] This imposter rule exception also applies if an imposter pretends to be **agent** of the named payee

          (b) **Fictitious payee rule** applies when maker, drawer, or his/her agent (employee) issues a note or a check to a fictitious payee—then maker, drawer, or employee forges the endorsement—subsequent parties can enforce the note or check against the maker or drawer

             1] Actually payee may be a real person as long as maker, drawer, or other person supplying name never intended for that payee to ever get payment

               EXAMPLE: R. Stewart submits a time card for a nonexistent employee and the employer issues the payroll check. Stewart forges the endorsement and transfers it to L. Reed. Reed wins against the employer even though the employer was unaware of the scheme at the time.

          (c) If person's negligence substantially contributes to the forgery that person is prevented from raising the defense of forgery and thus holder wins

             EXAMPLE: D. Wolter has a signature stamp and leaves it lying around. Unauthorized use of the stamp is not a defense against a holder as Wolter's negligence substantially contributed to the forgery. If the forger could be caught, Wolter could sue the forger for losses.

I. Additional Issues

1. Certain types of draft names come up—although they follow general rules of drafts, definitions are helpful

    a. Trade acceptance is a draft in which a seller of goods extends credit to buyer by drawing a draft on that buyer directing him/her to pay seller a sum of money on a specified date

          (1) Trade acceptance also requires signature of buyer on face of instrument—called acceptance—buyer is also called acceptor at this point

          (2) Then seller may negotiate trade acceptance at a discount to another party to receive immediate cash

          (3) Seller is normally both drawer and payee of a trade acceptance

    b. Banker's acceptance is a draft in which drawee and drawer are a bank

    c. Sight draft is one payable upon presentment to drawee

    d. Time draft is one payable at a specified date or payable a certain period of time after a specified date

    e. Money order is a draft purchased by one party to pay payee in which the third party is typically post office, a bank, or a company

  2. Definitions for certain types of checks are also helpful

    a. Traveler's check is purchased from a bank (or company)—drawer (traveler) must sign twice for purposes of identification (once at the time s/he purchases the check and again at the time s/he uses the check)—drawee is bank or company—payee is one who gets paid

          (1) Technically, drawee must be a bank to be a true "check"—if drawee is not a bank then traveler's check is actually a draft

    b. Cashier's check is a check in which drawer and drawee are the same bank with a separate party being the payee

          (1) This is still considered a "three-party" instrument even though drawer and drawee are same bank

    c. Certified check is a check that payor bank has agreed in advance to pay so that bank becomes primarily liable

    d. Teller's check (bank draft) is draft drawn by one bank on another bank

J. Banks

  1. Banks include savings and loan associations, credit unions, and trust companies

  2. Relationship between bank and depositor is debtor-creditor

    a. Even though the depositor has funds in the bank, a payee cannot force a drawee to make payment

    b. Only drawer has an action against drawee-bank for wrongfully dishonoring a check—based on contract between customer (drawer) and bank

    c. Bank required to report to IRS any transaction or series of related transactions greater than $10,000

          (1) Ordinary checks are exempted but cash and other types of checks such as cashier's checks come under reporting requirement

    d. Bank must report to IRS suspected crimes involving $1,000 or more in funds

  3. Checks

    a. Banks are not obligated to pay on a check presented more than six months after date

          (1) But they may pay in good faith and charge customer's account

    b. Even if check creates an overdraft, a bank may charge customer's account

    c. Bank is liable to drawer for damages caused by wrongful dishonor of a check

          (1) Wrongful dishonor may occur if the bank in error believes funds are insufficient when they are sufficient

    d. Payment of bad checks (e.g., forgery of drawer or altered checks)

          (1) Bank is liable to drawer for payment on bad checks unless drawer's negligence contributed because bank presumed to know signatures of its drawers

          (2) Bank cannot recover from a HDC to whom bank paid on a bad check

(3) If drawer fails to notify bank of forgery or alterations within thirty days of bank statement, the drawer is held liable on subsequent forgeries or alterations done in same way by same person

    (a) In any event, drawer must give notice of forgeries or alterations within one year to keep bank liable or else drawer is liable

        1] This applies to even nonrepeat cases as well as when bank was paying in bad faith

        EXAMPLE: G. Wilson forges the name of M. Gibson on a check in an artful way. A subsequent HDC cashes this check at the drawee bank. The bank is liable on this check and cannot recover from either the HDC or M. Gibson as long as Gibson notifies the bank of the forgery within one year. The loss falls on the bank based on the idea that the bank should know its drawer's signature.

    (b) Forgeries of endorsements are treated differently—depositor has three years to notify bank and also bank may charge check back to party that presented check to bank whether or not the party was a HDC

        1] Recall that one cashing check gave warranty that all signatures are genuine

        EXAMPLE: D issues a check to P. P loses the check which is found by X. X forges the endorsement and transfers it to H. Finally, H cashes the check at the drawee bank. D soon notifies the bank of the forgery. The bank may charge it back to H (whether or not a HDC) but not to D.

  e. Bank is not liable for early payment of postdated check unless drawer notified bank to not pay check until date on check

  f. Oral **stop payment order** is good for fourteen days; written stop payment order is good for six months and is renewable

    (1) Stop payment order must be given so as to give bank reasonable opportunity to act on it

    (2) Bank is liable to drawer if it pays after effective stop payment order only when drawer can prove that the bank's failure to obey the order caused drawer's loss. If drawer has no valid defense to justify dishonoring instrument, then bank has no liability for failure to obey stop payment order.

    EXAMPLE: W. Paisley buys a TV set from the Burke Appliance Store and pays for the set with a check. Later in the day Paisley finds a better model for the same price at another store. Paisley telephones his bank and orders the bank to stop payment on the check. If the bank mistakenly pays Paisley's check two days after receiving the stop payment order, the bank will not be liable if Paisley could not rightfully rescind his agreement with the Burke Appliance Store. With these facts, Paisley suffered no damages from the bank's mistake.

    (3) If drawer stops payment on the check, s/he is still liable to holder of check unless s/he has a valid defense (e.g., if holder qualifies as a holder in due course then drawer must be able to assert a real defense to free him/herself of liability)

  g. Bank is entitled to a depositor's endorsement on checks deposited with the bank

    (1) If missing, bank may supply endorsement to negotiate check

  h. Banks may choose which checks are charged to account first when several checks received in same day

K. Electronic Fund Transfer Act and Regulation E

1. Applied to consumer electronic fund transfers
2. For lost or stolen debit cards, customer is liable for

  a. Limit of $50 if notifies bank within two days of discovery of loss or theft
  b. Limit of $500 if notifies bank after two days, but before sixty days after unauthorized use appears on customer's bank statement
  c. Limit of $500 does not apply if fails to notify bank before sixty-day period
  d. Note how these rules are very different from those that apply to lost or stolen credit cards

3. Unsolicited debit cards may be sent to consumer only if the debit card is not functional but can be made functional at consumer's actual request
4. Regulates direct deposits to financial institutions
5. Bank is liable for failure to pay electronic fund transfer when customer has sufficient funds in account
6. Unauthorized use of electronic fund transfer is felony under federal law

    a. Banks and their officers must comply with strict rules for prevention or be subject to strict fines and/or imprisonment

L. Fund Transfers under UCC Article 4A

1. Applies to commercial electronic fund transfers

    a. Adopted by majority of states
    b. Does not apply to consumer transfers
    c. Applies to any method of transfer including electronic or mail

2. When party gives payment order to bank and that bank or another bank pays too much money or to wrong party, that bank in error is liable for error

    a. Then bank has burden of recovery for wrongfully paid amount

M. Transfer of Negotiable Documents of Title

1. Transfer of documents of title is very similar to transfer of negotiable instruments under commercial paper
2. Types of documents of title

    a. Bill of lading is a document issued by a carrier (a person engaged in the business of transporting or forwarding goods) and given to seller evidencing receipt of the goods for shipment
    b. A warehouse receipt is a document issued by a warehouseman (a person engaged in the business of storing goods for hire) and given to seller evidencing receipt of goods for storage

3. Form

    a. Document of title is negotiable if face of the document contains words of negotiability (order or bearer)

      (1) Document of title containing promise to deliver goods to the order of a named person is an order document

         (a) If person is named on face of document or, if there are endorsements, on back of document and last endorsement is a special endorsement, then document is an order document

            1] Proper negotiation requires delivery of document and endorsement by named individual(s)

      (2) Document of title containing a promise to deliver the goods to bearer is bearer document

         (a) If "bearer" is stated on face of document or, if there are endorsements on back of document and last endorsement is a blank endorsement, it is a bearer document

            1] Proper negotiation merely requires delivery of document

    b. Nonnegotiable (straight) documents of title are assigned, not negotiated

      (1) Assignee will never receive any better rights than assignor had

4. Due negotiation—document of title is "duly negotiated" when negotiated to a holder who takes it in good faith in the ordinary course of business without notice of a defense and pays value

    a. Value does not include payment of a preexisting (antecedent) debt—this is an important difference from value concept required to create a holder in due course for commercial paper

5. Holder by due negotiation acquires rights very similar to those acquired by a holder in due course

    a. These rights include

      (1) Title to document
      (2) Title to goods
      (3) All rights accruing under law of agency or estoppel, including rights to goods delivered after document was issued, and
      (4) The direct obligation of the issuer to hold or deliver the goods according to terms of document

b. A holder by due negotiation defeats similar defenses to those defeated by a holder in due course for commercial paper (personal but not real defenses)

c. A document of title procured by a thief upon placing stolen goods in a warehouse confers no rights in the underlying goods.

   (1) This defense is valid against subsequent holder to whom document of title has been duly negotiated

   (2) Therefore, original owner of goods can assert better title to goods than a holder who has received document through due negotiation

6. Rights acquired in absence of due negotiation

a. Transferee of a document, whether negotiable or nonnegotiable, to whom document has been delivered, but not duly negotiated, acquires title and rights which his/her transferor had or had actual authority to convey

7. Transferor for value warrants that

a. Document is genuine

b. S/he has no knowledge of any fact that would impair its validity or worth, and

c. His/her negotiation or transfer is rightful and fully effective with respect to document of title and goods it represents

MULTIPLE-CHOICE QUESTIONS (1-50)

1. Under the Negotiable Instruments Article of the UCC, an endorsement of an instrument "for deposit only" is an example of what type of endorsement?
- a. Blank.
- b. Qualified.
- c. Restrictive.
- d. Special.

2.

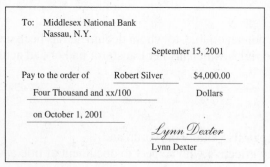

The above instrument is a
- a. Draft.
- b. Postdated check.
- c. Trade acceptance.
- d. Promissory note.

3. Which of the following statements regarding negotiable instruments is **not** correct?
- a. A certificate of deposit is a type of note.
- b. A check is a type of draft.
- c. A promissory note is a type of draft.
- d. A certificate of deposit is issued by a bank.

4. Based on the following instrument:

> May 19, 2001
>
> I promise to pay to the order of A. B. Shark $1,000 (one thousand and one hundred dollars) with interest thereon at the rate of 12% per annum.
>
> *T. T. Tile*
>
> T. T. Tile
>
> **Guaranty**
>
> I personally guaranty payment by T. T. Tile.
>
> *N. A. Abner*
>
> N. A. Abner

The instrument is a
- a. Promissory demand note.
- b. Sight draft.
- c. Check.
- d. Trade acceptance.

5. Under the Commercial Paper Article of the UCC, which of the following documents would be considered an order to pay?
- I. Draft
- II. Certificate of deposit

  - a. I only.
  - b. II only.
  - c. Both I and II.
  - d. Neither I nor II.

6. An instrument that is otherwise negotiable on its face states "Pay to Jenny Larson." Which of the following statements is(are) correct?
- I. It is negotiable if it is a check.
- II. It is negotiable if it is a draft drawn on a corporation.
- III. It is negotiable if it is a promissory note.

  - a. I only.
  - b. I and II only.
  - c. II and III only.
  - d. I, II, and III.

7. Under the Commercial Paper Article of the UCC, for a note to be negotiable it must
- a. Be payable to order or to bearer.
- b. Be signed by the payee.
- c. Contain references to all agreements between the parties.
- d. Contain necessary conditions of payment.

8. On February 15, 2001, P.D. Stone obtained the following instrument from Astor Co. for $1,000. Stone was aware that Helco, Inc. disputed liability under the instrument because of an alleged breach by Astor of the referenced computer purchase agreement. On March 1, 2001, Willard Bank obtained the instrument from Stone for $3,900. Willard had no knowledge that Helco disputed liability under the instrument.

> February 12, 2001
>
> Helco, Inc. promises to pay to Astor Co. or bearer the sum of $4,900 (four thousand four hundred and 00/100 dollars) on March 12, 2001 (maker may elect to extend due date to March 31, 2001) with interest thereon at the rate of 12% per annum.
>
> HELCO, INC.
>
> By: *A. J. Help*
>
> A. J. Help, President
>
> Reference: Computer purchase agreement dated February 12, 2001

The reverse side of the instrument is endorsed as follows:

> Pay to the order of Willard Bank, without recourse
>
> *P.D. Stone*
>
> P.D. Stone

The instrument is
- a. Nonnegotiable, because of the reference to the computer purchase agreement.
- b. Nonnegotiable, because the numerical amount differs from the written amount.
- c. Negotiable, even though the maker has the right to extend the time for payment.
- d. Negotiable, when held by Astor, but nonnegotiable when held by Willard Bank.

9. A draft made in the United States calls for payment in Canadian dollars.
- a. The draft is nonnegotiable because it calls for payment in money of another country.
- b. The draft is nonnegotiable because the rate of exchange may fluctuate thus violating the sum certain rule.

c. The instrument is negotiable if it satisfies all of the other elements of negotiability.

d. The instrument is negotiable only if it has the exchange rate written on the draft.

10. An instrument reads as follows:

$10,000	Ludlow, Vermont	February 1, 2001

I promise to pay to the order of Custer Corp. $10,000 within ten days after the sale of my two-carat diamond ring. I pledge the sale proceeds to secure my obligation hereunder.

R. Harris

R. Harris

Which of the following statements correctly describes the above instrument?

a. The instrument is nonnegotiable because it is **not** payable at a definite time.

b. The instrument is nonnegotiable because it is secured by the proceeds of the sale of the ring.

c. The instrument is a negotiable promissory note.

d. The instrument is a negotiable sight draft payable on demand.

11. Kline is holding a promissory note in which he is the payer and Breck is the promissor. One of the terms of the note states that payment is subject to the terms of the contract dated March 1 of the current year between Breck and Kline. Does this term destroy negotiability?

a. No, if the contract is readily available.

b. No, since the note can be enforced without regard to the mentioned contract.

c. No, as long as the terms in the mentioned contract are commercially reasonable.

d. Yes, since this term causes the note to have a conditional promise.

12. Based on the following instrument:

	May 19, 2001

I promise to pay to the order of A. B. Shark $1,000 (one thousand and one hundred dollars) with interest thereon at the rate of 12% per annum.

T. T. Tile

T. T. Tile

Guaranty

I personally guaranty payment by T. T. Tile.

N. A. Abner

N. A. Abner

The instrument is

a. Nonnegotiable even though it is payable on demand.

b. Nonnegotiable because the numeric amount differs from the written amount.

c. Negotiable even though a payment date is **not** specified.

d. Negotiable because of Abner's guaranty.

13. A note has an interest rate that varies based on the stated rate of 2% above the prime rate as determined by XYZ Bank in New York City. Under the Revised Article 3 of the Uniform Commercial Code, which of the following is true?

a. This interest rate provision destroys negotiability since it does not constitute a sum certain.

b. This note is not negotiable because the holder has to look outside the instrument to determine what the prime rate is.

c. The interest rate provision destroys negotiability because the prime rate can vary before the time the note comes due.

d. The interest rate provision is allowed in negotiable notes and does not destroy negotiability.

14. While auditing your client, Corbin Company, you see a check that is postdated and states "Pay to Corbin Company." You also see a note that is due in forty days and also says "Pay to Corbin Company." You note that both instruments contain all of the elements of negotiability except for possibly the ones raised by this fact pattern. Which of the following is(are) negotiable instruments?

a. The check.

b. The note.

c. Both the check and the note.

d. Neither the check nor the note.

15. Under the Revised Article 3 of the Uniform Code, which of the following is true if the maker of a note provides that payment must come out of a designated fund?

a. This is allowed even though the maker is not personally obligated to pay.

b. Since the instrument is not based on the general credit of the maker, the instrument is not negotiable.

c. The promise to pay is conditional; therefore, the note is not negotiable.

d. The instrument is not negotiable if the designated fund has insufficient funds.

16. Wyden holds a check that is written out to him. The check has the amount in words as five hundred dollars. The amount in figures on this check states $200. Which of the following is correct?

a. The check is cashable for $500.

b. The check is cashable for $200.

c. The check is not cashable because the amounts differ.

d. The check is not cashable because the amounts differ by more than 10%.

17. Under the Commercial Paper Article of the UCC, which of the following requirements must be met for a transferee of order paper to become a holder?

I. Possession
II. Endorsement of transferor

a. I only.

b. II only.

c. Both I and II.

d. Neither I nor II.

18. The following endorsements appear on the back of a negotiable promissory note payable to Lake Corp.

Pay to John Smith only
Frank Parker, President of Lake Corp.

John Smith

Pay to the order of Sharp, Inc. without recourse, but only if Sharp delivers computers purchased by Mary Harris by March 15, 2001.
Mary Harris

Sarah Sharp, President of Sharp, Inc.

Which of the following statements is correct?
    a.   The note became nonnegotiable as a result of Parker's endorsement.
    b.   Harris' endorsement was a conditional promise to pay and caused the note to be nonnegotiable.
    c.   Smith's endorsement effectively prevented further negotiation of the note.
    d.   Harris' signature was **not** required to effectively negotiate the note to Sharp.

19. A note is made payable to the order of Ann Jackson on the front. On the back, Ann Jackson signs it in blank and delivers it to Jerry Lin. Lin puts "Pay to Jerry Lin" above Jackson's endorsement. Which of the following statements is **false** concerning this note?
    a.   After Lin wrote "Pay to Jerry Lin," the note became order paper.
    b.   After Jackson endorsed the note but before Lin wrote on it, the note was bearer paper.
    c.   Lin needs to endorse this note to negotiate it further, even though he personally wrote "Pay to Jerry Lin" on the back.
    d.   The note is not negotiable because Lin wrote "Pay to Jerry Lin" instead of "Pay to the order of Jerry Lin."

20. You are examining some negotiable instruments for a client. Which of the following endorsements can be classified as a special restrictive endorsement?
    a.   Pay to Alex Ericson if he completes the contracted work within ten days, (signed) Stephanie Sene.
    b.   Pay to Alex Ericson without recourse (signed) Stephanie Sene.
    c.   For deposit only, (signed) Stephanie Sene.
    d.   Pay to Alex Ericson, (signed) Stephanie Sene.

21. On February 15, 2001, P.D. Stone obtained the following instrument from Astor Co. for $1,000. Stone was aware that Helco, Inc. disputed liability under the instrument because of an alleged breach by Astor of the referenced computer purchase agreement. On March 1, 2001, Willard Bank obtained the instrument from Stone for $3,900. Willard had no knowledge that Helco disputed liability under the instrument.

February 12, 2001

Helco, Inc. promises to pay to Astor Co. or bearer the sum of $4,900 (four thousand four hundred and 00/100 dollars) on March 12, 2001 (maker may elect to extend due date to March 31, 2001) with interest thereon at the rate of 12% per annum.

HELCO, INC.

By: *A. J. Help*

A. J. Help, President

Reference: Computer purchase agreement dated February 12, 2001

The reverse side of the instrument is endorsed as follows:

Pay to the order of Willard Bank, without recourse

P.D. Stone

P.D. Stone

Which of the following statements is correct?
    a.   Willard Bank **cannot** be a holder in due course because Stone's endorsement was without recourse.
    b.   Willard Bank must endorse the instrument to negotiate it.
    c.   Neither Willard Bank **nor** Stone are holders in due course.
    d.   Stone's endorsement was required for Willard Bank to be a holder in due course.

22. Under the Commercial Paper Article of the UCC, which of the following circumstances would prevent a person from becoming a holder in due course of an instrument?
    a.   The person was notified that payment was refused.
    b.   The person was notified that one of the prior endorsers was discharged.
    c.   The note was collateral for a loan.
    d.   The note was purchased at a discount.

23. One of the requirements needed for a holder of a negotiable instrument to be a holder in due course is the value requirement. Ruper is a holder of a $1,000 check written out to her. Which of the following would not satisfy the value requirement?
    a.   Ruper received the check from a tax client to pay off a four-month-old debt.
    b.   Ruper took the check in exchange for a negotiable note for $1,200 which was due on that day.
    c.   Ruper received the check in exchange for a promise to do certain specified services three months later.
    d.   Ruper received the check for a tax service debt for a close relative.

24. Larson is claiming to be a holder in due course of two instruments. One is a draft that is drawn on Picket Company and says "Pay to Brunt." The other is a check that says "Pay to Brunt." Both are endorsed by Brunt on the back and made payable to Larson. Larson gave value for and acted in good faith concerning both the draft and the check. Larson also claims to be ignorant of any adverse claims on either instrument which are not overdue or have not been dishonored. Which of the following is(are) true?

  I. Larson is a holder in due course of the draft.
  II. Larson is a holder in due course of the check.

    a.   I only.
    b.   II only.
    c.   Both I and II.
    d.   Neither I nor II.

25. In order to be a holder in due course, the holder, among other requirements, must give value. Which of the following will satisfy this value requirement?

  I. An antecedent debt.
  II. A promise to perform services at a future date.

    a.   I only.
    b.   II only.

c.   Both I and II.
d.   Neither I nor II.

26. Bond fraudulently induced Teal to make a note payable to Wilk, to whom Bond was indebted. Bond delivered the note to Wilk. Wilk negotiated the instrument to Monk, who purchased it with knowledge of the fraud and after it was overdue. If Wilk qualifies as a holder in due course, which of the following statements is correct?
   a.   Monk has the standing of a holder in due course through Wilk.
   b.   Teal can successfully assert the defense of fraud in the inducement against Monk.
   c.   Monk personally qualifies as a holder in due course.
   d.   Teal can successfully assert the defense of fraud in the inducement against Wilk.

27. To the extent that a holder of a negotiable promissory note is a holder in due course, the holder takes the note free of which of the following defenses?
   a.   Minority of the maker where it is a defense to enforcement of a contract.
   b.   Forgery of the maker's signature.
   c.   Discharge of the maker in bankruptcy.
   d.   Nonperformance of a condition precedent.

28. Under the Commercial Paper Article of the UCC, in a nonconsumer transaction, which of the following are real defenses available against a holder in due course?

	Material alteration	Discharge of bankruptcy	Breach of contract
a.	No	Yes	Yes
b.	Yes	Yes	No
c.	No	No	Yes
d.	Yes	No	No

29. On February 15, 2001, P.D. Stone obtained the following instrument from Astor Co. for $1,000. Stone was aware that Helco, Inc. disputed liability under the instrument because of an alleged breach by Astor of the referenced computer purchase agreement. On March 1, 2001, Willard Bank obtained the instrument from Stone for $3,900. Willard had no knowledge that Helco disputed liability under the instrument.

February 12, 2001

Helco, Inc. promises to pay to Astor Co. or bearer the sum of $4,900 (four thousand four hundred and 00/100 dollars) on March 12, 2001 (maker may elect to extend due date to March 31, 2001) with interest thereon at the rate of 12% per annum.

HELCO, INC.

By: *A. J. Help*
A. J. Help, President

Reference: Computer purchase agreement dated February 12, 2001

The reverse side of the instrument is endorsed as follows:

Pay to the order of Willard Bank, without recourse

P.D. Stone
P.D. Stone

If Willard Bank demands payment from Helco and Helco refuses to pay the instrument because of Astor's breach of the computer purchase agreement, which of the following statements would be correct?
   a.   Willard Bank is **not** a holder in due course because Stone was **not** a holder in due course.
   b.   Helco will **not** be liable to Willard Bank because of Astor's breach.
   c.   Stone will be the only party liable to Willard Bank because he was aware of the dispute between Helco and Astor.
   d.   Helco will be liable to Willard Bank because Willard Bank is a holder in due course.

30. Northup made out a negotiable promissory note that was payable to the order of Port. This promissory note was meant to purchase some furniture that Port used to own, but he lied to Northup when he claimed he still owned it. Port immediately negotiated the note to Johnson who knew about Port's lie. Johnson negotiated the note to Kenner who was a holder in due course. Kenner then negotiated the note back to Johnson. When Johnson sought to enforce the promissory note against Northup, she refused claiming fraud. Which of the following is correct?
   a.   Johnson, as a holder through a holder in due course, can enforce the promissory note.
   b.   Northup wins because Johnson does not have the rights of a holder in due course.
   c.   Northup wins because she has a real defense on this note.
   d.   Johnson's knowledge of the lie does not affect his rights on this note.

31. Goran wrote out a check to Ruz to pay for a television set he purchased at a flea market from Ruz. When Goran got home, he found out the box did not have the television set but some weights. Goran immediately gave his bank a stop payment order over the phone. He followed this up with a written stop payment order. In the meantime, Ruz negotiated the check to Schmidt who qualified as a holder in due course. Schmidt gave the check as a gift to Buck. When Buck tried to cash the check, the bank and Goran both refused to pay. Which of the following is correct?
   a.   Buck cannot collect on the check from the bank because Goran has a real defense.
   b.   Buck cannot collect on the check from Goran because Goran has a personal defense.
   c.   Buck can require the bank to pay because Buck is a holder through a holder in due course.
   d.   Buck can require Goran to pay on the check even though the check was a gift.

32. Under the Negotiable Instruments Article of the UCC, which of the following parties will be a holder but **not** be entitled to the rights of a holder in due course?
   a.   A party who, knowing of a real defense to payment, received an instrument from a holder in due course.
   b.   A party who found an instrument payable to bearer.
   c.   A party who received, as a gift, an instrument from a holder in due course.
   d.   A party who, in good faith and without notice of any defect, gave value for an instrument.

33. A holder in due course will take free of which of the following defenses?

a. Infancy, to the extent that it is a defense to a simple contract.
b. Discharge of the maker in bankruptcy.
c. A wrongful filling-in of the amount payable that was omitted from the instrument.
d. Duress of a nature that renders the obligation of the party a nullity.

34. Cobb gave Garson a signed check with the amount payable left blank. Garson was to fill in, as the amount, the price of fuel oil Garson was to deliver to Cobb at a later date. Garson estimated the amount at $700, but told Cobb it would be no more than $900. Garson did not deliver the fuel oil, but filled in the amount of $1,000 on the check. Garson then negotiated the check to Josephs in satisfaction of a $500 debt with the $500 balance paid to Garson in cash. Cobb stopped payment and Josephs is seeking to collect $1,000 from Cobb. Cobb's maximum liability to Josephs will be

a. $0
b. $ 500
c. $ 900
d. $1,000

35. A maker of a note will have a real defense against a holder in due course as a result of any of the following conditions **except**

a. Discharge in bankruptcy.
b. Forgery.
c. Fraud in the execution.
d. Lack of consideration.

36. Which of the following parties has(have) primary liability on a negotiable instrument?

I. Drawer of a check.
II. Drawee of a time draft before acceptance.
III. Maker of a promissory note.

a. I and II only.
b. II and III only.
c. I and III only.
d. III only.

37. Which of the following actions does **not** discharge a prior party to a commercial instrument?

a. Good faith payment or satisfaction of the instrument.
b. Cancellation of that prior party's endorsement.
c. The holder's oral renunciation of that prior party's liability.
d. The holder's intentional destruction of the instrument.

38. Under the Negotiable Instruments Article of the UCC, when an instrument is indorsed "Pay to John Doe" and signed "Faye Smith," which of the following statements is(are) correct?

	Payment of the instrument is guaranteed	The instrument can be further negotiated
a.	Yes	Yes
b.	Yes	No
c.	No	Yes
d.	No	No

39.

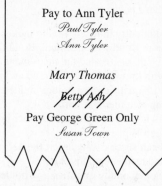

Susan Town, on receiving the above instrument, struck Betty Ash's endorsement. Under the Commercial Paper Article of the UCC, which of the endorsers of the above instrument will be completely discharged from secondary liability to later endorsers of the instrument?

a. Ann Tyler.
b. Mary Thomas.
c. Betty Ash.
d. Susan Town.

40. A subsequent holder of a negotiable instrument may cause the discharge of a prior holder of the instrument by any of the following actions **except**

a. Unexcused delay in presentment of a time draft.
b. Procuring certification of a check.
c. Giving notice of dishonor the day after dishonor.
d. Material alteration of a note.

41. A check has the following endorsements on the back:

Which of the following conditions occurring subsequent to the endorsements would discharge all of the endorsers?

a. Lack of notice of dishonor.
b. Late presentment.
c. Insolvency of the maker.
d. Certification of the check.

42. Robb, a minor, executed a promissory note payable to bearer and delivered it to Dodsen in payment for a stereo system. Dodsen negotiated the note for value to Mellon by delivery alone and without endorsement. Mellon endorsed the note in blank and negotiated it to Bloom for value. Bloom's demand for payment was refused by Robb because the note was executed when Robb was a minor. Bloom gave prompt notice of Robb's default to Dodsen and Mellon. None of the holders of the note were aware of Robb's minority. Which of the following parties will be liable to Bloom?

	Dodsen	Mellon
a.	Yes	Yes
b.	Yes	No
c.	No	No
d.	No	Yes

43. Vex Corp. executed a negotiable promissory note payable to Tamp, Inc. The note was collateralized by some of Vex's business assets. Tamp negotiated the note to Miller for value. Miller endorsed the note in blank and negotiated it to Bilco for value. Before the note became due, Bilco agreed to release Vex's collateral. Vex refused to pay Bilco when the note became due. Bilco promptly notified Miller and Tamp of Vex's default. Which of the following statements is correct?

    a.   Bilco will be unable to collect from Miller because Miller's endorsement was in blank.

    b.   Bilco will be able to collect from either Tamp or Miller because Bilco was a holder in due course.

    c.   Bilco will be unable to collect from either Tamp or Miller because of Bilco's release of the collateral.

    d.   Bilco will be able to collect from Tamp because Tamp was the original payee.

44. Under the Commercial Paper Article of the UCC, which of the following statements best describes the effect of a person endorsing a check "without recourse"?

    a.   The person has **no** liability to prior endorsers.

    b.   The person makes **no** promise or guarantee of payment on dishonor.

    c.   The person gives **no** warranty protection to later transferees.

    d.   The person converts the check into order paper.

45. A check is postdated to November 20 even though the check was written out on November 3 of the same year. Which of the following is correct under the Revised Article 3 of the Uniform Commercial Code?

    a.   The check is payable on demand on or after November 3 because part of the definition of a check is that it be payable on demand.

    b.   The check ceases to be demand paper and is payable on November 20.

    c.   The postdating destroys negotiability.

    d.   A bank that pays the check is automatically liable for early payment.

46. Stanley purchased a computer from Comp Electronics with a personal check. Later that day, Stanley saw a better deal on the computer so he orally stopped payment on the check with his bank. The bank, however, still paid Comp Electronics when the check was presented three days later. Which of the following is correct?

    a.   The bank is liable to Stanley for failure to follow the oral stop payment order.

    b.   The bank is not liable to Stanley because the stop payment order was not in writing.

    c.   The bank is not liable to Stanley if Comp Electronics qualifies as a holder in due course.

    d.   Comp Electronics is liable to Stanley to return the amount of the check.

47. A trade acceptance is an instrument drawn by a

    a.   Seller obligating the seller or designee to make payment.

    b.   Buyer obligating the buyer or designee to make payment.

    c.   Seller ordering the buyer or designee to make payment.

    d.   Buyer ordering the seller or designee to make payment.

48. Under the Documents of Title Article of the UCC, which of the following statements is(are) correct regarding a common carrier's duty to deliver goods subject to a negotiable bearer bill of lading?

  I.   The carrier may deliver the goods to any party designated by the holder of the bill of lading.

  II. A carrier who, without court order, delivers goods to a party claiming the goods under a missing negotiable bill of lading is liable to any person injured by the misdelivery.

    a.   I only.

    b.   II only.

    c.   Both I and II.

    d.   Neither I nor II.

49. Which of the following is **not** a warranty made by the seller of a negotiable warehouse receipt to the purchaser of the document?

    a.   The document transfer is fully effective with respect to the goods it represents.

    b.   The warehouseman will honor the document.

    c.   The seller has **no** knowledge of any facts that would impair the document's validity.

    d.   The document is genuine.

50. Under the UCC, a warehouse receipt

    a.   Will **not** be negotiable if it contains a contractual limitation on the warehouseman's liability.

    b.   May qualify as both a negotiable warehouse receipt and negotiable commercial paper if the instrument is payable either in cash or by the delivery of goods.

    c.   May be issued only by a bonded and licensed warehouseman.

    d.   Is negotiable if by its terms the goods are to be delivered to bearer or the order of a named person.

PROBLEMS

NOTE: These types of problems are no longer included in the CPA Examination but they have been retained because they are useful in developing skills to complete simulations.

Problem 1   (15 to 20 minutes)

Prince, Hall, & Charming, CPAs, has been retained to examine the financial statements of Hex Manufacturing Corporation. Shortly before beginning the examination for the year ended December 31, 2001, Mr. Prince received a telephone call from Hex's president indicating that he thought some type of embezzlement was occurring because the corporation's cash position was significantly lower than in prior years. The president then requested that Prince immediately undertake a special investigation to determine the amount of embezzlement, if any.

After a month of investigation, Prince uncovered an embezzlement scheme involving collusion between the head of payroll and the assistant treasurer. The following is a summary of Prince's findings:

• The head of payroll supplied the assistant treasurer with punched time cards for fictitious employees. The assistant treasurer prepared invoices, receiving reports, and purchase orders for fictitious suppliers. The assistant treasurer prepared checks for the fictitious employees and suppliers which were signed by the treasurer. Then, either the assistant treasurer or the head of payroll would endorse the checks and deposit them in various banks where they maintained accounts in the names of fictitious payees. All of the checks in question have cleared Omega Bank, the drawee.

• The embezzlement scheme had been operating for ten months and more than $120,000 had been embezzled by the time the scheme was uncovered. The final series of defalcations included checks payable directly to the head of payroll and the assistant treasurer. These checks included skillful forgeries of the treasurer's signature that were almost impossible to detect. This occurred while the treasurer was on vacation. These checks have also cleared Omega Bank, the drawee.

Required:

Answer the following, setting forth reasons for any conclusions stated.

Will Hex or Omega bear the loss with respect to the following categories of checks:

a. Those which were signed by the treasurer but payable to fictitious payees?

b. Those which include the forged signature of the treasurer?

Problem 2   (15 to 20 minutes)

River Oaks is a wholesale distributor of automobile parts. River Oaks received the promissory note shown below from First Auto, Inc., as security for payment of a $4,400 auto parts shipment. When River Oaks accepted the note as collateral for the First Auto obligation, River Oaks was aware that the maker of the note, Hillcraft, Inc., was claiming that the note was unenforceable because Alexco Co. had breached the license agreement under which Hillcraft had given the note. First Auto had acquired the note from Smith in exchange for repairing several cars owned by Smith. At the time First Auto received the note, First Auto was unaware of the dispute between Hillcraft and Alexco. Also, Smith, who paid Alexco $3,500 for the note, was unaware of Hillcraft's allegations that Alexco had breached the license agreement.

PROMISSORY NOTE
Date: __1/14/03__
___Hillcraft, Inc.___   promises to pay to ___Alexco Co. or bearer___   the sum of $4,400 ___Four Thousand and 00/100___ Dollars on or before_____May 15, 2004 (maker may elect to extend due date by 30 days)_____with interest thereon at the rate of 9 1/2% per annum.
Hillcraft, Inc.
By *P.J. Hill*
P.J. Hill, President
Reference: __Alexco Licensing Agreement__

The reverse side of the note was endorsed as follows:

Pay to the order of First Auto without recourse
E. Smith
E. Smith
Pay to the order of River Oaks Co.
First Auto
By *G. First*
G. First, President

First Auto is now insolvent and unable to satisfy its obligation to River Oaks. Therefore, River Oaks has demanded that Hillcraft pay $4,400, but Hillcraft has refused, asserting:

• The note is nonnegotiable because it references the license agreement and is not payable at a definite time or on demand.

• River Oaks is not a holder in due course of the note because it received the note as security for amounts owed by First Auto.

• River Oaks is not a holder in due course because it was aware of the dispute between Hillcraft and Alexco.

• Hillcraft can raise the alleged breach by Alexco as a defense to payment.

• River Oaks has no right to the note because it was not endorsed by Alexco.

• The maximum amount that Hillcraft would owe under the note is $4,000, plus accrued interest.

Required:

State whether each of Hillcraft's assertions are correct and give the reasons for your conclusions.

SIMULATION PROBLEMS

Simulation Problem 1   (10 to 15 minutes)

Instructions				
	Fact Pattern I	Fact Pattern II	Fact Pattern III	Fact Pattern IV

This simulation has four separate fact patterns, each followed by five legal conclusions relating to the fact pattern preceding those five numbered legal conclusions. Determine whether each conclusion is Correct or Incorrect.

	Fact Pattern I			
Instructions		Fact Pattern II	Fact Pattern III	Fact Pattern IV

An instrument purports to be a negotiable instrument. It otherwise fulfills all the elements of negotiability and it states "Pay to Rich Crane."

	Correct	*Incorrect*
1. It is negotiable if it is a check and Rich Crane has possession of the check.	O	O
2. It is negotiable if it is a draft drawn on a corporation.	O	O
3. It is negotiable if it is a promissory note due one year later with 5% interest stated on its face.	O	O
4. It is negotiable if it is a certificate of deposit.	O	O
5. It is negotiable even if it is a cashier's check.	O	O

		Fact Pattern II		
Instructions	Fact Pattern I		Fact Pattern III	Fact Pattern IV

Another instrument fulfills all of the elements of negotiability except possibly one, that is, the instrument does not identify any payee.

	Correct	*Incorrect*
6. The instrument is **not** negotiable if it is a draft.	O	O
7. The instrument is bearer paper if it is a check.	O	O
8. The instrument is negotiable if it is a promissory note.	O	O
9. The instrument is bearer paper if it is a promissory note.	O	O
10. The instrument is negotiable only if it also states the word "negotiable" on its face.	O	O

			Fact Pattern III	
Instructions	Fact Pattern I	Fact Pattern II		Fact Pattern IV

A promissory note states that the maker promises to pay to the order of ABC Company $10,000 plus interest at 2% above the prime rate of XYZ Bank in New York City one year from the date on the promissory note.

	Correct	*Incorrect*
11. The interest rate provision destroys negotiability because the prime rate can fluctuate during the year.	O	O
12. The interest rate provision destroys negotiability because one has to look outside the note to see what the prime rate of XYZ Bank is.	O	O
13. The maker is obligated to pay only the $10,000 because the amount of interest is not a sum certain.	O	O
14. The maker must pay $10,000 plus the judgment rate of interest because the amount of interest cannot be determined without referring to facts outside the instrument.	O	O
15. Any holder of this note could not qualify as a holder in due course because of the interest provision.	O	O

Instructions	Fact Pattern I	Fact Pattern II	Fact Pattern III	Fact Pattern IV

An individual fills out his personal check. He postdates the check for ten days later and notes on the face of the check that it is for "Payment for textbooks."

		Correct	*Incorrect*
16.	The instrument is demand paper because it is a check and is thus payable immediately.	○	○
17.	The check is not payable before the date on its face.	○	○
18.	If a bank pays on this check before its stated date, the bank is liable to the drawer.	○	○
19.	The notation "Payment for textbooks" destroys negotiability because it makes payment conditional.	○	○
20.	The notation "Payment for textbooks" does **not** destroy negotiability but only if the check was actually used to pay for textbooks.	○	○

Simulation Problem 2   (10 to 15 minutes)

Situation		
	Instrument 1	Instrument 2

During an audit of Trent Realty Corp.'s financial statements, Clark, CPA, reviewed two instruments.

	Instrument 1	
Situation		Instrument 2

Part a.

Instrument 1

$300,000	Belle, MD
	April 1, 2004

For value received, ten years after date, I promise to pay to the order of Dart Finance Co. Three Hundred Thousand and 00/100 dollars with interest at 9% per annum compounded annually until fully paid.

This instrument arises out of the sale of land located in MD.

It is further agreed that:

1.　　　　Maker will pay all costs of collection including reasonable attorney fees.
2.　　　　Maker may prepay the amount outstanding on any anniversary date of this instrument.

G. Evans
G. Evans

The following transactions relate to Instrument 1.

- On March 15, 2005, Dart endorsed the instrument in blank and sold it to Morton for $275,000.
- On July 10, 2005, Evans informed Morton that Dart had fraudulently induced Evans into signing the instrument.
- On August 15, 2005, Trent, which knew of Evans' claim against Dart, purchased the instrument from Morton for $50,000.

Items 1 through 5 relate to Instrument 1. For each item, select from List I the correct answer. An answer may be selected once, more than once, or not at all.

List I

A. Draft	E. Holder in due course	H. Nonnegotiable
B. Promissory Note	F. Holder with rights of a holder in due	I. Evans, Morton, and Dart
C. Security Agreement	course under the shelter provision	J. Morton and Dart
D. Holder	G. Negotiable	K. Only Dart

	(A)	(B)	(C)	(D)	(E)	(F)	(G)	(H)	(I)	(J)	(K)
1. Instrument 1 is a (type of instrument)	○	○	○	○	○	○	○	○	○	○	○
2. Instrument 1 is (negotiability)	○	○	○	○	○	○	○	○	○	○	○
3. Morton is considered a (type of ownership)	○	○	○	○	○	○	○	○	○	○	○
4. Trent is considered a (type of ownership)	○	○	○	○	○	○	○	○	○	○	○
5. Trent could recover on the instrument from [liable party(s)]	○	○	○	○	○	○	○	○	○	○	○

		Instrument 2
Situation	Instrument 1	

Part b.   ### Instrument 2

Front

To:	Pure Bank
	Upton, VT
	April 5, 2004

Pay to the order of M. West $1,500.00
One Thousand Five Hundred and 00/100 Dollars
on May 1, 2004

W. Fields
W. Fields

Back

M. West

Pay to C. Larr
T. Keetin

C. Larr
without recourse

Items 6 through 13 relate to Instrument 2. For each item, select from List II the correct answer. An answer may be selected once, more than once, or not at all.

<u>List II</u>

A.	Bearer paper	F.	Nonnegotiable
B.	Blank	G.	Note
C.	Check	H.	Order paper
D.	Draft	I.	Qualified
E.	Negotiable	J.	Special

		(A)	(B)	(C)	(D)	(E)	(F)	(G)	(H)	(I)	(J)
6.	Instrument 2 is a (type of instrument)	○	○	○	○	○	○	○	○	○	○
7.	Instrument 2 is (negotiability)	○	○	○	○	○	○	○	○	○	○
8.	West's endorsement makes the instrument (type of instrument)	○	○	○	○	○	○	○	○	○	○
9.	Keetin's endorsement makes the instrument (type of instrument)	○	○	○	○	○	○	○	○	○	○
10.	Larr's endorsement makes the instrument (type of instrument)	○	○	○	○	○	○	○	○	○	○
11.	West's endorsement would be considered (type of endorsement)	○	○	○	○	○	○	○	○	○	○
12.	Keetin's endorsement would be considered (type of endorsement)	○	○	○	○	○	○	○	○	○	○
13.	Larr's endorsement would be considered (type of endorsement)	○	○	○	○	○	○	○	○	○	○

1. c ___ ___	12. c ___ ___	22. c ___ ___	34. d ___ ___	45. b ___ ___
2. a ___ ___	13. d ___ ___	24. b ___ ___	35. d ___ ___	46. c ___ ___
3. c ___ ___	14. a ___ ___	25. a ___ ___	36. d ___ ___	47. c ___ ___
4. a ___ ___	15. a ___ ___	26. a ___ ___	37. c ___ ___	48. c ___ ___
5. a ___ ___	16. a ___ ___	27. d ___ ___	38. a ___ ___	49. b ___ ___
6. a ___ ___	17. c ___ ___	28. b ___ ___	39. c ___ ___	50. d ___ ___
7. a ___ ___	18. d ___ ___	29. d ___ ___	40. c ___ ___	
8. c ___ ___	19. d ___ ___	30. b ___ ___	41. d ___ ___	
9. c ___ ___	20. a ___ ___	31. d ___ ___	42. d ___ ___	
10. a ___ ___	21. b ___ ___	32. b ___ ___	43. c ___ ___	1st: ___/50 = ___%
11. d ___ ___	22. a ___ ___	33. c ___ ___	44. b ___ ___	2nd: ___/50 = ___%

MULTIPLE-CHOICE ANSWER EXPLANATIONS

B. Types of Commercial Paper

1.   (c)   This is a very common type of restrictive endorsement. Answer (a) is incorrect because a blank endorsement is one that does not specify any endorsee. Answer (b) is incorrect because a qualified endorsement is one in which the endorser disclaims liability to pay the holder or any subsequent endorser for the instrument if it is later dishonored. An example of this is the endorser putting in the words "without recourse" on the back of the instrument. Answer (d) is incorrect because a special endorsement refers to when the endorser indicates a specific person who needs to subsequently endorse it.

2.   (a)   This instrument is a draft because it is a three-party instrument where a drawer (Dexter) orders a drawee (Middlesex National Bank) to pay a fixed amount in money to the payee (Silver). Answer (b) is incorrect because in order for the instrument to qualify as a check, the instrument must be payable on demand. In this situation, the instrument held by Silver is a time draft which specifies the payment date as October 1, 2001. Answer (d) is incorrect because a promissory note is a two-party instrument in which one party promises to pay a fixed amount in money to the payee. Answer (c) is incorrect because a trade acceptance is a special type of draft in which a seller of goods extends credit to the buyer by drawing a draft on that buyer directing the buyer to pay a fixed amount in money to the seller on a specified date. The seller is therefore both the drawer and payee in a trade acceptance.

3.   (c)   Under the Revised Article 3 of the UCC, there are two basic categories of negotiable instruments (i.e., promissory notes and drafts). A certificate of deposit is a promissory note issued by a bank. A check is a draft drawn on a bank and payable on demand unless it is postdated.

4.   (a)   A promissory demand note is a two-party instrument in which the maker (T. T. Tile) promises to pay to the order of the payee (A. B. Shark) and the payment is made upon demand with no time period stated. N. A. Abner made a guaranty but it is still a two-party note. Answers (b), (c), and (d) are all incorrect because sight drafts, checks, and trade acceptances are all three-party instruments requiring a drawee.

5.   (a)   Drafts and checks are three-party instruments in which the drawer orders the drawee to pay the payee. Notes and certificates of deposit are two-party instruments in which the maker promises to pay the payee.

C. Requirements of Negotiability

6.   (a)   All negotiable instruments are required to be payable to order or bearer with the exception of checks. This instrument says "Pay to Jenny Larson"; therefore, it can only be negotiable if it is a check. All of these instruments in the question would be negotiable if they said "Pay to the order of Jenny Larson," including a check.

7.   (a)   One of the elements of negotiability is that the note be payable to order or to bearer. Under the revised UCC, this is true for all negotiable instruments except checks that do not need the words "to the order of" or "bearer." Answer (b) is incorrect because signing by the payee is a method of negotiation but is not a requirement to make the instrument negotiable. Answer (c) is incorrect because such references are not required. Answer (d) is incorrect because the elements of negotiability do not require the stating of any conditions of payment. In fact, such conditions can destroy negotiability.

8.   (c)   This promissory note is negotiable because it meets all of the requirements of negotiability. It is written and signed. It contains an unconditional promise to pay a fixed amount in money. It is payable at a definite time under the UCC even though the maker may extend the due date to March 31, 2001, because this option of the maker to extend the time is limited to a definite date. And finally, the instrument is payable to bearer because it states "Pay to Astor Co. or bearer." Answer (a) is incorrect because the reference to the computer purchase agreement does not condition payment on this agreement, it simply refers to it. Answer (b) is incorrect because when the words and numbers are contradictory, the written words control and thus, the instrument still contains a fixed amount. Answer (d) is incorrect because once an instrument is negotiable and remains unaltered, it is negotiable for all parties.

9.   (c)   The Revised Article 3 of the UCC allows a negotiable instrument to be payable in any medium of exchange of the US or a foreign government. Therefore, answer (a) is incorrect. Answer (b) is incorrect because negotiability is maintained despite the fact that rate of exchange can fluctuate. This is a fact of doing business internationally. Answer (d) is incorrect because the exchange rate can be determined readily.

10.   (a)   This instrument satisfies all of the requirements for negotiability except for the requirement that it be payable on demand or at a definite time. Since it is payable ten days after the sale of the maker's diamond ring, the time of payment is not certain as to the time of occurrence. Answer (b) is incorrect because a negotiable instrument may contain a promise to provide collateral. Answer (c) is incorrect because although it is a two-party note, it is not negotiable because it is not payable at a definite time. Answer (d) is incorrect because it is not negotiable and is not a draft. A draft requires a drawer ordering a drawee to pay the payee.

11. **(d)** Since this note is subject to the terms of another document, the promise in the note is conditional, causing negotiability to be destroyed. Answer (a) is incorrect because since one must look to a document outside of the note, this destroys negotiability. Answer (b) is incorrect because the note itself makes its promise conditioned on the contract. Thus, the contract cannot be ignored. Answer (c) is incorrect because the contract, which is outside of the note, must be examined. This destroys the note's negotiability.

12. **(c)** For a note to be negotiable, it must be written and signed by the maker, contain an unconditional promise to pay a fixed amount in money, be payable at a definite time or on demand, and be payable to order or to bearer. This note fulfills all of these requirements. It is therefore negotiable and does not require that the payment date be specified because it is payable on demand. Answer (a) is incorrect because the note fulfills all the requirements of negotiability. Answer (b) is incorrect because in cases of inconsistencies between words and figures, the words control. Answer (d) is incorrect because although the guaranty may make the note more desirable, it was already negotiable.

13. **(d)** Under the Revised Article 3 of the UCC, interest rates are allowed to be variable or fluctuate. Negotiability is not destroyed. Answer (a) is incorrect because the sum certain rule allows the interest rate to vary based on such things as the prime rate of interest of a given bank. Answer (b) is incorrect because negotiability is not destroyed by needing to resort to information outside of the negotiable instrument. Answer (c) is incorrect because it is allowed for the interest to vary while the negotiable instrument is still outstanding.

14. **(a)** Under the Revised Article 3 of the UCC, a check may be postdated and need not be payable to order. The words "Pay to Corbin Company" are allowed for checks. However, all negotiable instruments other than checks need to be payable to order or to bearer.

15. **(a)** Under the Revised Article 3 of the UCC, unlike under earlier versions, payment on a negotiable instrument may be designated to come from a particular source or fund. The maker or drawer does not have to be personally obligated. Therefore, answer (b) is incorrect. Answer (c) is incorrect because this provision is not deemed to make the instrument not negotiable for reason of a conditional promise. Answer (d) is incorrect because lack of payment due to insufficient funds does not destroy negotiability.

D. Interpretation of Ambiguities in Negotiable Instruments

16. **(a)** When the amount in words differs from the amount in figures on a negotiable instrument, the words control over the figures. Answer (b) is incorrect because the law has settled this ambiguity in favor of the words on negotiable instruments. Answer (c) is incorrect because the

instrument is still negotiable and can be cashed. Answer (d) is incorrect because there is no such rule involving 10%.

E. Negotiation

17. **(c)** Although negotiating bearer paper only requires delivery, negotiating order paper requires both delivery and endorsement by the transferor. Delivery requires that the holder get possession of the instrument.

18. **(d)** Since John Smith endorsed the instrument in blank (i.e., did not specify any endorsee) it became bearer paper. Since it was bearer paper in Harris's hands, she did not need to endorse it to negotiate it to the next party, Sharp. Answer (a) is incorrect because when Parker endorsed "Pay to John Smith only" he made the instrument require John Smith's signature to negotiate it further. Parker's endorsement will not restrict negotiations beyond John Smith's and it does not destroy negotiability. Answer (b) is incorrect as although conditions on the front generally destroy the negotiability of an instrument, conditions put into an endorsement do not. Answer (c) is incorrect because the wording "Pay to John Smith only" will not restrict further negotiation after John Smith. When John Smith endorsed it in blank, it became bearer paper.

19. **(d)** The words "Pay to the order of Jerry Lin" are not necessary because the note is already negotiable on its face where it was payable to the order of Ann Jackson. Answer (a) is not chosen because although when Jackson endorsed the note in blank, it became bearer paper, it was converted back to order paper when Lin put "Pay to Jerry Lin" above Jackson's endorsement. Answer (b) should not be chosen because when Jackson endorsed it without specifying any payee, the note became bearer paper. Answer (c) should not be chosen because it became order paper once "Pay to Jerry Lin" was written, whether he personally did it or not.

20. **(a)** This endorsement is special because it indicates "Pay to Alex Ericson" and it is restrictive because of the phrase "if he completes...." Answer (b) is incorrect because this endorsement is special and qualified. Answer (c) is incorrect because although it is restrictive, it is also a blank endorsement. Answer (d) is incorrect because although it is a special endorsement stating "Pay to Alex Ericson," it is not restrictive.

21. **(b)** Although the note was originally a bearer instrument, Stone endorsed it with a special endorsement when s/he indicated "Pay to the order of Willard Bank, without recourse" above the endorsement. This means that Willard Bank must endorse the note to negotiate it further. Answer (a) is incorrect because qualified endorsements such as "without recourse" disclaim some liability but do not prevent subsequent parties from becoming a holder in due course. Answer (c) is incorrect because although Stone is not a holder in due course because s/he had notice that the maker disputed liability under the note, Willard Bank is a holder in due course because Willard was unaware that Helco disputed liability on the note. Additionally, Willard meets the other requirements to be a holder in due course, because he was a holder of a negotiable note, gave value ($3,900) for it, took in good faith, and had no notice, not only of the alleged breach by Astor, but of any other relevant problems such as being overdue or having been dishonored.

Answer (d) is incorrect because the note was bearer paper when Stone received it and thus did not require an endorsement.

F. Holder in Due Course

22. (a)   To be a holder in due course, the holder must, among other things, take without notice that the instrument is overdue, has been dishonored, or that any person has a defense or claim to it. In this case, the person was notified that payment was refused. Answer (b) is incorrect because a prior endorser being discharged does not mean that person necessarily had a defense to the instrument. Answer (c) is incorrect because the use of a note as collateral does not prevent a holder from becoming a holder in due course. Answer (d) is incorrect because reasonable discounts are allowed and do not indicate bad faith or that a person has a defense or claim to the instrument.

23. (c)   An executory promise does not satisfy the value requirement to be a holder in due course until the promise is actually performed. Answer (a) is incorrect because Ruper received the check to pay off a previous debt owed to her. Taking in satisfaction of a previous debt constitutes value to be a holder in due course. Answer (b) is incorrect because she took the check in exchange for another negotiable instrument. The fact that the check was for less than the face value of the negotiable note does not violate the value requirements. Answer (d) is incorrect because taking the check to pay off an antecedent debt constitutes value whether the debtor was a relative or not.

24. (b)   In order to be a holder in due course, the individual must be a holder of a negotiable instrument as well as fulfilling the additional requirements referred to in the question. In this case, the draft is not negotiable because it is not payable to order or to bearer. However, the check is negotiable because checks do not have to be payable to order or to bearer to be negotiable.

25. (a)   Even though an antecedent debt would not be valid for the consideration requirement under contract law, it is valid for the value requirement under negotiable instruments law. A promise to perform services at a future date is an executory promise and is not value until actually performed.

G. Rights of a Holder in Due Course

26. (a)   Monk is not personally a HDC because although he was a holder of the negotiable note for which he gave value, he did not take in good faith because he had knowledge of the fraud before he purchased the note. Furthermore, he had notice that the note was overdue. Therefore, answer (c) can be ruled out. Answer (a) however, is correct because even though Monk was not a HDC, he obtained the instrument from Wilk who was a HDC. Therefore, Monk qualifies as a holder through a HDC and thus obtains all of the rights of a HDC. Answers (b) and (d) are incorrect because fraud in the inducement is a personal defense. Wilk, as a HDC, and Monk, as a holder through a HDC, both take the note free of personal defenses.

27. (d)   A holder in due course takes an instrument free of personal defenses but is subject to real defenses. Answer (d) is correct because it involves a breach of contract or nonperformance of a condition precedent which describes a personal defense. Answer (c) is incorrect because bankruptcy is a real defense. Answer (a) is incorrect because when a minor may disaffirm a contract, it is treated as a real defense. Answer (b) is incorrect because a forgery of a maker's or drawer's signature is a real defense.

28. (b)   Real defenses include bankruptcy and material alterations of the instrument. Material alterations include a change of any monetary amount. They also include changes in the interest rate, if any, on the instrument or changes in the date if the date affects when it is paid or the amount of interest to be paid. Personal defenses include the more typical defenses such as breach of contract, breach of warranty, and fraud in the inducement.

29. (d)   Helco is claiming breach of contract which is a personal defense. The general rule is that transfer of a negotiable instrument to a holder in due course cuts off all personal defenses against the holder in due course. Since Willard Bank is a holder in due course, Helco is liable to Willard Bank. Answer (a) is incorrect because Willard Bank meets all of the requirements to be a holder in due course. That is, Willard is a holder of a negotiable instrument, gave value, took in good faith, and took without notice of certain problems such as Helco's disputed liability. The fact that Stone was not a holder in due course does not change this. Answer (b) is incorrect because Willard Bank as a holder in due course wins against Helco's claim of Astor's breach. The breach of contract would only constitute a personal defense. Answer (c) is incorrect because Helco is liable to Willard Bank.

30. (b)   When a negotiable instrument is negotiated from a holder in due course to another holder, this other holder normally obtains the rights of a holder in due course. However, an important exception applies to this case. Since Johnson knew of the lie when he first acquired the note, he was not a HDC and cannot improve his status by reacquiring from a HDC. Answer (a) is incorrect because he did not qualify as a HDC due to his knowledge of the defense. Answer (c) is incorrect because fraud in the inducement is a personal, not real, defense. Answer (d) is incorrect because his knowledge of the lie prevents his becoming a HDC at first and prevents his later becoming a holder through a holder in due course.

31. (d)   Even though Buck did not personally qualify as a HDC, he was a holder through a holder in due course and can collect from the drawer despite the drawer's personal defense. Answer (a) is incorrect because Goran's defense is a personal defense. Also, the bank is permitted to follow the customer's stop payment order. Answer (b) is incorrect because Buck as a holder through a holder in due course can collect despite the personal defense. Answer (c) is incorrect because the bank is permitted to refuse payment and then Buck collects from the drawer.

32. (b)   A party who found an instrument payable to bearer is a holder but not a holder through a holder in due course. To be the latter, s/he must obtain a negotiable instrument from a holder in due course. If this had been the case, s/he would have obtained the rights of a holder in due course. However, since s/he found the instrument, it cannot be established that the previous holder was a holder in due course. Answer (a) is incorrect because s/he did receive the instrument from a holder in due course. S/he, therefore, does obtain the rights of a holder in due course even though s/he cannot be a holder in due course him/herself because of having notice of the defense on the instrument. Answer (c) is incorrect because the party received the instrument from a holder in due course and thus becomes a holder through a holder in due course. Answer (d) is incorrect because this party personally qualifies as a holder in due course, thereby obtaining those rights.

33.   (c)   An unauthorized completion of an incomplete instrument is a personal defense, and, as such, will not be valid against a HDC. Infancy (unless the instrument is exchanged for necessaries), bankruptcy of the maker, and extreme duress are all real defenses which are good against a HDC.

34.   (d)   Since Cobb left the amount blank on the signed check and Garson filled it in contrary to Cobb's instructions, this is a case of unauthorized completion which is a personal defense. Garson then negotiated the check to Josephs who is a holder in due course because he gave value for the negotiable instrument and took in good faith without notice of any problems. He gave value for the full $1,000 since cash and taking the check for a previous debt are both value under negotiable instrument law. Therefore, Josephs may collect the full $1,000 and win over the personal defense that Cobb has.

35.   (d)   A maker of a note may use real defenses against a holder in due course but not personal defenses. Lack of consideration is a personal defense. Discharge in bankruptcy, forgery, and fraud in the execution are all real defenses, which create a valid defense against a holder in due course.

H. Liability of Parties

36.   (d)   The maker of a note has primary liability on that note. No one has primary liability on a draft or check unless the drawee accepts it. This is true because although the drawee has been ordered by the drawer to pay, the drawee has not agreed to pay unless it accepts the draft or check.

37.   (c)   When there are multiple endorsers on a negotiable instrument, each is liable to subsequent endorsers or holders. Oral renunciation of a prior party's liability does not discharge that party's liability. Answer (a) is incorrect because once the primary party pays on the instrument, all endorsers are discharged from liability. Answer (b) is incorrect because cancellation of a prior party's endorsement does discharge that party's liability. Answer (d) is incorrect because when a holder intentionally destroys a negotiable instrument, the prior endorsers are discharged.

38.   (a)   When a negotiable instrument is indorsed and a specific person is indicated, the instrument is order paper and can be further negotiated by that person. Note also that payment of the instrument is guaranteed. If the primary party to the negotiable instrument does not pay, the indorser(s) are obligated to pay on the instrument when the holder demands payment or acceptance in a timely manner.

39.   (c)   Striking out the endorsement of a person discharges that person's secondary liability and discharges subsequent endorsers who have already endorsed. This does not, however, discharge any of the prior parties. Therefore,

in this case, Betty Ash is discharged from secondary liability to the later endorsers.

40.   (c)   Various acts or failures of a holder can cause a discharge of prior holders of an instrument. Among these are an unexcused delay in presenting an instrument, cancellation or renunciation of the instrument, fraudulent or material alteration, and certification of a check. Notice of dishonor generally should be given by midnight of the third business day after the dishonor or notice of the dishonor. Banks must give notice by midnight of the next banking day. In either case, answer (c) is correct. Answers (a), (b), and (d) are all incorrect because they are all acts that cause the discharge of prior holders.

41.   (d)   When a holder procures certification of a check, all prior endorsers are discharged. This is true because when a bank certifies a check, it has accepted the check and agreed to honor it as presented. Answers (a) and (b) are incorrect because although lack of notice of dishonor to other endorsers and late presentment of the instrument will normally discharge all endorsers, this is not true if the lack of notice of dishonor or the late presentment is excused. They can be excused in such cases as the delay is beyond the party's control or the presentment is waived. Furthermore in this fact pattern, Hopkins endorsed the check "payment guaranteed" and Quarry endorsed it "collection guaranteed." When words of guaranty are used, presentment or notice of dishonor are not required to hold the users liable. Answer (c) is incorrect because when the maker is insolvent the endorsers will likely be sought after for payment.

42.   (d)   Since Dodsen did not endorse the note, s/he gave transfer warranties and presentment warranties only to the immediate transferee (i.e., Mellon). Mellon gave these warranties to Bloom. Therefore although Mellon will be liable to Bloom, Dodsen will not be.

43.   (c)   Normally, Bilco could seek collection on the defaulted note from the previous endorsers, Tamp and Miller. However, in this case, Bilco agreed to release the collateral underlying this note. Since this materially affects the rights of Tamp and Miller to use this collateral, this act releases them. Answer (a) is incorrect because except for the release of the collateral, Bilco could have collected from his/her immediate transferor even without the endorsement. Answers (b) and (d) are incorrect because the release of the collateral releases Tamp and Miller.

44.   (b)   When a person endorses a negotiable instrument, s/he is normally secondarily liable to later endorsers. This liability means that the endorser can be required to make good on the instrument. If s/he endorses without recourse, the endorser can avoid this liability. Answer (a) is incorrect because the endorser is not liable to prior endorsers anyway whether or not s/he endorses without recourse. Answer (c) is incorrect because the endorser still gives the transferor's warranties with some modification. Answer (d) is incorrect because a check is converted into order paper only if the endorser also specifies a payee.

J. Banks

45.   (b)   Under the Revised Article 3, postdating a check does not destroy negotiability but makes the check properly payable on or after the date written on the check. Although the postdated check is not properly payable before the date on the instrument, if a bank pays it earlier, it is not liable unless the drawer had notified the bank that the check was postdated.

46. (c) If the bank fails to follow a stop payment order, it is liable to the customer only if the customer had a valid defense on the check and therefore suffers a loss. Comp Electronics, the payee, can qualify as a HDC and Stanley would have to pay anyway despite the stop payment order. Answer (a) is incorrect because the bank did not cause Stanley a loss. Answer (b) is incorrect because oral stop payment orders are valid for fourteen days. Answer (d) is incorrect because from the facts given, there is no evidence that Comp Electronics breached the contract.

M. Transfer of Negotiable Documents of Title

47. (c) A trade acceptance is a special type of draft in which a seller of goods extends credit to the buyer by drawing the draft on the buyer ordering the buyer to make payment to the seller on a specified date.

48. (c) A negotiable bearer bill of lading is a document of title that under the UCC allows the bearer the rights to the goods mentioned including the right to designate who will receive delivery of the goods. The carrier is required to deliver the goods to the holder of negotiable bearer bill of lading or to that holder's designee. The carrier is liable for any misdelivery for any damages caused.

49. (b) A person who negotiates a negotiable document of title for value extends the following warranties to the immediate purchaser: (1) negotiation by the transferor is rightful and fully effective with respect to the goods it represents, (2) the transferor has no knowledge of any facts that would impair the document's validity or worth, and (3) the document is genuine. However, the transferor of a negotiable warehouse receipt does not necessarily warrant that the warehouseman will honor the document.

50. (d) A negotiable warehouse receipt is a document issued as evidence of receipt of goods by a person engaged in the business of storing goods for hire. The warehouse receipt is negotiable if the face of the document contains the words of negotiability (order or bearer). Answer (a) is incorrect because the negotiability of the warehouse receipt is not destroyed by the inclusion of a contractual limitation on the warehouseman's liability. Answer (b) is incorrect because to qualify as commercial paper, the instrument must be payable only in money. If an instrument is payable in money or by the delivery of goods, it is a nonnegotiable instrument. Answer (c) is incorrect because the UCC does not state that only a bonded and licensed warehouseman can issue a warehouse receipt.

ANSWER OUTLINE

Problem 1   Fictitious Payee; Drawee Bank's Acceptance
                 of Check with Forgery of Drawer's Signature

a.   Checks paid to fictitious payees
        Hex will bear the ultimate loss on these items
           General Rule—forged signatures of drawers and
           forged endorsements are real defenses valid
           against holder in due course
        Exception—fictitious payees rule shifts loss to
        employer-drawer
           Rule states that real defense not created when
           agent or employee of the drawer with name of
           payee intending latter to have no such interest

b.   Checks containing forged signature of treasurer
        Forging of treasurer's signature is an unauthorized
        signature and not valid
        Bank is obligated to know the signatures of its cus-
        tomers and will bear the loss unless:
           Bank proves Hex contributed to forgery
           Bank proves Hex failed to exercise reasonable care
           and promptness in discovering unauthorized sig-
           natures on returned checks

UNOFFICIAL ANSWER

Problem 1   Fictitious Payee; Drawee Bank's Acceptance
                 of Check with Forgery of Drawer's Signature

a.   Checks paid to fictitious payees. Hex will bear the
ultimate loss on these items (the fictitious or nonexistent
"employees" and the fictitious suppliers). As a general rule,
forged signatures of drawers and forged endorsements are
real defenses which are valid even against a holder in due
course. However, when some of these activities are engaged
in by the employees of an employer-drawer of the checks, a
different rule is applied. Essentially, this rule negates these
real defenses in certain cases thereby shifting the loss to the
employer-drawer. The key rule is contained in the Uniform
Commercial Code's Article on Commercial Paper which
deals with "Imposters; Signature of Payee." In essence, this
rule makes the endorsement or signature of the agent or employee of the drawer (Hex) "effective" where the agent has
supplied the drawer the name of the payee intending the
latter to have no such interest.

As far as Omega is concerned, it will be treated as if it
had honored valid orders to pay and need not refund to Hex
the amounts it paid. The orders are valid since the forged
endorsements are not treated as unauthorized.

**b.   Checks which contain the forged signature of the
treasurer.** From the facts it is apparent that the treasurer
had the authority to sign checks and not the assistant treasurer or head of payroll. Thus, the forging of the treasurer's
signature was an "unauthorized signature" under the UCC.

As to these checks, the UCC provides that such signatures are wholly inoperative since the guilty parties had no
authority to sign the treasurer's or any other authorized
party's name as the drawer on behalf of Hex.

As between Hex and Omega, there is an obligation on
the part of the bank to know the signature of its drawer-
depositors. Since Omega has paid the items, it cannot re-
coup the loss from Hex. However, the bank has two possible ways to escape liability to Hex. First, it can resort to the
UCC section which imposes upon a customer to whom items
(checks) are returned, a duty to exercise reasonable care and

promptness in discovering and reporting unauthorized signatures. Another possibility is to establish negligence on the
part of Hex which substantially contributed to the forgeries.
Unless the bank can demonstrate that one of these exceptions applies, it will bear the loss.

ANSWER OUTLINE

Problem 2   Requisites for Negotiability; Transfer and
                 Negotiation; Holders and Holders in Due
                 Course; Liabilities and Rights

Hillcraft's assertion that the note is nonnegotiable is incor-
rect
   Reference to license agreement is okay because it does not
   make note subject to it
   Negotiability unaffected by maker's time extensions for a
   definite period of time
Hillcraft's assertion that River Oaks is not a HDC is incor-
rect
   Under UCC, value given when note is payment/security
   for antecedent debt
Hillcraft's assertion that River Oaks is not a HDC due to the
dispute is correct
   Holder isn't a HDC if takes note with notice of dispute
Hillcraft's assertion that it can raise the breach as a defense
is incorrect
   River Oaks has rights of HDC since took note from HDC
   River Oaks therefore does not take subject to Hillcraft's
   personal defense on note
Hillcraft's assertion that River Oaks has no right to the note
is incorrect
   Payee line on face makes it bearer paper
   Proper negotiation of bearer paper needs no endorsement
Hillcraft's assertion that its maximum liability is $4,000,
plus accrued interest, is correct
   Words take precedence over numbers if in conflict

UNOFFICIAL ANSWER

Problem 2   Requisites for Negotiability; Transfer and
                 Negotiation; Holders and Holders in Due
                 Course; Liabilities and Rights

Hillcraft's first assertion, that the note is nonnegotiable
because it references the license agreement and is not payable at a definite time or on demand, is incorrect. The note
is negotiable despite the reference to the license agreement
because it does not make the note subject to the terms of the
agreement; rather, the reference is regarded only as a recital
of its existence.

Also, Hillcraft's right to extend the time for payment
does not make the note nonnegotiable because the extension
period is for a definite period of time.

Hillcraft's second assertion, that River Oaks is not a
holder in due course (HDC) because it received the note as
security for an existing debt and, therefore, did not give
value for it, is incorrect. Under the UCC Commercial Paper
Article, a holder does give value for an instrument when it is
taken in payment of, or as security for, an antecedent claim.

Hillcraft's third assertion, that River Oaks is not a HDC
because River Oaks was aware of Alexco's alleged breach
of the license agreement, is correct. If a holder of a note is
aware of a dispute when it acquires the note, that holder
cannot be a HDC because it took with notice.

Hillcraft's fourth assertion, that it can raise the alleged breach by Alexco as a defense to payment of the note, is incorrect. Even though River Oaks is not a HDC under the UCC "shelter provision," it is entitled to the protection of a HDC because it took the instrument from First Auto, which was a HDC. Therefore, River Oaks did not take the note subject to Hillcraft's defense based on the alleged breach by Alexco. Hillcraft's defense is considered a personal defense and can only be used by Hillcraft against Alexco.

Hillcraft's fifth assertion, that River Oaks has no right to the note because it was not endorsed by Alexco, is incorrect. River Oaks acquired rights to the Hillcraft note without Alexco's endorsement because the note was a bearer instrument as a result of it being payable to "Alexco Company or bearer." A bearer instrument can be negotiated by delivery alone.

Hillcraft's final assertion, that the maximum amount Hillcraft would owe under the note is $4,000, plus accrued interest, is correct. If there is a conflict between a number written in numerals and also described by words, the words take precedence. Therefore, Hillcraft's maximum potential principal liability is $4,000 under the note.

SOLUTIONS TO SIMULATION PROBLEMS

Simulation Problem 1

1. **(C)** Even though the instrument states "Pay to Rich Crane," it is negotiable because a check does **not** have to be payable to order or bearer.

2. **(I)** A draft to be negotiable must be payable to order or to bearer. "Pay to the order of Rich Crane" would have made it negotiable.

3. **(I)** Promissory notes to be negotiable must be payable to order or to bearer.

4. **(I)** Certificates of deposit, unlike checks, must be payable to order or to bearer.

5. **(C)** A cashier's check is an actual check and thus does **not** have to be payable to order or to bearer.

6. **(I)** If an instrument does not name any payee, it is considered to be payable to bearer. Thus, negotiability is not destroyed.

7. **(C)** If no payee is named, it is bearer paper.

8. **(C)** Since no payee was named, it is bearer paper and thus negotiability is maintained.

9. **(C)** Like the cases of drafts, checks, and certificates of deposit, it is bearer paper.

10. **(I)** There is no such requirement to state "negotiable" on its face.

11. **(I)** The negotiability of an instrument is not destroyed simply because the interest rate used may fluctuate.

12. **(I)** Negotiability is not destroyed even if one has to look outside of the document to determine what the actual rate is.

13. **(I)** Even though the interest rate may fluctuate, the maker is still obligated to pay the $10,000 plus the interest.

14. **(I)** The maker must pay the $10,000 plus the interest described on the promissory note.

15. **(I)** Since this note is negotiable despite the possible fluctuation of the interest rate, a holder could qualify to be a holder in due course under those applicable rules.

16. **(I)** Normally a check is demand paper. However, when it is postdated, it is not payable until that date.

17. **(C)** The postdating overrides the normal characteristic that it is payable on demand.

18. **(I)** The bank is not liable unless the drawer has given the bank prior notice of the postdating.

19. **(I)** Notations on negotiable instruments that note what it is for do not put conditions on the payment and thus do not destroy negotiability.

20. **(I)** These notations can be ignored because they are not conditions of payment.

Simulation Problem 2

Part a.

1.   **(B)** Instrument 1 is a two-party instrument in which Evans promises to pay a fixed amount in money to Dart; therefore it qualifies as a promissory note. A promissory note may be payable on demand or at a specific point in time.

2.   **(G)** Instrument 1 meets the requirements of negotiability. It is written and signed by the maker. It contains an unconditional promise or order to pay a fixed amount in money, at a definite time or on demand. The document is also payable to order. The fact that it is payable on a certain date subject to acceleration does not destroy its negotiability.

3.   **(E)** To qualify as a holder in due course, an individual must be a holder of a properly negotiated negotiable instrument, give value for the instrument, and take the instrument in good faith and without notice that it is overdue, has been dishonored, or that any person has a defense or claim to it.

4.   **(F)** When a negotiable instrument is negotiated from a holder in due course to a second holder, the second holder usually acquires the rights of a holder in due course through the shelter provision. The shelter provision applies to holders who have not previously held the instrument with knowledge of any defenses.

5.   **(I)** A holder with rights of a holder in due course under the shelter provision obtains all the rights of a holder in due course. A holder in due course takes an instrument free of personal defenses, including fraud in the inducement. Therefore, Evans' claim that Dart had fraudulently induced Evans into signing the instrument would not prevent Trent from recovering from Evans. Trent would also be able to recover from Morton and Dart based on his holder in due course status.

Part b.

6.   **(D)** Instrument 2 is a draft because it is a three-party instrument where a drawer (Fields) orders a drawee (Pure Bank) to pay a fixed amount in money to the payee (West). It is not a check because it is not payable on demand.

7.   **(E)** The draft qualifies as a negotiable instrument as it meets all of the required elements of negotiability. The draft is written and signed by the drawer. It contains an unconditional order to pay a fixed amount in money. It is made payable to order and is payable at a definite time.

8.   **(A)** A blank endorsement which does not specify any endorsee converts order paper to bearer paper.

9.   **(H)** An endorsement which indicates the specific person to whom the endorsee wishes to negotiate the instrument is a special endorsement. The use of a special endorsement converts bearer paper into order paper.

10.   **(A)** Because Larr's endorsement does not specify any endorsee, the endorsement converts the order paper into bearer paper.

11.   **(B)** West's endorsement is a blank endorsement because it does not specify any endorsee.

12.   **(J)** Because Keetin's endorsement indicates a specific person to whom the instrument is being negotiated, the endorsement is a special endorsement.

13.   **(I)** Larr's endorsement is a qualified endorsement because Larr disclaimed liability by signing without recourse.

SECURED TRANSACTIONS

Overview

The concept of secured transactions is important to modern business. A creditor often requires some security from the debtor beyond a mere promise to pay. In general, the creditor may require the debtor to provide some collateral to secure payment on the debt. If the debt is not paid, the creditor then can resort to the collateral. Under revised Article 9 of the UCC, the collateral is generally personal property or fixtures. You need to understand the concept of attachment as discussed in this module. You also need to understand the important concept of perfection discussed in this module that allows a secured party to obtain greater rights over many third parties. Be sure to understand the three methods by which perfection can be accomplished. The examination also covers rules of priorities when competing interests exist in the same collateral.

A. Scope of Secured Transactions

1. This material is based on revised UCC Article 9 as well as its subsequent amendments now adopted by all states

2. Important definitions

    a. Secured party can be any creditor who has security interest in collateral of debtor

        (1) Creditor may be any of the following:

            (a) Lender

            (b) Seller

            (c) Cosigner

            (d) Buyer of accounts

            (e) Buyer of chattel paper

                1] Chattel paper consists of one or more writings that evidence debt that is secured by personal property

                    a] Often chattel paper is comprised of negotiable instrument along with security agreement

                2] Chattel paper may be tangible or electronic

        (2) Debtor is entity (or person) that owes either payment or some specified performance

        (3) Security interest is legal interest in collateral that secures either payment or debtor's specified performance of some obligation

        (4) Security agreement is transaction that creates security interest

    b. Types of collateral

        (1) Personal property

        (2) Fixtures

            (a) Personal property that has been attached permanently or relatively permanently to real property

        (3) Accounts

         (4) Investment property

            (a) Includes securities, securities accounts, commodities, or commodity accounts

        (5) Promissory note

        (6) Commercial tort claim

    c. Revised Article 9, as amended, of the UCC does **not** apply

        (1) If collateral is real property

        (2) To assignment of wage claims

        (3) To statutory liens

        (4) To checks, drafts, or certificates of deposit

B. Attachment of Security Interests

1. Attachment is a term used to describe the moment when security interest is enforceable against a debtor by the secured party

2. Security interest is said to attach when all of the following occur in any order (these are important)

    a. Secured party gives value (value is any consideration that supports any contract)

        (1) Preexisting claim (although not consideration) is value

        EXAMPLE: D already owes S $5,000 on a previous debt. Subsequently, D signs a security agreement giving S an interest in some furniture owned by D. Value has been given by S based on the previous debt.

        EXAMPLE: A bank grants a loan to allow B to purchase a washer and dryer. This extension of credit is a typical type of value.

    b. Debtor has rights in collateral

        (1) Debtor must have rights in collateral

            (a) Ownership interest suffices or having some right to possession of collateral but debtor is not required to have actual legal title

            EXAMPLE: M obtains a loan from a bank to purchase a sofa. She signs a security agreement granting the credit union a security interest in any sofa that she will buy with this loan. Attachment cannot occur until she buys a sofa. Note that the other two elements of attachment have occurred.

    c. And either

        (1) Collateral must be in possession of secured party by debtor's agreement (third party may possess if debtor agrees); or

        (2) Secured party must have "control" of collateral if it is investment property, deposit account, electronic chattel paper, or a letter-of-credit right; or

        (3) A record of security agreement must exist

            (a) Record may be in traditional writing or in electronic or other form that is retrievable in perceptible form

            (b) Security agreement must be signed or in case of electronic form, it must be authenticated

                1] Exception to need to sign or authenticate in case of pledge when secured party has possession or control of collateral

C. Perfecting a Security Interest

1. Entails steps **in addition to** attachment (with one exception discussed later) to give secured party priority over many other parties that may claim collateral

    a. Attachment focuses primarily on rights between creditor and debtor

    b. However, perfection focuses on rights between various **other parties** that may claim an interest in same collateral

        (1) Generally, perfecting a security interest gives (constructive) **notice to other parties** that the perfecting party claims an interest (security interest) in certain collateral

        (2) Only an attached security interest can be perfected

2. There are three primary ways that an attached security interest may be perfected—these are important

    a. Most security interests either can or must be perfected by filing financing statement(s) in the appropriate office

    b. Secured party takes possession of collateral, or in certain cases takes control

    c. In a few cases, security interest is perfected automatically upon attachment

3. Depending on the type of collateral there may be only one or several ways to perfect

4. Perfection by filing financing statement(s)

    a. These requirements are streamlined from previous law

        (1) Contents of financing statement

            (a) Debtor's name

                 1] Most jurisdictions now use electronic filing systems which mandate specific rules for use of names to avoid confusion

2]   Providing debtor's fictitious name or trade name normally not sufficient

(b) Indication of collateral covered

1]   Descriptions such as "all assets" are sufficient

(c) Name of secured party or agent

(d) Signature of debtor is no longer required if debtor approves

(e) Minor errors in financing statement do not invalidate it if they are not seriously misleading

(f) Law now allows that filing may be done either electronically or in writing

(2) Location of filing depends on state where individual debtor's residence is, not where collateral is

(a) If debtor is corporation or other chartered business, filing is accomplished in state where incorporated

(b) For other types of debtors, filing takes place where business is located

(3) Filings last for five years but can be continued with a continuation statement if filed within six months of expiration

(4) Financing statements can be refiled for each new five-year period

5. Perfection by secured party's control of collateral

a. This is the only way to perfect in cases of certificated securities, money, tangible chattel paper

EXAMPLE: P wishes to borrow money from a bank using several shares of stock that she owns. In addition to completing the three steps needed for attachment, the bank must possess the shares in order to perfect. Filing is not effective in this case.

(1) Electronic chattel paper must be perfected by filing or by control but not possession

(a) Secured party can have control of electronic chattel paper when there is only one authoritative copy

(2) Nonnegotiable instruments can be perfected either by filing or control

b. Possession by third parties is effective if all parties know of this

c. Perfection is accomplished by control rather than actual possession for investment property, deposit accounts, letter-of-credit rights

d. Secured party must use reasonable care to preserve collateral and may charge reasonable expenses to do so

6. Automatic perfection

a. Under the following conditions, perfection is accomplished by completing attachment with no further steps

(1) **Purchase money security interest in consumer goods**

(a) Purchase money security interest (PMSI) occurs in two important cases

1]   Seller retains security interest in same item sold on credit to secure payment

a]   Seller of software has the important PMSI

2]   Another party such as bank provides loan for and retains security interest in same item purchased by debtor

(b) "In consumer goods" means that goods are bought primarily for personal, family, or household purposes

EXAMPLE: B buys a refrigerator for his home from Friendly Appliance Dealer on credit. Friendly has B sign a written security agreement. Because all three elements needed for attachment took place, this is automatic perfection. This is true because the refrigerator is a purchase money security interest in consumer goods.

EXAMPLE: Same as previous example except that Second Intercity Bank provides the loan having B sign a security agreement. This is also a purchase money security interest in consumer goods. Perfection takes place when all three elements of attachment occur.

EXAMPLE: In the two examples above, if B had purchased the refrigerator for use in a restaurant, the collateral would be equipment. Therefore, automatic perfection would not occur. However, the secured party could file a financing statement to perfect the security interest in both cases.

   (c) Perfection by attachment does not occur for motor vehicles, trailers, or both—perfected by a lien on certificate of title filed with state

   (d) Automatic perfection is **not** effective against bona fide purchaser for value who buys goods from consumer for consumer use

      1] **Is effective,** however, if secured party had **filed**

EXAMPLE: B purchases a washer and dryer from Dear Appliances for use in his home giving Dear a security interest, then sells the washer and dryer to C for a fair price for C's household use. C is unaware of the security interest that Dear has in the washer and dryer. Dear's perfection on attachment is not effective against C.

EXAMPLE: Same example as above except that Dear had filed a financing statement. Dear wins because filing is effective even against a subsequent bona fide purchaser such as C even if he buys for consumer use.

*EXAMPLE: In the two examples above, if C had purchased the items from B for other than consumer use, C is **not** free of Dear's security interest. This is so because the rule only applies to bona fide purchasers for consumer use. The extra step of filing would not be needed.*

      2] **Is effective** if subsequent purchaser knows of security interest before buying

EXAMPLE: An appliance dealer sells a freezer to Jack for family use. Assume attachment has occurred. Jack then sells it to Cindy who is aware of the security interest that the dealer still has in the freezer. Even if Cindy is buying this for household use, she takes subject to the security interest.

  (2) Sale of promissory notes

  (3) Assignment of health care insurance to health care provider

  (4) Temporary automatic perfection for twenty days for instruments, certificated securities, negotiable documents, and proceeds of sale of perfected security interest

D. Other Issues under Secured Transactions

  1. After-acquired property and future goods are covered when parties agree to this

EXAMPLE: An agreement states that the collateral consists of all of debtor's furniture now located in his office as well as all office furniture subsequently acquired. The security interest in the new furniture cannot attach until the debtor acquires rights in the other office furniture.

    a. Typically used for inventory and accounts receivable when debtor also has rights to sell inventory and collect accounts (e.g., a floating lien)

      (1) Sometimes used for equipment

EXAMPLE: A, an automobile dealer, to obtain a loan, grants a bank a security interest covering "all automobiles now possessed and hereafter acquired." As the dealer obtains rights in the new inventory of automobiles, the security interest attaches as to those newly acquired automobiles.

    b. Certain restrictions exist if debtor buys consumer goods

      (1) An after acquired property clause applying to consumer goods is only effective against the consumer for ten days from date of purchase

  2. Although security interests in tort claims now come under revised Article 9, this security interest will not attach to an after-acquired commercial tort claim

  3. Computer software embedded in goods is treated as part of those goods and not as software

  4. Field warehousing is used to perfect security interest (analogous to possession or control)

    a. Debtor keeps inventory on his/her premises under control of third party such as bonded warehouseman or secured party's employee

    b. Secured party keeps control over inventory such as use of separate room or fenced-off portion with sign showing secured party's control

5. Consignments

   a. Consignment of security interest

     (1) If it is a "true consignment," consignee is simply a sales agent who does not own the goods but sells them for consignor

       (a) "True consignment" exists when

         1] Consignor retains title to goods
         2] Consignee has no obligation to buy goods
         3] Consignor has right to all proceeds (pays consignee commission)

         EXAMPLE: Manufacturer (consignor) gives possession of goods to a marketing representative (consignee) to sell those goods on commission.

       (b) To perfect his/her interest, a consignor must

         1] File a financing statement under secured transactions law and give notice to the consignee's creditors who have perfected security interests in the same type of goods

          a] Notice must contain description of the goods to be delivered and be given before the consignee receives possession of goods

          EXAMPLE: P delivers goods to A on consignment. The consignment is a "true consignment" in that P has title to the goods and pays A a commission for selling the goods. Any goods that are unsold are returned by A to P. A does not pay for any unsold goods. Creditors of A can assert claims against the goods that A possesses unless P has given notice to the creditors. The general way to accomplish this is by filing under the secured transactions law.

     (2) If it is not a true consignment because it is actually a **sale** from creditor to debtor in which debtor then owns the goods, look for a security agreement

       (a) Attachment and perfection occur as in typical secured transaction

E. Priorities

1. If more than one party claims a security interest in same collateral, rules of priority should be examined

2. Although the rules on priorities are complex with many exceptions, the following will give the general, important rules to prepare you for the exam

3. General rules of priorities

   a. If both parties have perfected, then first to either file or perfect generally has priority

     (1) This is true even if filing takes place before attachment

     EXAMPLE: K obtains a written security agreement on day one on collateral that D owns and possesses. On day two, K files a financing statement but does not loan the money (value) until day ten. L obtains a written security agreement on the same collateral on day three and gives value on day four and files on day six. K has priority because he filed first even though attachment and perfection did not occur until later (day ten). To test your understanding, note that for L, attachment took place on day four and perfection on day six.

     EXAMPLE: C obtains a security agreement from D on some jewelry that D owns. C loans D $1,000 and takes possession of the jewelry. The day before, D had signed a security agreement granting E a security interest in the same jewelry. E gives D $900 as a loan and files a financing statement one week later on the jewelry. C has priority over E since C perfected before E perfected and filed.

   b. Perfected security interests win over unperfected ones
   c. If neither is perfected, then the first to attach prevails although at least one party will be motivated to perfect
   d. General creditors (unsecured creditors) lose to secured creditors (perfected or unperfected)

4. Other principles on priorities

   a. Buyers in the ordinary course of business take free of any security interest whether perfected or not (be sure to know this one)

(1) In general, buying in the ordinary course of business means buying from inventory of a person or company that normally deals in those goods

(2) Buyer has priority even if s/he knows that security agreement exists but buyer must have possession

(3) Purpose is to allow purchasers to buy from merchants without fear of security agreements between merchants and other parties

> EXAMPLE: *S, a dealer in stereos, obtained financing from L by securing the loan with her inventory in stereos. B purchases one of the stereos from that inventory. B takes free of the security interest that L has in the inventory of S whether it is perfected or not.*

b. Distinguish between buyers in the ordinary course of business and the subsequent bona fide purchaser from consumers

(1) The latter defeats only a purchase money security interest in consumer goods (perfection on attachment) unless filing takes place—applies to sale by consumer to consumer

(2) The former applies whether buyer is consumer or not but seller is dealer in those goods

> EXAMPLE: *See previous example. The result is the same whether or not B was a consumer when he bought in the ordinary course of business from S.*

> EXAMPLE: *Refer again to the same example using S, L, and B. Now let's add on one more security interest in that B is buying the stereo on credit from S and for his own personal use. Attachment has occurred. There is perfection by attachment because between B and S, it is a purchase money security interest in consumer goods. If B sells the stereo to N, his neighbor, for consumer use, then N takes free of the perfected security interest (unless S had filed or N had notice of the security interest).*

c. In the case of a purchase money security interest, if the secured party files within ten days after the debtor receives the collateral, then this defeats other security interests by use of a ten-day grace period

(1) Note that this purchase money security interest (PMSI) does not require consumer goods

> EXAMPLE: *On August 1, B purchased some equipment from S on credit. All elements of attachment are satisfied on this date. On August 3, B borrows money from a bank using equipment purchased from S as collateral. Attachment is accomplished and a financing statement is correctly filed by the bank on August 3. On August 7, S then files a financing statement. Because of the ten-day grace period, S has priority over the bank.*

> EXAMPLE: *Same as above except that S files after the ten-day grace period or not at all. The bank has priority.*

(2) If inventory, no ten-day grace period is allowed for perfection to have priority

  (a) Party with purchase money security interest must give notice to other secured party

  (b) Party with purchase money security interest must perfect prior to debtor's taking possession

(3) Knowledge of preexisting security interest has no effect

d. Holder in due course of negotiable instruments wins over perfected or unperfected security interest

e. Security interest, perfected or unperfected, wins over subsequent perfected security interest if latter party **knew** of previous security interest

f. Possessor of negotiable document of title has priority over others

g. Lien creditor (e.g., repairman or contractor)

(1) Has priority over an unperfected security interest

  (a) Knowledge of security interest is immaterial

(2) Has priority over a security interest perfected after attachment of the lien unless it is a purchase money security interest perfected within the ten-day grace period

(3) A security interest perfected before the lien usually has priority

(4) Lien by statute (not by judgment or court order) has priority over a prior perfected security interest unless state statute expressly provides otherwise

> EXAMPLE: *A person such as a repairman, in the ordinary course of business, furnishes services or materials with respect to goods subject to a security interest. The repairman (artisan lien) has priority.*

h. Trustee in bankruptcy as a lien creditor

      (1) Trustee has the rights of a lien creditor from the date of filing of petition in bankruptcy

         (a) So has priority over a security interest perfected after date of filing petition unless it is a purchase money security interest perfected within the ten-day grace period

      (2) Trustee also takes the position of any existing lien creditor

F. Rights of Parties upon Default

1. If collateral consists of claims (e.g., receivables), the secured party has the right of collection from third parties

   a. Secured party may notify third party to pay secured party directly
   b. Secured party must account for any surplus and debtor is liable for any deficiency
   c. Secured party may deduct his/her reasonable expenses

2. Secured party may retain collateral already in his/her possession or may take possession or control from debtor

   a. May do so him/herself if s/he can without breach of the peace
   b. Otherwise, s/he must use judicial process to foreclose on collateral
   c. Secured party has duty to take reasonable care of collateral in his/her possession

      (1) Expenses to protect collateral are responsibility of debtor

3. If secured party proposes to satisfy obligation by retaining the collateral, s/he must

   a. Send written notice to debtor
   b. Must notify other secured parties (who have sent written notice of their interest), unless consumer goods
   c. Can only retain consumer goods if debtor has paid less than 60% of the purchase price or obligation

      (1) If 60% or more has been paid for a PMSI in consumer goods, secured party must sell collateral within ninety days after taking possession or be liable to the debtor unless debtor waives this right to sale **after** the default

4. Secured party may sell collateral

   a. May be a public or a private sale
   b. Must use commercially reasonable practices—this right cannot be waived by debtor
   c. Must sell within a reasonable time
   d. Must notify debtor of time and place of public sale or time after which private sale will occur unless collateral is perishable, threatens to decline in value, or is type sold on a recognized market

      (1) Must also notify other secured parties (who have sent written notice of their interest) unless collateral consists of consumer goods

   e. Secured party may buy at any public sale and also at a private sale if rights of debtor protected
   f. Subordinate claims are entitled to any surplus

      (1) Debtor is entitled to surplus (if any) after all claims and expenses are paid or is liable for deficiency (if any)

5. Debtor has right to redeem collateral before secured party disposes of it by paying

   a. Entire debt, and
   b. Secured party's reasonable expenses

6. Most remedies can be varied by agreement if reasonable

   a. Provision that secured party must account for any surplus to debtor cannot be varied by agreement

7. Good-faith purchaser (i.e., for value and with no knowledge of defects in sale) of collateral takes free of debtor's rights and any secured interest or lien subordinate to it

   a. Receives debtor's title

b.   If sale was improper, remedy of debtor is money damages against secured party who sold collateral, not against good-faith purchaser

G. Other Rights of Parties

1.   Debtor has right to request that creditor show proof of unpaid debt or request that creditor correct incorrect filings on collateral

a.   Creditor must either show that debt or filing is correct or make correction
b.   Creditor must do this within fourteen days or is liable for loss suffered as a result plus $500.

2.   When debtor pays debt in full, s/he has right to termination statement of creditor which creditor files or in some cases provides to debtor

a.   This provides notice that earlier filing has been satisfied

3.   After expenses are paid for repossessing collateral, storage, and reselling collateral, excess proceeds go to secured party, then to other lien holders

MULTIPLE-CHOICE QUESTIONS (1-30)

1. Under the Revised UCC Secured Transaction Article, when collateral is in a secured party's possession, which of the following conditions must also be satisfied to have attachment?

    a.   There must be a written security agreement.
    b.   The public must be notified.
    c.   The secured party must receive consideration.
    d.   The debtor must have rights to the collateral.

2. Under the Revised UCC Secured Transaction Article, which of the following after-acquired property may be attached to a security agreement given to a secured lender?

	Inventory	Equipment
a.	Yes	Yes
b.	Yes	No
c.	No	Yes
d.	No	No

3. Gardner Bank loaned Holland Company $20,000 to purchase some inventory to resell in its store. Gardner had Holland sign a security agreement that listed as collateral all present and future inventory of Holland as well as the proceeds of any sales of the inventory. Later, Boldon Company, who was aware of Gardner's security interest, extended credit to Holland but Holland failed to pay back either Gardner or Boldon. Boldon has sought to defeat the security interest pointing out that Gardner never filled out a financing statement. Which of the following is correct?

    a.   Gardner has an enforceable security interest that is valid against Holland and has priority over Boldon's interests.
    b.   Gardner does not have an enforceable security interest valid against Holland or against Boldon.
    c.   Gardner does have an enforceable security interest valid against Holland but not valid against Boldon.
    d.   Gardner does not have an enforceable security interest valid against Holland but does have one valid against Boldon.

4. Article 9 of the UCC which governs security interests has added some items that now are covered by security interests law. Which of the following is true?

    a.   Security interests in tort claims already assessed by a court of law are covered.
    b.   After-acquired commercial tort claims are covered.
    c.   Both a. and b.
    d.   Neither a. nor b.

5. Under the Revised Secured Transactions Article of the UCC, which of the following requirements is necessary to have a security interest attach?

	Debtor had rights in the collateral	Proper filing of a security agreement	Value given by the creditor
a.	Yes	Yes	Yes
b.	Yes	Yes	No
c.	Yes	No	Yes
d.	No	Yes	Yes

6. Under the Revised UCC Secured Transaction Article, which of the following events will always prevent a security interest from attaching?

    a.   Failure to have a written security agreement.

    b.   Failure of the creditor to have possession of the collateral.
    c.   Failure of the debtor to have rights in the collateral.
    d.   Failure of the creditor to give present consideration for the security interest.

7. Perfection of a security interest permits the secured party to protect its interest by

    a.   Avoiding the need to file a financing statement.
    b.   Preventing another creditor from obtaining a security interest in the same collateral.
    c.   Establishing priority over the claims of most subsequent secured creditors.
    d.   Denying the debtor the right to possess the collateral.

8. Under the Revised UCC Secured Transaction Article, what is the effect of perfecting a security interest by filing a financing statement?

    a.   The secured party can enforce its security interest against the debtor.
    b.   The secured party has permanent priority in the collateral even if the collateral is removed to another state.
    c.   The debtor is protected against all other parties who acquire an interest in the collateral after the filing.
    d.   The secured party has priority in the collateral over most creditors who acquire a security interest in the same collateral after the filing.

9. A secured creditor wants to file a financing statement to perfect its security interest. Under the Revised UCC Secured Transaction Article, which of the following must be included in the financing statement?

    a.   A listing or description of the collateral.
    b.   An after-acquired property provision.
    c.   The creditor's signature.
    d.   The collateral's location.

10. Which of the following transactions would illustrate a secured party perfecting its security interest by taking possession of the collateral?

    a.   A bank receiving a mortgage on real property.
    b.   A wholesaler borrowing to purchase inventory.
    c.   A consumer borrowing to buy a car.
    d.   A pawnbroker lending money.

11. Under the Revised UCC Secured Transaction Article, which of the following actions will best perfect a security interest in a negotiable instrument against any other party?

    a.   Filing a security agreement.
    b.   Taking possession of the instrument.
    c.   Perfecting by attachment.
    d.   Obtaining a duly executed financing statement.

12. Grey Corp. sells computers to the public. Grey sold and delivered a computer to West on credit. West executed and delivered to Grey a promissory note for the purchase price and a security agreement covering the computer. West purchased the computer for personal use. Grey did not file a financing statement. Is Grey's security interest perfected?

    a.   Yes, because Grey retained ownership of the computer.

b. Yes, because it was perfected at the time of attachment.
c. No, because the computer was a consumer good.
d. No, because Grey failed to file a financing statement.

13. In which of the following cases does a seller have automatic perfection of a security interest as soon as attachment takes place?

I. Purchase money security interest in consumer goods.
II. Purchase money security interest in inventory.
III. Purchase money security interest in equipment.

    a. I only.
    b. I and II only.
    c. II and III only.
    d. I, II and III.

14. Mars, Inc. manufactures and sells VCRs on credit directly to wholesalers, retailers, and consumers. Mars can perfect its security interest in the VCRs it sells without having to file a financing statement or take possession of the VCRs if the sale is made to

    a. Retailers.
    b. Wholesalers that sell to distributors for resale.
    c. Consumers.
    d. Wholesalers that sell to buyers in the ordinary course of business.

15. Under the Revised Secured Transaction Article of the UCC, which of the following purchasers will own consumer goods free of a perfected security interest in the goods?

    a. A merchant who purchases the goods for resale.
    b. A merchant who purchases the goods for use in its business.
    c. A consumer who purchases the goods from a consumer purchaser who gave the security interest.
    d. A consumer who purchases the goods in the ordinary course of business.

16. Under the Revised UCC Secured Transaction Article, what is the order of priority for the following security interests in store equipment?

I. Security interest perfected by filing on April 15, 2001.
II. Security interest attached on April 1, 2001.
III. Purchase money security interest attached April 11, 2001 and perfected by filing on April 20, 2001.

    a. I, III, II.
    b. II, I, III.
    c. III, I, II.
    d. III, II, I.

17. Noninventory goods were purchased and delivered on June 15, 2001. Several security interests exist in these goods. Which of the following security interests has priority over the others?

    a. Security interest in future goods attached June 10, 2001.
    b. Security interest attached June 15, 2001.
    c. Security interest perfected June 20, 2001.
    d. Purchase money security interest perfected June 24, 2001.

18. Under the Revised Secured Transaction Article of the UCC, what would be the order of priority for the following security interests in consumer goods?

I. Financing agreement filed on April 1.
II. Possession of the collateral by a creditor on April 10.
III. Financing agreement perfected on April 15.

    a. I, II, III.
    b. II, I, III.
    c. II, III, I.
    d. III, II, I.

19. A party who filed a security interest in inventory on April 1, 2001, would have a superior interest to which of the following parties?

    a. A holder of a mechanic's lien whose lien was filed on March 15, 2001.
    b. A holder of a purchase money security interest in after-acquired property filed on March 20, 2001.
    c. A purchaser in the ordinary course of business who purchased on April 10, 2001.
    d. A judgment lien creditor who filed its judgment on April 15, 2001.

20. W & B, a wholesaler, sold on credit some furniture to Broadmore Company, a retailer. W & B perfected its security interest by filing a financing statement. Lean purchased some furniture from Broadmore for his home. He was unaware of W & B's perfected security interest. McCoy purchased some furniture from Broadmore for her home. She was aware that Broadmore's inventory was subject to security interests since Broadmore was having financial problems and had to buy the furniture on credit. Norsome purchased some furniture from Broadmore for use in his business. Broadmore defaults on its loans from W & B, who wants to repossess the furniture purchased and delivered to Lean, McCoy, and Norsome. From which parties can W & B legally repossess the furniture?

    a. McCoy.
    b. Lean and McCoy.
    c. Norsome.
    d. None of these parties.

21. Rand purchased a sofa from Abby Department Store for use in her home. Abby had her sign a security agreement for the balance Rand owed. Rand did not pay the balance and sold the sofa to her neighbor, Gram, for use in his home. Gram did not realize that Rand had not paid off the balance. Abby filed a financing statement after Rand defaulted. This filing was also after Gram purchased the sofa from Rand. Which of the following is correct?

    a. Abby can repossess the sofa from Gram since it has a written security agreement covering the sofa.
    b. Abby can repossess the sofa from Gram since it perfected its security agreement by filing.
    c. Abby can repossess the sofa from Gram since it obtained automatic perfection.
    d. Abby has no right to repossess the sofa from Gram.

22. Wine purchased a computer using the proceeds of a loan from MJC Finance Company. Wine gave MJC a security interest in the computer. Wine executed a security agreement and financing statement, which was filed by MJC. Wine used the computer to monitor Wine's personal investments. Later, Wine sold the computer to Jacobs, for Jacobs' family use. Jacobs was unaware of MJC's security interest. Wine now is in default under the MJC loan. May MJC repossess the computer from Jacobs?

    a. No, because Jacobs was unaware of the MJC security interest.

b. No, because Jacobs intended to use the computer for family or household purposes.

c. Yes, because MJC's security interest was perfected before Jacobs' purchase.

d. Yes, because Jacobs' purchase of the computer made Jacobs personally liable to MJC.

23. Rally Co. has purchased some inventory from Kantar Corporation to sell to customers who will use the inventory primarily for consumer use. Which of the following is **not** correct?

    a. If Kantar sells the inventory to Rally on credit and takes out a security interest using the inventory as collateral, this a purchase money security interest.

    b. If Kantar sells the inventory to Rally on credit and takes out a security interest using the inventory as collateral, this is a purchase money security interest in consumer goods.

    c. If Kantar sells the inventory to Rally but Rally pays for it by getting a loan from a bank who takes out a security interest using the inventory as collateral, this is a purchase money security interest.

    d. If a customer purchases some inventory on credit from Rally for home use and signs a written security agreement presented by Rally that lists the inventory as collateral for the credit, this is a purchase money security interest in consumer goods.

24. On June 15, Harper purchased equipment for $100,000 from Imperial Corp. for use in its manufacturing process. Harper paid for the equipment with funds borrowed from Eastern Bank. Harper gave Eastern a security agreement and financing statement covering Harper's existing and after-acquired equipment. On June 21, Harper was petitioned involuntarily into bankruptcy under Chapter 7 of the Federal Bankruptcy Code. A bankruptcy trustee was appointed. On June 23, Eastern filed the financing statement. Which of the parties will have a superior security interest in the equipment?

    a. The trustee in bankruptcy, because the filing of the financing statement after the commencement of the bankruptcy case would be deemed a preferential transfer.

    b. The trustee in bankruptcy, because the trustee became a lien creditor before Eastern perfected its security interest.

    c. Eastern, because it had a perfected purchase money security interest without having to file a financing statement.

    d. Eastern, because it perfected its security interest within the permissible time limits.

Items 25 and 26 are based on the following:

Drew bought a computer for personal use from Hale Corp. for $3,000. Drew paid $2,000 in cash and signed a security agreement for the balance. Hale properly filed the security agreement. Drew defaulted in paying the balance of the purchase price. Hale asked Drew to pay the balance. When Drew refused, Hale peacefully repossessed the computer.

25. Under the Revised UCC Secured Transaction Article, which of the following remedies will Hale have?

    a. Obtain a deficiency judgment against Drew for the amount owed.

    b. Sell the computer and retain any surplus over the amount owed.

    c. Retain the computer over Drew's objection.

    d. Sell the computer without notifying Drew.

26. Under the Revised UCC Secured Transaction Article, which of the following rights will Drew have?

    a. Redeem the computer after Hale sells it.

    b. Recover the sale price from Hale after Hale sells the computer.

    c. Force Hale to sell the computer.

    d. Prevent Hale from selling the computer.

27. Under the Revised UCC Secured Transaction Article, which of the following statements is correct concerning the disposition of collateral by a secured creditor after a debtor's default?

    a. A good-faith purchaser for value and without knowledge of any defects in the sale takes free of any subordinate liens or security interests.

    b. The debtor may not redeem the collateral after the default.

    c. Secured creditors with subordinate claims retain the right to redeem the collateral after the collateral is sold to a third party.

    d. The collateral may only be disposed of at a public sale.

28. Bean defaulted on a promissory note payable to Gray Co. The note was secured by a piece of equipment owned by Bean. Gray perfected its security interest on May 29, 2001 Bean had also pledged the same equipment as collateral for another loan from Smith Co. after he had given the security interest to Gray. Smith's security interest was perfected on June 30, 2001. Bean is current in his payments to Smith. Subsequently, Gray took possession of the equipment and sold it at a private sale to Walsh, a good-faith purchaser for value. Walsh will take the equipment

    a. Free of Smith's security interest because Bean is current in his payments to Smith.

    b. Free of Smith's security interest because Walsh acted in good faith and gave value.

    c. Subject to Smith's security interest because the equipment was sold at a private sale.

    d. Subject to Smith's security interest because Smith is a purchase money secured creditor.

29. Under the Revised Secured Transactions Article of the UCC, which of the following remedies is available to a secured creditor when a debtor fails to make a payment when due?

	Proceed against the collateral	*Obtain a general judgment against the debtor*
a.	Yes	Yes
b.	Yes	No
c.	No	Yes
d.	No	No

30. In what order are the following obligations paid after a secured creditor rightfully sells the debtor's collateral after repossession?

  I. Debt owed to any junior security holder.
  II. Secured party's reasonable sale expenses.
  III. Debt owed to the secured party.

    a. I, II, III.
    b. II, I, III.
    c. II, III, I.
    d. III, II, I.

PROBLEMS

NOTE: These types of problems are no longer included in the CPA Examination but they have been retained because they are useful in developing skills to complete simulations.

Problem 1   (15 to 20 minutes)

Dunn & Co., CPAs, is auditing the 2003 financial statements of its client, Safe Finance. While performing the audit, Dunn learned of certain transactions that occurred during 2003 that may have an adverse impact on Safe's financial statements. The following transactions are of most concern to Dunn:

• On May 5, Safe sold certain equipment to Lux, who contemporaneously executed and delivered to Safe a promissory note and security agreement covering the equipment. Lux purchased the equipment for use in its business. On May 8, City Bank loaned Lux $50,000, taking a promissory note and security agreement from Lux that covered all of Lux's existing and after-acquired equipment. On May 11, Lux was involuntarily petitioned into bankruptcy under the liquidation provisions of the Bankruptcy Code and a trustee was appointed. On May 12, City filed a financing statement covering all of Lux's equipment. On May 14, Safe filed a financing statement covering the equipment it had sold to Lux on May 5.

• On July 10, Safe loaned $600,000 to Cam Corp., which used the funds to refinance existing debts. Cam duly executed and delivered to Safe a promissory note and a security agreement covering Cam's existing and after-acquired inventory of machine parts. On July 12, Safe filed a financing statement covering Cam's inventory of machine parts. On July 15, Best Bank loaned Cam $200,000. Contemporaneous with the loan, Cam executed and delivered to Best a promissory note and security agreement covering all of Cam's inventory of machine parts and any after-acquired inventory. Best had already filed a financing statement covering Cam's inventory on June 20, after Best agreed to make the loan to Cam. On July 14, Dix, in good faith, purchased certain machine parts from Cam's inventory and received delivery that same day.

Required:

Define a purchase money security interest. In separate paragraphs, discuss whether Safe has a priority security interest over

• The trustee in Lux's bankruptcy with regard to the equipment sold by Safe on May 5.
• City with regard to the equipment sold by Safe on May 5.
• Best with regard to Cam's existing and after-acquired inventory of machine parts.
• Dix with regard to the machine parts purchased on July 14 by Dix.

Problem 2   (15 to 20 minutes)

On February 20, 2004, Pine, Inc. ordered a specially manufactured computer system consisting of a disk drive and a central processing unit (CPU) from Xeon Corp., a seller of computers and other office equipment. A contract was signed and the total purchase price was paid to Xeon by Pine on the same date. The contract required Pine to pick up the computer system at Xeon's warehouse on March 9, 2004, but was silent as to when risk of loss passed to Pine. The computer system was completed on March 1, 2004, and set aside for Pine's contemplated pickup on March 9, 2004. On March 3, 2004, the disk drive was stolen from Xeon's warehouse. On March 9, 2004, Pine picked up the CPU. On March 15, 2004, Pine returned the CPU to Xeon for warranty repairs. On March 18, 2004, Xeon mistakenly sold the CPU to Meed, a buyer in the ordinary course of business.

On April 12, 2004, Pine purchased and received delivery of five word processors from Jensen Electronics Corp. for use in its business. The purchase price of the word processors was $15,000. Pine paid $5,000 down and executed an installment purchase note and a security agreement for the balance. The security agreement contained a description of the word processors. Jensen never filed a financing statement. On April 1, 2004, Pine had given its bank a security interest in all of its assets. The bank had immediately perfected its security interest by filing. Pine has defaulted on the installment purchase note.

Required:

Discuss the following assertions, indicating whether such assertions are correct and the reasons therefor.

• As of March 3, 2004, the risk of loss on the disk drive remained with Xeon.
• Meed acquired no rights in the CPU as a result of the March 18, 2004 transaction.
• Jensen's security interest in the word processors never attached and therefore, Jensen's security interest is not enforceable against Pine.
• Jensen has superior security interest to Pine's bank.

SIMULATION PROBLEM

Simulation Problem 1   (10 to 15 minutes)

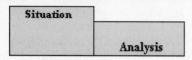

On January 2, 2004, Gray Interiors Corp., a retailer of sofas, contracted with Shore Furniture Co. to purchase 150 sofas for its inventory. The purchase price was $250,000. Gray paid $50,000 cash and gave Shore a note and security agreement for the balance. On March 1, 2004, the sofas were delivered. On March 10, 2004, Shore filed a financing statement.

On February 1, 2004, Gray negotiated a $1,000,000 line of credit with Float Bank, pledged its present and future inventory as security, and gave Float a security agreement. On February 20, 2004, Gray borrowed $100,000 from the line of credit. On March 5, 2004, Float filed a financing statement.

On April 1, 2004, Dove, a consumer purchaser in the ordinary course of business, purchased a sofa from Gray. Dove was aware of both security interests.

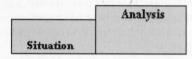

Items 1 through 6 refer to the fact pattern. For each item, determine whether (A), (B), or (C) is correct.

1. Shore's security interest in the sofas attached on
    - ○ A. January 2, 2004.
    - ○ B. March 1, 2004.
    - ○ C. March 10, 2004.

2. Shore's security interest in the sofas was perfected on
    - ○ A. January 2, 2004.
    - ○ B. March 1, 2004.
    - ○ C. March 10, 2004.

3. Float's security interest in Gray's inventory attached on
    - ○ A. February 1, 2004.
    - ○ B. March 1, 2004.
    - ○ C. March 5, 2004.

4. Float's security interest in Gray's inventory was perfected on
    - ○ A. February 1, 2004.
    - ○ B. February 20, 2004.
    - ○ C. March 5, 2004.

5. ○ A. Shore's security interest has priority because it was a purchase money security interest.
    ○ B. Float's security interest has priority because Float's financing statement was filed before Shore's.
    ○ C. Float's security interest has priority because Float's interest attached before Shore's.

6. ○ A. Dove purchased the sofa subject to Shore's security interest.
    ○ B. Dove purchased the sofa subject to both the Shore and Float security interests.
    ○ C. Dove purchased the sofa free of either the Shore or Float security interests.

MULTIPLE-CHOICE ANSWERS

1.	d	8.	d	15.	d	22.	c	29.	a
2.	a	9.	a	16.	c	23.	b	30.	c
3.	a	10.	d	17.	d	24.	d		
4.	a	11.	b	18.	a	25.	a		
5.	c	12.	b	19.	d	26.	c		
6.	c	13.	a	20.	d	27.	a	1st: __/30 = __%
7.	c	14.	c	21.	d	28.	b	2nd: __/30 = __%

MULTIPLE-CHOICE ANSWER EXPLANATIONS

B.   Attachment of Security Interests

1.   (d)   Under the Revised Article 9 on Secured Transactions, attachment of a security interest takes place when the secured party gives value, the debtor has rights in the collateral, and one of the following three is true:

    a.   The secured party must possess the collateral if the debtor agrees to it

    b.   The secured party must have control of certain types of collateral, or

    c.   The secured party must have a signed security agreement (or an authenticated electronic transmission).

2.   (a)   An after-acquired property clause in a security agreement allows the secured party's interest in such property to attach once the debtor acquires the property, without the need to make a new security agreement. These clauses are typically used for inventory and accounts receivable, and can also be used for equipment.

3.   (a)   The security interest did attach because there was a signed security agreement, Gardner gave value, and Holland had rights in the collateral. Upon attachment, Gardner's security interest is fully enforceable against Holland. Even though Gardner never perfected the security interest, it still has priority over Boldon's interests because Boldon was aware of the security interest.

4.   (a)   Security interests in tort claims are covered under the Revised UCC Secured Transactions Article; this is not true of after-acquired commercial tort claims.

5.   (c)   In order for attachment of a security interest to occur, three elements must take place. First, the secured party must give value, second, the debtor must have rights in the collateral, and third, there must be a security agreement. This security agreement may be oral if the secured party has possession or control of the collateral. Otherwise, it must be in writing and signed by the debtor. An exception to the signature requirement is made if it is an authenticated electronic transmission.

6.   (c)   In order for a security interest to attach, there must be a valid security agreement, the secured party must have given value, and the debtor must have rights in the collateral. If any one of these items is missing, attachment cannot take place. Answer (a) is incorrect because the security interest may be oral if the secured party has possession or control of the collateral. Answer (b) is incorrect because if the security agreement is in writing, the secured party does not need possession of the collateral to achieve attachment. Answer (d) is incorrect because the secured party must give value, not necessarily consideration. A preexisting claim, although not consideration, does count as value.

C.4.   Filing a Financing Statement

7.   (c)   Perfection of a security interest is important in that it establishes for a secured party priority over the claims that may be made by most subsequent secured creditors. Answer (a) is incorrect because there are three methods of obtaining perfection and one of them is filing a financing statement. Answer (b) is incorrect because subsequent creditors may still obtain security interests in the same collateral although they will normally obtain a lower priority. Answer (d) is incorrect because of times the debtor retains possession of the collateral.

8.   (d)   Perfection by filing a financing statement will not defeat all other parties who acquire an interest in the same collateral; rather, perfection by filing gives the secured party most possible rights in the collateral. Note, purchasers from a merchant in the ordinary course of business take the collateral free from any prior perfected security interest. The only time a purchaser would take the collateral subject to a prior perfected security interest would be when the purchaser knew that the merchant was selling the goods in violation of a financing statement. A creditor need not perfect the security interest in order to enforce it against the debtor. The filing of a financing statement does not protect the debtor's rights but rather the creditor's rights.

9.   (a)   Filing a financing statement is one method of perfecting a security interest in personal property. Under the Revised UCC Secured Transaction Article, a financing statement must include the following: the names of the debtor and creditor, and a listing or description of the collateral. An after-acquired property provision, the creditor's signature, and the collateral's location are not required to be included in the financing statement.

C.5.   Perfection by Possession

10.   (d)   One way to perfect a security interest is for the secured party to take possession of the collateral in addition to attaining attachment. A pawnbroker lending money is such a case. There is a security agreement which may be oral since the secured party has possession of the collateral. The secured party gives value by lending the money. The third step in attachment is that the debtor has rights in the collateral such as ownership. Since these steps constitute attachment, perfection is accomplished by the pawnbroker, the secured party, taking possession of the collateral. The secured transactions laws apply to security interests in personal property, not real property. The wholesaler (car buyer), not the secured party, will have possession of the collateral.

11.   (b)   In general, the best way to perfect a security interest in a negotiable instrument is to take possession of the instrument. This is true because negotiable instruments are easily negotiated to other holders who can become holders in due course. Answer (a) is incorrect because a holder can become a holder in due course even if a security agreement is filed. Answer (c) is incorrect because perfecting by attachment requires a purchase money security interest in consumer goods. Answer (d) is incorrect because this cannot even accomplish perfection until it is filed.

C.6. Automatic Perfection

12. (b)   Since West purchased the computer for personal use and the computer itself was the collateral for the security agreement, the fact pattern involves a purchase money security interest in consumer goods. Therefore, once attachment took place, perfection was automatic. Answer (c) is incorrect because since the computer was a consumer good, perfection was automatic upon attachment. Answer (d) is incorrect because filing a financing statement is not required for perfecting a purchase money security interest in consumer goods. Answer (a) is incorrect because retaining or obtaining possession, not ownership, by the secured party is a way to perfect. In any event, Grey Corp. did not retain either ownership or possession since they sold and delivered the computer to West.

13. (a)   Automatic perfection (perfection by attachment) takes place in the case of a purchase money security interest (PMSI) in consumer goods only. Answers (b), (c), and (d) are incorrect because they include PMSI in inventory or equipment which do not qualify for automatic perfection.

14. (c)   Mars holds a purchase money security interest in the goods sold, which allowed the buyers of these goods to secure the credit for their purchase. When a purchase money security interest is in consumer goods, the secured party (Mars) obtains perfection when attachment takes place without the need to file a financing statement or take possession or control of the collateral. Answers (a), (b), and (d) are incorrect because in those cases the goods comprise inventory, not consumer goods.

E. Priorities

15. (d)   Buyers in the ordinary course of business take goods free of any security interest whether perfected or not. The buyer can be, but need not be, a consumer. Answer (a) is incorrect because a merchant who purchases consumer goods for resale may not be buying in the ordinary course of business. Answer (b) is incorrect because the merchant who buys the consumer goods for use in his/her business may not be buying in the ordinary course of business. Answer (c) is incorrect because although a consumer can take goods free of a security interest when buying from another consumer, this requires certain facts along with a purchase money security interest in consumer goods. There are no facts in the question to show this.

16. (c)   In general, a purchase money security interest in noninventory has priority over nonpurchase money security interests if it was perfected within ten days after the debtor received the collateral. Item III, therefore, has the first priority because the purchase money security interest was perfected on April 20, 2001, which was within twenty days of the attachment. Item I has priority over Item II because the security interest in Item I was perfected, while the security interest in Item II was not.

17. (d)   A purchase money security interest in noninventory goods has a special rule. Since it was perfected within twenty days after the debtor got possession of the collateral, it has priority over all of the others. Answers (a) and (b) are incorrect because unperfected security interests have a lower priority than perfected security interests. Answer (c) is incorrect because although this security interest was perfected before the purchase money security interest, the latter has priority if perfected within twenty days of the debtor taking possession of the collateral.

18. (a)   Since security interest I was perfected first when the financing agreement was filed on April 1, it has the first priority. Security interest II was perfected on April 10 when the creditor took possession of the collateral. It has the second priority. Security interest III has the third priority since it was perfected last on April 15.

19. (d)   The party perfected by filing a security interest in inventory on April 1, 2001. S/he would therefore have priority over a judgment lien creditor who filed later on April 15, 2001. Answer (a) is incorrect because the mechanic's lien was filed on March 15 before the perfection of the security interest. Therefore, the mechanic's lien has priority over the perfected security interest. Answer (b) is incorrect because the holder of the purchase money security interest in after-acquired property filed and perfected before April 1. Answer (c) is incorrect because a purchaser in the ordinary course of business is free of other security interests even if they are perfected before s/he purchases the inventory.

20. (d)   Lean, McCoy, and Norsome all purchased the furniture in the ordinary course of business. As such, all three parties take free of the security interest even if it was perfected. This is true whether they purchased the furniture for consumer or business use and whether they knew of the security agreement or not.

21. (d)   Abby had a perfected security agreement because of the purchase money security interest in consumer goods. This, however, is not effective against a good-faith purchaser for value who buys from a consumer for consumer use as in the case of Gram. Perfection by filing is, however, effective in such a case but only if the filing is done before Gram purchases the sofa. Answer (a) is incorrect because the attachment of the written security interest makes it enforceable against Rand, not Gram. Answer (b) is incorrect because the filing of the financing statement took place after Gram bought the sofa. Answer (c) is incorrect because, although Abby did accomplish automatic perfection by way of the PMSI in consumer goods, this type of perfection was not effective against Gram because he was a good-faith purchaser for value who bought it from a consumer (Rand) for consumer use.

22. (c)   MJC obtained a security interest in the computer purchased by Wine and perfected it by filing. Even though when Jacobs later purchased it for consumer use he was unaware of MJC's security interest, MJC still has priority. This is true because the filing is constructive notice to all subsequent parties. MJC has priority and may repossess the computer even if Jacobs was unaware of the filed security interest. The filing gives MJC priority over Jacob despite his intended use for family. Jacobs is not personally liable to MJC because he made no contract and did not agree to take on liability with MJC.

23. (b) Because Kantar has a security interest in the inventory it sold and is also using the same inventory as collateral for the credit, this is a purchase money security interest. However, because the items Rally purchased are inventory, not consumer goods, in **Rally's** hands, this is not a PMSI in consumer goods. Answer (a) is not chosen because this does describe a PMSI since Kantar retained a security interest in the same items sold on credit to secure payment. Answer (c) is not chosen because a PMSI includes a third party giving a loan who retains a security interest in the same items purchased by the loan. Answer (d) is not chosen because this is a PMSI in consumer goods since the customer purchased the items for his/her home use.

24. (d) When a purchase money security interest uses noninventory as collateral, it has priority over prior competing interests as long as it is perfected within twenty days of the debtor obtaining possession of the collateral. Since the collateral in this fact pattern was equipment, and Eastern filed within twenty days, Eastern has priority over the trustee in bankruptcy. Perfection was not automatic since it was a purchase money security interest in equipment, not in consumer goods. Furthermore, since the secured party did not have possession of the collateral, the way to perfect this security interest is by filing a financing statement.

F. Rights of Parties upon Default

25. (a) After Hale repossesses the computer and sells it in a commercially reasonable fashion, Hale may obtain a deficiency judgment for the amount still owed after the proceeds from the sale pay the expenses of repossession and sale and the debt owed to Hale. Any remaining proceeds go to the debtor after repossession and sale expenses and secured parties are paid. For consumer goods, such as the personal computer in this fact pattern, the goods must be sold if the debtor has paid more than 60% of the debt secured by the consumer goods. In this fact pattern, Drew paid two-thirds of the debt. Hale must notify Drew in writing of the impending sale unless Drew had agreed otherwise in writing.

26. (c) Since Drew has paid two-thirds of the price, which is over 60% payment on the secured debt for consumer goods, Hale is obligated to sell the computer rather than keep it in satisfaction of the debt. The debtor may redeem before, not after, the sale. Hale may keep the proceeds needed to pay off repossession and sale expenses and the debt owed to Hale. Any excess would go to Drew. Hale has the right to sell the repossessed computer to pay off the secured debt unless Drew properly redeems the interest s/he has in the computer.

27. (a) Upon the debtor's default, the secured party may take possession of the collateral and sell it. A good-faith purchaser for value buys the collateral free of any liens or security interests. Answer (b) is incorrect because the debtor has the right to redeem the collateral before the secured party disposes of it. The debtor does this by paying the debt in full as well as the secured party's reasonable expenses. Answer (c) is incorrect as a good-faith purchaser of the collateral takes it free of the debtor's rights and any secured interest or lien subordinate to it. Answer (d) is incorrect because although the collateral may be disposed of by a public sale, it also may be disposed of by a private sale if the sale uses commercially reasonable practices.

28. (b) A good-faith purchaser for value at a private sale will take the property free from any security interest or subordinate liens in the property, but remains subject to security interests which are senior to that being discharged at the sale. In this case, Smith perfected his security interest later than Gray and has a subordinate interest in the property. Thus, Walsh takes the equipment free from this subordinate security interest. The fact that Bean is current in his payments to Smith would not affect Smith's interest in the property. As long as Walsh is a good-faith purchaser for value, it doesn't matter if the equipment is sold at a public or private sale. Smith is not a purchase money secured creditor since the proceeds of Smith's loan to Bean were not used to purchase the equipment acting as collateral.

29. (a) If the debtor defaults on the debt, the secured party may proceed against the collateral. This extra protection is one of the main reasons for having secured transactions. If the creditor chooses, s/he may obtain a general judgment against the debtor.

30. (c) Under the UCC, after a secured creditor rightfully sells the debtor's collateral after repossession, the secured party's reasonable sale expenses are paid first. Next, the debt owed to the secured party is paid. Any junior security holders then get paid to the extent of any money remaining.

ANSWER OUTLINE

Problem 1   Purchase Money Security Interest; Priority of
                  Bankruptcy Trustee; Purchase Money Secured
                  Party in Equipment and Buyer in Ordinary
                  Course of Business

Purchase Money Security Interest

Interest in personal property or fixtures

Secures payment or performance

Occurs when either

(1)   Seller retains interest in item sold on credit, or

(2)   Creditor retains interest in item purchased with
        loaned funds

Priorities

Safe has priority over trustee (i.e., lien creditor from date
of filing petition)

Generally, unperfected security interest is subordinate
to person becoming lien creditor before the security
interest is perfected

Safe as a purchase money secured party in equipment
has twenty-day grace period for filing

Safe filed within twenty-day grace period

Safe has priority over City

A purchase money security interest in equipment, if
perfected no later than the end of the twenty-day
grace period, prevails over a conflicting security interest

Safe filed within ten days of Lux's possession of the
equipment

Best has priority over Safe

If both conflicting security interests require filing to
be perfected, the first party to **file** has priority

Best filed before Safe

Dix has priority over Safe

A buyer in the ordinary course of business takes free
of prior perfected security interest

Dix qualifies as a buyer in the ordinary course of
business

UNOFFICIAL ANSWER

Problem 1   Purchase Money Security Interest; Priority of
                  Bankruptcy Trustee; Purchase Money Se-
                  cured Party in Equipment and Buyer in Ordi-
                  nary Course of Business

A purchase money security interest is an interest in personal property or fixtures that secures payment or performance of an obligation and that is (1) taken or retained by the
seller of the collateral to secure all or part of its price, or (2)
taken by a person who by making advances or incurring an
obligation gives value to enable the debtor to acquire rights
in or the use of collateral if such value is, in fact, so used.

Safe's security interest has priority over the rights of the
trustee in bankruptcy. The Revised UCC Article on Secured
Transactions states that a lien creditor includes a trustee in
bankruptcy from the date of the filing of the petition. Under
the general rule, an unperfected security interest is subordinate to the rights of a person who becomes a lien creditor
before the security interest is perfected. However, if the
secured party files with respect to a purchase money security
interest before or within twenty days after the debtor receives possession of the collateral, he takes priority over the
rights of a lien creditor that arise between the time the security interest attaches and the time of filing. Under the facts
of our case, Safe has a purchase money security interest in
the equipment because the security interest was taken by

Safe to secure the price. Therefore, because Safe filed a
financing statement on May 14 (within ten days after Lux
received possession of the equipment), it has a priority security interest over the trustee in bankruptcy (lien creditor)
whose claim arose between the time the security interest
attached (May 5) and the time of filing (May 14).

Safe has a priority security interest in the equipment
over City. A purchase money security interest in collateral
other than inventory has priority over a conflicting security
interest in the same collateral if the purchase money security
interest is perfected at the time the debtor receives possession of the collateral or within ten days thereafter. Because
Safe has a purchase money security interest in the equipment
that was perfected by filing a financing statement on May 14
(within ten days after Lux received possession of the equipment on May 5), Safe has a priority security interest over
City despite City's perfection of its security interest on May
12.

Best's security interest in the inventory has priority
over Safe's security interest. In general, conflicting perfected security interests rank according to priority in time of
filing or perfection. Priority dates from the time a filing is
first made covering the collateral or the time the security
interest is first perfected, whichever is earlier, provided that
there is no period thereafter when there is neither a filing nor
perfection. In this case, because both Best's and Safe's security interests were perfected by filing, the first to file
(Best) will have a priority security interest. The fact that
Best filed a financing statement prior to making the loan will
not affect Best's priority.

Safe will not have a priority security interest over Dix
because Dix is a buyer in the ordinary course of business
and will take free of Safe's perfected security interest. Dix
is a buyer in the ordinary course of business because Dix
acted in good faith when purchasing the machine parts in the
regular course of Cam's business. The Revised UCC Article
on Secured Transactions states that a buyer in the ordinary
course of business takes free of a security interest created by
his seller even though the security interest is perfected, and
even though the buyer knows of its existence. Therefore,
Dix will take the machine parts purchased from Cam's inventory on July 14, free from Safe's security interest, which
was perfected on July 12.

ANSWER OUTLINE

Problem 2   Risk of Loss; Rights under Entrusting of Pos-
                  session of Goods; Attachment of Security
                  Interests; Perfection of Security Interests

Correct, risk of loss remained with Xeon

When agreement is silent and seller is merchant, risk
passes to buyer when buyer receives goods

Incorrect, Meed did acquire rights in CPU

Entrusting situation: merchant acquires power to transfer
ownership and title

Entruster (Xeon) must be rightful owner

Merchant must deal in goods of like kind

Buyer must be in ordinary course of business

Incorrect, Jensen's security interest attached and is enforceable

Security interest in collateral attaches if

Secured party has security agreement, signed by debtor
containing description of collateral

May be oral if collateral is in secured party's posses-
sion
Secured party gave value
Debtor has rights in collateral
Incorrect, Jensen does not have superior interest to bank
Purchase money security interest is not in consumer
goods—no automatic perfection
Jensen must file to perfect
Bank has superior interest because it perfected; Jensen did
not

UNOFFICIAL ANSWER

Problem 2   Risk of Loss; Rights under Entrusting of Possession of Goods; Attachment of Security
Interests; Perfection of Security Interests

The assertion that as of March 3, 2004, the risk of loss
on the disk drive remained with Xeon is correct. Under the
UCC Sales Article, if the agreement between the parties is
otherwise silent, risk of loss passes to the buyer on the
buyer's receipt of the goods if the seller is a merchant. Under the facts, Xeon is a merchant because it sells computer
systems. Therefore, the risk of loss remained with Xeon
because the disk drive was never received by Pine.

The assertion that Meed acquired no rights in the CPU
as a result of the March 18, 2004, transaction is incorrect.
Under the UCC Sales Article, any entrusting of possession
of goods to a merchant who deals in goods of that kind gives
the merchant power to transfer all rights of the entruster to
the buyer in the ordinary course of business. Entrusting
includes any delivery and any acquiescence in retention of
possession regardless of any condition expressed between
the parties to the delivery or acquiescence, and regardless of
whether the possessor's disposition of the goods has been
such as to be larcenous under criminal law. For the merchant to acquire the power to transfer ownership and title,
the entruster must be the rightful owner. Under the facts of
this case, Pine had title at the time the CPU was returned to
Xeon for repairs and this constituted an entrusting that gave
Xeon the power to transfer all of Pine's rights in the CPU to
Meed.

The assertion that Jensen's security interest in the word
processors never attached and therefore Jensen's security
interest is not enforceable against Pine with respect to the
word processors is incorrect. A security interest in collateral
will attach if: the collateral is in the possession of the secured party under an agreement, or the debtor has signed a
security agreement that contains a description of the collateral; the secured party has given value; and the debtor has
rights in the collateral. Based on the facts, Jensen's security
interest attached on April 12, 2004, when Jensen sold and
Pine received the word processors and Jensen received a
security agreement executed by Pine that described the word
processors. On attachment, Jensen's security interest became enforceable against Pine.

The assertion that Jensen has a superior security interest
to Pine's bank is incorrect. Although Jensen has a purchase
money security interest to the extent the security interest is
taken by Jensen to secure the purchase price, Jensen's security interest will not be perfected by attachment alone. Jensen must file a financing statement to perfect its security
interest because the collateral involved is goods used for
business purposes and not consumer goods. Therefore, Jensen has an unperfected security interest in the word processors and the bank obtained a superior security interest by
perfecting.

SOLUTION TO SIMULATION QUESTION

Simulation Problem 1

1. **(B)** Gray gave Shore a security agreement on January 2. Shore also gave value but Gray did not receive the goods or have rights in them until March 1. Therefore, it was not until March 1 that attachment occurred.

2. **(C)** Perfection took place on March 10, when Shore filed the financing statement, since attachment had already been accomplished. Note that the filing was needed for perfection since this was not a purchase money security interest in consumer goods but in inventory.

3. **(A)** Float gave value by giving the $1,000,000 line of credit on February 1. On this same date, Gray gave Float a security agreement. Since Gray had rights in the collateral it already possessed, attachment took place on February 1 for that inventory possessed.

4. **(C)** Perfection occurred on March 5, when Float filed the financing statement, since attachment had already taken place previously.

5. **(B)** Generally, when two parties have perfected security interests in the same collateral, the first to either file or perfect has priority. When a purchase money security interest exists in the collateral, however, the general rule may vary, depending on whether the collateral is inventory or noninventory. In this case the collateral is inventory. A purchase money security interest in inventory may obtain priority over previously perfected conflicting security interests if (1) the purchase money security holder perfects his interest in the inventory at the time the debtor receives the inventory, and (2) the purchase money security holder provides written notice of his purchase money security interest and a description of the inventory to all holders of conflicting security interests who have filed financing statements covering the same type of inventory. If the purchase money security holder does not take these steps, the general rule applies. Answer (A) is incorrect because Shore did not take the necessary steps for its purchase money security interest to obtain priority. Answer (B) is correct because the general rule applies, and Float filed first. Answer (C) is incorrect because when both security interests are perfected, priority is not based on the order of attachment.

6. **(C)** A buyer in the ordinary course of business takes free of any security interests even if perfected and even if the buyer is aware of the security interests. Therefore, answers (A) and (B) are incorrect because Dove purchased the goods in the ordinary course of business.

BANKRUPTCY

Overview

The overall objective of bankruptcy law is to allow honest insolvent debtors to surrender most of their assets and obtain release from their debts. A secondary purpose is to give creditors fair opportunity to share in the debtor's limited assets in proportion to their claims.

Bankruptcy is typically tested by either a few multiple-choice questions or an essay question. These questions normally emphasize when involuntary and voluntary proceedings can be conducted, the federal exemp-

tions, the role of the trustee in bankruptcy, preferential transfers, priorities, and conditions under which debts may be discharged in bankruptcy. Although bankruptcy under Chapter 7 is emphasized on the CPA examination, you should also be familiar with the other portions of this module. Recently, for example, Chapter 11 on Business Reorganizations has received some increased treatment.

Various dollar amounts in this module have been increased so the dollar amounts in various textbooks may be too low under current bankruptcy law

A. Alternatives to Bankruptcy Proceedings

1. Creditors may choose to do nothing

    a. Expense of collection may exceed what creditors could recover
    b. Creditors may expect debtor to pull through

2. Creditors may rush to satisfy their claims individually through legal proceedings (i.e., legal judgments, garnishing of wages, etc.)

    a. Bankruptcy proceedings may result anyway, especially if some creditors are dissatisfied

3. Receiverships

    a. This provides for general administration of debtor's assets by a court appointee (a receiver) for benefit of all parties

4. Agreements can be used to avoid bankruptcy such as composition agreements with creditors whereby creditors agree to accept less

    a. Creditors who do not agree may force debtor into bankruptcy

B. Bankruptcy in General

1. Bankruptcy is based mostly on federal law
2. Bankruptcy provides a method of protecting creditors' rights and granting the debtor relief from his/her indebtedness

    a. Debtor is permitted to have a fresh start
    b. Creditors are treated more fairly according to the priorities stated in bankruptcy laws to effect an equitable distribution of debtor's property

C. Chapter 7 Voluntary Bankruptcy Petitions

1. Voluntary bankruptcy petition is a formal request by debtor for an order of relief

    a. Petition is filed with court along with list of debtor's assets and liabilities
    b. Debtor need not be insolvent—merely needs to state that s/he has debts
    c. Debtor is automatically given an order of relief upon filing of petition

        (1) Court may dismiss voluntary petition if petitioning debtor obligations are primarily consumer debts and granting of relief would be substantial abuse of Chapter 7—(debtor may then proceed under Chapter 13)

    d. Petition may be filed by husband and wife jointly

2. Any person, partnership, or corporation may file voluntary bankruptcy petition with some exceptions

    a. Insurance companies, banks, and savings and loans may not

D. Chapter 7 Involuntary Bankruptcy Petitions

1. Involuntary bankruptcy petition may be filed with bankruptcy court by creditors requesting an order for relief
2. Requirements to file petition

a. If there are fewer than twelve creditors, a single creditor may file the petition as long as his/her claim aggregates $11,625 in excess of any security s/he may hold

   (1) Claims must not be contingent

   (2) If necessary, more than one creditor may join together to have combined debts of more than $11,625 of unsecured claims

> EXAMPLE: Poor-R-Us Company is not paying its debts as they become due. Its creditors are A (owed $12,000), B (owed $7,000), and C (owed $5,000). A alone may file the involuntary petition to force the company into bankruptcy; however, if A does not wish to do so, neither B nor C **separately** may force the company into bankruptcy because of failure to meet the $11,625 test. B and C may join together to file the petition.

> EXAMPLE: XYZ Corporation is unable to pay current obligations. XYZ has three creditors: L (owed $12,000 which is secured by personal property), M (owed $24,000 of which one-half is secured), and N (owed $16,000 of which none is secured). L may not file an involuntary bankruptcy petition but can use the personal property to pay off the debt. Either M or N can file the petition.

b. If there are twelve or more creditors, then at least three must sign the petition and they must have claims that aggregate $11,625 in excess of any security held by them

   (1) Claims must not be contingent

   (2) Claims subject to bona fide dispute are not counted in above $11,625 tests

> EXAMPLE: Poor, Inc. is unable to meet its current obligations as they are becoming due because of severe business difficulties. It owes over $20,000 to a dozen different creditors. One of the unsecured creditors, Green, is owed $12,000. Green may not force Poor, Inc. into Chapter 7 bankruptcy because even though Green is owed more than $11,625, Green must be joined by two other creditors, even if their claims are very small.

> EXAMPLE: Same facts as above except that Poor, Inc. has only eleven creditors. Now Green alone may force Poor, Inc. into bankruptcy under Chapter 7.

c. Creditors who file petition in bankruptcy may need to post a bond that indemnifies debtor for losses caused by contesting petition to avoid frivolous petitions

   (1) Bankruptcy court may award damages including attorneys' fees to debtor who successfully challenges involuntary bankruptcy petition against creditors filing petition

      (a) If petition was made in bad faith, punitive damages may also be awarded

3. Exempt from involuntary bankruptcy are

a. Persons (individuals, partnerships, or corporations) owing less than $11,625

b. Farmers

c. Charitable organizations

4. When valid petition in bankruptcy is filed, it stops enforcement of most collections of debts and legal proceedings

> EXAMPLE: A judgment lien against property in the bankrupt's estate may not be enforced once the petition in bankruptcy is filed so that an orderly disposition of this debt and others can be accomplished.

a. Does not stop collection of alimony

5. Bankruptcy not available for deceased person's estate

a. But once bankruptcy has begun, it is not stopped if bankrupt (debtor) dies

6. An order of relief will be granted if the requirements for filing are met, and

a. The petition is uncontested; or

b. The petition is contested; and

   (1) The debtor is generally not paying his/her debts as they become due; or

   (2) During the 120 days preceding the filing of the petition, a custodian was appointed or took possession of substantially all of the property of the debtor

> EXAMPLE: Debtor assigns his property for the benefit of his creditor.

c. Note that the above rules involve a modified insolvency in the "equity sense" (i.e., debtor not paying debts as they become due). The rest of the Bankruptcy Act uses insolvency in the "bankruptcy sense" (i.e., liabilities exceed fair market value of all nonexempt assets). The use of insolvency in the equity sense for involuntary proceedings is important.

E. **Chapter 7 Bankruptcy Proceedings** (also called a liquidation or straight bankruptcy)

1. Take place under federal law

    a. An order of relief is sought
    b. Court appoints interim trustee
    c. Filing petition automatically stays other legal proceedings against debtor's estate until bankruptcy case is over or until court orders otherwise
    d. Debtor may regain property in possession of interim trustee by filing court approved bond

    EXAMPLE: Mortgage foreclosure by savings and loan will be suspended against debtor.

2. First creditors' meeting

    a. Debtor furnishes a schedule of assets, their locations, and a list of creditors
    b. Claims of debtors are deemed allowed unless objected to, in which case the court will determine their validity

        (1) Claims must be filed within six months of first creditors' meeting
        (2) Contingent and unliquidated claims are estimated
        (3) Any attorneys' fees above those ruled reasonable by court are disallowed when objected to by creditors

    c. Trustee may be elected by creditors in Chapter 7 proceeding

        (1) If no election requested by creditors, interim trustee appointed by court continues in office

3. Trustee—the representative of the estate

    a. Trustee has right to receive compensation for services rendered based on value of those services (rather than only on size of estate)
    b. Duties—to collect, liquidate, and distribute the estate, keeping accurate records of all transactions
    c. Trustee represents estate of bankrupt (debtor)
    d. Estate of debtor consists of

        (1) Property presently owned by debtor (as of the filing date)
        (2) Property owed to debtor by third parties that can be recovered by trustee
        (3) Income from property owned by estate after petition is filed
        (4) Property received by debtor within 180 days after filing of petition by following methods: inheritance, life insurance, divorce decree, property settlement with spouse, bequest, or devise

            (a) Part of estate of debtor even if debtor has right to receive above within 180 days after the filing of petition

        (5) Leases disguised as secured or unsecured installment sales contracts

            (a) Typically happens when lessee automatically owns "leased" property for no additional consideration or when lessee has option to buy "leased" property for nominal consideration, especially when leased property has a significant market value

                1] However, if agreement is a true lease, it is not part of the lessee's estate

                EXAMPLE: Y has been leasing property to Z under which Z may purchase the property for $10 at the expiration of the lease. It is estimated that the property will be worth $6,000, however, at that time. If Z takes out or is forced into Chapter 7 bankruptcy, this property will be included as part of Z's estate.

                EXAMPLE: Same facts as above except that Y perfects its security interest. Now Y can sell the property to satisfy Y's debt.

        (6) Property acquired by debtor, other than by methods listed above, after filing is considered "new estate" and not subject to creditors' claims in bankruptcy proceeding

4. Exemptions to which debtor is entitled

    a. Keeps any interests in joint tenancy property if those interests are exempt under other nonbankruptcy law, and

b. Debtor usually has option of choosing either

   (1) **Both** exemptions under state law and federal law other than under federal Bankruptcy Code

      (a) Typical state exemptions (limited in monetary value) include

         1] Small amount of money
         2] Residence
         3] Clothing
         4] Tools of trade
         5] Insurance

      (b) Examples of exemptions under federal nonbankruptcy law

         1] Veteran's benefits
         2] Social security benefits
         3] Unemployment compensation or benefits
         4] Disability benefits
         5] Alimony

   (2) Or, exemptions provided by federal Bankruptcy Code

      (a) Allowable federal exemptions include

         1] $17,425 equity in principal residence and burial plot
         2] $2,775 equity in one motor vehicle
         3] $1,750 in books and tools of one's trade
         4] $450 per item qualifying for personal, family, or home use (has an aggregate ceiling of $9,300)
         5] $1,150 in jewelry
         6] Dividends and life insurance up to $9,300
         7] Social security benefits
         8] Unemployment compensation
         9] Disability, illness, or unemployment benefits
        10] Alimony
        11] Veteran's benefits
        12] Prescribed health aids
        13] Public assistance
        14] Pensions and retirement benefits needed for support and ERISA qualified
        15] Lost earnings payments
        16] Wrongful death payments that bankrupted party depended on
        17] Wages up to maximum of specified formula (75% of person's disposable income or 30 times federal minimum wage
        18] Crime victim's compensation
        19] Interest in any property not to exceed $925 plus $8,725 of any unused portion of the homestead exemption (item [1] above); can be used to protect any type of property including cash
        20] Specified personal injury awards up to $17,425 (not to include pain and suffering or monetary loss)

c. Above exemptions doubled for married couples

5. Duties of trustee under Chapter 7 bankruptcy (i.e., a liquidation)

a. In general, to liquidate and sell assets owned to pay creditors based on priorities discussed later and to examine propriety of claims brought by creditors

   (1) Considers how best to sell, use, or lease property of estate to act in best interest of estate
   (2) Acquires all legal assets owed to estate for equitable distribution to creditors
   (3) Trustee makes interim reports and presents final accounting of the administration of the estate to the court

6. Powers of trustee

a. Trustee may take any legal action necessary to carry out duties

(1) Trustee may utilize any defense available to the debtor against third parties
(2) Trustee may continue or cease any legal action started by the debtor for the benefit of the estate

b. Trustee, with court approval, may employ professionals (e.g., accountants and lawyers) to assist trustee in carrying out duties that require professional expertise

(1) Employed professional must not hold any interest adverse to that of debtor (i.e., to avoid conflicts of interest)
(2) Employed professional has right to receive compensation for reasonable value of services performed

(a) Reasonable fee is based on amount and complexity of services rendered, not on size of estate

(3) Trustee, with court approval, may act in professional capacity if capable and be compensated separately for professional services rendered

c. Trustee must within sixty days of the order for relief assume or reject any executory contract, including leases, made by the debtor

(1) Any not assumed are deemed rejected
(2) Trustee must perform all obligations on lease of nonresidential property until lease is either assumed or rejected
(3) Rejection of a contract is a breach of contract and injured party may become an unsecured creditor
(4) Trustee may assign or retain leases if good for bankrupt's estate and if allowed under lease and state law
(5) Rejection or assumption of lease is subject to court approval

d. Trustee may set aside liens (those which arise automatically under law) if lien

(1) Becomes effective when bankruptcy petition is filed or when debtor becomes insolvent
(2) Is not enforceable against a bona fide purchaser when the petition is filed
(3) In the case of a security interest, is not perfected before filing of bankruptcy petition

e. Trustee **may set aside transfers made within one year prior** to the filing of the bankruptcy petition if

(1) The transfer was made with intent to hinder, delay, or defraud any creditor. The debtor need not be insolvent at time of transfer.
(2) Debtor received less than a reasonably equivalent value in exchange for such transfer or obligation and the debtor

(a) Was insolvent at the time, or became insolvent as a result of the transfer
(b) If the fact that the transfer was a fraudulent conveyance was the only grounds for avoiding the transfer; once avoided by trustee, transferee that gave value in good faith has a lien on property transferred to the extent of value given

f. Trustee may also set aside preferential transfers of nonexempt property to a creditor made within the **previous ninety days** while insolvent in the "bankruptcy sense"

(1) Preferential transfers are those made for **antecedent debts** that enable the creditor to receive more than s/he would have otherwise under a Chapter 7 liquidation proceeding

(a) Includes a security interest given by debtor to secure antecedent debt

EXAMPLE: Debtor paid off a loan to BB Bank sixty days before Debtor filed a bankruptcy petition. This is a preferential transfer.

EXAMPLE: Debtor gave CC Bank a security interest in some office furniture he owns to secure a previous loan CC Bank had granted him. This is a preferential transfer if Debtor gave the security interest within

ninety days of the filing of bankruptcy. The reason for this is that it gives the creditor (bank) greater rights than it had before.

EXAMPLE: Debtor prepaid some installments on an installment loan on equipment.

*EXAMPLE: Debtor made a gift to charity. This is **not** a transfer for an antecedent debt.*

(2) Preferential transfers **made to insiders** within the **previous twelve months** may be set aside

(a) Insiders are close blood relatives, officers, directors, controlling stockholders of corporations, or general partners of partnerships

EXAMPLE: S is a secured creditor of XYZ Co. that is in Chapter 7 bankruptcy. S is not an insider.

EXAMPLE: One year ago Herb purchased a car on credit from Ike. Thirty days before filing for bankruptcy, Herb, while insolvent, makes a payment to Ike concerning the auto. This is a preferential transfer. If Ike were Herb's brother, this preference could have been set aside if it had occurred, for example, 120 days before the filing of the petition while Herb was insolvent (insider preference).

(3) Exceptions to trustee's power to avoid preferential transfers

(a) A contemporaneous exchange between creditor and debtor whereby debtor receives new value

EXAMPLE: Herb, while insolvent, purchases a car for cash from Ike within ninety days of filing a petition in bankruptcy. The trustee could not avoid this transaction because Herb, the debtor, received present (i.e., contemporaneous) value (the car) for the cash transferred to Ike, the creditor. This is not a voidable preference.

(b) Transfer made in the ordinary course of business is not a voidable preference, nor is the perfected security interest that arises from it (if filed within forty-five days of creation of that debt)

EXAMPLE: Debtor pays the utility bill for the business.

(c) A security interest given by debtor to acquire property that is perfected within ten days after such security interest attaches

(d) A consumer debtor's payment of $600 or less to any creditor

7. Trustee may be sued or sue on behalf of estate

F. Claims

1. Property rights—where claimant has a property right, property is turned over to claimant, because not considered part of debtor's estate

a. Reclamation is a claim against specific property by a person claiming it to be his/hers

EXAMPLE: A person rented a truck for a week and in the meantime he becomes bankrupt. The lessor will make a reclamation.

b. Trust claim is made by beneficiary for trust property when the trustee is bankrupt

EXAMPLE: Trustee maintains a trust account for beneficiary under a trust set up in a will. Trustee becomes bankrupt. The trust account is not part of trustee's estate. The beneficiary may claim the trust account as his property.

c. Secured claim when creditor has a security interest (e.g., mortgage in property or security interest under UCC)

(1) As long as trustee does not successfully attack the security—basically, security interest must be without defects to prevail against trustee (i.e., perfected security interests)

(2) Secured status may be achieved by subrogation (e.g., surety is subrogated to creditor's collateral)

d. Setoffs are allowed to the extent the bankrupt and creditor have mutual debts whether unsecured or not

2. Filing of claims

a. All claims must be filed within six months after the first creditors' meeting

3. Proof of claims

a. Timely claims are deemed allowed unless creditor objects

        (1) Contingent and unliquidated claims may be estimated

    b. Claims below are not allowed if an objection is made

        (1) Unenforceable claims (by law or agreement)
        (2) Unmatured interest as of date of filing bankruptcy petition
        (3) Claims that may be offset
        (4) Property tax claim in excess of the property value
        (5) Insider or attorney claims in excess of reasonable value of services as determined by court
        (6) Alimony, maintenance, and support claims for amounts due after bankruptcy petition is filed (they are not dischargeable)
        (7) Landlord's damages for lease termination in excess of specified amounts
        (8) Damages for termination of an employment contract in excess of one year's wages
        (9) Certain employment tax claims

4. Priority of claims (be sure to know)

    a. Property rights (e.g., secured debts)

        (1) Technically, they are not a part of the priorities because they never become part of the bankrupt estate.

           (a) But security interests perfected before the ninety-day period (one year for insiders) can be thought of as having the highest priority up to the value of the collateral since it can be repossessed

    b. Unsecured claims are paid at each level of priority before any lower level is paid

        (1) If there are insufficient assets to pay any given level then assets are prorated at that level (the next levels get $0)

    c. Levels of priority

        (1) Administration costs

           (a) Includes fees to accountants, attorneys, trustees, and appraisers as well as expenses incurred only in recovering, preserving, selling, or discovering property that should be included in debtor's estate

              EXAMPLE: Bee, Ware, and Watch, a partnership of CPAs, performed professional services for Dee-Funct Company before it was forced into bankruptcy by its creditors. These fees are not put in the first priority but the last because they do not qualify as administration costs.

           (b) Also includes reasonable fees, salary, or wages needed for services such as operating the business after the bankruptcy action begins

        (2) Claims arising in ordinary course of debtor's business after involuntary bankruptcy petition is filed but before order for relief is entered
        (3) Wages of bankrupt's employees ($4,650 maximum each) accrued within ninety days before the petition in bankruptcy was filed (any excess is treated as a general claim)

           (a) This priority does not include officers' salaries

        (4) Contributions to employee benefit plans within the prior 180 days, limited to $4,650 per employee, reduced by amount received as wage preference
        (5) Claims on raising or storage of grain up to $4,650 for each individual
        (6) Consumer deposits for undelivered goods or services limited to $2,100 per individual
        (7) Alimony and child support
        (8) Taxes (federal, state, and local)
        (9) General (unsecured) creditors that filed timely proofs of claims

           (a) Includes amounts owed to secured creditors in excess of amount for which security sells

              EXAMPLE: X has been forced into Chapter 7 bankruptcy proceedings. X had assets that have been sold for $14,000 cash. Fees to accountants, attorneys, and the trustee total $3,000. Expenses to sell property total $1,000. Wages owed to two employees for the previous month's work are $4,500 and $4,000 respectively. Past taxes amount to $900 and two general creditors have claims amounting to $1,000 and $500 respectively. Under the priorities just given, the $3,000 and the $1,000 are administrative costs and are paid first. The *wages owed to the two employees are paid next leaving $1,500. The $900 in taxes is paid next, leaving $600. This must now be paid out proportionately; therefore, the general creditors received $400 and $200 respectively.*

(b) Unsecured claims filed late (unless excused) are paid after timely claims

G. Discharge of a Bankrupt

1. A discharge is the release of a debtor from all his/her debts not paid in bankruptcy except those not dischargeable

   a. Granting an order of relief to an individual is an automatic application for discharge
   b. Corporations and partnerships cannot receive a discharge

2. Debtor must be adjudged an "honest debtor" to be discharged
3. Acts that bar discharge of **all** debts

   a. Improper actions during bankruptcy proceeding

   (1) Making false claims against the estate
   (2) Concealing property
   (3) Transfer of property after filing with intent to defeat the law (i.e., fraudulent transfer)
   (4) Making any false entry in or on any document of account relating to bankrupt's affairs
   (5) These acts are also punishable by fines and imprisonment

   b. Failing to satisfactorily explain any loss of assets
   c. Refusing to obey court orders
   d. Removing or destroying property within twelve months prior to filing of petition with intent to hinder, delay, or defraud any creditor
   e. Destroying, falsifying, concealing, or failing to keep books of account or records unless such act is justified under the circumstances
   f. Being discharged in bankruptcy proceedings within the past six years
   g. "Substantial abuse" of bankruptcy by individual debtor with primarily consumer debts
   h. A preferential transfer does **not** bar discharge (but can be set aside)

H. Debts Not Discharged by Bankruptcy (even though general discharge allowed)

1. Taxes within three years of filing bankruptcy petition
2. Loans for payment of federal taxes
3. Unscheduled debts unless creditor had actual notice of proceedings (i.e., where bankrupt failed to list creditor and debt)

   EXAMPLE: In a petition in bankruptcy, a mistake was made so that a debt owed to ABC Company was listed as owed to XYZ Company. The debt to ABC is not discharged unless ABC somehow was aware of the mistake.

4. Alimony, separate maintenance, or child support
5. Liability due to theft or embezzlement
6. Debts arising from debtor's fraud about his/her financial condition or fraud in connection with purchase or sale of securities

   EXAMPLE: Obtaining credit using false information such as materially fraudulent financial statements that the creditor relied on.

7. Willful and/or malicious injuries to a person or property of another (intentional torts)

   a. Unintentional torts (i.e., negligence) and breaches of contract are dischargeable

8. Educational loans of a governmental unit or nonprofit institution which became due within prior five years unless liability would impose "undue hardship" on debtor or debtor's dependents
9. Governmental fines or penalties imposed within prior three years
10. Those from a prior bankruptcy proceeding in which the debtor waived discharge or was denied discharge
11. Liability incurred by driving while legally intoxicated
12. To avoid the practice of "loading up on luxury goods" before bankruptcy, there is a presumption of nondischargeability for

   a. Consumer debts to a single debtor of $1,150 or more for luxury goods or services

    b.   Certain cash advances based on consumer credit exceeding $1,150

13.   Any debt from violation of securities laws including those under Sarbanes-Oxley Act

I. Revocation of Discharge

1.   Discharge may be revoked if

    a.   Bankrupt committed fraud during bankruptcy proceedings unknown to creditors seeking revocation

        EXAMPLE: A bankrupt conceals assets in order to defraud creditors.

        (1) Must be applied for within one year of discharge

    b.   Bankrupt acquired rights or title to property of estate and fraudulently failed to report this
    c.   Bankrupt refused to obey lawful court order or refused to testify when not in violation of his/her constitutional right against self incrimination

J. Reaffirmation

1.   Debtor promises to pay a debt that will be discharged. The Code makes it difficult to reaffirm dischargeable debt.

    a.   To be enforceable, reaffirmation of dischargeable debt must satisfy the following conditions:

        (1) Reaffirmation must take place before discharge granted
        (2) Must be approved by bankruptcy court
        (3) Debtor is allowed sixty days to rescind reaffirmation once agreed to

           (a) Debtor must have received appropriate warnings from the court or attorney on effects of reaffirmation, and
           (b) If also involves consumer debt not secured by real property, court must approve new agreement as being in best interests of debtor and not imposing undue hardship on debtor

K. Business Reorganization—Chapter 11

1.   Goal is to keep financially troubled firm in business

    a.   It is an alternative to liquidation under Chapter 7 (straight bankruptcy)
    b.   In general, allows debtor to keep assets of business

2.   Can be initiated by debtor (voluntary) or creditors (involuntary)

    a.   Available to individuals, partnerships, or corporations including railroads. Other entities ineligible to be debtors under Chapter 7 are ineligible under Chapter 11.
    b.   If involuntary, same requirements must be met as needed to initiate a Chapter 7 involuntary proceeding

3.   Each class of similar creditors and shareholders creates separate committees to make master reorganization plan

    a.   Investigation of debtor's financial affairs is conducted
    b.   Committees meet together and negotiate reorganization plan if possible
    c.   If debtor's management capable of continuing business, no trustee is appointed
    d.   If debtor's management is not considered capable of running business, then trustee is appointed to conduct business
    e.   Approval of reorganization plan needs

        (1) Over 1/2 of creditors in each committee owed at least 2/3 of the total debt in that class, and
        (2) Acceptance of stockholders' holding at least 2/3 in amount of the stock
        (3) Complete reorganization plan can still be approved by court if court determines plan is fair even if some committees fail to approve it

4.   Important provision is court-supervised rehabilitation plan

    a.   Allows for continued operation of business unless court orders otherwise

    b.   Provides for payment of part or all of debts over extended period

        (1) Payment to creditors comes primarily from future income

    c.   Must divide claims into classes of similar claims and treat each class equally
    d.   Plan may provide for some creditors to receive stock in place of debt

        (1) Preferred shareholders may be converted to common shareholders
        (2) Common shareholders may forfeit shares of stock
        (3) Typically, claimants receive reduced amounts

5.   After court confirms plan and issues final decree

    a.   Debtor is discharged from debts that arose before confirmation of plan except those that were agreed to continue or will continue under Bankruptcy Code

        (1) New agreed-upon substituted debts are enforceable

6.   Court may convert Chapter 11 reorganization into Chapter 7 straight bankruptcy if fairer
7.   SEC has limited power to participate in bankruptcy reorganizations
8.   When debtor keeps and operates business, debtor has right to retain employees and professionals it used before reorganization

       EXAMPLE: Debtor, after a Chapter 11 reorganization, wishes to keep its CPA firm. This is permitted.

L. Debts Adjustment Plans—Chapter 13

1.   Most individuals are eligible if

    a.   Have regular income, and
    b.   Owe unsecured debts of less than $290,525, and
    c.   Owe secured debts of less than $871,550
    d.   Debt ceilings adjusted for inflation every three years

2.   Initiated when debtor files voluntary petition in bankruptcy court

    a.   Creditors may not file involuntary petition under Chapter 13
    b.   Petition normally includes composition or extension plan

        (1) Composition—creditors agree to accept less than full amounts due
        (2) Extension—provides debtor up to three years (five years if court approves) for payments to creditors

    c.   Filing of petition stays all collection and straight bankruptcy proceedings against debtor
    d.   Debtor has exclusive right to propose plan

        (1) If debtor does not file plan, creditors may force debtor into involuntary proceeding under Chapter 7

    e.   Plan will be confirmed or denied by court without approval of unsecured creditors

        (1) However, unsecured creditors must receive as much as they would get under Chapter 7, and

            (a) Either be paid in full, or
            (b) Have all debtor's disposable income committed to plan
            (c) Plan may put claims in different classifications but may not discriminate unfairly against any of designated classes

                1] Each claimant within same classification must receive same treatment

    f.   Court must appoint trustee in Chapter 13 cases
    g.   Debtor engaged in business may continue to operate that business subject to limitations imposed by court
    h.   Completion of plan discharges debtor from debts dischargeable
    i.   If composition were involved, then discharge bars another discharge for six years unless debtor paid 70% of debts covered

MULTIPLE-CHOICE QUESTIONS (1-29)

1. Which of the following statements is correct concerning the voluntary filing of a petition in bankruptcy?
   a. If the debtor has twelve or more creditors, the unsecured claims must total at least $11,625.
   b. The debtor must be insolvent.
   c. If the debtor has less than twelve creditors, the unsecured claims must total at least $11,625.
   d. The petition may be filed jointly by spouses.

2. A voluntary petition filed under the liquidation provisions of Chapter 7 of the Federal Bankruptcy Code
   a. Is **not** available to a corporation unless it has previously filed a petition under the reorganization provisions of Chapter 11 of the Federal Bankruptcy Code.
   b. Automatically stays collection actions against the debtor **except** by secured creditors.
   c. Will be dismissed unless the debtor has twelve or more unsecured creditors whose claims total at least $11,625.
   d. Does **not** require the debtor to show that the debtor's liabilities exceed the fair market value of assets.

3. On February 28, 2002, Master, Inc. had total assets with a fair market value of $1,200,000 and total liabilities of $990,000. On January 15, 2002, Master made a monthly installment note payment to Acme Distributors Corp., a creditor holding a properly perfected security interest in equipment having a fair market value greater than the balance due on the note. On March 15, 2002, Master voluntarily filed a petition in bankruptcy under the liquidation provisions of Chapter 7 of the Federal Bankruptcy Code. One year later, the equipment was sold for less than the balance due on the note to Acme.

If a creditor challenged Master's right to file, the petition would be dismissed
   a. If Master had less than twelve creditors at the time of filing.
   b. Unless Master can show that a reorganization under Chapter 11 of the Federal Bankruptcy Code would have been unsuccessful.
   c. Unless Master can show that it is unable to pay its debts in the ordinary course of business or as they come due.
   d. If Master is an insurance company.

4. Which of the following conditions, if any, must a debtor meet to file a voluntary bankruptcy petition under Chapter 7 of the Federal Bankruptcy Code?

	Insolvency	*Three or more creditors*
a.	Yes	Yes
b.	Yes	No
c.	No	Yes
d.	No	No

5. Brenner Corporation is trying to avoid bankruptcy but its four creditors are trying to force Brenner into bankruptcy. The four creditors are owed the following amounts:

Anteed Corporation	-	$5,000 of unsecured debt
Bounty Corporation	-	$4,500 of unsecured debt and
		$8,500 of secured debt
Courtney Corporation	-	$2,000 of unsecured debt
Dauntless Corporation	-	$1,000 of unsecured debt

Which of the creditors must sign the petition to force Brenner into bankruptcy?
   a. Bounty is sufficient.
   b. At least Anteed and Bounty are needed.
   c. At least Bounty, Courtney, and Dauntless are needed.
   d. All of these four creditors are needed.

Items 6 through 10 are based on the following:

Dart Inc., a closely held corporation, was petitioned involuntarily into bankruptcy under the liquidation provisions of Chapter 7 of the Federal Bankruptcy Code. Dart contested the petition.

Dart has not been paying its business debts as they became due, has defaulted on its mortgage loan payments, and owes back taxes to the IRS. The total cash value of Dart's bankruptcy estate after the sale of all assets and payment of administration expenses is $100,000.

Dart has the following creditors:

•   Fracon Bank is owed $75,000 principal and accrued interest on a mortgage loan secured by Dart's real property. The property was valued at and sold, in bankruptcy, for $70,000.

•   The IRS has a $12,000 recorded judgment for unpaid corporate income tax.

•   JOG Office Supplies has an unsecured claim of $3,000 that was timely filed.

•   Nanstar Electric Co. has an unsecured claim of $1,200 that was not timely filed.

•   Decoy Publications has a claim of $14,000, of which $2,000 is secured by Dart's inventory that was valued and sold, in bankruptcy, for $2,000. The claim was timely filed.

6. Which of the following statements would correctly describe the result of Dart's opposing the petition?
   a. Dart will win because the petition should have been filed under Chapter 11.
   b. Dart will win because there are **not** more than 12 creditors.
   c. Dart will lose because it is **not** paying its debts as they become due.
   d. Dart will lose because of its debt to the IRS.

7. Which of the following events will follow the filing of the Chapter 7 involuntary petition?

	A trustee will be appointed	*A stay against creditor collection proceedings will go into effect*
a.	Yes	Yes
b.	Yes	No
c.	No	Yes
d.	No	No

For **items 8 through 10** assume that the bankruptcy estate was distributed.

8. What dollar amount would Nanstar Electric Co. receive?
   a. $0
   b. $ 800
   c. $1,000
   d. $1,200

9. What total dollar amount would Fracon Bank receive on its secured and unsecured claims?
   a. $70,000
   b. $72,000

c. $74,000
d. $75,000

10. What dollar amount would the IRS receive?
   a. $0
   b. $ 8,000
   c. $10,000
   d. $12,000

11. Which of the following is **not** allowed as a federal exemption under the Federal Bankruptcy Code?
   a.   Some specified amount of equity in one motor vehicle.
   b.   Unemployment compensation.
   c.   Some specified amount of value in books and tools of one's trade.
   d.   All of the above are allowed.

12. Flax, a sole proprietor, has been petitioned involuntarily into bankruptcy under the Federal Bankruptcy Code's liquidation provisions. Simon & Co., CPAs, has been appointed trustee of the bankruptcy estate. If Simon also wishes to act as the tax return preparer for the estate, which of the following statements is correct?
   a.   Simon is prohibited from serving as both trustee and preparer under any circumstances because serving in that dual capacity would be a conflict of interest.
   b.   Although Simon may serve as both trustee and preparer, it is entitled to receive a fee only for the services rendered as a preparer.
   c.   Simon may employ itself to prepare tax returns if authorized by the court and may receive a separate fee for services rendered in each capacity.
   d.   Although Simon may serve as both trustee and preparer, its fees for services rendered in each capacity will be determined solely by the size of the estate.

13. Which of the following transfers by a debtor, within 90 days of filing for bankruptcy, could be set aside as a preferential payment?
   a.   Making a gift to charity.
   b.   Paying a business utility bill.
   c.   Borrowing money from a bank secured by giving a mortgage on business property.
   d.   Prepaying an installment loan on inventory.

Items 14 and 15 are based on the following:

On August 1, 2002, Hall filed a voluntary petition under Chapter 7 of the Federal Bankruptcy Code. Hall's assets are sufficient to pay general creditors 40% of their claims.

The following transactions occurred before the filing:

•   On May 15, 2002, Hall gave a mortgage on Hall's home to National Bank to secure payment of a loan National had given Hall two years earlier. When the loan was made, Hall's twin was a National employee.

•   On June 1, 2002, Hall purchased a boat from Olsen for $10,000 cash.

•   On July 1, 2002, Hall paid off an outstanding credit card balance of $500. The original debt had been $2,500.

14. The National mortgage was
   a.   Preferential, because National would be considered an insider.
   b.   Preferential, because the mortgage was given to secure an antecedent debt.

c.   Not preferential, because Hall is presumed insolvent when the mortgage was given.
d.   Not preferential, because the mortgage was a security interest.

15. The payment to Olsen was
   a.   Preferential, because the payment was made within ninety days of the filing of the petition.
   b.   Preferential, because the payment enabled Olsen to receive more than the other general creditors.
   c.   Not preferential, because Hall is presumed insolvent when the payment was made.
   d.   Not preferential, because the payment was a contemporaneous exchange for new value.

16. Under the liquidation provisions of Chapter 7 of the Federal Bankruptcy Code, a debtor will be denied a discharge in bankruptcy if the debtor
   a.   Fails to list a creditor.
   b.   Owes alimony and support payments.
   c.   Cannot pay administration expenses.
   d.   Refuses to satisfactorily explain a loss of assets.

17. On May 1, 2002, two months after becoming insolvent, Quick Corp., an appliance wholesaler, filed a voluntary petition for bankruptcy under the provisions of Chapter 7 of the Federal Bankruptcy Code. On October 15, 2001, Quick's board of directors had authorized and paid Erly $50,000 to repay Erly's April 1, 2001, loan to the corporation. Erly is a sibling of Quick's president. On March 15, 2002, Quick paid Kray $100,000 for inventory delivered that day.

Which of the following is **not** relevant in determining whether the repayment of Erly's loan is a voidable preferential transfer?
   a.   Erly is an insider.
   b.   Quick's payment to Erly was made on account of an antecedent debt.
   c.   Quick's solvency when the loan was made by Erly.
   d.   Quick's payment to Erly was made within one year of the filing of the bankruptcy petition.

18. Brook Corporation has filed for bankruptcy. Of the following debts Brook owes, indicate their priorities from the highest to the lowest.

   I. Federal taxes unpaid for the previous year.
   II. Wages of $3,000 owed to employees.
   III. Balance of $5,000 owed to a creditor that had a security interest. This creditor got paid fully by selling off the collateral except for this $5,000 deficiency.

   a.   I, II, III.
   b.   I, III, II.
   c.   II, I, III.
   d.   III, I, II.

19. Kessler Company has filed a voluntary bankruptcy petition. Kessler's debts include administration costs owed to accountants, attorneys, and appraisers. It also owes federal and state taxes. Kessler still owes various employees for the previous month's wages accrued before the petition was filed. None of these wages are owed to the officers and at most total $4,000 per employee. The company also owes several creditors for claims arising in the ordinary course of business. All of these latter claims arose before Kessler filed the bankruptcy petition. What are the priorities from highest to lowest of these listed debts and claims?

a. The claims arising in the ordinary course of business; the administration costs; the employees' wages; the federal and state taxes.

b. The administration costs; the employees' wages; the federal and state taxes; the claims arising in the ordinary course of business.

c. The federal and state taxes; the administration costs; the claims arising in the ordinary course of business; the employees' wages.

d. The claims arising in the ordinary course of business; the federal and state taxes; the administration costs; the employees' wages.

20. Which of the following acts will not bar a general discharge in bankruptcy?

a. The debtor tried to hide some property to prevent the estate from getting it.

b. The debtor intentionally injured a creditor during an argument about the bankruptcy proceedings.

c. The debtor is unwilling to explain satisfactorily why some assets are missing.

d. The debtor intentionally destroyed records of his assets.

21. Chapter 7 of the Federal Bankruptcy Code will deny a debtor a discharge when the debtor

a. Made a preferential transfer to a creditor.

b. Accidentally destroyed information relevant to the bankruptcy proceeding.

c. Obtained a Chapter 7 discharge ten years previously.

d. Is a corporation or a partnership.

22. Eckson was granted an order for relief after having filed a petition in bankruptcy. Which of the following actions would bar a general discharge in bankruptcy?

I. Ten months before the bankruptcy proceedings, Eckson had obtained credit from Cardinal Corporation by using false information on the credit application.

II. Six months before he filed the petition, Eckson removed a vehicle from his land with the intent to defraud a creditor.

III. During the bankruptcy proceedings, Eckson made a false entry on some records pertaining to his assets.

a. I only.

b. I and II only.

c. II and III only.

d. I, II, and III.

23. Which of the following acts by a debtor could result in a bankruptcy court revoking the debtor's discharge?

I. Failure to list one creditor.

II. Failure to answer correctly material questions on the bankruptcy petition.

a. I only.

b. II only.

c. Both I and II.

d. Neither I nor II.

24. Which of the following debts will **not** be discharged by bankruptcy even though a general discharge is allowed?

I. Debt owed to a corporation because the debtor was caught embezzling from it.

II. Money owed to a bank because the debtor was found to have committed fraud about her financial condition to get a loan.

III. Damages owed to a major customer because the debtor intentionally breached an important contract.

a. I only.

b. II only.

c. I and II only.

d. I, II, and III.

25. Which of the following claims will **not** be discharged in bankruptcy?

a. A claim that arises from alimony or maintenance.

b. A claim that arises out of the debtor's breach of contract.

c. A claim brought by a secured creditor that remains unsatisfied after the sale of the collateral.

d. A claim brought by a judgment creditor whose judgment resulted from the debtor's negligent operation of a motor vehicle.

26. By signing a reaffirmation agreement on April 15, 2002, a debtor agreed to pay certain debts that would be discharged in bankruptcy. On June 20, 2002, the debtor's attorney filed the reaffirmation agreement and an affidavit with the court indicating that the debtor understood the consequences of the reaffirmation agreement. The debtor obtained a discharge on August 25, 2002. The reaffirmation agreement would be enforceable only if it was

a. Made after discharge.

b. For debts aggregating less than $5,000.

c. Not for a household purpose debt.

d. Not rescinded before discharge.

27. Strong Corp. filed a voluntary petition in bankruptcy under the reorganization provisions of Chapter 11 of the Federal Bankruptcy Code. A reorganization plan was filed and agreed to by all necessary parties. The court confirmed the plan and a final decree was entered.

Which of the following statements best describes the effect of the entry of the court's final decree?

a. Strong Corp. will be discharged from all its debts and liabilities.

b. Strong Corp. will be discharged only from the debts owed creditors who agreed to the reorganization plan.

c. Strong Corp. will be discharged from all its debts and liabilities that arose before the date of confirmation of the plan.

d. Strong Corp. will be discharged from all its debts and liabilities that arose before the confirmation of the plan, except as otherwise provided in the plan, the order of confirmation, or the Bankruptcy Code.

28. Which of the following statements is correct with respect to the reorganization provisions of Chapter 11 of the Federal Bankruptcy Code?

a. A trustee must always be appointed.

b. The debtor must be insolvent if the bankruptcy petition was filed voluntarily.

c. A reorganization plan may be filed by a creditor anytime after the petition date.

d. The commencement of a bankruptcy case may be voluntary or involuntary.

29. Under Chapter 11 of the Federal Bankruptcy Code, which of the following would **not** be eligible for reorganization?

    a.   Retail sole proprietorship.
    b.   Advertising partnership.
    c.   CPA professional corporation.
    d.   Savings and loan corporation.

PROBLEMS

NOTE: These types of problems are no longer included in the CPA Examination but they have been retained because they are useful in developing skills to complete simulations.

Problem 1   (15 to 20 minutes)

On February 1, 2003, Drake, a sole proprietor operating a retail clothing store, filed a bankruptcy petition under the liquidation provisions of the Bankruptcy Code. For at least six months prior to the filing of the petition, Drake had been unable to pay current business and personal obligations as they came due. Total liabilities substantially exceeded the total assets. A trustee was appointed who has converted all of Drake's nonexempt property to cash in the amount of $96,000. Drake's bankruptcy petition reflects a total of $310,000 of debts, including the following:

- A judgment against Drake in the amount of $19,500 as a result of an automobile accident caused by Drake's negligence.
- Unpaid federal income taxes in the amount of $4,300 for the year 1998 (Drake filed an accurate tax return for 1998).
- A $3,200 obligation payable on June 1, 2003, described as being owed to Martin Office Equipment, when, in fact, the debt is owed to Bartin Computer Supplies (Bartin has no knowledge of Drake's bankruptcy and the time for filing claims has expired).
- Unpaid child support in the amount of $780 arising from a support order incorporated in Drake's 1997 divorce judgment.

Prior to the filing of the petition, Drake entered into the following transactions:

- January 13, 2003—paid Safe Bank $7,500, the full amount on an unsecured loan given by Safe on November 13, 2002 (Drake had used the loan proceeds to purchase a family automobile).
- October 21, 2002—conveyed to his brother, in repayment of a $2,000 debt, a painting that cost Drake $125 and which had a fair market value of $2,000.
- November 15, 2002—borrowed $23,000 from Home Savings and Loan Association, giving Home a first mortgage on Drake's residence, which has a fair market value of $100,000.
- November 9, 2002—paid $4,300 to Max Clothing Distributors for clothing delivered to Drake sixty days earlier (Drake had for several years purchased inventory from Max and his other suppliers on sixty-day credit terms).

Required:

Answer the following questions, setting forth reasons for any conclusions stated.

a. Will the four debts described above be discharged in Drake's bankruptcy?

b. What factors must the bankruptcy trustee show to set aside a transaction as a preferential transfer?

c. State whether each transaction entered into by Drake is a preferential or nonpreferential transfer.

Problem 2   (15 to 20 minutes)

Techno, Inc. is a computer equipment dealer. On February 3, 2003, Techno was four months behind in its payments to Allied Building Maintenance, Cleen Janitorial Services, Inc., and Jones and Associates, CPAs, all of whom provide monthly services to Techno. In an attempt to settle with these three creditors, Techno offered each of them a reduced lump-sum payment for the past due obligations and full payment for future services. These creditors rejected Techno's offer and on April 9, 2003, Allied, Cleen and Jones filed an involuntary petition in bankruptcy against Techno under the provisions of Chapter 7 of the Federal Bankruptcy Code. At the time of the filing, Techno's liability to the three creditors was $19,100, all of which was unsecured.

Techno, at the time of the filing, had liabilities of $229,000 (owed to twenty-three creditors) and assets with a fair market value of $191,000. During the entire year before the bankruptcy filing, Techno's liabilities exceeded the fair market value of its assets.

Included in Techno's liabilities was an installment loan payable to Dollar Finance Co., properly secured by cash registers and other equipment.

The bankruptcy court approved the involuntary petition.

On April 21, 2003, Dollar filed a motion for relief from automatic stay in bankruptcy court claiming it was entitled to take possession of the cash registers and other equipment securing its loan. Dollar plans to sell these assets immediately and apply the proceeds to the loan balance. The fair market value of the collateral is less than the loan balance and Dollar claims to lack adequate protection. Also, Dollar claims it is entitled to receive a priority distribution, before distribution to unsecured creditors, for the amount Techno owes Dollar less the proceeds from the sale of the collateral.

During the course of the bankruptcy proceeding, the following transactions were disclosed:

- On October 6, 2002, Techno paid its president $9,900 as repayment of an unsecured loan made to the corporation on September 18, 2000.
- On February 19, 2003, Techno paid $1,150 to Alexis Computers, Inc. for eight color computer monitors. These monitors were delivered to Techno on February 9, 2003, and placed in inventory.
- On January 12, 2003, Techno bought a new delivery truck from Maple Motors for $7,900 cash. On the date of the bankruptcy filing, the truck was worth $7,000.

Required:

Answer the following questions and give the reasons for your conclusions.

a. What circumstances had to exist to allow Allied, Cleen, and Jones to file an involuntary bankruptcy petition against Techno?

b. **1.** Will Dollar's motion for relief be granted?
2. Will Dollar's claim for priority be approved by the bankruptcy court?

c. Are the payments to Techno's president, Alexis, and Maple preferential transfers?

SIMULATION PROBLEMS

Simulation Problem 1   (10 to 15 minutes)

Situation		
	Analysis	Transactions

On April 1, 2004, Able Corp. was petitioned involuntarily into bankruptcy under the provisions of Chapter 7 of the Federal Bankruptcy Code.

When the petition was filed, Able had the following unsecured creditors:

Creditor	Amount owed
Cole	$12,000
Lake	2,000
Young	1,500
Thorn	1,000

The following transactions occurred before the bankruptcy petition was filed:

*   On January 15, 2004, Able paid Vista Bank the $1,000 balance due on an unsecured business loan.
*   On February 28, 2004, Able paid $1,000 to Owen, an officer of Able, who had lent Able money.
*   On March 1, 2004, Able bought a computer for use in its business from Core Computer Co. for $2,000 cash.

	Analysis	
Situation		Transactions

Part a.

Items 1 through 3 refer to the bankruptcy filing. For each item, determine whether the statement is True or False.

		True	*False*
1.	Able can file a voluntary petition for bankruptcy if it is solvent.	○	○
2.	Lake, Young, and Thorn can file a valid involuntary petition.	○	○
3.	Cole alone can file a valid involuntary petition.	○	○

		Transactions
Situation	Analysis	

Items 4 through 6 refer to the transactions that occurred before the filing of the involuntary bankruptcy petition. Assuming the bankruptcy petition was validly filed, for each item determine whether the statement is True or False.

		True	*False*
4.	The payment to Vista Bank would be set aside as a preferential transfer.	○	○
5.	The payment to Owen would be set aside as a preferential transfer.	○	○
6.	The purchase from Core Computer Co. would be set aside as a preferential transfer.	○	○

Simulation Problem 2   (10 to 15 minutes)

> Situation
>> Transactions

On March 15, 2004, Rusk Corporation was petitioned involuntarily into bankruptcy. At the time of the filing, Rusk had the following creditors:

- Safe Bank, for the balance due on the secured note and mortgage on Rusk's warehouse.
- Employee salary claims.
- 2002 federal income taxes due.
- Accountant's fees outstanding.
- Utility bills outstanding.

Prior to the bankruptcy filing, but while insolvent, Rusk engaged in the following transactions:

- On January 15, 2004, Rusk repaid all corporate directors' loans made to the corporation.
- On February 1, 2004, Rusk purchased raw materials for use in its manufacturing business and paid cash to the supplier.

> Transactions
>> Situation

Items 1 through 5 relate to Rusk's creditors and the February 1 and May 1 transactions. For each item, select from List I whether only statement I is correct, whether only statement II is correct, whether both statements I and II are correct, or whether neither statement I nor II is correct.

List I
A. I only.
B. II only.
C. Both I and II.
D. Neither I nor II.

                                                           (A) (B) (C) (D)

1.   I.   Safe Bank's claim will be the first paid of the listed claims because Safe is a secured creditor.
     II.   Safe Bank will receive the entire amount of the balance of the mortgage due as a secured creditor   O   O   O   O
          regardless of the amount received from the sale of the warehouse.

2.   I.   The employee salary claims will be paid in full after the payment of any secured party.
     II.   The employee salary claims up to $4,650 per claimant will be paid before payment of any general   O   O   O   O
          creditors' claims.

3.   I.   The claim for 2002 federal income taxes due will be paid as a secured creditor claim.
     II.   The claim for 2002 federal income taxes due will be paid prior to the general creditor claims.   O   O   O   O

4.   I.   The January 15 repayments of the directors' loans were preferential transfers even though the
          payments were made more than ten days before the filing of the petition.
     II.   The January 15 repayments of the directors' loans were preferential transfers because the   O   O   O   O
          payments were made to insiders.

5.   I.   The February 1 purchase and payment was **not** a preferential transfer because it was a transaction
          in the ordinary course of business.
     II.   The February 1 purchase and payment was a preferential transfer because it occurred within   O   O   O   O
          ninety days of the filing of the petition.

MULTIPLE-CHOICE ANSWERS

1. d __ __	8. a __ __	15. d __ __	21. d __ __	27. d __ __
2. d __ __	9. c __ __	16. d __ __	22. c __ __	28. d __ __
3. d __ __	10. d __ __	17. c __ __	23. b __ __	29. d __ __
4. d __ __	11. d __ __	18. c __ __	24. c __ __	
5. d __ __	12. c __ __	19. b __ __	25. a __ __	1st: __/29 = __%
6. c __ __	13. d __ __	20. b __ __	26. d __ __	2nd: __/29 = __%
7. a __ __	14. b __ __			

MULTIPLE-CHOICE ANSWER EXPLANATIONS

C. Chapter 7 Voluntary Bankruptcy Petitions

1.   (d)   Voluntary bankruptcy petition is a formal request by the debtor for an order of relief. This voluntary bankruptcy petition may be filed jointly by a husband and a wife. Answer (b) is incorrect because the debtor in a voluntary bankruptcy petition need not be insolvent but needs to state that s/he has debts. Answers (a) and (c) are incorrect because there is no requirement as to the minimum amount of the debtor's liabilities in a voluntary proceeding.

2.   (d)   Under Chapter 7 of the Federal Bankruptcy Code, a debtor may file a voluntary petition without showing that s/he is insolvent. S/he merely has to state the existence of debts. Therefore, the debtor is not required to show that liabilities exceed the fair market value of assets. Answer (a) is incorrect because a corporation may generally file a voluntary bankruptcy petition and there is not a requirement that it has previously filed under Chapter 11. Answer (b) is incorrect because when the debtor is automatically given an order for relief upon filing the petition, the actions to collect money by creditors are stayed. Secured creditors will resort to the collateral, however. Answer (c) is incorrect because the debtor is voluntarily going into bankruptcy and there is no requirement that twelve or more unsecured creditors be owed at least $11,625. Note that this requirement, as written, does not exist for an involuntary bankruptcy petition either.

3.   (d)   Most debtors may file a voluntary bankruptcy petition. Among those that may not are insurance companies, banks, and saving and loan associations. Answer (a) is incorrect because the number of creditors is not relevant for a voluntary bankruptcy petition. Answer (b) is incorrect because there is no need to show that a Chapter 11 bankruptcy would have been unsuccessful. Answer (c) is incorrect because the inability of the debtor to pay its debts as they become due is not relevant to a voluntary bankruptcy.

4.   (d)   A debtor may file a voluntary bankruptcy petition without showing that s/he is insolvent. The debtor may merely state that s/he has debts. There is also no requirement as to the number of creditors needed.

D. Chapter 7 Involuntary Bankruptcy Petitions

5.   (d)   Since there are fewer than twelve creditors, it is true that only one creditor is needed to file the petition. However, no one creditor is owed at least $11,625 of unsecured debt. Therefore, the claims can be aggregated to total at least $11,625 of unsecured debt. The only way this can be accomplished is by aggregating the claims of all four creditors. Note that Bounty Corporation is not enough because the secured debt is not counted in the total.

6.   (c)   When the debtor contests the petition s/he can still be forced into bankruptcy if the debtor is generally not paying his/her debts as they become due. Answer (a) is

incorrect because the petition may be filed under either Chapter 7 (straight bankruptcy) or Chapter 11 (business reorganization). When the bankruptcy is involuntary, Chapter 7 and Chapter 11 are alternatives and have the same requirements for filing against business debtors. Answer (b) is incorrect because although the rules are different when there are fewer than twelve creditors versus when there are twelve or more creditors, Dart can be forced into bankruptcy when Decoy Publications files the petition because Decoy is owed over $11,625 of unsecured debt. Answer (d) is incorrect because there is no exception for the IRS.

7.   (a)   Once a valid petition in bankruptcy is filed, this automatically stays other legal proceedings against the debtor's estate. Also, the court appoints an interim trustee.

8.   (a)   The bankruptcy estate contains $100,000 after the sale of all assets and payment of administration expenses. The secured debt of $70,000 to Fracon Bank and the secured debt of $2,000 to Decoy Publications are satisfied first. (This actually takes place as a higher priority over the administrative expenses.) Therefore, after paying this $72,000 there is $28,000 left. The $12,000 of unpaid income tax has the next highest priority of those listed. This leaves $16,000 for the general creditors who filed on time. There are three of these, that is, Fracon who is owed $5,000 in excess of what the sale of the property brought, JOG who is owed $3,000, and Decoy who is still owed $12,000 in excess of the security interest. These three creditors together are owed $20,000 ($5,000 + $3,000 + $12,000). Since this is more than the $16,000 left, these 3 general creditors' debts are prorated. The last priority of unsecured claimants who filed late get nothing. Therefore, Nanstar Electric gets $0.

9.   (c)   The bankruptcy estate contains $100,000 after the sale of all assets and payment of administration expenses. The secured debt of $70,000 to Fracon Bank and the secured debt of $2,000 to Decoy Publications are satisfied first. (This actually takes place as a higher priority over the administrative expenses.) Therefore, after paying this $72,000 there is $28,000 left. The $12,000 of unpaid income tax has the next highest priority of those listed. This leaves $16,000 for the general creditors who filed on time. There are three of these, that is, Fracon who is owed $5,000 in excess of what the sale of the property brought, JOG who is owed $3,000, and Decoy who is still owed $12,000 in excess of the security interest. These three creditors together are owed $20,000 ($5,000 + $3,000 + $12,000). Since this is more than the $16,000 left, these three general creditors' debts are prorated. Fracon Bank gets money from both the unsecured and secured claims. From the unsecured claim, Fracon receives a prorated share or

$$\frac{\$5,000}{\$5,000 + \$3,000 + \$12,000} \times \$16,000 = \$4,000$$

Add this prorated share of $4,000 to the $70,000 Fracon received from the sold property to arrive at $74,000.

10. (d) The bankruptcy estate contains $100,000 after the sale of all assets and payment of administration expenses. The secured debt of $70,000 to Fracon Bank and the secured debt of $2,000 to Decoy Publications are satisfied first. (This actually takes place as a higher priority over the administrative expenses.) Therefore, after paying this $72,000 there is $28,000 left. The $12,000 of unpaid income tax has the next highest priority of those listed.

E. Chapter 7 Bankruptcy Proceedings

11. (d) Federal exemptions allowed under the Federal Bankruptcy Code include $2,775 equity in one motor vehicle and $1,750 in books and tools of one's trade. They also include, among others, unemployment compensation.

12. (c) A trustee in bankruptcy has the power to employ court approved professionals, such as accountants and attorneys, to handle estate matters which require professional expertise. These professionals have the right to reimbursement for services rendered. A trustee is not deemed to have the appropriate expertise required to prepare tax returns; thus, a trustee may employ a CPA to perform this function. Simon, as trustee, has the power to employ himself to prepare tax returns if authorized by the court and may receive a separate fee for services rendered. Simon may serve as both trustee and preparer if authorized to do so by the court. Simon has the right to receive fees for services rendered as both a trustee and a preparer. The fee for services rendered in each capacity is determined on the basis of the value of the services rendered, not solely the size of the estate.

E.6.f.(3) Exceptions to Trustee's Power to Avoid Preferential Transfers

13. (d) Preferential transfers are payments made for antecedent debts which enable the creditor to receive more than s/he would under a Chapter 7 liquidation proceeding. A gift is not payment for an antecedent debt. Transfers made in the ordinary course of business are exceptions to the trustee's power to avoid a preferential transfer. A contemporaneous exchange between a creditor and the debtor whereby the debtor receives new value is not a preferential transfer. Prepaying an existing installment loan on inventory is making a payment on an antecedent debt which enables the creditor to receive more than s/he would in a liquidation proceeding.

14. (b) Under Chapter 7 of the Federal Bankruptcy Code, the trustee may set aside preferential transfers made to a creditor within ninety days prior to the filing of the petition for bankruptcy. Preferential transfers are those made for antecedent debts that allow the creditor to receive more than s/he would have under the bankruptcy law. All of these conditions were met for the National mortgage. Answer (a) is incorrect because National would not be considered an insider. Even though Hall's twin was a National employee, he was not an officer, director, or controlling stockholder of National. Furthermore, the preferential transfer was not made to him personally but to National Bank. Answer (c) is incorrect because to set aside a preferential transfer, the debtor must have made the transfer while he was insolvent in the bankruptcy sense. Therefore, if Hall was presumed insolvent when the mortgage was given, the trustee is able to set aside the preferential transfer. Note that insolvency is

irrelevant to whether a transfer is preferential or nonpreferential. Answer (d) is incorrect because when Hall gave National Bank the mortgage to secure payment of the two-year-old loan, this was a preferential transfer because it attempted to give National Bank more priority than it would have had as a general unsecured creditor.

15. (d) An exception to the trustee's powers to avoid preferential transfers is a contemporaneous exchange between the debtor and creditor for new values. When Hall paid the $10,000 cash, he received the boat he had purchased from Olsen. Therefore, this $10,000 payment was a contemporaneous exchange for new value. Answer (a) is incorrect because this fact pattern fits the contemporaneous exchange exception. It does not matter that the exchange occurred within ninety days of the filing. Answer (b) is incorrect because Olsen received the $10,000 cash in exchange for the boat. Olsen therefore has not been put in a better position than other general creditors, as Hall received new value for the cash. Answer (c) is incorrect because the issue of presumption of insolvency is not relevant when determining whether a transfer is preferential or nonpreferential.

16. (d) Improper actions during a bankruptcy that bar a discharge of all of the debts include concealing property and refusing to explain a loss of assets. Answer (a) is incorrect because this action means that this particular creditor's claim will not be discharged but does not bar a general discharge of the other debts. Answer (b) is incorrect because although alimony and support payments are not discharged themselves, their existence does not bar a general discharge. Answer (c) is incorrect because the inability to pay does not bar a general discharge.

17. (c) The trustee in bankruptcy may set aside preferential transfers made within ninety days before the filing of the bankruptcy petition while the debtor is insolvent. The time is extended to the previous twelve months if the preferential transfer was made to an insider. In this question, Quick's solvency when the loan was made by Erly is not relevant because this loan was made thirteen months before the filing of the petition for bankruptcy. Answer (a) is incorrect because since payment to Erly was made more than three months but less than twelve months before the filing, it is important that Erly is an insider. Answer (b) is incorrect because the definition of a preferential transfer incorporates transfers made for an antecedent debt. Answer (d) is incorrect because since Erly is an insider, it is relevant that the payment to Erly was made within one year of the filing of the bankruptcy petition.

F. Claims

18. (c) Of those listed, wages of the bankrupt's employees receive the highest priority for up to $4,650 each. Federal taxes have a low priority but are ahead of general creditors. Any deficiency for secured creditors after the collateral is sold is paid along with the general creditors.

19. (b) The highest priority includes the administration costs. Of those listed, the wages to employees up to $4,650 each accrued within ninety days before the petition was filed have the next priority. Federal and state taxes have the second lowest priority but are next because the claims in the ordinary course of business arose **before** the petition was filed and therefore get the lowest priority as general creditors.

G.   Discharge of a Bankrupt

20.   (b)   This is an intentional tort and the liability for these injuries would not be discharged in bankruptcy; however, this does not bar a general discharge of the debts. Answer (a) is incorrect because this is one of the prime acts that the law attempts to prevent. Answer (c) is incorrect because failing to satisfactorily explain a loss of assets can bar a general discharge. Answer (d) is incorrect because this is an act that can bar a general discharge.

21.   (d)   Corporations and partnerships cannot receive a discharge under Chapter 7 of the Federal Bankruptcy Code. Answer (a) is incorrect because although preferential transfers can be set aside, this would not prevent the discharge in bankruptcy. Answer (b) is incorrect because the rule is that destroying information relevant to the bankruptcy proceeding can bar a general discharge unless the act was justified under the circumstances. The accidental nature of the act in answer (b) is not a good case to bar the discharge. Answer (c) is incorrect because the rule states that the discharge is not allowed if the debtor has been discharged in bankruptcy within the past six years rather than ten years.

22.   (c)   Actions that bar a general discharge in bankruptcy include removing or destroying property within twelve months prior to filing the petition with an intent to hinder, delay, or defraud a creditor. Also included is making a false entry in a document related to the bankrupt's affairs. Obtaining credit by fraud involving the debtor's financial condition causes that debt to be nondischargeable. It, however, does not prevent a general discharge of all debts.

23.   (b)   The bankruptcy court can revoke the debtor's discharge if the debtor committed fraud during the bankruptcy proceedings, refused to obey lawful court orders, or failed to answer correctly material questions on the bankruptcy petition. Failure to list a creditor causes that creditor's debt not to be discharged but does not cause a revocation of the discharge.

H.   Debts Not Discharged by Bankruptcy

24.   (c)   There is a list of various types of debts that will not be discharged in bankruptcy, even though a general discharge is allowed. Among these are liabilities from theft, embezzlement, and committing fraud about one's financial condition. Note that liabilities from ordinary negligence or from breaches of contract, whether intentional or not, are dischargeable in bankruptcy.

25.   (a)   Debts that are not discharged in bankruptcy include alimony, separate maintenance, and child support. A claim from a breach of contract is a typical type of claim discharged. Any amount unsatisfied after sale of the collateral is paid along with the rest of the general creditors if sufficient funds remain after all of the other creditors are paid. These are discharged in bankruptcy. Although intentional torts are not dischargable in bankruptcy, claims based on mere negligence are.

J.   Reaffirmation

26.   (d)   To get debtors to reaffirm debts that have been discharged in bankruptcy, creditors must comply with certain procedures. In general, the reaffirmation must take place before the discharge is granted and it must be approved by the bankruptcy court. The debtor is given sixty days to rescind the reaffirmation after s/he agrees to it. Answer (a) is incorrect because it must be agreed to before discharge. Answer (b) is incorrect because there is no such limitation on the dollar amounts. Answer (c) is incorrect because the reaffirmation agreement is valid for almost all debt including household purpose debt.

K. Business Reorganization—Chapter 11

27.   (d)   Under the reorganization provisions of Chapter 11 of the Federal Bankruptcy Code, a court supervised rehabilitation plan is adopted. It typically allows for the continued operation of the business and provides for the payment of all or part of the debts over an extended period of time. The payments to the creditors often come largely from future earnings. Answer (a) is incorrect because the court typically does not discharge the debtor from all of its debts under a Chapter 11 bankruptcy but provides for payments of debts out of future earnings. Answer (b) is incorrect because the plans can apply to any creditors whether they were in the portion that agreed to the plan or not. Answer (c) is incorrect because the debtor under Chapter 11 is often required to pay all or part of the debts out of future earnings.

28.   (d)   The Chapter 11 bankruptcy petition may either be filed voluntarily by the debtor or filed by the creditors to force the debtor into bankruptcy. Answer (a) is incorrect because a trustee need not be appointed. Answer (b) is incorrect because the debtor need not be insolvent to file a voluntary bankruptcy petition. Answer (c) is incorrect because only the debtor has the right to file the reorganization plan during the first 120 days the order for relief occurs.

29.   (d)   Under Chapter 11 of the Federal Bankruptcy Code, individuals, partnerships, and corporations are eligible for reorganization. Savings and loan companies, banks, and insurance companies are not eligible.

ANSWER OUTLINE

Problem 1   Dischargeability of Debts in Bankruptcy; Preferential Transfer

a.   Judgment against Drake for auto accident is dischargeable
　　1998 unpaid federal income taxes are dischargeable
　　1998 taxes are not within three years of the filing
　　Obligation to Bartin is not dischargeable
　　　Debt was not included in bankruptcy petition
　　　Bartin did not know of Drake's bankruptcy before time for filing claim expired
　　Unpaid child support is not dischargeable

b.   Preferential transfer established if
　　Payment made within ninety days prior to filing
　　Antecedent debt owed by debtor
　　Debtor was insolvent
　　Benefited creditor
　　Creditor received more than it would in liquidation

c.   Payment to Safe is a preferential transfer
　　Transfer to Drake's brother is a preferential transfer
　　　Brother is an insider
　　　Payment made within one year of filing
　　Mortgage given to Home is not a preferential transfer
　　　Mortgage was not an antecedent debt
　　Payment to Max is not a preferential transfer
　　　Payment was made in ordinary course of business under ordinary terms

UNOFFICIAL ANSWER

Problem 1   Dischargeability of Debts in Bankruptcy; Preferential Transfer

a.   The judgment against Drake arising from this negligence is dischargeable in his bankruptcy.

　　The unpaid federal income taxes are also dischargeable because they became due and owing more than three years prior to the filing of the bankruptcy petition.

　　The obligation to Bartin will not be discharged because the debt was not included in Drake's bankruptcy petition schedules and the creditor did not have notice or actual knowledge of the bankruptcy in time to file a proof of claim.

　　The unpaid child support is not dischargeable in Drake's bankruptcy.

b.   To establish a preferential transfer that can be set aside, the bankruptcy trustee must show

　　•   A voluntary or involuntary transfer of nonexempt property to a creditor.

　　•   The transfer was made during the ninety days immediately preceding the bankruptcy filing (or within one year in the case of an "insider").

　　•   The transfer was on account of an antecedent debt.

　　•   The transfer was made while the debtor was insolvent.

　　•   The transfer allows the creditor to receive a greater percentage than would otherwise be received in the bankruptcy proceeding.

c.   The payment to Safe will be regarded as a preference and may be set aside by the trustee.

　　The transfer by Drake to his brother can be set aside as a preference since his brother would be considered an insider and payment was made within one year of filing.

　　Giving the mortgage to Home is not a preference because it was not on account of an antecedent debt.

　　The payment to Max is not a preference because it was made in the ordinary course of the business of Max and Drake under ordinary business terms.

ANSWER OUTLINE

Problem 2   Requirements for Involuntary Bankruptcy; Claims and Preferences—Secured Creditor; Preferential Transfer

a.   Involuntary bankruptcy petition against debtor having twelve or more creditors:
　　May be filed by three or more creditors having unsecured claims of at least $11,625
　　Debtor must not be paying undisputed debts as due

b.   **1.**   Dollar's motion for relief will be granted
　　　Dollar is entitled to take possession of collateral securing its loan
　　　　Secured creditor may take possession of collateral if there is no equity in it
　　　Dollar may sell collateral and apply proceeds to loan balance
　　2.   Bankruptcy court will not approve Dollar's claim for priority
　　　Dollar is entitled to the value of its collateral
　　　Dollar is an unsecured creditor for any deficiency

c.   Payment to Techno's president is a preferential transfer
　　President is an insider
　　Payment on unsecured loan during year preceding bankruptcy filing is preferential
　　Payment to Alexis is not a preferential transfer made in the ordinary course of business
　　Payment to Maple for truck is not a preferential transfer
　　Contemporaneous exchange for new value

UNOFFICIAL ANSWER

Problem 2   Requirements for Involuntary Bankruptcy; Claims and Preferences—Secured Creditor; Preferential Transfer

a.   An involuntary bankruptcy petition may be filed against a debtor having twelve or more creditors by at least three creditors having unsecured claims of at least $11,625, provided the debtor is not paying its undisputed debts as they become due.

b.   **1.**   Dollar's motion for relief will be granted. Dollar's claim that it is entitled to take possession of the collateral securing its loan is correct. Generally, a secured creditor is allowed to take possession of its collateral if there is no equity in it (that is, the debt balance exceeds the collateral's fair market value). Dollar would then be entitled to sell the collateral and apply the proceeds to the loan balance.

　　2.   Dollar's claim that is entitled to a priority distribution to the extent that the proceeds from the sale of its collateral are less than the loan balance will not be approved by the bankruptcy court. Dollar is entitled to the value of its collateral. As to any deficiency, Dollar will be treated as an unsecured creditor.

c.   The payment to Techno's president would be regarded as a preferential transfer. Because the president is an "insider," any payments made on the unsecured loan during the year preceding the bankruptcy filing would be considered a preferential transfer.

The payment to Alexis was not a preferential transfer because it was made in the ordinary course of business and under ordinary business terms.

The $7,900 payment to Maple for the truck was not a preferential transfer because it was not made on account of an antecedent debt, but as a contemporaneous exchange for new value.

SOLUTIONS TO SIMULATION PROBLEMS

Simulation Problem 1

1. **(T)** A debtor need not be insolvent to file a voluntary petition for bankruptcy. S/he merely needs to state that s/he has debts. Thus, Able could file even if solvent.

2. **(F)** In order to file a valid involuntary petition when there are fewer than twelve creditors, a single creditor may file the petition as long as s/he is owed at least $11,625 of unsecured debt. More than one creditor may be used to reach the $11,625 requirement. However, Lake, Young, and Thorn may not file a valid involuntary petition because they are collectively owed only $4,500.

3. **(T)** In order to file a valid involuntary petition when there are fewer than twelve creditors, a single creditor can file the petition as long as s/he is owed at least $11,625 of unsecured debt. Cole may file alone as s/he is owed $12,000.

4. **(T)** The trustee may set aside preferential transfers of nonexempt property to a creditor made within the previous ninety days while insolvent. The payment made to Vista Bank is a preferential transfer because it was made less than ninety days before April 1, 2004, the date the involuntary petition was filed.

5. **(T)** The trustee may set aside preferential transfers of nonexempt property to a creditor made within the previous ninety days while insolvent. If the creditor was an insider, the time period is extended to within one year prior to the filing of the bankruptcy petition. The payment to Owen is a preferential transfer because Owen, an officer of Able Corp., is an insider, and the payment was made within one year prior to the filing of the petition.

6. **(F)** The payment to Core is not a preferential transfer because contemporaneously, Able received new value; that is, the computer. A contemporaneous exchange between creditor and debtor whereby the debtor receives new value is an exception to the trustee's power to set aside as a preferential transfer.

Simulation Problem 2

1.   (A) Statement I is correct since secured creditors receive payments before unsecured creditors (up to the value of the collateral) or receive the collateral itself. Statement II is incorrect because a secured creditor gets paid first only up to the value of the security. Any debt above the value of the security is given the lowest priority along with the general creditors.

2.   (B) Statement I is incorrect and statement II is correct because employees have the highest priority after the secured creditor of all the ones listed in the question up to $4,650 per claimant, except for the accountants who are owed administrative costs.

3.   (B) Statement I is incorrect because there is no collateral backing the 2002 federal income tax claim. It will thus not be paid as a secured creditor. Statement II is correct because taxes (federal, state, or local) have a higher priority than the general creditors.

4.   (C) Statement I is correct because preferential transfers to insiders may be set aside when made within the previous **twelve** months. Thus, the January 15 repayment of corporate directors' loans are preferential transfers. Statement II is correct because the preferential transfer rule of ninety days is extended to twelve months in the case of insiders.

5.   (A) Both transfers in the ordinary course of business and contemporaneous exchanges between creditors and debtors (whereby the debtors receive new value) are exceptions to the trustee's power to avoid preferential transfers. In this case, Rusk had purchased raw materials for use in its manufacturing business and paid cash to the supplier. These facts constitute an exception to the trustee's power to avoid a preferential transfer. Statement II is incorrect because the purchase and payment constitute an exception to the preferential transfer avoiding powers.

DEBTOR-CREDITOR RELATIONSHIPS

Overview

The first part of this module discusses the rights and duties of debtors and creditors. One of the important areas is the idea of a lien. Note the different types of liens and their effects on debtors and creditors. Also covered are the concepts of composition agreements with creditors and assignments for the benefit of creditors. These can be used as alternatives to bankruptcy.

This module also discusses the concepts of guaranty and suretyship. These two are nearly the same concept. The main difference is that the guarantor is typically secondarily liable, whereas the surety is normally primarily liable. The rights and duties are otherwise almost the same for both the guarantors and the sureties.

A. Rights and Duties of Debtors and Creditors

1. Liens are creditors' claims on real or personal property to secure payment of debt or performance of obligations

2. Mechanic's lien or materialman's lien

   a. Statutory lien on real property to secure payment of debts for services or materials to improve real property

   > EXAMPLE: *Worker puts new roof on owner's building. Since the owner has not paid, the worker puts a lien on the building to secure payment. The worker may, after giving notice to the owner, foreclose on the property.*

3. Artisan's lien

   a. Occurs when one repairs or improves personal property for another and retains possession of that personal property

   > EXAMPLE: *A has a mechanic repair his car. Upon completion of the repairs, the mechanic retains possession of the car until A pays for the repairs.*

   b. Artisan's lien terminates when creditor receives or is offered payment or when s/he gives up possession of property

   c. Artisan's lien generally has priority over other liens or interests as long as creditor retains possession of the personal property

   d. If debtor does not pay, most statutes allow lienholder to give notice to owner and then to sell property

4. Innkeeper's lien allows hotel to keep possession of guest's baggage until hotel charges are paid

5. Attachment is a court-ordered seizure of property due to lack of payment **prior** to court judgment for past-due debt

   a. If creditor wins at trial, property is sold to pay off debt

   b. There are certain constitutional requirements to protect debtors because property is seized based on word of creditors

   c. Writ of attachment allows creditor to take possession of personal property to satisfy debt pursuant to successful legal action

6. Execution is remedy in which court order directs sheriff to seize debtor's property which can then be sold at judicial sale to pay off creditor.

   a. Any excess over debt owed is paid to debtor

   b. Many states provide homestead exemption so debtor can retain residence, often up to a specified dollar amount as well as furniture and vehicles up to a limit.

   > (1) Also, often allows retention by debtor of clothing, tools used in trade, pets, etc.

7. Garnishment allows creditor to seize money owed to debtor by third party after court judgment

   a. Garnishment involves seizing debtor's property possessed by third parties such as banks (debtor's bank account) or employers (debtor's wages)

   > EXAMPLE: *Creditor obtains a writ of garnishment from the court to collect from a bank $5,000 in the debtor's bank account.*

   b. State and federal laws limit amount of wages that can be garnished

   c. Creditors cannot garnish debtor's federal social security benefits

8. Judgment lien

     a. Occurs when awarded damages and files a lien against property to secure payment

     b. Debtor may fraudulently try to prevent creditor from satisfying a judgment

         (1) Examples include secret conveyances, debtor retaining possession after conveyance, or debtor retaining equitable interest after conveyance of property

             EXAMPLE: Debtor appears to sell all interest in some property but in fact names herself as the beneficiary as she conveys the legal title to the trustee.

9. Composition agreement with creditors (also called composition of creditors' agreement)

     a. Occurs by two or more creditors' agreement with debtor to accept less than full amount of debt as full satisfaction of debt

     b. Based on contract law so needs new consideration to be enforceable

         (1) New consideration is construed as two or more creditors each agreeing to accept less than full amount

             (a) Note that all creditors need not be part of agreement

             (b) Creditors need not be treated equally but treatment must be disclosed and agreed to by affected parties

         (2) Once debtor pays creditors at agreed rates, those debts are discharged

             (a) If debtor does not perform as agreed in composition agreement, creditors may choose to enforce either original debts or reduced debts under composition agreement.

             (b) Creditors not part of agreement are not bound by agreement and thus may resort to bankruptcy law or settle debt by own method

10. Assignment for the benefit of creditors

     a. Debtor voluntarily transfers all of his/her assets to an assignee (or trustee) to be sold for the benefit of creditors

     b. Assignee takes legal title

         (1) Debtor must cease all control of assets

         (2) Assignment is irrevocable

     c. No agreement between creditors is necessary

         (1) Creditors who accept assignment receive pro rata share of debt they are owed.

         (2) Dissatisfied creditors may file a petition in bankruptcy and assignments may be set aside

11. In homestead exemption

     a. In addition to providing exemptions against execution on debtor's assets, also provides exception for debtor's home so that unsecured creditors and trustees in bankruptcy may not satisfy debts from equity in debtor's home.

         (1) However, mortgage liens and IRS tax liens take priority over homestead exemption

12. Fair Debt Collection Practices Act restricts how creditors may collect debts

     a. Collection agencies are prevented from contacting debtor-consumer at inconvenient hours, inconvenient places, or at work if employer objects

     b. Collection agencies may not use methods that are abusive or misleading

     c. Debt collector must provide debtor written notice of amount of debt and to whom owed within five days of first communication

     d. When debtor contests validity of debt, collection attempts must cease until collector sends debtor verification

     e. Debt collectors must bring suit in court near debtors residence or in jurisdiction where contract signed

     f. If debt collector violates act, that person is liable for actual damages plus other damages such as court costs and attorneys' fees up to $1,000

g.   Federal Trade Commission enforces this act

   (1) May use cease and desist orders against debt collector
   (2) Civil lawsuits for damages are also allowed

h.   Act applies to collection agent collecting debt for another—does not apply if creditor collects own debt

13. Truth-in-Lending Act requires lenders and sellers to disclose credit terms on loans to consumer-debtors

a.   Disclosures include finance charges and annual percentage rate of interest charged
b.   Consumer has right to rescind credit within three days

14. Equal Credit Opportunity Act prohibits discrimination in consumer credit transactions based on marital status, sex, race, color, religion, national origin, age, or receipt of welfare, or because applicant has exercised legal rights

a.   If creditor denies or revokes credit or worsens credit terms, must provide notice to debtor of specific reasons for adverse action
b.   Provides for civil and criminal penalties

15. Fair Credit Reporting Act prohibits consumer reporting agencies from including in consumer reports any inaccurate or obsolete information

a.   Information includes creditworthiness, mode of living, character, reputation in general
b.   Consumer is allowed access to credit reports
c.   If consumer disagrees with information in report, agency must investigate and correct if appropriate

   (1) If dispute remains, consumer may file statement of his/her version that becomes part of permanent consumer's credit record.

16. Fair Credit Billing Act allows consumer to complain of billing errors and requires creditor to either explain or correct them

a.   If dispute remains, debtor may use lawsuit.

17. Fair Credit and Charge Card Disclosure Act requires disclosure of annual percentage rate, membership fee, etc. for credit or charge card solicitations or applications.

a.   Credit card holder's liability is limited to $50 per credit card for unauthorized charges due to lost or stolen credit cards

   (1) Additional limitation—not liable for any charges after holder notifies issuer

   EXAMPLE: Abel carelessly lost his credit card. He quickly notified the issuer. The person who found the card charged $100 on the card. All of this was after the issuer was notified that the card was lost. Abel is not liable for any of the unauthorized charges.

18. Bank debit cards

a.   Maximum liability of customer is $50 if s/he notifies bank within two days of debit card being lost or stolen

   (1) Failure to meet two-day notification period increases maximum liability to $500

b.   Maximum liability for customer greater than $500 if s/he fails to notify bank within sixty days of its showing up on bank statement of customer
c.   Banks are liable for wrongful dishonor for failure to pay electronic fund transfer when customer has sufficient funds in account

B. Nature of Suretyship and Guaranty

1.   In both suretyship and guaranty, third party promises to pay debt owed by debtor if debtor does not pay

a.   Third party's credit acts as security for debt to creditor

    b. Purpose of a suretyship agreement is to protect creditor by providing creditor with added security for obligation and to reduce creditor's risk of loss

        EXAMPLE: In order for D to obtain a loan from C, S (who has a good credit standing) promises to C that he, S, will pay debt if D does not.

  2. Suretyship and guaranty agreements involve three parties

    a. Creditor (C in above example)

       (1) Obligee of principal debtor

    b. Principal debtor (D in above example)

       (1) Has liability for debt owed to creditor

    c. Surety (S in above example) or guarantor

       (1) Promises to perform or pay debt of principal debtor
       (2) Also referred to as accommodation party or consignor

  3. Suretyship and guaranty contracts are similar but many courts distinguish them as such

    a. In strict suretyship, the surety promises to be responsible for the debt and is **primarily** liable for debt

       (1) Creditor can demand payment from surety when debt is due
       (2) Unconditional guaranty is the standard suretyship relationship in which there are no further conditions required for guarantor to be asked to pay if debtor does not

          EXAMPLE: G agreed in writing to act as surety when D took out a loan with C, the lender. If D does not pay, C may proceed directly against G. C need not try to collect from D first.

         (a) Creditor need not attempt collection from debtor first
         (b) Creditor need not give notice of debtor's default

    b. In contrast to suretyship, in guaranty contract, guarantor is normally **secondarily liable**

       (1) Guarantor can be required to pay debt only after debtor defaults and creditor demands payment from debtor
       (2) Sometimes guaranty contract requires creditor to both seek payment from debtor and bring suit if necessary

         (a) Called guarantor of collection

    c. Some courts treat guaranty and suretyship as same but for CPA exam, make distinctions given above

        NOTE: With those few exceptions noted in this outline, the rights and duties of both guarantors and sureties are essentially the same and the remainder of this outline will generally use surety and guarantor interchangeably.

  4. Examples of typical suretyship and guaranty arrangements

    a. Seller of goods on credit requires buyer to obtain a surety to guarantee payment for goods purchased
    b. Bank requires owners or directors of closely held corporation to act as sureties for loan to corporation
    c. Endorser of negotiable instrument agrees to pay if instrument not paid
    d. In order to transfer a check or note, transferor may be required to obtain a surety (accommodation endorser) to guarantee payment
    e. Purchaser of real property expressly assumes seller's mortgage on property (i.e., promises to pay mortgage debt)

       (1) Seller then has become surety

  5. Suretyship and guaranty contracts should satisfy elements of contracts in general

a. If surety's or guarantor's agreement arises at same time as the contract between creditor and debtor, no separate consideration is needed (consideration between creditor and debtor is still needed)

    (1) If creditor gave loan or credit before surety's promise, separate consideration is necessary to support surety's new promise

        EXAMPLE: C loaned $200,000 to D. Terms provided that the loan is callable by C with one month notice to D. C gave the agreed notice and exercised her right to call the loan. D requested a sixty-day extension. C agreed to the extension when S agreed to be a surety on this loan. There is consideration for the new surety agreement since C gave up the right to call the loan sooner.

        (a) Consideration need not be received by surety—often it is principal debtor that benefits

b. Guaranty's agreement to answer for debt or default of another must be in writing

    (1) Recall that under the Statute of Frauds under contract law, this is one of the types of contracts that must be in writing
    (2) However, if guarantor's promise is primarily for his/her own benefit, it need not be in writing

        EXAMPLE: S agrees to pay D's debt to D's creditor if he defaults. The main motive of S is to keep D in business to assure a steady supply of an essential component. S's agreement need not be in writing.

        EXAMPLE: A del credere agent is one who sells goods on credit to purchasers for the principal and agrees to pay the principal if the customers do not. Since his promise is primarily for his own benefit, it need not be in writing.

6. Third-party beneficiary contract is not a suretyship contract

a. Third-party beneficiary contract is one in which third party receives benefits from agreement made between promisor and promisee, although third person is not party to contract

    EXAMPLE: Father says: "Ship goods to my son and I will pay for them." This describes a third-party beneficiary contract, not a suretyship arrangement. Father is not promising to pay the debt of another, but rather engaging in an original promise to pay for goods that creditor delivers to son.

7. Indemnity contract is not a suretyship contract

a. An indemnity contract is between two parties (rather than three) whereby indemnitor makes a promise to a potential debtor, indemnitee, (not to creditor as in suretyship arrangement), to indemnify and reimburse debtor for payment of debt or for loss that may arise in future. Indemnitor pays because it has assumed risk of loss, not because of any default by principal debtor as in suretyship arrangement.

    EXAMPLE: Under terms of standard automobile collision insurance policy, insurance company agrees to indemnify automobile owner against damage to his/her car caused by collision.

8. Warranty (sometimes called guaranty) is not same as the type of guaranty under suretyship law

a. Warranties arise under, for example, real property law or sales law

    (1) Involve making representations as to facts, title, quality, etc. of property

9. Capacity to act as surety or guarantor

a. In general, individuals that have capacity to contract
b. Partnerships may act as sureties unless partnership agreement expressly prohibits it from entering into suretyship contracts
c. Individual partner normally has no authority to bind partnership as surety
d. Modern trend is that corporations may act as sureties

C. Creditor's Rights and Remedies

1. Against principal debtor

a. Creditor has right to receive payment or performance specified in contract
b. Creditor may proceed immediately against debtor upon default, unless contract states otherwise
c. When a debtor has more than one debt outstanding with same creditor and makes a part payment, debtor may give instructions as to which debt the payment is to apply

(1) If debtor gives no instructions, creditor is free to apply part payment to whichever debt s/he chooses; fact that one debt is guaranteed by surety and other is not makes no difference in absence of instructions by debtor

2. Against surety

   a. Creditor may proceed immediately against surety upon principal debtor's default

     (1) Unless contract requires it, it is not necessary to give surety notice of debtor's default

     (2) Since surety is immediately liable, s/he can be sued without creditor first attempting to collect from debtor

3. Against guarantor of collection

   a. A guarantor of collection's liability is conditioned on creditor notifying guarantor of debtor's default and creditor first attempting to collect from debtor

   b. Creditor must exhaust remedies by going against debtor before guarantor of collection's liability arises, even by lawsuit if necessary

4. On security (collateral) held by surety or creditor

   a. Upon principal debtor's default, creditor may resort to collateral to satisfy debt

     (1) If creditor does resort to collateral, any excess collateral or amount realized by its disposal over debt amount must be returned to principal debtor

     (2) If collateral is insufficient to pay debt, creditor may proceed against surety or debtor for balance due (deficiency)

   b. Creditor is not required to use collateral; creditor may instead proceed immediately against surety or principal debtor

D. Surety's and Guarantor's Rights and Remedies

1. When the debt or obligation for which surety has given promise is due

   a. Exoneration

     (1) Surety may require (by lawsuit if necessary) debtor to pay obligation if debtor is able before surety has paid

     (2) Exoneration is not available if creditor demands prompt performance from surety

   b. Surety may request creditor to resort first to collateral if surety can show collateral is seriously depreciating in value, or if surety can show undue hardship will otherwise result

2. When surety pays debt or obligation

   a. S/he is entitled to right of reimbursement from debtor

     (1) May recover only actual payments to creditor

     (2) Surety is entitled to resort to collateral as satisfaction of right of reimbursement

     (3) Surety's payment after having received notice of principal debtor's valid defense against creditor causes surety to lose right of reimbursement

   b. S/he has right of subrogation

     (1) Upon payment, surety obtains same rights against principal debtor that creditor had

       (a) That is, surety steps into creditor's shoes

       (b) If debtor is bankrupt, surety is subrogated to rights of creditor's priority in bankruptcy proceeding

         EXAMPLE: C, the creditor, required D, the debtor, to put up personal property as collateral on a loan and to also use S as a surety on the same loan. Upon D's default, C chooses to resort to S for payment. Upon payment, S may now sell the collateral under the right of subrogation because the creditor could have used the same right of sale of the collateral.

3. Creditor owes duty to surety to disclose, before surety agrees to contract, any information about material risks that are greater than surety aware of

    a.   Creditor must also disclose facts inquired by surety

E. Surety's and Guarantor's Defenses

1. Surety may generally exercise defenses on contract that would be available **to debtor**

    a.   Breach or failure of performance by **creditor**
    b.   Impossibility or illegality of performance
    c.   Creditor obtains debtor's promise by fraud, duress, or misrepresentation
    d.   Statute of limitations
    e.   Except that surety may not use debtor's **personal** defenses as discussed later

2. Surety may take advantage of **own** contractual defenses

    a.   Fraud or duress

       (1) If creditor obtains surety's promise by fraud or duress, contract is voidable at surety's option

          EXAMPLE: Creditor forces X to sign suretyship agreement at threat of great bodily harm.

       (2) If creditor gets principal debtor's promise using fraud or duress, then surety not liable

          (a) Exception: surety is liable if was aware of fraud or duress before s/he became surety

       (3) Fraud by principal debtor on surety to induce a suretyship agreement will **not** release surety if creditor has extended credit in good faith

          (a) But if creditor had knowledge of debtor's fraudulent representations, then surety may avoid liability

             EXAMPLE: Y asked Ace to act as surety on a loan from Bank. In order to induce Ace to act as surety, Y made fraudulent representations concerning its financial position to Ace. This fraud by Y will not release surety, Ace, if the creditor, Bank, had no knowledge of the fraud and extended credit in good faith. But if Bank had knowledge of Y's fraudulent representations, then Ace has a good defense and can avoid liability. Note that if Bank finds out about Y's fraudulent representations after Bank has extended credit, Ace has no defense.

    b.   Suretyship contract itself is void due to illegality
    c.   Incapacity of surety (e.g., surety is a minor)
    d.   Failure of consideration for suretyship contract

       (1) However, when surety's and principal debtor's obligations are incurred at same time, there is no need for any separate consideration beyond that supporting principal debtor's contract; if surety's undertaking is entered into subsequent to debtor's contract, it must be supported by separate consideration

    e.   Suretyship agreement is not in writing as required under Statute of Frauds
    f.   Creditor fails to notify surety of any material facts within creditor's knowledge concerning debtor's ability to perform

       EXAMPLE: Creditor's failure to report to surety that debtor has defaulted on several previous occasions.

       EXAMPLE: Creditor's failure to report to surety that debtor submitted fraudulent financial statements to surety to induce suretyship agreement.

    g.   Surety, in general, may use any obligations owed by creditor to surety as a setoff against any payments owed to creditor

       (1) True even if setoff arises from separate transaction

3. Acts of creditor or debtor materially affecting surety's obligations

    a.   Tender of performance by debtor or surety and refusal by creditor will discharge surety

       (1) However, tender of performance for obligation to pay money does not normally release principal debtor but stops accrual of interest on debt

    b.   Release of principal debtor from liability by creditor without consent of surety will also discharge surety's liability

    (1) But surety is not released if creditor specifically reserves his/her rights against surety

       (a) However, surety upon paying may then seek recovery from debtor

  c. Release of surety by creditor

    (1) Does **not** release principal debtor because liable whether or not surety is liable

  d. Proper performance by debtor or satisfaction of creditor through collateral will discharge surety

  e. Variance in terms and conditions of contract subsequent to surety's undertaking

    (1) Accommodation (noncompensated) surety is completely discharged for any change in contract made by creditor on terms required of principal debtor

    (2) Commercial (compensated) surety is completely released if modification in principal debtor's contract materially increases risk to surety

       (a) If risk not increased materially, then surety not released but his/her obligation is reduced by amount of loss due to modification

    (3) Surety may consent to modifications so that they are not defenses

    (4) Surety is not released if creditor modifies principal debtor's duties to be beneficial to surety (i.e., decreases surety's risk)

> *EXAMPLE: Creditor reduces interest rate on loan to principal debtor from 12% to 10%.*

    (5) Modifications that affect rights of sureties based on above principles

       (a) Extension of time on principal debtor's obligation
       (b) Change in amount, place, or manner of principal debtor's obligations
       (c) Modification of duties of principal debtor
       (d) Substitution of debtor's or delegation of debtor's obligation to another

          1] Note how this may result in change in risk to the surety

       (e) Release, surrender, destruction, or impairment of collateral by creditor before or after debtor's default releases surety by amount decreased

> *EXAMPLE: S is a surety on a $10,000 loan between Creditor and Debtor. Creditor is also holding $1,000 of Debtor's personal property as collateral on the $10,000 loan. Before the loan is paid, Creditor returns the collateral to Debtor. This action releases S from $1,000 of the $10,000 loan.*

> *EXAMPLE: S is a compensated surety for a loan between Debtor and Creditor. The loan had also been secured by collateral. Upon default, Creditor took possession of the collateral but let it get damaged by rain. The collateral was impaired by $500. Creditor also sought payment from S, the compensated surety. S may reduce his payment to Creditor by $500.*

    (6) In order to release surety, there must be an actual alteration or variance in terms of contract and not an option or election that principal debtor can exercise under express terms of original agreement which surety has guaranteed

> *EXAMPLE: Tenant and landlord entered into a two-year leasing agreement which expressly contained an option for an additional year which could be exercised by tenant, with X acting as surety on lease contract. If tenant exercises this option, X still remains bound as surety.*

4. Following are **not defenses of surety or guarantor**

  a. Personal defenses of principal debtor

    (1) Death of debtor or debtor's lack of capacity (e.g., debtor is a minor or was legally insane when contract was made)

    (2) Insolvency (or discharge in bankruptcy) of debtor

       (a) Possibility of debtor's insolvency is a primary reason for engaging in a surety arrangement

    (3) Personal debtor's setoffs

       (a) Unless debtor assigns them to surety

b. Creditor did not give notice to surety of debtor's default or creditor did not first proceed against principal debtor

(1) Unless a conditional guarantor and creditor violated condition

c. Creditor does not resort to collateral
d. Creditor delays in proceeding against debtor unless delay exceeds statute of limitations
e. When creditor is owed multiple debts by same debtor, creditor may choose to apply payment to any of the debts unless debtor directs otherwise—surety cannot direct which debt payment applies to

EXAMPLE: *Debtor owes two debts to Creditor. S is acting as a surety on one of these debts. When Debtor makes a payment, Creditor applies it to the debt on which S is not a surety since Debtor did not indicate which one. The surety has no defense from these facts and is not released.*

F. Cosureties

1. Cosureties exist when there is more than one surety for same obligation of principal debtor to same creditor

a. Not relevant whether or not cosureties are aware of each other or became cosureties at different times

(1) Must be sureties for same debtor for same obligation

b. Cosureties need not be bound for same amount; they can guarantee equal or unequal amounts of debt

(1) Collateral, if any, need not be held equally

c. Cosureties need not sign same document

2. Cosureties are jointly and severally liable to creditor

a. That is, creditor can proceed against any of the sureties jointly or against each one individually to extent surety has assumed liability
b. If creditor sues multiple sureties, s/he may recover in any proportion from each, but may only recover total amount of debtor's obligation
c. Proceeding against one or more sureties does not release remaining surety or sureties

3. Right of contribution exists among cosureties

a. Right of contribution arises when cosurety, in performance of debtor's obligation, pays more than his/her proportionate share of total liability, and thereby entitles cosurety to compel other cosureties to compensate him/her for excess amount paid (i.e., contribution from other cosureties for their pro rata share of liability)

4. Cosureties are only liable in contribution for their proportionate share

a. Cosurety's pro rata share is proportion that each surety's risk (i.e., amount each has personally guaranteed) bears to total amount of risk assumed by all sureties by using the following formula

$$\frac{\text{Dollar amount individual cosurety personally guaranteed}}{\text{Total dollar amount of risk assumed by all cosureties}}$$

EXAMPLE: *X and Y are cosureties for $5,000 and $10,000, respectively, of a $10,000 debt. Each is liable in proportion to amount each has personally guaranteed. Since X guaranteed $5,000 of debt and Y guaranteed $10,000 of debt, then X is individually liable for 1/3 ($5,000/$15,000) of debt and Y is individually liable for 2/3 ($10,000/$15,000) of debt. If debtor defaults on only $3,000 of debt, X is liable for $1,000 (1/3 x $3,000) and Y is liable for $2,000 (2/3 x $3,000). Although creditor may recover $3,000 from either, each cosurety has right of contribution from other cosurety.*

EXAMPLE: *Refer to the preceding example. If the creditor recovers all of the $3,000 debt from Y, then Y, under the right of contribution, can recover $1,000 from X so that each will end up paying his/her proportionate amount.*

5. Each cosurety is entitled to share in any collateral pledged (either held by creditor or other cosurety) in proportion to cosurety's liability for debtor's default

EXAMPLE: *If in above illustration, cosurety Y held collateral pledged by debtor worth $900, both cosureties X and Y would be entitled to share in collateral in proportion to their respective liabilities. X would be entitled to 1/3 ($5,000/$15,000) of $900 collateral, or $300; and Y would be entitled to 2/3 ($10,000/$15,000) of $900 collateral, or $600.*

6. Discharge or release of one cosurety by creditor results in a reduction of liability of remaining cosurety

    a. Remaining cosurety is released only to extent of released cosurety's pro rata share of debt liability (unless there is a reservation of rights by creditor against remaining cosurety)

        EXAMPLE: A and B are cosureties for $4,000 and $12,000, respectively, on a $12,000 debt. If creditor releases cosurety A, cosurety B is released to extent of cosurety A's liability. Each is liable in proportion to amount each has personally guaranteed. Since A guaranteed $4,000 of debt and B guaranteed $12,000 of debt, then A is individually liable for 1/4 ($4,000/$16,000) of debt and B is individually liable for 3/4 ($12,000/$16,000) of debt, that is, $9,000. Therefore, cosurety B is released of A's pro rata liability of $3,000 (1/4 x $12,000), and only remains a surety for $9,000 ($12,000 – $3,000) of debt.

7. A cosurety is not released from obligation to perform merely because another cosurety refuses to perform

    a. However, upon payment of full obligation, cosurety can demand a pro rata contribution from his/her nonperforming cosurety

    b. Cosurety is not released if other cosureties are **unable** to pay (i.e., dead, bankrupt)

        (1) In which case, modify the formula found at Section F.4.a. by taking those cosureties that cannot pay completely out of formula and use it with all remaining cosureties

8. Cosureties have rights of exoneration, reimbursement, and subrogation like any surety

G. Surety Bonds

1. An acknowledgment of an obligation to make good the performance by another of some act or responsibility

    a. Usually issued by companies which for a stated fee assume risk of performance by bonded party
    b. Performance of act or responsibility by bonded party discharges surety's obligation

2. Performance bonds are used to have surety guarantee completion of terms of contracts

    a. Construction bond guarantees builder's obligation to complete construction

        (1) If builder breaches contract, surety can be held liable for damages but not for specific performance (i.e., cannot be required to complete construction)

           (a) Surety may complete construction if chooses to

3. Fidelity bonds are forms of insurance that protects an employer against losses sustained due to acts of dishonest employees

    a. Any significant change in the employee's duties may serve to release the surety bonding company from its obligation

4. Surety bonding company retains right of subrogation against bonded party

MULTIPLE-CHOICE QUESTIONS (1-27)

1. A debtor may attempt to conceal or transfer property to prevent a creditor from satisfying a judgment. Which of the following actions will be considered an indication of fraudulent conveyance?

	Debtor remaining in possession after conveyance	Secret conveyance	Debtor retains an equitable benefit in the property conveyed
a.	Yes	Yes	Yes
b.	No	Yes	Yes
c.	Yes	Yes	No
d.	Yes	No	Yes

2. A homestead exemption ordinarily could exempt a debtor's equity in certain property from postjudgment collection by a creditor. To which of the following creditors will this exemption apply?

	Valid home mortgage lien	Valid IRS tax lien
a.	Yes	Yes
b.	Yes	No
c.	No	Yes
d.	No	No

3. Which of the following statements is(are) correct regarding debtors' rights?

I. State exemption statutes prevent all of a debtor's personal property from being sold to pay a federal tax lien.
II. Federal social security benefits received by a debtor are exempt from garnishment by creditors.

    a. I only.
    b. II only.
    c. Both I and II.
    d. Neither I nor II.

4. Under the Federal Fair Debt Collection Practices Act, which of the following would a collection service using improper debt collection practices be subject to?

    a. Abolishment of the debt.
    b. Reduction of the debt.
    c. Civil lawsuit for damages for violating the Act.
    d. Criminal prosecution for violating the Act.

5. Which of the following liens generally require(s) the lienholder to give notice of legal action before selling the debtor's property to satisfy the debt?

	Mechanic's lien	Artisan's lien
a.	Yes	Yes
b.	Yes	No
c.	No	Yes
d.	No	No

6. Which of the following prejudgment remedies would be available to a creditor when a debtor owns **no** real property?

	Writ of attachment	Garnishment
a.	Yes	Yes
b.	Yes	No
c.	No	Yes
d.	No	No

7. Which of the following events will release a non-compensated surety from liability to the creditor?

    a. The principal debtor was involuntarily petitioned into bankruptcy.
    b. The creditor failed to notify the surety of a partial surrender of the principal debtor's collateral.
    c. The creditor was adjudicated incompetent after the debt arose.
    d. The principal debtor exerted duress to obtain the surety agreement.

8. Which of the following involve(s) a suretyship relationship?

I. Transferee of a note requires transferor to obtain an accommodation endorser to guarantee payment.
II. The purchaser of goods agrees to pay for the goods but to have them shipped to another party.
III. The shareholders of a small, new corporation agree in writing to be personally liable on a corporate loan if the corporation defaults.

    a. I only.
    b. II only.
    c. I and II only.
    d. I and III only.

9. Reuter Bank loaned Sabean Corporation $500,000 in writing. As part of the agreement, Reuter required that the three owners of Sabean act as sureties on the loan. The corporation also required that some real estate owned by Sabean Corporation be used as collateral for 40% of the loan. The collateral and suretyship agreements were put in writing and signed by all relevant parties. When the $500,000 loan became due, which of the following rights does Reuter Bank have?

I. May demand payment of the full amount immediately from the sureties whether or not the corporation defaults on the loan.
II. May demand payment of the full amount immediately from the sureties even if Reuter does not attempt to recover any amount from the collateral.
III. May attempt to recover up to $200,000 from the collateral and the remainder from the sureties, even if the remainder is more than $300,000.
IV. Must first attempt to collect the debt from Sabean Corporation before it can resort to the sureties or the collateral.

    a. I and III only.
    b. II only.
    c. I, II, and III only.
    d. IV only.

10. Belmont acts as a surety for a loan to Diablo from Chaffin. In which of the following cases would Belmont be released from liability?

I. Diablo dies.
II. Diablo files bankruptcy.
III. Chaffin modifies Diablo's contract, increasing Diablo's risk of nonpayment.

    a. I only.
    b. III only.
    c. I and III only.
    d. I, II, and III.

11. A party contracts to guaranty the collection of the debts of another. As a result of the guaranty, which of the following statements is correct?

    a.   The creditor may proceed against the guarantor without attempting to collect from the debtor.

    b.   The guaranty must be in writing.

    c.   The guarantor may use any defenses available to the debtor.

    d.   The creditor must be notified of the debtor's default by the guarantor.

12. Sorus and Ace have agreed, in writing, to act as guarantors of collection on a debt owed by Pepper to Towns, Inc. The debt is evidenced by a promissory note. If Pepper defaults, Towns will be entitled to recover from Sorus and Ace unless

    a.   Sorus and Ace are in the process of exercising their rights against Pepper.

    b.   Sorus and Ace prove that Pepper was insolvent at the time the note was signed.

    c.   Pepper dies before the note is due.

    d.   Towns has **not** attempted to enforce the promissory note against Pepper.

13. Which of the following rights does a surety have?

	Right to compel the creditor to collect from the principal debtor	Right to compel the creditor to proceed against the principal debtor's collateral
a.	Yes	Yes
b.	Yes	No
c.	No	Yes
d.	No	No

14. Under the law of suretyship, which are generally among the rights that the surety may use?

  I.   Subrogation

 II.   Exoneration

III.   Reimbursement from debtor

    a.   I only.

    b.   III only.

    c.   I and II only.

    d.   I, II, and III.

15. Which of the following defenses would a surety be able to assert successfully to limit the surety's liability to a creditor?

    a.   A discharge in bankruptcy of the principal debtor.

    b.   A personal defense the principal debtor has against the creditor.

    c.   The incapacity of the surety.

    d.   The incapacity of the principal debtor.

16. Which of the following events will release a noncompensated surety from liability?

    a.   Release of the principal debtor's obligation by the creditor but with the reservation of the creditor's rights against the surety.

    b.   Modification by the principal debtor and creditor of their contract that materially increases the surety's risk of loss.

    c.   Filing of an involuntary petition in bankruptcy against the principal debtor.

    d.   Insanity of the principal debtor at the time the contract was entered into with the creditor.

17. Which of the following is **not** a defense that a surety may use to avoid payment of a debtor's obligation to a creditor?

    a.   The creditor had committed fraud against the debtor to induce the debtor to take on the debt with this creditor.

    b.   The creditor had committed fraud against the surety to induce the surety to guarantee the debtor's payment of a loan.

    c.   The statute of limitations has run on the debtor's obligation.

    d.   The debtor took out bankruptcy.

18. Which of the following acts always will result in the total release of a compensated surety?

    a.   The creditor changes the manner of the principal debtor's payment.

    b.   The creditor extends the principal debtor's time to pay.

    c.   The principal debtor's obligation is partially released.

    d.   The principal debtor's performance is tendered.

19. Green was unable to repay a loan from State Bank when due. State refused to renew the loan unless Green provided an acceptable surety. Green asked Royal, a friend, to act as surety on the loan. To induce Royal to agree to become a surety, Green fraudulently represented Green's financial condition and promised Royal discounts on merchandise sold at Green's store. Royal agreed to act as surety and the loan was renewed. Later, Green's obligation to State was discharged in Green's bankruptcy. State wants to hold Royal liable. Royal may avoid liability

    a.   If Royal can show that State was aware of the fraudulent representations.

    b.   If Royal was an uncompensated surety.

    c.   Because the discharge in bankruptcy will prevent Royal from having a right of reimbursement.

    d.   Because the arrangement was void at the inception.

20. Wright cosigned King's loan from Ace Bank. Which of the following events would release Wright from the obligation to pay the loan?

    a.   Ace seeking payment of the loan only from Wright.

    b.   King is granted a discharge in bankruptcy.

    c.   Ace is paid in full by King's spouse.

    d.   King is adjudicated mentally incompetent.

21. A distinction between a surety and a cosurety is that only a cosurety is entitled to

    a.   Reimbursement (Indemnification).

    b.   Subrogation.

    c.   Contribution.

    d.   Exoneration.

22. Ivor borrowed $420,000 from Lear Bank. At Lear's request, Ivor entered into an agreement with Ash, Kane, and Queen for them to act as cosureties on the loan. The agreement between Ivor and the cosureties provided that the maximum liability of each cosurety was: Ash, $84,000; Kane, $126,000; and Queen, $210,000. After making several payments, Ivor defaulted on the loan. The balance was $280,000. If Queen pays $210,000 and Ivor subsequently pays $70,000, what amounts may Queen recover from Ash and Kane?

a. $0 from Ash and $0 from Kane.
b. $42,000 from Ash and $63,000 from Kane.
c. $70,000 from Ash and $70,000 from Kane.
d. $56,000 from Ash and $84,000 from Kane.

23. Nash, Owen, and Polk are cosureties with maximum liabilities of $40,000, $60,000 and $80,000, respectively. The amount of the loan on which they have agreed to act as cosureties is $180,000. The debtor defaulted at a time when the loan balance was $180,000. Nash paid the lender $36,000 in full settlement of all claims against Nash, Owen, and Polk. The total amount that Nash may recover from Owen and Polk is
a. $0
b. $ 24,000
c. $ 28,000
d. $140,000

24. Ingot Corp. lent Flange $50,000. At Ingot's request, Flange entered into an agreement with Quill and West for them to act as compensated cosureties on the loan in the amount of $100,000 each. Ingot released West without Quill's or Flange's consent, and Flange later defaulted on the loan. Which of the following statements is correct?
a. Quill will be liable for 50% of the loan balance.
b. Quill will be liable for the entire loan balance.
c. Ingot's release of West will have **no** effect on Flange's and Quill's liability to Ingot.
d. Flange will be released for 50% of the loan balance.

25. Mane Bank lent Eller $120,000 and received securities valued at $30,000 as collateral. At Mane's request, Salem and Rey agreed to act as uncompensated cosureties on the loan. The agreement provided that Salem's and Rey's maximum liability would be $120,000 each.
   Mane released Rey without Salem's consent. Eller later defaulted when the collateral held by Mane was worthless and the loan balance was $90,000. Salem's maximum liability is
a. $30,000
b. $45,000
c. $60,000
d. $90,000

26. Lane promised to lend Turner $240,000 if Turner obtained sureties to secure the loan. Turner agreed with Rivers, Clark, and Zane for them to act as cosureties on the loan from Lane. The agreement between Turner and the cosureties provided that compensation be paid to each of the cosureties. It further indicated that the maximum liability of each cosurety would be as follows: Rivers $240,000, Clark $80,000, and Zane $160,000. Lane accepted the commitments of the sureties and made the loan to Turner. After paying ten installments totaling $100,000, Turner defaulted. Clark's debts, including the surety obligation to Lane on the Turner loan, were discharged in bankruptcy. Later, Rivers properly paid the entire outstanding debt of $140,000. What amount may Rivers recover from Zane?
a. $0
b. $56,000
c. $70,000
d. $84,000

27. Which of the following rights does one cosurety generally have against another cosurety?
a. Exoneration.
b. Subrogation.
c. Reimbursement.
d. Contribution.

PROBLEM

NOTE: These types of problems are no longer included in the CPA Examination but they have been retained because they are useful in developing skills to complete simulations.

Problem 1   (15 to 20 minutes)

Beach, a seventeen-year old minor, entered into an installment contract to purchase a travel agency from Reid. The purchase price included the fair market value of the tangible assets and an agreed-upon value for goodwill. At the time the contract was entered into, Beach misrepresented his age to Reid, claiming that he was nineteen. The age of majority in their jurisdiction was eighteen. Since Reid was unsure of Beach's financial position, Reid requested that Beach obtain a surety. Therefore, Beach entered into an agreement for Abel to act as a surety on the installment contract. Beach knowingly induced Abel to become a surety by supplying Abel with false financial statements.

The contract also provided that Reid was to receive a substantial payment in consideration of his agreement not to operate a travel agency within a one-mile radius of Beach's travel agency for a period of two years. After nineteen months, Reid opened a new travel agency across the street from Beach's business. Within one month thereafter, Beach lost nearly all of his clients to Reid and Beach defaulted on the installment payments, causing the entire amount owed to Reid to become due. Reid has brought an action against Beach and Abel to recover all monies due him.

Beach claims he is not liable on the contract since

•   He was only seventeen years old at the time the contract with Reid was signed.
•   The clause prohibiting Reid from competing with him is legally valid and therefore Reid's violation of such clause constitutes a breach of the sale contract.

Abel claims that he is not liable to Reid since

•   He was induced into becoming a surety by Beach's fraud.
•   Beach was seventeen years old at the time the contract with Reid was entered into.
•   Reid breached the sale contract by failing to comply with the express clause prohibiting competition with Beach.

Required:

Answer the following, setting forth reasons for any conclusions stated.

Assuming the contract is not divisible, discuss in separate paragraphs the assertions of Beach and Abel, indicating first whether such claims are correct.

SIMULATION PROBLEM

Simulation Problem 1   (10 to 15 minutes)

For each of the numbered words or phrases, select the one best phrase or sentence from the list A through J. Each response may be used only once.

    A.   Relationship whereby one person agrees to answer for the debt or default of another.
    B.   Requires certain contracts to be in writing to be enforceable.
    C.   Jointly and severally liable to creditor.
    D.   Promises to pay debt on default of principal debtor.
    E.   One party promises to reimburse debtor for payment of debt or loss if it arises.
    F.   Receives intended benefits of a contract.
    G.   Right of surety to require the debtor to pay before surety pays.
    H.   Upon payment of more than his/her proportionate share, each cosurety may compel other cosureties to pay their shares.
    I.   Upon payment of debt, surety may recover payment from debtor.
    J.   Upon payment, surety obtains same rights against debtor that creditor had.

	(A)	(B)	(C)	(D)	(E)	(F)	(G)	(H)	(I)	(J)
1. Indemnity contract	O	O	O	O	O	O	O	O	O	O
2. Suretyship contract	O	O	O	O	O	O	O	O	O	O
3. Surety	O	O	O	O	O	O	O	O	O	O
4. Third-party beneficiary	O	O	O	O	O	O	O	O	O	O
5. Cosurety	O	O	O	O	O	O	O	O	O	O
6. Statute of Frauds	O	O	O	O	O	O	O	O	O	O
7. Right of contribution	O	O	O	O	O	O	O	O	O	O
8. Reimbursement	O	O	O	O	O	O	O	O	O	O
9. Subrogation	O	O	O	O	O	O	O	O	O	O
10. Exoneration	O	O	O	O	O	O	O	O	O	O

1. a __ __	7. b __ __	13. d __ __	19. a __ __	25. b __ __
2. d __ __	8. d __ __	14. d __ __	20. c __ __	26. b __ __
3. b __ __	9. c __ __	15. c __ __	21. c __ __	27. d __ __
4. c __ __	10. b __ __	16. b __ __	22. b __ __	
5. a __ __	11. b __ __	17. d __ __	23. c __ __	1st: __/27 = __%
6. a __ __	12. d __ __	18. d __ __	24. a __ __	2nd: __/27 = __%

MULTIPLE-CHOICE ANSWER EXPLANATIONS

A. Rights and Duties of Debtors and Creditors

1. **(a)** Fraudulent conveyance of property is done with the intent to defraud a creditor, hinder or delay him/her, or put the property out of his/her reach. If the debtor maintains possession of the property, secretly transfers or hides the property, or retains an equitable interest in the property, then a fraudulent conveyance has occurred as all of the three actions prevent the creditor from receiving the full property.

2. **(d)** Although a homestead exemption can exempt a debtor's equity in certain property from postjudgment collection by a creditor, the collections to which it applies vary among the states. The best answer is that it does not apply to valid home mortgage liens or valid IRS tax liens.

3. **(b)** Under garnishment procedures, creditors may attach a portion of the debtor's wages to pay off a debt. There are legal limits as to how much of the wages can be garnished. Likewise, federal social security benefits are protected from garnishment by creditors. Therefore, statement II is correct. Statement I, however, is incorrect because federal tax liens can be used to sell a debtor's personal property to pay taxes.

4. **(c)** The Federal Fair Debt Collection Practices Act was passed to prevent debt collectors from using unfair or abusive collection methods. The Federal Trade Commission is charged with enforcement of this Act but aggrieved parties may also use a civil lawsuit against the debt collector who violates this Act. Answers (a) and (b) are incorrect because the remedy is a suit for damages or a suit for up to $1,000 for violation of the Act if damages are not proven. The remedy is not a reduction or abolishment of the debt. Answer (d) is incorrect because this Act does not provide for criminal prosecution.

5. **(a)** Liens are used by creditors to secure payment for services or materials, in the case of a mechanic's lien, or for repairs, in the case of an artisan's lien. They require that notice be given to the debtor before the creditor can sell the property to satisfy the debt.

6. **(a)** When a creditor wishes to collect a past-due debt from the debtor, s/he may use a writ of attachment. This is a prejudgment remedy in which the creditor is allowed to take into possession some personal property of the debtor prior to getting a judgment in a lawsuit for the past-due debt. The debtor may also wish to collect the debt by use of garnishment. This allows the creditor to obtain property of the debtor that is held by a third party. Typical examples include garnishing wages owed by the employer to the employee-debtor or garnishing the debtor's bank account. To avoid abuses, there are limitations on both of these remedies.

B. Nature of Suretyship and Guaranty

7. **(b)** Any acts of the creditor that materially affect the surety's obligation will release the surety. In this case, the surety was not notified that the creditor partially surrendered the principal debtor's collateral. The surety will not have this collateral as a possible partial protection and the law allows the noncompensated surety to be released. Answer (a) is incorrect—bankruptcy is a personal defense of the debtor and is not a defense for the surety. Answer (c) is incorrect because this is a debt that is voidable at the option of the creditor. Answer (d) is incorrect because there is a possible wrong against the debtor but this does not release the surety.

8. **(d)** Statement I illustrates a suretyship relationship in which the endorser of the note is the surety. Statement II illustrates a third-party beneficiary contract, not a suretyship relationship. The purchaser has agreed to pay for the goods as his/her own debt. The party to receive the goods is the third-party beneficiary. Statement III illustrates a suretyship relationship in which the shareholders are sureties.

C. Creditor's Rights and Remedies

9. **(c)** The creditor, Reuter Bank, has a lot of flexibility in remedies. Although Reuter may attempt to collect from Sabean when the loan is due, it is not required to but instead may resort to the sureties or to the collateral up to the 40% agreed upon, or both.

10. **(b)** When the creditor modifies the debtor's contract, increasing the surety's risk, the surety is released. Note that death of the principal debtor or the debtor's filing bankruptcy are personal defenses of the debtor that the surety cannot use. Such risks are some of the reasons creditors prefer sureties.

11. **(b)** Under the Statute of Frauds under contract law, a surety's (guarantor's) agreement to answer for the debt or default of another must be in writing. Answer (a) is incorrect, as a guarantor of collection's liability is conditioned on the creditor notifying the guarantor of the debtor's default and the creditor first attempting to collect from the debtor. Answer (c) is incorrect as the guarantor may not use the debtor's personal defenses, such as death or insolvency. Answer (d) is incorrect because it is the creditor that must notify the guarantor of the debtor's default, not vice versa.

12. **(d)** A guarantor's liability is conditioned on the creditor notifying the guarantor of the debtor's default and the creditor first attempting to collect from the debtor. In this case, if Towns has not attempted to collect against Pepper, then Towns would not yet be able to collect against Sorus and Ace. Answer (a) is incorrect because Sorus' and Ace's performance of the right of reimbursement from Pepper does not preclude Towns' recovery from Sorus and Ace. Answers (b) and (c) are incorrect because insolvency of the debtor and death of the debtor are not valid defenses of the guarantor against the creditor.

D.   Surety's and Guarantor's Rights and Remedies

13.   (d)   The surety is primarily liable on the debt of the principal debtor. Therefore, the creditor can seek payment directly from the surety as soon as the debt is due. For this reason, the surety cannot require the creditor to collect from the debtor nor can s/he compel the creditor to proceed against any collateral the principal debtor may have.

14.   (d)   Upon payment, the surety obtains the right of subrogation which is the ability to use the same rights the creditor had. Also, the surety may resort to the right of exoneration by requiring the debtor to pay when s/he is able if the creditor has not demanded immediate payment directly from the surety. If the surety has paid the debtor's obligation, the surety may attempt reimbursement from the debtor.

E.   Surety's and Guarantor's Defenses

15.   (c)   The surety may use his/her own defenses of incapacity of the **surety** or bankruptcy of the **surety** to limit his/her own liability. Although the surety may use most defenses that the **debtor** has to limit his/her (surety's) liability, the surety may not use the **personal** defenses of the debtor. These include the debtor's bankruptcy and the debtor's incapacity.

16.   (b)   A modification by the principal debtor and creditor in the terms and conditions of their original contract without the surety's consent will automatically release the surety if the surety's risk of loss is thereby materially increased. Note that a noncompensated surety is discharged even if the creditor does not change the surety's risk. However, a compensated surety is discharged only if the modification causes a material increase in risk. Answers (c) and (d) are incorrect because a surety may not exercise the principal debtor's personal defenses (i.e., insolvency and insanity). Answer (a) is incorrect because although a release of the principal debtor without the surety's consent will usually discharge the surety, there is no discharge if the creditor expressly reserves rights against the surety.

17.   (d)   Personal defenses that the debtor has such as bankruptcy or death of the debtor cannot be used by the surety to avoid payment of the debtor's obligation to the creditor. Answer (a) is incorrect because the surety may generally exercise the defenses on the contract that the debtor has against the creditor. Answer (b) is incorrect because the surety may take advantage of his/her own personal defenses such as fraud by the creditor against the surety. Answer (c) is incorrect because the surety generally may exercise the defenses on the contract that would be available to the debtor such as the running of the statute of limitations.

18.   (d)   A compensated surety will be released from an obligation to the creditor upon tender of performance by either the principal debtor or the surety. A compensated surety will also be completely released if modifications are made to the principal debtor's contract which materially increase risk to the surety. However, if the risk is not materially increased, the surety is not completely released but rather his/her obligation is reduced by the amount of loss due to modification. The surety also is not released if the modifications are beneficial to the surety. Answers (a) and (b) are incorrect because these modifications will not necessarily result in a material increase in the surety's risk or could even be beneficial to the surety. Answer (c) is incorrect because partial release of the principal debtor's obligation will result in partial release of the surety.

19.   (a)   Normally, fraud by the debtor on the surety to induce him/her to act as a surety will not release the surety. However, when the creditor is aware of the debtor's fraudulent misrepresentation, then the surety can avoid liability. Answer (b) is incorrect because the above principle is true whether the surety is compensated or not. Answer (c) is incorrect because the risk of bankruptcy is one of the reasons that the creditor desires a surety. Answer (d) is incorrect because fraudulent misrepresentations do not make a contract void but can make it voidable.

20.   (c)   Once the debt is paid by someone, both the principal debtor and the cosigner are released from obligations to pay the loan. Answer (a) is incorrect because the creditor may proceed against the cosigner without needing to proceed against the principal debtor. Answer (b) is incorrect because the possibility that the principal debtor may qualify for bankruptcy is one of the reasons that the creditor may desire a cosigner. Answer (d) is incorrect because even if the main debtor is adjudicated mentally incompetent, this can allow the main debtor to escape liability but not the cosigner.

F.   Cosureties

21.   (c)   A suretyship relationship exists when one party agrees to answer for the obligations of another. Cosureties exist when there is more than one surety guaranteeing the same obligation of the principal debtor. Both sureties and cosureties are entitled to reimbursement from the debtor if the surety pays the obligation. Sureties and cosureties both have the right of subrogation in that upon making payment, the surety has the same rights against the principal debtor that the creditor had. Both are also entitled to exoneration. Sureties and cosureties both may require the debtor to pay the obligation for which they have given promise if the debtor is able to do so. The right of contribution, however, exists only among cosureties. If a cosurety pays more than his/her proportionate share of the total liability, he/she is entitled to be compensated by the other cosureties for the excess amount paid.

22.   (b)   The right of contribution arises when one cosurety, in performance of the principal debtor's obligation, pays more than his/her proportionate share of the total liability. The right of contribution allows the performing cosurety to receive reimbursement from the other cosureties for their pro rata shares of the liability. The pro rata shares of the cosureties are determined as follows:

	Surety's pro rata share		Remaining liability		Surety's liability
Queen	(210,000/420,000)	x	210,000	=	105,000
Ash	(84,000/420,000)	x	210,000	=	42,000
Kane	(126,000/420,000)	x	210,000	=	63,000

Thus, Queen is entitled to receive $42,000 from Ash and $63,000 from Kane.

23.   (c)   A surety relationship is present when one party agrees to answer for the obligation of another. When there is more than one surety guaranteeing the same obligation of the principal debtor, the sureties become cosureties jointly and severally liable to the claims of the creditor. A right of contribution arises when one cosurety, in performance of the debtor's obligation, pays more than his proportionate share of the total liability. The right of contribution entitles the performing cosurety to reimbursement from the other cosureties for their pro rata shares of the liability. The pro rata shares of the cosureties are determined as follows:

	Surety's pro rata share		Remaining liability		Surety's liability
Nash	(40,000/180,000)	x	36,000	=	8,000
Owen	(60,000/180,000)	x	36,000	=	12,000
Polk	(80,000/180,000)	x	36,000	=	16,000

Thus, Nash is entitled to recover $12,000 from Owen and $16,000 from Polk for a total of $28,000.

24. (a) A discharge or release of one cosurety by a creditor results in a reduction of liability of the remaining cosurety. The remaining cosurety is released to the extent of the released cosurety's pro rata share of debt liability, unless there is a reservation of rights by the creditor against the remaining cosurety. Quill and West each had maximum liability of $100,000. Thus, Ingot's release of West will result in Quill's liability being reduced by West's pro rata share of the total debt liability, which was one-half. Therefore, Quill's liability has been reduced to $25,000 (i.e., 50% of the loan balance) due to the release of West as a cosurety. Answer (c) is therefore incorrect. Answer (d) is incorrect because the release of the cosurety does not release the principal debtor since the debtor's obligation is not affected in any way by Ingot's release of West. Answer (b) is incorrect because as discussed above, Quill's liability has been reduced due to Ingot's release of West.

25. (b) The discharge or release of one cosurety by the creditor results in a reduction of liability of the remaining cosurety. This reduction of liability is limited to the released cosurety's pro rata share of debt liability (unless there is a reservation of rights by the creditor against the remaining cosurety). Since Mane released Rey without reserving rights against Salem, Salem is released to the extent of Rey's pro rata share of the $90,000 liability. Salem's maximum liability can be calculated as follows:

Rey's %	$\dfrac{\$120,000}{\$240,000} = .50$
Loan balance	$ 90,000
x Rey's %	x .50
	$ 45,000
Loan balance	$ 90,000
Rey's pro rata share	(45,000)
Salem's maximum liability	$ 45,000

26. (b) The right of contribution arises when one cosurety, in performance of debtor's obligation, pays more than his proportionate share of the total liability. The right of contribution entitles the performing cosurety to reimbursement from the other cosureties for their pro rata shares of the liability. Since Clark's debts have been discharged in bankruptcy, River may only exercise his right of contribution against Zane, and may recover nothing from Clark. Zane's pro rata share of the remaining $140,000 would be determined as follows:

$$\dfrac{\text{Dollar amount guaranteed by Zane}}{\begin{array}{c}\text{Total amount of risk assumed by} \\ \text{remaining cosureties}\end{array}} \; x \; \begin{array}{c}\text{Remaining} \\ \text{obligation}\end{array}$$

$$\dfrac{160,000}{160,000 + 240,000} \; x \; 140,000 \; = \; 56,000$$

27. (d) Cosureties are jointly and severally liable to the creditor up to the amount of liability each agreed to. If a cosurety pays more than his/her proportionate share of the debt, s/he may seek contribution from the other cosureties for the excess. Answer (a) is incorrect because the right of exoneration refers to the surety requiring the debtor to pay the debt when able. Answer (b) is incorrect because subrogation refers to the right of the surety to obtain the same rights against the debtor that the creditor had, once the surety pays the creditor. Answer (c) is incorrect because the right of reimbursement allows the surety to recover payments from the debtor that the surety has made to the creditor.

ANSWER OUTLINE

Problem 1   Minority; Reasonable Covenant not to Compete; Surety's Defenses

Beach's minority defense is invalid
  Misrepresentation of age does not invalidate defense
  However, failure to disaffirm within reasonable time after reaching majority constitutes implied ratification
Beach's assertion that Reid's violation of noncompetition covenant constitutes breach is valid
  Noncompetition clause is reasonable in light of circumstances present
Abel's defense based on Beach's fraud is invalid
  Since Reid knew nothing of Beach's fraud, he has no duty to inform Abel
Abel's defense based on Beach's minority is invalid
  Surety cannot use minority of principal debtor as defense to payment
Abel's defense based on Reid's violation of noncompetition covenant is valid
  Surety may use material breach of underlying contract by creditor as defense to payment
  Reid's violation of noncompetition clause constitutes breach

UNOFFICIAL ANSWER

Problem 1   Minority; Reasonable Covenant not to Compete; Surety's Defenses

Beach's minority at the time the contract with Reid was entered into will not be a valid defense. Despite Beach's misrepresentation of his age, the agreement with Reid was voidable at Beach's option while Beach was a minor. However, Beach's use and operation of the travel agency for at least seven months after reaching majority constituted an implied ratification of the contract. Some states may construe Beach's mere failure to disaffirm the contract within a reasonable time after reaching majority to be a ratification of the contract. Furthermore, a small number of states provide that minority is not a defense where the minor has entered into a business contract.

Beach's assertion that he is not liable due to Reid's violation of the contract clause prohibiting Reid from competing with Beach is correct because violation of the non-competition covenant is a material breach of the contract. Since the case at issue involves the sale of a business including its goodwill, the legal validity of a clause prohibiting competition by the seller is determined by its reasonableness regarding the time and geographic area covered. Each case must be considered on its own facts, with a determination of what is reasonable under the particular circumstances. It appears that, according to the facts of this case, the prohibition against Reid's operating a competing travel agency within a one-mile radius of Beach's travel agency for two years is reasonable.

Abel's claim that he is not liable to Reid because of Beach's fraud in supplying him with false financial statements is incorrect. Although a creditor has a duty to disclose to the surety all material facts that would increase the surety's risk, the breach of such duty is not a valid defense of the surety if the creditor lacks knowledge of such facts. Therefore, unless Abel can show that Reid knew or had reason to know of the fraud committed by Beach, Abel will not be relieved of his surety undertaking.

Abel's claim that he is not liable to Reid because of Beach's minority is without merit. Beach's minority is a personal defense that in a proper case may be exercised only at Beach's option. Therefore, whether Beach has the power to disaffirm his contract with Reid will have no effect on Abel's surety obligations to Reid.

Abel's assertion that his liability to Reid will be discharged because of Reid's failure to comply with the express promise not to compete with Beach is correct. Unlike the defense of the principal debtor's minority, a material breach of the underlying contract between the principal debtor and creditor may be properly asserted by the surety. The creditor's failure to perform in accordance with the material terms of the underlying contract without justification will discharge the principal debtor's obligation to perform, thereby increasing the risk of the principal debtor's nonperformance. Thus, the surety will also be discharged from liability due to his own increased risk of loss on the surety contract. It seems clear that Reid's opening of a travel agency across the street from Beach's business after only nineteen months constituted a material breach of the sale contract. Therefore, Abel will be discharged from his surety obligation.

SOLUTION TO SIMULATION PROBLEM

Simulation Problem 1

1.   (E) An indemnity contract is not a suretyship contract. Instead it is a contract involving two parties in which the first party agrees to indemnify and reimburse the second party for covered debts or losses should they take place.

2.   (A) The suretyship contract involves three parties. The surety agrees with the creditor to pay for the debt or default if the debtor does not.

3.   (D) The surety is the party that agrees to pay the creditor if the debtor defaults.

4.   (F) When two parties make a contract that intends to benefit a third party, that party is a third-party beneficiary.

5.   (C) When two or more sureties agree to be sureties for the same obligation to the same creditor, they are known as co-sureties. They have joint and several liability.

6.   (B) The Statute of Frauds sets out rules that require certain contracts to be in writing, such as those in which a surety agrees to answer for the debt or default of another.

7.   (H) Cosureties are liable in contribution for their proportionate shares of the debt. If a cosurety pays more than this amount, s/he may seek contribution for the excess from the other cosureties.

8.   (I) The right of reimbursement is against the debtor to collect any amounts paid by the surety.

9.   (J) When the surety pays the creditor, it "steps into the shoes of the creditor" and obtains the same rights against the debtor that the creditor had.

10.   (G) If the debtor is able to pay, the surety may require the debtor to pay before the surety pays. This is called exoneration.

AGENCY

Overview

Agency is a relationship in which one party (agent) is authorized to act on behalf of another party (principal). The law of agency is concerned with the rights, duties, and liabilities of the parties in an agency relationship. Important to this relationship is the fact that the agent has a fiduciary duty to act in the best interest of the principal.

A good understanding of this module is important because partnership law is a special application of agency law.

The CPA exam emphasizes the creation and termination of the agency relationship, the undisclosed as well as the disclosed principal relationship, unauthorized acts or torts committed by the agent within the course and scope of the agency relationship and principal's liability for agent's unauthorized contracts.

A. Characteristics

1. Agency is a relationship between two parties, whereby one party (agent) agrees to act on behalf of the other party (principal). A contract is not required but is frequently present.

    a. Agent is subject to control of principal
    b. Agent is a fiduciary and must act for the benefit of principal
    c. Agent can be used for other purposes, but we are primarily concerned with agents that agree to act for the principal in business transactions with third parties
    d. Agent's specific authority is determined by the principal but generally agent has authority to bind the principal contractually with third parties

2. Employee (servant)

    a. Employee is a type of agent in which employee's physical conduct is subject to control by employer (master)

        (1) Employer is a type of principal and may be called such when the agent is an employee
        (2) Employer is generally liable for employee's torts if committed within course and scope of employment relationship

            (a) Known as doctrine of respondeat superior (vicarious liability)

                EXAMPLE: S is an employee of M. One day while delivering inventory for M, she negligently hits a third party with the delivery truck. Although S is liable because she committed the tort, M is also liable.

            (b) Course and scope of employment is defined broadly

                1] Note that this makes employer liable for torts of employee even if employer not actually negligent him/herself

                EXAMPLE: M, the employer, gives S $30 and asks him to go buy donuts for the employees who are working overtime. He takes his own car and injures a third party through his own negligence. The employer is also liable for this tort.

            (c) Employee need not be following instructions of employer (i.e., rule applies even if employee violated employer's instructions in committing tort)

                EXAMPLE: P works for Q delivering widgets. One rule that Q has is that all employees must look behind the truck before backing out after all deliveries. P violated this rule and injured R. Q is still liable even s/he though had taken steps to prevent this type of accident.

            (d) Contributory negligence (i.e., third party's negligence) is generally a defense for both the agent and his/her principal

                1] Some jurisdictions have adopted comparative negligence which means that defendant at fault pays but that amount of damages is determined by comparing each party's negligence

3. Independent contractor distinguished from employee

    a. Not subject to control of employer as to methods of work
    b. Not subject to regular supervision as an employee
    c. Employer controls results only (independent contractor controls the methods)
    d. Generally, employer is not liable for torts committed by independent contractor

    (1) Unless independent contractor is employed to do something inherently dangerous (e.g., blasting)

    (2) Unless employer was negligent in hiring independent contractor

  e. Independent contractor may also be an agent in certain cases

    EXAMPLE: A public accounting firm represents a client in tax court.

4. Examples of agents and agencies

  a. Power of attorney

    (1) Principal, in writing, grants authority to agent

      (a) Only principal need sign

    (2) Agent need not be an attorney but anyone with capacity to be agent

    (3) Power of attorney may grant general authority or restricted authority

  b. Broker—special agent acting for either buyer or seller in business transactions (e.g., real estate broker)

  c. Exclusive—only agent the principal may deal with for a certain purpose during life of the contract (e.g., real estate broker who has sole right to sell property except for personal sale by principal)

  d. Del credere—a sales agent who, prior to the creation and as a condition of the agency, guarantees the accounts of the customers to his/her principal (if the customers fail to pay)

    (1) Guarantee is not within the Statute of Frauds (i.e., it is not required to be in writing)

  e. E-agent is computer program or electronic method to take some action without specific human review

    EXAMPLE: P authorizes an on-line search to find the lowest price of a certain product found through on-line stores.

  f. Relationship resembling agency

    (1) Agency coupled with an interest—agent has an interest in subject matter through a security interest

      (a) For example, mortgagee with right to sell property on default of mortgagor

        1] Agreement stipulating agent is to receive profits or proceeds does not by itself create an agency coupled with an interest

      (b) Principal does not have the power to terminate agency coupled with an interest

      (c) Actually not an agency relationship because one who creates this relationship surrenders power—fact patterns may still use terms of principal and agent

5. Types of principals

  a. Disclosed—when the third party knows agent is acting for a principal and who the principal is

    (1) Principal becomes a party to authorized contracts made by the agent in the principal's name

    (2) Agent is not liable under contract

      EXAMPLE: Signed "Andy Andrews as agent for Pam Paringer."

      EXAMPLE: Signed "Pam Paringer, by Andy Andrews, agent."

      EXAMPLE: Signed "Pam Paringer, by Andy Andrews."

  b. Partially disclosed—when the third party knows or should know the agent is acting for a principal but does not know who the principal is

    (1) Both agent and principal are liable under the contract

      EXAMPLE: Signed, "Andy Andrews, agent."

      (a) Principal is liable for all parts of contract authorized by principal

      (b) Agent is liable for all of contract

      (c) Agent generally has same authority as if principal disclosed

  c. Undisclosed—when the third party has no notice that the agent is acting for a principal

(1) Both agent and principal are liable under authorized contracts if agent so intended to act for principal

> *EXAMPLE: Signed, "Andy Andrews."*

    (a) Similar to partially disclosed principal (i.e., principal is liable for parts of contract s/he authorized and agent is liable for all of contract)

    (b) Agent generally has same authority as if principal disclosed

6. Types of agents

   a. General agent—agent is given broad powers

   b. Special agent—authority of agent is limited in some significant way such as authority over one transaction

   c. Subagent

     (1) Generally, agents have no authority to hire subagents unless principal so authorizes

B. Methods of Creation

1. Appointment

   a. Express—by agreement between the principal and agent

     (1) Generally the agency contract need not be in writing in situations where the agent enters into agreements which themselves fall under the Statute of Frauds

> *EXAMPLE: A, in his capacity as agent of P, signs a contract for the sale of goods costing $600. Even though the sales contract must normally be in writing under the UCC version of the Statute of Frauds, the agency agreement between A and P need not be expressed in writing.*

       (a) But if agency contract cannot be completed within one year, it must be in writing

> *EXAMPLE: P agrees to pay A as his agent and to keep him as his agent for two years.*

       (b) In some states, agency contract needs to be written if agent is to buy or sell a specific piece of real estate named in agency contract

   b. Implied—based on customs and industry practices as to extent of agent's authority

2. Representation—principal represents to third party that someone is his/her agent

   a. Creates apparent (ostensible) authority

   b. Does not require reliance by third party

   c. Directed toward third party causing third party to believe (as opposed to implied appointment when agent is led to believe)

> *EXAMPLE: Principal writes to a third party that A is his agent and has authority. Even if A has no actual authority, he is an apparent agent.*

3. By estoppel—principal is not allowed to deny agency relationship when s/he causes third party to believe it exists

   a. Imposed by law rather than by agreement

   b. The third party must rely to his/her detriment on this appearance of agency before the principal is estopped from denying it

> *EXAMPLE: A, who is not an agent of P, bargained, while in P's presence with X, to buy goods for P. If P remains silent, he will not be able to deny the agency.*

4. Necessity—when a situation arises that makes it a matter of public policy to presume an agency relationship (e.g., in an emergency to contract for medical aid)

5. Ratification—approval after the fact of an unauthorized act done by an agent or one not yet an agent

   a. By affirming the act or by accepting the benefits of the act

   b. Other party to the contract can withdraw before principal ratifies

   c. Ratification is effective retroactively back to time of agent's act

   d. Undisclosed principal cannot ratify unauthorized acts of agent

   e. Requirements to be valid

(1) Act must be one that would have been valid if agent had been authorized (i.e., lawful and delegable)

   (a) Torts can be ratified, but not crimes

(2) Principal must have been in existence and competent when the act was done
(3) Principal must be aware of all material facts
(4) Act must be ratified in its entirety (i.e., cannot ratify the beneficial part and refuse the rest)

> EXAMPLE: Receptionist has no authority to contract for X Company but signs a service contract on behalf of X Company. Officers of X Company make use of service contract. The receptionist's act is ratified.

C. Authority

1. Actual authority

   a. Express—consists of all authority expressly given by the principal to his/her agent
   b. Implied—authority that can be reasonably implied from express authority and from the conduct of the principal

      (1) Includes authority to do what is customary under the circumstances

      > EXAMPLE: A has been engaged by P to be the general manager of P's retail store. A may buy and sell inventory in the business. She may also hire and fire the business employees. A may not, however, do such things as selling the business itself, selling the fixtures or the building, or advertising for the company to go into a complete new line or service.

2. Apparent (ostensible) authority—third party(ies) must have reasonable belief based on principal's representations

   a. For example, an agent insofar as third persons are concerned can do what the predecessor did or what agents in similar positions in the general business world are deemed authorized to do for their principals
   b. Secret limitations have no effect on third parties

   > EXAMPLE: Principal makes agent manager of his store but tells him not to purchase goods on his own. Agent has apparent authority to purchase as similar managers would.

   > EXAMPLE: P authorizes A to go to San Francisco to buy a piece of property to open up an office for P. P tells A to not pay more than $150,000. A makes a contract with T to buy some property for P. A signs the contract as agent for P but agrees to $160,000. T was unaware of the limitation on the purchase price. P is bound to the contract with T for the full $160,000.

   c. Apparent authority exists only for those who know of principal's representations whether directly or indirectly
   d. Agent has apparent authority after termination of agency until those with whom the agent has dealt are given actual notice; others who know of agency relationship require constructive notice

      (1) Notice may come from any source

3. Estoppel—not true authority, but an equitable doctrine to protect a third party who has detrimentally relied, by estopping the principal from denying the existence of authority

   a. Often indistinguishable from effects of apparent authority or ratification
   b. Only creates rights in the third party(ies)

   > EXAMPLE: A sells P's racehorse to T on P's behalf. P did not give authority, but since the racehorse continues to lose races, P does not object. When the horse begins to win races, P claims A never had authority to sell. If A does not have apparent authority and if P did not technically ratify, P can be estopped from denying the authority on equitable grounds.

D. Capacity to Be Agent or Principal

1. Principal must be able to give legal consent

   a. Minors (person under age of majority, that is, 18 or 21) can, in most jurisdictions, appoint an agent

      (1) But minor may disaffirm agency

   b. Unincorporated associations are not legal entities and therefore cannot appoint agents

      (1) Individual members will be responsible as principals if they appoint an agent

    c. If act requires some legal capacity (e.g., legal age to sell land), then principal must meet this requirement or agent cannot legally perform even if s/he has capacity. Capacity cannot be increased by appointment of an agent.

2. An agent must merely have sufficient mental and physical ability to carry out instructions of his/her principal

    a. Can bind principal even if agent is a minor or legally unable to act for self
    b. Corporations, unincorporated associations, and partnerships may act as agents
    c. A mental incompetent or an infant of tender years may not be an agent

E. Obligations and Rights

1. Principal's obligations to agent

    a. Compensate agent as per agreement, or, in the absence of an agreement, pay a reasonable amount for the agent's service
    b. Reimburse agent for reasonable expenses and indemnify agent against loss or liability for duties performed at the principal's direction which are not illegal
    c. Duty to cooperate with agent and assist him/her perform duties as agreed to between principal and agent
    d. Inform agent of risks (e.g., physical harm, pecuniary loss)
    e. May have remedies of discharging agent, restitution, damages, and accounting, or an injunction

2. Agent's obligations to principal

    a. Agent is a fiduciary and must act in the best interest of the principal and with loyalty
    b. Carry out instructions of principal exercising reasonable care and skill
    c. To account to the principal for profits and everything that rightfully belong to the principal and not commingle funds
    d. Duty not to compete or act adversely to principal

      (1) Includes not acting for oneself unless principal knows and agrees

    e. Give any information to principal that s/he would want or need to know
    f. After termination, must cease acting as agent

3. Principal's liability to third parties

    a. Disclosed principal is liable on contracts

      (1) Where agent has actual authority, implied authority, apparent authority, or contract is later ratified
      (2) Also held liable for any representations made by agent with authority to make them
      (3) Principal not liable where third party has any notice that agent is exceeding his actual authority

    b. Undisclosed or partially disclosed principal is liable unless

      (1) Third party holds agent responsible (third party has choice to hold principal liable once identity of principal becomes known)
      (2) Agent has already fully performed contract
      (3) Undisclosed principal is expressly excluded by contract
      (4) Contract is a negotiable instrument

        (a) Only fully disclosed (in instrument) principal is liable on a negotiable instrument

    c. If a writing is required under Statute of Frauds, principal will only be liable if contract is signed
    d. Principal has his/her own personal defenses (e.g., lack of capacity) and defenses on the contract (e.g., nonperformance by the third party)

      (1) Principal does not have agent's personal defenses (e.g., right of setoff where third party owes agent debt)

e.   Notice to agent is generally considered notice to the principal

4.   Agent's liability to third parties

a.   Agent is liable on contract when

(1)   Principal is undisclosed or partially disclosed

(a)   Agent is not relieved from liability until principal performs or third party elects to hold principal liable

(2)   S/he contracts in his/her own name
(3)   S/he guarantees principal's performance and principal fails
(4)   S/he signs a negotiable instrument and does not sign as an agent or does not include the principal's name (undisclosed principal)
(5)   S/he knows principal does not exist or is incompetent
(6)   S/he acts without authority

b.   Agent is not liable when

(1)   Principal is disclosed and agent signs all documents showing s/he is agent
(2)   Principal ratifies unauthorized act
(3)   Third party elects to hold partially disclosed or undisclosed principal liable

c.   Agent has his/her personal defenses (e.g., right of offset if third party owes him/her debt) and defenses on the contract (e.g., nonperformance by the third party)

(1)   Agent does not have principal's personal defenses (e.g., lack of capacity)

d.   Agent is liable if s/he does not deliver property received from third party for principal
e.   Agent is liable for his/her own crimes and torts

5.   Third party's liability to principal and agent

a.   Third party has no contractual liability to agent unless

(1)   Agent is a party to the contract (i.e., undisclosed or partially disclosed principal), or
(2)   Agent has an interest in the contract (e.g., agent invests in the contract)

b.   Third party is liable to disclosed, partially disclosed, and undisclosed principals

(1)   Third party has personal defenses against principal (e.g., lack of capacity), and defenses on the contract (e.g., nonperformance by principal)
(2)   Against undisclosed principal, third party also has personal defenses against agent

F.   Termination of Principal-Agent Relationship

1.   Acts of the parties

a.   By agreement

(1)   Time specified in original agreement (e.g., agency for one year)
(2)   Mutual consent
(3)   Accomplishment of objective (e.g., agency to buy a piece of land)

b.   Principal or agent may terminate agency

(1)   Party that terminates is liable for breach of contract if termination is before specified period of time

(a)   One still has power to terminate relationship even though s/he has no right to terminate (i.e., results in breach of contract)

EXAMPLE: A and P agree to be agent and principal for six months. P terminates A after two months. P is liable to A for breach of contract for the damages that this wrongful termination causes A. However, P does have the power to remove A's authority to act on behalf of P.

(2)   If either party breaches duties owed, other party may terminate agency without liability
(3)   If no time is specified in agency, then either party may terminate without liability

(4) Principal does not have power to terminate agency coupled with an interest

  c. Death of either agent or principal

  d. Agency coupled with an interest is irrevocable

    (1) Refers to cases in which agent has actual interest in property involved in this agency

2. Third parties who have dealt with agent or have known of agency must be given notice if agency terminated by acts of the parties

  a. Otherwise, agent still binds principal by apparent authority

  b. Constructive notice (e.g., publishing in a newspaper or a trade journal) is sufficient to third parties who have not previously dealt with agent

    EXAMPLE: P fired A, who had been P's agent for a few years. P published in the newspaper that A was no longer his agent. A subsequently made a contract with X purporting to bind P to the contract. X had never dealt with P and A before but was aware that A had been P's agent. X was not aware that A had been fired because he had not read the notice. X cannot hold P to the contract because of the constructive notice. X does not have to read it for the constructive notice to be valid.

  c. Actual notice (e.g., orally informing or sending a letter, etc.) must be given to third parties who have previously dealt with agent unless third party learns of termination from another source

    EXAMPLE: A, while acting as an agent of P, had previous dealings with T. P fires A but A makes a contract with T purporting to act as P's agent. T can still hold P liable unless he received actual notice of termination.

    EXAMPLE: Same as above except that the principal gave constructive notice. T may hold P liable.

    EXAMPLE: Same as above except that although P only gave constructive notice through a trade journal, T happened to read it. This qualifies as actual notice. Therefore, unlike above, T may not hold P liable.

3. Termination by operation of law

  a. If subject of agreement becomes illegal or impossible

  b. Death, insanity, or court determined incompetence of either party

    (1) Exception is an agency coupled with an interest

      EXAMPLE: If mortgagee has power to sell the property to recover his loan, this authority to sell as mortgagor's agent is not terminated by mortgagor's death.

  c. Bankruptcy of principal terminates the relationship

    (1) Bankruptcy of agent does not affect unless agent's solvency is needed for performance

  d. If terminated by operation of law, no notice need be given

MULTIPLE-CHOICE QUESTIONS (1-25)

1. Noll gives Carr a written power of attorney. Which of the following statements is correct regarding this power of attorney?

    a.   It must be signed by both Noll and Carr.

    b.   It must be for a definite period of time.

    c.   It may continue in existence after Noll's death.

    d.   It may limit Carr's authority to specific transactions.

2. A principal and agent relationship requires a

    a.   Written agreement.

    b.   Power of attorney.

    c.   Meeting of the minds and consent to act.

    d.   Specified consideration.

3. Lee repairs high-speed looms for Sew Corp., a clothing manufacturer. Which of the following circumstances best indicates that Lee is an employee of Sew and **not** an independent contractor?

    a.   Lee's work is not supervised by Sew personnel.

    b.   Lee's tools are owned by Lee.

    c.   Lee is paid weekly by Sew.

    d.   Lee's work requires a high degree of technical skill.

4. Harris, while delivering parts to a customer for his employer, negligently ran into and injured Wolfe. Harris had been asked by his employer to make these deliveries even though Harris was using his personal pickup truck. Neither Harris nor the employer had insurance to cover this injury. Which of the following is correct?

    a.   Wolfe can hold Harris liable but not the employer because Harris was driving his own vehicle.

    b.   Wolfe can hold the employer liable but not Harris because the employer had asked Harris to make the deliveries.

    c.   Wolfe can hold either Harris or the employer or both liable.

    d.   Wolfe can hold either Harris or the employer liable but not both.

5. Chiron employed Sherwin as a mechanic. Chiron has various rules that all employed mechanics must follow. One day a customer was injured severely when her car's brakes failed. It was shown that her car's brakes failed because Sherwin did not follow one of the specific rules of Chiron. Which of the following is correct?

    a.   Sherwin is liable to the customer but Chiron is not because the accident was caused by Sherwin breaking one of Chiron's specific rules.

    b.   The customer should sue Sherwin for fraud, not negligence, because Sherwin broke a rule of the employer.

    c.   The customer can hold Chiron liable but not Sherwin, because her contract to get the car repaired was with Chiron.

    d.   The customer may choose to recover damages from both Chiron and Sherwin.

6. Pine, an employee of Global Messenger Co., was hired to deliver highly secret corporate documents for Global's clients throughout the world. Unknown to Global, Pine carried a concealed pistol. While Pine was making a delivery, he suspected an attempt was being made to steal the pack-age, drew his gun and shot Kent, an innocent passerby. Kent will **not** recover damages from Global if

    a.   Global discovered that Pine carried a weapon and did nothing about it.

    b.   Global instructed its messengers **not** to carry weapons.

    c.   Pine was correct and an attempt was being made to steal the package.

    d.   Pine's weapon was unlicensed and illegal.

7. When an agent acts for an undisclosed principal, the principal will **not** be liable to third parties if the

    a.   Principal ratifies a contract entered into by the agent.

    b.   Agent acts within an implied grant of authority.

    c.   Agent acts outside the grant of actual authority.

    d.   Principal seeks to conceal the agency relationship.

8. Trent was retained, in writing, to act as Post's agent for the sale of Post's memorabilia collection. Which of the following statements is correct?

  I. To be an agent, Trent must be at least twenty-one years of age.

  II. Post would be liable to Trent if the collection was destroyed before Trent found a purchaser.

    a.   I only.

    b.   II only.

    c.   Both I and II.

    d.   Neither I nor II.

9. Blue, a used car dealer, appointed Gage as an agent to sell Blue's cars. Gage was authorized by Blue to appoint subagents to assist in the sale of the cars. Vond was appointed as a subagent. To whom does Vond owe a fiduciary duty?

    a.   Gage only.

    b.   Blue only.

    c.   Both Blue and Gage.

    d.   Neither Blue nor Gage.

10. Which of the following under agency law is **not** a type of authority that an agent might have?

    a.   Actual express.

    b.   Actual implied.

    c.   Resulting.

    d.   Apparent.

11. Which of the following actions requires an agent for a corporation to have a written agency agreement?

    a.   Purchasing office supplies for the principal's business.

    b.   Purchasing an interest in undeveloped land for the principal.

    c.   Hiring an independent general contractor to renovate the principal's office building.

    d.   Retaining an attorney to collect a business debt owed the principal.

12. Frost's accountant and business manager has the authority to

    a.   Mortgage Frost's business property.

    b.   Obtain bank loans for Frost.

    c.   Insure Frost's property against fire loss.

    d.   Sell Frost's business.

13. Ames, claiming to be an agent of Clar Corporation, makes a contract with Trimon in the name of Clar Corporation. Later, Clar Corporation, for the first time, learns what Ames has done and notifies Trimon of the truth that Ames was not an agent of Clar Corporation. Which of the following statements is incorrect?
a. Clar Corporation may ratify this contract if it does so with the entire contract.
b. Trimon may withdraw from the contract before Clar attempts to ratify it.
c. Clar Corporation may ratify this contract by performing under the contract without stating that it is ratifying.
d. Trimon may enforce this contract even if Clar Corporation does not wish to be bound.

14. Which of the following generally may ratify a contract that was agreed to by his/her agent without authority from the principal?

	Fully disclosed principal	Partially disclosed principal	Undisclosed principal
a.	Yes	Yes	Yes
b.	Yes	Yes	No
c.	Yes	No	No
d.	No	No	Yes

15. Beele authorized McDonald to be his agent to go to Denver and purchase some real estate that would be suitable to open up a branch office for Beele's business. He tells McDonald not to pay more than $125,000 for the real estate. McDonald contacts York to buy some real estate she owns. York calls Beele and Beele tells York that McDonald is his agent to buy the real estate. Nothing is mentioned about the $125,000 limitation. After negotiations between McDonald and York, McDonald signs a contract purchasing the real estate for $140,000. McDonald signed it indicating on the contract that he was signing as agent for Beele.

Further facts show that the real estate is worth $140,000. Which of the following is correct?
a. There is a fully enforceable contract between Beele and York for $140,000.
b. Beele may enforce the contract with York for $125,000.
c. There is no contract between Beele and York because McDonald did not have authority to purchase the real estate for $140,000.
d. York may require that Beele pay $140,000 because the real estate was worth $140,000 not $125,000.

16. Young Corp. hired Wilson as a sales representative for six months at a salary of $5,000 per month plus 6% of sales. Which of the following statements is correct?
a. Young does **not** have the power to dismiss Wilson during the six-month period without cause.
b. Wilson is obligated to act solely in Young's interest in matters concerning Young's business.
c. The agreement between Young and Wilson is **not** enforceable unless it is in writing and signed by Wilson.
d. The agreement between Young and Wilson formed an agency coupled with an interest.

17. Which of the following statement(s) concerning agency law is(are) true?

I. A contract is needed to have an agency relationship.
II. The agent owes a fiduciary duty to the principal.
III. The principal owes a fiduciary duty to the agent.
a. I and II only.
b. I and III only.
c. II only.
d. I, II, and III.

18. Easy Corp. is a real estate developer and regularly engages real estate brokers to act on its behalf in acquiring parcels of land. The brokers are authorized to enter into such contracts, but are instructed to do so in their own names without disclosing Easy's identity or relationship to the transaction. If a broker enters into a contract with a seller on Easy's behalf,
a. The broker will have the same actual authority as if Easy's identity has been disclosed.
b. Easy will be bound by the contract because of the broker's apparent authority.
c. Easy will **not** be liable for any negligent acts committed by the broker while acting on Easy's behalf.
d. The broker will **not** be personally bound by the contract because the broker has express authority to act.

19. An agent will usually be liable under a contract made with a third party when the agent is acting on behalf of a(n)

	Disclosed principal	Undisclosed principal
a.	Yes	Yes
b.	Yes	No
c.	No	Yes
d.	No	No

20. When a valid contract is entered into by an agent on the principal's behalf, in a nondisclosed principal situation, which of the following statements concerning the principal's liability is correct?

	The principal may be held liable once disclosed	The principal must ratify the contract to be held liable
a.	Yes	Yes
b.	Yes	No
c.	No	Yes
d.	No	No

21. Which of the following rights will a third party be entitled to after validly contracting with an agent representing an undisclosed principal?
a. Disclosure of the principal by the agent.
b. Ratification of the contract by the principal.
c. Performance of the contract by the agent.
d. Election to void the contract after disclosure of the principal.

22. Able, as agent for Baker, an undisclosed principal, contracted with Safe to purchase an antique car. In payment, Able issued his personal check to Safe. Able could not cover the check but expected Baker to give him cash to deposit before the check was presented for payment. Baker did not do so and the check was dishonored. Baker's identity became known to Safe. Safe may **not** recover from
a. Baker individually on the contract.
b. Able individually on the contract.
c. Baker individually on the check.
d. Able individually on the check.

23. Thorp was a purchasing agent for Ogden, a sole proprietor, and had the express authority to place purchase orders with Ogden's suppliers. Thorp placed an order with Datz, Inc. on Ogden's behalf after Ogden was declared incompetent in a judicial proceeding. Thorp was aware of Ogden's incapacity. Which of the following statements is correct concerning Ogden's liability to Datz?

    a.   Ogden will be liable because Datz was **not** informed of Ogden's incapacity.

    b.   Ogden will be liable because Thorp acted with express authority.

    c.   Ogden will **not** be liable because Thorp's agency ended when Ogden was declared incompetent.

    d.   Ogden will **not** be liable because Ogden was a nondisclosed principal.

24. Generally, an agency relationship is terminated by operation of law in all of the following situations **except** the

    a.   Principal's death.

    b.   Principal's incapacity.

    c.   Agent's renunciation of the agency.

    d.   Agent's failure to acquire a necessary business license.

25. Bolt Corp. dismissed Ace as its general sales agent and notified all of Ace's known customers by letter. Young Corp., a retail outlet located outside of Ace's previously assigned sales territory, had never dealt with Ace. Young knew of Ace as a result of various business contacts. After his dismissal, Ace sold Young goods, to be delivered by Bolt, and received from Young a cash deposit for 20% of the purchase price. It was not unusual for an agent in Ace's previous position to receive cash deposits. In an action by Young against Bolt on the sales contract, Young will

    a.   Lose, because Ace lacked any implied authority to make the contract.

    b.   Lose, because Ace lacked any express authority to make the contract.

    c.   Win, because Bolt's notice was inadequate to terminate Ace's apparent authority.

    d.   Win, because a principal is an insurer of an agent's acts.

PROBLEM

NOTE: These types of problems are no longer included in the CPA Examination but they have been retained because they are useful in developing skills to complete simulations.

Problem 1 (7 to 10 minutes)

John Nolan, a partner in Nolan, Stein, & Wolf partnership, transferred his interest in the partnership to Simon and withdrew from the partnership. Although the partnership will continue, Stein and Wolf have refused to admit Simon as a partner.

Subsequently, the partnership appointed Ed Lemon as its agent to market its various product lines. Lemon entered into a two-year written agency contract with the partnership which provided that Lemon would receive a 10% sales commission. The agency contract was signed by Lemon and, on behalf of the partnership, by Stein and Wolf.

After six months, Lemon was terminated without cause. Lemon asserts that

- He is an agent coupled with an interest.
- The agency relationship may not be terminated without cause prior to the expiration of its term.
- He is entitled to damages because of the termination of the agency relationship.

Required:

Answer the following, setting forth reasons for any conclusions stated.

Discuss the merits of Lemon's assertions.

SIMULATION PROBLEM

Simulation Problem 1   (10 to 15 minutes)

Situation
Relationships

Lace Computer Sales Corp. orally contracted with Banks, an independent consultant, for Banks to work part time as Lace's agent to perform Lace's customers' service calls. Banks, a computer programmer and software designer, was authorized to customize Lace's software to the customers' needs, on a commission basis, but was specifically told not to sell Lace's computers.

On March 15, Banks made a service call on Clear Co. to repair Clear's computer. Banks had previously called on Clear, customized Lace's software for Clear, and collected cash payments for the work performed. During the call, Banks convinced Clear to buy an upgraded Lace computer for a price much lower than Lace would normally charge. Clear had previously purchased computers from other Lace agents and had made substantial cash down payments to the agents. Clear had no knowledge that the price was lower than normal. Banks received a $1,000 cash down payment and promised to deliver the computer the next week. Banks never turned in the down payment and left town. When Clear called the following week to have the computer delivered, Lace refused to honor Clear's order.

Relationships
Situation

Items 1 through 5 relate to the relationships between the parties. For each item, select from List I whether only statement I is correct, whether only statement II is correct, whether both statements I and II are correct, or whether neither statement I nor II is correct.

List I
A. I only.
B. II only.
C. Both I and II.
D. Neither I nor II.

		(A)	(B)	(C)	(D)
1.	I. Lace's agreement with Banks had to be in writing for it to be a valid agency agreement.	○	○	○	○
	II. Lace's agreement with Banks empowered Banks to act as Lace's agent.				
2.	I. Clear was entitled to rely on Banks' implied authority to customize Lace's software.	○	○	○	○
	II. Clear was entitled to rely on Banks' express authority when buying the computer.				
3.	I. Lace's agreement with Banks was automatically terminated by Banks' sale of the computer.	○	○	○	○
	II. Lace must notify Clear before Banks' apparent authority to bind Lace will cease.				
4.	I. Lace is **not** bound by the agreement made by Banks with Clear.	○	○	○	○
	II. Lace may unilaterally amend the agreement made by Banks to prevent a loss on the sale of the computer to Clear.				
5.	I. Lace, as a disclosed principal, is solely contractually liable to Clear.	○	○	○	○
	II. Both Lace and Banks are contractually liable to Clear.				

MULTIPLE-CHOICE ANSWERS

1. d __ __	7. c __ __	13. d __ __	19. c __ __	25. c __ __
2. c __ __	8. d __ __	14. b __ __	20. b __ __	
3. c __ __	9. c __ __	15. a __ __	21. c __ __	
4. c __ __	10. c __ __	16. b __ __	22. c __ __	
5. d __ __	11. b __ __	17. c __ __	23. c __ __	1st: __/25 = __%
6. d __ __	12. c __ __	18. a __ __	24. c __ __	2nd: __/25 = __%

MULTIPLE-CHOICE ANSWER EXPLANATIONS

A. Characteristics

1. **(d)** A power of attorney is written authority conferred to an agent. It is conferred in a formal writing. A power of attorney can be general or it can grant the agent only restricted authority. Answer (a) is incorrect because the power of attorney must be signed only by the person granting such authority. Answer (b) is incorrect because the power of attorney does not have to be for a definite, specified time period. Answer (c) is incorrect because the death of the principal constitutes the termination of an agency relationship by operation of law.

2. **(c)** The relationship between a principal and agent is based upon the consent of both parties, also involving a meeting of the minds. Answer (d) is incorrect because specified consideration is not needed to create an agency relationship; the relationship between the principal and the agent need not be contractual. Answer (a) is incorrect because although the principal and agent relationship may be written, a written agreement is not required. Answer (b) is incorrect because power of attorney is not needed to create an agency relationship.

3. **(c)** An employee is generally subject to control as to the methods used to complete the work. An independent contractor is typically paid for the completion of the project rather than on an hourly, weekly, or monthly basis. Answer (a) is incorrect because supervision by Sew Corp. personnel shows an employment relationship. Answer (b) is incorrect because independent contractors typically provide their own tools. Answer (d) is incorrect because the work of both employees and independent contractors can require a high degree of skill.

A.2. Employee (Servant)

4. **(c)** Since Harris was acting within the scope of his employment when he negligently injured Wolfe, both Harris and his employer are liable. Wolfe can recover from either one or both. Answer (a) is incorrect because both are liable since Harris was acting within the scope of the employment. The ownership of the vehicle does not change this. Answer (b) is incorrect because Harris is liable for his own tort even though the employer can also be held liable. Answer (d) is incorrect because Wolfe may recover the full damages from either or may recover a portion of the damages from both.

5. **(d)** Because the repairs Sherwin did were within the scope of the employment, the employer is also liable. This is true even if the employer was diligent in creating excellent rules that were not followed by an employee. Answer (a) is incorrect because the repairs were within the scope of the employment. Answer (b) is incorrect because the customer can sue for negligence and hold both parties liable. Answer (c) is incorrect because the customer may recover from both under tort law.

6. **(d)** In general, the employer is not responsible for the crimes of the employee unless the employer aided or permitted the illegal activity, even if the activity was within the scope of the employment. Answer (a) is incorrect because if the employer did nothing to instruct the employee about the use of the weapon, this could help establish negligence on the part of the employer and would not prevent the use of the doctrine of respondeat superior, which makes employers liable for the tortious acts of their employees within the scope of the employment. Answer (b) is incorrect because the employer is liable for torts of the employee committed within the course and scope of the employment even if the employee was violating the employer's instructions. Answer (c) is incorrect because even if the employee's suspicions were correct, the shooting of an innocent passerby should establish at least negligence for which the employer and the employee are liable.

A.5. Types of Principals

7. **(c)** A principal, whether disclosed, partially disclosed, or undisclosed is liable on contracts where the agent has actual or apparent authority, or where the principal ratifies an agent's contract. Actual authority includes express or implied authority projected by the principal to the agent. Apparent authority of an agent is authority perceived by a third party based on the principal's representations. Therefore, apparent authority can exist only where there is a disclosed or a partially disclosed principal. It follows, then, that an undisclosed principal will **not** be liable to third parties if the agent acts outside the grant of **actual** authority.

B. Methods of Creation

8. **(d)** An agent must merely have sufficient mental and physical ability to carry out instructions of his/her principal. An agent can bind the principal even if the agent is a minor. If the memorabilia collection was destroyed before Trent found a purchaser, Post would not be liable to Trent. Upon the loss or destruction of the subject matter on which the agency relationship is based, the agency relationship is terminated.

9. **(c)** The fiduciary duty is an important duty owed by agents to their principals. Gage as Blue's agent was authorized by Blue to appoint subagents to assist in the sales transactions. Since Gage did appoint Vond as a subagent, legally Bond is an agent both of Blue and Gage. Therefore, Vond owes a fiduciary duty to both Blue and Gage making (a), (b), and (d) all incorrect.

10. **(c)** Resulting authority is not one of the types of authority that an agent might have. Answer (a) is not chosen because actual express authority is a common type of authority and consists of all authority expressly given by the principal to his/her agent. Answer (b) includes the authority that can be reasonably implied from the express authority and the conduct of the principal. Answer (d) is not chosen because even though a party was never authorized by a principal to be an agent, if the principal leads a third party to believe that the party did have authority, this is apparent agency.

11.   (b)   An agency agreement normally does not need to be in writing. Exceptions to this general rule include agency contracts that cannot be completed within one year and agreements whereby the agent is to buy specific real estate for the principal. This question incorporates the latter. Typical agency agreements need not be in writing; these would include purchasing office supplies, retaining an independent contractor to do renovation work, or hiring an attorney to collect a business debt.

12.   (c)   An agent has implied authority to do what is customary for agents of that type to do under the circumstances. It would be customary for one who is a principal's accountant and business manager to have authority to insure the principal's property against fire loss. Answers (a), (b), and (d) are incorrect because they involve authority that is beyond customary, ordinary authority.

B.5.   Ratification

13.   (d)   Since Ames had no express, implied, or actual authority, Trimon cannot enforce the contract. Answer (a) is not chosen because ratifications under agency law require that the contract be ratified in its entirety or not at all. Answer (b) is not chosen because until Clar ratifies the contract in its entirety, Trimon may withdraw from the contract since Ames had no authority to make the contract. Answer (c) is not chosen because ratification can be accomplished by actions as well as words.

14.   (b)   When the third party is aware that there is a principal, that principal, fully disclosed or partially disclosed, may generally ratify the contract when he or she is aware of all material facts and if ratification of the entire contract takes place.

C.   Authority

15.   (a)   Since Beele authorized McDonald to be his agent, the secret limitation has no effect on York. York may enforce the contract for the full $140,000. Answer (b) is incorrect because Beele authorized McDonald to be his agent. Even though his agent was instructed to pay at most $125,000 in the contract, this was a secret limitation that did not limit York who was unaware of it. Answer (c) is incorrect because McDonald was given authority to purchase real estate on Beele's behalf. The limitation on the dollar amount was not known by York and therefore does not limit her. Answer (d) is incorrect because although York can enforce the contract against Beele, it is because Beele gave authority to McDonald rather than how much the real estate is worth.

E.   Obligations and Rights

16.   (b)   As a fiduciary to the principal, an agent must act in the best interest of the principal. Therefore, the agent has an obligation to refrain from competing with or acting adversely to the principal, unless the principal knows and approves of such activity. Answer (c) is incorrect because the Statute of Frauds would not require that the described agency relationship be contained in a signed writing since it

is possible for the contract to be performed within one year. Answer (d) is incorrect because the mere right of the agent to receive a percentage of proceeds is not sufficient to constitute an agency coupled with an interest. In order to have an agency coupled with an interest, the agent must have either a property interest or a security interest in the subject matter of the agency relationship. Answer (a) is incorrect because in all agency relationships, except agencies coupled with an interest, the principal always has the power to dismiss the agent. However, the principal does not necessarily have the right to terminate the relationship. In certain situations the dismissed agent could sue for breach of contract.

17.   (c)   In an agency relationship, the agent owes a fiduciary duty to the principal but the principal does not owe a fiduciary duty to the agent. Also, even though there is often a contract between the principal and agent, this is not a requirement, for example, when the agent consents to act for the principal as a friend.

E.3.   Principal's Liability to Third Parties

18.   (a)   When the principal is undisclosed in an agency relationship, the agent generally has the same authority as if the principal were disclosed. The main difference is in the liability of the agent to third parties. Answer (b) is incorrect because the principal is liable on the contract because of the express authority given to the agent to make the contract on behalf of the principal. Apparent authority exists when the principal represents the agent to third parties to be his/her agent. In this case, the principal wished to be undisclosed. Answer (c) is incorrect because principal can be held liable for negligence committed by the agent within the course and scope of the agency. Answer (d) is incorrect because the agent can be held liable on the contract by third parties when the principal is undisclosed.

19.   (c)   An agent is liable to a third party on a contract when the principal is undisclosed or partially disclosed. If the principal is fully disclosed, the agent is not liable.

E.4.   Agent's Liability to Third Parties

20.   (b)   When an agent enters into a contract with a third person on behalf of an undisclosed principal, the agent is personally liable, unless the third person discovers the existence and identity of the principal and chooses to hold the principal to the contract instead of the agent. Ratification is the approval after the fact of an unauthorized act done by an agent or of an act done by someone who is not yet an agent. Undisclosed principals cannot ratify unauthorized acts of the agent.

21.   (c)   When a third party contracts with an agent representing an undisclosed principal, the agent is liable for performance of the contract. The third party is not entitled to disclosure of the principal. Answer (b) is incorrect because ratification of a contract by the principal is the approval required after the fact related to an unauthorized act by the agent or one not yet an agent. Answer (d) is incorrect because the third party generally is not allowed the option of voiding the contract after disclosure of the principal.

22.   (c)   One who issues a personal check is liable on it; however, any party or principal who is not disclosed on the check is not liable on the negotiable instrument. Answers (a) and (b) are incorrect because the third party can elect to hold either the agent or the principal liable when the agent makes a contract for an undisclosed principal. Answer (d) is incorrect because the party who signs a check is liable on it.

F. Termination of Principal-Agent Relationship

23. (c) The declaration of Ogden's incapacity constitutes the termination of the agency relationship by operation of law. When an agency relationship is terminated by operation of law, the agent's authority to enter into a binding agreement on behalf of the principal ceases. There is no requirement that notice be given to third parties when the agency relationship is terminated by operation of law. In this case, Ogden will not be liable to Datz because Thorp was without authority to enter into the contract. Answer (a) is incorrect because insanity of the principal terminates the agency relationship even though the third parties are unaware of the principal's insanity. Answer (b) is incorrect because Thorp's authority terminated upon the declaration of Ogden's incapacity. Answer (d) is incorrect because an undisclosed principal is liable unless the third party holds the agent responsible, the agent has fully performed the contract, the undisclosed principal is expressly excluded by contract or the contract is a negotiable instrument. However, Ogden will not be liable as Thorp was without authority to enter into the agreement.

24. (c) An agency relationship is terminated by operation of law if the subject of the agreement becomes illegal or impossible, the principal or the agent dies or becomes insane, or the principal becomes bankrupt. Answers (a), (b), and (d) are incorrect because they will cause the termination of an agency relationship by operation of law. Answer (c), agent's renunciation of the agency, will not cause the termination of an agency relationship.

25. (c) When the agency relationship is terminated by an act of the principal and/or agent, third parties are entitled to notice of the termination from the principal. Failure of the principal to give the required notice gives the agent apparent authority to act on behalf of the principal. Specifically, the principal must give actual notice to all parties who had prior dealings with the agent or principal. Constructive or public notice must be given to parties who knew of the existence of the agency relationship, but did not actually have business dealings with the agent or principal. Since Bolt Corp. did not give proper constructive notice to Young Corp., Ace had apparent authority to bind the principal and, therefore, Young Corp. will win. Accordingly, answer (a) is incorrect. Answer (b) is incorrect because although Ace lacked express authority, apparent authority was present due to the inadequacy of Bolt's notice. Answer (d) is incorrect because a principal is not an absolute insurer of his agent's acts. A principal is liable for his agent's torts only if the principal expressly authorizes the conduct or the tort is committed within the scope of the agent's employment.

ANSWER OUTLINE

Problem 1   Principal's Power and Right to Terminate
Agency

Lemon's first assertion is incorrect
   Agency coupled with an interest requires agent to have an
interest in property which is subject of agency
    Lemon's commission agreement does not qualify as an
agency coupled with an interest
Lemon's second assertion is incorrect
   Principal has the power to discharge the agent, although
the principal may not have the right to do so
Lemon's third assertion is correct
·   If principal wrongfully discharges agent, principal is li-
able for damages under breach of contract

UNOFFICIAL ANSWER

Problem 1   Principal's Power and Right to Terminate
Agency

    Lemon's first assertion that he is an agent coupled with
an interest is incorrect. An agency coupled with an interest
in the subject matter arises when the agent has an interest in
the property that is the subject of the agency. The fact that
Lemon entered into a two-year written agency agreement
with the partnership that would pay Lemon a commission
clearly will not establish an interest in the subject matter of
the agency. The mere expectation of profits to be realized or
proceeds to be derived from the sale of the partnership's
products is not sufficient to create an agency coupled with
an interest. As a result, the principal-agency relationship
may be terminated at any time.

    Lemon's second assertion that the principal-agency re-
lationship may not be terminated without cause prior to the
expiration of its term is incorrect. Where a principal-agency
relationship is based upon a contract to engage the agent for
a specified period of time, the principal may discharge the
agent despite the fact such discharge is wrongful. Although
the principal does not have the right to discharge the agent,
he does have the power to do so. Thus, Lemon may be discharged without cause.

    Lemon's third assertion that he is entitled to damages
because of the termination of the agency relationship is correct. Where a principal wrongfully discharges its agent, the
principal is liable for damages based on breach of contract.
Under the facts, Lemon's discharge by the partnership without cause constitutes a breach of contract for which Lemon
may recover damages.

SOLUTION TO SIMULATION PROBLEM

Simulation Problem 1

1. **(B)** Statement I is incorrect because normally an agency agreement need not be in writing unless the agency contract cannot be completed in one year. Statement II is correct because Lace authorized Banks to be Lace's agent.

2. **(A)** Statement I is correct because Banks was given actual, express authority by Lace to perform Lace's customers' service calls and to customize Lace's software to the customer's needs. As an extension to this actual, express authority, Clear can also rely on what is customary and ordinary for such an agent to be able to do under implied authority. Statement II is incorrect because Banks did not have express authority to sell the computer. In fact, Banks was told **not** to sell Lace's computers.

3. **(B)** Banks breached his/her fiduciary duty to Lace and breached his/her duty to follow instructions when s/he sold the computer. This, however, does not automatically terminate their agreement. Statement II is correct because Banks had dealt with Clear before as Lace's agent. Therefore, Clear must receive actual notice to terminate the apparent authority.

4. **(D)** Statement I is incorrect because Banks had apparent authority to sell the computer even though Banks did not have actual authority to do so. Statement II is incorrect because Lace is bound by the contract with Clear. Any modification of the contract must be made by both parties to the contract, not just one.

5. **(A)** Statement I is correct because since Lace was a disclosed principal, only Lace, the principal, is liable under the contract to Clear, the third party. Banks, the agent, is not. For the same reason, statement II is incorrect.

REGULATION OF EMPLOYMENT AND ENVIRONMENT

Overview

Issues on this topic are based on the Workers' Compensation Laws and Federal Social Security Rules including the Federal Insurance Contributions Act (FICA) and the Federal Unemployment Tax Act (FUTA). These laws supplement the law of agency. In this area, emphasis is placed on the impact that state and federal laws have on the regulation of employment.

To adequately understand these materials, you should emphasize the theory and purpose underlying the Workers' Compensation Laws. You should also focus on the effect that these laws have on employers and employees. Notice the changes these laws have made on common law.

Upon looking at the Federal Social Security Laws, emphasize the coverage and benefits of the respective programs.

Also, emphasize the various discrimination and environmental laws.

A. Federal Social Security Act

1. Main purpose of Act is as name implies (i.e., attainment of the social security of people in our society)

    a. Basic programs include

        (1) Old age insurance
        (2) Survivor's and disability insurance
        (3) Hospital insurance (Medicare)
        (4) Unemployment insurance

    b. Sources of financing for these programs

        (1) Old-age, survivor's, disability, and hospital insurance programs are financed out of taxes paid by employers, employees, and self-employed under provisions of Federal Insurance Contributions Act and Self-Employment Contributions Act
        (2) Unemployment insurance programs are financed out of taxes paid by employers under the Federal Unemployment Tax Act and various state unemployment insurance laws

2. Federal Insurance Contributions Act (FICA)

    a. Imposes social security tax on employees, self-employed, and employers
    b. Social security tax applies to compensation received that is considered to be wages
    c. In general, tax rates are same for both employer and employee

        (1) Rates changed from time to time

    d. Taxes are paid only up to base amount that is also changed frequently

        (1) If employee pays FICA tax on more than base amount, s/he has right to refund for excess

            (a) May happen when employee works for two or more employers

                1] These two or more employers do not get refunds

    e. FICA is also used to fund Medicare

        (1) Base rate on this Medicare portion has been set at a higher amount

    f. It is employer's duty to withhold employee's share of FICA from employee's wages and remit both employee's amount and employer's equal share to government

        (1) Employer subject to fines for failure to make timely FICA deposits

            (a) Also, employer subject to fine for failure to supply taxpayer identification number

        (2) Employer is required to match FICA contributions of employees on dollar-for-dollar basis
        (3) If employer neglects to withhold, employer may be liable for both employee's and employer's share of taxes (i.e., to pay double tax)

            (a) Once employer pays, s/he has right to collect employee's share from employee
            (b) Employer may voluntarily pay not only its share but also employee's share

           1] Employee's share is deductible by employer as additional compensation and is taxable to the employee as compensation

    (4) Employer is required to furnish employee with written statement of wages paid and FICA contributions withheld during calendar year

  g. Taxes paid by employer are deducted on tax return of employer

    (1) But employee may not deduct taxes paid on his/her tax return

  h. Neither pension plans nor any other programs may be substituted for FICA coverage

    (1) Individuals receiving payments from private pension plans may also receive social security payments

3. Self-Employment Contributions Act

  a. Self-employed persons are required to report their own taxable earnings and pay required social security tax

  b. Self-employment income is net earnings from self-employment

  c. Tax rates paid on self-employment income up to base amount

    (1) Since self-employed does not have employer to match the rate, tax rate is that of employer and employee combined

    (2) Base amount and tax rate are subject to amendment

    (3) Base rate is reduced by any wages earned during year because wages are subject to FICA

    (4) Self-employed can deduct half of FICA tax paid on his/her income tax form

4. Unemployment Insurance (Federal Unemployment Tax Act—FUTA)

  a. Tax is used to provide unemployment compensation benefits to workers who lose jobs and cannot find replacement work

  b. Federal unemployment tax must be paid by employer if employer employs one or more persons covered by act

    (1) Deductible as business expense on employer's federal income tax return

    (2) Not deductible by employee because not paid by employee

  c. Employer must also pay a state unemployment tax

    (1) An employer is entitled to credit against his/her federal unemployment tax for state unemployment taxes paid

    (2) State unemployment tax may be raised or lowered according to number of claims against employer

    (3) If employer pays a low state unemployment tax because of good employment record, then employer is entitled to additional credit against federal unemployment tax

5. Coverage under Social Security Act is mandatory for qualifying employees

  a. Person may not elect to avoid coverage

  b. Part-time and full-time employees are covered

  c. Compensation received must be "wages"

6. Definitions

  a. Wages—all compensation for employment

    (1) Include

      (a) Money wages

      (b) Contingent fees

      (c) Compensation in general even though not in cash

      (d) Base pay of those in the service

      (e) Bonuses and commissions

      (f) Most tips

        (g) Vacation and dismissal allowances

    (2) Exclude

        (a) Wages greater than base amount
        (b) Reimbursed travel expenses
        (c) Employee medical and hospital expenses paid by employer
        (d) Employee insurance premiums paid by employer
        (e) Payment to employee retirement plan by employer

b. Employee—person whose performance is subject to physical control by employer not only as to results but also as to methods of accomplishing those results

    (1) Partners, self-employed persons, directors of corporations, and independent contractors are not covered by unemployment compensation provisions since they are not "employees"

        (a) Are covered as self-employed persons for old-age, survivor's, and disability insurance program purposes

    (2) Independent contractor distinguished from an employee

        (a) Independent contractor not subject to control of employer or regular supervision as employee
        (b) That is, employer seeks results only and contractor controls method

          EXAMPLE: A builder of homes has only to produce the results.

    (3) Officers and directors of corporations are "employees" if they perform services and receive remuneration for these services from corporation

c. Employment—all service performed by employee for person employing him/her

    (1) Must be continuing or recurring work
    (2) Services from following are exempt from coverage

        (a) Student nurses
        (b) Certain public employees
        (c) Nonresident aliens

    (3) Services covered if performed by employee for employer without regard to residence or citizenship

        (a) Unless employer not connected with US

    (4) Domestic workers, agricultural workers, government employees, and casual workers are governed by special rules

d. Self-employment—carrying on trade or business either as individual or in partnership

    (1) Wages greater than base amount are excluded
    (2) Can be both employed (in one job) and self-employed (another business), but must meet requirements of trade or business (i.e., not a hobby, occasional investment, etc.)

e. Employer

    (1) For Federal Unemployment Tax Act (FUTA) need only employ one person or more for some portion of a day for twenty weeks, or pays $1,500 or more in wages in any calendar quarter
    (2) In general, may be individual, corporation, partnership, trust, or other entity

7. Old-age, survivor's, and disability insurance benefits

a. Availability of benefits depends upon attainment by individual of "insured status"

    (1) Certain lengths of working time are required to obtain insured status

b. An individual who is "fully insured" is eligible for following benefits

    (1) Survivor benefits for widow or widower and dependents

    (2) Benefits for disabled worker and his/her dependents

    (3) Old-age retirement benefits payable to retired worker and dependents

        (a) Reduced benefits for retirement at age sixty-two

    (4) Lump-sum death benefits

  c. Individual who is "currently insured" is eligible for following benefits

    (1) Limited survivor benefits

        (a) In general, limited to dependent minors or those caring for dependent minors

    (2) Benefits for disabled worker and his/her dependents

    (3) Lump-sum death benefits

    (4) Survivors or dependents need not have paid in program to receive benefits

    (5) Divorced spouses may receive benefits

  d. Amount of benefits defined by statute which changes from time to time and depends upon

    (1) Average monthly earnings, and

    (2) Relationship of beneficiary to retired, deceased, or disabled worker

        (a) For example, husband, wife, child, grandchild—may be entitled to different benefits

    (3) Benefits increased based on cost of living

    (4) Benefits increased for delayed retirement

8. Reduction of social security benefits

  a. Early retirement results in reduced benefits

    (1) Retirement age is increasing in steps

  b. Returning to work after retirement can affect social security benefits

    (1) Income from private pension plans, savings, investments, or insurance does not affect benefits because not earned income

    (2) Income from limited partnership is considered investment income rather than self-employment income

9. Unemployment benefits

  a. Eligibility for and amount of unemployment benefits governed by state laws

  b. Does not include self-employed

  c. Generally available only to persons unemployed through no fault of their own; however, not available to seasonal workers if paid on yearly basis (e.g., professional sports player in off-season)

  d. One must have worked for specified period of time and/or earned specified amount of wages

B. Workers' Compensation Act

1. Workers' compensation is a form of strict liability whereby employer is liable to employee for injuries or diseases sustained by employee which arise out of and in course of employment

  a. Employee is worker subject to control and supervision of employer

  b. Distinguish independent contractor

    (1) Details of work not supervised

    (2) Final result can of course be monitored (based on contract law)

2. Purpose

  a. To give employees and their dependents benefits for job-related injuries or diseases with little difficulty

    (1) Previously, employee had to sue employer for negligence to receive any benefits in form of damages

    (2) Employee usually cannot waive his/her right to benefits

b. Cost is passed on as an expense of production
c. **No fault need be shown**; payment is automatic upon satisfaction of requirements

  (1) Removes employer's common law defenses of

    (a) Assumption of risk
    (b) Negligence of a fellow employee—employer formerly could avoid liability by proving it was another employee's fault
    (c) Contributory negligence—injured employee was also negligent

3. Regulated by states

a. Except that federal government employees are covered by federal statute
b. Each state has its own statute

4. Generally, there are two types of statutes

a. Elective statutes

  (1) If employer rejects, s/he loses the three common law defenses against employee's common law suit for damages so most accept

b. Compulsory statutes

  (1) Require that all employers within coverage of statute provide benefits
  (2) Majority of states have compulsory coverage

5. Insurance used to provide benefits

a. In lieu of insurance policy, employer may assume liability for workers' compensation claims but must show proof of financial responsibility to carry own risk

6. Legislative scope

a. Workers' compensation coverage extends to all employees who are injured on the job or in the course of the employment (i.e., while acting in furtherance of employer's business purpose)
b. Coverage also extends to occupational diseases and preexisting diseases that are aggravated by employment
c. Coverage does not extend to employee while traveling to or from work
d. Out-of-state work may be covered if it meets above mentioned criteria
e. All states have workers' compensation law; most employees covered
f. Must be employee; coverage does not extend to independent contractors
g. Public employees are often covered

7. Legal action for damages

a. Employers covered by workers' compensation insurance are generally exempt from lawsuits by employees

  (1) If employee does not receive benefits covered under workers' compensation, s/he may sue insurance company that agreed to cover workers

b. Benefits under workers' compensation laws received by employee are in lieu of action for damages against employer and such a suit is barred

  (1) Employer assumes liability in exchange for employee giving up his/her common law rights to sue employer for damages caused by the job (e.g., suit based on negligence)
  (2) When employee is covered by workers' compensation law, his/her sole remedy against employer is that which is provided for under appropriate workers' compensation act
  (3) However, if employer **intentionally** injures employee, employee may proceed against employer based on intentional tort in addition to recovering under workers' compensation benefits

c. Employee is entitled to workers' compensation benefits **without regard to fault**

  (1) Negligence or even gross negligence of injured employee is not a bar to recovery

(2) Employee's negligence plays no role in determination of amount of benefits awarded

(3) Failure of employee to follow employer's rules is not a bar to recovery

(4) However, injuries caused by intentional self-infliction, or intoxication of employee, can bar recovery

d. When employer fails to provide workers' compensation insurance or when employer's coverage is inadequate, injured employee may sue in common law for damages, and employer cannot resort to usual common law defenses

(1) When employer uninsured, many states have a fund to pay employee for job-related injuries

(a) State then proceeds against uninsured company

(b) Penalties imposed

8. Actions against third parties

a. Employee's acceptance of workers' compensation benefits does not bar suit against third party whose negligence or unreasonably dangerous product caused injury

(1) If employee sues and recovers from third party, employer (or its insurance carrier) is entitled to compensation for workers' compensation benefits paid to employee

(a) Any recovery in excess of workers' compensation benefits received belongs to injured employee

(b) To the extent that recovery duplicates benefits already obtained from employer (or carrier), that employer (or carrier) is entitled to reimbursement from employee

EXAMPLE: Kraig, an employee of Badger Corporation, was injured in an auto accident while on the job. The accident was due to the negligence of Todd. Kraig can recover under workers' compensation and also fully recover from Todd in a civil court case. However, Kraig must reimburse the workers' compensation carrier to the extent the recovery from Todd duplicates benefits already obtained under workers' compensation laws.

b. If employee accepts workers' compensation benefits, employer (or its insurance carrier) is subrogated to rights of employee against third party who caused injury

(1) Therefore, if employee elects not to sue third party, employer (or its insurance carrier) obtains employee's right of action against third person

9. Claims

a. Employees are required to file claim forms on timely basis

10. Benefits

a. Medical

(1) Provides for medical care to injured or diseased employee

b. Disability

(1) This is partial wage continuation plan

c. Death

(1) Various plans and schedules provide payments to widow(er) and minor children

d. Special provisions

(1) Normally, statutes call for specific scheduled payments for loss of limb or eye

(2) Also, if employee's injury is of a nature that prevents his/her returning to his/her occupation, plan may pay cost of retraining

e. Normally not subject to waiver by employee

C. Torts of Employee

1. Employer is generally liable to third parties for torts of employee if committed within the course and scope of his/her employment

a. Note that third party may hold both liable up to full damages

D. Employee Safety

1. Occupational Safety and Health Act (OSHA)

   a. OSHA applies to almost all employers except federal government, state governments, and certain industries subject to other safety regulations
   b. Purpose of OSHA is to promote safety standards and job safety
   c. Occupational Safety and Health Administration (OSHA) administers this law

       (1) OSHA develops and enforces standards in work place on health and safety
       (2) OSHA investigates complaints and makes inspections of workplace

          (a) Employers can require OSHA to get search warrant for inspection

              1] Search warrant issued based on probable cause

                 a] High employee complaint rate can form probable cause

       (3) Employers required to keep records of job-related injuries and report serious accidents to OSHA
       (4) Employers required to comply with regulations set by OSHA
       (5) Employers are prohibited from discriminating against or discharging employees for exercising his/her rights under OSHA
       (6) OSHA may assess civil penalties for violations
       (7) Employers may be criminally liable if willful violation results in death of employee

          (a) Possible fine, imprisonment, or both

E. Employment Discrimination

1. Title VII of the Civil Rights Act of 1964 forbids discrimination in employment on the basis of race, color, religion, sex, or national origin

   a. Applies to employers and labor unions having fifteen or more employees whose business affects interstate commerce

       (1) By amendment, applies to federal, state, and local government employees

   b. Job discrimination applies to discrimination in hiring, promotion, transfers, firing, compensation, etc.
   c. Enforced by Equal Employment Opportunity Commission (EEOC) which is a federal government administrative agency, or by lawsuits of private individuals
   d. Not necessarily illegal to treat employees differently, but

       (1) Illegal discrimination occurs when employee treated differently than person of other race, color, religion, sex, or national origin
       (2) Illegal discrimination may occur when employer adopts rules that adversely affect a member of a protected class

           EXAMPLE: Rules requiring certain standards on weight, height, or strength

       (3) Illegal discrimination may be proven statistically to show pattern of discrimination
       (4) Defendant may have defenses to Title VII violations

          (a) Bona fide occupational qualification
          (b) Bona fide seniority or merit system
          (c) Professionally developed ability test
          (d) National security reasons

2. Age Discrimination in Employment Act

   a. Generally applies to individuals at least forty years old

       (1) Remedies for violations of Act

        (a) Monetary damages including back pay

        (b) Reinstatement

        (c) Promotion

   b. Applies to most businesses employing at least twenty people

   c. Generally prohibits mandatory retirement under age seventy

3. Vocational Rehabilitation Act of 1973 applies to employers with federal contracts over $2,500

   a. Employers required to take affirmative action to employ and advance qualified handicapped individuals

4. Americans with Disabilities Act (ADA)

   a. Applies to employers with at least fifteen employees

   b. Forbids companies and most other entities from discriminating against qualified persons with a disability in various employment decisions including hiring, firing, promotion, and pay

     (1) Qualified individual with disability means person who can perform essential functions of job either with or without reasonable accommodation

        (a) Reasonable accommodation may include acquiring new equipment, modifying facilities, restructuring jobs, modifying work schedules, etc. unless employer can show undue hardship based on significant expense or hardship

   c. ADA protects disabled persons from discrimination and guarantees them equal access to, among others,

     (1) Public services including public transportation and public accommodations

     (2) Public services operated by private entities

   d. Enforcement may be by attorney general or by private legal action

5. Pregnancy Discrimination Act

   a. Employers prohibited from discriminating against employees becoming pregnant or giving birth

     (1) Unmarried and married woman are covered

     (2) Employers' health and disability insurance must cover pregnancy the same as any other medical condition

6. Vietnam Era Veterans Readjustment Assistance Act

   a. Employers with federal contracts of $10,000 or more must take affirmative action in hiring and promoting qualified veterans of the Vietnam war or qualified disabled veterans

7. Discrimination based on religion

   a. Employer must accommodate employee's religious practices, beliefs, and observances unless it is an undue hardship on employer's business

8. Equal Pay Act

   a. Requires equal pay for equal work for both sexes

   b. Differences in pay may be based on merit, quality of work, seniority, shift differentials

   c. Enforced by Equal Employment Opportunity Commission (EEOC)

   d. To remedy violations, back pay may be required and wages of wronged employees must be raised to eliminate disparity

     (1) Other employees' wages may not be reduced instead

9. Affirmative Action

   a. Policies that

     (1) Encourage employers to correct present conditions or practices that cause discrimination, or

     (2) Provide for affirmative steps to increase in work forces the hiring of minorities and females

10. Family and Medical Leave Act

    a. Covers employees employed for at least twelve months for at least 1250 hours by employers having at least fifty employees

    b. Employees have right to up to twelve workweeks of leave during a twelve-month period for any of following reasons

       (1) Employee's own serious health problem
       (2) To care for serious health problem of parent, spouse, or child
       (3) Birth and care of baby
       (4) Child placed with employee for adoption or foster care

    c. Leave of twelve weeks may be done intermittently for cases of serious health problems of employee or his/her covered relatives

    d. Typically, leave is without pay

    e. When employee returns, s/he must get back same or equivalent position

    f. Returning employee cannot lose benefits due to leave

    g. Employers who deny these rights to employee are civilly liable for damages

11. Health Insurance Portability and Accountability Act

    a. Restricts using exclusions for preexisting conditions in employer sponsored group health insurance policies

12. Whistleblower Protection Act

    a. Federal law that protects federal employees from retaliation by employers for blowing the whistle on employers

    b. Majority of states also have laws that protect whistleblowers from employers' retaliation

F. Federal Fair Labor Standards Act

1. Applies to all businesses that affect interstate commerce
2. All covered employees must be paid at least "the minimum wage"

    a. Computer professionals have a much higher minimum wage

    b. Employees younger than twenty may be hired for a somewhat lower "opportunity wage" for ninety calendar days

3. Workers who work more than forty hours per week must be paid time and a half

    a. Regulates number of hours in standard work week

4. Some employees are not covered under some or all of the minimum wage and time-and-a-half provisions

    a. For example, professionals, executives, outside salespersons

5. Some employees must get at least minimum wage but are not covered by the overtime rules

    a. For example, taxi drivers, railroad employees

6. Employees may be paid based on various time bases such as hourly, weekly, monthly, etc.
7. Enforced by Department of Labor and may include fines and/or prison

G. National Labor Relations Act (Wagner Act)

1. Provides that employees have right to join, assist, or form labor organizations
2. Employers are required to bargain with union about work-related issues such as firing practices, working hours, retirement rules, safety conditions, and pay, including sick pay and vacation pay

H. Taft-Hartley Act

1. Prohibits certain unfair labor practices of unions such as secondary boycotts and featherbedding (requirements to pay employees for work not actually performed)
2. Provides for cooling-off period, in some cases, before a strike can take place

I.   Landrum-Griffin Act

1.   Requires extensive financial reporting involving unions
2.   Provides for civil and criminal action against misdeeds of union officers
3.   Provides for bill of rights for union members in conducting meetings and elections

J.   Federal Consolidated Budget Reconciliation Act (COBRA)

1.   Provides that when employee quits, s/he may keep same group health insurance coverage for eighteen months for that former employee and spouse

  a.   Former employee pays for it
  b.   Trade Act increases election period to keep same coverage

K. Pensions

1.   Employee Retirement Income Security Act (ERISA)

  a.   Does not require employer to set up pension plan
  b.   If employer does set up plan, it must meet certain standards

    (1) Generally, employee contributions to pension plan vest immediately
    (2) In general, employee's rights to employer's contributions to pension plan vest from five to seven years after beginning employment based on formulas in law
    (3) Standards on investment of funds are set up to avoid mismanagement
    (4) Employers cannot delay employee's participation in pension plan
    (5) Covered plans must give annual reports to employees in plan

2.   In noncontributory pension plan, employee does not pay but employer pays for all
3.   Maximum punishments for violations of Act by individuals increased to imprisonment of ten years and fine of $100,000—by entities, maximum fine is increased to $500,000
4.   Sarbanes-Oxley act requires administrators of employee benefit and profit sharing plans to provide participants and beneficiaries thirty-day advance notice of blackout periods when their rights are temporarily suspended to make changes in plan

  a.   Criminal penalties increased by significantly greater fines and longer imprisonment terms

    (1) Based on intent of reducing excesses of some corporations and holding officers and directors more accountable

  b.   Prohibits officers and directors from acquiring or transferring stock for services to corporation during blackout periods

L.   Worker Adjustment and Retraining Notification Act

1.   Provides that employers before they close a plant or have mass layoffs must give sixty days notice to employees as well as to state and local officials
2.   Act allows shorter notice period in case of emergencies or failing companies

M. Federal Employee Polygraph Protection Act

1.   Private employers may not require employees or prospective employees to take lie detector test or make adverse employment decisions based on such tests or refusals to take them

  a.   Act allows polygraph tests to be used by

    (1) Security services hiring employees to protect public health and safety
    (2) Employers that deal with national defense issues
    (3) Drug manufacturers and distributors

  b.   Government employers exempted
  c.   Private employer may use lie detector tests as part of investigation of economic loss when employer has reason to suspect individual

    (1) Employee cannot be disciplined based solely on test

(2) Employer is limited in topics of questions that violate privacy especially in topics not directly related to investigation of economic loss

N. Environmental Regulation

1. Under common law

a. Parties may be liable under doctrine of nuisance

(1) Based on party using property in manner that unreasonably interferes with another's right to use and enjoy property
(2) Typically, monetary damages is remedy rather than injunction
(3) Often, plaintiffs need to show their injury is distinct from harm of public in general

b. Businesses may be liable for negligence

(1) Plaintiff shows that his/her harm was caused by business polluter who failed to use reasonable care to prevent foreseeable harm

c. Businesses may be liable under strict liability if involved in ultrahazardous activities

EXAMPLE: B is in the business of transporting radioactive materials. Strict liability may be used which makes B liable for all damages it causes without the need to prove negligence.

2. Under federal statutory laws

a. Environmental Protection Agency (EPA)

(1) Administrative agency set up to ensure compliance with environmental protection laws
(2) EPA may enforce federal environmental laws by use of administrative orders and/or civil penalties

(a) May also refer criminal or civil actions to Department of Justice

(3) EPA also adopts regulations and conducts research on environment and effects of pollution
(4) Most environmental statutes provide for criminal liability

(a) Generally, corporate officers must be "blameworthy," based on ability to prevent or correct, to be criminally liable

(5) EPA generally uses civil suits more than criminal prosecutions because civil suits require preponderance of evidence to win but criminal convictions require proof beyond a reasonable doubt
(6) Private citizens may also sue violators or may sue EPA to enforce compliance with laws
(7) States may also sue violators

b. National Environmental Policy Act

(1) Requires all federal agencies consider environmental factors in all major decisions

(a) Requires preparation of environmental impact statement (EIS) when federal action or proposed laws significantly affect environment

1] Shows expected impact on environment
2] Describes adverse consequences of action that are unavoidable
3] Must examine alternatives to achieve goals
4] For EIS, environment means more than natural environment—can include aesthetic, cultural, and national heritage interests, etc.

(b) If agency finds no EIS is warranted, it must prepare and make available to public document called "Finding of No Significant Impact" with reasons for no action needed

c. Clean Air Act

(1) Provides that EPA set air quality standards for mobile sources, such as autos, and stationary sources, such as factories
(2) Regulates various toxic pollutants, including those that affect acid rain and ozone layer

   (3) Act allows private citizens to sue violators of Act

       (a) Those winning successful citizens' lawsuits can get attorneys' fees and court costs

   (4) Encourages and requires use of alternative fuels to help meet pollution goals
   (5) Federal government may force recall of automobiles violating emission regulations
   (6) EPA can assess stated civil penalties

       (a) When company finds it cost effective to violate Clean Air Act, EPA may wage penalty equal to benefit company received by not complying
       (b) Criminal fines and imprisonment for knowing violations

   (7) Amendments to Clean Air Act allow companies to trade some rights to pollute
   (8) Recent Supreme Court case says that Clean Air Act does not require EPA to consider cost in making air clean

d. Clean Water Act

   (1) EPA sets standards to reduce, eliminate, or prevent pollution of rivers, seas, ponds, wetlands, streams, etc.

       (a) For example, controls dredging or filling of rivers and wetlands

   (2) Owners of point sources such as floating vessels, pipes, ditches, and animal feeding operations must obtain permits which control water pollution

       (a) Nonpoint sources such as farms, forest lands, and mining are exempt

   (3) Broad in scope—includes regulation of discharge of heated water (e.g., by nuclear power plant or electric utilities)
   (4) Provides for fines and prison for neglect or knowing violations or endangerment (i.e., knowingly putting person in imminent danger of death or serious bodily harm)

e. Safe Drinking Water Act

   (1) Regulates safety of water supplied to homes by public water systems
   (2) Prohibits discharge of waste into wells for drinking water

f. Oil Pollution Act

   (1) Requires establishment of oil pollution cleanup contingency plans by tanker owners and operators to handle worst case spills under adverse weather conditions
   (2) Requires that new tankers have double hulls
   (3) Requires phase-in of double hulls on existing oil tankers and barges

g. Noise Control Act

   (1) Regulates noise pollution and encourages research on its effects
   (2) EPA establishes noise standards for products sold in US
   (3) Violations may result in fines, imprisonment, or injunctions

h. Resource Conservation and Recovery Act

   (1) Creates permit system to regulate businesses that store, use, or transport hazardous waste
   (2) Requires companies to keep strict records of hazardous waste from "cradle to grave" transport
   (3) Producers required to label and package correctly hazardous materials that are to be transported
   (4) Fines and prison for violators

       (a) Can be doubled for certain violations

   (5) Also, household waste regulated

i. Toxic Substances Control Act

   (1) Mandates testing and regulation of chemicals that pose unreasonable risk to health or environment

(a) Requires testing before marketing allowed

(2) Requires special labeling of toxic substances

j. Federal Insecticide, Fungicide, and Rodenticide Act

(1) Provides that pesticides and herbicides must be registered with EPA before sale
(2) EPA can

(a) Deny registration
(b) Certify them for general or restricted use
(c) Suspend registration if emergency or imminent danger

(3) Limits set for amount of pesticide residue permitted on crops for human or animal consumption
(4) Act has labeling requirements
(5) Violators subject to fine and imprisonment
(6) Private party may petition EPA to suspend or cancel registration

k. Federal Environmental Pesticide Control Act

(1) All who distribute pesticides must register them with EPA
(2) EPA uses cost-benefit analysis to decide to register pesticides rather than deciding if they will pose health hazard

l. Comprehensive Environmental, Compensation, and Liability Act (CERCLA)

(1) Often known as the Superfund legislation
(2) Levies taxes on manufacturers of certain dangerous chemicals
(3) Identifies hazardous waste sites needed to be cleaned up
(4) Regulates generation and transportation of hazardous substances

(a) Does not regulate petroleum or natural gas

(5) Government can impose broad liability for cleanup costs and environmental damages

(a) Parties have **joint and several liability** and include

1] **Current owners and operators** of site
2] **Past owners and operators** of site
3] Persons who **transported** waste to site
4] Persons who arranged to have waste transported

(b) With limited exceptions, the standard is based on **strict liability** for all cleanup costs
(c) One who is responsible for portion of waste can be liable for all cleanup costs
(d) Liability is retroactive under this statute
(e) Only three narrow defenses are allowed under this statute: acts of God, war, or unrelated third parties
(f) CERCLA does **not** make polluters liable to private parties; they generally use private suits under common law

m. Emergency Planning, and Community Right-to-Know Act

(1) Companies having specified amounts of extremely hazardous substances must notify state and local agencies and also must issue annual reports of releases of specified toxic chemicals that result from operations

(a) This information is available to public

n. International protection of ozone layer

(1) Many countries, including US, have agreed to reduce or eliminate certain chemicals believed to harm ozone layer

o. Nuclear Waste Policy Act

           (1) Creates national plan to dispose of highly radioactive nuclear waste
           (2) State may regulate emissions of radioactive particles under Clean Air Act

      p. Marine Protection, Research, and Sanctuaries Act

           (1) Regulates dumping into oceans
           (2) Establishing marine sanctuaries

      q. Endangered Species Act

           (1) Enforced by both EPA and Department of Commerce
           (2) Protects both endangered as well as threatened species

      r. Pollution Prevention Act

           (1) Provides incentives to industry to prevent some pollution from initially being formed

      s. SEC requires that companies report in financial statements their environmental liabilities

  3. Environmental Compliance Audits

      a. These are systematic, objective reviews designed to evaluate compliance with federal and state regulations and laws on environment

           (1) Some states have environmental audit privilege laws

      b. Purposes of audit

           (1) To discover violations or questionable practices to allow company to avoid litigation
           (2) Voluntary discovery to avoid criminal sanctions
           (3) To meet disclosure requirements under securities laws

O. Telephone Consumer Protection Act

  1. Restricts use of prerecorded messages
  2. Act requires that in order to use prerecorded messages, a live person must introduce prerecorded message and receive from telephoned person permission to play that message

      a. Act exempts calls by nonprofit organizations, calls made for emergencies, and call to businesses
      b. Act does not cover personal phone calls

P. Federal Telecommunications Act

  1. Prevents local or state governments from preventing entry of the growing telecommunications industry

Q. Identity Theft

  1. Increased penalties
  2. FTC is appointed to help victims of identity theft to restore credit and minimize impacts of identity theft

MULTIPLE-CHOICE QUESTIONS (1-44)

1. Taxes payable under the Federal Unemployment Tax Act (FUTA) are
    a. Calculated as a fixed percentage of all compensation paid to an employee.
    b. Deductible by the employer as a business expense for federal income tax purposes.
    c. Payable by employers for all employees.
    d. Withheld from the wages of all covered employees.

2. An unemployed CPA generally would receive unemployment compensation benefits if the CPA
    a. Was fired as a result of the employer's business reversals.
    b. Refused to accept a job as an accountant while receiving extended benefits.
    c. Was fired for embezzling from a client.
    d. Left work voluntarily without good cause.

3. After serving as an active director of Lee Corp. for twenty years, Ryan was appointed an honorary director with the obligation to attend directors' meetings with no voting power. In 2001, Ryan received an honorary director's fee of $5,000. This fee is
    a. Reportable by Lee as employee compensation subject to social security tax.
    b. Reportable by Ryan as self-employment income subject to social security self-employment tax.
    c. Taxable as "other income" by Ryan, **not** subject to any social security tax.
    d. Considered to be a gift **not** subject to social security self-employment or income tax.

4. Syl Corp. does **not** withhold FICA taxes from its employees' compensation. Syl voluntarily pays the entire FICA tax for its share and the amounts that it could have withheld from the employees. The employees' share of FICA taxes paid by Syl to the IRS is
    a. Deductible by Syl as additional compensation that is includible in the employees' taxable income.
    b. Not deductible by Syl because it does **not** meet the deductibility requirement as an ordinary and necessary business expense.
    c. A nontaxable gift to each employee, provided that the amount is less than $1,000 annually to each employee.
    d. Subject to prescribed penalties imposed on Syl for its failure to withhold required payroll taxes.

5. Social security benefits may include all of the following **except**
    a. Payments to divorced spouses.
    b. Payments to disabled children.
    c. Medicare payments.
    d. Medicaid payments.

6. Which of the following forms of income, if in excess of the annual exempt amount, will cause a reduction in a retired person's social security benefits?
    a. Annual proceeds from an annuity.
    b. Director's fees.
    c. Pension payments.
    d. Closely held corporation stock dividends.

7. Which of the following payments are deducted from an employee's salary?

	Unemployment compensation insurance	Worker's compensation insurance
a.	Yes	Yes
b.	Yes	No
c.	No	Yes
d.	No	No

8. Which of the following types of income is subject to taxation under the provisions of the Federal Insurance Contributions Act (FICA)?
    a. Interest earned on municipal bonds.
    b. Capital gains of $3,000.
    c. Car received as a productivity award.
    d. Dividends of $2,500.

9. Under the Federal Insurance Contributions Act (FICA), which of the following acts will cause an employer to be liable for penalties?

	Failure to supply taxpayer identification numbers	Failure to make timely FICA deposits
a.	Yes	Yes
b.	Yes	No
c.	No	Yes
d.	No	No

10. Which of the following parties generally is ineligible to collect workers' compensation benefits?
    a. Minors.
    b. Truck drivers.
    c. Union employees.
    d. Temporary office workers.

11. Kroll, an employee of Acorn, Inc., was injured in the course of employment while operating a forklift manufactured and sold to Acorn by Trell Corp. The forklift was defectively designed by Trell. Under the state's mandatory workers' compensation statute, Kroll will be successful in

	Obtaining workers' compensation benefits	A negligence action against Acorn
a.	Yes	Yes
b.	Yes	No
c.	No	Yes
d.	No	No

12. Which of the following provisions is basic to all workers' compensation systems?
    a. The injured employee must prove the employer's negligence.
    b. The employer may invoke the traditional defense of contributory negligence.
    c. The employer's liability may be ameliorated by a coemployee's negligence under the fellow-servant rule.
    d. The injured employee is allowed to recover on strict liability theory.

13. Workers' Compensation Acts require an employer to
    a. Provide coverage for all eligible employees.
    b. Withhold employee contributions from the wages of eligible employees.
    c. Pay an employee the difference between disability payments and full salary.
    d. Contribute to a federal insurance fund.

14. Generally, which of the following statements concerning workers' compensation laws is correct?
   a. The amount of damages recoverable is based on comparative negligence.
   b. Employers are strictly liable without regard to whether or **not** they are at fault.
   c. Workers' compensation benefits are **not** available if the employee is negligent.
   d. Workers' compensation awards are payable for life.

15. Workers' compensation laws provide for all of the following benefits **except**
   a. Burial expenses.
   b. Full pay during disability.
   c. The cost of prosthetic devices.
   d. Monthly payments to surviving dependent children.

16. Which of the following claims is(are) generally covered under workers' compensation statutes?

	Occupational disease	Employment aggravated preexisting disease
a.	Yes	Yes
b.	Yes	No
c.	No	Yes
d.	No	No

17. Under which of the following conditions is an on-site inspection of a workplace by an investigator from the Occupational Safety and Health Administration (OSHA) permissible?
   a. Only if OSHA obtains a search warrant after showing probable cause.
   b. Only if the inspection is conducted after working hours.
   c. At the request of employees.
   d. After OSHA provides the employer with at least twenty-four hours notice of the prospective inspection.

18. Which of the following Acts prohibit(s) an employer from discriminating among employees based on sex?

	Equal Pay Act	Title VII of the Civil Rights Act
a.	Yes	Yes
b.	Yes	No
c.	No	Yes
d.	No	No

19. Under the Age Discrimination in Employment Act, which of the following remedies is(are) available to a covered employee?

	Early Retirement	Back pay
a.	Yes	Yes
b.	Yes	No
c.	No	Yes
d.	No	No

20. Which of the following company policies would violate the Age Discrimination in Employment Act?
   a. The company will not hire any accountant below twenty-five years of age.
   b. The office staff must retire at age sixty-five or younger.
   c. Both of the above.
   d. None of the above.

21. Under the provisions of the Americans With Disabilities Act of 1990, in which of the following areas is a disabled person protected from discrimination?

	Public transportation	Privately operated public accommodations
a.	Yes	Yes
b.	Yes	No
c.	No	Yes
d.	No	No

22. Under the Americans with Disabilities Act, which is(are) true?
   I. The Act requires that companies with at least ten employees set up a specified plan to hire people with disabilities.
   II. The Act requires companies to make reasonable accommodations for disabled persons unless this results in undue hardship on the operations of the company.

   a. I only.
   b. II only.
   c. Both I and II.
   d. Neither I nor II.

23. The Americans With Disabilities Act has as a purpose to give remedies for discrimination to individuals with disabilities. Which of the following is(are) true of this Act?
   I. It protects most individuals with disabilities working for companies but only if the companies do not need to incur any expenses to modify the work environment to accommodate the disability.
   II. It may require a company to modify work schedules to accommodate persons with disabilities.
   III. It may require a company to purchase equipment at company expense to accommodate persons with disabilities.

   a. I only.
   b. I and II only.
   c. II and III only.
   d. III only.

24. Which of the following is **not** true under the Family and Medical Leave Act?
   a. An employee has a right to take a leave from work for the birth and care of her child for one month at half of her regular pay.
   b. An employee has a right to take a leave from work for twelve workweeks to care for his/her seriously ill parent.
   c. An employee, upon returning under the provisions of the Act, must get back the same or equivalent position in the company.
   d. This Act does not cover all employees.

25. The Family Medical Leave Act provides for
   I. Unpaid leave for the employee to care for a newborn baby.
   II. Unpaid leave for the employee to care for the serious health problem of his or her parent.
   III. Paid leave for the employee to care for a serious health problem of his or her spouse.

a. I only.
b. II only.
c. I and II but not III.
d. III but not I or II.

26. Under the Fair Labor Standards Act, which of the following pay bases may be used to pay covered, nonexempt employees who earn, on average, the minimum hourly wage?

	Hourly	Weekly	Monthly
a.	Yes	Yes	Yes
b.	Yes	Yes	No
c.	Yes	No	Yes
d.	No	Yes	Yes

27. Under the Fair Labor Standards Act, if a covered, nonexempt employee works consecutive weeks of forty-five, forty-two, thirty-eight, and thirty-three hours, how many hours of overtime must be paid to the employee?
a. 0
b. 7
c. 18
d. 20

28. Which of the following employee benefits is(are) exempt from the provisions of the National Labor Relations Act?

	Sick pay	Vacation pay
a.	Yes	Yes
b.	Yes	No
c.	No	Yes
d.	No	No

29. Under the Federal Consolidated Budget Reconciliation Act of 1985 (COBRA), when an employee voluntarily resigns from a job, the former employee's group health insurance coverage that was in effect during the period of employment with the company
a. Automatically ceases for the former employee and spouse, if the resignation occurred before normal retirement age.
b. Automatically ceases for the former employee's spouse, but continues for the former employee for an eighteen-month period at the former employer's expense.
c. May be retained by the former employee at the former employee's expense for at least eighteen months after leaving the company, but must be terminated for the former employee's spouse.
d. May be retained for the former employee and spouse at the former employee's expense for at least eighteen months after leaving the company.

30. Under the Employee Retirement Income Security Act of 1974 (ERISA), which of the following areas of private employer pension plans is(are) regulated?

	Employee vesting	Plan funding
a.	Yes	Yes
b.	Yes	No
c.	No	Yes
d.	No	No

31. Under the provisions of the Employee Retirement Income Security Act of 1974 (ERISA), which of the following statements is correct?

a. Employees are entitled to have an employer established pension plan.
b. Employers are prevented from unduly delaying an employee's participation in a pension plan.
c. Employers are prevented from managing retirement plans.
d. Employees are entitled to make investment decisions.

32. Under the Comprehensive Environmental Response, Compensation, and Liability Act (CERCLA), commonly known as Superfund, which of the following parties would be liable to the Environmental Protection Agency (EPA) for the expense of cleaning up a hazardous waste disposal site?

I. The current owner or operator of the site.
II. The person who transported the wastes to the site.
III. The person who owned or operated the site at the time of the disposal.

a. I and II.
b. I and III.
c. II and III.
d. I, II, and III.

33. Which of the following activities is(are) regulated under the Federal Water Pollution Control Act (Clean Water Act)?

	Discharge of heated water by nuclear power plants	Dredging of wetlands
a.	Yes	Yes
b.	Yes	No
c.	No	Yes
d.	No	No

34. Environmental Compliance Audits are used for which of the following purpose(s)?

I. To voluntarily discover violations to avoid criminal sanctions.
II. To discover violations to avoid civil litigation.
III. To meet disclosure requirements to the SEC under the securities laws.

a. I only.
b. I and II only.
c. II only.
d. I, II and III.

35. Which of the following is(are) true under the Federal Insecticide, Fungicide, and Rodenticide Act?

I. Herbicides and pesticides must be certified and can be used only for applications that are approved.
II. Herbicides and pesticides must be registered under the Act before companies can sell them.
III. Pesticides, when used on food crops, can only be used in quantities that are limited under the Act.

a. I only.
b. I and II only.
c. II and III only.
d. I, II, and III.

36. Under the Comprehensive Environmental Response, Compensation and Liability Act as amended by the Superfund Amendments, which of the following is(are) true?

I. The present owner of land can be held liable for cleanup of hazardous chemicals placed on the land by a previous owner.

II. An employee of a company that had control over the disposal of hazardous substances on the company's land can be held personally liable for cleanup costs.

    a.   I only.
    b.   II only.
    c.   Both I and II.
    d.   Neither I nor II.

37. The National Environmental Policy Act was passed to enhance and preserve the environment. Which of the following is **not** true?

    a.   The Act applies to all federal agencies.
    b.   The Act requires that an environmental impact statement be provided if any proposed federal legislation may significantly affect the environment.
    c.   Enforcement of the Act is primarily accomplished by litigation of persons who decide to challenge federal government decisions.
    d.   The Act provides generous tax breaks to those companies that help accomplish national environmental policy.

38. Under the federal statutes governing water pollution, which of the following areas is(are) regulated?

	Dredging of coastal or freshwater wetlands	Drinking water standards
a.	Yes	Yes
b.	Yes	No
c.	No	Yes
d.	No	No

39. The Clean Air Act provides for the enforcement of standards for

I. The emissions of radioactive particles from private nuclear power plants.

II. The emissions of pollution from privately owned automobiles.

III. The emissions of air pollution from factories.

    a.   I and II only.
    b.   I and III only.
    c.   II and III only.
    d.   I, II and III.

40. Under the Clean Air Act, which of the following statements is(are) correct regarding actions that may be taken against parties who violate emission standards?

I. The federal government may require an automobile manufacturer to recall vehicles that violate emission standards.

II. A citizens' group may sue to force a coal burning power plant to comply with emission standards.

    a.   I only.
    b.   II only.
    c.   Both I and II.
    d.   Neither I nor II.

41. The Environmental Protection Agency is an administrative agency in the federal government that aids in the protection of the environment. Which of the following is **not** a purpose or function of this agency?

    a.   It adopts regulations to protect the quality of water.
    b.   It aids private citizens to make cases for private civil litigation.
    c.   It may refer criminal matters to the Department of Justice.
    d.   It may refer civil cases to the Department of Justice.

42. Whenever a federal agency recommends actions or legislation that may affect the environment, the agency must prepare an environmental impact statement. Which of the following is **not** required in the environmental impact statement?

    a.   A description of the source of funds to accomplish the action without harming the environment.
    b.   An examination of alternate methods of achieving the goals of the proposed actions or legislation.
    c.   A description in detail of the proposed actions or legislation on the environment.
    d.   A description of any unavoidable adverse consequences.

43. Which of the following is(are) possible when a company violates the Clean Air Act?

I. The company can be assessed a criminal fine.

II. Officers of the company can be imprisoned.

III. The Environmental Protection Agency may assess a civil penalty equal to the savings of costs by the company for noncompliance.

    a.   I only.
    b.   I or II only.
    c.   III only.
    d.   I, II or III.

44. Green, a former owner of Circle Plant, caused hazardous waste pollution at the Circle Plant site two years ago. Sason purchased the plant and caused more hazardous waste pollution. It can be shown that 20% of the problem was caused by Green and that 80% of the problem was caused by Sason. Sason went bankrupt recently. The government wishes to clean up the site and hold Green liable. Which of the following is true?

    a.   The most Green can be held liable for is 20%.
    b.   Green is not liable for any of the cleanup costs since the site was sold.
    c.   Green is not liable for any of the cleanup costs because Green was responsible for less than half of the problem.
    d.   Green can be held liable for all the cleanup costs even if Sason has some funds.

PROBLEM

NOTE: These types of problems are no longer included in the CPA Examination but they have been retained because they are useful in developing skills to complete simulations.

Problem 1 (15 to 20 minutes)

Maple owns 75% of the common stock of Salam Exterminating, Inc. Maple is not an officer or employee of the corporation, and does not serve on its board of directors. Salam is in the business of providing exterminating services to residential and commercial customers.

Dodd performed exterminating services on behalf of Salam. Dodd suffered permanent injuries as a result of inhaling one of the chemicals used by Salam. This occurred after Dodd sprayed the chemical in a restaurant that Salam regularly services. Dodd was under the supervision of one of Salam's district managers and was trained by Salam to perform exterminating services following certain procedures, which he did. Later that day several patrons who ate at the restaurant also suffered permanent injuries as a result of inhaling the chemical. The chemical was manufactured by Ace Chemical Corp. and sold and delivered to Salam in a closed container. It was not altered by Salam. It has now been determined that the chemical was defectively manufactured and the injuries suffered by Dodd and the restaurant patrons were a direct result of the defect.

Salam has complied with an applicable compulsory workers' compensation statute by obtaining an insurance policy from Spear Insurance Co.

As a result of the foregoing, the following actions have been commenced:

• Dodd sued Spear to recover workers' compensation benefits.

• Dodd sued Salam based on negligence in training him.

• Dodd sued Ace based on strict liability in tort.

• The restaurant patrons sued Maple claiming negligence in not preventing Salam from using the chemical purchased from Ace.

Required:

Discuss the merits of the actions commenced by Dodd and the restaurant patrons, indicating the likely outcomes and your reasons therefor.

SIMULATION PROBLEM

Simulation Problem 1   (5 to 10 minutes)

For each of the numbered items, indicate: Yes, this item is considered to be wages under the Social Security Act, or No, this item is **not** considered to be wages under the Social Security Act.

		Yes	*No*
1.	Wages, paid in money, to a construction worker.	O	O
2.	Reimbursed normal travel expenses of a salesperson.	O	O
3.	Compensation not paid in cash.	O	O
4.	Commissions of a salesperson.	O	O
5.	Bonuses paid to employees.	O	O
6.	Employee insurance premiums paid by the employer.	O	O
7.	Wages paid to a secretary who is working part time.	O	O
8.	Vacation allowance pay given to employees who are working full time.	O	O
9.	Wages paid to a full-time secretary who wishes to elect not to be covered under the Social Security Act.	O	O
10.	Tips of a waitress.	O	O

MULTIPLE-CHOICE ANSWERS

1. b __ __	11. b __ __	21. a __ __	31. b __ __	41. b __ __
2. a __ __	12. d __ __	22. b __ __	32. d __ __	42. a __ __
3. b __ __	13. a __ __	23. c __ __	33. a __ __	43. d __ __
4. a __ __	14. b __ __	24. a __ __	34. d __ __	44. d __ __
5. d __ __	15. b __ __	25. c __ __	35. d __ __	
6. b __ __	16. a __ __	26. a __ __	36. c __ __	
7. d __ __	17. c __ __	27. b __ __	37. d __ __	
8. c __ __	18. a __ __	28. d __ __	38. a __ __	
9. a __ __	19. c __ __	29. d __ __	39. d __ __	1st: __/44 = __%
10. d __ __	20. b __ __	30. a __ __	40. c __ __	2nd: __/44 = __%

MULTIPLE-CHOICE ANSWER EXPLANATIONS

A. Federal Social Security Act

1. (b) Taxes payable under the Federal Unemployment Tax Act (FUTA) are used to provide unemployment compensation benefits to workers who lose jobs and cannot find replacement work. These taxes paid are deductible by the employer as a business expense for federal income tax purposes. Therefore, answer (b) is correct. Answer (c) is incorrect because only those employers who paid wages of $1,500 or more during any calendar quarter or who employed at least one employee for at least one day a week for twenty weeks must pay FUTA taxes. Answer (d) is incorrect because it is the employer, not the employee, who pays the taxes. Answer (a) is incorrect because the taxes payable under the FUTA are calculated as a fixed percentage of only the first $6,000 of wages of each employee.

2. (a) Unemployment compensation is intended for workers who lose jobs through no fault of their own and cannot find replacement work. Answer (a) is correct because a CPA fired as a result of the employer's business reversals is entitled to receive unemployment compensation. Answer (b) is incorrect because an accountant who refuses to accept replacement work offered him/her would not receive unemployment compensation. Answers (c) and (d) are incorrect because unemployment compensation is not intended for an employee whose actions led to his/her loss of a job.

3. (b) Directors' fees are generally treated as self-employment income and thus are subject to social security self-employment tax.

4. (a) Answer (a) is best since the nondeduction of the FICA tax **and** the payment of it by the employer effectively raises the income of the employee. Answer (d) is not correct because although the employer is required to withhold tax on wages and is liable for payment of such tax whether or not it is collected, the employer's liability can be relieved after showing the employee's related income tax liability has been paid. Therefore, since the employer has paid the taxes, the employer is not subject to penalty. Answer (c) is not correct since no mention is made of a gift. Answer (b) is not correct since no reference is made to wages not being an ordinary and necessary business expense.

5. (d) Social security benefits may include payments to spouses, including divorced spouses in some cases, and to children. It may also include medicare payments but not medicaid payments.

6. (b) **Earned** income in excess of the annual limitation will cause a reduction in a retired person's social security benefits. Answer (b) is therefore correct, since "director's fees" are considered earned income. Answers (a), (c), and (d) are incorrect because proceeds from an annuity, pension payments, and stock dividends are not considered earned income.

7. (d) Unemployment insurance tax must be paid by the employer if the employer employs one or more persons covered by the act. Payments for unemployment insurance are not deducted from employees' salaries. Workers' compensation is a form of strict liability whereby the employer is liable to the employee for injuries or diseases sustained by the employee which arise out of and in the course of employment. The insurance is paid by the employer and the cost is passed on as an expense of doing business. Thus, worker's compensation insurance also is not paid by the employee.

8. (c) Social security tax applies to wages, defined as all compensation for employment. Employment compensation does not have to be in the form of cash to be included in wages taxed under the Federal Insurance Contributions Act (FICA). Therefore, a car received as a productivity award is considered employment compensation subject to the social security tax and answers (a), (b), and (d) are incorrect, because these are not wages.

9. (a) Both a failure to supply taxpayer identification numbers and a failure to make timely FICA deposits would be violations of the Act. As all employees are required to participate in Social Security, their identification numbers must be supplied in order to track employment and cumulative FICA tax paid to the government. The Act also explicitly states that an employer's failure to collect and deposit taxes in a timely manner subjects him/her to penalties and interest.

B. Workers' Compensation Act

10. (d) Workers' compensation benefits arise out of a type of strict liability whereby employers are liable for injuries or diseases sustained by employees which arise from the scope of the employment. Temporary office workers are usually either independent contractors or are employees of a separate employment agency. Answer (a) is incorrect because the employment laws are especially meant to protect minors. Answer (b) is incorrect because truck drivers are not exempted. Answer (c) is incorrect because union affiliation does not create an exemption.

11.   (b)   Under workers' compensation laws, any employee injured during the course of employment is entitled to workers' compensation benefits regardless of fault, as long as the injury is not self-inflicted, and not the result of a fight or intoxication. However, acceptance of benefits under workers' compensation laws precludes an employee from suing the employer for damages in a civil court.

12.   (d)   Workers' compensation is a form of strict liability in which an employer is liable to employees for injuries or diseases sustained in the course of employment, without regard to fault. Answer (a) is incorrect because the injured employee is not required to establish employer negligence to recover a workers' compensation action. Answer (b) is incorrect because contributory negligence of the employee is not a valid defense in workers' compensation cases. The workers' compensation act removes the employer's common law defense of negligence of a fellow employee, therefore answer (c) is incorrect.

13.   (a)   Workers' Compensation Acts require an employer to provide coverage for all eligible employees. Furthermore, the employer is required to cover the cost of injuries to employees, and no amount is deducted from the employees' wages. Therefore, answer (b) is incorrect. Answer (c) is incorrect because under workers' compensation, the disability benefit payments are usually a percentage of weekly earnings. The employer does not have to make up the difference between the benefit payments and the employee's salary. Answer (d) is incorrect because a business covered under workers' compensation laws may be self-insured but it must show proof of financial responsibility to carry this risk.

14.   (b)   Most workers' compensation laws provide that the employer is strictly liable to an employee without regard to negligence of the employer or employee. Therefore, answers (a) and (c) are incorrect. Answer (d) is incorrect because worker's compensation awards may or may not be payable for life.

15.   (b)   The following are some examples of workers' compensation benefits: burial expenses, the cost of prosthetic devices, monthly payments to surviving dependent children, and **partial** wage continuation during disability.

16.   (a)   Both occupational disease and employment aggravated preexisting disease are covered by the statutes in that all consequences of an injury on the job, regardless of whether such injury was actually caused by an accident, are deemed to be "accidental" injuries resulting from employment. If any conditions in the workplace could have possibly contributed to or aggravated consequences, the doctrine of strict employer liability applies.

D. Employee Safety

17.   (c)   OSHA investigates complaints and makes inspections of the workplace. Employers can require that OSHA obtain a search warrant in most cases to conduct the search. Probable cause is needed to obtain a search warrant and complaints by employees can provide the needed probable cause. Answer (a) is incorrect because the employer can allow the search or give permission, in which cases, search warrants are not needed. Answer (b) is incorrect because inspections can be made during working hours. In fact, this may be the only or most effective time to conduct

the inspection. Answer (d) is incorrect because there is no requirement that OSHA give the employers advance notice of the inspections. Such a requirement would make many inspections less effective.

E. Employment Discrimination

18.   (a)   Under the Equal Pay Act, employers cannot pay some employees less money than that paid to employees of the opposite sex when equal work is performed. Under Title VII of the Civil Rights Act, employers cannot discriminate against a prospective employee on the basis of race, color, national origin, religion, or sex.

19.   (c)   The Age Discrimination in Employment Act does not specifically use the term "back pay" but the Act provides equitable relief as deemed appropriate and otherwise authorizes back pay. The Act does provide for employment reinstatement or promotion, but does not provide for early retirement.

20.   (b)   The Age Discrimination in Employment Act generally prohibits mandatory retirement under age seventy. Answers (a) and (c) are incorrect because the Act generally applies to individuals over forty years old. Answer (d) is incorrect because forced retirement under the age of seventy is generally prohibited under the Act.

21.   (a)   The Americans With Disabilities Act of 1990 prohibits all businesses with fifteen employees or more from considering a person's handicap when making a hiring decision. Also, the act requires businesses to make special accommodations available to handicapped employees and customers, unless the cost is too burdensome. Therefore, answer (a) is correct as the act covers both public transportation and privately operated public accommodations.

22.   (b)   The Americans with Disabilities Act provides the disabled with better access to employment, public accommodations, and transportation. The Act requires companies to make reasonable accommodations for the disabled unless this would cause undue hardship for the business. The Act does not require companies to set up a hiring plan.

23.   (c)   The Americans With Disabilities Act requires most companies and entities to not discriminate against qualified individuals with disabilities who can perform the essential functions of the job either with or without reasonable accommodation, unless the company can show undue hardship. Reasonable accommodation may include purchasing new equipment, modifying facilities, or modifying work schedules.

E.10.   Family and Medical Leave Act

24.   (a)   A covered employee has the right to a leave from work for specified reasons for twelve workweeks in a twelve-month period but typically receives leave without pay. Answer (b) is incorrect because it mentions one of the specified reasons allowed for a leave. Answer (c) is incorrect because an important right under the Act is to get back the same or similar position upon returning. Answer (d) is an incorrect response because not all employees are covered. To be covered employees must have worked for twelve months, for at least 1,250 hours in those twelve months, and be one of at least fifty employees.

25.   (c)   The Act provides for up to twelve workweeks of unpaid leave for the employee to care for serious health problems of his or her parent, spouse, or child. It also provides the same right to care for his or her newborn baby. Note that (d) is incorrect because it provides for paid leave to care for his or her spouse who is seriously ill.

F. Federal Fair Labor Standards Act

26.   (a)   The Fair Labor Standards Act allows employees to be paid on a piecework basis or salary. Workers must receive at least the equivalent of the minimum hourly rate, but the basis on which the workers are paid can be hourly, weekly, or monthly.

27.   (b)   The Fair Labor Standards Act requires overtime pay to be paid when hours worked in any given week exceed forty hours. Therefore, the additional five hours and two hours worked in the first two weeks constitute overtime.

G. National Labor Relations Act (Wagner Act)

28.   (d)   Among other fringe benefits, sick pay and vacation pay are subjects for collective bargaining. Therefore, sick pay and vacation pay are not exempt from the provisions of the National Labor Relations Act.

J. Federal Consolidated Budget Reconciliation Act

29.   (d)   Under the Federal Consolidated Budget Reconciliation Act of 1985 (COBRA), a former employee may retain group health coverage under the employer for him/herself and his/her spouse at the former employee's expense for at least eighteen months after leaving the company. Answer (a) is incorrect because the former employee and spouse may retain the coverage for at least eighteen months. Answers (b) and (c) are incorrect because not only the former employee but also the spouse may retain the coverage for eighteen months at the former employee's expense.

K. Pensions

30.   (a)   If a pension plan is established, employee contributions to the pension plan vest immediately. In addition, standards on investment of funds are set up to avoid mismanagement.

31.   (b)   The Employee Retirement Income Security Act of 1974 (ERISA) does not require an employer to establish a pension plan. Therefore, answer (a) is incorrect. If the employer does set up a plan, it must meet certain standards. These standards prevent employers from unduly delaying an employee's participation in a pension plan. Therefore, answer (b) is correct. Standards are also set up for the investment of funds to avoid mismanagement. However, employers are able to manage the retirement plans. Therefore, answer (c) is incorrect. Answer (d) is incorrect because ERISA provisions do not require that the employees make the investment decisions. This is a function of the particular company's plan.

N. Environmental Regulation

32.   (d)   CERCLA imposes environmental liability on a broad group of potentially responsible parties. The courts have included the following classes: (1) current owners and operators, (2) owners and operators at the time of waste disposal, (3) generators of hazardous waste, (4) transporters of hazardous waste, and (5) lenders who finance borrowers' hazardous waste sites.

33.   (a)   The Clean Water Act regulates the dredging or filling of wetlands. Without a permit, these are generally prohibited. The discharging of heated water by nuclear power plants is also regulated.

34.   (d)   All of the purposes listed are reasons to have an Environmental Compliance Audit. Since the environmental laws and regulations can be complex and may result in both criminal violations and civil liability, both statements I and II are correct. Statement III is also correct because problems with the environmental laws can be significant under the federal securities laws.

35.   (d)   The Federal Insecticide, Fungicide, and Rodenticide Act does have all three of the provisions. Herbicides and pesticides are required to be registered before they can be sold. Furthermore, they need to be used only for the purposes certified. Also, when used on food crops, the amount that can be used is limited.

36.   (c)   The provisions of the Comprehensive Environmental Response, Compensation, and Liability Act (CERCLA) as amended is very broad in scope. If the EPA cleans up the hazardous chemicals, it can recover the costs from any responsible party including present owners of the facility and any person who arranged for the disposal of the hazardous substance.

37.   (d)   The National Environmental Policy Act is centered around requiring the federal government and its agencies to consider the effects of its actions on the environment. It does not provide tax breaks to companies to accomplish environmental goals. Answer (a) is not chosen because it correctly states that the Act applies to all federal agencies. Answer (b) is not chosen because it is also correct. The Act does require an environmental impact statement if the environment may be significantly hurt. Answer (c) is not chosen because private litigation is the main way this Act is enforced.

38.   (a)   The Clean Water Act regulates the dredging of both coastal and freshwater wetlands. The Safe Drinking Water act regulates the safety of water supplied by public water systems to homes.

39.   (d)   The Clean Air Act regulates emissions into the air from automobiles, factories, and nuclear power plants. Note that emissions from the nuclear power plant are handled by the Clean Air Act rather than the Nuclear Waste Policy Act. The latter creates a national plan to dispose of highly radioactive nuclear waste.

40.   (c)   The Clean Air Act sets air quality standards for mobile sources such as autos, and for stationary sources such as power plants. The federal government has ways to encourage and require compliance, such as requiring manufacturers to recall vehicles that violate emission standards. The Act also allows private citizens to sue violators to enforce compliance.

41.   (b)   The Environmental Protection Agency (EPA) is an administrative agency designed to aid the federal government in national environmental policy. When citizens have private lawsuits about the environment, they would typically seek remedies by resorting to common law or statutory remedies. The Environmental Protection Agency was not set up to help in this manner. This agency does, however, adopt regulations on the environment. Therefore answer (a) is not chosen. Answers (c) and (d) are not chosen because the EPA does refer both criminal and civil cases over to the Department of Justice.

42. **(a)**   The environmental impact statement is not designed to show the cost or source of the funds for the actions or legislation being proposed. Answers (b), (c), and (d) are all not chosen because these are all required as part of the environmental impact statement.

43. **(d)**   The Clean Air Act provides for both criminal and civil penalties against violators. For criminal violations, both fines and prison are possible. Civil penalties can also be assessed by the EPA including an amount equal to any benefits in costs for not complying.

44. **(d)**   Green as a part owner is one of the parties that has joint and several liability for the cleanup costs. Even though Sason also has joint and several liability, Green can be held liable for any portion or all of the cleanup costs without regard to percent of responsibility. Answer (a) is incorrect because Green, having joint and several liability, can be held liable for all of the cleanup costs. Answer (b) is incorrect because past as well as present owners have potential liability. Answer (c) is incorrect because there is no such defense as having less than half of the responsibility.

ANSWER OUTLINE

Problem 1 Workers' Compensation; Definition of Employee; Strict Liability; Limited Liability of Shareholders

Dodd is entitled to workers' compensation from Spear
  Dodd is considered an employee because Salam had control over details of Dodd's work and Dodd was subject to Salam's supervision
Dodd will be unsuccessful in his negligence suit
  An employee who receives workers' compensation benefits cannot successfully maintain an action for negligence against his employer seeking additional compensation
Dodd will be successful in his action against Ace based on strict liability in tort
  Elements needed to prove strict tort liability are

  1. Product was unreasonably dangerous when it left the seller's hands
  2. Defect caused the injury
  3. Seller normally sells the product
  4. Product was not substantially changed before reaching the buyer

Maple is not liable to restaurant patrons based on negligence
  Shareholders of corporation are insulated from personal liability for negligence of corporation or corporation's employees

UNOFFICIAL ANSWER

Problem 1 Workers' Compensation; Definition of Employee; Strict Liability; Limited Liability of Shareholders

Dodd is entitled to recover workers' compensation benefits from Spear because Dodd was an employee of Salam, the injury was accidental, and the injury occurred out of and in the course of his employment with Salam. Based on the facts of this case, Dodd would be considered an employee and not an independent contractor because Salam had control over the details of Dodd's work by training Dodd to perform the services in a specified manner and Dodd was subject to Salam's supervision.

Dodd will be unsuccessful in his action against Salam based on negligence in training him because Dodd is an employee of Salam and Salam has complied with the applicable compulsory workers' compensation statute by obtaining workers' compensation insurance. Under workers' compensation, an employee who receives workers' compensation benefits cannot successfully maintain an action for negligence against his employer seeking additional compensation. Therefore, whether Salam was negligent in training Dodd is irrelevant.

Dodd's action against Ace based on strict liability in tort will be successful. Generally, in order to establish a cause of action based on strict liability in tort, it must be shown that: the product was in defective condition when it left the possession or control of the seller; the product was unreasonably dangerous to the consumer or user; the cause of the consumer's or user's injury was the defect; the seller engaged in the business of selling such a product; the product was one which the seller expected to, and did reach the consumer or user without substantial changes in the condition in which it was sold. Under the facts of this case, Ace will be liable based on strict liability in tort because all of the elements necessary to state such a cause of action have

been met. The fact that Dodd is entitled to workers' compensation benefits does not preclude Dodd from recovering based on strict liability in tort from a third party (Ace).

Maple will not be liable to the restaurant patrons based on negligence, because shareholders of a corporation are insulated from personal liability for the negligence of the corporation or the corporation's employees. This rule would apply even though Maple owned a controlling interest in the common stock of Salam. Therefore, whether Salam or Dodd was negligent is irrelevant.

SOLUTION TO SIMULATION PROBLEM

Simulation Problem 1

1. **(Y)** Under the Social Security Act, money wages are considered wages.

2. **(N)** Reimbursed travel expenses are generally excluded from wages.

3. **(Y)** Compensation whether in cash or not is generally considered to be wages.

4. **(Y)** Commissions are a method of compensation.

5. **(Y)** Bonuses are a method of compensation.

6. **(N)** Insurance premiums paid by employers for employees generally are excluded from wages.

7. **(Y)** Part-time employees are covered under this law.

8. **(Y)** Vacation allowance pay is another form of compensation.

9. **(Y)** Qualifying employees may not elect to avoid the Social Security Act.

10. **(Y)** Tips are another form of wages.

PROPERTY

Overview

Property entails items capable of being owned (i.e., the rights related to the ownership of things that society will recognize and enforce). Property is classified as real or personal, and as tangible or intangible. Protection of property and settlement of disputes concerning property is a major function of the legal system.

The candidate should be able to distinguish between personal and real property and between tenancies in common, joint tenancies, and tenancies by the entirety. The candidate also should understand that an instrument given primarily as security for real property is a mortgage and be able to distinguish between the legal results arising

from "assumption" of a mortgage and taking "subject to" a mortgage. Other questions concerning mortgages require basic knowledge of the concepts of novation, suretyship, subrogation, redemption, and purchase money mortgages.

Questions on deeds may distinguish between the legal implication of warranty deeds, quitclaim deeds, and special warranty deeds. Both mortgages and deeds should be publicly recorded, and the questions may require the candidate to identify a priority and explain constructive notice. The most important topics under lessor-lessee law are the Statute of Frauds, the effect of a sale of leased property, assignment, and subleasing.

A. Distinctions between Real and Personal Property

1. Real property (realty)—includes land and things attached to land in a relatively permanent manner

   EXAMPLE: A building is erected on a parcel of land. Both the land and the building are real property.

   a. Crops harvested are not real property because they are separate from land
   b. Growing crops are generally part of land and therefore realty

      (1) Growing crops can be sold separately from land in which case they are considered personal property

         (a) True whether buyer or seller will sever growing crops from land

2. Personal property (personalty)—property not classified as real property or a fixture

   a. May be either

      (1) Tangible—subject to physical possession

         EXAMPLE: Automobiles and books are tangible personal property.

      (2) Intangible—not subject to physical possession but subject to legal ownership

         EXAMPLE: Contractual rights to receive payment for automobiles sold are intangible personal property.

3. Fixture—item that was originally personal property but which is affixed to real property in relatively permanent fashion such that it is considered to be part of real property

   a. Several factors are applied in determining whether personal property that has been attached to real property is a fixture

      (1) Affixer's objective intent as to whether property is to be regarded as personalty or realty
      (2) Method and permanence of physical attachment to real property

         (a) If item cannot be removed without material injury to real property, it is generally held that item has become part of realty (i.e., a fixture)

      (3) Adaptability of use of personal property for purpose for which real property is used

         (a) If personal property is necessary or beneficial to use of real property, more likely that item is fixture
         (b) But if use or purpose of item is unusual for type of realty involved, it normally would be personal property

   b. Trade fixture is a fixture installed by tenant in connection with business on leased premises

      EXAMPLE: A tenant who is leasing premises for use as grocery store installs refrigeration unit on property. Refrigeration unit is integral to conducting of business for which tenant occupies premises and therefore qualifies as trade fixture.

      (1) Trade fixtures remain personal property, giving tenant right to remove these items upon expiration of lease

(a) If item is so affixed to real property that removing it would cause substantial damage, then it is considered part of realty

B. Personal Property Can Be Acquired By

1. Gift—a present, voluntary transfer of property without consideration

   a. Necessary elements

      (1) Donative intent by donor
      (2) Delivery
      (3) Acceptance by donee (usually presumed)

   b. Promise to make a gift is unenforceable because it is not a contract due to lack of consideration given by donee
   c. Inter vivos gift is made while donor is living and is irrevocable once completed
   d. Gift causa mortis is a conditional gift in contemplation of death and is automatically revoked if the donor does not die of impending illness or crisis causing gift

2. Will or intestate succession

   a. Property passes under terms of will that is valid at death
   b. If deceased has no valid will (i.e., dies intestate) then property passes under laws of state

3. Finding personal property

   a. Mislaid property

      (1) Happens when owner **voluntarily** puts the property somewhere but forgets to take it
      (2) Finder does **not** obtain title to mislaid property

         (a) Owner of premises becomes caretaker in case true owner of mislaid property comes back

   b. Lost property

      (1) Happens when owner **involuntarily** leaves property somewhere
      (2) Finder has title to lost property which is valid against all parties except the true owner

      EXAMPLE: *A loses his watch. B finds it but C attempts to take it from B even though both know it is not C's watch. B has the right to keep it from C.*

   c. Abandoned property

      (1) Generally, finder has title valid against all parties including owner that abandoned property

C. Bailments

1. Bailment exists when owner of personal property gives possession without giving title to another (bailee)—bailee has duty to either return personal property to bailor or to dispose of it as directed by owner
2. Requirements for creation

   a. Delivery of personal property to bailee
   b. Possession by bailee
   c. Bailee has duty to return property or dispose of property as directed by owner

3. Types of bailments

   a. For benefit of bailor (i.e., bailee takes care of bailor's property)
   b. For mutual benefit (i.e., bailee takes care of bailor's property for a fee)
   c. For benefit of bailee (i.e., bailor gratuitously allows bailee use of his/her property)

4. Bailee's duty of care

   a. Older view depended on the type of bailment (i.e., slight care if for benefit of bailor, ordinary care if for mutual benefit, extreme care if for benefit of bailee)
   b. Now general rule is bailee must take reasonable care in light of the facts and circumstances

       (1) Type of bailment is part of facts and is used to determine what is reasonable care

         (a) Bailee is absolutely liable for delivery to improper person

            1] But a receipt or ticket that is for identification of bailor entitles bailee to deliver bailed goods to holder of ticket without liability

  c. Bailee has absolute liability for unauthorized use of property

  d. Bailee usually cannot limit liability with exculpatory clauses

> *EXAMPLE: A coat check ticket often limits liability on its back side. If the ticket is to be just a means of identification, then the bailee's liability is not limited. If the bailor is aware of the liability limitations statement, liability may be limited if reasonable.*

5. Bailee has duty to use property as directed to fulfill purpose of bailment only

  a. Liable to bailor for misuse

  b. In cases of theft, destruction of property, or failing to return property, this constitutes tort of conversion

  c. Bailee may normally limit liability for his/her negligence but not for intentional conduct

6. Bailee is not an agent of bailor, so bailor is not responsible for bailee's actions

7. Bailments normally terminated by

  a. Fulfillment of purpose of bailment

  b. Agreement to terminate by both bailor and bailee

  c. Bailee using property inappropriately

8. Common carriers are licensed to provide transportation for public

  a. Liability is based on strict liability, so common carriers are liable for damage to goods being transported even if loss caused by third parties or by accidents

    (1) Exceptions—common carrier not liable for

      (a) Acts of shipper, such as improperly packing goods to be shipped
      (b) Acts of God, such as earthquakes
      (c) Acts of public enemies
      (d) Loss because of inherent nature of goods

    (2) Common carriers allowed to limit liability to dollar amount specified in contract

D. Intellectual Property and Computer Technology Rights

1. Two general but competing goals

  a. Incentives to create products and services

    (1) By granting property rights so creators have incentive to create and market

  b. Provide public access to intellectual property and computer ideas and uses

    (1) By limiting intellectual and computer technology rights so that public has access to this

2. Copyright law

  a. Protects original works (e.g., literary, musical, or artistic works)

    (1) Expressions of ideas are generally copyrightable—ideas may not by themselves be copyrighted

    (2) Amendments to Copyright Act protect computer programs

  b. Copyrights created after January 1, 1978, are valid for life of author plus seventy years

    (1) Are valid for 95 years from publication date when owned by publishing house, or 120 years from creation date, whichever expires first

  c. Registration of copyright not required because copyright begins when author puts expression in tangible form

        (1) Registration, however, gives copyright owner, in case of infringement, rights to statutory damages and attorneys' fees

   d. Works published after March 1, 1989, no longer need copyright notice on them

   e. Fair use doctrine allows use for limited purposes without violating copyright

        (1) Examples include portions for comment, news reporting, research, or teaching

> EXAMPLE: *Professor hands out copies of a portion of copyrighted work to each member of the class.*

   f. Consumer Software Copyright Act amends copyright law to include computer programs as creative works protected by federal copyright law

        (1) Covers not only portions of computer program readable by humans but also binary language portions normally read by computer

        (2) Covers general items in program such as its basic structure and organizations

   g. Remedies include stated statutory damages or actual damages including profits attributed to infringement of copyright—injunctions also allowed

        (1) Higher damages can be statutorily assessed for willful infringement

   h. Criminal penalties of fines and imprisonment are allowed for willful infringement

   i. No Electronic Theft Act (NET Act)

        (1) Act criminalizes copyright infringement over Internet whether or not for financial gain where retail value of copyrighted works exceeds $1,000

3. Patent Law

   a. Covers machines, processes, art, methods, composition of matter, new and useful improvements including genetically engineered plants or animals

   b. Mere ideas are not covered

        (1) But practical applications may be

   c. Invention must be novel, useful, and not obvious

   d. Patents administered by US Patent and Trademark Office

        (1) Inventor may not obtain patent if invention was on sale or in public use in US at least one year before attempt to obtain patent

   e. Generally, patents are valid for twenty years from when patent application was filed

        (1) By treaties, patents generally receive international protection for twenty years

        (2) Design patents are valid for fourteen years from date of issuance of patent

   f. Owner of patent must mark it using word patent to give notice to others

        (1) May also use Pat abbreviation

   g. US gives patent protection to first inventor to invent rather than first to file for that patent

        (1) Most countries give protection to the first to file the patent

   h. Earlier views of computer software often categorized it as based on ideas and thus not patentable—more recent authority and court decisions protect software and Internet business methods as patentable

> EXAMPLE: *Pratt Company patented a computer program that used mathematical formulas to constantly improve a curing process for synthetic rubber upon receiving feedback in the process. This computer program was patentable because Pratt did not attempt to patent the mathematical formula to exclude others from using the formula but patented the process.*

> EXAMPLE: *River.com Inc. receives a patent for the company storing customers' shipping (and billing information) with a one-click ordering system to reduce customers' need to reenter data on future orders.*

> EXAMPLE: *Dual Softie, Inc. receives a patent that allows purchasers of automobiles over Internet to select options wished on the auto.*

> EXAMPLE: *Silvernet, Inc. patents a system that pays individuals who respond to on-line surveys.*

i. Even when patent issued by US Patent Trade Office (PTO), PTO may reexamine and reject patent

   (1) Patent may be overturned or narrowed in case brought to court
   (2) Unlike earlier, computer-related patents focus now on whether they are novel and nonobvious rather than on whether they can be patented at all

j. Remedies include injunctions, damages including lost profits traceable to infringement, or assessment of reasonable royalties

   (1) If infringement is willful, inventor may be awarded treble damages and require infringer to also pay attorney's fees

k. US Supreme Court recently affirmed important part of patent law providing that one cannot escape liability for patent infringement by making only insubstantial changes to a patent and attempting to claim it to be a new patent

l. Paris convention—allows patent protection in many foreign countries

   (1) Most comprehensive agreement between nations involving intellectual property
   (2) Signed by nearly all industrialized countries and by many developing countries
   (3) Generally, allows a one-year grace period for inventors to file in other countries once inventor files for patent protection in first country

4. Trade Secrets Law

   a. No federal protection available under registration
   b. Alternative to protection by copyright or patent
   c. Protects formulas, patterns, devices or compilations of information that give business an advantage over competitors

      (1) Must be secret that others have difficulty in acquiring except by improper means
      (2) Owner must take reasonable steps to guard trade secret
      (3) Can cover computer hardware and software

   d. Remedies for violations include breach of contract, breach of fiduciary duties, wrongful appropriation of trade secret, injunction, theft, espionage

      (1) Civil law as well as criminal law may be used

   e. Trade secret protection by law may be lost if

      (1) Owner of trade secret fails to take steps to keep it secret, or
      (2) Other person independently discovers what was subject of trade secret

   f. Methods to help protect trade secret include

      (1) Licensing of software

         (a) Prohibit copying except for backup copies

      (2) Provide in license that it is terminated for any breach of confidentiality
      (3) Sell software in object code instead of source code
      (4) Have employees and buyers sign confidentiality agreements

5. Semiconductor Chip Protection Act

   a. Amends copyright laws
   b. Prohibits taking apart chips to copy them

      (1) Allows such act if used to create new chip rather than copy
      (2) Not prohibiting copying if design embodies the unoriginal or commonplace

   c. Protection is for ten years from time of registration or first commercial application, whichever is first
   d. Civil sanctions only—no criminal sanctions

6. Federal Counterfeit Access Device and Computer Fraud and Abuse Act has criminalized many intentional, unauthorized uses of computer to

a.   Obtain classified information to hurt US
b.   Collect credit or financial information protected by privacy laws

> *EXAMPLE: Obtaining credit card limits and credit card numbers by accessing credit card accounts.*

c.   Modify material financial data in computers
d.   Destroy or alter computer data to hurt rightful users

> *EXAMPLE: A person intentionally transfers a computer virus to a company computer.*

7.   Trademarks under Lanham Act

  a.   Purposes

   (1) To provide identification symbol for company's product
   (2) To guarantee consistent quality of all goods from same source
   (3) Advertising

  b.   Protection for trademark for distinctive graphics, words, shapes, packaging, or sounds

> *EXAMPLE: Coca-Cola has a trademark for its distinctive bottle.*

  c.   Marks normally need to be distinctive to be protected

   (1) Secondary meaning of things not inherently distinctive can develop to make them protectable

> *EXAMPLE: Microsoft registered "Windows" as a trademark when "Windows" acquired its secondary meaning.*

> *EXAMPLE: Windows store cannot be used as a trademark because it sells windows to put on homes and is thus generic rather than distinctive.*

  d.   Generic words like software cannot be protected

   (1) Many words that were once trademarks have become generic so are no longer protectable

> *EXAMPLE: Escalator was originally a brand name but is no longer protectable due to its generic use. Other examples are Yo-Yo and Dry Ice.*

> *EXAMPLE: Xerox takes out advertisements explaining that Xerox is not a verb, but instead say "copy" the document. Xerox is trying to protect its trademark by trying not to let the name grow into common usage.*

  e.   Trademark rights in US are obtained initially by its use in commerce

   (1) For distinctive marks, generally first seller to use trademark owns it
   (2) Company can register trademark

    (a) Although this is not required, provides constructive notice to others of claim of trademark

   (3) On-line company may register domain name as trademark with US Patent and Trademark Office

    (a) Various companies may use same trademark for different types of goods or services but only one company may register the domain name

> *EXAMPLE: Both Star Fences Inc. and Star Insurance Company wish to use Star.com. Only one may do so.*

  f.   Loss of trademark rights

   (1) Actual abandonment when not used in ordinary course of business

    (a) Presumption of abandonment if not used for three years unless owner can prove intent to use trademark

   (2) Constructive abandonment—Company allows trademark to lose its distinctiveness by frequent and common usage

  g.   Trademark infringement

   (1) Can infringe on trademark whether registered or not
   (2) Proof of infringement

    (a) Establish trademark is valid—federally registered mark is prima facie valid
    (b) Priority of usage

      (c) Violation against trademark if similarities will likely cause confusion in minds of prospective or actual purchasers

   h. Remedies for infringement

      (1) Injunction against use
      (2) Lost profits caused by confusion
      (3) Attorneys' fees in some situations

8. Other symbols under Lanham Act

   a. Certification mark

      (1) Used to certify characteristics such as origin by geographical location, origin by organization, mode of manufacture.

      EXAMPLE: Product XYZ receives the Good Housekeeping Seal of Approval.

   b. Collective mark

      (1) Used to identify that product or service is provided by certain collective group, union, or fraternal society.

      EXAMPLE: Product ABC indicates that it was manufactured by a unionized company.

   c. Service mark

      (1) Used to identify that services come from certain company or person

      EXAMPLE: All of the shops of a group of shops called The Green Roof Plaza have similar style of roofs painted in the same shade of green.

   d. Similar to trademarks, these additional three types of trade symbols need to be distinctive and not deceptive so that prospective customers do not confuse these products or services with others

      (1) Registration is not required but advisable because it provides federal protection for ten years

         (a) Renewable for as many additional ten-year periods as desired

9. Invasion of Privacy—Increased computer use puts on more pressure

   a. Computer Matching and Privacy Act

      (1) Regulates computer systems used to determine eligibility for various government programs such as student financial aid

   b. Right to Financial Privacy Act

      (1) Restricts government access to financial institution records without customer approval

   c. Family Educational Rights and Privacy Act

      (1) Grants adult students and parents of minors access and right to correct records at institutions of higher learning

10. Anticybersquatting Consumer Reform Act

   a. Federal law passed by Congress that amends Landham Act protecting trademarks
   b. Illegal to register or use domain name if

      (1) Domain name is identical or similar enough to confuse others with bad intent to profit from trademark

         (a) Bad faith includes using domain name to sell products or services
         (b) Also can include intent to harm goodwill of trademark

   c. Act applies to all domain names even those registered before Act
   d. Plaintiff may elect to sue either for actual damages (including profits) or statutory damages of $1,000 to $100,000

11. Counterfeit Access Device and Computer Fraud and Abuse Act

   a. Crime to obtain financial institution's financial records

   b. Crime to use cards, codes, counterfeit devices, etc. to obtain valuable items or to transfer funds without authorization

12. Information Infrastructure Protection Act

   a. Helps protect individuals or companies from another's unauthorized use of or access to computer's data

      (1) Law encompasses computer hackers, transmitting computer viruses or worms, etc.

13. Digital Millennium Copyright Act

   a. Federal law based on treaties with other countries to minimize pirating and distribution of copyrighted works

   b. Provides civil and criminal penalties against those that circumvent antipiracy protections or manufacture or sell such equipment to allow circumvention

   c. Internet Service Provider (ISP) is generally not liable for customers' copyright infringement unless ISP became aware of infringement and failed to correct problem

14. Uniform Computer Information Transactions Act (UCITA) requires that the following be in writing:

   a. Contracts for licensing of information rights for over $5,000

   b. Contracts for licensing of information services that cannot be performed within one year

   c. User agrees to contract by clicking, for example, on "I agree prompt button"

15. On-line dispute resolution is becoming increasingly used to resolve disputes

   a. Advantages include low cost, fast communication, and often no need to bring in third parties

   b. Disadvantage includes hard to enforce settlement because no court or sheriff involved

16. Internet Treaties

   a. Grants between many signing nations providing copyright protection for computer programs, producers' rights, performers' rights over the internet

      (1) Includes rental copies, transmissions over satellite, encrypted signals, and any type of media

E. Interests in Real Property

1. Present interests

   a. Fee simple absolute

      (1) Highest estate in law (has the most ownership rights)

      (2) May be transferred inter vivos (while living), by intestate succession (without will), or by will (testate at death)

      (3) May be subject to mortgages, state laws, etc.

        EXAMPLE: Most private residences are fee simple absolute estates although they are commonly subject to mortgage.

   b. Fee simple defeasible

      (1) Fee simple determinable—upon the happening of the stated event the estate automatically reverts to the grantor

        EXAMPLE: Conveyance to the holder of an interest was, "to A as long as A uses it for church purposes." The interest will revert back to the grantor or his heirs if the property is not used for church purposes.

      (2) Fee simple subject to condition subsequent—upon the happening of the stated event the grantor must take affirmative action to divest the grantee of the estate

        EXAMPLE: Conveyance to the holder of the interest was "to A, but if liquor is ever served on the premises, the grantor has right to enter the premises." The grantor has power of termination so as to repossess the premises.

    c.   Life interest—an interest whose duration is usually measured by the life of the holder but may be measured by lives of others

        EXAMPLE: Conveyance of land, "to A so long as she shall live."

        (1) Upon termination (death), property reverts to grantor or grantor's heirs, or to a named remainderman

        (2) Usual life interest can be transferred by deed only (i.e., not by a will because it ends on death)

        (3) Holder of a life interest (life tenant) is entitled to ordinary use and profits of land but may not commit waste (injure interests of remainderman)

            (a) Must maintain property (in reasonable state of repair)

            (b) May not misuse property

    d.   Leaseholds—see Lessor-Lessee at end of this module

2.   Future interest (holder of this interest has right to or possibility of possession in the future)

    a.   Reversion—future interest reverts back to transferor (or his/her heirs) at end of transferee's estate

        (1) Usually kept when conveying a life interest or an interest for a definite period of time

            EXAMPLE: X conveys, "to Y for life" or "to Y for ten years." X has a reversion.

    b.   Remainder—future interest is in a third party at the end of transferee's estate

        EXAMPLE: X conveys, "to Y for life, remainder to Z and her heirs."

3.   Concurrent interest—two or more persons (cotenants) have undivided interests and concurrent possessory rights in real or personal property—each has a nonexclusive right to possess whole property

    a.   Tenancy in common

        (1) A concurrent interest with no right of survivorship (interest passes to heirs, donee, or purchaser)

            EXAMPLE: A and B each own 1/2 of Greenacre as tenants in common. If B dies, then A still owns 1/2 and B's heirs own the other half.

        (2) Unless stated otherwise, multiple grantees are presumed to be tenants in common

        (3) Tenant in common may convey individual interest in the whole but cannot convey a specific portion of property

            (a) Unless there is a judicial partition to split up ownership

               1] Creditors may sue to compel a partition to satisfy individual's debts

    b.   Joint tenancy

        (1) A concurrent interest with all rights of ownership going to the surviving joint tenants (i.e., have rights of survivorship)

            (a) To create a joint tenancy, all of following unities are required: time, title, interest, and possession

            (b) Cannot be transferred by will because upon death, other cotenants own it

            (c) Corporation may not be joint tenant

             EXAMPLE: A and B each own 1/2 of Redacre as joint tenants. If B dies, A owns all of Redacre because of her right of survivorship. B's heirs do not receive any interest.

        (2) If rights in property conveyed without consent of others, new owner becomes a tenant in common rather than joint tenant; remaining cotenants are still joint tenants

            EXAMPLE: A, B, and C are joint tenants of Greenacre. A sells his interest to D without the consent of B and C. D is a tenant in common with a one-third interest in the whole. B and C are still joint tenants (with the right of survivorship) each having a one-third undivided interest.

    c.   Tenancy by the entirety

        (1) Joint interest held by husband and wife

(2) It is presumed when both spouses' names appear on title document

(3) To transfer, both must convey

(4) Each spouse has a right of survivorship

(5) Divorce creates a tenancy in common

4. Nonpossessory interests in land

    a. Easement is right to enter another's land and use it in limited way

    EXAMPLE: A is granted an easement to drive over a certain segment of B's land.

    (1) Methods of creation

       (a) Express grant in deed

       (b) Express reservation in deed

       EXAMPLE: S sells B some land whereby in the deed S reserves an easement to walk across the land.

       (c) By necessity

       EXAMPLE: A owns a piece of land that blocks B's access to any public road. B has the right to use A's land for access to the public road.

    b. Profit is right to enter another's land and remove items such as trees, grass, or gravel

    (1) Profits may be created by grant or by reservation

F. Contracts for Sale of Land

1. Generally precede transfers of land. Often includes escrows.

    EXAMPLE: An earnest money agreement. The purchaser puts the money down to show his seriousness while he investigates the title and arranges for a mortgage.

    a. Generally, agreement must

    (1) Be in writing and signed by party to be bound

       (a) To satisfy Statute of Frauds under contract law

    (2) Identify land and parties

    (3) Identify purpose

    (4) Contain terms or promises

    (5) Contain purchase price

    b. Assignable unless prohibited in contract

2. If not expressed, there is an implied promise that seller will provide a marketable title (implied warranty of marketability)

    a. A marketable title is one reasonably free from doubt. Does not contain such defects as breaks in chain of title, outstanding liens, or defective instruments in past (chain of title).

    (1) Zoning restrictions do not make a title unmarketable

    b. Agreement may provide for marketable or "insurable" title

    (1) Insurable title is one that a title insurance company will insure against defects, liens, and invalidity

    c. If title is not marketable, purchaser may

    (1) Rescind and recover any down payment

    (2) Sue for damages

    (3) Sue for specific performance with a reduction in price

3. Risk of loss before deed is conveyed (e.g., if house burns who bears the burden?)

    a. General rule is purchaser bears the risk of loss, subject to terms of the contract

    b. Courts may look to who has the most ownership rights and benefits (normally buyer)

    c. Either party can insure against risk of loss

G. Types of Deeds

1. Warranty deeds contain the following covenants (unconditional promises) by grantor

    a. Grantor has title and right to convey it
    b. Free from encumbrances except as disclosed in the deed

    EXAMPLE: O conveys by warranty deed Blackacre to P. There is a mortgage still unpaid on Blackacre. Unless O discloses this mortgage to P, O has violated the covenant that the deed be free from encumbrances.

    c. Quiet enjoyment—neither grantor nor third party with rightful claim will disturb grantee's possession

2. Bargain and sale deed (grant deeds)

    a. Generally, only covenants that grantor has done nothing to impair title (e.g., s/he has not created any encumbrances)
    b. Does not warrant against prior (before grantor's ownership) impairments

3. Quitclaim deed conveys only whatever interest in land the grantor has. No warranty of title is made by grantor.

    a. It is insurable, recordable, and mortgagable as with any other deed

H. Executing a Deed

1. Deed must have description of the real estate

    a. Purchase price not necessary in deed

2. There must be delivery for deed to be effective; there must be an intent on part of grantor to pass title (convey) to grantee

    a. Possession of the deed by grantee raises a presumption (rebuttable) of delivery
    b. A recorded deed raises a presumption (rebuttable) of delivery
    c. A deed given to a third party to give to grantee upon performance of a condition is a delivery in escrow

        (1) Escrow agent—intermediary between the two parties who holds deed until grantee pays, then gives deed to grantee and money to grantor

    d. Destruction of deed does not destroy title

I. Recording a Deed

1. Gives constructive notice to the world of grantee's ownership (this is important)

    a. Protects grantee (new owner) against subsequent purchasers

    EXAMPLE: X sells land to Y. Y records his deed. Later X sells land to Z. Z loses against Y because Y recorded the deed giving constructive notice of the prior sale.

        (1) However, deed is valid between immediate parties without recording

    b. Most recording statutes provide that subsequent purchaser (bona fide) who takes without notice of the first sale has priority

        (1) Under a notice-type statute, a subsequent bona fide (good-faith) purchaser, whether s/he records or not, wins over previous purchaser who did not record before that subsequent purchase

        EXAMPLE: A sells the same piece of property in a state having a notice-type statute to B and C in that order. B did not record the purchase. C is unaware of the sale to B and is thus a bona fide purchaser. C defeats B. Note that C should record the purchase or run the risk of another bona fide purchaser (i.e., D defeating C's claim).

        (2) Under a race-notice type (notice-race) statute, the subsequent bona fide purchaser wins over a previous purchaser only if s/he also records first (i.e., a "race" to file first)

        EXAMPLE: X sells some property to Y and then to Z, a good-faith purchaser. After the sale to Z, Y records the purchase and then Z records the purchase. Although Y wins in a state having a race-notice statute, Z wins in a state having a notice-type statute.

EXAMPLE: Same as above except that Z does not record, both results above are not affected.

    (3) Under a race statute, the first to record deed wins

  c. Notice refers to actual knowledge of prior sale or constructive knowledge (i.e., one is deemed to be aware of what is filed in records)

  d. To be a purchaser, one must give value that does not include antecedent debts

J. Title Insurance

1. Generally used to insure that title is good and to cover the warranties by seller

  a. Not required if contract does not require it

2. Without title insurance, purchaser's only recourse is against grantor and s/he may not be able to satisfy the damages

  a. Standard insurance policies generally insure against all defects of record and defects grantee may be aware of, but not defects disclosed by survey and physical inspection of premises

  b. Title insurance company is liable for any damages or expenses if there is a title defect or encumbrance that is insured against

    (1) Certain defects are not insured by the title policy

      (a) These exceptions must be shown on face of policy

  c. Title insurance does not pass to subsequent purchasers

K. Adverse Possession

1. Possessor of land who was not owner may acquire title if s/he holds it for the statutory period

  a. The statutory period is the running of the statute of limitations. Varies by state from five to twenty years.

  b. The statute begins to run upon the taking of possession

  c. True owner must commence legal action before statute runs or adverse possessor obtains title

  d. Successive possessors may tack (cumulate required time together)

    (1) Each possessor must transfer to the other. One cannot abandon or statute begins over again for the next possessor.

  e. True owner of a future interest (e.g., a remainder, is not affected by adverse possession)

EXAMPLE: X dies and leaves his property to A for life, remainder to B. A pays little attention to the property and a third party acquires it by adverse possession. When A dies, B is entitled to the property regardless of the adverse possession but the statute starts running against B.

2. Necessary elements

  a. Open and notorious possession

    (1) Means type of possession that would give reasonable notice to owner

  b. Hostile possession

    (1) Must indicate intentions of ownership

      (a) Does not occur when possession started permissively or as cotenants

      (b) Not satisfied if possessor acknowledges other's ownership

    (2) Color of title satisfies this requirement. When possession is taken under good-faith belief in a defective instrument or deed purporting to convey the land.

  c. Actual possession

    (1) Possession of land consistent with its normal use (e.g., farm land is being farmed)

  d. Continuous possession

    (1) Need not be constant, but possession as normally used

e. Exclusive possession

(1) Possession to exclusion of all others

L. Easement by Prescription

1. Person obtains right to use another's land (i.e., easement) in way similar to adverse possession
2. Same elements are used as for adverse possession except for exclusive possession—state laws require several years to obtain this

EXAMPLE: X cuts across Y's land for several years in such a way that s/he meets all of the same requirements as those needed for adverse possession except for exclusive possession. X obtains an easement to use the path even if Y later tries to stop X.

M. Mortgages

1. Lien on real property to secure payment of loan

a. Mortgage is an interest in real property and thus must satisfy Statute of Frauds

(1) Must be in writing and signed by party to be charged

(a) Party to be charged in this case is mortgagor (i.e., party taking out mortgage)

(2) Must include description of property and debt to be incurred

b. Debt is usually evidenced by a promissory note which is incorporated into mortgage
c. Mortgage must be delivered to mortgagee (i.e., lender)
d. Mortgage may be given to secure future advances
e. Purchase-money mortgage is created when seller takes a mortgage from buyer at time of sale

(1) Or lender furnishes money with which property is purchased

2. Mortgage may be recorded and receives the same benefits as recording a deed or recording an assignment of contract

a. Gives constructive notice of the mortgage

(1) But mortgage **is effective** between mortgagor and mortgagee and third parties, who have actual notice, even without recording

b. Protects mortgagee against subsequent mortgagees, purchasers, or other takers
c. Recording statutes for mortgages are like those used for recording deeds

(1) Under a notice-type statute, a subsequent good-faith mortgagee has priority over previous mortgagee who did not file

(a) This is true whether subsequent mortgagee files or not; but of course if s/he does not file, a subsequent good-faith mortgagee will have priority.

EXAMPLE: Banks A, B, and C, in that order, grant a mortgage to a property owner. None of these record the mortgage and none knows of the others. Between A and B, B has priority. However, C has priority over B.

EXAMPLE: Same facts as before, however, B does record before C grants the mortgage. B has priority over A again. B also has priority over C because now C has constructive notice of B and thus has lower priority.

(b) Notice is either actual notice or constructive notice based on recording

(2) Under a race-notice type (notice-race) statute, the subsequent good-faith mortgagee wins over a previous mortgagee only if s/he also records first
(3) Under a race statute, the first mortgagee to record mortgage wins
(4) First mortgage to have priority is satisfied in full (upon default) before next mortgage to have priority is satisfied

(a) Second mortgagee can require first mortgagee to resort to other property for payment if first mortgagee has other property available as security

3. When mortgaged property is sold the buyer may

a. Assume the mortgage

(1) If "assumed," the buyer becomes personally liable (mortgage holder is third-party beneficiary)

(2) Seller remains liable (unless released by mortgagee by a novation)

    (a) Mortgagee may hold either seller or buyer liable on mortgage

(3) Normally the mortgagee's consent is needed due to "due on sale clauses"

    (a) Terms of mortgage may permit acceleration of principal or renegotiation of interest rate upon transfer of the property

b. Take subject to the mortgage

(1) If buyer takes "subject to" then buyer accepts **no** liability for mortgage and seller is still primarily liable

(2) Mortgagee may still foreclose on the property even in the hands of buyer

    (a) Buyer may pay mortgage if s/he chooses to avoid foreclosure

(3) Mortgagee's consent to allow buyer to take subject to the mortgage is not needed unless stipulated in mortgage

c. Novation—occurs when purchaser assumes mortgage and mortgagee (lender) releases in writing the seller from the mortgage

> *EXAMPLE: O has mortgaged Redacre. He sells Redacre to T. T agrees to assume mortgage and mortgagee bank agrees in writing to substitute T as the only liable party in place of O. Because of this novation, O is no longer liable on the mortgage.*

4. Rights of parties

a. Mortgagor (owner, debtor) retains possession and right to use land

(1) May transfer land encumbered by mortgage

b. Mortgagee (creditor) has a lien on the land

(1) Even if mortgagor transfers land, it is still subject to the mortgage if it has been properly recorded

c. Mortgagee has right to assign mortgage to third party without mortgagors' consent

d. Upon mortgagor's default, mortgagee may assign mortgage to third parties or mortgagee may foreclose on the land

(1) Foreclosure requires judicial action that directs foreclosure sale

    (a) Court will refuse to confirm sale if price is so low as to raise a presumption of unfairness

    (b) However, court will not refuse to confirm sale merely because higher price might have been received at a later time

(2) Mortgagor usually can save real estate (redeem the property) by use of equity of redemption

    (a) Pays interest, debt, and expenses

    (b) Exists until foreclosure sale

    (c) Cannot be curtailed by prior agreement

(3) After foreclosure sale debtor has right of redemption if state law grants statutory right of redemption

    (a) Affords mortgagor one last chance to redeem property

    (b) Pays off loan within statutory period

(4) If mortgagee forecloses and sells property and mortgagor does not use equity of redemption or right of redemption

    (a) Mortgagee must return any excess proceeds from sale to mortgagor

        1] Equity above balance due does not give right to mortgagor to retain possession of property

      (b) If proceeds from sale are insufficient to pay note, mortgagor is still indebted to the mortgagee for deficiency

         1] Grantee of the mortgagor who **assumed** mortgage would also be liable for deficiency, but one who took **subject to** the mortgage would not be personally liable

5. Mortgage lenders are regulated by Real Estate Settlement Procedures Act (RESPA)

    a. Provides home buyers with extensive information about settlement process and helps protect them from high settlement fees

6. Deed of trust—also a nonpossessory lien on real property to secure a debt

    a. Like a mortgage, debtor retains possession of land and creditor has a lien on it
    b. Legal title is given to a trustee to hold

      (1) Upon default, trustee may sell the land for the benefit of creditor

7. Sale on contract

    a. Unlike a mortgage or a deed of trust, the seller retains title to property
    b. Purchaser takes possession and makes payments on the contract
    c. Purchaser gets title when debt fully paid

8. When mortgaged property is sold or destroyed, the proceeds from sale or insurance go to mortgagee with highest priority until it is completely paid, then the proceeds, if any, go to any mortgagees or other interest holders, with the next highest priority, etc.

N. Lessor-Lessee

1. A lease is a contract and a conveyance

    a. Contract is the primary source of rights and duties
    b. Contract must contain essential terms including description of leased premises
    c. May be oral if less than one year

2. Types of leaseholds

    a. Periodic tenancy

      (1) Lease is for a fixed time such as a month or year but it continues from period to period until proper notice of termination
      (2) Notice of termination normally must be given in the same amount of time as rent or tenancy period (i.e., if tenancy is from month to month then the landlord or tenant usually must give at least one month's notice)

    b. Tenancy for a term (also called tenancy for years)

      (1) Lease is for a fixed amount of time (e.g., lease of two years or six months)
      (2) Ends automatically at date of termination

    c. Tenancy at sufferance

      (1) Created when tenant remains in property after lease expires
      (2) Landlord has option of treating tenant as trespasser and ejecting him/her or treating him/her as tenant and collecting rent

    d. Tenancy at will

      (1) Property is leased for indefinite period of time
      (2) Either party may terminate lease at will

3. Lessor covenants (promises) and tenant's rights

    a. Generally, lessor's covenants are independent of lessee's rights; therefore, lessor's breach does not give lessee right to breach
    b. Right to possession—lessor makes premises available to lessee

(1) Residential lease for real estate entitles tenant to exclusive possession of property during period of lease unless otherwise agreed in lease

c. Quiet enjoyment—neither lessor nor a third party with a valid claim will evict lessee unless tenant has breached lease contract

d. Fitness for use—premises are fit for human occupation (i.e., warranty of habitability)

e. In general, if premises are destroyed through no fault of either party, then contract is terminated

EXAMPLE: Landlord's building is destroyed by a sudden flood. Tenant cannot hold landlord liable for loss of use of building.

f. Lessee may assign or sublease unless prohibited or restricted in lease

(1) Assignment is transfer by lessee of his/her entire interest reserving no rights

(a) Assignee is in privity of contract with lessor and lessor may proceed against him/her for rent and breaches under lease agreement

(b) Assignor (lessee) is still liable to lessor unless there is a novation or release

(c) Lease may have clause that requires consent of lessor for subleases

1] In which case, consent to each individual sublease is required
2] Lack of consent makes sublease voidable

(d) Clause prohibiting sublease does not prohibit assignment

(2) A sublease is the transfer by lessee of less than his/her entire interest (e.g., for three months during summer, then lessee returns to it in the fall)

(a) Lessee (sublessor) is still liable on lease

(b) Lessor has no privity with sublessee and can take no action against him/her for rent, but certain restrictions of original lease run with the land and are enforceable against sublessee

(c) Sublessee can assume obligations in sublease and be liable to pay landlord

(d) Clause prohibiting assignment does not prohibit sublease

g. Subject to lease terms, trade fixtures attached by lessee may be removed if can be removed without substantial damage to premises

h. Tenant can use premises for any legal purpose unless lease restricts

4. Lessee's duties and lessor's rights

a. Rent—due at end of term or period of tenancy unless otherwise agreed in lease

(1) No right to withhold rent even if lessor is in breach (unless so provided by lease or by statute)
(2) Nonpayment gives lessor right to sue for it or to bring an eviction suit or both

b. Lessee has obligation to make ordinary repairs. Lease or statute may make lessor liable.

(1) Structural repairs are lessor's duty

c. If tenant wrongfully retains possession after termination, lessor may

(1) Evict lessee, or
(2) Treat as holdover tenant and charge with fair rental value, or
(3) Tenancy becomes one of period-to-period, and lessee is liable for rent the same as in expired lease

5. Termination

a. Expiration of lease
b. Proper notice in a tenancy from period-to-period
c. Surrender by lessee and acceptance by lessor
d. Death of lessee terminates lease except for a lease for a period of years

(1) Death of lessor generally does not terminate lease

e. Eviction

        (1) Actual eviction—ousting directly

        (2) Constructive eviction—allowing conditions which make property unusable if lessor is liable for condition of premises

  f. Transfer of property does not affect tenancy

        (1) New owner cannot rightfully terminate lease unless old owner could have (e.g., breach by tenant)

            (a) However, if tenant purchases property then lease terminates

MULTIPLE-CHOICE QUESTIONS (1-42)

1. Which of the following items is tangible personal property?
    a.   Share of stock.
    b.   Trademark.
    c.   Promissory note.
    d.   Oil painting.

2. What is an example of property that can be considered either personal property or real property?
    a.   Air rights.
    b.   Mineral rights.
    c.   Harvested crops.
    d.   Growing crops.

3. Which of the following factors help determine whether an item of personal property is a fixture?
   I. Degree of the item's attachment to the property.
  II. Intent of the person who had the item installed.

    a.   I only.
    b.   II only.
    c.   Both I and II.
    d.   Neither I nor II.

4. Getty owned some personal property which was later found by Morris. Both Getty and Morris are claiming title to this personal property. In which of the following cases will Getty win over Morris?
   I. Getty had mislaid the property and had forgotten to take it with him.
  II. Getty had lost the property out of his van while driving down a road.
  III. Getty had abandoned the property but later changed his mind after Morris found it.

    a.   I only.
    b.   II only.
    c.   I and II only.
    d.   I, II, and III.

5. Rand discarded an old rocking chair. Stone found the rocking chair and, realizing that it was valuable, took it home. Later, Rand learned that Stone had the rocking chair and wanted it back. Rand subsequently put a provision in his will that his married daughter Walters will get the rocking chair. Who has the actual title to the rocking chair?

	Stone has title	Rand, while living, has title	Walters obtains title upon Rand's death
a.	No	Yes	Yes
b.	No	Yes	No
c.	Yes	Yes	Yes
d.	Yes	No	No

6. Which of the following standards of liability best characterizes the obligation of a common carrier in a bailment relationship?
    a.   Reasonable care.
    b.   Gross negligence.
    c.   Shared liability.
    d.   Strict liability.

7. Multicomp Company wishes to protect software it has developed. It is concerned about others copying this software and taking away some of its profits. Which of the following is true concerning the current state of the law?
    a.   Computer software is generally copyrightable.
    b.   To receive protection, the software must have a conspicuous copyright notice.
    c.   Software in human readable source code is copyrightable but in machine language object code is not.
    d.   Software can be copyrighted for a period not to exceed twenty years.

8. Which of the following is **not** correct concerning computer software purchased by Gultch Company from Softtouch Company? Softtouch originally created this software.
    a.   Gultch can make backup copies in case of machine failure.
    b.   Softtouch can typically copyright its software for at least seventy-five years.
    c.   If the software consists of compiled computer databases it cannot be copyrighted.
    d.   Computer programs are generally copyrightable.

9. Professor Bell runs off fifteen copies to distribute to his accounting class using his computer from a database in some software he had purchased for his personal research. The creator of this software is claiming a copyright. Which of the following is correct?
    a.   This is an infringement of a copyright since he bought the software for personal use.
    b.   This is not an infringement of a copyright since databases cannot be copyrighted.
    c.   This is not an infringement of a copyright because the copies were made using a computer.
    d.   This is not an infringement of a copyright because of the fair use doctrine.

10. Intellectual property rights included in software may be protected under which of the following?
    a.   Patent law.
    b.   Copyright law.
    c.   Both of the above.
    d.   None of the above.

11. Which of the following statements is **not** true of the law of trademarks in the United States?
    a.   Trademark law may protect distinctive shapes as well as distinctive packaging.
    b.   Trademark protection can be lost if the trademark becomes so popular that its use becomes commonplace.
    c.   Trademarks to receive protection need not be registered.
    d.   Trademarks are valid for twenty years after their formation.

12. Diane Trucco recently wrote a novel which is an excellent work of art. She wishes to copyright and publish this novel. Which of the following is correct?
    a.   Her copyright is valid for her life plus seventy years.
    b.   She must register her copyright to receive protection under the law.
    c.   She is required to put on a copyright notice to obtain a copyright.
    d.   All of the above are correct.

13. Long, Fall, and Pear own a building as joint tenants with the right of survivorship. Long gave Long's interest in the building to Green by executing and delivering a deed to Green. Neither Fall nor Pear consented to this transfer. Fall

and Pear subsequently died. After their deaths, Green's interest in the building would consist of
   a.   A 1/3 interest as a joint tenant.
   b.   A 1/3 interest as a tenant in common.
   c.   No interest because Fall and Pear did **not** consent to the transfer.
   d.   Total ownership due to the deaths of Fall and Pear.

14. What interest in real property generally gives the holder of that interest the right to sell the property?
   a.   Easement.
   b.   Leasehold.
   c.   License.
   d.   Fee simple.

15. Which of the following unities (elements) are required to establish a joint tenancy?

	Time	Title	Interest	Possession
a.	Yes	Yes	Yes	Yes
b.	Yes	Yes	No	No
c.	No	No	Yes	Yes
d.	Yes	No	Yes	No

16. Which of the following is not an interest that a person can have in real property?
   a.   Fee simple absolute.
   b.   Tenancy by default.
   c.   Life interest.
   d.   Remainder.

17. On July 1, 2001, Quick, Onyx, and Nash were deeded a piece of land as tenants in common. The deed provided that Quick owned 1/2 the property and Onyx and Nash owned 1/4 each. If Nash dies, the property will be owned as follows:
   a.   Quick 1/2, Onyx 1/2.
   b.   Quick 5/8, Onyx 3/8.
   c.   Quick 1/3, Onyx 1/3, Nash's heirs 1/3.
   d.   Quick 1/2, Onyx 1/4, Nash's heirs 1/4.

18. Brett conveys his real property by deed to his sister, Jan, for life with the remainder to go to his friend, Randy, for his life. Brett is still living. Randy died first and Jan died second. Who has title to this real property?
   a.   Brett.
   b.   Brett's heirs.
   c.   Jan's heirs.
   d.   Randy's heirs.

19. Court, Fell, and Miles own a parcel of land as joint tenants with right of survivorship. Court's interest was sold to Plank. As a result of the sale from Court to Plank
   a.   Fell, Miles, and Plank each own one-third of the land as joint tenants.
   b.   Fell and Miles each own one-third of the land as tenants in common.
   c.   Plank owns one third of the land as a tenant in common.
   d.   Plank owns one-third of the land as a joint tenant.

20. The following contains three fact patterns involving land. In which of the following is an easement involved?

   I.   O sells land to B in which O retains in the deed the right to use a roadway on B's newly purchased property.
   II. O sells land to B in which O in the deed has the right to cut and keep ten specified trees on the land sold.

   III. O sells land to B. O continues that year to use a roadway on B's newly purchased property when B is not looking.

   a.   I only.
   b.   I and II only.
   c.   II and III only.
   d.   I, II, and III.

21. A method of transferring ownership of real property that most likely would be considered an arm's-length transaction is transfer by
   a.   Inheritance.
   b.   Eminent domain.
   c.   Adverse possession.
   d.   Sale.

22. Which of the following elements must be contained in a valid deed?

	Purchase price	Description of the land
a.	Yes	Yes
b.	Yes	No
c.	No	Yes
d.	No	No

23. Which of the following warranties is(are) contained in a general warranty deed?

   I.   The grantor has the right to convey the property.
   II. The grantee will **not** be disturbed in possession of the property by the grantor or some third party's lawful claim of ownership.

   a.   I only.
   b.   II only.
   c.   Both I and II.
   d.   Neither I nor II.

24. For a deed to be effective between the purchaser and seller of real estate, one of the conditions is that the deed must
   a.   Contain the signatures of the seller and purchaser.
   b.   Contain the actual sales price.
   c.   Be delivered by the seller with an intent to transfer title.
   d.   Be recorded within the permissible statutory time limits.

Items 25 and 26 are based on the following:

   On February 1, Frost bought a building from Elgin, Inc. for $250,000. To complete the purchase, Frost borrowed $200,000 from Independent Bank and gave Independent a mortgage for that amount; gave Elgin a second mortgage for $25,000; and paid $25,000 in cash. Independent recorded its mortgage on February 2 and Elgin recorded its mortgage on March 12.

   The following transactions also took place:

   • On March 1, Frost gave Scott a $20,000 mortgage on the building to secure a personal loan Scott had previously made to Frost.

   • On March 10, Scott recorded this mortgage.

   • On March 15, Scott learned about both prior mortgages.

   • On June 1, Frost stopped making payments on all the mortgages.

- On August 1, the mortgages were foreclosed. Frost, on that date, owed Independent, $195,000; Elgin, $24,000; and Scott, $19,000.

A judicial sale of the building resulted in proceeds of $220,000 after expenses were deducted. The above transactions took place in a notice-race jurisdiction.

25. What amount of the proceeds will Scott receive?
  a. $0
  b. $ 1,000
  c. $12,500
  d. $19,000

26. Why would Scott receive this amount?
  a. Scott knew of the Elgin mortgage.
  b. Scott's mortgage was recorded before Elgin's and before Scott knew of Elgin's mortgage.
  c. Elgin's mortgage was first in time.
  d. After Independent is fully paid, Elgin and Scott share the remaining proceeds equally.

27. A purchaser who obtains real estate title insurance will
  a. Have coverage for the title exceptions listed in the policy.
  b. Be insured against all defects of record other than those excepted in the policy.
  c. Have coverage for title defects that result from events that happen after the effective date of the policy.
  d. Be entitled to transfer the policy to subsequent owners.

28. Which of the following is a defect in marketable title to real property?
  a. Recorded zoning restrictions.
  b. Recorded easements referred to in the contract of sale.
  c. Unrecorded lawsuit for negligence against the seller.
  d. Unrecorded easement.

29. Which of the following is not a necessary element for an individual to obtain title of a piece of real estate by adverse possession?
  a. Continuous possession.
  b. Possession that is to the exclusion of others.
  c. Possession permitted by the actual owner.
  d. Open and notorious possession.

30. Rake, twenty-five years ago, put a fence around a piece of land. At the time, Rake knew that fence not only surrounded his land but also a sizable piece of Howe's land. Every summer Rake planted a garden on this land surrounded by the fence. Howe recently sold all of his land to Cross. Cross has found out about the fence line and has asked Rake to either move the fence or pay Cross for the land in question. What is the result?
  a. Rake does not have to move the fence but must pay Cross for the land in question.
  b. Rake does not have to move the fence but must pay Howe for the land in question.
  c. Rake must move the fence.
  d. Rake must neither move the fence nor pay either party for the land in question.

31. Generally, which of the following federal acts regulate mortgage lenders?

	Real Estate Settlement Procedures Act (RESPA)	Federal Trade Commission Act
a.	Yes	Yes
b.	Yes	No
c.	No	Yes
d.	No	No

32. Gilmore borrowed $60,000 from Dix Bank. The loan was used to remodel a building owned by Gilmore as investment property and was secured by a second mortgage that Dix did not record. FCA Loan Company has a recorded first mortgage on the building. If Gilmore defaults on both mortgages, Dix
  a. Will **not** be entitled to any mortgage foreclosure sale proceeds, even if such proceeds are in excess of the amount owed to FCA.
  b. Will be unable to successfully claim any security interest in the building.
  c. Will be entitled to share in any foreclosure sale proceeds pro rata with FCA.
  d. Will be able to successfully claim a security interest that is subordinate to FCA's security interest.

33. Wilk bought an apartment building from Dix Corp. There was a mortgage on the building securing Dix's promissory note to Xeon Finance Co. Wilk took title subject to Xeon's mortgage. Wilk did not make the payments on the note due Xeon and the building was sold at a foreclosure sale. If the proceeds of the foreclosure sale are less than the balance due on the note, which of the following statements is correct regarding the deficiency?
  a. Xeon must attempt to collect the deficiency from Wilk before suing Dix.
  b. Dix will **not** be liable for any of the deficiency because Wilk assumed the note and mortgage.
  c. Xeon may collect the deficiency from either Dix or Wilk.
  d. Dix alone would be liable for the entire deficiency.

34. On April 6, Ford purchased a warehouse from Atwood for $150,000. Atwood had executed two mortgages on the property: a purchase money mortgage given to Lang on March 2, which was not recorded; and a mortgage given to Young on March 9, which was recorded the same day. Ford was unaware of the mortgage to Lang. Under the circumstances
  a. Ford will take title to the warehouse subject only to Lang's mortgage.
  b. Ford will take title to the warehouse free of Lang's mortgage.
  c. Lang's mortgage is superior to Young's mortgage because Lang's mortgage is a purchase money mortgage.
  d. Lang's mortgage is superior to Young's mortgage because Lang's mortgage was given first in time.

35. Which of the following conditions must be met to have an enforceable mortgage?
  a. An accurate description of the property must be included in the mortgage.
  b. A negotiable promissory note must accompany the mortgage.
  c. Present consideration must be given in exchange for the mortgage.
  d. The amount of the debt and the interest rate must be stated in the mortgage.

36. On February 1, Frost bought a building from Elgin, Inc. for $250,000. To complete the purchase, Frost borrowed $200,000 from Independent Bank and gave Independent a mortgage for that amount; gave Elgin a second mortgage for $25,000; and paid $25,000 in cash. Independent recorded its mortgage on February 2 and Elgin recorded its mortgage on March 12.

The following transactions also took place:

• On March 1, Frost gave Scott a $20,000 mortgage on the building to secure a personal loan Scott had previously made to Frost.

• On March 10, Scott recorded this mortgage.

• On March 15, Scott learned about both prior mortgages.

• On June 1, Frost stopped making payments on all the mortgages.

• On August 1, the mortgages were foreclosed. Frost, on that date, owed Independent, $195,000; Elgin, $24,000; and Scott, $19,000.

A judicial sale of the building resulted in proceeds of $220,000 after expenses were deducted. The above transactions took place in a notice-race jurisdiction.

Frost may redeem the property before the judicial sale only if

a. There is a statutory right of redemption.
b. It is probable that the sale price will result in a deficiency.
c. All mortgages are paid in full.
d. All mortgagees are paid a penalty fee.

37. A mortgagor's right of redemption will be terminated by a judicial foreclosure sale unless

a. The proceeds from the sale are not sufficient to fully satisfy the mortgage debt.
b. The mortgage instrument does not provide for a default sale.
c. The mortgagee purchases the property for market value.
d. The jurisdiction has enacted a statutory right of redemption.

38. Rich purchased property from Sklar for $200,000. Rich obtained a $150,000 loan from Marsh Bank to finance the purchase, executing a promissory note and a mortgage. By recording the mortgage, Marsh protects its

a. Rights against Rich under the promissory note.
b. Rights against the claims of subsequent bona fide purchasers for value.
c. Priority against a previously filed real estate tax lien on the property.
d. Priority against all parties having earlier claims to the property.

39. Which of the following provisions must be included to have an enforceable written residential lease?

	A description of the leased premises	A due date for the payment of rent
a.	Yes	Yes
b.	Yes	No
c.	No	Yes
d.	No	No

40. Which of the following rights is(are) generally given to a lessee of residual property?

I. A covenant of quiet enjoyment.

II. An implied warranty of habitability.

a. I only.
b. II only.
c. Both I and II.
d. Neither I nor II.

41. Which of the following methods of obtaining personal property will give the recipient ownership of the property?

	Lease	Finding abandoned property
a.	Yes	Yes
b.	Yes	No
c.	No	Yes
d.	No	No

42. Which of the following forms of tenancy will be created if a tenant stays in possession of the leased premises without the landlord's consent, after the tenant's one-year written lease expires?

a. Tenancy at will.
b. Tenancy for years.
c. Tenancy from period to period.
d. Tenancy at sufferance.

PROBLEM

NOTE: These types of problems are no longer included in the CPA Examination but they have been retained because they are useful in developing skills to complete simulations.

Problem 1 (15 to 20 minutes)

On March 2, 2003, Ash, Bale, and Rangel purchased an office building from Park Corp. as joint tenants with right of survivorship. There was an outstanding note and mortgage on the building, which they assumed. The note and mortgage named Park as the mortgagor (borrower) and Vista Bank as the mortgagee (lender). Vista has consented to the assumption.

Wein, Inc., a tenant in the office building, had entered into a ten-year lease dated May 8, 2000. The lease was silent regarding Wein's right to sublet. The lease provided for Wein to take occupancy on June 1, 2000, and that the monthly rent would be $5,000 for the entire ten-year term. On March 10, 2004, Wein informed Ash, Bale, and Rangel that it had agreed to sublet its office to Nord Corp. On March 17, 2004, Ash, Bale, and Rangel notified Wein of their refusal to consent to the sublet. The following assertions have been made:

- The sublet from Wein to Nord is void because Ash, Bale, and Rangel did not consent.
- If the sublet is not void, Ash, Bale, and Rangel have the right to hold either Wein or Nord liable for payment of the rent.

On April 4, 2004, Ash transferred his interest in the building to his spouse.

Required:

Answer the following, setting forth reasons for any conclusions stated.

a. For this item only, assume that Ash, Bale, and Rangel default on the mortgage note, that Vista forecloses, and a deficiency results. Discuss the personal liability of Ash, Bale, and Rangel to Vista and the personal liability of Park to Vista.

b. Discuss the assertions as to the sublet, indicating whether such assertions are correct and the reasons therefor.

c. For this item only, assume that Ash and Rangel died on April 20, 2004. Discuss the ownership interest(s) in the office building as of April 5, 2004, and April 21, 2004.

SIMULATION PROBLEM

Simulation Problem 1   (10 to 15 minutes)

Situation						
	Priority	Rationale	Sales Proceeds	Deficiency Fair	Deficiency Heath Finance	Deficiency Knox

On June 10, 1998, Bond sold real property to Edwards for $100,000. Edwards assumed the $80,000 recorded mortgage Bond had previously given to Fair Bank and gave a $20,000 purchase money mortgage to Heath Finance. Heath did not record this mortgage. On December 15, 1999, Edwards sold the property to Ivor for $115,000. Ivor bought the property subject to the Fair mortgage but did not know about the Heath mortgage. Ivor borrowed $50,000 from Knox Bank and gave Knox a mortgage on the property. Knox knew of the unrecorded Heath mortgage when its mortgage was recorded. Ivor, Edwards, and Bond defaulted on the mortgages. Fair, Heath, and Knox foreclosed and the property was sold at a judicial foreclosure sale for $60,000. At the time of the sale, the outstanding balance of principal and accrued interest on the Fair mortgage was $75,000. The Heath mortgage balance was $18,000 and the Knox mortgage was $47,500.

Fair, Heath, and Knox all claim that their mortgages have priority and should be satisfied first from the sale proceeds. Bond, Edwards, and Ivor all claim that they are not liable for any deficiency resulting from the sale.

The above transactions took place in a jurisdiction that has a notice-race recording statute and allows foreclosure deficiency judgments.

	Priority					
Situation		Rationale	Sales Proceeds	Deficiency Fair	Deficiency Heath Finance	Deficiency Knox

Part a.   Items 1 through 3. For each mortgage, select from List A the priority of that mortgage. A priority should be selected only once.

> *List A*
> A. First Priority.
> B. Second Priority.
> C. Third Priority.

	(A)	(B)	(C)
1. Knox Bank.	○	○	○
2. Heath Finance.	○	○	○
3. Fair Bank.	○	○	○

		Rationale				
Situation	Priority		Sales Proceeds	Deficiency Fair	Deficiency Heath Finance	Deficiency Knox

Part b.   Items 4 through 6. For each mortgage, select from List B the reason for its priority. A reason may be selected once, more than once, or not at all.

> *List B*
> A. An unrecorded mortgage has priority over any subsequently recorded mortgage.
> B. A recorded mortgage has priority over any unrecorded mortgage.
> C. The first recorded mortgage has priority over all subsequent mortgages.
> D. An unrecorded mortgage has priority over a subsequently recorded mortgage if the subsequent mortgagee knew of the unrecorded mortgage.
> E. A purchase money mortgage has priority over a previously recorded mortgage.

	(A)	(B)	(C)	(D)	(E)
4. Knox Bank.	○	○	○	○	○
5. Heath Finance.	○	○	○	○	○
6. Fair Bank.	○	○	○	○	○

			Sales Proceeds			
Situation	Priority	Rationale		Deficiency Fair	Deficiency Heath Finance	Deficiency Knox

Part c.   Items 7 through 9. For each mortgage, select from List C the amount of the sale proceeds that each mortgagee would be entitled to receive. An amount may be selected once, more than once, or not at all.

<u>List C</u>

A.	$0	E.	$42,000
B.	$12,500	F.	$47,500
C.	$18,000	G.	$60,000
D.	$20,000		

	(A)	(B)	(C)	(D)	(E)	(F)	(G)
7. Knox Bank.	○	○	○	○	○	○	○
8. Heath Finance.	○	○	○	○	○	○	○
9. Fair Bank.	○	○	○	○	○	○	○

Situation	Priority	Rationale	Sales Proceeds	Deficiency Fair	Deficiency Heath Finance	Deficiency Knox

Part d.   Items 10 through 12. Determine whether each party would be liable to pay a mortgage foreclosure deficiency judgment on the Fair Bank mortgage. If the party would be held liable, select from List D the reason for that party's liability. A reason may be selected once, more than once, or not at all.

<u>List D</u>

A. Original mortgagor.   C. Took subject to the mortgage.
B. Assumed the mortgage.   D. Not liable.

	(A)	(B)	(C)	(D)
10. Edwards.	○	○	○	○
11. Bond.	○	○	○	○
12. Ivor.	○	○	○	○

Situation	Priority	Rationale	Sales Proceeds	Deficiency Fair	Deficiency Heath Finance	Deficiency Knox

Part e.   For **items 13 through 15,** determine whether each party would be liable to pay a mortgage foreclosure deficiency judgment on the Heath Finance mortgage. If the party would be held liable, select from List E the reason for that party's liability. A reason may be selected once, more than once, or not at all.

<u>List E</u>

A. Original mortgagor.   C. Took subject to the mortgage.
B. Assumed the mortgage.   D. Not liable.

	(A)	(B)	(C)	(D)
13. Edwards.	○	○	○	○
14. Bond.	○	○	○	○
15. Ivor.	○	○	○	○

Situation	Priority	Rationale	Sales Proceeds	Deficiency Fair	Deficiency Heath Finance	Deficiency Knox

Part f.   For **items 16 through 18,** determine whether each party would be liable to pay a mortgage foreclosure deficiency judgment on the Knox Bank mortgage. If the party would be held liable, select from List F the reason for that party's liability. A reason may be selected once, more than once, or not at all.

<u>List F</u>

A. Original mortgagor.   C. Took subject to the mortgage.
B. Assumed the mortgage.   D. Not liable.

	(A)	(B)	(C)	(D)
16. Edwards.	○	○	○	○
17. Bond.	○	○	○	○
18. Ivor.	○	○	○	○

MULTIPLE-CHOICE ANSWERS

1.	d	__ __	10.	c	__ __	19.	c	__ __	28.	d	__ __
2.	d	__ __	11.	d	__ __	20.	a	__ __	29.	c	__ __
3.	c	__ __	12.	a	__ __	21.	d	__ __	30.	d	__ __
4.	c	__ __	13.	b	__ __	22.	c	__ __	31.	b	__ __
5.	d	__ __	14.	d	__ __	23.	c	__ __	32.	d	__ __
6.	d	__ __	15.	a	__ __	24.	c	__ __	33.	d	__ __
7.	a	__ __	16.	b	__ __	25.	d	__ __	34.	b	__ __
8.	c	__ __	17.	d	__ __	26.	b	__ __	35.	a	__ __
9.	d	__ __	18.	a	__ __	27.	b	__ __	36.	c	__ __

37.	d	__ __
38.	b	__ __
39.	b	__ __
40.	c	__ __
41.	c	__ __
42.	d	__ __
1st:	__/42 =	__%
2nd:	__/42 =	__%

MULTIPLE-CHOICE ANSWER EXPLANATIONS

A. Distinctions between Real and Personal Property

1. (d) Real property is land and objects attached to land in a relatively permanent manner; personal property is property not classified as real. Tangible property is subject to physical possession; intangible property cannot be physically possessed, but can be legally owned. Ownership of intangible property is often represented by a piece of paper, but the property itself is intangible. A share of stock is part ownership of a company; a trademark is ownership of the use of a particular mark, design, word, or picture, and a promissory note is ownership of the right to receive payment of a debt at a future date. These are all usually represented by a piece of paper, but are intangible. An oil painting is personal property subject to physical possession.

2. (d) Growing crops generally are part of the land and therefore considered real property. However, the crops can be sold separately from the land, in which case they are considered personal property under the UCC, whether the buyer or the seller will sever the growing crops later from the land. Answer (a) is incorrect because air rights are not discussed in the UCC as one of those that can be either. Answer (b) is incorrect because mineral rights are associated with land or realty. Answer (c) is incorrect because unlike growing crops that may be realty until sold in a contract, harvested crops are personal property separate from the realty.

B. Personal Property

3. (c) The factors used to determine whether an item of personal property is considered a fixture are (1) the affixer's intent, (2) the method and permanence of attachment, and (3) whether the personal property is customarily necessary to use the real property.

4. (c) When the owner mislays personal property and forgets to take it with him or her, the finder does not obtain title but the owner of the premise acts as caretaker in case the true owner comes back. In the case of lost property (involuntarily left), the finder obtains title; however, the true owner, Getty, wins over this title. In the case of abandoned property, the finder gets valid title that is even valid against Getty.

5. (d) When property is discarded with no intention of keeping ownership over it, it is considered abandoned property. In such cases, the one who finds and keeps the abandoned property becomes the owner with title that is good against all other parties, even the owner who abandoned it. Note that Walters cannot obtain title from Rand because Rand no longer owns the rocking chair.

C. Bailments

6. (d) The general rule for a bailee is to exercise reasonable care in light of the particular facts and circumstances. However, a common carrier holds itself out as a public delivery service, and is held to a very high standard for property placed in its care. Therefore, answer (d) is correct.

D. Intellectual Property and Computer Technology Rights

7. (a) Computer software is covered under the general copyright laws and is therefore usually copyrightable as an expression of ideas. Answer (b) is incorrect because copyrights in general do not need a copyright notice for works published after March 1, 1989. Answer (c) is incorrect because a recent court ruled that programs in both source codes, which are human readable, and in machine readable object code can be copyrighted. Answer (d) is incorrect because copyrights taken out by corporations or businesses are valid for 100 years from creation of the copyrighted item or seventy-five years from its publication, whichever is shorter.

8. (c) Computer databases are generally copyrightable as compilations. Answer (a) is not chosen because copies for archival purposes are allowed. Answer (b) is not chosen because in the case of corporations or businesses, the copyright is valid for the shorter of 100 years after the creation of the work or seventy-five years from its date of publication. Answer (d) is not chosen because computer programs are now generally recognized as copyrightable.

9. (d) Under the fair use doctrine, copyrighted items can be used for teaching, including distributing multiple copies for class use. Answer (a) is incorrect because although he originally purchased this software for personal use, he may still use it for his class, in which case, the fair use doctrine applies. Answer (b) is incorrect because databases can be copyrighted as derivative works. Answer (c) is incorrect because the use of the computer is not the issue but the fair use doctrine is.

10. (c) Both patent and copyright law are used under modern law to protect computer technology rights. Answer (a) is incorrect because copyright law now also protects software. Answer (b) is incorrect because modern law also protects software as patentable. Answer (d) is incorrect because modern law generally protects intellectual property rights in software under both patent law and copyright law.

11. **(d)** Trademarks are valid indefinitely until they are actually abandoned or the company allows the trademark to lose its distinctiveness. Answer (a) is not chosen because trademarks can protect many distinctive things such as shapes, packaging, or graphic designs. Answer (b) is not chosen because a company must take steps to keep the trademark distinctive or it can lose it through others' common usage. For example, elevator was once a trademark which has since been lost. Answer (c) is not chosen because although a company may register a trademark to better protect its legal rights, it may still receive protection without registering it by proving the facts.

12. **(a)** Since January 1, 1978, this is the life of a copyright. Answer (b) is incorrect because the copyright is valid when the author puts the work of art in tangible form. Answer (c) is incorrect because works published after March 1, 1989 no longer require a copyright notice placed on them. Answer (d) is incorrect because under current copyright law, (b) and (c) are no longer required.

E.   Interests in Real Property

13. **(b)** In a joint tenancy, each joint tenant has an equal and undivided interest in the property. Each joint tenant can transfer his/her interest in the property without the prior consent of the other joint tenants. When this occurs, the conveyance destroys the joint tenancy and creates a tenancy in common between the remaining joint tenants and the third party. When Long gave his/her interest in the building to Green, Green became a tenant in common with a 1/3 interest in the property. Therefore, answer (a) is incorrect. Answer (d) is incorrect because Green would have total interest in the building after the deaths of Fall and Pear only if Green had been a joint tenant rather than a tenant in common. Answer (c) is incorrect because a joint tenant may convey rights in property without the consent of other joint tenants.

14. **(d)** A fee simple is generally the most comprehensive interest that a person may have in property under the law of the United States. It allows the owner to sell it or to pass it on to heirs. Answer (a) is incorrect because an easement is not ownership of the land but the right to use it in a way such as using a roadway along with the owner. Answer (b) is incorrect because a leasehold gives the lessee the right to possess the premises under the lease but not the ownership of the premises. Answer (c) is incorrect because a license is permission given by the owner to use or occupy the real estate but not to own it.

15. **(a)** In a joint tenancy, each joint tenant has an equal and undivided interest in the property. Joint tenancy ownership consists of the unities of time, title, interest, and possession and carries with it the right of survivorship. Thus, all the elements listed in the question are required to establish a joint tenancy and answers (b), (c), and (d) are incorrect.

16. **(b)** A tenancy by default is not one of the recognized interests in real estate. Answer (a) is incorrect because a fee simple absolute is the highest estate recognized in American law. Answer (c) is incorrect because a life interest is an interest measured by the life of the holder or some other person. Answer (d) is incorrect because a remainder is the future interest that a third party acquires after the interest of a transferee terminates.

17. **(d)** In a tenancy in common, each tenant essentially owns an undivided fractional share of the property. Each tenant has the right to convey his/her interest in the property and if one of the tenants dies, that tenant's interest passes to his/her heirs. Therefore, if Nash dies, Nash's interest would pass to Nash's heirs and the ownership of the property would be as follows: Quick 1/2, Onyx 1/4, and Nash's heirs 1/4.

18. **(a)** Jan had title to the property when Brett granted it to her for her life. Randy never got title to it because he died before Jan's life estate terminated. When Jan died, her life estate terminated and the property reverted back to Brett, who was still living. Answer (b) is incorrect because Brett was still living. Answers (c) and (d) are incorrect because Jan and Randy had been granted life estates which automatically terminate upon their deaths.

19. **(c)** When rights in property held in joint tenancy are conveyed without the consent of the other joint tenants, the new owner becomes a tenant in common rather than a joint tenant. The remaining cotenants are still joint tenants. Thus, after the sale of land from Court to Plank without the consent of the others, Plank owns one third of the land as a tenant in common. Both Fell and Miles will continue to each own one third of the land as joint tenants.

20. **(a)** Fact pattern I involves an easement in which O reserves the right to use B's land in the deed to B. O does not any longer own the roadway but retains the right to use it. Fact pattern II is a profit rather than an easement in which O has the right to enter B's land to cut and keep the ten trees. Fact pattern III is not an easement because O has not retained nor has s/he been given the right to use the roadway. Note that this is not an easement by prescription in that the use is not open and notorious nor has it occurred for several years.

G. Types of Deeds

21. **(d)** An arm's-length transaction is a negotiation between unrelated parties acting in his/her interest. A way to test an arm's-length transaction is to consider what a disinterested third party would pay for the property. Answer (d) is correct because a sale involves the transfer of property for consideration in which a third party would generally negotiate and act in his/her interest. Answer (a) is incorrect because the property passes to a party as the decedent directs, subject to certain state limitations. Answer (b) is incorrect because eminent domain is the power of the government to take, with just compensation, private property for public use. Answer (c) is incorrect because adverse possession allows a person to gain title to real property if the person has continuously and openly occupied the land of another for a statutory period of time.

22. **(c)** In order for a deed to be valid, a description of the land must be included. The purchase price of the land need not be present to form a valid deed.

23. **(c)** A general warranty deed warrants that (1) the seller has title and the power to convey the property described in the deed, (2) the property is free from any encumbrances, except as disclosed in the deed, and (3) the grantee (purchaser) will not be disturbed in his/her possession of the property by the grantor (seller) or some third party's lawful claim of ownership. Thus, a general warranty deed would contain both of the warranties listed and answers (a), (b), and (d) are incorrect.

I. Recording a Deed

24.   (c)   In order for a deed to be effective between the purchaser and seller of real estate, the deed must be delivered by the seller with an intent to transfer title. Even though a deed may be executed it does not become effective until delivery is made with the proper intent. Answer (d) is incorrect because a deed need not be recorded in order for it to be valid between the seller and purchaser. Recordation of a deed is important because it gives constructive notice to all third parties of the grantee's ownership; however, it does not affect the resolution of any disputes between the grantor and the grantee. Answer (a) is incorrect since a deed need be signed by only the seller in order for it to be effective; it does not have to be signed by the purchaser. Answer (b) is incorrect since the form of a deed is very different from a contract for the sale of real property. There is no requirement that the deed must contain the actual sales price.

25.   (d)   Under a notice-race statute, if a mortgagee fails to record its mortgage, a subsequent mortgagee who records will have a superior security interest if s/he did not have notice of the prior mortgage. In this situation, Independent Bank was the first to record its mortgage and would receive the $195,000 owed it. Scott would then receive $19,000 because Scott recorded his/her mortgage before Elgin. Since Scott did not have knowledge of Elgin's mortgage until after Scott had recorded his/her mortgage, Scott would have priority over Elgin.

26.   (b)   Under a notice-race statute, a subsequent mortgagee (lender) who loans money without notice of a previous mortgage and records the mortgage first has priority over that previous mortgage. Thus, since Scott recorded his/her mortgage before Elgin and without knowledge of Elgin's mortgage, Scott would have priority in a notice-race jurisdiction. Answer (a) is incorrect because Scott did not know of Elgin's mortgage at the time Scott recorded his/her mortgage. Although Scott later learned about both prior mortgages, this would not affect Scott's priority over Elgin's mortgage. Answer (c) is incorrect because Elgin's mortgage would have priority only if it had been recorded before Scott's. Answer (d) is incorrect because Scott's mortgage had priority over Elgin's. Therefore, Scott would be entitled to receive the full $19,000 before Elgin received any of the proceeds from the judicial sale.

J. Title Insurance

27.   (b)   Title insurance insures against all defects of record and defects the grantee may be aware of. Any exceptions not insured by the title policy must be shown on the face of the policy. Answer (a) is incorrect because title exceptions are not insured by the title policy. Answer (c) is incorrect because title insurance covers only defects of record. Answer (d) is incorrect because title insurance does not pass to subsequent purchasers.

28.   (d)   Marketable title means that the title to real property is free from encumbrances, such as mortgages, easements, and liens and defects in the chain of title. However, there is an exception. Most courts hold that the seller's obligation to convey marketable title does not require the seller to convey the title free from recorded zoning restrictions,

visible public rights-of-way or recorded easements. An unrecorded easement, however, would be a defect in marketable title. Therefore, answer (d) is correct. An unrecorded lawsuit for negligence against the seller would not cause a defect in marketable title.

K. Adverse Possession

29.   (c)   One of the elements to obtain title to property by adverse possession is that the possession be hostile to the ownership interests of the actual owner. This does not occur when possession is permitted by the actual owner. All of the others are necessary elements to obtain ownership by adverse possession.

30.   (d)   Rake has fulfilled the elements necessary to gain title to this land in question by adverse possession. These are: (1) open and notorious possession, (2) hostile possession shown by the fence, (3) actual possession, (4) continuous possession, and (5) exclusive possession for twenty-five years. Note that it is considered continuous possession even though the gardening is only during the summer, because the fence is constantly there. Answers (a), (b), and (c) are incorrect because since Rake obtained title to the land in question, he does not have to move the fence or pay for the land.

M. Mortgages

31.   (b)   Congress enacted the Real Estate Settlement Procedures Act (RESPA) in 1974 to provide home buyers with more extensive information about the settlement process and to protect them from unnecessarily high settlement fees. The act applies to all federally related mortgage loans, and nearly all first mortgage loans. Therefore, the general purpose of this act is to regulate mortgage lenders.

The purpose of the Federal Trade Commission Act is to prevent unfair methods of competition and unfair or deceptive practices in commerce. It is a general consumer protection act, and regulates compliance with antitrust laws. Although it may apply to mortgage lenders, its general purpose is not to regulate mortgage lenders.

32.   (d)   Dix's second mortgage on Gilmore's property will allow Dix to claim a security interest subordinate to FCA's first mortgage security interest. Dix's failure to record the second mortgage will not affect their right to successfully enforce the mortgage against Gilmore. Therefore, answer (b) is incorrect. Answer (a) is incorrect because Dix would be entitled to receive mortgage foreclosure sale proceeds if such proceeds were in excess of the amount owed to FCA. Answer (c) is incorrect because FCA's first mortgage must be fully satisfied before any payments can be made to Dix.

33.   (d)   If a buyer takes a mortgage "subject to," then the buyer accepts no liability for the mortgage and the seller is still primarily liable. The mortgagor does not have to attempt to collect from the buyer first; he can go directly against the seller. Therefore, answer (d) is correct, and answers (a) and (c) are incorrect. Answer (b) is incorrect because Wilk did not **assume** the mortgage but bought the building **subject to** the mortgage.

34.   (b)   A purchaser of real estate takes title subject to any mortgage he was aware of or any mortgage that was recorded before the purchase. Ford, therefore, takes title to the warehouse subject to Young's mortgage, but free of

Lang's mortgage. Therefore, answer (b) is correct and answer (a) is incorrect. Answer (c) is incorrect because there is no such provision. Answer (d) is incorrect because the recording statutes change the first in time concept to encourage the recording of mortgages.

35. **(a)** To have an enforceable mortgage it must be in writing and must include a description of the property and debt to be incurred. Therefore, answer (a) is correct. Answer (b) is incorrect, because although debt is usually evidenced by a promissory note, this is not required to be. Answer (c) is incorrect because the promise to pay is adequate consideration. Answer (d) is incorrect because the amount of the debt and the interest rate are not required to be stated in the mortgage.

36. **(c)** A mortgagor has the right to redeem the mortgaged property after default and before a judicial sale by payment of all principal and interest due on the mortgage note. Thus, Frost may redeem the property only if all mortgages are paid in full prior to the judicial sale. Answer (a) is incorrect because the right of redemption is a right that occurs **after** the judicial sale. Most states allow a mortgagor a period of time, usually one year after the foreclosure sale, to reinstate the debt and mortgage by paying to the purchaser at the judicial sale the amount of the purchase price plus the statutory interest rate. Answer (b) is incorrect because Frost may redeem the property prior to the judicial sale by paying all mortgages in full without regard to the probable sale price of the property. Answer (d) is incorrect because Frost would not have to pay penalty fees to the mortgagees.

37. **(d)** After foreclosure of the mortgage, the mortgagor may redeem the property by payment of all principal and interest due on the mortgage note. However, the right of redemption will terminate at the time of the judicial foreclosure sale unless the jurisdiction has enacted a statutory right of redemption. Answers (a), (b), and (c) are incorrect because they do not affect when the mortgagor's right of redemption terminates.

38. **(b)** Recording a mortgage protects the mortgagee against **subsequent** mortgagees, purchasers, or other takers. Therefore, answers (a), (c), and (d) are incorrect because those answers involve parties with existing claims on the property.

N. Lessor-Lessee

39. **(b)** A residential lease agreement must contain the following essential elements: the parties involved, lease payment amount, lease term, and a description of the leased property. The omission of any of these terms will cause the agreement to fail for indefiniteness. The other terms of payment due date, liability insurance requirements, and responsibility for repairs are optional, but not required. They will not cause the contract to fail for indefiniteness.

40. **(c)** The lessee of residential property, although not the owner, generally has the right to possession of the property and the right to quiet enjoyment of the property. The right to quiet enjoyment means that neither the lessor nor a third party with a valid claim will evict the lessee unless the lessee has breached the lease contract. The lessee also has the implied warranty of habitability which means that s/he has the right to inhabit premises that are fit for human occupation.

41. **(c)** A lease is not a sale and does not involve a transfer of title. A lessee may have possession and control of the property but will not have ownership. When property is abandoned, the owner relinquishes possession and title of the property. Subsequent parties who acquire abandoned property with the intent to own it acquire title.

42. **(d)** A tenancy at sufferance is created when a tenant stays in possession of the leased property after the expiration of the lease without the landlord's consent. A tenant at sufferance is a trespasser and the landlord may evict the tenant by instituting legal proceedings. Answer (a) is incorrect because a tenancy at will is an agreement that is not for a fixed period but is terminable at the will of the landlord or tenant. In this situation, the tenant does not have the consent of the landlord to stay in possession of the property and a tenancy at will is not created. Answer (b) is incorrect because a tenancy for years is a tenancy that has a fixed beginning and end at the time of creation of the tenancy. Answer (c) is incorrect because a tenancy from period to period would only be created if the landlord allowed the tenant to remain in possession of the property.

ANSWER OUTLINE

Problem 1   Liability on Assumption of Mortgage; Sublet-
                 ting; Property Interests; Rights of Joint Ten-
                 ants and Tenants in Common

a.   Ash, Bale, and Rangel are personally liable to Vista
        They assumed the mortgage
        Park is also personally liable to Vista
            Assumption by third party does not relieve Park

b.   Assertion that the sublet is void is false
            A tenant may sublet unless stated otherwise in the
              lease
        Assertion that Wein or Nord is liable for rent is false
            Sublessee (Nord) is only liable to tenant (Wein)
                Tenant (Wein) is solely liable to landlord (Ash,
                  Bale, and Rangel)

c.   Ash's spouse becomes 1/3 tenant in common on April 4
            Transfer of joint tenant's interest without consent of
              other joint tenants precludes transferee from be-
              coming a joint tenant
            Rangel's death transfers his 1/3 interest to Bale
              through right of survivorship
                Bale has 2/3 interest and is now tenant in common
                  since he was the only joint tenant remaining
                  Ash's spouse remains 1/3 tenant in common

UNOFFICIAL ANSWER

Problem 1   Liability on Assumption of Mortgage; Sublet-
                 ting; Property Interests; Rights of Joint Ten-
                 ants and Tenants in Common

a.   Ash, Bale, and Rangel will be personally liable to Vista
for the deficiency resulting from the foreclosure sale because
they became the principal debtors when they assumed the
mortgage. Park will remain liable for the deficiency. Although Vista consented to the assumption of the mortgage
by Ash, Bale, and Rangel, such assumption does not relieve
Park from its obligation to Vista unless Park obtains a release from Vista or there is a novation.

b.   The assertion that the sublet from Wein to Nord is void
because Ash, Bale, and Rangel must consent to the sublet is
incorrect. Unless the lease provides otherwise, a tenant may
sublet the premises without the landlord's consent. Since
the lease was silent regarding Wein's right to sublet, Wein
may sublet to Nord without the consent of Ash, Bale, and
Rangel.

The assertion that if the sublet was not void Ash, Bale,
and Rangel have the right to hold either Wein or Nord liable
for payment of rent is incorrect. In a sublease, the sublessee/
subtenant (Nord) has no obligation to pay rent to the landlord (Ash, Bale, and Rangel).

The subtenant (Nord) is liable to the tenant (Wein), but
the tenant (Wein) remains solely liable to the landlord (Ash,
Bale, and Rangel) for the rent stipulated in the lease.

c.   Ash's inter vivos transfer of his 1/3 interest in the office
building to his spouse on April 4, resulted in his spouse obtaining a 1/3 interest in the office building as a tenant in
common. Ash's wife did not become a joint tenant with
Bale and Rangel because the transfer of a joint tenant's interest to an outside party destroys the joint tenancy nature of
the particular interest transferred. Bale and Rangel will remain as joint tenants with each other.

As of April 21, the office building was owned by Ash's
spouse who had a 1/3 interest as tenant in common and Bale
who had a 2/3 interest as tenant in common.

Ash's death on April 20, will have no effect on the
ownership of the office building because Ash had already
transferred all of his interest to his wife on April 4.

Rangel's death on April 20, resulted in his interest being acquired by Bale because of the right of survivorship
feature in a joint tenancy. Because there are no surviving
joint tenants, Bale will become a tenant in common who
owns 2/3 of the office building. Ash's spouse will not acquire any additional interest due to Rangel's death because
she was a tenant in common with Rangel.

SOLUTION TO SIMULATION PROBLEM

Simulation Problem 1

Part a.

1. **(C)** **2.** **(B)** **3.** **(A)** Under a notice-race recording statute, a subsequent mortgagee (lender) who loans money without notice of the previous mortgagee and records the mortgage first has priority over that previous mortgagee. Once a mortgagee records, this gives constructive notice to any subsequent parties who then cannot obtain priority over the one who recorded. In this fact pattern, Fair Bank was the first mortgagee. Since Fair Bank also recorded this mortgage first, Fair Bank has the first priority over the subsequent mortgagees. Therefore, the answer to number 3 is (A). Of the two remaining mortgagees, Heath Finance was next in time but did not record the mortgage. Knox Bank was third in time and did record. However, Knox is unable to gain priority over Heath because Knox, when it recorded, knew of the Heath mortgage. Therefore, Knox does not meet all of the rules necessary to have priority over Heath. Thus Heath has the second priority after Fair Bank and Knox has the third priority. Therefore, the answer to number 2 is (B) and number 1 is (C).

Part b.

4. **(D)** **5.** **(D)** **6.** **(C)** This part covers the reason for the priority that applies to each of the mortgagees. Reason (A) states that "an unrecorded mortgage has priority over any subsequently recorded mortgage." This is incorrect for all mortgagees and goes against the policy behind the recording statutes to encourage recording to warn subsequent parties of the previous mortgages. Reason (B) is not a correct statement. It states that "A recorded mortgage has priority over any unrecorded mortgage." In this fact pattern, Knox recorded but Heath did not; however, Knox still has a lower priority because Knox knew of the Heath mortgage when its mortgage was recorded. Reason (C) is the correct answer for Fair Bank. It states that "The first recorded mortgage has priority over all subsequent mortgages." This is true because once Fair Bank recorded, subsequent mortgagees had constructive notice of the Fair Bank mortgage and thus could not obtain priority. The correct answer to number 6 is therefore (C). Reason (D) states that "An unrecorded mortgage has priority over a subsequently recorded mortgage if the subsequent mortgagee knew of the unrecorded mortgage." In this fact pattern, the Heath mortgage was the unrecorded mortgage that still had a higher priority than the recorded Knox mortgage because Knox Bank knew of the Heath mortgage when its mortgage was recorded. Thus Knox never fulfilled the rule which would allow it as the subsequent mortgagee, to gain a higher priority. Therefore, reason (D) is the correct answer for both Knox Bank, number four, and Heath Finance, number 5, because the same rule determines the relative priority of these two parties. Note that reason (E) is not a correct statement for any of the mortgagees because there is no rule that gives purchase money mortgages priority over previously recorded mortgages.

Part c.

7. **(A)** **8.** **(A)** **9.** **(G)** Since Fair Bank has the highest priority, its mortgage will be satisfied first. Since the outstanding balance of the Fair Bank mortgage was greater than the $60,000 received at the judicial foreclosure, Fair Bank receives all of the $60,000 and Knox Bank and Heath Finance each receive nothing.

Part d.

10. **(B)** **11.** **(A)** **12.** **(D)** When a foreclosure sale does not provide enough money to pay off the mortgages, the mortgagee, in states that allow foreclosure deficiency judgments, will attempt to collect any deficiency from the parties involved. In this fact pattern, Bond is liable because s/he was the original mortgagor on the property and as such agreed to pay the mortgage. Thus, (A) is the correct answer for number 11. When Edwards later bought the property from Bond, s/he assumed the Fair Bank mortgage. Edwards, thus, became personally liable on the mortgage even though the seller, Bond, also remained liable. Therefore, (B) is the correct answer for number 10. When Ivor subsequently purchased the property from Edwards, Ivor purchased the property subject to the Fair Bank mortgage. In so doing, s/he did not accept any liability on the mortgage. Note that although reason (C) states "Took subject to the mortgage," the correct answer for number 12 is (D) "Not liable." This is true because the directions to part d. indicate that reasons (A), (B), or (C) are to be chosen as reasons **for liability** and (D) is to be chosen if the party is **not** liable.

Part e.

13. **(A)** **14.** **(D)** **15.** **(D)** When Edwards purchased the property, s/he gave a mortgage to Heath Finance. Therefore, (A) is the correct answer for number thirteen because as the original mortgagor on the Heath mortgage, s/he agreed to be liable on it. Bond is not liable on the Heath mortgage because s/he having owned the property earlier, never agreed to be liable on this mortgage. Therefore, the correct answer to number 14 is (D). Ivor is not liable on the Heath mortgage because s/he never had actual notice or constructive notice of the unrecorded mortgage, and never agreed to be liable on it. Therefore, the correct answer to number 15 is (D).

Part f.

16. **(D)** **17.** **(D)** **18.** **(A)** Since Ivor borrowed from Knox Bank and gave Knox a mortgage on the property, Ivor is liable as the original mortgagor, making (A) the correct reason for number 18. Both Edwards and Bond owned the property prior to the Knox mortgage and never agreed to be liable on it. Therefore, the correct answer to numbers 16 and 17 is (D).

INSURANCE

Overview

Insurance is a contract whereby the insurer (insurance company) indemnifies the insured (policyholder) against loss on designated property due to specified risks such as fire, storm, etc. The obligation of the insured under the insurance contract is the payment of the stipulated premium. Before an insured can recover under a property insurance policy, the policyholder must have an insurable interest in the property at the time it was damaged or destroyed. Basically, insurance is limited to providing protection against the risk of loss arising from a happening of events caused by the negligence of insured and negligence and intentional acts of third parties. Insurance does not protect against loss due to intentional acts of insured. Insurance contracts like others, require agreement, consideration, capacity, and legality.

Primary emphasis on the exam is placed upon knowledge of fire and casualty insurance. The exam has emphasized insurable interest, coinsurance and pro rata clauses, risks protected against, subrogation, and assignment of insurance contracts.

A. General Considerations

1. Insurance is the distribution of the cost of risk over a large number of individuals subject to the same risk, in order to reimburse the few who actually suffer from the risk
2. Insurance is designed to protect against large unexpected losses, not small everyday losses
3. Intentional acts of insured usually are not insurable (e.g., fire by arson, liability for assault and battery)

   a. Negligence or carelessness is insurable and is generally not a defense of the insurer
   b. Negligence of an insured's employees is also covered

4. Self-insurance is the periodic setting aside of money into a fund to provide for losses

   a. Not true insurance, because it is not a distribution of risk; it is preparation to meet possible losses

B. Insurance Contract

1. Similar to a common law contract. Must contain all essential elements (i.e., agreement, legality, capacity, and consideration)
2. Generally a unilateral contract where the insured prepays the premiums and the insurer promises to indemnify insured against loss
3. Insurance is generally binding at time of unconditional acceptance of the application and communication of this to insured

   a. The application is the offer, and issuance of the policy is acceptance
   b. A company agent (as opposed to an independent agent) usually has power to issue a temporarily binding slip that obligates the insurer during interim before issuance of policy
   c. Physical delivery of written policy is not necessary
   d. Insurer may require conditions to be met before policy becomes effective (e.g., pay a premium)

      (1) A general agent may accept a policy for insured

4. Policy may be voidable at option of insurer if there is

   a. Concealment—the insured failed to inform insurer at time of application of a fact material to insurer's risk

      EXAMPLE: *An applicant for auto insurance is unable to drive and does not so inform the insurer.*

      (1) Any matter specifically asked by insurer is by law material, and failure to disclose or a misleading answer is concealment
      (2) Need not disclose facts learned after making the contract

   b. Material misrepresentation by insured (e.g., nonexistent subject matter)

      (1) Representation acceptable if substantially true (e.g., value of subject matter does not have to be exact)

   c. Breach of warranty incorporated in the policy

      EXAMPLE: *An applicant for fire insurance warrants that a night watchman will be on duty at night at all times to check for fire. If he is not and a loss occurs, this may release the insurer.*

5. Statute of Frauds does not require insurance contract to be in writing because it may fall within the one-year rule (but usually is required by state statutes)

6. Insurable interest

   a. There must be a relationship between the insured and the insured event so that if the event occurs insured will suffer substantial loss

   b. In property, there must be both a legal interest and a possibility of pecuniary loss

      (1) Legal interest may be ownership or a security interest (e.g., general creditors do not have an insurable interest but judgment lien creditors and mortgagees do)

         EXAMPLE: G takes out a fire insurance policy on a building owned by A. G did this because he frequently does some business with A. Although A generally pays his bills as they are due, A owes G $20,000. G, as a general creditor only, has no insurable interest in A's building.

      (2) Insurable interest need not be present at inception of the policy so long as it is present at time of the loss

      (3) One can insure only to extent one has an insurable interest (e.g., mortgagee can insure only amount still due)

      (4) Contract to purchase or possession of property can give an insurable interest

      (5) Goods identified with contract create insurable interest

   c. For life insurance, one has an insurable interest in one's own life and the lives of close family relatives or individuals whose death could result in pecuniary loss

      (1) Company or person has insurable interest in key personnel or key employees

      (2) For life insurance, insurable interest need be present at inception of policy but not at time of death

         EXAMPLE: Same as example above except that G takes out a life insurance policy on A's life. G does not have an insurable interest.

         EXAMPLE: M and N are partners in a firm in which the skills of both M and N are important. M and N take out life insurance policies on each other. There are valid insurable interests for these policies.

         EXAMPLE: Same as previous example except that M and N terminate their partnership. They do not, however, terminate the life insurance policies on each other's lives. Upon M's death, N can collect on the life insurance policy.

   d. Insurance offered for identity fraud or identity theft

      (1) Typically covers fees paid to help restore bad credit trail left behind affecting person's name such as lost wages for work lost in correcting fraud, attorney's fees, reapplication fees, telephone charges

C. Subrogation

1. This is the right of insurer to step into the shoes of insured as to any cause of action relating to a third party whose conduct caused the loss

   EXAMPLE: While driving his car, X is hit by Y. If X's insurance company pays X, the insurance company is subrogated to X's claim against Y.

   a. Applies to accident, automobile collision, and fire policies

2. A general release of a third party, who caused the loss, by insured will release insurer from his/her obligation

   EXAMPLE: While driving his car, X is hit by Y. Y talks X into signing a statement that X releases Y from all liability. X will not be able to recover on his insurance. X's insurance company is released when Y is released.

   a. Because insurer's right of subrogation has been cut off

   b. A partial release will release insurer to that extent

D. Liability Insurance

1. Insurer agrees to protect insured against liability for accidental damage to persons or property

   a. Usually includes duty to defend in a lawsuit brought by third parties

   b. Intentional wrongs not covered (e.g., fraud)

   c. Insurer has no rights against insured for causing the loss because this is what the insurance is to protect against

2. Malpractice—a form of personal liability

    a. Used by accountants, doctors, lawyers

    b. Protects against liability for harm caused by errors or negligence in work

    c. Does not protect against intentional wrongs (e.g., fraud)

E. Fire Insurance

1. Generally covers direct fire damage and also damage as a result of fire such as smoke, water, or chemicals

2. Blanket policy applies to a class of property that may be changing (inventory) rather than a specific piece of property (specific policy)

3. Valued policy predetermines value of property that becomes the face value of the policy

4. Recovery limited to face value of policy

5. Unvalued (open) policy determines value of property at time of loss which is amount insured collects—maximum amount usually set

6. **Coinsurance clause**

    a. The insured agrees to maintain insurance equal to a specified percentage of the value of his/her property. Then when a loss occurs, insurer only pays a proportionate share if insured has not carried the specified percentage.

    b. Formula

$$\text{Total recovery} = \text{Actual loss} \times \frac{\text{Amount of insurance}}{\text{Coinsurance \% $\times$ FMV of property at time of loss}}$$

      EXAMPLE: Insured owns a building valued at $100,000. He obtains two insurance policies for $20,000 each and they both contain 80% coinsurance clauses. There is a fire and his loss is $40,000. He will only collect $20,000 ($10,000 each) on his insurance, calculated as follows:

$$\$40,000 \times \frac{\$20,000 + \$20,000}{80\% \text{ of } \$100,000}$$

    c. This formula is used even though the insured does not maintain insurance equal to specified coverage; in such cases, this formula provides a lower recovery than actual losses

      (1) Therefore, this encourages insured to insure property for amount up to fair market value multiplied by the specified coinsurance percentage

    d. Does not apply when insured property is totally destroyed

      EXAMPLE: On October 10, Harry's warehouse was totally destroyed by fire. At the time of the fire, the warehouse had a value of $500,000 and was insured against fire for $300,000. The policy contained an 80% coinsurance clause. Harry will recover $300,000, the face value of the policy, because total destruction occurred and the coinsurance clause would not apply. If the warehouse had been only partially destroyed, with damages amounting to $300,000, Harry would only recover $225,000 (based on the formula above), because the coinsurance clause would apply.

7. Pro rata clause

    a. Someone who is insured with multiple policies can only collect, from each insurer, the proportionate amount of the loss

      (1) Proportion is the amount insured by each insurer to total amount of insurance

        EXAMPLE: Insured incurs a loss due to fire on property and is entitled to a $10,000 recovery. The property is covered by two insurance policies, one for $8,000 from Company A and one for $12,000 from Company B. Consequently, total insurance coverage on the property was $20,000. Company A will be liable for 40% ($8,000/$20,000) of fire loss, that is, $4,000 (40% x $10,000). Company B will be liable for 60% ($12,000/$20,000) of fire loss, that is, $6,000 (60% x $10,000).

8. Proof of loss

    a. Insured must give insurer a statement of amount of loss, cause of loss, etc., within a specified time

      (1) Failure to comply will excuse insurer's liability unless performance is made impracticable (e.g., death of insured)

9. Mortgagor and mortgagee have insurable interests, and mortgagees usually require insurance for their protection

10. Fire policies are usually not assignable because risk may have changed

   a. Even if property is sold, there can be no assignment of insurance without insurer's consent
   b. A claim against an insurer may be assigned (e.g., house burns and insurance company has not yet paid)

MULTIPLE-CHOICE QUESTIONS (1-8)

1. Which of the following statements correctly describes the requirement of insurable interest relating to property insurance? An insurable interest
   a. Must exist when any loss occurs.
   b. Must exist when the policy is issued and when any loss occurs.
   c. Is created only when the property is owned in fee simple.
   d. Is created only when the property is owned by an individual.

2. In which of the following cases would Brown not have an insurable interest?
   a. Brown is a general creditor of Winfield Corporation which is having financial problems.
   b. Brown is a mortgagee on some real property purchased by Wilson.
   c. Brown, as an owner of Winfield Company, wishes to insure the life of an officer critical to Winfield.
   d. Brown wishes to take out a life insurance policy on his partner of a partnership in which both Brown and his partner have important skills for that partnership.

3. Which of the following parties has an insurable interest?

   I. A corporate retailer in its inventory.
   II. A partner in the partnership property.

   a. I only.
   b. II only.
   c. Both I and II.
   d. Neither I nor II.

4. Massaro is hit by Lux in a two-car accident that is later determined to be completely Lux's fault. Massaro's auto insurance policy paid her for the complete damages to her car and her person. Can Massaro's insurance company collect the amount it paid from another party?
   a. No, because Massaro's insurance company had been paid for the risk it took.
   b. Yes, it can recover from Lux or Lux's insurance company based on the right of subrogation.
   c. Yes, it can recover from Lux's insurance company, if insured, based on the right of contribution.
   d. Yes, it can recover from Lux or Lux's insurance company, if insured, based on the right of contribution.

5. On February 1, Papco Corp. entered into a contract to purchase an office building from Merit Company for $500,000 with closing scheduled for March 20. On February 2, Papco obtained a $400,000 standard fire insurance policy from Abex Insurance Company. On March 15, the office building sustained a $90,000 fire loss. On March 15, which of the following is correct?

   I. Papco has an insurable interest in the building.
   II. Merit has an insurable interest in the building.

   a. I only.
   b. II only.
   c. Both I and II.
   d. Neither I nor II.

6. Clark Corp. owns a warehouse purchased for $150,000 in 1995. The current market value is $200,000. Clark has the warehouse insured for fire loss with Fair Insurance Corp. and Zone Insurance Co. Fair's policy is for $150,000 and Zone's policy is for $75,000. Both policies contain the standard 80% coinsurance clause. If a fire totally destroyed the warehouse, what total dollar amount would Clark receive from Fair and Zone?
   a. $225,000
   b. $200,000
   c. $160,000
   d. $150,000

Items 7 and 8 are based on the following:

In 1997, Pod bought a building for $220,000. At that time, Pod purchased a $150,000 fire insurance policy with Owners Insurance Co. and a $50,000 fire insurance policy with Group Insurance Corp. Each policy contained a standard 80% coinsurance clause. In 2001, when the building had a fair market value of $250,000, it was damaged in a fire.

7. How much would Pod recover from Owners if the fire caused $180,000 in damage?
   a. $ 90,000
   b. $120,000
   c. $135,000
   d. $150,000

8. How much would Pod recover from Owners and Group if the fire totally destroyed the building?
   a. $160,000
   b. $200,000
   c. $220,000
   d. $250,000

PROBLEM

NOTE: These types of problems are no longer included in the CPA Examination but they have been retained because they are useful in developing skills to complete simulations.

Problem 1   (15 to 20 minutes)

On February 1, 2001, Tower and Perry, as tenants in common, purchased a two-unit apartment building for $250,000. They made a down payment of $100,000, and gave a $100,000 first mortgage to Midway Bank and a $50,000 second mortgage to New Bank.

New was aware of Midway's mortgage but, as a result of a clerical error, Midway did not record its mortgage until after New's mortgage was recorded.

At the time of purchase a $200,000 fire insurance policy was issued by Acme Insurance Co. to Tower and Perry. The policy contained an 80% coinsurance clause and a standard mortgagee provision.

Tower and Perry rented an apartment to Young under a month-to-month oral lease. They rented the other apartment to Zimmer under a three-year written lease.

On December 8, 2002, Perry died leaving a will naming the Dodd Foundation as the sole beneficiary of Perry's estate. The estate was distributed on January 15, 2003. That same date, the ownership of the fire insurance policy was assigned to Tower and Dodd with Acme's consent. On January 21, 2003, a fire caused $180,000 in structural damage to the building. At that time, its market value was $300,000 and the Midway mortgage balance was $80,000 including accrued interest. The New mortgage balance was $40,000 including accrued interest.

The fire made Young's apartment uninhabitable and caused extensive damage to the kitchen, bathrooms, and one bedroom of Zimmer's apartment. On February 1, 2003, Young and Zimmer moved out. The resulting loss of income caused a default on both mortgages.

On April 1, 2003, Acme refused to pay the fire loss claiming that the required insurable interest did not exist at the time of the loss and that the amount of the insurance was insufficient to provide full coverage for the loss. Tower and Dodd are involved in a lawsuit contesting the ownership of the building and the claims they have both made for any fire insurance proceeds.

On June 1, 2003, Midway and New foreclosed their mortgages and are also claiming any fire insurance proceeds that may be paid by Acme.

On July 1, 2003, Tower sued Zimmer for breach of the lease and is seeking to collect the balance of the lease term rent.

The above events took place in a notice-race statute jurisdiction.

Required:

Answer the following questions and give the reasons for your conclusions.

a.   Who had title to the building on January 21, 2003?

b.   Did Tower and/or Dodd have an insurable interest in the building when the fire occurred? If so, when would such an interest have arisen?

c.   Does Acme have to pay under the terms of the fire insurance policy? If so, how much?

d.   Assuming the fire insurance proceeds will be paid, what would be the order of payment to the various parties and in what amounts?

e.   Would Tower succeed in the suit against Zimmer?

SIMULATION PROBLEMS

Simulation Problem 1   (10 to 15 minutes)

Situation				
	Anderson vs. Harvest	**Anderson vs. Beach**	**Anderson vs. Edge**	**Foreclosure Proceeds**

On June 1, 2002, Anderson bought a one-family house from Beach for $240,000. At the time of the purchase, the house had a market value of $200,000 and the land was valued at $40,000. Anderson assumed the recorded $150,000 mortgage Beach owed Long Bank, gave a $70,000 mortgage to Rogers Loan Co., and paid $20,000 cash. Rogers did not record its mortgage. Rogers did not know about the Long mortgage.

Beach gave Anderson a quitclaim deed that failed to mention a recorded easement on the property held by Dalton, the owner of the adjacent piece of property. Anderson purchased a title insurance policy from Edge Title Insurance Co. Edge's policy neither disclosed nor excepted Dalton's easement.

On August 1, 2003, Anderson borrowed $30,000 from Forrest Finance to have a swimming pool dug. Anderson gave Forrest a $30,000 mortgage on the property. Forrest, knowing about the Long mortgage but not the Rogers mortgage, recorded its mortgage on August 10, 2003. After the digging began, Dalton sued to stop the work claiming violation of the easement. The court decided in Dalton's favor.

At the time of the purchase, Anderson had taken out two fire insurance policies; a $120,000 face value policy with Harvest Fire Insurance Co., and a $60,000 face value policy with Grant Fire Insurance Corp. Both policies contained a standard 80% coinsurance clause.

On December 1, 2003, a fire caused $180,000 damage to the house. At that time, the house had a market value of $250,000. Harvest and Grant refused to honor the policies, claiming that the house was underinsured.

Anderson made no mortgage payments after the fire and on April 4, 2004, after the house had been rebuilt, the mortgages were foreclosed. The balances due for principal and accrued interest were as follows: Long, $140,000; Rogers, $65,000; and Forrest, $28,000. At a foreclosure sale, the house and land were sold. After payment of all expenses, $200,000 of the proceeds remained for distribution. As a result of the above events, the following actions took place:

- Anderson sued Harvest and Grant for the face values of the fire insurance policies.
- Anderson sued Beach for failing to mention Dalton's easement in the quitclaim deed.
- Anderson sued Edge for failing to disclose Dalton's easement.
- Long, Rogers, and Forrest all demanded full payment of their mortgages from the proceeds of the foreclosure sale.

The preceding took place in a notice-race jurisdiction.

	Anderson vs. Harvest			
Situation		**Anderson vs. Beach**	**Anderson vs. Edge**	**Foreclosure Proceeds**

Part a.   Items 1 through 3 relate to Anderson's suit against Harvest and Grant. For each item, select from List I the dollar amount Anderson will receive.

List I

A.	$0	G.	$ 96,000
B.	$ 20,000	H.	$108,000
C.	$ 48,000	I.	$120,000
D.	$ 54,000	J.	$144,000
E.	$ 60,000	K.	$162,000
F.	$ 80,000	L.	$180,000

(A) (B) (C) (D) (E) (F) (G) (H) (I) (J) (K) (L)

1. What will be the dollar amount of Anderson's total fire insurance recovery?
   O O O O O O O O O O O O

2. What dollar amount will be payable by Harvest?
   O O O O O O O O O O O O

3. What dollar amount will be payable by Grant?
   O O O O O O O O O O O O

Situation	Anderson vs. Harvest	Anderson vs. Beach	Anderson vs. Edge	Foreclosure Proceeds

Part b. Items 4 through 6 relate to Anderson's suit against Beach. For each item, determine whether that statement is True or False.

	True	*False*
4. Anderson will win the suit against Beach.	O	O
5. A quitclaim deed conveys only the grantor's interest in the property.	O	O
6. A warranty deed protects the purchaser against any adverse title claim against the property.	O	O

Situation	Anderson vs. Harvest	Anderson vs. Beach	Anderson vs. Edge	Foreclosure Proceeds

Part c. Items 7 through 9 relate to Anderson's suit against Edge. For each item, determine whether that statement is True or False.

	True	*False*
7. Anderson will win the suit against Edge.	O	O
8. Edge's policy should insure against all title defects of record.	O	O
9. Edge's failure to disclose Dalton's easement voids Anderson's contract with Beach.	O	O

Situation	Anderson vs. Harvest	Anderson vs. Beach	Anderson vs. Edge	Foreclosure Proceeds

Part d. Items 10 through 12 relate to the demands Long, Rogers, and Forrest have made to have their mortgages satisfied out of the foreclosure proceeds. For each item, select from List II the dollar amount to be paid.

List II

A.	$0
B.	$ 28,000
C.	$ 32,000
D.	$ 65,000
E.	$107,000
F.	$135,000
G.	$140,000

	(A) (B) (C) (D) (E) (F) (G)
10. What dollar amount of the foreclosure proceeds will Long receive?	O O O O O O O
11. What dollar amount of the foreclosure proceeds will Rogers receive?	O O O O O O O
12. What dollar amount of the foreclosure proceeds will Forrest receive?	O O O O O O O

Simulation Problem 2   (10 to 15 minutes)

Situation	
	Analysis

On January 12, 2004, Frank, Inc. contracted in writing to purchase a factory building from Henderson for $250,000 cash. Closing took place on March 15, 2004. Henderson had purchased the building in 1997 for $225,000 and had, at that time, taken out a $180,000 fire insurance policy with Summit Insurance Co.

On January 15, 2004, Frank took out a $140,000 fire insurance policy with Unity Insurance Co. and a $70,000 fire insurance policy with Imperial Insurance, Inc.

On March 16, 2004, a fire caused $150,000 damage to the building. At that time the building had a market value of $250,000. All fire insurance policies contain a standard 80% coinsurance clause. The insurance carriers have refused any payment to Frank or Henderson alleging lack of insurable interest and insufficient coverage. Frank and Henderson have sued to collect on the policies.

	Analysis
Situation	

Items 1 through 6 relate to the suits by Frank and Henderson. For each item, determine whether the statement is True or False.

	True	*False*
1. Frank had an insurable interest at the time the Unity and Imperial policies were taken out.	○	○
2. Henderson had an insurable interest at the time of the fire.	○	○
3. Assuming Frank had an insurable interest, Frank's coverage would be insufficient under the Unity and Imperial coinsurance clauses.	○	○
4. Assuming Henderson had an insurable interest, Henderson's coverage would be insufficient under the Summit coinsurance clause.	○	○
5. Assuming only Frank had an insurable interest, Frank will recover $100,000 from Unity and $50,000 from Imperial.	○	○
6. Assuming only Henderson had an insurable interest, Henderson will recover $135,000 from Summit.	○	○

1.	a	__ __	3.	c	__ __	5.	c	__ __	7.	c	__ __	1st: __/8 = __%
2.	a	__ __	4.	b	__ __	6.	b	__ __	8.	b	__ __	2nd: __/8 = __%

MULTIPLE-CHOICE ANSWER EXPLANATIONS

B.6. Insurable Interest

1. (a) In the case of property insurance, the insurable interest must exist when the loss occurs. It need not exist when the policy is issued. Therefore, answer (b) is incorrect. Answers (c) and (d) are incorrect because there are no such requirements that the property be owned in fee simple or by individuals.

2. (a) To have an insurable interest in property, there must be both a legal interest and a possibility of pecuniary loss. Although a legal interest may involve ownership or a security interest, general creditors do not have the requisite interest to have an insurable interest. Answer (b) is incorrect because a mortgagee has an insurable interest for the mortgage balance still owed. Answer (c) is incorrect because Brown has an insurable interest in key company personnel whose death could result in pecuniary loss for Brown. Answer (d) is incorrect because Brown has an insurable interest in his partner whose death could cause him great monetary loss.

3. (c) An insurable interest in property exists if the insured has both a legal interest in the property and the possibility of incurring a pecuniary loss. The legal interest may be ownership or a security interest. A corporate retailer has an ownership interest in its inventory, and the possibility of incurring a monetary loss. A partner also has an ownership interest in partnership property, with the possibility of incurring a monetary loss.

C. Subrogation

4. (b) Once the insurance company pays its insured, Massaro, it steps into Massaro's shoes and obtains the same rights against third parties that Massaro had. Since Lux was at fault in this accident, the insurance company has rights against Lux as well as any insurance company that has insured Lux. Answer (a) is incorrect because the insurance company can nevertheless recover from third parties based on the right of subrogation. Answer (c) is incorrect because the insurance company has the right to collect from Lux as well as an insurer. Answer (d) is incorrect because the relevant concept is the right of subrogation, not contribution.

E. Fire Insurance

5. (c) An important element of a property insurance contract is the existence of an insurable interest. The insurable interest requirement is met when an entity has both a legal interest in the property and a possibility of monetary loss if the property is damaged. Since Merit still owns the office building at the time of the fire, they fulfill both these requirements. Papco also has an insurable interest which began on February 1 when they entered into the contract to purchase the building. Papco's legal interest results from their contract to purchase the building. Papco's monetary interest results from their potential loss of future use of the building. Thus, in this situation, both Papco and Merit have an insurable interest.

E.6. Coinsurance Clause

6. (b) Although Clark has insurance coverage exceeding the fair value of the warehouse, he may only recover the actual amount of his loss. The coinsurance clause does not apply when the insured property is totally destroyed. Fair Insurance will pay 150/225 of the $200,000 loss, or $133,333, while Zone Insurance will pay 75/225 of the $200,000 loss, or $66,667. Thus, Clark will receive a total of $200,000 from Fair and Zone.

7. (c) The recoverable loss is calculated using the coinsurance formula.

$$\text{Actual Loss} \times \frac{\text{Amount of insurance}}{\text{Coinsurance \% } \times \text{ FMV of property at time of loss}}$$

The amount recoverable from Owners is calculated as follows:

$$\$180,000 \times \frac{\$150,000}{80\% \times \$250,000} = \$135,000$$

8. (b) When property is covered by a coinsurance clause, the insured party agrees to maintain insurance equal to a given percentage of the value of the property, usually 80%. If the percentage of coverage is less than the specified percentage and partial destruction of the property occurs, then the insured will be liable for a portion of the loss. However, a coinsurance clause applies only when there has been partial destruction of property. If the insured property is totally destroyed, the coinsurance clause does not apply and the insured party will recover the face value of the insurance policy. Thus, Pod will recover $150,000 from Owners Insurance Co. and $50,000 from Group Insurance Co. for a total of $200,000.

ANSWER OUTLINE

Problem 1   Title of Real Estate; Insurable Interest; Re-
                   cording of Mortgage; Coinsurance Clause

a.   Tower and Perry owned property as tenants in common
         Either party may dispose of property by sale or on
           death
         On 1/21/03, Tower and Dodd are tenants in common,
           each owning one-half interest

b.   Both Tower and Dodd have insurable interest
         Tower's insurable interest arose when property pur-
           chased
         Dodd's insurable interest arose when Dodd inherited
           Perry's interest in house

c.   Acme must honor insurance policy and pay part of loss
         Amount of payment is determined by coinsurance
           formula

$$\frac{\text{Amount of coverage}}{\text{FMV x Coinsurance \%}} \quad \text{x} \quad \text{Amount of loss}$$

         Amount of recovery is

$$\frac{\$200,000}{\$300,000 \text{ x } .8} \quad \text{x} \quad \$180,000 \ = \ \$150,000$$

d.   In a race-notice statute jurisdiction, New's knowledge
         of Midway's first mortgage gives Midway priority
         over New
         Proceeds distributed as follows
             $80,000 to Midway because Midway is contingent
               beneficiary in policy
             $40,000 to New but not paid until Midway is paid
               in full
             $30,000 divided equally between Tower and Dodd
               as tenants in common

e.   Tower would not be able to collect rent from Zimmer
         Extensive damage to apartment
         Implied warranty of habitability breached by landlord
         Constructive eviction because premises no longer
           useful for intended purpose
         Constructive eviction releases both landlord and ten-
           ant from obligations under lease

UNOFFICIAL ANSWER

Problem 1   Title of Real Estate; Insurable Interest; Re-
                   cording of Mortgage; Coinsurance Clause

a.   Tower and Perry owned the property as tenants in common. This form of ownership allows either party to dispose
of his or her undivided interest by sale or on death. Any
person purchasing or inheriting Perry's interest would become a tenant in common with Tower. Thus, on January 21,
2003, Tower and Dodd are tenants in common, each owning
a one-half undivided interest in the house.

b.   Both Tower and Dodd have an insurable interest in the
house. Tower's interest arose when the property was purchased, continued when the insurance policy was purchased,
and still existed at the time of the fire loss.
         Dodd's interest arose when Dodd inherited Perry's in-
terest in the house. Acme's consent to the assignment of the
policy to Tower and Dodd entitles Dodd to a share of the
proceeds of the policy.

c.   Acme would have to honor the insurance contract and
pay part of the loss. Despite Tower and Perry not maintaining insurance coverage of 80% of the property's market
value, the coinsurance clause allows for a percentage of
recovery. The formula is as follows:

$$\frac{\text{Amount of coverage}}{\text{Actual market value x Coinsurance \%}} \quad \text{x} \quad \text{Amount of loss}$$

This would allow a recovery as follows:

$$\frac{\$200,000}{\$300,000 \text{ x } .8} \quad \text{x} \quad \$180,000 \ = \ \$150,000$$

d.   The conflict between Midway and New would be resolved in favor of Midway. In a notice-race statute jurisdiction, New's knowledge of Midway's first mortgage would
give Midway priority despite New's earlier filing. The insurance proceeds would be distributed as follows:

   • $80,000 to Midway representing the balance due on
the mortgage including accrued interest. This is due because
Midway as a mortgagee is included as a contingent beneficiary in the policy.
   • $40,000 to New for the same reasons as above but
not paid unless and until Midway is fully paid.
   • $30,000 to be divided equally between Tower and
Dodd as tenants in common.

e.   Tower would not be able to collect rent from Zimmer
for the balance of the term of the lease because Zimmer
moved as a result of the extensive fire damage to the apartment. The implied warranty of habitability would be considered breached by the landlord and a constructive eviction
of Zimmer would be deemed to have taken place because the
premises could no longer be used for their intended purpose.
Constructive eviction releases both the landlord and the tenant from their obligations under the lease.

SOLUTIONS TO SIMULATION PROBLEMS

Simulation Problem 1

Part a.

1. (K) In order to calculate the dollar amount of Anderson's total fire insurance recovery, use the coinsurance clause formula, adding together the amount of insurance for both Harvest and Grant, as follows:

$$\text{Recovery} = \text{Actual loss} \times \frac{\text{Amount of insurance}}{\text{Coinsurance \% x FMV of property at time of loss}}$$

$$\text{Recovery} = \$180,000 \times \frac{\$120,000 + \$60,000}{80\% \times \$250,000}$$

$$\text{Recovery} = \$162,000$$

2. (H) In order to calculate the dollar amount that will be payable to Harvest only, use the coinsurance clause formula.

$$\text{Recovery} = \$180,000 \times \frac{\$120,000}{80\% \times \$250,000}$$

$$\text{Recovery} = \$108,000$$

3. (D) In order to calculate the dollar amount payable to Grant only, use the same coinsurance clause formula.

$$\$180,000 \times \frac{\$60,000}{80\% \times \$250,000} = \$54,000$$

Part b.

4. (F) Since Beach had given Anderson a quitclaim deed, Anderson loses in the suit against Beach for failing to mention Dalton's easement in the quitclaim deed.

5. (T) Unlike a warranty deed, a quitclaim deed conveys only whatever interest in land the grantor has. No warranty concerning title or easements is given.

6. (T) A warranty deed contains covenants that generally protect the grantee against any adverse title claim against the property.

Part c.

7. (T) This statement is true because Edge failed to mention a recorded easement on the property. Note that when Edge failed to disclose the recorded easement, this allows Anderson to recover from Edge but does not void the contract between Anderson and the seller of the property.

8. (T) Standard title insurance policies generally insure against all title defects of record. This would be true of the title insurance policy that Anderson purchased from Edge.

9. (F) Since Edge failed to disclose the recorded easement, this allows Anderson to recover from Edge. However, it does not void the contract between Anderson and Beach.

Part d.

10. (G) Under a notice-race statute, the subsequent good-faith mortgagee wins over a previous mortgagee only if s/he also records first. In this fact pattern, Long has the first priority because its mortgage was recorded before mortgages were given to Forrest or Rogers. Since $200,000 remained to be distributed, Long gets all of its $140,000.

11. (C) Forrest has the second priority because although its mortgage was granted after Rogers, Rogers did not record its mortgage and Forrest was unaware of it when its mortgage was given. Therefore, Rogers has the third priority. After Long received his $140,000, there is $60,000 left. Forrest has second priority and will receive his full $28,000. Since there is not enough left to pay Rodgers the full $65,000, Rogers only gets the balance remaining of $32,000.

12. (B) Forrest has the second priority because although its mortgage was granted after Rogers, Rogers did not record its mortgage and Forrest was unaware of it when its mortgage was given. Therefore, Rogers has the third priority. After Long received his $140,000, there is $60,000 left. Forrest has second priority and will receive his full $28,000.

Simulation Problem 2

1. **(T)** In property, there must be both a legal interest and a possibility of pecuniary loss. This insurable interest need not be present at the inception of the policy so long as it is present at the time of loss. A contract to purchase or the possession of property can give an insurable interest. Frank had an insurable interest at the time the Unity and Imperial policies were taken out as Frank contracted to purchase the property prior to taking out the insurance policies.

2. **(F)** A contract to purchase or possession of the property can give an insurable interest. The closing of the sale of the property to Frank took place on March 15, 2004. At this point Henderson no longer had an insurable interest as he no longer had possession nor had he contracted to repurchase the property. Therefore, when the fire occurred on March 16, 2004, Henderson did not have an insurable interest.

3. **(F)** The recoverable loss is calculated using the coinsurance formula.

$$\text{Actual loss } \times \frac{\text{Amount of insurance}}{\text{Coinsurance \% x FMV of property at time of loss}}$$

The amount recoverable from Unity is calculated as follows:

$$\$150,000 \times \frac{\$140,000}{80\% \times \$250,000} = \$105,000$$

The amount recoverable from Imperial is calculated as follows:

$$\$150,000 \times \frac{\$70,000}{80\% \times \$250,000} = \$52,500$$

The total amount recoverable from the combined insurance policies is therefore sufficient to cover the loss.

4. **(T)** The recoverable loss is calculated using the coinsurance formula.

$$\text{Actual loss } \times \frac{\text{Amount of insurance}}{\text{Coinsurance \% x FMV of property at time of loss}}$$

The amount recoverable from Summit is calculated as follows:

$$\$150,000 \times \frac{\$180,000}{80\% \times \$250,000} = \$135,000$$

Thus, Henderson's coverage would be insufficient.

5. **(T)** The recoverable loss is calculated using the coinsurance formula.

$$\text{Actual loss } \times \frac{\text{Amount of insurance}}{\text{Coinsurance \% x FMV of property at time of loss}}$$

The amount recoverable from Unity is calculated as follows:

$$\$150,000 \times \frac{\$140,000}{80\% \times \$250,000} = \$105,000$$

The amount recoverable from Imperial is calculated as follows:

$$\$150,000 \times \frac{\$70,000}{80\% \times \$250,000} = \$52,500$$

Combined insurance policies are sufficient but only $150,000 can be recovered. Therefore, Frank can only recover proportionately from Unity and Imperial as follows:

$$\text{Unity} - \frac{140,000}{140,000 + 70,000} = 67\%$$

$$\text{Imperial} - \frac{70,000}{140,000 + 70,000} = 33\%$$

Therefore, Frank will receive $100,000 (67% x $150,000 loss) from Unity and $50,000 (33% x $150,000 loss) from Imperial.

6. **(T)** The recoverable loss is calculated using the coinsurance formula.

$$\text{Actual loss } \times \frac{\text{Amount of insurance}}{\text{Coinsurance \% x FMV of property at time of loss}}$$

The amount recoverable from Summit is calculated as follows:

$$\$150,000 \times \frac{\$180,000}{80\% \times \$250,000} = \$135,000$$

7 FEDERAL TAXATION

Introduction

Module 33/Individual Taxation (ITAX)

TAXES ON THE REGULATION EXAMINATION

Federal taxation is tested in the Regulation section of the exam. According to the AICPA's Content Specification Outline, federal taxation should account for about 60% of the Regulation section. Of this 60%, about 15% will test the federal income taxation of individuals, about 25% will test the federal income taxation of entities, about 10% will test income tax procedures and accounting issues, and about 10% will test the taxation of property transactions.

You will want to note that the Regulation exam contains only multiple-choice questions and simulations. Since the database for the Regulation exam is the income tax code and regulations, all simulations will involve taxation topics.

The multiple-choice questions test detailed application of the Internal Revenue Code and tax regulations. The instructions indicate that "answers should be based on the Internal Revenue Code and Tax Regulations in effect for the tax period specified in the item. If no tax period is specified, use the current Internal Revenue Code and Tax Regulations." On recent examinations, approximately 60% of the multiple-choice questions have specified the preceding taxable year, while the remaining 40% have no year specified.

As a practical matter, the examiners generally avoid testing on recent tax law changes, and have indicated that the **exam will generally cover federal tax regulations in effect 6 months before the date of the exam**. Also note that you are not expected to know amounts that change between years because of being indexed for inflation (e.g., the dollar amount of personal exemption, standard deduction, etc.).

The summary tax outlines presented in this chapter begin by emphasizing individual taxation. Because of numerous common concepts, partnership and corporate taxation are later presented in terms of their differences from individual taxation (i.e., learn individual taxes thoroughly and then learn the special rules of partnership and corporate taxation). Interperiod and intraperiod tax allocation questions are presented in Module 12, Deferred Taxes, of the Financial Accounting and Reporting Volume.

The property transactions outline has been inserted between individual taxation and the partnership and corporate tax outlines because property transactions are common to all types of taxpayers, and generally are tested within every tax problem, both PTAX and CTAX, as well as ITAX.

The next section presents a detailed outline of the individual tax formula, and outlines of two basic federal income tax returns: Form 1065—Partnership; and Form 1120—Corporation. These outlines are an intermediary step between the simple formula outline (below) and the outlines of the detailed rules.

Formula Outline for Individuals
Gross income
  – "Above the line" deductions
Adjusted gross income
  – Total itemized deductions (or standard deduction)
  – Exemptions
Taxable income
  x Tax rates
  – Tax credits
Tax liability

OVERVIEW OF FEDERAL TAX RETURNS

Problems requiring computation of taxable income require that you be familiar with the outlines below. The tax return outlines help you "pull together" all of the detailed tax rules. The schedule and form identification numbers are provided for reference only; they are not tested on the examination.

Review the outlines presented below. The outlines will introduce you to the topics tested on the exam and their relationship to final "tax liability."

Form 1040—Individuals

A. Income

1. Wages, salaries, tips, etc.
2. Interest (Sch. B)
3. Dividend income (Sch. B)
4. Income other than wages, dividends, and interest (The gross income reported on the schedules below is already reduced by corresponding deductible expenses. Only the net income [or loss] is reported on Form 1040.)

   a. State and local income tax refunds
   b. Alimony received
   c. Business income or loss (Sch. C)
   d. Capital gain or loss (Sch. D)
   e. Other gains or losses (Form 4797)
   f. Taxable IRA distributions, pensions, and annuities
   g. Rents, royalties, partnerships, S corporations, estates, trusts, etc. (Sch. E)
   h. Unemployment compensation, social security
   i. Other

B. Less "Above the Line" Deductions (also known as "Deductions **for** AGI")

1. One-half of self-employment tax
2. Moving expenses
3. Self-employed health insurance deduction
4. Medical savings account deduction
5. Payments to an individual retirement arrangement (IRA)
6. Payments to a Keogh retirement plan
7. Penalty on early withdrawal of savings
8. Student loan interest deduction
9. Alimony paid
10. Tuition and fees deduction

C. Adjusted Gross Income

D. Less Itemized Deductions (Sch. A), (or standard deduction), including

1. Medical and dental expenses
2. Taxes
3. Interest expense
4. Contributions
5. Casualty and theft losses
6. Miscellaneous

   a. Subject to 2% of AGI limitation
   b. Not subject to 2% of AGI limitation

E. Less Exemptions

F. Taxable Income

1. Find your tax in the tables, or
2. Use tax rate schedules

G. Additional Taxes

1. Alternative minimum tax (Form 6251)
2. Parents' election to report child's interest and dividends (Form 8814)
3. Lump-sum distribution from qualified retirement plans (Form 4972)

H. Less Tax Credits

1. General business credit

   a. Investment credit (Form 3468)
   b. Alcohol fuels credit
   c. Low-income housing credit
   d. Disabled access credit
   e. Employer social security credit

2. Credit for the elderly or the disabled (Sch. R)
3. Credit for child and dependent care expenses (Form 2441)
4. Child tax credit
5. Education credits (Form 8863)
6. Adoption credit (Form 8839)
7. Foreign tax credit (Form 1116)
8. Credit for prior year minimum tax

I. Tax Liability
J. Other Taxes

1. Self-employment tax (Sch. SE)
2. Advance earned income credit payments
3. Social security tax on unreported tip income (Form 4137)
4. Tax on IRAs and other retirement plans (Form 5329)
5. Household employment taxes (Sch. H)

K. Less Payments

1. Tax withheld on wages
2. Estimated tax payments
3. Earned income credit
4. Amount paid with an extension
5. Excess FICA paid
6. Credit for federal tax on special fuels (Form 4136)
7. Credit from a regulated investment company (Form 2439)

L. Amount Overpaid or Balance Due

Form 1065—Partnerships

A. Income

1. Gross sales less returns and allowances
2. Less cost of goods sold
3. Gross profit
4. Ordinary income from other partnerships and fiduciaries
5. Net farm profit
6. Ordinary gain or loss (including depreciation recapture)
7. Other

B. Less Deductions

1. Salaries and wages (other than to partners)
2. Guaranteed payments to partners
3. Rents
4. Interest expense

    5.   Taxes
    6.   Bad debts
    7.   Repairs
    8.   Depreciation
    9.   Depletion
   10.   Retirement plans
   11.   Employee benefit program contributions
   12.   Other

C.   Ordinary Income (Loss) from trade or business activity

D.   Schedule K (on partnership return) and **Schedule K-1** to be prepared for each partner

    1.   Ordinary income (loss) from trade or business activity
    2.   Income (loss) from rental real estate activity
    3.   Income (loss) from other rental activity
    4.   Portfolio income (loss)

        a.   Interest
        b.   Dividends
        c.   Royalties
        d.   Net short-term capital gain (loss)
        e.   Net long-term capital gain (loss)
        f.   Other portfolio income (loss)

    5.   Guaranteed payments
    6.   Net gain (loss) under Sec. 1231 (other than casualty or theft)
    7.   Other
    8.   Charitable contributions
    9.   Sec. 179 expense deduction
   10.   Deductions related to portfolio income
   11.   Other
   12.   Credits

        a.   Credit for income tax withheld
        b.   Low-income housing credit
        c.   Qualified rehabilitation expenditures related to rental real estate
        d.   Credits related to rental real estate activities

   13.   Other
   14.   a.   Net earnings (loss) from self-employment
        b.   Gross farming or fishing income
        c.   Gross nonfarm income

   15.   Tax preference items

        a.   Depreciation adjustment on property placed in service after 12/31/86
        b.   Tax-exempt private activity bond interest

   16.   Investment interest expense
   17.   Foreign income taxes

Form 1120—Corporations

A.   Gross Income

    1.   Gross sales less returns and allowances
    2.   Less cost of goods sold
    3.   Gross profit
    4.   Dividends
    5.   Interest
    6.   Gross rents
    7.   Gross royalties

8. Net capital gains
9. Ordinary gain or loss
10. Other income

B. Less Deductions

1. Compensation of officers
2. Salaries and wages (net of jobs credit)
3. Repairs
4. Bad debts
5. Rents
6. Taxes
7. Interest
8. Charitable contributions
9. Depreciation
10. Depletion
11. Advertising
12. Pension, profit-sharing plan contributions
13. Employee benefit programs
14. Other
15. Net operating loss deduction
16. Dividends received deduction

C. TAXABLE INCOME times tax rates
D. Less tax credits equals TAX LIABILITY

I. GROSS INCOME ON INDIVIDUAL RETURNS

This section outlines (1) gross income in general, (2) exclusions from gross income, (3) items to be included in gross income, (4) tax accounting methods, and (5) items to be included in gross income net of deductions (e.g., business income, sales and exchanges).

A. In General

1. **Gross income** includes all income from whatever source derived, unless specifically excluded

   a. Does not include a return of capital (e.g., if a taxpayer loans $6,000 to another and is repaid $6,500 at a later date, only the $500 difference is included in gross income)

   b. The income must be **realized** (i.e., there must be a transaction which gives rise to the income)

      (1) A mere appreciation in the value of property is not income (e.g., value of one's home increases $2,000 during year. Only if the house is sold will the increase in value be realized)

      (2) A transaction may be in the form of actual receipt of cash or property, accrual of a receivable, or sale or exchange

   c. The income must also be **recognized** (i.e., the transaction must be a taxable event, and not a transaction for which nonrecognition is provided in the Internal Revenue Code)

   d. An **assignment of income** will not be recognized for tax purposes

      (1) If income from property is assigned, it is still taxable to the owner of the property.

      EXAMPLE: X owns a building and assigns the rents to Y. The rents remain taxable to X, even though the rents are received by Y.

      (2) If income from services is assigned, it is still taxable to the person who earns it.

      EXAMPLE: X earns $200 per week. To pay off a debt owed to Y, he assigns half of it to Y. $200 per week remains taxable to X.

2. Distinction between exclusions, deductions, and credits

   a. **Exclusions**—income items which are not included in gross income

      (1) Exclusions must be specified by law. Remember, gross income includes all income except that specifically excluded.

      (2) Although exclusions are exempt from income tax, they may still be taxed under other tax rules (e.g., gifts may be subject to the gift tax).

   b. **Deductions**—amounts that are subtracted from income to arrive at adjusted gross income or taxable income

      (1) Deductions for adjusted gross income (above the line deductions)—amounts deducted from gross income to arrive at adjusted gross income

      (2) Itemized deductions (below the line deductions)—amounts deducted from adjusted gross income to arrive at taxable income

   c. **Credits**—amounts subtracted from the computed tax to arrive at taxes payable

B. Exclusions from Gross Income (not reported)

1. Payments received for **support** of minor children

   a. Must be children of the parent making the payments

   b. Decree of divorce or separate maintenance generally must specify the amount to be treated as child support, otherwise payments may be treated as alimony

2. **Property settlement** (division of capital) received in a divorce

3. **Annuities** and pensions are excluded to the extent they represent a return of capital

   a. Excluded portion of each payment is

   $$\frac{\text{Net cost of annuity}}{\text{Expected total annuity payments}} \times \text{Payment received}$$

   b. "Expected total annuity payments" is calculated by multiplying the annual return by

      (1) The number of years receivable if it is an annuity for a definite period

      (2) A life expectancy multiple (from IRS tables) if it is an annuity for life

c. Once this exclusion ratio is determined, it remains constant until the cost of the annuity is completely recovered. Any additional payments will be fully taxable.

> *EXAMPLE: Mr. Jones purchased an annuity contract for $3,600 that will pay him $1,500 per year beginning in 2003. His expected return under the contract is $10,800. Mr. Jones' exclusion ratio is $3,600 ÷ $10,800 = 1/3. For 2003, Mr. Jones will exclude $1,500 x 1/3 = $500; and will include the remaining $1,000 in gross income.*

d. If the taxpayer dies before total cost is recovered, unrecovered cost is allowed as a miscellaneous itemized deduction on the taxpayer's final tax return.

4. **Life insurance proceeds** (face amount of policy) are generally excluded if paid by reason of death

a. If proceeds are received in **installments,** amounts received in excess of pro rata part of face amount are taxable as interest

b. **Dividends** on unmatured insurance policies are excluded to the extent not in excess of cumulative premiums paid.

c. **Accelerated death benefits** received under a life insurance policy by a *terminally or chronically ill* individual are generally excluded from gross income

   (1) Similarly, if a portion of a life insurance contract on the life of a terminally or chronically ill individual is assigned or sold to a viatical settlement provider, proceeds received from the provider are excluded.

   (2) For a chronically ill individual, the exclusion is limited to the amount paid by the individual for unreimbursed long-term care costs. Payments made on a per diem basis, up to $220 per day, are excludable regardless of actual long-term care costs incurred.

d. All interest is taxable if proceeds are left with insurance company under agreement to pay only interest.

e. If insurance proceeds are paid for reasons other than death or under c. above, or if the policy was obtained by the beneficiary in exchange for valuable consideration from a person other than the insurance company, all proceeds in excess of cost are taxable. Annuity rules apply to installment payments.

> *EXAMPLE: Able was the owner and beneficiary of a $30,000 life insurance policy on Baker. Able sold the policy for $10,000 to Carr who subsequently paid $6,000 of premiums. If Baker died, Carr's gross income from the proceeds of the life insurance policy would total $30,000 – ($10,000 + $6,000) = $14,000.*

5. Certain **employee benefits** are excluded

a. **Group-term life insurance** premiums paid by employer (the **cost of up to $50,000** of insurance coverage is excluded). Exclusion not limited if beneficiary is the employer or a qualified charity.

b. Insurance premiums employer pays to fund an accident or health plan for employees are excluded.

c. **Accident and health benefits** provided by employer are excluded if benefits are for

   (1) Permanent injury or loss of bodily function
   (2) Reimbursement for medical care of employee, spouse, or dependents

      (a) Employee cannot take itemized deduction for reimbursed medical expenses
      (b) Exclusion may not apply to highly compensated individuals if reimbursed under a discriminatory self-insured medical plan

d. Employees of small businesses (50 or fewer employees) and self-employed individuals may qualify for a **medical savings account** (MSA) if covered under a high-deductible health insurance plan. An MSA is similar to an IRA, except used for health care.

   (1) Employer contributions to an employee's MSA are excluded from gross income (except if made through a cafeteria plan), and employee contributions are deductible for AGI.
   (2) Contributions are limited to 65% (75% for family coverage) of the annual health insurance deductible amount.
   (3) Earnings of an MSA are not subject to tax; distributions from an MSA used to pay qualified medical expenses are excluded from gross income.

e. **Meals or lodging** furnished for the convenience of the employer on the employer's premises are excluded.

   (1) For the convenience of the employer means there must be a noncompensatory reason such as the employee is required to be on duty during this period.

        (2) In the case of lodging, it also must be a condition of employment.

    f. Employer-provided educational assistance (e.g., payment of tuition, books, fees) derived from an employer's qualified **educational assistance program** is excluded up to maximum of **$5,250** per year. The exclusion applies to both undergraduate as well as graduate-level courses, but does not apply to assistance payments for courses involving sports, games, or hobbies, unless they involve the employer's business or are required as part of a degree program. Excludable assistance does not include tools or supplies that the employee retains after completion of the course, nor the cost of meals, lodging, or transportation.

    g. Employer payments to an employee for **dependent care assistance** are excluded from an employee's income if made under a written, nondiscriminatory plan. Maximum exclusion is **$5,000** per year ($2,500 for a married person filing a separate return).

    h. **Qualified adoption expenses** paid or incurred by an employer in connection with an employee's adoption of a child are excluded from the employee's gross income. For 2003, the maximum exclusion is **$10,160** per eligible child (including special needs children) and the exclusion is ratably phased out for modified AGI between $152,390 and $192,390.

    i. **Employee fringe benefits** are generally excluded if

        (1) **No additional-cost services**—for example, airline pass

        (2) **Employee discount** that is nondiscriminatory

        (3) **Working condition fringes**—excluded to the extent that if the amount had been paid by the employee, the amount would be deductible as an employee business expense

        (4) **De minimis fringes**—small value, impracticable to account for (e.g., coffee, personal use of copying machine)

        (5) **Qualified transportation fringes**

            (a) Up to $100 per month for 2003 can be excluded for employer-provided transit passes and transportation in a commuter highway vehicle if the transportation is between the employee's home and work place.

            (b) Up to $190 per month for 2003 can be excluded for employer-provided parking on or near the employer's place of business.

        (6) **Qualified moving expense reimbursement**—an individual can exclude any amount received from an employer as payment for (or reimbursement of) expenses which would be deductible as moving expenses if directly paid or incurred by the individual. The exclusion does not apply to any payment (or reimbursement of) an expense actually deducted by the individual in a prior taxable year.

    j. **Workers' compensation** is fully excluded if received for an occupational sickness or injury and is paid under a workers' compensation act or statute.

  6. Accident and health insurance benefits derived from policies **purchased by the taxpayer** are excluded, but not if the medical expenses were deducted in a prior year and the tax benefit rule applies.

  7. **Damages for physical injury or physical sickness** are excluded.

    a. If an action has its origin in a physical injury or physical sickness, then all damages therefrom (other than punitive damages) are excluded (e.g., damages received by an individual on account of a claim for loss due to a physical injury to such individual's spouse are excludible from gross income).

    b. Damages (other than punitive damages) received on account of a claim of wrongful death, and damages that are compensation for amounts paid for medical care (including medical care for emotional distress) are excluded.

    c. Emotional distress is not considered a physical injury or physical sickness. No exclusion applies to damages received from a claim of employment discrimination, age discrimination, or injury to reputation (even if accompanied by a claim of emotional distress).

    d. Punitive damages generally must be included in gross income, even if related to a physical injury or physical sickness.

  8. **Gifts, bequests, devises, or inheritances** are excluded.

    a. Income subsequently derived from property so acquired is not excluded (e.g., interest or rent).

    b. "Gifts" from employer except for noncash holiday presents are generally not excluded.

9. The receipt of **stock dividends** (or stock rights) is generally excluded from income (see page 504 for basis and holding period), but the FMV of the stock received will be included in income if the distribution.

    a. Is on preferred stock
    b. Is payable, at the election of any shareholder, in stock or property
    c. Results in the receipt of preferred stock by some common shareholders, and the receipt of common stock by other common shareholders
    d. Results in the receipt of property by some shareholders, and an increase in the proportionate interests of other shareholders in earnings or assets of the corporation

10. Certain **interest income** is excluded.

    a. Interest on obligations of a **state** or one of its political subdivisions (e.g., **municipal** bonds), the District of Columbia, and US possessions is generally **excluded** from income if the bond proceeds are used to finance traditional governmental operations.
    b. Other state and local government-issued obligations (private activity bonds) are generally fully taxable. An obligation is a private activity bond if (1) more than 10% of the bond proceeds are used (directly or indirectly) in a private trade or business and more than 10% of the principal or interest on the bonds is derived from, or secured by, money or property used in the trade or business, or (2) the lesser of 5% or $5 million of the bond proceeds is used (directly or indirectly) to make or finance loans to private persons or entities.
    c. The following bonds are **excluded from the private activity bond category** even though their proceeds are not used in traditional government operations. The interest from these bonds is excluded from income.

        (1) Qualified bonds issued for the benefit of schools, hospitals, and other charitable organizations
        (2) Bonds used to finance certain exempt facilities, such as airports, docks, wharves, mass commuting facilities, etc.
        (3) Qualified redevelopment bonds, small-issue bonds (i.e., bonds not exceeding $1 million), and student loan bonds
        (4) Qualified mortgage and veterans' mortgage bonds

    d. Interest on **US obligations** is **included** in income.

11. **Savings bonds for higher education**

    a. The accrued interest on Series EE US savings bonds that are redeemed by the taxpayer is excluded from gross income to the extent that the aggregate redemption proceeds (principal plus interest) are used to finance the higher education of the taxpayer, taxpayer's spouse, or dependents.

        (1) The bonds must be issued after December 31, 1989, to an individual age twenty-four or older at the bond's issue date.
        (2) The purchaser of the bonds must be the sole owner of the bonds (or joint owner with his or her spouse). Married taxpayers must file a joint return to qualify for the exclusion.
        (3) The redemption proceeds must be used to pay qualified higher education expenses (i.e., tuition and required fees less scholarships, fellowships, and employer-provided educational assistance) at an accredited university, college, junior college, or other institution providing postsecondary education, or at an area vocational education school.
        (4) If the redemption proceeds exceed the qualified higher education expenses, only a pro rata amount of interest can be excluded.

            EXAMPLE: During 2003, a married taxpayer redeems Series EE bonds receiving $6,000 of principal and $4,000 of accrued interest. Assuming qualified higher education expenses total $9,000, accrued interest of $3,600 ($9,000/$10,000 x $4,000) can be excluded from gross income.

    b. If the taxpayer's modified AGI exceeds a specified level, the exclusion is subject to phaseout as follows:

        | | *2003* |
Filing status	*AGI phaseout range*
Married filing jointly	$87,750 – $117,750
Single (including head of household)	$58,500 – $ 73,500

(1) The reduction of the exclusion is computed as

$$\left(\frac{\text{Excess AGI}}{\substack{\$15,000 \\ (\$30,000 \text{ for joint returns})}}\right) \times \left(\begin{array}{c}\text{Otherwise} \\ \text{excludable} \\ \text{interest}\end{array}\right) = \text{Reduction}$$

(2) If the taxpayer's modified AGI exceeds the applicable phaseout range, no exclusion is available.

> EXAMPLE: *Assume the joint return of the married taxpayer in the above example has modified AGI of $107,750 for 2003. The reduction would be ($20,000/$30,000) x $3,600 = $2,400. Thus, of the $4,000 of interest received, a total of $1,200 could be excluded from gross income.*

12. **Scholarships and fellowships**

   a. A **degree candidate** can exclude the amount of a scholarship or fellowship that is used for tuition and course-related fees, books, supplies, and equipment. Amounts used for other purposes including room and board are included in income.

   b. Amounts received as a grant or a tuition reduction that represent payment for teaching, research, or other services are not excludable.

   c. Nondegree students may not exclude any part of a scholarship or fellowship grant.

13. Political contributions received by candidates' campaign funds are excluded from income, but included if put to personal use.

14. Rental value of parsonage or cash rental allowance for a parsonage is excluded by a minister.

15. **Discharge of indebtedness** normally results in income to debtor, but may be **excluded** if

   a. A discharge of certain student loans pursuant to a loan provision providing for discharge if the individual works in a certain profession for a specified period of time

   b. A discharge of a corporation's debt by a shareholder (treated as a contribution to capital)

   c. The discharge is a gift

   d. The discharge is a purchase money debt reduction (treat as a reduction of purchase price)

   e. Debt is discharged in a bankruptcy proceeding, or debtor is insolvent both before and after discharge

      (1) If debtor is insolvent before but solvent after discharge of debt, income is recognized to the extent that the FMV of assets exceeds liabilities after discharge

      (2) The amount excluded from income in e. above must be applied to reduce tax attributes in the following order

         (a) NOL for taxable year and loss carryovers to taxable year

         (b) General business credit

         (c) Minimum tax credit

         (d) Capital loss of taxable year and carryovers to taxable year

         (e) Reduction of the basis of property

         (f) Passive activity loss and credit carryovers

         (g) Foreign tax credit carryovers to or from taxable year

      (3) Instead of reducing tax attributes in the above order, taxpayer may elect to first reduce the basis of depreciable property

16. **Lease improvements.** Increase in value of property due to improvements made by lessee are excluded from lessor's income unless improvements are made in lieu of fair value rent.

17. **Foreign earned income exclusion.** An individual meeting either a bona fide residence test or a physical presence test may elect to exclude up to $80,000 of income earned in a foreign country for calendar year 2003 (and thereafter). Qualifying taxpayers also may elect to exclude additional amounts based on foreign housing costs.

   a. To qualify, an individual must be a (1) US citizen who is a foreign resident for an uninterrupted period that includes an entire taxable year (bona fide residence test), or (2) US citizen or resident present in a foreign country for at least 330 full days in any twelve-month period (physical presence test).

   b. An individual who elects to exclude the housing cost amount can exclude only the lesser of (1) the housing cost amount attributable to employer-provided amounts, or (2) the individual's foreign earned income for the year.

    c. Housing cost amounts not provided by an employer can be deducted for AGI, but deduction is limited to the excess of the taxpayer's foreign earned income over the applicable foreign earned income exclusion.

C. Items to Be Included in Gross Income

    Gross income includes all income from any source except those specifically excluded. The more common items of gross income are listed below. Those items requiring a detailed explanation are discussed on the following pages.

1. Compensation for services, including wages, salaries, bonuses, commissions, fees, and tips

    a. Property received as compensation is included in income at FMV on date of receipt.

    b. Bargain purchases by an employee from an employer are included in income at FMV less price paid.

    c. Life insurance premiums paid by employer must be included in an employee's gross income except for group-term life insurance coverage of $50,000 or less.

    d. Employee expenses paid or reimbursed by the employer unless the employee has to account to the employer for these expenses and they would qualify as deductible business expenses for employee.

    e. **Tips** must be included in gross income

        (1) If an individual receives less than $20 in tips while working for one employer during one month, the tips do not have to be reported to the employer, but the tips must be included in the individual's gross income when received

        (2) If an individual receives $20 or more in tips while working for one employer during one month, the individual must report the total amount of tips to the employer by the tenth day of the following month for purposes of withholding of income tax and social security tax. Then the total amount of tips must be included in the individual's gross income for the month in which reported to the employer.

2. Gross income derived from business or profession
3. Distributive share of partnership or S corporation income
4. Gain from the sale or exchange of real estate, securities, or other property
5. Rents and royalties
6. Dividends
7. **Interest** including

    a. Earnings from savings and loan associations, mutual savings banks, credit unions, etc.

    b. Interest on bank deposits, corporate or US government bonds, and treasury bills

        (1) Interest from US obligations is included, while interest on state and local obligations is generally excluded.

        (2) If a taxpayer elects to amortize the bond premium on taxable bonds acquired after 1987, any bond premium amortization is treated as an offset against the interest earned on the bond. The amortization of bond premium reduces taxable income (by offsetting interest income) as well as the bond's basis.

    c. **Interest on tax refunds**

    d. Imputed interest from interest-free and low-interest loans

        (1) Borrower is treated as making imputed interest payments (subject to the same deduction restrictions as actual interest payments) which the lender reports as interest income.

(2) Lender is treated as making gifts (for personal loans) or paying salary or dividends (for business-related loans) to the borrower.

(3) Rate used to impute interest is tied to average yield on certain federal securities; if the federal rate is greater than the interest rate charged on a loan (e.g., a low-interest loan), impute interest only for the excess.

   (a) For demand loans, the deemed transfers are generally treated as occurring at the end of each year, and will fluctuate with interest rates.

   (b) For term loans, the interest payments are determined at the date of the loan and then allocated over the term of the loan; lender's payments are treated as made on date of loan.

(4) No interest is imputed to either the borrower or the lender for any day on which the aggregate amount of loans between such individuals (and their spouses) does not exceed $10,000.

(5) For any day that the aggregate amount of loans between borrower and lender (and their spouses) does not exceed $100,000, imputed interest is limited to borrower's "net investment income"; no interest is imputed if borrower's net investment income does not exceed $1,000.

EXAMPLE: Parents make a $200,000 interest-free demand loan to their unmarried daughter on January 1, 2003. Assume the average federal short-term rate is 6% for 2003. If the loan is outstanding for the entire year, under Step 1, the daughter is treated as making a $12,000 ($200,000 x 6%) interest payment on 12/31/03, which is included as interest income on the parents' 2003 tax return. Under Step 2, the parents are treated as making a $12,000 gift to their daughter on 12/31/03. (Note that the gift will be offset by annual exclusions totaling $22,000 for gift tax purposes as discussed in Module 37.)

8. **Alimony** and separate maintenance payments

   a. Alimony is included in the recipient's gross income and is deductible toward AGI by the payor. In order for a payment to be considered as alimony, the payment must

      (1) Be made **pursuant to a decree** of divorce or written separation instrument
      (2) Be made in **cash** and received **by or on behalf** of the payee's spouse
      (3) **Terminate upon death** of the recipient
      (4) Not be made to a member of the same household at the time the payments are made
      (5) Not be made to a person with whom the taxpayer is filing a joint return
      (6) Not be characterized in the decree or written instrument as other than alimony

   b. **Alimony recapture** may occur if payments sharply decline in the second or third years. This is accomplished by making the payor report the recaptured alimony from the first and second years as income (and allowing the payee to deduct the same amount) in the third year.

      (1) Recapture for the second year occurs to the extent that the alimony paid in the second year exceeds the third-year alimony by more than $15,000.
      (2) Recapture for the first year occurs to the extent that the alimony paid in the first year exceeds the average alimony paid in the second year (reduced by the recapture for that year) and third year by more than $15,000.
      (3) Recapture will not apply to any year in which payments terminate as a result of the death of either spouse or the remarriage of the payee.
      (4) Recapture does not apply to payments that may fluctuate over three years or more and are not within the control of the payor spouse (e.g., 20% of the net income from a business).

      EXAMPLE: If a payor makes alimony payments of $50,000 in 2001 and no payments in 2002 or 2003, $50,000 – $15,000 = $35,000 will be recaptured in 2003 (assuming none of the exceptions apply).

      EXAMPLE: If a payor makes alimony payments of $50,000 in 2001, $20,000 in 2002, and nothing in 2003, the recapture amount for 2002 is $20,000 – $15,000 = $5,000. The recapture amount for 2001 is $50,000 – ($15,000 + $7,500) = $27,500. The $7,500 is the average payments for 2002 and 2003 after reducing the $20,000 year 2002 payment by the $5,000 of recapture for 2002. The recapture amounts for 2001 and 2002 total $32,500 and are reported in 2003.

   c. Any amounts specified as **child support** are not treated as alimony.

      (1) Child support is not gross income to the payee and is not deductible by the payor.
      (2) If the decree or instrument specifies both alimony and child support, but **less is paid than required,** then amounts are first allocated to child support, with any remainder allocated to alimony.

    (3) If a specified amount of alimony is to be reduced upon the happening of some **contingency relating to a child,** then an amount equal to the specified reduction will be treated as child support rather than alimony.

> *EXAMPLE: A divorce decree provides that payments of $1,000 per month will be reduced by $400 per month when a child reaches age twenty-one. Here, $400 of each $1,000 monthly payment will be treated as child support.*

9. **Social security,** pensions, annuities (other than excluded recovery of capital)

    a. Up to 50% of social security retirement benefits may be included in gross income if the taxpayer's provisional income (AGI + tax-exempt income + 50% of the social security benefits) exceeds a threshold that is $32,000 for a joint return, $0 for married taxpayers filing separately, and $25,000 for all other taxpayers. The amount to be included in gross income is the lesser of

        (1) 50% of the social security benefits, or
        (2) 50% of the excess of the taxpayer's provisional income over the base amount.

> *EXAMPLE: A single taxpayer with AGI of $20,000 received tax-exempt interest of $2,000 and social security benefits of $7,000. The social security to be included in gross income is the lesser of*
>
> $1/2\ (\$\ 7,000) = \$3,500;\ or$
> $1/2\ (\$25,500 - \$25,000) = \$250.$

    b. **Up to 85%** of social security retirement benefits may be included in gross income for taxpayers with provisional income above a higher second threshold that is $44,000 for a joint return, $0 for married taxpayers filing separately, and $34,000 for all other taxpayers. The amount to be included in gross income is the lesser of

        (1) 85% of the taxpayer's social security benefits, or
        (2) The sum of (a) 85% of the excess of the taxpayer's provisional income above the applicable higher threshold amount plus (b) the smaller of (i) the amount of benefits included under a. above, or (ii) $4,500 for single taxpayers or $6,000 for married taxpayers filing jointly.

    c. **Rule of thumb:** Social security retirement benefits are fully excluded by low-income taxpayers (i.e., provisional income less than $25,000); 85% of benefits must be included in gross income by high-income taxpayers (i.e., provisional income greater than $60,000).

    d. **Lump-sum distributions** from qualified pension, profit-sharing, stock bonus, and Keogh plans (but not IRAs) may be eligible for special tax treatment.

        (1) The portion of the distribution allocable to pre-1974 years is eligible for long-term capital gain treatment.
        (2) If the employee was born before 1936, the employee may elect ten-year averaging.
        (3) Alternatively, the distribution may be rolled over tax-free (within sixty days) to a traditional IRA, but subsequent distributions from the IRA will be treated as ordinary income.

10. **Income in respect of a decedent** is income that would have been income of the decedent before death but was not includible in income under the decedent's method of accounting (e.g., installment payments that are paid to a decedent's estate after his/her death). Such income has the same character as it would have had if the decedent had lived and must be included in gross income by the person who receives it.

11. Employer supplemental unemployment benefits or strike benefits from union funds

12. Fees, including those received by an executor, administrator, director, or for jury duty or precinct election board duty

13. Income from discharge of indebtedness unless specifically excluded (see page 394)

14. **Stock options**

    a. An **incentive stock option** receives favorable tax treatment.

        (1) The option must meet certain technical requirements to qualify.
        (2) No income is recognized by employee when option is granted or exercised.
        (3) If employee holds the stock acquired through exercise of the option at least two years from the date the option was granted, and holds the stock itself at least one year, the

            (a) Employee's realized gain will be long-term capital gain
            (b) Employer receives no deduction

(4) If the holding period requirements above are not met, the employee has ordinary income to the extent that the FMV at date of exercise exceeds the option price.

    (a) Remainder of gain is short-term or long-term capital gain.

    (b) Employer receives a deduction equal to the amount employee reports as ordinary income.

(5) An incentive stock option may be treated as a nonqualified stock option if a corporation so elects at the time the option is issued.

b. A **nonqualified stock option** is included in income when received if option has a determinable FMV.

(1) If option has no ascertainable FMV when received, then income arises when option is exercised; to the extent of the difference between the FMV when exercised and the option price.

(2) Amount recognized (at receipt or when exercised) is treated as ordinary income to employee; employer is allowed a deduction equal to amount included in employee's income.

c. An **employee stock purchase plan** that does not discriminate against rank and file employees

(1) No income when employee receives or exercises option

(2) If the employee holds the stock at least two years after the option is granted and at least one year after exercise, then

    (a) Employee has ordinary income to the extent of the lesser of

        1] FMV at time option granted over option price, or
        2] FMV at disposition over option price

    (b) Capital gain to the extent realized gain exceeds ordinary income

(3) If the stock is not held for the required time, then

    (a) Employee has ordinary income at the time of sale for the difference between FMV when exercised and the option price. This amount also increases basis.

    (b) Capital gain or loss for the difference between selling price and increased basis

15. **Prizes and awards** are generally taxable.

a. Prizes and awards received for religious, charitable, scientific, educational, artistic, literary, or civic achievement can be excluded only if the recipient

(1) Was selected without any action on his/her part,

(2) Is not required to render substantial future services, and

(3) Designates that the prize or award is to be transferred by the payor to a governmental unit or a tax-exempt charitable, educational, or religious organization

(4) The prize or award is excluded from the recipient's income, but no charitable deduction is allowed for the transferred amount.

b. **Employee achievement awards** are excluded from an employee's income if the cost to the employer of the award does not exceed the amount allowable as a deduction (generally from $400 to $1,600; see page 403).

(1) The award must be for length of service or safety achievement and must be in the form of tangible personal property (cash does not qualify).

(2) If the cost of the award exceeds the amount allowable as a deduction to the employer, the employee must include in gross income the greater of

    (a) The portion of cost not allowable as a deduction to the employer, or

    (b) The excess of the award's FMV over the amount allowable as a deduction.

16. **Tax benefit rule.** A recovery of an item deducted in an earlier year must be included in gross income to the extent that a tax benefit was derived from the prior deduction of the recovered item.

a. A tax benefit was derived if the previous deduction reduced the taxpayer's income tax.

b. A recovery is excluded from gross income to the extent that the previous deduction did not reduce the taxpayer's income tax.

(1) A deduction would not reduce a taxpayer's income tax if the taxpayer was subject to the alternative minimum tax in the earlier year and the deduction was not allowed in computing AMTI (e.g., state income taxes).

(2) A recovery of state income taxes, medical expenses, or other items deductible on Schedule A (Form 1040) will be excluded from gross income if an individual did not itemize deductions for the year the item was paid.

> EXAMPLE: Individual X, a single taxpayer, did not itemize deductions but instead used the standard deduction of $4,750 for 2003. In 2004, a refund of $300 of 2003 state income taxes is received. X would exclude the $300 refund from income in 2004.

> EXAMPLE: Individual Y, a single taxpayer, had total itemized deductions of $4,800 for 2003, including $800 of state income taxes. In 2004, a refund of $400 of 2003 state income taxes is received. Y must include $50 ($4,800 – $4,750) of the refund in income for 2004.

17. Embezzled or other illegal income
18. **Gambling winnings**
19. **Unemployment compensation** is fully included in gross income by the recipient.

D. Tax Accounting Methods

Tax accounting methods often affect the period in which an item of income or deduction is recognized. Note that the classification of an item is not changed, only the time for its inclusion in the tax computation.

1. Cash method or accrual method is commonly used.

   a. **Cash method** recognizes income when first received or constructively received; expenses are deductible when paid.

      (1) **Constructive receipt** means that an item is unqualifiedly available without restriction (e.g., interest on bank deposit is income when credited to account).

      (2) Not all receipts are income (e.g., loan proceeds, return of investment); not all payments are deductible (e.g., loan repayment, expenditures benefiting future years generally must be capitalized and deducted over cost recovery period).

   b. The cash method cannot generally be used if inventories are necessary to clearly reflect income, and cannot generally be used by C corporations, partnerships that have a C corporation as a partner, tax shelters, and certain tax-exempt trusts. However, the following may use the cash method:

      (1) A qualified personal service corporation (e.g., corporation performing services in health, law, engineering, accounting, actuarial science, performing arts, or consulting) if at least 95% of stock is owned by specified shareholders including employees.

      (2) An entity (other than a tax shelter) if for every year it has average annual gross receipts of **$5 million or less** for any prior three-year period and provided it does not have inventories for sale to customers.

      (3) A **small business taxpayer** with average annual gross receipts of **$1 million or less** for any prior three-year period (ending after December 17, 1998) can use the cash method and is excepted from the requirements to account for inventories and use the accrual method for purchases and sales of merchandise.

      (4) A **small business taxpayer** is eligible to use the cash method of accounting if, in addition to having average gross receipts of more than $1 million and less than $10 million, the business meets any one of three requirements.

         (a) The principal business activity is **not** retailing, wholesaling, manufacturing, mining, publishing, or sound recording;

         (b) The principal business activity is the provision of services, or custom manufacturing; or

         (c) Regardless of the principal business activity, a taxpayer may use the cash method with respect to any separate business that satisfies (a) or (b) above.

      (5) A taxpayer using the accrual method who meets the requirements in (3) or (4) can change to the cash method but must treat merchandise inventory as a material or supply that is not incidental (i.e., only deductible in the year actually consumed or used in the taxpayer's business).

c. **Accrual method** must be used by taxpayers (other than small business taxpayers) for purchases and sales when inventories are required to clearly reflect income.

(1) **Income** is recognized when "all events" have occurred that fix the taxpayer's right to receive the item of income and the amount can be determined with reasonable accuracy.

(2) An **expense** is deductible when "all events" have occurred that establish the fact of the liability and the amount can be determined with reasonable accuracy. The all-events test is not satisfied until **economic performance** has taken place.

(a) For property or services to be provided **to the taxpayer,** economic performance occurs when the property or services are actually provided by the other party.

(b) For property or services to be provided **by the taxpayer,** economic performance occurs when the property or services are physically provided by the taxpayer.

(3) An exception to the economic performance rule treats certain **recurring items of expense** as incurred in advance of economic performance provided

(a) The all-events test, without regard to economic performance, is satisfied during the tax year;

(b) Economic performance occurs within a reasonable period (but in no event more than 8.5 months after the close of the tax year);

(c) The item is recurring in nature and the taxpayer consistently treats items of the same type as incurred in the tax year in which the all-events test is met; and

(d) Either the amount is not material or the accrual of the item in the year the all-events test is met results in a better matching against the income to which it relates.

2. **Special rules** regarding methods of accounting

a. **Rents and royalties received in advance** are included in gross income in the year received under both the cash and accrual methods.

(1) A **security deposit** is included in income when not returned to tenant.

(2) An amount called a "security deposit" that may be used as final payment of rent is considered to be advance rent and included in income when received.

EXAMPLE: In 2003, a landlord signed a five-year lease. During 2003, the landlord received $5,000 for that year's rent, and $5,000 as advance rent for the last year (2007) of the lease. All $10,000 will be included in income for 2003.

b. Dividends are included in gross income in the year received under both the cash and accrual methods.

c. No advance deduction is generally allowed for accrual method taxpayers for estimated or contingent expenses; the obligation must be "fixed and determinable."

3. The **installment method** applies to gains (not losses) from the disposition of property where at least one payment is to be received after the year of sale. The installment method does not change the character of the gain to be reported (e.g., ordinary, capital, etc.), and is required unless the taxpayer makes a negative election to report the full amount of gain in year of sale.

a. The installment method **cannot be used** for property held for sale in the ordinary course of business (except time-share units, residential lots, and property used or produced in farming), and cannot be used for sales of stock or securities traded on an established securities market.

b. The amount to be reported in each year is determined by the formula

$$\frac{\text{Gross profit}}{\text{Total contract price}} \quad \text{x} \quad \text{Amount received in year}$$

(1) **Contract price** is the selling price reduced by the seller's liabilities that are assumed by the buyer, to the extent not in excess of the seller's basis in the property.

EXAMPLE: Taxpayer sells property with a basis of $80,000 to buyer for a selling price of $150,000. As part of the purchase price, buyer agrees to assume a $50,000 mortgage on the property and pay the remaining $100,000 in 10 equal annual installments together with adequate interest.

The contract price is $100,000 ($150,000 – $50,000); the gross profit is $70,000 ($150,000 – $80,000); and the gross profit ratio is 70% ($70,000 ÷ $100,000). Thus, $7,000 of each $10,000 payment is reported as gain from the sale.

> *EXAMPLE: Assume the same facts as above except that the seller's basis is $30,000. The contract price is $120,000 ($150,000 – mortgage assumed but only to extent of seller's basis of $30,000); the gross profit is $120,000 ($150,000 – $30,000); and the gross profit ratio is 100% ($120,000 ÷ $120,000). Thus, 100% of each $10,000 payment is reported as gain from the sale. In addition, the amount by which the assumed mortgage exceeds the seller's basis ($20,000) is deemed to be a payment in year of sale. Since the gross profit ratio is 100%, all $20,000 is reported as gain in the year the mortgage is assumed.*

    (2) Any depreciation recapture under Secs. 1245, 1250, and 291 must be included in income in the year of sale. Amount of recapture included in income is treated as an increase in the basis of the property for purposes of determining the gross profit ratio. Remainder of gain is spread over installment payments.

    (3) If installment obligations are pledged as security for a loan, the net proceeds of the loan are treated as payments received on the installment obligations.

    (4) Installment obligations arising from nondealer sales of property used in the taxpayer's trade or business or held for the production of rental income (e.g., factory building, warehouse, office building, apartment building) are subject to an interest charge on the tax that is deferred on such sales to the extent that the amount of deferred payments arising from all dispositions of such property during a taxable year and outstanding as of the close of the taxable year exceeds $5,000,000. This provision does not apply to installment sales of property if the sales price does not exceed $150,000, to sales of personal use property, and to sales of farm property.

4. **Percentage-of-completion** method can be used for contracts that are not completed within the year they are started.

    a. Percentage-of-completion method recognizes income each year based on the percentage of the contract completed that year.

    b. Taxpayer may elect not to recognize income or account for costs from a contract for a tax year if less than 10% of the estimated total contract costs have been incurred as of the end of the year.

E. Business Income and Deductions

1. **Gross income** for a business includes sales less cost of goods sold plus other income. In computing cost of goods sold

    a. Inventory is generally valued at (1) cost, or (2) market, whichever is lower

    b. Specific identification, FIFO, and LIFO are allowed

    c. If LIFO is used for taxes, it must also be used on books

    d. Lower of cost or market cannot be used with LIFO

2. All **ordinary** (customary and not a capital expenditure) and **necessary** (appropriate and helpful) **expenses** incurred in a trade or business are deductible.

    a. Business expenses that violate public policy (fines or illegal kickbacks) are not deductible.

    b. No deduction or credit is allowed for any amount paid or incurred in carrying on a trade or business that consists of trafficking in controlled substances. However, this limitation does not alter the definition of gross income (i.e., sales less cost of goods sold).

    c. Business expenses must be reasonable.

        (1) If salaries are excessive (unreasonable compensation), they may be disallowed as a deduction to the extent unreasonable.

        (2) Reasonableness of compensation issue generally arises only when the relationship between the employer and employee exceeds that of the normal employer-employee relationship (e.g., employee is also a shareholder).

        (3) Use test of what another enterprise would pay under similar circumstances to an unrelated employee.

    d. In the case of an individual, any charge (including taxes) for basic local telephone service with respect to the **first telephone line** provided to any residence of the taxpayer shall be treated as a nondeductible personal expense. Disallowance does not apply to charges for long-distance calls, charges for equipment rental, and optional services provided by a telephone company, or charges attributable to additional telephone lines to a taxpayer's residence other than the first telephone line.

e. **Uniform capitalization rules** generally require that all costs incurred (both direct and indirect) in manufacturing or constructing real or personal property, or in purchasing or holding property for sale, must be capitalized as part of the cost of the property.

(1) These costs become part of the basis of the property and are recovered through depreciation or amortization, or are included in inventory and recovered through cost of goods sold as an off-set to selling price.

(2) The rules apply to inventory, noninventory property produced or held for sale to customers, and to assets or improvements to assets constructed by a taxpayer for the taxpayer's own use in a trade or business or in an activity engaged in for profit.

(3) Taxpayers subject to the rules are required to capitalize not only direct costs, but also most indirect costs that benefit the assets produced or acquired for resale, including general, administrative, and overhead costs.

(4) Retailers and wholesalers must include in inventory all costs incident to purchasing and storing inventory such as wages of employees responsible for purchasing inventory, handling, processing, repackaging and assembly of goods, and off-site storage costs. These rules do not apply to "small retailers and wholesalers" (i.e., a taxpayer who acquires personal property for resale if the taxpayer's average annual gross receipts for the three preceding taxable years do not exceed $10,000,000).

(5) Interest must be capitalized if the debt is incurred or continued to finance the construction or production of real property, property with a recovery period of twenty years, property that takes more than two years to produce, or property with a production period exceeding one year and a cost exceeding $1 million.

(6) The capitalization rules do not apply to research and experimentation expenditures, property held for personal use, and to free-lance authors, photographers, and artists.

f. **Business meals, entertainment, and travel**

(1) Receipts must be maintained for all lodging expenditures and for other expenditures of **$75** or more except transportation expenditures where receipts are not readily available.

(2) Adequate contemporaneous records must be maintained for business meals and entertainment to substantiate the amount of expense, for example, who, when, where, and why (the 4 W's).

(3) Business meals and entertainment must be directly related or associated with the active conduct of a trade or business to be deductible. The taxpayer or a representative must be present to satisfy this requirement.

(4) The amount of the otherwise allowable deduction for business meals or entertainment must be reduced by 50%. This **50% reduction rule** applies to all food, beverage, and entertainment costs (even though incurred in the course of travel away from home) after determining the amount otherwise deductible. The 50% reduction rule will not apply if

(a) The full value of the meal or entertainment is included in the recipient's income or excluded as a fringe benefit.

(b) An employee is reimbursed for the cost of a meal or entertainment (the 50% reduction rule applies to the party making the reimbursement).

(c) The cost is for a traditional employer-paid employee recreation expense (e.g., a company Christmas party).

(d) The cost is for samples and other promotional activities made available to the public.

(e) The expense is for a sports event that qualifies as a charitable fund-raising event.

(f) The cost is for meals or entertainment sold for full consideration.

(5) The cost of a ticket to any entertainment activity is limited (prior to the 50% reduction rule) to its face value.

(6) No deduction is generally allowed for expenses with respect to an entertainment, recreational, or amusement facility.

(a) Entertainment facilities include yachts, hunting lodges, fishing camps, swimming pools, etc.

(b) If the facility or club is used for a business purpose, the related out-of-pocket expenditures are deductible even though depreciation, etc. of the facility is not deductible.

(7) No deduction is allowed for dues paid to country clubs, golf and athletic clubs, airline clubs, hotel clubs, and luncheon clubs. Dues are generally deductible if paid to professional organizations (accounting, medical, and legal associations), business leagues, trade associations, chambers of commerce, boards of trade, and civic and public service organizations (Kiwanis, Lions, Elks).

(8) **Transportation and travel expenses** are deductible if incurred in the active conduct of a trade or business.

    (a) Deductible transportation expenses include local transportation between two job locations, but excludes commuting expenses between residence and job.

    (b) Deductible travel expenses are those incurred while temporarily "away from tax home" overnight including meals, lodging, transportation, and expenses incident to travel (clothing care, etc.).

        1] Travel expenses to and from domestic destination are fully deductible if business is the primary purpose of trip.

        2] Actual automobile expenses can be deducted, or beginning January 1, 2003, taxpayers can use standard mileage rate of 36¢/mile for all business miles (plus parking and tolls).

        3] No deduction is allowed for travel as a form of education. This rule applies when a travel expense would otherwise be deductible only on the ground that the travel itself serves educational purposes.

        4] No deduction is allowed for expenses incurred in attending a convention, seminar, or similar meeting for investment purposes.

g. Deductions for **business gifts** are limited to **$25** per recipient each year.

(1) Advertising and promotional gifts costing $4 or less are not limited.

(2) Gifts of tangible personal property costing $400 or less are deductible if awarded as an employee achievement award for length of service or safety achievement.

(3) Gifts of tangible personal property costing $1,600 or less are deductible if awarded as an employee achievement award under a qualified plan for length of service or safety achievement.

    (a) Plan must be written and nondiscriminatory.

    (b) Average cost of all items awarded under the plan during the tax year must not exceed $400.

h. **Bad debts** are generally deducted in the year they become worthless.

(1) There must have been a valid "debtor-creditor" relationship.

(2) A **business bad debt** is one that is incurred in the trade or business of the lender.

    (a) Deductible against ordinary income (toward AGI)

    (b) Deduction allowed for partial worthlessness

(3) Business bad debts must be deducted under the specific charge-off method (the reserve method generally cannot be used).

    (a) A deduction is allowed when a specific debt becomes partially or totally worthless.

    (b) A bad debt deduction is available for accounts or notes receivable only if the amount owed has already been included in gross income for the current or a prior taxable year. Since receivables for services rendered of a **cash method** taxpayer have not yet been included in gross income, the receivables cannot be deducted when they become uncollectible.

(4) A **nonbusiness bad debt** (not incurred in trade or business) can only be deducted

    (a) If totally worthless

    (b) As a short-term capital loss

(5) Guarantor of debt who has to pay takes same deduction as if the loss were from a direct loan

    (a) Business bad debt if guarantee related to trade, business, or employment

    (b) Nonbusiness bad debt if guarantee entered into for profit but not related to trade or business

    i. A **hobby** is an activity not engaged in for profit (e.g., stamp or card collecting engaged in for recreation and personal pleasure).

      (1) Special rules generally limit the deduction of hobby expenses to the amount of hobby gross income. No net loss can generally be deducted for hobby activities.

      (2) Hobby expenses are deductible as itemized deductions in the following order:

        (a) First deduct taxes, interest, and casualty losses pertaining to the hobby.

        (b) Then other hobby operating expenses are deductible to the extent they do not exceed hobby gross income reduced by the amounts deducted in (a). Out-of-pocket expenses are deducted before depreciation. These hobby expenses are aggregated with other miscellaneous itemized deductions that are subject to the 2% of AGI floor.

      (3) An activity is presumed to be for profit (not a hobby) if it produces a net profit in at least three out of five consecutive years (two out of seven years for horses).

3. **Net operating loss (NOL)**

    a. A net operating loss is generally a business loss but may occur even if an individual is not engaged in a separate trade or business (e.g., a NOL created by a personal casualty loss).

    b. A NOL may be carried **back two years** and carried **forward twenty years** to offset taxable income in those years.

      (1) Carryback is first made to the second preceding year.

      (2) Taxpayer may elect not to carryback and only carryforward twenty years.

      (3) A three-year carryback period is permitted for the portion of the NOL that relates to casualty and theft losses of individual taxpayers, and to NOLs that are attributable to presidentially declared disasters and are incurred by taxpayers engaged in farming or by a small business.

      (4) A *small business* is any trade or business (including one conducted by a corporation, partnership, or sole proprietorship) with average annual gross receipts of $5 million or less for the three-year tax period preceding the loss year.

    c. For NOLs arising in tax years ending in 2001 and 2002, the two-year (or three-year) carryback is extended to five years. However, a taxpayer may make an irrevocable election to waive the five-year carryback period, and carry back only two years (or three years if applicable).

    d. The following cannot be included in the computation of a NOL:

      (1) Any NOL carryforward or carryback from another year

      (2) Excess of capital losses over capital gains. Excess of nonbusiness capital losses over nonbusiness capital gains even if overall gains exceed losses

      (3) Personal exemptions

      (4) Excess of nonbusiness deductions (usually itemized deductions) over nonbusiness income

        (a) The standard deduction is treated as a nonbusiness deduction.

        (b) Contributions to a self-employed retirement plan are considered nonbusiness deductions.

        (c) Casualty losses (even if personal) are considered business deductions.

        (d) Dividends and interest are nonbusiness income; salary and rent are business income.

      (5) Any remaining loss is a NOL and must be carried back first, unless election is made to carryforward only.

> *EXAMPLE: George, single with no dependents, started his own delivery business and incurred a loss from the business for 2003. In addition, he earned interest on personal bank deposits of $1,800. After deducting his itemized deductions for interest and taxes of $9,000, and his personal exemption of $3,050, the loss shown on George's Form 1040 was $20,300. George's net operating loss would be computed as follows:*

Taxable income		$(20,300)
Nonbusiness deductions	$9,000	
Nonbusiness income	−1,800	7,200
Personal exemption		3,050
Net operating loss		$(10,050)

4. Limitation on deductions for **business use of home**. To be deductible

    a. A portion of the home must be used exclusively and regularly as the *principal place of business*, or as a meeting place for patients, clients, or customers.

      (1) Exclusive use rule does not apply to the portion of the home used as a day care center and to a place of regular storage of business inventory or product samples if the home is the sole fixed location of a trade or business selling products at retail or wholesale.

      (2) If an employee, the exclusive use must be for the convenience of the employer.

      (3) A home office qualifies as a taxpayer's *principal place of business* if

         (a) It is the place where the primary income-generating functions of the trade or business are performed; or

         (b) The office is used to conduct administrative or management activities of the taxpayer's business, and there is no other fixed location of the business where substantial administrative or management activities are performed. Activities that are administrative or managerial in nature include billing customers, clients, or patients; keeping books and records; ordering supplies; setting up appointments; and forwarding orders or writing reports.

  b. Deduction is limited to the excess of gross income derived from the business use of the home over deductions otherwise allowable for taxes, interest, and casualty losses.

  c. Any business expenses not allocable to the use of the home (e.g., wages, transportation, supplies) must be deducted before home use expenses.

  d. Any business use of home expenses that are disallowed due to the gross income limitation can be carried forward and deducted in future years subject to the same restrictions.

    EXAMPLE: Taxpayer uses 10% of his home exclusively for business purposes. Gross income from his business totaled $750, and he incurred the following expenses:

	Total	*10% Business*
Interest	*4,000*	*$400*
Taxes	*2,500*	*250*
Utilities, insurance	*1,500*	*150*
Depreciation	*2,000*	*200*

    Since total deductions for business use of the home are limited to business gross income, the taxpayer can deduct the following for business use of his home: $400 interest; $250 taxes; $100 utilities and insurance; and $0 depreciation (operating expenses such as utilities and insurance must be deducted before depreciation). The remaining $50 of utilities and insurance, and $200 of depreciation can be carried forward and deducted in future years subject to the same restrictions.

5. Loss deductions incurred in a trade or business, or in the production of income, are limited to the amount a taxpayer has "**at risk**."

  a. Applies to all activities except the leasing of personal property by a closely held corporation (5 or fewer individuals own more than 50% of stock)

  b. Applies to individuals and closely held regular corporations

  c. Amount "at risk" includes

      (1) The cash and adjusted basis of property contributed by the taxpayer, and

      (2) Liabilities for which the taxpayer is personally liable; excludes nonrecourse debt.

  d. For real estate activities, a taxpayer's amount at risk includes "qualified" nonrecourse financing secured by the real property used in the activity.

      (1) Nonrecourse financing is qualified if it is borrowed from a lender engaged in the business of making loans (e.g., bank, savings and loan) provided that the lender is not the promoter or seller of the property or a party related to either; or is borrowed from or guaranteed by any federal, state, or local government or instrumentality thereof.

      (2) Nonrecourse financing obtained from a qualified lender who has an equity interest in the venture is treated as an amount at risk, as long as the terms of the financing are commercially reasonable.

      (3) The nonrecourse financing must not be convertible, and no person can be personally liable for repayment.

  e. Excess losses can be carried over to subsequent years (no time limit) and deducted when the "at risk" amount has been increased.

  f. Previously allowed losses will be recaptured as income if the amount at risk is reduced below zero.

6. **Losses and credits from passive activities** may generally only be used to offset income from (or tax allocable to) passive activities. Passive losses may not be used to offset active income (e.g., wages, salaries, professional fees, etc.) or portfolio income (e.g., interest, dividends, annuities, royalties, etc.).

EXAMPLE: Ken has salary income, a loss from a partnership in whose business Ken does not materially participate, and income from a limited partnership. Ken may offset the partnership loss against the income from the limited partnership, but not against his salary income.

EXAMPLE: Robin has dividend and interest income of $40,000 and a passive activity loss of $30,000. The passive activity loss cannot be offset against the dividend and interest income.

   a. Applies to individuals, estates, trusts, closely held C corporations, and personal service corporations

     (1) A closely held C corporation is one with five or fewer shareholders owning more than 50% of stock.

     (2) Personal service corporation is an incorporated service business with more than 10% of its stock owned by shareholder-employees.

   b. **Passive activity** is any activity that involves the conduct of a trade or business in which the taxpayer does "not materially participate," any rental activity, and any limited partnership interest.

     (1) Material participation is the taxpayer's involvement in an activity on a regular, continuous, and substantial basis considering such factors as time devoted, physical duties performed, and knowledge of or experience in the business.

     (2) Passive activity does not include (1) a working interest in any oil or gas property that a taxpayer owns directly or through an entity that does not limit the taxpayer's liability, (2) operating a hotel or transient lodging if significant services are provided, or (3) operating a short-term equipment rental business.

   c. **Losses** from passive activities may be deducted only against income from passive activities.

     (1) If there is insufficient passive activity income to absorb passive activity losses, the excess losses are carried forward indefinitely to future years.

     (2) If there is insufficient passive activity income in subsequent years to fully absorb the loss carryforwards, the unused losses from a passive activity may be deducted when the taxpayer's entire interest in the activity that gave rise to the unused losses is finally disposed of in a fully taxable transaction.

     (3) Other dispositions

       (a) A transfer of a taxpayer's interest in a passive activity by reason of the taxpayer's death results in suspended losses being allowed (to the decedent) to the extent they exceed the amount of the step-up in basis allowed.

       (b) If the disposition is by gift, the suspended losses are added to the basis of the gift property. If less than 100% of an interest is transferred by gift, an allocable portion of the suspended losses is added to the basis of the gift.

       (c) An installment sale of a passive interest triggers the recognition of suspended losses in the ratio that the gain recognized in each year bears to the total gain on sale.

       (d) If a formerly passive activity becomes an active one, suspended losses are allowed against income from the now active business (if the activity remains the same).

   d. **Credits** from passive activities can only be used to offset the tax liability attributable to passive activity income.

     (1) Excess credits are carried forward indefinitely (subject to limited carryback during the phase-in period).

     (2) Excess credits (unlike losses) cannot be used in full in the year in which the taxpayer's entire passive activity interest is disposed of. Instead, excess credits continue to be carried forward.

     (3) Credits allowable under the passive activity limitation rules are also subject to the general business credit limitation.

   e. Although a **rental activity** is defined as a passive activity regardless of the property owner's participation in the operation of the rental property, a special rule permits an individual to offset up to

$25,000 of income that is **not** from passive activities by losses or credits from rental real estate if the individual **actively participates** in the rental real estate activity.

(1) "Active participation" is less stringent than "material participation" and is met if the taxpayer personally operates the rental property; or, if a rental agent operates the property, the taxpayer participates in management decisions or arranges for others to provide services.

(2) An individual is not considered to actively participate in a rental real estate activity unless the individual's interest in the activity (including any interest owned by the individual's spouse) was at least 10% of the value of all interests in the activity throughout the year.

(3) The active participation requirement must be met in both the year that the loss arises and the year in which the loss is allowed.

(4) For losses, the $25,000 amount is reduced by 50% of AGI in excess of $100,000 and fully phased out when AGI exceeds $150,000. For this purpose, AGI is computed before including taxable social security, before deducting IRA contributions, and before the exclusion of interest from Series EE bonds used for higher education.

(5) For low-income housing and rehabilitation credits, the $25,000 amount is reduced by 50% of AGI in excess of $200,000 and fully phased out when AGI exceeds $250,000.

f. If a taxpayer meets certain eligibility requirements, losses and credits from rental real estate activities in which the taxpayer materially participates are not subject to the passive loss limitations. This provision applies to individuals and closely held C corporations.

(1) Individuals are eligible if (a) more than half of all the personal services they perform during the year are for real property trades or businesses in which they materially participate, and (b) they perform more than 750 hours of service per year in those real estate activities. On a joint return, this relief is available if either spouse separately satisfies the requirements.

(2) Closely held C corporations are eligible if more than 50% of their gross receipts for the taxable year are derived from real property trades or businesses in which the corporation materially participated.

(3) Suspended losses from any rental real property that is not treated as passive by the above provision are treated as losses from a former passive activity. The deductibility of these suspended losses is limited to income from the activity; they are not allowed to offset other income.

g. The passive activity limitation rules do not apply to losses disallowed under the at risk rules.

F. Depreciation, Depletion, and Amortization

Depreciation is an allowance for the exhaustion, wear and tear of property used in a trade or business, or of property held for the production of income. The depreciation class of property is generally determined by reference to its Asset Depreciation Range (ADR) guideline class. Taxpayers must determine annual deductions based on the applicable property class, depreciation method, and averaging convention.

1. For property placed in service prior to 1981, the basis of property reduced by salvage value was recovered over its useful life using the straight-line, declining balance, or sum-of-the-years' digits method. Whether an accelerated method of depreciation could be used depended on the classification and useful life of the property, and whether it was new or used when acquired. The Accelerated Cost Recovery System (ACRS) was used to recover the basis of depreciable property placed in service after 1980 and before 1987.

2. **Modified Accelerated Cost Recovery System (MACRS)**

a. MACRS is **mandatory** for most depreciable property placed in service **after 1986**.

b. Salvage value is completely ignored under MACRS; the method of cost recovery and the recovery period are the same for both new and used property.

c. **Recovery property** includes all property other than land, intangible assets, and property the taxpayer elects to depreciate under a method not expressed in terms of years (e.g., units of production or income forecast methods). Recovery property placed in service after 1986 is divided into six classes of personal property based on ADR midpoint life and into two classes of real property. Each class is assigned a recovery period and a depreciation method. Recovery deductions for the first six classes are based on the declining balance method, switching to the straight-line method to maximize deductions.

(1) **3-year, 200% class.** Includes property with an ADR midpoint of four years or less (except for autos and light trucks) and certain horses

(2) **5-year, 200% class.** Includes property with an ADR midpoint of more than four and less than ten years. Also included are autos and light trucks, computers and peripheral equipment, office machinery (typewriters, calculators, copiers, etc.)

(3) **7-year, 200% class.** Includes property with an ADR midpoint of at least ten and less than sixteen years. Also included are property having no ADR midpoint and not classified elsewhere, and office furniture and fixtures (desks, files, etc.)

(4) **10-year, 200% class.** Includes property with an ADR midpoint of at least sixteen and less than twenty years

(5) **15-year, 150% class.** Includes property with an ADR midpoint of at least twenty years and less than twenty-five years

(6) **20-year, 150% class.** Includes property with an ADR midpoint of twenty-five years or more, other than real property with an ADR midpoint of 27.5 years or more

(7) **27 1/2-year, straight-line class.** Includes residential rental property (i.e., a building or structure with 80% or more of its rental income from dwelling units)

(8) **39-year, straight-line class.** Includes any property that is neither residential real property nor property with a class life of less than 27.5 years

d. Instead of using the declining balance method for three-year through twenty-year property, taxpayers can elect to use the straight-line method over the MACRS class life. This is an annual class-by-class election.

e. Instead of using the 200% declining balance method for three-year through ten-year property, taxpayers can elect to use the 150% declining balance method. This is an annual class-by-class election.

f. An **alternative depreciation system** (ADS) provides for straight-line depreciation over the property's ADS class life (twelve years for personal property with no ADS class life, and forty years for real property).

(1) A taxpayer may elect to use the alternative system for any class of property placed in service during a taxable year. For real property, the election is made on a property-by-property basis.

(2) Once made, the election is irrevocable and continues to apply to that property for succeeding years, but does not apply to similar property placed in service in a subsequent year, unless a new election is made.

(3) The alternative system must be used for foreign use property, property used 50% or more for personal use, and for purposes of computing earnings and profits.

g. An **averaging convention** is used to compute depreciation for the taxable year in which property is placed in service or disposed of under both the regular MACRS and alternative depreciation system.

(1) **Personal property** is treated as placed in service or disposed of at the midpoint of the taxable year, resulting in a **half-year** of depreciation for the year in which the property is placed in service or disposed of. However, no depreciation is allowed for personal property disposed of in the same taxable year in which it was placed in service.

EXAMPLE: A calendar-year taxpayer purchased machinery (5-year, 200% class) for $10,000 in January 2003. Because of the averaging convention, the depreciation for 2003 will be ($10,000 x 40% x 1/2) = $2,000.

(2) A **midquarter** convention must be used if more than 40% of all personal property is placed in service during the last quarter of the taxpayer's taxable year. Under this convention, property is treated as placed in service (or disposed of) in the middle of the quarter in which placed in service (or disposed of).

EXAMPLE: In January 2003 a calendar-year taxpayer purchased machinery for $10,000. In December 2003 the taxpayer purchased additional machinery for $30,000. All machinery was assigned to the 5-year, 200% class. No other depreciable assets were purchased during the year.

Since the machinery placed in service during the last three months of the year exceeded 40% of the depreciable basis of all personal property placed in service during the taxable year, all machinery is depreciated under the midquarter convention. The taxpayer may claim 3.5 quarters depreciation on the machinery acquired in January ($10,000 x 40% x 3.5/4 = $3,500), and only 1/2 quarter of depreciation for the machinery acquired in December ($30,000 x 40% x .5/4 = $1,500).

(3) **Real property** is treated as placed in service or disposed of in the middle of a month, resulting in a **half-month** of depreciation for the month disposed of or placed in service.

> EXAMPLE: *A calendar-year taxpayer purchased a warehouse (39-year property) for $150,000 and placed it in service on March 26, 2003. Because of the mid-month convention, the depreciation for 2003 will be ($150,000 x 9.5/468 months) = $3,045.*

h. The cost of **leasehold improvements** made by a lessee must be recovered over the MACRS recovery period of the underlying property without regard to the lease term. Upon the expiration of the lease, any unrecovered adjusted basis in abandoned leasehold improvements will be treated as a loss.

i. **Sec. 179 expense election.** A taxpayer (other than a trust or estate) may annually elect to treat the cost of qualifying depreciable property as an expense rather than a capital expenditure.

(1) Qualifying property is generally recovery property that is tangible personal property acquired by purchase from an unrelated party for use in the active conduct of a trade or business. Off-the-shelf computer software with a useful life of more than one year is treated as qualifying property that may be expensed.

(2) The maximum cost that can be expensed is **$100,000 for 2003** but is reduced dollar-for-dollar by the cost of qualifying property that is placed in service during the taxable year that exceeds $400,000.

(3) The amount of expense deduction is further limited to the taxable income derived from the active conduct by the taxpayer of any trade or business. Any expense deduction disallowed by this limitation is carried forward to the succeeding taxable year.

(4) If property is converted to nonbusiness use at any time, the excess of the amount expensed over the MACRS deductions that would have been allowed must be recaptured as ordinary income in the year of conversion.

j. **Additional first-year depreciation.** Taxpayers may deduct additional first-year depreciation on qualified property acquired after September 10, 2001, and before September 11, 2004, if placed in service before January 1, 2005. The allowance is available for new property that is depreciable under MACRS and has a recovery period of twenty years or less, or is qualified leasehold improvement property. A taxpayer may elect not to use additional first-year depreciation with respect to any class of property.

(1) Additional first-year depreciation is allowed for both regular tax and alternative minimum tax (AMT) in the year the property is placed in service, and no AMT adjustment is necessary. Similarly, if additional first-year depreciation is claimed, no AMT adjustment is required on regular MACRS deductions.

(2) The Sec. 179 expense election is computed prior to the additional first-year depreciation allowance. The regular MACRS deduction is computed after reducing adjusted basis by any Sec. 179 expense election and the additional first-year depreciation allowance.

(3) The additional first-year depreciation rate is 30% for property acquired before May 6, 2003, while a 50% rate applies to property acquired after May 5, 2003. A taxpayer may elect to use the old 30% rate for property acquired after May 5, 2003.

> EXAMPLE: *A calendar-year taxpayer purchases new equipment (5-year, 200% class) for $403,000 during June 2003 and elects to take the maximum Sec. 179 expense. The Sec. 179 expense deduction would be computed first and would total $100,000 – ($403,000 – $400,000) = $97,000. Second, additional first-year depreciation would be computed and would total ($403,000 – $97,000) x 50% = $153,000. Third, regular MACRS depreciation would be computed and would total [$403,000 – ($97,000 + $153,000)] x 2/5 x 1/2 = $30,600. As a result the adjusted basis of the equipment would be computed as follows:*

Cost	$403,000
Sec. 179 expense deduction	(97,000)
Additional first-year depreciation	(153,000)
MACRS depreciation	(30,600)
Adjusted basis	$122,400

k. For a passenger automobile first placed in service after September 10, 2001, the amount of MACRS (including expensing) deductions is limited to $3,060 in the year placed in service ($10,710 if 50% additional first-year depreciation is taken), $4,900 for the second year, $2,950 for the third year, and $1,775 for each year thereafter. These amounts are indexed for inflation.

(1) These limits are reduced to reflect personal use [e.g., if auto is used 30% for personal use and 70% for business use, limits are (70% x $3,060) = $2,142 for the year of acquisition, (70% x $4,900) = $3,430 for the second year, etc.].

(2) If automobile is not used more than 50% for business use, MACRS is limited to straight-line depreciation over five years.

    (a) Use of the automobile for income-producing purposes is not counted in determining whether the more than 50% test is met, but is considered in determining the amount of allowable depreciation.

      EXAMPLE: An automobile is used 40% in a business, 35% for production of income, and 25% for personal use. The 200% declining balance method cannot be used because business use is not more than 50%. However, depreciation limited to the straight-line method is allowed based on 75% of use.

    (b) If the more than 50% test is met in year of acquisition, but business use subsequently falls to 50% or less, MACRS deductions in excess of five-year straight-line method are recaptured.

l. Transportation property other than automobiles (e.g., airplanes, trucks, boats, etc.), entertainment property (including real property), any computer or peripheral equipment not used exclusively at a regular business establishment, and cellular telephones and similar telecommunications equipment are subject to the same more than 50% business use requirement and consequent restrictions on depreciation as are applicable to automobiles.

(1) Failure to use these assets more than 50% for business purposes will limit the deductions to the straight-line method.

(2) If the more than 50% test is met in year of acquisition, but business use subsequently falls to 50% or less, MACRS deductions in excess of the applicable straight-line method are recaptured.

3. **Depletion**

  a. Depletion is allowed on timber, minerals, oil, and gas, and other exhaustible natural resources or wasting assets.

  b. There are two basic methods to compute depletion for the year.

    (1) **Cost** method divides the adjusted basis by the total number of recoverable units and multiplies by the number of units sold (or payment received for, if cash basis) during the year.

      (a) Adjusted basis is cost less accumulated depletion (not below zero).

        EXAMPLE: Land cost $10,050,000 of which $50,000 is the residual value of the land. There are 1,000,000 barrels of oil recoverable. If 10,000 barrels were sold, cost depletion would be ($10,000,000 ÷ 1,000,000 barrels) x 10,000 = $100,000.

    (2) **Percentage** method uses a specified percentage of gross income from the property during the year.

      (a) Deduction may not exceed 50% of the taxable income (before depletion) from the property.

      (b) May be taken even after costs have been recovered and there is no basis

      (c) May be used for domestic oil and gas wells by "independent producer" or royalty owner; cannot be used for timber

      (d) The percentage is a statutory amount and generally ranges from 5% to 20% depending on the mineral.

4. **Amortization** is allowed for several special types of capital expenditures

  a. A corporation's or partnership's organizational expenses can be amortized over sixty or more months. Otherwise deductible only when corporation or partnership is dissolved.

  b. **Business investigation and start-up costs** are deductible in the year paid or incurred if the taxpayer is currently in a similar line of business as the start-up business. If not in a similar line of business and the new business is

    (1) Acquired by the taxpayer, then investigation and start-up costs are capitalized and may be amortized over not less than sixty months beginning with the month that business begins

    (2) Not acquired by the taxpayer, then investigation costs are not deductible

    c. Pollution control facilities can be amortized over sixty months if installed on property that was placed in operation prior to 1976. The pollution control investment must not increase output, capacity, or the useful life of the asset.

    d. Patents and copyrights may be amortized over their useful life.

        (1) Seventeen years for patents; life of author plus fifty years for copyrights

        (2) If become obsolete early, deduct in that year

    e. Research and experimental expenses may be amortized over sixty months or more. Alternatively, may be expensed at election of taxpayer if done so for year in which such expenses are first incurred or paid.

    f. Intangible assets for which the Code does not specifically provide for amortization are amortizable over their useful lives.

5. **Sec. 197 intangibles**

    a. Most **acquired intangible assets** are to be amortized over a fifteen-year period, beginning with the month in which the intangible is acquired (the treatment of self-created intangible assets is not affected). Sec. 197 applies to most intangibles acquired either in stand-alone transactions or as part of the acquisition of a trade or business.

    b. An amortizable Sec. 197 intangible is any qualifying intangible asset which is acquired by the taxpayer, and which is held in connection with the conduct of a trade or business. Qualifying intangibles include goodwill, going concern value, workforce, information base, know-how, customer-based intangibles, government licenses and permits, franchises, trademarks, and trade names.

    c. Certain assets qualify as Sec. 197 intangibles only if acquired in connection with the acquisition of a trade or business or substantial portion thereof. These include covenants not to compete, computer software, film, sound recordings, video tape, patents, and copyrights.

    d. Certain intangible assets are expressly excluded from the definition of Sec. 197 intangibles including many types of financial interests, instruments, and contracts; interests in a corporation, partnership, trust, or estate; interests in land; professional sports franchises; and leases of tangible personal property.

    e. No loss can be recognized on the disposition of a Sec. 197 intangible if the taxpayer retains other Sec. 197 intangibles acquired in the same transaction or a series of transactions. Any disallowed loss is added to the basis of remaining Sec. 197 intangibles and recovered through amortization.

II. "ABOVE THE LINE" DEDUCTIONS

    "Above the line" deductions are taken from gross income to determine adjusted gross income. Adjusted gross income is important, because it may affect the amount of allowable charitable contributions, medical expenses, casualty losses, and miscellaneous itemized deductions. The deductions that reduce gross income to arrive at adjusted gross income are

1. Business deductions of a self-employed person (see Business Income and Deductions, page 401)
2. Losses from sale or exchange of property (discussed in Sales and Other Dispositions and in Capital Gains and Losses, pages 503 and 510)
3. Deductions attributable to rents and royalties
4. One-half of self-employment tax
5. Moving expenses
6. Contributions to self-employed retirement plans and IRAs
7. Deduction for interest on education loans
8. Penalties for premature withdrawals from time deposits
9. Alimony payments
10. Jury duty pay remitted to employer

A. The treatment of **reimbursed employee business expenses** depends on whether the employee makes an adequate accounting to the employer and returns amounts in excess of substantiated expenses.

    1. Per diem reimbursements at a rate not in excess of the federal per diem rate and 36 cents per mile are deemed to satisfy the substantiation requirement if employee provides time, place, and business purpose of expenses.

2. If the employee **makes an adequate accounting** to employer and reimbursements equal expenses, or if the employee substantiates expenses and returns any excess reimbursement, the reimbursements are excluded from gross income and the expenses are not deductible.

3. If the employee **does not make an adequate accounting** to the employer or does not return excess reimbursements, the total amount of reimbursement is included in the employee's gross income and the related employee expenses are deductible as miscellaneous itemized deductions subject to the 50% limitation for business meals and entertainment and the 2% of AGI floor (same as for unreimbursed employee business expenses).

B. Expenses attributable to **property held for the production of rents or royalties** are deductible "above the line."

1. **Rental of vacation home**

    a. If there is any personal use, the **amount deductible** is

       (1) $\dfrac{\text{No. of days rented}}{\text{Total days used}} \times \text{Total expenses} = \text{Amount deductible}$

       (2) Personal use is by taxpayer or any other person to whom a fair rent is not charged.

    b. **If used as a residence,** amount deductible is further limited to rental income less deductions otherwise allowable for interest, taxes, and casualty losses.

       (1) Used as a residence if personal use exceeds greater of fourteen days or 10% of number of days rented

       (2) These limitations do not apply if rented or held for rental for a continuous twelve-month period with no personal use.

       EXAMPLE: Use house as a principal residence and then begin to rent in June. As long as rental continues for twelve consecutive months, limitations do not apply in year converted to rental.

    c. If used as a residence (above) and **rented for less than fifteen days** per year, then income therefrom is not reported and rental expense deductions are not allowed.

       EXAMPLE: Taxpayer rents his condominium for 120 days for $2,000 and uses it himself for 60 days. The rest of the year it is vacant. His expenses are

Mortgage interest	$1,800
Real estate taxes	600
Utilities	300
Maintenance	300
Depreciation	2,000
	$5,000

       Taxpayer may deduct the following expenses:

	Rental expense	Itemized deduction
Mortgage interest	$1,200	$600
Real estate taxes	400	200
Utilities	200	--
Maintenance	200	--
Depreciation	--	--
	$2,000	$800

       Taxpayer may not deduct any depreciation because his rental expense deductions are limited to rental income when he has made personal use of the condominium in excess of the fourteen-day or 10% rule.

C. A **self-employed** individual can **deduct one-half of the self-employment tax paid** for the taxable year (e.g., if the amount of self-employment tax that an individual taxpayer must pay for 2003 is $7,710, the individual can deduct 50% x $7,710 = $3,855 in arriving at AGI).

D. A **self-employed** individual can **deduct 100%** for 2003 of the **premiums for medical insurance** for the individual, spouse, and dependents in arriving at AGI.

1. This deduction cannot exceed the individual's net earnings from the trade or business with respect to which the plan providing for health insurance was established. For purposes of this limitation, an S corporation more-than-two-percent shareholder's earned income is determined exclusively by reference to the shareholder's wages received from the S corporation.

2. No deduction is allowed if the self-employed individual or spouse is eligible to participate in an employer's subsidized health plan. The determination of whether self-employed individuals or their spouses are eligible for employer-paid health benefits is to be made on a calendar month basis.

3. Any medical insurance premiums not deductible under the above rules are deductible as an itemized medical expense deduction from AGI.
4. The deduction does not reduce the income base for purposes of the self-employment tax.

E. Moving Expenses

1. The distance between the former residence and new job (d_2) must be **at least fifty miles** farther than from the former residence to the former job (d_1) (i.e., $d_2 - d_1 \geq 50$ miles). If no former job, new job must be at least fifty miles from former residence.
2. Employee must be **employed** at least thirty-nine weeks out of the twelve months following the move. Self-employed individual must be employed seventy-eight weeks out of the twenty-four months following the move (in addition to thirty-nine weeks out of first twelve months). Time test does not have to be met in case of death, taxpayer's job at new location ends because of disability, or taxpayer is laid off for other than willful misconduct.
3. **Deductible** moving expenses include the costs of moving household goods and personal effects from the old to the new residence, and the costs of traveling (including lodging) from the old residence to the new residence.
4. **Nondeductible** moving expenses include the costs of meals, househunting trips, temporary lodging in the general location of the new work site, expenses incurred in selling an old house or buying a new house, and expenses in settling a lease on an old residence or acquiring a lease on a new residence.

F. Contributions to Certain Retirement Plans

1. Contributions to an **Individual Retirement Account** (IRA)

   a. If neither the taxpayer nor the taxpayer's spouse is an active participant in an employer-sponsored retirement plan or a Keogh plan, there is no phaseout of IRA deductions.

      (1) The maximum deduction for an individual's contributions to an IRA is generally the lesser of

         (a) **$3,000,** or
         (b) 100% of compensation (including alimony)

      (2) For married taxpayers filing a joint return, up to $3,000 can be deducted for contributions to the IRA of each spouse (even if one spouse is not working), provided that the combined earned income of both spouses is at least equal to the amounts contributed to the IRAs.

   b. For 2003, the IRA deduction for individuals who are active participants in an employer retirement plan or a Keogh plan is proportionately phased out for married individuals filing jointly with AGI between $60,000 and $70,000, and for single individuals with AGI between $40,000 and $50,000.

      (1) An individual will not be considered an active participant in an employer plan merely because the individual's spouse is an active participant for any part of the plan year.
      (2) The maximum deductible IRA contribution for an individual who is not an active participant, but whose spouse is, will be proportionately phased out at a combined AGI between $150,000 and $160,000.

   c. Under the **phaseout rule,** the $3,000 maximum deduction is reduced by a percentage equal to adjusted gross income in excess of the lower AGI amount (above) divided by $10,000. The deduction limit is rounded to the next lowest multiple of $10.

      (1) A taxpayer whose AGI is not above the applicable phaseout range can make a $200 deductible contribution regardless of the proportional phaseout rule. This $200 minimum applies separately to taxpayer and taxpayer's spouse.
      (2) A taxpayer who is partially or totally prevented from making deductible IRA contributions can make **nondeductible IRA contributions**.
      (3) Total IRA contributions (whether deductible or not) are subject to the $3,000 or 100% of compensation limit.

      EXAMPLE: For 2003, a single individual who has compensation income (and AGI) of $46,000 and who is an active participant in an employer-sponsored retirement plan would be subject to a limit reduction of $1,800 computed as follows: $3,000 x [($46,000 – $40,000) ÷ $10,000)] = $1,800. Thus, the individual's deductible IRA contribution would be limited to $3,000 – $1,800 = $1,200. However, the individual could make nondeductible IRA contributions of up to $1,800 more.

EXAMPLE: For 2003, a single individual who has compensation income (and AGI) of $49,600 and who is an active participant in an employer-sponsored retirement plan would normally be limited to an IRA deduction of $3,000 – [($49,600 – $40,000) ÷ $10,000] x $3,000 = $120. However, because of the special rule in (2) above, a $200 IRA contribution deduction is allowable.

    d. For tax years 2002 through 2005, an individual at least age 50 before the close of the taxable year can make an additional "catch-up" contribution of $500 to an IRA. Thus, for 2003, the maximum IRA contribution and deduction for an individual at least age 50 is $3,000 + $500 = $3,500.

    e. The 10% penalty tax on early withdrawals (pre-age 59 1/2) does not apply to amounts withdrawn for "qualified higher education expenses" and "first-time homebuyer expenses" ($10,000 lifetime cap), nor to distributions made to unemployed individuals for health insurance premiums, and distributions to the extent that deductible medical expenses exceed 7.5% of AGI.

       (1) Qualified higher education expenses include tuition, fees, books, supplies, and equipment for postsecondary education for the taxpayer, taxpayer's spouse, or any child or grandchild of the taxpayer or the taxpayer's spouse

       (2) Qualified first-time homebuyer distributions must be used in 120 days to buy, build, or rebuild a first home that is a principal residence for the taxpayer or taxpayer's spouse. Acquisition costs include reasonable financing or other closing costs.

2. Contributions to a **Roth IRA** are not deductible, but qualified distributions of earnings are tax-free. Individuals making contributions to a Roth IRA can still make contributions to a deductible or nondeductible IRA, but maximum contributions to all IRAs is limited to $3,000 for 2003. ($3,500 if the individual is at least age 50).

    a. Eligibility for a Roth IRA is phased out for single taxpayers with AGI between $95,000 and $110,000, and for joint filers with AGI between $150,000 and $160,000.

    b. Unlike traditional IRAs contributions may be made to Roth IRAs even after the individual reaches age 70 1/2.

    c. Qualified distributions from a Roth IRA are not included in gross income and are not subject to the 10% early withdrawal penalty. A qualified distribution is a distribution that is made after the five-year period beginning with the first tax year for which a contribution was made and the distribution is made (1) after the individual reaches age 59 1/2, (2) to a beneficiary (or the individual's estate) after the individual's death, (3) after the individual becomes disabled, or (4) for the first-time homebuyer expenses of the individual, individual's spouse, children, grandchildren, or ancestors ($10,000 lifetime cap).

    d. Nonqualified distributions are includible in income to the extent attributable to earnings and generally subject to the 10% early withdrawal penalty. Distributions are deemed to be made from contributed amounts first.

    e. Taxpayers with AGI of less than $100,000 can convert assets in traditional IRAs to a Roth IRA at any time without paying the 10% tax on early withdrawals, although the deemed distributions of IRA assets will be included in income.

3. Contributions can be made to an **education IRA** (Coverdell Education Savings Account) of up to $2,000 per beneficiary (until the beneficiary reaches age eighteen), to pay the costs of a beneficiary's higher education.

    a. Contributions are not deductible, but withdrawals to pay the cost of a beneficiary's education expenses are tax-free.

    b. Any earnings of an education IRA that are distributed but are not used to pay a beneficiary's education expenses must be included in the distributee's gross income and are subject to a 10% penalty tax.

    c. Under a special rollover provision, the amount left in an education IRA before the beneficiary reaches age 30 can be rolled over to another family member's education IRA without triggering income taxes or penalties.

    d. Eligibility is phased out for single taxpayers with modified AGI between $95,000 and $110,000, and for married taxpayers with modified AGI between $190,000 and $220,000.

    e. For tax years beginning after December 31, 2001, expenses that may be paid tax-free from an education IRA have been expanded to include expenses for enrollment (including room and board, uniforms, transportation, computers, and Internet access services) in elementary or secondary schools, whether public, private, or religious. Furthermore, taxpayers may take advantage of the exclusion for distributions from education IRAs, the Hope and lifetime learning credits, and the qualified tuition program in the same year.

4. **Self-employed** individuals (sole proprietors and partners) may contribute to a qualified retirement plan (called H.R.-10 or Keogh Plan).

   a. The maximum contribution and deduction to a defined-contribution self-employed retirement plan is the lesser of

      (1) $40,000, or 100% of earned income for 2003
      (2) The definition of "earned income" includes the retirement plan and self-employment tax deductions (i.e., earnings from self-employment must be reduced by the retirement plan contribution and the self-employment tax deduction for purposes of determining the maximum deduction).

   b. A taxpayer may elect to treat contributions made up until the due date of the tax return (including extensions) as made for the taxable year for which the tax return is being filed, if the retirement plan was established by the end of that year.

5. An employer's contributions to an employee's **simplified employee pension (SEP) plan** are deductible by the employer, limited to the lesser of 15% of compensation (up to a compensation ceiling of $200,000 for 2003) or $40,000. Thus, an employer's maximum contribution to, and deduction for, an employee's SEP for 2003 is $200,000 x 15% = $30,000.

   a. SEP may contain a salary reduction provision allowing an employee to take a reduced salary and to have the reduction (up to $12,000 for 2003) deposited in the plan as an employer contribution.
   b. The employer's SEP contributions (including up to $12,000 of employee salary reduction contributions) are excluded from the employee's gross income.
   c. In addition, the employee may make deductible IRA contributions subject to the IRA phaseout rules (discussed in 2.c. above).

6. A **savings incentive match plan for employees (SIMPLE)** is not subject to the nondiscrimination rules (including top-heavy provisions) and certain other complex requirements generally applicable to qualified plans, and may be structured as an IRA or as a 401(k) plan.

   a. Limited to employers with 100 or fewer employees who received at least $5,000 in compensation from the employer in the preceding year.

      (1) Plan allows employees to make elective contributions of up to $6,500 of their pretax salaries per year (expressed as a percentage of compensation, not a fixed dollar amount) and requires employers to match a portion of the contributions.
      (2) Eligible employees are those who earned at least $5,000 in any two prior years and who may be expected to earn at least $5,000 in the current year.

   b. Employers must satisfy one of two contribution formulas.

      (1) Matching contribution formula generally requires an employer to match the employee contribution dollar-for-dollar up to 3% of the employee's compensation for the year.
      (2) Alternatively, an employer can make a nonelective contribution of 2% of compensation for each eligible employee who has at least $5,000 of compensation from the employer during the year.

   c. Contributions to the plan are immediately vested, but a 25% penalty applies to employee withdrawals made within two years of the date the employee began participating in the plan.

G. Deduction for Interest on Education Loans

1. An individual is allowed to deduct **up to $2,500** for interest on qualified education loans. However, the deduction is not available if the individual is claimed as a dependent on another taxpayer's return.
2. A *qualified education loan* is any debt incurred to pay the qualified higher education expenses of the taxpayer, taxpayer's spouse, or dependents (as of the time the debt was incurred), and the education expenses must relate to a period when the student was enrolled on at least a half-time basis. However, any debt owed to a related party is not a qualified educational loan (e.g., education debt owed to family member).

3. Qualified education expenses include such costs as tuition, fees, room, board, and related expenses.

4. The deduction is phased out for single taxpayers with modified AGI between $50,000 and $65,000, and for married taxpayers with modified AGI between $100,000 and $130,000.

H. Deduction for Qualified Tuition and Related Expenses

1. For tax years beginning after 2001, individuals will be allowed to deduct qualified higher education expenses in arriving at AGI. For 2002 and 2003, the maximum deduction is limited to $3,000.

2. Taxpayers with AGI up to $65,000 ($130,000 for married filing jointly) can claim the deduction. Taxpayers with AGI above these levels, married individuals filing separately, and an individual who can be claimed as a dependent are not entitled to any deduction.

3. *Qualified tuition and related expenses* means tuition and fees required for enrollment of the taxpayer, taxpayer's spouse, or dependent at a postsecondary educational institution. Such term does not include expenses with respect to any course involving sports, games, or hobbies, or any noncredit course, unless such course is part of the individual's degree program. Also excluded are nonacademic fees such as student activity fees, athletic fees, and insurance expenses.

4. The deduction is allowed for expenses paid during the tax year, in connection with enrollment during the year or in connection with an academic term beginning during the year or the first three months of the following year.

5. If a taxpayer takes a Hope credit or lifetime learning credit with respect to a student, the qualified higher education expenses of that student for the year are not deductible under this provision.

I. Penalties for Premature Withdrawals from Time Deposits

1. Full amount of interest is included in gross income.

2. Forfeited interest is then subtracted "above the line."

J. Alimony or Separate Maintenance Payments Are Deducted "Above the Line."

K. Jury Duty Pay Remitted to Employer

1. An employee is allowed to deduct the amount of jury duty pay that was surrendered to an employer in return for the employer's payment of compensation during the employee's jury service period.

2. Both regular compensation and jury duty pay must be included in gross income.

III. ITEMIZED DEDUCTIONS FROM ADJUSTED GROSS INCOME

Itemized deductions reduce adjusted gross income, and are sometimes referred to as "below the line" deductions because they are deducted from adjusted gross income. Itemized deductions (or a standard deduction) along with personal exemptions are subtracted from adjusted gross income to arrive at taxable income.

A taxpayer will itemize deductions only if the taxpayer's total itemized deductions exceed the applicable standard deduction that is available to nonitemizers. The amount of the standard deduction is based on the filing status of the taxpayer, whether the taxpayer is a dependent, and is indexed for inflation. Additional standard deductions are allowed for age and blindness.

	Filing status	Basic standard deduction 2003
a)	Married, filing jointly; or surviving spouse	$9,500
b)	Married, filing separately	4,750
c)	Head of household	7,000
d)	Single	4,750

A dependent's basic standard deduction is limited to the lesser of (1) the basic standard deduction for single taxpayers of $4,750 for 2003; or (2) the greater of (a) $750, or (b) the dependent's earned income plus $250.

An unmarried individual who is not a surviving spouse, and is either age sixty-five or older or blind, receives an additional standard deduction of $1,150 for 2003. The standard deduction is increased by $2,300 for 2003 if the individual is both elderly and blind. The increase is $950 for 2003 for each married individual who is age sixty-five or older or blind. The increase for a married individual who is both elderly and blind is $1,900 for 2003. An elderly or blind individual who may be claimed as a dependent on another taxpayer's return may claim the basic standard deduction plus the additional standard deduction(s). For example, for 2003 an unmarried dependent, age sixty-five, with only unearned income would have a standard deduction of $750 + $1,150 = $1,900.

The major itemized deductions are outlined below. It should be remembered that some may be deducted in arriving at AGI if they are incurred by a self-employed taxpayer in a trade or business, or for the production of rents or royalties.

A. Medical and Dental Expenses

1. Medical and dental expenses paid by taxpayer for himself, spouse, or dependent (relationship, support, and citizenship tests are met) are deductible in year of payment, if not reimbursed by insurance, employer, etc. A child of divorced or separated parents is treated as a dependent of both parents for this purpose.

2. Computation—unreimbursed medical expenses (including *prescribed* medicine and insulin, and medical insurance premiums) are deducted to the extent **in excess of 7.5%** of adjusted gross income.

   EXAMPLE: Ralph and Alice Jones, who have Adjusted Gross Income of $20,000, paid the following medical expenses: $900 for hospital and doctor bills (above reimbursement), $250 for prescription medicine, and $600 for medical insurance. The Joneses would compute their medical expense deduction as follows:

Prescribed medicine	$ 250
Hospital, doctors	900
Medical insurance	600
	$1,750
Less 7.5% of AGI	−1,500
Medical expense deduction	$250

3. Deductible medical care does not include **cosmetic surgery** or other procedures, unless the surgery or procedure is necessary to ameliorate a deformity arising from, or directly related to, a congenital abnormality, a personal injury resulting from an accident or trauma, or a disfiguring disease. In addition, to be deductible, the procedure must promote proper body function or prevent or treat illness or disease (e.g., LASIK and radial keratotomy are deductible; teeth whitening is not deductible).

   a. Cosmetic surgery is defined as any procedure directed at improving the patient's appearance and does not meaningfully promote the proper function of the body or prevent or treat illness or disease.

   b. If expenses for cosmetic surgery are not deductible under this provision, then amounts paid for insurance coverage for such expenses are not deductible, and an employer's reimbursement of such expenses under a health plan is not excludable from the employee's gross income.

4. Expenses incurred by physically handicapped individuals for **removal of structural barriers** in their residences to accommodate their handicapped condition are fully deductible as medical expenses. Qualifying expenses include constructing entrance or exit ramps, widening doorways and hallways, the installation of railings and support bars, and other modifications.

5. **Capital expenditures** for special equipment (other than in 4. above) installed for medical reasons in a home or automobile are deductible as medical expenses to the extent the expenditures exceed the increase in value of the property.

6. **Deductible** medical expenses include

   a. Fees for doctors, surgeons, dentists, osteopaths, ophthalmologists, optometrists, chiropractors, chiropodists, podiatrists, psychiatrists, psychologists, and Christian Science practitioners

   b. Fees for hospital services, therapy, nursing services (including nurses' meals you pay for), ambulance hire, and laboratory, surgical, obstetrical, diagnostic, dental, and X-ray services

   c. Meals and lodging provided by a hospital during medical treatment, and meals and lodging provided by a center during treatment for alcoholism or drug addiction

   d. Amounts paid for lodging (but not meals) while away from home primarily for medical care provided by a physician in a licensed hospital or equivalent medical care facility. Limit is $50 per night for each individual.

   e. Medical and hospital insurance premiums

   f. *Prescribed* medicines and insulin

   g. Transportation for needed medical care. Actual auto expenses can be deducted, or taxpayer can use standard rate of 12¢/mile beginning January 1, 2003 (plus parking and tolls).

   h. Special items and equipment, including false teeth, artificial limbs, eyeglasses, hearing aids, crutches, guide dogs, motorized wheelchairs, hand controls on a car, and special telephones for deaf

7. Items **not deductible** as medical expenses include

    a. Bottled water, maternity clothes, and diaper service

    b. Household help, and care of a normal and healthy baby by a nurse (but a portion may qualify for child or dependent care tax credit)

    c. Toothpaste, toiletries, cosmetics, etc.

    d. Program to stop smoking or lose weight (unless prescribed to alleviate a specific illness)

    e. Trip, social activities, or health club dues for general improvement of health

    f. Nonprescribed medicines and drugs (e.g., over-the-counter medicines)

    g. Illegal operation or treatment

    h. Funeral and burial expenses

8. Reimbursement of expenses deducted in an earlier year may have to be included in gross income in the period received under the tax benefit rule.

9. Reimbursement in excess of expenses is includible in income to the extent the excess reimbursement was paid by policies provided by employer.

B. Taxes

1. The following taxes are **deductible as a tax** in year paid if they are imposed on the taxpayer:

    a. **Income tax** (state, local, or foreign)

        (1) The deduction for state and local taxes includes amounts withheld from salary, estimated payments made during the year, and payments made during the year on a tax for a prior year.

        (2) A refund of a prior year's taxes is not offset against the current year's deduction, but is generally included in income under the tax benefit rule.

    b. **Real property taxes** (state, local, or foreign) are deductible by the person on whom the taxes are imposed.

        (1) When real property is sold, the deduction is apportioned between buyer and seller on a daily basis within the real property tax year, even if parties do not apportion the taxes at the closing.

        (2) **Assessments** for improvements (e.g., special assessments for streets, sewers, sidewalks, curbing) are generally not deductible, but instead must be added to the basis of the property. However, the portion of an assessment that is attributable to repairs or maintenance, or to meeting interest charges on the improvements, is deductible as taxes.

    c. **Personal property taxes** (state or local, not foreign) are deductible if ad valorem (i.e., assessed in relation to the value of property). A motor vehicle tax based on horsepower, weight, or model year is not deductible.

2. The following taxes are **deductible only as an expense** incurred in a trade or business or in the production of income (above the line):

    a. Social security and other employment taxes paid by employer

    b. Federal excise taxes on automobiles, tires, telephone service, and air transportation

    c. Customs duties and gasoline taxes

    d. State and local taxes not deductible as such (stamp or cigarette taxes) or charges of a primarily regulatory nature (licenses, etc.)

    e. Sales taxes incurred on the acquisition or disposition of property are treated as part of the cost of the acquired property or as a reduction in the amount realized on the disposition.

3. The following taxes are **not deductible:**

    a. Federal income taxes

    b. Federal, state, or local estate or gift taxes

    c. Social security and other federal employment taxes paid by employee (including self-employment taxes)

    d. Social security and other employment taxes paid by an employer on the wages of an employee who only performed domestic services (i.e., maid, etc.)

C. Interest Expense

1. The classification of interest expense is generally determined by tracing the use of the borrowed funds. Interest expense is not deductible if loan proceeds were used to produce tax-exempt income (e.g., purchase municipal bonds).

2. No deduction is allowed for prepaid interest; it must be capitalized and deducted in the future period(s) to which it relates. However, an individual may elect to deduct *mortgage points* when paid if the points represent interest and mortgage proceeds were used to buy, build, or substantially improve a principal residence. Otherwise points must be capitalized and deducted over the term of the mortgage.

3. **Personal interest.** No deduction is allowed for personal interest.

   a. Personal interest **includes** interest paid or incurred to purchase an asset for personal use, credit card interest for personal purchases, interest incurred as an employee, and interest on income tax underpayments.

   b. Personal interest **excludes** qualified residence interest, investment interest, interest allocable to a trade or business (other than as an employee), interest incurred in a passive activity, and interest on deferred estate taxes.

      EXAMPLE: X, a self-employed consultant, finances a new automobile used 80% for business and 20% for personal use. X would treat 80% of the interest as deductible business interest expense (toward AGI), and 20% as nondeductible personal interest.

      EXAMPLE: Y, an employee, finances a new automobile used 80% for use in her employer's business and 20% for personal use. All of the interest expense on the auto loan would be considered nondeductible personal interest.

4. **Qualified residence interest.** The disallowance of personal interest above does not apply to interest paid or accrued on acquisition indebtedness or home equity indebtedness secured by a security interest perfected under local law on the taxpayer's principal residence or a second residence owned by the taxpayer.

   a. **Acquisition indebtedness.** Interest is deductible on up to $1,000,000 ($500,000 if married filing separately) of loans secured by the residence if such loans were used to acquire, construct, or substantially improve the home.

      (1) Acquisition indebtedness is reduced as principal payments are made and cannot be restored or increased by refinancing the home.

      (2) If the home is refinanced, the amount qualifying as acquisition indebtedness is limited to the amount of acquisition debt existing at the time of refinancing plus any amount of the new loan that is used to substantially improve the home.

   b. **Home equity indebtedness.** Interest is deductible on up to $100,000 ($50,000 if married filing separately) of loans secured by the residence (other than acquisition indebtedness) regardless of how the loan proceeds are used (e.g., automobile, education expenses, medical expenses, etc.). The amount of home equity indebtedness cannot exceed the FMV of the home as reduced by any acquisition indebtedness.

      EXAMPLE: Allan purchased a home for $380,000, borrowing $250,000 of the purchase price that was secured by a fifteen-year mortgage. In 2003, when the home was worth $400,000 and the balance of the first mortgage was $230,000, Allan obtained a second mortgage on the home in the amount of $120,000, using the proceeds to purchase a car and to pay off personal loans. Allan may deduct the interest on the balance of the first mortgage acquisition indebtedness of $230,000. However, Allan can deduct interest on only $100,000 of the second mortgage as qualified residence interest because it is considered home equity indebtedness (i.e., the loan proceeds were not used to acquire, construct, or substantially improve a home). The interest on the remaining $20,000 of the second mortgage is nondeductible personal interest.

   c. The term "residence" includes houses, condominiums, cooperative housing units, and any other property that the taxpayer uses as a dwelling unit (e.g., mobile home, motor home, boat, etc.).

   d. In the case of a residence used partly for rental purposes, the interest can only be qualified residence interest if the taxpayer's personal use during the year exceeds the greater of fourteen days or 10% of the number of days of rental use (unless the residence was not rented at any time during the year).

   e. Qualified residence interest does not include interest on unsecured home improvement loans, but does include mortgage prepayment penalties.

5. **Investment interest.** The deduction for investment interest expense for noncorporate taxpayers is limited to the amount of net investment income. Interest disallowed is carried forward indefinitely and is allowed only to the extent of net investment income in a subsequent year.

EXAMPLE: For 2003, a single taxpayer has investment interest expense of $40,000 and net investment income of $24,000. The deductible investment interest expense for 2003 is limited to $24,000, with the remaining $16,000 carried forward and allowed as a deduction to the extent of net investment income in subsequent years.

a. Investment interest expense is interest paid or accrued on indebtedness properly allocable to property held for investment, including

(1) Interest expense allocable to portfolio income, and

(2) Interest expense allocable to a trade or business in which the taxpayer does not materially participate, if that activity is not treated as a passive activity

b. Investment interest expense excludes interest expense taken into account in determining income or loss from a passive activity, interest allocable to rental real estate in which the taxpayer actively participates, qualified residence interest, and personal interest.

c. Net investment income includes

(1) Interest, rents, and royalties in excess of any related expenses, and

(2) The net gain (all gains minus all losses) on the sale of investment property, but only to the extent that the net gain exceeds the net capital gain (i.e., net LTCG in excess of net STCL).

d. A taxpayer may elect to treat qualified **dividend income** and **net capital gain** (i.e., an excess of net LTCG over net STCL) as investment income. However, if this election is made, a taxpayer must reduce the amount of qualified dividend income and net capital gain otherwise eligible for reduced maximum tax rates by the amount included as investment income.

EXAMPLE: Assume a taxpayer has the following items of income and expense for 2003:

Interest income	*$ 15,000*
Net long-term capital gain	*18,000*
Investment interest expense	*25,000*

The taxpayer's deduction for investment interest expense is generally limited to $15,000 for 2003 unless the taxpayer elects to include a portion of the net LTCG in the determination of the investment interest expense limitation. If the taxpayer elects to treat $10,000 of the net LTCG as investment income, all of the taxpayer's investment interest expense will be deductible. But by doing this, $10,000 of the net LTCG will be taxed at ordinary tax rates, leaving only the remaining $8,000 of net LTCG to be taxed at preferential rates.

e. Only investment expenses (e.g., rental fees for safety deposit box rental, investment counseling fees, subscriptions to investment periodicals) remaining after the 2% of AGI limitation are used in computing net investment income.

f. Income and expenses taken into account in computing the income or loss from a passive activity are excluded from net investment income.

D. Charitable Contributions

Contributions to qualified domestic charitable organizations are deductible in the year actually paid or donated (for both accrual- and cash-basis taxpayers) with some carryover allowed. A "pledge" is *not* a payment. Charging the contribution on your credit card *does constitute payment*.

1. **Qualified organizations** include

a. A state, a US possession or political subdivision, or the District of Columbia if made exclusively for public purposes

b. A community chest, corporation, foundation, etc., operated exclusively for charitable, religious, educational, scientific, or literary purposes, or for the prevention of cruelty to children or animals, or for fostering national or international amateur sports competition (unless they provide facilities or equipment)

(1) No part of the earnings may inure to any individual's benefit

(2) May not attempt to influence legislation or intervene in any political campaign

c. Church, synagogue, or other religious organizations

d. War veterans' organizations

e. Domestic fraternal societies operating under the lodge system (only if contribution used exclusively for the charitable purposes listed in b. above)

f. Nonprofit cemetery companies if the funds are irrevocably dedicated to the perpetual care of the cemetery as a whole, and not a particular lot or mausoleum crypt

2. Dues, fees, or assessments paid to qualified organizations are deductible to the extent that payments exceed benefits received. Dues, fees, or assessments are not deductible if paid to veterans' organizations, lodges, fraternal organizations, and country clubs

3. Out-of-pocket expenses to maintain a **student** (domestic or foreign) in a taxpayer's home are deductible (limited to $50/month for each month the individual is a full-time student) if

   a. Student is in 12th or lower grade and not a dependent or relative
   b. Based on written agreement between taxpayer and qualified organization
   c. Taxpayer receives no reimbursement

4. Payments to qualified organizations for goods or services are deductible to the extent the amount paid exceeds the fair market value of benefits received.

5. A taxpayer who makes a payment to or for the benefit of a college or university and is thereby entitled to purchase tickets to athletic events is allowed to deduct 80% of the payment as a charitable contribution. Any payment that is attributable to the actual cost of tickets is not deductible as a charitable contribution.

6. Unreimbursed out-of-pocket expenses incurred while rendering services to a charitable organization without compensation are deductible, including actual auto expenses or a standard rate of 14¢ per mile may be used for 2002 and 2003.

7. No charitable deduction is allowed for any **contribution of $250 or more** unless the donor obtains written acknowledgment from the donee including a good faith estimate of the value of any goods or services provided to the donor in exchange for the contribution. Canceled checks are not sufficient substantiation for contributions of $250 or more.

8. **Nondeductible** contributions include contributions to/for/of

   a. Civic leagues, social clubs, and foreign organizations
   b. Communist organizations, chambers of commerce, labor unions
   c. The value of the taxpayer's time or services
   d. The use of property, or less than an entire interest in property
   e. Blood donated
   f. Tuition or amounts in place of tuition
   g. Payments to a hospital for care of particular patients
   h. "Sustainer's gift" to retirement home
   i. Raffles, bingo, etc. (but may qualify as gambling loss)
   j. Fraternal societies if the contributions are used to defray sickness or burial expenses of members
   k. Political organizations
   l. Travel, including meals and lodging (e.g., trip to serve at charity's national meeting), if there is any significant element of personal pleasure, recreation, or vacation involved

9. Contributions of property to qualified organizations are **deductible**

   a. At fair market value when FMV is below basis
   b. At basis when fair market value exceeds basis and property would result in short-term capital gain or ordinary income if sold (e.g., gain would be ordinary because of depreciation recapture or if property is inventory)
   c. If contributed property is *capital gain property* that would result in LTCG if sold (i.e., generally investment property and personal-use property held more than one year), the amount of contribution is the property's FMV. However, if the contributed property is *tangible personal capital gain property* and its use is unrelated to the charity's activity, the amount of contribution is restricted to the property's basis.
   d. Appraisal fees on donated property are a miscellaneous itemized deduction.

10. The overall limitation for contribution deductions is **50%** of adjusted gross income (before any net operating loss carryback). A second limitation is that contributions of long-term capital gain property

to charities in Section 10.a. below (where gain is not reduced) are limited to **30%** of AGI. A third limitation is that some contributions to certain charities are limited to **20%** of AGI or a lesser amount.

   a. Contributions to the following are taken first and may be taken up to **50%** of AGI limitation

      (1) Public charities

         (a) Churches
         (b) Educational organizations
         (c) Tax-exempt hospitals
         (d) Medical research
         (e) States or political subdivisions
         (f) US or District of Columbia

      (2) All private operating foundations, that is, foundations that spend their income directly for the active conduct of their exempt activities (e.g., public museums)

      (3) Certain private nonoperating foundations that distribute proceeds to public and private operating charities

   b. Deductions for contributions of **long-term capital gain property** (when the gain is not to be reduced) to organizations in Section 10.a. above are limited to **30%** of adjusted gross income; but, taxpayer may elect to reduce all appreciated long-term capital gain property by the potential gain and not be subject to this 30% limitation.

   c. Deductions for contributions to charities that do not qualify in Section 10.a. above (generally private nonoperating foundations) are subject to special limitations.

      (1) The deduction limitation for gifts of

         (a) Ordinary income property is the lesser of (1) 30% of AGI, or (2) (50% x AGI) – gifts to charities in Section 10.a. above

         (b) Capital gain property is lesser of (1) 20% of AGI, or (2) (30% x AGI) – gifts of long-term capital gain property to charities in Section 10.a. above where no reduction is made for appreciation

      (2) These deductions are taken after deductions to organizations in Section 10.a. above without the 30% limitation on capital gain property in Section 10.b. above.

> *EXAMPLE: An individual with AGI of $9,000 made a contribution of capital gain appreciated property with a FMV of $5,000 to a church, and gave $2,000 cash to a private nonoperating foundation. Since the contribution to the church (before the 30% limit) exceeds 50% of AGI, no part of the contribution to the foundation is deductible this year. Assuming no election is made to reduce the contribution of the capital gain property by the amount of its appreciation, the current deduction for the contribution to the church is limited to 30% x $9,000 = $2,700.*

11. Contributions in excess of the 50%, 30%, or 20% limitation can be carried forward for **five years** and remain subject to the 50%, 30%, or 20% limitation in the carryforward years.

> *EXAMPLE: Ben's adjusted gross income is $50,000. During the year he gave his church $2,000 cash and land (held for investment more than one year) having a fair market value of $30,000 and a basis of $22,000. Ben also gave $5,000 cash to a private foundation to which a 30% limitation applies.*
>
> *Since Ben's contributions to an organization to which the 50% limitation applies (disregarding the 30% limitation for capital gain property) exceed $25,000 (50% of $50,000), his contribution to the private foundation is not deductible this year. The $2,000 cash donated to the church is deducted first. The donation for the gift of land is not required to be reduced by the appreciation in value, but is limited to $15,000 (30% x $50,000). Thus, Ben may deduct only $17,000 ($2,000 + $15,000). The unused portion of the land contribution ($15,000) and the gift to the private foundation ($5,000) are carried over to the next year, still subject to their respective 30% limitations.*
>
> *Alternatively, Ben may elect to reduce the value of the land by its appreciation of $8,000 and not be subject to the 30% limitation for capital gain property. In such case, his current deduction would be $25,000 ($2,000 cash + $22,000 land + $1,000 cash to private foundation), but only the remaining $4,000 cash to the private foundation would be carried over to the next year.*

E. Personal Casualty and Theft Gains and Losses

Gains and losses from casualties and thefts of **property held for personal use** are not subject to the Sec. 1231 netting process. Instead, personal casualty and theft gains and losses are **separately netted,** without regard to the holding period of the converted property.

1. A **casualty loss** must be identifiable, damaging to property, and sudden, unexpected, or unusual. Casualty losses **include**

    a. Damage from a fire, storm, accident, mine cave-in, sonic boom, or loss from vandalism

    b. Damage to trees and shrubs if there is a decrease in the total value of the real estate

    c. A loss on personal residence that has been rendered unsafe by reason of a disaster declared by the President and has been ordered demolished or relocated by a state or local government.

2. Losses **not deductible** as casualties include

    a. Losses from the breakage of china or glassware through handling or by a family pet

    b. Disease, termite, or moth damage

    c. Expenses incident to casualty (temporary quarters, etc.)

    d. Progressive deterioration through a steadily operating cause and damage from normal process. Thus, the steady weakening of a building caused by normal or usual wind and weather conditions is not a casualty loss.

    e. Losses from nearby disaster (property value reduced due to location near a disaster area)

    f. Loss of future profits from, for example, ice storm damage to standing timber that reduces the rate of growth or the quality of future timber. To qualify as a casualty, the damage must actually result in existing timber being rendered unfit for use.

3. Casualty loss is deductible in the year the loss occurs.

    a. Theft loss is deductible in the year the loss is discovered.

    b. Loss in a federally declared disaster area is deductible either in the year loss occurs or the preceding year (by filing an amended return).

4. The **amount of loss** is the lesser of (1) the decrease in the FMV of the property resulting from the casualty, or (2) the adjusted basis of the property. The amount of loss must be reduced by

    a. Any insurance or reimbursement, and

    b. $100 floor for each separate nonbusiness casualty

5. An individual is not permitted to deduct a casualty loss for damage to **insured property** not used in a trade or business or in a transaction entered into for profit unless the individual files a timely insurance claim with respect to the loss. Casualty insurance premiums are considered a personal expense and are not deductible.

6. If personal casualty and theft **gains exceed losses** (after the $100 floor for each loss), then all gains and losses are treated as capital gains and losses.

    EXAMPLE: An individual incurred a $5,000 personal casualty gain, and a $1,000 personal casualty loss (after the $100 floor) during the current taxable year. Since there was a net gain, the individual will report the gain and loss as a $5,000 capital gain and a $1,000 capital loss.

7. If losses **(after the $100 floor for each loss) exceed gains,** the losses (1) offset gains, and (2) are an ordinary deduction from AGI to the extent **in excess of 10% of AGI.**

    EXAMPLE: An individual had AGI of $40,000 (before casualty gains and losses), and also had a personal casualty loss of $12,000 (after the $100 floor) and a personal casualty gain of $3,000. Since there was a personal casualty net loss, the net loss will be deductible as an itemized deduction of [$12,000 – $3,000 – (10% x $40,000)] = $5,000.

    EXAMPLE: Frank Jones' lakeside cottage, which cost him $13,600 (including $1,600 for the land) on April 30, 1988, was partially destroyed by fire on July 12, 2003. The value of the property immediately before the fire was $46,000 ($24,000 for the building and $22,000 for the land), and the value immediately after the fire was $36,000. He collected $7,000 from the insurance company. It was Jones' only casualty for 2003 and his AGI was $25,000. Jones' casualty loss deduction from the fire would be $400, computed as follows:

Value of entire property before fire	$46,000
Value of entire property after fire	–36,000
Decrease in fair market value of entire property	$10,000
Adjusted basis (cost in this case)	$13,600
Loss sustained (lesser of decrease in FMV or adjusted basis)	$10,000
Less insurance recovery	–7,000
Casualty loss	$ 3,000
Less $100 limitation	– 100
Loss after $100 limitation	$ 2,900
Less 10% of AGI	2,500
Casualty loss deduction	$ 400

A CHARITABLE CONTRIBUTION FLOWCHART FOR INDIVIDUALS

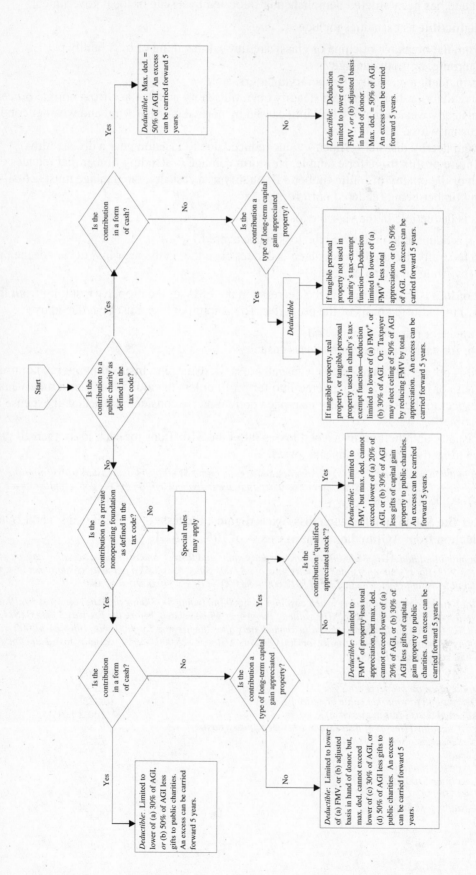

Start

Is the contribution to a public charity as defined in the tax code?

Yes →

Is the contribution in a form of cash?

Yes → *Deductible:* Max. ded. = 50% of AGI. An excess can be carried forward 5 years.

No →

Is the contribution a type of long-term capital gain appreciated property?

No → *Deductible:* Deduction limited to lower of (a) FMV, or (b) adjusted basis in hand of donor. Max. ded. = 50% of AGI. An excess can be carried forward 5 years.

Yes → **Deductible**

If tangible personal property not used in charity's tax-exempt function—Deduction limited to lower of (a) FMV* less total appreciation, or (b) 50% of AGI. An excess can be carried forward 5 years.

If tangible property, real property, or tangible personal property used in charity's tax-exempt function—Deduction limited to lower of (a) FMV*, or (b) 30% of AGI. Or: Taxpayer may elect ceiling of 50% of AGI by reducing FMV by total appreciation. An excess can be carried forward 5 years.

No →

Is the contribution to a private nonoperating foundation as defined in the tax code?

No → Special rules may apply

Yes →

Is the contribution in a form of cash?

Yes → *Deductible:* Limited to lower of (a) 30% of AGI, or (b) 50% of AGI less gifts to public charities. An excess can be carried forward 5 years.

No →

Is the contribution a type of long-term capital gain appreciated property?

No → *Deductible:* Limited to lower of (a) FMV, or (b) adjusted basis in hand of donor, but, max. ded. cannot exceed lower of (c) 30% of AGI, or (d) 50% of AGI less gifts to public charities. An excess can be carried forward 5 years.

Yes →

Is the contribution "qualified appreciated stock"?

Yes → *Deductible:* Limited to FMV, but max. ded. cannot exceed lower of (a) 20% of AGI, or (b) 30% of AGI less gifts of capital gain property to public charities. An excess can be carried forward 5 years.

No → *Deductible:* Limited to FMV* of property less total appreciation, but max. ded. cannot exceed lower of (a) 20% of AGI, or (b) 30% of AGI less gifts of capital gain property to public charities. An excess can be carried forward 5 years.

AGI = *adjusted gross income.*
FMV = *fair market value.*
The FMV of depreciable property given to a charitable organization must be reduced by the potential ordinary gain generated by depreciation recapture.

F. Miscellaneous Deductions

1. The following miscellaneous expenses are only deductible to the extent they (in the aggregate) **exceed 2% of AGI**.

   a. **Outside salesman expenses** include all business expenses of an employee who principally solicits business for his/her employer while away from the employer's place of business.

   b. All **unreimbursed employee expenses** including

      (1) Employee **education** expenses if

         (a) Incurred to maintain or improve skills required in employee's present job, or to meet requirements to keep job

         (b) Deductible expenses include unreimbursed transportation, travel, tuition, books, supplies, etc.

         (c) Education expenses are not deductible if required to meet minimum educational requirements in employee's job, or the education qualifies the employee for a new job (e.g., CPA review course) even if a new job is not sought

         (d) Travel as a form of education is not deductible

      (2) **Other deductible unreimbursed employee expenses** include

         (a) Transportation and travel (including 50% of meals and entertainment)

         (b) Uniforms not adaptable to general use

         (c) Employment agency fees to secure employment in same occupation

         (d) Subscription to professional journals

         (e) Dues to professional societies, union dues, and initiation fees

         (f) Physical examinations required by employer

         (g) A college professor's research, lecturing, and writing expenses

         (h) Amounts teacher pays to a substitute

         (i) Surety bond premiums

         (j) Malpractice insurance premiums

         (k) A research chemist's laboratory breakage fees

         (l) Small tools and supplies

   c. Tax counsel, assistance, and tax return preparation fees

   d. Expenses for the production of income other than those incurred in a trade or business or for production of rents and royalties (e.g., investment counsel fees, clerical help, safe-deposit box rent, legal fees to collect alimony, etc.)

2. The following miscellaneous expenses are **not subject to the 2% floor**, but instead are **deductible in full**.

   a. Gambling losses to the extent of gambling winnings

   b. Impairment-related work expenses for handicapped employees

   c. Estate tax related to income in respect of a decedent

   d. Certain adjustments when a taxpayer restores amounts held under a claim of right

   e. Certain costs of cooperative housing corporations

   f. Certain expenses of short sales

   g. The balance of an employee's investment in an annuity contract where the employee dies before recovering the entire investment

3. Examples of **nondeductible expenses** include

   a. Fees and licenses, such as auto licenses, marriage licenses, and dog tags

   b. Home repairs, insurance, rent

   c. Personal legal expenses

   d. Life insurance

   e. Burial expenses

   f. Capital expenditures

   g. Illegal bribes and kickbacks

   h. Fines and tax penalties

   i. Collateral

    j.   Commuting to and from work

    k.   Professional accreditation fees

    l.   Bar examination fees and incidental expenses in securing admission to the bar

    m. Medical and dental license fees paid to obtain initial licensing

    n.   Campaign expenses of a candidate for any office are not deductible, nor are registration fees for primary elections, even if taxpayer is the incumbent of the office to be contested.

    o.   Cost of midday meals while working late (except while traveling away from home)

    p.   Political contributions

G. An individual whose AGI exceeds a threshold amount of $139,500 for 2003 is required to reduce the amount of allowable itemized deductions by 3% of the excess over the threshold amount. The threshold amount is $69,750 for 2003 for a married person filing separately.

    1.   Itemized deductions **subject to reduction** include taxes, qualified residence interest, charitable contributions, miscellaneous itemized deductions (other than gambling).

    2.   The reduction is determined after first taking into account the other limitations that determine how much of a particular type of expense may be deducted (e.g., the 2% floor for miscellaneous itemized deductions).

    3.   Itemized deductions **not subject to reduction** include medical, investment interest, casualty and theft losses, and gambling losses.

    4.   The **reduction cannot exceed 80%** of allowable itemized deductions, not counting medical expenses, investment interest, casualty losses, and gambling losses (to the extent of gambling income).

    5.   This limitation does not apply for purposes of computing the alternative minimum tax (i.e., itemized deductions that are otherwise allowed in computing AMTI are not reduced by this limitation).

EXAMPLE:

	Allen	*Baker*
Adjusted gross income for 2003	*$230,000*	*$230,000*
Medical expenses	*$ 0*	*$ 17,000*
State income tax	*6,000*	*3,000*
Real estate taxes	*10,000*	*0*
Charitable contributions	*4,000*	*0*
Reduction limitation, lesser of		
* [($230,000 – $139,500) x 3%]*		
* or ($20,000 x 80%)*	*(2,715)*	
* ($3,000 x 80%)*		*(2,400)*
Total itemized deductions	*$ 17,285*	*17,600*
Taxable income before		
* personal exemptions*	*$212,715*	*$212,400*

IV. EXEMPTIONS

    Personal exemptions are similar to itemized deductions in that they are deducted from adjusted gross income. Personal exemptions are allowed for the taxpayer, spouse, and dependent if the dependent is a US citizen or resident.

    1.   The personal exemption amount is $3,050 for 2003.

    2.   The deduction for personal exemptions is reduced or even eliminated if AGI exceeds certain threshold amounts. Once AGI exceeds these thresholds, personal exemptions are reduced by 2% for each $2,500 ($1,250 for a married person filing separately) or fraction thereof by which AGI exceeds the thresholds.

        a.   The AGI threshold amounts are as follows:

	2003
Joint return; or surviving spouse	$209,250
Married filing separately	104,625
Head of household	174,400
Single	139,500

        b.   Since the reduction is 2% for each $2,500 ($1,250 for a married person filing separately) or fraction thereof by which AGI exceeds the threshold, all personal exemptions are completely eliminated when AGI exceeds the thresholds by more than $122,500.

EXAMPLE

	Single	Joint return
Adjusted gross income for 2003	$ 230,000	$ 230,000
Threshold	(139,500)	(209,250)
Excess	$ 90,500	$ 20,750
Personal exemption(s) before phaseout	$ 3,050	$6,100
Percentage reduction		
$90,500/$2,500 x 2%	74%	
$20,750/$2,500 x 2%		18%
Phaseout	(2,257)	(1,098)
Personal exemption(s) after phaseout	$ 793	$ 5,002

3. Personal exemption for **taxpayer**

   a. Full exemption even if birth or death occurred during the year
   b. No personal exemption for taxpayer if eligible to be claimed as a dependent on another taxpayer's return

4. Exemption for **spouse**

   a. Exemption on joint return
   b. Not allowed if divorced or legally separated at end of year
   c. If a separate return is filed, taxpayer may claim spouse exemption only if the spouse had no gross income and was not the dependent of another taxpayer.

5. Exemptions for **dependents**

   a. Full exemption even if death or birth occurred during the year
   b. Each dependent must meet **five tests**.

      (1) **Joint return.** Dependent cannot file a joint return, unless filed solely for refund of tax withheld.
      (2) **Member of household or related.** Dependent must either live with the taxpayer for the entire year or be related (closer than cousin).

         (a) *Related* includes ancestors, descendants, brothers and sisters, uncles and aunts, nephews and nieces, half and step relationships, and in-laws.
         (b) Relationships established by marriage are not ended by death or divorce.
         (c) A person temporarily absent for vacation, school, or sickness, or indefinitely confined in a nursing home meets the member of household test.
         (d) A person who died during the year but was a member of household until death, and a child who is born during the year and is a member of household for the rest of year, meet the member of household requirement.

      (3) **Citizenship.** Dependent must be a citizen, resident, or national of US, or a resident of Canada or Mexico.
      (4) **Gross income.** Dependent had less than $3,050 for 2003 of gross income.

         (a) Does not apply to child of taxpayer under the age of nineteen at end of year.
         (b) Does not apply to child of taxpayer if a full-time student at least five months during year and under age twenty-four at end of year.
         (c) Gross income does not include tax-exempt income (e.g., nontaxable social security).

      (5) **Support.** Taxpayer must furnish over one-half of support.

         (a) Includes food, clothing, FMV of lodging, medical, education, recreation, and certain capital expenses.
         (b) Excludes life insurance premiums, funeral expenses, nontaxable scholarships, income and social security taxes paid from a dependent's own income.

      NOTE: A phrase that may be used as a device to remember the five dependency tests is—Joe Must Come Get Supper.

   c. A **multiple support agreement** can be used if no single taxpayer furnishes more than 50% of the support of a dependent. Then any taxpayer (who meets the other requirements) contributing **more than 10%** can claim the dependent provided others furnishing more than 10% agree not to claim the dependent as an exemption.
   d. Child of divorced or separated parents

(1) Treated as receiving over one-half of support from custodial parent (i.e., parent who has custody for the greater part of the year)

(2) Noncustodial parent will be treated as providing over one-half of support if

    (a) Custodial parent signs a written declaration waiving the right to claim such child as a dependent, and the written declaration is attached to the noncustodial parent's return, or

    (b) Pre–1985 divorce decree or written agreement entitles that parent to the exemptions and that parent provides $600 or more for the child's support.

V. TAX COMPUTATION

A. Tax Tables

1. Tax tables contain precomputed tax liability based on taxable income.

    a. AGI less itemized deductions and exemptions
    b. Filing status

      (1) Single
      (2) Head of household
      (3) Married filing separately
      (4) Married filing joint return (even if only one had income)
      (5) Surviving spouse (qualifying widow[er] with dependent child)

2. Tax tables must be used by taxpayers unless taxable income is $100,000 or more.

B. Tax Rate Schedules

1. For 2003 the tax rates for individuals are as follows:

Tax rate	Joint return surviving spouse	Married filing separately
10%	$ 0 – $ 14,000	$ 0 – $ 7,000
15%	$ 14,001 – $ 56,800	$ 7,001 – $ 28,400
25%	$ 56,801 – $114,650	$ 28,401 – $ 57,325
28%	$114,651 – $174,700	$ 57,326 – $ 87,350
33%	$174,701 – $311,950	$ 87,351 – $155,975
35%	$311,951 and over	$155,976 and over

Tax rate	Head of household	Single
10%	$ 0 – $ 10,000	$ 0 – $ 7,000
15%	$ 10,001 – $ 38,050	$ 7,001 – $ 28,400
25%	$ 38,051 – $ 98,250	$ 28,401 – $ 68,800
28%	$ 98,251 – $159,100	$ 68,801 – $143,500
33%	$159,101 – $311,950	$143,501 – $311,950
35%	$311,951 and over	$311,951 and over

2. **Income of children under age fourteen.** The earned income of a child of any age and the unearned income of a child fourteen years or older as of the end of the taxable year is taxed at the child's own marginal rate. However, the **unearned income in excess of $1,500** (for 2003) of a child under age fourteen is generally taxed at the rates of the child's parents.

    a. The amount taxed at the parents' rates equals the child's unearned income less the sum of (1) any penalty for early withdrawal of savings, (2) $750, and (3) the greater of $750 or the child's itemized deductions directly connected with the production of unearned income.

      (1) Directly connected itemized deductions are those expenses incurred to produce or collect income, or maintain property that produces unearned income, including custodian fees, service fees to collect interest and dividends, and investment advisory fees. These are deductible as miscellaneous itemized deductions subject to a 2% of AGI limitation.

      (2) The amount taxed at the parents' rates cannot exceed the child's taxable income.

      EXAMPLE: Janie (age 11) is claimed as a dependent on her parents' return and in 2003 receives dividend income of $10,000, and has no itemized deductions. The amount of Janie's income taxed at her parents' tax rates is $8,500 [$10,000 – ($750 + $750)].

      EXAMPLE: Brian (age 12) is claimed as a dependent on his parents' return and in 2003 receives interest income of $15,000 and has itemized deductions of $1,200 that are directly connected to the production of the interest income. The amount of Brian's income taxed at his parents' tax rates is $13,050 [$15,000 – ($750 + $1,200)].

> *EXAMPLE: Kerry (age 10) is claimed as a dependent on her parents' return and in 2003 receives interest income of $12,000, has an early withdrawal penalty of $350, and itemized deductions of $400 that are directly connected to the production of the interest income. The amount of Kerry's income taxed at her parents' tax rates is $10,150 [$12,000 – ($350 + $750 + $750)].*

    b. A child's tax liability on unearned income taxed at the parents' rates is the child's share of the increase in tax (including alternative minimum tax) that would result from adding to the parents' taxable income the unearned income of their children under age fourteen.

    c. If the child's parents are divorced, the custodial parent's taxable income will be used in determining the child's tax liability.

    d. If child's parents are divorced and both parents have custody, the taxable income of the parent having custody for the greater portion of the calendar year will be used in determining the child's tax liability.

3. **Reporting unearned income of a child on parent's return.** Parents may elect to include on their return the unearned income of their child under age fourteen whose income consists solely of interest and dividends and is between $750 and $7,500 (for 2003).

    a. The child is treated as having no gross income and does not have to file a tax return for the year the election is made.

    b. The electing parents must include the child's gross income in excess of $1,500 on their return for the tax year, resulting in the taxation of that income at the parents' highest marginal rate. Also, the parents must report additional tax liability equal to the lesser of (1) $112.50, or (2) 15% of the child's income in excess of $750.

    c. The election cannot be made if estimated tax payments were made for the tax year in the child's name and social security number, or if the child is subject to backup withholding.

C. Filing Status

1. Married persons (married at year-end or at time of death of spouse) can file joint return or separate returns.

2. **Qualifying widow(er) with dependent child** (i.e., surviving spouse) may use joint tax rates for the two years following the year in which the spouse died.

    a. Surviving spouse must have been eligible to file a joint return in the year of the spouse's death.

    b. Dependent child, stepchild, adopted child, or foster child must live in household with surviving spouse.

    c. Surviving spouse must provide more than 50% of costs of maintaining household that was the main home of the child for the entire year.

3. **Head of household** status applies to an unmarried person (other than a qualifying widow(er) with dependent child) who provides more than 50% of costs of maintaining household for more than one-half the year for

    a. Taxpayer's unmarried child, stepchild, grandchild, or adopted child (who need not be a dependent), or

    b. Relative (closer than cousin) who is a dependent; including a married child or married descendant

    c. Parents need not live with head of household, but parents' household must be maintained by taxpayer (e.g., nursing home) and parents must qualify as taxpayer's dependents

    d. Unmarried requirement is satisfied if spouses are living apart under a separate maintenance decree.

4. **Cost of maintaining household**

    a. *Includes* rent, mortgage interest, taxes, insurance on home, repairs, utilities, and food eaten in the home.

    b. *Excludes* the cost of clothing, education, medical expenses, vacations, life insurance, transportation, rental value of home, value of taxpayer's services.

D. Alternative Minimum Tax (AMT)

1. The alternative minimum tax for noncorporate taxpayers is computed by applying a two-tiered rate schedule to a taxpayer's alternative minimum tax base. A 26% rate applies to the first $175,000 of a taxpayer's alternative minimum taxable income (AMTI) in excess of the exemption amount. A 28% rate applies to AMTI greater than $175,000 ($87,500 for married taxpayers filing separately) above

the exemption amount. This tax applies to the extent that a taxpayer's AMT exceeds the amount of regular tax.

2. A taxpayer's AMT is generally the amount by which the applicable percentage (26% or 28%) of AMTI as reduced by an exemption amount and reduced by the AMT foreign tax credit exceeds the amount of a taxpayer's regular tax as reduced by the regular tax foreign tax credit.

3. AMT computation formula

$$
\begin{array}{l}
\text{Regular taxable income}\\
\underline{+\ (-)\quad\text{Adjustments}}\\
\underline{+\qquad\text{Tax preferences}}\\
=\ \text{Alternative minimum taxable income}\\
\underline{-\qquad\text{Exemption amount}}\\
=\ \text{Alternative minimum tax base}\\
\underline{\times\qquad\text{26\% or 28\%}}\\
=\ \text{Tentative before foreign tax credit}\\
\underline{-\qquad\text{AMT foreign tax credit}}\\
=\ \text{Tentative minimum tax}\\
\underline{-\qquad\text{Regular tax liability (reduced by regular tax foreign tax credit)}}\\
\underline{=\ \text{AMT (if positive)}}
\end{array}
$$

4. **Exemption.** AMTI is offset by an exemption. However, the AMT exemption amount is phased out at the rate of 25% of AMTI between certain specified levels.

Filing status	AMT exemption	Phaseout range
Married filing jointly;		
Surviving Spouse	$58,000	$150,000 – $382,000
Single; Head of Household	$40,250	$112,500 – $273,500
Married filing separately	$29,000	$ 75,000 – $191,000

In the case of a child under the age of fourteen, the AMT exemption (normally $40,250) is limited to the child's earned income plus $5,600 (for 2003).

5. **Adjustments.** In determining AMTI, taxable income must be computed with various adjustments. Example of adjustments include

a. For real property placed in service after 1986 and before 1999, the difference between regular tax depreciation and straight-line depreciation over forty years.

b. For personal property placed in service after 1986, the difference between regular tax depreciation and depreciation using the 150% declining balance method (switching to straight-line when necessary to maximize the deduction)

c. Excess of stock's FMV over amount paid upon exercise of incentive stock options.

d. The medical expense deduction is computed using a 10% floor (instead of the 7.5% floor used for regular tax)

e. No deduction is allowed for home mortgage interest if the loan proceeds were not used to buy, build, or improve the home

f. No deduction is allowed for personal, state, and local taxes, and for miscellaneous itemized deductions subject to the 2% floor for regular tax purposes

g. No deduction is allowed for personal exemptions and the standard deduction

h. For long-term contracts, the excess of income under the percentage-of-completion method over the amount reported using the completed-contract method

i. The installment method cannot be used for sales of dealer property

6. **Preference items.** The following are examples of preference items added to taxable income (as adjusted above) in computing AMTI:

a. Tax-exempt interest on certain private activity bonds reduced by related interest expense that is disallowed for regular tax purposes

b. Accelerated depreciation on real property and leased personal property placed in service before 1987—excess of accelerated depreciation over straight-line

c. The excess of percentage of depletion over the property's adjusted basis

d. 42% of the amount of excluded gain from Sec. 1202 small business stock (7% of the excluded gain for sales or exchanges on or after May 6, 2003)

7. **Regular tax credits.** Generally, an individual's tax credits are allowed to reduce regular tax liability, but only to the extent that regular income tax liability exceeds tentative minimum tax liability.

    a. However, personal nonrefundable credits are allowed to the extent of the sum of (1) regular tax liability (reduced by the foreign tax credit), plus (2) the alternative minimum tax (i.e., the excess of the tentative minimum tax over the regular tax) determined without regard to the AMT foreign tax credit.

    b. These nonrefundable personal credits include the dependent care credit, the credit for the elderly and disabled, the adoption credit, the child tax credit, and the HOPE and lifetime learning credits.

    EXAMPLE: For 2003, the Millers' regular tax liability (before credits) is $3,000, and their tentative minimum tax is $4,000. The Millers may claim up to $4,000 of nonrefundable personal credits to offset both their regular tax and their AMT.

8. **Minimum tax credit.** The amount of AMT paid (net of exclusion preferences) is allowed as a credit against regular tax liability in future years.

    a. The amount of the AMT credit to be carried forward is the excess of the AMT paid over the AMT that would be paid if AMTI included only exclusion preferences (e.g., disallowed itemized deductions and the preferences for excess percentage of depletion, tax-exempt interest, and charitable contributions).

    b. The credit can be carried forward indefinitely, but not carried back.

    c. The AMT credit can only be used to reduce regular tax liability, **not** future AMT liability.

E. Other Taxes

1. **Social security** (FICA) tax is imposed on both employers and employees (withheld from wages). The FICA tax has two components: old age, survivor, and disability insurance (OASDI) and medicare hospital insurance (HI). The OASDI rate is 6.2% and the HI rate is 1.45%, resulting in a combined rate of 7.65%. For 2003, the OASDI portion (6.2%) is capped at $87,000, while the HI portion (1.45%) applies to all wages.

2. **Federal unemployment** (FUTA) tax is imposed only on employers at a rate of 6.2% of the first $7,000 of wages paid to each employee. A credit of up to 5.4% is available for unemployment taxes paid to a state, leaving a net federal tax of 0.8%.

3. **Self-employment** tax is imposed on individuals who work for themselves (e.g., sole proprietor, independent contractor, partner). The combined self-employment tax rate is 15.3%, of which the medicare portion is 2.9%.

    a. The full self-employment tax (15.3%) is capped at $87,000 for 2003, while the medicare portion (2.9%) applies to all self-employment earnings.

    b. Income from self-employment generally includes all items of business income less business deductions. Does not include personal interest, dividends, rents, capital gains and losses, and gains and losses on the disposition of business property.

    c. Wages subject to FICA tax are deducted from $87,000 for 2003 in determining the amount of income subject to self-employment tax.

    d. No tax if net earnings from self-employment are less than $400.

    e. A deduction equal to one-half of the self-employment tax rate (7.65%) multiplied by the taxpayer's self-employment income (without regard to this deduction) is allowed in computing the taxpayer's net earnings from self-employment.

        (1) This deemed deduction is allowed in place of deducting one-half of the amount of self-employment tax that is actually paid.

        (2) The purpose of this deduction is to allow the amount on which the self-employment tax is based to be adjusted downward to reflect the fact that employees do not pay FICA tax on the amount of the FICA tax that is paid by their employers.

    EXAMPLE: A taxpayer has self-employment income of $50,000 before the deemed deduction for 2003. The deemed deduction is $50,000 x 7.65% = $3,825, resulting in net earnings from self-employment of $50,000 – $3,825 = $46,175 and a self-employment tax of $46,175 x 15.30% = $7,065. In computing AGI, the taxpayer is allowed to deduct one-half of the self-employment tax actually paid, $7,065 x 50% = $3,533.

    EXAMPLE: A taxpayer has self-employment income of $100,000 before the deemed deduction for 2003. The deemed deduction is $100,000 x 7.65% = $7,650, resulting in net earnings from self-employment of $100,000 – $7,650 = $92,350. The taxpayer's self-employment tax will be ($87,000 x 15.3%) + [($92,350 – $87,000) x 2.9%] = $13,466. In computing AGI, the taxpayer is allowed to deduct one-half of the self-employment tax actually paid, $13,466 x 50% = $6,733.

VI. TAX CREDITS/ESTIMATED TAX PAYMENTS

Tax credits directly reduce tax liability. The tax liability less tax credits equals taxes payable. Taxes that have already been withheld on wages and estimated tax payments are credited against tax liability without limitation, even if the result is a refund due to the taxpayer.

A. General Business Credit

1. It is comprised of the (1) investment credit (energy, rehabilitation, and reforestation), (2) work opportunity credit, (3) welfare-to-work credit, (4) alcohol fuels credit, (5) research credit, (6) low-income housing credit, (7) enhanced oil recovery credit, (8) disabled access credit, (9) renewable resources electricity production credit, (10) empowerment zone employment credit, (11) Indian employment credit, (12) employer social security credit, (13) orphan drug credit, (14) new markets tax credit, (15) small-employer pension plan startup cost credit, and (16) the employer-provided child care credit.

2. The general business credit is allowed to the extent of "net income tax" less the greater of (1) the tentative minimum tax or (2) 25% of "net regular tax liability" above $25,000.

   a. "Net income tax" means the amount of the regular income tax plus the alternative minimum tax, and minus nonrefundable tax credits (except the alternative minimum tax credit).
   b. "Net regular tax liability" is the taxpayer's regular tax liability reduced by nonrefundable tax credits (except the alternative minimum tax credit).

   EXAMPLE: An individual (not subject to the alternative minimum tax) has a net income tax of $65,000. The individual's general business credit cannot exceed $65,000 – [25% x ($65,000 – $25,000)] = $55,000.

3. A general business credit in excess of the limitation amount is carried back one year and forward twenty years.

B. Business Energy Credit

1. The business energy credit is **10%** for qualified investment in property that uses solar, geothermal, or ocean thermal energy. The property must be constructed by the taxpayer, or if acquired, the taxpayer must be the first person to use the property.
2. The recoverable basis of energy property must be reduced by 50% of the amount of business energy credit.

C. Credit for Rehabilitation Expenditures

1. Special investment credit (in lieu of regular income tax credits and energy credits) for qualified expenditures incurred to substantially rehabilitate old buildings. Credit percentages are (1) 10% for nonresidential buildings placed in service before 1936 (other than certified historic structures), and (2) 20% for residential and nonresidential certified historic structures.
2. **To qualify** for credit on other than certified historic structures

   a. 75% of external walls must remain in place as external or internal walls
   b. 50% or more of existing external walls must be retained in place as external walls
   c. 75% or more of existing internal structural framework must be retained in place

3. A building's recoverable basis must be reduced by 100% of the amount of rehabilitation credit.

D. Work Opportunity Credit

1. Credit is generally 40% of the first $6,000 of qualified first year wages paid to each qualified new employee who begins work before January 1, 2004. For qualified summer youth employees, the credit is 40% of the first $3,000 of wages for services performed during any ninety-day period between May 1 and September 15.
2. Qualified new employees include a (1) qualified IV-A recipient, (2) qualified veteran, (3) qualified ex-felon, (4) high-risk youth, (5) vocational rehabilitation referral, (6) qualified summer youth employee, and, (7) qualified food stamp recipient.
3. Employer's deduction for wages is reduced by the amount of credit.
4. Taxpayer may elect not to claim credit (to avoid reducing wage deduction).

E. Welfare-to-Work Credit

1. Credit is available for wages paid to long-term family assistance recipients who begin work before January 1, 2004.

2. The amount of credit is 35% of the first $10,000 of qualified first-year wages and 50% of the first $10,000 of qualified second-year wages.
3. The employer's deduction for wages is reduced by the amount of credit.
4. The work opportunity credit is not available for an employee in the same year that the welfare-to-work credit is taken with respect to the employee.

F. Alcohol Fuels Credit

1. A ten cents per gallon tax credit is allowed for the production of up to fifteen million gallons per year of ethanol by an eligible small ethanol producer (i.e., one having a production capacity of up to thirty million gallons of alcohol per year).
2. The tax credit for ethanol blenders is sixty cents per gallon for 190 or greater proof ethanol and forty-five cents per gallon for 150 to 190 proof ethanol.

G. Low-Income Housing Credit

1. The amount of credit for owners of low-income housing projects depends upon (1) whether the taxpayer acquires existing housing or whether the housing is newly constructed or rehabilitated, and (2) whether or not the housing project is financed by tax-exempt bonds or other federally subsidized financing. The applicable credit rates are the appropriate percentages issued by the IRS for the month in which the building is placed in service.
2. The amount on which the credit is computed is the portion of the total depreciable basis of a qualified housing project that reflects the portion of the housing units within the project that are occupied by qualified low-income individuals.
3. The credit is claimed each year (for a ten-year period) beginning with the year that the property is placed in service. The first-year credit is prorated to reflect the date placed in service.

H. Disabled Access Credit

1. A tax credit is available to an eligible small business for expenditures incurred to make the business accessible to disabled individuals. The amount of this credit is equal to 50% of the amount of the eligible access expenditures for a year that exceed $250 but do not exceed $10,250.
2. An eligible small business is one that either (1) had gross receipts for the preceding tax year that did not exceed $1 million, or (2) had no more than 30 full-time employees during the preceding tax year, and (3) elects to have this credit apply.
3. Eligible access expenditures are amounts incurred to comply with the requirements of the Americans with Disabilities Act of 1990 and include amounts incurred for the purpose of removing architectural, communication, physical, or transportation barriers that prevent a business from being accessible to, or usable by, disabled individuals; amounts incurred to provide qualified readers to visually impaired individuals, and amounts incurred to acquire or modify equipment or devices for disabled individuals. Expenses incurred in connection with new construction are not eligible for the credit.
4. This credit is included as part of the general business credit; no deduction or credit is allowed under any other Code provision for any amount for which a disabled access credit is allowed.

I. Empowerment Zone Employment Credit

1. The credit is generally equal to 20% of the first $15,000 of wages paid to each employee who is a resident of a designated empowerment zone and performs substantially all services within the zone in an employer's trade or business.
2. The deduction for wages must be reduced by the amount of credit.

J. Employer Social Security Credit

1. Credit allowed to food and beverage establishments for the employer's portion of FICA tax (7.65%) attributable to reported tips in excess of those tips treated as wages for purposes of satisfying the minimum wage provisions of the Fair Labor Standards Act.
2. No deduction is allowed for any amount taken into account in determining the credit.

K. Employer-Provided Child Care Credit

1. For tax years beginning after December 31, 2001, employers who provide child care facilities to their employees during normal working hours are eligible for a credit equal to 25% of qualified child care

expenditures, and 10% of qualified child care resource and referral expenditures. The maximum credit is $150,000 per year, and is subject to a ten-year recapture rule.

2. *Qualified child care expenditures* include amounts paid to acquire, construct, and rehabilitate property which is to be used as a qualified child care facility (e.g., training costs of employees, scholarship programs, compensation for employees with high levels of child care training).

3. To prevent a double benefit, the basis of qualifying property is reduced by the amount of credit, and the amount of qualifying expenditures that would otherwise be deductible must be reduced by the amount of credit.

L. Credit for the Elderly and the Disabled

1. Eligible taxpayers are those who are either (1) 65 or older or (2) permanently and totally disabled.

   a. Permanent and total disability is the inability to engage in substantial gainful activity for a period that is expected to last for a continuous twelve-month period.

   b. Married individuals must file a joint return to claim the credit unless they have not lived together at all during the year.

   c. Credit cannot be claimed if Form 1040A or 1040EZ is filed.

2. Credit is **15%** of an initial amount reduced by certain amounts excluded from gross income and AGI in excess of certain levels. The amount of credit is limited to the amount of tax liability.

   a. Initial amount varies with filing status.

      (1) $5,000 for single or joint return where only one spouse is 65 or older
      (2) $7,500 for joint return where both spouses are 65 or older
      (3) $3,750 for married filing a separate return
      (4) Limited to disability income for taxpayers under age 65

   b. Reduced by annuities, pensions, social security, or disability income that is excluded from gross income

   c. Also reduced by 50% of the excess of AGI over

      (1) $7,500 if single
      (2) $10,000 if joint return
      (3) $5,000 for married individual filing separate return

   EXAMPLE: H, age 67, and his wife, W, age 65, file a joint return and have adjusted gross income of $12,000. H received social security benefits of $2,000 during the year. The computation of their credit would be as follows:

Initial amount		$7,500
Less: social security	$2,000	
50% of AGI over $10,000	1,000	3,000
Balance		4,500
		x 15%
Amount of credit (limited to tax liability)		$ 675

M. Child Care Credit

1. For 2003, the credit may vary from **20% to 35%** of the amount paid for qualifying household and dependent care expenses incurred to enable taxpayer to be gainfully employed or look for work. Credit is 35% if AGI is $15,000 or less, but is reduced by 1 percentage point for each $2,000 (or portion thereof) of AGI in excess of $15,000 (but not reduced below 20%).

   EXAMPLE: Able, Baker, and Charlie have AGIs of $10,000, $20,000, and $50,000 respectively, and each incurs child care expenses of $2,000. Able's child care credit is $700 (35% x $2,000); Baker's credit is $640 (32% x $2,000); and Charlie's credit is $400 (20% x $2,000).

2. **Eligibility** requirements include

   a. Expenses must be incurred to enable taxpayer to be gainfully employed

   b. Married taxpayer must file joint return. If divorced or separated, credit available to parent having custody longer time during year

   c. Taxpayer must furnish more than half the cost of maintaining a household that is the principal residence of both taxpayer and **qualifying individual,** who is

      (1) Dependent under thirteen years of age, or
      (2) Dependent or spouse who is physically or mentally incapable of self-care

d. **Qualifying expenses** are those incurred for care of qualifying individual and for household services that were partly for care of qualifying individual to enable taxpayer to work or look for work

(1) Expenses incurred outside taxpayer's household qualify only if incurred for a qualifying individual who regularly spends at least eight hours each day in taxpayer's household

(2) Payments to taxpayer's child under age nineteen do not qualify

(3) Payments to a relative do not qualify if taxpayer is entitled to a dependency exemption for that relative

3. **Maximum amount of expenses** that qualify for credit is the least of

a. Actual expenses incurred, or

b. **$3,000** for one, **$6,000** for two or more qualifying individuals, or

c. Taxpayer's earned income (or spouse's earned income if smaller)

d. If spouse is a student or incapable of self-care and thus has little or no earned income, spouse is treated as being gainfully employed and having earnings of not less than $250 per month for one, $500 per month for two or more qualifying individuals

EXAMPLE: Husband and wife have earned income of $15,000 each, resulting in AGI of $30,000. They have one child, age 3. They incurred qualifying household service expenses of $1,500 and child care expenses at a nursery school of $2,200.

Household expenses	*$1,500*
Add child care outside home	*2,200*
Total employment-related expenses	*$3,700*
Maximum allowable expenses	*$3,000*
Credit = 27% x $3,000	*$ 810*

N. Foreign Tax Credit

1. Foreign income taxes on US taxpayers can either be deducted or used as a credit at the option of the taxpayer each year.

2. The credit is limited to the overall limitation of

$$\frac{\text{TI from all foreign countries}}{\text{Taxable income + Exemptions}} \text{ x (US tax – Credit for elderly)}$$

3. The limitation must be computed separately for passive income (i.e., dividends, interest, royalties, rents, and annuities).

4. Foreign tax credit in excess of the overall limitation is subject to a two-year carryback and a five-year carryforward.

5. There is no limitation if foreign taxes are used as a deduction.

O. Earned Income Credit

1. The earned income credit is a **refundable** tax credit for eligible low-income workers. Earned income includes wages, salaries, and other employee compensation (including union strike benefits), plus earnings from self-employment (after the deduction for one-half self-employment taxes). Earned income excludes income from pensions and annuities, and investment income such as interest and dividends.

2. For 2003, the earned income credit is allowed at a rate of 34% of the first $7,490 of earned income for taxpayers with one qualifying child, and is allowed at a rate of 40% on the first of $10,510 of earned income for taxpayers with two or more qualifying children. The maximum credit is reduced by 15.98% (21.06% for two or more qualifying children) of the amount of which earned income (or AGI if greater) exceeds $13,730 ($14,730 for married taxpayers filing jointly).

3. To be eligible for the credit an individual must

a. Have earned income and a return that covers a twelve-month period

b. Maintain a household for more than half the year for a qualifying child in the US

c. Have a filing status other than married filing a separate return

d. Not be a qualifying child of another person

e. Not claim the exclusion for foreign earned income

f. Not have disqualified income in excess of $2,600

4. A **qualifying child** must be

   a. The individual's son, daughter, adopted child, grandchild, stepson, stepdaughter, descendant of a stepchild, or foster child.

   b. Under age nineteen, or a full-time student under age twenty-four, or permanently and totally disabled.

5. **Disqualified income** includes both taxable and tax-exempt interest, dividends, net rental and royalty income, net capital gain income, and net passive income.

6. A **reduced earned income credit** is available to an individual who does not have qualifying children if (1) the individual's principal place of abode for more than half the tax year is in the US, (2) the individual (or spouse) is at least age twenty-five (but under sixty-five) at the end of the tax year, and (3) the individual does not qualify as a dependency exemption on another taxpayer's return. For 2003, the maximum credit is 7.65% of the first $4,990 of earned income, and is reduced by 7.65% of earned income (or AGI if greater) in excess of $6,240 ($7,240 for married taxpayers filing jointly).

7. The earned income credit is refundable if the amount of credit exceeds the taxpayer's tax liability. Individuals with qualifying children who expect a refund because of the earned income credit may arrange to have up to 60% of the credit added to paychecks.

P. Credit for Adoption Expenses

1. A nonrefundable credit of up to $10,160 (for 2003) for qualified adoption expenses incurred for each eligible child (including a child with special needs).

   a. An *eligible child* is an individual who has not attained the age of 18 as of the time of the adoption, or who is physically or mentally incapable of self-care. A *child with special needs* must be a citizen or resident of the US.

   b. Married taxpayers generally must file a joint return to claim the credit.

   c. The credit is phased out ratably for modified AGI between $152,390 and $192,390.

2. *Qualified adoption expenses* are taken into account in the year the adoption becomes final and include all reasonable and necessary adoption fees, court costs, attorney fees, and other expenses that are directly related to the legal adoption by the taxpayer of an eligible child. However, expenses incurred in carrying out a surrogate parenting arrangement or in adopting a spouse's child do not qualify for the credit.

3. Any portion of the credit not allowed because of the limitation based on tax liability may be carried forward for up to five years.

Q. Child Tax Credit (CTC)

1. The amount of the credit is $1,000 per qualifying child for 2003.

2. A *qualifying child* is a US citizen or resident who is a child, descendant, stepchild, or eligible foster child for whom the taxpayer may claim a dependency exemption and who is less than seventeen years old as of the close of the calendar year in which the tax year of the taxpayer begins.

3. The child tax credit begins to phase out when modified adjusted gross income reaches $110,000 for joint filers, $55,000 for married taxpayers filing separately, and $75,000 for single taxpayers and heads of households. The credit is reduced by $50 for each $1,000, or fraction thereof, of modified AGI above the thresholds.

4. The CTC is refundable to the extent of 10% of the taxpayer's earned income in excess of $10,500 (for 2003), up to the per child credit amount of $1,000 per child. Taxpayers with more than two children may calculate the refundable portion of the credit using the excess of their social security taxes (i.e., taxpayer's share of FICA taxes and one-half of self-employment taxes) over their earned income credit, if it results in a larger amount. The amount of refundable CTC reduces the amount of nonrefundable CTC.

R. Hope Scholarship Credit

1. For the *first two years* of a postsecondary school program, qualifying taxpayers may elect to take a nonrefundable tax credit of 100% for the first $1,000 of qualified tuition and related expenses (not room and board), and a 50% credit for the next $1,000 of such expenses, for a total credit of up to $1,500 a year per student.

2. The credit is available on a *per student basis* and covers tuition payments for the taxpayer as well as the taxpayer's spouse and dependents.

    a. To be eligible for the credit, the student must be enrolled on at least a half-time basis for one academic period during the year.

    b. If a student is claimed as a dependent of another taxpayer, only that taxpayer may claim the education credit for the student's qualified tuition and related expenses. However, if the taxpayer is eligible to, but does **not** claim the student as a dependent, only the student may claim the education credit for the student's qualified tuition and related expenses.

3. The credit is phased out for single taxpayers with modified AGI between $41,000 and $51,000, and for joint filers with a modified AGI between $83,000 and $103,000.

4. For a tax year, a taxpayer may elect only one of the following with respect to one student: (1) the Hope credit, or (2) the lifetime learning credit.

S. Lifetime Learning Credit

1. A nonrefundable 20% tax credit is available for up to $10,000 (for tax years beginning after 12/31/02) of qualified tuition and related expenses per year for graduate and undergraduate courses at an eligible educational institution.

2. The credit may be claimed for an unlimited number of years, is available on a *per taxpayer basis*, covers tuition payments for the taxpayer, spouse, and dependents.

3. Similar to the Hope credit, if a student is claimed as a dependent of another taxpayer, only that taxpayer may claim the education credit for the student's qualified tuition and related expenses. However, if the taxpayer is eligible to, but does **not** claim the student as a dependent, only the student may claim the education credit for the student's qualified tuition and related expenses.

4. The credit is phased out for single taxpayers with a modified AGI between $41,000 and $51,000, and for joint filers with modified AGI between $83,000 and $103,000.

5. For a tax year, a taxpayer may elect only one of the following with respect to one student: (1) the Hope credit, or (2) the lifetime learning credit.

EXAMPLE: Alan paid qualified tuition and related expenses for his dependent, Betty, to attend college. Assuming all other relevant requirements are met, Alan may claim either a Hope Scholarship credit or lifetime learning credit with respect to his dependent, Betty, but not both.

EXAMPLE: Cathy paid $2,000 in qualified tuition and related expenses for her dependent, Doug, to attend college. Also during the year, Cathy paid $600 in qualified tuition to attend a continuing education course to improve her job skills. Assuming all relevant requirements are met, Cathy may claim the Hope Scholarship credit for the $2,000 paid for her dependent, Doug, and a lifetime learning credit for the $600 of qualified tuition that she paid for the continuing education course to improve her job skills.

*EXAMPLE: The facts are the same as in the preceding example, except that Cathy paid $3,500 in qualified tuition and related expenses for her dependent, Doug, to attend college. Although a Hope Scholarship credit is available only with respect to the first $2,000 of qualified tuition and related expenses paid with respect to Doug, Cathy **cannot** add the $1,500 of excess expenses to her $600 of qualified tuition in computing the amount of her lifetime learning credit.*

*EXAMPLE: Ernie has one dependent, Frank. During the current year, Ernie paid qualified tuition and related expenses for Frank to attend college. Although Ernie is eligible to claim Frank as a dependent on Ernie's federal income tax return, Ernie does **not** do so. Therefore, assuming all other relevant requirements are met, Frank is allowed an education credit on Frank's federal income tax return for his qualified tuition and related expenses paid by Ernie, and Ernie is not allowed an education credit with respect to Frank's education expenses. The result would be the same if Frank had paid his qualified tuition expenses himself.*

T. Estimated Tax Payments

1. An individual whose regular and alternative minimum tax liability is not sufficiently covered by withholding on wages must pay estimated tax in quarterly installments or be subject to penalty.

2. Quarterly payments of estimated tax are due by the 15th day of the 4th, 6th, and 9th month of the taxable year, and by the 15th day of the 1st month of the following year.

3. For 2003, individuals (other than high-income individuals) will incur no penalty if the amount of tax withheld plus estimated payments are at least equal to the lesser of

    a. 90% of the current year's tax,

    b. 90% of the tax determined by annualizing current-year taxable income through each quarter, or

    c. 100% of the prior year's tax

4. For 2003, high-income individuals must use 110% (instead of 100%) if they base their estimates on their prior year's tax. A person is a high-income individual if the AGI shown on the individual's return for the preceding tax year exceeds $150,000 ($75,000 for a married individual filing separately).

5. The penalty is based on the difference between the required annual payment (i.e., lesser of a., b., or c. above) and the amount paid.

6. Generally no penalty if

a. Total tax due was less than $1,000;

b. Taxpayer had no tax liability for prior year (i.e., total tax was zero), prior year was a twelve-month period, and taxpayer was a US citizen or resident for entire year; or,

c. IRS waives penalty because failure to pay was the result of casualty, disaster, or other unusual circumstances.

VII. FILING REQUIREMENTS

A. Form 1040 must generally be filed if gross income at least equals the sum of the taxpayer's standard deduction plus personal exemptions allowable (e.g., generally $4,750 + $3,050 = $7,800 for single taxpayer for 2003).

1. The additional standard deduction for age ($1,150 for 2003) is included in determining an individual's filing requirement; the additional standard deduction for blindness and dependency exemptions are not included.

*EXAMPLE: A single individual age 65 and blind who **cannot** be claimed as a dependency exemption by another taxpayer must file a return for 2003 if the individual's gross income is at least $4,750 + $3,050 + $1,150 = $8,950*

2. An individual who can be claimed as a dependency exemption by another taxpayer must file a return if the individual either has (1) unearned income in excess of the sum of $750 plus any additional standard deductions allowed for age and blindness, or (2) total gross income in excess of the individual's standard deduction (i.e., earned income plus $250 up to the normal amount of the basic standard deduction—$4,700 for single taxpayer—plus additional standard deductions for age and blindness).

EXAMPLE: A single individual age 65 who can be claimed as a dependency exemption by another taxpayer must file a return for 2003 if the individual has unearned income (e.g., interest and dividends) in excess of $750 + $1,150 = $1,900.

3. Self-employed individual must file if net earnings from self-employment are **$400** or more.

4. A married individual filing separately must file if gross income is $3,050 or more.

B. Return must be filed by 15th day of 4th calendar month following close of taxable year.

C. An automatic four-month extension of time for filing the return can be obtained by filing Form 4868 by the due date of the return, and paying any estimated tax due.

VIII. TAX PROCEDURES

A. Audit and Appeal Procedures

1. Taxpayer makes determination of tax when return is filed.

2. Examination of questionable returns may be conducted by correspondence, in an IRS office (i.e., office audit), or at taxpayer's place of business (i.e., field audit).

3. If taxpayer does not agree with the changes proposed by the examiner and the examination was made in an IRS office or by correspondence, the taxpayer may request a meeting with the examiner's supervisor.

4. If no agreement is reached, or if the examination was conducted in the field, the IRS will send the taxpayer a copy of the examination report and a letter stating the proposed changes (**thirty-day letter**).

5. A taxpayer has thirty days to (1) accept deficiency, (2) appeal the examiner's findings, or (3) may disregard the thirty-day letter and wait for a statutory notice of deficiency (**ninety-day letter**).

6. If taxpayer has appealed and agreement is not reached at appellate level of IRS, a ninety-day letter is sent.

7. Taxpayer has ninety days to file a petition in the Tax Court.

a. Assessment and collection are prohibited so long as the taxpayer can petition the Tax Court. Payment of deficiency is not required before going to Tax Court.

b. If a petition is not filed within ninety days, the tax deficiency is assessed and the amount is subject to collection if not paid within ten days.

B. Assessments

1. The normal period for assessment of a tax deficiency is **three years** after the due date of the return or three years after the return is filed, whichever is later.
2. The assessment period is extended to **six years** if gross income omissions exceed 25% of the gross income stated on the return.
3. There is no time limit for assessment if no return is filed, if the return is fraudulent, or if there is a willful attempt to evade taxes.
4. Assessment period (normally three years) is suspended for 150 days after timely mailing of deficiency notice (90-day letter) to taxpayer.
5. Within sixty days after making the assessment, the IRS is required to provide a notice and demand for payment. If tax is not paid, the tax may be collected by levy or by court proceedings started within ten years of assessment.

C. Collection from Transferees and Fiduciaries

1. Transferee provisions are a method of collecting a predetermined tax that the transferor taxpayer cannot pay.
2. Generally transferor must be insolvent, or no longer in existence (e.g., corporation was dissolved).
3. Generally transferees are liable only to the extent of property received from the transferor taxpayer.

D. Closing Agreement and Compromise

1. A closing agreement is a final determination of tax liability that is binding on both the IRS and taxpayer.
2. A compromise is a writing-down of the tax liability. The IRS has broad authority to compromise in the event that doubt exists as to the existence of actual tax liability or because of the taxpayer's inability to pay.

E. Claims for Refund

1. An income tax refund claim is made on Form 1040X. Form 843 should be used to file a refund claim for taxes other than income taxes. Form 1045 may be used to file for a tentative adjustment or refund of taxes when an overpayment of taxes for a prior year results from the carryback of a current year's net operating loss.
2. Period for filing refund claims
   a. Refund claim must be filed within **three years** from date return was filed, or **two years** from payment of tax, whichever is later. If return filed before due date, the return is treated as filed on due date.
   b. Three-year period is extended to seven years for claims resulting from bad debts or worthless securities.
   c. If refund claim results from a carryback (e.g., NOL), the three-year period begins with the return for the year in which the carryback arose.
3. Suit for refund
   a. Only recourse from IRS's disallowance of refund claim is to begin suit in court within two years of notice of disallowance.
   b. If IRS fails to act on refund claim within six months, the taxpayer may treat it as disallowed.

F. Interest

1. Interest is allowed on overpayments from date of overpayment to thirty days before date of refund check.
   a. If an overpayment, amounts of tax withheld and estimated payments are deemed paid on due date of return.
   b. No interest is allowed if refund is made within forty-five days of later of (1) return due date or (2) actual filing of return.
2. For underpayments of tax, the interest rate is equal to the three-month Treasury bill rate plus three percentage points. For overpayments, the interest rate is equal to the federal short-term rate plus two percentage points.

G. Taxpayer Penalties

1. Penalties may be imposed for late filing or failure to file, and late payment of tax.

   a. **Late filing** or failure to file penalty is 5% of the net tax due per month (up to 25%).

   b. **Late payment** of tax penalty is 1% of the net tax due per month (up to 25%).

      (1) For any month to which both of the above apply, the late filing penalty is reduced by the late payment penalty so that the maximum is 5% per month (up to 25%)

      (2) For returns not filed within sixty days of due date (including extensions), the IRS may assess a minimum late filing penalty which is the lesser of $100 or the amount of net tax due.

2. An **accuracy-related penalty of 20%** of the underpayment applies if the underpayment of tax is attributable to one or more of the following: (1) negligence or disregard of rules and regulations, (2) any substantial understatement of income tax, (3) any substantial valuation overstatement, (4) any substantial overstatement of pension liabilities, or (5) any substantial gift or estate tax valuation understatement.

   a. Accuracy-related penalty does not apply if the underpayment is due to reasonable cause, or there is adequate disclosure and the position has a reasonable basis for being sustained.

   b. **Negligence penalty** applies to any careless, reckless, or intentional disregard of rules or regulations, and any failure to make a reasonable attempt to comply with the provisions of the tax law. Penalty is imposed only on the portion of tax liability due to negligence, and can be avoided by adequate disclosure of a position that has a reasonable basis.

   c. **Substantial understatement of income tax penalty** applies if the understatement exceeds the greater of (1) 10% of the tax due, or (2) $5,000 ($10,000 for most corporations). Penalty can be avoided by adequate disclosure of a position that has a reasonable basis, or if there is substantial authority for the position taken.

   d. **Substantial overstatement penalty** may be imposed if the value (or adjusted basis) of property stated on the return is 200% or more of the amount determined to be correct.

      (1) Penalty applies to the extent resulting income tax underpayment exceeds $5,000 ($10,000 for most corporations).

      (2) Penalty is applied at a 40% rate if gross overvaluation is 400% or more of the amount determined to be correct.

   e. **Substantial overstatement of pension liabilities penalty** applies if the amount of stated pension liabilities is 200% or more of the amount determined to be correct. Penalty is 40% if misstatement is 400% or more, but penalty is not applicable if resulting underpayment is $1,000 or less.

   f. **Gift or estate tax valuation misstatement penalty** applies if the value of property on a gift or estate return is 50% or less of the amount determined to be correct.

      (1) Penalty is 40% if valuation used is 25% or less of amount determined to be correct.

      (2) No penalty if resulting understatement of tax is $5,000 or less.

3. **Civil fraud penalty** is 75% of the portion of underpayment attributable to fraud. The accuracy-related penalty does not apply to the portion of underpayment subject to the fraud penalty.

IX. SOURCES OF FEDERAL TAX AUTHORITY

A. The Internal Revenue Code (IRC) is the basic foundation of federal tax law, and represents a codification of the federal tax laws of the United States.

1. A series of self-contained revenue acts were first codified into an organized framework with the Internal Revenue Code of 1939. Subsequently, the 1939 IRC was reorganized and replaced with the 1954 IRC. In 1986, the Code's name was changed to the IRC of 1986, and has been frequently amended since then (e.g., Jobs and Growth Tax Relief Reconciliation Act of 2003).

2. The Internal Revenue Code of 1986 is actually Title 26 of the United States Code, and is generally divided into an orderly framework as follows: Subtitles; Chapters; Subchapters; Parts; Subparts; Sections; and Subsections.

3. **Subtitles** are denoted with a capital letter, with most pertaining to a general area of tax law as follows:

Subtitle	Topic
A	Income Taxes
B	Estate and Gift Taxes
C	Employment Taxes
D	Miscellaneous Excise Taxes
E	Alcohol, Tobacco, and Certain Other Excise Taxes
F	Procedure and Administration
G	The Joint Committee on Taxation
H	Financing of Presidential Election Campaigns
I	Trust Fund Code
J	Coal Industry Health Benefits
K	Group Health Plan Requirements

4. Each subtitle generally contains a number of **chapters** that are numbered in ascending order throughout the Code. Each chapter generally contains the tax rules that relate to a more narrowly defined area of law than is addressed by a subtitle. For example, Subtitle A—Income Taxes is divided as follows:

Chapter	Topic
1	Normal Taxes and Surtaxes
2	Tax on Self-Employment Income
3	Withholding of Tax on Nonresident Aliens and Foreign Corporations
4	[Repealed]
5	[Repealed]
6	Consolidated Returns

5. Chapters of the IRC are further divided into **subchapters** with each subchapter pertaining to a more narrowly defined area of tax law than is addressed by a chapter. For example, Chapter 1, Normal Taxes and Surtaxes includes Subchapter C—corporate distributions and adjustments, Subchapter K—partners and partnerships, and Subchapter S—tax treatment of S corporations and shareholders.

6. Subchapters are generally divided into **parts,** which are then frequently divided into subparts. Additionally, subparts are divided into **sections** that represent the organizational division of the Internal Revenue Code to which persons dealing with tax matters most often refer (e.g., Sec. 351 transfers to a controlled corporation, Sec. 1231 gains and losses, Sec. 1245 recapture).

7. Code sections are often divided into smaller divisions that may include subsections, paragraphs, subparagraphs, and clauses. Sections are denoted by numbers (1, 2, 3, etc.), subsections by lowercase letters (a, b, c, etc.), paragraphs by numbers (1, 2, 3, etc.), subparagraphs by capital letters (A, B, C, etc.), and clauses by lowercase roman numerals (i, ii, iii, etc.). This organizational scheme is important because the IRC contains many cross references which indicate the scope or limit the application of a provision.

EXAMPLE: Sec. 7701 is a definitional section that begins. "When used in title..." and then goes on to provide a series of definitions. As a result, a definition found in Sec. 7701 applies to all of the Internal Revenue of Code of 1986.

EXAMPLE: Code Sec. 311(b) provides a gain recognition rule that applies to a corporation when it distributes appreciated property to a shareholder. However, its application is limited in that it only applies to distributions described in Subpart A (i.e., Code Secs. 301 through 307). Code Sec. 311(b)'s position within the overall Code framework is as follows:

Title: Internal Revenue Code of 1986
   Subtitle A: Income Taxes
      Chapter 1: Normal taxes and surtaxes
         Subchapter C: Corporate distributions and adjustments
            Part I: Distributions by corporations
               Subpart B: Effects on corporation
                  Section 311: Tax liability of corporation on distributions
                     Subsection (b): Distributions of appreciated property
                        Paragraph (1): In general. If—
                           Subparagraph (A): "a corporation distributes property...in a distribution to which Subpart A applies..."

B. The IRC gives the Treasury Department or its delegate (the Commissioner of Internal Revenue) the authority to issue Regulations to provide administrative interpretation of the tax law. These regulations may be separated into two broad categories: legislative and interpretive. **Legislative regulations** are those issued by the IRS under a specific grant of authority to prescribe the operating rules for a statute (e.g., "the

Secretary shall prescribe such regulations as he may deem necessary," or "under regulations prescribed by the Secretary") and have the force and effect of law. The consolidated tax return regulations are an example of legislative regulations. In contrast, **interpretive regulations** are issued pursuant to the general rule-making authority granted to the IRS under Sec. 7805(a) and provide guidance regarding the IRS's interpretation of a statute. Although interpretive regulations do not have the force and effect of law, they are generally accorded substantial weight by the courts.

1. Regulations may also be categorized as proposed, temporary, or final regulations. Regulations are generally issued as **Proposed regulations** allowing interested parties a period of time of at least thirty days to comment and suggest changes. As a result of the comments received, the IRS may make changes to a proposed regulation before being published as a final regulation. Proposed regulations do not carry the same authority as temporary or final regulations. **Temporary regulations** are generally issued following recent tax legislation to provide interim guidance until final regulations are adopted. Temporary regulations (issued after 11/20/88) must be concurrently issued as proposed regulations, and these temporary regulations expire no later than three years from date of issue. Prior to its expiration, a temporary regulation is given the same weight as a final regulation. **Final regulations** are issued after public comments on proposed regulations are evaluated. Final regulations supersede any existing temporary regulations.

2. Regulations are organized in a sequential system with numbers preceding and following a decimal point. The numbers preceding the decimal point indicate the type of regulation or applicable are of tax law to which they pertain, while the numbers immediately following a decimal point indicate the IRC section being interpreted. Some of the more common prefixes include

Number	Type
1	Income Tax
20	Estate Tax
25	Gift Tax
301	Administrative and Procedural Matters
601	Procedural Rules

    The numbers and letters to the right of the section number indicate the regulation number and smaller divisions of the regulation (e.g., paragraph, subparagraph). These regulation numbers and paragraphs do not necessarily correspond to the subsection of the Code being interpreted. For example, Reg. 1.267(d)-1(a)(4) provides four examples of the application of Code Sec. 267(d) concerning the determination of recognized gain where a loss was previously disallowed. The citation represents subparagraph (4) or paragraph (a) of the first regulation interpreting Code Sec. 267(d). The citation of temporary regulation includes a "T" which indicates the nature of the regulation as temporary. For example, 1.45D-1T is a temporary regulation that explains the rules and conditions for claiming the new markets tax credit of Code Sec. 45.

C. **Revenue rulings** have less force and effect than regulations, but are second to regulations as important administrative sources of federal tax law. A revenue ruling gives the IRS's interpretation of how the Code and regulations apply to a specific fact situation, and therefore indicates how the IRS will treat similar transactions. Revenue rulings can be relied upon as authority by all taxpayers, and are published in the Internal Revenue Bulletin and later in the Cumulative Bulletin. The current status of a revenue ruling can be checked in the most current index to the Cumulative Bulletin. **Revenue procedures** announce administrative practices followed by the IRS, and are published in the Internal Revenue Bulletin and later in the Cumulative Bulletin. Revenue procedures provide guidelines that taxpayers must meet in order to obtain a revenue ruling, and also indicate areas in which the IRS will not issue revenue rulings. A **private letter ruling** is a written statement issued to the taxpayer who requested advice concerning a specific transaction. Although issued only to a specific taxpayer, private letter rulings are useful because they indicate how the IRS may treat a similar transaction, and are included in the list of substantial authority upon which a taxpayer may rely to avoid certain statutory penalties.

MULTIPLE-CHOICE QUESTIONS (1-219)

1. Richard Brown, who retired on May 31, 2003, receives a monthly pension benefit of $700 payable for life. His life expectancy at the date of retirement is ten years. The first pension check was received on June 15, 2003. During his years of employment, Brown contributed $12,000 to the cost of his company's pension plan. How much of the pension amounts received may Brown exclude from taxable income for the years 2003, 2004, and 2005?

	2003	*2004*	*2005*
a.	$0	$0	$0
b.	$4,900	$4,900	$4,900
c.	$ 700	$1,200	$1,200
d.	$4,900	$8,400	$8,400

2. Fuller was the owner and beneficiary of a $200,000 life insurance policy on a parent. Fuller sold the policy to Decker, for $25,000. Decker paid a total of $40,000 in premiums. Upon the death of the parent, what amount must Decker include in gross income?
- a. $0
- b. $135,000
- c. $160,000
- d. $200,000

3. Seymour Thomas named his wife, Penelope, the beneficiary of a $100,000 (face amount) insurance policy on his life. The policy provided that upon his death, the proceeds would be paid to Penelope with interest over her present life expectancy, which was calculated at twenty-five years. Seymour died during 2003, and Penelope received a payment of $5,200 from the insurance company. What amount should she include in her gross income for 2003?
- a. $ 200
- b. $1,200
- c. $4,200
- d. $5,200

4. Under a "cafeteria plan" maintained by an employer,
- a. Participation must be restricted to employees, and their spouses and minor children.
- b. At least three years of service are required before an employee can participate in the plan.
- c. Participants may select their own menu of benefits.
- d. Provision may be made for deferred compensation other than 401(k) plans.

5. David Autrey was covered by an $80,000 group-term life insurance policy of which his wife was the beneficiary. Autrey's employer paid the entire cost of the policy, for which the uniform annual premium was $8 per $1,000 of coverage. Autrey died during 2003, and his wife was paid the $80,000 proceeds of the insurance policy. What amount of group-term life insurance proceeds must be included in gross income by Autrey's widow?
- a. $0
- b. $30,000
- c. $50,000
- d. $80,000

6. Howard O'Brien, an employee of Ogden Corporation, died on June 30, 2003. During July, Ogden made employee death payments (which do not represent the proceeds of life insurance) of $10,000 to his widow, and $10,000 to his fifteen-year-old son. What amounts should be included in gross income by the widow and son in their respective tax returns for 2003?

	Widow	*Son*
a.	$ 5,000	$ 5,000
b.	$ 5,000	$10,000
c.	$ 7,500	$ 7,500
d.	$10,000	$10,000

7. John Budd files a joint return with his wife. Budd's employer pays 100% of the cost of all employees' group-term life insurance under a qualified plan. Under this plan, the maximum amount of tax-free coverage that may be provided for Budd by his employer is
- a. $100,000
- b. $ 50,000
- c. $ 10,000
- d. $ 5,000

8. During the current year Hal Leff sustained a serious injury in the course of his employment. As a result of this injury, Hal received the following payments during the year:

Workers' compensation	$2,400
Reimbursement from his employer's accident and health plan for medical expenses paid by Hal and not deducted by him	1,800
Damages for physical injuries	8,000

The amount to be included in Hal's gross income for the current year should be
- a. $12,200
- b. $ 8,000
- c. $ 1,800
- d. $0

9. James Martin received the following compensation and fringe benefits from his employer during 2003:

Salary	$50,000
Year-end bonus	10,000
Medical insurance premiums paid by employer	1,000
Reimbursement of qualified moving expenses	5,000

What amount of the preceding payments should be included in Martin's 2003 gross income?
- a. $60,000
- b. $61,000
- c. $65,000
- d. $66,000

10. On February 1, 2003, Hall learned that he was bequeathed 500 shares of common stock under his father's will. Hall's father had paid $2,500 for the stock in 1999. Fair market value of the stock on February 1, 2003, the date of his father's death, was $4,000 and had increased to $5,500 six months later. The executor of the estate elected the alternate valuation date for estate tax purposes. Hall sold the stock for $4,500 on June 1, 2003, the date that the executor distributed the stock to him. How much income should Hall include in his 2003 individual income tax return for the inheritance of the 500 shares of stock that he received from his father's estate?
- a. $5,500
- b. $4,000
- c. $2,500
- d. $0

11. In 2003, Gail Judd received the following dividends from:

Benefit Life Insurance Co., on Gail's life insurance policy (Total dividends received have not yet exceeded accumulated premiums paid) $100

Safe National Bank, on bank's common stock   300

Roe Mfg. Corp., a Delaware corporation, on preferred stock   500

What amount of dividend income should Gail report in her 2003 income tax return?

    a. $900

    b. $800

    c. $500

    d. $300

12. Amy Finch had the following cash receipts during 2003:

Dividend from a mutual insurance company on a life insurance policy $500

Dividend on listed corporation stock; payment date by corporation was 12/30/02, but Amy received the dividend in the mail on 1/2/03   875

Total dividends received to date on the life insurance policy do not exceed the aggregated premiums paid by Amy. How much should Amy report for dividend income for 2003?

    a. $1,375

    b. $ 875

    c. $ 500

    d. $0

13. Jack and Joan Mitchell, married taxpayers and residents of a separate property state, elect to file a joint return for 2003 during which they received the following dividends:

	Received by	
	Jack	Joan
Alert Corporation (a qualified, domestic corporation)	$400	$ 50
Canadian Mines, Inc. (a Canadian company)		300
Eternal Life-Mutual Insurance Company (dividends on life insurance policy)	200	

Total dividends received to date on the life insurance policy do not exceed cumulative premiums paid. For 2003, what amount should the Mitchells report on their joint return as dividend income?

    a. $550

    b. $600

    c. $750

    d. $800

14. During 2000, Karen purchased 100 shares of preferred stock of Boling Corp. for $5,500. During 2003, Karen received a stock dividend of ten additional shares of Boling Corp. preferred stock. On the date the preferred stock was distributed, it had a fair market value of $60 per share. What is Karen's basis in the ten shares of preferred stock that she received as a dividend?

    a. $0

    b. $500

    c. $550

    d. $600

15. Micro Corp., a calendar-year accrual-basis corporation, purchased a five-year, 8%, $100,000 taxable corporate bond for $108,530 on July 1, 2003, the date the bond was issued. The bond paid interest semiannually. Micro elected to amortize the bond premium. For Micro's 2003 tax return, the bond premium amortization for 2003 should be

I. Computed under the constant yield to maturity method.

II. Treated as an offset to the interest income on the bond.

    a.   I only.

    b.   II only.

    c.   Both I and II.

    d.   Neither I nor II.

16. In a tax year where the taxpayer pays qualified education expenses, interest income on the redemption of qualified US Series EE Bonds may be excluded from gross income. The exclusion is subject to a modified gross income limitation and a limit of aggregate bond proceeds in excess of qualified higher education expenses. Which of the following is(are) true?

I. The exclusion applies for education expenses incurred by the taxpayer, the taxpayer's spouse, or any person whom the taxpayer may claim as a dependent for the year.

II. "Otherwise qualified higher education expenses" must be reduced by qualified scholarships not includible in gross income.

    a.   I only.

    b.   II only.

    c.   Both I and II.

    d.   Neither I nor II.

17. During 2003 Kay received interest income as follows:

On US Treasury certificates $4,000

On refund of 2001 federal income tax   500

The total amount of interest subject to tax in Kay's 2003 tax return is

    a. $4,500

    b. $4,000

    c. $ 500

    d. $0

18. Charles and Marcia are married cash-basis taxpayers. In 2003, they had interest income as follows:

- $500 interest on federal income tax refund.
- $600 interest on state income tax refund.
- $800 interest on federal government obligations.
- $1,000 interest on state government obligations.

What amount of interest income is taxable on Charles and Marcia's 2003 joint income tax return?

    a. $ 500

    b. $1,100

    c. $1,900

    d. $2,900

19. Clark bought Series EE US Savings Bonds in 2003. Redemption proceeds will be used for payment of college tuition for Clark's dependent child. One of the conditions that must be met for tax exemption of accumulated interest on these bonds is that the

    a.   Purchaser of the bonds must be the sole owner of the bonds (or joint owner with his or her spouse).

    b.   Bonds must be bought by a parent (or both parents) and put in the name of the dependent child.

    c.   Bonds must be bought by the owner of the bonds before the owner reaches the age of twenty-four.

    d.   Bonds must be transferred to the college for redemption by the college rather than by the owner of the bonds.

20. Daniel Kelly received interest income from the following sources in 2003:

New York Port Authority bonds	$1,000
Puerto Rico Commonwealth bonds	1,800

What portion of such interest is tax exempt?

a. $0
b. $1,000
c. $1,800
d. $2,800

21. In 2003 Uriah Stone received the following interest payments:

- Interest of $400 on refund of federal income tax for 2001.
- Interest of $300 on award for personal injuries sustained in an automobile accident during 2000.
- Interest of $1,500 on municipal bonds.
- Interest of $1,000 on United States savings bonds (Series HH).

What amount, if any, should Stone report as interest income on his 2003 tax return?

a. $0
b. $ 700
c. $1,700
d. $3,200

22. For the year ended December 31, 2003, Don Raff earned $1,000 interest at Ridge Savings Bank on a certificate of deposit scheduled to mature in 2005. In January 2004, before filing his 2003 income tax return, Raff incurred a forfeiture penalty of $500 for premature withdrawal of the funds. Raff should treat this $500 forfeiture penalty as a

a. Reduction of interest earned in 2003, so that only $500 of such interest is taxable on Raff's 2003 return.
b. Deduction from 2004 adjusted gross income, deductible only if Raff itemizes his deductions for 2004.
c. Penalty **not** deductible for tax purposes.
d. Deduction from gross income in arriving at 2004 adjusted gross income.

23. Which payment(s) is(are) included in a recipient's gross income?

I. Payment to a graduate assistant for a part-time teaching assignment at a university. Teaching is not a requirement toward obtaining the degree.
II. A grant to a Ph.D. candidate for his participation in a university-sponsored research project for the benefit of the university.

a. I only.
b. II only.
c. Both I and II.
d. Neither I nor II.

24. Majors, a candidate for a graduate degree, received the following scholarship awards from the university in 2003:

- $10,000 for tuition, fees, books, and supplies required for courses.
- $2,000 stipend for research services required by the scholarship.

What amount of the scholarship awards should Majors include as taxable income in 2003?

a. $12,000
b. $10,000
c. $ 2,000
d. $0

25. In July 1988, Dan Farley leased a building to Robert Shelter for a period of fifteen years at a monthly rental of $1,000 with no option to renew. At that time the building had a remaining estimated useful life of twenty years.

Prior to taking possession of the building, Shelter made improvements at a cost of $18,000. These improvements had an estimated useful life of twenty years at the commencement of the lease period. The lease expired on June 30, 2003, at which point the improvements had a fair market value of $2,000. The amount that Farley, the landlord, should include in his gross income for 2003 is

a. $ 6,000
b. $ 8,000
c. $10,000
d. $18,500

26. Bob and Sue Stewart were divorced in 2001. Under the terms of their divorce decree, Bob paid alimony to Sue at the rate of $50,000 in 2001, $20,000 in 2002, and nothing in 2003. What amount of alimony recapture must be included in Bob's gross income for 2003?

a. $0
b. $23,283
c. $30,000
d. $32,500

27. Which of the following conditions must be present in a post-1984 divorce agreement for a payment to qualify as deductible alimony?

I. Payments must be in cash.
II. The payment must end at the recipient's death

a. I only.
b. II only.
c. Both I and II.
d. Neither I nor II.

28. Darr, an employee of Sorce C corporation, is not a shareholder. Which of the following would be included in a taxpayer's gross income?

a. Employer-provided medical insurance coverage under a health plan.
b. A $10,000 gift from the taxpayer's grandparents.
c. The fair market value of land that the taxpayer inherited from an uncle.
d. The dividend income on shares of stock that the taxpayer received for services rendered.

29. With regard to the inclusion of social security benefits in gross income for the 2003 tax year, which of the following statements is correct?

a. The social security benefits in excess of modified adjusted gross income are included in gross income.
b. The social security benefits in excess of one half the modified adjusted gross income are included in gross income.
c. Eighty-five percent of the social security benefits is the maximum amount of benefits to be included in gross income.
d. The social security benefits in excess of the modified adjusted gross income over $32,000 are included in gross income.

30. Perle, a dentist, billed Wood $600 for dental services. Wood paid Perle $200 cash and built a bookcase for Perle's office in full settlement of the bill. Wood sells comparable bookcases for $350. What amount should Perle include in taxable income as a result of this transaction?
- a. $0
- b. $200
- c. $550
- d. $600

31. John and Mary were divorced in 2002. The divorce decree provides that John pay alimony of $10,000 per year, to be reduced by 20% on their child's 18th birthday. During 2003, John paid $7,000 directly to Mary and $3,000 to Spring College for Mary's tuition. What amount of these payments should be reported as income in Mary's 2003 income tax return?
- a. $ 5,600
- b. $ 8,000
- c. $ 8,600
- d. $10,000

32. Clark filed Form 1040EZ for the 2002 taxable year. In July 2003, Clark received a state income tax refund of $900, plus interest of $10, for overpayment of 2002 state income tax. What amount of the state tax refund and interest is taxable in Clark's 2003 federal income tax return?
- a. $0
- b. $ 10
- c. $900
- d. $910

33. Hall, a divorced person and custodian of her twelve-year-old child, submitted the following information to the CPA who prepared her 2003 return:

The divorce agreement, executed in 2000, provides for Hall to receive $3,000 per month, of which $600 is designated as child support. After the child reaches age eighteen, the monthly payments are to be reduced to $2,400 and are to continue until remarriage or death. However, for the year 2003, Hall received a total of only $5,000 from her former husband. Hall paid an attorney $2,000 in 2003 in a suit to collect the alimony owed.

What amount should be reported in Hall's 2003 return as alimony income?
- a. $28,800
- b. $ 5,000
- c. $ 3,000
- d. $0

34. Lee, an attorney, uses the cash receipts and disbursements method of reporting. In 2003, a client gave Lee 500 shares of a listed corporation's stock in full satisfaction of a $10,000 legal fee the client owed to Lee. This stock had a fair market value of $8,000 on the date it was given to Lee. The client's basis for this stock was $6,000. Lee sold the stock for cash in January 2004. In Lee's 2003 income tax return, what amount of income should be reported in connection with the receipt of the stock?
- a. $10,000
- b. $ 8,000
- c. $ 6,000
- d. $0

35. In 1999, Ross was granted an incentive stock option (ISO) by her employer as part of an executive compensation package. Ross exercised the ISO in 2001 and sold the stock in 2003 at a gain. Ross was subject to regular tax for the year in which the
- a.   ISO was granted.
- b.   ISO was exercised.
- c.   Stock was sold.
- d.   Employer claimed a compensation deduction for the ISO.

36. Ed and Ann Ross were divorced in January 2003. In accordance with the divorce decree, Ed transferred the title in their home to Ann in 2003. The home, which had a fair market value of $150,000, was subject to a $50,000 mortgage that had twenty more years to run. Monthly mortgage payments amount to $1,000. Under the terms of settlement, Ed is obligated to make the mortgage payments on the home for the full remaining twenty-year term of the indebtedness, regardless of how long Ann lives. Ed made twelve mortgage payments in 2003. What amount is taxable as alimony in Ann's 2003 return?
- a. $0
- b. $ 12,000
- c. $100,000
- d. $112,000

37. Income in respect of a cash-basis decedent
- a.   Covers income earned and collected after a decedent's death.
- b.   Receives a stepped-up basis in the decedent's estate.
- c.   Includes a bonus earned before the taxpayer's death but not collected until after death.
- d.   Must be included in the decedent's final income tax return.

38. The following information is available for Ann Drury for 2003:

Salary	$36,000
Premiums paid by employer on group-term life insurance in excess of $50,000	500
Proceeds from state lottery	5,000

How much should Drury report as gross income on her 2003 tax return?
- a. $36,000
- b. $36,500
- c. $41,000
- d. $41,500

39. Mr. and Mrs. Alvin Charak took a foster child, Robert, into their home in 2003. A state welfare agency paid the Charaks $3,900 during the year for related expenses. Actual expenses incurred by the Charaks during 2003 in caring for Robert amounted to $3,000. The remaining $900 was spent by the Charaks in 2003 towards their own personal expenses. How much of the foster child payments is taxable income to the Charaks in 2003?
- a. $0
- b. $ 900
- c. $2,900
- d. $3,900

40. Pierre, a headwaiter, received tips totaling $2,000 in December 2002. On January 5, 2004, Pierre reported this tip income to his employer in the required written statement.

At what amount, and in which year, should this tip income be included in Pierre's gross income?

- a. $2,000 in 2003.
- b. $2,000 in 2004.
- c. $1,000 in 2003, and $1,000 in 2004.
- d. $ 167 in 2003, and $1,833 in 2004.

41. With regard to the alimony deduction in connection with a 2003 divorce, which one of the following statements is correct?

- a. Alimony is deductible by the payor spouse, and includible by the payee spouse, to the extent that payment is contingent on the status of the divorced couple's children.
- b. The divorced couple may be members of the same household at the time alimony is paid, provided that the persons do not live as husband and wife.
- c. Alimony payments must terminate on the death of the payee spouse.
- d. Alimony may be paid either in cash or in property.

42. In 2003, Joan accepted and received a $10,000 award for outstanding civic achievement. Joan was selected without any action on her part, and no future services are expected of her as a condition of receiving the award. What amount should Joan include in her 2003 adjusted gross income in connection with this award?

- a. $0
- b. $ 4,000
- c. $ 5,000
- d. $10,000

43. In 2003, Emil Gow won $5,000 in a state lottery. Also in 2003, Emil spent $400 for the purchase of lottery tickets. Emil elected the standard deduction on his 2003 income tax return. The amount of lottery winnings that should be included in Emil's 2003 taxable income is

- a. $0
- b. $2,000
- c. $4,600
- d. $5,000

44. Lake Corp., an accrual-basis calendar-year corporation, had the following 2003 receipts:

2004 advanced rental payments where the lease ends in 2005	$125,000
Lease cancellation payment from a five-year lease tenant	50,000

Lake had no restrictions on the use of the advanced rental payments and renders no services. What amount of income should Lake report on its 2003 tax return?

- a. $0
- b. $ 50,000
- c. $125,000
- d. $175,000

45. Paul Bristol, a cash-basis taxpayer, owns an apartment building. The following information was available for 2003:

- An analysis of the 2003 bank deposit slips showed recurring monthly rents received totaling $50,000.
- On March 1, 2003, the tenant in apartment 2B paid Bristol $2,000 to cancel the lease expiring on December 31, 2003.
- The lease of the tenant in apartment 3A expired on December 31, 2003, and the tenant left improve-

ments valued at $1,000. The improvements were not in lieu of any rent required to have been paid.

In computing net rental income for 2003, Bristol should report gross rents of

- a. $50,000
- b. $51,000
- c. $52,000
- d. $53,000

46. Emil Gow owns a two-family house that has two identical apartments. Gow lives in one apartment and rents out the other. In 2003, the rental apartment was fully occupied and Gow received $7,200 in rent. During the year ended December 31, 2003, Gow paid the following:

Real estate taxes	$6,400
Painting of rental apartment	800
Annual fire insurance premium	600

In 2003, depreciation for the entire house was determined to be $5,000. What amount should Gow include in his adjusted gross income for 2003?

- a. $2,900
- b. $ 800
- c. $ 400
- d. $ 100

47. Amy Finch had the following cash receipts during 2003:

Net rent on vacant lot used by a car dealer (lessee pays all taxes, insurance, and other expenses on the lot)	$6,000
Advance rent from lessee of above vacant lot, such advance to be applied against rent for the last two months of the five-year lease in 2007	1,000

How much should Amy include in her 2003 taxable income for rent?

- a. $7,000
- b. $6,800
- c. $6,200
- d. $6,000

48. Royce Rentals, Inc., an accrual-basis taxpayer, reported rent receivable of $25,000 and $35,000 in its 2003 and 2002 balance sheets, respectively. During 2003, Royce received $50,000 in rent payments and $5,000 in nonrefundable rent deposits. In Royce's 2003 corporate income tax return, what amount should Royce include as rent revenue?

- a. $45,000
- b. $50,000
- c. $55,000
- d. $65,000

49. John Budd is single, with no dependents. During 2003, John received wages of $11,000 and state unemployment compensation benefits of $2,000. He had no other source of income. The amount of state unemployment compensation benefits that should be included in John's 2003 adjusted gross income is

- a. $2,000
- b. $1,000
- c. $ 500
- d. $0

50. A cash-basis taxpayer should report gross income

- a. Only for the year in which income is actually received in cash.
- b. Only for the year in which income is actually received whether in cash or in property.

c.   For the year in which income is either actually or constructively received in cash only.

d.   For the year in which income is either actually or constructively received, whether in cash or in property.

51. Which of the following taxpayers may use the cash method of accounting?

a.   A tax shelter.

b.   A qualified personal service corporation.

c.   A C corporation with annual gross receipts of $50,000,000.

d.   A manufacturer with annual gross receipts of $3,000,000.

52. In 2003, Stewart Corp. properly accrued $5,000 for an income item on the basis of a reasonable estimate. In 2004, after filing its 2003 federal income tax return, Stewart determined that the exact amount was $6,000. Which of the following statements is correct?

a.   No further inclusion of income is required as the difference is less than 25% of the original amount reported and the estimate had been made in good faith.

b.   The $1,000 difference is includible in Stewart's 2004 income tax return.

c.   Stewart is required to notify the IRS within 30 days of the determination of the exact amount of the item.

d.   Stewart is required to file an amended return to report the additional $1,000 of income.

53. Axis Corp. is an accrual-basis calendar-year corporation. On December 13, 2003, the Board of Directors declared a 2% of profits bonus to all employees for services rendered during 2003 and notified them in writing. None of the employees own stock in Axis. The amount represents reasonable compensation for services rendered and was paid on March 13, 2004. Axis' bonus expense may

a.   Not be deducted on Axis' 2003 tax return because the per share employee amount **cannot** be determined with reasonable accuracy at the time of the declaration of the bonus.

b.   Be deducted on Axis' 2003 tax return.

c.   Be deducted on Axis' 2004 tax return.

d.   Not be deducted on Axis' tax return because payment is a disguised dividend.

54. On December 1, 2002, Michaels, a self-employed cash-basis taxpayer, borrowed $100,000 to use in her business. The loan was to be repaid on November 30, 2003. Michaels paid the entire interest of $12,000 on December 1, 2002. What amount of interest was deductible on Michaels' 2003 income tax return?

a. $12,000

b. $11,000

c. $ 1,000

d. $0

55. Blair, CPA, uses the cash receipts and disbursements method of reporting. In 2003, a client gave Blair 100 shares of a listed corporation's stock in full satisfaction of a $5,000 accounting fee the client owed Blair. This stock had a fair market value of $4,000 on the date it was given to Blair. The client's basis for this stock was $3,000. Blair sold the stock for cash in January 2004. In Blair's 2003 return, what amount of income should be reported in connection with the receipt of the stock?

a. $0

b. $3,000

c. $4,000

d. $5,000

56. Unless the Internal Revenue Service consents to a change of method, the accrual method of tax reporting is generally mandatory for a sole proprietor when there are

	Accounts receivable for services rendered	Year-end merchandise inventories
a.	Yes	Yes
b.	Yes	No
c.	No	No
d.	No	Yes

57. Alex Burg, a cash-basis taxpayer, earned an annual salary of $80,000 at Ace Corp. in 2003, but elected to take only $50,000. Ace, which was financially able to pay Burg's full salary, credited the unpaid balance of $30,000 to Burg's account on the corporate books in 2003, and actually paid this $30,000 to Burg on January 30, 2004. How much of the salary is taxable to Burg in 2003?

a. $50,000

b. $60,000

c. $65,000

d. $80,000

58. Dr. Berger, a physician, reports on the cash basis. The following items pertain to Dr. Berger's medical practice in 2003:

Cash received from patients in 2003	$200,000
Cash received in 2003 from third-party reimbursers for services provided by Dr. Berger in 2002	30,000
Salaries paid to employees in 2003	20,000
Year-end 2003 bonuses paid to employees in 2004	1,000
Other expenses paid in 2003	24,000

What is Dr. Berger's net income for 2003 from his medical practice?

a. $155,000

b. $156,000

c. $185,000

d. $186,000

59. Which of the following taxpayers may use the cash method of accounting for tax purposes?

a.   Partnership that is designated as a tax shelter.

b.   Retail store with $2 million inventory, and $9 million average annual gross receipts.

c.   An international accounting firm.

d.   C corporation manufacturing exercise equipment with average annual gross receipts of $8 million.

60. The uniform capitalization method must be used by

I.   Manufacturers of tangible personal property.

II.   Retailers of personal property with $2 million dollars in average annual gross receipts for the three preceding years.

a.   I only.

b.   II only.

c.   Both I and II.

d.   Neither I nor II.

61. Mock operates a retail business selling illegal narcotic substances. Which of the following item(s) may Mock deduct in calculating business income?

I. Cost of merchandise.
II. Business expenses other than the cost of merchandise.

   a. I only.
   b. II only.
   c. Both I and II.
   d. Neither I nor II.

62. Banks Corp., a calendar-year corporation, reimburses employees for properly substantiated qualifying business meal expenses. The employees are present at the meals, which are neither lavish nor extravagant, and the reimbursement is not treated as wages subject to withholdings. For 2003, what percentage of the meal expense may Banks deduct?

   a. 0%
   b. 50%
   c. 80%
   d. 100%

63. Which of the following costs is not included in inventory under the Uniform Capitalization rules for goods manufactured by the taxpayer?

   a. Research.
   b. Warehousing costs.
   c. Quality control.
   d. Taxes excluding income taxes.

64. Under the uniform capitalization rules applicable to property acquired for resale, which of the following costs should be capitalized with respect to inventory if **no** exceptions are met?

	Marketing costs	Off-site storage costs
a.	Yes	Yes
b.	Yes	No
c.	No	No
d.	No	Yes

65. In the case of a corporation that is **not** a financial institution, which of the following statements is correct with regard to the deduction for bad debts?

   a. Either the reserve method or the direct charge-off method may be used, if the election is made in the corporation's first taxable year.
   b. On approval from the IRS, a corporation may change its method from direct charge-off to reserve.
   c. If the reserve method was consistently used in prior years, the corporation may take a deduction for a reasonable addition to the reserve for bad debts.
   d. A corporation is required to use the direct charge-off method rather than the reserve method.

66. Ram Corp.'s operating income for the year ended December 31, 2003, amounted to $100,000. Included in Ram's 2003 operating expenses is a $6,000 insurance premium on a policy insuring the life of Ram's president. Ram is beneficiary of this policy. In Ram's 2003 tax return, what amount should be deducted for the $6,000 life insurance premium?

   a. $6,000
   b. $5,000
   c. $1,000
   d. $0

67. Jason Budd, CPA, reports on the cash basis. In April 2002, Budd billed a client $3,500 for the following professional services:

Personal estate planning	$2,000
Personal tax return preparation	1,000
Compilation of business financial statements	500

No part of the $3,500 was ever paid. In April 2003, the client declared bankruptcy, and the $3,500 obligation became totally uncollectible. What loss can Budd deduct on his 2003 tax return for this bad debt?

   a. $0
   b. $ 500
   c. $1,500
   d. $3,500

68. Earl Cook, who worked as a machinist for Precision Corp., loaned Precision $1,000 in 2000. Cook did not own any of Precision's stock, and the loan was not a condition of Cook's employment by Precision. In 2003, Precision declared bankruptcy, and Cook's note receivable from Precision became worthless. What loss can Cook claim on his 2003 income tax return?

   a. $0
   b. $ 500 long-term capital loss.
   c. $1,000 short-term capital loss.
   d. $1,000 business bad debt.

69. During the 2003 holiday season, Palo Corp. gave business gifts to seventeen customers. These gifts, which were not of an advertising nature, had the following fair market values:

4	at	$ 10
4	at	25
4	at	50
5	at	100

How much of these gifts was deductible as a business expense for 2003?

   a. $840
   b. $365
   c. $140
   d. $0

70. Jennifer, who is single, has the following items of income and deduction for 2003:

Salary	$30,000
Itemized deductions (all attributable to a personal casualty loss when a hurricane destroyed her residence)	45,000
Personal exemption	3,050

What is the amount of Jennifer's net operating loss for 2003?

   a. $0
   b. $15,000
   c. $18,050
   d. $45,000

71. Robin Moore, a self-employed taxpayer, reported the following information for 2003:

Income:	Dividends from investments	$ 500
	Net short-term capital gain on sale of investment	1,000
Deductions:	Net loss from business	(6,000)
	Personal exemption	(3,050)
	Standard deduction	(4,750)

What is the amount of Moore's net operating loss for 2003?
- a. $4,500
- b. $5,000
- c. $6,000
- d. $9,250

72. Destry, a single taxpayer, reported the following on his US Individual Income Tax Return Form 1040:

Income	
Wages	$ 5,000
Interest on savings account	1,000
Net rental income	4,000
Deductions	
Personal exemption	$ 3,050
Standard deduction	4,750
Net business loss	16,000
Net short-term capital loss	2,000

What is Destry's net operating loss that is available for carryback or carryforward?
- a. $ 7,000
- b. $ 9,000
- c. $12,750
- d. $16,000

73. Cobb, an unmarried individual, had an adjusted gross income of $200,000 in 2003 before any IRA deduction, taxable social security benefits, or passive activity losses. Cobb incurred a loss of $30,000 in 2003 from rental real estate in which he actively participated. What amount of loss attributable to this rental real estate can be used in 2003 as an offset against income from nonpassive sources?
- a. $0
- b. $12,500
- c. $25,000
- d. $30,000

74. The rule limiting the allowability of passive activity losses and credits applies to
- a. Partnerships.
- b. S corporations.
- c. Personal service corporations.
- d. Widely held C corporations.

75. Don Wolf became a general partner in Gata Associates on January 1, 2003, with a 5% interest in Gata's profits, losses, and capital. Gata is a distributor of auto parts. Wolf does not materially participate in the partnership business. For the year ended December 31, 2003, Gata had an operating loss of $100,000. In addition, Gata earned interest of $20,000 on a temporary investment. Gata has kept the principal temporarily invested while awaiting delivery of equipment that is presently on order. The principal will be used to pay for this equipment. Wolf's passive loss for 2003 is
- a. $0
- b. $4,000
- c. $5,000
- d. $6,000

76. With regard to the passive loss rules involving rental real estate activities, which one of the following statements is correct?
- a. The term "passive activity" includes any rental activity without regard as to whether or not the taxpayer materially participates in the activity.

- b. Gross investment income from interest and dividends **not** derived in the ordinary course of a trade or business is treated as passive activity income that can be offset by passive rental activity losses when the "active participation" requirement is **not** met.
- c. Passive rental activity losses may be deducted only against passive income, but passive rental activity credits may be used against tax attributable to nonpassive activities.
- d. The passive activity rules do **not** apply to taxpayers whose adjusted gross income is $300,000 or less.

77. If an individual taxpayer's passive losses and credits relating to rental real estate activities cannot be used in the current year, then they may be carried
- a. Back two years, but they cannot be carried forward.
- b. Forward up to a maximum period of twenty years, but they cannot be carried back.
- c. Back two years or forward up to twenty years, at the taxpayer's election.
- d. Forward indefinitely or until the property is disposed of in a taxable transaction.

78. Aviation Corp. manufactures model airplanes for children. During 2003, Aviation purchased $203,000 of production machinery to be used in its business. For 2003, Aviation's taxable income before any Sec. 179 expense deduction was $7,000. What is the maximum amount of Sec. 179 expense election Aviation will be allowed to deduct for 2003 and the maximum amount of Sec. 179 expense election that can carryover to 2004?

	Expense	*Carryover*
a.	$ 7,000	$15,000
b.	$ 7,000	$18,000
c.	$22,000	$0
d.	$25,000	$0

79. Which of the following conditions must be satisfied for a taxpayer to expense, in the year of purchase, under Internal Revenue Code Section 179, the cost of new or used tangible depreciable personal property?

I. The property must be purchased for use in the taxpayer's active trade or business.
II. The property must be purchased from an unrelated party.

- a. I only.
- b. II only.
- c. Both I and II.
- d. Neither I nor II.

80. Krol Corp., a calendar-year taxpayer, purchased furniture and fixtures for use in its business and placed the property in service on November 1, 2003. The furniture and fixtures cost $56,000 and represented Krol's only acquisition of depreciable property during the year. Krol did **not** take additional first-year depreciation and did **not** elect to expense any part of the cost of the property under Sec. 179. What is the amount of Krol Corp.'s depreciation deduction for the furniture and fixtures under the Modified Accelerated Cost Recovery System (MACRS) for 2003?

a. $ 2,000
b. $ 2,667
c. $ 8,000
d. $16,000

81. On June 29, 2003, Sullivan purchased and placed into service an apartment building costing $360,000 including $30,000 for the land. What was Sullivan's MACRS deduction for the apartment building in 2003?

a. $7,091
b. $6,500
c. $6,000
d. $4,583

82. Data Corp., a calendar-year corporation, purchased and placed into service office equipment during November 2003. No other equipment was placed into service during 2003. Under the general MACRS depreciation system, what convention must Data use?

a. Full-year.
b. Half-year.
c. Midquarter.
d. Midmonth.

83. Under the modified accelerated cost recovery system (MACRS) of depreciation for property placed in service after 1986,

a. Used tangible depreciable property is excluded from the computation.
b. Salvage value is ignored for purposes of computing the MACRS deduction.
c. No type of straight-line depreciation is allowable.
d. The recovery period for depreciable realty must be at least 27.5 years.

84. With regard to depreciation computations made under the general MACRS method, the half-year convention provides that

a. One-half of the first year's depreciation is allowed in the year in which the property is placed in service, regardless of when the property is placed in service during the year, and a half-year's depreciation is allowed for the year in which the property is disposed of.
b. The deduction will be based on the number of months the property was in service, so that one-half month's depreciation is allowed for the month in which the property is placed in service and for the month in which it is disposed of.
c. Depreciation will be allowed in the first year of acquisition of the property only if the property is placed in service **no** later than June 30 for calendar-year corporations.
d. Depreciation will be allowed in the last year of the property's economic life only if the property is disposed of after June 30 of the year of disposition for calendar-year corporations.

85. In 2003, Roe Corp. purchased and placed in service a machine to be used in its manufacturing operations. This machine cost $201,000. What portion of the cost may Roe elect to treat as an expense rather than as a capital expenditure?

a. $20,000
b. $21,000
c. $24,000
d. $25,000

86. Easel Co. has elected to reimburse employees for business expenses under a nonaccountable plan. Easel does not require employees to provide proof of expenses and allows employees to keep any amount not spent. Under the plan, Mel, an Easel employee for a full year, gets $400 per month for business automobile expenses. At the end of the year Mel informs Easel that the only business expense incurred was for business mileage of 12,000 at a rate of 36 cents per mile, the IRS standard mileage rate at the time. Mel encloses a check for $660 to refund the overpayment to Easel. What amount should be reported in Mel's gross income for the year?

a. $0
b. $480
c. $4,320
d. $4,800

87. Adams owns a second residence that is used for both personal and rental purposes. During 2003, Adams used the second residence for 50 days and rented the residence for 200 days. Which of the following statements is correct?

a. Depreciation may not be deducted on the property under any circumstances.
b. A rental loss may be deducted if rental-related expenses exceed rental income.
c. Utilities and maintenance on the property must be divided between personal and rental use.
d. All mortgage interest and taxes on the property will be deducted to determine the property's net income or loss

88. Charles Gilbert, a corporate executive, incurred business-related unreimbursed expenses in 2003 as follows:

Entertainment	$900
Travel	700
Education	400

Assuming that Gilbert does not itemize deductions, how much of these expenses should he deduct on his 2003 tax return?

a. $0
b. $ 700
c. $1,300
d. $1,600

89. James, a calendar-year taxpayer, was employed and resided in Boston. On February 4, 2003, James was permanently transferred to Florida by his employer. James worked full-time for the entire year. In 2003, James incurred and paid the following unreimbursed expenses in relocating.

Lodging and travel expenses while moving	$1,000
Meals while in route to Florida	300
Cost of insuring household goods and personal effects during move	200
Cost of shipping household pets to new home	100
Costs of moving household furnishings and personal effects	3,000

What amount was deductible as moving expenses on James' 2003 tax return?

a. $4,600
b. $4,500
c. $4,300
d. $4,000

90. Martin Dawson, who resided in Detroit, was unemployed for the last six months of 2002. In January 2003, he moved to Houston to seek employment, and obtained a full-time job there in February. He kept this job for the balance of the year. Martin paid the following expenses in 2003 in connection with his move:

Rental of truck to move his personal belongings to Houston	$ 800
Penalty for breaking the lease on his Detroit apartment	300
Total	$1,100

How much can Martin deduct in 2003 for moving expenses?

    a. $0
    b. $ 300
    c. $ 800
    d. $1,100

91. Richard Putney, who lived in Idaho for five years, moved to Texas in 2003 to accept a new position. His employer reimbursed him in full for all direct moving costs, but did not pay for any part of the following indirect moving expenses incurred by Putney:

Househunting trips to Texas	$800
Temporary housing in Texas	900

How much of the indirect expenses can be deducted by Putney as moving expenses?

    a. $0
    b. $ 900
    c. $1,500
    d. $1,700

92. Which one of the following statements concerning Roth IRAs is **not** correct?

    a.   The maximum annual contribution to a Roth IRA is reduced if adjusted gross income exceeds certain thresholds.
    b.   Contributions to a Roth IRA are not deductible.
    c.   An individual is allowed to make contributions to a Roth IRA even after age 70½.
    d.   A contribution to a Roth IRA must be made by the due date for filing the individual's tax return for the year (including extensions).

93. What is the maximum amount of adjusted gross income that a taxpayer may have and still qualify to roll over the balance from a traditional individual retirement account (IRA) into a Roth IRA?

    a. $ 50,000
    b. $ 80,000
    c. $100,000
    d. $150,000

94. Which one of the following statements concerning an education IRA (Coverdell Education Savings Account) is **not** correct?

    a.   Contributions to an education IRA are not deductible.
    b.   A taxpayer may contribute up to $2,000 in 2003 to an education IRA to pay the costs of the designated beneficiary's higher education.
    c.   Eligibility for an education IRA is phased out if adjusted gross income exceeds certain threshold levels.
    d.   Contributions can be made to an education IRA on behalf of a beneficiary until the beneficiary reaches age twenty-one.

95. For 2003, Val and Pat White (both age 40) filed a joint return. Val earned $35,000 in wages and was covered by his employer's qualified pension plan. Pat was unemployed and received $5,000 in alimony payments for the first four months of the year before remarrying. The couple had no other income. Each contributed $3,000 to an IRA account. The allowable IRA deduction on their 2003 joint tax return is

    a. $6,000
    b. $4,000
    c. $3,000
    d. $2,000

96. Davis, a sole proprietor with no employees, has a Keogh profit-sharing plan to which he may contribute 15% of his annual earned income. For this purpose, "earned income" is defined as net self-employment earnings reduced by the

    a.   Deductible Keogh contribution.
    b.   Self-employment tax.
    c.   Self-employment tax and one-half of the deductible Keogh contribution.
    d.   Deductible Keogh contribution and one-half of the self-employment tax.

97. Ronald Birch, who is single and age 28, earned a salary of $40,000 in 2003 as a plumber employed by Lupo Company. Birch was covered for the entire year 2003 under Lupo's qualified pension plan for employees. In addition, Birch had a net income of $15,000 from self-employment in 2003. What is the maximum amount that Birch can deduct in 2003 for contributions to an individual retirement account (IRA)?

    a. $3,000
    b. $2,000
    c. $1,500
    d. $0

98. Sol and Julia Crane (both age 43) are married and filed a joint return for 2003. Sol earned a salary of $80,000 in 2003 from his job at Troy Corp., where Sol is covered by his employer's pension plan. In addition, Sol and Julia earned interest of $3,000 in 2003 on their joint savings account. Julia is not employed, and the couple had no other income. On July 15, 2003, Sol contributed $3,000 to an IRA for himself, and $3,000 to an IRA for his spouse. The allowable IRA deduction in the Cranes' 2003 joint return is

    a. $0
    b. $3,000
    c. $4,000
    d. $6,000

99. Paul and Lois Lee, both age fifty, are married and filed a joint return for 2003. Their 2003 adjusted gross income was $85,000, including Paul's $75,000 salary. Lois had no income of her own. Neither spouse was covered by an employer-sponsored pension plan. What amount could the Lees contribute to IRAs for 2003 to take advantage of their maximum allowable IRA deduction in their 2003 return?

    a. $3,000
    b. $3,500
    c. $6,000
    d. $7,000

100. In 2003, deductible contributions to a defined contribution qualified retirement plan on behalf of a self-employed individual whose income from self-employment is $50,000 are limited to

a. $ 2,000
b. $11,000
c. $40,000
d. $50,000

101. Which allowable deduction can be claimed in arriving at an individual's 2003 adjusted gross income?

    a.   Charitable contribution.
    b.   Foreign income taxes.
    c.   Tax return preparation fees.
    d.   Self-employed health insurance deduction.

102. Which one of the following statements concerning the deduction for interest on qualified education loans is **not** correct?

    a.   The deduction is available even if the taxpayer does not itemize deductions.
    b.   The deduction only applies to the first sixty months of interest payments.
    c.   Qualified education expenses include tuition fees, room, and board.
    d.   The educational expenses must relate to a period when the student was enrolled on at least a half-time basis.

103. Dale received $1,000 in 2003 for jury duty. In exchange for regular compensation from her employer during the period of jury service, Dale was required to remit the entire $1,000 to her employer in 2003. In Dale's 2003 income tax return, the $1,000 jury duty fee should be

    a.   Claimed in full as an itemized deduction.
    b.   Claimed as an itemized deduction to the extent exceeding 2% of adjusted gross income.
    c.   Deducted from gross income in arriving at adjusted gross income.
    d.   Included in taxable income without a corresponding offset against other income.

104. During 2003, George (age ten and claimed as a dependency exemption by his parents) received dividend income of $3,700, and had wages from an after-school job of $1,700. What is the amount that will be reported as George's taxable income for 2003?

    a. $0
    b. $ 650
    c. $3,450
    d. $4,700

105. Which of the following requirements must be met in order for a single individual to qualify for the additional standard deduction?

	Must be age 65 or older or blind	*Must support dependent child or aged parent*
a.	Yes	Yes
b.	No	No
c.	Yes	No
d.	No	Yes

106. Carroll, an unmarried taxpayer with an adjusted gross income of $100,000, incurred and paid the following unreimbursed medical expenses for the year:

Doctor bills resulting from a serious fall	$5,000
Cosmetic surgery that was necessary to correct a congenital deformity	$15,000

Carroll had no medical insurance. For regular income tax purposes, what was Carroll's maximum allowable medical

expense deduction, after the applicable threshold limitation, for the year?

    a. $0
    b. $12,500
    c. $15,000
    d. $20,000

107. Charlene and Gene Blair are married and filed a joint return for 2003. Their medical related expenditures for 2003 included the following:

Medical insurance premiums	$ 800
Medicines prescribed by doctors	450
Aspirin and over-the-counter cold capsules	80
Unreimbursed doctor fees	1,000
Transportation to and from doctors	150
Emergency room fee	500

The emergency room fee related to an injury incurred by the Blair's son, Eric, during a visit to their home. The Blairs graciously paid the bill; however, they provided no other support for Eric during the year. For 2003, Eric earned $12,000 as a self-employed house painter. Assuming the Blairs' adjusted gross income was $30,000, what amount of medical expenses can the Blairs deduct as an itemized deduction for 2003?

    a. $0
    b. $ 150
    c. $ 650
    d. $1,750

108. Tom and Sally White, married and filing joint income tax returns, derive their entire income from the operation of their retail stationery shop. Their 2003 adjusted gross income was $100,000. The Whites itemized their deductions on Schedule A for 2003. The following unreimbursed cash expenditures were among those made by the Whites during 2003:

Repair and maintenance of motorized wheelchair for physically handicapped dependent child	$ 600
Tuition, meals, lodging at special school for physically handicapped dependent child in an institution primarily for the availability of medical care, with meals and lodging furnished as necessary incidents to that care	8,000

Without regard to the adjusted gross income percentage threshold, what amount may the Whites claim in their 2003 return as qualifying medical expenses?

    a. $8,600
    b. $8,000
    c. $ 600
    d. $0

109. In 2003, Wells paid the following expenses:

Premiums on an insurance policy against loss of earnings due to sickness or accident	$3,000
Physical therapy after spinal surgery	2,000
Premium on an insurance policy that covers reimbursement for the cost of prescription drugs	500

In 2003, Wells recovered $1,500 of the $2,000 that she paid for physical therapy through insurance reimbursement from a group medical policy paid for by her employer. Disregarding the adjusted gross income percentage threshold, what amount could be claimed on Wells' 2003 income tax return for medical expenses?

    a. $4,000
    b. $3,500
    c. $1,000
    d. $ 500

110. Mr. and Mrs. Sloan incurred the following expenses on December 15, 2003, when they adopted a child:

Child's medical expenses	$5,000
Legal expenses	8,000
Agency fee	3,000

Before consideration of any "floor" or other limitation on deductibility, what amount of the above expenses may the Sloans deduct on their 2003 joint income tax return?

a. $16,000
b. $13,000
c. $11,000
d. $ 5,000

111. Ruth and Mark Cline are married and will file a joint 2003 income tax return. Among their expenditures during 2003 were the following discretionary costs that they incurred for the sole purpose of improving their physical appearance and self-esteem:

Face-lift for Ruth, performed by a licensed surgeon	$5,000
Hair transplant for Mark, performed by a licensed surgeon	3,600

Disregarding the adjusted gross income percentage threshold, what total amount of the aforementioned doctors' bills may be claimed by the Clines in their 2003 return as qualifying medical expenses?

a. $0
b. $3,600
c. $5,000
d. $8,600

112. During 2003, Scott charged $4,000 on his credit card for his dependent son's medical expenses. Payment to the credit card company had not been made by the time Scott filed his income tax return in 2004. However, in 2003, Scott paid a physician $2,800 for the medical expenses of his wife, who died in 2002. Disregarding the adjusted gross income percentage threshold, what amount could Scott claim in his 2003 income tax return for medical expenses?

a. $0
b. $2,800
c. $4,000
d. $6,800

113. Which one of the following expenditures qualifies as a deductible medical expense for tax purposes?

a. Diaper service.
b. Funeral expenses.
c. Nursing care for a healthy baby.
d. Premiums paid for Medicare B supplemental medical insurance.

114. Jon Stenger, a cash-basis taxpayer, had adjusted gross income of $35,000 in 2003. During the year he incurred and paid the following medical expenses:

Drugs and medicines prescribed by doctors	$ 300
Health insurance premiums	750
Doctors' fees	2,550
Eyeglasses	75
	$3,675

Stenger received $900 in 2003 as reimbursement for a portion of the doctors' fees. If Stenger were to itemize his deductions, what would be his allowable net medical expense deduction?

a. $0
b. $ 150
c. $1,050
d. $2,475

115. During 2003, Mr. and Mrs. Benson provided substantially all the support, in their own home, for their son John, age twenty-six, and for Mrs. Benson's cousin Nancy, age seventeen. John had $3,900 of income for 2003, and Nancy's income was $2,500. The Bensons paid the following medical expenses during the year:

Medicines and drugs:	
For themselves	$400
For John	500
For Nancy	100
Doctors:	
For themselves	600
For John	900
For Nancy	200

What is the total amount of medical expenses (before application of any limitation rules), that would enter into the calculation of itemized deductions on the Bensons' 2003 tax return?

a. $1,000
b. $1,300
c. $2,400
d. $2,700

116. All of the following taxes are deductible as itemized deductions by a self-employed taxpayer **except:**

a. Foreign real estate taxes
b. Foreign income taxes
c. Personal property taxes
d. One-half of self-employment taxes

117. Matthews was a cash-basis taxpayer whose records showed the following:

2003 state and local income taxes withheld	$1,500
2003 state estimated income taxes paid December 30, 2003	400
2003 federal income taxes withheld	2,500
2003 state and local income taxes paid April 17, 2004	300

What total amount was Matthews entitled to claim for taxes on her 2003 Schedule A of Form 1040?

a. $4,700
b. $2,200
c. $1,900
d. $1,500

118. In 2002, Farb, a cash-basis individual taxpayer, received an $8,000 invoice for personal property taxes. Believing the amount to be overstated by $5,000, Farb paid the invoiced amount under protest and immediately started legal action to recover the overstatement. In June 2003, the matter was resolved in Farb's favor, and he received a $5,000 refund. Farb itemizes his deductions on his tax returns. Which of the following statements is correct regarding the deductibility of the property taxes?

a. Farb should deduct $8,000 in his 2002 income tax return and should report the $5,000 refund as income in his 2003 income tax return.
b. Farb should **not** deduct any amount in his 2002 income tax return and should deduct $3,000 in his 2003 income tax return.
c. Farb should deduct $3,000 in his 2002 income tax return.

d. Farb should **not** deduct any amount in his 2002 income tax return when originally filed, and should file an amended 2002 income tax return in 2003.

119. In 2003, Burg paid $8,000 to the tax collector of Sun City for realty taxes on a two-family house owned in joint-tenancy between Burg and his mother. Of this amount, $3,800 covered back taxes for 2002, and $4,200 covered 2003 taxes. Burg resides on the second floor of the house, and his mother resides on the first floor. In Burg's itemized deductions on his 2003 return, what amount was Burg entitled to claim for realty taxes?

    a. $0
    b. $4,000
    c. $4,200
    d. $8,000

120. Sara Harding is a cash-basis taxpayer who itemized her deductions. The following information pertains to Sara's state income taxes for the taxable year 2003:

Withheld by employer in 2003		$2,000
Payments on 2003 estimate:		
4/15/03	$300	
6/15/03	300	
9/15/03	300	
1/15/04	300	1,200
Total paid and withheld		$3,200
Actual tax, per state return		3,000
Overpayment		$ 200

There was no balance of tax or refund due on Sara's 2002 state tax return. How much is deductible for state income taxes on Sara's 2003 federal income tax return?

    a. $2,800
    b. $2,900
    c. $3,000
    d. $3,200

121. During 2003, Jack and Mary Bronson paid the following taxes:

Taxes on residence (for period January 1 to September 30, 2003)	$2,700
State motor vehicle tax on value of the car	360

The Bronsons sold their house on June 30, 2003, under an agreement in which the real estate taxes were not prorated between the buyer and sellers. What amount should the Bronsons deduct as taxes in calculating itemized deductions for 2003?

    a. $1,800
    b. $2,160
    c. $2,700
    d. $3,060

122. George Granger sold a plot of land to Albert King on July 1, 2003. Granger had not paid any realty taxes on the land since 2001. Delinquent 2002 taxes amounted to $600, and 2003 taxes amounted to $700. King paid the 2002 and 2003 taxes in full in 2003, when he bought the land. What portion of the $1,300 is deductible by King in 2003?

    a. $ 353
    b. $ 700
    c. $ 962
    d. $1,300

123. During 2003 Mr. and Mrs. West paid the following taxes:

Property taxes on residence	$1,800
Special assessment for installation of a sewer system in their town	1,000
State personal property tax on their automobile	600
Property taxes on land held for long-term appreciation	300

What amount can the Wests deduct as property taxes in calculating itemized deductions for 2003?

    a. $2,100
    b. $2,700
    c. $3,100
    d. $3,700

124. Alex and Myra Burg, married and filing joint income tax returns, derive their entire income from the operation of their retail candy shop. Their 2003 adjusted gross income was $50,000. The Burgs itemized their deductions on Schedule A for 2003. The following unreimbursed cash expenditures were among those made by the Burgs during 2003:

State income tax	$1,200
Self-employment tax	7,650

What amount should the Burgs deduct for taxes in their itemized deductions on Schedule A for 2003?

    a. $1,200
    b. $3,825
    c. $5,025
    d. $7,650

125. The 2003 deduction by an individual taxpayer for interest on investment indebtedness is

    a. Limited to the investment interest paid in 2003.
    b. Limited to the taxpayer's 2003 interest income.
    c. Limited to the taxpayer's 2003 net investment income.
    d. Not limited.

126. The Browns borrowed $20,000, secured by their home, to purchase a new automobile. At the time of the loan, the fair market value of their home was $400,000, and it was unencumbered by other debt. The interest on the loan qualifies as

    a. Deductible personal interest.
    b. Deductible qualified residence interest.
    c. Nondeductible interest.
    d. Investment interest expense.

127. On January 2, 2000, the Philips paid $50,000 cash and obtained a $200,000 mortgage to purchase a home. In 2003 they borrowed $15,000 secured by their home, and used the cash to add a new room to their residence. That same year they took out a $5,000 auto loan.

The following information pertains to interest paid in 2003:

Mortgage interest	$17,000
Interest on room construction loan	1,500
Auto loan interest	500

For 2003, how much interest is deductible, prior to any itemized deduction limitations?

    a. $17,000
    b. $17,500
    c. $18,500
    d. $19,000

128. Jackson owns two residences. The second residence, which has never been used for rental purposes, is the only residence that is subject to a mortgage. The following expenses were incurred for the second residence in 2003:

Mortgage interest	$5,000
Utilities	1,200
Insurance	6,000

For regular income tax purposes, what is the maximum amount allowable as a deduction for Jackson's second residence in 2003?

     a. $6,200 in determining adjusted gross income.
     b. $11,000 in determining adjusted gross income.
     c. $5,000 as an itemized deduction.
     d. $12,200 as an itemized deduction.

129. Robert and Judy Parker made the following payments during 2003:

Interest on a life insurance policy loan (the loan proceeds were used for personal use)	$1,200
Interest on home mortgage for period January 1 to October 4, 2003	3,600
Penalty payment for prepayment of home mortgage on October 4, 2003	900

How much can the Parkers utilize as interest expense in calculating itemized deductions for 2003?

     a. $5,700
     b. $4,620
     c. $4,500
     d. $3,600

130. Charles Wolfe purchased the following long-term investments at par during 2003:

$20,000 general obligation bonds of Burlington County (wholly tax-exempt)
$10,000 debentures of Arrow Corporation

Wolfe financed these purchases by obtaining a $30,000 loan from the Union National Bank. For the year 2003, Wolfe made the following interest payments:

Union National Bank	$3,600
Interest on home mortgage	3,000
Interest on credit card charges (items purchased for personal use)	500

What amount can Wolfe utilize as interest expense in calculating itemized deductions for 2003?

     a. $3,000
     b. $4,200
     c. $5,400
     d. $7,100

131. During 2003, William Clark was assessed a deficiency on his 2001 federal income tax return. As a result of this assessment he was required to pay $1,120 determined as follows:

Additional tax	$900
Late filing penalty	60
Negligence penalty	90
Interest	70

What portion of the $1,120 would qualify as itemized deductions for 2003?

     a. $0
     b. $ 14
     c. $150
     d. $220

132. Smith, a single individual, made the following charitable contributions during the current year. Smith's adjusted gross income is $60,000.

Donation to Smith's church	$5,000
Artwork donated to the local art museum. Smith purchased it for $2,000 four months ago. A local art dealer appraised it for	3,000
Contribution to a needy family	1,000

What amount should Smith deduct as a charitable contribution?

     a. $5,000
     b. $7,000
     c. $8,000
     d. $9,000

133. Stein, an unmarried taxpayer, had adjusted gross income of $80,000 for the year and qualified to itemize deductions. Stein had no charitable contribution carryovers and only made one contribution during the year. Stein donated stock, purchased seven years earlier for $17,000, to a tax-exempt educational organization. The stock was valued at $25,000 when it was contributed. What is the amount of charitable contributions deductible on Stein's current year income tax return?

     a. $17,000
     b. $21,000
     c. $24,000
     d. $25,000

134. Moore, a single taxpayer, had $50,000 in adjusted gross income for 2003. During 2003 she contributed $18,000 to her church. She had a $10,000 charitable contribution carryover from her 2002 church contributions. What was the maximum amount of properly substantiated charitable contributions that Moore could claim as an itemized deduction for 2003?

     a. $10,000
     b. $18,000
     c. $25,000
     d. $28,000

135. Spencer, who itemizes deductions, had adjusted gross income of $60,000 in 2003. The following additional information is available for 2003:

Cash contribution to church	$4,000
Purchase of art object at church bazaar (with a fair market value of $800 on the date of purchase)	1,200
Donation of used clothing to Salvation Army (fair value evidenced by receipt received)	600

What is the maximum amount Spencer can claim as a deduction for charitable contributions in 2003?

     a. $5,400
     b. $5,200
     c. $5,000
     d. $4,400

136. Ruth Lewis has adjusted gross income of $100,000 for 2003 and itemizes her deductions. On September 1, 2003, she made a contribution to her church of stock held for investment for two years that cost $10,000 and had a fair market value of $70,000. The church sold the stock for $70,000 on the same date. Assume that Lewis made no other contributions during 2003 and made no special election in regard to this contribution on her 2003 tax return. How much should Lewis claim as a charitable contribution deduction for 2003?

     a. $50,000
     b. $30,000
     c. $20,000
     d. $10,000

137. On December 15, 2003, Donald Calder made a contribution of $500 to a qualified charitable organization, by charging the contribution on his bank credit card. Calder paid the $500 on January 20, 2004, upon receipt of the bill from the bank. In addition, Calder issued and delivered a promissory note for $1,000 to another qualified charitable organization on November 1, 2003, which he paid upon maturity six months later. If Calder itemizes his deductions, what portion of these contributions is deductible in 2003?

- a. $0
- b. $ 500
- c. $1,000
- d. $1,500

138. Under a written agreement between Mrs. Norma Lowe and an approved religious exempt organization, a ten-year-old girl from Vietnam came to live in Mrs. Lowe's home on August 1, 2003, in order to be able to start school in the US on September 3, 2003. Mrs. Lowe actually spent $500 for food, clothing, and school supplies for the student during 2003, without receiving any compensation or reimbursement of costs. What portion of the $500 may Mrs. Lowe deduct on her 2003 income tax return as a charitable contribution?

- a. $0
- b. $200
- c. $250
- d. $500

139. During 2003, Vincent Tally gave to the municipal art museum title to his private collection of rare books that was assessed and valued at $60,000. However, he reserved the right to the collection's use and possession during his lifetime. For 2003, he reported an adjusted gross income of $100,000. Assuming that this was his only contribution during the year, and that there were no carryovers from prior years, what amount can he deduct as contributions for 2003?

- a. $0
- b. $30,000
- c. $50,000
- d. $60,000

140. Jimet, an unmarried taxpayer, qualified to itemize 2003 deductions. Jimet's 2003 adjusted gross income was $30,000 and he made a $2,000 cash donation directly to a needy family. In 2003, Jimet also donated stock, valued at $3,000, to his church. Jimet had purchased the stock four months earlier for $1,500. What was the maximum amount of the charitable contribution allowable as an itemized deduction on Jimet's 2003 income tax return?

- a. $0
- b. $1,500
- c. $2,000
- d. $5,000

141. Taylor, an unmarried taxpayer, had $90,000 in adjusted gross income for 2003. During 2003, Taylor donated land to a church and made no other contributions. Taylor purchased the land in 1992 as an investment for $14,000. The land's fair market value was $25,000 on the day of the donation. What is the maximum amount of charitable contribution that Taylor may deduct as in itemized deduction for the land donation for 2003?

- a. $25,000
- b. $14,000
- c. $11,000
- d. $0

142. In 2003, Joan Frazer's residence was totally destroyed by fire. The property had an adjusted basis and a fair market value of $130,000 before the fire. During 2003, Frazer received insurance reimbursement of $120,000 for the destruction of her home. Frazer's 2003 adjusted gross income was $70,000. Frazer had no casualty gains during the year. What amount of the fire loss was Frazer entitled to claim as an itemized deduction on her 2003 tax return?

- a. $ 2,900
- b. $ 8,500
- c. $ 8,600
- d. $10,000

143. Alex and Myra Burg, married and filing joint income tax returns, derive their entire income from the operation of their retail candy shop. Their 2003 adjusted gross income was $50,000. The Burgs itemized their deductions on Schedule A for 2003. The following unreimbursed cash expenditures were among those made by the Burgs during 2003:

> Repair of glass vase accidentally broken in home by dog;
> vase cost $500 in 2000; fair value $600 before accident
> and $200 after accident $90

Without regard to the $100 "floor" and the adjusted gross income percentage threshold, what amount should the Burgs deduct for the casualty loss in their itemized deductions on Schedule A for 2003?

- a. $0
- b. $ 90
- c. $300
- d. $400

144. Hall, a divorced person and custodian of her twelve-year-old child, filed her 2003 federal income tax return as head of a household. During 2003 Hall paid a $490 casualty insurance premium on her personal residence. Hall does not rent out any portion of the home, nor use it for business.

The casualty insurance premium of $490 is

- a. Allowed as an itemized deduction subject to the $100 floor and the 10% of adjusted gross income floor.
- b. Allowed as an itemized deduction subject to the 2% of adjusted gross income floor.
- c. Deductible in arriving at adjusted gross income.
- d. Not deductible in 2003.

Items 145 and 146 are based on the following selected 2003 information pertaining to Sam and Ann Hoyt, who filed a joint federal income tax return for the calendar year 2003. The Hoyts had adjusted gross income of $34,000 and itemized their deductions for 2003. Among the Hoyts' cash expenditures during 2003 were the following:

> $2,500 repairs in connection with 2003 fire damage to the Hoyt residence. This property has a basis of $50,000. Fair market value was $60,000 before the fire and $55,000 after the fire. Insurance on the property had lapsed in 2002 for nonpayment of premium.
> $800 appraisal fee to determine amount of fire loss.

145. What amount of fire loss were the Hoyts entitled to deduct as an itemized deduction on their 2003 return?

- a. $5,000
- b. $2,500
- c. $1,600
- d. $1,500

146. The appraisal fee to determine the amount of the Hoyts' fire loss was
   a.   Deductible from gross income in arriving at adjusted gross income.
   b.   Subject to the 2% of adjusted gross income floor for miscellaneous itemized deductions.
   c.   Deductible after reducing the amount by $100.
   d.   Not deductible.

147. Which of the following is **not** a miscellaneous itemized deduction?
   a.   Legal fee for tax advice related to a divorce.
   b.   IRA trustee's fees that are separately billed and paid.
   c.   Appraisal fee for a charitable contribution.
   d.   Check-writing fees for a personal checking account.

148. Hall, a divorced person and custodian of her twelve-year-old child, submitted the following information to the CPA who prepared her 2003 return:

   The divorce agreement, executed in 2000, provides for Hall to receive $3,000 per month, of which $600 is designated as child support. After the child reaches eighteen, the monthly payments are to be reduced to $2,400 and are to continue until remarriage or death. However, for the year 2003, Hall received a total of only $5,000 from her former husband. Hall paid an attorney $2,000 in 2003 in a suit to collect the alimony owed.

The $2,000 legal fee that Hall paid to collect alimony should be treated as
   a.   A deduction in arriving at adjusted gross income.
   b.   An itemized deduction subject to the 2% of adjusted gross income floor.
   c.   An itemized deduction **not** subject to the 2% of adjusted gross income floor.
   d.   A nondeductible personal expense.

149. Hall, a divorced person and custodian of her twelve-year-old child, submitted the following information to the CPA who prepared her 2003 return:

   During 2003, Hall spent a total of $1,000 for state lottery tickets. Her lottery winnings in 2003 totaled $200. Hall's lottery transactions should be reported as follows:

| | | Schedule A—itemized deductions | |
| | | Other miscellaneous deductions | |
	Other income on page 1	Subject to 2% AGI floor	Not subject to 2% AGI floor
a.	$0	$0	$0
b.	$200	$0	$200
c.	$200	$200	$0
d.	$200	$0	$0

150. Joel Rich is an outside salesman, deriving his income solely from commissions, and personally bearing all expenses without reimbursement of any kind. During 2003, Joel paid the following expenses pertaining directly to his activities as an outside salesman:

Travel	$10,000
Secretarial	7,000
Telephone	1,000

How should these expenses be deducted in Joel's 2003 return?

	From gross income, in arriving at adjusted gross income	As itemized deductions
a.	$18,000	$0
b.	$11,000	$ 7,000
c.	$10,000	$ 8,000
d.	$0	$18,000

151. Magda Micale, a public school teacher with adjusted gross income of $10,000, paid the following items in 2003 for which she received no reimbursement:

Initiation fee for membership in teachers' union	$100
Dues to teachers' union	180
Voluntary unemployment benefit fund contributions to union-established fund	72

How much can Magda claim in 2003 as allowable miscellaneous deductions on Schedule A of Form 1040?
   a. $ 80
   b. $280
   c. $252
   d. $352

152. Harold Brodsky is an electrician employed by a contracting firm. His adjusted gross income is $25,000. During the current year he incurred and paid the following expenses:

Use of personal auto for company business (reimbursed by employer for $200)	$300
Specialized work clothes	550
Union dues	600
Cost of income tax preparation	150
Preparation of will	100

If Brodsky were to itemize his personal deductions, what amount should he claim as miscellaneous deductible expenses?
   a. $ 800
   b. $ 900
   c. $1,500
   d. $1,700

153. Which items are **not** subject to the phaseout of the amount of certain itemized deductions that may be claimed by high-income individuals?
   a.   Qualified residence interest.
   b.   Charitable contributions.
   c.   Investment interest expenses.
   d.   Real estate taxes.

154. For 2003, Dole's adjusted gross income exceeds $500,000. After the application of any other limitation, itemized deductions are reduced by
   a.   The **lesser** of 3% of the excess of adjusted gross income over the applicable amount or 80% of **certain** itemized deductions.
   b.   The **lesser** of 3% of the excess of adjusted gross income over the applicable amount or 80% of **all** itemized deductions.
   c.   The **greater** of 3% of the excess of adjusted gross income over the applicable amount or 80% of **certain** itemized deductions.
   d.   The **greater** of 3% of the excess of adjusted gross income over the applicable amount or 80% of **all** itemized deductions.

155. Which one of the following is **not** included in determining the total support of a dependent?

a. Fair rental value of dependent's lodging.
b. Medical insurance premiums paid on behalf of the dependent.
c. Birthday presents given to the dependent.
d. Nontaxable scholarship received by the dependent.

156. In 2003, Smith, a divorced person, provided over one-half the support for his widowed mother, Ruth, and his son, Clay, both of whom are US citizens. During 2003, Ruth did not live with Smith. She received $9,000 in social security benefits. Clay, a full-time graduate student, and his wife lived with Smith. Clay had no income but filed a joint return for 2003, owing an additional $500 in taxes on his wife's income. How many exemptions was Smith entitled to claim on his 2003 tax return?

a. 4
b. 3
c. 2
d. 1

157. Jim and Kay Ross contributed to the support of their two children, Dale and Kim, and Jim's widowed parent, Grant. For 2003, Dale, a twenty-year-old full-time college student, earned $4,500 from a part-time job. Kim, a twenty-three-year-old bank teller, earned $12,000. Grant received $5,000 in dividend income and $4,000 in nontaxable social security benefits. Grant, Dale, and Kim are US citizens and were over one-half supported by Jim and Kay. How many exemptions can Jim and Kay claim on their 2003 joint income tax return?

a. Two
b. Three
c. Four
d. Five

158. Joe and Barb are married, but Barb refuses to sign a 2003 joint return. On Joe's separate 2003 return, an exemption may be claimed for Barb if

a. Barb was a full-time student for the entire 2003 school year.
b. Barb attaches a written statement to Joe's income tax return, agreeing to be claimed as an exemption by Joe for 2003.
c. Barb was under the age of nineteen.
d. Barb had **no** gross income and was **not** claimed as another person's dependent in 2003.

159. Al and Mary Lew are married and filed a joint 2003 income tax return in which they validly claimed the $3,050 personal exemption for their dependent seventeen-year-old daughter, Doris. Since Doris earned $5,400 in 2003 from a part-time job at the college she attended full-time, Doris was also required to file a 2003 income tax return. What amount was Doris entitled to claim as a personal exemption in her 2003 individual income tax return?

a. $0
b. $ 750
c. $3,050
d. $4,750

160. During 2003 Robert Moore, who is fifty years old and unmarried, maintained his home in which he and his widower father, age seventy-five, resided. His father had $3,500 interest income from a savings account and also received $2,400 from social security during 2003. Robert provided 60% of his father's total support for 2003. What is Robert's filing status for 2003, and how many exemptions should he claim on his tax return?

a. Head of household and two exemptions.
b. Single and two exemptions.
c. Head of household and one exemption.
d. Single and one exemption.

161. John and Mary Arnold are a childless married couple who lived apart (alone in homes maintained by each) the entire year 2003. On December 31, 2003, they were legally separated under a decree of separate maintenance. Which of the following is the only filing status choice available to them when filing for 2003?

a. Single.
b. Head of household.
c. Married filing separate return.
d. Married filing joint return.

162. Albert and Lois Stoner, age sixty-six and sixty-four, respectively, filed a joint tax return for 2003. They provided all of the support for their blind nineteen-year-old son, who has no gross income. Their twenty-three-year-old daughter, a full-time student until her graduation on June 14, 2003, earned $3,000, which was 40% of her total support during 2003. Her parents provided the remaining support. The Stoners also provided the total support of Lois' father, who is a citizen and lifelong resident of Peru. How many exemptions can the Stoners claim on their 2003 income tax return?

a. 4
b. 5
c. 6
d. 7

163. Jim Planter, who reached age sixty-five on January 1, 2003, filed a joint return for 2003 with his wife Rita, age fifty. Mary, their twenty-one-year-old daughter, was a full-time student at a college until her graduation on June 2, 2003. The daughter had $6,500 of income and provided 25% of her own support during 2003. In addition, during 2003 the Planters were the sole support for Rita's niece, who had no income. How many exemptions should the Planters claim on their 2003 tax return?

a. 2
b. 3
c. 4
d. 5

164. In 2003, Sam Dunn provided more than half the support for his wife, his father's brother, and his cousin. Sam's wife was the only relative who was a member of Sam's household. None of the relatives had any income, nor did any of them file an individual or a joint return. All of these relatives are US citizens. Which of these relatives should be claimed as a dependent or dependents on Sam's 2003 return?

a. Only his wife.
b. Only his father's brother.
c. Only his cousin.
d. His wife, his father's brother, and his cousin.

165. In 2003, Alan Kott provided more than half the support for his following relatives, none of whom qualified as a member of Alan's household:

Cousin
Niece
Foster parent

None of these relatives had any income, nor did any of these relatives file an individual or joint return. All of these relatives are US citizens. Which of these relatives could be claimed as a dependent on Alan's 2003 return?

a. No one.
b. Niece.
c. Cousin.
d. Foster parent.

166. Sara Hance, who is single and lives alone in Idaho, has no income of her own and is supported in full by the following persons:

	Amount of support	Percent of total
Alma (an unrelated friend)	$2,400	48
Ben (Sara's brother)	2,150	43
Carl (Sara's son)	450	9
	$5,000	100

Under a multiple support agreement, Sara's dependency exemption can be claimed by

a. No one.
b. Alma.
c. Ben.
d. Carl.

167. Mr. and Mrs. Vonce, both age sixty-two, filed a joint return for 2003. They provided all the support for their daughter, who is nineteen, legally blind, and who has no income. Their son, age twenty-one and a full-time student at a university, had $6,200 of income and provided 70% of his own support during 2003. How many exemptions should Mr. and Mrs. Vonce have claimed on their 2003 joint income tax return?

a. 2
b. 3
c. 4
d. 5

168. Which of the following is(are) among the requirements to enable a taxpayer to be classified as a "qualifying widow(er)"?

I. A dependent has lived with the taxpayer for six months.
II. The taxpayer has maintained the cost of the principal residence for six months.

a. I only.
b. II only.
c. Both I and II.
d. Neither I nor II.

169. For head of household filing status, which of the following costs are considered in determining whether the taxpayer has contributed more than one-half the cost of maintaining the household?

	Insurance on the home	Rental value of home
a.	Yes	Yes
b.	No	No
c.	Yes	No
d.	No	Yes

170. A husband and wife can file a joint return even if

a. The spouses have different tax years, provided that both spouses are alive at the end of the year.
b. The spouses have different accounting methods.
c. Either spouse was a nonresident alien at any time during the tax year, provided that at least one spouse makes the proper election.
d. They were divorced before the end of the tax year.

171. Emil Gow's wife died in 2001. Emil did not remarry, and he continued to maintain a home for himself and his dependent infant child during 2002 and 2003, providing full support for himself and his child during these years. For 2001, Emil properly filed a joint return. For 2003, Emil's filing status is

a. Single.
b. Head of household.
c. Qualifying widower with dependent child.
d. Married filing joint return.

172. Nell Brown's husband died in 2000. Nell did not remarry, and continued to maintain a home for herself and her dependent infant child during 2001, 2002, and 2003, providing full support for herself and her child during these three years. For 2000, Nell properly filed a joint return. For 2003, Nell's filing status is

a. Single.
b. Married filing joint return.
c. Head of household.
d. Qualifying widow with dependent child.

173. Mrs. Irma Felton, by herself, maintains her home in which she and her unmarried son reside. Her son, however, does not qualify as her dependent. Mrs. Felton's husband died in 2002. What is Mrs. Felton's filing status for 2003?

a. Single.
b. Qualifying widow with dependent child.
c. Head of household.
d. Married filing jointly.

174. Poole, forty-five years old and unmarried, is in the 15% tax bracket. He had 2003 adjusted gross income of $20,000. The following information applies to Poole:

Medical expenses	$6,500
Standard deduction	4,750
Personal exemption	3,050

Poole wishes to minimize his income tax. What is Poole's 2003 total income tax?

a. $3,000
b. $1,830
c. $1,793
d. $1,568

175. Which of the following itemized deductions are deductible when computing the alternative minimum tax for individuals?

a. State income taxes
b. Home equity mortgage interest when the loan proceeds were used to purchase an auto
c. Unreimbursed employee expenses in excess of 2% of adjusted gross income
d. Gambling losses.

176. Randy Lowe reported the following items in computing his regular federal income tax for 2003:

Personal exemption	$3,050
Itemized deduction for state taxes	1,500
Cash charitable contributions	1,250
Net long-term capital gain	700
Excess of accelerated depreciation over straight-line depreciation on real property placed in service prior to 1987	600
Tax-exempt interest from private activity bonds	400

What are the amounts of tax preference items and adjustments that must be added to or subtracted from regular taxable income in order to compute Lowe's alternative minimum taxable income for 2003?

	Preferences	Adjustments
a.	$1,000	$4,550
b.	$1,000	$5,800
c.	$1,700	$4,550
d.	$2,250	$5,250

177. In 2002, Karen Miller had an alternative minimum tax liability of $20,000. This was the first year that she paid an alternative minimum tax. When she recomputed her 2002 alternative minimum tax using only exclusion preferences and adjustments, her alternative minimum tax was $9,000. For 2003, Karen had a regular tax liability of $50,000 and a tentative minimum tax of $45,000. What is the amount of Karen's unused minimum tax credit from 2003 that will carry over to 2004?

a. $0
b. $4,000
c. $5,000
d. $6,000

178. In 2003, Don Mills, a single taxpayer, had $70,000 in taxable income before personal exemptions. Mills had no tax preferences. His itemized deductions were as follows:

State and local income taxes	$5,000
Home mortgage interest on loan to acquire residence	6,000
Miscellaneous deductions that exceed 2% of adjusted gross income	2,000

What amount did Mills report as alternative minimum taxable income before the AMT exemption?

a. $72,000
b. $75,000
c. $77,000
d. $83,000

179. An individual's alternative minimum tax adjustments include

	Net long-term capital gain in excess of net short-term capital loss	Home equity interest expense where loan proceeds not used to buy, build, or improve home
a.	Yes	Yes
b.	Yes	No
c.	No	Yes
d.	No	No

180. The credit for prior year alternative minimum tax liability may be carried

a. Forward for a maximum of five years.
b. Back to the three preceding years or carried forward for a maximum of five years.
c. Back to the three preceding years.
d. Forward indefinitely.

181. The alternative minimum tax (AMT) is computed as the

a. Excess of the regular tax over the tentative AMT.
b. Excess of the tentative AMT over the regular tax.
c. The tentative AMT plus the regular tax.
d. Lesser of the tentative AMT or the regular tax.

182. The following information pertains to Joe Diamond, a cash-method sole proprietor for 2003:

Gross receipts from business	$150,000
Interest income from personal investments	10,000
Cost of goods sold	80,000
Other business operating expenses	40,000

What amount of net earnings from self-employment would be multiplied by the applicable self-employment tax rate to compute Diamond's self-employment tax for 2003?

a. $25,410
b. $27,705
c. $30,000
d. $40,000

183. Freeman, a single individual, reported the following income in the current year:

Guaranteed payment from services rendered to a partnership	$50,000
Ordinary income from an S corporation	$20,000

What amount of Freeman's income is subject to self-employment tax?

a. $0
b. $20,000
c. $50,000
d. $70,000

184. Rich is a cash-basis self-employed air-conditioning repairman with 2003 gross business receipts of $20,000. Rich's cash disbursements were as follows:

Air conditioning parts	$2,500
Yellow Pages listing	2,000
Estimated federal income taxes on self-employment income	1,000
Business long-distance telephone calls	400
Charitable contributions	200

What amount should Rich report as net self-employment income?

a. $15,100
b. $14,900
c. $14,100
d. $13,900

185. The self-employment tax is

a. Fully deductible as an itemized deduction.
b. Fully deductible in determining net income from self-employment.
c. One-half deductible from gross income in arriving at adjusted gross income.
d. Not deductible.

186. An employee who has had social security tax withheld in an amount greater than the maximum for a particular year, may claim

a. Such excess as either a credit or an itemized deduction, at the election of the employee, if that excess resulted from correct withholding by two or more employers.
b. Reimbursement of such excess from his employers, if that excess resulted from correct withholding by two or more employers.

c. The excess as a credit against income tax, if that excess resulted from correct withholding by two or more employers.

d. The excess as a credit against income tax, if that excess was withheld by one employer.

187. Alex Berger, a retired building contractor, earned the following income during 2003:

Director's fee received from Keith Realty Corp. $ 600
Executor's fee received from the estate of his deceased sister 7,000

Berger's gross income from self-employment for 2003 is

a. $0
b. $ 600
c. $7,000
d. $7,600

188. Smith, a retired corporate executive, earned consulting fees of $8,000 and director's fees of $2,000 in 2003. Smith's gross income from self-employment for 2003 is

a. $0
b. $ 2,000
c. $ 8,000
d. $10,000

189. Which one of the following credits is not a component of the general business credit?

a. Disabled access credit.
b. Employer social security credit.
c. Foreign tax credit.
d. Welfare-to-work credit.

190. Which of the following credits is a combination of several tax credits to provide uniform rules for the current and carryback-carryover years?

a. General business credit.
b. Foreign tax credit.
c. Minimum tax credit.
d. Enhanced oil recovery credit.

191. Melvin Crane is sixty-six years old, and his wife, Matilda, is sixty-five. They filed a joint income tax return for 2003, reporting an adjusted gross income of $16,550, on which they owed a tax of $60. They received $3,000 from social security benefits in 2003. How much can they claim on Form 1040 in 2003, as a credit for the elderly?

a. $0
b. $ 60
c. $255
d. $675

192. Nora Hayes, a widow, maintains a home for herself and her two dependent preschool children. In 2003, Nora's earned income and adjusted gross income was $44,000. During 2003, Nora paid work-related expenses of $6,000 for a housekeeper to care for her children. How much can Nora claim for child care credit in 2003?

a. $0
b. $ 960
c. $1,200
d. $2,100

193. Robert and Mary Jason, filing a joint tax return for 2003, had a tax liability of $9,000 based on their tax table income and three exemptions. Robert and Mary had earned income of $30,000 and $22,000, respectively, during 2003. In order for Mary to be gainfully employed, the Jasons in-

curred the following employment-related expenses for their four-year-old son John in 2003:

Payee	Amount
Union Day Care Center	$2,500
Acme Home Cleaning Service	500
Wilma Jason, babysitter (Robert Jason's mother)	1,000

Assuming that the Jasons do not claim any other credits against their tax, what is the amount of the child care tax credit they should report on their tax return for 2003?

a. $500
b. $600
c. $ 700
d. $1,050

194. To qualify for the child care credit on a joint return, at least one spouse must

	Have an adjusted gross income of $10,000 or less	Be gainfully employed when related expenses are incurred
a.	Yes	Yes
b.	No	No
c.	Yes	No
d.	No	Yes

195. Sunex Co., an accrual-basis, calendar-year domestic C corporation, is taxed on its worldwide income. In the current year, Sunex's US tax liability on its domestic and foreign-source income is $60,000 and no prior year foreign income taxes have been carried forward. Which factor(s) may affect the amount of Sunex's foreign tax credit available in its current year corporate income tax return?

	Income source	The foreign tax rate
a.	Yes	Yes
b.	Yes	No
c.	No	Yes
d.	No	No

196. The following information pertains to Wald Corp.'s operations for the year ended December 31, 2003:

Worldwide taxable income	$300,000
US source taxable income	180,000
US income tax before foreign tax credit	96,000
Foreign nonbusiness-related interest earned	30,000
Foreign income taxes paid on nonbusiness-related interest earned	12,000
Other foreign source taxable income	90,000
Foreign income taxes paid on other foreign source taxable income	27,000

What amount of foreign tax credit may Wald claim for 2003?

a. $28,800
b. $36,600
c. $38,400
d. $39,000

197. Foreign income taxes paid by a corporation

a. May be claimed either as a deduction or as a credit, at the option of the corporation.
b. May be claimed only as a deduction.
c. May be claimed only as a credit.
d. Do **not** qualify either as a deduction or as a credit.

198. Which of the following credits can result in a refund even if the individual had **no** income tax liability?

a. Credit for prior year minimum tax.
b. Credit for the elderly or the disabled.

c. Earned income credit.

d. Child and dependent care credit.

199. Kent qualified for the earned income credit in 2003. This credit could result in a

    a. Refund even if Kent had no tax withheld from wages.

    b. Refund only if Kent had tax withheld from wages.

    c. Carryback or carryforward for any unused portion.

    d. Subtraction from adjusted gross income to arrive at taxable income.

200. Which one of the following statements is correct with regard to the earned income credit?

    a. The credit is available only to those individuals whose earned income is equal to adjusted gross income.

    b. For purposes of the earned income test, "earned income" includes workers' compensation benefits.

    c. The credit can result in a refund even if the individual had **no** tax withheld from wages.

    d. The credit is available on a tax return that covers less than twelve months.

201. Which of the following tax credits **cannot** be claimed by a corporation?

    a. Foreign tax credit.

    b. Earned income credit.

    c. Alternative fuel production credit.

    d. General business credit.

202. Which one of the following statements is correct regarding the credit for adoption expenses?

    a. The credit for adoption expenses is a refundable credit.

    b. The maximum credit is $5,000 for the adoption of a child with special needs.

    c. Qualified adoption expenses are taken into account in the year that the adoption becomes final.

    d. An eligible child is an individual who has not attained the age of twenty-one as of the time of adoption.

203. Which one of the following statements is **not** correct with regard to the child tax credit?

    a. The credit is $600 per qualifying child for tax years beginning in 2003.

    b. The amount of credit is reduced if modified adjusted gross income exceeds certain thresholds.

    c. To qualify for the credit, a dependent child must be less than sixteen years old.

    d. A qualifying child must be a US citizen or resident.

204. Which one of the following statements concerning the Hope scholarship credit is **not** correct?

    a. The credit is available for the first two years of postsecondary education program.

    b. The credit is available on a per student basis.

    c. To be eligible for the credit, the student must be enrolled full-time for at least one academic period during the year.

    d. If a parent claims a child as a dependent, any qualified expenses paid by the child are deemed to be paid by the parent.

205. Which one of the following statements concerning the lifetime learning credit is **not** correct?

    a. The credit is 20% of the first $10,000 of qualified tuition and related expenses for 2003.

    b. Qualifying expenses include the cost of tuition for graduate courses at an eligible educational institution.

    c. The credit may be claimed for an unlimited number of years.

    d. The credit is available on a per student basis.

206. Chris Baker's adjusted gross income on her 2002 tax return was $160,000. The amount covered a twelve-month period. For the 2003 tax year, Baker may avoid the penalty for the underpayment of estimated tax if the timely estimated tax payments equal the required annual amount of

    I. 90% of the tax on the return for the current year, paid in four equal installments.

    II. 100% of prior year's tax liability, paid in four equal installments.

    a. I only.

    b. II only.

    c. Both I and II.

    d. Neither I nor II.

207. Krete, an unmarried taxpayer, had income exclusively from wages. By December 31, 2003, Krete's employer had withheld $16,000 in federal income taxes and Krete had made no estimated tax payments. On April 15, 2004, Krete timely filed an extension request to file her individual tax return and paid $300 of additional taxes. Krete's 2003 income tax liability was $16,500 when she timely filed her return on April 30, 2004, and paid the remaining income tax liability balance. What amount would be subject to the penalty for the underpayment of estimated taxes?

    a. $0

    b. $ 200

    c. $ 500

    d. $16,500

208. John Smith is the executor of his father's estate. His father, a calendar-year taxpayer, died on July 15, 2003. As executor of his father's estate, John is required to file a final income tax return Form 1040 for his father's 2003 tax year. What is the due date of his father's 2003 federal income tax return assuming John does not file for an extension?

    a. November 1, 2003.

    b. November 15, 2003.

    c. March 15, 2004.

    d. April 15, 2004.

209. Ray Birch, age sixty, is single with no dependents. Birch's only income is from his occupation as a self-employed plumber. Birch must file a return for 2003 if his net earnings from self-employment are at least

    a. $ 400

    b. $ 750

    c. $2,950

    d. $4,750

210. Jackson Corp., a calendar-year corporation, mailed its 2002 tax return to the Internal Revenue Service by certified mail on Thursday, March 13, 2003. The return, postmarked March 13, 2003, was delivered to the Internal Revenue Service on March 18, 2003. The statute of limitations on Jackson's corporate tax return begins on

a. December 31, 2002.
b. March 13, 2003.
c. March 16, 2003.
d. March 18, 2003.

211. A calendar-year taxpayer files an individual tax return for 2002 on March 20, 2003. The taxpayer neither committed fraud nor omitted amounts in excess of 25% of gross income on the tax return. What is the latest date that the Internal Revenue Service can assess tax and assert a notice of deficiency?

a. March 20, 2006.
b. March 20, 2005.
c. April 15, 2006.
d. April 15, 2005.

212. Harold Thompson, a self-employed individual, had income transactions for 2002 (duly reported on his return filed in April 2003) as follows:

Gross receipts	$400,000
Less cost of goods sold and deductions	320,000
Net business income	$ 80,000
Capital gains	36,000
Gross income	$116,000

In November 2003, Thompson discovers that he had inadvertently omitted some income on his 2002 return and retains Mann, CPA, to determine his position under the statute of limitations. Mann should advise Thompson that the six-year statute of limitations would apply to his 2002 return only if he omitted from gross income an amount in excess of

a. $ 20,000
b. $ 29,000
c. $100,000
d. $109,000

213. If a taxpayer omits from his or her income tax return an amount that exceeds 25% of the gross income reported on the return, the Internal Revenue Service can issue a notice of deficiency within a maximum period of

a. Three years from the date the return was filed, if filed before the due date.
b. Three years from the date the return was due, if filed by the due date.
c. Six years from the date the return was filed, if filed before the due date.
d. Six years from the date the return was due, if filed by the due date.

214. A claim for refund of erroneously paid income taxes, filed by an individual before the statute of limitations expires, must be submitted on Form

a. 1139
b. 1045
c. 1040X
d. 843

215. If an individual paid income tax in 2003 but did **not** file a 2003 return because his income was insufficient to require the filing of a return, the deadline for filing a refund claim is

a. Two years from the date the tax was paid.
b. Two years from the date a return would have been due.
c. Three years from the date the tax was paid.
d. Three years from the date a return would have been due.

216. A married couple filed their joint 2001 calendar-year return on March 15, 2002, and attached a check for the balance of tax due as shown on the return. On June 15, 2003, the couple discovered that they had failed to include $2,000 of home mortgage interest in their itemized deductions. In order for the couple to recover the tax that they would have saved by using the $2,000 deduction, they must file an amended return no later than

a. December 31, 2004.
b. March 15, 2005.
c. April 15, 2005.
d. June 15, 2005.

217. Richard Baker filed his 2002 individual income tax return on April 15, 2003. On December 31, 2003, he learned that 100 shares of stock that he owned had become worthless in 2002. Since he did not deduct this loss on his 2002 return, Baker intends to file a claim for refund. This refund claim must be filed not later than April 15,

a. 2004
b. 2006
c. 2009
d. 2010

218. A taxpayer filed his income tax return after the due date but neglected to file an extension form. The return indicated a tax liability of $50,000 and taxes withheld of $45,000. On what amount would the penalties for late filing and late payment be computed?

a. $0
b. $ 5,000
c. $45,000
d. $50,000

219. An accuracy-related penalty applies to the portion of tax underpayment attributable to

I. Any substantial gift or estate tax valuation understatement

II. Any substantial income tax valuation overstatement.

a. I only.
b. II only.
c. Both I and II.
d. Neither I nor II.

SIMULATION PROBLEMS

Simulation Problem 1   (10 to 15 minutes)

Situation
    Tax Treatment

Cole, a newly licensed CPA, opened an office in 2003 as a sole practitioner engaged in the practice of public accountancy. Cole reports on the cash basis for income tax purposes. Listed below are Cole's 2003 business and nonbusiness transactions, as well as possible tax treatments.

Tax Treatment
Situation

For each of Cole's transactions (**Items 1 through 20**), select the appropriate tax treatment. A tax treatment may be selected once, more than once, or not at all.

Tax treatments

A. Taxable as interest income in Schedule B—Interest and Dividend Income.
B. Taxable as other income on page 1 of Form 1040.
C. Not taxable.
D. Deductible on page 1 of Form 1040 to arrive at adjusted gross income.
E. Deductible in Schedule A—Itemized Deductions, subject to threshold of 7.5% of adjusted gross income.
F. Deductible in Schedule A—Itemized Deductions, subject to threshold of 10% of adjusted gross income and additional threshold of $100.
G. Deductible in full in Schedule A—Itemized Deductions (cannot be claimed as a credit).

H. Deductible in Schedule B—Interest and Dividend Income.
I. Deductible in Schedule C—Profit or Loss from Business.
J. Deductible in Schedule D—Capital Gains or Losses.
K. Deductible in Schedule E—Supplemental Income and Loss.
L. Deductible in Form 4797—Sales of Business Property.
M. Claimed in Form 1116—Foreign Tax Credit, or in Schedule A—Itemized Deductions, at taxpayer's option.
N. Based on gross self-employment income.
O. Based on net earnings from self-employment.
P. Not deductible.

Transactions	(A)	(B)	(C)	(D)	(E)	(F)	(G)	(H)	(I)	(J)	(K)	(L)	(M)	(N)	(O)	(P)
1. Fees received for jury duty.	○	○	○	○	○	○	○	○	○	○	○	○	○	○	○	○
2. Interest income on mortgage loan receivable.	○	○	○	○	○	○	○	○	○	○	○	○	○	○	○	○
3. Penalty paid to bank on early withdrawal of savings.	○	○	○	○	○	○	○	○	○	○	○	○	○	○	○	○
4. Write-offs of uncollectible accounts receivable from accounting practice.	○	○	○	○	○	○	○	○	○	○	○	○	○	○	○	○
5. Cost of attending review course in preparation for the Uniform CPA Examination.	○	○	○	○	○	○	○	○	○	○	○	○	○	○	○	○
6. Fee for the biennial permit to practice as a CPA.	○	○	○	○	○	○	○	○	○	○	○	○	○	○	○	○
7. Costs of attending CPE courses in fulfillment of state board requirements.	○	○	○	○	○	○	○	○	○	○	○	○	○	○	○	○
8. Contribution to a qualified Keogh retirement plan.	○	○	○	○	○	○	○	○	○	○	○	○	○	○	○	○
9. Loss sustained from nonbusiness bad debt.	○	○	○	○	○	○	○	○	○	○	○	○	○	○	○	○
10. Loss sustained on sale of "Small Business Corporation" (Section 1244) stock.	○	○	○	○	○	○	○	○	○	○	○	○	○	○	○	○
11. Taxes paid on land owned by Cole and rented out as a parking lot.	○	○	○	○	○	○	○	○	○	○	○	○	○	○	○	○
12. Interest paid on installment purchases of household furniture.	○	○	○	○	○	○	○	○	○	○	○	○	○	○	○	○
13. Alimony paid to former spouse who reports the alimony as taxable income.	○	○	○	○	○	○	○	○	○	○	○	○	○	○	○	○

	Transactions	(A)	(B)	(C)	(D)	(E)	(F)	(G)	(H)	(I)	(J)	(K)	(L)	(M)	(N)	(O)	(P)
14.	Personal medical expenses charged on credit card in December 2003 but not paid until January 2004.	O	O	O	O	O	O	O	O	O	O	O	O	O	O	O	O
15.	Personal casualty loss sustained.	O	O	O	O	O	O	O	O	O	O	O	O	O	O	O	O
16.	State inheritance tax paid on bequest received.	O	O	O	O	O	O	O	O	O	O	O	O	O	O	O	O
17.	Foreign income tax withheld at source on dividend received.	O	O	O	O	O	O	O	O	O	O	O	O	O	O	O	O
18.	Computation of self-employment tax.	O	O	O	O	O	O	O	O	O	O	O	O	O	O	O	O
19.	One-half of self-employment tax paid with 2003 return filed in April 2004.	O	O	O	O	O	O	O	O	O	O	O	O	O	O	O	O
20.	Insurance premiums paid on Cole's life.	O	O	O	O	O	O	O	O	O	O	O	O	O	O	O	O

Simulation Problem 2   (10 to 15 minutes)

Situation
Tax Treatment

Green is self-employed as a human resources consultant and reports on the cash basis for income tax purposes. Listed below are Green's 2003 business and nonbusiness transactions, as well as possible tax treatments.

Tax Treatment
Situation

For each of Green's transactions (**Items 1 through 25**), select the appropriate tax treatment. A tax treatment may be selected once, more than once, or not at all.

Tax treatments

A. Taxable as other income on Form 1040.
B. Reported in Schedule B—Interest and Dividend Income.
C. Reported in Schedule C as trade or business income.
D. Reported in Schedule E—Supplemental Income and Loss.
E. Not taxable.
F. Fully deductible on Form 1040 to arrive at adjusted gross income.
G. Fifty percent deductible on Form 1040 to arrive at adjusted gross income.
H. Reported in Schedule A—Itemized Deductions (deductibility subject to threshold of 7.5% of adjusted gross income).
I. Reported in Schedule A—Itemized Deductions (deductibility subject to threshold of 2% of adjusted gross income).

J. Reported in Form 4562—Depreciation and Amortization and deductible in Schedule A—Itemized Deductions (deductibility subject to threshold of 2% of adjusted gross income).
K. Reported in Form 4562—Depreciation and Amortization, and deductible in Schedule C—Profit or Loss from Business.
L. Fully deductible in Schedule C—Profit or Loss from Business.
M. Partially deductible in Schedule C—Profit or Loss from Business.
N. Reported in Form 2119—Sale of Your Home, and deductible in Schedule D—Capital Gains and Losses.
O. Not deductible.

Transactions

	(A)	(B)	(C)	(D)	(E)	(F)	(G)	(H)	(I)	(J)	(K)	(L)	(M)	(N)	(O)
1. Retainer fees received from clients.	○	○	○	○	○	○	○	○	○	○	○	○	○	○	○
2. Oil royalties received.	○	○	○	○	○	○	○	○	○	○	○	○	○	○	○
3. Interest income on general obligation state and local government bonds.	○	○	○	○	○	○	○	○	○	○	○	○	○	○	○
4. Interest on refund of federal taxes.	○	○	○	○	○	○	○	○	○	○	○	○	○	○	○
5. Death benefits from term life insurance policy on parent.	○	○	○	○	○	○	○	○	○	○	○	○	○	○	○
6. Interest income on US Treasury bonds.	○	○	○	○	○	○	○	○	○	○	○	○	○	○	○
7. Share of ordinary income from an investment in a limited partnership reported in Form 1065, Schedule K-1.	○	○	○	○	○	○	○	○	○	○	○	○	○	○	○
8. Taxable income from rental of a townhouse owned by Green.	○	○	○	○	○	○	○	○	○	○	○	○	○	○	○
9. Prize won as a contestant on a TV quiz show.	○	○	○	○	○	○	○	○	○	○	○	○	○	○	○
10. Payment received for jury service.	○	○	○	○	○	○	○	○	○	○	○	○	○	○	○
11. Dividends received from mutual funds that invest in tax-free government obligations.	○	○	○	○	○	○	○	○	○	○	○	○	○	○	○
12. Qualifying medical expenses not reimbursed by insurance.	○	○	○	○	○	○	○	○	○	○	○	○	○	○	○
13. Personal life insurance premiums paid by Green.	○	○	○	○	○	○	○	○	○	○	○	○	○	○	○
14. Expenses for business-related meals where clients were present.	○	○	○	○	○	○	○	○	○	○	○	○	○	○	○

Transactions	(A)	(B)	(C)	(D)	(E)	(F)	(G)	(H)	(I)	(J)	(K)	(L)	(M)	(N)	(O)
15. Depreciation on personal computer purchased in 2003 used for business.	○	○	○	○	○	○	○	○	○	○	○	○	○	○	○
16. Business lodging expenses, while out of town.	○	○	○	○	○	○	○	○	○	○	○	○	○	○	○
17. Subscriptions to professional journals used for business.	○	○	○	○	○	○	○	○	○	○	○	○	○	○	○
18. Self-employment taxes paid.	○	○	○	○	○	○	○	○	○	○	○	○	○	○	○
19. Qualifying contributions to a simplified employee pension plan.	○	○	○	○	○	○	○	○	○	○	○	○	○	○	○
20. Election to expense business equipment purchased in 2003.	○	○	○	○	○	○	○	○	○	○	○	○	○	○	○
21. Qualifying alimony payments made by Green.	○	○	○	○	○	○	○	○	○	○	○	○	○	○	○
22. Subscriptions for investment-related publications.	○	○	○	○	○	○	○	○	○	○	○	○	○	○	○
23. Interest expense on a home-equity line of credit for an amount borrowed to finance Green's business.	○	○	○	○	○	○	○	○	○	○	○	○	○	○	○
24. Interest expense on a loan for an auto used 75% for business.	○	○	○	○	○	○	○	○	○	○	○	○	○	○	○
25. Loss on sale of residence.	○	○	○	○	○	○	○	○	○	○	○	○	○	○	○

Simulation Problem 3   (10 to 15 minutes)

Situation	
	Deductibility

Facts: Mark Smith is an employee of Patton Corporation. Additionally, Smith operates a consulting business as a sole proprietor and owns an apartment building. Smith made the expenditures listed below during 2003.

	Deductibility
Situation	

For each of the following items, indicate whether each expenditure is deductible for AGI, from AGI (not subject to 2% limitation), from AGI (subject to 2% limitation), or not deductible.

	For AGI (A)	*From AGI (No 2%)* (B)	*From AGI (2% Floor)* (C)	*Not ded.* (D)
1. Smith paid the medical expenses of his mother-in-law. Although Smith provided more than half of her support, she does not qualify as Smith's dependent because she had gross income of $5,000.	O	O	O	O
2. Smith paid the real estate taxes on his rental apartment building.	O	O	O	O
3. Smith paid state sales taxes of $1,500 on an automobile that he purchased for personal use.	O	O	O	O
4. Smith paid the real estate taxes on his mother-in-law's home. She is the owner of the home.	O	O	O	O
5. Smith paid $1,500 of interest on credit card charges. The charges were for items purchased for personal use.	O	O	O	O
6. Smith paid an attorney $500 to prepare Smith's will.	O	O	O	O
7. Smith incurred $750 of expenses for business meals and entertainment in his position as an employee of Patton Corporation. Smith's expenses were not reimbursed.	O	O	O	O
8. Smith paid self-employment taxes of $3,000 as a result of earnings from the consulting business that he conducts as a sole proprietor.	O	O	O	O
9. Smith made a contribution to his self-employed retirement plan (Keogh Plan).	O	O	O	O
10. Smith had gambling losses totaling $2,500 for the year. He is including a lottery prize of $5,000 in his gross income this year.	O	O	O	O

Simulation Problem 4   (10 to 15 minutes)

Situation	
	Tax Treatment

The Internal Revenue Service is auditing Oate's 2002 Form 1040—Individual Income Tax Return. During 2003, Oate, an unmarried custodial parent, had one dependent three-year-old child and worked for a CPA firm. For 2003, Oate, who had adjusted gross income of $40,000, qualified to itemize deductions and was subject to federal income tax liability.

	Tax Treatment
Situation	

For **items 1 through 9,** select from the following list of tax treatments the appropriate tax treatment. A tax treatment may be selected once, more than once, or not at all.

Selections

A. Not deductible on Form 1040.

B. Deductible in full on Schedule A—Itemized Deductions.

C. Deductible in Schedule A—Itemized Deductions subject to a limitation of 50% of adjusted gross income.

D. Deductible in Schedule A—Itemized Deductions as miscellaneous deduction subject to a threshold of 2% of adjusted gross income.

E. Deductible in Schedule A—Itemized Deductions as miscellaneous deductions not subject to a threshold of 2% adjusted gross income.

F. Deductible on Schedule E—Supplemental Income and Loss.

G. A credit is allowable.

(A) (B) (C) (D) (E) (F) (G)

1. In 2003, Oate paid $2,000 interest on the $25,000 home equity mortgage on her vacation home, which she used exclusively for personal use. The mortgage is secured by Oate's vacation home, and the loan proceeds were used to purchase an automobile.   ○ ○ ○ ○ ○ ○ ○

2. For 2003, Oate had a $30,000 cash charitable contribution carryover from her 2002 cash donation to the American Red Cross. Oate made no additional charitable contributions in 2003.   ○ ○ ○ ○ ○ ○ ○

3. During 2003, Oate had investment interest expense that did not exceed her net investment income.   ○ ○ ○ ○ ○ ○ ○

4. Oate's 2003 lottery ticket losses were $450. She had no gambling winnings.   ○ ○ ○ ○ ○ ○ ○

5. During 2003, Oate paid $2,500 in real property taxes on her vacation home, which she used exclusively for personal use.   ○ ○ ○ ○ ○ ○ ○

6. In 2003, Oate paid a $500 premium for a homeowner's insurance policy on her principal residence.   ○ ○ ○ ○ ○ ○ ○

7. For 2003, Oate paid $1,500 to an unrelated babysitter to care for her child while she worked.   ○ ○ ○ ○ ○ ○ ○

8. In 2003, Oate paid $4,000 interest on the $60,000 acquisition mortgage of her principal residence. The mortgage is secured by Oate's home.   ○ ○ ○ ○ ○ ○ ○

9. During 2003, Oate paid $3,600 real property taxes on residential rental property in which she actively participates. There was no personal use of the rental property.   ○ ○ ○ ○ ○ ○ ○

Simulation Problem 5   (10 to 15 minutes)

Situation		
	Adjusted Gross Income	Exemptions

Frank and Dale Cumack are married and filing a joint 2003 income tax return. During 2003, Frank, sixty-five, was retired from government service and Dale, fifty-five, was employed as a university instructor. In 2003, the Cumacks contributed all of the support to Dale's father, Jacques, an unmarried French citizen and French resident who had no gross income.

	Adjusted Gross Income	
Situation		Exemptions

Part a.

For **items 1 through 10,** select the correct amount of income, loss, or adjustment to income that should be recognized on page 1 of the Cumacks' 2003 Form 1040—Individual Income Tax Return to arrive at the adjusted gross income for each separate transaction. A tax treatment may be selected once, more than once, or not at all.

Any information contained in an item is unique to that item and is not to be incorporated in your calculations when answering other items.

Selections

A. $0	D. $3,000	F. $4,000	I. $10,000	K. $ 30,000
B. $1,000	E. $3,500	G. $5,000	J. $25,000	L. $125,000
C. $2,000		H. $9,000		M. $150,000

(A) (B) (C) (D) (E) (F) (G) (H) (I) (J) (K) (L) (M)

1. During 2003, Dale received a $30,000 cash gift from her aunt. ○ ○ ○ ○ ○ ○ ○ ○ ○ ○ ○ ○ ○

2. Dale contributed $3,500 to her traditional Individual Retirement Account (IRA) on January 15, 2003. In 2003, she earned $60,000 as a university instructor. During 2003 the Cumacks were not active participants in an employer's qualified pension or annuity plan. ○ ○ ○ ○ ○ ○ ○ ○ ○ ○ ○ ○ ○

3. In 2003, the Cumacks received a $1,000 federal income tax refund. ○ ○ ○ ○ ○ ○ ○ ○ ○ ○ ○ ○ ○

4. During 2003, Frank, a 50% partner in Diske General Partnership, received a $4,000 guaranteed payment from Diske for services that he rendered to the partnership that year. ○ ○ ○ ○ ○ ○ ○ ○ ○ ○ ○ ○ ○

5. In 2003, Frank received $10,000 as beneficiary of his deceased brother's life insurance policy. ○ ○ ○ ○ ○ ○ ○ ○ ○ ○ ○ ○ ○

6. Dale's employer pays 100% of the cost of all employees' group-term life insurance under a qualified plan. Policy cost is $5 per $1,000 of coverage. Dale's group-term life insurance coverage equals $450,000. ○ ○ ○ ○ ○ ○ ○ ○ ○ ○ ○ ○ ○

7. In 2003, Frank won $5,000 at a casino and had $2,000 in gambling losses. ○ ○ ○ ○ ○ ○ ○ ○ ○ ○ ○ ○ ○

8. During 2003, the Cumacks received $1,000 interest income associated with a refund of their prior years' federal income tax. ○ ○ ○ ○ ○ ○ ○ ○ ○ ○ ○ ○ ○

9. In 2003, the Cumacks sold their first and only residence for $400,000. They purchased their home in 1989 for $50,000 and have lived there since then. There were no other capital gains, losses, or capital loss carryovers. The Cumacks do not intend to buy another residence. ○ ○ ○ ○ ○ ○ ○ ○ ○ ○ ○ ○ ○

10. In 2003, Zeno Corp. declared a stock dividend and Dale received one additional share of Zeno common stock for three shares of Zeno common stock that she held. The stock that Dale received had a fair market value of $9,000. There was no provision to receive cash instead of stock. ○ ○ ○ ○ ○ ○ ○ ○ ○ ○ ○ ○ ○

Situation	Adjusted Gross Income	Exemptions

Part b.

Frank and Dale Cumack are married and filing a joint 2003 income tax return. During 2003, Frank, sixty-five, was retired from government service and Dale, fifty-five, was employed as a university instructor. In 2003, the Cumacks contributed all of the support to Dale's father, Jacques, an unmarried French citizen and French resident who had no gross income.

For **item 11,** determine whether the Cumacks overstated, understated, or correctly determined the number of both personal and dependency exemptions.

Selections

    O. Overstated the number of both personal and dependency exemptions.
    U. Understated the number of both personal and dependency exemptions.
    C. Correctly determined the number of both personal and dependency
       exemptions.

                                                                               (O) (U) (C)

11. The Cumacks claimed three exemptions on their 2003 joint income tax return.   ○ ○ ○

Additional Simulations

    Appendix A—Simulation 3 involves Individual Taxation
    Appendix A—Simulation 4 involves Individual Taxation

MULTIPLE-CHOICE ANSWERS

1. c __ __	46. c __ __	91. a __ __	136. b __ __	181. b __ __
2. b __ __	47. a __ __	92. d __ __	137. b __ __	182. b __ __
3. b __ __	48. a __ __	93. c __ __	138. b __ __	183. c __ __
4. c __ __	49. a __ __	94. d __ __	139. a __ __	184. a __ __
5. a __ __	50. d __ __	95. a __ __	140. b __ __	185. c __ __
6. d __ __	51. b __ __	96. d __ __	141. a __ __	186. c __ __
7. b __ __	52. b __ __	97. d __ __	142. a __ __	187. b __ __
8. d __ __	53. b __ __	98. b __ __	143. a __ __	188. d __ __
9. a __ __	54. b __ __	99. d __ __	144. d __ __	189. c __ __
10. d __ __	55. c __ __	100. c __ __	145. d __ __	190. a __ __
11. b __ __	56. d __ __	101. d __ __	146. b __ __	191. b __ __
12. b __ __	57. d __ __	102. b __ __	147. d __ __	192. c __ __
13. c __ __	58. d __ __	103. c __ __	148. b __ __	193. b __ __
14. d __ __	59. c __ __	104. c __ __	149. b __ __	194. b __ __
15. c __ __	60. a __ __	105. c __ __	150. d __ __	195. a __ __
16. c __ __	61. a __ __	106. b __ __	151. a __ __	196. b __ __
17. a __ __	62. b __ __	107. b __ __	152. b __ __	197. a __ __
18. c __ __	63. a __ __	108. a __ __	153. c __ __	198. c __ __
19. a __ __	64. d __ __	109. c __ __	154. a __ __	199. a __ __
20. d __ __	65. d __ __	110. d __ __	155. d __ __	200. c __ __
21. c __ __	66. d __ __	111. a __ __	156. c __ __	201. b __ __
22. d __ __	67. a __ __	112. d __ __	157. b __ __	202. c __ __
23. c __ __	68. c __ __	113. d __ __	158. d __ __	203. c __ __
24. c __ __	69. b __ __	114. b __ __	159. a __ __	204. c __ __
25. a __ __	70. b __ __	115. d __ __	160. d __ __	205. d __ __
26. d __ __	71. c __ __	116. d __ __	161. a __ __	206. a __ __
27. c __ __	72. a __ __	117. c __ __	162. a __ __	207. a __ __
28. d __ __	73. a __ __	118. a __ __	163. c __ __	208. d __ __
29. c __ __	74. c __ __	119. d __ __	164. b __ __	209. a __ __
30. c __ __	75. c __ __	120. b __ __	165. b __ __	210. c __ __
31. b __ __	76. a __ __	121. b __ __	166. c __ __	211. c __ __
32. b __ __	77. d __ __	122. a __ __	167. b __ __	212. d __ __
33. d __ __	78. a __ __	123. b __ __	168. d __ __	213. d __ __
34. b __ __	79. c __ __	124. a __ __	169. c __ __	214. c __ __
35. c __ __	80. a __ __	125. c __ __	170. b __ __	215. a __ __
36. a __ __	81. b __ __	126. b __ __	171. c __ __	216. c __ __
37. c __ __	82. c __ __	127. c __ __	172. c __ __	217. d __ __
38. d __ __	83. b __ __	128. c __ __	173. c __ __	218. b __ __
39. b __ __	84. a __ __	129. c __ __	174. c __ __	219. c __ __
40. b __ __	85. c __ __	130. a __ __	175. d __ __	
41. c __ __	86. d __ __	131. a __ __	176. a __ __	
42. d __ __	87. c __ __	132. b __ __	177. d __ __	
43. d __ __	88. a __ __	133. c __ __	178. c __ __	
44. d __ __	89. c __ __	134. c __ __	179. c __ __	1st: __/219 = __%
45. c __ __	90. c __ __	135. c __ __	180. d __ __	2nd: __/219 = __%

MULTIPLE-CHOICE ANSWER EXPLANATIONS

I.B.3. Annuities

1. **(c)** The requirement is to determine the pension (annuity) amounts excluded from income during 2003, 2004, and 2005. Brown's contribution of $12,000 will be recovered pro rata over the life of the annuity. Under this rule, $100 per month (12,000 ÷ 120 months) is excluded from income.

	Received	Excluded	Included
2003	$4,900	$ 700	$4,200
2004	8,400	1,200	7,200
2005	8,400	1,200	7,200

I.B.4. Life Insurance Proceeds

2. **(b)** The requirement is to determine the amount of life insurance proceeds that must be included in gross in-

come by Decker, on the death of Fuller's parent. Life insurance proceeds paid because of the insured person's death are generally excluded from gross income. However, the exclusion generally does not apply if the insurance policy was obtained by the beneficiary in exchange for valuable consideration from a person other than the insurance company. Here, Decker purchased the policy from Fuller for $25,000 and paid an additional $40,000 in premiums, so Decker must include in gross income the excess of insurance proceeds over his investment in the policy [$200,000 – ($25,000 + $40,000) = $135,000.

3. **(b)** The requirement is to determine the amount of life insurance payments to be included in a widow's gross income. Life insurance proceeds paid by reason of death are excluded from income if paid in a lump sum or in installments. If the payments are received in installments, the principal amount of the policy divided by the number of annual payments is excluded each year. Therefore, $1,200 of the $5,200 insurance payment is included in Penelope's gross income.

Annual installment	$ 5,200
Principal amount ($100,000 ÷ 25)	– 4,000
Gross income	$ 1,200

I.B.5. Employee Benefits

4. **(c)** The requirement is to determine the correct statement regarding a "cafeteria plan" maintained by an employer. Cafeteria plans are employer-sponsored benefit packages that offer employees a choice between taking cash and receiving qualified benefits (e.g., accident and health insurance, group-term life insurance, coverage under a dependent care or group legal services program). Thus, employees "may select their own menu of benefits." If an employee chooses qualified benefits, they are excluded from the employee's gross income to the extent allowed by law. If an employee chooses cash, it is includible in the employee's gross income as compensation. Answer (a) is incorrect because participation is restricted to employees only. Answer (b) is incorrect because there is no minimum service requirement that must be met before an employee can participate in a plan. Answer (d) is incorrect because deferred compensation plans other than 401(k) plans are not included in the definition of a cafeteria plan.

5. **(a)** The requirement is to determine the amount of group-term life insurance proceeds that must be included in gross income by Autrey's widow. Life insurance proceeds paid by reason of death are generally excluded from gross income. Note that although only the cost of the first $50,000 of group-term insurance coverage can be excluded from gross income during the employee's life, the entire amount of insurance proceeds paid by reason of death will be excluded from the beneficiary's income.

6. **(d)** The requirement is to determine the amount of employee death payments to be included in gross income by the widow and the son. The $5,000 employee death benefit exclusion was repealed for decedents dying after August 20, 1996.

7. **(b)** The requirement is to determine the maximum amount of tax-free group-term life insurance coverage that can be provided to an employee by an employer. The cost of the first $50,000 of group-term life insurance coverage provided by an employer will be excluded from an employee's income.

8. **(d)** The requirement is to determine the amount to be included in Hal's gross income for the current year. All three amounts that Hal received as a result of his injury are excluded from gross income. Benefits received as workers' compensation and compensation for damages for physical injuries are always excluded from gross income. Amounts received from an employer's accident and health plan as reimbursement for medical expenses are excluded so long as the medical expenses are not deducted as itemized deductions.

9. **(a)** James Martin's gross income consists of

Salary	$50,000
Bonus	10,000
	$60,000

Medical insurance premiums paid by an employer are excluded from an employee's gross income. Additionally, qualified moving expense reimbursements are an employee fringe benefit and can be excluded from gross income. This means that an employee can exclude an amount paid by an employer as payment for (or reimbursement of) expenses that would be deductible as moving expenses if directly paid or incurred by the employee.

I.B.8. Gifts and Inheritances

10. **(d)** The requirement is to determine how much income Hall should include in his 2003 tax return for the inheritance of stock which he received from his father's estate. Since the definition of gross income excludes property received as a gift, bequest, devise, or inheritance, Hall recognizes no income upon receipt of the stock. Since the executor of his father's estate elected the alternate valuation date (August 1), and the stock was distributed to Hall before that date (June 1), Hall's basis for the stock would be its $4,500 FMV on June 1. Since Hall also sold the stock on June 1 for $4,500, Hall would have no gain or loss resulting from the sale.

I.B.9. Stock Dividends

11. **(b)** The requirement is to determine the amount of dividend income that should be reported by Gail Judd. The $100 dividend on Gail's life insurance policy is treated as a reduction of the cost of insurance (because total dividends have not yet exceeded accumulated premiums paid) and is excluded from gross income. Thus, Gail will report the $300 dividend on common stock and the $500 dividend on preferred stock, a total of $800 as dividend income for 2003.

12. **(b)** The requirement is to determine the amount of dividend income to be reported on Amy's 2003 return. Dividends are included in income at earlier of actual or constructive receipt. When corporate dividends are paid by mail, they are included in income for the year in which received. Thus, the $875 dividend received 1/2/03 is included in income for 2003. The $500 dividend on a life insurance policy from a mutual insurance company is treated as a reduction of the cost of insurance and is excluded from gross income.

13. **(c)** The requirement is to determine the amount of dividends to be reported by the Mitchells on a joint return. The amount of dividends would be ($400 + $50 + $300) = $750. The $200 dividend on the life insurance policy is not gross income, but is considered a reduction of the cost of the policy.

14. **(d)** The requirement is to determine Karen's basis in the 10 shares of preferred stock received as a stock dividend. Generally, stock dividends are nontaxable, and a taxpayer's basis for original stock is allocated to the dividend stock in proportion to fair market values. However, any stock that is distributed **on** preferred stock results in a taxable stock dividend. The amount to be included in the shareholder's income is the stock's fair market value on date of distribution. Similarly, the shareholder's basis for the dividend shares will be equal to their fair market value on date of distribution (10 x $60 = $600).

I.B.10. Interest Income

15. (c) The requirement is to determine the correct statement(s) regarding the amortization of bond premium on a taxable bond. The amount of premium amortization on taxable bonds acquired by the taxpayer after 1987 is treated as an offset to the amount of interest income reported on the bond. The method of calculating the annual amortization is determined by the date the bond was issued, as opposed to the acquisition date. If the bond was issued after September 27, 1985, the amortization must be calculated under the constant yield to maturity method. Otherwise, the amortization must be made ratably over the life of the bond. Under the constant yield to maturity method, the amortizable bond premium is computed on the basis of the taxpayer's yield to maturity, using the taxpayer's basis for the bond, and compounding at the close of each accrual period.

16. (c) The requirement is to determine whether two statements are true concerning the exclusion of interest income on US Series EE Bonds that are redeemed to pay for higher education. The accrued interest on US Series EE savings bonds that are redeemed by a taxpayer is excluded from gross income to the extent that the aggregate redemption proceeds (principal plus interest) are used to finance the higher education of the taxpayer, taxpayer's spouse, or dependents. Qualified higher educational expenses include tuition and fees, but not room and board or the cost of courses involving sports, games, or hobbies that are not part of a degree program. In determining the amount of available exclusion, qualified educational expenses must be reduced by qualified scholarships that are exempt from tax, and any other nontaxable payments such as veteran's educational assistance and employer-provided educational assistance.

17. (a) The requirement is to determine the amount of interest subject to tax in Kay's 2003 tax return. Interest must generally be included in gross income, unless a specific statutory provision provides for its exclusion (e.g., interest on municipal bonds). Interest on US Treasury certificates and on a refund of federal income tax would be subject to tax on Kay's 2003 tax return.

18. (c) The requirement is to determine the amount of interest income taxable on Charles and Marcia's joint income tax return. A taxpayer's income includes interest on state and federal income tax refunds and interest on federal obligations, but excludes interest on state obligations. Here, their joint taxable income must include the $500 interest on federal income tax refund, $600 interest on state income tax refund, and $800 interest on federal government obligations, but will exclude the $1,000 tax-exempt interest on state government obligations. Although a refund of federal income tax would be excluded from gross income, any interest on a refund must be included in gross income.

19. (a) The requirement is to determine the condition that must be met for tax exemption of accumulated interest on Series EE US Savings Bonds. An individual may be able to exclude from income all or a part of the interest received on the redemption of Series EE US Savings Bonds. To qualify, the bonds must be issued after December 31, 1989, the purchaser of the bonds must be the sole owner of the bonds (or joint owner with his or her spouse), and the owner(s) must be at least twenty-four years old before the bond's issue date. To exclude the interest the redemption

proceeds must be used to pay the tuition and fees incurred by the taxpayer, spouse, or dependents to attend a college or university or certain vocational schools.

20. (d) The requirement is to determine the amount of tax-exempt interest. Interest on obligations of a state or one of its political subdivisions (e.g., New York Port Authority bonds), or a possession of the US (e.g., Puerto Rico Commonwealth bonds) is tax-exempt.

21. (c) Stone will report $1,700 of interest income. Interest on FIT refunds, personal injury awards, US savings bonds, and most other sources is fully taxable. However, interest on state or municipal bonds is generally not taxable.

22. (d) The requirement is to determine how Don Raff's $500 interest forfeiture penalty should be reported. An interest forfeiture penalty for making a premature withdrawal from a certificate of deposit should be deducted from gross income in arriving at adjusted gross income in the year in which the penalty is incurred, which in this case is 2004.

I.B.12. Scholarships and Fellowships

23. (c) The requirement is to determine which payment(s) must be included in a recipient's gross income. A candidate for a degree can exclude amounts received as a scholarship or fellowship if, according to the conditions of the grant, the amounts are used for the payment of tuition and fees, books, supplies, and equipment required for courses at an educational institution. All payments received for services must be included in income, even if the services are a condition of receiving the grant or are required of all candidates for the degree. Here, the payment to a graduate assistant for a part-time teaching assignment and the grant to a Ph.D. candidate for participation in research are payments for services and must be included in income.

24. (c) The requirement is to determine the amount of scholarship awards that Majors should include as taxable income in 2003. Only a candidate for a degree can exclude amounts received as a scholarship award. The exclusion available to degree candidates is limited to amounts received for the payment of tuition and fees, books, supplies, and equipment required for courses at the educational institution. Since Majors is a candidate for a graduate degree, Majors can exclude the $10,000 received for tuition, fees, books, and supplies required for courses. However, the $2,000 stipend for research services required by the scholarship must be included in taxable income for 2003.

I.B.16. Lease Improvements

25. (a) The requirement is to determine a lessor's 2003 gross income. A lessor excludes from income any increase in the value of property caused by improvements made by the lessee, unless the improvements were made in lieu of rent. In this case, there is no indication that the improvements were made in lieu of rent. Therefore, for 2003, Farley should only include the six rent payments in income: 6 x $1,000 = $6,000.

I.C. Items to Be Included in Gross Income

26. (d) The requirement is to determine the amount of alimony recapture that must be included in Bob's gross income for 2003. Alimony recapture may occur if alimony payments sharply decline in the second and third years that payments are made. The payor must report the recaptured alimony as gross income in the third year, and the payee is allowed a deduction for the same amount. Recapture for the second year (2002) occurs to the extent that the alimony paid in the second year ($20,000) exceeds the alimony paid in the third year ($0) by more than $15,000 [i.e., $20,000 – ($0 + $15,000) = $5,000 of recapture].

Recapture for the first year (2001) occurs to the extent that the alimony paid in the first year ($50,000) exceeds the *average alimony* paid in the second and third years by more than $15,000. For this purpose, the alimony paid in the second year ($20,000) must be reduced by the amount of recapture for that year ($5,000).

First year (2001) payment		$50,000
Second year (2002) payment		
($20,000 – $5,000)	$15,000	
Third year (2003) payment	+ 0	
Total	$15,000	
	÷ 2	(7,500)
		(15,000)
Recapture for first year (2001)		$ 27,500

Thus, the total recapture to be included in Bob's gross income for 2003 is $5,000 + $27,500 = $32,500.

27. (c)   The requirement is to determine which conditions must be present in a post-1984 divorce agreement for a payment to qualify as deductible alimony. In order for a payment to be deductible by the payor as alimony, the payment must be made in cash or its equivalent, the payment must be received by or on behalf of a spouse under a divorce or separation instrument, the payments must terminate at the recipient's death, and must not be designated as other than alimony (e.g., child support).

28. (d)   The requirement is to determine which of the following would be included in gross income by Darr who is an employee of Sorce C corporation. The definition of gross income includes income from whatever source derived and would include the dividend income on shares of stock that Darr received for services rendered. However, items specifically excluded from gross income include amounts received as a gift or inheritance, as well as employer-provided medical insurance coverage under a health plan.

29. (c)   The requirement is to determine the correct statement regarding the inclusion of social security benefits in gross income for 2003. A maximum of 85% of social security benefits may be included in gross income for high-income taxpayers. Thus, no matter how high a taxpayer's income, 85% of the social security benefits is the maximum amount of benefits to be included in gross income.

30. (c)   The requirement is to determine the amount that Perle should include in taxable income as a result of performing dental services for Wood. An exchange of services for property or services is sometimes called bartering. A taxpayer must include in income the amount of cash and the fair market value of property or services received in exchange for the performance of services. Here, Perle's taxable income should include the $200 cash and the bookcase with a comparable value of $350, a total of $550.

31. (b)   The requirement is to determine the amount of payments to be included in Mary's income tax return for 2003. Alimony must be included in gross income by the payee and is deductible by the payor. In order to be treated

as alimony, a payment must be made in cash and be received by or paid on behalf of the former spouse. Amounts treated as child support are not alimony; they are neither deductible by the payor, nor taxable to the payee. Payments will be treated as child support to the extent that payments will be reduced upon the happening of a contingency relating to a child (e.g., the child attaining a specified age, marrying, becoming employed). Here, since future payments will be reduced by 20% on their child's 18th birthday, the total cash payments of $10,000 ($7,000 paid directly to Mary plus the $3,000 of tuition paid on Mary's behalf) must be reduced by 20% and result in $8,000 of alimony income for Mary. The remaining $2,000 is treated as child support and is not taxable.

32. (b)   The requirement is to determine the amount of interest for overpayment of 2002 state income tax and state income tax refund that is taxable in Clark's 2003 federal income tax return. The $10 of interest income on the tax refund is taxable and must be included in gross income. On the other hand, a state income tax refund is included in gross income under the "tax benefit rule" only if the refunded amount was deducted in a prior year and the deduction provided a benefit because it reduced the taxpayer's federal income tax. The payment of state income taxes will not result in a "benefit" if an individual does not itemize deductions, or is subject to the alternative minimum tax for the year the taxes are paid. Individuals who file Form 1040EZ are not allowed to itemize deductions and must use the standard deduction. Since state income taxes are only allowed as an itemized deduction and Clark did not itemize for 2002 (he used Form 1040EZ), his $900 state income tax refund is nontaxable and is excluded from taxable income.

33. (d)   The requirement is to determine the amount to be reported in Hall's 2003 return as alimony income. If a divorce agreement specifies both alimony and child support, but less is paid than required, then payments are first allocated to child support, with only the remainder in excess of required child support to be treated as alimony. Pursuant to Hall's divorce agreement, $3,000 was to be paid each month, of which $600 was designated as child support, leaving a balance of $2,400 per month to be treated as alimony. However, during 2003, only $5,000 was paid to Hall by her former husband which was less than the $36,000 required by the divorce agreement. Since required child support payments totaled $600 x 12 = $7,200 for 2003, all $5,000 of the payments actually received by Hall during 2003 is treated as child support, with nothing remaining to be reported as alimony.

34. (b)   The requirement is to determine the amount of income to be reported by Lee in connection with the receipt of stock for services rendered. Compensation for services rendered that is received by a cash method taxpayer must be included in income at its fair market value on the date of receipt.

35. (c)   The requirement is to determine when Ross was subject to "regular tax" with regard to stock that was acquired through the exercise of an incentive stock option. There are no tax consequences when an incentive stock option is granted to an employee. When the option is exercised, any excess of the stock's FMV over the option price is a tax preference item for purposes of the employee's alternative minimum tax. However, an employee is not subject to regular tax until the stock acquired through exercise of the option is sold.

If the employee holds the stock acquired through exercise of the option at least two years from the date the option was granted (and holds the stock itself at least one year), the employee's realized gain is treated as long-term capital gain in the year of sale, and the employer receives no compensation deduction. If the preceding holding period rules are not met at the time the stock is sold, the employee must report ordinary income to the extent that the stock's FMV at date of exercise exceeded the option price, with any remaining gain reported as long-term or short-term capital gain. As a result, the employer receives a compensation deduction equal to the amount of ordinary income reported by the employee.

36. **(a)** The requirement is to determine the amount that is taxable as alimony in Ann's return. In order to be treated as alimony, a payment must be made in cash and be received by or on behalf of the payee spouse. Furthermore, cash payments must be required to terminate upon the death of the payee spouse to be treated as alimony. In this case, the transfer of title in the home to Ann is not a cash payment and cannot be treated as alimony. Although the mortgage payments are cash payments made on behalf of Ann, the payments are not treated as alimony because they will be made throughout the full twenty-year mortgage period and will not terminate in the event of Ann's death.

37. **(c)** The requirement is to determine the correct statement with regard to income in respect of a cash basis decedent. Income in respect of a decedent is income earned by a decedent before death that was not includible in the decedent's final income tax return because of the decedent's method of accounting (e.g., receivables of a cash basis decedent). Such income must be included in gross income by the person who receives it and has the same character (e.g., ordinary or capital) as it would have had if the decedent had lived.

38. **(d)** The requirement is to determine the amount of gross income. Drury's gross income includes the $36,000 salary, the $500 of premiums paid by her employer for group-term life insurance coverage in excess of $50,000, and the $5,000 proceeds received from a state lottery.

39. **(b)** The requirement is to determine the amount of foster child payments to be included in income by the Charaks. Foster child payments are excluded from income to the extent they represent reimbursement for expenses incurred for care of the foster child. Since the payments ($3,900) exceeded the expenses ($3,000), the $900 excess used for the Charaks' personal expenses must be included in their gross income.

40. **(b)** The requirement is to determine the amount and the year in which the tip income should be included in Pierre's gross income. If an individual receives less than $20 in tips during one month while working for one employer, the tips do not have to be reported to the employer and the tips are included in the individual's gross income when received. However, if an individual receives $20 or more in tips during one month while working for one employer, the individual must report the total amount of tips to that employer by the tenth day of the next month. Then the tips are included in gross income for the month in which they are reported to the employer. Here, Pierre received $2,000 in tips during December 2003 that he reported to his employer in January 2004. Thus, the $2,000 of tips will be included in Pierre's gross income for 2004.

41. **(c)** The requirement is to determine the correct statement regarding the alimony deduction in connection with a 2003 divorce. To be considered alimony, cash payments must terminate on the death of the payee spouse. Answer (a) is incorrect because alimony payments cannot be contingent on the status of the divorced couple's children. Answer (b) is incorrect because the divorced couple cannot be members of the same household at the time the alimony is paid. Answer (d) is incorrect because only cash payments can be considered alimony.

42. **(d)** The requirement is to determine the amount of a $10,000 award for outstanding civic achievement that Joan should include in her 2003 adjusted gross income. An award for civic achievement can be excluded from gross income only if the recipient was selected without any action on his/her part, is not required to render substantial future services as a condition of receiving the award, and designates that the award is to be directly transferred by the payor to a governmental unit or a tax-exempt charitable, educational, or religious organization. Here, since Joan accepted and actually received the award, the $10,000 must be included in her adjusted gross income.

43. **(d)** The requirement is to determine the amount of lottery winnings that should be included in Gow's taxable income. Lottery winnings are gambling winnings and must be included in gross income. Gambling losses are deductible from AGI as a miscellaneous deduction (to the extent of winnings) not subject to the 2% of AGI floor if a taxpayer itemizes deductions. Since Gow elected the standard deduction for 2003, the $400 spent on lottery tickets is not deductible. Thus, all $5,000 of Gow's lottery winnings are included in his taxable income.

I.C.5. Rents and Royalties

44. **(d)** The requirement is to determine the amount of advance rents and lease cancellation payments that should be reported on Lake Corp.'s 2003 tax return. Advance rental payments must be included in gross income when received, regardless of the period covered or whether the taxpayer uses the cash or accrual method. Similarly, lease cancellation payments are treated as rent and must be included in income when received, regardless of the taxpayer's method of accounting.

45. **(c)** The requirement is to determine the amount to be reported as gross rents. Gross rents include the $50,000 of recurring rents plus the $2,000 lease cancellation payment. The $1,000 of lease improvements are excluded from income since they were **not** required in lieu of rent.

46. **(c)** The requirement is to determine the amount of net rental income that Gow should include in his adjusted gross income. Since Gow lives in one of two identical apartments, only 50% of the expenses relating to both apartments can be allocated to the rental unit.

Rent	$7,200
Less:	
Real estate taxes (50% x $6,400)	(3,200)
Painting of rental apartment	(800)
Fire insurance (50% x $600)	(300)
Depreciation (50% x $5,000)	(2,500)
Net rental income	$ 400

47. (a)   The requirement is to determine the amount of rent income to be reported on Amy's 2003 return. Both the $6,000 of rent received for 2003, as well as the $1,000 of advance rent received in 2003 for the last two months of the lease must be included in income for 2003. Advance rent must be included in income in the year received regardless of the period covered or the accounting method used.

48. (a)   The requirement is to determine the amount to be reported as rent revenue in an accrual-basis taxpayer's tax return for 2003. An accrual-basis taxpayer's rent revenue would consist of the amount of rent earned during the taxable year plus any advance rent received. Advance rents must be included in gross income when received under both the cash and accrual methods, even though they have not yet been earned. In this case, Royce's rent revenue would be determined as follows:

Rent receivable 12/31/02	$35,000
Rent receivable 12/31/03	25,000
Decrease in receivables	(10,000)
Rent collections during 2003	50,000
Rent deposits	5,000
Rent revenue for 2003	$45,000

The rent deposits must be included in gross income for 2003 because they are nonrefundable deposits.

I.C.19.   Unemployment Compensation

49. (a)   The requirement is to determine the amount of state unemployment benefits that should be included in adjusted gross income. All unemployment compensation benefits received must be included in gross income.

I.D.   Tax Accounting Methods

50. (d)   The requirement is to determine the correct statement regarding the reporting of income by a cash-basis taxpayer. A cash-basis taxpayer should report gross income for the year in which income is either actually or constructively received, whether in cash or in property. Constructive receipt means that an item of income is unqualifiedly available to the taxpayer without restriction (e.g., interest on bank deposit is income when credited to account).

51. (b)   The requirement is to determine which taxpayer may use the cash method of accounting. The cash method cannot generally be used if inventories are necessary to clearly reflect income, and cannot generally be used by C corporations, partnerships that have a C corporation as a partner, tax shelters, and certain tax-exempt trusts. Taxpayers permitted to use the cash method include a qualified personal service corporation, an entity (other than a tax shelter) if for every year it has average gross receipts of $5 million or less for any prior three-year period (and provided it does not have inventories), and a small taxpayer with average annual gross receipts of $1 million or less for any prior three-year period may use the cash method and is excepted from the requirement to account for inventories

52. (b)   The requirement is to select the correct statement regarding the $1,000 of additional income determined by Stewart, an accrual method corporation. Under the accrual method, income generally is reported in the year earned. If an amount is included in gross income on the basis of a reasonable estimate, and it is later determined that the exact amount is more, then the additional amount is included in income in the tax year in which the determination of the exact amount is made. Here, Stewart properly accrued $5,000 of income for 2003, and discovered that the exact amount was $6,000 in 2004. Therefore, the additional $1,000 of income is properly includible in Stewart's 2004 income tax return.

53. (b)   The requirement is to determine the correct statement regarding Axis Corp.'s deduction for its employees bonus expense. An accrual-method taxpayer can deduct compensation (including a bonus) when there is an obligation to make payment, the services have been performed, and the amount can be determined with reasonable accuracy. It is not required that the exact amount of compensation be determined during the taxable year. As long as the computation is known and the liability is fixed, accrual is proper even though the profits upon which the compensation are based are not determined until after the end of the year.

Although compensation is generally deductible only for the year in which the compensation is paid, an exception is made for accrual method taxpayers so long as payment is made within 2 1/2 months after the end of the year. Here, since the services were performed, the method of computation was known, the amount was reasonable, and payment was made by March 15, 2004, the bonus expense may be deducted on Axis Corp.'s 2003 tax return. Note that the bonus could not be a disguised dividend because none of the employees were shareholders.

54. (b)   The requirement is to determine the amount of the 2002 interest payment of $12,000 that was deductible on Michaels' 2003 income tax return. Generally, there is no deduction for prepaid interest. When a taxpayer pays interest for a period that extends beyond the end of the tax year, the interest paid in advance must be spread over the period to which it applies. Michaels paid $12,000 of interest during 2002 that relates to the period beginning December 1, 2002, and ending November 30, 2003. Therefore, 1/12 x $12,000 = $1,000 of interest was deductible for 2002, and 11/12 x $12,000 = $11,000 was deductible for 2003.

55. (c)   The requirement is to determine the amount of income to be reported in Blair's 2003 return for the stock received in satisfaction of a client fee owed to Blair. Since Blair is a cash method taxpayer, the amount of income to be recognized equals the $4,000 fair market value of the stock on date of receipt. Note that the $4,000 of income is reported by Blair in 2003 when the stock is received; not in 2004 when the stock is sold.

56. (d)   The requirement is to determine whether the accrual method of tax reporting is mandatory for a sole proprietor when there are accounts receivable for services rendered, or year-end merchandise inventories. A taxpayer's taxable income should be computed using the method of accounting by which the taxpayer regularly computes income in keeping the taxpayer's books. Either the cash or the accrual method generally can be used so long as the method is consistently applied and clearly reflects income. However, when the production, purchase, or sale of merchandise is an income producing factor, inventories must be maintained to clearly reflect income. If merchandise inventories are necessary to clearly determine income, only the accrual method of tax reporting can be used for purchases and sales.

57. (**d**)   The requirement is to determine the amount of salary taxable to Burg in 2003. Since Burg is a cash-basis taxpayer, salary is taxable to Burg when actually or constructively received, whichever is earlier. Since the $30,000 of unpaid salary was unqualifiedly available to Burg during 2003, Burg is considered to have constructively received it. Thus, Burg must report a total of $80,000 of salary for 2003; the $50,000 actually received plus $30,000 constructively received.

58. (**d**)   The requirement is to determine the 2003 medical practice net income for a cash basis physician. Dr. Berger's income consists of the $200,000 received from patients and the $30,000 received from third-party reimbursers during 2003. His 2003 deductions include the $20,000 of salaries and $24,000 of other expenses paid in 2003. The year-end bonuses will be deductible for 2004.

59. (**c**)   The requirement is to determine which taxpayer may use the cash method of accounting for tax purposes. The cash method generally cannot be used (and the accrual method must be used to measure sales and cost of goods sold) if inventories are necessary to clearly determine income. Additionally, the cash method generally cannot generally be used by (1) a corporation (other than an S corporation), (2) a partnership with a corporation as a partner, and (3) a tax shelter. However, this prohibition against the use of the cash method in the preceding sentence does not apply to a farming business, a qualified personal service corporation (e.g., a corporation performing services in health, law, engineering, architecture, accounting, actuarial science, performing arts, or consulting), and a corporation or partnership (that is not a tax shelter) that does not have inventories and whose average annual gross receipts for the most recent three-year period do not exceed $5 million.

I.E.   Business Income and Deductions

60. (**a**)   Uniform capitalization rules generally require that all costs incurred (both direct and indirect) in manufacturing or constructing real or personal property, or in purchasing or holding property for sale, must be capitalized as part of the cost of the property. However, these rules do not apply to a "small retailer or wholesaler" who acquires personal property for resale if the retailer's or wholesaler's average annual gross receipts for the three preceding taxable years do not exceed $10 million.

61. (**a**)   The requirement is to determine whether the cost of merchandise, and business expenses other than the cost of merchandise, can be deducted in calculating Mock's business income from a retail business selling illegal narcotic substances. Generally, business expenses that are incurred in an illegal activity are deductible if they are ordinary and necessary, and reasonable in amount. Under a special exception, no deduction or credit is allowed for any amount that is paid or incurred in carrying on a trade or business which consists of trafficking in controlled substances. However, this limitation that applies to expenditures in connection with the illegal sale of drugs does not alter the normal definition of gross income (i.e., sales minus cost of goods

sold). As a result, in arriving at gross income from the business, Mock may reduce total sales by the cost of goods sold, and thus is allowed to deduct the cost of merchandise in calculating business income.

62. (**b**)   The requirement is to determine the percentage of business meals expense that Banks Corp. can deduct for 2003. Generally, only 50% of business meals and entertainment is deductible. When an employer reimburses its employees' substantiated qualifying business meal expenses, the 50% limitation on deductibility applies to the employer.

63. (**a**)   The requirement is to determine which of the costs is **not** included in inventory under the Uniform Capitalization (UNICAP) rules for goods manufactured by a taxpayer. UNICAP rules require that specified overhead items must be included in inventory including factory repairs and maintenance, factory administration and officers' salaries related to production, taxes (other than income taxes), the costs of quality control and inspection, current and past service costs of pension and profit-sharing plans, and service support such as purchasing, payroll, and warehousing costs. Nonmanufacturing costs such as selling, advertising, and research and experimental costs are not required to be included in inventory.

64. (**d**)   If no exceptions are met, the uniform capitalization rules generally require that all costs incurred in purchasing or holding inventory for resale must be capitalized as part of the cost of the inventory. Costs that must be capitalized with respect to inventory include the costs of purchasing, handling, processing, repackaging and assembly, and off-site storage. An off-site storage facility is one that is not physically attached to, and an integral part of, a retail sales facility. Service costs such as marketing, selling, advertising, and general management are immediately deductible and need not be capitalized as part of the cost of inventory.

65. (**d**)   The requirement is to determine the correct statement regarding the deduction for bad debts in the case of a corporation that is not a financial institution. Except for certain small banks that can use the experience method of accounting for bad debts, all taxpayers (including those that previously used the reserve method) are required to use the direct charge-off method of accounting for bad debts.

66. (**d**)   The requirement is to determine the amount of life insurance premium that can be deducted in Ram Corp.'s income tax return. Generally, no deduction is allowed for expenditures that produce tax-exempt income. Here, no deduction is allowed for the $6,000 life insurance premium because Ram is the beneficiary of the policy, and the proceeds of the policy will be excluded from Ram's income when the officer dies.

67. (**a**)   The requirement is to determine the amount of bad debt deduction for a cash-basis taxpayer. Accounts receivable resulting from services rendered by a cash-basis taxpayer have a zero tax basis, because the income has not yet been reported. Thus, failure to collect the receivable results in a nondeductible loss.

68. (**c**)   The requirement is to determine the loss that Cook can claim as a result of the worthless note receivable in 2003. Cook's $1,000 loss will be treated as a nonbusiness bad debt, deductible as a short-term capital loss. The loss is

not a business bad debt because Cook was not in the business of lending money, nor was the loan required as a condition of Cook's employment. Since Cook owned no stock in Precision, the loss could **not** be deemed to be a loss from worthless stock, deductible as a long-term capital loss.

69.   (b)   The requirement is to determine the amount of gifts deductible as a business expense. The deduction for business gifts is limited to $25 per recipient each year. Thus, Palo Corporation's deduction for business gifts would be [(4 x $10) + (13 x $25)] = $365.

I.E.3 Net Operating Loss (NOL)

70.   (b)   The requirement is to determine Jennifer's net operating loss (NOL) for 2003. Jennifer's personal casualty loss of $45,000 incurred as a result of the destruction of her personal residence is allowed as a deduction in the computation of her NOL and is subtracted from her salary income of $30,000, to arrive at a NOL of $15,000. No deduction is allowed for personal and dependency exemptions in the computation of a NOL.

71.   (c)   The requirement is to determine the amount of net operating loss (NOL) for a self-employed taxpayer for 2003. A NOL generally represents a loss from the conduct of a trade or business and can generally be carried back two years and forward twenty years to offset income in the carryback and carryforward years. Since a NOL generally represents a business loss, an individual taxpayer's personal exemptions and an excess of nonbusiness deductions over nonbusiness income cannot be subtracted in computing the NOL. Nonbusiness deductions generally include itemized deductions as well as the standard deduction if the taxpayer does not itemize. In this case, the $4,750 standard deduction offsets the $1,500 of nonbusiness income received in the form of dividends and short-term capital gain, but the excess ($3,250) cannot be included in the NOL computation. Thus, the taxpayer's NOL simply consists of the $6,000 business loss.

72.   (a)   The requirement is to determine Destry's net operating loss (NOL). A net operating loss generally represents a loss from the conduct of a trade or business and can generally be carried back two years and forward twenty years to offset income in the carryback and carryforward years. Since a NOL generally represents a business loss, an individual taxpayer's personal exemption and an excess of nonbusiness deductions (e.g., standard deduction) over nonbusiness income (e.g., interest from savings account) cannot be subtracted in computing the NOL. Similarly, no deduction is allowed for a net capital loss. As a result, Destry's NOL consists of his net business loss of $16,000 reduced by his business income of $5,000 from wages and $4,000 of net rental income, resulting in a NOL of $7,000.

I.E.6. Losses and Credits from Passive Activities

73.   (a)   The requirement is to determine the amount of Cobb's rental real estate loss that can be used as an offset against income from nonpassive sources. Losses from passive activities may generally only be used to offset income from other passive activities. Although a rental activity is defined as a passive activity regardless of the owner's participation in the operation of the rental property, a special rule permits an individual to offset up to $25,000 of income that is not from passive activities by losses from a rental real

estate activity if the individual actively participates in the rental real estate activity. However, this special $25,000 allowance is reduced by 50% of the taxpayer's AGI in excess of $100,000, and is fully phased out when AGI exceeds $150,000. Since Cobb's AGI is $200,000, the special $25,000 allowance is fully phased out and no rental loss can be offset against income from nonpassive sources.

74.   (c)   The requirement is to determine the entity to which the rules limiting the allowability of passive activity losses and credits applies. The passive activity limitations apply to individuals, estates, trusts, closely held C corporations, and personal service corporations. Application of the passive activity loss limitations to personal service corporations is intended to prevent taxpayers from sheltering personal service income by creating personal service corporations and acquiring passive activity losses at the corporate level. A personal service corporation is a corporation (1) whose principal activity is the performance of personal services, and (2) such services are substantially performed by owner-employees. Since passive activity income, losses, and credits from partnerships and S corporations flow through to be reported on the tax returns of the owners of such entities, the passive activity limitations are applied at the partner and shareholder level, rather than to partnerships and S corporations themselves.

75.   (c)   The requirement is to determine Wolf's passive loss resulting from his 5% general partnership interest in Gata Associates. A partnership is a pass-through entity and its items of income and loss pass through to partners to be included on their tax returns. Since Wolf does not materially participate in the partnership's auto parts business, Wolf's distributable share of the loss from the partnership's auto parts business is classified as a passive activity loss. Portfolio income or loss must be excluded from the computation of the income or loss resulting from a passive activity, and must be separately passed through to partners.

Portfolio income includes all interest income, other than interest income derived in the ordinary course of a trade or business. Interest income derived in the ordinary course of a trade or business includes only interest income on loans and investments made in the ordinary course of a trade or business of lending money, and interest income on accounts receivable arising in the ordinary course of a trade or business. Since the $20,000 of interest income derived by the partnership resulted from a temporary investment, the interest income must be classified as portfolio income and cannot be netted against the $100,000 operating loss from the auto parts business. Thus, Wolf will report a passive activity loss of $100,000 x 5% = $5,000; and will report portfolio income of $20,000 x 5% = $1,000.

76.   (a)   The requirement is to determine the correct statement regarding the passive loss rules involving rental real estate activities. By definition, any rental activity is a passive activity without regard as to whether or not the taxpayer materially participates in the activity. Answer (b) is incorrect because interest and dividend income not derived in the ordinary course of business is treated as **portfolio** income, and **cannot** be offset by passive rental activity losses when the "active participation" requirement is **not** met. Answer (c) is incorrect because passive rental activity credits **cannot** be used to offset the tax attributable to **nonpassive** activities. Answer (d) is incorrect because the passive activity rules contain no provision that excludes tax-payers below a certain income level from the limitations imposed by the passive activity rules.

77.   (d)   The requirement is to determine the correct statement regarding an individual taxpayer's passive losses and credits relating to rental real estate activities that cannot be currently deducted. Generally, losses and credits from passive activities can only be used to offset income from (or tax allocable to) passive activities. If there is insufficient passive activity income (or tax) to absorb passive activity losses and credits, the unused losses and credits are carried forward indefinitely or until the property is disposed of in a taxable transaction. Answers (a) and (c) are incorrect because unused passive losses and credits are never carried back to prior taxable years. Answer (b) is incorrect because there is no maximum carryforward period.

I.F.   Depreciation, Depletion, and Amortization

78.   (a)   The requirement is to determine the maximum amount of Sec. 179 expense election that Aviation Corp. will be allowed to deduct for 2003, and the maximum amount of expense election that it can carry over to 2004. Sec. 179 permits a taxpayer to elect to treat up to $25,000 of the cost of qualifying depreciable personal property as an expense rather than as a capital expenditure. However, the $25,000 maximum is reduced dollar-for-dollar by the cost of qualifying property placed in service during the taxable year that exceeds $200,000. Here, the maximum amount that can be expensed is $25,000 – ($203,000 – $200,000) = $22,000 for 2003. However, this amount is further limited as a deduction for 2003 to Aviation's taxable income of $7,000 before the Sec. 179 expense deduction. The remainder ($22,000 – $7,000 = $15,000) that is not currently deductible because of the taxable income limitation can be carried over and will be deductible subject to the taxable income limitation in 2004.

79.   (c)   The requirement is to determine which conditions must be satisfied to enable a taxpayer to expense the cost of new or used tangible depreciable personal property under Sec. 179. Taxpayers may elect to expense up to $25,000 of the cost of new or used tangible depreciable personal property placed in service during the taxable year. To qualify, the property must be acquired by purchase from an unrelated party for use in the taxpayer's active trade or business. The maximum cost that can be expensed ($25,000 for 2003) is reduced dollar-for-dollar by the cost of qualifying property that is placed in service during the year that exceeds $200,000. Additionally, the amount that can be expensed is further limited to the aggregate taxable income derived from the active conduct of any trade or business of the taxpayer.

80.   (a)   The requirement is to determine the MACRS deduction for the furniture and fixtures placed in service during 2003. The furniture and fixtures qualify as seven-year property and under MACRS will be depreciated using the 200% declining balance method. Normally, a half-year convention applies to the year of acquisition. However, the midquarter convention must be used if more than 40% of all personal property is placed in service during the last quarter of the taxpayer's taxable year. Since this was Krol's only acquisition of personal property and the property was placed in service during the last quarter of Krol's calendar year, the

mid-quarter convention must be used. Under this convention, property is treated as placed in service during the middle of the quarter in which placed in service. Since the furniture and fixtures were placed in service in November, the amount of allowable MACRS depreciation is limited to $56,000 x 2/7 x 1/8 = $2,000.

81.   (b)   The requirement is to determine Sullivan's MACRS deduction for the apartment building in 2003. The MACRS deduction for residential real property placed in service during 2003 must be determined using the mid-month convention (i.e., property is treated as placed in service at the midpoint of the month placed in service) and the straight-line method of depreciation over a 27.5-year recovery period. Here, the $360,000 cost must first be reduced by the $30,000 allocated to the land, to arrive at a basis for depreciation of $330,000. Since the building was placed in service on June 29, the mid-month convention results in 6.5 months of depreciation for 2003. The MACRS deduction for 2003 is [$330,000 x (6.5 months)/(27.5 x 12 months)] = $6,500.

82.   (c)   The requirement is to determine the depreciation convention that must be used when a calendar-year taxpayer's only acquisition of equipment during the year occurs during November. Generally, a half-year convention applies to depreciable personal property, and a mid-month convention applies to depreciable real property. Under the half-year convention, a half-year of depreciation is allowed for the year in which property is placed in service, regardless of when the property is placed in service during the year, and a half-year of depreciation is allowed for the year in which the property is disposed of. However, a taxpayer must instead use a midquarter convention if more than 40% of all depreciable personal property acquired during the year is placed in service during the last quarter of the taxable year. Under this convention, property is treated as placed in service (or disposed of) in the middle of the quarter in which placed in service (or disposed of). Since Data Corp. is a calendar-year taxpayer and its only acquisition of depreciable personal property was placed in service during November (i.e., the last quarter of its taxable year), it must use the midquarter convention, and will only be allowed a half-quarter of depreciation of its office equipment for 2003.

83.   (b)   The requirement is to determine the correct statement regarding the modified accelerated cost recovery system (MACRS) of depreciation for property placed in service after 1986. Under MACRS, salvage value is completely ignored for purposes of computing the depreciation deduction, which results in the recovery of the entire cost of depreciable property. Answer (a) is incorrect because used tangible depreciable property is depreciated under MACRS. Answer (c) is incorrect because the cost of some depreciable realty must be depreciated using the straight-line method. Answer (d) is incorrect because the cost of some depreciable realty is included in the ten-year (e.g., single purpose agricultural and horticultural structures) and twenty-year (e.g., farm buildings) classes.

84.   (a)   The requirement is to determine the correct statement regarding the half-year convention under the general MACRS method. Under the half-year convention that generally applies to depreciable personal property, one-half of the first year's depreciation is allowed in the year in which the property is placed in service, regardless of when the property is placed in service during the year, and a half-year's depreciation is allowed for the year in which the property is disposed of, regardless of when the property is disposed of during the year. Answer (b) is incorrect because allowing one-half month's depreciation for the month that property is placed in service or disposed of is known as the "midmonth convention."

85. **(c)** The requirement is to determine the portion of the $201,000 cost of the machine that can be treated as an expense for 2003. Sec. 179 permits a taxpayer to elect to treat up to $25,000 of the cost of qualifying depreciable personal property as an expense rather than as a capital expenditure. However, the $25,000 maximum is reduced dollar-for-dollar by the cost of qualifying property placed in service during the taxable year that exceeds $200,000. Here, the maximum amount that can be expensed is [$25,000 – ($201,000 – $200,000)] = $24,000.

II. "Above the Line" Deductions

86. **(d)** The requirement is to determine the amount to be reported in Mel's gross income for the $400 per month received for business automobile expenses under a nonaccountable plan from Easel Co. Reimbursements and expense allowances paid to an employee under a nonaccountable plan must be included in the employee's gross income and are reported on the employee's W-2. The employee must then complete Form 2106 and itemize to deduct business-related expenses such as the use of an automobile.

87. **(c)** The requirement is to determine the correct statement regarding a second residence that is rented for 200 days and used 50 days for personal use. Deductions for expenses related to a dwelling that is also used as a residence by the taxpayer may be limited. If the taxpayer's personal use exceeds the greater of 14 days, or 10% of the number of days rented, deductions allocable to rental use are limited to rental income. Here, since Adams used the second residence for 50 days and rented the residence for 200 days, no rental loss can be deducted. All expenses related to the property, including utilities and maintenance, must be allocated between personal use and rental use. Answer (d) is incorrect because only the mortgage interest and taxes allocable to rental use would be deducted in determining the property's net rental income or loss. Answer (a) is incorrect, since depreciation on the property could be deducted if Adams' gross rental income exceeds allocable out-of-pocket rental expenses.

88. **(a)** The requirement is to determine the amount of unreimbursed employee expenses that can be deducted by Gilbert if he does not itemize deductions. Gilbert cannot deduct any of the expenses listed if he does not itemize deductions. The unreimbursed employee business expenses are deductible only as itemized deductions, subsequent to the 2% of AGI floor.

II.E.   Moving Expenses

89. **(c)** The requirement is to determine the amount of moving expense that James can deduct for 2003. Direct moving expenses are deductible if closely related to the start of work at a new location and a distance test (i.e., distance from new job to former residence is at least fifty miles further than distance from old job to former residence) and a time test (i.e., employed at least thirty-nine weeks out of

twelve months following move) are met. Since both tests are met, James' unreimbursed lodging and travel expenses ($1,000), cost of insuring household goods and personal effects during move ($200), cost of shipping household pets ($100), and cost of moving household furnishings and personal effects ($3,000) are deductible. Indirect moving expenses such as premove househunting, temporary living expenses, and meals while moving are not deductible.

90. **(c)** The requirement is to determine Martin's deductible moving expenses. Moving expenses are deductible if closely related to the start of work at a new location and a distance (i.e., new job must be at least fifty miles from former residence) and time (i.e., employed at least thirty-nine weeks out of twelve months following move) tests are met. Here, both tests are met and Martin's $800 cost of moving his personal belongings is deductible. However, the $300 penalty for breaking his lease is not deductible.

91. **(a)** Only the direct costs incurred for transporting a taxpayer, his or her family, and their household goods and personal effects from their former residence to their new residence can qualify as deductible moving expenses. The indirect moving expense costs incurred for meals while in transit, house hunting, temporary lodging, to sell or purchase a home, and to break or acquire a lease are not deductible.

II.F.   Contributions to Certain Retirement Plans

92. **(d)** The requirement is to determine the incorrect statement concerning a Roth IRA. The maximum annual contribution to a Roth IRA is subject to reduction if the taxpayer's adjusted gross income exceeds certain thresholds. Unlike a traditional IRA, contributions are not deductible and can be made even after the taxpayer reaches age 70½. The contribution must be made by the due date of the taxpayer's tax return (**not** including extensions).

93. **(c)** The requirement is to determine the maximum amount of adjusted gross income that a taxpayer may have and still qualify to roll over a traditional IRA into a Roth IRA. A conversion or rollover of a traditional IRA to a Roth IRA can occur if the taxpayer's AGI does not exceed $100,000, the taxpayer is not married filing a separate return, and the rollover occurs within sixty days of the IRA distribution. For purposes of the determining eligibility, the $100,000 AGI ceiling is determined by including taxable social security and is determined before the exclusions for interest on Series EE bonds used for higher education, employer provided adoption assistance, and foreign earned income. The IRA conversion or rollover amount is not taken into account in determining the $100,000 AGI ceiling.

94. **(d)** The requirement is to determine which statement concerning an education IRA is not correct. Contributions to an education IRA are not deductible, but withdrawals of earnings will be tax-free if used to pay the qualified higher education expenses of the designated beneficiary. The maximum amount that can be contributed to an education IRA for 2003 is limited to $2,000, but the annual contribution is phased out by adjusted gross income in excess of certain thresholds. Contributions generally cannot be made to an education IRA after the date on which the designated beneficiary reaches age eighteen.

95. **(a)** The requirement is to determine the Whites' allowable IRA deduction on their 2003 joint return. For married taxpayers filing a joint return for 2003, up to $3,000 can be deducted for contributions to the IRA of each spouse (even if one spouse is not working), provided that the combined earned income of both spouses is at least equal to the amounts contributed to the IRAs. Even though Val is covered by his employer's qualified pension plan, the Whites are eligible for the maximum deduction because their gross income of $35,000 + $5,000 = $40,000 does not exceed the base amount ($60,000) at which the maximum $3,000 deduction would be reduced. Also note that Pat's $5,000 of taxable alimony payments is treated as compensation for purposes of qualifying for an IRA deduction. Since they each contributed $3,000 to an IRA account, the allowable deduction on their joint return is $6,000.

96. (d) The requirement is to determine the definition of "earned income" for purposes of computing the annual contribution to a Keogh profit-sharing plan by Davis, a sole proprietor. A self-employed individual may contribute to a qualified retirement plan called a Keogh plan. The maximum contribution to a Keogh profit-sharing plan is the lesser of $40,000 or 25% of earned income. For this purpose, "earned income" is defined as net earnings from self-employment (i.e., business gross income minus allowable business deductions) reduced by the deduction for one-half of the self-employment tax, and the deductible Keogh contribution itself.

97. (d) A single individual with AGI over $50,000 for 2003 would only be entitled to an IRA deduction if the taxpayer is not covered by a qualified employee pension plan.

98. (b) The requirement is to determine the allowable IRA deduction on the Cranes' 2003 joint return. Since Sol is covered by his employer's pension plan, Sol's contribution of $3,000 is proportionally phased out as a deduction by AGI between $60,000 and $70,000. Since the Cranes' AGI exceeded $70,000, no deduction is allowed for Sol's contribution. Although Julia is not employed, $3,000 can be contributed to her IRA because the combined earned income on the Cranes' return is at least $6,000. The maximum IRA deduction for an individual who is not covered by an employer plan, but whose spouse is, is proportionally phased out for AGI between $150,000 and $160,000. Since Julia is not covered by an employer plan and the Cranes' AGI is below $150,000, the $3,000 contribution to Julia's IRA is fully deductible for 2003.

99. (d) The requirement is to determine the Lees' maximum IRA contribution and deduction on a joint return for 2003. Since neither taxpayer was covered by an employer-sponsored pension plan, there is no phaseout of the maximum deduction due to the level of their adjusted gross income. For married taxpayers filing a joint return, up to $3,000 can be deducted for contributions to the IRA of each spouse (even if one spouse is not working), provided that the combined earned income of both spouses is at least equal to the amounts contributed to the IRAs. Additionally, an individual at least age 50 can make a special catch-up contribution of $500 for 2003, resulting in an increased maximum contribution and deduction of $3,500 for 2003. Thus, the Lees may contribute and deduct a maximum of $7,000 to their individual retirement accounts for 2003, with a maximum of $3,500 placed into each account.

100. (c) The maximum deduction for contributions to a defined contribution self-employed retirement plan is limited to the lesser of $40,000, or 100% of self-employment income for 2003.

101. (d) The requirement is to determine which allowable deduction can be claimed in arriving at an individual's adjusted gross income. One hundred percent of a self-employed individual's health insurance premiums are deductible in arriving at an individual's adjusted gross income for 2003. Charitable contributions, foreign income taxes (if not used as a credit), and tax return preparation fees can be deducted only from adjusted gross income if an individual itemizes deductions.

II.G. Deduction for Interest on Education Loan

102. (b) The requirement is to determine the incorrect statement concerning the deduction for interest on qualified education loans. For a tax year beginning in 2003, an individual is allowed to deduct up to $2,500 for interest on qualified education loans in arriving at AGI. The deduction is subject to an income phase-out and the loan proceeds must have been used to pay for the qualified higher education expenses (e.g., tuition, fees, room, board) of the taxpayer, spouse, or a dependent (at the time the debt was incurred). The education expenses must relate to a period when the student was enrolled on at least a half-time basis. The sixty-month limitation was repealed for tax years beginning after 2001.

103. (c) The requirement is to determine how Dale should treat her $1,000 jury duty fee that she remitted to her employer. Fees received for serving on a jury must be included in gross income. If the recipient is required to remit the jury duty fees to an employer in exchange for regular compensation, the remitted jury duty fees are allowed as a deduction from gross income in arriving at adjusted gross income.

III. Itemized Deductions from Adjusted Gross Income

104. (c) The requirement is to determine George's taxable income. George's adjusted gross income consists of $3,700 of dividends and $1,700 of wages. Since George is eligible to be claimed as a dependency exemption by his parents, there will be no personal exemption on George's return and his basic standard deduction is limited to the greater of $750, or George's earned income of $1,700, plus $250. Thus, George's taxable income would be computed as follows:

Dividends	$ 3,700
Wages	1,700
AGI	$ 5,400
Exemption	0
Std. deduction	(1,950)
Taxable income	$ 3,450

105. (c) The item asks you to determine the requirements that must be met in order for a single individual to qualify for the additional standard deduction. A single individual who is age sixty-five or older or blind is eligible for an additional standard deduction ($1,150 for 2003). Two additional standard deductions are allowed for an individual who is age sixty-five or older **and** blind. It is not required that an individual support a dependent child or aged parent in order to qualify for an additional standard deduction.

III.A. Medical and Dental Expenses

106. (b) The requirement is to determine Carroll's maximum medical expense deduction after the applicable threshold limitation for the year. An individual taxpayer's unreimbursed medical expenses are deductible to the extent in excess of 7.5% of the taxpayer's adjusted gross income. Although the cost of cosmetic surgery is generally not deductible, the cost is deductible if the cosmetic surgery or procedure is necessary to ameliorate a deformity related to a congenital abnormality or personal injury resulting from an accident, trauma, or disfiguring disease. Here, Carroll's deduction is ($5,000 + $15,000) − ($100,000 x 7.5%) = $12,500.

107. (b) The requirement is to determine the Blairs' itemized deduction for medical expenses for 2003. A taxpayer can deduct the amounts paid for the medical care of himself, spouse, or dependents. The Blairs' qualifying medical expenses include the $800 of medical insurance premiums, $450 of prescribed medicines, $1,000 of unreimbursed doctor's fees, and $150 of transportation related to medical care. These expenses, which total $2,400, are deductible to the extent they exceed 7.5% of adjusted gross income, and result in a deduction of $150. Note that nonprescription medicines, including aspirin and over-the-counter cold capsules, are not deductible. Additionally, the Blairs cannot deduct the emergency room fee they paid for their son because they did not provide more than half of his support and he therefore does not qualify as their dependent.

108. (a) The requirement is to determine the amount the Whites may deduct as qualifying medical expenses without regard to the adjusted gross income percentage threshold. The Whites' deductible medical expenses include the $600 spent on repair and maintenance of the motorized wheelchair and the $8,000 spent for tuition, meals, and lodging at the special school for their physically handicapped dependent child. Payment for meals and lodging provided by an institution as a necessary part of medical care is deductible as a medical expense if the main reason for being in the institution is to receive medical care. Here, the item indicates that the Whites' physically handicapped dependent child was in the institution primarily for the availability of medical care, and that meals and lodging were furnished as necessary incidents to that care.

109. (c) The requirement is to determine the amount Wells can deduct as qualifying medical expenses without regard to the adjusted gross income percentage threshold. Wells' deductible medical expenses include the $500 premium on the prescription drug insurance policy and the $500 unreimbursed payment for physical therapy. The earnings protection policy is not considered medical insurance because payments are not based on the amount of medical expenses incurred. As a result, the $3,000 premium is a nondeductible personal expense.

110. (d) The requirement is to determine the amount of expenses incurred in connection with the adoption of a child that can be deducted by the Sloans on their 2003 joint return. A taxpayer can deduct the medical expenses paid for a child at the time of adoption if the child qualifies as the taxpayer's dependent when the medical expenses are paid. Additionally, if a taxpayer pays an adoption agency for medical expenses the adoption agency already paid, the tax-

payer is treated as having paid those expenses. Here, the Sloans can deduct the child's medical expenses of $5,000 that they paid. On the other hand, the legal expenses of $8,000 and agency fee of $3,000 incurred in connection with the adoption are treated as nondeductible personal expenses. However, the Sloans will qualify to claim a nonrefundable tax credit of up to $10,160 for these qualified adoption expenses.

111. (a) The requirement is to determine the amount that can be claimed by the Clines in their 2003 return as qualifying medical expenses. No medical expense deduction is allowed for cosmetic surgery or similar procedures, unless the surgery or procedure is necessary to ameliorate a deformity related to a congenital abnormality or personal injury resulting from an accident, trauma, or disfiguring disease. Cosmetic surgery is defined as any procedure that is directed at improving a patient's appearance and does not meaningfully promote the proper function of the body or prevent or treat illness or disease. Thus, Ruth's face-lift and Mark's hair transplant do not qualify as deductible medical expenses in 2003.

112. (d) The requirement is to determine the amount that Scott can claim as deductible medical expenses. The medical expenses incurred by a taxpayer for himself, spouse, or a dependent are deductible when paid or charged to a credit card. The $4,000 of medical expenses for his dependent son are deductible by Scott in 2003 when charged on Scott's credit card. It does not matter that payment to the credit card issuer had not been made when Scott filed his return. Expenses paid for the medical care of a decedent by the decedent's spouse are deductible as medical expenses in the year they are paid, whether the expenses are paid before or after the decedent's death. Thus, the $2,800 of medical expenses for his deceased spouse are deductible by Scott when paid in 2003, even though his spouse died in 2002.

113. (d) The requirement is to determine which expenditure qualifies as a deductible medical expense. Premiums paid for Medicare B supplemental medical insurance qualify as a deductible expense. Diaper service, funeral expenses, and nursing care for a healthy baby are not deductible as medical expenses.

114. (b) The requirement is to determine Stenger's net medical expense deduction for 2003. It would be computed as follows:

Prescription drugs	$ 300
Medical insurance premiums	750
Doctors ($2,550 − $900)	1,650
Eyeglasses	75
	$2,775
Less 7.5% of AGI ($35,000)	2,625
Medical expense deduction for 2003	$ 150

115. (d) The requirement is to determine the total amount of deductible medical expenses for the Bensons before the application of any limitation rules. Deductible medical expenses include those incurred by a taxpayer, taxpayer's spouse, dependents of the taxpayer, or any person for whom the taxpayer could claim a dependency exemption except that the person had gross income of $3,050 or more, or filed a joint return. Thus, the Bensons may deduct medical expenses incurred for themselves, for John (i.e., no dependency exemption only because his gross income is $3,050 or more), and for Nancy (i.e., a dependent of the Bensons).

III.B. Taxes

116. (d) The requirement is to determine the tax that is not deductible as an itemized deduction. One-half of a self-employed taxpayer's self-employment tax is deductible from gross income in arriving at adjusted gross income. Foreign real estate taxes, foreign income taxes, and personal property taxes can be deducted as itemized deductions from adjusted gross income.

117. (c) The requirement is to determine the amount that Matthews can deduct as taxes on her 2003 Schedule A of Form 1040. An individual's state and local income taxes are deductible as an itemized deduction, while federal income taxes are not deductible. For a cash-basis taxpayer, state and local taxes are deductible for the year in which paid or withheld. As a result, Matthew's deduction for 2003 consists of her state and local taxes withheld of $1,500 and the December 30 estimated payment of $400. The state and local income taxes that Matthews paid in April 2004 will be deductible for 2004.

118. (a) The requirement is to determine the correct statement regarding Farb, a cash-basis individual taxpayer who paid an $8,000 invoice for personal property taxes under protest in 2002, and received a $5,000 refund of the taxes in 2003. If a taxpayer receives a refund or rebate of taxes deducted in an earlier year, the taxpayer must generally include the refund or rebate in income for the year in which received. Here, Farb should deduct $8,000 in his 2002 income tax return and should report the $5,000 refund as income in his 2003 income tax return.

119. (d) The requirement is to determine the amount of itemized deduction for realty taxes that can be deducted by Burg. Generally, an individual's payment of state, local, or foreign real estate taxes is deductible as an itemized deduction if the individual is the owner of the property on which the taxes are imposed. Because the property is jointly-owned by Burg, he is individually liable for the entire amount of realty taxes and may deduct the entire payment on his return. Even back taxes can be deducted by Burg as long as he was the owner of the property during the period of time to which the back taxes are related.

120. (b) The requirement is to determine Sara's deduction for state income taxes in 2003. Sara's deduction would consist of the $2,000 withheld by her employer in 2003, plus the three estimated payments (3 x $300 = $900) actually paid during 2003, a total of $2,900. Note that the 1/15/04 estimated payment would be deductible for 2004.

121. (b) The requirement is to determine the amount of **taxes** deductible as an itemized deduction. The $360 vehicle tax based on value is deductible as a personal property tax. The real property tax of $2,700 must be apportioned between the Bronsons and the buyer for tax purposes even though they did not actually make an apportionment. Since the house was sold June 30, while the taxes were paid to September 30, the Bronsons would deduct 6/9 x $2,700 = $1,800. The buyer would deduct the remaining $900.

122. (a) The requirement is to determine what portion of the $1,300 of realty taxes is deductible by King in 2003. The $600 of delinquent taxes charged to the seller and paid by King are not deductible, but are added to the cost of the property. The $700 of taxes for 2003 are apportioned between the seller and King according to the number of days that each held the property during the year. King's deduction would be

$$\frac{184}{365} \times \$700 = \$353$$

123. (b) The requirement is to determine the amount of property taxes deductible as itemized deductions. The property taxes on the residence and the land held for appreciation, together with the personal property taxes on the auto are deductible. The special assessment is not deductible, but would be added to the basis of the residence.

124. (a) The requirement is to determine the amount the Burgs should deduct for taxes in their itemized deductions. The $1,200 of state income tax paid by the Burgs is deductible as an itemized deduction. However, the $7,650 of self-employment tax is not deductible as an itemized deduction. Instead, 50% x $7,650 = $3,825 of self-employment tax is deductible from gross income in arriving at the Burgs' adjusted gross income.

III.C. Interest Expense

125. (c) The requirement is to determine the correct statement regarding an individual taxpayer's deduction for interest on investment indebtedness. The deduction for interest expense on investment indebtedness is limited to the taxpayer's net investment income. Net investment income includes such income as interest, dividends, and short-term capital gains, less any related expenses.

126. (b) The requirement is to determine the correct statement regarding the interest on the Browns' $20,000 loan that was secured by their home and used to purchase an automobile. Qualified residence interest consists of interest on acquisition indebtedness and home equity indebtedness. Interest on home equity indebtedness loans of up to $100,000 is deductible as qualified residence interest if the loans are secured by a taxpayer's principal or second residence regardless of how the loan proceeds are used. The amount of home equity indebtedness cannot exceed the fair market value of a home as reduced by any acquisition indebtedness. Since the Browns' home had a FMV of $400,000 and was unencumbered by other debt, the interest on the $20,000 home equity loan is deductible as qualified residence interest.

127. (c) The requirement is to determine how much interest is deductible by the Philips for 2003. Qualified residence interest includes the interest on acquisition indebtedness. Such interest is deductible on up to $1 million of loans secured by a principal or second residence if the loans were used to purchase, construct, or substantially improve a home. Here, the Philips' original mortgage of $200,000 as well as the additional loan of $15,000 qualify as acquisition indebtedness, and the resulting $17,000 + $1,500 = $18,500 of interest is deductible. On the other hand, the $500 of interest on the auto loan is considered personal interest and not deductible.

128. (c) The requirement is to determine the maximum amount allowable as a deduction for Jackson's second residence. Qualified residence interest includes acquisition indebtedness and home equity indebtedness on the taxpayer's principal residence and a second residence. Here, the $5,000 of mortgage interest on the second residence is qualified residence interest and is deductible as an itemized deduction. In contrast, the $1,200 of utilities expense and $6,000 of insurance expense are nondeductible personal expenses.

129. (c) The requirement is to determine the amount of interest expense deductible as an itemized deduction. The $3,600 of home mortgage interest, and the $900 mortgage prepayment penalty are fully deductible as interest expense in computing itemized deductions. The $1,200 interest on the life insurance policy is not deductible since it is classified as personal interest.

130. (a) The requirement is to determine the amount of interest deductible as an itemized deduction. Since 2/3 of the loan proceeds were used to purchase tax-exempt bonds, 2/3 of the bank interest is nondeductible. The remaining 1/3 of the bank interest ($1,200) is related to the purchase of the Arrow debentures and is classified as investment interest deductible to the extent of net investment income ($0). The $3,000 of home mortgage interest is fully deductible as qualified residence interest. The interest on credit card charges is personal interest and is not deductible.

131. (a) None of the items listed relating to the tax deficiency for 2001 are deductible. The interest on the tax deficiency is considered personal interest and is not deductible. The additional federal income tax, the late filing penalty, and the negligence penalty are also not deductible.

III.D.   Charitable Contributions

132. (b) The requirement is to determine the amount that Smith should deduct as a charitable contribution. If appreciated property is contributed, the amount of contribution is generally the property's FMV if a sale of the property would result in a long-term capital gain. Here, the art object worth $3,000 was purchased for $2,000 just four months earlier. Since its holding period did not exceed twelve months, a sale of the art object would result in only a short-term capital gain, and the amount of allowable contribution deduction is limited to its $2,000 cost basis. Additionally, the donation of $5,000 cash to Smith's church is deductible but no deduction is available for the $1,000 contribution to a needy family. To be deductible, a contribution must be made to a qualifying organization.

133. (c) The requirement is to determine the amount of charitable contributions deductible on Stein's current year income tax return. The donation of appreciated stock held more than twelve months is a contribution of intangible, long-term capital gain appreciated property. The amount of contribution is the stock's FMV of $25,000, but is limited in deductibility for the current year to 30% of AGI. Thus, the current year deduction is limited to 30% x $80,000 = $24,000. The remaining $1,000 of contributions can be carried forward for up to five years, subject to the 30% limitation in the carryforward years.

134. (c) The requirement is to determine the maximum amount of properly substantiated charitable contributions that Moore could claim as an itemized deduction for 2003. Moore gave $18,000 to her church during 2003 and had a $10,000 charitable contribution carryover from 2002, resulting in a total of $28,000 of contributions. Since an individual's deduction for charitable contributions cannot ex-

ceed an overall limitation of 50% of adjusted gross income, Moore's charitable contribution deduction for 2003 is limited to ($50,000 AGI x 50%) = $25,000. Since Moore's 2003 contributions will be deducted before her carryforward from 2002, Moore will carry over $3,000 of her 2002 contributions to 2004.

135. (c) The requirement is to determine the maximum amount that Spencer can claim as a deduction for charitable contributions in 2003. The cash contribution of $4,000 to church and the $600 fair market value of the used clothing donated to Salvation Army are fully deductible. However, the deduction for the art object is limited to the $400 excess of its cost ($1,200) over its fair market value ($800).

136. (b) The requirement is to determine Lewis' charitable contribution deduction. The donation of appreciated stock held more than twelve months is a contribution of intangible, long-term capital gain appreciated property. The amount of contribution is the stock's FMV of $70,000, but is limited in deductibility for 2003 to 30% of AGI. Thus, the 2003 deduction is $100,000 x 30% = $30,000. The amount of contribution in excess of the 30% limitation ($70,000 – $30,000 = $40,000) can be carried forward for up to five years, subject to the 30% limitation in the carryforward years.

137. (b) The requirement is to determine the amount of contributions deductible in 2003. Charitable contributions are generally deductible in the year actually paid. The $500 charge to his bank credit card made on December 15, 2003, is considered a payment, and is deductible for 2003. The $1,000 promissory note delivered on November 1, 2003, is not considered a contribution until payment of the note upon maturity in 2004.

138. (b) The requirement is to determine the amount of student expenses deductible as a charitable contribution. A taxpayer may deduct as a charitable contribution up to $50 per **school month** of unreimbursed expenses incurred to maintain a student (in the 12th or lower grade) in the taxpayer's home pursuant to a written agreement with a qualified organization. Since the student started school in September, the amount deductible as a charitable contribution is $50 x 4 = $200.

139. (a) Vincent Tally is not entitled to a deduction for contributions in 2003 because he did not give up his entire interest in the book collection. By reserving the right to use and possess the book collection for his lifetime, Vincent Tally has not made a completed gift. Therefore, no deduction is available. The contribution will be deductible when his entire interest in the books is transferred to the art museum.

140. (b) The requirement is to determine the maximum amount of charitable contribution allowable as an itemized deduction on Jimet's 2003 income tax return. If appreciated property is contributed, the amount of contribution is generally the property's FMV if the property would result in a long-term capital gain if sold. If not, the amount of contribution for appreciated property is generally limited to the property's basis. Here, the stock worth $3,000 was purchased for $1,500 just four months earlier. Since its holding period did not exceed twelve months, a sale of the stock would result in a short-term capital gain, and the amount of allowable contribution deduction is limited to the stock's basis of $1,500. Additionally, to be deductible, a contribution must be made to a qualifying **organization**. As a result, the $2,000 cash given directly to a needy family is not deductible.

141. **(a)** The requirement is to determine the maximum amount of charitable contribution deductible as an itemized deduction on Taylor's tax return for 2003. The donation of appreciated land purchased for investment and held for more than twelve months is a contribution of real capital gain property (property that would result in long-term capital gain if sold). The amount of contribution is the land's FMV of $25,000, limited in deductibility for the current year to 30% of AGI. In this case, since 30% of AGI would be 30% x $90,000 = $27,000, the full amount of the land contribution ($25,000) is deductible for 2003.

III.E. Personal Casualty and Theft Gains and Losses

142. **(a)** The requirement is to determine the amount of the fire loss to her personal residence that Frazer can claim as an itemized deduction. The amount of a personal casualty loss is computed as the lesser of (1) the adjusted basis of the property ($130,000), or (2) the decline in the property's fair market value resulting from the casualty ($130,000 – $0 = $130,000); reduced by any insurance recovery ($120,000), and a $100 floor. Since Frazer had no casualty gains during the year, the net casualty loss is then deductible as an itemized deduction to the extent that it exceeds 10% of adjusted gross income.

Fire loss	$ 130,000
Insurance proceeds	(120,000)
$100 floor	(100)
10% of $70,000 AGI	(7,000)
Casualty loss itemized deduction	$ 2,900

143. **(a)** The requirement is to determine the amount the Burgs should deduct for the casualty loss (repair of glass vase accidentally broken by their dog) in their itemized deductions. A casualty is the damage, destruction, or loss of property resulting from an identifiable event that is sudden, unexpected, or unusual. Deductible casualty losses may result from earthquakes, tornadoes, floods, fires, vandalism, auto accidents, etc. However, a loss due to the accidental breakage of household articles such as glassware or china under normal conditions is not a casualty loss. Neither is a loss due to damage caused by a family pet.

144. **(d)** The requirement is to determine the proper treatment of the $490 casualty insurance premium. Casualty insurance premiums on an individual's personal residence are considered nondeductible personal expenses. Even though a casualty is actually incurred during the year, no deduction is available for personal casualty insurance premiums.

145. **(d)** The requirement is to determine the amount of the fire loss damage to their personal residence that the Hoyts can deduct as an itemized deduction. The amount of a nonbusiness casualty loss is computed as the lesser of (1) the adjusted basis of the property, or (2) the property's decline in FMV; reduced by any insurance recovery, and a $100 floor. If an individual has a net casualty loss for the year, it is then deductible as an itemized deduction to the extent that it exceeds 10% of adjusted gross income.

Lesser of:			
Adjusted basis	=	$50,000	
Decline in FMV			
($60,000 – $55,000)	=	$ 5,000	$ 5,000
Reduce by:			
Insurance recovery			(0)
$100 floor			(100)
10% of $34,000 AGI			(3,400)
Casualty loss itemized deduction			$ 1,500

Note that the $2,500 spent for repairs is not included in the computation of the loss.

146. **(b)** The requirement is to determine the proper treatment for the $800 appraisal fee that was incurred to determine the amount of the Hoyts' fire loss. The appraisal fee is considered an expense of determining the Hoyts' tax liability; it is not a part of the casualty loss itself. Thus, the appraisal fee is deductible as a miscellaneous itemized deduction subject to a 2% of adjusted gross income floor.

III.F. Miscellaneous Deductions

147. **(d)** The requirement is to determine which item is **not** a miscellaneous itemized deduction. A legal fee for tax advice related to a divorce, IRA trustee's fees that are separately billed and paid, and an appraisal fee for valuing a charitable contribution qualify as miscellaneous itemized deductions subject to the 2% of AGI floor. On the other hand, the check writing fees for a personal checking account are a personal expense and not deductible.

148. **(b)** The requirement is to determine the proper treatment of the $2,000 legal fee that was incurred by Hall in a suit to collect the alimony owed her. The $2,000 legal fee is considered an expenditure incurred in the production of income. Expenses incurred in the production of income are deductible as miscellaneous itemized deductions subject to the 2% of adjusted gross income floor.

149. **(b)** The requirement is to determine the proper reporting of Hall's lottery transactions. Hall's lottery winnings of $200 must be reported as other income on page 1 of Hall's Form 1040. Hall's $1,000 expenditure for state lottery tickets is deductible as a miscellaneous itemized deduction not subject to the 2% of AGI floor, but is limited in amount to the $200 of lottery winnings included in Hall's gross income.

150. **(d)** The requirement is to determine how expenses pertaining to business activities should be deducted by an outside salesman. An outside salesman is an employee who principally solicits business for his employer while away from the employer's place of business. All unreimbursed business expenses of an outside salesman are deducted as miscellaneous itemized deductions, subject to a 2% of AGI floor. Deductible expenses include business travel, secretarial help, and telephone expenses.

151. **(a)** The requirement is to determine the amount that can be claimed as miscellaneous itemized deductions. Both the initiation fee and the union dues are fully deductible. The voluntary benefit fund contribution is not deductible. Miscellaneous itemized deductions are generally deductible only to the extent they exceed 2% of AGI. In this case the deductible amount is $80 [$280 – (.02 x $10,000)].

152. **(b)** The requirement is to compute the amount of miscellaneous itemized deductions. The cost of uniforms not adaptable to general use (specialized work clothes), union dues, unreimbursed auto expenses, and the cost of income tax preparation are all miscellaneous itemized deductions. The preparation of a will is personal in nature, and is not deductible. Thus, the computation of Brodsky's miscellaneous itemized deductions in excess of the 2% of AGI floor is as follows:

Unreimbursed auto expenses	$ 100
Specialized work clothes	550
Union dues	600
Cost of income tax preparation	150
	$1,400
Less (2% x $25,000)	(500)
Deduction allowed	$ 900

III.G.   Reduction of Itemized Deductions

153. (c) The requirement is to determine the item that is not subject to the phaseout of itemized deductions for high-income individuals. An individual whose adjusted gross income exceeds a threshold amount ($139,500 for 2003) is required to reduce the amount of allowable itemized deductions by 3% of the excess of adjusted gross income over the threshold amount. All itemized deductions are subject to this reduction **except** medical expenses, nonbusiness casualty losses, investment interest expense, and gambling losses.

154. (a) The requirement is to determine the correct statement regarding the reduction in itemized deductions. For an individual whose AGI exceeds a threshold amount, the amount of otherwise allowable itemized deductions is reduced by the lesser of (1) 3% of the excess of AGI over the threshold amount, or (2) 80% of certain itemized deductions. The itemized deductions that are subject to reduction include taxes, qualified residence interest, charitable contributions, and miscellaneous itemized deductions (other than gambling losses). The reduction of these itemized deductions can not exceed 80% of the amount that is otherwise allowable.

IV.   Exemptions

155. (d) The requirement is to determine which item is not included in determining the total support of a dependent. Support includes food, clothing, FMV of lodging, medical, recreational, educational, and certain capital expenditures made on behalf of a dependent. Excluded from support is life insurance premiums, funeral expenses, nontaxable scholarships, and income and social security taxes paid from a dependent's own income.

156. (c) The requirement is to determine the number of exemptions that Smith was entitled to claim on his 2003 tax return. Smith will be allowed one exemption for himself and one exemption for his dependent mother. Smith is entitled to an exemption for his mother because he provided over half of her support, and her gross income ($0) was less than $3,050. Note that her $9,000 of social security benefits is excluded from her gross income, and that she did not have to live with Smith because she is related to him. No exemption is available to Smith for his son, Clay, because his son filed a joint return on which there was a tax liability.

157. (b) The requirement is to determine how many exemptions Jim and Kay can claim on their 2003 joint income tax return. Jim and Kay are entitled to one personal exemp-

tion each on their joint return. They also are entitled to one exemption for Dale since they provided more than half of Dale's support, and Dale was a full-time student under age twenty-four not subject to the $3,050 gross income test. However, no dependency exemptions are available for Kim and Grant because they each had gross income of at least $3,050.

158. (d) The requirement is to determine the requirements which must be satisfied in order for Joe to claim an exemption for his spouse on Joe's separate return for 2003. An exemption can be claimed for Joe's spouse on Joe's separate 2003 return only if the spouse had **no** gross income and was **not** claimed as another person's dependent in 2003.

159. (a) The requirement is to determine the amount of personal exemption on a dependent's tax return. No personal exemption is allowed on an individual's tax return if the individual can be claimed as a dependency exemption by another taxpayer.

160. (d) The requirement is to determine Robert's filing status and the number of exemptions that he should claim. Robert's father does not qualify as Robert's dependent because his father's gross income (interest income of $3,500) was not less than $3,050. Social security is not included in the gross income test. Since his father does not qualify as his dependent, Robert does not qualify for head-of-household filing status. Thus, Robert will file as single with one exemption.

161. (a) The requirement is to determine the filing status of the Arnolds. Since they were legally separated under a decree of separate maintenance on the last day of the taxable year and do not qualify for head-of-household status, they must each file as single.

162. (a) Mr. and Mrs. Stoner are entitled to one exemption each. They are entitled to one exemption for their daughter since they provided over 50% of her support, and she was a full-time student under age twenty-four not subject to the $3,050 gross income test. An exemption can be claimed for their son because they supported him, and he made less than $3,050 in gross income. No exemption is allowable for Mrs. Stoner's father since he was neither a US citizen nor resident of the US, Canada, or Mexico. There is no additional exemption for being age sixty-five or older.

163. (c) The requirement is to determine the number of exemptions the Planters may claim on their joint tax return. There is one exemption for Mr. Planter, and one exemption for his spouse. In addition there is one dependency exemption for their daughter, and one dependency exemption for the niece. The dependency gross income test does not apply to their daughter since she was under age twenty-four and a full-time student for some part of at least five calendar months. There is no additional exemption for being age sixty-five or older.

164. (b) The requirement is to determine which of the relatives can be claimed as a dependent (or dependents) on Sam's 2003 return. A taxpayer's own spouse is never a dependent of the taxpayer. Although a personal exemption is generally available for a taxpayer's spouse on the taxpayer's return, it is not a "dependency exemption." Generally, a dependency exemption is available for a dependent if (1) the taxpayer furnishes more than 50% of the dependent's support, (2) the dependent's gross income is less than $3,050, (3) the dependent is of specified relationship to the taxpayer or lives in the taxpayer's household for the entire year, (4) the dependent is a US citizen or resident of the US, Canada, or Mexico, and (5) the dependent does not file a joint return. Here, the support, gross income, US citizen, and joint return tests are met with respect to both Sam's cousin and his father's brother (i.e., Sam's uncle). However, Sam's cousin is not of specified relationship to Sam as defined in the IRC, and could only be claimed as a dependent if the cousin lived in Sam's household for the entire year. Since Sam's cousin did not live in Sam's household, Sam cannot claim a dependency exemption for his cousin. On the other hand, Sam's uncle is of specified relationship to Sam as defined in the IRC and can be claimed as a dependency exemption by Sam.

165. **(b)** The requirement is to determine which relative could be claimed as a dependent. One of the requirements that must be satisfied to claim a person as a dependent is that the person must be (1) of specified relationship to the taxpayer, or (2) a member of the taxpayer's household. Cousins and foster parents are not of specified relationship and only qualify if a member of the taxpayer's household. Since Alan's cousin and foster parent do not qualify as members of Alan's household, only Alan's niece can be claimed as a dependent.

166. **(c)** The requirement is to determine who can claim Sara's dependency exemption under a multiple support agreement. A multiple support agreement can be used if (1) no single taxpayer furnishes more than 50% of a dependent's support, and (2) two or more persons, each of whom would be able to take the exemption but for the support test, together provide more than 50% of the dependent's support. Then, any taxpayer who provides more than 10% of the dependent's support can claim the dependent if (1) the other persons furnishing more than 10% agree not to claim the dependent as an exemption, and (2) the other requirements for a dependency exemption are met. One of the other requirements that must be met is that the dependent be related to the taxpayer or live in the taxpayer's household. Alma is not eligible for the exemption because Sara is unrelated to Alma and did not live in Alma's household. Carl is not eligible for the exemption because he provided only 9% of Sara's support. Ben is eligible to claim the exemption for Sara under a multiple support agreement because Ben is related to Sara and has provided more than 10% of her support.

167. **(b)** The requirement is to determine the number of exemptions allowable in 2003. Mr. and Mrs. Vonce are entitled to one exemption each. They are also entitled to one exemption for their dependent daughter since they provided over one half of her support and she had less than $3,050 of gross income. An exemption is not available for their son because he provided over one half of his own support.

V.C.   Filing Status

168. **(d)** The requirement is to determine which statements (if any) are among the requirements to enable a taxpayer to be classified as a "qualifying widow(er)." Qualifying widow(er) filing status is available for the two years following the year of a spouse's death if (1) the surviving spouse was eligible to file a joint return in the year of the spouse's death, (2) does not remarry before the end of the current year, and (3) the surviving spouse pays **over 50%** of the cost of maintaining a household that is the principal home for the **entire year** of the surviving spouse's dependent child.

169. **(c)** The requirement is to determine which items are considered in determining whether an individual has contributed more than one half the cost of maintaining the household for purposes of head of household filing status. The cost of maintaining a household includes such costs as rent, mortgage interest, taxes, insurance on the home, repairs, utilities, and food eaten in the home. The cost of maintaining a household does **not** include the cost of clothing, education, medical treatment, vacations, life insurance, transportation, the rental value of a home an individual owns, or the value of an individual's services or those of any member of the household.

170. **(b)** The requirement is to determine the correct statement regarding the filing of a joint tax return. A husband and wife can file a joint return even if they have different accounting methods. Answer (a) is incorrect because spouses must have the same tax year to file a joint return. Answer (c) is incorrect because if either spouse was a nonresident alien at any time during the tax year, **both** spouses must elect to be taxed as US citizens or residents for the entire tax year. Answer (d) is incorrect because taxpayers cannot file a joint return if divorced before the end of the year.

171. **(c)** The requirement is to determine Emil Gow's filing status for 2003. Emil should file as a "Qualifying widower with dependent child" (i.e., surviving spouse) which will entitle him to use the joint return tax rates. This filing status is available for the two taxable years following the year of a spouse's death if (1) the surviving spouse was eligible to file a joint return in the year of the spouse's death, (2) does not remarry before the end of the current tax year, and (3) the surviving spouse pays over 50% of the cost of maintaining a household that is the principal home for the entire year of the surviving spouse's dependent child.

172. **(c)** The requirement is to determine Nell's filing status for 2003. Nell qualifies as a head of household because she is unmarried and maintains a household for her infant child. Answer (a) is incorrect because although Nell is single, head of household filing status provides for lower tax rates. Answer (b) is incorrect because Nell is unmarried at the end of 2003. Since Nell's spouse died in 2000, answer (d) is incorrect because the filing status of a "qualifying widow" is only available for the two years following the year of the spouse's death.

173. **(c)** Mrs. Felton qualifies as a head of household because she is both unmarried and maintains a household for her unmarried child. The unmarried child for whom she maintains a household need not qualify as her dependent in order for Mrs. Felton to claim the head-of-household status. Answer (b) is incorrect because in order for Mrs. Felton to qualify, her son must qualify as a dependent, which he does not. Although Mrs. Felton would have qualified as married filing jointly, answer (d), in 2002 (the year of her husband's death), the problem requirement is her 2003 status. Answer (a), single, is incorrect because although the widow is single, head of household filing status provides for lower tax rates.

174. (c) The requirement is to determine the 2003 income tax for Poole, an unmarried taxpayer in the 15% bracket with $20,000 of adjusted gross income. To determine Poole's taxable income, his adjusted gross income must be reduced by the greater of his itemized deductions or a standard deduction, and a personal exemption. Since Poole's medical expenses of $6,500 are deductible to the extent in excess of 7.5% of his AGI of $20,000, his itemized deductions of $5,000 exceed his available standard deduction of $4,750. Poole's tax computation is as follows:

Adjusted gross income		$20,000
Less:		
Itemized deductions	$5,000	
Personal exemption	3,050	8,050
Taxable income		$12,000
Tax rate		x 15%
Income tax		$ 1,793

V.D.   Alternative Minimum Tax (AMT)

175. (d) The requirement is to determine the itemized deduction that is deductible when computing an individual's alternative minimum tax (AMT). For purposes of computing an individual's AMT, no deduction is allowed for personal, state, and local income taxes, and miscellaneous itemized deductions subject to the 2% of adjusted gross income threshold. Similarly, no deduction is allowed for home mortgage interest if the loan proceeds were not used to buy, build, or substantially improve the home.

176. (a) The requirement is to determine the amount of tax preferences and adjustments that must be included in the computation of Randy's alternative minimum tax. The tax preferences include the $600 of excess depreciation on real property placed in service prior to 1987, and the $400 of tax-exempt interest on private activity bonds. These must be added to regular taxable income in arriving at alternative minimum taxable income (AMTI). The adjustments include the $3,050 personal exemption and $1,500 of state income taxes that are deductible in computing regular taxable income but are not deductible in computing AMTI.

177. (d) The requirement is to determine the amount of Karen's unused alternative minimum tax credit that will carry over to 2004. The amount of alternative minimum tax paid by an individual that is attributable to timing preferences and adjustments is allowed as a tax credit (i.e., minimum tax credit) that can be applied against regular tax liability in future years. The minimum tax credit is computed as the excess of the AMT actually paid over the AMT that would have been paid if AMTI included only exclusion preferences and adjustments (e.g., disallowed itemized deductions, excess percentage depletion, tax-exempt private activity bond interest). Since the minimum tax credit can only be used to reduce future regular tax liability, the credit can only reduce regular tax liability to the point at which it equals the taxpayer's tentative minimum tax. In this case, Karen's payment of $20,000 of alternative minimum tax in 2002 generates a minimum tax credit of $20,000 – $9,000 = $11,000 which is carried forward to 2003. Since Karen's 2003 regular tax liability of $50,000 exceeded her tentative minimum tax of $45,000, $5,000 of Karen's minimum tax credit would be used to reduce her 2003 tax liability to

$45,000. Therefore, $11,000 – $5,000 = $6,000 of unused minimum tax credit would carry over to 2004.

178. (c) The requirement is to determine the amount that Mills should report as alternative minimum taxable income (AMTI) before the AMT exemption. Certain itemized deductions, although allowed for regular tax purposes, are not deductible in computing an individual's AMTI. As a result, no AMT deduction is allowed for state, local, and foreign income taxes, real and personal property taxes, and miscellaneous itemized deductions subject to the 2% of AGI floor. Also, the deduction for medical expenses is computed using a 10% floor (instead of the 7.5% floor used for regular tax), and no deduction is allowed for qualified residence interest if the mortgage proceeds were **not** used to buy, build, or substantially improve the taxpayer's principal residence or a second home. Additionally, no AMT deduction is allowed for personal exemptions and the standard deduction.

Here, Mills' $5,000 of state and local income taxes and $2,000 of miscellaneous itemized deductions that were deducted for regular tax purposes must be added back to his $70,000 of regular taxable income before personal exemption to arrive at Mills' AMTI before AMT exemption of ($70,000 + $5,000 + $2,000)= $77,000. Note that no adjustment was necessary for the mortgage interest because the mortgage loan was used to acquire his residence.

179. (c) The requirement is to determine whether a net capital gain and home equity interest expense are adjustments for purposes of computing the alternative minimum tax. Although an excess of net long-term capital gain over net short-term capital loss may be subject to a reduced maximum tax rate, the excess is neither a tax preference nor an adjustment in computing the alternative minimum tax. On the other hand, home equity interest expense where the home equity loan proceeds were not used to buy, build, or improve the home is an adjustment because the interest expense, although deductible for regular tax purposes, is not deductible for purposes of computing an individual's alternative minimum tax.

180. (d) The requirement is to determine the proper treatment for the credit for prior year alternative minimum tax (AMT). The amount of AMT paid by an individual taxpayer that is attributable to timing differences can be carried forward indefinitely as a minimum tax credit to offset the individual's future regular tax liability (not future AMT liability). The amount of AMT credit to be carried forward is the excess of the AMT actually paid over the AMT that would have been paid if AMTI included only exclusion preferences (e.g., disallowed itemized deductions, preferences for excess percentage depletion, and tax-exempt private activity bond interest).

181. (b) The requirement is to determine the correct statement regarding the computation of the alternative minimum tax (AMT). A taxpayer is subject to the AMT only if the taxpayer's tentative AMT exceeds the taxpayer's regular tax. Thus, the alternative minimum tax is computed as the excess of the tentative AMT over the regular tax.

V.E.   Other Taxes

182. (b) The requirement is to determine the amount of net earnings from self-employment that would be multiplied by the self-employment tax rate to compute Diamond's self-employment tax for 2003. Since self-employment earnings generally represent earnings derived from a trade or business carried on as a sole proprietor, the $10,000 of interest income from personal investments would be excluded from the computation. On the other hand, a self-employed taxpayer is allowed a deemed deduction equal to 7.65% of self-employment earnings in computing the amount of net earnings upon which the tax is based. The purpose of this deemed deduction is to reflect the fact that employees do not pay FICA tax on the corresponding 7.65% FICA tax paid by their employers.

Gross receipts from business	$150,000
Cost of goods sold	(80,000)
Operating expenses	(40,000)
Self-employment earnings	$ 30,000
Less deemed deduction (100%- 7.65%)	x 92.35%
Net earnings to be multiplied by self-employment tax rate	$ 27,705

183. (c) The requirement is to determine the amount of Freeman's income that is subject to self-employment tax. The self-employment tax is imposed on self-employment income to provide Social Security and Medicare benefits for self-employed individuals. Self-employment income includes an individual's net earnings from a trade or business carried on as sole proprietor or as an independent contractor. The term also includes a partner's distributive share of partnership ordinary income or loss from trade or business activities, as well as guaranteed payments received by a partner for services rendered to a partnership. Self-employment income excludes gains and losses from the disposition of property used in a trade or business, as well as a shareholder's share of ordinary income from an S corporation

184. (a) The requirement is to determine the amount of Rich's net self-employment income. Income from self-employment generally includes all items of business income less business deductions. Excluded from the computation would be estimated income taxes on self-employment income, charitable contributions, investment income, and gains and losses on the disposition of property used in a trade or business. An individual's charitable contributions can only be deducted as an itemized deduction. Rich's net self-employment income would be

Business receipts	$20,000
Air conditioning parts	(2,500)
Yellow Pages listing	(2,000)
Business telephone calls	(400)
	$15,100

185. (c) The requirement is to determine the correct statement regarding the self-employment tax. The self-employment tax is imposed at a rate of 15.3% on individuals who work for themselves (e.g., sole proprietor, independent contractor, partner). One-half of an individual's self-employment tax is deductible from gross income in arriving at adjusted gross income.

186. (c) The requirement is to determine the correct statement with regard to social security tax (FICA) withheld in an amount greater than the maximum for a particular year. If an individual works for more than one employer, and combined wages exceed the maximum used for FICA purposes, too much FICA tax will be withheld. In such case, since the excess results from correct withholding by two or more employers, the excess should be claimed as a credit against income tax. Answer (a) is incorrect because

the excess cannot be used as an itemized deduction. Answer (b) is incorrect because if employers withhold correctly, no reimbursement can be obtained from the employers. Answer (d) is incorrect because if the excess FICA tax withheld results from incorrect withholding by any one employer, the employer must reimburse the excess and it cannot be claimed as a credit against tax.

187. (b) The requirement is to determine Berger's gross income from self-employment for 2003. Self-employment income represents the net earnings of an individual from a trade or business carried on as a proprietor or partner, or from rendering services as an independent contractor. The director's fee is self-employment income since it is related to a trade or business, and Berger is not an employee. Fees received by a fiduciary (e.g., executor) are generally not related to a trade or business and not self-employment income. However, executor's fees may constitute self-employment if the executor is a professional fiduciary or carries on a trade or business in the administration of an estate.

188. (d) The requirement is to determine Smith's gross income from self-employment. Self-employment income represents the net earnings of an individual from a trade or business carried on as a sole proprietor or partner, or from rendering services as an independent contractor (i.e., not an employee). The $8,000 consulting fee and the $2,000 of director's fees are self-employment income because they are related to a trade or business and Smith is not an employee.

VI.A. General Business Credit

189. (c) The requirement is to determine which credit is not a component of the general business credit. The general business credit is a combination of several credits that provide uniform rules for current and carryback-carryover years. The general business credit is composed of the investment credit, work opportunity credit, welfare-to-work credit, alcohol fuels credit, research credit, low-income housing credit, enhanced oil recovery credit, disabled access credit, renewable electricity production credit, empowerment zone employment credit, Indian employment credit, employer social security credit, orphan drug credit, the new markets credit, the small employer pension plan start-up costs credit, and the employer-provided child care facilities credit. A general business credit in excess of the limitation amount is carried back one year and forward twenty years to offset tax liability in those years.

190. (a) The requirement is to determine which tax credit is a combination of credits to provide for uniform rules for the current and carryback-carryover years. The general business credit is composed of the investment credit, work opportunity credit, welfare-to-work credit, alcohol fuels credit, research credit, low-income housing credit, enhanced oil recovery credit, disabled access credit, renewable electricity production credit, empowerment zone employment credit, Indian employment credit, employer social security credit, orphan drug credit, the new markets credit, the small employer pension plan start-up costs credit, and the employer-provided child care facilities credit. A general business credit in excess of the limitation amount is carried back one year and forward twenty years to offset tax liability in those years.

VI.K. Credit for the Elderly and the Disabled

191. (b)   The requirement is to determine the amount that can be claimed as a credit for the elderly. The amount of credit (limited to tax liability) is 15% of an initial amount reduced by social security and 50% of AGI in excess of $10,000. Here, the credit is the lesser of (1) the taxpayers' tax liability of $60, or (2) 15% [$7,500 – $3,000 – (.50)($16,550 – $10,000)] = $184.

VI.L. Child Care Credit

192. (c)   The requirement is to compute Nora's child care credit for 2003. Since she has two dependent preschool children, all $6,000 paid for child care qualifies for the credit. The credit is 35% of qualified expenses, but is reduced by one percentage point for each $2,000 (or fraction thereof) of AGI over $15,000 down to a minimum of 20%. Since Nora's AGI is $44,000, her credit is 20% x $6,000 = $1,200.

193. (b)   The requirement is to determine the amount of the child care credit allowable to the Jasons. The credit is from 20% to 35% of certain dependent care expenses limited to the lesser of (1) $3,000 for one qualifying individual, $6,000 for two or more; (2) taxpayer's earned income, or spouse's if smaller; or (3) actual expenses. The $2,500 paid to the Union Day Care Center qualifies, as does the $1,000 paid to Wilma Jason. Payments to relatives qualify if the relative is not a dependent of the taxpayer. Since Robert and Mary Jason only claimed three exemptions, Wilma was not their dependent. The $500 paid to Acme Home Cleaning Service does not qualify since it is *completely* unrelated to the care of their child. To qualify, expenses must be at least partly for the care of a qualifying individual. Since qualifying expenses exceed $3,000, the Jasons' credit is 20% x $3,000 = $600.

194. (b)   The requirement is to determine the qualifications for the child care credit that at least one spouse must satisfy on a joint return. The child care credit is a percentage of the amount paid for qualifying household and dependent care expenses incurred to enable an individual to be gainfully employed or look for work. To qualify for the child care credit on a joint return, at least one spouse must be gainfully employed or be looking for work when the related expenses are incurred. Note that it is not required that at least one spouse be gainfully employed, but only needs to be looking for work when the expenses are incurred. Additionally, at least one spouse must have earned income during the year. However, there is no limit as to the maximum amount of earned income or adjusted gross income reported on the joint return.

VI.M. Foreign Tax Credit

195. (a)   The requirement is to determine which factor(s) may affect the amount of Sunex's foreign tax credit available in its current year corporate income tax return. Since US taxpayers are subject to US income tax on their worldwide income, they are allowed a credit for the income taxes paid to foreign countries. The applicable foreign tax rate will affect the amount of foreign taxes paid, and thereby affect the amount available as a foreign tax credit. Additionally, since the amount of credit that can be currently used cannot exceed the amount of US tax attributable to the foreign-source income, the income source will affect the

amount of available foreign tax credit for the current year if the limitation based on the amount of US tax is applicable.

196. (b)   The requirement is to determine the amount of foreign tax credit that Wald Corp. may claim for 2003. Since US taxpayers are subject to US income tax on their worldwide income, they are allowed a credit for the income taxes paid to foreign countries. However, the amount of credit that can be currently used cannot exceed the amount of US tax that is attributable to the foreign income. This foreign tax credit limitation can be expressed as follows:

$$\frac{\text{Foreign TI}}{\text{Worldwide TI}} \text{ x (US tax) = Foreign tax credit limitation}$$

One limitation must be computed for foreign source passive income (e.g., interest, dividends, royalties, rents, annuities), with a separate limitation computed for all other foreign source taxable income.

In this case, the foreign income taxes paid on other foreign source taxable income of $27,000 is fully usable as a credit in 2003 because it is less than the applicable limitation amount (i.e., the amount of US tax attributable to the income).

$$\frac{\$90,000}{\$300,000} \text{ x (\$96,000) = \$28,800}$$

On the other hand, the credit for the $12,000 of foreign income taxes paid on non-business-related interest is limited to the amount of US tax attributable to the foreign interest income, $9,600.

$$\frac{\$30,000}{\$300,000} \text{ x (\$96,000) = \$9,600}$$

Thus, Wald Corp.'s foreign tax credit for 2003 totals $27,000 + $9,600 = $36,600. The $12,000 – $9,600 = $2,400 of unused foreign tax credit resulting from the application of the limitation on foreign taxes attributable to foreign source interest income can be carried back two years and forward five years to offset US income tax in those years.

197. (a)   The requirement is to determine the correct statement regarding a corporation's foreign income taxes. Foreign income taxes paid by a corporation may be claimed either as a credit or as a deduction, at the option of the corporation.

VI.N. Earned Income Credit

198. (c)   The requirement is to determine the credit that can result in a refund even if an individual had no income tax liability. The earned income credit is a refundable credit and can result in a refund even if the individual had no tax withheld from wages.

199. (a)   The requirement is to choose the correct statement regarding Kent's earned income credit. The earned income credit could result in a refund even if Kent had no tax withheld from wages. Since the credit is refundable, answer (c) is incorrect because there will never be any unused credit to carry back or forward. Answer (d) is incorrect because the credit is a direct subtraction from the computed tax.

200. (c)   The requirement is to determine the correct statement regarding the earned income credit. The earned income credit is a refundable credit and can result in a refund even if the individual had no tax withheld from wages.

To qualify, an individual must have earned income, but the amount of earned income does not have to equal adjusted gross income. For purposes of the credit, earned income excludes workers' compensation benefits. Additionally, the credit is available only if the tax return covers a full twelve-month period.

201. (b) The requirement is to determine the tax credit that cannot be claimed by a corporation. The foreign tax credit, alternative fuel production credit, and general business credit may be claimed by a corporation. The earned income credit cannot be claimed by a corporation; it is available only to individuals.

VI.O. Credit for Adoption Expenses

202. (c) The requirement is to determine the correct statement regarding the credit for adoption expenses. The adoption expenses credit is a nonrefundable credit for up to $10,160 (for 2003) of expenses (including special needs children) incurred to adopt an eligible child. An eligible child is one who is under eighteen years of age at time of adoption, or physically or mentally incapable of self-care. Qualified adoption expenses are taken as a credit in the year the adoption becomes final.

VI.P. Child Tax Credit

203. (c) The requirement is to determine the incorrect statement concerning the child tax credit. Individual taxpayers are permitted to take a tax credit based solely on the number of their dependent children under age seventeen. The amount of the credit is $600 per qualifying child, but is subject to reduction if adjusted gross income exceeds certain income levels. A qualifying child must be a US citizen or resident.

VI.Q. Hope Scholarship Credit

204. (c) The requirement is to determine the incorrect statement concerning the Hope scholarship credit. The Hope scholarship credit provides for a maximum credit of $1,500 per year (100% of the first $1,000, plus 50% of the next $1,000 of tuition expenses) for the first two years of postsecondary education. The credit is available on a per student basis and covers tuition paid for the taxpayer, spouse, and dependents. To be eligible, the student must be enrolled on at least a part-time basis for one academic period during the year. If a parent claims a child as a dependent, only the parent can claim the credit and any qualified expenses paid by the child are deemed paid by the parent.

VI.R. Lifetime Learning Credit

205. (d) The requirement is to determine the incorrect statement concerning the lifetime learning credit. The lifetime learning credit provides a credit of 20% of up to $10,000 of tuition and fees paid by a taxpayer for one or more students for graduate and undergraduate courses at an eligible educational institution. The credit may be claimed for an unlimited number of years, is available on a per taxpayer basis, and covers tuition paid for the taxpayer, spouse, and dependents.

VI.S. Estimated Tax Payments

206. (a) The requirement is to determine which statement(s) describe how Baker may avoid the penalty for the underpayment of estimated tax for the 2003 tax year. An individual whose regular and alternative minimum tax liability is not sufficiently covered by withholding from wages must pay estimated tax in quarterly installments or be subject to penalty. Individuals will incur no underpayment penalty for 2003 if the amount of tax withheld plus estimated payments are at least equal to the lesser of (1) 90% of the current year's tax; (2) 100% of the prior year's tax; or (3) 90% of the tax determined by annualizing current year taxable income through each quarter. However, note that for 2003, high-income individuals (i.e., individuals whose adjusted gross income for the preceding year exceeds $150,000) must use 110% (instead of 100%) if they wish to base their estimated tax payments on their prior year's tax liability.

207. (a) The requirement is to determine what amount would be subject to penalty for the underpayment of estimated taxes. A taxpayer will be subject to an underpayment of estimated tax penalty if the taxpayer did not pay enough tax either through withholding or by estimated tax payments. For 2003, there will be no penalty if the total tax shown on the return less the amount paid through withholding (including excess social security tax withholding) is less than $1,000. Additionally, for 2003, individuals will incur no penalty if the amount of tax withheld plus estimated payments are at least equal to the lesser of (1) 90% of the current year's tax (determined on the basis of actual income or annualized income), or (2) 100% of the prior year's tax. In this case, since the tax shown on Krete's return ($16,500) less the tax paid through withholding ($16,000) was less than $1,000, there will be no penalty for the underpayment of estimated taxes.

VII. Filing Requirements

208. (d) The requirement is to determine the original due date for a decedent's federal income tax return. The final return of a decedent is due on the same date the decedent's return would have been due had death not occurred. An individual's federal income tax return is due on the 15th day of the fourth calendar month following the close of the tax year (e.g., April 15 for a calendar-year taxpayer).

209. (a) The requirement is to determine Birch's filing requirement. A self-employed individual must file an income tax return if net earnings from self-employment are $400 or more.

VIII.B. Assessments

210. (c) The requirement is to determine the date on which the statute of limitations begins for Jackson Corp.'s 2002 tax return. Generally, any tax that is imposed must be assessed within three years of the filing of the return, or if later, the due date of the return. Since Jackson Corp.'s 2002 return was filed on March 13, 2003, and the return was due on March 15, 2003, the statute of limitations expires on March 15, 2006. This means that the statute of limitations begins on March 16, 2003.

211. (c) The requirement is to determine the latest date that the IRS can assert a notice of deficiency for a 2002 calendar-year return if the taxpayer neither committed fraud nor omitted amounts in excess of 25% of gross income. The normal period for assessment is the later of three years after a return is filed, or three years after the due date of the return. Since the 2002 calendar-year return was filed on March 20, 2003, and was due on April 15, 2003, the IRS must assert a deficiency no later than April 15, 2006.

212. (d) A six-year statute of limitations applies if gross income omitted from the return exceeds 25% of the gross income reported on the return. For this purpose, gross income of a business includes total gross receipts before subtracting cost of goods sold and deductions. Thus, a six-year statute of limitations will apply to Thompson if he omitted from gross income an amount in excess of ($400,000 + $36,000) x 25% = $109,000.

213. (d) The requirement is to determine the maximum period during which the IRS can issue a notice of deficiency if the gross income omitted from a taxpayer's return exceeds 25% of the gross income reported on the return. A **six-year** statute of limitations applies if gross income omitted from the return exceeds 25% of the gross income reported on the return. Additionally, a tax return filed **before** its due date is treated as filed **on** its due date. Thus, if a return is filed before its due date, and the gross income omitted from the return exceeds 25% of the gross income reported on the return, the IRS has **six** years from the due date of the return to issue a notice of deficiency.

VIII.E. Claims for Refund

214. (c) The requirement is to determine the form that must be filed by an individual to claim a refund of erroneously paid income taxes. Form 1040X, Amended US Individual Income Tax Return, should be used to claim a refund of erroneously paid income taxes. Form 843 should be used to file a refund claim for taxes other than income taxes. Form 1139 may be used by a corporation to file for a tentative adjustment or refund of taxes when an overpayment of taxes for a prior year results from the carryback of a current year's net operating loss or net capital loss. Form 1045 may be used by taxpayers other than corporations to apply for similar adjustments.

215. (a) The requirement is to determine the date by which a refund claim must be filed if an individual paid income tax during 2003 but did not file a tax return. An individual must file a claim for refund within three years from the date a return was filed, or two years from the date of payment of tax, whichever is later. If no return was filed, the claim for refund must be filed within two years from the date that the tax was paid.

216. (c) The requirement is to determine the date by which a taxpayer must file an amended return to claim a refund of tax paid on a calendar-year 2001 return. A taxpayer must file an amended return to claim a refund within three years from the date a return was filed, or two years from the date of payment of tax, whichever is later. If a return is filed before its due date, it is treated as filed on its due date. Thus, the taxpayer's 2001 calendar-year return that was filed on March 15, 2002, is treated as filed on April 15, 2002. Therefore, an amended return to claim a refund must be filed not later than April 15, 2005.

217. (d) The requirement is to determine the date by which a refund claim due to worthless security must be filed. The normal three-year statute of limitations is extended to seven years for refund claims resulting from bad

debts or worthless securities. Since the securities became worthless during 2002, and Baker's 2002 return was filed on April 15, 2003, Baker's refund claim must be filed no later than April 15, 2010.

VIII.G. Taxpayer Penalties

218. (b) The requirement is to determine the amount on which the penalties for late filing and late payment would be computed. The late filing and late payment penalties are based on the amount of net tax due. If a taxpayer's tax return indicated a tax liability of $50,000, and $45,000 of taxes were withheld, the late filing and late payment penalties would be based on the $5,000 of tax that is owed.

219. (c) An accuracy-related penalty equal to 20% of the underpayment of tax may be imposed if the underpayment of tax is attributable to one or more of the following: (1) negligence or disregard of the tax rules and regulations; (2) any substantial understatement of income tax; (3) any substantial valuation overstatement; (4) any substantial overstatement of pension liabilities; or (5) any substantial gift or estate tax valuation understatement. The penalty for gift or estate tax valuation understatement may apply if the value of property on a gift or estate tax return is 50% or less of the amount determined to be correct. The penalty for a substantial income tax valuation overstatement may apply if the value (or adjusted basis) of property is 200% or more of the amount determined to be correct.

SOLUTIONS TO SIMULATION PROBLEMS

Simulation Problem 1

Transactions	(A)	(B)	(C)	(D)	(E)	(F)	(G)	(H)	(I)	(J)	(K)	(L)	(M)	(N)	(O)	(P)
1. Fees received for jury duty.	○	●	○	○	○	○	○	○	○	○	○	○	○	○	○	○
2. Interest income on mortgage loan receivable.	●	○	○	○	○	○	○	○	○	○	○	○	○	○	○	○
3. Penalty paid to bank on early withdrawal of savings.	○	○	○	●	○	○	○	○	○	○	○	○	○	○	○	○
4. Write-offs of uncollectible accounts receivable from accounting practice.	○	○	○	○	○	○	○	○	○	○	○	○	○	○	○	●
5. Cost of attending review course in preparation for the Uniform CPA Examination.	○	○	○	○	○	○	○	○	○	○	○	○	○	○	○	●
6. Fee for the biennial permit to practice as a CPA.	○	○	○	○	○	○	○	○	●	○	○	○	○	○	○	○
7. Costs of attending CPE courses in fulfillment of state board requirements.	○	○	○	○	○	○	○	○	●	○	○	○	○	○	○	○
8. Contribution to a qualified Keogh retirement plan.	○	○	○	●	○	○	○	○	○	○	○	○	○	○	○	○
9. Loss sustained from nonbusiness bad debt.	○	○	○	○	○	○	○	●	○	○	○	○	○	○	○	○
10. Loss sustained on sale of "Small Business Corporation" (Section 1244) stock.	○	○	○	○	○	○	○	○	○	○	○	●	○	○	○	○
11. Taxes paid on land owned by Cole and rented out as a parking lot.	○	○	○	○	○	○	○	○	○	○	●	○	○	○	○	○
12. Interest paid on installment purchases of household furniture.	○	○	○	○	○	○	○	○	○	○	○	○	○	○	○	●
13. Alimony paid to former spouse who reports the alimony as taxable income.	○	○	○	●	○	○	○	○	○	○	○	○	○	○	○	○
14. Personal medical expenses charged on credit card in December 2003 but not paid until January 2004.	○	○	○	○	●	○	○	○	○	○	○	○	○	○	○	○
15. Personal casualty loss sustained.	○	○	○	○	○	●	○	○	○	○	○	○	○	○	○	○
16. State inheritance tax paid on bequest received.	○	○	○	○	○	○	○	○	○	○	○	○	○	○	○	●
17. Foreign income tax withheld at source on dividend received.	○	○	○	○	○	○	○	○	○	○	○	○	●	○	○	○
18. Computation of self-employment tax.	○	○	○	○	○	○	○	○	○	○	○	○	○	○	●	○
19. One-half of self-employment tax paid with 2003 return filed in April 2004.	○	○	○	●	○	○	○	○	○	○	○	○	○	○	○	○
20. Insurance premiums paid on Cole's life.	○	○	○	○	○	○	○	○	○	○	○	○	○	○	○	●

Explanation of solutions

1. **(B)** Fees received for jury duty represent compensation for services and must be included in gross income. Since there is no separate line for jury duty fees, they are taxable as other income on page 1 of Form 1040.

2. **(A)** Interest income on a mortgage loan receivable must be included in gross income and is taxable as interest income in Schedule B—Interest and Dividend Income.

3. **(D)** An interest forfeiture penalty for making an early withdrawal from a certificate of deposit is deductible on page 1 of Form 1040 to arrive at adjusted gross income.

4. **(P)** The problem indicates that Cole is a CPA reporting on the cash basis. Accounts receivable resulting from services rendered by a cash-basis taxpayer have a zero tax basis, because the income has not yet been reported. Therefore, the write-offs of zero basis uncollectible accounts receivable from Cole's accounting practice are not deductible.

5. **(P)** An educational expense that is part of a program of study that can qualify an individual for a new trade or business is not deductible. This is true even if the individual is not seeking a new job. In this case, the cost of attending a review course in preparation for the CPA examination is a nondeductible personal expense since it qualifies Cole for a new profession.

6. **(I)** Licensing and regulatory fees paid to state or local governments are an ordinary and necessary trade or business expense and are deductible by a sole proprietor on Schedule C—Profit or Loss from Business. Since Cole is a cash method tax payor, he can deduct the fee for the biennial permit to practice when paid in 2003.

7. **(I)** All trade or business expenses of a self-employed individual are deductible on Schedule C—Profit or Loss from Business. Education must meet certain requirements before the related expenses can be deducted. Generally, deductible education expenses must not be a part of a program that will qualify the individual for a new trade or business and must (1) be required by an employer or by law to keep the individual's present position, or (2) maintain or improve skills required in the individual's present work. In this case, Cole already is a CPA and is fulfilling state CPE requirements, so his education costs of attending CPE courses are deductible in Schedule C—Profit or Loss from Business.

8. **(D)** Contributions to a self-employed individual's qualified Keogh retirement plan are deductible on page 1 of Form 1040 to arrive at adjusted gross income. The maximum deduction for contributions to a defined contribution Keogh retirement plan is limited to the lesser of $40,000, or 100 % of self-employment income.

9. **(J)** A loss sustained from a nonbusiness bad debt is always classified as a short-term capital loss. Therefore, Cole's nonbusiness bad debt is deductible in Schedule D—Capital Gains or Losses.

10. **(L)** A loss sustained on the sale of Sec. 1244 stock is generally deductible as an ordinary loss, with the amount of ordinary loss deduction limited to $50,000. On a joint return, the limit is increased to $100,000, even if the stock was owned by only one spouse. The ordinary loss resulting from the sale of Sec. 1244 stock is deductible in Form 4797—Sales of Business Property. To the extent that a loss on Sec. 1244 stock exceeds the applicable $50,000 or $100,000 limit, the loss is deductible as a capital loss in Schedule D—Capital Gains or Losses. Similarly, if Sec. 1244 stock is sold at a gain, the gain would be reported as a capital gain in Schedule D if the stock is a capital asset.

11. **(K)** Rental income and expenses related to rental property are generally reported in Schedule E. Here, the taxes paid on land owned by Cole and rented out as a parking lot are deductible in Schedule E—Supplemental Income and Loss. Schedule E also is used to report the income or loss from royalties, partnerships, S corporations, estates, and trusts.

12. **(P)** The interest paid on installment purchases of household furniture is considered personal interest and is not deductible. Personal interest is any interest that is not qualified residence interest, investment interest, passive activity interest, or business interest. Personal interest generally includes interest on car loans, interest on income tax, installment plan interest, credit card finance charges, and late payment charges by a utility.

13. **(D)** Alimony paid to a former spouse who reports the alimony as taxable income is deductible on page 1 of Form 1040 to arrive at adjusted gross income.

14. **(E)** Personal medical expenses are generally deductible as an itemized deduction subject to a 7.5% of AGI threshold for the year in which they are paid. Additionally, an individual can deduct medical expenses charged to a credit card in the year the charge is made. It makes no difference when the amount charged is actually paid. Here, Cole's personal medical expenses charged on a credit card in December 2003 but not paid until January 2004 are deductible for 2003 in Schedule A—Itemized Deductions, subject to a threshold of 7.5% of adjusted gross income.

15. **(F)** If an individual sustains a personal casualty loss, it is deductible in Schedule A—Itemized Deductions subject to a threshold of $100 and an additional threshold of 10% of adjusted gross income.

16. **(P)** State inheritance taxes paid on a bequest that was received are not deductible. Other taxes not deductible in computing an individual's federal income tax include federal estate and gift taxes, federal income taxes, and social security and other employment taxes paid by an employee.

17. **(M)** An individual can deduct foreign income taxes as an itemized deduction or can deduct foreign income taxes as a tax credit. Cole's foreign income tax withheld at source on foreign dividends received can be claimed in Form 1116—Foreign Tax Credit, or in Schedule A—Itemized Deductions, at Cole's option.

18. **(O)** A self-employed individual is subject to a self-employment tax if the individual's net earnings from self-employment are at least $400.

19. **(D)** An individual's self-employment tax is computed in Schedule SE and is added as an additional tax in arriving at the individual's total tax. One-half of the computed self-employment tax is allowed as a deduction in arriving at adjusted gross income. Here, one-half of Cole's self-employment tax for 2003 is deductible for 2003 on page 1 of Form 1040 to arrive at adjusted gross income, even though the tax was not paid until the return was filed in April 2004.

20. **(P)** Insurance premiums paid on Cole's life are classified as a personal expense and are not deductible.

Simulation Problem 2

Transactions	(A)	(B)	(C)	(D)	(E)	(F)	(G)	(H)	(I)	(J)	(K)	(L)	(M)	(N)	(O)
1. Retainer fees received from clients.	○	○	●	○	○	○	○	○	○	○	○	○	○	○	○
2. Oil royalties received.	○	○	○	●	○	○	○	○	○	○	○	○	○	○	○
3. Interest income on general obligation state and local government bonds.	○	○	○	○	●	○	○	○	○	○	○	○	○	○	○
4. Interest on refund of federal taxes.	○	●	○	○	○	○	○	○	○	○	○	○	○	○	○
5. Death benefits from term life insurance policy on parent.	○	○	○	○	○	○	●	○	○	○	○	○	○	○	○
6. Interest income on US Treasury bonds.	○	●	○	○	○	○	○	○	○	○	○	○	○	○	○
7. Share of ordinary income from an investment in a limited partnership reported in Form 1065, Schedule K-1.	○	○	○	●	○	○	○	○	○	○	○	○	○	○	○
8. Taxable income from rental of a townhouse owned by Green.	○	○	○	●	○	○	○	○	○	○	○	○	○	○	○
9. Prize won as a contestant on a TV quiz show.	●	○	○	○	○	○	○	○	○	○	○	○	○	○	○
10. Payment received for jury service.	●	○	○	○	○	○	○	○	○	○	○	○	○	○	○
11. Dividends received from mutual funds that invest in tax-free government obligations.	○	○	○	○	●	○	○	○	○	○	○	○	○	○	○
12. Qualifying medical expenses not reimbursed by insurance.	○	○	○	○	○	○	○	●	○	○	○	○	○	○	○
13. Personal life insurance premiums paid by Green.	○	○	○	○	○	○	○	○	○	○	○	○	○	○	●
14. Expenses for business-related meals where clients were present.	○	○	○	○	○	○	○	○	○	○	○	○	●	○	○
15. Depreciation on personal computer purchased in 2003 used for business.	○	○	○	○	○	○	○	○	○	○	●	○	○	○	○
16. Business lodging expenses, while out of town.	○	○	○	○	○	○	○	○	○	○	●	○	○	○	○
17. Subscriptions to professional journals used for business.	○	○	○	○	○	○	○	○	○	○	●	○	○	○	○
18. Self-employment taxes paid.	○	○	○	○	○	●	○	○	○	○	○	○	○	○	○
19. Qualifying contributions to a simplified employee pension plan.	○	○	○	○	○	●	○	○	○	○	○	○	○	○	○
20. Election to expense business equipment purchased in 2003.	○	○	○	○	○	○	○	○	○	●	○	○	○	○	○
21. Qualifying alimony payments made by Green.	○	○	○	○	○	●	○	○	○	○	○	○	○	○	○
22. Subscriptions for investment-related publications.	○	○	○	○	○	○	○	○	●	○	○	○	○	○	○
23. Interest expense on a home-equity line of credit for an amount borrowed to finance Green's business.	○	○	○	○	○	○	○	○	○	○	○	●	○	○	○
24. Interest expense on a loan for an auto used 75% for business.	○	○	○	○	○	○	○	○	○	○	○	○	●	○	○
25. Loss on sale of residence.	○	○	○	○	○	○	○	○	○	○	○	○	○	○	●

Explanation of solutions

1. **(C)** All trade or business income and deductions of a self-employed individual are reported on Schedule C—Profit or Loss from Business. Retainer fees received from clients is reported in Schedule C as trade or business income.

2. **(D)** Income derived from royalties is reported in Schedule E—Supplemental Income and Loss. Schedule E also is used to report the income or loss from rental real estate, partnerships, S corporations, estates, and trusts.

3. **(E)** Interest from general obligation state and local government bonds is tax-exempt and is excluded from gross income.

4. **(B)** The interest income on a refund of federal income taxes must be included in gross income and is reported in Schedule B—Interest and Dividend Income. The actual refund of federal income taxes itself is excluded from gross income.

5. **(E)** Life insurance proceeds paid by reason of death are generally excluded from gross income. Here, the death benefits received by Green from a term life insurance policy on the life of Green's parent are not taxable.

6. **(B)** Interest income from US Treasury bonds and treasury bills must be included in gross income and is reported in Schedule B—Interest and Dividend Income.

7. **(D)** A partner's share of a partnership's ordinary income that is reported to the partner on Form 1065, Schedule K-1 must be included in the partner's gross income and is reported in Schedule E—Supplemental Income and Loss.

8. **(D)** The taxable income from the rental of a townhouse owned by Green must be included in gross income and is reported in Schedule E—Supplemental Income and Loss.

9. **(A)** A prize won as a contestant on a TV quiz show must be included in gross income. Since there is no separate line on Form 1040 for prizes, they are taxable as other income on Form 1040.

10. **(A)** Fees received for jury duty represent compensation for services and must be included in gross income. Since there is no separate line for jury duty fees, they are taxable as other income on Form 1040.

11. **(E)** An investor in a mutual fund may receive several different kinds of distributions including ordinary dividends, capital gain distributions, tax-exempt interest dividends, and return of capital distributions. A mutual fund may pay tax-exempt interest dividends to its shareholders if it meets certain requirements. These dividends are paid from the tax-exempt state and local obligation interest earned by the fund and retain their tax-exempt character when reported by the shareholder. Thus, Green's dividends received from mutual funds that invest in tax-free government obligations are not taxable.

12. **(H)** Qualifying medical expenses not reimbursed by insurance are deductible in Schedule A as an itemized deduction to the extent in excess of 7.5% of adjusted gross income.

13. **(O)** Personal life insurance premiums paid on Green's life are classified as a personal expense and not deductible.

14. **(M)** All trade or business expenses of a self-employed individual are deductible on Schedule C—Profit or Loss from Business. However, only 50% of the cost of business meals and entertainment is deductible. Therefore, Green's expenses for business-related meals where clients were present are partially deductible in Schedule C.

15. **(K)** The deduction for depreciation on listed property (e.g., automobiles, cellular telephones, computers, and property used for entertainment etc.) is computed on Form 4562—Depreciation and Amortization. Since Green's personal computer was used in his business as a self-employed consultant, the amount of depreciation computed on Form 4562 is then deductible in Schedule C—Profit or Loss from Business.

16. **(L)** Lodging expenses while out of town on business are an ordinary and necessary business expense and are fully deductible by a self-employed individual in Schedule C—Profit or Loss from Business.

17. **(L)** The cost of subscriptions to professional journals used for business are an ordinary and necessary business expense and are fully deductible by a self-employed individual in Schedule C—Profit or Loss from Business.

18. **(G)** An individual's self-employment tax is computed in Schedule SE and is added as an additional tax in arriving at the individual's total tax liability. One-half of the computed self-employment tax is then allowed as a deduction on Form 1040 in arriving at adjusted gross income.

19. **(F)** Qualifying contributions to a self-employed individual's simplified employee pension plan are deductible on page 1 of Form 1040 to arrive at adjusted gross income.

20. **(K)** For 2003, Sec. 179 permits a taxpayer to elect to treat up to $100,000 of the cost of qualifying depreciable personal business property as an expense rather than as a capital expenditure. In this case, Green's election to expense business equipment would be computed on Form 4562—Depreciation and Amortization, and then would be deductible in Schedule C—Profit or Loss from Business.

21. **(F)** Qualifying alimony payments made by Green to a former spouse are fully deductible on Form 1040 to arrive at adjusted gross income.

22. **(I)** The costs of subscriptions for investment publications are not related to Green's trade or business, but instead are considered expenses incurred in the production of portfolio income and are reported as miscellaneous itemized deductions in Schedule A—Itemized Deductions. These investment expenses are deductible to the extent that the aggregate of expenses in this category exceed 2% of adjusted gross income.

23. **(L)** The nature of interest expense is determined by using a tracing approach (i.e., the nature depends upon how the loan proceeds were used). Since the interest expense on Green's home-equity line of credit was for a loan to finance Green's business, the best answer is to treat the interest as a business expense fully deductible in Schedule C—Profit or Loss from Business.

24. **(M)** The interest expense on a loan for an auto used by a self-employed individual in a trade or business is deductible as a business expense. Since Green's auto was used 75% for business, only 75% of the interest expense is deductible in Schedule C—Profit or Loss from Business. The remaining 25% is considered personal interest expense and is not deductible.

25. **(O)** The loss resulting from the sale of Green's personal residence is not deductible because the property was held for personal use. Only losses due to casualty or theft are deductible for personal use property.

Simulation Problem 3

	For AGI (A)	From AGI (No 2%) (B)	From AGI (2% Floor) (C)	Not ded. (D)
1. Smith paid the medical expenses of his mother-in-law. Although Smith provided more than half of her support, she does not qualify as Smith's dependent because she had gross income of $5,000.	○	●	○	○
2. Smith paid the real estate taxes on his rental apartment building.	●	○	○	○
3. Smith paid state sales taxes of $1,500 on an automobile that he purchased for personal use.	○	○	○	●
4. Smith paid the real estate taxes on his mother-in-law's home. She is the owner of the home.	○	○	○	●
5. Smith paid $1,500 of interest on credit card charges. The charges were for items purchased for personal use.	○	○	○	●
6. Smith paid an attorney $500 to prepare Smith's will.	○	○	○	●
7. Smith incurred $750 of expenses for business meals and entertainment in his position as an employee of Patton Corporation. Smith's expenses were not reimbursed.	○	○	●	○
8. Smith paid self-employment taxes of $3,000 as a result of earnings from the consulting business that he conducts as a sole proprietor.	●	○	○	○
9. Smith made a contribution to his self-employed retirement plan (Keogh Plan).	●	○	○	○
10. Smith had gambling losses totaling $2,500 for the year. He is including a lottery prize of $5,000 in his gross income this year.	○	●	○	○

Explanation of solutions

1. **(B)** Deductible medical expenses include amounts paid for the diagnosis, cure, relief, treatment or prevention of disease of the taxpayer, spouse, and dependents. The term **dependent** includes any person who qualifies as a dependency exemption, or would otherwise qualify as a dependency exemption except that the gross income and joint return tests are not met. Therefore, the medical expenses of Smith's mother-in-law are properly deductible from Smith's AGI and are not subject to the 2% limitation.

2. **(A)** Expenses attributable to property held for the production of rents or royalties are properly deductible "above the line." "Above the line" deductions are subtracted from gross income to determine adjusted gross income. Therefore, expenses incurred from a passive activity such as Smith's rental apartment building are deductible for AGI.

3. **(D)** State sales tax paid on an automobile purchased for personal use is not deductible. However, if the automobile had been purchased for business use, the sales tax incurred in its acquisition would be treated as part of the cost of the automobile and could be recovered through depreciation.

4. **(D)** Real estate (real property) taxes are deductible only if imposed on property owned by the taxpayer. Since Smith's mother-in-law is the legal owner of the house, Smith cannot deduct his payment of those real estate taxes.

5. **(D)** No deduction is allowed for personal interest.

6. **(D)** Personal legal expenses are not a deductible expense. Only legal counsel obtained for advice concerning tax matters or incurred in the production of income are deductible. Therefore, Smith cannot deduct the $500 incurred to prepare his will.

7. **(C)** Unreimbursed employee expenses including business meals and entertainment (subject to the 50% rule) are deductible to the extent they exceed 2% of AGI. Therefore, $375 ($750 x 50%) is deductible from AGI, subject to the 2% floor.

8. **(A)** An individual is allowed to deduct one half of the self-employment tax paid for the taxable year in the computation of AGI. Therefore, $1,500 is deductible for AGI.

9. **(A)** Contributions by self-employed individuals to a qualified retirement plan (Keogh Plan) are a deduction for AGI.

10. **(B)** Gambling losses to the extent of gambling winnings are categorized as miscellaneous deductions not subject to the 2% floor. Therefore, the $2,500 of Smith's gambling losses would be deductible in full since he properly included his $5,000 winnings in his gross income for 2003.

Simulation Problem 4

                                              (A) (B) (C) (D) (E) (F) (G)

1. In 2003, Oate paid $2,000 interest on the $25,000 home equity mortgage on her vacation home, which she used exclusively for personal use. The mortgage is secured by Oate's vacation home, and the loan proceeds were used to purchase an automobile.
    ○ ● ○ ○ ○ ○ ○

2. For 2003, Oate had a $30,000 cash charitable contribution carryover from her 2002 cash donation to the American Red Cross. Oate made no additional charitable contributions in 2003.
    ○ ○ ● ○ ○ ○ ○

3. During 2003, Oate had investment interest expense that did not exceed her net investment income.
    ○ ● ○ ○ ○ ○ ○

4. Oate's 2003 lottery ticket losses were $450. She had no gambling winnings.
    ● ○ ○ ○ ○ ○ ○

5. During 2003, Oate paid $2,500 in real property taxes on her vacation home, which she used exclusively for personal use.
    ○ ● ○ ○ ○ ○ ○

6. In 2003, Oate paid a $500 premium for a homeowner's insurance policy on her principal residence.
    ● ○ ○ ○ ○ ○ ○

7. For 2003, Oate paid $1,500 to an unrelated babysitter to care for her child while she worked.
    ○ ○ ○ ○ ○ ○ ●

8. In 2003, Oate paid $4,000 interest on the $60,000 acquisition mortgage of her principal residence. The mortgage is secured by Oate's home.
    ○ ● ○ ○ ○ ○ ○

9. During 2002, Oate paid $3,600 real property taxes on residential rental property in which she actively participates. There was no personal use of the rental property.
    ○ ○ ○ ○ ○ ● ○

Explanation of solutions

   1. **(B)** Interest expense on home equity indebtedness is deductible on up to $100,000 of home equity loans secured by a first or second residence regardless of how the loan proceeds were used.

   2. **(C)** Contributions in excess of applicable percentage limitations can be carried forward for up to five tax years. Here, the $30,000 of charitable contribution carryover from 2002 is deductible as an itemized deduction for 2003 subject to a limitation of 50% of AGI.

   3. **(B)** Investment interest expense is deductible as an itemized deduction to the extent of net investment income. Since Oate's investment interest expense did not exceed her net investment income, it is deductible in full.

   4. **(A)** Gambling losses (including lottery ticket losses) are deductible as an itemized deduction to the extent of the gambling winnings included in gross income. Since Oate had no gambling winnings, the losses are not deductible.

   5. **(B)** State, local, or foreign real estate taxes imposed on the taxpayer for property held for personal use are fully deductible as an itemized deduction.

   6. **(A)** A premium for a homeowner's insurance policy on a principal residence is a nondeductible personal expense.

   7. **(G)** Payments to an unrelated babysitter to care for her child while Oate worked would qualify for the child and dependent care credit. For 2007, the credit may vary from 20% to 35% of up to $3,000 ($6,000 for two or more qualifying individuals) of qualifying household and dependent care expenses incurred to enable the taxpayer to be gainfully employed or look for work.

   8. **(B)** Interest expense on acquisition indebtedness is deductible on up to $1 million of loans secured by the residence if such loans were used to acquire, construct, or substantially improve a principal residence or a second residence.

   9. **(F)** An expense incurred in the production of rental income (e.g., interest, taxes, depreciation, insurance, utilities) are deductible on Schedule E and are included in the computation of net rental income or loss.

Simulation Problem 5

Part a.

		(A)	(B)	(C)	(D)	(E)	(F)	(G)	(H)	(I)	(J)	(K)	(L)	(M)
1.	During 2003, Dale received a $30,000 cash gift from her aunt.	●	○	○	○	○	○	○	○	○	○	○	○	○
2.	Dale contributed $3,500 to her traditional Individual Retirement Account (IRA) on January 15, 2003. In 2003, she earned $60,000 as a university instructor. During 2003 the Cumacks were not active participants in an employer's qualified pension or annuity plan.	○	○	○	○	●	○	○	○	○	○	○	○	○
3.	In 2003, the Cumacks received a $1,000 federal income tax refund.	●	○	○	○	○	○	○	○	○	○	○	○	○
4.	During 2003, Frank, a 50% partner in Diske General Partnership, received a $4,000 guaranteed payment from Diske for services that he rendered to the partnership that year.	○	○	○	○	○	●	○	○	○	○	○	○	○
5.	In 2003, Frank received $10,000 as beneficiary of his deceased brother's life insurance policy.	●	○	○	○	○	○	○	○	○	○	○	○	○
6.	Dale's employer pays 100% of the cost of all employees' group-term life insurance under a qualified plan. Policy cost is $5 per $1,000 of coverage. Dale's group-term life insurance coverage equals $450,000.	○	○	●	○	○	○	○	○	○	○	○	○	○
7.	In 2003, Frank won $5,000 at a casino and had $2,000 in gambling losses.	○	○	○	○	○	○	●	○	○	○	○	○	○
8.	During 2003, the Cumacks received $1,000 interest income associated with a refund of their prior years' federal income tax.	○	●	○	○	○	○	○	○	○	○	○	○	○
9.	In 2003, the Cumacks sold their first and only residence for $400,000. They purchased their home in 1989 for $50,000 and have lived there since then. There were no other capital gains, losses, or capital loss carryovers. The Cumacks do not intend to buy another residence.	●	○	○	○	○	○	○	○	○	○	○	○	○
10.	In 2003, Zeno Corp. declared a stock dividend and Dale received one additional share of Zeno common stock for three shares of Zeno common stock that she held. The stock that Dale received had a fair market value of $9,000. There was no provision to receive cash instead of stock.	●	○	○	○	○	○	○	○	○	○	○	○	○

Explanation of solutions

1. (**$0**) Amounts received as a gift are fully excluded from gross income.

2. (**$3,500**) The maximum deduction for contributions to a traditional IRA by an individual at least age 50 is the lesser of $3,500, or 100% of compensation for 2003. Since the Cumacks were not active participants in an employer's qualified pension or annuity plan, there is no phaseout of the maximum deduction based on AGI.

3. (**$0**) Since federal income taxes are not deductible in computing a taxpayer's federal income tax liability, a refund of federal income taxes is excluded from gross income.

4. (**$4,000**) Guaranteed payments are partnership payments to partners for services rendered or for the use of capital without regard to partnership income. A guaranteed payment is deductible by the partnership, and the receipt of a guaranteed payment must be included in the partner's gross income, and is reported as self-employment income in the computation of the partner's self-employment tax.

5. (**$0**) The proceeds of life insurance policies paid by reason of death of the insured are generally excluded from the beneficiary's gross income.

6. (**$2,000**) An employer's payment of the cost of the first $50,000 of coverage for group-term life insurance can be excluded from an employee's gross income. Since Dale's employer provided group-term insurance of $450,000, and the cost of coverage was $5 per $1,000 of coverage, $5 x 400 = $2,000, must be included in Dale's gross income.

7. (**$5,000**) Gambling winnings must be included in gross income. Gambling losses cannot be offset against gambling winnings, but instead are deducted from AGI as a miscellaneous itemized deduction limited in amount to the gambling winnings included in gross income.

8.   (**$1,000**) Although a federal income tax refund can be excluded from gross income, interest on the refund must be included in gross income.

9.   (**$0**) Up to $250,000 of gain can be excluded from gross income if an individual owned and occupied a residence as a principal residence for an aggregate of at least two of the five years preceding sale. The excludable gain is increased to $500,000 for married individuals filing jointly if either spouse meets the ownership requirement, and both spouses meet the use requirement.

10. (**$0**) Stock dividends are generally excluded from gross income because a shareholder's relative interest in earnings and assets is unaffected.

Part b.

		(O) (U) (C)
11.	The Cumacks claimed three exemptions on their 2003 joint income tax return.	● ○ ○

Explanation of solution

11.   (**O**) To qualify as a dependency exemption, a dependent must be a US citizen or resident of the US, Canada, or Mexico. Since Dale's father, Jacques, is both a French citizen and French resident, he does not qualify as a dependency exemption even though the Cumacks provided all of his support.

TRANSACTIONS IN PROPERTY

A. Sales and Other Dispositions

A sale or other disposition is a transaction that generally gives rise to the recognition of gain or loss. Gains or losses may be categorized as ordinary or capital. If an exchange is nontaxable, the recognition of gain or loss is generally deferred until a later sale of the newly acquired property. This is accomplished by giving the property received the basis of the old property exchanged.

1. The **basis of property** to determine gain or loss is generally its cost or purchase price.

   a. The **cost** of property is the amount paid for it in cash or the FMV of other property, plus expenses connected with the purchase such as abstract of title fees, installation of utility services, legal fees (including title search, contract, and deed fees), recording fees, surveys, transfer taxes, owner's title insurance, and any amounts the seller owes that the buyer agrees to pay (e.g., back taxes and interest, recording or mortgage fees, charges for improvements or repairs, sales commissions).

   b. If property is acquired subject to a debt, or the purchaser assumes a debt, this debt is also included in cost.

   EXAMPLE: Susan purchased a parcel of land by paying cash of $30,000 and assuming a mortgage of $60,000. She also paid $400 for a title insurance policy on the land. Susan's basis for the land is $90,400.

   c. If **acquired by gift**, the basis for gain is the basis of the donor (transferred basis) increased by any gift tax paid attributable to the net appreciation in the value of the gift.

      (1) Basis for loss is lesser of gain basis (above), or FMV on date of gift.

      (2) Because of this rule, no gain or loss is recognized when use of the basis for computing loss results in a gain, and use of the basis for computing gain results in a loss.

      EXAMPLE: Jill received a boat from her father as a gift. Father's adjusted basis was $10,000 and FMV was $8,000 at date of gift. Jill's basis for gain is $10,000, while her basis for loss is $8,000. If Jill later sells the boat for $9,200, no gain or loss will be recognized.

      (3) The increase in basis for gift tax paid is limited to the amount (not to exceed the gift tax paid) that bears the same ratio to the amount of gift tax paid as the net appreciation in value of the gift bears to the amount of the gift.

         (a) The amount of gift is reduced by any portion of the $11,000 annual exclusion allowable with respect to the gift.

         (b) Where more than one gift of a present interest is made to the same donee during a calendar year, the $11,000 exclusion is applied to gifts in chronological order.

      EXAMPLE: Tom received a gift of property with a FMV of $101,000 and an adjusted basis of $71,000. The donor paid a gift tax of $18,000 on the transfer. Tom's basis for the property would be $77,000 determined as follows:

$$\$71,000 \ basis + \left[\ \$18,000 \ gift \ tax \ \ x \ \ \frac{(\$101,000 \ FMV \ - \ \$71,000 \ basis)}{(\$101,000 \ FMV \ - \ \$11,000 \ exclusion)} \ \right] = \$77,000$$

   d. If **acquired from decedent**, basis is property's FMV on date of decedent's death, or alternate valuation date (generally six months after death).

      (1) Use FMV on date of disposition if alternate valuation is elected and property is distributed, sold, or otherwise disposed of during six-month period following death.

      EXAMPLE: Ann received 100 shares of stock as an inheritance from her uncle Henry, who died January 20, 2003. The stock had a FMV of $40,000 on January 20, and a FMV of $30,000 on July 20, 2003. The stock's FMV was $34,000 on June 15, 2003, the date the stock was distributed to Ann.

      If the alternate valuation is not elected, or no estate tax return is filed, Ann's basis for the stock is its FMV of $40,000 on the date of Henry's death. If the alternate valuation is elected, Ann's basis will be the stock's $34,000 FMV on June 15 (the date of distribution) since the stock was distributed to Ann within six months after the decedent's death.

      (2) FMV rule not applicable to appreciated property acquired by the decedent by gift within one year before death if such property then passes from the donee-decedent to the original donor or donor's spouse. The basis of such property to the original donor (or spouse) will be the adjusted basis of the property to the decedent immediately before death.

e.   The basis of **stock received as a dividend** depends upon whether it was included in income when received.

(1)   If included in income, basis is its FMV at date of distribution.

(2)   If nontaxable when received, the basis of shareholder's original stock is allocated between the dividend stock and the original stock in proportion to their relative FMVs. The holding period of the dividend stock includes the holding period of the original stock.

EXAMPLE: T owns 100 shares of XYZ Corp. common stock that was acquired in 2000 for $12,000. In 2003, T received a nontaxable distribution of 10 XYZ Corp. preferred shares. At date of distribution the FMV of the 100 common shares was $15,000, and the FMV of the 10 preferred shares was $5,000. The portion of the $12,000 basis allocated to the preferred and common shares would be

$$Preferred = \frac{\$5,000}{\$20,000} \; (\$12,000) \; = \; \$3,000$$

$$Common = \frac{\$15,000}{\$20,000} \; (\$12,000) \; = \; \$9,000$$

f.   The basis of **stock rights** depends upon whether they were included in income when received.

(1)   If rights were nontaxable and allowed to expire, they are deemed to have no basis and no loss can be deducted.

(2)   If rights were nontaxable and exercised or sold

(a)   Basis is zero if FMV of rights is less than 15% of FMV of stock, unless taxpayer elects to allocate basis

(b)   If FMV of rights at date of receipt is at least 15% of FMV of stock, or if taxpayer elects, basis is

$$\frac{FMV \text{ of rights}}{FMV \text{ of rights} + FMV \text{ stock}} \quad x \quad \left(\begin{array}{c} \text{Basis in} \\ \text{stock} \end{array} \right)$$

(3)   If rights were taxable and included in income, basis is their FMV at date of distribution.

g.   Detailed rules for basis are included in following discussions of exchanges and involuntary conversions.

2.   In a **sale**, the gain or loss is generally the difference between

a.   The cash or fair market value received, and the adjusted basis of the property sold

b.   If the property sold is mortgaged (or encumbered by any other debt) and the buyer assumes or takes the property subject to the debt

(1)   Include the amount of the debt in the amount realized because the seller is relieved of the obligation

EXAMPLE: Property with a $10,000 mortgage, and a basis of $15,000, is sold for $10,000 cash and buyer assumes the mortgage. The amount realized is $20,000, and the gain is $5,000.

(2)   If the amount of the mortgage exceeds basis, use the same rules.

EXAMPLE: Property with a $15,000 mortgage, and a basis of $10,000, is given away subject to the mortgage. The amount realized is $15,000, and the gain is $5,000.

c.   Casual sellers of property (as opposed to dealers) reduce selling price by any selling expenses.

3.   In a **taxable exchange,** the gain or loss is the difference between the adjusted basis of the property exchanged and the FMV of the property received. The basis of property received in a taxable exchange is its FMV.

4.   **Nontaxable exchanges** generally are not taxed in the current period. Questions concerning nontaxable exchanges often require a determination of the basis of property received, and the effect of boot on the recognition of gain.

a.   **Like-kind exchange**—an exchange of business or investment property for property of a like-kind

(1)   Does not apply to property held for personal use, inventory, stocks, bonds, notes, intangible evidences of ownership, and interests in a partnership

(2) Property held for business use may be exchanged for investment property or vice versa.
(3) Like-kind means "same class of property."

   (a) Real property must be exchanged for real property; personal property must be exchanged
       for personal property within the same General Asset Class or within the same Product
       Class. For example

       1] Land held for investment exchanged for apartment building
       2] Real estate exchanged for a lease on real estate to run thirty years or more
       3] Truck exchanged for a truck

   (b) Exchange of personal property for real property does not qualify.
   (c) Exchange of US real property for foreign real property does not qualify.

(4) To qualify as a like-kind exchange (1) the property to be received must be identified within
    forty-five days after the date on which the old property is relinquished, and (2) the exchange
    must be completed within 180 days after the date on which the old property is relinquished,
    but not later than the due date of the tax return (including extensions) for the year that the old
    property is relinquished.
(5) The **basis of like-kind property received** is the basis of like-kind property given.

   (a) + Gain recognized
   (b) + Basis of boot given (money or property not of a like-kind)
   (c) − Loss recognized
   (d) − FMV of boot received

(6) If unlike property (i.e., boot) is received, its basis will be its FMV on the date of the exchange.
(7) If property is exchanged solely for other like-kind property, no gain or loss is recognized. The
    basis of the property received is the same as the basis of the property transferred.
(8) If boot (money or property not of a like-kind) is given, no gain or loss is generally recognized.
    However, gain or loss is recognized if the boot given consists of property with a FMV differ-
    ent from its basis.

   *EXAMPLE: Land held for investment plus shares of stock are exchanged for investment real estate with a FMV of
   $13,000. The land transferred had an adjusted basis of $10,000 and FMV of $11,000; the stock had an adjusted
   basis of $5,000 and FMV of $2,000. A $3,000 loss is recognized on the transfer of stock. The basis of the acquired
   real estate is $12,000 ($10,000 + $5,000 basis of boot given − $3,000 loss recognized).*

(9) **If boot is received**

   (a) Any realized gain is recognized to the extent of the lesser of (1) the realized gain, or (2)
       the FMV of the boot received
   (b) No loss is recognized due to the receipt of boot

   *EXAMPLE: Land held for investment with a basis of $10,000 was exchanged for other investment real estate
   with a FMV of $9,000, an automobile with a FMV of $2,000, and $1,500 in cash. The realized gain is $2,500.
   Even though $3,500 of "boot" was received, the recognized gain is only $2,500 (limited to the realized gain).
   The basis of the automobile (unlike property) is its FMV $2,000; while the basis of the real estate acquired is
   $9,000 ($10,000 + $2,500 gain recognized − $3,500 boot received).*

(10) **Liabilities** assumed (or liabilities to which property exchanged is subject) on either or both
     sides of the exchange are treated as boot.

   (a) Boot received—if the liability was assumed by the other party
   (b) Boot given—if the taxpayer assumed a liability on the property acquired
   (c) If liabilities are assumed on both sides of the exchange, they are offset to determine the
       net amount of boot given or received.

   *EXAMPLE: A owns investment land with an adjusted basis of $50,000, FMV of $70,000, but which is subject
   to a mortgage of $15,000. B owns investment land with an adjusted basis of $60,000, FMV of $65,000, but
   which is subject to a mortgage of $10,000. A and B exchange real estate investments with A assuming B's
   $10,000 mortgage, and B assuming A's $15,000 mortgage. The computation of realized gain, recognized
   gain, and basis for the acquired real estate for both A and B is as follows:*

	A		*B*
FMV of real estate received	$65,000		$70,000
+ Liability on old real estate assumed by other party (boot received)	15,000	(1)	10,000
Amount realized on the exchange	$80,000		$80,000
– Adjusted basis of old real estate transferred	–50,000		– 60,000
– Liability assumed by taxpayer on new real estate (boot given)	–10,000	(2)	– 15,000
Gain realized	$20,000		$ 5,000
Gain recognized (1) minus (2)	$ 5,000		$ --
Basis of old real estate transferred	$50,000		$60,000
+ Gain recognized	5,000		--
– Liability on old real estate assumed by other party (boot received)	–15,000		– 10,000
Basis of new real estate acquired	$50,000		$65,000

(d) Boot given in the form of an assumption of a liability does **not** offset boot received in the form of cash or unlike property; however, boot given in the form of cash or unlike property does offset boot received in the form of a liability assumed by the other party.

> *EXAMPLE: Assume the same facts as above except that the mortgage on B's old real estate was $6,000, and that A paid B cash of $4,000 to make up the difference. The tax effects to A remain unchanged. However, since the $4,000 cash cannot be offset by the liability assumed by B, B must recognize a gain of $4,000, and will have a basis of $69,000 for the new real estate.*

(11) If within two years after a like-kind exchange between related persons [as defined in Sec. 267(b)] either person disposes of the property received in the exchange, any gain or loss that was not recognized on the exchange must be recognized (subject to the loss limitation rules for related persons) as of the date that the property was disposed of. This gain recognition rule does not apply if the subsequent disposition was the result of the death of one of the persons, an involuntary conversion, or where neither the exchange nor the disposition had tax avoidance as one of its principal purposes.

b. **Involuntary conversions**

(1) Occur when money or other property is received for property that has been destroyed, damaged, stolen, or condemned (even if property is transferred only under threat or imminence of condemnation).

(2) If payment is received and gain is realized, taxpayer may **elect not to recognize gain** if converted property is replaced with property of similar or related use.

(a) Gain is recognized only to the extent that the amount realized exceeds the cost of the replacement.

(b) The **replacement** must be purchased within a **period** beginning with the earlier of the date of disposition or the date of threat of condemnation, and ending two years after the close of the taxable year in which gain is first **realized** (three years for condemned business or investment real property, other than inventory or property held primarily for resale).

(c) **Basis of replacement property** is the cost of the replacement decreased by any gain not recognized.

> *EXAMPLE: Taxpayer had unimproved real estate (with an adjusted basis of $20,000) which was condemned by the county. The county paid him $24,000 and he reinvested $21,000 in unimproved real estate. $1,000 of the $4,000 realized gain would not be recognized. His tax basis in the new real estate would be $20,000 ($21,000 cost – $1,000 deferred gain).*

> *EXAMPLE: Assume the same facts as above except the taxpayer reinvested $25,000 in unimproved real estate. None of the $4,000 realized gain would be recognized. His basis in the new real estate would be $21,000 ($25,000 cost – $4,000 deferred gain).*

(3) If property is converted directly into property similar or related in service or use, complete nonrecognition of gain is mandatory. The basis of replacement property is the same as the property converted.

(4) The meaning of **property similar or related in service or use** is more restrictive than "like-kind."

(a) For an owner-user—property must be functionally the same and have same end use (business vehicle must be replaced by business vehicle that performs same function).

(b) For a lessor—property must perform same services for **lessor** (lessor could replace a rental manufacturing plant with a rental-wholesale grocery warehouse even though tenant's functional use differs).

(c) A purchase of at least 80% of the stock of a corporation whose property is similar or related in service or use also qualifies.

(d) More liberal "like-kind" test applies to real property held for business or investment (other than inventory or property held primarily for sale) that is converted by seizure, condemnation, or threat of condemnation (e.g., improved real estate could be replaced with unimproved real estate).

(5) If property is not replaced within the time limit, an amended return is filed to recognize gain in the year realized.

(6) Losses on involuntary conversions are recognized whether the property is replaced or not. However, a loss on condemnation of property held for personal use (e.g., personal residence) is not deductible.

c. **Sale or exchange of principal residence**

(1) An individual may **exclude** from income up to **$250,000** of gain that is realized on the sale or exchange of a residence, if the individual owned and occupied the residence as a principal residence for an aggregate of *at least two of the five years* preceding the sale or exchange. The amount of excludable gain is increased to **$500,000** for married individuals filing jointly if either spouse meets the ownership requirement, and both spouses meet the use requirement.

(a) The exclusion replaces the gain rollover rules and the one-time $125,000 exclusion formerly available to eligible individuals age fifty-five or older.

(b) Gain in excess of the $250,000 (or $500,000) exclusion must be included in income even though the sale proceeds are reinvested in another principal residence.

(2) The exclusion is determined on an individual basis.

(a) A single individual who otherwise qualifies for the exclusion is entitled to exclude up to $250,000 of gain even though the individual marries someone who has used the exclusion within two years before the marriage.

(b) In the case of married taxpayers who do not share a principal residence but file joint returns, a $250,000 exclusion is available for a qualifying sale or exchange of each spouse's principal residence.

(3) Special rules apply to divorced taxpayers.

(a) If a residence is transferred to a taxpayer incident to a divorce, the time during which the taxpayer's spouse or former spouse owned the residence is added to the taxpayer's period of ownership.

(b) A taxpayer who owns a residence is deemed to use it as a principal residence while the taxpayer's spouse or former spouse is given use of the residence under the terms of a divorce or separation.

(4) A taxpayer's period of ownership of a residence includes the period during which the taxpayer's deceased spouse owned the residence.

(5) Tenant-stockholders in a cooperative housing corporation can qualify to exclude gain from the sale of the stock.

(6) If the taxpayer does not meet the two-year ownership or use requirements, a pro rata amount of the $250,000 or $500,000 exclusion applies if the sale or exchange is due to a change in place of employment, health, or unforeseen circumstances. To satisfy the change in employment condition, the taxpayer must be required to move at least fifty miles from his former place of employment, or if previously unemployed at least fifty miles from his former residence. To satisfy the change of health condition, the taxpayer must be instructed to relocate by a physician for health reasons (e.g., advanced age-related infirmities, severe allergies,

emotional problems). Unforeseen circumstances include natural or man-made disasters such as war or acts of terrorism, cessation of employment, death, divorce or legal separation, and multiple births from the same pregnancy.

> *EXAMPLE: Harold, an unmarried taxpayer, purchased a home in a suburb of Chicago on October 1, 2001. Eighteen months later his employer transferred him to St. Louis and Harold sold his home for a gain of $200,000. Since Harold sold his home because of a change in place of employment and had owned and used the home as a principal residence for eighteen months, the exclusion of his gain is limited to $250,000 x 18/24 = $187,500.*

(7) A loss from the sale of personal residence is not deductible.

d. **Exchange of insurance policies.** No gain or loss is recognized on an exchange of certain life, endowment, and annuity contracts to allow taxpayers to obtain better insurance.

5. **Sales and exchanges of securities**

a. Stocks and bonds are not included under like-kind exchanges
b. Exchange of stock of same corporation

(1) Common for common, or preferred for preferred is nontaxable
(2) Common for preferred, or preferred for common is taxable, unless exchange qualifies as a recapitalization (see page 581)

c. Exercise of conversion privilege in convertible stock or bond is generally nontaxable.
d. The first-in, first-out (FIFO) method is used to determine the basis of securities sold unless the taxpayer can specifically identify the securities sold and uses specific identification.

e. **Capital gains exclusion for small business stock**

(1) A noncorporate taxpayer can exclude 50% of capital gains resulting from the sale of qualified small business stock held for more than five years.
(2) To qualify, the stock must be acquired directly (or indirectly through a pass-through entity) at its original issuance.
(3) A qualified small business is a C corporation with $50 million or less of capitalization. Generally, personal service, banking, leasing, investing, real estate, farming, mineral extraction, and hospitality businesses do not qualify as eligible small businesses.
(4) Gains eligible for exclusion are limited to the greater of $10 million, or 10 times the investor's stock basis.

    (a) 42% of the excluded gain is treated as a tax preference item for AMT purposes.
    (b) Only gains net of exclusion are included in determining the investment interest expense and capital loss limitations.

f. **Rollover of capital gain from publicly traded securities**

(1) An individual or C corporation may elect to roll over an otherwise currently taxable capital gain from the sale of publicly traded securities if the sale proceeds are used to purchase common stock or a partnership interest in a specialized small business investment company (SSBIC) within sixty days of the sale of the securities.
(2) An SSBIC is a partnership or corporation licensed by the Small Business Administration under the Small Business Investment Act of 1958 as in effect on May 13, 1993.
(3) The amount of gain eligible for rollover is limited to $50,000 per year for individuals (lifetime cap of $500,000) and $250,000 per year for corporations (lifetime cap of $1 million).
(4) The taxpayer's basis in the SSBIC stock or partnership interest must be reduced by the gain that is rolled over.

g. **Market discount bonds**

(1) Gain on the disposition of a bond (including a tax-exempt bond) that was acquired for a price that was less than the principal amount of the bond is treated as taxable interest income to the extent of the accrued market discount for bonds purchased after April 30, 1993.
(2) Accrued market discount is the difference between the bond's cost basis and its redemption value at maturity amortized over the remaining life of the bond.

h.   **Wash sales**

(1)   Wash sale occurs when stock or securities (or options to acquire stock or securities) are sold at a loss and within **thirty days before or after the sale**, substantially identical stock or securities (or options to acquire them) in the same corporation are purchased.

(2)   Wash sale loss is not deductible, but is added to the basis of the new stock.

(3)   Wash sale rules do not apply to gains.

> *EXAMPLE: C purchased 100 shares of XYZ Corporation stock for $1,000. C later sold the stock for $700, and within thirty days acquired 100 shares of XYZ Corporation stock for $800. The loss of $300 on the sale of stock is not recognized. However, the unrecognized loss of $300 is added to the $800 cost of the new stock to arrive at the basis for the new stock of $1,100. The holding period of the new stock includes the period of time the old stock was held.*

(4)   Does not apply to dealers in stock and securities where loss is sustained in ordinary course of business.

i.   **Worthless stock and securities**

(1)   Treated as a capital loss as if sold on the last day of the taxable year they become worthless.

(2)   Treated as an ordinary loss if stock and securities are those of an **80% or more owned corporate subsidiary** that derived more than 90% of its gross receipts from active-type sources.

6.   **Losses on deposits in insolvent financial institutions**

a.   Loss resulting from a nonbusiness deposit in an insolvent financial institution is generally treated as a nonbusiness bad debt deductible as a short-term capital loss (STCL) in the year in which a final determination of the amount of loss can be made.

b.   As an alternative, if a reasonable estimate of the amount of loss can be made, an individual may elect to

(1)   Treat the loss as a personal casualty loss subject to the $100 floor and 10% of AGI limitation. Then no bad debt deduction can be claimed.

(2)   In lieu of (1) above, treat up to $20,000 as a miscellaneous itemized deduction subject to the 2% of AGI floor if the deposit was not federally insured. Then remainder of loss is treated as a STCL.

> *EXAMPLE: An individual with no capital gains and an AGI of $70,000, incurred a loss on a federally insured deposit in a financial institution of $30,000. The individual may treat the loss as a $30,000 STCL subject to the $3,000 net capital loss deduction limitation, with the remaining $27,000 carried forward as a STCL; or, may treat the loss as a personal casualty loss and an itemized deduction of [($30,000 – $100) – (10% x $70,000)] = $22,900. If the deposit had **not** been federally insured, the individual could also have taken a miscellaneous itemized deduction of [$20,000 – (2% x $70,000)] = $18,600, with the remaining $10,000 treated as a STCL (i.e., $3,000 net capital loss deduction and a $7,000 STCL carryover).*

7.   **Losses, expenses, and interest between related taxpayers**

a.   **Loss is disallowed** on the sale or exchange of property to a related taxpayer.

(1)   Transferee's basis is cost; holding period begins when transferee acquires property.

(2)   On a later resale, any gain recognized by the transferee is reduced by the disallowed loss (unless the transferor's loss was from a wash sale, in which case no reduction is allowed).

(3)   **Related taxpayers** include

(a)   Members of a family, including spouse, brothers, sisters, ancestors, and lineal descendents

(b)   A corporation and a more than 50% shareholder

(c)   Two corporations which are members of the same controlled group

(d)   A person and an exempt organization controlled by that person

(e)   Certain related individuals in a trust, including the grantor or beneficiary and the fiduciary

(f)   A C corporation and a partnership if the same persons own more than 50% of the corporation, and more than 50% of the capital and profits interest in the partnership

(g)   Two S corporations if the same persons own more than 50% of each

(h)   An S corporation and a C corporation if the same persons own more than 50% of each

> *EXAMPLE: During August 2002, Bob sold stock with a basis of $4,000 to his brother Ray for $3,000, its FMV. During June 2003, Ray sold the stock to an unrelated taxpayer for $4,500. Bob's loss of $1,000 is disallowed; Ray recognizes a STCG of ($4,500 – $3,000) – $1,000 disallowed loss = $500.*

(4) **Constructive stock ownership rules** apply in determining if taxpayers are related. For purposes of determining stock ownership

    (a) Stock owned, directly or indirectly, by a corporation, partnership, estate, or trust is considered as being owned proportionately by its shareholders, partners, or beneficiaries.

    (b) An individual is considered as owning the stock owned, directly or indirectly, by his brothers and sisters (whole or half blood), spouse, ancestors, and lineal descendants.

    (c) An individual owning stock in a corporation [other than by (b) above] is considered as owning the stock owned, directly or indirectly, by his partner.

b. The disallowed loss rule in a. above does not apply to transfers between spouses, or former spouses incident to divorce, as discussed below.

c. Any loss from the sale or exchange of property between corporations that are members of the same **controlled group** is deferred (instead of disallowed) until the property is sold outside the group. Use controlled group definition found in Module 36, D.2., but substitute "more than 50%" for "at least 80%."

> *EXAMPLE: Mr. Gudjob is the sole shareholder of X Corp. and Y Corp. During 2002, X Corp. sold nondepreciable property with a basis of $8,000 to Y Corp. for $6,000, its FMV. During 2003, Y Corp. sold the property to an unrelated taxpayer for $6,500. X Corp.'s loss in 2002 is deferred. In 2003, X Corp. recognizes the $2,000 of deferred loss, and Y Corp. recognizes a gain of $500.*

d. An accrual-basis payor is effectively placed on the cash method of accounting for purposes of deducting accrued interest and other expenses owed to a related cash-basis payee.

    (1) No deduction is allowable until the year the amount is actually paid.

    (2) This rule applies to pass-through entities (e.g., a partnership and **any** partner; two partnerships if the same persons own more than 50% of each; an S corporation and **any** shareholder) in addition to the related taxpayers described in a.(3) above, but does not apply to guaranteed payments to partners. This rule also applies to a personal service corporation and **any** employee-owner.

> *EXAMPLE: A calendar-year S corporation accrued a $500 bonus owed to an employee-shareholder in 2003 but did not pay the bonus until February 2004. The $500 bonus will be deductible by the S corporation in 2004, when the employee-shareholder reports the $500 as income.*

8. **Transfer between spouses**

a. No gain or loss is generally recognized on the transfer of property from an individual to (or in trust for the benefit of)

    (1) A spouse (other than a nonresident alien spouse), or

    (2) A former spouse (other than a nonresident alien former spouse), if the transfer is related to the cessation of marriage, or occurs within one year after marriage ceases

b. Transfer is treated as if it were a gift from one spouse to the other.

c. Transferee's basis in the property received will be the transferor's basis (even if FMV is less than the property's basis).

> *EXAMPLE: H sells property with a basis of $6,000 to his spouse, W, for $8,000. No gain is recognized to H, and W's basis for the property is $6,000. W's holding period includes the period that H held the property.*

d. If property is transferred to a **trust** for the benefit of a spouse or former spouse (incident to divorce)

    (1) Gain is recognized to the extent that the amount of liabilities assumed exceeds the total adjusted basis of property transferred.

    (2) Gain or loss is recognized on the transfer of installment obligations.

9. Gain from the sale or exchange of property will be entirely ordinary gain (no capital gain) if the property is depreciable in hands of transferee and the sale or exchange is between

a. A person and a more than 50% owned corporation or partnership

b. A taxpayer and any trust in which such taxpayer or spouse is a beneficiary, unless such beneficiary's interest is a remote contingent interest

c. Constructive ownership rules apply; use rules in Section 7.a.(4)(a) and (b) above

B. Capital Gains and Losses

1. Capital gains and losses result from the "sale or exchange of capital assets." The term **capital assets** includes investment property and property held for personal use. The term specifically **excludes**

   a. Stock in trade, inventory, or goods held primarily for sale to customers in the normal course of business

   b. Depreciable or real property used in a trade or business

   c. Copyrights or artistic, literary, etc., compositions created by the taxpayer

      (1) They are capital assets only if purchased by the taxpayer.
      (2) Patents are generally capital assets in the hands of the inventor.

   d. Accounts or notes receivable arising from normal business activities

   e. US government publications acquired other than by purchase at regular price

   f. Supplies of a type regularly used or consumed by a taxpayer in the ordinary course of the taxpayer's trade or business

2. Whether short-term or long-term depends upon the **holding period**

   a. Long-term if held more than one year

   b. The day property was acquired is excluded and the day it is disposed of is included.

   c. Use calendar months (e.g., if held from January 4 to January 4 it is held exactly one year)

   d. If stock or securities which are traded on an established securities market (or other property regularly traded on an established market) are sold, any resulting gain or loss is recognized on the date the trade is executed (transaction date) by both cash and accrual taxpayers.

   e. The holding period of property received in a nontaxable exchange (e.g., like-kind exchange, involuntary conversion) includes the holding period of the property exchanged, if the property that was exchanged was a capital asset or Sec. 1231 asset.

   f. If the basis of property to a prior owner carries over to the present owner (e.g., gift), the holding period of the prior owner "tacks on" to the present owner's holding period.

   g. If using the lower FMV on date of gift to determine loss, then holding period begins when the gift is received.

      EXAMPLE: X purchased property on July 14, 2002, for $10,000. X made a gift of the property to Z on June 10, 2003, when its FMV was $8,000. Since Z's basis for gain is $10,000, Z's holding period for a disposition at a gain extends back to July 14, 2002. Since Z's $8,000 basis for loss is determined by reference to FMV at June 10, 2003, Z's holding period for a disposition at a loss begins on June 11.

   h. Property acquired from a decedent is always given long-term treatment, regardless of how long the property was held by the decedent or beneficiary, and is treated as property held more than twelve months.

3. Computation of capital gains and losses for **all taxpayers**

   a. First net STCG with STCL and net LTCG with LTCL to determine

      (1) Net short-term capital gain or loss (NSTCG or NSTCL)
      (2) Net long-term capital gain or loss (NLTCG or NLTCL)

   b. Then net these two together to determine whether there is a net capital gain or loss (NCG or NCL)

4. The following rules apply to **individuals:**

   a. Capital gains offset capital losses, with any remaining net capital gains included in gross income.

   b. Net capital gains are subject to tax at various rates, depending on the type of assets sold or exchanged and length of time the assets were held.

      (1) Capital gain from assets held one year or less is taxed at the taxpayer's regular tax rates (up to 35%).

      (2) Capital gain from the sale of collectibles held more than twelve months (e.g., antiques, metals, gems, stamps, coins) is taxed at a maximum rate of 28%.

      (3) Capital gain attributable to unrecaptured depreciation on Sec. 1250 property held more than twelve months is taxed at a maximum rate of 25%.

(4) For tax years ending on or after May 6, 2003, the capital gain from assets held more than twelve months (other than from collectibles and unrecaptured depreciation on SEC. 1250 property) may be taxed at one of the following rates:

    (a) 20% (or 10% for individuals in the 10% or 15% tax brackets) for sales and exchanges prior to May 6, 2003.

    (b) 15% (or 5% for individuals in the 10% or 15% tax brackets) for sales and exchanges after May 5, 2003.

    (c) 8% for individuals in the 10% or 15% tax brackets for assets held more than five years and sold or exchanged prior to May 6, 2003.

(5) For installment sales of assets held more than twelve months, the date an installment payment is received (not the date the asset was sold) determines the capital gains rate that should be applied

c. Gains and losses (including carryovers) within each of the rate groups are netted to arrive at a net gain or loss. A net loss in any rate group is applied to reduce the net gain in the highest rate group first (e.g., a net short-term capital loss is applied to reduce any net gain from the 28% group, then the 25% group, and finally to reduce gain from the 15% group).

EXAMPLE: Kim, who is in the 35% tax bracket, had the following capital gains and losses for calendar-year 2003:

Net short-term capital loss	*$(1,500)*
28% group—collectibles net gain	*900*
25% group—unrecaptured Sec. 1250 net gain	*2,000*
15% group—net gain	*5,000*
Net capital gain	*$ 6,400*

In this case, the NSTCL of $1,500 first offsets the $900 of collectibles gain, and then offsets $600 of the unrecaptured Sec. 1250 gain. As a result of this netting procedure, Kim has $1,400 of unrecaptured Sec. 1250 gain that will be taxed at a rate of 25%, and $5,000 of capital gain that will be taxed at a rate of 15%.

d. If there is a **net capital loss** the following rules apply:

(1) A net capital loss is a deduction in arriving at AGI, but limited to the lesser of

    (a) $3,000 ($1,500 if married filing separately), or
    (b) The excess of capital losses over capital gains

(2) Both a NSTCL and a NLTCL are used dollar-for-dollar in computing the capital loss deduction.

EXAMPLE: An individual had $2,000 of NLTCL and $500 of NSTCL for 2003. The capital losses are combined and the entire net capital loss of $2,500 is deductible in computing the individual's AGI.

(3) Short-term losses are used before long-term losses. The amount of net capital loss that exceeds the allowable deduction may be carried over for an unlimited period of time. Capital loss carryovers retain their identity; short-term losses carry over as short-term losses, and long-term losses carry over as long-term losses in the 28% group. Losses remaining unused on a decedent's final return are extinguished and provide no tax benefit.

EXAMPLE: An individual has a $4,000 STCL and a $5,000 LTCL for 2003. The $9,000 net capital loss results in a capital loss deduction of $3,000 for 2003, while the remainder is a carryover to 2004. Since $3,000 of the STCL would be used to create the capital loss deduction, there is a $1,000 STCL carryover and a $5,000 LTCL carryover to 2004. The $5,000 LTCL carryover would first offset gains in the 28% group.

(4) For purposes of determining the amount of excess net capital loss that can be carried over to future years, the taxpayer's net capital loss for the year is reduced by the lesser of (1) $3,000 ($1,500 if married filing separately), or (2) adjusted taxable income.

    (a) Adjusted taxable income is taxable income increased by $3,000 ($1,500 if married filing separately) and the amount allowed for personal exemptions.

    (b) An excess of deductions allowed over gross income is taken into account as negative taxable income.

    EXAMPLE: For 2003, a single individual with no dependents had a net capital loss of $8,000, and had allowable deductions that exceeded gross income by $4,000. For 2003, the individual is entitled to a net capital loss deduction of $3,000, and will carry over a net capital loss of $5,950 to 2004. This amount represents the 2003 net capital loss of $8,000 reduced by the lesser of (1) $3,000, or (2) – $4,000 + $3,000 + $3,050 personal exemption = $2,050.

5. **Corporations** have special capital gain and loss rules.

    a.   Capital losses are only allowed to offset capital gains, not ordinary income.

    b.   A **net capital loss** is carried back three years, and forward five years to offset capital gains in those years. All capital loss carrybacks and carryovers are treated as **short-term** capital losses.

        EXAMPLE: A corporation has a NLTCL of $8,000 and a NSTCG of $2,000, resulting in a net capital loss of $6,000 for 2003. The $6,000 NLTCL is not deductible for 2003, but is first carried back as a STCL to 2000 to offset capital gains. If not used up in 2000, the STCL is carried to 2001 and 2002, and then forward to 2004, 2005, 2006, 2007, and 2008 to offset capital gains in those years.

    c.   Although an alternative tax computation still exists for a corporation with a net capital gain, the alternative tax computation applies the highest corporate rate (35%) to a net capital gain and thus provides no benefit.

C. Personal Casualty and Theft Gains and Losses

Gains and losses from casualties and thefts of property held for personal use are separately netted, without regard to the holding period of the converted property.

1.   If gains exceed losses (after the $100 floor for each loss), then all gains and losses are treated as capital gains and losses, short-term or long-term depending upon holding period.

    EXAMPLE: An individual incurred a $25,000 personal casualty gain, and a $15,000 personal casualty loss (after the $100 floor) during the current taxable year. Since there was a net gain, the individual will report the gain and loss as a $25,000 capital gain and a $15,000 capital loss.

2.   If losses (after the $100 floor for each loss) exceed gains, the losses (1) offset gains, and (2) are an ordinary deduction from AGI to the extent in excess of 10% of AGI.

    EXAMPLE: An individual had AGI of $40,000 (before casualty gains or losses), and also had a personal casualty loss of $25,000 (after the $100 floor) and a personal casualty gain of $15,000. Since there was a net personal casualty loss, the net loss will be deductible as an itemized deduction of [$25,000 – $15,000 – (10% x $40,000)] = $6,000.

D. Gains and Losses on Business Property

Although property used in a business is excluded from the definition of "capital assets," Sec. 1231 extends capital gain and loss treatment to business assets if the gains from these assets exceed losses. However, before Sec. 1231 becomes operative, Sections 1245, 1250, and 291 provide for recapture of depreciation (i.e., gain is taxed as ordinary income to the extent of certain depreciation previously deducted).

1.   All gains and losses are **ordinary** on business property **held one year or less**.

2.   **Section 1231**

    a.   All property included must have been held for **more than one year**.

        (1) Section 1231 gains and losses include those from

            (a) Sale or exchange of property used in trade or business (or held for production of rents or royalties) and which is not

                1]   Inventory
                2]   A copyright or artistic composition

            (b) Casualty, theft, or condemnation of

                1]   Property used in trade or business
                2]   Capital assets held in connection with a trade or business, or a transaction entered into for profit

            (c) Infrequently encountered items such as cut timber, coal and domestic iron ore, livestock, and unharvested crop

    b.   The combining of Sec. 1231 gains and losses is accomplished in **two steps**. **First**, net all casualty and theft gains and losses on property held for more than one year.

        (1) If the losses exceed gains, treat them all as ordinary losses and gains and do not net them with other Sec. 1231 gains and losses.

        (2) If the gains exceed losses, the net gain is combined with other Sec. 1231 gains and losses.

c. **Second**, net all other Sec. 1231 gains and losses (except casualty and theft net loss per above).

   (1) Include casualty and theft net gain
   (2) Include gains and losses from condemnations (other than condemnations on nonbusiness, non-income-producing property)
   (3) Include gains and losses from the sale or exchange of property used in trade or business

d. If losses exceed gains, treat all gains and losses as ordinary.

e. If gains exceed losses, treat the Sec. 1231 net gain as a long-term capital gain.

   EXAMPLE: Taxpayer has a gain of $10,000 from the sale of land used in his business, a loss of $4,000 on the sale of depreciable property used in his business, and a $2,000 (noninsured) loss when a car used in his business was involved in a collision.

   The net gain or loss from casualty or theft is the $2,000 loss. The net casualty loss of $2,000 is treated as an ordinary loss and not netted with other Sec. 1231 gains and losses.

   The $10,000 gain is netted with the $4,000 loss resulting in a net Sec. 1231 gain of $6,000, which is then treated as a long-term capital gain.

f. Net Sec. 1231 gain will be treated as ordinary income (instead of LTCG) to the extent of nonrecaptured net Sec. 1231 losses for the five most recent taxable years.

   (1) Losses are deemed recaptured in the chronological order in which they arose
   (2) Any Sec. 1231 gain recharacterized as ordinary income consists first of gain in the 28% group, then gain in the 25% group, and finally gain the 20% group

   EXAMPLE: Corp. X, on a calendar year, has a net Sec. 1231 gain of $10,000 for 2003. For the years 1998 through 2002, Corp. X had net Sec. 1231 losses totaling $8,000. Of the $10,000 net Sec. 1231 gain for 2003, the first $8,000 will be treated as ordinary income, with only the remaining $2,000 treated as long-term capital gain.

3. **Section 1245 Recapture**

   a. Requires the recapture as **ordinary income** of all gain attributable to

      (1) **Post-1961 depreciation** on the disposition of Sec. 1245 property
      (2) **Post-1980 recovery deductions** on the disposition of Sec. 1245 recovery property (including amount expensed under Sec. 179 expense election)

   b. **Sec. 1245 property** generally includes depreciable tangible and intangible **personal property,** for example

      (1) Desks, machines, equipment, cars, and trucks
      (2) Special purpose structures, storage facilities, and other property (but not buildings and structural components); for example, oil and gas storage tanks, grain storage bins and silos, and escalators and elevators

   c. **Sec. 1245 recovery property** means **all** ACRS recovery property placed in service after 1980 and **before 1987** other than nineteen-year real property that is classified as real residential rental property, real property used outside the US, subsidized low-income housing, and real property for which a straight-line election was made.

   NOTE: If the cost of nineteen-year nonresidential real property placed in service before 1987 was recovered using the prescribed percentages of ACRS, the gain on disposition is ordinary income to extent of all ACRS deductions. Such recapture is not limited to the excess of accelerated depreciation over straight-line. However, if the straight-line method was elected for nineteen-year real property, there is no recapture and all gain is Sec. 1231 gain.

   d. Sec. 1245 does not apply to real residential rental property and nonresidential real property placed in service after 1986 because only straight-line depreciation is allowable.

   e. Upon the disposition of property subject to Sec. 1245, any recognized gain will be ordinary income to the extent of all depreciation or post-1980 cost recovery deductions.

      (1) Any remaining gain after recapture will be Sec. 1231 gain if property held more than one year.

      EXAMPLE: Megan sold equipment used in her business for $11,000. The equipment had cost $10,000 and $6,000 of depreciation had been taken, resulting in an adjusted basis of $4,000. Megan's recognized gain is $11,000 – $4,000 = $7,000. Since the equipment was Sec. 1245 property, the gain must be recognized as Sec. 1245 ordinary income to the extent of the $6,000 of depreciation deducted. The remaining $1,000 gain ($7,000 gain – $6,000 ordinary income) is recognized as Sec. 1231 gain.

EXAMPLE: Assume the same facts as in the preceding example, except the equipment was sold for $9,000. Megan's recognized gain would be $9,000 – $4,000 = $5,000. Now, since the $6,000 of depreciation deducted exceeds the recognized gain of $5,000, the amount of Sec. 1245 ordinary income would be limited to the recognized gain of $5,000. There would be no Sec. 1231 gain.

EXAMPLE: Assume the same facts as in the first example, except the equipment was sold for only $3,500. Megan's sale of the equipment now results in a recognized loss of $3,500 – $4,000 = ($500). Since there is loss, there would be no Sec. 1245 depreciation recapture and the $500 loss would be classified as a Sec. 1231 loss.

    (2) If the disposition is not by sale, use FMV of property (instead of selling price) to determine gain.

        (a) When boot is received in a like-kind exchange, Sec. 1245 will apply to the recognized gain.

        EXAMPLE: Taxpayer exchanged his old machine (adjusted basis of $2,500) for a smaller new machine worth $5,000 and received $1,000 cash. Depreciation of $7,500 had been taken on the old machine. The realized gain of $3,500 ($6,000 – $2,500) will be recognized to the extent of the $1,000 boot, and will be treated as ordinary income as the result of Sec. 1245.

        (b) Sec. 1245 recapture does not apply to transfers by gift (including charitable contributions) or transfers at death.

4. **Section 1250 Recapture**

  a. Applies to all real property (e.g., buildings and structural components) that is not Sec. 1245 recovery property.

    (1) If Sec. 1250 property was held twelve months or less, gain on disposition is recaptured as ordinary income to extent of all depreciation (including straight-line).

    (2) If Sec. 1250 property was held more than twelve months, gain is recaptured as ordinary income to the extent of post-1969 **additional depreciation** (generally depreciation in excess of straight-line).

    *EXAMPLE: An office building with an adjusted basis of $200,000 was sold by **individual X** in 2003 for $350,000. The property had been purchased for $300,000 in 1980 and $100,000 of depreciation had been deducted. Straight-line depreciation would have totaled $70,000.*

Total gain ($350,000 – $200,000)	*$150,000*
Post-1969 additional depreciation recaptured as ordinary income	*(30,000)*
Remainder is Sec. 1231 gain	*$120,000*

5. **Section 291 Recapture**

  a. The ordinary income element on the disposition of Sec. 1250 property by **corporations** is increased by 20% of the additional amount that would have been ordinary income if the property had instead been Sec. 1245 property or Sec. 1245 recovery property.

  *EXAMPLE: Assuming the same facts as in the above example except that the building was sold by **Corporation X** in 2003, the computation of gain would be*

Total gain ($350,000 – $200,000)	*$150,000*
Post-1969 additional depreciation recaptured as ordinary income	*(30,000)**
Additional ordinary income—20% of $70,000 (the additional amount that would have been ordinary income if the property were Sec. 1245 property)	*(14,000)**
Remainder is Sec. 1231 gain	*$106,000*

  * *All $44,000 ($30,000 + $14,000) of recapture is referred to as Sec. 1250 ordinary income.*

6. **Summary of Gains and Losses on Business Property.** The treatment of gains and losses (other than personal casualty and theft) on property held for **more than one year** is summarized in the following **four steps** (also enumerated on flowchart at end of this section):

  a. Separate all recognized gains and losses into four categories

    (1) Ordinary gain and loss
    (2) Sec. 1231 casualty and theft gains and losses
    (3) Sec. 1231 gains and losses other than by casualty or theft
    (4) Gains and losses on capital assets (other than by casualty or theft)

NOTE: (2) and (3) are only temporary classifications and all gains and losses will ultimately receive ordinary or capital treatment.

b. Any gain (casualty or other) on Sec. 1231 property is treated as ordinary income to extent of Sec. 1245, 1250, and 291 depreciation recapture.

c. After depreciation recapture, any remaining Sec. 1231 casualty and theft gains and losses on business property are netted.

   (1) If losses exceed gains—the losses and gains receive ordinary treatment
   (2) If gains exceed losses—the net gain is combined with other Sec. 1231 gains and losses in d. below

d. After recapture, any remaining Sec. 1231 gains and losses (other than by casualty or theft), are combined with any net casualty or theft gain from c. above.

   (1) If losses exceed gains—the losses and gains receive ordinary treatment
   (2) If gains exceed losses—the net gain receives LTCG treatment (except ordinary income treatment to extent of nonrecaptured net Sec. 1231 losses for the five most recent tax years)

   EXAMPLE: *Taxpayer incurred the following transactions during the current taxable year:*

Loss on condemnation of land used in business held fifteen months	$ (500)
Loss on sale of machinery used in business held two months	(1,000)
Bad debt loss on loan made three years ago to friend	(2,000)
Gain from insurance reimbursement for tornado damage to business property held ten years	3,000
Loss on sale of business equipment held three years	(4,000)
Gain on sale of land held four years and used in business	5,000

   The gains and losses would be treated as follows: Note that the loss on machinery is ordinary because it was not held more than one year.

		Sec. 1231		Other		Capital	
	Ordinary	Casualty		Sec. 1231		L-T	S-T
	$(1,000)	$3,000		$ (500)			$(2,000)*
				(4,000)			
				5,000			
		$3,000	→	3,000			
				$3,500	→	$3,500	
	$(1,000)					$3,500	$(2,000)

   * A nonbusiness bad debt is always treated as a STCL.

TAX TREATMENT OF GAINS AND LOSSES (OTHER THAN PERSONAL CASUALTY AND THEFT) ON PROPERTY HELD MORE THAN ONE YEAR

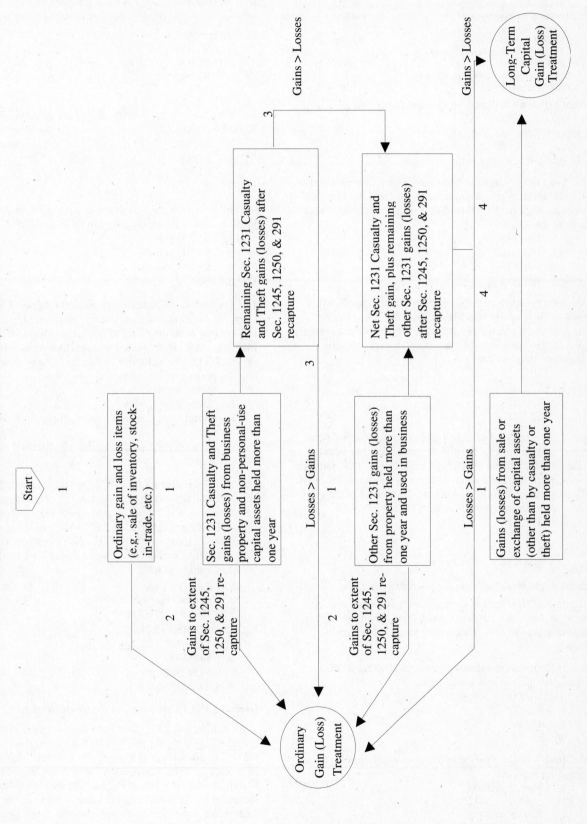

MULTIPLE-CHOICE QUESTIONS (1-63)

1. Ralph Birch purchased land and a building which will be used in connection with Birch's business. The costs associated with this purchase are as follows:

Cash down payment	$ 40,000
Mortgage on property	350,000
Survey costs	2,000
Title and transfer taxes	2,500
Charges for hookup of gas, water, and sewer lines	3,000
Back property taxes owed by the seller that were paid by Birch	5,000

What is Birch's tax basis for the land and building?
- a. $ 44,500
- b. $394,500
- c. $397,500
- d. $402,500

2. Fred Berk bought a plot of land with a cash payment of $40,000 and a purchase money mortgage of $50,000. In addition, Berk paid $200 for a title insurance policy. Berk's basis in this land is
- a. $40,000
- b. $40,200
- c. $90,000
- d. $90,200

3. Smith made a gift of property to Thompson. Smith's basis in the property was $1,200. The fair market value at the time of the gift was $1,400. Thompson sold the property for $2,500. What was the amount of Thompson's gain on the disposition?
- a. $0
- b. $1,100
- c. $1,300
- d. $2,500

4. Julie received a parcel of land as a gift from her Aunt Agnes. At the time of the gift, the land had a fair market value of $81,000 and an adjusted basis of $21,000. This was the only gift that Julie received from Agnes during 2003. If Agnes paid a gift tax of $14,000 on the transfer of the gift to Julie, what tax basis will Julie have for the land?
- a. $21,000
- b. $31,000
- c. $33,000
- d. $80,000

Items 5 and 6 are based on the following data:

In 2000 Iris King bought shares of stock as an investment, at a cost of $10,000. During 2002, when the fair market value was $8,000, Iris gave the stock to her daughter, Ruth.

5. If Ruth sells the shares of stock in 2003 for $7,000, Ruth's recognized loss would be
- a. $3,000
- b. $2,000
- c. $1,000
- d. $0

6. Ruth's holding period of the stock for purposes of determining her loss
- a. Started in 2000.
- b. Started in 2002.
- c. Started in 2003.
- d. Is irrelevant because Ruth received the stock for no consideration of money or money's worth.

Items 7 through 9 are based on the following data:

Laura's father, Albert, gave Laura a gift of 500 shares of Liba Corporation common stock in 2003. Albert's basis for the Liba stock was $4,000. At the date of this gift, the fair market value of the Liba stock was $3,000.

7. If Laura sells the 500 shares of Liba stock in 2003 for $5,000, her basis is
- a. $5,000
- b. $4,000
- c. $3,000
- d. $0

8. If Laura sells the 500 shares of Liba stock in 2003 for $2,000, her basis is
- a. $4,000
- b. $3,000
- c. $2,000
- d. $0

9. If Laura sells the 500 shares of Liba stock in 2003 for $3,500, what is the reportable gain or loss in 2003?
- a. $3,500 gain.
- b. $ 500 gain.
- c. $ 500 loss.
- d. $0.

10. On June 1, 2003, Ben Rork sold 500 shares of Kul Corp. stock. Rork had received this stock on May 1, 2003, as a bequest from the estate of his uncle, who died on March 1, 2003. Rork's basis was determined by reference to the stock's fair market value on March 1, 2003. Rork's holding period for this stock was
- a. Short-term.
- b. Long-term.
- c. Short-term if sold at a gain; long-term if sold at a loss.
- d. Long-term if sold at a gain; short-term if sold at a loss.

11. Fred Zorn died on January 5, 2003, bequeathing his entire $2,000,000 estate to his sister, Ida. The alternate valuation date was validly elected by the executor of Fred's estate. Fred's estate included 2,000 shares of listed stock for which Fred's basis was $380,000. This stock was distributed to Ida nine months after Fred's death. Fair market values of this stock were

At the date of Fred's death	$400,000
Six months after Fred's death	450,000
Nine months after Fred's death	480,000

Ida's basis for this stock is
- a. $380,000
- b. $400,000
- c. $450,000
- d. $480,000

Items 12 and 13 are based on the following data:

On March 1, 2003, Lois Rice learned that she was bequeathed 1,000 shares of Elin Corp. common stock under the will of her uncle, Pat Prevor. Pat had paid $5,000 for the Elin stock in 1998. Fair market value of the Elin stock on March 1, 2003, the date of Pat's death, was $8,000 and had increased to $11,000 six months later. The executor of Pat's estate elected the alternative valuation for estate tax purposes. Lois sold the Elin stock for $9,000 on May 1, 2003, the date that the executor distributed the stock to her.

12. Lois' basis for gain or loss on sale of the 1,000 shares of Elin stock is
   a. $ 5,000
   b. $ 8,000
   c. $ 9,000
   d. $11,000

13. Lois should treat the 1,000 shares of Elin stock as a
   a. Short-term Section 1231 asset.
   b. Long-term Section 1231 asset.
   c. Short-term capital asset.
   d. Long-term capital asset.

Items 14 and 15 are based on the following data:

In January 2003, Joan Hill bought one share of Orban Corp. stock for $300. On March 1, 2003, Orban distributed one share of preferred stock for each share of common stock held. This distribution was nontaxable. On March 1, 2003, Joan's one share of common stock had a fair market value of $450, while the preferred stock had a fair market value of $150.

14. After the distribution of the preferred stock, Joan's bases for her Orban stocks are

	Common	Preferred
a.	$300	$0
b.	$225	$ 75
c.	$200	$100
d.	$150	$150

15. The holding period for the preferred stock starts in
   a. January 2003.
   b. March 2003.
   c. September 2003.
   d. December 2003.

16. On July 1, 1999, Lila Perl paid $90,000 for 450 shares of Janis Corp. common stock. Lila received a nontaxable stock dividend of 50 new common shares in August 2003. On December 20, 2003, Lila sold the 50 new shares for $11,000. How much should Lila report in her 2003 return as long-term capital gain?
   a. $0
   b. $ 1,000
   c. $ 2,000
   d. $11,000

17. Tom Gow owned a parcel of investment real estate that had an adjusted basis of $25,000 and a fair market value of $40,000. During 2003, Gow exchanged his investment real estate for the items of property listed below.

Land to be held for investment (fair market value)	$35,000
A small sailboat to be held for personal use (fair market value)	3,000
Cash	2,000

What is Tom Gow's recognized gain and basis in his new investment real estate?

	Gain recognized	Basis for real estate
a.	$2,000	$22,000
b.	$2,000	$25,000
c.	$5,000	$25,000
d.	$5,000	$35,000

18. In a "like-kind" exchange of an investment asset for a similar asset that will also be held as an investment, no tax-

able gain or loss will be recognized on the transaction if both assets consist of
   a. Convertible debentures.
   b. Convertible preferred stock.
   c. Partnership interests.
   d. Rental real estate located in different states.

19. Leker exchanged a van that was used exclusively for business and had an adjusted tax basis of $20,000 for a new van. The new van had a fair market value of $15,000, and Leker also received $3,000 in cash. What was Leker's tax basis in the acquired van?
   a. $20,000
   b. $17,000
   c. $12,000
   d. $ 5,000

20. Pat Leif owned an apartment house that he bought in 1990. Depreciation was taken on a straight-line basis. In 2003, when Pat's adjusted basis for this property was $200,000, he traded it for an office building having a fair market value of $600,000. The apartment house has 100 dwelling units, while the office building has 40 units rented to business enterprises. The properties are **not** located in the same city. What is Pat's reportable gain on this exchange?
   a. $400,000 Section 1250 gain.
   b. $400,000 Section 1231 gain.
   c. $400,000 long-term capital gain.
   d. $0.

21. On July 1, 2003, Riley exchanged investment real property, with an adjusted basis of $160,000 and subject to a mortgage of $70,000, and received from Wilson $30,000 cash and other investment real property having a fair market value of $250,000. Wilson assumed the mortgage. What is Riley's recognized gain in 2003 on the exchange?
   a. $ 30,000
   b. $ 70,000
   c. $ 90,000
   d. $100,000

22. On October 1, 2003, Donald Anderson exchanged an apartment building having an adjusted basis of $375,000 and subject to a mortgage of $100,000 for $25,000 cash and another apartment building with a fair market value of $550,000 and subject to a mortgage of $125,000. The property transfers were made subject to the outstanding mortgages. What amount of gain should Anderson recognize in his tax return for 2003?
   a. $0
   b. $ 25,000
   c. $125,000
   d. $175,000

23. The following information pertains to the acquisition of a six-wheel truck by Sol Barr, a self-employed contractor:

Cost of original truck traded in	$20,000
Book value of original truck at trade-in date	4,000
List price of new truck	25,000
Trade-in allowance for old truck	6,000
Business use of both trucks	100%

The basis of the new truck is
   a. $27,000
   b. $25,000
   c. $23,000
   d. $19,000

24. An office building owned by Elmer Bass was condemned by the state on January 2, 2002. Bass received the
condemnation award on March 1, 2003. In order to qualify
for nonrecognition of gain on this involuntary conversion,
what is the last date for Bass to acquire qualified replacement property?

    a.   August 1, 2004.
    b.   January 2, 2005.
    c.   March 1, 2006.
    d.   December 31, 2006.

25. In March 2003, Davis, who is single, purchased a new
residence for $200,000. During that same month he sold his
former residence for $380,000 and paid the realtor a $20,000
commission. The former residence, his first home, had cost
$65,000 in 1980. Davis added a bathroom for $5,000 in
1999. What amount of gain is recognized from the sale of
the former residence on Davis' 2003 tax return?

    a. $160,000
    b. $ 90,000
    c. $ 40,000
    d. $0

26. The following information pertains to the sale of Al and
Beth Oran's principal residence:

Date of sale	February 2003
Date of purchase	October 1986
Net sales price	$760,000
Adjusted basis	$170,000

Al and Beth owned their home jointly and had occupied it as
their principal residence since acquiring the home in 1986.
In June 2003, the Orans bought a condo for $190,000 to be
used as their principal residence. What amount of gain must
the Orans recognize on their 2003 joint return from the sale
of their residence?

    a. $ 90,000
    b. $150,000
    c. $340,000
    d. $400,000

27. Ryan, age fifty-seven, is single with no dependents. In
January 2003, Ryan's principal residence was sold for the
net amount of $400,000 after all selling expenses. Ryan
bought the house in 1990 and occupied it until sold. On the
date of sale, the house had a basis of $180,000. Ryan does
not intend to buy another residence. What is the maximum
exclusion of gain on sale of the residence that may be
claimed in Ryan's 2003 income tax return?

    a. $250,000
    b. $220,000
    c. $125,000
    d. $0

28. Miller, an individual calendar-year taxpayer, purchased
100 shares of Maples Inc. common stock for $10,000 on
July 10, 2002, and an additional fifty shares of Maples Inc.
common stock for $4,000 on December 24, 2002. On Janu-
ary 8, 2003, Miller sold the 100 shares purchased on July 10,
2002, for $7,000. What is the amount of Miller's recognized
loss for 2003 and what is the basis for her remaining fifty
shares of Maples Inc. stock?

    a. $3,000 recognized loss; $4,000 basis for her re-
        maining stock.
    b. $1,500 recognized loss; $5,500 basis for her re-
        maining stock.

    c. $1,500 recognized loss; $4,000 basis for her re-
        maining stock.
    d. $0 recognized loss; $7,000 basis for her remaining
        stock.

29. Smith, an individual calendar-year taxpayer, purchased
100 shares of Core Co. common stock for $15,000 on De-
cember 15, 2002, and an additional 100 shares for $13,000
on December 30, 2002. On January 3, 2003, Smith sold the
shares purchased on December 15, 2002, for $13,000. What
amount of loss from the sale of Core stock is deductible on
Smith's 2002 and 2003 income tax returns?

	2002	*2003*
a.	$0	$0
b.	$0	$2,000
c.	$1,000	$1,000
d.	$2,000	$0

30. On March 10, 2003, James Rogers sold 300 shares of
Red Company common stock for $4,200. Rogers acquired
the stock in 2000 at a cost of $5,000.

    On April 4, 2003, he repurchased 300 shares of Red
Company common stock for $3,600 and held them until
July 18, 2003, when he sold them for $6,000.

    How should Rogers report the above transactions for
2003?

    a.   A long-term capital loss of $800.
    b.   A long-term capital gain of $1,000.
    c.   A long-term capital gain of $1,600.
    d.   A long-term capital loss of $800 and a short-term
        capital gain of $2,400.

31. Murd Corporation, a domestic corporation, acquired a
90% interest in the Drum Company in 1999 for $30,000.
During 2003, the stock of Drum was declared worthless.
What type and amount of deduction should Murd take for
2003?

    a.   Long-term capital loss of $1,000.
    b.   Long-term capital loss of $15,000.
    c.   Ordinary loss of $30,000.
    d.   Long-term capital loss of $30,000.

32. If an individual incurs a loss on a nonbusiness deposit
as the result of the insolvency of a bank, credit union, or
other financial institution, the individual's loss on the nonbusiness deposit may be deducted in any one of the following ways **except:**

    a.   Miscellaneous itemized deduction
    b.   Casualty loss
    c.   Short-term capital loss
    d.   Long-term capital loss

Items 33 and 34 are based on the following:

    Conner purchased 300 shares of Zinco stock for
$30,000 in 1999. On May 23, 2003, Conner sold all the
stock to his daughter Alice for $20,000, its then fair market
value. Conner realized no other gain or loss during 2003.
On July 26, 2003, Alice sold the 300 shares of Zinco for
$25,000.

33. What amount of the loss from the sale of Zinco stock
can Conner deduct in 2003?

    a. $0
    b. $ 3,000
    c. $ 5,000
    d. $10,000

34. What was Alice's recognized gain or loss on her sale?
a. $0.
b. $5,000 long-term gain.
c. $5,000 short-term loss.
d. $5,000 long-term loss.

35. In 2003, Fay sold 100 shares of Gym Co. stock to her son, Martin, for $11,000. Fay had paid $15,000 for the stock in 2000. Subsequently in 2003, Martin sold the stock to an unrelated third party for $16,000. What amount of gain from the sale of the stock to the third party should Martin report on his 2003 income tax return?
a. $0
b. $1,000
c. $4,000
d. $5,000

36. Among which of the following related parties are losses from sales and exchanges not recognized for tax purposes?
a. Mother-in-law and daughter-in-law.
b. Uncle and nephew.
c. Brother and sister.
d. Ancestors, lineal descendants, and all in-laws.

37. On May 1, 2003, Daniel Wright owned stock (held for investment) purchased two years earlier at a cost of $10,000 and having a fair market value of $7,000. On this date he sold the stock to his son, William, for $7,000. William sold the stock for $6,000 to an unrelated person on July 1, 2003. How should William report the stock sale on his 2003 tax return?
a. As a short-term capital loss of $1,000.
b. As a long-term capital loss of $1,000.
c. As a short-term capital loss of $4,000.
d. As a long-term capital loss of $4,000.

38. Al Eng owns 50% of the outstanding stock of Rego Corp. During 2003, Rego sold a trailer to Eng for $10,000, the trailer's fair value. The trailer had an adjusted tax basis of $12,000, and had been owned by Rego and used in its business for three years. In its 2003 income tax return, what is the allowable loss that Rego can claim on the sale of this trailer?
a. $0
b. $2,000 capital loss.
c. $2,000 Section 1231 loss.
d. $2,000 Section 1245 loss.

39. For a cash basis taxpayer, gain or loss on a year-end sale of listed stock arises on the
a. Trade date.
b. Settlement date.
c. Date of receipt of cash proceeds.
d. Date of delivery of stock certificate.

40. Lee qualified as head of a household for 2003 tax purposes. Lee's 2003 taxable income was $100,000, exclusive of capital gains and losses. Lee had a net long-term loss of $8,000 in 2003. What amount of this capital loss can Lee offset against 2003 ordinary income?
a. $0
b. $3,000
c. $4,000
d. $8,000

41. For the year ended December 31, 2003, Sol Corp. had an operating income of $20,000. In addition, Sol had capital gains and losses resulting in a net short-term capital gain of $2,000 and a net long-term capital loss of $7,000. How much of the excess of net long-term capital loss over net short-term capital gain could Sol offset against ordinary income for 2003?
a. $5,000
b. $3,000
c. $1,500
d. $0

42. In 2003, Nam Corp., which is not a dealer in securities, realized taxable income of $160,000 from its business operations. Also, in 2003, Nam sustained a long-term capital loss of $24,000 from the sale of marketable securities. Nam did not realize any other capital gains or losses since it began operations. In Nam's income tax returns, what is the proper treatment for the $24,000 long-term capital loss?
a. Use $3,000 of the loss to reduce 2003 taxable income, and carry $21,000 of the long-term capital loss forward for five years.
b. Use $6,000 of the loss to reduce 2003 taxable income by $3,000, and carry $18,000 of the long-term capital loss forward for five years.
c. Use $24,000 of the long-term capital loss to reduce 2003 taxable income by $12,000.
d. Carry the $24,000 long-term capital loss forward for five years, treating it as a short-term capital loss.

43. For assets acquired in 2003, the holding period for determining long-term capital gains and losses is more than
a. 18 months.
b. 12 months.
c. 9 months.
d. 6 months.

44. On July 1, 2003, Kim Wald sold an antique for $12,000 that she had bought for her personal use in 2001 at a cost of $15,000. In her 2003 return, Kim should treat the sale of the antique as a transaction resulting in
a. A nondeductible loss.
b. Ordinary loss.
c. Short-term capital loss.
d. Long-term capital loss.

45. Paul Beyer, who is unmarried, has taxable income of $30,000 exclusive of capital gains and losses and his personal exemption. In 2003, Paul incurred a $1,000 net short-term capital loss and a $5,000 net long-term capital loss. His capital loss carryover to 2004 is
a. $0
b. $1,000
c. $3,000
d. $5,000

46. Capital assets include
a. A corporation's accounts receivable from the sale of its inventory.
b. Seven-year MACRS property used in a corporation's trade or business.
c. A manufacturing company's investment in US Treasury bonds.
d. A corporate real estate developer's unimproved land that is to be subdivided to build homes, which will be sold to customers.

47. Joe Hall owns a limousine for use in his personal service business of transporting passengers to airports. The limousine's adjusted basis is $40,000. In addition, Hall owns his personal residence and furnishings, that together cost him $280,000. Hall's capital assets amount to
- a. $320,000
- b. $280,000
- c. $ 40,000
- d. $0

48. In 2003, Ruth Lee sold a painting for $25,000 that she had bought for her personal use in 1997 at a cost of $10,000. In her 2003 return, Lee should treat the sale of the painting as a transaction resulting in
- a. Ordinary income.
- b. Long-term capital gain.
- c. Section 1231 gain.
- d. No taxable gain.

49. In 2003, a capital loss incurred by a married couple filing a joint return
- a. Will be allowed only to the extent of capital gains.
- b. Will be allowed to the extent of capital gains, plus up to $3,000 of ordinary income.
- c. Will be allowed to the extent of capital gains, plus up to $6,000 of ordinary income.
- d. Is **not** an allowable loss.

50. Platt owns land that is operated as a parking lot. A shed was erected on the lot for the related transactions with customers. With regard to capital assets and Section 1231 assets, how should these assets be classified?

	Land	*Shed*
a.	Capital	Capital
b.	Section 1231	Capital
c.	Capital	Section 1231
d.	Section 1231	Section 1231

51. In 1999, Iris King bought a diamond necklace for her own use, at a cost of $10,000. In 2003, when the fair market value was $12,000, Iris gave this necklace to her daughter, Ruth. No gift tax was due. This diamond necklace is a
- a. Capital asset.
- b. Section 1231 asset.
- c. Section 1245 asset.
- d. Section 1250 asset.

52. Which of the following is a capital asset?
- a. Delivery truck.
- b. Personal-use recreation equipment.
- c. Land used as a parking lot for customers.
- d. Treasury stock, at cost.

53. Don Mott was the sole proprietor of a high-volume drug store which he owned for fifteen years before he sold it to Dale Drug Stores, Inc. in 2003. Besides the $900,000 selling price for the store's tangible assets and goodwill, Mott received a lump sum of $30,000 in 2003 for his agreement not to operate a competing enterprise within ten miles of the store's location for a period of six years. The $30,000 will be taxed to Mott as
- a. $30,000 ordinary income in 2003.
- b. $30,000 short-term capital gain in 2003.
- c. $30,000 long-term capital gain in 2003.
- d. Ordinary income of $5,000 a year for six years.

54. In June 2003, Olive Bell bought a house for use partially as a residence and partially for operation of a retail gift shop. In addition, Olive bought the following furniture:

Kitchen set and living room pieces for the residential portion	$ 8,000
Showcases and tables for the business portion	12,000

How much of this furniture comprises capital assets?
- a. $0
- b. $ 8,000
- c. $12,000
- d. $20,000

55. An individual's losses on transactions entered into for personal purposes are deductible only if
- a. The losses qualify as casualty or theft losses.
- b. The losses can be characterized as hobby losses.
- c. The losses do not exceed $3,000 ($6,000 on a joint return).
- d. No part of the transactions was entered into for profit.

56. Evon Corporation, which was formed in 2000, had $50,000 of net Sec. 1231 gain for its 2003 calendar year. Its net Sec. 1231 gains and losses for its three preceding tax years were as follows:

Year	*Sec. 1231 results*
2000	Gain of $10,000
2001	Loss of $15,000
2002	Loss of $20,000

As a result, Evon Corporation's 2003 net Sec. 1231 gain would be characterized as
- a. A net long-term capital gain of $50,000.
- b. A net long-term capital gain of $35,000 and ordinary income of $15,000.
- c. A net long-term capital gain of $25,000 and ordinary income of $25,000.
- d. A net long-term capital gain of $15,000 and ordinary income of $35,000.

57. Which one of the following would **not** be Sec. 1231 property even though held for more than twelve months?
- a. Business inventory.
- b. Unimproved land used for business.
- c. Depreciable equipment used in a business.
- d. Depreciable real property used in a business.

58. Vermont Corporation distributed packaging equipment that it no longer needed to Michael Jason who owns 20% of Vermont's stock. The equipment, which was acquired in 1998, had an adjusted basis of $2,000 and a fair market value of $9,000 at the date of distribution. Vermont had properly deducted $6,000 of straight-line depreciation on the equipment while it was used in Vermont's manufacturing activities. What amount of ordinary income must Vermont recognize as a result of the distribution of the equipment?
- a. $0
- b. $3,000
- c. $6,000
- d. $7,000

59. Tally Corporation sold machinery that had been used in its business for a loss of $22,000 during 2003. The machinery had been purchased and placed in service sixteen months earlier. For 2003, the $22,000 loss will be treated as a
- a   Capital loss.
- b.   Sec. 1245 loss.

   c.   Sec. 1231 loss.
   d.   Casualty loss because the machinery was held less than two years.

60. On January 2, 2001, Bates Corp. purchased and placed into service seven-year MACRS tangible property costing $100,000. On July 31, 2003, Bates sold the property for $102,000, after having taken $47,525 in MACRS depreciation deductions. What amount of the gain should Bates recapture as ordinary income?

   a. $0
   b. $ 2,000
   c. $47,525
   d. $49,525

61. Thayer Corporation purchased an apartment building on January 1, 2000, for $200,000. The building was depreciated using the straight-line method. On December 31, 2003, the building was sold for $220,000, when the asset balance net of accumulated depreciation was $170,000. On its 2003 tax return, Thayer should report

   a.   Section 1231 gain of $42,500 and ordinary income of $7,500.
   b.   Section 1231 gain of $44,000 and ordinary income of $6,000.
   c.   Ordinary income of $50,000.
   d.   Section 1231 gain of $50,000.

62. For the year ended December 31, 2003, McEwing Corporation, a calendar-year corporation, reported book income before income taxes of $120,000. Included in the determination of this amount were the following gain and losses from property that had been held for more than one year:

Loss on sale of building depreciated on the straight-line method	$(7,000)
Gain on sale of land used in McEwing's business	16,000
Loss on sale of investments in marketable securities	(8,000)

For the year ended December 31, 2003, McEwing's taxable income was

   a. $113,000
   b. $120,000
   c. $125,000
   d. $128,000

63. David Price owned machinery which he had acquired in 2002 at a cost of $100,000. During 2003, the machinery was destroyed by fire. At that time it had an adjusted basis of $86,000. The insurance proceeds awarded to Price amounted to $125,000, and he immediately acquired a similar machine for $110,000.

   What should Price report as ordinary income resulting from the involuntary conversion for 2003?

   a. $14,000
   b. $15,000
   c. $25,000
   d. $39,000

SIMULATION PROBLEM

Simulation Problem 1   (5 to 10 minutes)

Tax Treatment

    Classify the gains and losses resulting from the following independent transactions. For each transaction (**Items 1 through 12**), select the appropriate tax treatment. A tax treatment may be selected once, more than once, or not at all.

Tax treatment

A. Long-term capital gain   F. Sec. 1231 loss
B. Long-term capital loss   G. Ordinary income
C. Short-term capital gain   H. Ordinary loss
D. Short-term capital loss   I. Not deductible
E. Sec. 1231 gain

Transaction	(A)	(B)	(C)	(D)	(E)	(F)	(G)	(H)	(I)
1. Gain from sale of business inventory held thirteen months.	O	O	O	O	O	O	O	O	O
2. Gain from sale of personal residence held three years.	O	O	O	O	O	O	O	O	O
3. Gain from sale of unimproved land used as business parking lot and held seventeen months.	O	O	O	O	O	O	O	O	O
4. Loss from sale of eight-year-old boat held for personal use.	O	O	O	O	O	O	O	O	O
5. Gain from sale of lot held as investment for eleven months.	O	O	O	O	O	O	O	O	O
6. Casualty gain on personal residence held ten years (this was taxpayer's only casualty during year).	O	O	O	O	O	O	O	O	O
7. Casualty loss on truck used in business and held seven months.	O	O	O	O	O	O	O	O	O
8. Loss from nonbusiness bad debt that was outstanding two years.	O	O	O	O	O	O	O	O	O
9. Loss from sale of factory building held twenty-two months.	O	O	O	O	O	O	O	O	O
10. Loss from sale of business warehouse held four months.	O	O	O	O	O	O	O	O	O
11. Collection of cash method taxpayer's accounts receivable.	O	O	O	O	O	O	O	O	O
12. Gain from sale of unimproved land used as parking lot for business and held nine months.	O	O	O	O	O	O	O	O	O

MULTIPLE-CHOICE ANSWERS

1.	d	15.	a	29.	a	43.	b	57.	a
2.	d	16.	c	30.	c	44.	a	58.	c
3.	c	17.	c	31.	c	45.	c	59.	c
4.	c	18.	d	32.	d	46.	c	60.	c
5.	c	19.	b	33.	a	47.	b	61.	b
6.	b	20.	d	34.	a	48.	b	62.	b
7.	b	21.	d	35.	b	49.	b	63.	a
8.	b	22.	b	36.	c	50.	d		
9.	d	23.	c	37.	a	51.	a		
10.	b	24.	d	38.	c	52.	b		
11.	c	25.	c	39.	a	53.	a		
12.	c	26.	a	40.	b	54.	b		
13.	d	27.	b	41.	d	55.	a	1st: __/63 = __%
14.	b	28.	b	42.	d	56.	d	2nd: __/63 = __%

MULTIPLE-CHOICE ANSWER EXPLANATIONS

A.1. Basis of Property

1. (d) The requirement is to determine Birch's tax basis for the purchased land and building. The basis of property acquired by purchase is a cost basis and includes not only the cash paid and liabilities incurred, but also includes certain settlement fees and closing costs such as abstract of title fees, installation of utility services, legal fees (including title search, contract, and deed fees), recording fees, surveys, transfer taxes, owner's title insurance, and any amounts the seller owes that the buyer agrees to pay, such as back taxes and interest, recording or mortgage fees, charges for improvements or repairs, and sales commissions.

2. (d) The requirement is to determine the basis for the purchased land. The basis of the land consists of the cash paid ($40,000), the purchase money mortgage ($50,000), and the cost of the title insurance policy ($200), a total of $90,200.

A.1.c. Acquired by Gift

3. (c) The requirement is to determine the amount of gain recognized by Thompson resulting from the sale of appreciated property received as a gift. A donee's basis for appreciated property received as a gift is generally the same as the donor's basis. Since Smith had a basis for the property of $1,200 and Thompson sold the property for $2,500, Thompson must recognize a gain of $1,300.

4. (c) The requirement is to determine Julie's basis for the land received as a gift. A donee's basis for gift property is generally the same as the donor's basis, increased by any gift tax paid that is attributable to the property's net appreciation in value. That is, the amount of gift tax that can be added is limited to the amount that bears the same ratio as the property's net appreciation bears to the amount of taxable gift. For this purpose, the amount of gift is reduced by any portion of the $11,000 annual exclusion that is allowable with respect to the gift. Thus, Julie's basis is $21,000 + [$14,000 ($81,000 – 21,000) / ($81,000 – $11,000)] = $33,000.

5. (c) The requirement is to determine Ruth's recognized loss if she sells the stock received as a gift for $7,000. Since the stock's FMV ($8,000) was less than its basis ($10,000) at date of gift, Ruth's basis for computing a loss is the stock's FMV of $8,000 at date of gift. As a result, Ruth's recognized loss is $8,000 – $7,000 = $1,000.

6. (b) The requirement is to determine Ruth's holding period for stock received as a gift. If property is received as a gift, and the property's FMV on date of gift is used to determine a loss, the donee's holding period begins when the gift was received. Thus, Ruth's holding period starts in 2002.

7. (b) The requirement is to determine the basis of the Liba stock if it is sold for $5,000. If property acquired by gift is sold at a gain, its basis is the donor's basis ($4,000), increased by any gift tax paid attributable to the net appreciation in value of the gift ($0).

8. (b) The requirement is to determine the basis of the Liba stock if it is sold for $2,000. If property acquired by gift is sold at a loss, its basis is the lesser of (1) its gain basis ($4,000 above), or (2) its FMV at date of gift ($3,000).

9. (d) The requirement is to determine the amount of reportable gain or loss if the Liba stock is sold for $3,500. No gain or loss is recognized on the sale of property acquired by gift if the basis for loss ($3,000 above) results in a gain and the basis for gain ($4,000 above) results in a loss.

A.1.d. Acquired from Decedent

10. (b) The requirement is to determine the holding period for stock received as a bequest from the estate of a deceased uncle. Property received from a decedent is deemed to be held long-term regardless of the actual period of time that the decedent or beneficiary actually held the property and is treated as held for more than twelve months.

11. (c) The requirement is to determine Ida's basis for stock inherited from a decedent. The basis of property received from a decedent is generally the property's FMV at date of the decedent's death, or FMV on the alternate valuation date (six months after death). Since the executor of Zorn's estate elected to use the alternate valuation for estate tax purposes, the stock's basis to Ida is its $450,000 FMV six months after Zorn's death.

NOTE: If the stock had been distributed to Ida within six months of Zorn's death, the stock's basis would be its FMV on date of distribution.

12. (c) The requirement is to determine Lois' basis for gain or loss on the sale of Elin stock acquired from a decedent. Since the alternate valuation was elected for Prevor's estate, but the stock was distributed to Lois within six months of date of death, Lois' basis is the $9,000 FMV of the stock on date of distribution (5/1/03).

13. (d) The requirement is to determine how Lois should treat the shares of Elin stock. The stock should be treated as a capital asset held long-term since (1) property acquired from a decedent is considered to be held for more than twelve months regardless of its actual holding period, and (2) the stock is an investment asset in Lois' hands. The stock is not a Sec. 1231 asset because it was not held for use in Lois' trade or business.

A.1.e. Stock Received as a Dividend

14. (b) The requirement is to determine the basis for the common stock and the preferred stock after the receipt of a nontaxable preferred stock dividend. Joan's original common stock basis must be allocated between the common stock and the preferred stock according to their relative fair market value.

Common stock (FMV)	$450
Preferred stock (FMV)	150
Total value	$600

The ratio of the common stock to total value is $450/$600 or 3/4. This ratio multiplied by the original common stock basis of $300 results in a basis for the common stock of $225. The basis of the preferred stock would be ($150/$600 x $300) = $75.

15. (a) The requirement is to determine the holding period for preferred stock that was received in a nontaxable distribution on common stock. Since the tax basis of the preferred stock is determined in part by the basis of the common stock, the holding period of the preferred stock includes the holding period of the common stock (i.e., the holding period of the common stock tacks on to the preferred stock). Thus, the holding period of the preferred stock starts when the common stock was acquired, January 2003.

16. (c) The requirement is to determine the amount of long-term capital gain to be reported on the sale of fifty shares of stock received as a nontaxable stock dividend. After the stock dividend, the basis of each share would be determined as follows:

$$\frac{\$90,000}{450 + 50} = \$180 \text{ per share}$$

Since the holding period of the new shares includes the holding period of the old shares, the sale of the fifty new shares for $11,000 results in a LTCG of $2,000 [$11,000 – (50 shares x $180)].

A.4.a. Like-Kind Exchange

17. (c) The requirement is to determine Gow's recognized gain and basis for the investment real estate acquired in a like-kind exchange. In a like-kind exchange of property held for investment, a realized gain ($15,000 in this case) will be recognized only to the extent of unlike property (i.e., boot) received. Here the unlike property consists of the $2,000 cash and $3,000 FMV of the sailboat received, re-

sulting in the recognition of $5,000 of gain. The basis of the acquired like-kind property reflects the deferred gain resulting from the like-kind exchange, and is equal to the basis of the property transferred ($25,000), increased by the amount of gain recognized ($5,000), and decreased by the amount of boot received ($2,000 +$3,000), or $25,000.

18. (d) The requirement is to determine which exchange qualifies for nonrecognition of gain or loss as a like-kind exchange. The exchange of business or investment property solely for like-kind business or investment property is treated as a nontaxable exchange. Like-kind means "the same class of property." Real property must be exchanged for real property, and personal property must be exchanged for personal property. Here, the exchange of rental real estate is an exchange of like-kind property, even though the real estate is located in different states. The like-kind exchange provisions do not apply to exchanges of stocks, bonds, notes, convertible securities, the exchange of partnership interests, and property held for personal use.

19. (b) The requirement is to determine the basis for Leker's new van. The exchange of Leker's old van with a basis of $20,000 that was used exclusively for business, for a new van worth $15,000 plus $3,000 cash qualified as a like-kind exchange. Since it is a like-kind exchange, Leker's realized loss of $20,000 – ($15,000 + $3,000) = $2,000 cannot be recognized, but instead is reflected in the basis of the new van. The new van's basis is the adjusted basis of Leker's old van of $20,000 reduced by the $3,000 of cash boot received, resulting in a basis of $17,000.

20. (d) The requirement is to determine the reportable gain resulting from the exchange of an apartment building for an office building. No gain or loss is recognized on the exchange of business or investment property for property of a like-kind. The term "like-kind" means the same class of property (i.e., real estate must be exchanged for real estate, personal property exchanged for personal property). Thus, the exchange of an apartment building for an office building qualifies as a like-kind exchange. Since no boot (money or unlike property) was received, the realized gain of $600,000 – $200,000 = $400,000 is not recognized.

21. (d) The requirement is to determine the amount of recognized gain resulting from a like-kind exchange of investment property. In a like-kind exchange, gain is recognized to the extent of the lesser of (1) "boot" received, or (2) gain realized.

FMV of property received	$ 250,000
Cash received	30,000
Mortgage assumed	70,000
Amount realized	$ 350,000
Basis of property exchanged	(160,000)
Gain realized	$ 190,000

Since the "boot" received includes both the cash and the assumption of the mortgage, gain is recognized to the extent of the $100,000 of "boot" received.

22. (b) The requirement is to determine the amount of gain recognized to Anderson on the like-kind exchange of apartment buildings. Anderson's realized gain is computed as follows:

FMV of building received		$550,000
Mortgage on old building		100,000
Cash received		25,000
Amount realized		$675,000
Less:		
Basis of old building	$375,000	
Mortgage on new building	125,000	500,000
Realized gain		$175,000

Since the boot received in the form of cash cannot be offset against boot given in the form of an assumption of a mortgage, the realized gain is recognized to the extent of the $25,000 cash received.

23. (c) The requirement is to determine the basis of a new truck acquired in a like-kind exchange. The basis of the new truck is the book value (i.e., adjusted basis) of the old truck of $4,000 plus the additional cash paid of $19,000 (i.e., the list price of the new truck of $25,000 less the trade-in allowance of $6,000).

A.4.b. Involuntary Conversions

24. (d) The requirement is to determine the end of the replacement period for nonrecognition of gain following the condemnation of real property. For a condemnation of real property held for productive use in a trade or business or for investment, the replacement period ends three years after the close of the taxable year in which the gain is first realized. Since the gain was realized in 2003, the replacement period ends December 31, 2006.

A.4.c. Sale or Exchange of Residence

25. (c) The requirement is to determine the amount of gain from the sale of the former residence that is recognized on Davis' 2003 return. An individual may exclude from income up to $250,000 of gain that is realized on the sale or exchange of a residence, if the individual owned and occupied the residence as a principal residence for an aggregate of at least two of the five years preceding the sale or exchange. Davis' former residence cost $65,000 and he had made improvements costing $5,000, resulting in a basis of $70,000. Since Davis sold his former residence for $380,000 and paid a realtor commission of $20,000, the net amount realized from the sale was $360,000. Thus, Davis realized a gain of $360,000 – $70,000 = $290,000. Since Davis qualifies to exclude $250,000 of the gain from income, the remaining $40,000 of gain is recognized and included in Davis' income for 2003.

26. (a) The requirement is to determine the amount of gain to be recognized on the Orans' 2003 joint return from the sale of their residence. An individual may exclude from income up to $250,000 of gain that is realized on the sale or exchange of a residence, if the individual owned and occupied the residence as a principal residence for an aggregate of at least two of the five years preceding the sale or exchange. The amount of excludable gain is increased to $500,000 for married individuals filing jointly if either spouse meets the ownership requirement, and both spouses meet the use requirement. Here, the Orans realized a gain of $760,000 – $170,000 = $590,000, and qualify to exclude $500,000 of the gain from income. The remaining $90,000 of gain is recognized and taxed to the Orans for 2003.

27. (b) The requirement is to determine the maximum exclusion of gain on the sale of Ryan's principal residence.

An individual may exclude from income up to $250,000 of gain that is realized on the sale or exchange of a residence, if the individual owned and occupied the residence as a principal residence for an aggregate of at least two of the five years preceding the sale or exchange. Since Ryan meets the ownership and use requirements, and realized a gain of $400,000 – $180,000 = $220,000, all of Ryan's gain will be excluded from his gross income.

A.5. Sales and Exchanges of Securities

28. (b) The requirement is to determine Miller's recognized loss and the basis for her remaining fifty shares of Maples Inc. stock. No loss can be deducted on the sale of stock if substantially identical stock is purchased within thirty days before or after the sale. Any loss that is not deductible because of this rule is added to the basis of the new stock. If the taxpayer acquires less than the number of shares sold, the amount of loss that cannot be recognized is determined by the ratio of the number of shares acquired to the number of shares sold. Miller purchased 100 shares of Maples stock for $10,000 and sold the stock on January 8, 2003, for $7,000, resulting in a loss of $3,000. However, only half of the loss can be deducted by Miller because on December 24, 2002 (within thirty days before the January 8, 2003 sale), Miller purchased an additional 50 shares of Maples stock. Since only $1,500 of the loss can be recognized, the $1,500 of loss not recognized is added to the basis of Miller's remaining 50 shares resulting in a basis of $4,000 + $1,500 = $5,500.

29. (a) The requirement is to determine the amount of loss from the sale of Core stock that is deductible on Smith's 2002 and 2003 income tax returns. No loss can be deducted on the sale of stock if substantially identical stock is purchased within thirty days before or after the sale. Any loss that is not deductible because of this rule is added to the basis of the new stock. In this case, Smith purchased 100 shares of Core stock for $15,000 and sold the stock on January 3, 2003, for $13,000, resulting in a loss of $2,000. However, the loss cannot be deducted by Smith because on December 30, 2002 (within thirty days prior to the January 3, 2003 sale), Smith purchased an additional 100 shares of Core stock. Smith's disallowed loss of $2,000 is added to the $13,000 cost of the 100 Core shares acquired on December 30 resulting in a tax basis of $15,000 for those shares.

30. (c) The purchase of substantially identical stock within thirty days of the sale of stock at a loss is known as a wash sale. The $800 loss incurred in the wash sale ($5,000 basis less $4,200 amount realized) is disallowed. The basis of the replacement (substantially identical) stock is its cost ($3,600) plus the disallowed wash sale loss ($800). The holding period of the replacement stock includes the holding period of the wash sale stock. The amount realized ($6,000) less the basis ($4,400) results in a long-term gain of $1,600.

31. (c) Worthless securities generally receive capital loss treatment. However, if the loss is incurred by a corporation on its investment in an affiliated corporation (80% or more ownership), the loss is treated as an ordinary loss.

A.6. Losses on Deposits in Insolvent Financial Institutions

32. (d) A loss resulting from a nonbusiness deposit in an insolvent financial institution is generally treated as a nonbusiness bad debt deductible as a short-term capital loss. However, subject to certain limitations, an individual may elect to treat the loss as a casualty loss or as a miscellaneous itemized deduction.

A.7. Losses, Expenses, and Interest between Related Taxpayers

33.   (a)   The requirement is to determine the amount of the $10,000 loss that Conner can deduct from the sale of stock to his daughter, Alice. Losses are disallowed on sales or exchanges of property between related taxpayers, including members of a family. For this purpose, the term *family* includes an individual's spouse, brothers, sisters, ancestors, and lineal descendants (e.g., children, grandchildren, etc.). Since Conner sold the stock to his daughter, no loss can be deducted.

34.   (a)   The requirement is to determine the recognized gain or loss on Alice's sale of the stock that she had purchased from her father. Losses are disallowed on sales or exchanges of property between related taxpayers, including family members. Any gain later realized by the related transferee on the subsequent disposition of the property is not recognized to the extent of the transferor's disallowed loss. Here, her father's realized loss of $30,000 – $20,000 = $10,000 was disallowed because he sold the stock to his daughter, Alice. Her basis for the stock is her cost of $20,000. On the subsequent sale of the stock, Alice realizes a gain of $25,000 – $20,000 = $5,000. However, this realized gain of $5,000 is not recognized because of her father's disallowed loss of $10,000.

35.   (b)   The requirement is to determine the amount of gain from the sale of stock to a third party that Martin should report on his 2003 income tax return. Losses are disallowed on sales of property between related taxpayers, including family members. Any gain later realized by the transferee on the disposition of the property is not recognized to the extent of the transferor's disallowed loss. Here, Fay's realized loss of $15,000 – $11,000 = $4,000 is disallowed because she sold the stock to her son, Martin. Martin's basis for the stock is his cost of $11,000. On the subsequent sale of the stock to an unrelated third party, Martin realizes a gain of $16,000 – $11,000 = $5,000. However, this realized gain of $5,000 is recognized only to the extent that it exceeds Fay's $4,000 disallowed loss, or $1,000.

36.   (c)   The requirement is to determine among which of the related individuals are losses from sales and exchanges not recognized for tax purposes. No loss deduction is allowed on the sale or exchange of property between members of a family. For this purpose, an individual's *family* includes only brothers, sisters, half-brothers and half-sisters, spouse, ancestors (parents, grandparents, etc.) and lineal descendants (children, grandchildren, etc.) Since in-laws and uncles are excluded from this definition of a family, a loss resulting from a sale or exchange with an uncle or between in-laws would be recognized.

37.   (a)   Losses are disallowed on sales between related taxpayers, including family members. Thus, Daniel's loss of $3,000 is disallowed on the sale of stock to his son, William. William's basis for the stock is his $7,000 cost. Since William's stock basis is determined by his cost (not by reference to Daniel's cost), there is no "tack-on" of Daniel's holding

period. Thus, a later sale of the stock for $6,000 on July 1 generates a $1,000 STCL for William.

38.   (c)   The requirement is to determine the amount of loss that Rego Corp. can deduct on a sale of its trailer to a 50% shareholder. Losses are disallowed on transactions between related taxpayers, including a corporation and a shareholder owning more than 50% of its stock. Since Al Eng owns only 50% (not more than 50%), the loss is recognized by Rego. Since the trailer was held for more than one year and used in Rego's business, the $2,000 loss is a Sec. 1231 loss. Answer (d) is incorrect because Sec. 1245 only applies to gains.

B. Capital Gains and Losses

39.   (a)   The requirement is to determine when gain or loss on a year-end sale of listed stock arises for a cash basis taxpayer. If stock or securities that are traded on an established securities market are sold, any resulting gain or loss is recognized on the trade date (i.e., the date on which the trade is executed) by both cash and accrual method taxpayers.

40.   (b)   The requirement is to determine the amount of an $8,000 net long-term capital loss that can be offset against Lee's taxable income of $100,000. An individual's net capital loss can be offset against ordinary income up to a maximum of $3,000 ($1,500 if married filing separately). Since a net capital loss offsets ordinary income dollar for dollar, Lee has a $3,000 net capital loss deduction for 2003 and a long-term capital loss carryover of $5,000 to 2004 .

41.   (d)   The requirement is to determine the amount of excess of net long-term capital loss over net short-term capital gain that Sol Corp. can offset against ordinary income. A corporation's net capital loss cannot be offset against ordinary income. Instead, a net capital loss is generally carried back three years and forward five years as a STCL to offset capital gains in those years.

42.   (d)   The requirement is to determine the proper treatment for a $24,000 NLTCL for Nam Corp. A corporation's capital losses can only be used to offset capital gains. If a corporation has a net capital loss, the net capital loss cannot be currently deducted, but must be carried back three years and forward five years as a STCL to offset capital gains in those years. Since Nam had not realized any capital gains since it began operations, the $24,000 LTCL can only be carried forward for five years as a STCL.

43.   (b)   The requirement is to determine the holding period for determining long-term capital gains and losses. Long-term capital gains and losses result if capital assets are held more than twelve months.

44.   (a)   The requirement is to determine the treatment for the sale of the antique by Wald. Since the antique was held for personal use, the sale of the antique at a loss is not deductible.

45.   (c)   The requirement is to determine the capital loss carryover to 2004 . The NSTCL and the NLTCL result in a net capital loss of $6,000. LTCLs are deductible dollar for dollar, the same as STCLs. Since an individual can deduct a net capital loss up to a maximum of $3,000, the net capital loss of $6,000 results in a capital loss deduction of $3,000 for 2003, and a long-term capital loss carryover to 2004 of $3,000.

B.1. Capital Assets

46. **(c)** The requirement is to determine the item that is included in the definition of capital assets. The definition of capital assets includes property held as an investment and would include a manufacturing company's investment in US Treasury bonds. In contrast, the definition specifically excludes accounts receivable arising from the sale of inventory, depreciable property used in a trade or business, and property held primarily for sale to customers in the ordinary course of a trade or business.

47. **(b)** The requirement is to determine the amount of Hall's capital assets. The definition of capital assets includes investment property and property held for personal use (e.g., personal residence and furnishings), but excludes property used in a trade or business (e.g., limousine).

48. **(b)** The requirement is to determine the proper treatment for the gain recognized on the sale of a painting that was purchased in 1997 and held for personal use. The definition of "capital assets" includes investment property and property held for personal use (if sold at a gain). Because the painting was held for more than one year, the gain from the sale of the painting must be reported as a long-term capital gain. Note that if personal-use property is sold at a loss, the loss is not deductible.

49. **(b)** The requirement is to determine the correct treatment for a capital loss incurred by a married couple filing a joint return for 2003. Capital losses first offset capital gains, and then are allowed as a deduction of up to $3,000 against ordinary income, with any unused capital loss carried forward indefinitely. Note that a married taxpayer filing separately can only offset up to $1,500 of net capital loss against ordinary income.

50. **(d)** The requirement is to determine the proper classification of land used as a parking lot and a shed erected on the lot for customer transactions. The definition of capital assets includes investment property and property held for personal use, but excludes any property used in a trade or business. The definition of Sec. 1231 assets generally includes business assets held more than one year. Since the land and shed were used in conjunction with a parking lot business, they are properly classified as Sec. 1231 assets.

51. **(a)** The requirement is to determine the classification of Ruth's diamond necklace. The diamond necklace is classified as a capital asset because the definition of "capital asset" includes investment property and *property held for personal use*. Answers (b), (c), and (d) are incorrect because Sec. 1231 generally includes only assets used in a trade or business, while Sections 1245 and 1250 only include depreciable assets.

52. **(b)** The requirement is to determine which asset is a capital asset. The definition of capital assets includes personal-use property, but excludes property used in a trade or business (e.g., delivery truck, land used as a parking lot). Treasury stock is not considered an asset, but instead is treated as a reduction of stockholders' equity.

53. **(a)** The requirement is to determine how a lump sum of $30,000 received in 2003, for an agreement not to operate a competing enterprise, should be treated. A covenant not to compete is not a capital asset. Thus, the $30,000 received as consideration for such an agreement must be reported as ordinary income in the year received.

54. **(b)** The requirement is to determine the amount of furniture classified as capital assets. The definition of capital assets includes investment property and property held for personal use (e.g., kitchen and living room pieces), but excludes property used in a trade or business (e.g., showcases and tables).

C. Personal Casualty and Theft Gains and Losses

55. **(a)** The requirement is to determine the correct statement regarding the deductibility of an individual's losses on transactions entered into for personal purposes. An individual's losses on transactions entered into for personal purposes are deductible only if the losses qualify as casualty or theft losses. Answer (b) is incorrect because hobby losses are not deductible. Answers (c) and (d) are incorrect because losses (other than by casualty or theft) on transactions entered into for personal purposes are not deductible.

D. Gains and Losses on Business Property

56. **(d)** The requirement is to determine the characterization of Evon Corporation's $50,000 of net Sec. 1231 gain for its 2003 tax year. Although a net Sec. 1231 gain is generally treated as a long-term capital gain, it instead must be treated as ordinary income to the extent of the taxpayer's nonrecaptured net Sec. 1231 losses for its five preceding taxable years. Here, since the nonrecaptured net Sec. 1231 losses for 2001 and 2002 total $35,000, only $15,000 of the $50,000 net Sec. 1231 gain will be treated as a long-term capital gain.

57. **(a)** The requirement is to determine which item would not be characterized as Sec. 1231 property. Sec. 1231 property generally includes both depreciable and nondepreciable property used in a trade or business or held for the production of income if held for more than twelve months. Specifically excluded from Sec. 1231 is inventory and property held for sale to customers, as well as accounts and notes receivable arising in the ordinary course of a trade or business.

58. **(c)** The requirement is to determine the amount of ordinary income that must be recognized by Vermont Corporation from the distribution of the equipment to a shareholder. When a corporation distributes appreciated property, it must recognize gain just as if it had sold the property for its fair market value. As a result Vermont must recognize a gain of $9,000 – $2,000 = $7,000 on the distribution of the equipment. Since the distributed property is depreciable personality, the gain is subject to Sec. 1245 recapture as ordinary income to the extent of the $6,000 of straight-line depreciation deducted by Vermont. The remaining $1,000 of gain would be treated as Sec. 1231 gain.

59. **(c)** The requirement is to determine the nature of a loss resulting from the sale of business machinery that had been held sixteen months. Property held for use in a trade or business is specifically excluded from the definition of capital assets, and if held for more than one year is considered Sec. 1231 property. Answer (b) is incorrect because Sec. 1245 only applies to gains.

60.   (c)   The requirement is to determine the amount of gain from the sale of property that must be recaptured as ordinary income. A gain from the disposition of seven-year tangible property is subject to recapture under Sec. 1245 which recaptures gain to the extent of all depreciation previously deducted. Here, Bates' gain from the sale of the property is determined as follows:

Selling price		$102,000
Cost	$100,000	
Depreciation	− 47,525	
Adjusted basis		− 52,475
Gain		$ 49,525

Under Sec. 1245, Bates Corp's gain is recaptured as ordinary income to the extent of the $47,525 deducted as depreciation. The remaining $2,000 of gain would be classified as Sec. 1231 gain.

61.   (b)   The requirement is to determine the proper treatment of the $50,000 gain on the sale of the building, which is Sec. 1250 property. Sec. 1250 recaptures gain as ordinary income to the extent of "excess" depreciation (i.e., depreciation deducted in excess of straight-line). The total gain less any depreciation recapture is Sec. 1231 gain. Since straight-line depreciation was used, there is no recapture under Sec. 1250. However, Sec. 291 requires that the amount of ordinary income on the disposition of Sec. 1250 property by corporations be increased by 20% of the additional amount that would have been ordinary income if the property had instead been Sec. 1245 property. If the building had been Sec. 1245 property the amount of recapture would have been $30,000 ($200,000 − $170,000). Thus, the Sec. 291 ordinary income is $30,000 x 20% = $6,000. The remaining $44,000 is Sec. 1231 gain.

62.   (b)   The requirement is to determine McEwing Corporation's taxable income given book income plus additional information regarding items that were included in book income. The loss on sale of the building ($7,000) and gain on sale of the land ($16,000) are Sec. 1231 gains and losses. The resulting Sec. 1231 net gain of $9,000 is then treated as LTCG and will be offset against the LTCL of $8,000 resulting from the sale of investments. Since these items have already been included in book income, McEwing's taxable income is the same as its book income, $120,000.

63.   (a)   The realized gain resulting from the involuntary conversion ($125,000 insurance proceeds − $86,000 adjusted basis = $39,000) is recognized only to the extent that the insurance proceeds are not reinvested in similar property ($125,000 − $110,000 = $15,000). Since the machinery was Sec. 1245 property, the recognized gain of $15,000 is recaptured as ordinary income to the extent of the $14,000 of depreciation previously deducted. The remaining $1,000 is Sec. 1231 gain.

SOLUTIONS TO SIMULATION PROBLEM

Simulation Problem 1

Transaction	(A)	(B)	(C)	(D)	(E)	(F)	(G)	(H)	(I)
1. Gain from sale of business inventory held thirteen months.	○	○	○	○	○	○	●	○	○
2. Gain from sale of personal residence held three years.	●	○	○	○	○	○	○	○	○
3. Gain from sale of unimproved land used as business parking lot and held seventeen months.	○	○	○	○	●	○	○	○	○
4. Loss from sale of eight-year old boat held for personal use.	○	○	○	○	○	○	○	○	●
5. Gain from sale of lot held as investment for eleven months.	○	○	●	○	○	○	○	○	○
6. Casualty gain on personal residence held ten years (this was taxpayer's only casualty during year).	●	○	○	○	○	○	○	○	○
7. Casualty loss on truck used in business and held seven months.	○	○	○	○	○	○	○	●	○
8. Loss from nonbusiness bad debt that was outstanding two years.	○	○	○	●	○	○	○	○	○
9. Loss from sale of factory building held twenty-two months.	○	○	○	○	○	●	○	○	○
10. Loss from sale of business warehouse held four months.	○	○	○	○	○	○	○	●	○
11. Collection of cash method taxpayer's accounts receivable.	○	○	○	○	○	○	●	○	○
12. Gain from sale of unimproved land used as parking lot for business and held nine months.	○	○	○	○	○	○	●	○	○

Explanation of solutions

1. (G) Inventory is neither a Sec. 1231 asset nor a capital asset.

2. (A) Capital assets include personal use property.

3. (E) Sec. 1231 includes gain from nondepreciable business property held more than one year.

4. (I) Loss from sale of personal use property is not deductible.

5. (C) Capital assets include investment property.

6. (A) A net personal casualty gain is treated as a capital gain.

7. (H) Ordinary loss because the business truck was not held for more than one year.

8. (D) Loss from nonbusiness bad debt is always treated as a short-term capital loss.

9. (F) Business property held more than one year.

10. (H) Ordinary because property must be held more than one year to be a Sec. 1231 loss.

11. (G) Accounts receivable are neither Sec. 1231 assets nor capital assets.

12. (G) Ordinary loss because business land not held for more than one year.

PARTNERSHIPS

Partnerships are organizations of two or more persons to carry on business activities for profit. For tax purposes, partnerships also include a syndicate, joint venture, or other unincorporated business through which any business or financial operation is conducted. Partnerships do not pay any income tax, but instead act as a conduit to pass through tax items to the partners. Partnerships file an informational return (Form 1065), and partners report their share of partnership ordinary income or loss and other items on their individual returns. The nature or character (e.g., taxable, nontaxable) of income or deductions is not changed by the pass-through nature of the partnership.

A. Entity Classification

1. Eligible business entities (a business entity other than an entity automatically classified as a corporation) may choose how they will be classified for federal tax purposes by filing Form 8832. A business entity with at least two members can choose to be classified as either an association taxable as a corporation or as a partnership. A business entity with a single member can choose to be classified as either an association taxable as a corporation or disregarded as an entity separate from its owner.

    a. An eligible business entity that does not file Form 8832 will be classified under default rules. Under default rules, an eligible business entity will be classified as a partnership if it has two or more members, or disregarded as an entity separate from its owner if it has a single owner.

    b. Once an entity makes an election, a different election cannot be made for sixty months unless there is more than a 50% ownership change and the IRS consents.

2. **General partnerships** exist when two or more partners join together and do not specifically provide that one or more partners is a limited partner. Since each general partner has unlimited liability, creditors can reach the personal assets of a general partner to satisfy partnership debts, including a malpractice judgment against the partnership even though the partner was not personally involved in the malpractice.

3. **Limited partnerships** have two classes of partners, with at least one general partner (who has the same rights and responsibilities as a partner in a general partnership) and at least one limited partner. A limited partner generally cannot participate in the active management of the partnership, and in the event of losses, generally can lose no more than his or her own capital contribution. A limited partnership is often the preferred entity of choice for real estate ventures requiring significant capital contributions.

4. **Limited liability partnerships** differ from general partnerships in that with an LLP, a partner is not liable for damages resulting from the negligence, malpractice, or fraud committed by other partners. However, each partner is personally liable for his or her own negligence, malpractice, or fraud. LLPs are often used by service providers such as architects, accountants, attorneys, and physicians.

5. **Limited liability companies** that do not elect to be treated as an association taxable as a corporation are subject to the rules applicable to partnerships (a single-member LLC would be disregarded as an entity separate from its owner). An LLC combines the nontax advantage of limited liability for each and every owner of the entity, with the tax advantage of pass-through treatment, and the flexibility of partnership taxation. The LLC structure is generally available to both nonprofessional service providers as well as capital-intensive companies.

6. **Electing large partnerships** are partnerships that have elected to be taxed under a simplified reporting system that does not require as much separate reporting to partners as does a regular partnership. For example, charitable contributions are deductible by the partnership (subject to a 10% of taxable income limitation), and the Sec. 179 expense election is deducted in computing partnership ordinary income and not separately passed through to partners. To qualify, the partnership must not be a service partnership nor engaged in commodity trading, must have at least 100 partners, and must file an election to be taxed as an electing large partnership. A partnership will cease to be an electing large partnership if it has fewer than 100 partners for a taxable year.

7. **Publicly traded partnerships** are partnerships whose interests are traded on an established securities exchange or in a secondary market and are generally taxed as C corporations.

B. Partnership Formation

1.   As a general rule, **no gain or loss** is recognized by a partner when there is a contribution of property to the partnership in exchange for an interest in the partnership. There are three situations where gain must be recognized.

   a.   A partner must recognize gain when property is contributed which is subject to a liability, and the resulting decrease in the partner's individual liability exceeds the partner's partnership basis.

   (1) The excess of liability over adjusted basis is generally treated as a capital gain from the sale or exchange of a partnership interest.
   (2) The gain will be treated as ordinary income to the extent the property transferred was subject to depreciation recapture under Sec. 1245 or 1250.

   EXAMPLE: A partner acquires a 20% interest in a partnership by contributing property worth $10,000 but with an adjusted basis of $4,000. There is a mortgage of $6,000 that is assumed by the partnership. The partner must recognize a gain of $800, and has a zero basis for the partnership interest, calculated as follows:

Adjusted basis of contributed property	$ 4,000
Less: portion of mortgage allocated to other partners (80% x $6,000)	(_4,800_)
Partner's basis (not reduced below 0)	$_____0_

   b.   Gain will be recognized on a contribution of property to a partnership in exchange for an interest therein if the partnership would be an investment company if incorporated.
   c.   Partner must recognize compensation income when an interest in partnership capital is received in exchange for **services rendered**.

   EXAMPLE: X received a 10% capital interest in the ABC Partnership in exchange for services rendered. On the date X was admitted to the partnership, ABC's net assets had a basis of $30,000 and a FMV of $50,000. X must recognize compensation income of $5,000.

2.   Property contributed to the partnership has the same **basis** as it had in the contributing partner's hands (a transferred basis).

   a.   The basis for the partner's partnership interest is increased by the adjusted basis of property contributed.
   b.   No gain or loss is generally recognized by the partnership upon the contribution.

3.   The **partnership's holding period** for contributed property includes the period of time the property was held by the partner.
4.   A **partner's holding period** for a partnership interest includes the holding period of property contributed, if the contributed property was a capital asset or Sec. 1231 asset in the contributing partner's hands.
5.   Although not a separate taxpaying entity, the partnership must make most elections as to the tax treatment of partnership items. For example, the partnership must select a taxable year and various accounting methods which can differ from the methods used by its partners. Partnership elections include an overall method of accounting, inventory method, the method used to compute depreciation, and the election to expense depreciable assets under Sec. 179.

C. Partnership Income and Loss

1.   Since a partnership is not a separate taxpaying entity, but instead acts as a conduit to pass-through items of income and deduction to individual partners, the partnership's reporting of income and deductions requires a two-step approach.

   a.   **First,** all items having special tax characteristics (i.e., subject to partial or full exclusion, % or dollar limitation, etc.) must be segregated and taken into account separately by each partner so that any special tax characteristics are preserved.

   (1) These special items are listed separately on Schedule K of the partnership return and include

      (a) Capital gains and losses
      (b) Sec. 1231 gains and losses
      (c) Charitable contributions
      (d) Foreign income taxes
      (e) Sec. 179 expense deduction for recovery property (limited to $25,000 for 2003)

      (f) Interest, dividend, and royalty income
      (g) Interest expense on investment indebtedness
      (h) Net income (loss) from rental real estate activity
      (i) Net income (loss) from other rental activity

  b. **Second,** all remaining items (since they have no special tax characteristics) are ordinary in nature and are netted in the computation of partnership ordinary income or loss from trade or business activities

    (1) Frequently encountered ordinary income and deductions include

      (a) Sales less cost of goods sold
      (b) Business expenses such as wages, rents, bad debts, and repairs
      (c) Guaranteed payments to partners
      (d) Depreciation
      (e) Amortization (over sixty months or more) of partnership organization expenses—Note that syndication fees (expenses of selling partnership interests) are neither deductible nor amortizable
      (f) Sec. 1245, 1250, etc., recapture
      (g) See Form 1065 outline at beginning of chapter for more detail

2. The **character** of any gain or loss recognized on the disposition of property is generally determined by the nature of the property in the hands of the partnership. However, for contributed property, the character may be based on the nature of the property to the contributing partner before contribution.

  a. If a partner contributes **unrealized receivables,** the partnership will recognize ordinary income or loss on the subsequent disposition of the unrealized receivables.

  b. If the property contributed was **inventory** property to the contributing partner, any gain or loss recognized by the partnership on the disposition of the property within five years will be treated as ordinary income or loss.

  c. If the contributed property was a **capital asset,** any loss later recognized by the partnership on the disposition of the property within five years will be treated as a capital loss to the extent of the contributing partner's unrecognized capital loss at the time of contribution. This rule applies to losses only, not to gains.

3. A person sitting for the examination should be able to calculate a partnership's ordinary income by adjusting partnership book income (or partnership book income by adjusting ordinary income).

EXAMPLE: A partnership's accounting income statement discloses net income of $75,000 (i.e., book income). The three partners share profit and losses equally. Supplemental data indicate the following information has been included in the computation of net income:

	DR.	CR.
Net sales		$160,000
Cost of goods sold	$ 88,000	
Tax-exempt income		1,500
Sec. 1231 casualty gain		9,000
Section 1231 gain (other than casualty)		6,000
Section 1250 gain		20,000
Long-term capital gain		7,500
Short-term capital loss	6,000	
Guaranteed payments ($8,000 per partner)	24,000	
Charitable contributions	9,000	
Advertising expense	2,000	
	$129,000	$204,000

Partnership ordinary income is $66,000, computed as follows:

Book income		$ 75,000
Add:		
Charitable contributions	$ 9,000	
Short-term capital loss	6,000	15,000
		$ 90,000

Deduct:		
Tax-exempt income	$ 1,500	
Sec. 1231 casualty gain	9,000	
Section 1231 gain (other than casualty)	6,000	
Long-term capital gain	7,500	24,000
Partnership ordinary income		$ 66,000

Each partner's share of partnership ordinary income is $22,000.

4. Three sets of rules may limit the amount of partnership loss that a partner can deduct.

 a. A partner's distributive share of partnership ordinary loss and special loss items is deductible by the partner only to the extent of the **partner's basis** for the partnership interest at the end of the taxable year [Sec. 704(d)].

 (1) The pass-through of loss is considered to be the last event during the partnership's taxable year; all positive basis adjustments are made prior to determining the amount of deductible loss.

 (2) Unused losses are carried forward and can be deducted when the partner obtains additional basis for the partnership interest.

 EXAMPLE: *A partner who materially participates in the partnership's business has a distributive share of partnership capital gain of $200 and partnership ordinary loss of $3,000, but the partner's basis in the partnership is only $2,400 before consideration of these items. The partner can deduct $2,600 of the ordinary loss ($2,400 of beginning basis + $200 net capital gain). The remaining $400 of ordinary loss must be carried forward.*

 b. The deductibility of partnership losses is also limited to the amount of the partner's **at-risk basis** [Sec. 465].

 (1) A partner's at-risk basis is generally the same as the partner's regular partnership basis with the exception that liabilities are included in at-risk basis only if the partner is personally liable for such amounts.

 (2) Nonrecourse liabilities are generally excluded from at-risk basis.

 (3) Qualified nonrecourse real estate financing is included in at-risk basis.

 c. The deductibility of partnership losses may also be subject to the **passive activity loss limitations** [Sec. 469]. Passive activity losses are deductible only to the extent of the partner's income from other passive activities (see Module 33).

 (1) Passive activities include (a) any partnership trade or business in which the partner does not materially participate, and (b) any rental activity.

 (2) A limited partnership interest generally fails the material participation test.

 (3) To qualify for the $25,000 exception for active participation in a rental real estate activity, a partner (together with spouse) must own at least 10% of the value of the partnership interests.

D. Partnership Agreements

1. A partner's distributive share of income or loss is generally determined by the partnership agreement. Such agreement can have different ratios for income or loss, and may agree to allocate other items (e.g., credits and deductions) in varying ratios

 a. Special allocations must have **substantial economic effect**.

 (1) Economic effect is measured by an analysis of the allocation on the partners' capital accounts. The special allocation (a) must be reflected in the partners' capital accounts, (b) liquidation distributions must be based upon the positive capital account balances of partners, and (c) there must be a deficit payback agreement wherein partners agree to restore any deficit capital account balances.

 (2) An allocation's economic effect will **not** be substantial if the net change recorded in the partners' capital accounts does not differ substantially from what would have been recorded without the special allocation, and the total tax liability of all partners is less.

 b. If no allocation is provided, or if the allocation of an item does not have substantial economic effect, the partners' distributive shares of that item shall be determined by the ratio in which the partners generally divide the income or loss of the partnership.

c. **If property is contributed** by a partner to a partnership, related items of income, deduction, gain, or loss must be allocated among partners in a manner that reflects the difference between the property's tax basis and its fair market value at the time of contribution.

> EXAMPLE: *Partner X contributes property with a tax basis of $1,000 and a fair market value of $10,000 to the XYZ Partnership. If the partnership subsequently sells the property for $12,000, the first $9,000 of gain must be allocated to X, with the remaining $2,000 of gain allocated among partners according to their ratio for sharing gains.*

(1) If property contributed to a partnership is distributed within seven years to a partner other than the partner who contributed such property, the contributing partner must recognize the precontribution gain or loss to the extent that the precontribution gain or loss would be recognized if the partnership had sold the property for its fair market value at the time of distribution.

(2) The above recognition rule will not generally apply if other property of a like-kind to the contributed property is distributed to the contributing partner no later than the earlier of (1) the 180th day after the date on which the originally contributed property was distributed to another partner, or (2) the due date (without extension) for the contributing partner's return for the tax year in which the original distribution of property occurred.

d. If there was any change in the ownership of partnership interests during the year, distributive shares of partnership interest, taxes, and payments for services or for the use of property must be allocated among partners by assigning an appropriate share of each item to each day of the partnership's taxable year.

> EXAMPLE: *Z becomes a 40% partner in calendar-year Partnership XY on December 1. Previously, X and Y each had a 50% interest. Partnership XY uses the cash method of accounting and on December 31 pays $10,000 of interest expense that relates to its entire calendar year. Z's distributive share of the interest expense will be ($10,000 ÷ 365 days) x 31 days x 40% = $340.*

2. **Distributable shares** of income and guaranteed payments are reported by partners for their taxable year during which the end of the partnership fiscal year occurs. All items, including guaranteed payments, are deemed to pass through on the last day of the partnership's tax year.

a. **Guaranteed payments** are payments to a partner determined without regard to income of the partnership. Guaranteed payments are deductible by the partnership and reported as income by the partners.

> EXAMPLE: *Z (on a calendar-year) has a 20% interest in a partnership that has a fiscal year ending May 31. Z received a guaranteed payment for services rendered of $1,000 a month from 6/1/02 to 12/31/02 and $1,500 a month from 1/1/03 to 5/31/03. After deducting the guaranteed payment, the partnership had ordinary income of $50,000 for its fiscal year ended 5/31/03. Z must include $24,500 in income on Z's calendar-year 2003 return ($50,000 x 20%) + ($1,000 x 7) + ($1,500 x 5).*

b. Partners are generally not considered to be employees for purposes of employee fringe benefits (e.g., cost of $50,000 of group-term life insurance, exclusion of premiums or benefits under an employer accident or health plan, etc.). A partner's fringe benefits are deductible by the partnership as guaranteed payments and must be included in a partner's gross income.

3. **Family partnerships** are subject to special rules because of their potential use for tax avoidance.

a. If the business is primarily service oriented (capital is not a material income-producing factor), a family member will be considered a partner only if the family member shares in the management or performs needed services.

b. Capital is not a material income-producing factor if substantially all of the gross income of the business consists of fees, commissions, or other compensation for personal services (e.g., accountants, architects, lawyers).

c. A family member is generally considered a partner if the family member actually owns a capital interest in a business in which capital is a material income-producing factor.

d. Where a capital interest in a partnership in which capital is a material income-producing factor is treated as created by gift, the distributive shares of partnership income of the donor and donee are determined by first making a reasonable allowance for services rendered to the partnership, and then allocating the remainder according to the relative capital interests of the donor and donee.

E. Partner's Basis in Partnership

1. A partner's **original basis** is generally determined by the manner in which the partnership interest was acquired (e.g., contribution of property, compensation for services, purchase, gift, received from decedent).

2. As the partnership operates, the partner's basis for the partnership interest increases or decreases.

    a. A partner's basis is increased by the adjusted basis of any subsequent capital contributions.
    b. Also, a partner's basis is **increased** by any distributive share of

        (1) Partnership ordinary income
        (2) Capital gains and other special income items
        (3) Tax-exempt income of the partnership
        (4) The excess of the deduction for depletion over the partnership's basis of the property subject to depletion

    c. A partner's basis is **decreased** (but not below zero) by

        (1) The amount of money and the adjusted basis of other property distributed to the partner
        (2) The partner's distributive share of partnership ordinary loss and special expense items, as well as nondeductible items not properly chargeable to capital
        (3) The amount of the partner's deduction for depletion on oil and gas wells

        EXAMPLE: In the example in Section 3. on page 534, one partner's tax basis (who had a $15,000 tax basis at the beginning of the year) would be $40,000 at the end of the year, calculated as shown below.

Beginning partnership basis		$15,000
Add:		
Distributive share of partnership ordinary income	22,000	
Tax-exempt income	500	
Sec. 1231 casualty gain	3,000	
Section 1231 gain (other than casualty)	2,000	
Long-term capital gain	2,500	30,000
		$45,000
Less:		
Short-term capital loss	$ 2,000	
Charitable contributions	3,000	5,000
Ending partnership basis		$40,000

    d. **Changes in liabilities** affect a partner's basis.

        (1) An **increase** in the **partnership's liabilities** (e.g., loan from a bank, increase in accounts payable) increases each partner's basis in the partnership by each partner's share of the increase.
        (2) Any **decrease** in the **partnership's liabilities** is considered to be a distribution of money to each partner and reduces each partner's basis in the partnership by each partner's share of the decrease.
        (3) Any **decrease** in a partner's **individual liability** by reason of the assumption by the partnership of such individual liabilities is considered to be a distribution of money to the partner by the partnership (i.e., partner's basis is reduced).
        (4) Any **increase** in a partner's **individual liability** by reason of the assumption by the partner of partnership liabilities is considered to be a contribution of money to the partnership by the partner. Thus, the partner's basis is increased.

        EXAMPLE: The XYZ partnership owns a warehouse with an adjusted basis of $120,000 subject to a mortgage of $90,000. Partner X (one of three equal partners) has a basis for his partnership interest of $75,000. If the partnership transfers the warehouse and mortgage to Partner X as a current distribution, X's basis for his partnership interest immediately following the distribution would be $15,000, calculated as follows:

Beginning basis	$ 75,000
Individual assumption of mortgage	+ 90,000
	$165,000
Distribution of warehouse	−120,000
Partner's share of decrease in partnership's liabilities	− 30,000
Basis after distribution	$ 15,000

        EXAMPLE: Assume in the example above that one of the other one-third partners had a basis of $75,000 immediately before the distribution. What would the partner's basis be immediately after the distribution to Partner X? $45,000 (i.e., $75,000 less 1/3 of the $90,000 decrease in partnership liabilities).

e. A partner's basis for the partnership is adjusted in the following order: (1) increased for all income items (including tax-exempt income); (2) decreased for distributions; and (3) decreased by deductions and losses (including nondeductible items not charged to capital).

> *EXAMPLE: A partner with a basis of $50 for his partnership interest at the beginning of the partnership year receives a $30 cash distribution during the year and is allocated a $60 distributive share of partnership ordinary loss, and an $8 distributive share of capital gain. In determining the extent to which the ordinary loss is deductible by the partner, the partner's partnership basis of $50 is first increased by the $8 of capital gain and reduced by the $30 cash distribution to $28, so that his deductible ordinary loss is limited to his remaining basis of $28.*

F. Transactions with Controlled Partnerships

1. If a person engages in a transaction with a partnership other than as a member of such partnership, any resulting gain or loss is generally recognized. However, if the transaction involves a **more than 50% owned partnership,** one of three special rules may apply. Constructive ownership rules [page 509, Sections 7.a.(4)(a) and (b)] apply in determining whether a transaction involves a more than 50% owned partnership.

a. **No losses** are deductible from sales or exchanges of property between a partnership and a person owning (directly or indirectly) more than 50% of the capital or profits interests in such partnership, or between two partnerships in which the same persons own (directly or indirectly) more than 50% of the capital or profits interests. A gain later realized on a subsequent sale by the transferee will not be recognized to the extent of the disallowed loss.

> *EXAMPLE: Partnership X is owned by three **equal** partners, A, B, and C, who are brothers. Partnership X sells property at a loss of $5,000 to C. Since C owns a more than 50% interest in the partnership (i.e., C constructively owns his brothers' partnership interests), the $5,000 loss is disallowed to Partnership X.*

> *EXAMPLE: Assume the same facts as in the above example. C later resells the property to Z, an unrelated taxpayer, at a gain of $6,000. C's realized gain of $6,000 will not be recognized to the extent of the $5,000 disallowed loss to the Partnership X.*

b. If a person related to a partner does not indirectly own a more than 50% partnership interest, a transaction between the related person and the partnership is treated as occurring between the related person and the partners individually.

> *EXAMPLE: X owns 100% of X Corp. and also owns a 25% interest in WXYZ Partnership. X Corp. sells property at a $1,200 loss to the WXYZ Partnership. Since X Corp. is related to partner X (i.e., X owns more than 50% of X Corp.), the transaction is treated as if it occurred between X Corp. and partners W, X, Y, and Z individually. Therefore, the loss disallowed to X Corp. is $1,200 x 25% = $300.*

c. A **gain** recognized on a sale or exchange of property between a partnership and a person owning (directly or indirectly) more than 50% of the capital or profits interests in such partnership, or between two partnerships in which the same persons own (directly or indirectly) more than 50% of the capital or profits interests, will be treated as **ordinary income** if the property is **not a capital asset** in the hands of the transferee.

> *EXAMPLE: Assume the same facts as in the preceding example. Further assume that F is the father of W, Y, and Z. F sells investment property to Partnership WXYZ at a gain of $10,000. If the property will not be a capital asset to Partnership WXYZ, F must report the $10,000 gain as ordinary income because F constructively owns a more than 50% partnership interest (i.e., F constructively owns his children's partnership interests).*

d. A **gain** recognized on a sale or exchange of property between a partnership and a person owning (directly or indirectly) more than 50% of the capital or profits interests in such partnership will be treated as **ordinary income** if the property is **depreciable property** in the hands of the transferee.

G. Taxable Year of Partnership

1. When a partnership adopts (or attempts to change) its taxable year, it is subject to the following restrictions:

a. A partnership must adopt the taxable year used by one or more of its partners owning an aggregate interest of more than 50% in profits and capital (but only if the taxable year used by such partners has been the same for the lesser of three taxable years or the period the partnership has existed).

> *EXAMPLE: A partnership is formed by a corporation (which receives a 55% partnership interest) and five individuals (who each receive a 9% partnership interest). The corporation has a fiscal year ending June 30, while the individuals have a calendar year. The partnership must adopt a fiscal year ending June 30.*

    b.   If partners owning a more than 50% interest in partnership profits and capital do not have the same year-end, the partnership must adopt the same taxable year as used by all of its principal partners (i.e., a partner with a 5% or more interest in capital or profits).

    c.   If its principal partners have different taxable years, the partnership must adopt the taxable year that results in the least aggregate deferral of income to partners.

2.   A different taxable year than the year determined above can be used by a partnership if a **valid business purpose** can be established and IRS permission is received. The business purpose test will be met if a partnership receives at least 25% of its gross receipts in the last two months of a twelve-month period, and this "25% test" has been satisfied for three consecutive years.

    EXAMPLE: Partnership X is owned by three equal partners—A, B, and C, who use a calendar year. Partnership X has received at least 25% of its gross receipts during the months of June and July for each of the last three years. Partnership X may be allowed to change to a fiscal year ending July 31.

3.   A partnership that otherwise would be required to adopt or change its tax year (normally to the calendar year) may **elect to use a fiscal year if the election does not result in a deferral period longer than three months,** or, if less, the deferral period of the year currently in use.

    a.   The "deferral period" is the number of months between the close of the fiscal year elected and the close of the required year (e.g., if a partnership elects a tax year ending September 30 and a tax year ending December 31 is required, the deferral period of the year ending September 30 is three months).

    b.   A partnership that elects a tax year other than a required year must make a "required payment" which is in the nature of a refundable, noninterest-bearing deposit that is intended to compensate the government for the revenue lost as a result of tax deferral. The required payment is due on May 15 each year and is recomputed for each subsequent year.

4.   The **taxable year** of a partnership ordinarily **will not close** as a result of the death or entry of a partner, or the liquidation or sale of a partner's interest. But the partnership's taxable year closes as to **the partner** whose **entire interest** is sold or liquidated. Additionally, the partnership tax year closes with respect to a deceased partner as of date of death.

    EXAMPLE: A partner sells his entire interest in a calendar-year partnership on March 31. His pro rata share of partnership income up to March 31 is $15,000. Since the partnership year closes with respect to him at the time of sale, the $15,000 is includible in his income and increases the basis of his partnership interest for purposes of computing gain or loss on the sale. However, the partnership's taxable year does not close as to its remaining partners.

    EXAMPLE: X (on a calendar year) is a partner in the XYZ Partnership that uses a June 30 fiscal year. X died on April 30, 2003. Since the partnership year closes with respect to X at his death, X's final return for the period January 1 through April 30 will include his share of partnership income for the period beginning July 1, 2002, and ending April 30, 2003. His share of partnership income for May and June 2003 will be reported by his estate or other successor in interest.

H. Partnership's Use of Cash Method

1.   The cash method cannot generally be used if inventories are necessary to clearly reflect income and cannot generally be used by tax shelters and partnerships that have a C corporation as a partner.

2.   Any partnership (other than a tax shelter) can use the cash method if for every year it has average gross receipts of **$5 million or less** for any prior three-year period and does not have inventories for sale to customers.

3.   A small partnership with average annual gross receipts of **$1 million or less** for any prior three-year period can use the cash method and is excepted from the requirements to account for inventories and use the accrual method for purchases and sales of merchandise.

I. Termination or Continuation of Partnership

1.   A partnership will terminate when it no longer has at least two partners.

2.   A partnership and its taxable year will terminate for all partners if there is a sale or exchange of 50% or more of the **total interests** in partnership capital and profits within a twelve-month period.

    a.   Sales or exchanges of at least 50% during any twelve-month period cause a termination.

    EXAMPLE: The calendar-year ABC Partnership has three equal partners, A, B, and C. B sold his interest to D on November 1, 2002, and C sold his interest to E on April 1, 2003. The ABC Partnership is considered terminated on April 1 because at least 50% of the total interests have been sold within a twelve-month period.

b.   If the same partnership interest is sold more than once during a twelve-month period, the sale is counted only once.

> EXAMPLE: The calendar-year RST Partnership has three equal partners, R, S, and T. T sold his interest to X on December 1, 2002, and X sold his interest to Y on May 1, 2003. The RST Partnership is not terminated because multiple sales of the same partnership interest are counted only once.

3.   In a **merger** of partnerships, the resulting partnership is a continuation of the merging partnership whose partners have a more than 50% interest in the resulting partnership.

> EXAMPLE: Partnerships AB and CD merge on April 1, forming the ABCD Partnership in which the partners' interests are as follows: Partner A, 30%; B, 30%; C, 20%; and D, 20%. Partnership ABCD is a continuation of the AB Partnership. The CD Partnership is considered terminated and its taxable year closed on April 1.

4.   In a **division** of a partnership, a resulting partnership is a continuation of the prior partnership if the resulting partnership's partners had a more than 50% interest in the prior partnership.

> EXAMPLE: Partnership ABCD is owned as follows: A, 40%; and B, C, and D each own a 20% interest. The partners agree to separate and form two partnerships—AC and BD. Partnership AC is a continuation of ABCD. BD is considered a new partnership and must adopt a taxable year, as well as make any other necessary tax accounting elections.

J. Sale of a Partnership Interest

1.   Since a partnership interest is usually a capital asset, the sale of a partnership interest generally results in **capital gain or loss**.

    a.   Gain is excess of amount realized over the adjusted basis for the partnership interest.

    b.   Include the selling partner's share of partnership liabilities in the amount realized because the selling partner is relieved of them.

> EXAMPLE: Miller sold her partnership interest to Carter for $150,000 cash, plus Carter's assumption of Miller's $60,000 share of partnership liabilities. The amount realized by Miller on the sale of her partnership interest is $150,000 + $60,000 = $210,000.

2.   **Gain is ordinary** (instead of capital) to extent attributable to unrealized receivables or appreciated inventory (Sec. 751 items).

    a.   The term **unrealized receivables** generally refers to the accounts receivable of a cash method taxpayer, but for this purpose also includes any potential recapture under Secs. 1245, 1250, and 1252.

    b.   The term **inventory** includes all assets except capital assets and Section 1231 assets.

> EXAMPLE: X has a 40% interest in the XY Partnership. Partner X sells his 40% interest to Z for $50,000. X's basis in his partnership is $22,000 and the cash-method partnership had the following receivables and inventory:
>
> | | Adjusted basis | Fair market value |
> |---|---|---|
> | Accounts receivable | 0 | $10,000 |
> | Inventory | 4,000 | 10,000 |
> | Potential Sec. 1250 recapture | 0 | 10,000 |
> | | $4,000 | $30,000 |
>
> X's total gain is $28,000 (i.e., $50,000 – $22,000). Since the Sec. 1250 recapture is treated as "unrealized receivables" and the inventory is appreciated, X will recognize ordinary income to the extent that his selling price attributable to Sec. 751 items ($30,000 x 40% = $12,000) exceeds his basis in those items ($4,000 x 40% = $1,600), that is, $10,400. The remainder of X's gain ($28,000 – $10,400 = $17,600) will be treated as capital gain.

K. Pro Rata Distributions from Partnership

1.   Partnership recognizes no gain or loss on a distribution.

2.   If a single distribution consists of **multiple items of property,** the distributed property reduces the partner's basis for the partnership interest in the **following order:**

    a.   Money,

    b.   Adjusted basis of unrealized receivables and inventory, and

    c.   Adjusted basis of other property.

3.   Partner recognizes **gain** only to the extent **money received exceeds the partner's partnership basis**.

    a.   Relief from liabilities is deemed a distribution of money.

    b.   Gain is capital except for gain attributable to unrealized receivables and substantially appreciated inventory.

    c.   The receipt of property (other than money) will not cause the recognition of gain.

EXAMPLE: Casey had a basis of $9,000 for his partnership interest at the time that he received a nonliquidating partnership distribution consisting of $5,000 cash and other property with a basis of $3,000 and a FMV of $8,000. No gain is recognized by Casey since the cash received did not exceed his partnership basis. Casey's $9,000 basis for his partnership interest is first reduced by the $5,000 cash, and then reduced by the $3,000 basis of other property, to $1,000. Casey will have a basis for the other property received of $3,000.

4. Partner recognizes **loss** only upon **complete liquidation** of a partnership interest through receipt of only money, unrealized receivables, or inventory.

   a. The amount of loss is the basis for the partner's partnership interest less the money and the partnership's basis in the unrealized receivables and inventory received by the partner.
   b. The loss is generally treated as a capital loss.
   c. If property other than money, unrealized receivables, or inventory is distributed in complete liquidation of a partner's interest, no loss can be recognized.

EXAMPLE: Day had a basis of $20,000 for his partnership interest before receiving a distribution in complete liquidation of his interest. The liquidating distribution consisted of $6,000 cash and inventory with a basis of $11,000. Since Day's liquidating distribution consisted of only money and inventory, Day will recognize a loss on the liquidation of his partnership interest. The amount of loss is the $3,000 difference between the $20,000 basis for his partnership interest, and the $6,000 cash and the $11,000 basis for the inventory received. Day will have an $11,000 basis for the inventory.

EXAMPLE: Assume the same facts as in the preceding example except that Day's liquidating distribution consists of $6,000 cash and a parcel of land with a basis of $11,000. Since the liquidating distribution now includes property other than money, receivables, and inventory, no loss can be recognized on the liquidation of Day's partnership interest. The basis for Day's partnership interest is first reduced by the $6,000 cash to $14,000. Since no loss can be recognized, the parcel of land must absorb all of Day's unrecovered partnership basis. As a result, the land will have a basis of $14,000.

5. In **nonliquidating (current) distributions,** a partner's basis in distributed property is generally the same as the partnership's former basis in the property; but is **limited** to the basis for the partner's partnership interest less any money received.

EXAMPLE: Sara receives a current distribution from her partnership at a time when the basis for her partnership interest is $10,000. The distribution consists of $7,000 cash and Sec. 1231 property with an adjusted basis of $5,000 and a FMV of $9,000. No gain is recognized by Sara since the cash received did not exceed her basis. After being reduced by the cash, her partnership basis of $3,000 is reduced by the basis of the property (but not below zero). Her basis for the property is limited to $3,000.

6. **If multiple properties are distributed** in a liquidating distribution, or if the partnership's basis for distributed properties exceed the partner's basis for the partnership interest, the partner's basis for the partnership interest is allocated in the following order:

   a. Basis is first allocated to unrealized receivables and inventory items in an amount equal to their adjusted basis to the partnership. If the basis for the partner's interest to be allocated to the assets is less than the total basis of these properties to the partnership, a **basis decrease** is required,and is determined under (1) below.
   b. To the extent a partner's basis is not allocated to assets under a. above, basis is allocated to other distributed properties by assigning to each property its adjusted basis in the hands of the partnership, and then increasing or decreasing the basis to the extent required in order for the adjusted basis of the distributed properties to equal the remaining basis for the partner's partnership interest.

      (1) A **basis decrease** is allocated

         (a) First to properties with unrealized depreciation in proportion to their respective amounts of unrealized depreciation (but only to the extent of each property's unrealized depreciation), and
         (b) Then in proportion to the respective adjusted basis of the distributed properties.

EXAMPLE: A partnership distributes two items of property (A and B) that are neither unrealized receivables nor inventory to Baker in liquidation of his partnership interest that has a basis of $20.

	Partnership basis	*FMV*
Property A	*$15*	*$15*
Property B	*15*	*5*
Total	*$30*	*$20*

Basis is first allocated $15 to A and $15 to B (their adjusted bases to the partnership). A $10 basis decrease is required because the assets' bases of $30 exceeds Baker's basis for his partnership interest of $20. The $10 decrease is allocated to B to the extent of its unrealized depreciation. Thus, Baker has a basis of $15 for property A and a basis of $5 for property B.

(2) A **basis increase** is allocated

(a) First to properties with unrealized appreciation in proportion to their respective amounts of unrealized appreciation (but only to the extent of each property's unrealized appreciation), and

(b) Then in proportion to the relative FMVs of the distributed properties.

EXAMPLE: A partnership distributes two items of property (C and D) that are neither unrealized receivables nor inventory to Alan in liquidation of his partnership interest that has a basis of $55.

	Partnership basis	FMV
Property C	$ 5	$40
Property D	10	10
Total	$15	$50

Basis is first allocated $5 to C and $10 to D (their adjusted bases to the partnership). The $40 basis increase (Alan's $55 basis less the partnership's basis for the assets $15) is then allocated to C to the extent of its unrealized appreciation of $35, with the remaining $5 of basis adjustment allocated according to the relative FMV of C and D [i.e., $4 to C (for a total basis of $44) and $1 to D (for a total basis of $11)]

7. Payments made in liquidation of the interest of a retiring or deceased partner are generally treated as partnership distributions made in exchange for the partner's interest in partnership property. Such payments generally result in capital gain or loss to the retiring or deceased partner.

a. However, payments made to a retiring or deceased general partner in a partnership in which capital is **not** a material income-producing factor must be reported as ordinary income by the partner to the extent such payments are for the partner's share of unrealized receivables or goodwill (unless the partnership agreement provides for a payment with respect to goodwill).

b. Amounts treated as ordinary income by the retiring or deceased partner are either deductible by the partnership (treated as guaranteed payments), or reduce the income allocated to remaining partners (treated as a distributive share of partnership income).

c. Capital is **not** a material income-producing factor if substantially all of the gross income of the business consists of fees, commissions, or other compensation for personal services (e.g., accountants, doctors, dentists, lawyers).

L. Non-Pro-Rata Distributions from Partnership

1. A non-pro-rata (disproportionate) distribution occurs when

a. A distribution is disproportionate as to a partner's share of unrealized receivables or substantially appreciated inventory. Inventory is **substantially appreciated** if its FMV exceeds 120% of its basis.

(1) Partner may receive more than the partner's share of these assets, or

(2) Partner may receive more than the partner's share of other assets, in effect giving up a share of unrealized receivables or substantially appreciated inventory

b. The partner may recognize gain or loss.

(1) The gain or loss is the difference between the FMV of what is received and the basis of what is given up.

(2) The gain or loss is limited to the disproportionate amount of unrealized receivables or substantially appreciated inventory that is received or given up.

(3) The character of the gain or loss depends upon the character of the property given up.

c. The partnership may similarly recognize gain or loss when there is a disproportionate distribution with respect to substantially appreciated inventory or unrealized receivables.

EXAMPLE: A, B, and C each own a one-third interest in a partnership. The partnership has the following assets:

	Adjusted basis	FMV
Cash	$ 6,000	$ 6,000
Inventory	6,000	12,000
Land	9,000	18,000
	$21,000	$36,000

Assume that A has a $7,000 basis for his partnership interest and that all inventory is distributed to A in liquidation of his partnership interest. He is treated as having exchanged his 1/3 interest in the cash and the land for a 2/3 increased interest in the substantially appreciated inventory. He has a gain of $3,000. He received $8,000 (2/3 x $12,000) of inventory for his basis of $2,000 (1/3 x $6,000) in cash and $3,000 (1/3 x $9,000) of land. The gain is capital if the land *was a capital asset. The partnership is treated as having received $8,000 (FMV of A's 1/3 share of cash and land) in exchange for inventory with a basis of $4,000 (basis of inventory distributed in excess of A's 1/3 share). Thus, the partnership will recognize ordinary income of $4,000.*

M. Optional Adjustment to Basis of Partnership Property

1. On a distribution of property to a partner, or on a sale by a partner of a partnership interest, the partnership may elect to adjust the basis of its assets to **prevent any inequities** that otherwise might occur. Once an election is made, it applies to all similar transactions unless IRS approves revocation of the election.

2. Upon the **distribution of partnership property,** the basis of remaining partnership property will be adjusted for **all** partners.

   a. Increased by

      (1) The amount of gain recognized to a distributee partner, and
      (2) The excess of the partnership's basis in the property distributed over the basis of that property in the hands of distributee partner

      EXAMPLE: If election were made under facts in the example on page 540, $2,000 of basis that otherwise would be lost will be allocated to remaining partnership Sec. 1231 property.

   b. Decreased by

      (1) The amount of loss recognized to a distributee partner, and
      (2) The excess of basis of property in hands of distributee over the prior basis of that property in the partnership

3. Upon the **sale or exchange of a partnership interest,** the basis of partnership property to the **transferee** (not other partners) will be

   a. Increased by the excess of the basis of the transferee's partnership interest over the transferee's share of the adjusted basis of partnership property
   b. Decreased by the excess of transferee's share of adjusted basis of partnership property over the basis for the transferee's partnership interest

      EXAMPLE: Assume X sells his 40% interest to Z for $80,000 when the partnership balance sheet reflects the following:

      XY Partnership

Assets	Basis	FMV
Accounts Receivable	$ 0	$100,000
Real Property	30,000	100,000
Capital		
X (40%)		$ 80,000
Y (60%)		120,000

      Z will have a basis for his partnership interest of $80,000, while his share of the adjusted basis of partnership property will only be $12,000. If the partnership elects to adjust the basis of partnership property, it will increase the basis of its assets by $68,000 ($80,000 – $12,000) solely for the benefit of Z. The basis of the receivables will increase from 0 to $40,000 with the full adjustment allocated to Z. When the receivables are collected, Y will have $60,000 of income and Z will have none. The basis of the real property will increase by $28,000 to $58,000, so that Z's share of the basis will be $40,000 (i.e., $12,000 + $28,000).

MULTIPLE-CHOICE QUESTIONS (1-69)

1. At partnership inception, Black acquires a 50% interest in Decorators Partnership by contributing property with an adjusted basis of $250,000. Black recognizes a gain if

I. The fair market value of the contributed property exceeds its adjusted basis.

II. The property is encumbered by a mortgage with a balance of $100,000.

     a.   I only.
     b.   II only.
     c.   Both I and II.
     d.   Neither I nor II.

2. On June 1, 2003, Kelly received a 10% interest in Rock Co., a partnership, for services contributed to the partnership. Rock's net assets at that date had a basis of $70,000 and a fair market value of $100,000. In Kelly's 2003 income tax return, what amount must Kelly include as income from transfer of the partnership interest?
     a. $ 7,000 ordinary income.
     b. $ 7,000 capital gain.
     c. $10,000 ordinary income.
     d. $10,000 capital gain.

3. Ola Associates is a limited partnership engaged in real estate development. Hoff, a civil engineer, billed Ola $40,000 in 2003 for consulting services rendered. In full settlement of this invoice, Hoff accepted a $15,000 cash payment plus the following:

	Fair market value	Carrying amount on Ola's books
3% limited partnership interest in Ola	$10,000	N/A
Surveying equipment	7,000	$3,000

What amount should Hoff, a cash-basis taxpayer, report in his 2003 return as income for the services rendered to Ola?
     a. $15,000
     b. $28,000
     c. $32,000
     d. $40,000

4. The following information pertains to property contributed by Gray on July 1, 2003, for a 40% interest in the capital and profits of Kag & Gray, a partnership:

As of June 30, 2003

Adjusted basis	Fair market value
$24,000	$30,000

After Gray's contribution, Kag & Gray's capital totaled $150,000. What amount of gain was reportable in Gray's 2003 return on the contribution of property to the partnership?
     a. $0
     b. $ 6,000
     c. $30,000
     d. $36,000

5. The holding period of a partnership interest acquired in exchange for a contributed capital asset begins on the date
     a.   The partner is admitted to the partnership.
     b.   The partner transfers the asset to the partnership.
     c.   The partner's holding period of the capital asset began.
     d.   The partner is first credited with the proportionate share of partnership capital.

6. The following information pertains to Carr's admission to the Smith & Jones partnership on July 1, 2003:

     Carr's contribution of capital: 800 shares of Ed Corp. stock bought in 1990 for $30,000; fair market value $150,000 on July 1, 2003.
     Carr's interest in capital and profits of Smith & Jones: 25%.
     Fair market value of net assets of Smith & Jones on July 1, 2003, after Carr's admission: $600,000.

Carr's gain in 2003 on the exchange of the Ed Corp. stock for Carr's partnership interest was
     a. $120,000 ordinary income.
     b. $120,000 long-term capital gain.
     c. $120,000 Section 1231 gain.
     d. $0.

7. The holding period of property acquired by a partnership as a contribution to the contributing partner's capital account
     a.   Begins with the date of contribution to the partnership.
     b.   Includes the period during which the property was held by the contributing partner.
     c.   Is equal to the contributing partner's holding period prior to contribution to the partnership.
     d.   Depends on the character of the property transferred.

8. On September 1, 2003, James Elton received a 25% capital interest in Bredbo Associates, a partnership, in return for services rendered plus a contribution of assets with a basis to Elton of $25,000 and a fair market value of $40,000. The fair market value of Elton's 25% interest was $50,000. How much is Elton's basis for his interest in Bredbo?
     a. $25,000
     b. $35,000
     c. $40,000
     d. $50,000

9. Basic Partnership, a cash-basis calendar-year entity, began business on February 1, 2003. Basic incurred and paid the following in 2003:

Filing fees incident to the creation of the partnership	$ 3,600
Accounting fees to prepare the representations in offering materials	12,000

Basic elected to amortize costs. What was the maximum amount that Basic could deduct on the 2003 partnership return?
     a. $11,000
     b. $ 3,300
     c. $ 2,860
     d. $ 660

10. Thompson's basis in Starlight Partnership was $60,000 at the beginning of the year. Thompson materially participates in the partnership's business. Thompson received $20,000 in cash distributions during the year. Thompson's share of Starlight's current operations was a $65,000 ordinary loss and a $15,000 net long-term capital gain. What is the amount of Thompson's deductible loss for the period?
     a. $15,000
     b. $40,000
     c. $55,000
     d. $65,000

11. In computing the ordinary income of a partnership, a deduction is allowed for

   a.   Contributions to recognized charities.

   b.   The first $100 of dividends received from qualifying domestic corporations.

   c.   Short-term capital losses.

   d.   Guaranteed payments to partners.

12. Which of the following limitations will apply in determining a partner's deduction for that partner's share of partnership losses?

	At-risk	Passive loss
a.	Yes	No
b.	No	Yes
c.	Yes	Yes
d.	No	No

13. Dunn and Shaw are partners who share profits and losses equally. In the computation of the partnership's 2003 book income of $100,000, guaranteed payments to partners totaling $60,000 and charitable contributions totaling $1,000 were treated as expenses. What amount should be reported as ordinary income on the partnership's 2003 return?

   a. $100,000

   b. $101,000

   c. $160,000

   d. $161,000

14. The partnership of Martin & Clark sustained an ordinary loss of $84,000 in 2003. The partnership, as well as the two partners, are on a calendar-year basis. The partners share profits and losses equally. At December 31, 2003, Clark, who materially participates in the partnership's business, had an adjusted basis of $36,000 for his partnership interest, before consideration of the 2003 loss. On his individual income tax return for 2003, Clark should deduct a(n)

   a.   Ordinary loss of $36,000.

   b.   Ordinary loss of $42,000.

   c.   Ordinary loss of $36,000 and a capital loss of $6,000.

   d.   Capital loss of $42,000.

15. The partnership of Felix and Oscar had the following items of income during the taxable year ended December 31, 2003.

Income from operations	$156,000
Tax-exempt interest income	8,000
Dividends from foreign corporations	6,000
Net rental income	12,000

What is the total ordinary income of the partnership for 2003?

   a. $156,000

   b. $174,000

   c. $176,000

   d. $182,000

16. A guaranteed payment by a partnership to a partner for services rendered, may include an agreement to pay

  I.   A salary of $5,000 monthly without regard to partnership income.

 II.   A 25% interest in partnership profits.

   a.   I only.

   b.   II only.

   c.   Both I and II.

   d.   Neither I nor II.

17. Chris, a 25% partner in Vista partnership, received a $20,000 guaranteed payment in 2003 for deductible services rendered to the partnership. Guaranteed payments were not made to any other partner. Vista's 2003 partnership income consisted of

Net business income before guaranteed payments	$80,000
Net long-term capital gains	10,000

What amount of income should Chris report from Vista Partnership on her 2003 tax return?

   a. $37,500

   b. $27,500

   c. $22,500

   d. $20,000

18. On January 2, 2003, Arch and Bean contribute cash equally to form the JK Partnership. Arch and Bean share profits and losses in a ratio of 75% to 25%, respectively. For 2003, the partnership's ordinary income was $40,000. A distribution of $5,000 was made to Arch during 2003. What amount of ordinary income should Arch report from the JK Partnership for 2003?

   a. $ 5,000

   b. $10,000

   c. $20,000

   d. $30,000

19. Guaranteed payments made by a partnership to partners for services rendered to the partnership, that are deductible business expenses under the Internal Revenue Code, are

  I.   Deductible expenses on the US Partnership Return of Income, Form 1065, in order to arrive at partnership income (loss).

 II.   Included on Schedule K-1 to be taxed as ordinary income to the partners.

   a.   I only.

   b.   II only.

   c.   Both I and II.

   d.   Neither I nor II.

20. The method used to depreciate partnership property is an election made by

   a.   The partnership and must be the same method used by the "principal partner."

   b.   The partnership and may be any method approved by the IRS.

   c.   The "principal partner."

   d.   Each individual partner.

21. Under the Internal Revenue Code sections pertaining to partnerships, guaranteed payments are payments to partners for

   a.   Payments of principal on secured notes honored at maturity.

   b.   Timely payments of periodic interest on bona fide loans that are **not** treated as partners' capital.

   c.   Services or the use of capital without regard to partnership income.

   d.   Sales of partners' assets to the partnership at guaranteed amounts regardless of market values.

22. Dale's distributive share of income from the calendar-year partnership of Dale & Eck was $50,000 in 2003. On December 15, 2003, Dale, who is a cash-basis taxpayer, received a $27,000 distribution of the partnership's 2003 income, with the $23,000 balance paid to Dale in February

2004. In addition, Dale received a $10,000 interest-free loan from the partnership in 2003. This $10,000 is to be offset against Dale's share of 2004 partnership income. What total amount of partnership income is taxable to Dale in 2003?

    a. $27,000
    b. $37,000
    c. $50,000
    d. $60,000

23. At December 31, 2002, Alan and Baker were equal partners in a partnership with net assets having a tax basis and fair market value of $100,000. On January 1, 2003, Carr contributed securities with a fair market value of $50,000 (purchased in 2001 at a cost of $35,000) to become an equal partner in the new firm of Alan, Baker, and Carr. The securities were sold on December 15, 2003, for $47,000. How much of the partnership's capital gain from the sale of these securities should be allocated to Carr?

    a. $0
    b. $ 3,000
    c. $ 6,000
    d. $12,000

24. Gilroy, a calendar-year taxpayer, is a partner in the firm of Adams and Company which has a fiscal year ending June 30. The partnership agreement provides for Gilroy to receive 25% of the ordinary income of the partnership. Gilroy also receives a guaranteed payment of $1,000 monthly which is deductible by the partnership. The partnership reported ordinary income of $88,000 for the year ended June 30, 2003, and $132,000 for the year ended June 30, 2004. How much should Gilroy report on his 2003 return as total income from the partnership?

    a. $25,000
    b. $30,500
    c. $34,000
    d. $39,000

25. On December 31, 2002, Edward Baker gave his son, Allan, a gift of a 50% interest in a partnership in which capital is a material income-producing factor. For the year ended December 31, 2003, the partnership's ordinary income was $100,000. Edward and Allan were the only partners in 2003. There were no guaranteed payments to partners. Edward's services performed for the partnership were worth a reasonable compensation of $40,000 for 2003. Allan has never performed any services for the partnership. What is Allan's distributive share of partnership income for 2003?

    a. $20,000
    b. $30,000
    c. $40,000
    d. $50,000

Items 26 and 27 are based on the following:

    Jones and Curry formed Major Partnership as equal partners by contributing the assets below.

	Asset	Adjusted basis	Fair market value
Jones	Cash	$45,000	$45,000
Curry	Land	30,000	57,000

The land was held by Curry as a capital asset, subject to a $12,000 mortgage, that was assumed by Major.

26. What was Curry's initial basis in the partnership interest?

    a. $45,000
    b. $30,000
    c. $24,000
    d. $18,000

27. What was Jones' initial basis in the partnership interest?

    a. $51,000
    b. $45,000
    c. $39,000
    d. $33,000

Items 28 and 29 are based on the following:

    Flagg and Miles are each 50% partners in Decor Partnership. Each partner had a $200,000 tax basis in the partnership on January 1, 2003. Decor's 2003 net business income before guaranteed payments was $45,000. During 2003, Decor made a $7,500 guaranteed payment to Miles for deductible services rendered.

28. What total amount from Decor is includible in Flagg's 2003 tax return?

    a. $15,000
    b. $18,750
    c. $22,500
    d. $37,500

29. What is Miles's tax basis in Decor on December 31, 2003?

    a. $211,250
    b. $215,000
    c. $218,750
    d. $222,500

30. Peters has a one-third interest in the Spano Partnership. During 2003, Peters received a $16,000 guaranteed payment, which was deductible by the partnership, for services rendered to Spano. Spano reported a 2003 operating loss of $70,000 before the guaranteed payment. What is(are) the net effect(s) of the guaranteed payment?

  I. The guaranteed payment decreases Peters' tax basis in Spano by $16,000.
  II. The guaranteed payment increases Peters' ordinary income by $16,000.

    a. I only.
    b. II only.
    c. Both I and II.
    d. Neither I nor II.

31. Dean is a 25% partner in Target Partnership. Dean's tax basis in Target on January 1, 2003, was $20,000. At the end of 2003, Dean received a nonliquidating cash distribution of $8,000 from Target. Target's 2003 accounts recorded the following items:

Municipal bond interest income	$12,000
Ordinary income	40,000

What was Dean's tax basis in Target on December 31, 2003?

    a. $15,000
    b. $23,000
    c. $25,000
    d. $30,000

32. On January 4, 2003, Smith and White contributed $4,000 and $6,000 in cash, respectively, and formed the Macro General Partnership. The partnership agreement allocated profits and losses 40% to Smith and 60% to White.

In 2003, Macro purchased property from an unrelated seller for $10,000 cash and a $40,000 mortgage note that was the general liability of the partnership. Macro's liability

a. Increases Smith's partnership basis by $16,000.
b. Increases Smith's partnership basis by $20,000.
c. Increases Smith's partnership basis by $24,000.
d. Has **no** effect on Smith's partnership basis.

33. Gray is a 50% partner in Fabco Partnership. Gray's tax basis in Fabco on January 1, 2003, was $5,000. Fabco made no distributions to the partners during 2003, and recorded the following:

Ordinary income	$20,000
Tax exempt income	8,000
Portfolio income	4,000

What is Gray's tax basis in Fabco on December 31, 2003?

a. $21,000
b. $16,000
c. $12,000
d. $10,000

34. On January 1, 2003, Kane was a 25% equal partner in Maze General Partnership, which had partnership liabilities of $300,000. On January 2, 2003, a new partner was admitted and Kane's interest was reduced to 20%. On April 1, 2003, Maze repaid a $100,000 general partnership loan. Ignoring any income, loss, or distributions for 2003, what was the **net** effect of the two transactions for Kane's tax basis in Maze partnership interest?

a. Has **no** effect.
b. Decrease of $35,000.
c. Increase of $15,000.
d. Decrease of $75,000.

35. Lee inherited a partnership interest from Dale. The adjusted basis of Dale's partnership interest was $50,000, and its fair market value on the date of Dale's death (the estate valuation date) was $70,000. What was Lee's original basis for the partnership interest?

a. $70,000
b. $50,000
c. $20,000
d. $0

36. Which of the following should be used in computing the basis of a partner's interest acquired from another partner?

	Cash paid by transferee to transferor	Transferee's share of partnership liabilities
a.	No	Yes
b.	Yes	No
c.	No	No
d.	Yes	Yes

37. Hall and Haig are equal partners in the firm of Arosa Associates. On January 1, 2003, each partner's adjusted basis in Arosa was $40,000. During 2003 Arosa borrowed $60,000, for which Hall and Haig are personally liable. Arosa sustained an operating loss of $10,000 for the year ended December 31, 2003. The basis of each partner's interest in Arosa at December 31, 2003, was

a. $35,000
b. $40,000
c. $65,000
d. $70,000

38. Doris and Lydia are sisters and also are equal partners in the capital and profits of Agee & Nolan. The following information pertains to 300 shares of Mast Corp. stock sold by Lydia to Agee & Nolan.

Year of purchase	1997
Year of sale	2003
Basis (cost)	$9,000
Sales price (equal to fair market value)	$4,000

The amount of long-term capital loss that Lydia recognized in 2003 on the sale of this stock was

a. $5,000
b. $3,000
c. $2,500
d. $0

39. In March 2003, Lou Cole bought 100 shares of a listed stock for $10,000. In May 2003, Cole sold this stock for its fair market value of $16,000 to the partnership of Rook, Cole & Clive. Cole owned a one-third interest in this partnership. In Cole's 2003 tax return, what amount should be reported as short-term capital gain as a result of this transaction?

a. $6,000
b. $4,000
c. $2,000
d. $0

40. Kay Shea owns a 55% interest in the capital and profits of Dexter Communications, a partnership. In 2003, Kay sold an oriental lamp to Dexter for $5,000. Kay bought this lamp in 1997 for her personal use at a cost of $1,000 and had used the lamp continuously in her home until the lamp was sold to Dexter. Dexter purchased the lamp as an investment. What is Kay's reportable gain in 2003 on the sale of the lamp to Dexter?

a. $4,000 ordinary income.
b. $4,000 long-term capital gain.
c. $2,200 ordinary income.
d. $1,800 long-term capital gain.

41. Gladys Peel owns a 50% interest in the capital and profits of the partnership of Peel and Poe. On July 1, 2003, Peel bought land the partnership had used in its business for its fair market value of $10,000. The partnership had acquired the land five years ago for $16,000. For the year ended December 31, 2003, the partnership's net income was $94,000 after recording the $6,000 loss on the sale of land. Peel's distributive share of ordinary income from the partnership for 2003 was

a. $47,000
b. $48,500
c. $49,000
d. $50,000

42. Under Section 444 of the Internal Revenue Code, certain partnerships can elect to use a tax year different from their required tax year. One of the conditions for eligibility to make a Section 444 election is that the partnership must

a. Be a limited partnership.
b. Be a member of a tiered structure.
c. Choose a tax year where the deferral period is **not** longer than three months.
d. Have less than seventy-five partners.

43. Which one of the following statements regarding a partnership's tax year is correct?

  a. A partnership formed on July 1 is required to adopt a tax year ending on June 30.

  b. A partnership may elect to have a tax year other than the generally required tax year if the deferral period for the tax year elected does **not** exceed three months.

  c. A "valid business purpose" can **no** longer be claimed as a reason for adoption of a tax year other than the generally required tax year.

  d. Within thirty days after a partnership has established a tax year, a form must be filed with the IRS as notification of the tax year adopted.

44. Without obtaining prior approval from the IRS, a newly formed partnership may adopt

  a. A taxable year which is the same as that used by one or more of its partners owning an aggregate interest of more than 50% in profits and capital.

  b. A calendar year, only if it comprises a twelve-month period.

  c. A January 31 year-end if it is a retail enterprise, and all of its principal partners are on a calendar year.

  d. Any taxable year that it deems advisable to select.

45. Irving Aster, Dennis Brill, and Robert Clark were partners who shared profits and losses equally. On February 28, 2003, Aster sold his interest to Phil Dexter. On March 31, 2003, Brill died, and his estate held his interest for the remainder of the year. The partnership continued to operate and for the fiscal year ending June 30, 2003, it had a profit of $45,000. Assuming that partnership income was earned on a pro rata monthly basis and that all partners were calendar-year taxpayers, the distributive shares to be included in 2003 gross income should be

  a. Aster $10,000, Brill $0, Estate of Brill $15,000, Clark $15,000, and Dexter $5,000.

  b. Aster $10,000, Brill $11,250, Estate of Brill $3,750, Clark $15,000, and Dexter $5,000.

  c. Aster $0, Brill $11,250, Estate of Brill $3,750, Clark $15,000, and Dexter $15,000.

  d. Aster $0, Brill $0, Estate of Brill $15,000, Clark $15,000, and Dexter $15,000.

46. On January 3, 2003, the partners' interests in the capital, profits, and losses of Able Partnership were

	% of capital profits and losses
Dean	25%
Poe	30%
Ritt	45%

On February 4, 2003, Poe sold her entire interest to an unrelated person. Dean sold his 25% interest in Able to another unrelated person on December 20, 2003. No other transactions took place in 2003. For tax purposes, which of the following statements is correct with respect to Able?

  a. Able terminated as of February 4, 2003.

  b. Able terminated as of December 20, 2003.

  c. Able terminated as of December 31, 2003.

  d. Able did **not** terminate.

47. Curry's sale of her partnership interest causes a partnership termination. The partnership's business and financial operations are continued by the other members. What is(are) the effect(s) of the termination?

 I. There is a deemed distribution of assets to the remaining partners and the purchaser.

 II. There is a hypothetical recontribution of assets to a new partnership.

  a. I only.

  b. II only.

  c. Both I and II.

  d. Neither I nor II.

48. Cobb, Danver, and Evans each owned a one-third interest in the capital and profits of their calendar-year partnership. On September 18, 2003, Cobb and Danver sold their partnership interests to Frank, and immediately withdrew from all participation in the partnership. On March 15, 2004, Cobb and Danver received full payment from Frank for the sale of their partnership interests. For tax purposes, the partnership

  a. Terminated on September 18, 2003.

  b. Terminated on December 31, 2003.

  c. Terminated on March 15, 2004.

  d. Did **not** terminate.

49. Partnership Abel, Benz, Clark & Day is in the real estate and insurance business. Abel owns a 40% interest in the capital and profits of the partnership, while Benz, Clark, and Day each owns a 20% interest. All use a calendar year. At November 1, 2003, the real estate and insurance business is separated, and two partnerships are formed: Partnership Abel & Benz takes over the real estate business, and Partnership Clark & Day takes over the insurance business. Which one of the following statements is correct for tax purposes?

  a. Partnership Abel & Benz is considered to be a continuation of Partnership Abel, Benz, Clark & Day.

  b. In forming Partnership Clark & Day, partners Clark and Day are subject to a penalty surtax if they contribute their entire distributions from Partnership Abel, Benz, Clark & Day.

  c. Before separating the two businesses into two distinct entities, the partners must obtain approval from the IRS.

  d. Before separating the two businesses into two distinct entities, Partnership Abel, Benz, Clark & Day must file a formal dissolution with the IRS on the prescribed form.

50. Under which of the following circumstances is a partnership that is not an electing large partnership considered terminated for income tax purposes?

 I. Fifty-five percent of the total interest in partnership capital and profits is sold within a twelve-month period.

 II. The partnership's business and financial operations are discontinued.

  a. I only.

  b. II only.

  c. Both I and II.

  d. Neither I nor II.

51. David Beck and Walter Crocker were equal partners in the calendar-year partnership of Beck & Crocker. On July 1, 2002, Beck died. Beck's estate became the successor in interest and continued to share in Beck & Crocker's profits until Beck's entire partnership interest was liquidated on

April 30, 2003. At what date was the partnership considered terminated for tax purposes?

a. April 30, 2003.
b. December 31, 2003.
c. July 31, 2003.
d. July 1, 2003.

52. On December 31, 2003, after receipt of his share of partnership income, Clark sold his interest in a limited partnership for $30,000 cash and relief of all liabilities. On that date, the adjusted basis of Clark's partnership interest was $40,000, consisting of his capital account of $15,000 and his share of the partnership liabilities of $25,000. The partnership has no unrealized receivables or appreciated inventory. What is Clark's gain or loss on the sale of his partnership interest?

a. Ordinary loss of $10,000.
b. Ordinary gain of $15,000.
c. Capital loss of $10,000.
d. Capital gain of $15,000.

Items 53 and 54 are based on the following:

The personal service partnership of Allen, Baker & Carr had the following cash basis balance sheet at December 31, 2002:

Assets	Adjusted basis per books	Market value
Cash	$102,000	$102,000
Unrealized accounts receivable	--	420,000
Totals	$102,000	$522,000
Liability and Capital		
Note payable	$ 60,000	$ 60,000
Capital accounts:		
Allen	14,000	154,000
Baker	14,000	154,000
Carr	14,000	154,000
Totals	$102,000	$522,000

Carr, an equal partner, sold his partnership interest to Dole, an outsider, for $154,000 cash on January 1, 2003. In addition, Dole assumed Carr's share of the partnership's liability.

53. What was the total amount realized by Carr on the sale of his partnership interest?

a. $174,000
b. $154,000
c. $140,000
d. $134,000

54. What amount of ordinary income should Carr report in his 2003 income tax return on the sale of his partnership interest?

a. $0
b. $ 20,000
c. $ 34,000
d. $140,000

55. On April 1, 2003, George Hart, Jr. acquired a 25% interest in the Wilson, Hart and Company partnership by gift from his father. The partnership interest had been acquired by a $50,000 cash investment by Hart, Sr. on July 1, 1997. The tax basis of Hart, Sr.'s partnership interest was $60,000 at the time of the gift. Hart, Jr. sold the 25% partnership interest for $85,000 on December 17, 2003. What type and amount of capital gain should Hart, Jr. report on his 2003 tax return?

a. A long-term capital gain of $25,000.

b. A short-term capital gain of $25,000.
c. A long-term capital gain of $35,000.
d. A short-term capital gain of $35,000.

56. On June 30, 2003, James Roe sold his interest in the calendar-year partnership of Roe & Doe for $30,000. Roe's adjusted basis in Roe & Doe at June 30, 2003, was $7,500 before apportionment of any 2003 partnership income. Roe's distributive share of partnership income up to June 30, 2003, was $22,500. Roe acquired his interest in the partnership in 1997. How much long-term capital gain should Roe report in 2003 on the sale of his partnership interest?

a. $0
b. $15,000
c. $22,500
d. $30,000

57. Stone and Frazier decided to terminate the Woodwest Partnership as of December 31. On that date, Woodwest's balance sheet was as follows:

Cash	$2,000
Land (adjusted basis)	$2,000
Capital—Stone	$3,000
Capital—Frazier	$1,000

The fair market value of the equipment was $3,000. Frazier's outside basis in the partnership was $1,200. Upon liquidation, Frazier received $1,500 in cash. What gain should Frazier recognize?

a. $0
b. $250
c. $300
d. $500

58. Curry's adjusted basis in Vantage Partnership was $5,000 at the time he received a nonliquidating distribution of land. The land had an adjusted basis of $6,000 and a fair market value of $9,000 to Vantage. What was the amount of Curry's basis in the land?

a. $9,000
b. $6,000
c. $5,000
d. $1,000

59. Hart's adjusted basis in Best Partnership was $9,000 at the time he received the following nonliquidating distribution of partnership property:

Cash	$ 5,000
Land	
Adjusted basis	7,000
Fair market value	10,000

What was the amount of Hart's basis in the land?

a. $0
b. $ 4,000
c. $ 7,000
d. $10,000

60. Day's adjusted basis in LMN Partnership interest is $50,000. During the year Day received a nonliquidating distribution of $25,000 cash plus land with an adjusted basis of $15,000 to LMN, and a fair market value of $20,000. How much is Day's basis in the land?

a. $10,000
b. $15,000
c. $20,000
d. $25,000

Items 61 and 62 are based on the following:

The adjusted basis of Jody's partnership interest was $50,000 immediately before Jody received a current distribution of $20,000 cash and property with an adjusted basis to the partnership of $40,000 and a fair market value of $35,000.

61. What amount of taxable gain must Jody report as a result of this distribution?
- a. $0
- b. $ 5,000
- c. $10,000
- d. $20,000

62. What is Jody's basis in the distributed property?
- a. $0
- b. $30,000
- c. $35,000
- d. $40,000

63. On June 30, 2003, Berk retired from his partnership. At that time, his capital account was $50,000 and his share of the partnership's liabilities was $30,000. Berk's retirement payments consisted of being relieved of his share of the partnership liabilities and receipt of cash payments of $5,000 per month for eighteen months, commencing July 1, 2003. Assuming Berk makes no election with regard to the recognition of gain from the retirement payments, he should report income of

	2003	2004
a.	$13,333	$26,667
b.	20,000	20,000
c.	40,000	--
d.	--	40,000

64. The basis to a partner of property distributed "in kind" in complete liquidation of the partner's interest is the
- a. Adjusted basis of the partner's interest increased by any cash distributed to the partner in the same transaction.
- b. Adjusted basis of the partner's interest reduced by any cash distributed to the partner in the same transaction.
- c. Adjusted basis of the property to the partnership.
- d. Fair market value of the property.

Items 65 and 66 are based on the following data:

Mike Reed, a partner in Post Co., received the following distribution from Post:

	Post's basis	Fair market value
Cash	$11,000	$11,000
Inventory	5,000	12,500

Before this distribution, Reed's basis in Post was $25,000.

65. If this distribution were nonliquidating, Reed's basis for the inventory would be
- a. $14,000
- b. $12,500
- c. $ 5,000
- d. $ 1,500

66. If this distribution were in complete liquidation of Reed's interest in Post, Reed's recognized gain or loss resulting from the distribution would be
- a. $7,500 gain.
- b. $9,000 loss

- c. $1,500 loss.
- d. $0

67. In 1998, Lisa Bara acquired a one-third interest in Dee Associates, a partnership. In 2003, when Lisa's entire interest in the partnership was liquidated, Dee's assets consisted of the following: cash, $20,000 and tangible property with a basis of $46,000 and a fair market value of $40,000. Dee has no liabilities. Lisa's adjusted basis for her one-third interest was $22,000. Lisa received cash of $20,000 in liquidation of her entire interest. What was Lisa's recognized loss in 2003 on the liquidation of her interest in Dee?
- a. $0.
- b. $2,000 short-term capital loss.
- c. $2,000 long-term capital loss.
- d. $2,000 ordinary loss.

68. For tax purposes, a retiring partner who receives retirement payments ceases to be regarded as a partner
- a. On the last day of the taxable year in which the partner retires.
- b. On the last day of the particular month in which the partner retires.
- c. The day on which the partner retires.
- d. Only after the partner's entire interest in the partnership is liquidated.

69. John Albin is a retired partner of Brill & Crum, a personal service partnership. Albin has not rendered any services to Brill & Crum since his retirement in 2002. Under the provisions of Albin's retirement agreement, Brill & Crum is obligated to pay Albin 10% of the partnership's net income each year. In compliance with this agreement, Brill & Crum paid Albin $25,000 in 2003. How should Albin treat this $25,000?
- a. Not taxable.
- b. Ordinary income.
- c. Short-term capital gain.
- d. Long-term capital gain.

SIMULATION PROBLEMS

Simulation Problem 1   (5 to 10 minutes)

Situation		
	Partner's Basis	Concepts

During 2003, Adams, a general contractor, Brinks, an architect, and Carson, an interior decorator, formed the Dex Home Improvement General Partnership by contributing the assets below.

	Asset	Adjusted basis	Fair market value	% of partner share in capital, profits & losses
Adams	Cash	$40,000	$40,000	50%
Brinks	Land	$12,000	$21,000	20%
Carson	Inventory	$24,000	$24,000	30%

The land was a capital asset to Brinks, subject to a $5,000 mortgage, which was assumed by the partnership.

	Partner's Basis	
Situation		Concepts

For items 1 and 2, determine and select the initial basis of the partner's interest in Dex.

1. Brinks' initial basis in Dex is
    a. $21,000
    b. $12,000
    c. $ 8,000

2. Carson's initial basis in Dex is
    a. $25,500
    b. $24,000
    c. $19,000

During 2003, the Dex Partnership breaks even but decides to make distributions to each partner.

		Concepts
Situation	Partner's Basis	

For items 3 through 8, determine whether the statement is True or False.

		True	*False*
3.	A nonliquidating cash distribution may reduce the recipient partner's basis in his partnership interest below zero.	○	○
4.	A nonliquidating distribution of unappreciated inventory reduces the recipient partner's basis in his partnership interest.	○	○
5.	In a liquidating distribution of property other than money, where the partnership's basis of the distributed property exceeds the basis of the partner's interest, the partner's basis in the distributed property is limited to his predistribution basis in the partnership interest.	○	○
6.	Gain is recognized by the partner who receives a nonliquidating distribution of property, where the adjusted basis of the property exceeds his basis in the partnership interest before the distribution.	○	○
7.	In a nonliquidating distribution of inventory, where the partnership has no unrealized receivables or appreciated inventory, the basis of inventory that is distributed to a partner cannot exceed the inventory's adjusted basis to the partnership.	○	○
8.	The partnership's nonliquidating distribution of encumbered property to a partner who assumes the mortgage, does not affect the other partners' bases in their partnership interests.	○	○

Additional Simulation

Appendix A—Simulation 5 involves Partnership Taxation

MULTIPLE-CHOICE ANSWERS

1. d __ __	16. a __ __	31. c __ __	46. b __ __	61. a __ __
2. c __ __	17. a __ __	32. a __ __	47. c __ __	62. b __ __
3. c __ __	18. d __ __	33. a __ __	48. a __ __	63. d __ __
4. a __ __	19. c __ __	34. b __ __	49. a __ __	64. b __ __
5. c __ __	20. b __ __	35. a __ __	50. c __ __	65. c __ __
6. d __ __	21. c __ __	36. d __ __	51. a __ __	66. b __ __
7. b __ __	22. c __ __	37. c __ __	52. d __ __	67. c __ __
8. b __ __	23. d __ __	38. d __ __	53. a __ __	68. d __ __
9. d __ __	24. c __ __	39. a __ __	54. d __ __	69. b __ __
10. c __ __	25. b __ __	40. b __ __	55. a __ __	
11. d __ __	26. c __ __	41. d __ __	56. a __ __	
12. c __ __	27. a __ __	42. c __ __	57. c __ __	
13. b __ __	28. b __ __	43. b __ __	58. c __ __	
14. a __ __	29. c __ __	44. a __ __	59. b __ __	1st: __/69= __%
15. a __ __	30. b __ __	45. b __ __	60. b __ __	2nd: __/69= __%

MULTIPLE-CHOICE ANSWER EXPLANATIONS

B. Partnership Formation

1.   (d)   The requirement is to determine which statements are correct regarding Black's recognition of gain on transferring property with an adjusted basis of $250,000 in exchange for a 50% partnership interest. Generally, no gain is recognized when appreciated property is transferred to a partnership in exchange for a partnership interest. However, gain will be recognized if the transferred property is incumbered by a mortgage, and the partnership's assumption of the mortgage results in a decrease in the transferor's individual liabilities that exceeds the basis of the property transferred. Here, the basis of the property transferred is $250,000, and the net decrease in Black's individual liabilities is $50,000 (i.e., $100,000 x 50%), so no gain is recognized.

2.   (c)   The requirement is to determine the amount that must be included on Kelly's 2003 income tax return as the result of the receipt of a 10% partnership interest in exchange for services. A taxpayer must recognize ordinary income when a capital interest in a partnership is received as compensation for services rendered. The amount of ordinary income to be included on Kelly's 2003 return is the fair market value of the partnership interest received ($100,000 x 10% = $10,000).

3.   (c)   The requirement is to determine the amount that Hoff, a cash-basis taxpayer, should report as income for the services rendered to Ola Associates. A cash-basis taxpayer generally reports income when received, unless constructively received at an earlier date. The amount of income to be reported is the amount of money, plus the fair market value of other property received. In this case, Hoff must report a total of $32,000, which includes the $15,000 cash, the $10,000 FMV of the limited partnership interest, and the $7,000 FMV of the surveying equipment received. Note that since Hoff is a cash-basis taxpayer, he would not report income at the time that he billed Ola $40,000, nor would he be entitled to a bad debt deduction when he accepts $32,000 of consideration in full settlement of his $40,000 invoice.

4.   (a)   The requirement is to determine the amount of gain reportable in Gray's return as a result of Gray's contribution of property in exchange for a 40% partnership interest. Generally, no gain or loss is recognized on the contribution of property in exchange for a partnership interest.

Note that this nonrecognition rule applies even though the value of the partnership capital interest received (40% x $150,000 = $60,000) exceeds the fair market value of the property contributed ($30,000).

5.   (c)   The requirement is to determine the correct statement regarding the holding period for a partnership interest acquired in exchange for a contributed capital asset. The holding period for a partnership interest that is acquired through a contribution of property depends upon the nature of the contributed property. If the contributed property was a capital asset or Sec. 1231 asset to the contributing partner, the holding period of the acquired partnership interest includes the period of time that the capital asset or Sec. 1231 asset was held by the partner. For all other contributed property, a partner's holding period for a partnership interest begins when the partnership interest is acquired.

6.   (d)   The requirement is to determine the amount of gain recognized on the exchange of stock for a partnership interest. Generally no gain or loss is recognized on the transfer of property to a partnership in exchange for a partnership interest. Since Carr's gain is not recognized, there will be a carryover basis of $30,000 for the stock to the partnership, and Carr will have a $30,000 basis for the 25% partnership interest received.

7.   (b)   The requirement is to determine the holding period for property acquired by a partnership as a contribution to the contributing partner's capital account. Generally no gain or loss is recognized on the contribution of property to a partnership in exchange for a capital interest. Since the partnership's basis for the contributed property is determined by reference to the contributing partner's former basis for the property (i.e., a transferred basis), the partnership's holding period includes the period during which the property was held by the contributing partner.

8.   (b)   The requirement is to determine Elton's basis for his 25% interest in the Bredbo partnership. Since Elton received a capital interest with a FMV of $50,000 in exchange for property worth $40,000 and services, Elton must recognize compensation income of $10,000 ($50,000 − $40,000) on the transfer of services for a capital interest. Thus, Elton's basis for his partnership interest consists of the $25,000 basis of assets transferred plus the $10,000 of income recognized on the transfer of services, a total of $35,000.

9. **(d)** The requirement is to determine the maximum amount of filing fees and accounting fees that Basic could deduct on the 2003 partnership return. The filing fees incident to the creation of the partnership are *organizational expenditures* that can be amortized over not less than sixty months beginning with the month that business begins if an election is made with the partnership's first tax return. Since Basic is a calendar-year partnership and began business in February, there would be eleven months of amortization for 2003, resulting in a maximum deduction of $3,600 x 11/60 = $660. The accounting fees to prepare the representations in offering materials are considered syndication fees. *Syndication fees* include the costs connected with the issuing and marketing of partnership interests such as commissions, professional fees, and printing costs. These costs must be capitalized and can neither be amortized nor depreciated.

C. Partnership Income and Loss

10. **(c)** The requirement is to determine the amount of loss that Thompson can deduct as a result of his interest in the Starlight Partnership. A partner's distributive share of partnership losses is generally deductible to the extent of the tax basis for the partner's partnership interest at the end of the year. All positive basis adjustments and all reductions for distributions must be taken into account before determining the amount of deductible loss. Here, Thompson's basis of $60,000 at the beginning of the year would be increased by the $15,000 of net long-term capital gain, reduced by the $20,000 cash distribution, to $55,000. As a result, Thompson's deduction of the ordinary loss for the current year is limited to $55,000 which reduces the basis for his partnership interest to zero. He cannot deduct the remaining $10,000 of ordinary loss currently, but will carry it forward and deduct it when he has sufficient basis for his partnership interest.

11. **(d)** The requirement is to determine the item that is deductible in the computation of the ordinary income of a partnership. Guaranteed payments to partners are always deductible in computing a partnership's ordinary income. Contributions to recognized charities and short-term capital losses cannot be deducted in computing a partnership's ordinary income because they are subject to special limitations and must be separately passed through so that any applicable limitations can be applied at the partner level. Similarly, dividends are an item of portfolio income and must be separately passed through to partners in order to retain its character as portfolio income when reported on partners' returns.

12. **(c)** The requirement is to determine whether the at-risk and passive activity loss limitations apply in determining a partner's deduction for that partner's share of partnership losses. A partner's distributive share of partnership losses is generally deductible by the partner to the extent of the partner's basis in the partnership at the end of the taxable year. Additionally, the deductibility of partnership losses is limited to the amount of the partner's at-risk basis, and will also be subject to the passive activity loss limitations if they are applicable. Note that the at-risk and passive activity loss limitations apply at the partner level, rather than at the partnership level.

13. **(b)** The requirement is to determine the amount to be reported as ordinary income on the partnership's return given partnership book income of $100,000. The $60,000 of guaranteed payments to partners were deducted in computing partnership book income and are also deductible in computing partnership ordinary income. However, the $1,000 charitable contribution deducted in arriving at partnership book income must be separately passed through to partners on Schedule K-1 and cannot be deducted in computing partnership ordinary income. Thus, the partnership's ordinary income is $100,000 + $1,000 = $101,000.

14. **(a)** The requirement is to determine the amount and type of partnership loss to be deducted on Clark's individual return. Since a partnership functions as a pass-through entity, the nature of a loss as an ordinary loss is maintained when passed through to partners. However, the amount of partnership loss that can be deducted by a partner is limited to a partner's tax basis in the partnership at the end of the partnership taxable year. Thus, Clark's distributive share of the ordinary loss ($42,000) is only deductible to the extent of $36,000. The remaining $6,000 of loss would be carried forward by Clark and could be deducted after his partnership basis has been increased.

15. **(a)** The requirement is to determine the ordinary income of the partnership. Income from operations is considered ordinary income. The net rental income and the dividends from foreign corporations are separately allocated to partners and must be excluded from the computation of the partnership's ordinary income. Tax-exempt income remains tax-exempt and must also be excluded from the computation of ordinary income. Thus, ordinary income only consists of the income from operations of $156,000.

D. Partnership Agreements

16. **(a)** The requirement is to determine the correct statement(s) concerning agreements for guaranteed payments. Guaranteed payments are payments made to a partner for services or for the use of capital if the payments are determined *without regard to the amount of partnership income.* Guaranteed payments are deductible by a partnership in computing its ordinary income or loss from trade or business activities, and must be reported as self-employment income by the partner receiving payment. A payment that represents a 25% interest in partnership profits could not be classified as a guaranteed payment because the payment is conditioned on the partnership having profits.

17. **(a)** The requirement is to determine the amount of income that Chris should report as a result of her 25% partnership interest. A partnership is a pass-through entity and its items of income and deduction pass through to be reported on partners' returns even though not distributed. The amount to be reported by Chris consists of her guaranteed payment, plus her 25% share of the partnership's business income and capital gains. Since Chris's $20,000 guaranteed payment is for deductible services rendered to the partnership, it must be subtracted from the partnership's net business income before guaranteed payments of $80,000 to determine the amount of net business income to be allocated among partners. Chris's reportable income from the partnership includes

Guaranteed payment	$20,000
Business income [($80,000 – $20,000) x 25%]	15,000
Net long-term capital gain ($10,000 x 25%)	2,500
	$37,500

18. (d) The requirement is to determine Arch's share of the JK Partnership's ordinary income for 2003. A partnership functions as a pass-through entity and its items of income and deduction are passed through to partners according to their profit and loss sharing ratios, which may differ from the ratios used to divide capital. Here, Arch's distributive share of the partnership's ordinary income is $40,000 x 75% = $30,000. Note that Arch will be taxed on his $30,000 distributive share of ordinary income even though only $5,000 was distributed to him.

19. (c) The requirement is to determine whether the statements regarding partners' guaranteed payments are correct. Guaranteed payments made by a partnership to partners for services rendered are an ordinary deduction in computing a partnership's ordinary income or loss from trade or business activities on page 1 of Form 1065. Partners must report the receipt of guaranteed payments as ordinary income (self-employment income) and that is why the payments also must be separately listed on Schedule K and Schedule K-1.

20. (b) The requirement is to determine the correct statement regarding a partnership's election of a depreciation method. The method used to depreciate partnership property is an election made by the partnership and may be any method approved by the IRS. The partnership is not restricted to using the same method as used by its "principal partner." Since the election is made at the partnership level, and not by each individual partner, partners are bound by whatever depreciation method that the partnership elects to use.

21. (c) The requirement is to determine the correct statement regarding guaranteed payments to partners. Guaranteed payments are payments made to partners for their services or for the use of capital without regard to the amount of the partnership's income. Guaranteed payments are deductible by the partnership in computing its ordinary income or loss from trade of business activities, and must be reported as self-employment income by the partners receiving payment.

22. (c) The requirement is to determine the total amount of partnership income that is taxable to Dale in 2003. A partnership functions as a pass-through entity and its items of income and deduction are passed through to partners on the last day of the partnership's taxable year. Income and deduction items pass through to be reported by partners even though not actually distributed during the year. Here, Dale is taxed on his $50,000 distributive share of partnership income for 2003, even though $23,000 was not received until 2004. The $10,000 interest-free loan does not effect the pass-through of income for 2003, and the $10,000 offset against Dale's distributive share of partnership income for 2004 will not effect the pass-through of that income in 2003.

23. (d) The requirement is to determine the amount of the partnership's capital gain from the sale of securities to be allocated to Carr. Normally, the entire amount of precontribution gain would be allocated to Carr. However, in this case the allocation to Carr is limited to the partnership's

recognized gain resulting from the sale, $47,000 selling price – $35,000 basis = $12,000.

24. (c) The requirement is to determine the amount that Gilroy should report for 2003 as total income from the partnership. Gilroy's income will consist of his share of the partnership's ordinary income for the fiscal year ending June 30, 2003 (the partnership year that ends within his year), plus the twelve monthly guaranteed payments that he received for that period of time.

25% x $88,000	=	$22,000
12 x $ 1,000	=	12,000
Total income	=	$34,000

25. (b) The requirement is to determine Allan's distributive share of the partnership income. In a family partnership, services performed by family members must first be reasonably compensated before income is allocated according to the capital interests of the partners. Since Edward's services were worth $40,000, Allan's distributive share of partnership income is ($100,000 – $40,000) x 50% = $30,000.

26. (c) The requirement is to determine Curry's initial basis for the 50% partnership interest received in exchange for a contribution of property subject to a $12,000 mortgage that was assumed by the partnership. Generally, no gain or loss is recognized on the contribution of property in exchange for a partnership interest. As a result, Curry's initial basis for the partnership interest received consists of the $30,000 adjusted basis of the land contributed to the partnership, less the net reduction in Curry's individual liability resulting from the partnership's assumption of the $12,000 mortgage. Since Curry received a 50% partnership interest, the net reduction in Curry's individual liability is $12,000 x 50% = $6,000. As a result, Curry's basis for the partnership interest is $30,000 – $6,000 = $24,000.

27. (a) The requirement is to determine Jones' initial basis for the 50% partnership interest received in exchange for a contribution of cash of $45,000. Since partners are individually liable for their share of partnership liabilities, an increase in partnership liabilities increases a partner's basis in the partnership by the partner's share of the increase. Jones' initial basis consists of the $45,000 of cash contributed, increased by the increase in Jones' individual liability resulting from the partnership's assumption of Curry's mortgage ($12,000 x 50% = $6,000). Thus, Jones' initial basis for the partnership interest is $45,000 + $6,000 = $51,000.

28. (b) The requirement is to determine the total amount includible in Flagg's 2003 tax return as a result of Flagg's 50% interest in the Decor Partnership. Decor's net business income of $45,000 would be reduced by the guaranteed payment of $7,500, resulting in $37,500 of ordinary income that would pass through to be reported on partners' returns. Here, Flagg's share of the includible income would be $37,500 x 50% = $18,750.

29. (c) The requirement is to determine Miles's tax basis for his 50% interest in the Decor Partnership on December 31, 2003. The basis for a partner's partnership interest is increased by the partner's distributive share of partnership income that is taxed to the partner. Here, Decor's net business income of $45,000 would be reduced by the guaranteed payment of $7,500, resulting in $37,500 of ordinary income that would pass through to be reported on partners' returns and increase the basis of their partnership interests. Here, Miles's beginning tax basis for the partnership interest of $200,000 would be increased by Miles's distributive share of ordinary income ($37,500 x 50% = $18,750), to $218,750.

30. **(b)** The requirement is to determine the net effect(s) of the $16,000 guaranteed payment made to Peters by the Spano Partnership who reported an operating loss of $70,000 before deducting the guaranteed payment. A guaranteed payment is a partnership payment made to a partner for services or for the use of capital if the payment is determined without regard to the amount of partnership income. A guaranteed payment is deductible by a partnership in computing its ordinary income or loss from trade or business activities and must be reported as self-employment income by the partner receiving the payment, thereby increasing Peters' ordinary income by $16,000. However, since Peters has only a one-third interest in the Spano Partnership, the $16,000 of guaranteed payment deducted by Spano would have the effect of reducing Peters' tax basis in Spano by only one-third of $16,000.

E. Partner's Basis in Partnership

31. **(c)** The requirement is to determine the basis for Dean's 25% partnership interest at December 31, 2003. A partner's basis for a partnership interest is increased or decreased by the partner's distributive share of all partnership items. Basis is increased by the partner's distributive share of all income items (including tax-exempt income) and is decreased by all loss and deduction items (including nondeductible items) and distributions received from the partnership. In this case, Dean's beginning basis of $20,000 would be increased by the pass-through of his distributive share of the partnership's ordinary income ($40,000 x 25% = $10,000) and municipal bond interest income ($12,000 x 25% = $3,000), and would be decreased by the $8,000 cash nonliquidating distribution that he received.

32. **(a)** The requirement is to determine the effect of a $40,000 increase in partnership liabilities on the basis for Smith's 40% partnership interest. Since partners are individually liable for their share of partnership liabilities, a change in the amount of partnership liabilities affects a partner's basis for a partnership interest. When partnership liabilities increase, it is effectively treated as if each partner individually borrowed money and then made a capital contribution of the borrowed amount. As a result, an increase in partnership liabilities increases each partner's basis in the partnership by each partner's share of the increase. Here, Smith's basis is increased by his 40% share of the mortgage (40% x $40,000 = $16,000).

33. **(a)** The requirement is to determine Gray's tax basis for a 50% interest in the Fabco Partnership. The basis for a partner's partnership interest is increased by the partner's distributive share of all partnership items of income and is decreased by the partner's distributive share of all loss and deduction items. Here, Gray's beginning basis of $5,000 would be increased by Gray's 50% distributive share of ordinary income ($10,000), tax-exempt income ($4,000), and portfolio income ($2,000), resulting in an ending basis of $21,000 for Gray's Fabco partnership interest.

34. **(b)** The requirement is to determine the net effect of the two transactions on Kane's tax basis for his Maze partnership interest. A partner's basis for a partnership interest consists of the partner's capital account plus the partner's share of partnership liabilities. A decrease in a partner's share of partnership liabilities is considered to be a deemed distribution of money and reduces a partner's basis for the partnership interest. Here, Kane's partnership interest was reduced from 25% to 20% on January 2, resulting in a reduction in Kane's share of liabilities of 5% x $300,000 = $15,000. Subsequently, on April 1, when there was a $100,000 repayment of partnership loans, there was a further reduction in Kane's share of partnership liabilities of 20% x $100,000 = $20,000. Thus, the net effect of the reduction of Kane's partnership interest to 20% from 25%, and the repayment of $100,000 of partnership liabilities would be to reduce Kane's basis for the partnership interest by $15,000 + $20,000 = $35,000.

35. **(a)** The requirement is to determine the original basis of Lee's partnership interest that was received as an inheritance from Dale. The basis of property received from a decedent is generally its fair market value as of date of death. Since fair market value on the date of Dale's death was used for estate tax purposes, Lee's original basis is $70,000.

36. **(d)** The requirement is to determine whether cash paid by a transferee, and the transferee's share of partnership liabilities are to be included in computing the basis of a partner's interest acquired from another partner. When an existing partner sells a partnership interest, the consideration received by the transferor partner, and the basis of the transferee's partnership interest includes both the cash actually paid by the transferee to the transferor, as well as the transferee's assumption of the transferor's share of partnership liabilities.

37. **(c)** The requirement is to determine the basis of each partner's interest in Arosa at December 31, 2003. Since there are two equal partners, each partner's adjusted basis in Arosa of $40,000 on January 1, 2003, would be increased by 50% of the $60,000 loan and would be decreased by 50% of the $10,000 operating loss. Thus, each partner's basis in Arosa at December 31, 2003, would be $40,000 + $30,000 liability – $5,000 loss = $65,000.

F. Transactions with Controlled Partnerships

38. **(d)** The requirement is to determine the amount of long-term capital loss recognized by Lydia from the sale of stock to Agee & Nolan. A loss is disallowed if incurred in a transaction between a partnership and a person owning (directly or constructively) more than a 50% capital or profits interest. Although Lydia directly owns only a 50% partnership interest, she constructively owns her sister's 50% partnership interest. Since Lydia directly and constructively has a 100% partnership interest, her $5,000 loss is disallowed.

39. **(a)** The requirement is to determine the amount to be reported as short-term capital gain on Cole's sale of stock to the partnership. If a person engages in a transaction with a partnership other than as a partner of such partnership, any resulting gain is generally recognized just as if the transaction had occurred with a nonpartner. Here, Cole's gain of $16,000 – $10,000 = $6,000 is fully recognized. Since the stock was not held for more than twelve months, Cole's $6,000 gain is treated as a short-term capital gain.

40. (b)   The requirement is to determine the amount and nature of Kay's gain from the sale of the lamp to Admor. A gain that is recognized on a sale of property between a partnership and a person owning a more than 50% partnership interest will be treated as ordinary income if the property is not a capital asset in the hands of the transferee. Although Kay has a 55% partnership interest, the partnership purchased the lamp as an investment (i.e., a capital asset), and Kay's gain will solely depend on how she held the lamp. Since she used the lamp for personal use, Kay has a $5,000 – $1,000 = $4,000 long-term capital gain.

41. (d)   The requirement is to determine Peel's distributive share of ordinary income from the partnership. Although the $6,000 loss that was deducted in arriving at the partnership's net income would also be deductible for tax purposes, it must be separately passed through to partners because it is a Sec. 1231 loss. Thus, the $6,000 loss must be added back to the $94,000 of partnership net income and results in partnership ordinary income of $100,000. Peel's share is $100,000 x 50% = $50,000.

G.   Taxable Year of Partnership

42. (c)   The requirement is to determine the correct statement regarding a partnership's eligibility to make a Sec. 444 election. A partnership must generally adopt the same taxable year as used by its one or more partners owning an aggregate interest of more than 50% in partnership profits and capital. However, under Sec. 444, a partnership can instead elect to adopt a fiscal year that does not result in a deferral period of longer than three months. The deferral period is the number of months between the end of its selected year and the year that it generally would be required to adopt. For example, a partnership that otherwise would be required to adopt a taxable year ending December 31, could elect to adopt a fiscal year ending September 30. The deferral period would be the months of October, November, and December. The partnership is not required to be a limited partnership, be a member of tiered structure, or have less than seventy-five partners.

43. (b)   The requirement is to determine the correct statement regarding a partnership's tax year. A partnership must generally determine its taxable year in the following order: (1) it must adopt the taxable year used by its one or more partners owning an aggregate interest of more than 50% in profits and capital; (2) if partners owning a more than 50% interest in profits and capital do not have the same year-end, the partnership must adopt the same taxable year as used by all of its principal partners; and (3) if principal partners have different taxable years, the partnership must adopt the taxable year that results in the least aggregate deferral of income to partners.

A different taxable year other than the year determined above can be used by a partnership if a valid business purpose can be established and IRS permission is received. Alternatively, a partnership can elect to use a tax year (other than one required under the general rules in the first paragraph), if the election does not result in a deferral of income of more than three months. The deferral period is the number of months between the close of the elected tax year and the close of the year that would otherwise be required under the general rules. Thus, a partnership that would otherwise

be required to adopt a tax year ending December 31 could elect to adopt a fiscal year ending September 30 (three-month deferral), October 31 (two-month deferral), or November 30 (one-month deferral). Note that a partnership that makes this election must make "required payments" which are in the nature of refundable, noninterest-bearing deposits that are intended to compensate the Treasury for the revenue lost as a result of the deferral period.

44. (a)   A newly formed partnership must adopt the same taxable year as is used by its partners owning a more than 50% interest in profits and capital. If partners owning more than 50% do not have the same taxable year, a partnership must adopt the same taxable year as used by all of its principal partners (i.e., partners with a 5% or more interest in capital and profits). If its principal partners have different taxable years, a partnership must adopt the tax year that results in the least aggregate deferral of income to partners.

45. (b)   The requirement is to determine the distributive shares of partnership income for the partnership fiscal year ended June 30, 2003, to be included in gross income by Aster, Brill, Estate of Brill, Clark, and Dexter. Clark was a partner for the entire year and is taxed on his distributive 1/3 share ($45,000 x 1/3 = $15,000). Since Aster sold his entire partnership interest to Dexter, the partnership tax year closes with respect to Aster on February 28. As a result, Aster's distributive share is $45,000 x 1/3 x 8/12 = $10,000. Dexter's distributive share is $45,000 x 1/3 / 4/12 = $5,000.

Additionally, a partnership tax year closes with respect to a deceased partner as of date of death. Since Brill died on March 31, the distributive share to be included in Brill's 2003 Form 1040 would be $45,000 x 1/3 x 9/12 = $11,250. Since Brill's estate held his partnership interest for the remainder of the year, the estate's distributive share of income is $45,000 x 1/3 x 3/12 = $3,750.

I.   Termination or Continuation of Partnership

46. (b)   The requirement is to determine the correct statement regarding the termination of the Able Partnership. A partnership is terminated for tax purposes when there is a sale or exchange of 50% or more of the total interests in partnership capital and profits within any twelve-month period. Since Poe sold her 30% interest on February 4, 2003, and Dean sold his 25% partnership interest on December 20, 2003, there has been a sale of 55% of the total interests within a twelve-month period and the Able Partnership is terminated on December 20, 2003.

47. (c)   The requirement is to determine which statements are correct concerning the termination of a partnership. A partnership will terminate when there is a sale of 50% or more of the total interests in partnership capital and profits within any twelve-month period. When this occurs, there is a deemed distribution of assets to the remaining partners and the purchaser, and a hypothetical recontribution of these same assets to a new partnership.

48. (a)   The requirement is to determine the date on which the partnership terminated for tax purposes. The partnership was terminated on September 18, 2003, the date on which Cobb and Danver sold their partnership interests to Frank, since on that date there was a sale of 50% or more of the total interests in partnership capital and profit.

49.   (a)   The requirement is to determine the correct statement concerning the division of Partnership Abel, Benz, Clark, & Day into two partnerships. Following the division of a partnership, a resulting partnership is deemed to be a continuation of the prior partnership if the resulting partnership's partners had a more than 50% interest in the prior partnership. Here, as a result of the division, Partnership Abel & Benz is considered to be a continuation of the prior partnership because its partners (Abel and Benz) owned more than 50% of the interests in the prior partnership (i.e., Abel 40% and Benz 20%).

50.   (c)   The requirement is to determine under which circumstances a partnership, other than an electing large partnership, is considered terminated for income tax purposes. A partnership will be terminated when (1) there are no longer at least two partners, (2) no part of any business, financial operation, or venture of the partnership continues to be carried on by any of its partners in a partnership, or (3) within a twelve-month period there is a sale or exchange of 50% or more of the total interest in partnership capital and profits.

51.   (a)   The requirement is to determine the date on which the partnership was terminated. A partnership generally does not terminate for tax purposes upon the death of a partner, since the deceased partner's estate or successor in interest continues to share in partnership profits and losses. However, the Beck and Crocker Partnership was terminated when Beck's entire partnership interest was liquidated on April 30, 2003, since there no longer were at least two partners and the business ceased to exist as a partnership.

J.   Sale of a Partnership Interest

52.   (d)   The requirement is to determine the amount and character of gain or loss recognized on the sale of Clark's partnership interest. A partnership interest is a capital asset and a sale generally results in capital gain or loss, except that ordinary income must be reported to the extent of the selling partner's share of unrealized receivables and appreciated inventory. Here, Clark realized $55,000 from the sale of his partnership interest ($30,000 cash + relief from his $25,000 share of partnership liabilities). Since the partnership had no unrealized receivables or appreciated inventory and the basis of Clark's interest was $40,000, Clark realized a capital gain of $55,000 – $40,000 = $15,000 from the sale.

53.   (a)   The requirement is to determine the total amount realized by Carr on the sale of his partnership interest. The total amount realized consists of the amount of cash received plus the buyer's assumption of Carr's share of partnership liabilities. Thus, the total amount realized is $154,000 + ($60,000 x 1/3) = $174,000.

54.   (d)   The requirement is to determine the amount of ordinary income that Carr should report on the sale of his partnership interest. Although the sale of a partnership interest generally results in capital gain or loss, ordinary income must be recognized to the extent of the selling partner's share of unrealized receivables and appreciated inventory. Here, Carr must report ordinary income to the extent of his 1/3 share of the unrealized accounts receivable of $420,000, or $140,000.

55.   (a)   The requirement is to determine the amount and type of capital gain to be reported by Hart, Jr. from the sale

of his partnership interest. Since the partnership interest was acquired by gift from Hart, Sr., Jr.'s basis would be the same as Sr.'s basis at date of gift, $60,000. Since Jr.'s basis is determined from Sr.'s basis, Jr.'s holding period includes the period the partnership interest was held by Sr. Thus, Hart, Jr. will report a LTCG of $85,000 – $60,000 = $25,000.

56.   (a)   The requirement is to determine the amount of LTCG to be reported by Roe on the sale of his partnership interest. Roe's basis for his partnership interest of $7,500 must first be increased by his $22,500 distributive share of partnership income, to $30,000. Since the selling price also was $30,000, Roe will report no gain or loss on the sale of his partnership interest.

K.   Pro Rata Distributions from Partnership

57.   (c)   The requirement is to determine Frazier's recognized gain resulting from the cash received in liquidation of his partnership interest. A distributee partner will recognize any realized gain or loss resulting from the complete liquidation of the partner's interest if only cash is received. Since Frazier's basis for his partnership interest was $1,200 and he received $1,500 cash, Frazier must recognize a $300 capital gain.

58.   (c)   The requirement is to determine the basis for land acquired in a nonliquidating partnership distribution. Generally, no gain or loss is recognized on the distribution of partnership property to a partner. As a result, the partner's basis for distributed property is generally the same as the partnership's former basis for the property (a transferred basis). However, since the distribution cannot reduce the basis for the partner's partnership interest below zero, the distributed property's basis to the partner is limited to the partner's basis for the partnership interest before the distribution. In this case, Curry's basis for the land will be limited to the $5,000 basis for his partnership interest before the distribution.

59.   (b)   The requirement is to determine Hart's basis for the land received in a nonliquidating partnership distribution. If both cash and noncash property are received in a single distribution, the basis for the partner's partnership interest is first reduced by the cash, before being reduced by noncash property. Although a partner's basis for noncash property is generally the same as the partnership's basis for the property ($7,000 in this case), the partner's basis for distributed property will be limited to the partner's basis for the partnership interest reduced by any cash received in the same distribution. Here, the $9,000 basis of Hart's partnership interest is first reduced by the $5,000 cash received, with the remaining basis of $4,000 allocated as basis for the land received.

60.   (b)   The requirement is to determine Day's basis in the land received in a nonliquidating distribution. If both cash and noncash property are received in a single distribution, the basis for the partner's partnership interest is first reduced by the cash, before the noncash property. Since partnership distributions are generally nontaxable, a distributee partner's basis for distributed property is generally the same as the partnership's former basis for the property (a transferred basis). Here, the basis of Day's partnership interest of $50,000 is first reduced by the $25,000 of cash received, and then reduced by the $15,000 adjusted basis of the land, to $10,000. Day's basis for the land received is $15,000.

61. (a)   The requirement is to determine the amount of taxable gain that Jody must report as the result of a current distribution of cash and property from her partnership. No loss can be recognized as a result of a proportionate current (nonliquidating) distribution, and gain will be recognized only if the amount of cash received exceeds the basis for the partner's partnership interest. If both cash and noncash property are received in a single distribution, the basis for the partner's interest is first reduced by the cash, before noncash property. Since the $20,000 cash received does not exceed the $50,000 basis of Jody's partnership interest immediately before the distribution, no gain is recognized.

62. (b)   The requirement is to determine the basis of property received in a current distribution. If both cash and noncash property are received in a single distribution, the basis for the partner's partnership interest is first reduced by the cash, before being reduced by noncash property. Although a partner's basis for distributed property is generally the same as the partnership's basis for the property ($40,000 in this case), the partner's basis for distributed property will be limited to the partner's basis for the partnership interest reduced by any money received in the same distribution. Here, the $50,000 basis of Jody's partnership interest is first reduced by the $20,000 of cash received, with the remaining basis of $30,000 allocated as the basis for the property received.

63. (d)   The requirement is to determine the amount of income from the receipt of retirement payments to be reported by Berk in 2003 and 2004. Payments to a retiring partner are generally treated as received in exchange for the partner's interest in partnership property. As such, they are generally treated under the rules that apply to liquidating distributions. Retirement payments are not deductible by the partnership as guaranteed payments and are not treated as distributive shares of income. Under the rules for liquidating distributions, the $5,000 per month cash payments are treated as a reduction of the basis for Berk's partnership interest, and result in gain to the extent in excess of basis. Berk's $80,000 basis for his partnership interest ($50,000 capital + $30,000 share of liabilities) would first be reduced by the relief from $30,000 of liabilities to $50,000. Next, the $30,000 of cash payments received during 2002 (6 x $5,000) would reduce Berk's basis to $20,000 and result in no gain to be reported for 2003. Finally, the $60,000 of payments for 2004 (12 x $5,000) would exceed his remaining basis and result in Berk's reporting of $40,000 of capital gain for 2004.

64. (b)   The requirement is to determine the correct statement regarding the basis of property to a partner that is distributed "in-kind" in complete liquidation of the partner's interest. In a complete liquidation of a partner's interest in a partnership, the in-kind property distributed will have a basis equal to the adjusted basis of the partner's partnership interest reduced by any money received in the same distribution. Generally, in a liquidating distribution, the basis for a partnership interest is (1) first reduced by the amount of money received, (2) then reduced by the partnership's basis for any unrealized receivables and inventory received, (3) with any remaining basis for the partnership interest allocated to other

property received in proportion to their adjusted bases (not FMV) to the partnership.

65. (c)   The requirement is to determine the basis of the inventory received in a nonliquidating partnership distribution of cash and inventory. Here, the $25,000 basis of Reed's partnership interest would first be reduced by the $11,000 of cash received, and then reduced by the $5,000 basis of the inventory to $9,000. Reed's basis for the inventory received is $5,000.

66. (b)   The requirement is to determine Reed's recognized gain or loss resulting from the cash and inventory received in complete liquidation of Reed's partnership interest. A distributee partner can recognize loss only upon the complete liquidation of the partner's interest through the receipt of only money, unrealized receivables, or inventory. Since Reed received only money and inventory, the amount of recognized loss is the $9,000 difference between the $25,000 basis of his partnership interest and the $11,000 of cash and $5,000 basis for the inventory received.

67. (c)   The requirement is to determine the amount of loss recognized by Lisa on the complete liquidation of her one-third partnership interest. A distributee partner can recognize loss only upon the complete liquidation of the partner's interest through receipt of only money, unrealized receivables, or inventory. Since Lisa only received cash, the amount of recognized loss is the $2,000 difference between the $22,000 adjusted basis of her partnership interest and the $20,000 of cash received. Since a partnership interest is a capital asset and Lisa acquired her one-third interest in 1998, Lisa has a $2,000 long-term capital loss.

68. (d)   The requirement is to determine when a retiring partner who receives retirement payments ceases to be regarded as a partner. A retiring partner continues to be a partner for income tax purposes until the partner's entire interest has been completely liquidated through distributions or payments.

69. (b)   The requirement is to determine the treatment for the payments received by Albin. Payments made by a personal service partnership to a retired partner that are determined by partnership income are distributive shares of partnership income, regardless of the period over which they are paid. Thus, they are taxable to Albin as ordinary income.

SOLUTIONS TO SIMULATION PROBLEM

Problem 1

1.   (c) The requirement is to determine Brinks' initial basis for his 20% partnership interest received in exchange for a contribution of property subject to a $5,000 mortgage. Generally, no gain or loss is recognized on the contribution of property in exchange for a partnership interest. As a result, Brinks' initial basis for the partnership interest received consists of the $12,000 basis of the land contributed to the partnership, less the net reduction in Brinks' individual liability resulting from the partnership's assumption of the mortgage. Since Brinks received a 20% partnership interest, the net reduction in Brinks' individual liability equals $5,000 x 80% = $4,000. As a result, Brinks' basis for the partnership interest is $12,000 – $4,000 = $8,000.

2.   (a) The requirement is to determine Carson's initial basis for his 30% partnership interest received in exchange for a contribution of inventory. Since partners are individually liable for their share of partnership liabilities, an increase in partnership liabilities increases a partner's basis in the partnership by the partner's share of the increase. Carson's initial basis is the $24,000 adjusted basis of the inventory contributed, increased by the increase in his individual liability resulting from the partnership's assumption of Brinks' mortgage ($5,000 x 30% = $1,500). Thus, Carson's initial basis for the partnership interest is $24,000 + $1,500 = $25,500.

		True	*False*
3.	A nonliquidating cash distribution may reduce the recipient partner's basis in his partnership interest below zero.	○	●
4.	A nonliquidating distribution of unappreciated inventory reduces the recipient partner's basis in his partnership interest.	●	○
5.	In a liquidating distribution of property other than money, where the partnership's basis of the distributed property exceeds the basis of the partner's interest, the partner's basis in the distributed property is limited to his predistribution basis in the partnership interest.	●	○
6.	Gain is recognized by the partner who receives a nonliquidating distribution of property, where the adjusted basis of the property exceeds his basis in the partnership interest before the distribution.	○	●
7.	In a nonliquidating distribution of inventory, where the partnership has no unrealized receivables or appreciated inventory, the basis of inventory that is distributed to a partner cannot exceed the inventory's adjusted basis to the partnership.	●	○
8.	The partnership's nonliquidating distribution of encumbered property to a partner who assumes the mortgage, does not affect the other partners' bases in their partnership interests.	○	●

Explanation of solutions

3.   (F) A partner can never have a negative basis for a partnership interest. Partnership distributions can only reduce a partner's basis to zero.

4.   (T) Partnership distributions are generally nontaxable and reduce the recipient partner's basis by the adjusted basis of the property distributed.

5.   (T) A liquidating distribution of property other than money generally does not cause the distributee partner to recognize gain. As a result, the distributee partner's basis in the distributed property is limited to the partner's predistribution basis for the partnership interest.

6.   (F) Gain is recognized by a distributee partner only if the amount of money distributed exceeds the partner's predistribution basis for the partnership interest. Distributions of property other than money never result in the recognition of gain by the distributee partner.

7.   (T) Generally, a nonliquidating distribution of inventory is not taxable, and the adjusted basis for the inventory carries over to the distributee partner. As a result, the distributee partner's basis for the inventory cannot exceed the inventory's adjusted basis to the partnership.

8.   (F) Since partners are individually liable for partnership liabilities, a decrease in partnership liabilities will decrease the basis for a partner's partnership interest by the partner's share of the decrease. Thus, if a distributee partner assumes a mortgage on encumbered property, the other partners' bases in their partnership interests will be decreased by their share of the decrease in partnership liabilities.

CORPORATIONS

Corporations are separate taxable entities, organized under state law. Although corporations may have many of the same income and deduction items as individuals, corporations are taxed at different rates and some tax rules are applied differently. There also are special provisions applicable to transfers of property to a corporation, and issuance of stock.

A. Transfers to a Controlled Corporation (Sec. 351)

1. **No gain or loss** is recognized if property is transferred to a corporation solely in exchange for stock and immediately after the exchange those persons transferring property control the corporation.

   a. **Property** includes everything but services.

   b. **Control** means ownership of at least 80% of the total combined voting power and 80% of each class of nonvoting stock.

   c. **Receipt of boot** (e.g., cash, short-term notes, securities, etc.) will cause recognition of gain (but not loss).

      (1) Corporation's assumption of liabilities is treated as boot only if there is a tax avoidance purpose, or no business purpose.

      (2) Shareholder recognizes gain if liabilities assumed by corporation exceed the total basis of property transferred by the shareholder.

2. **Shareholder's basis for stock** = Adjusted basis of property transferred

   a. + Gain recognized

   b. – Boot received (assumption of liability always treated as boot for purposes of determining stock basis)

3. **Corporation's basis for property** = Transferor's adjusted basis + Gain recognized to transferor.

   EXAMPLE: Individuals A, B, & C form ABC Corp. and make the following transfer to their corporation:

Item transferred	A	B	C
Property – FMV	$10,000	$8,000	$ --
– Adjusted basis	1,500	3,000	--
Liability assumed by ABC Corp.	2,000	--	--
Services	--	--	1,000
Consideration received			
Stock (FMV)	$ 8,000	$7,600	$1,000
Two-year note (FMV)	--	400	--
Gain recognized to shareholder	$ 500[a]	$ 400[b]	$1,000[c]
Basis of stock received	--	3,000	1,000
Basis of property to corp.	2,000	3,400	1,000[d]

   a   Liability in excess of basis: $2,000 – $1,500 = $500
   b   Assumes B elects out of the installment method
   c   Ordinary compensation income
   d   Expense or asset depending on nature of services rendered

B. Section 1244—Small Business Corporation (SBC) Stock

1. Sec. 1244 stock permits shareholders to deduct an **ordinary loss** on sale or worthlessness of stock.

   a. Shareholder must be the original holder of stock, and an individual or partnership.

   b. Stock can be common or preferred, voting or nonvoting, and must have been issued for money or property (other than stock or securities)

   c. Ordinary loss limited to **$50,000 ($100,000** on joint return); any excess is treated as a capital loss.

   d. The corporation during the five-year period before the year of loss, received less than 50% of its total gross receipts from royalties, rents, dividends, interest, annuities, and gains from sales or exchanges of stock or securities.

      EXAMPLE: Jim (married and filing a joint return) incurred a loss of $120,000 from the sale of Sec. 1244 stock during 2003. $100,000 of Jim's loss is deductible as an ordinary loss, with the remaining $20,000 treated as a capital loss.

2. If Sec. 1244 stock is received in exchange for property whose FMV is less than its adjusted basis, the stock's basis is reduced to the FMV of the property to determine the amount of ordinary loss.

   EXAMPLE: Joe made a Sec. 351 transfer of property with an adjusted basis of $20,000 and a FMV of $16,000 in exchange for Sec. 1244 stock. The basis of Joe's stock is $20,000, but solely for purposes of Sec. 1244 the stock's basis is reduced to

$16,000.   If Joe subsequently sold his stock for $15,000, $1,000 of his loss would be treated as an ordinary loss under Sec. 1244, with the remaining $4,000 treated as a capital loss.

3. For purposes of determining the amount of ordinary loss, increases in basis through capital contributions or otherwise are treated as allocable to stock which is not Sec. 1244 stock.

   EXAMPLE: Jill acquired 100 shares of Sec. 1244 stock for $10,000. Jill later made a $2,000 contribution to the capital of the corporation, increasing her stock basis to $12,000. Jill subsequently sold the 100 shares for $9,000. Of Jill's $3,000 loss, ($10,000 ÷ $12,000) x $3,000 = $2,500 qualifies as an ordinary loss under Sec. 1244, with the remaining ($2,000 ÷ $12,000) x $3,000 = $500 treated as a capital loss.

4. SBC is any domestic corporation whose aggregate amount of money and adjusted basis of other property received for stock, as a contribution to capital, and as paid-in surplus, does not exceed $1,000,000. If more than $1 million of stock is issued, up to $1 million of qualifying stock can be designated as Sec. 1244 stock.

C. Variations from Individual Taxation

1. Filing and payment of tax

   a. A corporation generally must file a Form 1120 every year even though it has no taxable income. A short-form Form 1120-A may be filed if gross receipts, total income, and total assets are each less than $500,000.

   b. The return must be filed by the fifteenth day of the third month following the close of its taxable year (e.g., March 15 for calendar-year corporation).

      (1) An automatic six-month extension may be obtained by filing Form 7004.
      (2) Any balance due on the corporation's tax liability must be paid with the request for extension.

   c. Estimated tax payments must be made by every corporation whose estimated tax is expected to be $500 or more. A corporation's estimated tax is its expected tax liability (including alternative minimum tax) less its allowable tax credits.

      (1) Quarterly payments are due on the fifteenth day of the fourth, sixth, ninth, and twelfth months of its taxable year (April 15, June 15, September 15, and December 15 for a calendar-year corporation). Any balance due must be paid by the due date of the return.
      (2) No penalty for underpayment of estimated tax will be imposed if payments at least equal the lesser of

         (a) 100% of the current year's tax (determined on the basis of actual income or annualized income), or
         (b) 100% of the preceding year's tax (if the preceding year was a full twelve months and showed a tax liability).

      (3) A corporation with $1 million or more of taxable income in any of its three preceding tax years (i.e., **large corporation**) can use its preceding year's tax only for its first installment and must base its estimated payments on 100% of its current year's tax to avoid penalty.
      (4) If any amount of tax is not paid by the original due date, interest must be paid from the due date until the tax is paid.
      (5) A failure-to-pay tax delinquency penalty will be owed if the amount of tax paid by the original due date of the return is less than 90% of the tax shown on the return. The failure-to-pay penalty is imposed at a rate of 0.5% per month (or fraction thereof), with a maximum penalty of 25%.

2. Corporations are subject to

   a. **Regular tax rates**

	Taxable income	Rate
(1)	$0-$50,000	15%
(2)	$50,001-$75,000	25
(3)	$75,001-$10 million	34
(4)	Over $10 million	35

   (5) The less-than-34% brackets are phased out by adding an additional tax of 5% of the excess of taxable income over $100,000, up to a maximum additional tax of $11,750.

(6) The 34% bracket is phased out for corporations with taxable income in excess of $15 million by adding an additional 3% of the excess of taxable income over $15 million, up to a maximum additional tax of $100,000.

b. Certain personal service corporations are not eligible to use the less-than-35% brackets and their taxable income is taxed at a flat 35% rate.

c. **Alternative minimum tax (AMT)**

(1) **Computation.** The AMT is generally the amount by which 20% of alternative minimum taxable income (AMTI) as reduced by an exemption and the alternative minimum tax foreign tax credit, exceeds the regular tax (i.e., regular tax liability reduced by the regular tax foreign tax credit). AMTI is equal to taxable income computed with specified adjustments and increased by tax preferences.

(2) **Exemption.** AMTI is offset by a $40,000 exemption. However, the exemption is reduced by 25% of AMTI over $150,000, and completely phased out once AMTI reaches $310,000.

(3) **AMT formula**

```
        Regular taxable income before NOL deduction
   +    Tax preference items
  +(–)  Adjustments (other than ACE and NOL deduction)
        Pre-ACE alternative minimum taxable income (AMTI)
  +(–)  ACE adjustment [75% of difference between pre-ACE AMTI and adjusted current earnings (ACE)]
    –   AMT NOL deduction [limited to 90% of pre-NOL AMTI]
        Alternative minimum taxable income (AMTI)
    –   Exemption ($40,000 less 25% of AMTI over $150,000)
        Alternative minimum tax base
   x    20% rate
        Tentative AMT before foreign tax credit
    –   AMT foreign tax credit (limited to 90% of pre-credit AMT)
        Tentative minimum tax (TMT)
    –   Regular income tax (less regular tax foreign tax credit)
        Alternative minimum tax (if positive)
```

(4) **Preference items.** The following are examples of items added to regular taxable income in computing pre-ACE AMTI:

(a) Tax-exempt interest on private activity bonds (net of related expenses)
(b) Excess of accelerated over straight-line depreciation on real property and leased personal property placed in service before 1987
(c) The excess of percentage depletion deduction over the property's adjusted basis
(d) The excess of intangible drilling costs using a ten-year amortization over 65% of net oil and gas income

(5) **Adjustments.** The following are examples of adjustments to regular taxable income in computing pre-ACE AMTI:

(a) For real property placed in service after 1986 and before 1999, the difference between regular tax depreciation and straight-line depreciation over forty years
(b) For personal property placed in service after 1986, the difference between regular tax depreciation and depreciation using the 150% declining balance method
(c) The installment method cannot be used for sales of inventory-type items
(d) Income from long-term contracts must be determined using the percentage of completion method

(6) **Adjusted current earnings (ACE).** ACE is a concept based on a corporation's earnings and profits, and is calculated by making adjustments to pre-ACE AMTI.

AMTI before ACE adjustment and NOL deduction

Add: Tax-exempt income on municipal bonds (less expenses)
           Tax-exempt life insurance death benefits (less expenses)
           70% dividends-received deduction

Deduct: Depletion using cost depletion method
           Depreciation using ADS straight-line for all property (this adjustment eliminated for property
             placed in service after 1993)

Other: Capitalize organizational expenditures and circulation expenses
           Add increase (subtract decrease) in LIFO recapture amount (i.e., excess of FIFO value over
             LIFO basis)
           Installment method cannot be used for nondealer sales of property
           <u>Amortize intangible drilling costs over five years</u>

Adjusted current earnings (ACE)
<u>– Pre-ACE AMTI</u>
Balance (positive or negative)
<u>x 75%</u>
<u>ACE adjustment (positive or negative)</u>

EXAMPLE: Acme, Inc. has adjusted current earnings of $100,000 and alternative minimum taxable income (before this adjustment) of $60,000. Since adjusted current earnings exceeds pre-ACE AMTI by $40,000, 75% of this amount must be added to Acme's AMTI. Thus, Acme's AMTI for the year is $90,000 [$60,000 + ($40,000 x 75%)].

  (a) The ACE adjustment can be positive or negative, but a negative ACE adjustment is limited in amount to prior years' net positive ACE adjustments.

  (b) The computation of ACE is not the same as the computation of a corporation's E&P. For example, federal income taxes, penalties and fines, and the disallowed portion of business meals and entertainment would be deductible in computing E&P, but are not deductible in computing ACE.

(7) **Minimum tax credit.** The amount of AMT paid is allowed as a credit against regular tax liability in future years.

  (a) The credit can be carried forward indefinitely, but not carried back.

  (b) The AMT credit can only be used to reduce regular tax liability, not future AMT liability.

(8) **Small corporation exemption.** A corporation is exempt from the corporate AMT for its first tax year (regardless of income levels). After the first year, it is exempt from AMT if it passes a gross receipts test. It is exempt for its second year if its first year's gross receipts do not exceed $5 million. To be exempt for its third year, the corporation's average gross receipts for the first two years must not exceed $7.5 million. To be exempt for the fourth year (and subsequent years), the corporation's average gross receipts for all prior three-year periods must not exceed $7.5 million.

EXAMPLE: Zero Corp., a calendar-year corporation, was formed on January 2, 2000, and had gross receipts for its first four taxable years as follows:

Year	*Gross receipts*
2000	*$ 4,500,000*
2001	*9,000,000*
2002	*8,000,000*
2003	*6,500,000*

Zero is automatically exempt from AMT for 2000. It is exempt for 2001 because its gross receipts for 2000 do not exceed $5 million. Zero also is exempt for 2002 because its average gross receipts for 2000-2001 do not exceed $7.5 million. Similarly, it is exempt for 2003 because its average gross receipts for 2000-2002 do not exceed $7.5 million. However, Zero will lose its exemption from AMT for 2004 and all subsequent years because its average gross receipts for 2001-2003 exceed $7.5 million.

  d. See subsequent discussion for penalty taxes on

    (1) Accumulated earnings

    (2) Personal holding companies

3. **Gross income** for a corporation is quite similar to the rules for an individual taxpayer. However, there are a few differences.

  a. A corporation does not recognize gain or loss on the **issuance of its own stock** (including treasury stock), or on the lapse or acquisition of an option to buy or sell its stock (including treasury stock).

     (1) It generally recognizes gain (but not loss) if it distributes appreciated property to its shareholders.

     (2) **Contributions to capital** are excluded from a corporation's gross income, whether received from shareholders or nonshareholders.

        (a) If property is received from a shareholder, the shareholder recognizes no gain or loss, the shareholder's basis for the contributed property transfers to the corporation, and the shareholder's stock basis is increased by the basis of the contributed property.

        (b) If property is received as a capital contribution from a nonshareholder, the corporation's basis for the contributed property is zero.

           1] If money is received, the basis of property purchased within one year afterwards is reduced by the money contributed.

           2] Any money not used reduces the basis of the corporation's existing property beginning with depreciable property.

  b. No gain or loss is recognized on the **issuance of debt**.

     (1) Premium or discount on bonds payable is amortized as income or expense over the life of bonds.

     (2) Ordinary income/loss is recognized by a corporation on the repurchase of its bonds, determined by the relationship of the repurchase price to the net carrying value of the bonds (issue price plus or minus the discount or premium amortized).

     (3) Interest earned and gains recognized in a bond sinking fund are income to the corporation.

  c. Gains are treated as ordinary income on sales to or from a more than 50% shareholder, or between corporations which are more than 50% owned by the same individual, if the property is subject to depreciation in the hands of the buyer.

4. Deductions for a corporation are much the same as for individuals. However, there are some major differences.

  a. Adjusted gross income is not applicable to corporations.

  b. **Organizational expenditures** may be amortized over **sixty months** or longer if elected in the tax return for the year in which the corporation begins business, otherwise deductible only in the year of liquidation.

     (1) The election must be made by the due date for filing the tax return (including extensions) for the tax year in which the corporation begins business, and applies to expenditures incurred before the end of the tax year in which the corporation begins business (even if the amounts have not yet been paid by a cash-method corporation).

     (2) Amortization period starts with the month that the corporation begins business.

     (3) Organizational expenditures include expenses of temporary directors and organizational meetings, state fees for incorporation, accounting and legal service costs incident to incorporation (e.g., drafting bylaws, minutes of organizational meetings, and terms of original stock certificates).

     (4) Expenditures connected with issuing or selling shares of stock, or listing stock on an exchange are neither deductible nor amortizable. Expenditures connected with the transfer of an asset to the corporation must be capitalized as part of the cost of the asset.

  c. The deduction for **charitable contributions** is **limited to 10% of taxable income** before the contributions deduction, the dividends received deduction, a net operating loss carryback (but after carryover), and a capital loss carryback (but after carryover).

     (1) Generally the same rules apply for valuation of contributed property as for individuals except

        (a) Deduction for donations of inventory and other appreciated ordinary income-producing property is the donor's basis plus one-half of the unrealized appreciation but limited to twice the basis, provided

           1] Donor is a corporation (but not an S corporation)

           2] Donee must use property for care of ill, needy, or infants

3] Donor must obtain a written statement from the donee that the use requirement has been met

4] No deduction allowed for unrealized appreciation that would be ordinary income under recapture rules

(b) Deduction for donation of appreciated scientific personal property to a college or university is the donor's basis plus one-half the unrealized appreciation but limited to twice the basis, provided

1] Donor is a corporation (but not an S corporation, personal holding company, or service organization)

2] Property was constructed by donor and contributed within two years of substantial completion, and donee is original user of property

3] Donee must use property for research or experimentation

4] Donor must obtain a written statement from the donee that the use requirement has been met

5] No deduction allowed for unrealized appreciation that would be ordinary income under recapture rules

(2) Contributions are deductible in period paid (subject to 10% limitation) unless corporation is an accrual method taxpayer and then deductible (subject to 10% limitation) when authorized by board of directors if payment is made within 2 1/2 months after tax year end, and corporation elects to deduct contributions when authorized.

(3) Excess contributions over the 10% limitation may be carried forward for up to five years.

EXAMPLE: The books of a calendar-year, accrual method corporation for 2003 disclose net income of $350,000 after deducting a charitable contribution of $50,000. The contribution was authorized by the Board of Directors on December 24, 2003, and was actually paid on January 31, 2004. The allowable charitable contribution deduction for 2003 (if the corporation elects to deduct it when accrued) is $40,000, calculated as follows: ($350,000 + $50,000) x .10 = $40,000. The remaining $10,000 is carried forward for up to five years.

d. A **100% DRD** for dividends received from affiliated (i.e., at least 80% owned) corporations if a consolidated tax return is not filed.

(1) If a consolidated tax return is filed, intercompany dividends are eliminated and not included in consolidated gross income.

(2) See Section D. for discussion of affiliated corporations

e. An **80% dividends received deduction** (DRD) is allowed for qualified dividends from taxable domestic unaffiliated corporations that are **at least 20% owned**.

(1) DRD may be **limited to 80% of taxable income** before the 80% dividends received deduction, the net operating loss deduction, and a capital loss carryback.

EXAMPLE: A corporation has income from sales of $20,000 and dividend income of $10,000, along with business expenses of $22,000. Since taxable income before the DRD would be $8,000 (less than the dividend income), the DRD is limited to $6,400 (80% x $8,000). Thus, taxable income would be $1,600 ($8,000 – $6,400).

(2) Exception: The 80% of **taxable income limitation does not apply** if the full 80% DRD creates or increases a net operating loss.

EXAMPLE: In the example above, assume that all facts are the same except that business expenses are $22,001. Since the full DRD ($8,000) would create a $1 net operating loss ($7,999 – $8,000), the taxable income limitation would not apply and the full DRD ($8,000) would be allowed.

f. Only a **70% dividends received deduction** (instead of 80%) is allowed for qualified dividends from taxable domestic unaffiliated corporations that are **less than 20% owned**.

(1) A 70% of taxable income limitation (instead of 80%) and a limitation exception for a net operating loss apply as in e.(1) and (2) above.

(2) If dividends are received from both 20% owned corporations and corporations that are less than 20% owned, the 80% DRD and 80% DRD limitation for dividends received from 20% owned corporations is computed first. Then the 70% DRD and 70% DRD limitation is computed for dividends received from less than 20% owned corporations. For purposes of com-

puting the 70% DRD limitation, taxable income is reduced by the total amount of dividends received from 20% owned corporations.

EXAMPLE: A corporation has taxable income before the dividends received deduction of $100,000. Included in taxable income are $65,000 of dividends from a 20% owned corporation and $40,000 of dividends from a less than 20% owned corporation. First, the 80% DRD for dividends received from the 20% owned corporation is computed. That deduction equals $52,000 [i.e., the lesser of 80% of the dividends received (80% x $65,000), or 80% of taxable income (80% x $100,000)].

Second, the 70% DRD for the dividends received from the less than 20% owned corporation is computed. That deduction is $24,500 [i.e., the lesser of 70% of the dividends received (70% x $40,000), or 70% of taxable income after deducting the amount of dividends from the 20% owned corporation (70% x [$100,000 – $65,000])]. Thus, the total dividends received deduction is $52,000 + $24,500 = $76,500.

g. A portion of a corporation's 80% (or 70%) DRD will be disallowed if the dividends are directly attributable to **debt-financed portfolio stock**.

   (1) "Portfolio stock" is any stock (except stock of a corporation if the taxpayer owns at least 50% of the voting power and at least 50% of the total value of such corporation).

   (2) The DRD percentage for debt-financed portfolio stock = [80% (or 70%) x (100% – average % of indebtedness on the stock)].

   EXAMPLE: P, Inc. purchased 25% of T, Inc. for $100,000, paying with $50,000 of its own funds and $50,000 borrowed from its bank. During the year P received $9,000 in dividends from T, and paid $5,000 in interest expense on the bank loan. No principal payments were made on the loan during the year. If the stock were not debt financed, P's DRD would be $9,000 x 80% = $7,200. However, because half of the stock investment was debt financed, P's DRD is $9,000 x [80% x (100% – 50%)] = $3,600.

   (3) The reduction in the DRD cannot exceed the interest deduction allocable to the portfolio stock indebtedness.

   EXAMPLE: Assume the same facts as above except that the interest expense on the bank loan was only $3,000. The reduction in the DRD would be limited to the $3,000 interest deduction on the loan. The DRD would be ($9,000 x 80%) – $3,000 = $4,200.

h. **No DRD** is allowed if the dividend paying stock is held **less than forty-six days** during the ninety-day period that begins forty-five days before the stock becomes ex-dividend. In the case of preferred stock, no DRD is allowed if the dividends received are for a period or periods in excess of 366 days and the stock has been held for less than ninety-one days during the 180-day period that begins ninety days before the stock becomes ex-dividend.

i. The **basis of stock** held by a corporation must be reduced by the nontaxed portion of a nonliquidating **extraordinary dividend** received with respect to the stock, unless the corporation has held the stock for more than two years before the dividend is announced. To the extent the nontaxed portion of an extraordinary dividend exceeds the adjusted basis of the stock, the excess is recognized as gain for the taxable year in which the extraordinary dividend is received.

   (1) The nontaxed portion of a dividend is generally the amount that is offset by the DRD.

   (2) A dividend is considered "extraordinary" when it equals or exceeds 10% (5% for preferred stock) of the stock's adjusted basis (or FMV if greater on the day preceding the ex-dividend date).

   (3) Aggregation of dividends

      (a) All dividends received that have ex-dividend dates that occur within a period of 85 consecutive days are treated as one dividend.

      (b) All dividends received within 365 consecutive days are treated as extraordinary dividends if they in total exceed 20% of the stock's adjusted basis.

   (4) This provision is not applicable to dividends received from an affiliated corporation, and does not apply if the stock was held during the entire period the paying corporation (and any predecessor) was in existence.

   EXAMPLE: Corporation X purchased 30% of the stock of Corporation Y for $10,000 during June 2003. During December 2003, X received a $20,000 dividend from Y. X sold its Y stock for $5,000 in March 2004.

   Because the dividend from Y is an extraordinary dividend, the nontaxed portion (equal to the DRD allowed to X) $20,000 x 80% = $16,000 has the effect of reducing the Y stock basis from $10,000 to $0, with the remaining $6,000 recognized as gain for 2003. At time of sale, the excess of sale proceeds over the reduced stock basis $5,000 – $0 = $5,000 is also recognized as gain.

j. **Losses** in the ordinary course of business are deductible.

    (1) Loss is **disallowed** if the sale or exchange of property is between

        (a) A corporation and a more than 50% shareholder,

        (b) A C corporation and an S corporation if the same persons own more than 50% of each, or

        (c) A corporation and a partnership if the same persons own more than 50% of the corporation, and more than 50% of the capital and profits interest in the partnership.

        (d) In the event of a disallowed loss, the transferee on subsequent disposition only recognizes gain to the extent it exceeds the disallowed loss.

    (2) Any loss from the sale or exchange of property between corporations that are members of the same **controlled group** is **deferred** (instead of disallowed) until the property is sold outside the group. See controlled group definition in Section D.2., except substitute "more than 50%" for "at least 80%."

    (3) An accrual method C corporation is effectively placed on the cash method of accounting for purposes of deducting accrued interest and other expenses owed to a related cash method payee. No deduction is allowable until the year the amount is actually paid.

      EXAMPLE: A calendar-year corporation accrues $10,000 of salary to an employee (a 60% shareholder) during 2003, but does not make payment until February 2004. The $10,000 will be deductible by the corporation and reported as income by the employee-shareholder in 2004.

    (4) **Capital losses** are deductible only to the extent of capital gains (i.e., may not offset ordinary income).

        (a) Unused capital losses are carried back three years and then carried forward five years to offset capital gains.

        (b) All corporate capital loss carrybacks and carryforwards are treated as **short-term**.

    (5) Bad debt losses are treated as ordinary deductions.

    (6) Casualty losses are treated the same as for an individual except

        (a) There is no $100 floor

        (b) If property is completely destroyed, the amount of loss is the property's adjusted basis

        (c) A partial loss is measured the same as for an individual's nonbusiness loss (i.e., the lesser of the decrease in FMV, or the property's adjusted basis)

    (7) A corporation's **net operating loss** is computed the same way as its taxable income.

        (a) The dividends received deduction is allowed without limitation.

        (b) No deduction is allowed for a NOL carryback or carryover from other years.

        (c) A NOL is generally carried back two years and forward twenty years to offset taxable income in those years. However, a three-year carryback is permitted for the portion of a NOL that is attributable to a presidentially declared disaster and is incurred by a small business corporation (i.e., a corporation whose average annual gross receipts are $5 million or less for the three-tax-year period preceding the loss year). A corporation may elect to forego carryback and only carry forward twenty years.

        (d) For NOLs arising in tax years ending in 2001 and 2002, the carryback period is extended to five years. However, a corporation can make an irrevocable election to waive the five-year carryback period, and carry back only two years (or three years if applicable).

k. Depreciation and depletion computations are same as for individuals.

l. Research and development expenditures of a corporation (or individual) may be treated under one of three alternatives

    (1) Currently expensed in year paid or incurred

    (2) Amortized over a period of sixty months or more if life not determinable

    (3) Capitalized and depreciated over determinable life

m. Contributions to a pension or profit sharing plan

    (1) Defined benefit plans

(a) Maximum deductible contribution is actuarially determined.

(b) There also are minimum funding standards.

(2) Defined contribution plans

(a) **Maximum deduction** for contributions to qualified profit-sharing or stock bonus plans is generally limited to 25% of the compensation paid or accrued during the year to covered employees.

(b) If more than 25% is paid, the excess can be carried forward as part of the contributions of succeeding years to the extent needed to bring the deduction up to 25%.

5. In working a corporate problem, certain calculations must be made in a specific order [e.g., charitable contributions (CC) must be computed before the dividends received deduction (DRD)]. The following memory device is quite helpful:

> Gross income
>   – Deductions (except CC and DRD)
> _____
> Taxable income before CC and DRD
>   – CC (limited to 10% of TI before CC, DRD,
>   capital loss carryback, and NOL carryback)
> _____
> Taxable income before DRD
>   – DRD (may be limited* to 80% (or 70%) of TI before
>   DRD, capital loss carryback, and NOL carryover or carryback)
> _____
> Taxable income
>   x Applicable rates
> _____
> Tax liability before tax credits
>   – Tax credits
> _____
> Tax liability
> _____

> * *Limitation not applicable if full 80% (or 70%) of dividends received creates or increases an NOL.*

6. A person sitting for the CPA examination should be able to **reconcile book and taxable income**.

a. If you begin with book income to calculate taxable income, make the following adjustments:

(1) **Increase book income** by

(a) Federal income tax expense

(b) Excess of capital losses over capital gains because a net capital loss is not deductible

(c) Income items in the tax return not included in book income (e.g., prepaid rents, royalties, interest)

(d) Charitable contributions in excess of the 10% limitation

(e) Expenses deducted on the books but not on the tax return (e.g., amount of business gifts in excess of $25, nondeductible life insurance premiums paid, 50% of business meals and entertainment)

(2) **Deduct from book income**

(a) Income reported on the books but not on the tax return (e.g., tax-exempt interest, life insurance proceeds)

(b) Expenses deducted on the tax return but not on the books (e.g., MACRS depreciation above straight-line, charitable contribution carryover)

(c) The dividends received deduction

b. When going from taxable income to book income, the above adjustments would be reversed.

c. **Schedule M-1** of Form 1120 provides a reconciliation of income per books with taxable income before the NOL and DRD. There are two types of Schedule M-1 items:

(1) Permanent differences (e.g., tax-exempt interest)

(2) Temporary differences—items reflected in different periods (e.g., accelerated depreciation on tax return and straight-line on books)

> EXAMPLE: *A corporation discloses that it had net income after taxes of $36,000 per books. Included in the computation were deductions for charitable contributions of $10,000, a net capital loss of $5,000, and federal income taxes paid of $9,000. What is the corporation's TI?*

Net income per books after tax	$36,000
Nondeductible net capital loss	+ 5,000
Federal income tax expense	+ 9,000
Charitable contributions	+10,000
Taxable income before CC	$60,000
CC (limited to 10% x 60,000)	– 6,000
Taxable income	$54,000

d. **Schedule M-2** of Form 1120 analyzes changes in a corporation's Unappropriated Retained Earnings per books between the beginning and end of the year.

Balance at beginning of year	
Add:	Net income per books
	Other increases
Less:	Dividends to shareholders
	Other decreases (e.g., addition to reserve for contingencies)
Balance at end of year	

D. Affiliated and Controlled Corporations

1. An **affiliated group** is a parent-subsidiary chain of corporations in which **at least 80%** of the combined voting power and total value of all stock (except nonvoting preferred) are owned by includible corporations.

a. They may elect to file a consolidated return. Election is binding on all future returns.

b. If affiliated corporations file a consolidated return, intercompany dividends are eliminated in the consolidation process. If separate tax returns are filed, dividends from affiliated corporations are eligible for a 100% dividends received deduction.

c. Possible advantages of a consolidated return include the deferral of gain on intercompany transactions and offsetting operating/capital losses of one corporation against the profits/capital gains of another.

EXAMPLE: P Corp. owns 80% of the stock of A Corp., 40% of the stock of B Corp., and 45% of the stock of C Corp. A Corp. owns 40% of the stock of B Corp. A consolidated tax return could be filed by P, A, and B.

EXAMPLE: Parent and Subsidiary file consolidated tax returns using a calendar year. During 2003, Subsidiary paid a $10,000 dividend to Parent. Also during 2003, Subsidiary sold land with a basis of $20,000 to Parent for its FMV of $50,000. During 2004, Parent sold the land to an unrelated taxpayer for $55,000.

The intercompany dividend is eliminated in the consolidation process and is excluded from consolidated taxable income. Additionally, Subsidiary's $30,000 of gain from the sale of land to Parent is deferred for 2003. The $30,000 will be included in consolidated taxable income for 2004 when Parent reports $5,000 of income from the sale of that land to the unrelated taxpayer.

2. A **controlled group** of corporations is limited to an aggregate of $75,000 of taxable income taxed at less than 35%, one $250,000 accumulated earnings credit, one $25,000 Sec. 179 expense deduction, etc. There are three basic types of controlled groups.

a. **Parent-subsidiary**—Basically same as P-S group eligible to file consolidated return, except ownership requirement is 80% of combined voting power **or** total value of stock. Affiliated corporations are subject to the controlled group limitations if the corporations file separate tax returns.

b. **Brother-sister**—Two or more corporations at least 80% owned by five or fewer individuals, estates, or trusts, who also own more than 50% of each corporation when counting only identical ownership in each corporation. The 80% test is applied by including only the shares of those shareholders that hold stock in each corporation of the group being tested. The percentage tests are based on voting power **or** total value.

EXAMPLE:	*Individual*	*Corporations*		*Stock considered*
	shareholder	*W*	*X*	*for 50% test*
	A	*30%*	*20%*	*20%*
	B	*5*	*40*	*5%*
	C	*30*	*35*	*30%*
	D	*15*	*5*	*5%*
	E	*20*	*--*	*--*
		100%	*100%*	*60%*

Corporations W and X are a controlled group since five or fewer individuals own at least 80% of each, and also own more than 50% when counting only identical ownership.

EXAMPLE:

Individual	Corporations		*Stock considered*
shareholder	*Y*	*Z*	*for 50% test*
F	79%	100%	79%
G	*21%*	*--*	*--*
	100%	*100%*	*79%*

Y and Z are not a controlled group because the 80% test is not met for Corporation Y. Since G owns no stock in Z, G's stock in Y cannot be added to F's Y stock for purposes of applying the 80% test.

    c.   **Combined**—The parent in a P-S group is also a member of a brother-sister group of corporations.

       EXAMPLE: Individual H owns 100% of the stock of Corporations P and Q. Corporation P owns 100% of the stock of Corporation S. P, S, and Q are members of one controlled group.

E.   Dividends and Distributions

    1.   **Ordinary corporate distributions**

       a.   Corporate distributions of property to shareholders on their stock are subject to a **three-step** treatment.

          (1)   Dividend—to be included in gross income
          (2)   Return of stock basis—nontaxable and reduces shareholder's basis for stock
          (3)   Gain—to extent distribution exceeds shareholder's stock basis

       b.   The **amount** of distribution to a shareholder is the cash plus the FMV of other property received, reduced by liabilities assumed.

       c.   A shareholder's tax **basis** for distributed property is the property's FMV at date of distribution (not reduced by liabilities).

       d.   A **dividend** is a distribution of property by a corporation to its shareholders out of

          (1)   Earnings and profits of the current taxable year (CEP), computed at the end of the year, without regard to the amount of earnings and profits at the date of distribution; or,
          (2)   Earnings and profits accumulated after February 28, 1913 (AEP).

          EXAMPLE: Corporation X has earnings and profits of $6,000 and makes a $10,000 distribution to its sole shareholder, A, who has a stock basis of $3,000. The $10,000 distribution to A will be treated as a dividend of $6,000, a nontaxable return of stock basis of $3,000, and a capital gain of $1,000.

       e.   The **distributing corporation recognizes gain** on the distribution of appreciated property as if such property were sold for its FMV.

       EXAMPLE: A corporation distributes property with a FMV of $10,000 and a basis of $3,000 to a shareholder. The corporation recognizes a gain of $10,000 – $3,000 = $7,000.

          (1)   If the distributed property is subject to a liability (or if the distributee assumes a liability) and the FMV of the distributed property is less than the amount of liability, then the gain is the difference between the amount of liability and the property's basis.

          EXAMPLE: A corporation distributes property with a FMV of $10,000 and a basis of $3,000 to a shareholder, who assumes a liability of $12,000 on the property. The corporation recognizes a gain of $12,000 – $3,000 = $9,000.

          (2)   The type of gain recognized (e.g., ordinary, Sec. 1231, capital) depends on the nature of the property distributed (e.g., recapture rules may apply).

    2.   **Earnings and profits**

       a.   **Current earnings and profits** (CEP) are **similar to book income**, but are computed by making adjustments to taxable income.

          (1)   Add—tax-exempt income, dividends received deduction, excess of MACRS depreciation over depreciation computed under ADS, etc..
          (2)   Deduct—federal income taxes, net capital loss, excess charitable contributions, expenses relating to tax-exempt income, penalties, etc.

       b.   **Accumulated earnings and profits** (AEP) represent the sum of prior years' CEP, reduced by distributions and net operating loss of prior years.

       c.   CEP are increased by the gain recognized on a distribution of appreciated property (excess of FMV over basis).

d. Distributions reduce earnings and profits (but not below zero) by

(1) The amount of money

(2) The face amount (or issue price if less) of obligations of the distributing corporation, and

(3) The adjusted basis (or FMV if greater) of other property distributed

(4) Above reductions must be adjusted by any liability assumed by the shareholder, or the amount of liability to which the property distributed is subject.

> EXAMPLE: Z Corp. has two 50% shareholders, B Corp. and Mr. C. Z Corp. distributes a parcel of land (held for investment) to each shareholder. Each parcel of land has a FMV of $12,000 with a basis of $8,000 and each shareholder assumes a liability of $3,000 on the property received. Z Corp. will recognize a gain of $4,000 on the distribution of each property.
>
> | | *B Corp.* | *Mr. C* |
> |---|---|---|
> | *Dividend ($12,000 – $3,000)* | *$ 9,000* | *$ 9,000* |
> | *Tax basis for property received* | *12,000* | *12,000* |
> | *Effect (before tax) on Z's earnings & profits:* | | |
> | *Increased by gain (FMV-basis)* | *4,000* | *4,000* |
> | *Increased by liabilities distributed* | *3,000* | *3,000* |
> | *Decreased by FMV of property distributed* | *(12,000)* | *(12,000)* |

3. **Stock redemptions**

a. A stock redemption is **treated as an exchange,** generally resulting in capital gain or loss treatment to the shareholder if at least one of the following five tests is met. Constructive stock ownership rules generally apply in determining whether the following tests are met:

(1) The redemption is not essentially equivalent to a dividend (this has been interpreted by Revenue Rulings to mean that a redemption must reduce a shareholder's right to vote, share in earnings, and share in assets upon liquidation; and after the redemption the shareholder's stock ownership [both direct and constructive] must not exceed 50%), or

(2) The redemption is substantially disproportionate (i.e., after redemption, shareholder's percentage ownership is less than 80% of shareholder's percentage ownership prior to redemption, and less than 50% of shares outstanding), or

(3) All of the shareholder's stock is redeemed, or

(4) The redemption is from a noncorporate shareholder in a partial liquidation, or

(5) The distribution is a redemption of stock to pay death taxes under Sec. 303.

b. If none of the above tests are met, the redemption proceeds are treated as an ordinary Sec. 301 distribution, **taxable as a dividend** to the extent of the distributing corporation's earnings and profits.

c. A corporation cannot deduct amounts paid or incurred in connection with a redemption of its stock (except for interest expense on loans used to purchase stock).

4. **Complete liquidations**

a. Amounts received by **shareholders** in liquidation of a corporation are treated as received in exchange for stock, generally resulting in capital gain or loss. Property received will have a basis equal to FMV.

b. A **liquidating corporation** generally recognizes gain or loss on the sale or distribution of its assets in complete liquidation.

(1) If a distribution, gain or loss is computed as if the distributed property were sold to the distributee for FMV.

(2) If distributed property is subject to a liability (or a shareholder assumes a liability) in excess of the basis of the distributed property, FMV is deemed to be not less than the amount of liability.

c. **Distributions to related persons**

(1) No loss is generally recognized to a liquidating corporation on the distribution of property to a related person if

(a) The distribution is not pro rata, or

(b) The property was acquired by the liquidating corporation during the five-year period ending on the date of distribution in a Sec. 351 transaction or as a contribution to capital.

This includes any property whose basis is determined by reference to the adjusted basis of property described in the preceding sentence.

(2) Related person is a shareholder who owns (directly or constructively) more than 50% of the corporation's stock.

d. Carryover basis property

(1) If a corporation acquires property in a Sec. 351 transaction or as a contribution to capital at any time after the date that is two years before the date of the adoption of the plan of complete liquidation, any loss resulting from the property's sale, exchange, or distribution can be recognized only to the extent of the decline in value that occurred subsequent to the date that the corporation acquired the property.

(2) The above rule applies only where the loss is not already completely disallowed by c.(1) above, and is intended to apply where there is no clear and substantial relationship between the contributed property and the conduct of the corporation's business. If the contributed property is actually used in the corporation's business, the above rule should not apply if there is a business purpose for placing the property in the corporation.

EXAMPLE: A shareholder makes a capital contribution of property unrelated to the corporation's business with a basis of $15,000 and a FMV of $10,000 on the contribution date. Within two years the corporation adopts a plan of liquidation and sells the property for $8,000. The liquidating corporation's recognized loss will be limited to $10,000 – $8,000 = $2,000.

e. Liquidation of subsidiary

(1) **No gain or loss** is recognized to a **parent corporation** under Sec. 332 on the receipt of property in complete liquidation of an **80% or more owned subsidiary**. The subsidiary's basis for its assets along with all tax accounting attributes (e.g., earnings and profits, NOL and charitable contribution carryforwards) will transfer to the parent corporation.

(2) **No gain or loss** is recognized to a **subsidiary corporation** on the distribution of property to its parent if Sec. 332 applies to the parent corporation.

    (a) If the subsidiary has debt outstanding to the parent, nonrecognition also applies to property distributed in satisfaction of the debt.

    (b) Gain (but not loss) is recognized on the distribution of property to minority (20% or less) shareholders.

(3) Nonrecognition does not extend to minority shareholders. A minority shareholder's gain or loss will be recognized under the general rule at 4.a. on the preceding page.

EXAMPLE: Parent Corp. owns 80% of Subsidiary Corp., with the remaining 20% of Subsidiary stock owned by Alex. Parent's basis in its Subsidiary stock is $100,000, while Alex has a basis for her Subsidiary stock of $15,000. Subsidiary Corp. is to be liquidated and will distribute to Parent Corp. assets with a FMV of $200,000 and a basis of $150,000, and will distribute to Alex assets with a FMV of $50,000 and a basis of $30,000. Subsidiary has an unused capital loss carryover of $10,000. The tax effects of the liquidation will be as follows:

> *Parent Corp. will not recognize gain on the receipt of Subsidiary's assets in complete liquidation, since Subsidiary is an at least 80%-owned corporation. The basis of Subsidiary's assets to Parent will be their transferred basis of $150,000, and Parent will inherit Subsidiary's unused capital loss carryover of $10,000.*

> *Alex will recognize a gain of $35,000 ($50,000 FMV – $15,000 stock basis) from the liquidation. Alex's tax basis for Subsidiary's assets received in the liquidation will be their FMV of $50,000.*

> *Subsidiary Corp. will not recognize gain on the distribution of its asses to Parent Corp., but will recognize a gain of $20,000 ($50,000 FMV – $30,000 basis) on the distribution of its assets to Alex.*

5. Stock purchases treated as asset acquisitions

    a. An acquiring corporation that has purchased at least 80% of a target corporation's stock within a twelve-month period may elect under Sec. 338 to have the purchase of stock treated as an acquisition of assets.

    b. Old target corporation is deemed to have sold all its assets on the acquisition date, and is treated as a new corporation that has purchased those assets on the day after the acquisition date.

      (1) Acquisition date is the date on which at least 80% of the target's stock has been acquired by purchase within a twelve-month period.

      (2) Gain or loss is generally recognized to old target corporation on deemed sale of assets.

(3) The deemed sales price for the target corporation's assets is generally the FMV of the target's assets as of the close of the acquisition date.

F. Personal Holding Company and Accumulated Earnings Taxes

1. Personal holding companies (PHC) are subject to a penalty tax on undistributed PHC income to discourage taxpayers from accumulating their investment income in a corporation taxed at lower than individual rates.

   a. A **personal holding company** is any corporation (except certain banks, financial institutions, and similar corporations) that meets two requirements.

      (1) During anytime in the last half of the tax year, five or fewer individuals own more than 50% of the value of the outstanding **stock** directly or indirectly, **and**

      (2) The corporation receives at least 60% of its adjusted ordinary gross **income** as "personal holding company income" (e.g., dividends, interest, rents, royalties, and other passive income)

   b. Taxed

      (1) At ordinary corporate rates on taxable income, plus

      (2) 15% tax rate on undistributed PHC income (for tax years beginning after 12/31/02)

   c. The PHC tax

      (1) Is **self-assessing** (i.e., computed on Sch. PH and attached to Form 1120); a six-year statute of limitations applies if no Sch. PH is filed

      (2) May be avoided by dividend payments sufficient in amount to reduce undistributed PHC income to zero

   d. The PHC tax is computed as follows:

      Taxable Income
      + Dividends-received deduction
      + Net operating loss deduction (except NOL of immediately preceding year allowed without a dividends-received deduction)
      – Federal and foreign income taxes
      – Charitable contributions in excess of 10% limit
      – Net capital loss
      – Net LTCG over NSTCL (net of tax)
      Adjusted Taxable Income
      – Dividends paid during taxable year
      – Dividends paid within 2 1/2 months after close of year (limited to 20% of dividends actually paid during year)
      – Dividend carryover
      – Consent dividends
      Undistributed PHC Income
      x   15%
      Personal Holding Company Tax

   e. **Consent dividends** are hypothetical dividends that are treated as if they were paid on the last day of the corporation's taxable year. Since they are not actually distributed, shareholders increase their stock basis by the amount of consent dividends included in their gross income.

   f. PHC tax liability for a previous year (but not interest and penalties) may be avoided by payment of a deficiency dividend within ninety days of a "determination" by the IRS that the corporation was a PHC for a previous year.

2. Corporations may be subject to an **accumulated earnings tax** (AET), in addition to regular income tax, if they accumulate earnings beyond reasonable business needs in order to avoid a shareholder tax on dividend distributions.

   a. The tax is not self-assessing, but is based on the IRS' determination of the existence of tax avoidance intent.

   b. AET may be imposed without regard to the number of shareholders of the corporation, but does not apply to personal holding companies.

   c. **Accumulated earnings credit** is allowed for greater of

(1) $250,000 ($150,000 for personal service corporations) minus the accumulated earnings and profits at end of prior year, or

(2) Reasonable needs of the business (e.g., expansion, working capital, to retire debt, etc.).

d.   Balance of accumulated taxable income is taxed at 15% tax rate (for tax years beginning after 12/31/02)

e.   The AET may be avoided by dividend payments sufficient in amount to reduce accumulated taxable income to zero.

f.   The accumulated earnings tax is computed as follows:

```
Taxable Income
   +    Dividends-received deduction
   +    NOL deduction
   −    Federal and foreign income taxes
   −    Excess charitable contributions (over 10% limit)
   −    Net capital loss
   −    Net LTCG over net STCL (net of tax)
Adjusted Taxable Income
   −    Dividends paid during last 9 1/2 months of tax year and 2 1/2 months after close
   −    Consent dividends
   −    Accumulated earnings credit
Accumulated Taxable Income
   x    15%
Accumulated Earnings Tax
```

G. S Corporations

An S corporation generally pays no corporate income taxes. Instead, it functions as a pass-through entity (much like a partnership) with its items of income, gain, loss, deduction, and credit passed through and directly included in the tax computations of its shareholders. Electing small business corporations are designated as S corporations; all other corporations are referred to as C corporations.

1. **Eligibility** requirements for S corporation status

    a.   Domestic corporation

    b.   An S corporation may own any percent of the stock of a C corporation, and 100% of the stock of a qualified subchapter S subsidiary.

        (1)   An S corporation cannot file a consolidated return with an affiliated C corporation.

        (2)   A *qualified subchapter S subsidiary* (QSSS) is any domestic corporation that qualifies as an S corporation and is 100% owned by an S corporation parent, which elects to treat it as a QSSS. A QSSS is not treated as a separate corporation and all of its assets, liabilities, and items of income, deduction, and credit are treated as belonging to the parent S corporation.

    c.   Only **one class of stock** issued and outstanding. A corporation will not be treated as having more than one class of stock solely because of differences in voting rights among the shares of common stock (i.e., both voting and nonvoting common stock may be outstanding).

    d.   **Shareholders** must be individuals, estates, or trusts created by will (only for a two-year period), voting trusts, an Electing Small Business Trust (ESBT), a Qualified Subchapter S Trust (QSST), or a trust all of which is treated as owned by an individual who is a citizen or resident of the US (i.e., Subpart E trust).

        (1)   A QSST and a Subpart E trust may continue to be a shareholder for two years beginning with the date of death of the deemed owner.

        (2)   Code Sec. 401(a) qualified retirement plan trusts and Code Sec. 501(c) charitable organizations that are exempt from tax under Code Sec. 501(a) are eligible to be shareholders of an S corporation. The S corporation's items of income and deduction will flow through to the tax-exempt shareholder as unrelated business taxable income (UBIT).

    e.   No nonresident alien shareholders

    f.   Number of shareholders **limited to 75**

        (1)   Husband and wife (and their estates) are counted as one shareholder.

        (2)   Each beneficiary of a voting trust is considered a shareholder.

      (3) If a trust is treated as owned by an individual, that individual (not the trust) is treated as the shareholder.

2. An **election must be filed** anytime in the preceding taxable year or on or before the fifteenth day of the third month of the year for which effective.

    a. All shareholders on date of election, plus any shareholders who held stock during the taxable year but before the date of election, must consent to the election.

       (1) If an election is made on or before the fifteenth day of the third month of taxable year, but either (1) a shareholder who held stock during the taxable year and before the date of election does not consent to the election, or (2) the corporation did not meet the eligibility requirements during the part of the year before the date of election, then the election is treated as made for the following taxable year.

       (2) An election made after the fifteenth day of the third month of the taxable year is treated as made for the following year.

    b. A newly formed corporation's election will be timely if made within two and one-half months of the first day of its taxable year (e.g., a calendar-year corporation formed on August 6, 2003, could make an S corporation election that would be effective for its 2003 calendar year if the election is filed on or before October 20, 2003).

    c. A valid election is effective for all succeeding years until terminated.

    d. The IRS has the authority to waive the effect of an invalid election caused by a corporation's inadvertent failure to qualify as a small business corporation or to obtain required shareholder consents (including elections regarding qualified subchapter S trusts), or both. Additionally, the IRS may treat late-filed subchapter S elections as timely filed if there is reasonable cause justifying the late filing.

3. **LIFO recapture.** A C corporation using LIFO that converts to S status must recapture the excess of the inventory's value using a FIFO cost flow assumption over its LIFO tax basis as of the close of its last tax year as a C corporation.

    a. The LIFO recapture is included in the C corporation's gross income and the tax attributable to its inclusion is payable in four equal installments.

    b. The first installment must be paid by the due date of the tax return for the last C corporation year, with the three remaining installments due by the due dates of the tax returns for the three succeeding taxable years.

4. A corporation making an S election is generally required to **adopt or change to (1) a year ending December 31,** or (2) a fiscal year that is the same as the fiscal year used by shareholders owning more than 50% of the corporation's stock.

    a. An S corporation may use a different fiscal year if a valid business purpose can be established (i.e., natural business year) and IRS permission is received. The business purpose test will be met if an S corporation receives at least 25% of its gross receipts in the last two months of the selected fiscal year, and this 25% test has been satisfied for three consecutive years.

    EXAMPLE: An S corporation, on a calendar year, has received at least 25% of its gross receipts during the months of May and June for each of the last three years. The S corporation may be allowed to change to a fiscal year ending June 30.

    b. An S corporation that otherwise would be required to adopt or change its tax year (normally to the calendar year) may elect to use a fiscal year if the election does not result in a deferral period longer than three months, or, if less, the deferral period of the year currently in use.

       (1) The "deferral period" is the number of months between the close of the fiscal year elected and the close of the required year (e.g., if an S corporation elects a tax year ending September 30 and a tax year ending December 31 is required, the deferral period of the year ending September 30 is three months).

       (2) An S corporation that elects a tax year other than a required year must make a "required payment" which is in the nature of a refundable, noninterest-bearing deposit that is intended to

compensate the government for the revenue lost as a result of tax deferral. The required payment is due on May 15 each year and is recomputed for each subsequent year.

5. An S corporation must **file Form 1120S** by the fifteenth day of the third month following the close of its taxable year (e.g., March 15 for a calendar-year S corporation).

  a. An automatic six-month extension may be obtained by filing Form 7004.
  b. Estimated tax payments must be made if estimated tax liability (e.g., built-in gains tax, excess net passive income tax) is expected to be $500 or more.

6. **Termination** of S corporation status may be caused by

  a. Shareholders owning **more than 50%** of the shares of stock of the corporation consent to **revocation** of the election.

    (1) A revocation made on or before the fifteenth day of the third month of the taxable year is generally effective on the first day of such taxable year.
    (2) A revocation made after the fifteenth day of the third month of the taxable year is generally effective as of the first day of the following taxable year.
    (3) Instead of the dates mentioned above, a revocation may specify an effective date on or after the date on which the revocation is filed.

    EXAMPLE: For a calendar-year S corporation, a revocation not specifying a revocation date that is made on or before 3/15/03 is effective as of 1/1/03. A revocation not specifying a revocation date that is made after 3/15/03 is effective as of 1/1/04. If a revocation is filed 3/11/03 and specifies a revocation date of 7/1/03, the corporation ceases to be an S corporation on 7/1/03.

  b. The corporation's **failing to satisfy any of the eligibility requirements** listed in 1. Termination is effective on the date an eligibility requirement is failed.

  EXAMPLE: A calendar-year S corporation with common stock outstanding issues preferred stock on April 1, 2003. Since its S corporation status terminates on April 1, it must file an S corporation tax return (Form 1120S) for the period January 1 through March 31, and a C corporation tax return (Form 1120) for the period April 1 through December 31, 2003. Both tax returns would be due by March 15, 2004.

  c. Passive investment income exceeding 25% of gross receipts for three consecutive taxable years if the corporation has subchapter C earnings and profits at the end of each of those years.

    (1) Subchapter C earnings and profits are earnings and profits accumulated during a taxable year for which the corporation was a C corporation.
    (2) Termination is effective as of the first day of the taxable year beginning after the third consecutive year of passive investment income in excess of 25% of gross receipts.

    EXAMPLE: An S corporation with subchapter C earnings and profits had passive investment income in excess of 25% of its gross receipts for its calendar years 2001, 2002, and 2003. Its S corporation status would terminate 1/1/04.

  d. Generally once terminated, S corporation status can be reelected only after five non-S-corporation years.

    (1) The corporation can request IRS for an earlier reelection.
    (2) IRS may treat an inadvertent termination as if it never occurred.

7. An **S corporation** generally pays no federal income taxes, but may have to pay a tax on its built-in gain, or on its excess passive investment income if certain conditions are met (see page 580).

  a. The S corporation is treated as a **pass-through entity;** the character of any item of income, expense, gain, loss, or credit is determined at the corporate level, and passes through to shareholders, retaining its identity.
  b. An S corporation must recognize gain on the distribution of appreciated property (other than its own obligations) to its shareholders. Gain is recognized in the same manner as if the property had been sold to the distributee at its FMV.

  EXAMPLE: An S corporation distributes property with a FMV of $900 and an adjusted basis of $100 to its sole shareholder. Gain of $800 will be recognized by the corporation. The character of the gain will be determined at the corporate level, and passed through and reported by its shareholder. The shareholder is treated as receiving a $900 distribution, subject to the distribution rules discussed on page 579.

c.   Expenses and interest owed to any cash-method shareholder are deductible by an accrual-method S corporation only when paid.

> *EXAMPLE: An accrual-method calendar-year S corporation accrues $2,000 of salary to a cash-method employee (a 1% shareholder) during 2003, but does not make payment until February 2004. The $2,000 will be deductible by the corporation in 2004, and reported by the shareholder-employee as income in 2004.*

d.   An S corporation will not generate any earnings and profits. All items are reflected in adjustments to the basis of shareholders' stock and/or debt.

e.   S corporations must make estimated tax payments for the tax liability attributable to the built-in gains tax, excess passive investment income tax, and the tax due to investment credit recapture.

f.   The provisions of subchapter C apply to an S corporation, except where inconsistent with subchapter S. For example, an S corporation can use Secs. 332 and 337 to liquidate an acquired subsidiary, and can make a Sec. 338 election if otherwise qualified.

8.   A **shareholder** of an S corporation must separately take into account (for the shareholder's taxable year in which the taxable year of the S corporation ends) (1) the shareholder's pro rata share of the corporation's items of income (including tax-exempt income), loss, deduction, or credit the separate treatment of which could affect the tax liability of **any** shareholder, plus (2) the shareholder's pro rata share of all remaining items which are netted together into "ordinary income (loss) from trade or business activity."

a.   Some of the **items which must be separately passed through** to retain their identity include

   (1)   Net long-term capital gain (loss)
   (2)   Net short-term capital gain (loss)
   (3)   Net gain (loss) from Sec. 1231 casualty or theft
   (4)   Net gain (loss) from other Sec. 1231 transactions
   (5)   Tax-exempt interest
   (6)   Charitable contributions
   (7)   Foreign income taxes
   (8)   Depletion
   (9)   Investment interest expense
   (10)   Dividend, interest, and royalty income
   (11)   Net income (loss) from real estate activity
   (12)   Net income (loss) from other rental activity

b.   All separately stated items plus the ordinary income or loss are allocated on a **per share, per day basis** to anyone who was a shareholder during the year. Items are allocated to shareholders' stock (both voting and nonvoting) but not to debt.

   (1)   The per share, per day rule will not apply if

      (a)   A shareholder's interest is completely terminated and all affected shareholders consent to allocate items as if the corporation's taxable year consisted of two years, the first of which ends on the date the shareholder's interest was terminated. The closing of the books method applies only to the affected shareholders. *Affected shareholders* include the shareholder whose interest was terminated and shareholders to whom the terminating shareholder transferred shares during the year.

      > *EXAMPLE: Assume in the above example that the S corporation had net income of $40,000 for the month of January. If both Alan and Betty consent, $40,000 would be allocated to Alan, and $325,000 would be allocated to Betty.*

      (b)   An S corporation's election is terminated on other than the first day of the taxable year, and all shareholders during the S short year and all persons who were shareholders on the first day of the C short year consent to allocate items using the corporation's financial accounting records.

      > *EXAMPLE: Bartec Corporation, with ordinary income of $365,000 for calendar year 2003, had its S status terminated on February 1, 2003, when the Post Partnership became a shareholder. Assuming Bartec's shareholders do **not** elect to allocate items using Bartec's financial accounting records, the ordinary income for calendar year 2003 of $365,000 would be allocated on a daily basis between Bartec's S short year and its C short year. Thus, the amount of income to be reported on Bartec's S return would be $365,000/365 days (31 days) = $31,000. The remaining $365,000 – $31,000 = $334,000 of ordinary income would be reported on Bartec's C return for 2003.*

(2) The per share, per day rule **cannot** be used if

    (a) There is a sale or exchange of 50% or more of the stock of the corporation during an S termination year. Financial accounting records must be used to allocate items.

    (b) A Sec. 338 election is made. Then the gains and losses resulting from the Sec. 338 election must be reported on a C corporation return.

c. A shareholder who disposes of stock in an S corporation is treated as the shareholder for the day of disposition. A shareholder who dies is treated as the shareholder for the day of the shareholder's death.

> *EXAMPLE: Alan owned 100% of a calendar-year S corporation's stock on January 1, 2003. Alan sold all his stock to Betty on January 31. Assuming the S corporation had $365,000 of ordinary income for the entire 2003 calendar year, the amount allocated to Alan would be $31,000 (31 days x $1,000 per day), and the amount allocated to Betty would be $334,000 (334 days x $1,000 per day).*

9. Three sets of rules may limit the amount of S corporation loss that a shareholder can deduct.

a. A shareholder's allocation of the aggregate **losses and deductions** of an S corporation can be deducted by the shareholder to the extent of the **shareholder's basis for stock plus basis of any debt** owed the shareholder by the corporation [Sec. 1366 (d)].

    (1) An excess of loss over combined basis for stock and debt can be carried forward indefinitely and deducted when there is basis to absorb it.

> *EXAMPLE: An S corporation incurred losses totaling $50,000. Its sole shareholder (who materially participates in the business and is at-risk) had a stock basis of $30,000 and debt with a basis of $15,000. The shareholder's loss deduction is limited to $45,000. The losses first reduce stock basis to zero, then debt basis is reduced to zero. The excess loss of $5,000 can be carried forward and deducted when there is basis to absorb it.*

    (2) Once reduced, the basis of debt is later increased (but not above its original basis) by *net undistributed income.*

> *EXAMPLE: An S corporation incurred a loss of $20,000 for 2002. Its sole shareholder (who materially participates in the business and is at-risk) had a stock basis of $10,000 and debt with a basis of $15,000. The pass-through of the $20,000 loss would first reduce stock basis to zero, and then reduce debt basis to $5,000.*
>
> *Assume that for 2003, the same S corporation had ordinary income of $10,000, and made a $4,000 cash distribution to its shareholder during the year. The first $4,000 of basis increase resulting from the pass-through of income would be allocated to stock in order to permit the $4,000 distribution to be nontaxable. The remaining basis increase (net **un**distributed income of $6,000) would restore debt basis to $11,000 (from $5,000).*

b. The deductibility of S corporation losses is also limited to the amount of the shareholder's **at-risk basis** at the end of the taxable year [Sec. 465].

    (1) A shareholder's amount at-risk includes amounts borrowed and reloaned to the S corporation if the shareholder is personally liable for repayment of the borrowed amount, or has pledged property not used in the activity as security for the borrowed amount.

    (2) A shareholder's amount at-risk does not include any debt of the S corporation to any person other than the shareholder, even if the shareholder guarantees the debt.

c. The deductibility of S corporation losses may also be subject to the **passive activity loss limitations** [Sec. 469]. Passive activity losses are deductible only to the extent of the shareholder's income from other passive activities (See Module 33).

    (1) Passive activities include (a) any S corporation trade or business in which the shareholder does not materially participate, and (b) any rental activity.

    (2) If a shareholder "actively participates" in a rental activity and owns (together with spouse) at least 10% of the value of an S corporation's stock, up to $25,000 of rental losses may be deductible against earned income and portfolio income.

10. A shareholder's S corporation **stock basis** is **increased** by all income items (including tax-exempt income), plus depletion in excess of the basis of the property subject to depletion; **decreased** by all loss and deduction items, nondeductible expenses not charged to capital, and the shareholder's deduction for depletion on oil and gas wells; and **decreased** by distributions that are excluded from gross income. Stock basis is **adjusted in the following order:**

a. Increased for all income items

b. Decreased for distributions that are excluded from gross income

c.   Decreased for nondeductible, noncapital items
d.   Decreased for deductible expenses and losses

> *EXAMPLE: An S corporation has tax-exempt income of $5,000, and an ordinary loss from business activity of $6,000 for calendar year 2003. Its sole shareholder had a stock basis of $2,000 on January 1, 2003. The $5,000 of tax-exempt income would pass through to the shareholder, increasing the shareholder's stock basis to $7,000, and would permit the pass-through and deduction of the $6,000 of ordinary loss, reducing the shareholder's stock basis to $1,000.*

> *EXAMPLE: An S corporation had an ordinary loss from business activity of $6,000 and made a $7,000 cash distribution to its sole shareholder during calendar year 2003. The sole shareholder had a stock basis of $8,000 on January 1, 2003. The $7,000 cash distribution would be nontaxable and would reduce stock basis to $1,000. As a result, only $1,000 of the $6,000 ordinary loss would be allowable as a deduction to the shareholder for 2003. The remaining $5,000 of ordinary loss would be carried forward and deducted by the shareholder when there is stock basis to absorb it.*

11.   The **treatment of distributions** (Cash + FMV of other property) to shareholders is determined as follows:

a.   Distributions are **nontaxable** to the extent of the Accumulated Adjustments Account (AAA) and are applied to **reduce the AAA and the shareholder's stock basis**.

   (1)   The AAA represents the cumulative total of undistributed net income items for S corporation taxable years beginning after 1982.
   (2)   If there is more than one distribution during the year, a pro rata portion of each distribution is treated as made from the AAA.
   (3)   The AAA can have a negative balance if expenses and losses exceed income.
   (4)   No adjustment is made to the AAA for tax-exempt income and related expenses, and Federal taxes attributable to a year in which the corporation was a C corporation. Tax-exempt income and related expenses are reflected in the corporation's Other Adjustments Account (OAA).
   (5)   For purposes of determining the treatment of a distribution, the amount in the AAA at the close of any taxable year is determined without regard to any **net negative adjustment** (i.e., the excess of reductions over increases to the AAA for the taxable year) for such taxable year.

b.   Distributions in excess of the AAA are treated as **ordinary dividends** to the extent of the corporation's **accumulated earnings and profits (AEP).** These amounts represent earnings and profits that were accumulated (and never taxed to shareholders) during C corporation taxable years.

c.   Distributions are next **nontaxable** to the extent of **remaining stock basis** and are applied to reduce the OAA and paid-in capital.

d.   Distributions **in excess of stock basis** are treated as **gain** from the sale of stock.

> *EXAMPLE: A calendar-year S corporation had subchapter C accumulated earnings and profits of $10,000 at December 31, 2002. During calendar year 2003, the corporation had net income of $20,000, and distributed $38,000 to its sole shareholder on June 20, 2003. Its shareholder had a stock basis of $15,000 at January 1, 2003.*
> *The $20,000 of net income passes through and is includible in gross income by the shareholder for 2003. The shareholder's stock basis is increased by the $20,000 of income (to $35,000), as is the AAA which is increased to $20,000. Of the $38,000 distribution, the first $20,000 is nontaxable and (1) reduces stock basis to $15,000, and (2) the AAA to zero; the next $10,000 of distribution is reported as dividend income (no effect on stock basis); while the remaining $8,000 of distribution is nontaxable and reduces stock basis to $7,000.*

12.   Health and accident insurance premiums and other **fringe benefits** paid by an S corporation on behalf of a more than 2% shareholder-employee are deductible by the S corporation as compensation and includible in the shareholder-employee's gross income on Form W-2.

13.   An S corporation (that previously was a C corporation) is taxed on its **net recognized built-in gain** if the gain is (1) attributable to an excess of the FMV of its assets over their aggregate adjusted basis as of the beginning of its first taxable year as an S corporation, and (2) is recognized within **ten years** after the effective date of its S corporation election.

a.   This provision generally applies to C corporations that make an S corporation election after December 31, 1986.

b.   To determine the tax, (1) take the lesser of (a) the net recognized built-in gain for the taxable year, or (b) taxable income determined as if the corporation were a C corporation (except the NOL and dividends-received deductions are not allowed); (2) subtract any NOL and capital loss carryforwards from C corporation years; (3) multiply the resulting amount by the highest corporate tax rate (currently 35%); and (4) subtract any general business credit carryovers from C corporation years and the special fuels tax credit.

c.   Any net recognized built-in gain that escapes the built-in gains tax because of the taxable income limitation is carried forward and is subject to the built-in gains tax to the extent the corporation subsequently has other taxable income (that is not already subject to the built-in gains tax) for any taxable year within the ten-year recognition period.

d.   Recognized built-in gain **does not include** gain from the disposition of an asset if

(1) The asset was not held by the corporation when its S election became effective (e.g., an asset was purchased after the first day of its S election), or

(2) The gain is attributable to appreciation that occurred after the S election became effective (e.g., an asset is sold for a gain of $1,000, but $600 of its appreciation occurred after the first day of its S election; the corporation would be taxed on only $400 of gain).

e.   The total amount of net recognized built-in gain that will be taxed to an S corporation is limited to the aggregate net unrealized built-in gain when the S election became effective.

f.   The **built-in gains tax** that is paid by an S corporation is **treated as a loss** sustained by the S corporation during the taxable year. The character of the loss is determined by allocating the loss proportionately among the recognized built-in gains giving rise to such tax.

EXAMPLE: For 2003, an S corporation has taxable income of $100,000, which includes a $40,000 long-term capital gain that is also a recognized built-in gain. Since its recognized built-in gain of $40,000 is less than its taxable income, its built-in gains tax for 2003 is $40,000 x 35% = $14,000. Since the built-in gain was a long-term capital gain, the built-in gains tax paid of $14,000 is treated as a long-term capital loss. As a result, a net long-term capital gain of $26,000 ($40,000 LTCG – $14,000 LTCL) passes through to shareholders for 2003.

EXAMPLE: For 2003, an S corporation has taxable income of $10,000, which includes a $40,000 long-term capital gain that is also a recognized built-in gain. Since its taxable income of $10,000 is less than its recognized built-in gain of $40,000, its built-in gains tax for 2003 is limited to $10,000 x 35% = $3,500. As a result, a net long-term capital gain of $40,000 – $3,500 = $36,500 passes through to shareholders for 2003.

The remaining $30,000 of untaxed recognized built-in gain would be suspended and carried forward to 2004, where it would again be treated as a recognized built-in gain. If the S corporation has at least $30,000 of taxable income in 2004 that is not already subject to the built-in gains tax, the suspended gain from 2003 will be taxed. As a result, the amount of built-in gains tax paid by the S corporation for 2004 will be $30,000 x 35% = $10,500, and will pass through to shareholders as a long-term capital loss, since the original gain in 2003 was a long-term capital gain.

14. If an S corporation has subchapter C accumulated earnings and profits, and its **passive investment income exceeds 25% of gross receipts,** a tax is imposed at the highest corporate rate on the lesser of (1) excess net passive income (ENPI), or (2) taxable income.

a. $$\text{ENPI} = \binom{\text{Net passive}}{\text{income}} \times \left(\frac{\text{Passive investment income} - (25\% \text{ of Gross receipts})}{\text{Passive investment income}} \right)$$

b.   **Passive investment income** means gross receipts derived from dividends, interest, royalties, rents, annuities, and gains from the sale or exchange of stock or securities. However, dividends from an affiliated C corporation subsidiary are not treated as passive investment income to the extent the dividends are attributable to the earnings and profits derived from the active conduct of a trade or business by the C corporation.

c.   The tax paid reduces the amount of passive investment income passed through to shareholders

EXAMPLE: An S corporation has gross receipts of $80,000, of which $50,000 is interest income. Expenses incurred in the production of this passive income total $10,000. The ENPI is $24,000.

$$\text{ENPI} = (\$50,000 - \$10,000) \times \left(\frac{\$50,000 - (25\% \times \$80,000)}{\$50,000} \right) = \$24,000$$

H. Corporate Reorganizations

Certain exchanges, usually involving the exchange of one corporation's stock for the stock or property of another, result in deferral of gain or loss.

1.   There are seven different **types** of reorganizations which generally result in nonrecognition treatment.

a.   Type A—statutory mergers or consolidations

(1) Merger is one corporation absorbing another by operation of law

(2) Consolidation is two corporations combining in a new corporation, the former ones dissolving

b.   Type B—the use of solely voting stock of the acquiring corporation (or its parent) to acquire at least 80% of the voting power and 80% of each class of nonvoting stock of the target corporation

        (1) No boot can be used by the acquiring corporation to acquire the target's stock

        (2) Results in the acquisition of a controlled subsidiary

   c. Type C—the use of solely voting stock of the acquiring corporation (or its parent) to acquire substantially all of the target's properties

        (1) In determining whether the acquisition is made for solely voting stock, the assumption by the acquiring corporation of a liability of the target corporation, or the fact that the property acquired is subject to a liability is disregarded.

        (2) "Substantially all" means at least 90% of the FMV of the target's net assets, and at least 70% of its gross assets.

        (3) The target (acquired) corporation must distribute the consideration it receives, as well as all of its other properties, in pursuance of the plan of reorganization.

   d. Type D—a transfer by a corporation of part or all of its assets to another if immediately after the transfer the transferor corporation, or its shareholders, control the transferee corporation (i.e., own at least 80% of the voting power and at least 80% of each class of nonvoting stock)

        (1) Although it may be acquisitive, this type of reorganization is generally used to divide a corporation.

        (2) Generally results in a spin-off, split-off, or split-up.

   e. Type E—a recapitalization to change the capital structure of a single corporation (e.g., bondholders exchange old bonds for new bonds or stock)

   f. Type F—a mere change in identity, form, or place of organization (e.g., name change, change of state of incorporation)

   g. Type G—a transfer of assets by an insolvent corporation or pursuant to bankruptcy proceedings, with the result that former creditors often become the owners of the corporation

2. For the reorganization to be tax-free, it must meet one of the above definitions and the exchange must be made under a plan or reorganization involving the affected corporations as parties to the reorganization. It generally must satisfy the judicial doctrines of continuity of shareholder interest, business purpose, and continuity of business enterprise.

   a. **Continuity of shareholder interest**—The shareholders of the transferor (acquired) corporation must receive stock in the transferee (acquiring) corporation at least equal in value to 50% of the value of all of the transferor's formerly outstanding stock.

   b. **Continuity of business enterprise**—The transferor's historic business must be continued, or a significant portion (e.g., 1/3) of the transferor's historic assets must be used in a business.

3. **No gain or loss** is generally recognized to a **transferor corporation** on the transfer of its property pursuant to a plan of reorganization.

   a. The **transferee corporation's basis for property** received equals the transferor's basis plus gain recognized (if any) to the transferor.

   b. Gain is recognized on the distribution to shareholders of any property other than stock or securities of a party to the reorganization (e.g., property the transferor retained and did not transfer to the acquiring corporation), as if such property were sold for its FMV.

4. No gain or loss is recognized by a corporation on the disposition of stock or securities in another corporation that is a party to the reorganization.

   a. No gain or loss is generally recognized on the distribution of stock or securities of a controlled subsidiary in a qualifying spin-off, split-off, or split-up. However, the distributing corporation must recognize gain on the distribution of its subsidiary's stock if immediately after the distribution, any person holds a 50% or greater interest in the distributing corporation or a distributed subsidiary that is attributable to stock acquired by purchase during the five-year period ending on date of distribution.

   b. Gain is recognized on the distribution of appreciated boot property.

5. If a **shareholder receives boot** in a reorganization, gain is recognized (but not loss).

a. Boot includes the FMV of an excess of principal (i.e., face) amount of securities received over the principal amount of securities surrendered.

> *EXAMPLE: In a recapitalization, a bondholder exchanges a bond with a face amount and basis of $1,000, for a new bond with a face amount of $1,500 and a fair market value of $1,575. Since an excess face amount of security ($500) has been received, the bondholder's realized gain of $575 will be recognized to the extent of the fair market value of the excess [($500/$1,500) x $1,575] = $525.*

b. Recognized gain will be treated as a dividend to the extent of the shareholder's ratable share of earnings and profits of the acquired corporation if the receipt of boot has the effect of the distribution of a dividend.

   (1) Whether the receipt of boot has the effect of a dividend is determined by applying the Sec. 302(b) redemption tests based on the shareholder's stock interest in the acquiring corporation (i.e., as if only stock had been received, and then the boot was used to redeem the stock that was not received).

   (2) The receipt of boot will generally not have the effect of a dividend, and will thus result in capital gain.

6. A shareholder's **basis for stock and securities received** equals the basis of stock and securities surrendered, plus gain recognized, and minus boot received.

> *EXAMPLE: Pursuant to a merger of Corporation T into Corporation P, Smith exchanged 100 shares of T that he had purchased for $1,000, for 80 shares of P having a FMV of $1,500 and also received $200 cash. Smith's realized gain of $700 is recognized to the extent of the cash received of $200, and is treated as a capital gain. Smith's basis for his P stock is $1,000 ($1,000 + $200 recognized gain – $200 cash received).*

7. **Carryover of tax attributes**

a. The tax attributes of the acquired corporation (e.g., NOL carryovers, earnings and profits, accounting methods, etc.) generally carry over to the acquiring corporation in an acquisitive reorganization.

b. The amount of an **acquired corporation's NOL** carryovers that can be utilized by the acquiring corporation for its first taxable year ending after the date of acquisition is **limited by Sec. 381** to

$$\text{Acquiring corporation's TI before NOL deduction} \quad \text{x} \quad \frac{\text{Days after acquisition date}}{\text{Total days in taxable year}}$$

> *EXAMPLE: Corporation P (on a calendar year) acquired Corporation T in a statutory merger on October 19, 2003, with the former T shareholders receiving 60% of P's stock. If T had an NOL carryover of $70,000, and P has taxable income (before an NOL deduction) of $91,500, the amount of T's $70,000 NOL carryover that can be deducted by P for 2003 would be*

$$\$91,500 \ x \ \frac{73}{365} \ = \ \$18,300$$

c. If there is a **more than 50% change in ownership** of a loss corporation, the taxable income for any year of the new loss (or surviving) corporation may be reduced by an NOL carryover from the old loss corporation only to the extent of the value of the old loss corporation's stock on the date of the ownership change multiplied by the "long-term tax-exempt rate" (**Sec. 382 limitation**).

   (1) An ownership change has occurred when the percentage of stock owned by an entity's 5% or more shareholders has increased by more than 50 percentage points relative to the lowest percentage owned by such shareholders at any time during the preceding three-year testing period.

   (2) For the year of acquisition, the Sec. 382 limitation amount is available only to the extent allocable to days after the acquisition date.

$$\text{Sec. 382 limitation} \quad \text{x} \quad \frac{\text{Days after acquisition date}}{\text{Totals days in taxable year}}$$

> *EXAMPLE: If T's former shareholders received only 30% of P's stock in the preceding example, there would be a more than 50 percentage point change in ownership of T Corporation, and T's NOL carryover would be subject to a Sec. 382 limitation. If the FMV of T's stock on October 19, 2003, was $500,000 and the long-term tax-exempt rate were 5%, the Sec. 382 limitation for 2003 would be ($500,000 x 5%) x (73/365 days) = $5,000.*
>
> *Thus, only $5,000 of T's NOL carryover could be deducted by P for 2003. The remaining $70,000 – $5,000 = $65,000 of T's NOL would be carried forward by P and could be used to offset P's taxable income for 2004 to the extent of the Sec. 382 limitation (i.e., $500,000 x 5% = $25,000).*

MULTIPLE-CHOICE QUESTIONS (1-164)

1. Alan, Baker, and Carr formed Dexter Corporation during 2003. Pursuant to the incorporation agreement, Alan transferred property with an adjusted basis of $30,000 and a fair market value of $45,000 for 450 shares of stock, Baker transferred cash of $35,000 in exchange for 350 shares of stock, and Carr performed services valued at $25,000 in exchange for 250 shares of stock. Assuming the fair market value of Dexter Corporation stock is $100 per share, what is Dexter Corporation's tax basis for the property received from Alan?

    a. $0
    b. $30,000
    c. $45,000
    d. $65,000

2. Clark and Hunt organized Jet Corp. with authorized voting common stock of $400,000. Clark contributed $60,000 cash. Both Clark and Hunt transferred other property in exchange for Jet stock as follows:

| | | Other property | |
	Adjusted basis	Fair market value	Percentage of Jet stock acquired
Clark	$ 50,000	$100,000	40%
Hunt	120,000	240,000	60%

What was Clark's basis in Jet stock?

    a. $0
    b. $100,000
    c. $110,000
    d. $160,000

3. Adams, Beck, and Carr organized Flexo Corp. with authorized voting common stock of $100,000. Adams received 10% of the capital stock in payment for the organizational services that he rendered for the benefit of the newly formed corporation. Adams did not contribute property to Flexo and was under no obligation to be paid by Beck or Carr. Beck and Carr transferred property in exchange for stock as follows:

	Adjusted basis	Fair market value	Percentage of Flexo stock acquired
Beck	5,000	20,000	20%
Carr	60,000	70,000	70%

What amount of gain did Carr recognize from this transaction?

    a. $40,000
    b. $15,000
    c. $10,000
    d. $0

4. Jones incorporated a sole proprietorship by exchanging all the proprietorship's assets for the stock of Nu Co., a new corporation. To qualify for tax-free incorporation, Jones must be in control of Nu immediately after the exchange. What percentage of Nu's stock must Jones own to qualify as "control" for this purpose?

    a. 50.00%
    b. 51.00%
    c. 66.67%
    d. 80.00%

5. Feld, the sole stockholder of Maki Corp., paid $50,000 for Maki's stock in 1997. In 2003, Feld contributed a parcel of land to Maki but was not given any additional stock for this contribution. Feld's basis for the land was $10,000, and its fair market value was $18,000 on the date of the transfer of title. What is Feld's adjusted basis for the Maki stock?

    a. $50,000
    b. $52,000
    c. $60,000
    d. $68,000

6. Rela Associates, a partnership, transferred all of its assets, with a basis of $300,000, along with liabilities of $50,000, to a newly formed corporation in return for all of the corporation's stock. The corporation assumed the liabilities. Rela then distributed the corporation's stock to its partners in liquidation. In connection with this incorporation of the partnership, Rela recognizes

    a. No gain or loss on the transfer of its assets nor on the assumption of Rela's liabilities by the corporation.
    b. Gain on the assumption of Rela's liabilities by the corporation.
    c. Gain or loss on the transfer of its assets to the corporation.
    d. Gain, but **not** loss, on the transfer of its assets to the corporation.

7. Roberta Warner and Sally Rogers formed the Acme Corporation on October 1, 2003. On the same date Warner paid $75,000 cash to Acme for 750 shares of its common stock. Simultaneously, Rogers received 100 shares of Acme's common stock for services rendered. How much should Rogers include as taxable income for 2003 and what will be the basis of her stock?

	Taxable income	Basis of stock
a.	$0	$0
b.	$0	$10,000
c.	$10,000	$0
d.	$10,000	$10,000

8. Jackson, a single individual, inherited Bean Corp. common stock from Jackson's parents. Bean is a qualified small business corporation under Code Sec. 1244. The stock cost Jackson's parents $20,000 and had a fair market value of $25,000 at the parents' date of death. During the year, Bean declared bankruptcy and Jackson was informed that the stock was worthless. What amount may Jackson deduct as an ordinary loss in the current year?

    a. $0
    b. $ 3,000
    c. $20,000
    d. $25,000

9. Which of the following is **not** a requirement for stock to qualify as Sec. 1244 small business corporation stock?

    a. The stock must be issued to an individual or to a partnership.
    b. The stock was issued for money or property (other than stock and securities).
    c. The stock must be common stock.
    d. The issuer must be a domestic corporation.

10. During the current year, Dinah sold Sec. 1244 small business corporation stock that she owned for a loss of $125,000. Assuming Dinah is married and files a joint income tax return for 2003, what is the character of Dinah's recognized loss from the sale of the stock?

a. $125,000 capital loss.
b. $25,000 capital loss; $100,000 ordinary loss.
c. $75,000 capital loss; $50,000 ordinary loss.
d. $0 capital loss; $125,000 ordinary loss.

11. Nancy, who is single, formed a corporation during 1999 using a tax-free asset transfer that qualified under Sec. 351. She transferred property having an adjusted basis of $80,000 and a fair market value of $60,000, and in exchange received Sec. 1244 small business corporation stock. During February 2003, Nancy sold all of her stock for $35,000. What is the amount and character of Nancy's recognized loss resulting from the sale of the stock in 2003?
   a. $0 ordinary loss; $45,000 capital loss.
   b. $25,000 ordinary loss; $10,000 capital loss.
   c. $25,000 ordinary loss; $20,000 capital loss.
   d. $45,000 ordinary loss; $0 capital loss.

12. A civil fraud penalty can be imposed on a corporation that underpays tax by
   a. Omitting income as a result of inadequate record-keeping.
   b. Failing to report income it erroneously considered **not** to be part of corporate profits.
   c. Filing an incomplete return with an appended statement, making clear that the return is incomplete.
   d. Maintaining false records and reporting fictitious transactions to minimize corporate tax liability.

13. Bass Corp., a calendar-year C corporation, made qualifying 2002 estimated tax deposits based on its actual 2001 tax liability. On March 15, 2003, Bass filed a timely automatic extension request for its 2002 corporate income tax .return. Estimated tax deposits and the extension payment totaled $7,600. This amount was 95% of the total tax shown on Bass' final 2002 corporate income tax return. Bass paid $400 additional tax on the final 2002 corporate income tax return filed before the extended due date. For the 2002 calendar year, Bass was subject to pay

I.   Interest on the $400 tax payment made in 2003.
II. A tax delinquency penalty.

   a. I only.
   b. II only.
   c. Both I and II.
   d. Neither I nor II.

14. Edge Corp., a calendar-year C corporation, had a net operating loss and zero tax liability for its 2003 tax year. To avoid the penalty for underpayment of estimated taxes, Edge could compute its first quarter 2004 estimated income tax payment using the

	Annualized income method	*Preceding year method*
a.	Yes	Yes
b.	Yes	No
c.	No	Yes
d.	No	No

15. A corporation's tax year can be reopened after all statutes of limitations have expired if

I.   The tax return has a 50% nonfraudulent omission from gross income.
II. The corporation prevails in a determination allowing a deduction in an open tax year that was taken erroneously in a closed tax year.

a. I only.
b. II only.
c. Both I and II.
d. Neither I nor II.

16. A corporation's penalty for underpaying federal estimated taxes is
   a. Not deductible.
   b. Fully deductible in the year paid.
   c. Fully deductible if reasonable cause can be established for the underpayment.
   d. Partially deductible.

17. Blink Corp., an accrual-basis calendar-year corporation, carried back a net operating loss for the tax year ended December 31, 2002. Blink's gross revenues have been under $500,000 since inception. Blink expects to have profits for the tax year ending December 31, 2003. Which method(s) of estimated tax payment can Blink use for its quarterly payments during the 2003 tax year to avoid underpayment of federal estimated taxes?

I.   100% of the preceding tax year method
II. Annualized income method

   a. I only.
   b. Both I and II.
   c. II only.
   d. Neither I nor II.

18. When computing a corporation's income tax expense for estimated income tax purposes, which of the following should be taken into account?

	Corporate tax credits	*Alternative minimum tax*
a.	No	No
b.	No	Yes
c.	Yes	No
d.	Yes	Yes

19. Finbury Corporation's taxable income for the year ended December 31, 2002, was $2,000,000 on which its tax liability was $680,000. In order for Finbury to escape the estimated tax underpayment penalty for the year ending December 31, 2003, Finbury's 2003 estimated tax payments must equal at least
   a. 90% of the 2003 tax liability.
   b. 93% of the 2003 tax liability.
   c. 100% of the 2003 tax liability.
   d. The 2002 tax liability of $680,000.

20. Kisco Corp.'s taxable income for 2003 before taking the dividends received deduction was $70,000. This includes $10,000 in dividends from a 15%-owned taxable domestic corporation. Given the following tax rates, what would Kisco's income tax be before any credits?

Taxable income partial rate table	*Tax rate*
Up to $50,000	15%
Over $50,000 but not over $75,000	25%

   a. $10,000
   b. $10,750
   c. $12,500
   d. $15,750

21. Green Corp. was incorporated and began business in 2001. In computing its alternative minimum tax for 2002, it determined that it had adjusted current earnings (ACE) of $400,000 and alternative minimum taxable income (prior to the ACE adjustment) of $300,000. For 2003, it had adjusted current earnings of $100,000 and alternative minimum taxable income (prior to the ACE adjustment) of $300,000. What is the amount of Green Corp.'s adjustment for adjusted current earnings that will be used in calculating its alternative minimum tax for 2003?

- a. $ 75,000
- b. $ (75,000)
- c. $(100,000)
- d. $(150,000)

22. Eastern Corp., a calendar-year corporation, was formed during 2002. On January 3, 2003, Eastern placed five-year property in service. The property was depreciated under the general MACRS system. Eastern did not elect to use the straight-line method. The following information pertains to Eastern:

Eastern's 2003 taxable income	$300,000
Adjustment for the accelerated depreciation taken on 2003 5-year property	1,000
2003 tax-exempt interest from private activity bonds	5,000

What was Eastern's 2003 alternative minimum taxable income before the adjusted current earnings (ACE) adjustment?

- a. $306,000
- b. $305,000
- c. $304,000
- d. $301,000

23. If a corporation's tentative minimum tax exceeds the regular tax, the excess amount is

- a. Carried back to the first preceding taxable year.
- b. Carried back to the third preceding taxable year.
- c. Payable in addition to the regular tax.
- d. Subtracted from the regular tax.

24. Rona Corp.'s 2003 alternative minimum taxable income was $200,000. The exempt portion of Rona's 2003 alternative minimum taxable income was

- a. $0
- b. $12,500
- c. $27,500
- d. $52,500

25. A corporation's tax preference items that must be taken into account for 2003 alternative minimum tax purposes include

- a. Use of the percentage-of-completion method of accounting for long-term contracts.
- b. Casualty losses.
- c. Tax-exempt interest on private activity bonds.
- d. Capital gains.

26. In computing its 2003 alternative minimum tax, a corporation must include as an adjustment

- a. The dividends received deduction.
- b. The difference between regular tax depreciation and straight-line depreciation over forty years for real property placed in service in 1998.
- c. Charitable contributions.
- d. Interest expense on investment property.

27. A corporation will not be subject to the alternative minimum tax for calendar year 2003 if

- a. The corporation's net assets do not exceed $7.5 million.
- b. The corporation's average annual gross receipts do not exceed $10 million.
- c. The corporation has less then ten shareholders.
- d. 2003 is the corporation's first tax year.

28. Bradbury Corp., a calendar-year corporation, was formed on January 2, 2000, and had gross receipts for its first four taxable years as follows:

Year	Gross receipts
2000	$4,500,000
2001	9,000,000
2002	9,500,000
2003	6,500,000

What is the first taxable year that Bradbury Corp. is **not exempt** from the alternative minimum tax (AMT)?

- a. 2001
- b. 2002
- c. 2003
- d. Bradbury is exempt from AMT for its first four taxable years.

29. Which of the following entities must include in gross income 100% of dividends received from unrelated taxable domestic corporations in computing regular taxable income?

	Personal service corporations	Personal holding companies
a.	Yes	Yes
b.	No	No
c.	Yes	No
d.	No	Yes

30. Andi Corp. issued $1,000,000 face amount of bonds in 1995 and established a sinking fund to pay the debt at maturity. The bondholders appointed an independent trustee to invest the sinking fund contributions and to administer the trust. In 2003, the sinking fund earned $60,000 in interest on bank deposits and $8,000 in net long-term capital gains. All of the trust income is accumulated with Andi's periodic contributions so that the aggregate amount will be sufficient to pay the bonds when they mature. What amount of trust income was taxable to Andi in 2003?

- a. $0
- b. $ 8,000
- c. $60,000
- d. $68,000

31. The following information pertains to treasury stock sold by Lee Corp. to an unrelated broker in 2003:

Proceeds received	$50,000
Cost	30,000
Par value	9,000

What amount of capital gain should Lee recognize in 2003 on the sale of this treasury stock?

- a. $0
- b. $ 8,000
- c. $20,000
- d. $30,500

32. During 2003, Ral Corp. exchanged 5,000 shares of its own $10 par common stock for land with a fair market value of $75,000. As a result of this exchange, Ral should report in its 2003 tax return

a. $25,000 Section 1245 gain.
b. $25,000 Section 1231 gain.
c. $25,000 ordinary income.
d. No gain.

33. Pym, Inc., which had earnings and profits of $100,000, distributed land to Kile Corporation, a stockholder, as a dividend in kind. Pym's adjusted basis for this land was $3,000. The land had a fair market value of $12,000 and was subject to a mortgage liability of $5,000, which was assumed by Kile Corporation. The dividend was declared and paid during November 2003.

How much of the distribution would be reportable by Kile as a dividend, before the dividends received deduction?
    a. $0
    b. $ 3,000
    c. $ 7,000
    d. $12,000

34. Which of the following costs are amortizable organizational expenditures?
    a.   Professional fees to issue the corporation's stock.
    b.   Commissions paid by the corporation to underwriters for stock issue.
    c.   Printing costs to issue the corporation's stock.
    d.   Expenses of temporary directors meetings.

35. Brown Corp., a calendar-year taxpayer, was organized and actively began operations on July 1, 2003, and incurred the following costs:

Legal fees to obtain corporate charter	$40,000
Commission paid to underwriter	25,000
Other stock issue costs	10,000

Brown wishes to amortize its organizational costs over the shortest period allowed for tax purposes. In 2003, what amount should Brown deduct for the amortization of organizational expenses?
    a. $8,000
    b. $7,500
    c. $5,000
    d. $4,000

36. The costs of organizing a corporation
    a.   May be deducted in full in the year in which these costs are incurred even if paid in later years.
    b.   May be deducted only in the year in which these costs are paid.
    c.   May be amortized over a period of not less than sixty months even if these costs are capitalized on the company's books.
    d.   Are nondeductible capital expenditures.

37. Silo Corp. was organized on March 1, 2003, began doing business on September 1, 2003, and elected to file its income tax return on a calendar-year basis. The following qualifying organizational expenditures were incurred in organizing the corporation:

July 1, 2003	$3,000
September 3, 2003	6,000

The maximum allowable deduction for amortization of organizational expenditures for 2003 is
    a. $ 600
    b. $ 700
    c. $ 900
    d. $1,500

38. During 2003, Jackson Corp. had the following income and expenses:

Gross income from operations	$100,000
Dividend income from taxable domestic 20%-owned corporations	10,000
Operating expenses	35,000
Officers' salaries	20,000
Contributions to qualified charitable organizations	8,000
Net operating loss carryforward from 2002	30,000

What is the amount of Jackson Corp.'s charitable contribution carryover to 2004?
    a. $0
    b. $2,500
    c. $5,500
    d. $6,300

39. In 2003, Cable Corp., a calendar-year C corporation, contributed $80,000 to a qualified charitable organization. Cable's 2003 taxable income before the deduction for charitable contributions was $820,000 after a $40,000 dividends received deduction. Cable also had carryover contributions of $10,000 from the prior year. In 2003, what amount can Cable deduct as charitable contributions?
    a. $90,000
    b. $86,000
    c. $82,000
    d. $80,000

40. If a corporation's charitable contributions exceed the limitation for deductibility in a particular year, the excess
    a.   Is **not** deductible in any future or prior year.
    b.   May be carried back or forward for one year at the corporation's election.
    c.   May be carried forward to a maximum of five succeeding years.
    d.   May be carried back to the third preceding year.

41. Tapper Corp., an accrual-basis calendar-year corporation, was organized on January 2, 2003. During 2003, revenue was exclusively from sales proceeds and interest income. The following information pertains to Tapper:

Taxable income before charitable contributions for the year ended December 31, 2003	$500,000
Tapper's matching contribution to employee-designated qualified universities made during 2003	10,000
Board of Directors' authorized contribution to a qualified charity (authorized December 1, 2003, made February 1, 2004)	30,000

What is the maximum allowable deduction that Tapper may take as a charitable contribution on its tax return for the year ended December 31, 2003?
    a. $0
    b. $10,000
    c. $30,000
    d. $40,000

42. Lyle Corp. is a distributor of pharmaceuticals and sells only to retail drug stores. During 2003, Lyle received unsolicited samples of nonprescription drugs from a manufacturer. Lyle donated these drugs in 2003 to a qualified exempt organization and deducted their fair market value as a charitable contribution. What should be included as gross income in Lyle's 2003 return for receipt of these samples?
    a.   Fair market value.
    b.   Net discounted wholesale price.
    c. $25 nominal value assigned to gifts.
    d. $0.

43. During 2003, Nale Corp. received dividends of $1,000 from a 10%-owned taxable domestic corporation. When Nale computes the maximum allowable deduction for contributions in its 2003 return, the amount of dividends to be included in the computation of taxable income is
   a. $0
   b. $ 200
   c. $ 300
   d. $1,000

44. Gero Corp. had operating income of $160,000, after deducting $10,000 for contributions to State University, but not including dividends of $2,000 received from nonaffiliated taxable domestic corporations.

In computing the maximum allowable deduction for contributions, Gero should apply the percentage limitation to a base amount of
   a. $172,000
   b. $170,400
   c. $170,000
   d. $162,000

45. Norwood Corporation is an accrual-basis taxpayer. For the year ended December 31, 2003, it had book income before tax of $500,000 after deducting a charitable contribution of $100,000. The contribution was authorized by the Board of Directors in December 2003, but was not actually paid until March 1, 2004. How should Norwood treat this charitable contribution for tax purposes to minimize its 2003 taxable income?
   a. It cannot claim a deduction in 2003, but must apply the payment against 2004 income.
   b. Make an election claiming a deduction for 2003 of $50,000 and carry the remainder over a maximum of five succeeding tax years.
   c. Make an election claiming a deduction for 2003 of $60,000 and carry the remainder over a maximum of five succeeding tax years.
   d. Make an election claiming a 2003 deduction of $100,000.

46. In 2003, Best Corp., an accrual-basis calendar-year C corporation, received $100,000 in dividend income from the common stock that it held in a 15%-owned domestic corporation. The stock was not debt-financed, and was held for over a year. Best recorded the following information for 2003:

Loss from Best's operations	$ (10,000)
Dividends received	100,000
Taxable income (before dividends received deduction)	$ 90,000

Best's dividends received deduction on its 2003 tax return was
   a. $100,000
   b. $ 80,000
   c. $ 70,000
   d. $ 63,000

47. In 2003, Acorn, Inc. had the following items of income and expense:

Sales	$500,000
Cost of sales	250,000
Dividends received	25,000

The dividends were received from a corporation of which Acorn owns 30%. In Acorn's 2003 corporate income tax

return, what amount should be reported as income before special deductions?
   a. $525,000
   b. $505,000
   c. $275,000
   d. $250,000

48. The corporate dividends received deduction
   a. Must exceed the applicable percentage of the recipient shareholder's taxable income.
   b. Is affected by a requirement that the investor corporation must own the investee's stock for a specified minimum holding period.
   c. Is unaffected by the percentage of the investee's stock owned by the investor corporation.
   d. May be claimed by S corporations.

49. In 2003, Ryan Corp. had the following income:

Income from operations	$300,000
Dividends from unrelated taxable domestic corporations less than 20% owned	2,000

Ryan had no portfolio indebtedness. In Ryan's 2003 taxable income, what amount should be included for the dividends received?
   a. $ 400
   b. $ 600
   c. $1,400
   d. $1,600

50. In 2003, Daly Corp. had the following income:

Profit from operations	$100,000
Dividends from 20%-owned taxable domestic corporation	1,000

In Daly's 2003 taxable income, how much should be included for the dividends received?
   a. $0
   b. $ 200
   c. $ 800
   d. $1,000

51. Cava Corp., which has **no** portfolio indebtedness, received the following dividends in 2003:

From a mutual savings bank	$1,500
From a 20%-owned unaffiliated domestic taxable corporation	7,500

How much of these dividends qualifies for the 80% dividends received deduction?
   a. $9,000
   b. $7,500
   c. $1,500
   d. $0

52. During 2003, Stark Corp. reported gross income from operations of $350,000 and operating expenses of $400,000. Stark also received dividend income of $100,000 (not included in gross income from operations) from an investment in a taxable domestic corporation in which it owns 10% of the stock. Additionally, Stark had a net operating loss carryover from 2002 of $30,000. What is the amount of Stark Corp.'s net operating loss for 2003?
   a. $0
   b. $(20,000)
   c. $(30,000)
   d. $(50,000)

53. A C corporation's net capital losses are
   a.   Carried forward indefinitely until fully utilized.
   b.   Carried back three years and forward five years.
   c.   Deductible in full from the corporation's ordinary income.
   d.   Deductible from the corporation's ordinary income only to the extent of $3,000.

54. For the year ended December 31, 2002, Taylor Corp. had a net operating loss of $200,000. Taxable income for the earlier years of corporate existence, computed without reference to the net operating loss, was as follows:

	Taxable income
1997	$ 5,000
1998	$10,000
1999	$20,000
2000	$30,000
2001	$40,000

If Taylor makes **no** special election to waive a net operating loss carryback period, what amount of net operating loss will be available to Taylor for the year ended December 31, 2003?
   a. $200,000
   b. $130,000
   c. $110,000
   d. $ 95,000

55. When a corporation has an unused net capital loss that is carried back or carried forward to another tax year,
   a.   It retains its original identity as short-term or long-term.
   b.   It is treated as a short-term capital loss whether or not it was short-term when sustained.
   c.   It is treated as a long-term capital loss whether or not it was long-term when sustained.
   d.   It can be used to offset ordinary income up to the amount of the carryback or carryover.

56. For the year ended December 31, 2003, Haya Corp. had gross business income of $600,000 and expenses of $800,000. Contributions of $5,000 to qualified charities were included in expenses. In addition to the expenses, Haya had a net operating loss carryover of $9,000. What was Haya's net operating loss for 2003?
   a. $209,000
   b. $204,000
   c. $200,000
   d. $195,000

57. Dorsett Corporation's income tax return for 2003 shows deductions exceeding gross income by $56,800. Included in the tax return are the following items:

Net operating loss deduction (carryover from 2002)	$15,000
Dividends received deduction	6,800

What is Dorsett's net operating loss for 2003?
   a. $56,800
   b. $50,000
   c. $41,800
   d. $35,000

58. Ram Corp.'s operating income for the year ended December 31, 2003, amounted to $100,000. Also in 2003, a machine owned by Ram was completely destroyed in an accident. This machine's adjusted basis immediately before the casualty was $15,000. The machine was not insured and had no salvage value.

In Ram's 2003 tax return, what amount should be deducted for the casualty loss?
   a. $ 5,000
   b. $ 5,400
   c. $14,900
   d. $15,000

59. For the first taxable year in which a corporation has qualifying research and experimental expenditures, the corporation
   a.   Has a choice of either deducting such expenditures as current business expenses, or capitalizing these expenditures.
   b.   Has to treat such expenditures in the same manner as they are accounted for in the corporation's financial statements.
   c.   Is required to deduct such expenditures currently as business expenses or lose the deductions.
   d.   Is required to capitalize such expenditures and amortize them ratably over a period of not less than sixty months.

60. For the year ended December 31, 2003, Kelly Corp. had net income per books of $300,000 before the provision for federal income taxes. Included in the net income were the following items:

Dividend income from a 5%-owned domestic taxable corporation (taxable income limitation does not apply and there is no portfolio indebtedness)	$50,000
Bad debt expense (represents the increase in the allowance for doubtful accounts)	80,000

Assuming no bad debt was written off, what is Kelly's taxable income for the year ended December 31, 2003?
   a. $250,000
   b. $330,000
   c. $345,000
   d. $380,000

61. For the year ended December 31, 2003, Maple Corp.'s book income, before federal income tax, was $100,000. Included in this $100,000 were the following:

Provision for state income tax	$1,000
Interest earned on US Treasury Bonds	6,000
Interest expense on bank loan to purchase US Treasury Bonds	2,000

Maple's taxable income for 2003 was
   a. $ 96,000
   b. $ 97,000
   c. $100,000
   d. $101,000

62. For the year ended December 31, 2003, Dodd Corp. had net income per books of $100,000. Included in the computation of net income were the following items:

Provision for federal income tax	$27,000
Net long-term capital loss	5,000
Keyman life insurance premiums (corporation is beneficiary)	3,000

Dodd's 2003 taxable income was
   a. $127,000
   b. $130,000
   c. $132,000
   d. $135,000

63. For the year ended December 31, 2003, Bard Corp.'s income per accounting records, before federal income taxes, was $450,000 and included the following:

State corporate income tax refunds	$ 4,000
Life insurance proceeds on officer's death	15,000
Net loss on sale of securities bought for investment in 2001	20,000

Bard's 2003 taxable income was

    a. $435,000
    b. $451,000
    c. $455,000
    d. $470,000

64. Dewey Corporation's book income before federal income taxes was $520,000 for the year ended December 31, 2003. Dewey was incorporated during 2003 and began business in June. Organization costs of $260,000 were expensed for financial statement purposes during 2003. For tax purposes these costs are being written off over the minimum allowable period. For the year ended December 31, 2003, Dewey's taxable income was

    a. $520,000
    b. $489,900
    c. $747,900
    d. $778,000

65. Bishop Corporation reported taxable income of $700,000 on its federal income tax return for calendar year 2003. Selected information for 2003 is available from Bishop's records as follows:

Provision for federal income tax per books	$280,000
Depreciation claimed on the tax return	130,000
Depreciation recorded in the books	75,000
Life insurance proceeds on death of corporate officer	100,000

Bishop reported net income per books for 2003 of

    a. $855,000
    b. $595,000
    c. $575,000
    d. $475,000

66. For the year ended December 31, 2003, Ajax Corporation had net income per books of $1,200,000. Included in the determination of net income were the following items:

Interest income on municipal bonds	$ 40,000
Damages received from settlement of patent infringement lawsuit	200,000
Interest paid on loan to purchase municipal bonds	8,000
Provision for federal income tax	524,000

What should Ajax report as its taxable income for 2003?

    a. $1,492,000
    b. $1,524,000
    c. $1,684,000
    d. $1,692,000

67. For its taxable year 2003, Farve Corp. had net income per books of $80,000, which included municipal bond interest of $5,000, dividend income of $10,000, a deduction for a net capital loss of $6,000, a deduction for business meals of $4,000, and a deduction for federal income taxes of $18,000. What is the amount of income that would be shown on the last line of Schedule M-1 (Reconciliation of Income [Loss] Per Books with Income [Loss] Per Return) of Farve Corp.'s corporate income tax return for 2003?

    a. $ 90,000
    b. $ 93,000

    c. $ 99,000
    d. $101,000

68. In 2003, Starke Corp., an accrual-basis calendar-year corporation, reported book income of $380,000. Included in that amount was $50,000 municipal bond interest income, $170,000 for federal income tax expense, and $2,000 interest expense on the debt incurred to carry the municipal bonds. What amount should Starke's taxable income be as reconciled on Starke's Schedule M-1 of Form 1120, US Corporation Income Tax Return?

    a. $330,000
    b. $500,000
    c. $502,000
    d. $550,000

69. Would the following expense items be reported on Schedule M-1 of the corporation income tax return (Form 1120) showing the reconciliation of income per books with income per return?

	Lodging expenses for executive out-of-town travel	*Deduction for a net capital loss*
a.	Yes	Yes
b.	No	No
c.	Yes	No
d.	No	Yes

70. In the reconciliation of income per books with income per return

    a.   Only temporary differences are considered.
    b.   Only permanent differences are considered.
    c.   Both temporary and permanent differences are considered.
    d.   Neither temporary nor permanent differences are considered.

71. Media Corp. is an accrual-basis, calendar-year C corporation. Its 2003 reported book income included $6,000 in municipal bond interest income. Its expenses included $1,500 of interest incurred on indebtedness used to carry municipal bonds and $8,000 in advertising expense. What is Media's net M-1 adjustment on its 2003 Form 1120, US Corporation Income Tax Return, to reconcile to its 2003 taxable income?

    a. $(4,500)
    b. $ 1,500
    c. $ 3,500
    d. $ 9,500

72. Barbaro Corporation's retained earnings at January 1, 2003, was $600,000. During 2003 Barbaro paid cash dividends of $150,000 and received a federal income tax refund of $26,000 as a result of an IRS audit of Barbaro's 2000 tax return. Barbaro's net income per books for the year ended December 31, 2003, was $274,900 after deducting federal income tax of $183,300. How much should be shown in the reconciliation Schedule M-2, of Form 1120, as Barbaro's retained earnings at December 31, 2003?

    a. $443,600
    b. $600,900
    c. $626,900
    d. $750,900

73. Olex Corporation's books disclosed the following data for the calendar year 2003:

Retained earnings at beginning of year	$50,000
Net income for year	70,000
Contingency reserve established at end of year	10,000
Cash dividends paid during year	8,000

What amount should appear on the last line of reconciliation Schedule M-2 of Form 1120?

- a. $102,000
- b. $120,000
- c. $128,000
- d. $138,000

74. Bank Corp. owns 80% of Shore Corp.'s outstanding capital stock. Shore's capital stock consists of 50,000 shares of common stock issued and outstanding. Shore's 2003 net income was $140,000. During 2003, Shore declared and paid dividends of $60,000. In conformity with generally accepted accounting principles, Bank recorded the following entries in 2003:

	Debit	Credit
Investment in Shore Corp. common stock	$112,000	
Equity in earnings of subsidiary		$112,000
Cash	48,000	
Investment in Shore Corp. common stock		48,000

In its 2003 consolidated tax return, Bank should report dividend revenue of

- a. $48,000
- b. $14,400
- c. $ 9,600
- d. $0

75. In 2003, Portal Corp. received $100,000 in dividends from Sal Corp., its 80%-owned subsidiary. What net amount of dividend income should Portal include in its 2003 consolidated tax return?

- a. $100,000
- b. $ 80,000
- c. $ 70,000
- d. $0

76. Potter Corp. and Sly Corp. file consolidated tax returns. In January 2002, Potter sold land, with a basis of $60,000 and a fair value of $100,000, to Sly for $100,000. Sly sold the land in June 2003 for $125,000. In its 2003 and 2002 tax returns, what amount of gain should be reported for these transactions in the consolidated return?

	2003	2002
a.	$25,000	$40,000
b.	$25,000	$0
c.	$40,000	$25,000
d.	$65,000	$0

77. When a consolidated return is filed by an affiliated group of includible corporations connected from inception through the requisite stock ownership with a common parent

- a. Intercompany dividends are excludable to the extent of 80%.
- b. Operating losses of one member of the group offset operating profits of other members of the group.
- c. Each of the subsidiaries is entitled to an alternative minimum tax exemption.
- d. Each of the subsidiaries is entitled to an accumulated earnings tax credit.

78. Dana Corp. owns stock in Seco Corp. For Dana and Seco to qualify for the filing of consolidated returns, at least what percentage of Seco's total voting power and total value of stock must be directly owned by Dana?

	Total voting power	Total value of stock
a.	51%	51%
b.	51%	80%
c.	80%	51%
d.	80%	80%

79. Consolidated returns may be filed

- a. Either by parent-subsidiary corporations or by brother-sister corporations.
- b. Only by corporations that formally request advance permission from the IRS.
- c. Only by parent-subsidiary affiliated groups.
- d. Only by corporations that issue their financial statements on a consolidated basis.

80. Parent Corporation and Subsidiary Corporation file consolidated returns on a calendar-year basis. In January 2002, Subsidiary sold land, which it had used in its business, to Parent for $50,000. Immediately before this sale, Subsidiary's basis for the land was $30,000. Parent held the land primarily for sale to customers in the ordinary course of business. In July 2003, Parent sold the land to Adams, an unrelated individual. In determining consolidated taxable income for 2003, how much should Subsidiary take into account as a result of the 2002 sale of the land from Subsidiary to Parent?

- a. $0
- b. $20,000
- c. $30,000
- d. $50,000

81. At the beginning of the year, Westwind, a C corporation, had a deficit of $45,000 in accumulated earnings and profits. For the current year, Westwind reported earnings and profits of $15,000. Westwind distributed $12,000 during the year. What was the amount of Westwind's accumulated earnings and profits deficit at year-end?

- a. $(30,000)
- b. $(42,000)
- c. $(45,000)
- d. $(57,000)

82. At the beginning of the year, Cable, a C corporation, had accumulated earnings and profits of $100,000. Cable reported the following items on its current year tax return:

Taxable income	$50,000
Federal income taxes paid	5,000
Current year charitable contributions in excess of 10% limitation	1,000
Net capital loss for current year	2,000

What is Cable's accumulated earnings and profits at the end of the year?

- a. $142,000
- b. $145,000
- c. $147,000
- d. $150,000

83. On January 1, 2003, Locke Corp., an accrual-basis, calendar-year C corporation, had $30,000 in accumulated earnings and profits. For 2003, Locke had current earnings and profits of $20,000 and made two $40,000 cash distributions to its shareholders, one in April and one in September of 2003. What amount of the 2003 distributions is classified as dividend income to Locke's shareholders?

a. $0
b. $20,000
c. $50,000
d. $80,000

84. Chicago Corp., a calendar-year C corporation, had accumulated earnings and profits of $100,000 as of January 1, 2003 and had a **deficit** in its current earnings and profits for the entire 2003 tax year in the amount of $140,000. Chicago Corp. distributed $30,000 cash to its shareholders on December 31, 2003. What would be the balance of Chicago Corp.'s accumulated earnings and profits as of January 1, 2004?

a. $0
b. $(30,000)
c. $(40,000)
d. $(70,000)

85. Salon, Inc. distributed cash and personal property to its sole shareholder. Using the following facts, determine the amount of gain that would be recognized by Salon, Inc. as the result of making the distribution to its shareholder?

Item	Amount
Cash	$20,000
Personal property:	
Fair market value	6,000
Adjusted basis	3,000
Liability on property assumed by shareholder	10,000

a. $ 3,000
b. $ 4,000
c. $ 7,000
d. $23,000

86. Kent Corp. is a calendar-year, accrual-basis C corporation. In 2003, Kent made a nonliquidating distribution of property with an adjusted basis of $150,000 and a fair market value of $200,000 to Reed, its sole shareholder. The following information pertains to Kent:

Reed's basis in Kent stock at January 1, 2003	$500,000
Accumulated earnings and profits at January 1, 2003	125,000
Current earnings and profits for 2003	60,000

What was taxable as dividend income to Reed for 2003?

a. $ 60,000
b. $150,000
c. $185,000
d. $200,000

87. Ridge Corp., a calendar-year C corporation, made a nonliquidating cash distribution to its shareholders of $1,000,000 with respect to its stock. At that time, Ridge's current and accumulated earnings and profits totaled $750,000 and its total paid-in capital for tax purposes was $10,000,000. Ridge had no corporate shareholders. Ridge's cash distribution

I.   Was taxable as $750,000 of dividend income to its shareholders.
II. Reduced its shareholders' adjusted bases in Ridge stock by $250,000.

a. I only.
b. II only.
c. Both I and II.
d. Neither I nor II.

88. Tour Corp., which had earnings and profits of $400,000, made a nonliquidating distribution of property to its shareholders in 2003 as a dividend in kind. This property, which had an adjusted basis of $30,000 and a fair market value of $20,000 at date of distribution, did not constitute assets used in the active conduct of Tour's business. How much loss did Tour recognize on this distribution?

a. $30,000
b. $20,000
c. $10,000
d. $0

89. On January 1, 2003, Kee Corp., a C corporation, had a $50,000 deficit in earnings and profits. For 2003 Kee had current earnings and profits of $10,000 and made a $30,000 cash distribution to its stockholders. What amount of the distribution is taxable as dividend income to Kee's stockholders?

a. $30,000
b. $20,000
c. $10,000
d. $0

90. Dahl Corp. was organized and commenced operations in 1994. At December 31, 2003, Dahl had accumulated earnings and profits of $9,000 before dividend declaration and distribution. On December 31, 2003, Dahl distributed cash of $9,000 and a vacant parcel of land to Green, Dahl's only stockholder. At the date of distribution, the land had a basis of $5,000 and a fair market value of $40,000. What was Green's taxable dividend income in 2003 from these distributions?

a. $ 9,000
b. $14,000
c. $44,000
d. $49,000

91. Pym, Inc. which had earnings and profits of $100,000, distributed land to Alex Rowe, a stockholder, as a dividend in kind. Pym's adjusted basis for this land was $3,000. The land had a fair market value of $12,000 and was subject to a mortgage liability of $5,000, which was assumed by Rowe. The dividend was declared and paid during November 2003. How much of the distribution was taxable to Rowe as a dividend?

a. $9,000
b. $7,000
c. $4,000
d. $3,000

92. On June 30, 2003, Ral Corporation had retained earnings of $100,000. On that date, it sold a plot of land to a noncorporate stockholder for $50,000. Ral had paid $40,000 for the land in 1995, and it had a fair market value of $80,000 when the stockholder bought it. The amount of dividend income taxable to the stockholder in 2003 is

a. $0
b. $10,000
c. $20,000
d. $30,000

93. On December 1, 2003, Gelt Corporation declared a dividend and distributed to its sole shareholder, as a dividend in kind, a parcel of land that was not an inventory asset. On the date of the distribution, the following data were available:

Adjusted basis of land	$ 6,500
Fair market value of land	14,000
Mortgage on land	5,000

For the year ended December 31, 2003, Gelt had earnings and profits of $30,000 without regard to the dividend distribution. By how much should the dividend distribution reduce the earnings and profits for 2003?

    a. $ 1,500
    b. $ 6,500
    c. $ 9,000
    d. $14,000

94. Two unrelated individuals, Mark and David, each own 50% of the stock of Pike Corporation, which has accumulated earnings and profits of $250,000. Because of his inactivity in the business in recent years, Mark has decided to retire from the business and wishes to sell his stock. Accordingly, Pike will distribute cash of $500,000 in redemption of all of the stock owned by Mark. If Mark's adjusted basis for his stock at date of redemption is $300,000, what will be the tax effect of the redemption to Mark?

    a. $125,000 dividend
    b. $200,000 dividend
    c. $200,000 capital gain
    d. $250,000 dividend

95. How does a noncorporate shareholder treat the gain on a redemption of stock that qualifies as a partial liquidation of the distributing corporation?

    a.   Entirely as capital gain.
    b.   Entirely as a dividend.
    c.   Partly as capital gain and partly as a dividend.
    d.   As a tax-free transaction.

96. In 2003, Kara Corp. incurred the following expenditures in connection with the repurchase of its stock from shareholders to avert a hostile takeover:

Interest on borrowings used to repurchase stock	$100,000
Legal and accounting fees in connection with the repurchase	400,000

The total of the above expenditures deductible in 2003 is

    a. $0
    b. $100,000
    c. $400,000
    d. $500,000

97. A corporation was completely liquidated and dissolved during 2003. The filing fees, professional fees, and other expenditures incurred in connection with the liquidation and dissolution are

    a.   Deductible in full by the dissolved corporation.
    b.   Deductible by the shareholders and not by the corporation.
    c.   Treated as capital losses by the corporation.
    d.   Not deductible either by the corporation or shareholders.

98. What is the usual result to the shareholders of a distribution in complete liquidation of a corporation?

    a.   No taxable effect.
    b.   Ordinary gain to the extent of cash received.
    c.   Ordinary gain or loss.
    d.   Capital gain or loss.

99. Par Corp. acquired the assets of its wholly owned subsidiary, Sub Corp., under a plan that qualified as a tax-free complete liquidation of Sub. Which of the following of Sub's unused carryovers may be transferred to Par?

	Excess charitable contributions	Net operating loss
a.	No	Yes
b.	Yes	No
c.	No	No
d.	Yes	Yes

100. Kappes Corp. distributed marketable securities in a pro rata redemption of its stock in a complete liquidation. These securities, which had been purchased in 1996 for $150,000, had a fair market value of $100,000 when distributed. What loss does Kappes recognize as a result of the distribution?

    a. $0.
    b. $50,000 long-term capital loss.
    c. $50,000 Section 1231 loss.
    d. $50,000 ordinary loss.

101. When a parent corporation completely liquidates its 80%-owned subsidiary, the parent (as stockholder) will ordinarily

    a.   Be subject to capital gains tax on 80% of the long-term gain.
    b.   Be subject to capital gains tax on 100% of the long-term gain.
    c.   Have to report any gain on liquidation as ordinary income.
    d.   Not recognize gain or loss on the liquidating distributions.

102. Lark Corp. and its wholly owned subsidiary, Day Corp., both operated on a calendar year. In January 2003, Day adopted a plan of complete liquidation. Two months later, Day paid all of its liabilities and distributed its remaining assets to Lark. These assets consisted of the following:

Cash	$50,000
Land (at cost)	10,000

Fair market value of the land was $30,000. Upon distribution of Day's assets to Lark, all of Day's capital stock was canceled. Lark's basis for the Day stock was $7,000. Lark's recognized gain in 2003 on receipt of Day's assets in liquidation was

    a. $0
    b. $50,000
    c. $53,000
    d. $73,000

103. On June 1, 2003, Green Corp. adopted a plan of complete liquidation. The liquidation was completed within a twelve-month period. On August 1, 2003, Green distributed to its stockholders installment notes receivable that Green had acquired in connection with the sale of land in 2002. The following information pertains to these notes:

Green's basis	$ 90,000
Fair market value	162,000
Face amount	185,000

How much gain must Green recognize in 2003 as a result of this distribution?

    a. $0
    b. $23,000
    c. $72,000
    d. $95,000

104. Carmela Corporation had the following assets on January 2, 2003, the date on which it adopted a plan of complete liquidation:

	Adjusted basis	Fair market value
Land	$ 75,000	$150,000
Inventory	43,500	66,000
Totals	$118,500	$216,000

The land was sold on June 30, 2003, to an unrelated party at a gain of $75,000. The inventory was sold to various customers during 2003 at an aggregate gain of $22,500. On December 10, 2003, the remaining asset (cash) was distributed to Carmela's stockholders, and the corporation was liquidated. What is Carmela's recognized gain in 2003?

- a. $0
- b. $22,500
- c. $75,000
- d. $97,500

105. Mintee Corp., an accrual-basis calendar-year C corporation, had no corporate shareholders when it liquidated in 2003. In cancellation of all their Mintee stock, each Mintee shareholder received in 2003 a liquidation distribution of $2,000 cash and land with a tax basis of $5,000 and a fair market value of $10,500. Before the distribution, each shareholder's tax basis in Mintee stock was $6,500. What amount of gain should each Mintee shareholder recognize on the liquidating distribution?

- a. $0
- b. $ 500
- c. $4,000
- d. $6,000

106. Edge Corp. met the stock ownership requirements of a personal holding company. What sources of income must Edge consider to determine if the income requirements for a personal holding company have been met?

I. Interest earned on tax-exempt obligations.
II. Dividends received from an unrelated domestic corporation.

- a. I only.
- b. II only.
- c. Both I and II.
- d. Neither I nor II.

107. Kane Corp. is a calendar-year domestic personal holding company. Which deduction(s) must Kane make from 2003 taxable income to determine undistributed personal holding company income prior to the dividend-paid deduction?

	Federal income taxes	Net long-term capital gain less related federal income taxes
a.	Yes	Yes
b.	Yes	No
c.	No	Yes
d.	No	No

108. Dart Corp., a calendar-year domestic C corporation, is not a personal holding company. For purposes of the accumulated earnings tax, Dart has accumulated taxable income for 2003. Which step(s) can Dart take to eliminate or reduce any 2003 accumulated earnings tax?

I. Demonstrate that the "reasonable needs" of its business require the retention of all or part of the 2003 accumulated taxable income.

II. Pay dividends by March 15, 2004.

- a. I only.
- b. II only.
- c. Both I and II.
- d. Neither I nor II.

109. The accumulated earnings tax can be imposed

- a. On both partnerships and corporations.
- b. On companies that make distributions in excess of accumulated earnings.
- c. On personal holding companies.
- d. Regardless of the number of stockholders in a corporation.

110. Zero Corp. is an investment company authorized to issue only common stock. During the last half of 2003, Edwards owned 240 of the 1,000 outstanding shares of stock in Zero. Another 560 shares of stock outstanding were owned, twenty shares each, by twenty-eight shareholders who are neither related to each other nor to Edwards. Zero could be a personal holding company if the remaining 200 shares of common stock were owned by

- a. An estate where Edwards is the beneficiary.
- b. Edwards' brother-in-law.
- c. A partnership where Edwards is not a partner.
- d. Edwards' cousin.

111. Arbor Corp. has nine common stockholders. Arbor derives all of its income from investments in stocks and securities, and regularly distributes 51% of its taxable income as dividends to its stockholders. Arbor is a

- a. Regulated investment company.
- b. Personal holding company.
- c. Corporation subject to the accumulated earnings tax.
- d. Corporation subject to tax on income not distributed to stockholders.

112. Kari Corp., a manufacturing company, was organized on January 2, 2003. Its 2003 federal taxable income was $400,000 and its federal income tax was $100,000. What is the maximum amount of accumulated taxable income that may be subject to the accumulated earnings tax for 2003 if Kari takes only the minimum accumulated earnings credit?

- a. $300,000
- b. $150,000
- c. $ 50,000
- d. $0

113. The following information pertains to Hull, Inc., a personal holding company, for the year ended December 31, 2003:

Undistributed personal holding company income	$100,000
Dividends paid during 2003	20,000
Consent dividends reported in the 2003 individual income tax returns of the holders of Hull's common stock, but **not** paid by Hull to its stockholders	10,000

In computing its 2003 personal holding company tax, what amount should Hull deduct for dividends paid?

- a. $0
- b. $10,000
- c. $20,000
- d. $30,000

114. Benson, a singer, owns 100% of the outstanding capital stock of Lund Corp. Lund contracted with Benson, specifying that Benson was to perform personal services for Magda Productions, Inc., in consideration of which Benson was to receive $50,000 a year from Lund. Lund contracted with Magda, specifying that Benson was to perform personal services for Magda, in consideration of which Magda was to pay Lund $1,000,000 a year. Personal holding company income will be attributable to

    a.   Benson only.
    b.   Lund only.
    c.   Magda only.
    d.   All three contracting parties.

115. The personal holding company tax

    a.   Qualifies as a tax credit that may be used by partners or stockholders to reduce their individual income taxes.
    b.   May be imposed on both corporations and partnerships.
    c.   Should be self-assessed by filing a separate schedule with the regular tax return.
    d.   May be imposed regardless of the number of equal stockholders in a corporation.

116. The accumulated earnings tax does **not** apply to

    a.   Corporations that have more than 100 stockholders.
    b.   Personal holding companies.
    c.   Corporations filing consolidated returns.
    d.   Corporations that have more than one class of stock.

117. The personal holding company tax may be imposed

    a.   As an alternative tax in place of the corporation's regularly computed tax.
    b.   If more than 50% of the corporation's stock is owned, directly or indirectly, by more than ten stockholders.
    c.   If at least 60% of the corporation's adjusted ordinary gross income for the taxable year is personal holding company income, and the stock ownership test is satisfied.
    d.   In conjunction with the accumulated earnings tax.

118. The accumulated earnings tax

    a.   Should be self-assessed by filing a separate schedule along with the regular tax return.
    b.   Applies only to closely held corporations.
    c.   Can be imposed on S corporations that do not regularly distribute their earnings.
    d.   Cannot be imposed on a corporation that has undistributed earnings and profits of less than $150,000.

119. Kee Holding Corp. has eighty unrelated equal stockholders. For the year ended December 31, 2003, Kee's income comprised the following:

Net rental income	$ 1,000
Commissions earned on sales of franchises	3,000
Dividends from taxable domestic corporations	90,000

Deductible expenses for 2003 totaled $10,000. Kee paid no dividends for the past three years. Kee's liability for personal holding company tax for 2003 will be based on

    a. $12,000
    b. $11,000
    c. $ 9,000
    d. $0

120. The accumulated earnings tax

    a.   Depends on a stock ownership test based on the number of stockholders.
    b.   Can be avoided by sufficient dividend distributions.
    c.   Is computed by the filing of a separate schedule along with the corporation's regular tax return.
    d.   Is imposed when the entity is classified as a personal holding company.

121. Where passive investment income is involved, the personal holding company tax may be imposed

    a.   On both partnerships and corporations.
    b.   On companies whose gross income arises solely from rentals, if the lessors render no services to the lessees.
    c.   If more than 50% of the company is owned by five or fewer individuals.
    d.   On small business investment companies licensed by the Small Business Administration.

122. In determining accumulated taxable income for the purpose of the accumulated earnings tax, which one of the following is allowed as a deduction?

    a.   Capital loss carryover from prior year.
    b.   Dividends received deduction.
    c.   Net operating loss deduction.
    d.   Net capital loss for current year.

123. The minimum accumulated earnings credit is

    a. $150,000 for all corporations.
    b. $150,000 for nonservice corporations only.
    c. $250,000 for all corporations.
    d. $250,000 for nonservice corporations only.

124. Daystar Corp. which is not a mere holding or investment company, derives its income from consulting services. Daystar had accumulated earnings and profits of $45,000 at December 31, 2002. For the year ended December 31, 2003, it had earnings and profits of $115,000 and a dividends-paid deduction of $15,000. It has been determined that $20,000 of the accumulated earnings and profits for 2003 is required for the reasonable needs of the business. How much is the allowable accumulated earnings credit at December 31, 2003?

    a. $105,000
    b. $205,000
    c. $150,000
    d. $250,000

125. Stahl, an individual, owns 100% of Talon, an S corporation. At the beginning of the year, Stahl's basis in Talon was $65,000. Talon reported the following items from operations during the current year:

Ordinary loss	$10,000
Municipal interest income	6,000
Long-term capital gain	4,000
Short-term capital loss	9,000

What was Stahl's basis in Talon at year-end?

    a. $50,000
    b. $55,000
    c. $56,000
    d. $61,000

126. Baker, an individual, owned 100% of Alpha, an S corporation. At the beginning of the year, Baker's basis in

Alpha Corp. was $25,000. Alpha realized ordinary income during the year in the amount of $1,000 and a long-term capital loss in the amount of $3,000 for this year. Alpha distributed $30,000 in cash to Baker during the year. What amount of the $30,000 cash distribution is taxable to Baker?

    a. $0
    b. $ 4,000
    c. $ 7,000
    d. $30,000

127. Lane Inc., an S corporation, pays single coverage health insurance premiums of $4,800 per year and family coverage premiums of $7,200 per year. Mill is a 10% shareholder-employee in Lane. On Mill's behalf, Lane pays Mill's family coverage under the health insurance plan. What amount of insurance premiums is includible in Mill's gross income?

    a. $0
    b. $ 720
    c. $4,800
    d. $7,200

128. Beck Corp. has been a calendar-year S corporation since its inception on January 2, 1999. On January 1, 2003, Lazur and Lyle each owned 50% of the Beck stock, in which their respective tax bases were $12,000 and $9,000. For the year ended December 31, 2003, Beck had $81,000 in ordinary business income and $10,000 in tax-exempt income. Beck made a $51,000 cash distribution to each shareholder on December 31, 2003. What was Lazur's tax basis in Beck after the distribution?

    a. $ 1,500
    b. $ 6,500
    c. $52,500
    d. $57,500

129. Graphite Corp. has been a calendar-year S corporation since its inception on January 2, 1999. On January 1, 2003, Smith and Tyler each owned 50% of the Graphite stock, in which their respective bases were $12,000 and $9,000. For the year ended December 31, 2003, Graphite had $80,000 in ordinary business income and $6,000 in tax-exempt income. Graphite made a $53,000 cash distribution to each shareholder on December 31, 2003. What total amount of income from Graphite is includible in Smith's 2003 adjusted gross income?

    a. $96,000
    b. $93,000
    c. $43,000
    d. $40,000

130. Dart Corp., a calendar-year S corporation, had 60,000 shares of voting common stock and 40,000 shares of nonvoting common stock issued and outstanding. On February 23, 2003, Dart filed a revocation statement with the consent of shareholders holding 30,000 shares of its voting common stock and 5,000 shares of its nonvoting common stock. Dart's S corporation election

    a.   Did not terminate.
    b.   Terminated as of January 1, 2003.
    c.   Terminated on February 24, 2003.
    d.   Terminated as of January 1, 2004.

131. Which one of the following statements concerning the eligibility requirements for S corporations is **not** correct?

    a.   An S corporation is permitted to own 90% of the stock of a C corporation.

    b.   An S corporation is permitted to own 100% of the stock of another S corporation.
    c.   An S corporation is permitted to be a partner in a partnership.
    d.   A partnership is permitted to be a shareholder of an S corporation.

132. Dart Corp., a calendar-year corporation, was formed in 1993 and made an S corporation election in 1996 that is still in effect. Its books and records for 2003 reflect the following information:

Accumulated earnings and profits at 1/1/03	$90,000
Accumulated adjustments account at 1/1/03	50,000
Ordinary income for 2003	200,000

Dart Corp. is solely owned by Robert, whose basis in Dart's stock was $100,000 on January 1, 2003. During 2003, Dart distributed $310,000 to Robert. What is the amount of the $310,000 distribution that Robert must report as dividend income for 2003 assuming no special elections were made with regard to the distribution?

    a. $0
    b. $ 60,000
    c. $ 90,000
    d. $140,000

133. Village Corp., a calendar-year corporation, began business in 1996. Village made a valid S Corporation election on September 5, 2003, with the unanimous consent of its shareholders. The eligibility requirements for S status continued to be met throughout 2003. On what date did Village's S status become effective?

    a.   January 1, 2003.
    b.   January 1, 2004.
    c.   September 5, 2003.
    d.   September 5, 2004.

134. A shareholder's basis in the stock of an S corporation is increased by the shareholder's pro rata share of income from

	Tax-exempt interest	Taxable interest
a.	No	No
b.	No	Yes
c.	Yes	No
d.	Yes	Yes

135. Zinco Corp. was a calendar-year S corporation. Zinco's S status terminated on April 1, 2003, when Case Corp. became a shareholder. During 2003 (365-day calendar year), Zinco had nonseparately computed income of $310,250. If no election was made by Zinco, what amount of the income, if any, was allocated to the S short year for 2003?

    a. $77,563
    b. $77,350
    c. $76,500
    d. $0

136. Bristol Corp. was formed as a C corporation on January 1, 1992, and elected S corporation status on January 1, 2000. At the time of the election, Bristol had accumulated C corporation earnings and profits that have not been distributed. Bristol has had the same twenty-five shareholders throughout its existence. In 2003 Bristol's S election will terminate if it

    a.   Increases the number of shareholders to seventy-five.

b. Adds a decedent's estate as a shareholder to the existing shareholders.

c. Takes a charitable contribution deduction.

d. Has passive investment income exceeding 90% of gross receipts in each of the three consecutive years ending December 31, 2002.

137. As of January 1, 2003, Kane owned all the 100 issued shares of Manning Corp., a calendar-year S corporation. On the 40th day of 2003, Kane sold twenty-five of the Manning shares to Rodgers. For the year ended December 31, 2003 (a 365-day calendar year), Manning had $73,000 in nonseparately stated income and made no distributions to its shareholders. What amount of nonseparately stated income from Manning should be reported on Kane's 2003 tax return?

a. $56,900
b. $56,750
c. $54,750
d. $48,750

138. On February 10, 2003, Ace Corp., a calendar-year corporation, elected S corporation status and all shareholders consented to the election. There was no change in shareholders in 2003. Ace met all eligibility requirements for S status during the preelection portion of the year. What is the earliest date on which Ace can be recognized as an S corporation?

a. February 10, 2002.
b. February 10, 2003.
c. January 1, 2002.
d. January 1, 2003.

139. An S corporation has 30,000 shares of voting common stock and 20,000 shares of nonvoting common stock issued and outstanding. The S election can be revoked voluntarily with the consent of the shareholders holding, on the day of the revocation,

	Shares of voting stock	Shares of nonvoting stock
a.	0	20,000
b.	7,500	5,000
c.	10,000	16,000
d.	20,000	0

140. The Haas Corp., a calendar-year S corporation, has two equal shareholders. For the year ended December 31, 2003, Haas had income of $60,000, which included $50,000 from operations and $10,000 from investment interest income. There were no other transactions that year. Each shareholder's basis in the stock of Haas will increase by

a. $50,000
b. $30,000
c. $25,000
d. $0

141. Which of the following conditions will prevent a corporation from qualifying as an S Corporation?

a. The corporation owns 100% of the stock of a C corporation.

b. The corporation is a partner in a partnership.

c. 30% of the corporation's stock is held by a voting trust.

d. The corporation has common voting stock and preferred nonvoting stock outstanding.

142. If an S corporation has **no** accumulated earnings and profits, the amount distributed to a shareholder

a. Must be returned to the S corporation.

b. Increases the shareholder's basis for the stock.

c. Decreases the shareholder's basis for the stock.

d. Has no effect on the shareholder's basis for the stock.

143. A corporation that has been an S corporation from its inception may

	Have both passive and nonpassive income	Be owned by a bankruptcy estate
a.	No	Yes
b.	Yes	No
c.	No	No
d.	Yes	Yes

144. Bern Corp., an S corporation, had an ordinary loss of $36,500 for the year ended December 31, 2003. At January 1, 2003, Meyer owned 50% of Bern's stock. Meyer held the stock for forty days in 2003 before selling the entire 50% interest to an unrelated third party. Meyer's basis for the stock was $10,000. Meyer was a full-time employee of Bern until the stock was sold. Meyer's share of Bern's 2003 loss was

a. $0
b. $ 2,000
c. $ 4,000
d. $18,300

145. A calendar-year corporation whose status as an S corporation was terminated during 2003 must wait how many years before making a new S election, in the absence of IRS consent to an earlier election?

a. Can make a new S election for calendar year 2003.

b. Must wait three years.

c. Must wait five years.

d. Must wait six years.

146. Which one of the following will render a corporation ineligible for S corporation status?

a. One of the stockholders is a decedent's estate.

b. One of the stockholders is a bankruptcy estate.

c. The corporation has both voting and nonvoting common stock issued and outstanding.

d. The corporation has eighty stockholders.

147. With regard to S corporations and their stockholders, the "at risk" rules applicable to losses

a. Depend on the type of income reported by the S corporation.

b. Are subject to the elections made by the S corporation's stockholders.

c. Take into consideration the S corporation's ratio of debt to equity.

d. Apply at the shareholder level rather than at the corporate level.

148. An S corporation may deduct

a. Foreign income taxes.

b. A net Section 1231 loss.

c. Investment interest expense.

d. The amortization of organizational expenditures.

149. An S corporation's accumulated adjustments account, which measures the amount of earnings that may be distributed tax-free

a. Must be adjusted downward for the full amount of federal income taxes attributable to any taxable year in which the corporation was a C corporation.

b. Must be adjusted upward for the full amount of federal income taxes attributable to any taxable year in which the corporation was a C corporation.

c. Must be adjusted upward or downward for only the federal income taxes affected by capital gains or losses, respectively, for any taxable year in which the corporation was a C corporation.

d. Is not adjusted for federal income taxes attributable to a taxable year in which the corporation was a C corporation.

150. If a calendar-year S corporation does **not** request an automatic six-month extension of time to file its income tax return, the return is due by
   a. January 31.
   b. March 15.
   c. April 15.
   d. June 30.

151. An S corporation is **not** permitted to take a deduction for
   a. Compensation of officers.
   b. Interest paid to individuals who are not stockholders of the S corporation.
   c. Charitable contributions.
   d. Employee benefit programs established for individuals who are not stockholders of the S corporation.

152. An S corporation may
   a. Have both common and preferred stock outstanding.
   b. Have a partnership as a shareholder.
   c. Have a nonresident alien as a shareholder.
   d. Have as many as seventy-five shareholders.

153. Which of the following is **not** a requirement for a corporation to elect S corporation status (Subchapter S)?
   a. Must be a member of a controlled group.
   b. Must confine stockholders to individuals, estates, and certain qualifying trusts.
   c. Must be a domestic corporation.
   d. Must have only one class of stock.

154. Brooke, Inc., an S corporation, was organized on January 2, 2003, with two equal stockholders who materially participate in the S corporation's business. Each stockholder invested $5,000 in Brooke's capital stock, and each loaned $15,000 to the corporation. Brooke then borrowed $60,000 from a bank for working capital. Brooke sustained an operating loss of $90,000 for the year ended December 31, 2003. How much of this loss can each stockholder claim on his 2003 income tax return?
   a. $ 5,000
   b. $20,000
   c. $45,000
   d. $50,000

155. Jaxson Corp. has 200,000 shares of voting common stock issued and outstanding. King Corp. has decided to acquire 90% of Jaxson's voting common stock solely in exchange for 50% of its voting common stock and retain Jaxson as a subsidiary after the transaction. Which of the following statements is true?

   a. King must acquire 100% of Jaxson stock for the transaction to be a tax-free reorganization.
   b. The transaction will qualify as a tax-free reorganization.
   c. King must issue at least 60% of its voting common stock for the transaction to qualify as a tax-free reorganization.
   d. Jaxson must surrender assets for the transaction to qualify as a tax-free reorganization.

156. Ace Corp. and Bate Corp. combine in a qualifying reorganization and form Carr Corp., the only surviving corporation. This reorganization is tax-free to the

	Shareholders	*Corporations*
a.	Yes	Yes
b.	Yes	No
c.	No	Yes
d.	No	No

157. In a type B reorganization, as defined by the Internal Revenue Code, the

   I. Stock of the target corporation is acquired solely for the voting stock of either the acquiring corporation or its parent.
   II. Acquiring corporation must have control of the target corporation immediately after the acquisition.

   a. I only.
   b. II only.
   c. Both I and II.
   d. Neither I nor II.

158. Pursuant to a plan of corporate reorganization adopted in July 2003, Gow exchanged 500 shares of Lad Corp. common stock that he had bought in January 2001 at a cost of $5,000 for 100 shares of Rook Corp. common stock having a fair market value of $6,000. Gow's recognized gain on this exchange was
   a. $1,000 long-term capital gain.
   b. $1,000 short-term capital gain.
   c. $1,000 ordinary income.
   d. $0

159. Which one of the following is a corporate reorganization as defined in the Internal Revenue Code?
   a. Mere change in place of organization of one corporation.
   b. Stock redemption.
   c. Change in depreciation method from accelerated to straight-line.
   d. Change in inventory costing method from FIFO to LIFO.

160. With regard to corporate reorganizations, which one of the following statements is correct?
   a. A mere change in identity, form, or place of organization of one corporation does **not** qualify as a reorganization.
   b. The reorganization provisions **cannot** be used to provide tax-free treatment for corporate transactions.
   c. Securities in corporations **not** parties to a reorganization are always "boot."
   d. A "party to the reorganization" does **not** include the consolidated company.

161. Which one of the following is **not** a corporate reorganization as defined in the Internal Revenue Code?

    a.   Stock redemption.

    b.   Recapitalization.

    c.   Mere change in identity.

    d.   Statutory merger.

162. Claudio Corporation and Stellar Corporation both
report on a calendar-year basis. Claudio merged into Stellar
on June 30, 2003. Claudio had an allowable net operating
loss carryover of $270,000. Stellar's taxable income for the
year ended December 31, 2003, was $360,000 before con-
sideration of Claudio's net operating loss carryover. Claudio's fair market value before the merger was $1,500,000.
The federal long-term tax-exempt rate is 5%. As a result of
the merger, Claudio's former shareholders own 10% of
Stellar's outstanding stock. How much of Claudio's net
operating loss carryover can be used to offset Stellar's 2003
taxable income?

    a. $ 38,014

    b. $ 75,000

    c. $180,000

    d. $181,967

163. In 2000, Celia Mueller bought a $1,000 bond issued
by Disco Corporation for $1,100. Instead of paying off the
bondholders in cash, Disco issued 100 shares of preferred
stock in 2003 for each bond outstanding. The preferred
stock had a fair market value of $15 per share. What is the
recognized gain to be reported by Mueller in 2003?

    a. $0.

    b. $400 dividend.

    c. $400 long-term capital gain.

    d. $500 long-term capital gain.

164. On April 1, 2003, in connection with a recapitalization
of Oakbrook Corporation, Mary Roberts exchanged 500
shares that cost her $95,000 for 1,000 shares of new stock
worth $91,000 and bonds in the principal amount of $10,000
with a fair market value of $10,500. What is the amount of
Roberts' recognized gain during 2003?

    a. $0

    b. $ 6,500

    c. $10,000

    d. $10,500

SIMULATION PROBLEMS
Simulation Problem 1   (35 to 40 minutes)

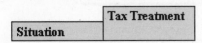

The following adjusted accounts appeared in the records of Oak Corp., an accrual-basis corporation, for the year ended December 31, 2003. Numbers in brackets refer to the items in *Additional information*.

Revenues and gains		
Net sales	$900,000	[1]
Dividends	20,000	[2]
Interest	8,000	[3]
Gain on sale of stock	10,000	[4]
Equity in earnings of Tech Partnership	60,000	[5]
Keyman life insurance proceeds	250,000	[6]
Tax refund	5,000	[7]
Total	1,253,000	
Costs and expenses		
Cost of goods sold	525,000	[8]
Salaries and wages	200,000	[9]
Doubtful accounts	20,000	[10]
Taxes	90,000	[11]
Interest	25,000	[12]
Contributions	18,000	[13]
Depreciation	80,000	[14]
Other	33,000	[15]
Federal income tax	65,000	[16]
Total	1,056,000	
Net income	$ 197,000	

Additional information

[1] Trade accounts receivable at December 31, 2003, and at December 31, 2002, amounted to $330,000 and $200,000, respectively.

[2] Dividends were declared and paid in 2003 by an unrelated taxable domestic corporation whose securities are traded on a major stock exchange.

[3] Interest revenue comprises interest on municipal bonds issued in 1990 and purchased by Oak in the open market in 2002.

[4] Gain on sale of stock arose from the following purchase and sale of stock in an unrelated corporation listed on a major stock exchange:

Bought in 2000	Cost	$12,000
Sold in 2003	Proceeds of sale	22,000

[5] Oak owns 50% of Tech Partnership. The other 50% is owned by an unrelated individual. Tech reported the following tax information to Oak:

Oak's share of:

Partnership ordinary income	$ 79,000
Net long-term capital loss	(19,000)

[6] Oak owned the keyman life insurance policy, paid the premiums, and was the direct beneficiary. The proceeds were collected on the death of Oak's controller.

[7] The tax refund arose from Oak's overpayment of federal income tax on the 2002 return.

[8] Cost of goods sold relates to Oak's net sales.

[9] Salaries and wages includes officers' compensation of $75,000.

[10] Doubtful accounts expense represents an addition to Oak's allowance for doubtful accounts based on an aging schedule whereby Oak "reserves" all accounts receivable over 120 days for book purposes. The balance in Oak's allowance for doubtful accounts was $142,000 at December 31, 2003. Actual bad debts written off in 2003 amounted to $11,000.

[11] Taxes comprise payroll taxes and property taxes.

[12] Interest expense resulted from borrowing for working capital purposes.

[13] Contributions were all paid in 2003 to State University, specifically designated for the purchase of lab equipment.

[14] Oak has always used straight-line depreciation for both book and tax purposes.

[15] Other expenses include premiums of $15,000 on the keyman life insurance policy covering the controller.

[16] Federal income tax is the amount estimated and accrued before preparation of the return.

For **items 1 through 16** indicate the amount, **if any,** that should be included in the computation of Oak's 2003 federal taxable income. Any possible optional treatment should be resolved in a manner that will minimize Oak's 2003 taxable income. On the CPA exam, a list of numeric answers would be provided for the candidate to select from.

Simulation Problem 2   (10 to 15 minutes)

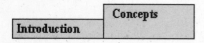

Given below are terms appearing in the federal income tax code, regulations and explanations.

A. Accumulated earnings tax
B. Capital assets
C. Capital contribution
D. Claim of right
E. Consent divided
F. Constructive dividend
G. Constructive receipt
H. Deficiency dividend
I. Dividends paid deduction

J. Dividends received deduction
K. Earned income
L. Exchanged basis
M. Excise tax
N. Fair market value
O. Head of household
P. Nontaxable exchange
Q. Passive income
R. Personal holding company

S. Personal holding company tax
T. Personal service corporation
U. Portfolio income
V. Regulated investment company
W. Sec. 1231 assets
X. Surviving spouse
Y. Taxable exchange
Z. Transferred basis

Indicate your choice of the best term applying to each of the statements below. Each term may be selected once, more than once, or not at all.

1. A corporation whose income was derived solely from dividends, interest, and royalties, and during the last six months of its year more than 50% of the value of its outstanding stock is owned by five or fewer individuals.

2. The basis used to determine gain on sale of property that was received as a gift.

3. The trade-in of production machinery for new production machinery by a corporation, when the corporation pays additional cash.

4. An unmarried individual whose filing status enables the taxpayer to use a set of income tax rates that are lower than those applicable to other unmarried individuals, but are higher than those applicable to married persons filing a joint return.

5. If income is unqualifiedly available, it will be subject to the income tax even though it is not physically in the taxpayer's possession.

6. A special tax imposed on corporations that accumulate their earnings beyond the reasonable needs of the business.

7. The classification of income from interest, dividends, annuities, and certain royalties.

8. The classification of depreciable assets and real estate used in a trade or business and held for more than one year.

9. This deduction attempts to mitigate the triple taxation that would occur if one corporation paid dividends to a corporate shareholder who, in turn, distributed such amounts to its individual shareholders.

10. Sale of property to a corporation by a shareholder for a selling price that is in excess of the property's fair market value.

	(A)	(B)	(C)	(D)	(E)	(F)	(G)	(H)	(I)	(J)	(K)	(L)	(M)	(N)	(O)	(P)	(Q)	(R)	(S)	(T)	(U)	(V)	(W)	(X)	(Y)	(Z)
1.																										
2.	O	O	O	O	O	O	O	O	O	O	O	O	O	O	O	O	O	O	O	O	O	O	O	O	O	O
3.	O	O	O	O	O	O	O	O	O	O	O	O	O	O	O	O	O	O	O	O	O	O	O	O	O	O
4.	O	O	O	O	O	O	O	O	O	O	O	O	O	O	O	O	O	O	O	O	O	O	O	O	O	O
5.	O	O	O	O	O	O	O	O	O	O	O	O	O	O	O	O	O	O	O	O	O	O	O	O	O	O
6.	O	O	O	O	O	O	O	O	O	O	O	O	O	O	O	O	O	O	O	O	O	O	O	O	O	O
7.	O	O	O	O	O	O	O	O	O	O	O	O	O	O	O	O	O	O	O	O	O	O	O	O	O	O
8.	O	O	O	O	O	O	O	O	O	O	O	O	O	O	O	O	O	O	O	O	O	O	O	O	O	O
9.	O	O	O	O	O	O	O	O	O	O	O	O	O	O	O	O	O	O	O	O	O	O	O	O	O	O
10.	O	O	O	O	O	O	O	O	O	O	O	O	O	O	O	O	O	O	O	O	O	O	O	O	O	O

Simulation Problem 3 (15 to 25 minutes)

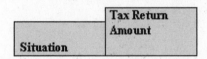

The following adjusted revenue and expense accounts appeared in the accounting records of Aviator, Inc., an accrual-basis taxpayer, for the year ended December 31, 2003:

Revenues	
Net sales	$2,000,000
Dividends	50,000
Interest	22,000
Gains on the sale of stock	20,000
Total	$2,092,000
Expenses	
Cost of goods sold	$1,000,000
Salaries and wages	400,000
Interest	25,000
Contributions	40,000
Depreciation (see note)	260,000
Losses on the sale of stock	30,000
Total	$1,755,000
Net Income	$ 337,000

NOTE: *There is no Sec. 1245, Sec. 1250, or Sec. 291 recapture.*

Additional information

(1) The dividends were received from a taxable domestic corporation, whose stock is traded on a major stock exchange.

(2) Interest expense consists of: $20,000 interest on funds borrowed for working capital and $5,000 interest on funds borrowed to purchase municipal bonds.

(3) Interest revenue consists of interest earned on

Corporate bonds purchased in 2002	$20,000
Municipal bonds purchased in 2003	2,000

(4) Contributions of $40,000 were made to qualified charitable organizations.

(5) On January 2, 2003, Aviator, Inc. commenced active operations. In connection with creating the business, Aviator incurred the following organizational expenditures:

Legal fees	$30,000
State incorporation fees	20,000
Brokers commission on the sale of stock	15,000

Aviator is amortizing the deductible expenses over the minimum allowable period. The expenditures were erroneously excluded from the accounts shown above.

(6) Gains from the sale of stock arose from the following sales of stock of unrelated corporations:

Tech. Corp (bought February 2003; sold April 2003)	$15,000
Major Corp (bought June 1999; sold September 2003)	5,000

(7) All losses from the sale of stock are classified as long-term capital losses.

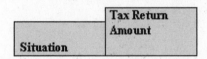

For **items 1 through 7** record the appropriate amount as it would appear on the Aviator, Inc. corporate tax return. On the exam, a list of numeric answers would be presented for the candidate to select from.

1. What is the amount of interest expense that Aviator, Inc. can deduct on its tax return?

2. What is the amount of interest income that must be included in Aviator's gross income?

3. What is the allowable amount of organizational expenditures that is deductible on Aviator's tax return?

4. How much of the capital gains must be included in Aviator's gross income?

5. How much of the capital losses can be deducted on Aviator's tax return?

6. What is the amount of Aviator's dividends received deduction?

7. What is Aviator's maximum charitable contributions deduction?

Simulation Problem 4   (40 to 50 minutes)

Situation	
	Tax Return Amounts

Following is Ral Corp.'s condensed income statement, before federal income tax, for the year ended December 31, 2003:

Sales		$1,000,000
Cost of sales		700,000
Gross profit		300,000
Operating expenses		220,000
Operating income		80,000
Other income (loss):		
Interest	$ 5,200	
Dividends	19,200	
Net long-term capital loss	(6,400)	18,000
Income before federal income tax		$ 98,000

Additional information
Interest arose from the following sources:

US Treasury notes	$ 3,000
Municipal arbitrage bonds	2,000
Other municipal bonds	200
Total interest	$5,200

Dividends arose from the following sources:

Taxable domestic corporation	Date stock acquired	Percent owned by Ral	
Clove Corp.	7/1/97	30.0	$ 7,000
Ramo Corp.	9/1/99	10.0	6,000
Sol Corp. (stock sold 1/10/04)	12/1/03	5.0	1,000
Real Estate Investment Trust	6/1/02	1.0	2,700
Mutual Fund Corp. (capital gains dividends only)	4/1/01	0.1	400
Money Market Fund (invests only in interest/paying securities)	3/1/00	0.1	2,100
Total dividends			$19,200

Operating expenses include the following:

Bonus of $5,000 paid to Ral's sales manager on January 31, 2004. This bonus was based on a percentage of Ral's 2003 sales and was computed on January 25, 2004, under a formula in effect in 2003.

Estimate of $10,000 for bad debts. Actual bad debts for the year amounted to $8,000.

Keyman life insurance premiums of $4,000. Ral is the beneficiary of the policies.

State income taxes of $12,000.

During 2003, Ral made estimated federal income tax payments of $25,000. These payments were debited to prepaid tax expense on Ral's books.

Ral does not exercise significant influence over Clove and accordingly did **not** use the equity method of accounting for this investment.

Ral declared and paid dividends of $11,000 during 2003.

Corporate income tax rates are as follows:

Taxable income					Of the
over	but not over	Pay	+	% on excess	amount over/
$ 0 /	$ 50,000	$ 0		15%	$ 0
50,000 /	75,000	7,500		25	50,000
75,000 /	100,000	13,750		34	75,000
100,000 /	335,000	22,250		39	100,000

Ral was not subject to the alternative minimum tax in 2003.

	Tax Return Amounts
Situation	

Items 1 through 14 below pertain to the computation of Ral Corp.'s 2003 federal income tax. For each item, select the appropriate amount. An amount may be selected once, more than once, or not at all.

Amount

A.	$0	J.	$ 3,000	S.	$ 6,400
B.	$ 280	K.	$ 3,200	T.	$ 7,000
C.	$ 320	L.	$ 4,000	U.	$ 8,000
D.	$ 1,000	M.	$ 4,200	V.	$10,000
E.	$ 1,470	N.	$ 4,800	W.	$11,000
F.	$ 1,680	O.	$ 4,900	X.	$12,000
G.	$ 1,890	P.	$ 5,000	Y.	$13,750
H.	$ 2,000	Q.	$ 5,200	Z.	$22,250
I.	$ 2,200	R.	$ 5,600		

Item for Ral's 2003 Federal Income Tax

1. Amount of deduction for manager's $5,000 bonus for 2003.

2. Deduction for bad debts for 2003.

3. Deduction for keyman life insurance premiums for 2003.

4. Deduction for state income taxes for 2003.

5. Amount of interest to be included in gross income for 2003.

6. Dividends received deduction for dividends received from Clove Corp.

7. Dividends received deduction for dividends received from Ramo Corp.

8. Dividends received deduction for dividends received from Sol Corp.

9. Dividends received deduction for dividends received from Real Estate Investment Trust.

10. Dividends received deduction for dividends received from Mutual Fund Corp.

11. Dividends received deduction for dividends received from Money Market Fund.

12. Deduction for the $11,000 of dividends paid by Ral to its shareholders.

13. Deduction for net capital loss for 2003.

14. Ral's federal income tax for 2003 if taxable income were $100,000.

	(A)	(B)	(C)	(D)	(E)	(F)	(G)	(H)	(I)	(J)	(K)	(L)	(M)	(N)	(O)	(P)	(Q)	(R)	(S)	(T)	(U)	(V)	(W)	(X)	(Y)	(Z)
1.	○	○	○	○	○	○	○	○	○	○	○	○	○	○	○	○	○	○	○	○	○	○	○	○	○	○
2.	○	○	○	○	○	○	○	○	○	○	○	○	○	○	○	○	○	○	○	○	○	○	○	○	○	○
3.	○	○	○	○	○	○	○	○	○	○	○	○	○	○	○	○	○	○	○	○	○	○	○	○	○	○
4.	○	○	○	○	○	○	○	○	○	○	○	○	○	○	○	○	○	○	○	○	○	○	○	○	○	○
5.	○	○	○	○	○	○	○	○	○	○	○	○	○	○	○	○	○	○	○	○	○	○	○	○	○	○
6.	○	○	○	○	○	○	○	○	○	○	○	○	○	○	○	○	○	○	○	○	○	○	○	○	○	○
7.	○	○	○	○	○	○	○	○	○	○	○	○	○	○	○	○	○	○	○	○	○	○	○	○	○	○
8.	○	○	○	○	○	○	○	○	○	○	○	○	○	○	○	○	○	○	○	○	○	○	○	○	○	○
9.	○	○	○	○	○	○	○	○	○	○	○	○	○	○	○	○	○	○	○	○	○	○	○	○	○	○
10.	○	○	○	○	○	○	○	○	○	○	○	○	○	○	○	○	○	○	○	○	○	○	○	○	○	○
11.	○	○	○	○	○	○	○	○	○	○	○	○	○	○	○	○	○	○	○	○	○	○	○	○	○	○
12.	○	○	○	○	○	○	○	○	○	○	○	○	○	○	○	○	○	○	○	○	○	○	○	○	○	○
13.	○	○	○	○	○	○	○	○	○	○	○	○	○	○	○	○	○	○	○	○	○	○	○	○	○	○
14.	○	○	○	○	○	○	○	○	○	○	○	○	○	○	○	○	○	○	○	○	○	○	○	○	○	○

Simulation Problem 5   (5 to 10 minutes)

Situation	
	Tax Return Amounts

Lan Corp., an accrual-basis calendar-year repair service corporation, was formed and began business on January 6, 2003. Lan's valid S corporation election took effect retroactively on January 6, 2003. Since the question requires a numeric answer, a list of numeric amounts would be provided for the candidate to select from.

	Tax Return Amounts
Situation	

For **items 1 through 4,** determine the amount, if any, using the fact pattern for each item.

1.   Assume the following facts:

Lan's 2003 books recorded the following items:

Gross receipts	$7,260
Interest income on investments	50
Charitable contributions	1,000
Supplies	1,120

What amount of net business income should Lan report on its 2003 Form 1120S, US Income Tax Return for an S Corporation, Schedule K?

2.   Assume the following facts:

As of January 6, 2003, Taylor and Barr each owned 100 shares of the 200 issued shares of Lan stock. On January 31, 2003, Taylor and Barr each sold twenty shares to Pike. No election was made to terminate the tax year. Lan had net business income of $14,400 for the year ended December 31, 2003, and made no distributions to its shareholders. Lan's 2003 calendar year had 360 days.

What amount of net business income should have been reported on Pike's 2003 Schedule K-1 from Lan? (2003 is a 360-day tax year.) Round the answer to the nearest hundred.

3.   Assume the following facts:

Pike purchased forty Lan shares on January 31, 2003, for $4,000. Lan made no distributions to shareholders, and Pike's 2003 Schedule K-1 from Lan reported

Ordinary business loss	$(1,000)
Municipal bond interest income	150

What was Pike's basis in his Lan stock at December 31, 2003?

4.   Assume the following facts:

On January 6, 2003, Taylor and Barr each owned 100 shares of the 200 issued shares of Lan stock. Taylor's basis in Lan shares on that date was $10,000. Taylor sold all of his Lan shares to Pike on January 31, 2003, and Lan made a valid election to terminate its tax year. Taylor's share of ordinary income from Lan prior to the sale was $2,000. Lan made a cash distribution of $3,000 to Taylor on January 30, 2003.

What was Taylor's basis in Lan shares for determining gain or loss from the sale to Pike?

Additional Simulation
    Appendix A—Simulation 2 involves Partnership Taxation

MULTIPLE-CHOICE ANSWERS

1. c			29. a			57. c			85. c			113. d			141. d		
2. c			30. d			58. d			86. c			114. b			142. c		
3. d			31. a			59. a			87. c			115. c			143. d		
4. d			32. d			60. c			88. d			116. b			144. b		
5. c			33. c			61. c			89. c			117. c			145. c		
6. a			34. d			62. d			90. c			118. d			146. d		
7. d			35. d			63. c			91. b			119. d			147. d		
8. a			36. c			64. c			92. d			120. b			148. d		
9. c			37. a			65. c			93. a			121. c			149. d		
10. b			38. c			66. d			94. c			122. d			150. b		
11. c			39. b			67. d			95. a			123. d			151. c		
12. d			40. c			68. c			96. b			124. a			152. d		
13. a			41. d			69. d			97. a			125. c			153. a		
14. b			42. a			70. c			98. d			126. b			154. b		
15. b			43. d			71. a			99. d			127. d			155. b		
16. a			44. a			72. d			100. b			128. b			156. a		
17. c			45. c			73. a			101. d			129. d			157. c		
18. d			46. d			74. d			102. a			130. a			158. d		
19. c			47. c			75. d			103. c			131. d			159. a		
20. b			48. b			76. d			104. d			132. b			160. c		
21. b			49. b			77. b			105. d			133. b			161. a		
22. a			50. b			78. b			106. b			134. d			162. a		
23. c			51. b			79. c			107. a			135. c			163. a		
24. c			52. b			80. b			108. c			136. d			164. b		
25. c			53. b			81. b			109. c			137. b					
26. b			54. d			82. a			110. a			138. d					
27. d			55. b			83. c			111. b			139. c			1st: __/164 = __%		
28. c			56. d			84. c			112. c			140. b			2nd: __/164= __%		

MULTIPLE-CHOICE ANSWER EXPLANATIONS

A. Transfers to a Controlled Corporation

1. **(c)** The requirement is to determine Dexter Corporation's tax basis for the property received in the incorporation from Alan. Since Alan and Baker are the only transferors of property and they, in the aggregate, own only 800 of the 1,050 shares outstanding immediately after the incorporation, Sec. 351 does not apply to provide nonrecognition treatment for Alan's transfer of property. As a result, Alan is taxed on his realized gain of $15,000, and Dexter Corporation has a cost (i.e., FMV) basis of $45,000 for the transferred property.

2. **(c)** The requirement is to determine Clark's basis for the Jet Corp. stock received in exchange for a contribution of cash and other property. Generally, no gain or loss is recognized if property is transferred to a corporation solely in exchange for stock, if immediately after the transfer, the transferors of property are in control of the corporation. Since Clark and Hunt both transferred property solely in exchange for stock, and together own all of the corporation's stock, their realized gains on the "other property" transferred are not recognized. As a result, Clark's basis for his Jet stock is equal to the $60,000 of cash plus the $50,000 adjusted basis of other property transferred, or $110,000. Hunt's basis for his Jet stock is equal to the $120,000 adjusted basis of the other property that he transferred.

3. **(d)** The requirement is to determine Carr's recognized gain on the transfer of appreciated property in connection with the organization of Flexo Corp. No gain or loss is recognized if property is transferred to a corporation solely in exchange for stock, if the transferors of property are in

control of the corporation immediately after the exchange. "Control" means that the transferors of property must, in the aggregate, own at least 80% of the corporation's stock immediately after the exchange. Since both Beck and Carr transferred property in exchange for stock, and in the aggregate they own 90% of Flexo's stock immediately after the exchange, the requirements for nonrecognition are met.

4. **(d)** The requirement is to determine the percentage of Nu's stock that Jones must own to qualify for a tax-free incorporation. No gain or loss is recognized if property is transferred to a corporation solely in exchange for stock and the transferor(s) are in control of the corporation immediately after the exchange. For this purpose, the term "control" means the ownership of at least 80% of the combined voting power of stock entitled to vote, and at least 80% of each class of nonvoting stock.

5. **(c)** The requirement is to determine Feld's stock basis following the contribution of a parcel of land to his solely owned corporation. When a shareholder makes a contribution to the capital of a corporation, no gain or loss is recognized to the shareholder, the corporation has a transferred (carryover) basis for the property, and the shareholder's original stock basis is increased by the adjusted basis of the additional property contributed. Here, Feld's beginning stock basis of $50,000 is increased by the $10,000 basis for the contributed land, resulting in a stock basis of $60,000.

6. **(a)** The requirement is to determine whether gain or loss is recognized on the incorporation of Rela Associates (a partnership). No gain or loss is recognized if property is transferred to a corporation solely in exchange for stock, if immediately after the transfer, the transferor is in control of the corporation. For purposes of determining whether consideration other than stock (boot) has been received, the assumption of liabilities by the transferee corporation is not to be treated as the receipt of money or other property by the transferor. Thus, Rela Associates recognizes no gain or loss on the transfer of its assets and liabilities to a newly formed corporation in return for all of the corporation's stock.

Also note that no gain or loss will be recognized by Rela Associates on the distribution of the corporation's stock to its partners in liquidation, and no gain or loss will be recognized by the partners when they receive the corporation's stock in liquidation of their partnership interests.

7.   (d)   The requirement is to determine the taxable income to Rogers and the basis of her stock. Since services are excluded from the definition of "property," Rogers' transfer does not fall under the nonrecognition provision of Sec. 351. Rogers must report $10,000 of compensation income and the basis for the stock is $10,000, the amount reported as income.

B.   Sec. 1244 Stock

8.   (a)   The requirement is to determine the amount of ordinary loss that Jackson can deduct as a result of the worthlessness of the Bean Corp. stock that he inherited from his parents. Sec. 1244 permits a shareholder to deduct an ordinary loss of up to $50,000 per year ($100,000 if married filing jointly) if qualifying stock is sold, exchanged, or becomes worthless. The qualifying stock must have been issued in exchange for money or other property and must have been issued to the individual or partnership sustaining the loss. Ordinary loss treatment is not available if the shareholder sustaining the loss was **not** the original holder of the stock. As a result, an individual who acquires stock by purchase, gift, or inheritance from another shareholder is not entitled to ordinary loss treatment. Since Jackson inherited the Bean stock from his parents, Jackson does not qualify for ordinary loss treatment and his $25,000 loss will be recognized as a long-term capital loss.

9.   (c)   The requirement is to determine which statement is **not** a requirement for stock to qualify as Sec. 1244 small business corporation stock. To qualify as Sec. 1244 small business corporation stock, the stock must be issued by a domestic corporation to an individual or partnership in exchange for money or property (other than stock or securities). Any type of stock can qualify, whether common or preferred, voting or nonvoting.

10.   (b)   The requirement is to determine the character of Dinah's recognized loss from the sale of Sec. 1244 stock to be reported on her joint income tax return for 2003. Sec. 1244 permits an individual to deduct an ordinary loss on the sale or worthlessness of stock. The amount of ordinary loss deduction is annually limited to $50,000 ($100,000 for a married taxpayer filing a joint return), with any excess loss treated as a capital loss. Since Dinah is married filing a joint return, her ordinary loss is limited to $100,000, with the remaining $25,000 recognized as a capital loss.

11.   (c)   The requirement is to determine the amount and character of Nancy's recognized loss resulting from the sale of Sec. 1244 stock for $35,000 in 2003. Sec. 1244 permits a single individual to annually deduct up to $50,000 of ordinary loss from the sale or exchange of small business corporation stock. Since Nancy acquired her stock in a tax-free asset transfer under Sec. 351, her stock's basis is $80,000 and the sale of the stock for $35,000 results in a loss of $45,000. However, because the property that Nancy transferred in exchange for the stock had an adjusted basis ($80,000) in excess of its fair market value ($60,000), the stock's basis must be reduced by the excess ($20,000) for purposes of determining the amount that can be treated as an ordinary loss. Thus, the amount of ordinary loss is limited to $60,000 – $35,000=$25,000, with the remaining loss ($45,000 – $25,000 = $20,000) treated as a capital loss.

C.1.   Filing and Payment of Tax

12.   (d)   The requirement is to determine the correct statement concerning the imposition of a civil fraud penalty on a corporation. If part of a tax underpayment is the result of fraud, a fraud penalty equal to 75% of the portion of the underpayment attributable to fraud will be assessed. Fraud differs from simple, honest mistakes and negligence. Fraud involves a taxpayer's actual, deliberate, or intentional wrongdoing with the specific purpose to evade a tax believed to be owing. Examples of conduct from which fraud may be inferred include keeping a double set of books; making false entries or alterations, false invoices or documents; destroying books or records; and, concealing assets or covering up sources of income. Answers (a), (b), and (c) are incorrect because omitting income as a result of inadequate recordkeeping, erroneously failing to report income, and filing an incomplete return with a statement attached making clear that the return is incomplete, do not constitute deliberate actions with the specific intent of evading tax.

13.   (a)   The requirement is to determine whether Bass Corp. has to pay interest on the $400 tax payment made in 2003 and/or a tax delinquency penalty. A corporation is generally required to make estimated tax payments and to pay all of its remaining tax liability on or before the original due date of its tax return. Filing for an extension of time to file the tax return does not extend the time to pay the tax liability. If any amount of tax is not paid by the original due date, interest must be paid from the due date until the tax is paid. Additionally, a failure-to-pay tax delinquency penalty will be owed if the amount of tax paid by the original due date of the return is less than 90% of the tax shown on the return. The failure-to-pay penalty is imposed at a rate of 0.5% per month (or fraction thereof), with a maximum penalty of 25%. The penalty is imposed on the amount of unpaid tax at the beginning of the month for which the penalty is being computed. Bass Corp. is not subject to the failure-to-pay delinquency penalty because it paid in 95% of the total tax shown on its return by the original due date of the return.

14.   (b)   The requirement is to determine whether Edge Corp. could compute its first quarter 2004 estimated income tax payment using the annualized income method and/or the preceding year method. A corporation generally must pay four installments of estimated tax, each equal to 25% of its required annual payment. A penalty for the underpayment of estimated taxes can be avoided if a corporation's quarterly estimated payments are at least equal to the least of (1) 100% of the tax shown on the current year's tax return, (2) 100% of the tax that would be due by placing the current year's income for specified monthly periods on an annualized basis, or (3) 100% of the tax shown on the corporation's return for the preceding year. However, the preceding year's tax liability cannot be used to determine estimated payments if no tax liability existed in the preceding year or a short-period tax return was filed for the preceding year.

15. (b) The requirement is to determine which statements are correct in regard to the reopening of a tax year after the statute of limitations have expired. The statute of limitations stipulate a time limit for the government's assessment of tax or a taxpayer's claim for refund. The normal period for the statute of limitations is the later of three years after a return is filed, or three years after the due date of the return. A six-year statute of limitations will apply if the gross income omitted from the return exceeds 25% of the gross income reported on the return. If a taxpayer's return was false or fraudulent with the intent to evade tax, or the taxpayer engaged in a willful attempt to evade tax, there is no statute of limitations. If a tax return has a 50% non-fraudulent omission from gross income, there would be a six-year statute of limitations. However, once the six-year period expired, the year could not be reopened. In contrast, a closed year can be reopened if a corporation prevails in a determination allowing a deduction in an open year that the taxpayer erroneously had taken in a closed tax year. This special rule for the reopening of a tax year is intended to prevent the double inclusion of an item of income, or the double allowance of a deduction or credit that would otherwise occur.

16. (a) Even though a corporation's penalty for underpaying federal estimated taxes is in the nature of interest, it is treated as an addition to tax, and as such, the penalty is not deductible.

17. (c) The requirement is to determine which methods of estimated tax payment can be used by Blink Corp. to avoid the penalty for underpayment of federal estimated taxes. Generally, to avoid a penalty for the underpayment of estimated taxes a corporation's quarterly estimated payments must be at least equal to the least of (1) 100% of the tax shown on the current year's tax return, (2) 100% of the tax that would be due by placing income for specified monthly periods on an annualized basis, or (3) 100% of the tax shown on the corporation's return for the preceding year, provided the preceding year showed a positive tax liability and consisted of twelve months. In this case, Blink cannot base its estimated payments on its preceding year because Blink had a net operating loss for 2002.

18. (d) The requirement is to indicate whether corporate tax credits and the alternative minimum tax must be taken into account for purposes of computing a corporation's estimated income tax payments. A corporation must make estimated tax payments unless its tax liability can reasonably be expected to be less than $500. A corporation's estimated tax is its expected tax liability (including the alternative minimum tax) less its allowable tax credits.

19. (c) The requirement is to determine the minimum estimated tax payments that must be made by Finbury Corporation to avoid the estimated tax underpayment penalty for 2003. Since Finbury is a large corporation (i.e., a corporation with taxable income of $1,000,000 or more in any of its

three preceding tax years), its estimated tax payments must be at least equal to 100% of its 2003 tax liability.

C.2.a. Corporate Tax Rates

20. (b) The requirement is to determine Kisco's income tax before credits given $70,000 of taxable income before a dividends received deduction that included a $10,000 dividend from a 15%-owned taxable domestic corporation. Since the $10,000 dividend would be eligible for a 70% dividends received deduction, Kisco's taxable income would be reduced by $7,000, resulting in taxable income of $63,000. The computation of tax would be

$50,000	x	15%	=	$ 7,500
$13,000	x	25%	=	3,250
		Tax	=	$10,750

C.2.c. Alternative Minimum Tax (AMT)

21. (b) The requirement is to determine the adjustment for adjusted current earnings (ACE) that will be used in the computation of Green Corp.'s alternative minimum tax for 2003. The ACE adjustment is equal to 75% of the difference between ACE and pre-ACE alternative minimum taxable income (AMTI). The ACE adjustment can be positive or negative, but a negative ACE adjustment is limited in amount to prior years' net positive ACE adjustments. For 2002, Green had a positive ACE adjustment of ($400,000 – $300,000) x 75% = $75,000. For 2003, Green's ACE is less than its pre-ACE AMTI leading to a negative ACE adjustment of ($100,000 – $300,000) x 75% = $150,000. However, this negative ACE adjustment is allowed only to the extent of $75,000, the amount of Green's net positive adjustment for prior years.

22. (a) The requirement is to determine Eastern's alternative minimum taxable income before the adjusted current earnings (ACE) adjustment. The starting point for computing a corporation's alternative minimum taxable income (AMTI) is its regular taxable income, which is then increased by tax preferences, and increased or decreased by specified adjustments. One tax preference that must be added to a corporation's regular taxable income is the amount of tax-exempt interest from private activity bonds. One adjustment that must be made to convert regular taxable income to AMTI is the adjustment for depreciation on personal business property placed in service after 1986. For regular tax purposes, Eastern utilized the general MACRS depreciation system and would have used the 200% declining balance method for computing regular tax depreciation on the five-year property placed in service during 2003. However, for AMT purposes, depreciation on five-year property must be computed using the 150% declining balance method. In this case, it means that Eastern's regular tax depreciation exceeded its allowable AMT depreciation by $1,000, and this amount must be added back to regular taxable income to arrive at AMTI. Thus, Eastern's AMTI (before ACE adjustment) is its regular taxable income of $300,000, plus its $5,000 of tax-exempt interest from private activity bonds and $1,000 of depreciation adjustment, or $306,000.

23. (c) The requirement is to determine the correct statement regarding the amount of excess of a corporation's tentative minimum tax over its regular tax. If a corporation's tentative minimum tax exceeds its regular tax, the excess represents the corporation's alternative minimum tax and is payable in addition to its regular tax.

24.   (c)   The requirement is to determine the exempt portion of Rona Corp.'s alternative minimum taxable income (AMTI). A corporation is allowed an exemption of $40,000 in computing its AMTI. However, the $40,000 exemption is reduced by 25% of the corporation's AMTI in excess of $150,000. Here, the amount of exemption is $40,000 – [($200,000 – $150,000) x 25%] = $27,500.

25.   (c)   The requirement is to determine which item is a tax preference that must be included in the computation of a corporation's alternative minimum tax (AMT) for 2003. Tax-exempt interest on private activity bonds is a tax preference item. Answer (a) is incorrect because it is the excess of income under the percentage-of-completion method over the amount reported using the completed-contract method that is a positive adjustment in computing the AMT. Answer (b) is incorrect because a deduction for casualty losses is allowed in the computation of AMT. Answer (d) is incorrect because capital gains are not a preference item in computing the AMT.

26.   (b)   For real property that was placed in service before January 1, 1999, an AMT adjustment is necessary because for AMT purposes, real property must be depreciated using the straight-line method over a forty-year recovery period, rather than the thirty-nine year or twenty-seven and one-half year recovery period used for regular tax purposes. However, note that this *adjustment has been eliminated for real property first placed in service after December 31, 1998.* The dividends received deduction, charitable contributions, and investment interest expense are neither adjustments nor tax preference items.

27.   (d)   The requirement is to determine when a corporation will not be subject to the alternative minimum tax (AMT) for 2003. A corporation is exempt from AMT for its first tax year. After the first year, a corporation is exempt from AMT for each year that it passes a gross receipts test. A corporation is exempt for its second year if its gross receipts for the first year did not exceed $5 million. For all subsequent years, a corporation is exempt if its average annual gross receipts for the testing period do not exceed $7.5 million. Exemption from the AMT is not based on asset size nor number of shareholders.

28.   (c)   A corporation is exempt from the corporate AMT for its first tax year. It is exempt for its second year if its first year's gross receipts were $5 million or less. To be exempt for its third year, the corporation's average gross receipts for the first two years must be $7.5 million or less. To be exempt for the fourth year (and subsequent years), the corporation's average gross receipts for all prior three-year periods also must be $7.5 million or less. Here, Bradbury is exempt for 2002 because its average gross receipts for 2000-2001 were $6.75 million. However, Bradbury loses its exemption for 2003 and all subsequent years because its average gross receipts for 2000-2002 exceed $7.5 million ($7.67 million).

C.3.   Gross Income

29.   (a)   The requirement is to indicate whether personal service corporations and personal holding companies must include 100% of dividends received from unrelated taxable domestic corporations in gross income in computing regular taxable income. Since the question concerns **gross income,** not taxable income, no part of the dividend income would be offset by a dividends received deduction. Therefore, both personal service corporations and personal holding companies must include 100% of dividends received from unrelated taxable domestic corporations in gross income.

30.   (d)   The requirement is to determine the amount of bond sinking fund trust income taxable to Andi Corp. in 2003. Since the trust income will be accumulated and benefit Andi Corp. by reducing the amount of future contributions that Andi must make to the bond sinking fund, all of the trust income, consisting of $60,000 of interest and $8,000 of long-term capital gain, is taxable to Andi Corp.

31.   (a)   The requirement is to determine the amount of capital gain recognized by Lee Corp. on the sale of its treasury stock. A corporation will never recognize gain or loss on the receipt of money or other property in exchange for its stock, including treasury stock.

32.   (d)   The requirement is to determine the amount of gain to be recognized by Ral Corp. when it issues its stock in exchange for land. No gain or loss is ever recognized by a corporation on the receipt of money or other property in exchange for its own stock (including treasury stock).

33.   (c)   The requirement is to determine the amount of dividend reportable by a corporate distributee on a property distribution. The amount of dividend to be reported by a corporate distributee is the FMV of the property less any liability assumed. Kile's dividend would be $12,000, reduced by the liability of $5,000 = $7,000.

C.4.b.   Organizational Expenditures

34.   (d)   The requirement is to determine which costs are amortizable organizational expenditures. A corporation's organizational expenditures can be amortized over a period of not less than sixty months, beginning with the month that business begins. Organizational expenditures include fees for accounting and legal services incident to incorporation (e.g., fees for drafting corporate charter, bylaws, terms of stock certificates), expenses of organizational meetings and of temporary directors meetings, and fees paid to the state of incorporation. However, the costs incurred in issuing and selling stock and securities (e.g., professional fees to issue stock, printing costs, underwriting commissions) do not qualify as organizational expenditures and are not tax deductible.

35.   (d)   The requirement is to determine the maximum amount of Brown Corp.'s deduction for the amortization of organizational expenditures. A corporation's organizational expenditures can be amortized over a period of not less than sixty months, beginning with the month that the corporation begins business. Brown's amortizable organizational expenditures include the $40,000 of legal fees to obtain a corporate charter, but exclude underwriting commissions and other stock issue costs. These underwriting commissions and other stock issue costs are not deductible, and merely reduce Brown's paid-in capital. Since Brown began active business operations in July, Brown's maximum amortization deduction is $40,000 x 6/60 = $4,000.

36.   (c)   The requirement is to determine the correct statement regarding the costs of organizing a corporation. A corporation's organizational expenditures (e.g., legal fees for drafting the corporate charter, bylaws, and terms of original stock certificates, necessary accounting services, expenses of temporary directors, fees paid to the state of incorporation) are incidental to the creation of the corporation and have value throughout the life of the corporation. For tax purposes, a corporation may elect to amortize its organization costs over a period of not less than sixty months. The election is made by attaching a statement to the corporation's tax return for the tax year in which the corporation begins business, and amortization begins with the month that the corporation begins business.

37. (a) The requirement is to determine the maximum deduction for amortization of organizational expenditures for a calendar-year corporation. A corporation's organizational expenditures can be amortized ratably over a period of not less than sixty months, beginning with the month in which the corporation begins business. Since the organizational expenditures total $9,000 and the corporation began business in September, the maximum amount of amortization for 2003 would be ($9,000 x 4/60) = $600.

C.4.c.   Charitable Contributions

38. (c) The requirement is to determine the amount of Jackson Corp.'s charitable contributions carryover to 2004. A corporation's charitable contributions deduction is limited to 10% of its taxable income computed before the deduction for charitable contributions, the dividends received deduction, and before deductions for a NOL carryback and capital loss carryback. Although the limitation is computed before deducting NOL and capital loss carrybacks, NOL and capital loss carryforwards are deducted in arriving at the contribution base amount. Thus, of the $8,000 given to charitable organizations during 2003, $2,500 can be currently deducted, leaving $5,500 to be carried over to 2004.

Gross income from operations	$100,000
Dividend income	10,000
Operating expenses	(35,000)
Officers' salaries	(20,000)
NOL carryover from 2002	(30,000)
TI before contributions and DRD	$ 25,000
	x 10%
Contributions deduction for 2003	$ 2,500

39. (b) The requirement is to determine the amount that Cable Corp. can deduct for charitable contributions for 2003. A corporation's charitable contribution deduction is limited to 10% of its taxable income computed before the charitable contribution and dividends received deductions. Since Cable's taxable income of $820,000 already included a $40,000 dividends received deduction, $40,000 must be added back to arrive at Cable's contribution base of $860,000. Thus, Cable's maximum contribution deduction for 2003 would be limited to $860,000 x 10% = $86,000. Cable would deduct the $80,000 contributed during 2003, plus $6,000 of its $10,000 carryover from 2002. This means that Cable will have a $4,000 contributions carryover from 2002 to 2004.

40. (c) The requirement is to select the correct statement regarding a corporation's charitable contributions in excess of the limitation for deductibility in a particular year. Charitable contributions in excess of the 10% of taxable income limitation may be carried forward to a maximum of five succeeding years. The contributions actually made during a later year plus any carryforwards are also subject to a 10% limitation. Contributions actually made during a taxable year are deducted before carryforwards.

41. (d) The requirement is to determine the **maximum** charitable contribution deduction that Tapper Corp. may take on its 2003 return. Since Tapper is an accrual method calendar-year corporation, it can deduct contributions actually made during 2003, plus Tapper can elect to deduct any contribution authorized by its board of directors during 2003, so long as the contribution is subsequently made no later than 2 1/2 months after the end of the tax year. Thus, to maximize its deduction for 2003, Tapper can deduct both the $10,000 contribution made during 2003 as well as the $30,000 contribution authorized during 2003 and paid on February 1, 2004. The total ($40,000) is deductible for 2003 since it is less than the limitation amount ($500,000 x 10% = $50,000).

42. (a) The requirement is to determine the amount to be included as gross income in Lyle Corp.'s 2003 return for the receipt of nonprescription drug samples that were later donated to an exempt organization. When unsolicited samples of items that are normally inventoried and sold in the ordinary course of business are received from a supplier, and later donated as a charitable contribution, the fair market value of the items received must be included in gross income. The taxpayer is then allowed a charitable contribution deduction equal to the fair market value of the items donated.

43. (d) The requirement is to determine the portion of the dividends received of $1,000 that is to be included in taxable income when Nale Corp. computes its maximum allowable deduction for contributions. A corporation's maximum allowable deduction for charitable contributions is limited to 10% of its taxable income before the charitable contributions and dividends received deductions. Thus, Nale must include all $1,000 of dividends in its taxable income for purposes of computing its maximum allowable deduction for contributions.

44. (a) The requirement is to determine the contribution base for purposes of computing Gero Corp.'s charitable contributions deduction. A corporation's contribution base is its taxable income before the charitable contributions deduction, the dividends received deduction, and before deductions for NOL and capital loss carrybacks. Since Gero had operating income of $160,000 after deducting $10,000 of contributions, its contribution base would be $160,000 + $10,000 + $2,000 dividends = $172,000.

45. (c) The requirement is to determine the maximum charitable contribution deduction for 2003. Since Norwood is an accrual-basis calendar-year corporation, it can elect to deduct a contribution authorized by its board of directors during 2003, so long as the contribution is subsequently paid no later than two and one-half months after year-end (i.e., by March 15th). Thus, to maximize its deduction for 2003, Norwood can elect to deduct the $10,000 contribution authorized during 2003 and paid on March 1, 2004, but its deduction is limited to 10% of taxable income before the charitable contribution deduction. The maximum amount deductible for 2003 is

Book income	$500,000
+ Charitable contribution	100,000
TI before CC deduction	$600,000
	x 10%
Maximum CC deduction	$ 60,000

The remaining $40,000 can be carried over a maximum of five years.

C.4.e.   Dividends Received Deduction (DRD)

46. **(d)**   The requirement is to determine Best Corp.'s dividends received deduction for the $100,000 of dividends received from an unrelated domestic corporation. Dividends received from less than 20%-owned corporations are generally eligible for a 70% DRD (i.e., 70% x dividend). However, if the corporation's taxable income before the DRD is less than the amount of dividend, the DRD will be limited to 70% of taxable income, unless the full DRD (70% x dividend) creates or increases a net operating loss. Here, since taxable income before the DRD ($90,000) is less than the amount of dividends ($100,000), and the full DRD (70% x $100,000 = $70,000) would not create a NOL, the DRD is limited to 70% x $90,000 = $63,000.

47. **(c)**   The requirement is to determine the amount to be reported as income before special deductions on Acorn's tax return. A corporation's taxable income before special deductions generally includes all income and all deductions except for the dividends received deduction. Thus, Acorn's income before special deductions would include the sales of $500,000 and dividend income of $25,000, less the cost of sales of $250,000, a total of $275,000.

48. **(b)**   The requirement is to determine the correct statement regarding the corporate dividends received deduction (DRD). To qualify for a DRD, the investor corporation must own the investee's stock for more than forty-five days (ninety days for preferred stock if the dividends received are in arrears for more than one year). Answer (a) is incorrect because the DRD may be limited to the applicable percentage of the investor corporation's taxable income. Answer (c) is incorrect because a 70% DRD applies to dividends from less-than-20%-owned corporations, an 80% DRD applies to dividends from unaffiliated corporations that are at least 20%-owned, while a 100% DRD applies to dividends from corporations that are at least 80%-owned when a consolidated tax return is not filed.

49. **(b)**   The requirement is to determine the amount of dividends to be included in Ryan Corp.'s taxable income. Since the dividends were received from less than 20%-owned taxable domestic corporations, they are eligible for a 70% dividends received deduction. Thus, the amount of dividends to be included in taxable income is $2,000 – (70% x $2,000) = $600.

50. **(b)**   The requirement is to determine the amount of dividends to be included in Daly Corp.'s **taxable income** for 2003. Since the dividends were received from 20%-owned taxable domestic corporations, they are eligible for an 80% dividends received deduction. Thus, the amount of dividends to be included in taxable income is $1,000 – (80% x $1,000) = $200.

51. **(b)**   The requirement is to determine the amount of dividends that qualifies for the 80% dividends received deduction. Only dividends received from taxable domestic unaffiliated corporations that are at least 20%-owned qualify for the 80% dividends received deduction ($7,500). So-called "dividends" paid by mutual savings banks are reported as interest, and are not eligible for the dividends received deduction.

C.4.j.   Losses

52. **(b)**   The requirement is to determine Stark Corp.'s net operating loss (NOL) for 2003. A NOL carryover from 2002 would not be allowed in computing the 2003 NOL. In contrast, a dividends received deduction (DRD) is allowed in computing a NOL since a corporation's DRD is not subject to limitation if it creates or increases a NOL. Stark Corp.'s NOL would be computed as follows:

Gross income from operations	$ 350,000
Dividend income	100,000
Less operating expenses	(400,000)
TI before DRD	$ 50,000
DRD (70% x $100,000)	(70,000)
Net operating loss for 2003	$ (20,000)

53. **(b)**   The requirement is to determine the proper treatment of a C corporation's net capital losses. A corporation's capital losses can only be used to offset capital gains. If a corporation has a net capital loss, it cannot be currently deducted, but instead must be carried back three years and forward five years as a STCL to offset capital gains in those years.

54. **(d)**   The requirement is to determine the amount of Taylor Corp.'s 2002 net operating loss (NOL) that is available for use in its 2003 return. A net operating loss is generally carried back two years and forward twenty years to offset taxable income in the carryback and carryforward years. However, for NOLs arising in tax years ending in 2001 and 2002, a five-year carryback is available. Since Taylor Corp. made no election to waive a carryback period, the 2002 NOL would be used to offset Taylor's 1997 through 2001 taxable income in the five carryback years (a total of $105,000) leaving $200,000 – $105,000 = $95,000 to be carried forward as an NOL deduction in its 2003 return.

55. **(b)**   The requirement is to determine the correct statement regarding the carryback or carryforward of an unused net capital loss. A corporation's unused net capital loss is carried back three years and forward for up to five years to offset capital gains in the carryback and carryforward years. An unused net capital loss is always carried back and forward as a short-term capital loss whether or not it was short-term when sustained.

56. **(d)**   The requirement is to determine Haya Corporation's net operating loss (NOL) for 2003. A deduction for a net operating loss carryover is not allowed in computing a NOL. Furthermore, a deduction for charitable contributions is generally not allowed, since the charitable contributions deduction is limited to 10% of taxable income before the charitable contributions and dividends received deductions. Thus, Haya's NOL for 2003 would be computed as follows:

Gross income	$ 600,000
Less expenses	(800,000)
	$(200,000)
Add back contributions included in expenses	5,000
NOL for 2003	$(195,000)

57. **(c)**   The requirement is to determine the NOL for 2003 given that deductions in the tax return exceed gross income by $56,800. In computing the NOL for 2003, the DRD of $6,800 would be fully allowed, but the $15,000 NOL deduction (carryover from 2002) would not be allowed. $56,800 – $15,000 = $41,800.

58. **(d)** The requirement is to determine the amount of casualty loss deduction available to Ram Corp. due to the complete destruction of its machine. If business property is completely destroyed, the amount of casualty loss deduction is the property's adjusted basis immediately before the casualty. Note that the "$100 floor" and "10% of adjusted gross income" limitations that apply to personal casualty losses, do not apply to business casualty losses.

C.4.l. R&D Expenditures

59. **(a)** The requirement is to determine the proper treatment for qualifying research and experimentation expenditures. A taxpayer can elect to deduct qualifying research and experimentation expenditures as a current expense if the taxpayer so elects for the first taxable year in which the expenditures are incurred. Otherwise, the taxpayer must capitalize the expenditures. Then, if the capitalized costs are not subject to depreciation (because there is no determinable life), the taxpayer can amortize them over a period of sixty months or longer.

C.6. Reconcile Book and Taxable Income

60. **(c)** The requirement is to determine Kelly Corp.'s taxable income given net income per books of $300,000, that included $50,000 of dividend income and an $80,000 deduction for bad debt expense. Since the dividends were received from a 5%-owned taxable domestic corporation, they are eligible for a 70% dividends received deduction ($50,000 x 70% = $35,000). Since no bad debts were actually written off and the reserve method cannot be used for tax purposes, the $80,000 of bad debt expense per books is not deductible for tax purposes and must be added back to book income to arrive at taxable income. Kelly's taxable income is $300,000 – $35,000 + $80,000 = $345,000.

61. **(c)** The requirement is to determine Maple Corp.'s taxable income given book income before federal income taxes of $100,000. The provision for state income taxes of $1,000 that was deducted per books is also an allowable deduction in computing taxable income. The interest earned on US Treasury Bonds of $6,000 that was included in book income must also be included in computing taxable income. The $2,000 of interest expense on the bank loan to purchase the US Treasury Bonds was deducted per books and is also an allowable deduction in computing taxable income, because the interest income from the obligations is taxable. Since there are no differences between the book and tax treatment of these items, taxable income is the same as book income before federal income taxes, $100,000.

62. **(d)** The requirement is to determine Dodd Corp.'s taxable income given net income per books of $100,000. The $27,000 provision for federal income tax deducted per books is not deductible in computing taxable income. The $5,000 net capital loss deducted per books is not deductible in computing taxable income because a corporation can only use capital losses to offset capital gains. The life insurance premiums of $3,000 deducted per books are not deductible in computing taxable income because life insurance proceeds are excluded from gross income. Thus, Dodd Corp.'s taxable income is $100,000 + $27,000 + $5,000 + $3,000 = $135,000.

63. **(c)** The requirement is to determine Bard Corp.'s taxable income given book income of $450,000. No ad-

justment is necessary for the $4,000 of state corporate income tax refunds since they were included in book income and would also be included in taxable income due to the "tax benefit rule" (i.e., an item of deduction that reduces a taxpayer's income tax for a prior year must be included in gross income if later recovered). The life insurance proceeds of $15,000 must be subtracted from book income because they were included in book income, but would be excluded from taxable income. The net capital loss of $20,000 that was subtracted in computing book income must be added back to book income because a net capital loss is not deductible in computing taxable income. Thus, Bard Corp.'s taxable income would be $450,000 – $15,000 + $20,000 = $455,000.

64. **(c)** The requirement is to determine Dewey Corporation's taxable income, given that organization costs of $258,000 were deducted as an expense in arriving at book income of $520,000. For tax purposes, organizational expenditures can be amortized over a minimum period of sixty months, beginning with the month in which the corporation begins business. Since Dewey began business in June, the allowable amortization for 2003 would be $258,000 x 7/60 = $30,100. Thus, adding back the $258,000 deduction for organization expense to book income, and subtracting the $30,100 of allowable amortization for tax purposes results in taxable income of $520,000 + $258,000 – $30,100 = $747,900.

65. **(c)** The requirement is to determine net income per books given TI of $700,000.

Taxable income	$700,000
Provision for federal income tax	– 280,000
Depreciation on tax return	+ 130,000
Depreciation per books	– 75,000
Life insurance proceeds	+ 100,000
Net income per books	$575,000

The provision for federal income tax is not deductible in computing TI but must be deducted per books. The life insurance proceeds are tax exempt, but must be included per books.

66. **(d)** The requirement is to compute Ajax's taxable income given book income of $1,200,000 and items included in the computation of book income. Book income must be adjusted for the tax-exempt interest (net of related expenses) and the provision for federal income tax:

Book income	$1,200,000
Municipal bond interest	(40,000)
Nondeductible interest expense (to produce tax-exempt interest income)	8,000
Provision for federal income tax	524,000
Taxable income	$1,692,000

The damages received for patent infringement that were included in book income are similarly included in taxable income, so no adjustment is necessary.

C.6.c. Schedule M-1

67. **(d)** The requirement is to determine the amount of income to be shown on the last line of Farve Corp.'s Schedule M-1 for 2003. Schedule M-1 provides a reconciliation of income reported per books with income reported on the tax return. Generally, items of income and deduction whose book and tax treatment differ, result in Schedule M-1 items. However, since Schedule M-1 reconciles to taxable income before the dividends received and net operating loss deductions, the dividends received deduction will not be a reconciling item on Schedule M-1. In this case, Farve Corp.'s $80,000 of book income would be increased by the $18,000 of federal income tax, $6,000 of net capital loss, and 50% of the $4,000 of business meals which were deducted per books, but are not deductible for tax purposes. Book income would be reduced by the $5,000 of municipal bond interest that is tax-exempt.

68. **(c)** The requirement is to determine Starke Corp.'s taxable income as reconciled on Schedule M-1 of Form 1120. Schedule M-1 provides a reconciliation of a corporation's book income with its taxable income before the dividends received and net operating loss deductions. Starke reported book income of $380,000 that included $50,000 of municipal bond interest income, and deductions for $170,000 of federal income tax expense and $2,000 of interest expense incurred to carry the municipal bonds. Since municipal bond interest is tax-exempt, the $50,000 of interest income must be subtracted from book income, and the $2,000 of interest expense incurred to carry the municipal bonds is not deductible and must be added back to book income. Similarly, the $170,000 of federal income tax expense is not deductible and must be added back to book income. Thus, Starke's taxable income is $380,000 – $50,000 + $2,000 + $170,000 = $502,000.

69. **(d)** The requirement is to determine whether lodging expenses for out-of-town travel and the deduction of a net capital loss would be reported on Schedule M-1 of the US corporate income tax return (Form 1120). Schedule M-1 generally provides a reconciliation of a corporation's income per books with the corporation's taxable income before the NOL and dividends received deductions. Since a net capital loss deducted per books would not be deductible for tax purposes, the net capital loss would be added back to book income on Schedule M-1. However, since out-of-town lodging expenses are deductible for both book and tax purposes, the expenses would not appear on Schedule M-1.

70. **(c)** The reconciliation of income per books with income per return is accomplished on Schedule M-1 of Form 1120. Both temporary differences (e.g., accelerated depreciation on tax return and straight-line on books) and permanent differences (e.g., tax-exempt interest) must be considered to convert book income to taxable income.

71. **(a)** The requirement is to determine Media Corporation's net M-1 adjustment on its 2003 Form 1120. Generally, items of income and deduction whose book and tax treatment differ result in Schedule M-1 adjustments that reconcile income reported per books with taxable income. Media reported book income that included $6,000 in municipal bond interest income, and deductions that included $1,500 of interest expense incurred on debt to carry the municipal bonds, and $8,000 in advertising expense. Since municipal bond interest is tax-exempt, the $6,000 of interest income must be subtracted from book income. Additionally, since the $1,500 of interest expense to carry the municipal bonds is an expense incurred in the production of exempt income, it is not tax deductible and must be added back to book income. On the other hand, the $8,000 of advertising expense is deductible for book as well as taxable income purposes, and no Schedule M-1 adjustment is necessary. Thus, Media's net Schedule M-1 adjustment to reconcile

book income to taxable income is $1,500 – $6,000 = ($4,500).

C.6.d. Schedule M-2

72. **(d)** The requirement is to determine the amount to be shown on Schedule M-2 of Form 1120 as Barbaro's retained earnings at December 31, 2003. Beginning with the balance at January 1, 2003, the end of year balance would be computed as follows:

Balance, 1/1/03	$600,000
Net income for year	+ 274,900
Federal income tax refund	+ 26,000
Cash dividends	– 150,000
Balance, 12/31/03	$750,900

73. **(a)** The requirement is to determine the amount that should appear on the last line of Schedule M-2 of Form 1120. Schedule M-2 is an "Analysis of Unappropriated Retained Earnings Per Books." Its first line is the balance at the beginning of the year and its last line is the balance at the end of the year. The end-of-year balance would be computed as follows:

Retained earnings, beginning	$ 50,000
Net income for year	+ 70,000
Contingency reserve	– 10,000
Cash dividends	– 8,000
Retained earnings, end of year	$102,000

D. Affiliated and Controlled Corporations

74. **(d)** The requirement is to determine the amount of dividend revenue to be reported on Bank Corp.'s consolidated tax return for the $48,000 of dividends received from Bank Corp.'s 80%-owned subsidiary, Shore Corp. Instead of filing separate tax returns, an affiliated group of corporations (i.e., corporations connected through 80% or more stock ownership) can elect to file a consolidated tax return. If a consolidated return is filed, dividends received from affiliated group members are eliminated in the consolidation process, and are not reported on the consolidated tax return.

75. **(d)** The requirement is to determine the amount of net dividend income received from an affiliated corporation that should be included in Portal Corporation's 2003 consolidated tax return. When dividends are received from an affiliated corporation (i.e., at least 80%-owned subsidiary) during a consolidated return year, the intercompany dividends are eliminated in the consolidation process and are not included in gross income.

76. **(d)** The requirement is to determine the amount of gain to be reported in the 2003 and 2002 consolidated tax returns. Generally, gains and losses on intercompany transactions during consolidated return years are deferred and reported in subsequent years when a restoration event occurs. Since Potter and Sly filed a consolidated tax return for 2002, Potter's gain on the sale of land to Sly in 2002 is deferred and will be reported when Sly sells the land outside of the affiliated group in 2003. Thus, the 2002 consolidated return will report no gain with regard to the land, while the 2003 consolidated return will report the aggregate amount of gain, $125,000 – $60,000 = $65,000.

77. **(b)** The requirement is to determine the correct statement regarding an affiliated group of includible corporations filing a consolidated return. One of the advantages of filing a consolidated return is that operating losses of one member of the group offset operating profits of other members of the group. Answer (a) is incorrect because intercompany dividends are eliminated in the consolidation process and are excluded from the return. Answers (c) and (d) are incorrect because an affiliated group of includible corporations is also a controlled group and is therefore limited to one alternative minimum tax exemption and one accumulated earnings credit.

78. **(d)**   The requirement is to determine the stock ownership requirement that must be satisfied to enable Dana Corp. to elect to file a consolidated tax return that includes Seco Corp. For Dana and Seco to qualify for filing a consolidated tax return, Dana must directly own stock possessing at least 80% of the total voting power, and at least 80% of the total value of Seco stock.

79. **(c)**   The requirement is to determine the correct statement regarding the filing of consolidated returns. The election to file consolidated returns is limited to affiliated corporations. Affiliated corporations are parent-subsidiary corporations that are connected through stock ownership wherein at least 80% of the combined voting power and value of all stock (except the common parent's) is directly owned by other includible corporations. Answer (a) is incorrect because brother-sister corporations are not affiliated corporations. Answer (b) is incorrect because no advance permission is required. Answer (d) is incorrect because an affiliated group's election to file consolidated returns is independent of its issuing financial statements on a consolidated basis.

80. **(b)**   The requirement is to determine the amount of gain for 2003 that Subsidiary should take into account as a result of the 2002 sale of land to Parent. Since Parent and Subsidiary are filing consolidated tax returns, the $20,000 of gain to Subsidiary in 2002 is not recognized, but instead is deferred and recognized when the land is sold outside the affiliated group in 2003.

E.   Dividends and Distributions

81. **(b)**   The requirement is to determine Westwind's accumulated earnings and profits at year-end. Here, Westwind had a beginning deficit of $45,000, had current earnings and profits of $15,000, and distributed $12,000 cash during the year. As a result, Westwind's beginning deficit of $45,000 would be reduced by the $3,000 of current earnings and profits that were not distributed, resulting in a deficit of $42,000 at the end of the year.

82. **(a)**   The requirement is to determine Cable's accumulated earnings and profits (AEP) at the end of the year. Cable's beginning AEP of $100,000 would be increased by its earnings and profits for the current tax year (CEP). The starting point for computing Cable's CEP would be its taxable income of $50,000. Taxable income would be reduced by the $5,000 of federal income taxes paid, and would also be reduced by the $1,000 of current year charitable contributions which would not be allowed as a deduction in computing taxable income because of the 10% of taxable income limitation. Additionally, CEP would be reduced by the current year net capital loss of $2,000 which would not be allowed as a deduction in computing current year taxable income because a corporation cannot deduct a net capital loss. As a result, Cable's CEP is $50,000 – ($5,000 + $1,000 +

$2,000) = $42,000, and its AEP at the end of the current year is $100,000 + $42,000 = $142,000.

83. **(c)**   The requirement is to determine the amount of the 2003 distributions classified as dividend income to Locke's shareholders. A corporation's distributions to shareholders on their stock are treated as a dividend to the extent of a corporation's current earnings and profits and/or accumulated earnings and profits. Here, the $80,000 distributed to shareholders would be treated as a dividend to the extent of Locke's current ($20,000) and accumulated ($30,000) earnings and profits, or $50,000.

84. **(c)**   The requirement is to determine the balance of Chicago Corp.'s accumulated earnings and profits (AEP) at January 1, 2004. The AEP beginning balance of $100,000 would be reduced by the 2003 deficit of ($140,000), resulting in a deficit of ($40,000). Since distributions only pay out a corporation's positive AEP, and neither create nor increase a deficit in AEP, the AEP deficit of ($40,000) is not affected by the $30,000 distributed to shareholders.

85. **(c)**   The requirement is to determine the amount of gain recognized by Salon, Inc. as a result of the distribution of property and liability to its sole shareholder. Generally, a corporation must recognize gain when it distributes appreciated property to a shareholder. The gain is measured by treating the corporation as if it had sold the property to the shareholder for its fair market value. However, if there is a liability on the property that is assumed by the shareholder and the amount of liability exceeds the property's fair market value, then the amount of liability is used to measure the gain. Here, Salon's recognized gain would total $10,000 liability – $3,000 basis = $7,000.

86. **(c)**   The requirement is to determine the amount received from Kent Corp. that is taxable as dividend income to Reed for 2003. The term "dividend" means any distribution of property made by a corporation to its shareholders out of its current earnings and profits and/or accumulated earnings and profits. For distributions of property other than cash, the amount of distribution is the property's fair market value reduced by any liabilities that are assumed or liabilities to which the property is subject. In this case, the amount of distribution made by Kent Corp. to Reed is the property's fair market value of $200,000. This $200,000 of distribution is taxable as dividend income to Reed to the extent of Kent Corp.'s current earnings and profits ($60,000) and accumulated earnings and profits ($125,000), a total of $185,000. Note that this answer assumes that the gain that was recognized by Kent Corp. on the distribution ($200,000 FMV – $150,000 adjusted basis = $50,000) has already been included in the amount provided as Kent's current earnings and profits for 2003. This assumption can be made because the item indicates "Current earnings and profits for 2003," not "Current earnings and profits before the distribution." Also, note that the portion of the distribution that is not a dividend ($200,000 – $185,000 = $15,000) is a nontaxable return of Reed's stock basis, and reduces stock basis from $500,000 to $485,000.

87. **(c)**   The requirement is to determine which statements are correct concerning Ridge Corp.'s cash distribution of $1,000,000 to its shareholders with respect to its stock. A corporation's distributions to shareholders on their stock will be taxed as dividend income to the extent of the corporation's current and accumulated earnings and profits. Any distributions in excess of earnings and profits are treated as a nontaxable return of stock basis, with any distributions in excess of a shareholder's stock basis treated as capital gain. Therefore, $750,000 of the distribution to Ridge's shareholders was taxable as a dividend, with the remaining $250,000 treated as a nontaxable return of stock basis.

88.   (d)   The requirement is to determine the amount of loss recognized by Tour Corporation on the nonliquidating distribution of property to shareholders. Although a gain would be recognized, no loss can be recognized on nonliquidating corporate distributions to shareholders.

89.   (c)   The requirement is to determine the amount taxable as a dividend to Kee's shareholders for 2003. Corporate distributions of property to shareholders on their stock are taxed as dividends to the extent of accumulated and/or current earnings and profits. Even though a corporation has an accumulated deficit in earnings and profits for prior years ($50,000 in this case), a distribution will nevertheless be taxed as a dividend to the extent of the corporation's earnings and profits for the current taxable year when measured at the end of the year. Thus, the $30,000 distribution will be taxed as a dividend to the extent of the current earnings and profits for 2003 of $10,000.

90.   (c)   The requirement is to determine the amount of taxable dividend income resulting from Dahl Corp.'s distribution of cash and land to Green. The amount of distribution received by Green equals the amount of cash ($9,000) plus the FMV of the land ($40,000), a total of $49,000. This $49,000 will be taxable as dividend income to Green to the extent that it is paid out of Dahl Corp.'s current and accumulated earnings and profits. Dahl had accumulated earnings and profits of $9,000 before consideration of the dividend declaration and distribution. Since a distributing corporation recognizes gain on the distribution of appreciated property, Dahl must recognize a gain of $40,000 – $5,000 = $35,000 on the distribution of the land. This $35,000 of gain increases Dahl Corp.'s available earnings and profits from $9,000 to $44,000. Thus, Green's $49,000 distribution will be taxed as a dividend to the extent of $44,000.

91.   (b)   The requirement is to determine the amount of the taxable dividend for an individual shareholder on a property distribution. A distributee shareholder is considered to have received a dividend equal to the fair market value of the property distributed less any liabilities assumed. In this case, Rowe received a taxable dividend of $7,000 ($12,000 – $5,000).

92.   (d)   The requirement is to determine the amount of dividend income taxable to the shareholder. If a corporation sells property to a shareholder for less than fair market value, the shareholder is considered to have received a constructive dividend to the extent of the difference between the fair market value of the property and the price paid. Thus, the shareholder's dividend income is $80,000 – $50,000 = $30,000.

93.   (a)   Distributions of property to shareholders reduce earnings and profits (E&P) by the greater of the property's adjusted basis, or its FMV at date of distribution. E&P must be adjusted by any gain recognized to the distributing corporation, and any liabilities to which the property being dis-

tributed is subject. Gelt Corporation would recognize a gain of $7,500 on the distribution (i.e., $14,000 FMV – $6,500 basis). The adjustments to E&P (before tax) would be

	E&P
Gain recognized	$ 7,500
Distribution of property (FMV)	(14,000)
Distribution of liability	5,000
Net decrease in E&P (before tax)	$ (1,500)

E.3.   Stock Redemptions

94.   (c)   The requirement is to determine the tax effect of Mark's stock redemption. Since the redemption is a complete redemption of all of Mark's stock ownership, the redemption proceeds of $500,000 qualify for exchange treatment. Thus, Mark will report a capital gain of $500,000 – $300,000 = $200,000.

95.   (a)   The requirement is to determine how the gain resulting from a stock redemption should be treated by a noncorporate shareholder if the redemption qualifies as a partial liquidation of the distributing corporation. A corporate stock redemption is treated as an exchange, generally resulting in capital gain or loss treatment to a shareholder if the redemption meets any one of five tests. Redemptions qualifying for exchange treatment include (1) a redemption that is not essentially equivalent to a dividend, (2) a redemption that is substantially disproportionate, (3) a redemption that completely terminates a shareholder's interest, (4) a redemption of a noncorporate shareholder in a partial liquidation, and (5) a redemption to pay death taxes. If none of the above five tests are met, the redemption proceeds are generally treated as a dividend.

96.   (b)   The requirement is to determine the amount of interest and legal and accounting fees that were incurred in connection with Kara Corp.'s stock repurchase that is deductible for 2003. No deduction is allowed for any amount paid or incurred by a corporation in connection with the redemption of its stock, except for interest expense on loans to repurchase stock. Thus, the $100,000 of interest expense on loans used to repurchase stock is deductible, while the $400,000 of legal and accounting fees incurred in connection with the repurchase of stock is not deductible.

E.4.   Complete Liquidations

97.   (a)   The requirement is to determine the correct statement regarding the expenses incurred in completely liquidating and dissolving a corporation. The general expenses incurred in the complete liquidation and dissolution of a corporation are deductible by the corporation as ordinary and necessary business expenses. These expenses include filing fees, professional fees, and other expenditures incurred in connection with the liquidation and dissolution.

98.   (d)   The requirement is to determine the usual result to the shareholders of a distribution in complete liquidation of a corporation. Amounts received by shareholders in complete liquidation of a corporation are treated as received in exchange for stock, generally resulting in capital gain or loss because the stock was held as an investment. Because liquidating distributions are generally treated as received in a taxable exchange, any property received by shareholders will have a basis equal to fair market value.

99. (d) The requirement is to determine whether the unused carryovers for excess charitable contributions and net operating loss of a wholly owned subsidiary carryover to a parent corporation as a result of a tax-free complete liquidation of the subsidiary. When a parent corporation completely liquidates its 80% or more owned subsidiary under Sec. 332, the liquidation is treated as a mere change in form and the parent corporation will not recognize any gain or loss on the receipt of liquidating distributions from its subsidiary. Similarly, the subsidiary corporation will not recognize any gain or loss on distributions to its parent corporation. As a result, there will be a carryover basis for all of the subsidiary's assets that are received by the parent corporation, as well as a carryover of all of the subsidiary's tax attributes to the parent corporation. The subsidiary's tax attributes that carryover to the parent include such items as earnings and profits, capital loss carryovers, accounting methods, and tax credit carryovers, as well as unused excess charitable contributions, and net operating losses.

100. (b) The requirement is to determine the amount of Kappes Corp.'s recognized loss resulting from the distribution of marketable securities in complete liquidation. Generally, a corporation will recognize gain or loss on the distribution of its property in complete liquidation just as if the property were sold to the distributee for its fair market value. Since the marketable securities were a capital asset and held for more than one year, the distribution results in a long-term capital loss of $150,000 – $100,000 = $50,000.

101. (d) When a parent corporation liquidates its 80% or more owned subsidiary, the parent corporation (as stockholder) will ordinarily not recognize any gain or loss on the receipt of liquidating distributions from its subsidiary.

102. (a) The requirement is to determine the recognized gain to Lark Corp. on the complete liquidation of its wholly owned subsidiary, Day Corp. No gain or loss will be recognized by a parent corporation (Lark Corp.) on the receipt of property in complete liquidation of an 80% or more owned subsidiary (Day Corp.).

103. (c) The requirement is to determine the amount of gain to be recognized by Green Corp. as a result of the distribution of installment notes in the process of liquidation. A corporation generally recognizes gain on the distribution of appreciated property in the process of liquidation. Thus, Green Corp. must recognize gain on the distribution of the notes to the extent that the FMV of the notes ($162,000) exceeds the basis of the notes ($90,000), or $72,000.

104. (d) The requirement is to determine Carmela's recognized gain from the sale of assets during a complete liquidation. Gain or loss is generally recognized by a corporation on the sale of property following the adoption of a plan of complete liquidation even if the corporation then distributes all of its assets within twelve months after the plan of liquidation is adopted. Carmela would recognize gain on the land of $75,000 ($150,000 – $75,000) and on the inventory of $22,500 ($66,000 – $43,500).

105. (d) The requirement is to determine the amount of gain that each Mintee Corp. shareholder should recognize as a result of a liquidating distribution from Mintee. Amounts received by noncorporate shareholders in complete liquidation of a corporation are treated as received in exchange for stock, generally resulting in capital gain or loss because the stock was held as an investment. Here the amount realized by each shareholder consists of $2,000 cash plus the $10,500 FMV of the land, for a total of $12,500. Since each shareholder's stock basis was $6,500, each shareholder has a gain of $12,500 – $6,500 = $6,000.

G. Personal Holding Company and Accumulated Earnings Taxes

106. (b) The requirement is to determine what sources of income that Edge Corp. must consider to determine whether the income requirements for a personal holding company have been met. A corporation is a personal holding company if (1) five or fewer individuals own more than 50% of its stock at any time during the last half of its taxable year, and (2) at least 60% of its adjusted gross income is personal holding company income (e.g., dividends, interest, rent). The computation of the personal holding company income requirement includes only items that are included in gross income. Since interest on tax-exempt obligations would be excluded from gross income, tax-exempt interest would not be considered in determining whether the income requirement is met.

107. (a) The requirement is to determine which deduction(s) can be subtracted from taxable income in arriving at a corporation's undistributed personal holding company income (UPHCI). A series of adjustments must be made to a corporation's taxable income in order to arrive at UPHCI. These adjustments include the deduction of federal income taxes (including AMT and foreign income taxes), and the deduction for a net capital gain (i.e., the excess of NLTCG over NSTCL) less the amount of federal income taxes attributable to the net capital gain. This deduction prevents a personal holding company from paying the PHC tax on its net long-term capital gains.

108. (c) The requirement is to determine which step(s) Dart Corp. can take to eliminate or reduce any 2003 accumulated earnings tax (AET). The AET is a penalty tax that can be imposed (in addition to regular income tax) on a corporation if it accumulates earnings in excess of reasonable business needs. To avoid the AET, Dart can demonstrate that the reasonable needs of its business require the retention of all or part of the 2003 accumulated taxable income. Additionally, Dart can reduce its accumulated taxable income by paying a dividend to its shareholders. For this purpose, any dividends paid within the first 2 1/2 months of the tax year are treated as if paid on the last day of the preceding tax year. Thus, Dart's payment of dividends by March 15, 2004, would reduce its exposure to the AET for 2003.

109. (d) The requirement is to determine the correct statement regarding the accumulated earnings tax (AET). The AET is a penalty tax that can be imposed on a corporation if it accumulates earnings in excess of reasonable business needs, regardless of the number of shareholders that the corporation has. Answer (a) is incorrect because the AET cannot be imposed on partnerships. Answer (b) is incorrect because a corporation that distributes all of its accumulated earnings would not be subject to the AET. Answer (c) is incorrect because the AET cannot be imposed on personal holding companies.

110. (a)   The requirement is to determine whose ownership of the remaining 200 shares of common stock could make Zero Corp. (with 1,000 outstanding shares) a personal holding company. A corporation is a personal holding company if (1) at least 60% of its adjusted ordinary gross income is derived from investment sources (e.g., interest, dividends, royalties), and (2) five or fewer individuals own more than 50% of the value of its stock at any time during the last half of its taxable year. In determining whether the more than 50% stock ownership requirement is met, the constructive ownership rules of Sec. 544 apply. Under these rules, an individual is considered as owning the stock owned by his family including only brothers and sisters, spouse, ancestors, and lineal descendants. Additionally, stock owned by a corporation, partnership, estate, or trust is considered as being owned proportionately by its shareholders, partners, or beneficiaries. Here, Edwards directly owns 240 shares and if he were the beneficiary of an estate that owned 200 shares, Edwards would directly and constructively own 440 shares. Then with four other unrelated shareholders, each owning twenty shares, there would be five shareholders who directly or constructively own 520 shares, more than 50% of the corporation's outstanding stock.

111. (b)   The requirement is to determine the status of Arbor Corp. A corporation is a personal holding company (PHC) if (1) five or fewer individuals own more than 50% of its stock during the last half of its taxable year, and (2) at least 60% of its adjusted gross income is derived from investment sources (e.g., dividends, interest, rents). Although the amount of dividends paid to its shareholders may affect the computation of the PHC tax, the amount of dividends paid has no effect on the determination of PHC status. Answer (a) is incorrect because a regulated investment company is a status obtained by registering under the Investment Company Act of 1940, and is not determined by the facts and circumstances present for any given year. Answer (c) is incorrect because the accumulated earnings tax does not apply to personal holding companies. Answer (d) is incorrect because all of Arbor's taxable income is subject to regular federal income tax.

112. (c)   The requirement is to determine the maximum amount of accumulated taxable income that may be subject to the accumulated earnings tax for 2003 if Kari Corp. takes only the minimum accumulated earnings credit. Since Kari is a manufacturing company that was first organized in 2003, it is entitled to a minimum accumulated earnings credit of $250,000. To determine its potential exposure to the accumulated earnings tax, its 2003 taxable income of $400,000 must be reduced by its federal income taxes of $100,000 and its minimum accumulated earnings credit of $250,000, to arrive at its maximum exposure of $50,000.

113. (d)   The requirement is to determine the amount that Hull, Inc. can deduct for dividends paid in the computation of its personal holding company (PHC) tax. The PHC tax is a penalty tax imposed at a 15% tax rate on a corporation's undistributed personal holding company income. A PHC is allowed a dividends paid deduction that is subtracted from its adjusted taxable income in arriving at its undistributed personal holding company income. Hull's dividends paid deduction consists of the $20,000 of dividends actually paid to its shareholders during 2003, plus the $10,000 of consent dividends reported in its shareholders' individual income tax returns for 2003.

Consent dividends are hypothetical dividends that are treated as if they were paid on the last day of the corporation's tax year. Since consent dividends are taxable to shareholders but not actually distributed, shareholders increase their stock basis by the amount of consent dividends included in their gross income. The consent dividend procedure has the same result as an actual dividend distribution, followed by the shareholders making a capital contribution of the dividend back to the corporation.

114. (b)   The requirement is to determine the taxpayer to whom the personal holding company (PHC) income will be attributed. A corporation will be classified as a personal holding company if (1) it is more than 50% owned by five or fewer individuals, and (2) at least 60% of the corporation's adjusted ordinary gross income is PHC income. PHC income is generally passive income and includes dividends, interest, adjusted rents, adjusted royalties, compensation for the use of corporate property by a 25% or more shareholder, and certain personal service contracts involving a 25% or more shareholder. An amount received from a personal service contract is classified as PHC income if (1) some person other than the corporation has the right to designate, by name or by description, the individual who is to perform the services, and (2) the person so designated is (directly or constructively) a 25% or more shareholder. Here, since Benson owns 100% of Lund Corp. and Lund Corp. contracted with Magda specifying that Benson is to perform personal services for Magda, the income from the personal service contract will be personal holding company income to Lund Corp.

115. (c)   The requirement is to determine the correct statement regarding the personal holding company (PHC) tax. The PHC tax should be self-assessed by filing a separate schedule 1120-PH along with the regular tax return Form 1120. Answer (a) is incorrect because the PHC tax is a penalty tax imposed in addition to regular federal income taxes. Answer (b) is incorrect because the PHC tax can only be imposed on corporations. Answer (d) is incorrect because the PHC tax can only be imposed if five or fewer individuals own more than 50% of the value of a corporation's stock. Thus, if a corporation's stock is owned by ten or more equal unrelated shareholders, the corporation cannot be a PHC.

116. (b)   The requirement is to determine the correct statement regarding the accumulated earnings tax (AET). The AET does not apply to corporations that are personal holding companies. Answer (a) is incorrect because the AET can apply regardless of the number of shareholders that a corporation has. Answers (c) and (d) are incorrect because the AET applies to corporations that accumulate earnings in excess of their reasonable business needs and is not dependent upon whether a corporation files a consolidated return or the number of classes of stock that a corporation has.

117. (c)   The requirement is to determine the correct statement concerning the personal holding company (PHC) tax. The personal holding company tax may be imposed if at least 60% of the corporation's adjusted ordinary gross income for the taxable year is personal holding company income, and the stock ownership test is satisfied. Answer (b) is incorrect because the stock ownership test is met if more than 50% of the corporation's stock is owned, directly or indirectly, by **five or fewer** stockholders. Answer (a) is incorrect because the PHC tax is a penalty tax imposed in addition to the regular corporate income tax. Answer (d) is incorrect because the PHC tax takes precedent over the accumulated earnings tax. The accumulated earnings tax does not apply to a personal holding company.

118. (d) The requirement is to determine the correct statement concerning the accumulated earnings tax (AET). Answer (d), "The accumulated earnings tax can **not** be imposed on a corporation that has undistributed earnings and profits of less than $150,000," is correct because every corporation (even a personal service corporation) is eligible for an accumulated earnings credit of at least $150,000. Answer (a) is incorrect because the AET is not self-assessing, but instead is assessed by the IRS after finding a tax avoidance intent on the part of the taxpayer. Answer (b) is incorrect because the AET may be imposed regardless of the number of shareholders that a corporation has. Answer (c) is incorrect because the AET cannot be imposed on a corporation for any year in which an S corporation election is in effect because an S corporation's earnings pass through and are taxed to shareholders regardless of whether the earnings are actually distributed.

119. (d) The requirement is to determine the amount on which Kee Holding Corp.'s liability for personal holding company (PHC) tax will be based. To be classified as a personal holding company, a corporation must meet both a "stock ownership test" and an "income test." The "stock ownership test" requires that more than 50% of the stock must be owned (directly or indirectly) by five or fewer individuals. Since Kee has eighty unrelated equal shareholders, the stock ownership test is not met. Thus, Kee is not a personal holding company and has no liability for the PHC tax.

120. (b) The accumulated earnings tax (AET) can be avoided by sufficient dividend distributions. The imposition of the AET does not depend on a stock ownership test, nor is it self-assessing requiring the filing of a separate schedule attached to the regular tax return. The AET cannot be imposed on personal holding companies.

121. (c) The personal holding company (PHC) tax may be imposed if more than 50% of a corporation's stock is owned by five or fewer individuals. The PHC tax cannot be imposed on partnerships. Additionally, small business investment companies licensed by the Small Business Administration are excluded from the tax. If a corporation's gross income arises solely from rents, the rents will not be PHC income (even though no services are rendered to lessees) and thus, the PHC tax cannot be imposed.

122. (d) A net capital loss for the current year is allowed as a deduction in determining accumulated taxable income for purposes of the accumulated earnings tax. A capital loss carryover from a prior year, a dividends received deduction, and a net operating loss deduction would all be added back to taxable income in arriving at accumulated taxable income.

123. (d) The minimum accumulated earnings credit is $250,000 for nonservice corporations; $150,000 for service corporations.

124. (a) The requirement is to determine Daystar's allowable accumulated earnings credit for 2003. The credit is the greater of (1) the earnings and profits of the tax year retained for reasonable business needs of $20,000; or (2) $150,000 less the accumulated earnings and profits at the end of the preceding year of $45,000. Thus, the credit is $150,000 – $45,000 = $105,000.

H.   S Corporations

125. (c) The requirement is to determine Stahl's basis for his S corporation stock at the end of the year. A shareholder's basis for S corporation stock is increased by the pass-through of all income items (including tax-exempt income) and is decreased by distributions that are excluded from the shareholder's gross income, as well as the pass-through of all loss and deduction items (including nondeductible items). Here, Stahl's beginning stock basis of $65,000 is increased by the $6,000 of municipal interest income and $4,000 of long-term capital gain, and is decreased by the ordinary loss of $10,000 and short-term capital loss of $9,000, resulting in a stock basis of $56,000 at the end of the year.

126. (b) The requirement is to determine the amount of the $30,000 distribution from an S corporation that is taxable to Baker. If an S corporation has no accumulated earnings and profits from C years, distributions to shareholders are generally nontaxable and reduce a shareholder's stock basis. To the extent that distributions exceed stock basis, they result in capital gain. A shareholder's basis for S corporation stock is first increased by the pass through of income, then reduced by distributions that are excluded from gross income, and finally reduced by the pass through of losses and deductions. Here, Baker's beginning stock basis of $25,000 would first be increased by the pass through of the $1,000 of ordinary income, to $26,000. Then the $30,000 cash distribution would be a nontaxable return of stock basis to the extent of $26,000, with the remaining $4,000 in excess of stock basis taxable to Baker as capital gain. Baker will not be able to deduct the long-term capital loss of $3,000 this year because the cash distribution reduced his stock basis to zero. Instead, the $3,000 loss will be carried forward and will be available as a deduction when Baker has sufficient basis to absorb the loss.

127. (d) The requirement is to determine the amount of the $7,200 of health insurance premiums paid by Lane, Inc. (an S corporation) to be included in gross income by Mill. Compensation paid by an S corporation includes fringe benefit expenditures made on behalf of officers and employees owning more than 2% of the S corporation' stock. Since Mill is a 10% shareholder-employee, Mill's compensation income reported on his W-2 from Lane must include the $7,200 of health insurance premiums paid by Lane for health insurance covering Mill, his spouse, and dependents. Note that Mill may qualify to deduct 100% of the $7,200 for AGI as a self-employed health insurance deduction.

128. (b) The requirement is to determine Lazur's tax basis for the Beck Corp. stock after the distribution. A shareholder's basis for stock of an S corporation is increased by the pass-through of all income items (including tax-exempt income) and is decreased by distributions that are excluded from the shareholder's gross income. Here, Lazur's beginning basis of $12,000 is increased by his 50% share of Beck's ordinary business income ($40,500) and tax-exempt income ($5,000) and is decreased by the $51,000 cash distribution excluded from his gross income, resulting in a stock basis of $6,500.

129. (d)   The requirement is to determine the amount of income from Graphite Corp. (an S corporation) that should be included in Smith's 2003 adjusted gross income. An S corporation is a pass-through entity and its items of income and deduction flow through to be reported on shareholders' returns. Since Smith is a 50% shareholder, half of the ordinary business income ($80,000 x 50% = $40,000) and half of the tax-exempt interest ($6,000 x 50% = $3,000) would pass through to Smith. Since the income passed through to Smith would retain its character, Smith must include the $40,000 of ordinary income in gross income, while the $3,000 of tax-exempt interest retains its exempt characteristic and would be excluded from Smith's gross income. Smith's $12,000 of stock basis at the beginning of the year would be increased by the pass-through of the $40,000 of ordinary income as well as the $3,000 of tax-exempt income, to $55,000. As a result, the $53,000 cash distribution received by Smith would be treated as a nontaxable return of stock basis and would reduce the basis of Smith's stock to $2,000.

130. (a)   The requirement is to determine the effect of the revocation statement on Dart Corp.'s S corporation election. A revocation of an S election will be effective if it is signed by shareholders owning more than 50% of the S corporation's outstanding stock. For this purpose, both voting and nonvoting shares are counted. Here Dart Corp. has a total of 100,000 shares outstanding. As a result, the revocation statement consented to by shareholders holding a total of 40,000 shares, would not be effective and would not terminate Dart Corp.'s S corporation election.

131. (d)   The requirement is to determine the incorrect statement regarding S corporation eligibility requirements. The eligibility requirements restrict S corporation shareholders to individuals (other than nonresident aliens), estates, and certain trusts. Partnerships and C corporations are not permitted to own stock in an S corporation. However, an S corporation is permitted to be a partner in a partnership, and may own any percentage of stock of a C corporation, as well as own 100% of the stock of a qualified subchapter S subsidiary.

132. (b)   The requirement is to determine the portion of the $310,000 distribution that must be reported as dividend income by Robert. Distributions from an S corporation are generally treated as first coming from its accumulated adjustment account (AAA), and then are treated as coming from its accumulated earnings and profits (AEP). A positive balance in an S corporation's AAA is generally nontaxable when distributed because it represents amounts that have already been taxed to shareholders during S years. In contrast, an S corporation's AEP represents earnings accumulated during C years that have never been taxed to shareholders, and must be reported as dividend income when received. In this case, the beginning balance in the AAA and shareholder stock basis must first be increased by the pass through of the $200,000 of ordinary income that is taxed to Robert for 2003. This permits the first $250,000 of the distribution to be nontaxable and will reduce the balance in the AAA to zero and Robert's stock basis to $50,000. The remaining $60,000 of distribution is a distribution of the corporation's AEP and must be reported as dividend income by Robert.

133. (b)   The requirement is to determine the date on which Village Corp.'s S status became effective. A subchapter S election that is filed on or before the 15th day of the third month of a corporation's taxable year is generally effective as of the beginning of the taxable year in which filed. If the S election is filed after the 15th day of the third month, the election is generally effective as of the first day of the corporation's next taxable year. Here, Village Corp. uses a calendar year and its S election was filed on September 5, 2003, which is beyond the 15th day of the third month of the taxable year (March 15). As a result, Village's subchapter S status becomes effective as of the first day of its next taxable year, January 1, 2004.

134. (d)   The requirement is to determine whether a shareholder's basis in the stock of an S corporation is increased by the shareholder's pro rata share of tax-exempt interest and taxable interest. An S corporation is a pass through entity and its items of income and deduction pass through to be reported on shareholder returns. As a result, a shareholder's S corporation stock basis is increased by the pass through of all items of income, including both taxable as well as tax-exempt interest. An S shareholder's stock basis must be increased by tax-exempt interest in order to permit a later distribution of that interest to be nontaxable.

135. (c)   The requirement is to determine the amount of income that should be allocated to Zinco Corp.'s short S year when its S election is terminated on April 1, 2003. When a corporation's subchapter S election is terminated during a taxable year, its income for the entire year must be allocated between the resulting S short year and C short year. If no special election is made, the income must be allocated on a daily basis between the S and C short years. In this case, the daily income equals $310,250/365 days = $850 per day. Since the election was terminated on April 1, there would be ninety days in the S short year, and $850 x 90 = $76,500 of income would be allocated to the tax return for the S short year to be passed through and taxed to shareholders.

136. (d)   The requirement is to determine the correct statement regarding the termination of an S election. Answer (d) is correct because an S election will be terminated if an S corporation has passive investment income in excess of 25% of gross receipts for three consecutive taxable years, if the corporation also has subchapter C accumulated earnings and profits at the end of each of those three years. Answer (a) is incorrect because an S corporation is permitted to have a maximum of seventy-five shareholders. Answer (b) is incorrect because a decedent's estate may be a shareholder of an S corporation. Answer (c) is incorrect because S corporations are allowed to make charitable contributions. Contributions separately pass through to shareholders and can be deducted as charitable contributions on shareholder returns.

137. (b)   The requirement is to determine the amount of income from Manning (an S corporation) that should be reported on Kane's 2003 tax return. An S corporation's tax items are allocated to shareholders on a per share, per day basis. Since Manning had income of $73,000 for its entire year, its per day income is $73,000/365 = $200. Since there are 100 shares outstanding, Manning's daily income per share is $200/100 = $2. Since Kane sold twenty-five of his shares on the 40th day of 2003 and held his remaining seventy-five shares throughout the year, the amount of income to be reported on Kane's 2003 return would be determined as follows:

75 shares	x	$2	x	365 days	=	$54,750
25 shares	x	$2	x	40 days	=	2,000
						$56,750

138. (d) The requirement is to determine the earliest date on which Ace Corp. (a calendar-year corporation) can be recognized as an S corporation. Generally, an S election will be effective as of the first day of a taxable year if the election is made on or before the 15th day of the third month of the taxable year. Since there was no change in shareholders during the year, all of Ace's shareholders consented to the election, and Ace met all eligibility requirements during the preelection portion of the year, its election filed on February 10, 2003, is effective as of January 1, 2003. Note that if either a shareholder who held stock during the taxable year and before the date of election did not consent to the election, or the corporation did not meet the eligibility requirements before the date of election, then an otherwise valid election would be treated as made for the following taxable year.

139. (c) The requirement is to determine the number of shares of voting and nonvoting stock that must be owned by shareholders making a revocation of an S election. A revocation of an S election may be filed by shareholders owning more than 50% of an S corporation's outstanding stock. For this purpose, both voting and nonvoting shares are counted. In this case, since the S corporation has a total of 50,000 voting and nonvoting shares outstanding, the shareholders consenting to the revocation must own more than 25,000 shares.

140. (b) The requirement is to determine the amount of increase for each shareholder's basis in the stock of Haas Corp., a calendar-year S corporation, for the year ended December 31, 2003. An S corporation shareholder's basis for stock is increased by the pass through of all S corporation income items (including tax-exempt income), and is decreased by all loss and deduction items, as well as nondeductible expenses not charged to capital. Since Haas has two equal shareholders, each shareholder's stock basis will be increased by 50% of the operating income of $50,000, and 50% of the interest income of $10,000, resulting in an increase for each shareholder of $30,000.

141. (d) The requirement is to determine the condition that will prevent a corporation from qualifying as an S corporation. Certain eligibility requirements must be satisfied before a corporation can make a subchapter S election. Generally, in order to be an S corporation, a corporation must have only one class of stock outstanding and have no more than seventy-five shareholders, who are either individuals, estates, or certain trusts. An S corporation may own any percentage of the stock of a C corporation, and 100% of the stock of a qualified subchapter S subsidiary.

142. (c) The requirement is to determine the correct statement regarding distributions to shareholders by an S corporation that has no accumulated earnings and profits. S corporations do not generate any earnings and profits, but may have accumulated earnings and profits from prior years

as a C corporation. If accumulated earnings and profits are distributed to shareholders, the distributions will be taxed as dividend income to the shareholders. However, if an S corporation has no accumulated earnings and profits, distributions are generally nontaxable and reduce a shareholder's basis for stock. To the extent distributions exceed stock basis, they result in capital gain.

143. (d) The requirement is to determine whether a corporation that has been an S corporation from its inception may have both passive and nonpassive income, and be owned by a bankruptcy estate. To qualify as an S corporation, a corporation must have seventy-five or fewer shareholders who are individuals (other than nonresident aliens), certain trusts, or estates (including bankruptcy estates). If a corporation has been an S corporation since its inception, there is no limitation on the amount or type of income that it generates, and it can have both passive and nonpassive income.

144. (b) The requirement is to determine Meyer's share of an S corporation's $36,500 ordinary loss. An S corporation's items of income and deduction are allocated on a daily basis to anyone who was a shareholder during the taxable year. Here, the $36,500 ordinary loss would be divided by 365 days to arrive at a loss of $100 per day. Since Meyer held 50% of the S corporation's stock for forty days, Meyer's share of the loss would be ($100 x 50%) x 40 days = $2,000.

145. (c) The requirement is to determine the period that a calendar-year corporation must wait before making a new S election following the termination of its S status during 2003. Generally, following the revocation or termination of an S election, a corporation must wait five years before reelecting subchapter S status unless the IRS consents to an earlier election.

146. (d) The requirement is to determine which will render a corporation ineligible for S corporation status. Answer (d) is correct because an S corporation is limited to seventy-five shareholders. Answers (a) and (b) are incorrect because a decedent's estate and a bankruptcy estate are allowed as S corporation shareholders. Although an S corporation may only have one class of stock issued and outstanding, answer (c) is incorrect because a difference in voting rights among outstanding common shares is not treated as having more than one class of stock outstanding.

147. (d) The requirement is to determine the correct statement with regard to the application of the "at-risk" rules to S corporations and their shareholders. The at-risk rules limit a taxpayer's deduction of losses to the amount that the taxpayer can actually lose (i.e., generally the amount of cash and the adjusted basis of property invested by the taxpayer, plus any liabilities for which the taxpayer is personally liable). The at-risk rules apply to S corporation shareholders rather than at the corporate level, with the result that the deduction of S corporation losses is limited to the amount of a shareholder's at-risk investment. The application of the at-risk rules does not depend on the type of income reported by the S corporation, are not subject to any elections made by S corporation shareholders, and are applied without regard to the S corporation's ratio of debt to equity.

148. **(d)**   The requirement is to determine the item that may be deducted by an S corporation. Items having no special tax characteristics can be netted together in the computation of the S corporation's ordinary income or loss, with only the net amount passed through to shareholders. Thus, only ordinary items (e.g., amortization of organizational expenditures) can be deducted by an S corporation. Answer (a) is incorrect because foreign income taxes must be separately passed through to shareholders so that the shareholders can individually elect to treat the payment of foreign income taxes as a deduction or as a credit. Answer (b) is incorrect because a net Sec. 1231 loss must be separately passed through to shareholders so that the Sec. 1231 netting process can take place at the shareholder level. Answer (c) is incorrect because investment interest expense must be separately passed through to shareholders so the deduction limitation (i.e., limited to net investment income) can be applied at the shareholder level.

149. **(d)**   The requirement is to determine the correct statement regarding an S corporation's Accumulated Adjustments Account (AAA). An S corporation that has accumulated earnings and profits must maintain an AAA. The AAA represents the cumulative balance of all items of the undistributed net income and deductions for S corporation years beginning after 1982. The AAA is generally increased by all income items and is decreased by distributions and all loss and deduction items except no adjustment is made for tax-exempt income and related expenses, and no adjustment is made for federal income taxes attributable to a taxable year in which the corporation was a C corporation. The payment of federal income taxes attributable to a C corporation year would decrease an S corporation's accumulated earnings and profits (AEP). Note that the amounts represented in the AAA differ from AEP. A positive AEP balance represents earnings and profits accumulated in C corporation years that have never been taxed to shareholders. A positive AAA balance represents income from S corporation years that has already been taxed to shareholders but not yet distributed. An S corporation will not generate any earnings and profits for taxable years beginning after 1982.

150. **(b)**   The requirement is to determine the due date of a calendar-year S corporation's tax return. An S corporation must file its federal income tax return (Form 1120-S) by the 15th day of the third month following the close of its taxable year. Thus, a calendar-year S corporation must file its tax return by March 15, if an automatic six-month extension of time is not requested.

151. **(c)**   The requirement is to determine the item for which an S corporation is not permitted a deduction. Compensation of officers, interest paid to nonshareholders, and employee benefits for nonshareholders are deductible by an S corporation in computing its ordinary income or loss. However, charitable contributions, since they are subject to percentage limitations at the shareholder level, must be separately stated and are not deductible in computing an S corporation's ordinary income or loss.

152. **(d)**   An S corporation may have as many as seventy-five shareholders. However, an S corporation cannot have both common and preferred stock outstanding because an S corporation is limited to a single class of stock. Similarly, a partnership is not permitted to be a shareholder in an S corporation because all S corporation shareholders must be

individuals, estates, or certain trusts. Additionally, an S corporation cannot have a nonresident alien as a shareholder.

153. **(a)**   The requirement is to determine which is **not** a requirement for a corporation to elect S corporation status. An S corporation must generally have only one class of stock, be a domestic corporation, and confine shareholders to individuals, estates, and certain trusts. An S corporation need **not** be a member of a controlled group.

154. **(b)**   The requirement is to determine the amount of loss from an S corporation that can be deducted by each of two equal shareholders. An S corporation loss is passed through to shareholders and is deductible to the extent of a shareholder's basis for stock plus the basis for any debt owed the shareholder by the corporation. Here, each shareholder's allocated loss of $45,000 ($90,000 ÷ 2) is deductible to the extent of stock basis of $5,000 plus debt basis of $15,000, or $20,000. The remainder of the loss ($25,000 for each shareholder) can be carried forward indefinitely by each shareholder and deducted when there is basis to absorb it.

I. Corporate Reorganizations

155. **(b)**   The requirement is to determine the correct statement regarding King Corp.'s acquisition of 90% of Jaxson Corp.'s voting common stock solely in exchange for 50% of King Corp.'s voting common stock. The acquisition by one corporation, in exchange **solely** for part of its voting stock, of stock of another corporation qualifies as a tax-free type B reorganization if immediately after the acquisition, the acquiring corporation is in control of the acquired corporation. The term **control** means the ownership of at least 80% of the acquired corporation's stock. Since King Corp. will use solely its voting stock to acquire 90% of Jaxson Corp. the acquisition will qualify as a tax-free type B reorganization. Answer (c) is incorrect because there is no requirement concerning the minimum percentage of King Corp. stock that must be used. Answer (d) is incorrect because a type B reorganization involves the acquisition of stock, not assets.

156. **(a)**   The requirement is to determine whether a qualifying reorganization is tax-free to the corporations and their shareholders. Corporate reorganizations are generally nontaxable. As a result, a corporation will not recognize gain or loss on the transfer of its assets, and shareholders do not recognize gain or loss when they exchange stock and securities in parties to the reorganization. Here, Ace and Bate combine and form Carr, the only surviving corporation. This qualifies as a consolidation (Type A reorganization) and is tax-free to Ace and Bate on the transfer of their assets to Carr, and also is tax-free to the shareholders when they exchange their Ace and Bate stock for Carr stock. Similarly, the reorganization is tax-free to Carr when it issues its shares to acquire the Ace and Bate assets.

157. **(c)**   The requirement is to determine whether the statements are applicable to type B reorganizations. In a type B reorganization, the acquiring corporation must use solely voting stock to acquire control of the target corporation immediately after the acquisition. The stock that is used to make the acquisition can be solely voting stock of the acquiring corporation, or solely voting stock of the parent corporation that is in control of the acquiring corporation, but not both. If a subsidiary uses its parent's stock to make the acquisition, the target corporation becomes a second-tier subsidiary of the parent corporation.

158. (d) The requirement is to determine Gow's recognized gain resulting from the exchange of Lad Corp. stock for Rook Corp. stock pursuant to a plan of corporate reorganization. No gain or loss is recognized to a shareholder if stock in one party to a reorganization (Lad Corp.) is exchanged **solely** for stock in another corporation (Rook Corp.) that is a party to the reorganization.

159. (a) The requirement is to determine the item that is defined in the Internal Revenue Code as a corporate reorganization. Corporate reorganizations generally receive nonrecognition treatment. Sec. 368 of the Internal Revenue Code defines seven types of reorganization, one of which is listed. An "F" reorganization is a mere change in identity, form, or place of organization of one corporation. A stock redemption is not a reorganization but instead results in dividend treatment or qualifies for exchange treatment. A change of depreciation method or inventory method is a change of an accounting method.

160. (c) The requirement is to determine the correct statement concerning corporate reorganizations. Answer (b) is incorrect because the reorganization provisions do provide for tax-free treatment for certain corporate transactions. Specifically, shareholders will not recognize gain or loss when they exchange stock or securities in a corporation that is a party to a reorganization solely for stock or securities in such corporation, or in another corporation that is also a party to the reorganization. Thus, securities in corporations not parties to the reorganization are always treated as "boot." Answer (d) is incorrect because the term "a party to the reorganization" includes a corporation resulting from the reorganization (i.e., the consolidated company). Answer (a) is incorrect because a mere change in identity, form, or place of organization of one corporation qualifies as a Type F reorganization.

161. (a) The requirement is to determine which is not a corporate reorganization. A corporate reorganization is specifically defined in Sec. 368 of the Internal Revenue Code. Sec. 368 defines seven types of reorganization, of which 3 are present in this item: Type A, a statutory merger; Type E, a recapitalization; and, Type F, a mere change in identity, form, or place of organization. Answer (a), a stock redemption, is the correct answer because it is not a reorganization as defined by Sec. 368 of the Code.

162. (a) The requirement is to determine the amount of Claudio's net operating loss (NOL) carryover that can be used to offset Stellar's 2003 taxable income. The amount of Claudio's NOL ($270,000) that can be utilized by Stellar for 2003 is limited by Sec. 381 to the taxable income of Stellar for its full taxable year (before a NOL deduction) multiplied by the fraction

$$\frac{\text{Days after acquisition date}}{\text{Total days in the taxable year}}$$

This limitation is 185/365 days x $360,000 = $182,466. Additionally, since there was a more than fifty percentage point change in the ownership of Claudio, Sec. 382 limits the amount of Claudio's NOL carryover that can be utilized by Stellar to the fair market value of Claudio multiplied by

the federal long-term tax-exempt rate. $1,500,000 x 5% = $75,000. However, for purposes of applying this limitation for the year of acquisition, the limitation amount is only available to the extent allocable to the days in Stellar's taxable year after the acquisition date.

$$\$75{,}000 \times 185/365 \text{ days} = \$38{,}014$$

NOTE: The remainder of Claudio's NOL ($270,000 – $38,014 = $231,986) can be carried forward and used to offset Stellar's taxable income (subject to the Sec. 382 limitation) in carryforward years.

163. (a) The requirement is to determine the recognized gain to be reported by Mueller on the exchange of her Disco bond for Disco preferred stock. The issuance by Disco Corporation of its preferred stock in exchange for its bonds is a nontaxable "Type E" reorganization (i.e., a recapitalization). Since Mueller did not receive any boot, no part of her $400 realized gain is recognized.

164. (b) The requirement is to determine the amount of recognized gain in a recapitalization. Since a recapitalization is a reorganization, a realized gain will be recognized to the extent that consideration other than stock or securities is received, including the FMV of an excess principal amount of securities received over the principal amount of securities surrendered. Since no securities were surrendered, the entire $10,500 FMV of the securities received by Roberts is treated as boot. However, in this case, Roberts recognized gain is limited to her realized gain ($91,000 + $10,500) – $95,000 = $6,500.

SOLUTIONS TO SIMULATION PROBLEMS

Simulation Problem 1

1. **($900,000)** The problem states that Oak Corp. is an accrual-basis corporation. Since the net sales are already stated on an accrual basis, no adjustment is necessary for beginning and ending trade accounts receivable.

2. **($6,000)** The $20,000 of dividends received from an unrelated taxable domestic corporation are eligible for a dividends received deduction. Since the stock was traded on a "major stock exchange," it should be assumed that Oak owned less than 20% of the dividend-paying corporation and that the dividends qualify for a 70% DRD ($20,000 x 70% = $14,000).

3. **($0)** The $8,000 of interest income from municipal bonds is excluded from Oak's gross income.

4. **($0)** Oak's $10,000 of LTCG is offset by Oak's share of the partnership's LTCL.

5. **($79,000)** The $60,000 of earnings from the Tech Partnership represents the netting of Oak's share of the partnership's ordinary income of $79,000 and LTCL of $19,000. Since the $19,000 LTCL is a special loss item, it cannot be netted against ordinary income but instead must be reported as LTCL and be combined with Oak's $10,000 of LTCG. The resulting net LTCL of $9,000 ($19,000 LTCL – $10,000 LTCG) is not currently deductible, but instead must be carried back three years and forward five years to offset capital gains in the carryback and carryforward years.

6. **($0)** The $250,000 of life insurance proceeds resulting from the death of Oak's controller are excluded from Oak's gross income.

7. **($0)** The $5,000 refund of Oak's 2002 federal income tax is excluded from Oak's gross income because Oak's payment of federal income tax was not deductible.

8. **($525,000)** The cost of goods sold is already stated on the accrual basis and no adjustment is necessary.

9. **($125,000)** Since officers' compensation must be separately stated on Oak's tax return, the $75,000 of officers' compensation must be subtracted from salaries and wages, and separately deducted.

10. **($11,000)** Oak's deduction for bad debts is limited to the $11,000 of accounts receivable actually written off during the year.

11. **($90,000)** The payroll taxes and property taxes are fully deductible and no adjustment is necessary.

12. **($25,000)** The interest expense incurred for working capital purposes is fully deductible and no adjustment is necessary.

13. **($5,000)** The deduction for the $18,000 of charitable contributions is limited to 10% of Oak's taxable income before the charitable contributions and dividends received deductions. Before computing this limitation, it is necessary to first consider any remaining adjustments. After considering all remaining adjustments, the calculation of the charitable contributions deduction is computed as follows:

(1)	Sales (net)	$900,000	
	Dividends	20,000	
(5)	Partnership ordinary income	79,000	
	Total income		$999,000
(8)	Cost of goods sold	525,000	
(9)	Salaries and wages	125,000	
(9)	Officers' compensation	75,000	
(10)	Bad debts	11,000	
(11)	Taxes	90,000	
(12)	Interest	25,000	
(14)	Depreciation	80,000	
(15)	Other Expenses	18,000	
	Total deductions		(949,000)
	Taxable income before charitable contributions and		
	dividends received deductions		$ 50,000

The maximum deduction allowed for charitable contributions is limited to 10% of taxable income before the charitable contribution deduction and the dividends received deduction. Therefore, $5,000 will be the maximum deduction allowed for Oak Corp. in 2003. The excess contributions ($18,000 – $5,000 = $13,000) will be carried forward for a period of five years.

14. **($80,000)** Since straight-line depreciation is used for both book and tax purposes, no adjustment is necessary.

15. **($18,000)** The $33,000 of other expenses must be reduced by the $15,000 of premiums paid on the keyman life insurance policy covering Oak's controller. No deduction is allowed for life insurance premiums on a policy for which Oak is the beneficiary.

16. **($0)** The provision for federal income tax is not deductible in computing taxable income.

Simulation Problem 2

1. **(R)** To be classified as a personal holding company, a corporation must meet two requirements: (1) the corporation must receive at least 60% of its adjusted ordinary gross income as "personal holding company income" such as dividends, interest, rents, royalties, and other passive income; and (2) the corporation must have more than 50% of the value of its outstanding stock directly or indirectly owned by five or fewer individuals during any time in the last half of the tax year.

2. **(Z)** The transferred basis, equal to the basis of the donor plus any gift tax paid attributable to the net appreciation in the value of the gift, is the basis used to determine gain on sale of property that was received as a gift.

3. **(P)** A like-kind exchange, the exchange of business or investment property for property of a like-kind, qualifies as a nontaxable exchange. Thus, the exchange of production machinery for new production machinery when boot (money) is given is a nontaxable exchange.

4. **(O)** Head of household filing status applies to unmarried persons not qualifying for surviving spouse status who maintain a household for more than one-half of the taxable year for a dependent. The tax rates applicable to the head of household status are lower than those applicable to individuals filing as single, but are higher than rates applicable to married individuals filing a joint return.

5. **(G)** Under the doctrine of constructive receipt, income is includable in gross income and subject to income tax for the taxable year in which that income is made unqualifiedly available to the taxpayer without restriction, even though not physically in the taxpayer's possession.

6. **(A)** Corporations may be subject to an accumulated earnings tax, in addition to regular income tax, if a corporation accumulates earnings beyond reasonable business needs in order to avoid shareholder tax on dividend distributions.

7. **(U)** Portfolio income is defined as income from interest, dividends, annuities, and certain royalties.

8. **(W)** Section 1231 assets include depreciable assets and real estate used in a trade or business and held for more than one year.

9. **(J)** The dividends received deduction was enacted by Congress to mitigate the triple taxation that occurs when one corporation pays dividends to a corporate stockholder who, in turn, distributes such amounts to its individual stockholders.

10. **(F)** A constructive dividend results when a shareholder is considered to have received a dividend from a corporation, although the corporation did not specifically declare a dividend. This situation may occur when a shareholder/employee receives an excessive salary from a corporation, when there is a loan to a shareholder where there is no intent to repay the amount loaned, or when a corporation purchases shareholder property for an amount in excess of the property's fair market value. Constructive dividends often result when a transaction between a shareholder and corporation is not an arm's-length transaction.

Simulation Problem 3

1. **($20,000)** Interest on funds borrowed for working capital is deductible. However, interest incurred on borrowed funds to purchase municipal bonds is not deductible because the resulting income is exempt from tax.

2. **($20,000)** Interest earned on corporate bonds must be included in gross income. However, interest earned on municipal bonds is excluded.

3. **($10,000)** Expenditures incurred in creating a corporation may be amortized over a period of not less than sixty months. However, expenditures connected with selling or issuing stock are neither deductible nor amortizable. Therefore, only the legal fees and state incorporation fees are amortized over not less than sixty months. The amount to be deducted on the corporate tax return will equal $10,000 (30,000 + 20,000)/60 x 12 months.

4. **($20,000)** All of the capital gains would be included in Aviator's gross income.

5. **($20,000)** Corporate capital losses can only be deducted to the extent of capital gains. Therefore, only $20,000 of capital losses can be deducted on the Aviator, Inc. tax return. Since this is Aviator's first year of existence, the excess of capital losses over capital gains ($10,000) will then be carried forward five years as a short-term capital loss, to offset capital gains.

6. **($35,000)** The dividends received deduction will be based on 70% of its dividends received, since Aviator, Inc. owns less than 20% of the dividend-paying corporation.

7. **($38,000)** A charitable contributions deduction is limited to a maximum of 10% of taxable income before the dividends received deduction and a charitable contributions deduction. Therefore, taxable income before these deductions needs to be calculated to determine the maximum allowable deduction. Taxable income is computed as follows:

Sales	$2,000,000
Dividends	50,000
Interest revenue	20,000
Gains on the sale of stock	20,000
Cost of goods sold	(1,000,000)
Salaries and wages	(400,000)
Depreciation	(260,000)
Losses on the sale of stock	(20,000)
Organizational expenditures	(10,000)
Interest expense	(20,000)
	$ 380,000

The charitable contributions deduction will be limited to $38,000 ($380,000 x 10%). The excess not allowed ($40,000 – $38,000 = $2,000) will be carried forward for up to five years.

Simulation Problem 4

1. **(P; $5,000)** Ral is an accrual method taxpayer, the payment was based on a formula in effect for 2003, and the sales manager had performed the services in 2003.

2. **(U; $8,000)** Since taxpayers are required to use the direct charge-off method in computing taxable income, only the $8,000 of actual bad debts for 2003 can be deducted.

3. **(A; $0)** Since Ral is the beneficiary of the policies and the eventual proceeds will be excluded from gross income, the premium cannot be deducted in computing taxable income.

4. **(X; $12,000)** State income taxes are deductible in computing federal taxable income.

5. **(P; $5,000)** The $3,000 interest on US Treasury notes and $2,000 interest on municipal arbitrage bonds is taxable, while the $200 interest on municipal bonds is nontaxable.

6. **(R; $5,600)** Since Clove is at least 20% owned, the $7,000 of dividends are eligible for an 80% dividends received deduction.

7. **(M; $4,200)** Since Ramo is less than 20% owned, the $6,000 of dividends are eligible for an 70% dividends received deduction.

8. **(A; $0)** No dividends received deduction is allowed because the stock was not held for more than forty-five days.

9. **(A; $0)** No dividends received deduction is allowed because a real estate investment trust (REIT) is a pass-through entity with only one level of tax paid (by its shareholders).

10. **(A; $0)** The $400 of capital gains dividends pass through as capital gains and are not eligible for a dividends received deduction.

11. **(A; $0)** No dividends received deduction is allowed because Money Market Fund derived all of its income from investments in "interest paying securities," not dividend paying stocks.

12. **(A; $0)** No federal income tax deduction is allowed for corporate dividend payments to its own shareholders.

13. **(A; $0)** Ral's net capital loss is $6,400 – $400 capital gains dividends = $6,000. However, a corporation cannot deduct a net capital loss. Instead, it is carried back three years and forward five years to offset capital gains in those years.

14. **(Z; $22,250)** The tax rate schedule indicates that the tax on $100,000 of taxable income is $22,250.

Simulation Problem 5

For **items 1 through 4,** candidates were asked to determine the amount for Lan Corp. (an accrual-basis calendar-year S corporation), using the fact pattern for each item.

   1.   **($6,140)** The requirement is to determine the amount of net business income that Lan should report on Schedule K of Form 1120S. The term "net business income" corresponds to an S corporation's "ordinary income (loss) from trade or business activities." The computation of this amount excludes any item that must be separately stated and passed through to shareholders in order to retain the item's special tax characteristics. Here, the interest income on investments is portfolio income and must be separately stated and passed through to shareholders as interest income. Similarly, the charitable contributions must be separately stated and passed through to shareholders in order to apply the appropriate percentage limitations at the shareholder level. As a result, Lan's net business income consists of its $7,200 of gross receipts reduced by the $1,120 of supplies expense, or $6,140.

   2.   **($2,700)** The requirement it to determine the amount of net business income to be reported on Pike's 2003 Schedule K-1 from Lan. If there is no election to terminate the tax year following the sale of stock, the income of an S corporation for the entire taxable year is allocated per share, per day to anyone who was a shareholder during the year. Lan was formed on January 6, 2003, and its tax year consists of 360 days. So its net business income per share, per day would be $14,400 ÷ 200 shares ÷ 360 days = $.20. Since Pike purchased his forty shares on January 31, he is considered to own his stock for a total of 334 days during the year (counting February 1 as the first day). Thus, the amount of net business income to be reported on Pike's Schedule K-1 is (40 shares x 334 days x $.20) = $2,672. Since the instructions indicated that the answer should be rounded to the nearest hundred, the correct answer is $2,700.

   3.   **($3,150)** The requirement is to determine Pike's basis for his Lan stock at December 31, 2003, assuming that he had purchased the stock for $4,000. An S corporation's items of income and deduction pass through to be reported on shareholder returns even though no distributions are made. As a result, a shareholder's S corporation stock basis is increased by the pass through of all income items (including tax-exempt income), and is decreased by all loss and deduction items (including nondeductible expenses). In this case, Pike's beginning basis of $4,000 would be increased by the $150 of municipal bond interest income, and decreased by the $1,000 of ordinary business loss.

   4.   **($9,000)** The requirement is to determine Taylor's basis in Lan shares for determining gain or loss from the sale of stock to Pike. Taylor's beginning stock basis of $10,000 must be increased by his $2,000 share of the ordinary income from Lan prior to the sale, and must be decreased by the $3,000 nontaxable cash distribution that Taylor received. Recall that distributions by S corporations without accumulated earnings and profits are treated as a return of stock basis and are excluded from gross income.

I. GIFT AND ESTATE TAXATION

The federal gift tax is an excise tax (imposed on donor) on the transfer of property by gift during a person's lifetime. The federal estate tax is an excise tax on the transfer of property upon death. The Tax Reform Act of 1976 combined these taxes into a **unified transfer tax** rate schedule that applies to both life and death transfers. To remove relatively small gifts and estates from the imposition of tax, a **unified transfer tax credit** of **$345,800** is allowed for 2003 against gift and estate taxes. This is equivalent to an **exemption** of the first **$1,000,000** of taxable gifts or taxable estate from the unified transfer tax.

A. The Gift Tax

1. **Gift Tax Formula**

Gross gifts (cash plus FMV of property at date of gift)		$xxx
Less:		
One-half of gifts treated as given by spouse	$ x	
Annual exclusion (up to $11,000 per donee)	x	
Unlimited exclusion for tuition or medical expenses paid on behalf of donee	x	
Unlimited exclusion for gifts to political organizations	x	
Charitable gifts (remainder of charitable gifts after annual exclusion)	x	
Marital deduction (remainder of gifts to spouse after annual exclusion)	x	xx
Taxable gifts for current year		$ xx
Add: Taxable gifts for prior years		x
Total taxable gifts		$ xx
Unified transfer tax on total taxable gifts		$ xx
Less: Unified transfer tax on taxable gifts made prior to current year		x
Unified transfer tax for current year		$ xx
Unified transfer tax credit	$ xx	
Less: Unified transfer tax credit used in prior years	x	x
Net gift tax liability		$ xx

2. A **gift** occurs when a transfer becomes complete and is measured by its fair market value on that date. A gift becomes **complete** when the donor has relinquished dominion and control and no longer has the power to change its disposition, whether for the donor's benefit or for the benefit of another.

   a.   The creation of joint ownership in property is treated as a gift to the extent the donor's contribution exceeds the donor's retained interest.

   b.   The creation of a joint bank account is not a gift; but a gift results when the noncontributing tenant withdraws funds.

3. Gross gifts less the following deductions equal taxable gifts:

   a.   **Annual exclusion**—of up to $11,000 (for 2003) per donee is allowed for gifts of present interests (not future interests). A **present interest** is an unrestricted right to the immediate use, possession, or enjoyment of property or the income from property. A **future interest** includes reversions, remainders, and other interests that are limited to commence in use, possession, or enjoyment at some future date or time.

     (1) Trusts for minors (Sec. 2503(c) trusts) allow parents and other donors to obtain an annual exclusion for gifts to trusts for children under age twenty-one even though the trust does not distribute its income annually. To qualify, the trust must provide

      (a) Until the beneficiary reaches age twenty-one, the trustee **may** pay the income and/or the underlying assets to the beneficiary, and,

      (b) Any income and assets not distributed must pass to the beneficiary when the beneficiary reaches age twenty-one. If the beneficiary dies before age twenty-one, the income and underlying assets are either payable to the beneficiary's estate, or are payable to any person the minor may appoint if the minor possesses a general power of appointment over the trust property.

     (2) **Crummey** trusts allow a donor to obtain an annual exclusion upon funding a discretionary trust. This type of trust is more flexible than a Sec. 2503(c) trust because the beneficiary can be of any age and the trust can terminate at any age. To qualify, a beneficiary must have the power to demand a distribution equal to the lesser of the donor's annual exclusion ($11,000), or the beneficiary's pro rata share of the amount transferred to the trust each year.

b. **Gift-splitting**—a gift by either spouse to a third party may be treated as made one-half by each, if both spouses consent to election. Gift-splitting has the advantage of using the other spouse's annual exclusion and unified transfer tax credit.

> EXAMPLE: *H is married and has three sons. H could give $22,000 per year to each of his sons without making a tax-able gift if H's spouse (W) consents to gift-splitting.*

	H	W
Gifts	$66,000	
Gift-splitting	(33,000)	$33,000
Annual exclusion (3 x $11,000)	(33,000)	(33,000)
Taxable gifts	$_____0	$_____0

c. **Educational and medical exclusion**—an unlimited exclusion is available for amounts **paid on behalf of a donee** (1) as tuition to an educational organization, or (2) to a health care provider for medical care of donee

d. **Political gifts**—an unlimited exclusion is available for the transfer of money or other property to a political organization.

e. **Charitable gifts**—(net of annual exclusion) are deductible without limitation

f. **Marital deduction**—is allowed without limitation for gifts to a donor's spouse

    (1) The gift must not be a terminable interest (i.e., donee spouse's interest ends at death with no control over who receives remainder).

    (2) If donor elects, a gift of **qualified terminable interest** property (i.e., property placed in trust with income to donee spouse for life and remainder to someone else at donee spouse's death) will qualify for the marital deduction if the income is paid at least annually to spouse and the property is not subject to transfer during the donee spouse's lifetime.

    (3) The marital deduction for gifts to an alien spouse is limited to $110,000 per year.

4. The **tax computation** reflects the **cumulative nature** of the gift tax. A tax is first computed on lifetime taxable gifts, then is reduced by the tax on taxable gifts made in prior years in order to tax the current year's gifts at applicable marginal rates. Any available transfer tax credit is then subtracted to arrive at the gift tax liability.

5. A **gift tax return** must be filed on a calendar-year basis, with the return due and tax paid on or before April 15th of the following year.

a. A donor who makes a gift to charity is not required to file a gift tax return if the entire value of the donated property qualifies for a gift tax charitable deduction.

b. If the donor dies, the gift tax return for the year of death is due not later than the due date for filing the decedent's federal estate tax return (generally nine months after date of death).

6. The **basis of property acquired by gift**

a. Basis for gain—basis of donor plus gift tax attributable to appreciation

b. Basis for loss—lesser of gain basis or FMV at date of gift

c. The increase in basis for gift tax paid is limited to the amount (not to exceed the gift tax paid) that bears the same ratio to the amount of gift tax paid as the net appreciation in value of the gift bears to the amount of the gift.

    (1) The amount of gift is reduced by any portion of the $11,000 annual exclusion allowable with respect to the gift.

    (2) Where more than one gift of a present interest is made to the same donee during a calendar year, the $11,000 exclusion is applied to gifts in chronological order.

> EXAMPLE: *Joan received property with a FMV of $60,000 and an adjusted basis of $80,000 as a gift. The donor paid a gift tax of $12,000 on the transfer. Since the property was not appreciated in value, no gift tax can be added in the basis computation. Joan's basis for computing a gain is $80,000, while her basis for computing a loss is $60,000.*

B. The Estate Tax

1. Estate Tax Formula

Gross estate (cash plus FMV of property at date of death, or alternate valuation date)		$xxx
Less:		
Funeral expenses	$x	
Administrative expenses	x	
Debts and mortgages	x	
Casualty losses	x	
Charitable bequests (unlimited)	x	
Marital deduction (unlimited)	x	xx
Taxable estate		$xxx
Add: Post-76 adjusted taxable gifts		xx
Total taxable life and death transfers		$xxx
Unified transfer tax on total transfers		$ xx
Less:		
Unified transfer tax on post-76 taxable gifts	$x	
Unified transfer tax credit	x	
State death, foreign death, and prior transfer tax credits	x	x
Net estate tax liability		$ xx

2. **Gross estate** includes the FMV of all property in which the decedent had an interest at time of death.

a. **Jointly held property**

(1) If property was held by tenancy in common, only the FMV of the decedent's share is included.

(2) Include one-half the FMV of community property, and one-half the FMV of property held **by spouses** in joint tenancy or tenancy by the entirety.

(3) Include one-half of FMV if the property held by two persons in joint tenancy was acquired by gift, bequest, or inheritance (1/3 if held by three persons, etc.)

(4) If property held in joint tenancy was acquired by purchase by **other than spouses,** include the FMV of the property multiplied by the percentage of total cost furnished by the decedent.

b. The FMV of transfers with retained life estates and revocable transfers are included in the gross estate.

c. Include the FMV of transfers intended to take effect at death (i.e., the donee can obtain enjoyment only by surviving the decedent, and the decedent prior to death had a reversionary interest of more than 5% of the value of the property).

d. Include any property over which the decedent had a **general power of appointment** (i.e., decedent could appoint property in favor of decedent, decedent's estate, or creditors of decedent or decedent's estate).

e. Include the value of life insurance proceeds from policies payable to the estate, and policies over which the decedent possessed an "incident of ownership" (e.g., right to change beneficiary).

f. Income in respect of a decedent

3. Property is included at **FMV** at **date of decedent's death**; or executor may elect to use FMV at **alternate valuation date** (generally a date six months subsequent to death), if such election will reduce both the gross estate and the federal estate tax liability.

a. If alternate valuation is elected, but property is disposed of within six months of death, then use FMV on date of disposition.

b. Election is irrevocable and applies to all property in estate; cannot be made on an individual property basis.

4. **Estate tax deductions** include funeral expenses, administrative expenses, debts and mortgages, casualty losses during the estate administration, charitable bequests (no limit), and an unlimited marital deduction for the FMV of property passing to a surviving spouse.

a. A terminable interest granted to surviving spouse will not generally qualify for marital deduction.

b. If executor elects, the FMV of "qualified terminable interest property" is eligible for the marital deduction if the income from the property is paid at least annually to spouse and the property is not subject to transfer during the surviving spouse's lifetime.

    c. Property passing to a surviving spouse who is not a US citizen is not eligible for the estate tax marital deduction, except for property passing to an alien spouse through a qualified domestic trust (QDT).

    d. Property passing from a nonresident alien to a surviving spouse who is a US citizen is eligible for the estate tax marital deduction.

5. Post-76 taxable gifts are added back to the taxable estate at date of gift FMV. Any gift tax paid is *not* added back.

6. A unified transfer tax is computed on total life and death transfers, then is reduced by the tax already paid on post-76 gifts, the unified transfer tax credit, state death tax credit (limited to table amount), foreign death tax credit, and prior transfer tax credit (i.e., percentage of estate tax paid on the transfer to the present decedent from a transferor who died within past ten years).

7. An **estate tax return** must be filed if the decedent's **gross estate exceeds $1,000,000** in 2003. The return must be filed within **nine months** of decedent's death, unless an extension of time has been granted.

8. The **basis of property acquired from a decedent** is generally the FMV at date of decedent's death, or the alternate valuation date if elected for estate tax purposes.

    a. Use FMV on date of disposition if alternate valuation is elected and property is distributed, sold, or otherwise disposed of during the six-month period following death.

    b. FMV rule does not apply to appreciated property acquired by the decedent by gift within one year before death if such property then passes from the donee-decedent to the original donor or donor's spouse. The basis of such property to the original donor (or spouse) will be the adjusted basis of the property to the decedent immediately before death.

    EXAMPLE: Son gives property with FMV of $40,000 (basis of $5,000) to terminally ill father within one year before father's death. The property is included in father's estate at FMV of $40,000. If property passes to son or son's spouse, basis will remain at $5,000. If passed to someone else, the property's basis will be $40,000.

II. GENERATION-SKIPPING TAX

    This tax is imposed in addition to the federal gift and estate taxes (i.e., unified transfer tax) and is designed to prevent individuals from escaping an entire generation of gift and estate taxes by transferring property to, or in trust for the benefit of, a person that is two or more generations younger than the donor or transferor.

A. The tax approximates the unified transfer tax that would be imposed if property were actually transferred to each successive generation, and is imposed on taxable distributions, taxable terminations, and direct skips to someone at least two generations below that of the donor or transferor.

1. A taxable distribution is a distribution out of a trust's income or corpus to a beneficiary at least two generations below that of the grantor (unless the grandchild's parent is deceased and was a lineal descendant of the grantor) while an older generation beneficiary has an interest in the trust.

2. A taxable termination means that by reason of death, expiration of time, or otherwise, the interest of a nonskip person terminates (i.e., someone less than two generations below the donor or transferor) and a skip person (i.e., someone at least two generations below the donor or transferor) becomes the recipient of the trust property or the only beneficiary.

3. A direct skip occurs when one or more generations are bypassed altogether and property is transferred directly to, or in trust for, a skip person.

B. The generation-skipping transfer tax is imposed at a flat rate that equals the maximum unified transfer tax rate of 49% for 2003.

C. Exemptions available

1. A $1,120,000 exemption per transferor for 2003.

2. An unlimited exemption is available for a direct skip to a grandchild if the grandchild's parent is deceased and was a lineal descendant of the transferor.

III. INCOME TAXATION OF ESTATES AND TRUSTS

    Although estates and trusts are separate taxable entities, they will not pay an income tax if they distribute all of their income to beneficiaries. In this respect they act as a conduit, since the income taxed to beneficiaries will have the same character as it had for the estate or trust.

A. An estate or trust must **file** US Fiduciary Income Tax Return Form 1041 if it has **gross income of $600 or more**.

1. Return is due by the 15th day of the fourth month following the close of the estate or trust's taxable year.
2. A **trust must adopt a calendar year** as its taxable year. An estate may adopt a calendar year or any fiscal year.
3. For 2003, estate and trusts are taxed as follows:

   a. First $1,900 of taxable income is taxed at 15%
   b. Over $1,900 but not over $4,500 is taxed at 25%
   c. Over $4,500 but not over $6,850 is taxed at 28%
   d. Over $6,850 but not over $9,350 is taxed at 33%
   e. Over $9,350 is taxed at 35%

4. The alternative minimum tax applies to estates and trusts and is computed in the same manner as for individuals. The AMT exemption for an estate or trust is $22,500.
5. Estates and trusts are generally required to make estimated tax payments using the rules applicable to individuals. However, estates do not have to make estimated payments for taxable years ending within two years of the decedent's death.

B.   Classification of Trusts

1. **Simple trust** is one that (1) is required to distribute all of its income to beneficiaries each year, (2) cannot make charitable contributions, and (3) makes no distribution of trust corpus (i.e., principal) during the year.
2. **Complex trust** is one in which (1) the trustee has discretion whether to distribute or accumulate its income, (2) may make charitable contributions, and (3) may distribute trust corpus.

C.   Computation of Estate or Trust Taxable Income

1. **Gross income** for an estate or trust is generally the same as for individual taxpayers.

   a. Generally no gain or loss is recognized on the transfer of property to beneficiaries to satisfy specific bequests.
   b. Gain or loss is recognized on the transfer of property to beneficiaries in lieu of cash to satisfy specific cash bequests.

2. **Allowable deductions** for an estate or trust are generally the same as for an individual taxpayer.

   a. A personal **exemption** is allowed.

      (1) $600 for estate
      (2) $300 for simple trust (i.e., a trust required to distribute all income currently)
      (3) $100 for a complex trust (i.e., a trust other than a simple trust)

   b. Charitable contributions can be deducted without limitation if paid out of income.

      (1) Contributions are not deductible to the extent paid out of tax-exempt income.
      (2) Only complex trusts can make charitable contributions.

   c. Expenses incurred in the production of tax exempt income are not deductible.
   d. Capital losses offset capital gains and a net capital loss of up to $3,000 can be deducted with the remainder carried forward.
   e. Medical and funeral expenses of a decedent are not allowed as deductions on estate's income tax return Form 1041. However, if medical expenses are paid within twelve months of the decedent's death, they are deductible on the decedent's final Form 1040, if the estate's executor waives the deduction on the decedent's estate tax return
   f. Any unused capital loss and NOL carryovers from the decedent's final Form 1040 are not allowed as deductions.

3. An **income distribution deduction** is allowed for distributions of income to beneficiaries.

a. **Distributable net income (DNI)** is the maximum amount of deduction for distributions to beneficiaries in any taxable year and also determines the amounts and character of the income reported by the beneficiaries.

b. Generally, DNI is the same as the estate's or trust's taxable income computed before the income distribution deduction with the following modifications:

   (1) Add

    (a) Personal exemption
    (b) Any net capital loss deduction (limited to $3,000)
    (c) Tax exempt interest (reduced by related nondeductible expenses)

   (2) Subtract

    (a) Net capital gains allocable to corpus
    (b) Extraordinary dividends and taxable stock dividends allocated to corpus of simple trust

c. Deduction will be the lesser of DNI or the amount distributed to beneficiaries (i.e., taxable income required to be distributed, plus other amount of taxable income distributed).

D. Treatment of Simple Trust and Beneficiaries

1. Income is taxed to beneficiaries, not to trust.
2. Beneficiaries are taxed on the income required to be distributed (up to DNI), even though not actually distributed during the year.
3. Income passes through to beneficiaries retaining its characteristics (e.g., tax-exempt income passes through retaining its exempt status).
4. If multiple beneficiaries, DNI is prorated in proportion to the amount of required distribution to each beneficiary.

E. Treatment of Complex Trust and Beneficiaries

1. A two-tier income distribution system is used.

   a. First tier: Distributions of the first tier are income amounts that are required to be distributed and include distributions that can be paid out of income or corpus, to the extent paid out of income.
   b. Second tier: Distributions of the second tier are all other amounts that are actually paid during the year or are required to be paid.

2. DNI is first allocated to distributions in the first tier. Any remaining DNI is prorated to distributions in the second tier.

   EXAMPLE: A trust has DNI of $9,000. The trust instrument requires that $6,000 of income be distributed annually to Alan. Further, it permits distributions to Baker and Carr of income or corpus in the trustee's discretion. For the current year, the trustee distributes $6,000 to Alan, $4,000 to Baker, and $2,000 to Carr.

   Since Alan's distribution is a first tier distribution, all $6,000 distributed is taxable to Alan. This leaves only $3,000 of DNI to be allocated to the second tier distributions to Baker and Carr. Since DNI would be allocated in proportion to the amounts distributed, $2,000 of Baker's distribution and $1,000 of Carr's distribution would be taxable.

F. Grantor Trusts are trusts over which the grantor (or grantor's spouse) retain substantial control. The income from a grantor trust is generally taxed to the grantor, not to the trust or beneficiaries. A grantor trust generally exists if any of the following conditions are present:

1. Trust income will, or in the grantor's or nonadverse party's discretion may be, distributed to the grantor or grantor's spouse (or used to pay life insurance premiums of either).
2. The grantor (or nonadverse party) has the power to revoke the trust.
3. The grantor (or grantor's spouse) holds a reversionary interest worth more than 5% of trust corpus.
4. The grantor (or nonadverse party) can deal with trust property in a nonfiduciary capacity (e.g., purchase trust assets for less than adequate consideration or borrow trust property at below market rate).
5. The grantor (or grantor's spouse) or nonadverse party controls the beneficial enjoyment of the trust (e.g., ability to change beneficiaries).

G. Termination of Estate or Trust

1. An estate or trust is not entitled to a personal exemption on its final return.

2. Any unused carryovers (e.g., NOL or capital loss) are passed through to beneficiaries for use on their individual tax returns.

3. Any excess deductions for its final year are passed through to beneficiaries and can be deducted as miscellaneous itemized deductions.

IV. EXEMPT ORGANIZATIONS

A. Types of Organizations

1. Tax-exempt organizations are listed by class of organization in the Internal Revenue Code. Generally, an exempt organization serves some common good, is operated as a not-for-profit entity, its net earnings do not inure for the benefit of specified individuals, and the organization does not exert undue political influence. To obtain exempt status, the organization must be one of those specifically identified in the Code, and generally must apply for and receive an exemption.

2. **Sec. 501(c)(3) organizations** (religious, educational, charitable, etc.) generally must apply for exemption by filing Form 1023 within fifteen months from the end of the month in which they were organized. To qualify, (1) the organization must meet an organizational and operational test, (2) no part of the organization's net earnings can inure to the benefit of private shareholders or individuals, and (3) the organization cannot, as a substantial part of its activities, attempt to influence legislation (unless it elects an exception permitting certain lobby expenditures) or directly participate to any extent in a political campaign for or against any candidate for public office.

    a. Some organizations do not have to file for exemption (e.g., churches or an organization [other than a private foundation] normally having annual gross receipts of not more than $5,000). They automatically are exempt if they meet the requirements of Sec. 501(c)(3).

    b. The **organizational test** requires the articles of organization limit the organization's purposes to one or more exempt purposes described in Sec. 501(c)(3), and must not expressly empower the organization to engage in activities that are not in furtherance of its one or more exempt purposes, except as an insubstantial part of its activities.

    c. The **operational test** requires that an exempt organization be operated exclusively for an exempt purpose. An organization will be considered to be operated exclusively for an exempt purpose only if it engages primarily in activities that accomplish its exempt purpose. An organization will not be so regarded if more than an insubstantial part of its activities is not in furtherance of an exempt purpose.

IRC 501	*Type of Organization*	*Description*
(c) (1)	Federal and Regulated Agencies	Federal Credit Unions, FDIC, Federal Land Bank
(c) (2)	Title Holding Corporation for Exempt Organization	Corporation holding title to fraternity or sorority house
(c) (3)	Religious, Educational, Charitable, Scientific, Literary, Testing for Public Safety, Foster National or International Amateur Sports Competition, Prevention of Cruelty to Children or Animals Organizations	Activities of a nature implied by description of class of organization (e.g., church, school, museum, zoo, planetarium, Red Cross, Boy Scouts of America)
(c) (4)	Civic Leagues, Social Welfare Organizations, and Local Associations of Employees	Promotion of community welfare (e.g., community association, volunteer fire companies, garden club, League of Women Voters)
(c) (5)	Labor, Agricultural, and Horticultural Organizations	Educational or instructive, to improve conditions of work, and to improve products and efficiency (e.g., teacher's association)
(c) (6)	Business Leagues, Chamber of Commerce, Real Estate Boards, etc.	Improvement of business conditions of one or more lines of business (e.g., trade of professional associations, Chambers of Commerce)
(c) (7)	Social and Recreation Clubs	Recreation and social activities (e.g., Country Club, Sailing Club, Tennis Club)
(c) (8)	Fraternal Beneficiary Societies and Associations	Lodge providing for payment of life, sickness, accident, or other benefits to members
(c) (9)	Voluntary Employees' Beneficiary Associations	Providing for payment of life, sickness, accident or other benefits to members

(c)(10)	Domestic Fraternal Societies and Associations	Lodge devoting its net earnings to charitable, fraternal, and other specified purposes, but no life, sickness, or accident benefits to members
(c)(11)	Teachers' Retirement Fund Associations	Payment of retirement benefits to teachers
(c)(12)	Benevolent Life Insurance Associations, Mutual or Cooperative Telephone Companies, etc.	Activities of a mutually beneficial nature
(c)(13)	Cemetery Companies	Operated for benefit of lot owners who purchase lots for burial
(c)(14)	State Chartered Credit Unions	Loans to members
(c)(15)	Mutual Insurance Companies or Associations	Providing insurance to members substantially at cost
(c)(16)	Farmers Cooperative Organizations to Finance Crop Operations	Financing of crop operations in conjunction with activities of marketing or purchasing association
(c)(17)	Supplemental Unemployment Benefit Trusts	Payment of supplemental unemployment compensation benefits
(c)(19)	Member of Armed Forces Post or Organization	Veterans of Foreign Wars (VFW)
(d)	Religious and Apostolic Associations	Communal religious community that conducts business activities. Members must include pro rata share of organization's income in their gross income
(e)	Cooperative Hospital Service Organizations	Performs cooperative service for hospitals (e.g., centralized purchasing organization)
(k)	Child Care Organizations	Provides care for children

    d. **Inurement** is private benefit provided to insiders who have the institutional opportunity to direct the organization's resources to themselves, to entities in which they have an interest, or to family members. Inurement issues may arise because of excessive compensation, payment of excessive rent, receipt of less than fair value from sales of property, and inadequately secured loans.

    e. An organization (other than churches and private foundations) can elect to replace the substantial part of activities test with a limit defined in terms of expenditures for influencing legislation. **Attempting to influence legislation** includes (1) any attempt to influence any legislation through an effort to affect the opinions of the general public (i.e., grassroots lobbying), and (2) any attempt to influence any legislation through communication with any member or employee of a legislative body, or with any government official or employee who may participate in the formulation of legislation (i.e., direct lobbying).

        (1) Attempting to influence legislation does **not** include appearing before or communicating with any legislative body with respect to a possible decision of that body that might affect the powers, duties, exempt status, or the deduction of contributions to the organization.

        (2) If the election to be subject to the lobbying expenditures limits (instead of the substantial part of activities test) is made, an organization will not lose its exempt status unless it normally makes lobbying expenditures in excess of 150% of lobbying nontaxable amount or normally makes grassroots expenditures in excess of 150% of grassroots nontaxable amount.

        (3) If the election is made, an organization will be subject to a 25% excise tax on the excess of its lobbying and grassroots expenditures over the lobbying and grassroots nontaxable amounts.

3. **Private foundations** are Sec. 501(c)(3) organizations other than churches, educational organizations, hospitals or medical research organizations operated in conjunction with hospitals, endowment funds operated for the benefit of certain state and municipal colleges and universities, governmental units, and publicly supported organizations.

    a. An organization is **publicly supported** if it normally receives at least one-third of its total support from governmental units and the general public (e.g., support received in the form of gifts, grants, contributions, membership fees, gross receipts from admissions, sales of merchandise, etc.)

    b. Private foundations may be subject to taxes based on investment income, self-dealing, failure to distribute income, excess business holdings, investments that jeopardize charitable purposes, and taxable expenditures. The initial taxes (with the exception of the tax on investment income) are imposed because the organization engages in prohibited transactions. Additional taxes are imposed if the prohibited transactions are not corrected with a specified period.

4. **Feeder organizations** do not qualify for tax-exempt status. A feeder organization carries on a trade or business for the benefit of an exempt organization and remits its profits to the exempt organization.

B. Filing Requirements

1. Most exempt organizations must file an **annual information return** Form 990 (Return of Organization Exempt from Income Tax). Organizations **not** required to file Form 990 include churches, federal agencies, organizations whose annual gross receipts do not exceed $25,000, and private foundations.
2. Exempt organizations with **unrelated business income** must file Form 990-T (Exempt Organization Business Income Tax Return) if the organization has gross income of at least $1,000 from an unrelated trade or business. Form 990-T may be required even though Form 990 is not required.
3. **Private foundations** must annually file Form 990-PF (Return of Private Foundation). If an organization is subject to any of the excise taxes imposed on private foundations, Form 4720 (Return of Certain Excise Taxes on Charities and Other Persons) must be filed with Form 990-PF.

C. Unrelated Business Income (UBI)

1. **UBI** is income from a business that is (1) **regularly carried on**, and (2) is **unrelated** to the organization's exempt purpose. A business is substantially related only if the activity (not its proceeds) contributes importantly to the accomplishment of the exempt purposes of the organization.
2. Income derived from debt-financed property unrelated to the exempt function of the organization is included in UBI. The amount of such income to be included in UBI is based on the proportion of average acquisition indebtedness to the property's average adjusted basis.
3. Income from commercial product advertising in journals and other publications is generally UBI.
4. Activities specifically treated as resulting in **related income** (not UBI) include

   a. An activity where substantially all work is performed without compensation (e.g., a church runs a second-hand clothing store with all work performed by volunteers).
   b. A trade or business carried on for the convenience of students or members of a charitable, religious, or scientific organization (e.g., university bookstore).
   c. The sale of merchandise received as gifts or contributions.
   d. Income from dividends, interest, annuities, and royalties. However, such income will be included in UBI if it results from debt-financed investments.
   e. Income derived from renting real property. However, income derived from renting personal property is considered UBI unless the personal property is leased with the real property and personal property rents do not exceed 10% of total rents.
   f. Conducting bingo games if the games are not in violation of any state or local law, and are conducted in a jurisdiction that ordinarily confines bingo games to exempt organizations.

5. UBI is **taxed to the extent in excess of $1,000**. UBI is taxed at regular corporate rates if the organization is a corporation, taxed at rates applicable to trusts if the organization is a trust.

V. INCOME TAX RETURN PREPARERS

A. Preparer—an individual who prepares for compensation, or who employs one or more persons to prepare for compensation, an income tax return, or a substantial portion of return.

1. Preparer need **not** be enrolled to practice before the Internal Revenue Service.
2. Compensation—must be received and can be implied or explicit (e.g., a person who does neighbor's return and receives a gift has not been compensated. Accountant who prepares individual return of the president of a company, for which he performs the audit, for no additional fee as part of a prior agreement **has** been compensated [implied])

B. AICPA Statement on Standards for Tax Services

1. **Tax Return Positions**

   a. With respect to tax return positions, a CPA

      (1) Should not recommend a position unless there is a **realistic possibility of it being sustained** administratively or judicially on its merits if challenged.

(2) Should not prepare or sign a tax return if the CPA knows the return takes a position that the CPA could not recommend under a. above.

(3) Notwithstanding a. and b., a CPA may recommend a position that is not frivolous so long as the position is adequately disclosed on the return or claim for refund. A frivolous position is one which is knowingly advanced in bad faith and is patently improper (e.g., a return position that is contrary to a clear, unambiguous statute).

(4) Should advise the client of the potential penalty consequences of any recommended tax position.

b. A CPA should not recommend a tax position that exploits the IRS audit process, or serves as a mere arguing position advanced solely to obtain leverage in bargaining with the IRS.

c. A CPA has both the right and the responsibility to be an advocate for the client.

2. **Realistic Possibility Standard**

a. The CPA should consider the weight of each authority (e.g., Code, Regs., court decisions, well-reasoned treaties, article in professional tax publications, etc.) in determining whether this standard is met, and may rely on well-reasoned treatises and articles in recognized professional tax publications.

b. Realistic possibility of success may require as much as a **one-third likelihood** of success.

c. The realistic possibility standard is less stringent than the "more likely than not" and "substantial authority" standards, but is more strict than the "reasonable basis" standard.

3. **Answers to Questions on Returns**

a. A CPA should make a reasonable effort to obtain from the client and provide appropriate answers to all questions on a tax return before signing as preparer.

b. When reasonable grounds for omitting an answer exist, the CPA is not required to provide an explanation on the return of the reason for omission. Reasonable grounds for omitting an answer include

(1) Information is not readily available and the answer is not significant in terms of taxable income or tax liability.

(2) Uncertainty as to meaning of question.

(3) Answer is voluminous and return states that data will be supplied upon examination.

4. **Procedural Aspects of Preparing Returns**

a. A CPA may in good faith rely without verification upon information furnished by the client or by third parties, and is not required to audit, examine, or review books, records, or documents in order to independently verify the taxpayer's information.

(1) However, the CPA should not ignore implications of information furnished and should make reasonable inquires if information appears incorrect, incomplete, or inconsistent.

(2) When feasible, the CPA should refer to the client's past returns.

b. Where the IRS imposes a condition for deductibility or other treatment of an item (e.g., requires supporting documentation), the CPA should make appropriate inquiries to determine whether the condition for deductibility has been met.

c. When preparing a tax return, a CPA should consider information known from the tax return of another client if that information is relevant to the return being prepared, and such consideration does not violate any rule regarding confidentiality.

5. **Use of Estimates**

a. Where data is missing (e.g., result of a fire, computer failure), estimates of the missing data may be made by the client.

b. A CPA may prepare a tax return using estimates if it is impracticable to obtain exact data, and the estimated amounts are reasonable.

c. An estimate should not imply greater accuracy than actually exists (e.g., estimate $1,000 rather than $999.32).

6. **Departure from Position Previously Concluded in an IRS Proceeding or Court Decision**

   a. Unless the taxpayer is bound to a specified treatment in the later year, such as by a formal closing agreement, the treatment of an item as part of concluding an IRS proceeding or as part of a court decision in a prior year, does not restrict the CPA from recommending a different tax treatment in a later year's return.

   b. Court decisions, rulings, or other authorities more favorable to the taxpayer's current position may have developed since the prior proceeding was concluded or the prior court decision was rendered.

7. **Knowledge of Error: Return Preparation**

   a. The term "error" as used here includes any position, omission, or method of accounting that, at the time the return is filed, fails to meet the standards as outlined in 1. and 2. above. An error does not include an item that has an insignificant effect on the client's tax liability.

   b. A CPA should inform a client promptly upon becoming aware of a material error in a previously filed return or upon becoming aware of a client's failure to file a required return. A CPA

   (1) Should recommend (either orally or in writing) measures to be taken.
   (2) Is not obligated to inform the IRS of the error, and may not do so without the client's permission, except where required by law.

   c. If the CPA is requested to prepare the client's current return, and the client has not taken appropriate action to correct an error in a prior year's return, the CPA should consider whether to continue a professional relationship with the client or withdraw.

8. **Knowledge of Error: Administrative Proceedings**

   a. When a CPA is representing a client in an IRS proceeding (e.g., examination, appellate conference) with respect to a return that contains an error of which the CPA has become aware, the CPA should promptly inform the client and recommend measures to be taken.

   b. The CPA should request the client's permission to disclose the error to the IRS, and lacking such permission, should consider whether to withdraw from representing the client.

9. **Form and Content of Advice to Clients**

   a. No standard format is required in communicating written or oral advice to a client.

   b. Written, rather than oral, communications are recommended for important, unusual, or complicated transactions.

   c. A CPA may choose to communicate with a client when subsequent developments affect previous advice. Such communication is only required when the CPA undertakes this obligation by specific agreement with the client.

C. Preparer Penalties

1. If (1) any part of an understatement of liability with respect to a return or refund claim is due to a position that has no **realistic possibility of success**, (2) the return preparer knew (or reasonably should have known) of that position, and (3) that position was not disclosed or was frivolous, then the preparer is subject to a $250 penalty unless there is reasonable cause for the understatement and the preparer acted in good faith.

   a. Realistic possibility of success may require as much as a one-third likelihood of success.
   b. A frivolous position is one that is knowingly advanced in bad faith and is patently improper.

2. If any part of an understatement of liability with respect to a return or refund claim is due (1) to a willful attempt to understate tax liability by a return preparer with respect to the return or claim, or (2) to any reckless or intentional disregard of rules or regulations, the preparer is subject to a penalty of $1,000.

   a. The $1,000 penalty is reduced by the penalty paid in 1. above.
   b. Rules and regulations include the Internal Revenue Code, Treasury Regulations, and Revenue Rulings.

3. Additional penalties may be imposed on preparers if they fail to fulfill the following requirements (unless failure is due to reasonable cause):

   a. Preparer must sign returns done for compensation.
   b. Preparer must provide a copy of the return or refund claim to the taxpayer no later than when the preparer presents a copy of the return to the taxpayer for signing.
   c. Returns and claims for refund must contain the social security number of preparer and identification number of preparer's employer or partnership (if any).
   d. Preparer must either keep a list of those for whom returns were filed with specified information, or copies of the actual returns, for three years.
   e. Employers of return preparers must retain a listing of return preparers and place of employment for three years.
   f. Preparer must not endorse or negotiate a refund check issued to a taxpayer.
   g. Preparer must not disclose information furnished in connection with the preparation of a tax return, unless for quality or peer review, or under an administrative order by a regulatory agency.

MULTIPLE-CHOICE QUESTIONS (1-82)

1. Steve and Kay Briar, US citizens, were married for the entire 2003 calendar year. In 2003, Steve gave a $30,000 cash gift to his sister. The Briars made no other gifts in 2003. They each signed a timely election to treat the $30,000 gift as made one-half by each spouse. Disregarding the unified credit and estate tax consequences, what amount of the 2003 gift is taxable to the Briars?

   a. $20,000
   b. $10,000
   c. $8,000
   d. $0

2. In 2003, Sayers, who is single, gave an outright gift of $50,000 to a friend, Johnson, who needed the money to pay medical expenses. In filing the 2003 gift tax return, Sayers was entitled to a maximum exclusion of

   a. $0
   b. $10,000
   c. $11,000
   d. $50,000

3. During 2003, Blake transferred a corporate bond with a face amount and fair market value of $20,000 to a trust for the benefit of her sixteen-year old child. Annual interest on this bond is $2,000, which is to be accumulated in the trust and distributed to the child on reaching the age of twenty-one. The bond is then to be distributed to the donor or her successor-in-interest in liquidation of the trust. Present value of the total interest to be received by the child is $8,710. The amount of the gift that is excludable from taxable gifts is

   a. $20,000
   b. $11,000
   c. $8,710
   d. $0

4. Under the unified rate schedule for 2003,

   a. Lifetime taxable gifts are taxed on a noncumulative basis.
   b. Transfers at death are taxed on a noncumulative basis.
   c. Lifetime taxable gifts and transfers at death are taxed on a cumulative basis.
   d. The gift tax rates are 5% higher than the estate tax rates.

5. Which of the following requires filing a gift tax return, if the transfer exceeds the available annual gift tax exclusion?

   a. Medical expenses paid directly to a physician on behalf of an individual unrelated to the donor.
   b. Tuition paid directly to an accredited university on behalf of an individual unrelated to the donor.
   c. Payments for college books, supplies, and dormitory fees on behalf of an individual unrelated to the donor.
   d. Campaign expenses paid to a political organization.

6. On July 1, 2003, Vega made a transfer by gift in an amount sufficient to require the filing of a gift tax return. Vega was still alive in 2004. If Vega did **not** request an extension of time for filing the 2003 gift tax return, the due date for filing was

   a. March 15, 2004.
   b. April 15, 2004.
   c. June 15, 2004.
   d. June 30, 2004.

7. Jan, an unmarried individual, gave the following outright gifts in 2003:

Donee	Amount	Use by donee
Jones	$15,000	Down payment on house
Craig	12,000	College tuition
Kande	5,000	Vacation trip

Jan's 2003 exclusions for gift tax purposes should total

   a. $27,000
   b. $25,000
   c. $22,000
   d. $ 9,000

8. When Jim and Nina became engaged in April 2003, Jim gave Nina a ring that had a fair market value of $50,000. After their wedding in July 2003, Jim gave Nina $75,000 in cash so that Nina could have her own bank account. Both Jim and Nina are US citizens. What was the amount of Jim's 2003 marital deduction?

   a. $ 64,000
   b. $ 75,000
   c. $114,000
   d. $125,000

9. Raff created a joint bank account for himself and his friend's son, Dave. There is a gift to Dave when

   a. Raff creates the account.
   b. Raff dies.
   c. Dave draws on the account for his own benefit.
   d. Dave is notified by Raff that the account has been created.

10. Fred and Ethel (brother and sister), residents of a non-community property state, own unimproved land that they hold in joint tenancy with rights of survivorship. The land cost $100,000 of which Ethel paid $80,000 and Fred paid $20,000. Ethel died during 2003 when the land was worth $300,000, and $240,000 was included in Ethel's gross estate. What is Fred's basis for the property after Ethel's death?

   a. $140,000
   b. $240,000
   c. $260,000
   d. $300,000

11. Bell, a cash-basis calendar-year taxpayer, died on June 1, 2003. In 2003, prior to her death, Bell incurred $2,000 in medical expenses. The executor of the estate paid the medical expenses, which were a claim against the estate, on July 1, 2003. If the executor files the appropriate waiver, the medical expenses are deductible on

   a. The estate tax return.
   b. Bell's final income tax return.
   c. The estate income tax return.
   d. The executor's income tax return.

12. If the executor of a decedent's estate elects the alternate valuation date and none of the property included in the gross estate has been sold or distributed, the estate assets must be valued as of how many months after the decedent's death?

   a. 12
   b. 9

c.   6

d.   3

13. What amount of a decedent's taxable estate is effectively tax-free if the maximum unified estate and gift credit is taken during 2003?

   a. $ 625,000

   b. $ 650,000

   c. $ 675,000

   d. $1,000,000

14. Which of the following credits may be offset against the gross estate tax to determine the net estate tax of a US citizen dying during 2003?

	Unified credit	Credit for gift taxes paid on gifts made after 1976
a.	Yes	Yes
b.	No	No
c.	No	Yes
d.	Yes	No

15. Fred and Amy Kehl, both US citizens, are married. All of their real and personal property is owned by them as tenants by the entirety or as joint tenants with right of survivorship. The gross estate of the first spouse to die

   a.   Includes 50% of the value of all property owned by the couple, regardless of which spouse furnished the original consideration.

   b.   Includes only the property that had been acquired with the funds of the deceased spouse.

   c.   Is governed by the federal statutory provisions relating to jointly held property, rather than by the decedent's interest in community property vested by state law, if the Kehls reside in a community property state.

   d.   Includes one-third of the value of all real estate owned by the Kehls, as the dower right in the case of the wife or curtesy right in the case of the husband.

16. In connection with a "buy-sell" agreement funded by a cross-purchase insurance arrangement, business associate Adam bought a policy on Burr's life to finance the purchase of Burr's interest. Adam, the beneficiary, paid the premiums and retained all incidents of ownership. On the death of Burr, the insurance proceeds will be

   a.   Includible in Burr's gross estate, if Burr owns 50% or more of the stock of the corporation.

   b.   Includible in Burr's gross estate only if Burr had purchased a similar policy on Adam's life at the same time and for the same purpose.

   c.   Includible in Burr's gross estate, if Adam has the right to veto Burr's power to borrow on the policy that Burr owns on Adam's life.

   d.   Excludible from Burr's gross estate.

17. Following are the fair market values of Wald's assets at the date of death:

Personal effects and jewelry	$150,000
Land bought by Wald with Wald's funds five years prior to death and held with Wald's sister as joint tenants with right of survivorship	800,000

The executor of Wald's estate did not elect the alternate valuation date. The amount includible as Wald's gross estate in the federal estate tax return is

   a. $150,000

b. $550,000

c. $800,000

d. $950,000

18. Which one of the following is a valid deduction from a decedent's gross estate?

   a.   State inheritance taxes.

   b.   Income tax paid on income earned and received after the decedent's death.

   c.   Federal estate taxes.

   d.   Unpaid income taxes on income received by the decedent before death.

19. Eng and Lew, both US citizens, died in 2003. Eng made taxable lifetime gifts of $100,000 that are **not** included in Eng's gross estate. Lew made no lifetime gifts. At the dates of death, Eng's gross estate was $850,000, and Lew's gross estate was $950,000. A federal estate tax return must be filed for

	Eng	Lew
a.	No	No
b.	No	Yes
c.	Yes	No
d.	Yes	Yes

20. With regard to the federal estate tax, the alternate valuation date

   a.   Is required to be used if the fair market value of the estate's assets has increased since the decedent's date of death.

   b.   If elected on the first return filed for the estate, may be revoked in an amended return provided that the first return was filed on time.

   c.   Must be used for valuation of the estate's liabilities if such date is used for valuation of the estate's assets.

   d.   Can be elected only if its use decreases both the value of the gross estate and the estate tax liability.

21. Proceeds of a life insurance policy payable to the estate's executor, as the estate's representative, are

   a.   Includible in the decedent's gross estate only if the premiums had been paid by the insured.

   b.   Includible in the decedent's gross estate only if the policy was taken out within three years of the insured's death under the "contemplation of death" rule.

   c.   Always includible in the decedent's gross estate.

   d.   Never includible in the decedent's gross estate.

22. Ross, a calendar-year, cash-basis taxpayer who died in June 2003, was entitled to receive a $10,000 accounting fee that had not been collected before the date of death. The executor of Ross' estate collected the full $10,000 in July 2003. This $10,000 should appear in

   a.   Only the decedent's final individual income tax return.

   b.   Only the estate's fiduciary income tax return.

   c.   Only the estate tax return.

   d.   Both the fiduciary income tax return and the estate tax return.

Items 23 and 24 are based on the following data:

Alan Curtis, a US citizen, died on March 1, 2003, leaving an adjusted gross estate with a fair market value of $1,400,000 at the date of death. Under the terms of Alan's will, $375,000 was bequeathed outright to his widow, free of all estate and inheritance taxes. The remainder of Alan's estate was left to his mother. Alan made no taxable gifts during his lifetime.

23. Disregarding extensions of time for filing, within how many months after the date of Alan's death is the federal estate tax return due?

    a.   2 1/2
    b.   3 1/2
    c.   9
    d.   12

24. In computing the taxable estate, the executor of Alan's estate should claim a marital deduction of

    a. $ 250,000
    b. $ 375,000
    c. $ 700,000
    d. $1,025,000

25. In 1998, Edwin Ryan bought 100 shares of a listed stock for $5,000. In June 2003, when the stock's fair market value was $7,000, Edwin gave this stock to his sister, Lynn. No gift tax was paid. Lynn died in October 2003, bequeathing this stock to Edwin, when the stock's fair market value was $9,000. Lynn's executor did not elect the alternate valuation. What is Edwin's basis for this stock after he inherits it from Lynn's estate?

    a. $0
    b. $5,000
    c. $7,000
    d. $9,000

26. The generation-skipping transfer tax is imposed

    a.   Instead of the gift tax.
    b.   Instead of the estate tax.
    c.   At the highest tax rate under the unified transfer tax rate schedule.
    d.   When an individual makes a gift to a grandparent.

27. Under the terms of the will of Melvin Crane, $10,000 a year is to be paid to his widow and $5,000 a year is to be paid to his daughter out of the estate's income during the period of estate administration. No charitable contributions are made by the estate. During 2003, the estate made the required distributions to Crane's widow and daughter and for the entire year the estate's distributable net income was $12,000. What amount of the $10,000 distribution received from the estate must Crane's widow include in her gross income for 2003?

    a. $0
    b. $ 4,000
    c. $ 8,000
    d. $10,000

Items 28 and 29 are based on the following:

Lyon, a cash-basis taxpayer, died on January 15, 2003. In 2003, the estate executor made the required periodic distribution of $9,000 from estate income to Lyon's sole heir. The following pertains to the estate's income and disbursements in 2003:

2003 Estate Income
  $20,000   Taxable interest
    10,000   Net long-term capital gains allocable to corpus

2003 Estate Disbursements
   $5,000   Administrative expenses attributable to taxable income

28. For the 2003 calendar year, what was the estate's distributable net income (DNI)?

    a. $15,000
    b. $20,000
    c. $25,000
    d. $30,000

29. Lyon's executor does not intend to file an extension request for the estate fiduciary income tax return. By what date must the executor file the Form 1041, US Fiduciary Income Tax Return, for the estate's 2003 calendar year?

    a.   March 15, 2004.
    b.   April 15, 2004.
    c.   June 15, 2004.
    d.   September 15, 2004.

30. A distribution from estate income, that was **currently** required, was made to the estate's sole beneficiary during its calendar year. The maximum amount of the distribution to be included in the beneficiary's gross income is limited to the estate's

    a.   Capital gain income.
    b.   Ordinary gross income.
    c.   Distributable net income.
    d.   Net investment income.

31. A distribution to an estate's sole beneficiary for the 2003 calendar year equaled $15,000, the amount currently required to be distributed by the will. The estate's 2003 records were as follows:

Estate income
$40,000   Taxable interest

Estate disbursements
$34,000   Expenses attributable to taxable interest

What amount of the distribution was taxable to the beneficiary?

    a. $40,000
    b. $15,000
    c. $ 6,000
    d. $0

32. With regard to estimated income tax, estates

    a.   Must make quarterly estimated tax payments starting no later than the second quarter following the one in which the estate was established.
    b.   Are exempt from paying estimated tax during the estate's first two taxable years.
    c.   Must make quarterly estimated tax payments only if the estate's income is required to be distributed currently.
    d.   Are not required to make payments of estimated tax.

33. A complex trust is a trust that

    a.   Must distribute income currently, but is prohibited from distributing principal during the taxable year.
    b.   Invests only in corporate securities and is prohibited from engaging in short-term transactions.
    c.   Permits accumulation of current income, provides for charitable contributions, or distributes principal during the taxable year.
    d.   Is exempt from payment of income tax since the tax is paid by the beneficiaries.

34. The 2003 standard deduction for a trust or an estate in the fiduciary income tax return is

a. $0
b. $650
c. $750
d. $800

35. Which of the following fiduciary entities are required to use the calendar year as their taxable period for income tax purposes?

	Estates	Trusts (except those that are tax exempt)
a.	Yes	Yes
b.	No	No
c.	Yes	No
d.	No	Yes

36. Ordinary and necessary administration expenses paid by the fiduciary of an estate are deductible
a. Only on the fiduciary income tax return (Form 1041) and never on the federal estate tax return (Form 706).
b. Only on the federal estate tax return and never on the fiduciary income tax return.
c. On the fiduciary income tax return only if the estate tax deduction is waived for these expenses.
d. On both the fiduciary income tax return and on the estate tax return by adding a tax computed on the proportionate rates attributable to both returns.

37. An executor of a decedent's estate that has only US citizens as beneficiaries is required to file a fiduciary income tax return, if the estate's gross income for the year is at least
a. $ 400
b. $ 500
c. $ 600
d. $1,000

38. The charitable contribution deduction on an estate's fiduciary income tax return is allowable
a. If the decedent died intestate.
b. To the extent of the same adjusted gross income limitation as that on an individual income tax return.
c. Only if the decedent's will specifically provides for the contribution.
d. Subject to the 2% threshold on miscellaneous itemized deductions.

39. On January 1, 2003, Carlt created a $300,000 trust that provided his mother with a lifetime income interest starting on January 1, 2003, with the remainder interest to go to his son. Carlt expressly retained the power to revoke both the income interest and the remainder interest at any time. Who will be taxed on the trust's 2003 income?
a. Carlt's mother.
b. Carlt's son.
c. Carlt.
d. The trust.

40. Astor, a cash-basis taxpayer, died on February 3. During the year, the estate's executor made a distribution of $12,000 from estate income to Astor's sole heir and adopted a calendar year to determine the estate's taxable income. The following additional information pertains to the estate's income and disbursements for the year:

Estate income

| Taxable interest | $65,000 |
| Net long-term capital gains allocable to corpus | 5,000 |

Estate disbursements

| Administrative expenses attributable to taxable income | 14,000 |
| Charitable contributions from gross income to a public charity, made under the terms of the will | 9,000 |

For the calendar year, what was the estate's distributable net income (DNI)?
a. $39,000
b. $42,000
c. $58,000
d. $65,000

41. For income tax purposes, the estate's initial taxable period for a decedent who died on October 24
a. May be either a calendar year, or a fiscal year beginning on the date of the decedent's death.
b. Must be a fiscal year beginning on the date of the decedent's death.
c. May be either a calendar year, or a fiscal year beginning on October 1 of the year of the decedent's death.
d. Must be a calendar year beginning on January 1 of the year of the decedent's death.

42. The private foundation status of an exempt organization will terminate if it
a. Becomes a public charity.
b. Is a foreign corporation.
c. Does **not** distribute all of its net assets to one or more public charities.
d. Is governed by a charter that limits the organization's exempt purposes.

43. Which of the following exempt organizations must file annual information returns?
a. Churches.
b. Internally supported auxiliaries of churches.
c. Private foundations.
d. Those with gross receipts of less than $5,000 in each taxable year.

44. To qualify as an exempt organization other than a church or an employees' qualified pension or profit-sharing trust, the applicant
a. Cannot operate under the "lodge system" under which payments are made to its members for sick benefits.
b. Need **not** be specifically identified as one of the classes on which exemption is conferred by the Internal Revenue Code, provided that the organization's purposes and activities are of a nonprofit nature.
c. Is barred from incorporating and issuing capital stock.
d. Must file a written application with the Internal Revenue Service.

45. To qualify as an exempt organization, the applicant
a. May be organized and operated for the primary purpose of carrying on a business for profit, provided that all of the organization's net earnings are turned over to one or more tax exempt organizations.

b.   Need **not** be specifically identified as one of the classes upon which exemption is conferred by the Internal Revenue Code, provided that the organization's purposes and activities are of a nonprofit nature.

c.   Must **not** be classified as a social club.

d.   Must **not** be a private foundation organized and operated exclusively to influence legislation pertaining to protection of the environment.

46. Carita Fund, organized and operated exclusively for charitable purposes, provides insurance coverage, at amounts substantially below cost, to exempt organizations involved in the prevention of cruelty to children. Carita's insurance activities are

a.   Exempt from tax.

b.   Treated as unrelated business income.

c.   Subject to the same tax provisions as those applicable to insurance companies.

d.   Considered "commercial-type" as defined by the Internal Revenue Code.

47. The filing of a return covering unrelated business income

a.   Is required of all exempt organizations having at least $1,000 of unrelated business taxable income for the year.

b.   Relieves the organization of having to file a separate annual information return.

c.   Is **not** necessary if all of the organization's income is used exclusively for charitable purposes.

d.   Must be accompanied by a minimum payment of 50% of the tax due as shown on the return, with the balance of tax payable six months later.

48. A condominium management association wishing to be treated as a homeowners association and to qualify as an exempt organization for a particular year

a.   Need **not** file a formal election.

b.   Must file an election as of the date the association was organized.

c.   Must file an election at the beginning of the association's first taxable year.

d.   Must file a separate election for each taxable year no later than the due date of the return for which the election is to apply.

49. An organization wishing to qualify as an exempt organization

a.   Is prohibited from issuing capital stock.

b.   Is limited to three prohibited transactions a year.

c.   Must **not** have non-US citizens on its governing board.

d.   Must be of a type specifically identified as one of the classes on which exemption is conferred by the Code.

50. Which one of the following statements is correct with regard to exempt organizations?

a.   An organization is automatically exempt from tax merely by meeting the statutory requirements for exemptions.

b.   Exempt organizations that are required to file annual information returns must disclose the identity of all substantial contributors, in addition to the amount of contributions received.

c.   An organization will automatically forfeit its exempt status if any executive or other employee of the organization is paid compensation in excess of $150,000 per year, even if such compensation is reasonable.

d.   Exempt status of an organization may **not** be retroactively revoked.

51. To qualify as an exempt organization, the applicant

a.   Must fall into one of the specific classes upon which exemption is conferred by the Internal Revenue Code.

b.   **Cannot**, under any circumstances, be a foreign corporation.

c.   **Cannot**, under any circumstances, engage in lobbying activities.

d.   **Cannot** be exclusively a social club.

52. To qualify as an exempt organization,

a.   A written application need **not** be filed if no applicable official form is provided.

b.   No employee of the organization is permitted to receive compensation in excess of $100,000 per year.

c.   The applicant must be of a type specifically identified as one of the classes upon which exemption is conferred by the Code.

d.   The organization is prohibited from issuing capital stock.

53. Hope is a tax-exempt religious organization. Which of the following activities is(are) consistent with Hope's tax-exempt status?

I.   Conducting weekend retreats for business organizations.

II.   Providing traditional burial services that maintain the religious beliefs of its members.

a.   I only.

b.   II only.

c.   Both I and II.

d.   Neither I nor II.

54. The organizational test to qualify a public service charitable entity as tax-exempt requires the articles of organization to

I. Limit the purpose of the entity to the charitable purpose.

II. State that an information return should be filed annually with the Internal Revenue Service.

a.   I only.

b.   II only.

c.   Both I and II.

d.   Neither I nor II.

55. Which of the following activities regularly conducted by a tax-exempt organization will result in unrelated business income?

I. Selling articles made by handicapped persons as part of their rehabilitation, when the organization is involved exclusively in their rehabilitation.

II. Operating a grocery store almost fully staffed by emotionally handicapped persons as part of a therapeutic program.

a.   I only.

b.   II only.

c. Both I and II.

d. Neither I nor II.

56. An organization that operates for the prevention of cruelty to animals will fail to meet the operational test to qualify as an exempt organization if

	The organization engages in insubstantial nonexempt activities	*The organization directly participates in any political campaign*
a.	Yes	Yes
b.	Yes	No
c.	No	Yes
d.	No	No

57. Which one of the following statements is correct with regard to unrelated business income of an exempt organization?

a. An exempt organization that earns any unrelated business income in excess of $100,000 during a particular year will lose its exempt status for that particular year.

b. An exempt organization is not taxed on unrelated business income of less than $1,000.

c. The tax on unrelated business income can be imposed even if the unrelated business activity is intermittent and is carried on once a year.

d. An unrelated trade or business activity that results in a loss is excluded from the definition of unrelated business.

58. Which of the following activities regularly carried out by an exempt organization will **not** result in unrelated business income?

a. The sale of laundry services by an exempt hospital to other hospitals.

b. The sale of heavy-duty appliances to senior citizens by an exempt senior citizen's center.

c. Accounting and tax services performed by a local chapter of a labor union for its members.

d. The sale by a trade association of publications used as course materials for the association's seminars that are oriented towards its members.

59. If an exempt organization is a corporation, the tax on unrelated business taxable income is

a. Computed at corporate income tax rates.

b. Computed at rates applicable to trusts.

c. Credited against the tax on recognized capital gains.

d. Abated.

60. During 2003, Help, Inc., an exempt organization, derived income of $15,000 from conducting bingo games. Conducting bingo games is legal in Help's locality and is confined to exempt organizations in Help's state. Which of the following statements is true regarding this income?

a. The entire $15,000 is subject to tax at a lower rate than the corporation income tax rate.

b. The entire $15,000 is exempt from tax on unrelated business income.

c. Only the first $5,000 is exempt from tax on unrelated business income.

d. Since Help has unrelated business income, Help automatically forfeits its exempt status for 2003.

61. Which of the following statements is correct regarding the unrelated business income of exempt organizations?

a. If an exempt organization has any unrelated business income, it may result in the loss of the organization's exempt status.

b. Unrelated business income relates to the performance of services, but **not** to the sale of goods.

c. An unrelated business does **not** include any activity where all the work is performed for the organization by unpaid volunteers.

d. Unrelated business income tax will **not** be imposed if profits from the unrelated business are used to support the exempt organization's charitable activities.

62. An incorporated exempt organization subject to tax on its 2003 unrelated business income

a. Must make estimated tax payments if its tax can reasonably be expected to be $100 or more.

b. Must comply with the Code provisions regarding installment payments of estimated income tax by corporations.

c. Must pay at least 70% of the tax due as shown on the return when filed, with the balance of tax payable in the following quarter.

d. May defer payment of the tax for up to nine months following the due date of the return.

63. If an exempt organization is a charitable trust, then unrelated business income is

a. Not subject to tax.

b. Taxed at rates applicable to corporations.

c. Subject to tax even if such income is less than $1,000.

d. Subject to tax only for the amount of such income in excess of $1,000.

64. With regard to unrelated business income of an exempt organization, which one of the following statements is true?

a. If an exempt organization has any unrelated business income, such organization automatically forfeits its exempt status for the particular year in which such income was earned.

b. When an unrelated trade or business activity results in a loss, such activity is excluded from the definition of unrelated business.

c. If an exempt organization derives income from conducting bingo games, in a locality where such activity is legal, and in a state that confines such activity to nonprofit organizations, then such income is exempt from the tax on unrelated business income.

d. Dividends and interest earned by all exempt organizations always are excluded from the definition of unrelated business income.

65. Which of the following acts constitute(s) grounds for a tax preparer penalty?

I. Without the taxpayer's consent, the tax preparer disclosed taxpayer income tax return information under an order from a state court.

II. At the taxpayer's suggestion, the tax preparer deducted the expenses of the taxpayers' personal domestic help as a business expense on the taxpayer's individual tax return.

a. I only.
b. II only.
c. Both I and II.
d. Neither I nor II.

66. Vee Corp. retained Water, CPA, to prepare its 2003 income tax return. During the engagement, Water discovered that Vee had failed to file its 1998 income tax return. What is Water's professional responsibility regarding Vee's unfiled 1998 income tax return?

a. Prepare Vee's 1998 income tax return and submit it to the IRS.
b. Advise Vee that the 1998 income tax return has not been filed and recommend that Vee ignore filing its 1998 return since the statute of limitations has passed.
c. Advise the IRS that Vee's 1998 income tax return has not been filed.
d. Consider withdrawing from preparation of Vee's 2003 income tax return until the error is corrected.

67. To avoid tax return preparer penalties for a return's understated tax liability due to an intentional disregard of the regulations, which of the following actions must a tax preparer take?

a. Audit the taxpayer's corresponding business operations.
b. Review the accuracy of the taxpayer's books and records.
c. Make reasonable inquiries if the taxpayer's information is incomplete.
d. Examine the taxpayer's supporting documents.

68. Kopel was engaged to prepare Raff's 2003 federal income tax return. During the tax preparation interview, Raff told Kopel that he paid $3,000 in property taxes in 2003. Actually, Raff's property taxes amounted to only $600. Based on Raff's word, Kopel deducted the $3,000 on Raff's return, resulting in an understatement of Raff's tax liability. Kopel had no reason to believe that the information was incorrect. Kopel did not request underlying documentation and was reasonably satisfied by Raff's representation that Raff had adequate records to support the deduction. Which of the following statements is correct?

a. To avoid the preparer penalty for willful understatement of tax liability, Kopel was obligated to examine the underlying documentation for the deduction.
b. To avoid the preparer penalty for willful understatement of tax liability, Kopel would be required to obtain Raff's representation in writing.
c. Kopel is **not** subject to the preparer penalty for willful understatement of tax liability because the deduction that was claimed was more than 25% of the actual amount that should have been deducted.
d. Kopel is **not** subject to the preparer penalty for willful understatement of tax liability because Kopel was justified in relying on Raff's representation.

69. A penalty for understated corporate tax liability can be imposed on a tax preparer who fails to

a. Audit the corporate records.
b. Examine business operations.
c. Copy all underlying documents.

d. Make reasonable inquiries when taxpayer information appears incorrect.

70. A tax return preparer is subject to a penalty for knowingly or recklessly disclosing corporate tax return information, if the disclosure is made

a. To enable a third party to solicit business from the taxpayer.
b. To enable the tax processor to electronically compute the taxpayer's liability.
c. For peer review.
d. Under an administrative order by a state agency that registers tax return preparers.

71. A tax return preparer may disclose or use tax return information without the taxpayer's consent to

a. Facilitate a supplier's or lender's credit evaluation of the taxpayer.
b. Accommodate the request of a financial institution that needs to determine the amount of taxpayer's debt to it, to be forgiven.
c. Be evaluated by a quality or peer review.
d. Solicit additional nontax business.

72. Which, if any, of the following could result in penalties against an income tax return preparer?

I. Knowing or reckless disclosure or use of tax information obtained in preparing a return.
II. A willful attempt to understate any client's tax liability on a return or claim for refund.

a. Neither I nor II.
b. I only.
c. II only.
d. Both I and II.

73. Clark, a professional tax return preparer, prepared and signed a client's 2003 federal income tax return that resulted in a $600 refund. Which one of the following statements is correct with regard to an Internal Revenue Code penalty Clark may be subject to for endorsing and cashing the client's refund check?

a. Clark will be subject to the penalty if Clark endorses and cashes the check.
b. Clark may endorse and cash the check, without penalty, if Clark is enrolled to practice before the Internal Revenue Service.
c. Clark may endorse and cash the check, without penalty, because the check is for less than $500.
d. Clark may endorse and cash the check, without penalty, if the amount does **not** exceed Clark's fee for preparation of the return.

74. A CPA who prepares clients' federal income tax returns for a fee must

a. File certain required notices and powers of attorney with the IRS before preparing any returns.
b. Keep a completed copy of each return for a specified period of time.
c. Receive client documentation supporting all travel and entertainment expenses deducted on the return.
d. Indicate the CPA's federal identification number on a tax return only if the return reflects tax due from the taxpayer.

75. A CPA owes a duty to

a. Provide for a successor CPA in the event death or disability prevents completion of an audit.

b.   Advise a client of errors contained in a previously filed tax return.

c.   Disclose client fraud to third parties.

d.   Perform an audit according to GAAP so that fraud will be uncovered.

76. In general, if the IRS issues a thirty-day letter to an individual taxpayer who wishes to dispute the assessment, the taxpayer

a.   May, without paying any tax, immediately file a petition that would properly commence an action in Tax Court.

b.   May ignore the thirty-day letter and wait to receive a ninety-day letter.

c.   Must file a written protest within ten days of receiving the letter.

d.   Must pay the taxes and then commence an action in federal district court.

77. A CPA will be liable to a tax client for damages resulting from all of the following actions **except**

a.   Failing to timely file a client's return.

b.   Failing to advise a client of certain tax elections.

c.   Refusing to sign a client's request for a filing extension.

d.   Neglecting to evaluate the option of preparing joint or separate returns that would have resulted in a substantial tax savings for a married client.

78. According to the profession's standards, which of the following statements is correct regarding the standards a CPA should follow when recommending tax return positions and preparing tax returns?

a.   A CPA may recommend a position that the CPA concludes is frivolous as long as the position is adequately disclosed on the return.

b.   A CPA may recommend a position in which the CPA has a good faith belief that the position has a realistic possibility of being sustained if challenged.

c.   A CPA will usually **not** advise the client of the potential penalty consequences of the recommended tax return position.

d.   A CPA may sign a tax return as preparer knowing that the return takes a position that will **not** be sustained if challenged.

79. According to the standards of the profession, which of the following statements is(are) correct regarding the action to be taken by a CPA who discovers an error in a client's previously filed tax return?

 I.   Advise the client of the error and recommend the measures to be taken.

II.   Withdraw from the professional relationship regardless of whether or not the client corrects the error.

a.   I only.

b.   II only.

c.   Both I and II.

d.   Neither I nor II.

80. According to the profession's ethical standards, a CPA preparing a client's tax return may rely on unsupported information furnished by the client, without examining underlying information, unless the information

a.   Is derived from a pass-through entity.

b.   Appears to be incomplete on its face.

c.   Concerns dividends received.

d.   Lists charitable contributions.

81. Which of the following acts by a CPA will **not** result in a CPA incurring an IRS penalty?

a.   Failing, without reasonable cause, to provide the client with a copy of an income tax return.

b.   Failing, without reasonable cause, to sign a client's tax return as preparer.

c.   Understating a client's tax liability as a result of an error in calculation.

d.   Negotiating a client's tax refund check when the CPA prepared the tax return.

82. According to the standards of the profession, which of the following sources of information should a CPA consider before signing a client's tax return?

 I.   Information actually known to the CPA from the tax return of another client.

II.   Information provided by the client that appears to be correct based on the client's returns from prior years.

a.   I only.

b.   II only.

c.   Both I and II.

d.   Neither I nor II.

SIMULATION PROBLEMS

Simulation Problem 1   (10 to 20 minutes)

Situation		
	Type of Gift	Generation Skipping Tax

During 2003, various clients went to Rowe, CPA, for tax advice concerning possible gift tax liability on transfers they made throughout 2003.

	Type of Gift	
Situation		Generation Skipping Tax

Part a.

For each client, indicate whether the transfer of cash, the income interest, or the remainder interest is a gift of a present interest, a gift of a future interest, or not a completed gift.

Answer List

P.   Present Interest

F.   Future Interest

N.   Not Completed

Assume the following facts:

Cobb created a $500,000 trust that provided his mother with an income interest for her life and the remainder interest to go to his sister at the death of his mother. Cobb expressly retained the power to revoke both the income interest and the remainder interest at any time.

Items to be answered

		(P)	(F)	(N)
1.	The income interest at the trust's creation.	○	○	○
2.	The remainder interest at the trust's creation.	○	○	○

Kane created a $100,000 trust that provided her nephew with the income interest until he reached forty-five years of age. When the trust was created, Kane's nephew was twenty-five. The income distribution is to start when Kane's nephew is twenty-nine. After Kane's nephew reaches the age of forty-five, the remainder interest is to go to Kane's niece.

		(P)	(F)	(N)
3.	The income interest.	○	○	○

During 2003, Hall, an unmarried taxpayer, made a $10,000 cash gift to his son in May and a further $12,000 cash gift to him in August.

		(P)	(F)	(N)
4.	The cash transfers.	○	○	○

During 2003, Yeats transferred property worth $20,000 to a trust with the income to be paid to her twenty-two-year-old niece Jane. After Jane reaches the age of thirty, the remainder interest is to be distributed to Yeats' brother. The income interest is valued at $9,700 and the remainder interest at $10,300.

		(P)	(F)	(N)
5.	The income interest.	○	○	○
6.	The remainder interest.	○	○	○

Tom and Ann Curry, US citizens, were married for the entire 2003 calendar year. Tom gave a $40,000 cash gift to his uncle, Grant. The Currys made no other gifts to Grant in 2003. Tom and Ann each signed a timely election stating that each made one-half of the $40,000 gift.

		(P)	(F)	(N)
7.	The cash transfers.	○	○	○

Murry created a $1,000,000 trust that provided his brother with an income interest for ten years, after which the remainder interest passes to Murry's sister. Murry retained the power to revoke the remainder interest at any time. The income interest was valued at $600,000.

		(P)	(F)	(N)
8.	The income interest.	○	○	○
9.	The remainder interest.	○	○	○

Situation	Type of Gift	Generation Skipping Tax

Part b.

For **item 10,** determine whether the transfer is subject to the generation skipping tax, the gift tax, or both taxes. Disregard the use of any exclusions and the unified credit.

Answer List

A.   Generation Skipping Tax

B.   Gift Tax

C.   Both Taxes

(A) (B) (C)

10.   Martin's daughter, Kim, has one child, Dale. During 2003, Martin made an outright $5,000,000 gift to Dale.   ○   ○   ○

Simulation Problem 2   (5 to 10 minutes)

Introduction	
	Preparer's Responsibility

A CPA sole practitioner has tax preparers' responsibilities when preparing tax returns for clients.

	Preparer's Responsibility
Introduction	

Items 1 through 9 each represent an independent factual situation in which a CPA sole practitioner has prepared and signed the taxpayer's income tax return. For each item, select from the following list the correct response regarding the tax preparer's responsibilities. A response may be selected once, more than once, or not at all.

Answer List

P.   The tax preparer's action constitutes an act of tax preparer misconduct subject to the Internal Revenue Code penalty.

E.   The Internal Revenue Service will examine the facts and circumstances to determine whether the reasonable cause exception applies; the good-faith exception applies; or both exceptions apply.

N.   The tax preparer's action does **not** constitute an act of tax preparer misconduct.

		(P)	(E)	(N)
1.	The tax preparer disclosed taxpayer income tax return information under an order from a state court, without the taxpayer's consent.	○	○	○
2.	The tax preparer relied on the advice of an advisory preparer to calculate the taxpayer's tax liability. The tax preparer believed that the advisory preparer was competent and that the advice was reasonable. Based on the advice, the taxpayer had understated income tax liability.	○	○	○
3.	The tax preparer did **not** charge a separate fee for the tax return preparation and paid the taxpayer the refund shown on the tax return less a discount. The tax preparer negotiated the actual refund check for the tax preparer's own account after receiving power of attorney from the taxpayer.	○	○	○
4.	The tax preparer relied on information provided by the taxpayer regarding deductible travel expenses. The tax preparer believed that the taxpayer's information was correct but inquired about the existence of the travel expense records. The tax preparer was satisfied by the taxpayer's representations that the taxpayer had adequate records for the deduction. Based on this information, the income tax liability was understated.	○	○	○
5.	The taxpayer provided the tax preparer with a detailed check register to compute business expenses. The tax preparer knowingly overstated the expenses on the income tax return.	○	○	○
6.	The tax preparer disclosed taxpayer income tax return information during a quality review conducted by CPAs. The tax preparer maintained a record of the review.	○	○	○
7.	The tax preparer relied on incorrect instructions on an IRS tax form that were contrary to the regulations. The tax preparer was **not** aware of the regulations or the IRS announcement pointing out the error. The understatement was immaterial as a result of the isolated error.	○	○	○
8.	The tax preparer used income tax return information without the taxpayer's consent to solicit additional business.	○	○	○
9.	The tax preparer knowingly deducted the expenses of the taxpayer's personal domestic help as wages paid in the taxpayer's business on the taxpayer's income tax return.	○	○	○

Simulation Problem 3   (10 to 20 minutes)

Situation		
	Estate Tax Treatment I	Estate Tax Treatment II

Before his death, Remsen, a US citizen, made cash gifts of $7,000 each to his four sisters. In 2003 Remsen also paid $2,000 in tuition directly to his grandchild's university on the grandchild's behalf. Remsen made no other lifetime transfers. Remsen died on January 9, 2003, and was survived by his wife and only child, both of whom were US citizens. The Remsens did not live in a community property state.

At his death Remsen owned

Cash	$650,000
Marketable securities (fair market value)	900,000
Life insurance policy with Remsen's wife named as the beneficiary (fair market value)	500,000

Under the provisions of Remsen's will, the net cash, after payment of executor's fees and medical and funeral expenses, was bequeathed to Remsen's son. The marketable securities were bequeathed to Remsen's spouse. During 2003 Remsen's estate paid

Executor fees to distribute the decedent's property (deducted on the fiduciary tax return)	$15,000
Decedent's funeral expenses	12,000

The estate's executor extended the time to file the estate tax return.

On December 3, 2003, the estate's executor paid the decedent's outstanding $10,000 medical expenses and filed the extended estate tax return.

	Estate Tax Treatment I	
Situation		Estate Tax Treatment II

Part a.

For **items 1 through 5,** identify the federal estate tax treatment for each item. A response may be selected once, more than once, or not at all.

Answer List

F. Fully includible in Remsen's gross estate.
P. Partially includible in Remsen's gross estate.
N. Not includible in Remsen's gross estate.

	(F)	(P)	(N)
1. What is the estate tax treatment of the $7,000 cash gift to each sister?	○	○	○
2. What is the estate tax treatment of the life insurance proceeds?	○	○	○
3. What is the estate treatment of the marketable securities?	○	○	○
4. What is the estate tax treatment of the $2,000 tuition payment?	○	○	○
5. What is the estate tax treatment of the $650,000 cash?	○	○	○

Situation	Estate Tax Treatment I	Estate Tax Treatment II

Part b.

For **items 6 through 10,** identify the federal estate tax treatment for each item. A response may be selected once, more than once, or not at all.

Answer List

G. Deductible from Remsen's gross estate to arrive at Remsen's taxable estate.
I. Deductible on Remsen's 2003 individual income tax return.
E. Deductible on either Remsen's estate tax return or Remsen's 2003 individual income tax return.
N. Not deductible on either Remsen's estate tax return or Remsen's 2003 individual income tax return.

		(G)	(I)	(E)	(N)
6.	What is the estate tax treatment of the executor's fees?	○	○	○	○
7.	What is the estate tax treatment of the cash bequest to Remsen's son?	○	○	○	○
8.	What is the estate tax treatment of the life insurance proceeds paid to Remsen's spouse?	○	○	○	○
9.	What is the estate tax treatment of the funeral expenses?	○	○	○	○
10.	What is the estate treatment of the $10,000 of medical expenses incurred before the decedent's death and paid by the executor on December 3, 2003?	○	○	○	○

Simulation Problem 4   (10 to 20 minutes)

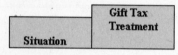

Scott Lane, an unmarried US citizen, made no lifetime transfers prior to 2003. During 2003, Lane made the following transfers:

- Gave an $11,000 cash gift to Kamp, a close friend.
- Made two separate $10,000 cash gifts to his only child.
- Created an **irrevocable** trust beginning in 2003 that provided his aunt with an income interest to be paid for the next five years. The remainder interest is to pass to Lane's sole cousin. The income interest is valued at $26,000 and the remainder interest is valued at $74,000.
- Paid $25,000 tuition directly to his grandchild's university on his grandchild's behalf.
- Created an **irrevocable** trust that provided his brother with a lifetime income interest beginning in 2005, after which a remainder interest passes to their sister.
- Created a **revocable** trust with his niece as the sole beneficiary. During 2003, the niece received $12,000 interest income from the trust.

For **items 1 through 7,** determine whether the tax transactions are fully taxable, partially taxable, or not taxable to Lane in 2003 for gift tax purposes after considering the gift tax annual exclusion. Ignore the unified credit when answering the items. An answer may be selected once, more than once, or not at all.

Gift Tax Treatments

F.   Fully taxable to Lane in 2003 for gift tax purposes.
P.   Partially taxable to Lane in 2003 for gift tax purposes.
N.   Not taxable to Lane in 2003 for gift tax purposes.

		(F)	(P)	(N)
1.	What is the gift tax treatment of Lane's gift to Kamp?	O	O	O
2.	What is the gift tax treatment of Lane's cash gifts to his child?	O	O	O
3.	What is the gift tax treatment of the trust's income interest to Lane's aunt?	O	O	O
4.	What is the gift tax treatment of the trust's remainder interest to Lane's cousin?	O	O	O
5.	What is the gift tax treatment of the tuition payment to Lane's grandchild's university?	O	O	O
6.	What is the gift tax treatment of the trust's income interest to Lane's brother?	O	O	O
7.	What is the gift tax treatment of the $12,000 interest income that Lane's niece received from the revocable trust?	O	O	O

Additional Simulation

Appendix A—Simulation 1 involves Estate and Gift Taxation

MULTIPLE-CHOICE ANSWERS

1.	c	__ __	18.	d	__ __	35.	d	__ __	52.	c	__ __	69.	d	__ __
2.	c	__ __	19.	a	__ __	36.	c	__ __	53.	b	__ __	70.	a	__ __
3.	d	__ __	20.	d	__ __	37.	c	__ __	54.	a	__ __	71.	c	__ __
4.	c	__ __	21.	c	__ __	38.	c	__ __	55.	d	__ __	72.	d	__ __
5.	c	__ __	22.	d	__ __	39.	c	__ __	56.	c	__ __	73.	a	__ __
6.	b	__ __	23.	c	__ __	40.	b	__ __	57.	b	__ __	74.	b	__ __
7.	a	__ __	24.	b	__ __	41.	a	__ __	58.	d	__ __	75.	b	__ __
8.	b	__ __	25.	b	__ __	42.	a	__ __	59.	a	__ __	76.	b	__ __
9.	c	__ __	26.	c	__ __	43.	c	__ __	60.	b	__ __	77.	c	__ __
10.	c	__ __	27.	c	__ __	44.	d	__ __	61.	c	__ __	78.	b	__ __
11.	b	__ __	28.	a	__ __	45.	d	__ __	62.	b	__ __	79.	a	__ __
12.	c	__ __	29.	b	__ __	46.	a	__ __	63.	d	__ __	80.	b	__ __
13.	d	__ __	30.	c	__ __	47.	a	__ __	64.	c	__ __	81.	c	__ __
14.	d	__ __	31.	c	__ __	48.	d	__ __	65.	b	__ __	82.	c	__ __
15.	a	__ __	32.	b	__ __	49.	d	__ __	66.	d	__ __			
16.	d	__ __	33.	c	__ __	50.	b	__ __	67.	c	__ __	1st: __/82 = __%
17.	d	__ __	34.	a	__ __	51.	a	__ __	68.	d	__ __	2nd: __/82 = __%

MULTIPLE-CHOICE ANSWER EXPLANATIONS

I.A. Gift Tax

1. **(c)** The requirement is to determine the amount of the $30,000 gift that is taxable to the Briars. Steve and Kay (his spouse) elected to split the gift made to Steve's sister, so each is treated as making a gift of $15,000. Since both Steve and Kay would be eligible for an $11,000 exclusion, each will have made a taxable gift of $15,000 – $11,000 exclusion = $4,000.

2. **(c)** The requirement is to determine the maximum exclusion available on Sayers' 2003 gift tax return for the $50,000 gift to Johnson who needed the money to pay medical expenses. The first $11,000 of gifts made to a donee during calendar year 2003 (except gifts of future interests) is excluded in determining the amount of the donor's taxable gifts for the year. Note that Sayers does not qualify for the unlimited exclusion for medical expenses paid on behalf of a donee, because Sayers did not pay the $50,000 to a medical care provider on Johnson's behalf.

3. **(d)** The requirement is to determine the amount of gift that is excludable from taxable gifts. Since the interest income resulting from the bond transferred to the trust will be accumulated and distributed to the child in the future upon reaching the age of twenty-one, the gift (represented by the $8,710 present value of the interest to be received by the child at age twenty-one) is a gift of a future interest and is not eligible to be offset by an annual exclusion.

4. **(c)** The requirement is to determine the correct statement regarding the unified transfer tax rate schedule. The unified transfer tax rate schedule applies on a cumulative basis to both life and death transfers. During a person's lifetime, a tax is first computed on cumulative lifetime taxable gifts, then is reduced by the tax on taxable gifts made in prior years in order to tax the current year's gifts at applicable marginal rates. At death, a unified transfer tax is computed on total life and death transfers, then is reduced by the tax already paid on post-1976 gifts, the unified transfer tax credit, state death taxes, foreign death taxes, and prior transfer taxes.

5. **(c)** The requirement is to determine which gift requires the filing of a gift tax return when the amount transferred exceeds the available annual gift tax exclusion. A gift in the form of payments for college books, supplies, and dormitory fees on behalf of an individual unrelated to the donor requires the filing of a gift tax return if the amount of payments exceeds the $11,000 annual exclusion. In contrast, no gift tax return need be filed for medical expenses or college tuition paid on behalf of a donee, and campaign expenses paid to a political organization, because there are unlimited exclusions available for these types of gifts after the annual exclusion has been used.

6. **(b)** The requirement is to determine the due date for filing a 2003 gift tax return (Form 709). A gift tax return must be filed on a calendar-year basis, with the return due and tax paid on or before April 15th of the following year. If the donor subsequently dies, the gift tax return is due not later than the date for filing the federal estate tax return (generally nine months after date of death). Here, since Vega was still living in 2004, the due date for filing the 2003 gift tax return is April 15, 2004.

7. **(a)** The requirement is to determine Jan's total exclusions for gift tax purposes. In computing a donor's gift tax, the first $11,000 of gifts made to a donee during calendar year 2003 is excluded in determining the amount of the donor's taxable gifts. Thus, $11,000 of the $15,000 given to Jones, $11,000 of the $12,000 given to Craig, and all $5,000 given to Kande can be excluded, resulting in a total exclusion of $27,000. Note that Jan's gift to Craig does not qualify for the unlimited exclusion of educational gifts paid on behalf of a donee, because the amount was paid directly to Craig. All $12,000 could have been excluded if Jan had made the tuition payment directly to the college.

8. **(b)** The requirement is to determine the amount of Jim's gift tax marital deduction. An unlimited marital deduction is allowed for gift tax purposes for gifts to a donee, who at the time of the gift is the donor's spouse. Thus, Jim's gift of $75,000 to Nina made after their wedding is eligible for the marital deduction, whereas the gift of the $50,000 engagement ring does not qualify because Jim and

Nina were not married at date of gift. The gift tax annual exclusion of $11,000 applies to multiple gifts to the same donee in chronological order, reducing the taxable gift of the engagement ring to $50,000 – $11,000 = $39,000. Since there is no remaining annual exclusion to reduce the gift of the $75,000 bank account, it would be completely offset by a marital deduction of $75,000.

9.   (c)   The requirement is to determine when a gift occurs in conjunction with Raff's creation of a joint bank account for himself and his friend's son, Dave. A gift does not occur when Raff opens the joint account and deposits money into it. Instead, a gift results when the noncontributing tenant (Dave) withdraws money from the account for his own benefit.

I.B.   Estate Tax

10.   (c)   The requirement is to determine Fred's basis for the property after the death of the joint tenant (Ethel). When property is held in joint tenancy by other than spouses, the property's fair market value is included in a decedent's estate to the extent of the percentage that the decedent contributed toward the purchase. Since Ethel furnished 80% of the land's purchase price, 80% of its $300,000 fair market value, or $240,000 is included in Ethel's estate. Thus, Fred's basis is $240,000 plus the $20,000 of purchase price that he furnished, a total of $260,000.

11.   (b)   The requirement is to determine the correct treatment of medical expenses paid by the executor of Bell's estate if the executor files the appropriate waiver. The executor may elect to treat medical expenses paid by the decedent's estate for the decedent's medical care as paid by the decedent at the time the medical services were provided. To qualify for this election, the medical expenses must be paid within the one-year period after the decedent's death, and the executor must attach a waiver to the decedent's Form 1040 indicating that the expenses will not be claimed as a deduction on the decedent's estate tax return. Here, since Bell died during 2003, and the medical services were provided and paid for by Bell's estate during 2003, the medical expenses are deductible on Bell's final income tax return for 2003 provided that the executor attaches the appropriate waiver.

12.   (c)   If the executor of a decedent's estate elects the alternate valuation date and none of the assets have been sold or distributed, the estate assets must be included in the decedent's gross estate at their FMV as of six months after the decedent's death.

13.   (d)   The requirement is to determine the amount of a decedent's taxable estate that is effectively tax-free if the maximum unified estate and gift credit is taken. The maximum unified estate and gift tax credit is $345,800 for 2003. Due to the graduated structure of the tax, this credit is the equivalent of an exemption of $1,000,000 and effectively permits $1,000,000 of taxable estate to be free of tax.

14.   (d)   The requirement is to determine which of the credits may be offset against the gross estate tax in determining the net estate tax of a US citizen for 2003. In computing the net estate tax of a US citizen, the gross estate tax may be offset by the unified transfer tax credit, and credits for state death taxes, foreign death taxes, and prior transfer taxes. For 2003, a unified transfer tax credit of $345,800 is allowed against gift and estate taxes and is equivalent to an exemption of the first $1,000,000 of taxable gifts or taxable estate from the unified transfer tax. Only taxable gifts made after 1976 are added back to a donor's taxable estate in arriving at the tax base for the application of the unified transfer tax at death. To the extent these taxable gifts exceeded the exemption equivalent of the unified credit and required the payment of a gift tax during the donor's lifetime, such tax is then subtracted from a donor's tentative estate tax at death in arriving at the gross estate tax. Thus, although post-1976 gift taxes reduce the net estate tax, they are not subtracted as a tax credit from the gross estate tax.

15.   (a)   The requirement is to determine the correct statement with regard to the gross estate of the first spouse to die when property is owned by them as tenants by the entirety or as joint tenants with right of survivorship. Under the general rule for joint tenancies, 100% of the value of jointly held property is included in a deceased tenant's gross estate except to the extent that the surviving tenants can prove that they contributed to the cost of the property. However, under a special rule applicable to spouses who own property as tenants by the entirety or as joint tenants with right of survivorship, the gross estate of the first spouse to die automatically includes 50% of the value of the jointly held property, regardless of which spouse furnished the original consideration for the purchase of the property.

16.   (d)   The requirement is to determine the amount of insurance proceeds included in Burr's gross estate with regard to a policy on Burr's life purchased by Adam in connection with a "buy-sell" agreement funded by a cross-purchase insurance arrangement. The gross estate of a decedent includes the proceeds of life insurance on the decedent's life if (1) the insurance proceeds are payable to the estate, (2) the proceeds are payable to another for the benefit of the estate, or (3) the decedent possessed an incident of ownership in the policy. An "incident of ownership" not only means ownership of the policy in a legal sense, but also includes the power to change beneficiaries, to revoke an assignment, to pledge the policy for a loan, or to surrender or cancel the policy. Here, since the policy owned by Adam on Burr's life was not payable to or for the benefit of Burr's estate, and Burr had no incident of ownership in the policy, the full amount of insurance proceeds would be excluded from Burr's gross estate.

17.   (d)   The requirement is to determine the amount includible as Wald's gross estate for federal estate tax purposes. If an executor does not elect the alternate valuation date, all property in which the decedent possessed an ownership interest at time of death is included in the decedent's gross estate at its fair market value at date of death. If property was held in joint tenancy and was acquired by purchase by other than spouses, the property's total fair market value will be included in the decedent's gross estate except to the extent that the surviving tenant can prove that he/she contributed toward the purchase. Since Wald purchased the land with his own funds, the land's total fair market value ($800,000) must be included in Wald's gross estate together with Wald's personal effects and jewelry ($150,000), resulting in a gross estate of $950,000.

18.   (d)   The requirement is to determine the item that is deductible from a decedent's gross estate. Unpaid income taxes on income received by the decedent before death would be a liability of the estate and would be deductible from the gross estate. State inheritance taxes, income tax paid on income earned and received after the decedent's death, and federal estate taxes are not deductible in computing a decedent's taxable estate. Note that although state inheritance taxes are not deductible in computing a decedent's taxable estate, a limited tax credit is allowed for state death taxes in computing the net estate tax payable.

19. **(a)** The requirement is to determine whether federal estate tax returns must be filed for the estates of Eng and Lew. For a decedent dying during 2003, a federal estate tax return (Form 706) must be filed if the decedent's gross estate exceeds $1,000,000. If a decedent made taxable lifetime gifts such that the decedent's unified transfer tax credit was used to offset the gift tax, the $1,000,000 exemption amount must be reduced by the amount of taxable lifetime gifts to determine whether a return is required to be filed.

Since Lew made no lifetime gifts and the value of Lew's gross estate was only $950,000, no federal estate tax return is required to be filed for Lew's estate. In Eng's case, the $1,000,000 exemption is reduced by Eng's $100,000 of taxable lifetime gifts to $900,000. However, since Eng's gross estate totaled only $850,000, no federal estate tax return is required to be filed for Eng's estate.

20. **(d)** The requirement is to determine the correct statement regarding the use of the alternate valuation date in computing the federal estate tax. An executor of an estate can elect to use the alternate valuation date (the date six months after the decedent's death) to value the assets included in a decedent's gross estate only if its use decreases both the value of the gross estate and the amount of estate tax liability. Answer (a) is incorrect because the alternate valuation date cannot be used if its use increases the value of the gross estate. Answer (b) is incorrect because the use of the alternate valuation date is an irrevocable election. Answer (c) is incorrect because the alternate valuation date is only used to value an estate's assets, not its liabilities.

21. **(c)** The requirement is to determine when the proceeds of life insurance payable to the estate's executor, as the estate's representative, are includible in the decedent's gross estate. The proceeds of life insurance on the decedent's life are always included in the decedent's gross estate if (1) they are receivable by the estate, (2) the decedent possessed any incident of ownership in the policy, or (3) they are receivable by another (e.g., the estate's executor) for the benefit of the estate.

22. **(d)** The requirement is to determine the proper income and estate tax treatment of an accounting fee earned by Ross before death, that was subsequently collected by the executor of Ross' estate. Since Ross was a calendar-year, cash-method taxpayer, the income would not be included on Ross' final individual income tax return because payment had not been received. Since the accounting fee would not be included in Ross' final income tax return because of Ross' cash method of accounting, the accounting fee would be "income in respect of a decedent." For estate tax purposes, income in respect of a decedent will be included in the decedent's gross estate at its fair market value on the appropriate valuation date. For income tax purposes, the income tax basis of the decedent (zero) transfers over to the estate or beneficiary who collects the fee. The recipient of the income must classify it in the same manner (i.e., ordi-

nary income) as would have the decedent. Thus, the accounting fee must be included in Ross' gross estate and must also be included in the estate's fiduciary income tax return (Form 1041) because the fee was collected by the executor of Ross' estate.

23. **(c)** The requirement is to determine within how many months after the date of Alan's death his federal estate tax return should be filed. The federal estate tax return (Form 706) must be filed and the tax paid within nine months of the decedent's death, unless an extension of time has been granted.

24. **(b)** The requirement is to determine the amount of marital deduction that can be claimed in computing Alan's taxable estate. In computing the taxable estate of a decedent, an unlimited marital deduction is allowed for the portion of the decedent's estate that passes to the decedent's surviving spouse. Since $375,000 was bequeathed outright to Alan's widow, Alan's estate will receive a marital deduction of $375,000.

25. **(b)** The requirement is to determine Edwin's basis for the stock inherited from Lynn's estate. A special rule applies if a decedent (Lynn) acquires appreciated property as a gift within one year of death, and this property passes to the donor (Edwin) or donor's spouse. Then the donor's (Edwin's) basis is the basis of the property in the hands of the decedent (Lynn) before death. Since Lynn had received the stock as a gift, Lynn's basis before death ($5,000) becomes the basis of the stock to Edwin.

II. Generation-Skipping Tax

26. **(c)** The requirement is to determine the correct statement regarding the generation-skipping transfer tax. The generation-skipping transfer tax is imposed as a separate tax in addition to the federal gift and estate taxes, and is designed to prevent an individual from escaping an entire generation of gift and estate taxes by transferring property to a person that is two or more generations *below* that of the transferor. The tax is imposed at the highest tax rate (50%) under the unified transfer tax rate schedule.

III. Income Taxation of Estates and Trusts

27. **(c)** The requirement is to determine the amount of the estate's $10,000 distribution that must be included in gross income by Crane's widow. The maximum amount that is taxable to beneficiaries is limited to the estate's distributable net income (DNI). Since distributions to multiple beneficiaries exceed DNI, the estate's $12,000 of DNI must be prorated to distributions to determine the portion of each distribution that must be included in gross income. Since distributions to the widow and daughter totaled $15,000, the portion of the $10,000 distribution that must be included in the widow's gross income equals ($10,000/$15,000) x $12,000 = $8,000.

28. **(a)** The requirement is to determine the estate's distributable net income (DNI). An estate's DNI generally is its taxable income before the income distribution deduction, increased by its personal exemption, any net capital loss deduction, and tax-exempt interest (reduced by related nondeductible expenses), and decreased by any net capital gains allocable to corpus. Here, the estate's DNI is the

$20,000 of taxable interest reduced by the $5,000 of administrative expenses attributable to taxable income, or $15,000.

29. (b)   The requirement is to determine the due date for the Fiduciary Income Tax Return (Form 1041) for the estate's 2003 calendar year. Form 1041 is due on the 15th day of the fourth month following the end of the tax year. Thus, an estate's calendar-year return is generally due on April 15th of the following year.

30. (c)   The requirement is to determine the maximum amount to be included in the beneficiary's gross income for a distribution from estate income that was currently required. Distributable net income (DNI) is the maximum amount of distributions that can be taxed to beneficiaries as well as the maximum amount of distributions deduction for an estate.

31. (c)   The requirement is to determine the amount of the estate's $15,000 distribution that is taxable to the sole beneficiary. The maximum amount that is taxable to the beneficiary is limited to the estate's distributable net income (DNI). An estate's DNI is generally its taxable income before the income distribution deduction, increased by its exemption, a net capital loss deduction, and tax-exempt interest (reduced by related nondeductible expenses), and decreased by any net capital gains allocable to corpus. Here, the estate's DNI is its taxable interest of $40,000, reduced by the $34,000 of expenses attributable to taxable interest, or $6,000.

32. (b)   The requirement is to determine the correct statement regarding an estate's estimated income taxes. Trusts and estates must make quarterly estimated tax payments, except that an estate is exempt from making estimated tax payments for taxable years ending within two years of the decedent's death.

33. (c)   The requirement is to determine the correct statement regarding a complex trust. A simple trust is one that (1) is required to distribute all of its income to designated beneficiaries every year, (2) has no beneficiaries that are qualifying charitable organizations, and (3) makes no distributions of trust corpus (i.e., principal) during the year. A complex trust is any trust that is not a simple trust. Answer (a) is incorrect because a complex trust is not required to distribute income currently, nor is it prohibited from distributing trust principal. Answer (b) is incorrect because there are no investment restrictions imposed on a complex trust. Answer (d) is incorrect because an income tax is imposed on a trust's taxable income.

34. (a)   The requirement is to determine the amount of **standard deduction** for a trust or an estate in the fiduciary income tax return (Form 1041). No standard deduction is available for a trust or an estate on the fiduciary income tax return. On the other hand, a personal exemption is allowed for an estate or trust on the fiduciary income tax return. The personal exemption is $600 for an estate, $300 for a simple trust (i.e., a trust required to distribute all income currently), and $100 for a complex trust (i.e., a trust other than a simple trust).

35. (d)   The requirement is to indicate whether estate and trusts are required to use the calendar year as their taxable year. All trusts (except those that are tax exempt) are generally required to use the calendar year for tax purposes.

In contrast, an estate may adopt the calendar year, or any fiscal year as its taxable year.

36. (c)   The requirement is to determine the proper treatment for ordinary and necessary administrative expenses paid by the fiduciary of an estate. Ordinary and necessary administrative expenses paid by the fiduciary of an estate can be deducted on either the estate's fiduciary income tax return, or on the estate's federal estate tax return. Although the expenses cannot be deducted twice, they can be allocated between the two returns in any manner that the fiduciary sees fit. If the administrative expenses are to be deducted on the fiduciary income tax return, the potential estate tax deduction must be waived for these expenses.

37. (c)   The requirement is to determine when a fiduciary income tax return for a decedent's estate must be filed. The executor of a decedent's estate that has only US citizens as beneficiaries is required to file a fiduciary income tax return (Form 1041) if the estate's gross income is $600 or more. The return is due on or before the 15th day of the fourth month following the close of the estate's taxable year.

38. (c)   The requirement is to determine the correct statement regarding the charitable contribution deduction on an estate's fiduciary income tax return (Form 1041). An estate is allowed a deduction for a contribution to a charitable organization if (1) the decedent's will specifically provides for the contribution, and (2) the recipient is a qualified charitable organization. The amount allowed as a charitable deduction is not subject to any percentage limitations, but must be paid from amounts included in the estate's gross income for the year of contribution.

39. (c)   The requirement is to determine who will be taxed on the trust's 2003 income. During 2003, Carlt created a trust providing a lifetime income interest for his mother, with a remainder interest to go to his son, but he expressly retained the power to revoke both the income interest and remainder interest at any time. When the grantor of a trust retains substantial control over the trust, such as the power to revoke the income and remainder interests, the trust income will be taxed to the grantor and not to the trust or beneficiaries.

40. (b)   The requirement is to determine the estate's distributable net income (DNI). An estate's DNI generally is its taxable income before the income distribution deduction, increased by its personal exemption, any net capital loss deduction, and tax-exempt income (reduced by related expenses), and decreased by any net capital gain allocable to corpus. Here, the estate's DNI is the $65,000 of taxable interest, reduced by the $14,000 of administrative expenses attributable to taxable income and the $9,000 of charitable contributions. Charitable contributions are allowed as a deduction if made under the terms of the decedent's will and are paid to qualified charitable organizations from amounts included in the estate's gross income.

41. (a)   The requirement is to determine the correct statement for income tax purposes regarding the initial taxable period for the estate of a decedent who died on October 24. For income tax purposes, a decedent's estate is allowed to adopt a calendar year or any fiscal year beginning on the date of the decedent's death. Answer (b) is incorrect because an estate may adopt a calendar year and is not restricted to a fiscal year. Answer (c) is incorrect because the estate's first tax year would begin on October 24, not October 1. Answer (d) is incorrect because an estate is not restricted to a calendar year, and if it adopted a calendar year, its initial year would begin with the date of the decedent's death (October 24).

IV.A.1. Tax-Exempt Organizations

42.   (a)   The requirement is to determine what will terminate the private foundation status of an exempt organization. The private foundation status of an exempt organization will terminate if it becomes a public charity. Answer (b) is incorrect because a private foundation can be organized as a foreign corporation. Answer (c) is incorrect because private foundations are not required to distribute their assets to public charities. Answer (d) is incorrect because a private foundation's exempt purposes are already severely restricted by the Code.

43.   (c)   The requirement is to determine which exempt organizations must file annual information returns. Private foundations must file annual information returns specifically stating items of gross income, receipts, and disbursements, and such other information as may be required. In contrast, churches, religious groups, and exempt organizations other than private foundations are required to file an information return only if their gross receipts are more than $25,000.

44.   (d)   Organizations that can qualify as exempt organizations are listed in Sec. 501 of the Internal Revenue Code, and can take the form of a trust or corporation. To receive exempt status, the organization must file a written application with the IRS. In no event will exempt status be conferred upon an organization unless the organization is one of those types of organizations specifically listed in the Code. A fraternal benefit society must operate under the lodge system. An organization operating under the lodge system carries on its activities under a form of organization that comprises local branches chartered by a parent organization and can be established to provide its members with sick benefits.

45.   (d)   The requirement is to determine the correct statement regarding qualification as an exempt organization. To qualify as an exempt organization, the applicant must not be a private foundation organized and operated exclusively to influence legislation pertaining to protection of the environment. Exempt status is specifically denied to organizations if a substantial part of their activities consists of "carrying on propaganda, or otherwise attempting, to influence legislation," if expenditures exceed certain amounts. Answer (a) is incorrect because an exempt organization cannot be organized for the primary purpose of carrying on a business for profit. Answer (b) is incorrect because an organization must be one of those classes upon which exemption is specifically conferred by the Internal Revenue Code. Answer (c) is incorrect because a social club organized for recreation will qualify for exemption if substantially all of the activities of the club are for such purposes and none of the profits inure to the benefit of any shareholder.

46.   (a)   The requirement is to determine the proper tax treatment of Carita Fund's insurance activities. An otherwise qualifying exempt organization will instead be subject to tax if a substantial part of its activities consists of providing commercial-type insurance. Sec. 501(m)(3) provides

that "commercial-type insurance" does not include insurance provided at substantially below cost to a class of charitable recipients. Since Carita Fund was organized and operated exclusively for charitable purposes, and provided below cost insurance coverage to exempt organizations involved in the prevention of cruelty to children, its insurance activities are exempt from tax. The insurance activities do not constitute unrelated business income because the insurance activities were substantially related to the performance of the fund's exempt purpose. Answer (c) is incorrect because Carita Fund qualifies as an exempt organization.

47.   (a)   The filing of a return covering unrelated business income (Form 990-T) is required of all exempt organizations having at least $1,000 of unrelated business taxable income for the year. However, this does not relieve the organization of having to file a separate information return (Form 990) if it is otherwise required to file. Answer (c) is incorrect because in determining whether income is unrelated business income, the exempt organization's need for the income or the use it makes of the profits is irrelevant. Answer (d) is incorrect because the tax on unrelated business income of exempt organizations must be paid in full with the return.

48.   (d)   A condominium management association wishing to be treated as a homeowners association and thereby qualify as an exempt organization for a particular year must file a separate election for each taxable year no later than the due date of the tax return for which the election is to apply.

49.   (d)   An organization wishing to qualify as an exempt organization must be of a type specifically identified as one of the classes on which exemption is conferred by the Code. In no event will exempt status be conferred upon an organization unless the organization is one of those listed. Furthermore, in order to receive exempt status, the organization must file an application with the Internal Revenue Service. Answer (a) is incorrect since an exempt organization may be organized as a corporation. Answer (b) is incorrect because an exempt organization may lose its exempt status by engaging in any prohibited transaction. Answer (c) is incorrect because non-US citizens may be on an exempt organization's governing board.

50.   (b)   The requirement is to determine the correct statement regarding exempt organizations. With the exception chiefly of churches, an exempt organization (other than a private foundation) must nevertheless file an annual information return specifically stating items of gross income, receipts, and disbursements unless its gross receipts are normally not more than $25,000. An exempt organization required to file a return must annually report the total amount of contributions received as well as the identity of substantial contributors.

   Answer (a) is incorrect because an organization can only achieve exempt status by filing an application for exemption with the Internal Revenue Service. Answer (c) is incorrect because there is no limitation on the amount of compensation that can be paid to an employee if the compensation is reasonable. Answer (d) is incorrect because exempt status can be retroactively revoked if an organization's character, purposes, or methods of operation are other than as stated in the application for exemption.

51.   (a)   The requirement is to determine the correct statement regarding qualification as an exempt organization. To qualify as an exempt organization, the applicant for exemption must fall into one of the specified classes of organizations that are listed in Sec. 501 as being exempt from tax. Answer (d) is incorrect because a social club can be an exempt organization as long as substantially all its activities are for such purposes and no part of its net earnings inures to the benefit of any private shareholder. Answer (c) is incorrect because most exempt organizations are permitted specified levels of lobbying expenditures, and can even elect to be subject to a tax equal to 25% of their excess lobbying expenditures to prevent loss of exempt status. Answer (b) is incorrect because foreign corporations can qualify as exempt organizations.

52.   (c)   Organizations that can qualify as exempt organizations are listed in Sec. 501 of the Internal Revenue Code. An exempt organization can take the form of a trust or a corporation. In order to receive exempt status, the organization must file an application with the Internal Revenue Service. In no event will exempt status be conferred upon an organization unless the organization is one of those listed in the Code. Answer (b) is incorrect because there is no limitation on the amount of salary that can be paid an employee.

IV.A.2.   Sec. 501(c)(3) Organizations

53.   (b)   The requirement is to determine which of the activities is(are) consistent with Hope's tax-exempt status as a religious organization. An exempt organization must be operated exclusively for its exempt purpose, and other activities not in furtherance of its exempt purpose must be only an insubstantial part of its activities. A religious organization's providing traditional burial services that maintain the religious beliefs of its members would be consistent with its tax-exempt status as a religious organization. However, conducting recreational functions such as weekend retreats conducted for business organizations ordinarily would not be consistent with the tax-exempt status of a religious organization unless there were tightly scheduled religious activities and only limited free time for incidental recreation activities.

54.   (a)   The requirement is to determine which statements are correct in regard to the organizational test to qualify a public service charitable entity as tax-exempt. The term "articles of organization" includes the trust instrument, corporate charter, articles of association, or any other written instruments by which an organization is created. To satisfy the organizational test, the articles of organization (1) must limit the organization's purposes to one or more exempt purposes described in Sec. 501(c)(3); and, (2) must not expressly empower the organization to engage in activities that are not in furtherance of one or more exempt purposes, except as an insubstantial part of its activities.

55.   (d)   The requirement is to determine which of two activities (if any) will result in unrelated business income. Unrelated business income (UBI) is income derived from a trade or business, the conduct of which is not substantially related to the exercise or performance of an organization's exempt purpose. For a trade or business to be related, the conduct of the business activity must have a causal relationship to the achievement of the organization's exempt purpose. Selling articles made by handicapped persons as part

of their rehabilitation would be substantially related to the exempt purpose of an organization exclusively involved in their rehabilitation. Similarly, operating a grocery store almost fully staffed by emotionally handicapped persons as part of a therapeutic program to allow the persons to become involved with society, assume responsibility, and to exercise business judgment, would be substantially related to the rehabilitation purposes of the exempt organization.

56.   (c)   The operational test requires that an exempt organization be operated exclusively for an exempt purpose. An organization will be considered to be operated exclusively for an exempt purpose only if it engages primarily in activities that accomplish its exempt purpose. An organization will not be so regarded if more than an insubstantial part of its activities is not in furtherance of an exempt purpose. Thus, an organization that engages in insubstantial nonexempt activities will not fail the operational test. In contrast, an organization that operates for the prevention of cruelty to animals will fail the operational test if it directly participates in any political campaign.

IV.C.   Unrelated Business Income (UBI)

57.   (b)   The requirement is to determine the correct statement with regard to the unrelated business income of an exempt organization. An exempt organization is not taxed on unrelated business income of less than $1,000. Answer (a) is incorrect because the amount of unrelated business income will not cause the loss of exempt status. Answer (c) is incorrect because the tax will not apply to a business activity that is not regularly carried on. Answer (d) is incorrect because a loss from an unrelated trade or business activity is allowed in computing unrelated business taxable income.

58.   (d)   The requirement is to determine which one of the listed activities will not result in unrelated business income. Unrelated business income (UBI) is income derived from any trade or business, the conduct of which is not substantially related to the exercise or performance of an organization's exempt purpose. For a trade or business to be "related," the conduct of the business activity must have a causal relationship to the achievement of the exempt purpose. A business activity will be "substantially related" only if the causal relationship is a substantial one. Assuming that the development and improvement of its members is one of the purposes for which a trade association is granted an exemption, the sale of publications used as course materials for the association's seminars for its members would be substantially related.

Answer (a) is incorrect because even though a special rule permits an exempt hospital to perform services at cost for other hospitals with facilities to serve not more than 100 inpatients, the permitted services are limited to data processing, purchasing, warehousing, billing and collection, food, clinical, industrial engineering, laboratory, printing, communications, record center, and personnel services. Answer (b) is incorrect because even though an exempt senior citizen's center may operate a beauty parlor and barber shop for its members, selling major appliances to its members has been held to generate unrelated business income. Answer (c) is incorrect because the performance of accounting and tax services for its members would be unrelated to the exempt purpose of a labor union.

59. **(a)** The requirement is to determine the correct statement with regard to an exempt organization's unrelated business taxable income when the exempt organization is a corporation. An exempt organization's unrelated business income in excess of $1,000 is taxed at regular corporate income tax rates if the organization is a corporation. An exempt organization must be a trust in order for its unrelated business income to be taxed at the rates applicable to trusts.

60. **(b)** The requirement is to determine the correct statement regarding an exempt organization's income of $15,000 derived from conducting bingo games. If an exempt organization derives income from conducting bingo games, in a locality where such activity is legal, and in a state that confines such activity to nonprofit organizations, then such income is exempt from the tax on unrelated business income. Answer (d) is incorrect because unrelated business income will not cause the revocation or forfeiture of an organization's exempt status.

61. **(c)** The requirement is to determine the correct statement regarding the unrelated business income of exempt organizations. A tax-exempt organization may be subject to tax on its unrelated business income if the organization conducts a trade or business that is not substantially related to the exempt purpose of the organization, and the trade or business is regularly carried on by the organization. For an exempt organization, an unrelated business does not include any activity where all the work is performed for the organization by unpaid volunteers. Answer (a) is incorrect because although unrelated business income may result in a tax, it will not result in the loss of the organization's exempt status. Answer (b) is incorrect because the term "business" is broadly defined to include any activity conducted for the production of income through the sale of merchandise or the performance of services. Answer (d) is incorrect because using a trade or business to provide financial support for the organization's exempt purpose will not prevent an activity from being classified as an unrelated trade or business and being subject to the tax on unrelated business income.

62. **(b)** The requirement is to determine the correct statement regarding an exempt organization's payment of estimated taxes on its unrelated business income. An exempt organization subject to tax on its unrelated business income must comply with the Code provisions regarding installment payments of estimated income tax by corporations. This means that an exempt organization must make quarterly estimated tax payments if it expects its estimated tax on its unrelated business income to be $500 or more. Answers (c) and (d) are incorrect because any tax on unrelated business income must be paid in full by the due date of the exempt organization's return.

63. **(d)** The requirement is to determine the correct statement regarding the taxability of unrelated business income (UBI) to an exempt organization that is a charitable trust. Answer (c) is incorrect because an exempt organization that is a charitable trust is subject to tax on its UBI only to the extent that its UBI exceeds $1,000. Answers (a) and (b) are incorrect because an exempt organization with UBI in excess of $1,000 is subject to tax at rates applicable to trusts if it is organized as a charitable trust.

64. **(c)** Unrelated business income (UBI) is gross income derived from any trade or business the conduct of

which is not substantially related to the exercise or performance of an organization's exempt purpose. Although dividends and interest are generally excluded from UBI, they will be included if they result from debt-financed investments. Answer (d) is incorrect because it states that dividends and interest are always **excluded** from UBI. Answer (a) is incorrect because the Code only imposes a tax on UBI, it does not revoke an organization's exempt status. Answer (b) is incorrect because a net operating loss is allowed in computing unrelated business taxable income. Answer (c) is correct because Code Sec. 513(f) specifically excludes from UBI an exempt organization's conducting bingo games where such activity is legal.

V. Income Tax Return Preparers

65. **(b)** The requirement is to determine which acts constitute(s) grounds for a tax preparer penalty. A return preparer will be subject to penalty if the preparer knowingly or recklessly discloses information furnished in connection with the preparation of a tax return, unless such information is furnished for quality or peer review, under an administrative order by a regulatory agency, or pursuant to an order of a court. Additionally, a return preparer will be subject to penalty if any part of an understatement of liability with respect to a return or refund claim is due to the preparer's willful attempt to understate tax liability, or to any reckless or intentional disregard of rules and regulations.

66. **(d)** The requirement is to determine Water's responsibility regarding Vee's unfiled 1998 income tax return. A CPA should promptly inform the client upon becoming aware of the client's failure to file a required return for a prior year. However, the CPA is not obligated to inform the IRS and the CPA may not do so without the client's permission, except where required by law. If the CPA is requested to prepare the current year's return (2003) and the client has not taken action to file the return for the earlier year (1998), the CPA should consider whether to withdraw from preparing the current year's return and whether to continue a professional relationship with the client. Also, note that the normal statue of limitations for the assessment of a tax deficiency is three years after the due date of the return or three years after the return is filed, whichever is later. Thus, the statute of limitations is still open with regard to 1998 since there is no time limit for the assessment of tax if no tax return was filed.

67. **(c)** The requirement is to determine which action a tax return preparer must take to avoid tax preparer penalties for a return's understated tax liability due to a taxpayer's intentional disregard of regulations. A return preparer may, in good faith, rely without verification upon information furnished by the client or by third parties, and is not required to audit, examine, or review books, records, or documents in order to independently verify the taxpayer's information. However, the preparer should not ignore the implications of information furnished and should make reasonable inquiries if the furnished information appears incorrect, incomplete, or inconsistent.

68. **(d)** According to the Statements on Standards for Tax Services, in preparing a tax return a CPA may in good faith rely upon information furnished by the client or third parties without further verification.

69. **(d)** The requirement is to determine the correct statement regarding the imposition of a preparer penalty for understated corporate tax liability. A return preparer may in good faith rely without verification upon information furnished, and is not required to audit, examine, or review books, records, or documents in order to independently verify a taxpayer's information. However, the preparer should not ignore the implications of information furnished and should make reasonable inquiries if information appears incorrect, incomplete, or inconsistent.

70. **(a)** A tax return preparer is subject to a penalty for knowingly or recklessly disclosing corporate tax return information, if the disclosure is made to enable a third party to solicit business from the taxpayer. Taxpayer return information can be disclosed by the preparer without penalty if the disclosure is made to enable the tax processor to electronically compute the taxpayer's liability, for purposes of the tax return preparer's peer review, or if the disclosure is made under an administrative order by a state agency that registers tax return preparers.

71. **(c)** The requirement is to determine the correct statement regarding a tax return preparer's disclosure or use of tax return information without the taxpayer's consent. Generally, a tax return preparer who knowingly or recklessly discloses **any** information furnished to him in connection with the preparation of a return, or uses any such information other than to prepare, or to assist in preparing a return, is guilty of a misdemeanor, and upon conviction may be subject to fine and/or imprisonment. A limited exception permits the disclosure or use of tax return information for purposes of being evaluated by quality or peer reviews.

72. **(d)** A penalty of up to $1,000 may be assessed against a tax return preparer who knowingly or recklessly discloses or uses any tax return information other than to prepare, or assist in preparing a return. Additionally, a penalty of $1,000 will be assessed against a return preparer who willfully attempts to understate any client's tax liability on a return or claim for refund.

73. **(a)** Under Internal Revenue Code Section 6695(f) any person who is an income tax return preparer who endorses or otherwise negotiates any check which is issued to a taxpayer shall pay a penalty of $500.

74. **(b)** A CPA who prepares a federal income tax return for a fee must keep a completed copy of the return for a minimum of three years. Answer (a) is incorrect because prior to preparing a tax return the CPA would not be required to file certain notices and powers of attorney with the IRS. Answer (c) is incorrect because a CPA would only be required to ask the client if documentation of these expenses exists. The CPA would not have to actually receive and examine this documentation. Answer (d) is incorrect because the CPA's federal identification number would be required on any federal income tax return prepared for a fee.

75. **(b)** A CPA generally does owe a duty to inform a client that there are errors in a previously filed tax return so that the client may file an amended tax return. Answer (a) is incorrect because the client chooses his/her own CPA. Answer (c) is incorrect because CPAs are not required to disclose fraud by the client but are usually engaged to give an opinion on the fairness of the financial statements. An-

swer (d) is incorrect because although the CPA has a duty to perform an audit in accordance with GAAS and consistent with GAAP, the CPA is not under a duty to discover fraud in the audit unless the fraud would have been uncovered in the process of an ordinary audit or unless the CPA agreed to greater responsibility to uncover fraud.

76. **(b)** If the IRS issues a thirty-day letter to an individual taxpayer who wishes to dispute the assessment, the taxpayer may ignore the thirty-day letter and wait to receive a ninety-day letter. Answer (a) is incorrect because a taxpayer must receive a ninety-day letter before a petition can be filed in Tax Court. Answer (c) is incorrect because a taxpayer has a thirty-day period during which to file a written protest. Answer (d) is incorrect because a taxpayer is not required to pay the taxes and commence an action in federal district court.

Generally, upon the receipt of a thirty-day letter, a taxpayer who wishes to dispute the findings has thirty days to (1) request a conference with an appeals officer or file a written protest letter, or (2) may elect to do nothing during the thirty-day period and await a ninety-day letter. The taxpayer would then have ninety days to file a petition with the Tax Court. Alternatively, a taxpayer may choose to pay the additional taxes and file a claim for refund. When the refund claim is disallowed, the taxpayer could then commence an action in federal district court.

77. **(c)** A CPA will be liable to a tax client for damages resulting from the following activities: (1) failure to file a client's return on a timely basis, (2) gross negligence or fraudulent conduct resulting in client losses, (3) erroneous advice or failure to advise client of certain tax elections, and (4) wrongful disclosure or use of confidential information. A CPA will not be liable to a tax client for refusing to sign a client's request for a filing extension, therefore answer (c) is correct.

78. **(b)** According to the Statements on Standards for Tax Services, a CPA should not recommend a position unless there is a realistic possibility of it being sustained if it is challenged. Furthermore, a CPA should not prepare or sign an income tax return if the CPA knows that the return takes a position that will not be sustained if challenged. Therefore, answer (d) is incorrect. Also, a CPA should advise the client of the potential penalty consequences of any recommended tax position. Therefore, answer (c) is incorrect. Answer (a) is incorrect as a CPA may not recommend a position that is frivolous even if the position is adequately disclosed on the return.

79. **(a)** While performing services for a client, a CPA may become aware of an error in a previously filed return. The CPA should advise the client of the error (as required by the Statements on Standards for Tax Services) and the measures to be taken. It is the client's responsibility to decide whether to correct the error. In the event that the client does not correct an error, or agree to take the necessary steps to change from an erroneous method of accounting, the CPA should consider whether to continue a professional relationship with the client.

80. **(b)** A CPA may in good faith rely without verification upon information furnished by the client when preparing the client's tax return. However, the CPA should not ignore implications of information furnished and should make reasonable inquiries if information appears incorrect, incomplete, or inconsistent.

81.   (c)   Answer (a) is incorrect because IRC §6695(a) imposes a $50 penalty upon income tax return preparers who fail to furnish a copy of the return to the taxpayer. Answer (b) is incorrect because IRC §6695(b) imposes a $50 penalty upon income tax return preparers who fail to sign a return, unless the failure is due to reasonable cause. Answer (d) is incorrect because IRC §6695(f) imposes a $500 penalty upon income tax return preparers who endorse or otherwise negotiate a client's tax refund checks. There is no code section imposing a penalty for the understating of a client's tax liability due to an error in calculation.

82.   (c)   A CPA should consider both: (1) information actually known to the CPA from the tax return of another client; and (2) information provided by the client that appears to be correct based on the client's returns from prior years. In preparing or signing a return, a CPA may in good faith rely without verification upon information furnished by the client or by third parties. However, the CPA should not ignore the implications of information furnished and should make reasonable inquires if the information furnished appears to be incorrect, incomplete, or inconsistent either on its face or on the basis of other facts known to the CPA.

SOLUTIONS TO SIMULATION PROBLEMS

Simulation Problem 1

A gift occurs when a transfer becomes complete and is measured by its fair market value on that date. A gift becomes **complete** when the donor has relinquished dominion and control and no longer has the power to change its disposition, whether for the donor's benefit or for the benefit of another. An annual exclusion of up to $11,000 is available for gifts of a present interest. A **present interest** is an unrestricted right to the immediate use, possession, or enjoyment of property or the income from property. A **future interest** includes reversions, remainders, and other interests that are limited to commence in use, possession, or enjoyment at some future date or time. Gifts of future interests do not qualify for the annual exclusion.

Part a.

For items 1 through 9, candidates were asked to determine whether the transfer of cash, an income interest, or a remainder interest represents a gift of a present interest (P), a gift of a future interest (F), or not a completed gift (N).

1. **(N)** Since Cobb expressly retained the power to revoke the income interest transferred to his mother at any time, he has not relinquished dominion and control and the transfer of the income interest is not a completed gift.

2. **(N)** Since Cobb expressly retained the power to revoke the remainder interest transferred to his sister at any time, he has not relinquished dominion and control and the transfer of the remainder interest is not a completed gift.

3. **(F)** Kane's transfer of an income interest to a nephew and a remainder interest to a niece are completed gifts because Kane has relinquished dominion and control. Since Kane's nephew was twenty-five years of age when the trust was created, but income distributions will not begin until the nephew is age twenty-nine, the transfer of the income interest is a gift of future interest and does not qualify for the annual exclusion.

4. **(P)** Since Hall's gifts of cash to his son were outright gifts, they are gifts of a present interest and qualify for the annual exclusion.

5. **(P)** Yeats' gift of the income interest to her twenty-two-year-old niece is a gift of a present interest qualifying for the annual exclusion since Jane has the unrestricted right to immediate enjoyment of the income. The fact that the value of the income interest does not exceed $11,000 does not affect its nature (i.e., completed gift of a present interest).

6. **(F)** Yeats' gift of the remainder interest to her brother is a completed gift of a future interest since the brother cannot enjoy the property or any of the income until Jane reaches age thirty.

7. **(P)** Tom's gift of $40,000 cash to his uncle is an outright gift of a present interest and qualifies for the annual exclusion. Since gift-splitting was elected and Tom and Ann would each receive an $11,000 annual exclusion, Tom and Ann each made a taxable gift of $20,000 – $11,000 exclusion = $9,000.

8. **(P)** Murry's gift of the income interest to his brother is a completed gift because Murry has relinquished dominion and control. It is a gift of a present interest qualifying for the annual exclusion since his brother has the unrestricted right to immediate enjoyment of the income.

9. **(N)** Since Murry retained the right to revoke the remainder interest transferred to his sister at any time, the transfer of the remainder interest does not result in a completed gift.

Part b.

For item 10, candidates were asked to determine whether the transfer is subject to the generation-skipping tax (A), the gift tax (B), or both taxes (C).

10. **(C)** Since Martin made an outright gift of $5,000,000 to Dale, the transfer is a gift of a present interest and is subject to the gift tax. Since Dale happens to be Martin's grandchild, the gift also is subject to the generation-skipping tax. The generation-skipping tax on the transfer of property is imposed in addition to federal gift and estates taxes and is designed to prevent individuals from escaping an entire generation of gift and estate taxes by transferring property to, or in trust for the benefit of, a person that is two or more generations younger than the donor or transferor. The tax approximates the unified transfer tax that would be imposed if the property were actually transferred to each successive generation.

Simulation Problem 2

For **items 1 through 9,** candidates were asked to determine for each item whether (P) the tax preparer's action constitutes an act of tax preparer misconduct subject to the Internal Revenue Code penalty; (E) the IRS will examine the facts and circumstances to determine whether the reasonable cause exception applies, the good faith exception applies, or both exceptions apply; or, (N) the tax preparer's action does not constitute an act of tax preparer misconduct.

1.   (N) A return preparer will be subject to penalty if the preparer knowingly or recklessly discloses information furnished in connection with the preparation of a tax return, unless such information is furnished for quality or peer review, under an administrative order by a regulatory agency, or pursuant to an order of a court.

2.   (E) The reasonable cause and good faith exception applies if the return preparer relied in good faith on the advice of an advisory preparer who the return preparer had reason to believe was competent to render such advice.

3.   (P) A return preparer will be subject to penalty if the preparer endorses or otherwise negotiates (directly or through an agent) any refund check issued to a taxpayer (other than the preparer) if the preparer was the preparer of the return or claim for refund which gave rise to the refund check.

4.   (N) A return preparer may in good faith rely without verification upon information furnished by the client or third parties, and is not required to audit, examine, or review books, records, or documents in order to independently verify the taxpayer's information. If the IRS requires supporting documentation as a condition for deductibility, the return preparer should make appropriate inquiries to determine whether the condition has been met.

5.   (P) A return preparer will be subject to penalty if there is a willful attempt in any manner to understate the tax liability of any taxpayer. A preparer is considered to have willfully attempted to understate liability if the preparer disregards information furnished by the taxpayer to wrongfully reduce the tax liability of the taxpayer.

6.   (N) A return preparer will be subject to penalty if the preparer knowingly or recklessly discloses information furnished in connection with the preparation of a tax return, unless such information is furnished for quality or peer review, under an administrative order by a regulatory agency, or pursuant to an order of a court.

7.   (E) Under these facts, a position taken on a return which is consistent with incorrect instructions does not satisfy the realistic possibility standard. However, if the preparer relied on the incorrect instructions and was not aware of the announcement or regulations, the reasonable cause and good faith exception may apply depending upon the facts and circumstances.

8.   (P) A return preparer will be subject to penalty if the preparer knowingly or recklessly discloses information furnished in connection with the preparation of a tax return, unless such information is furnished for quality or peer review, under an administrative order by a regulatory agency, or pursuant to an order of a court.

9.   (P) A return preparer will be subject to penalty if there is a willful attempt in any manner to understate the tax liability of any taxpayer or there is a reckless or intentional disregard of rules or regulations. The penalty will apply if a preparer knowingly deducts the expenses of the taxpayer's domestic help as wages paid in the taxpayer's business.

Simulation Problem 3

Part a.

For **items 1 through 5,** candidates were asked to identify the federal tax treatment for each item by indicating whether the item was fully includible in Remsen's gross estate (F), partially includible in Remsen's gross estate (P), or not includible in Remsen's gross estate (N).

1. **(N)** Generally, gifts made before death are not includible in the decedent's gross estate, even though the gifts were made within three years of death.

2. **(F)** The gross estate includes the value of all property in which the decedent had a beneficial interest at time of death. Here, the life insurance proceeds must be included in Remsen's gross estate because the problem indicates that Remsen was the owner of the policy.

3. **(F)** The fair market value of the marketable securities must be included in Remsen's gross estate because Remsen was the owner of the securities at time of death.

4. **(N)** Generally, gifts made before death are not includible in the decedent's gross estate.

5. **(F)** The $650,000 cash that Remsen owned must be included in Remsen's gross estate.

Part b.

For **items 6 through 10,** candidates were asked to identify the federal tax treatment for each item by indicating whether the item was deductible from Remsen's gross estate to arrive at Remsen's taxable estate (G), deductible on Remsen's 2003 individual income tax return (I), deductible on either Remsen's estate tax return or Remsen's 2003 individual income tax return (E), or not deductible on either Remsen's estate tax return or Remsen's 2003 individual income tax return (N).

6. **(N)** The $15,000 of executor's fees to distribute the decedent's property are deductible on **either** the federal estate tax return (Form 706) or the estate's fiduciary income tax return (Form 1041). Such expenses **cannot** be deducted twice. Since the problem indicates that these expenses were deducted on the fiduciary tax return (Form 1041), they cannot be deducted on the estate tax return.

7. **(N)** A decedent's gross estate is reduced by funeral and administrative expenses, debts and mortgages, casualty and theft losses, charitable bequests, and a marital deduction for the value of property passing to the decedent's surviving spouse. There is no deduction for bequests to beneficiaries other than the decedent's surviving spouse.

8. **(G)** Generally, property included in a decedent's gross estate will be eligible for an unlimited marital deduction if the property passes to the decedent's surviving spouse. Here, the life insurance proceeds paid to Remsen's spouse were included in Remsen's gross estate because Remsen owned the policy, and are deductible from Remsen's gross estate as part of the marital deduction in arriving at Remsen's taxable estate.

9. **(G)** Funeral expenses are deductible only on the estate tax return and include a reasonable allowance for a tombstone, monument, mausoleum, or burial lot.

10. **(E)** The executor of a decedent's estate may elect to treat medical expenses paid by the estate for the decedent's medical care as paid by the decedent at the time the medical services were provided. To qualify for this election, the medical expenses must be paid within the one-year period after the decedent's death, and the executor must attach a waiver to the decedent's Form 1040 indicating that the expenses will not be claimed as a deduction on the decedent's estate tax return. In this case, the medical expenses qualify for the election because Remsen died on January 9, 2003, and the expenses were paid on December 3, 2003.

Simulation Problem 4

For **items 1 through 7,** candidates were asked to identify the federal gift tax treatment for each item by indicating whether the item is fully taxable (F), partially taxable (P), or not taxable (N) to Lane in 2003 for gift tax purposes after considering the gift tax annual exclusion.

1. **(N)** There is no taxable gift because the $11,000 cash gift is a gift of a present interest and is fully offset by an $11,000 annual exclusion.

2. **(P)** The $20,000 of cash gifts given to his child would be partially offset by a $11,000 annual exclusion, resulting in a taxable gift of $9,000.

3. **(P)** The gift of the income interest valued at $26,000 to his aunt is a gift of a present interest and would be partially offset by an $11,000 annual exclusion, resulting in a taxable gift of $15,000.

4. **(F)** Since the remainder interest will pass to Lane's cousin after the expiration of five years, the gift of the remainder interest is a gift of a future interest and is not eligible for an annual exclusion. As a result, the $74,000 value of the remainder interest is fully taxable.

5. **(N)** An unlimited exclusion is available for medical expenses and tuition paid on behalf of a donee. Since Lane paid the $25,000 of tuition directly to his grandchild's university on his grandchild's behalf, the gift is fully excluded and not subject to gift tax.

6. **(F)** Since Lane created the irrevocable trust in 2003 but his brother will not begin receiving the income until 2005, the gift of the income interest to his brother is a gift of a future interest and cannot be offset by an annual exclusion. As a result, the gift is fully taxable for gift tax purposes.

7. **(P)** The creation of a revocable trust is not a completed gift and trust income is taxable to the grantor (Lane). As a result, a gift occurs only as the trust income is actually paid to the beneficiary. Here, the $12,000 of interest income received by the niece during 2003 is a gift of a present interest and would be partially offset by an $11,000 annual exclusion.

SIMULATION 1

Topic—Estate and Gift Taxation   (25 to 30 minutes)

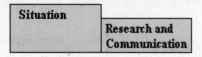

Glen Moore inherited stock from his mother, Ruth. She had died on September 1, 2003, when the stock had a fair market value of $150,000. Ruth had acquired the stock on May 15, 2003, at a cost of $120,000. Ruth's estate was too small to require the filing of a federal estate tax return. Moore wants to know how much gross income he must report because of the receipt of his inheritance in 2003. Additionally, Glen would like to know how much gain he will have to report if he sells the stock for $165,000 in January 2004. and whether his gain will qualify as a long-term capital gain.

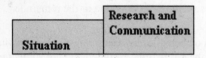

Use the Internal Revenue Code to research the answer to Glen's questions, and prepare a memo for your firm's client files indicating the results of your research.

SOLUTION TO SIMULATION 1

Keywords you might have used include, "inheritance," "basis," "holding period," and "capital gains and losses."

TO: Client Tax File

FROM: [*your name*]

DATE: [*today's date*]

Facts

Glen Moore inherited stock when his mother, Ruth, died on September 1, 2003. The stock had cost Ruth $120,000 on May 15, 2003, and had a fair market value of $150,000 on the date of her death. Ruth's estate was too small to require the filing of a Federal estate tax return. Moore may sell the stock for $165,000 in January 2004.

Issues

How much gross income must Moore report for 2003 because of his stock inheritance?
What amount and type of gain will Moore report if he sells the stock for $165,000 in January 2004?

Conclusion

The receipt of the stock will be excluded from Moore's gross income. The sale of the stock for $165,000 would result in a $15,000 long-term capital gain in 2004.

Support

Moore will be able to exclude the receipt of the stock from gross income since Code Sec. 102(a) provides that gross income does **not** include the value of property acquired by gift, bequest, devise, or inheritance. Sec. 1014(a)(1) provides that the basis of property acquired from a decedent shall be its fair market value at the date of decedent's death, which in this case is $150,000. Since the stock is being held as an investment and qualifies as a capital asset under Sec. 1221, a sale of the stock for $165,000 in January 2004 would result in a capital gain of $15,000. In regard to holding period, Sec. 1223(11) provides that if property is acquired from a decedent and its basis is determined under Sec. 1014, and the property is sold within one year after death, then the property shall be considered to have been held for more than one year. Finally, Sec. 1222 provides that the term "long-term capital gain" means gain from sale or exchange of a capital asset held for more than one year. As a result, Moore's gain of $165,000 – $150,000 = $15,000 would be reported as a long-term capital gain if the stock were sold in January 2004.

Action to Be Taken

Prepare letter and review results with client.

SIMULATION 2   (30 to 35 minutes)

Topic—Corporate Taxation

Situation			
	Tax Return Amounts	Deductibility	Research

Kimberly Corp. is a calendar-year accrual-basis corporation that commenced operations on January 1, 2000. The following adjusted accounts appear on Kimberly's records for the year ended December 31, 2003. Kimberly is not subject to the uniform capitalization rules.

Revenues and gains	
Gross sales	$2,000,000
Dividends:	
30%-owned domestic corporation	10,000
XYZ Corp.	10,000
Interest:	
US treasury bonds	26,000
Municipal bonds	25,000
Insurance proceeds	40,000
Gain on sale:	
Unimproved lot (1)	20,000
XYZ stock (2)	5,000
State franchise tax refund	14,000
Total	2,150,000
Costs and expenses	
Cost of goods sold	350,000
Salaries and wages	470,000
Depreciation:	
Real property	50,000
Personal property (3)	100,000
Bad debt (4)	10,000
State franchise tax	25,000
Vacation expense	10,000
Interest expense (5)	16,000
Life insurance premiums	20,000
Federal income taxes	200,000
Entertainment expense	20,000
Other expenses	29,000
Total	1,300,000
Net income	$ 850,000

Additional information

(1) Gain on the sale of unimproved lot: Purchased in 2001 for use in business for $50,000. Sold in 2003 for $70,000. Kimberly has never had any Sec. 1231 losses.

(2) Gain on sale of XYZ Stock: Purchased in 2000.

(3) Personal Property: The book depreciation is the same as tax depreciation for all the property that was placed in service before January 1, 2003. The book depreciation is straight-line over the useful life, which is the same as class life. Company policy is to use the half-year convention per books for personal property. Furniture and fixtures costing $56,000 were placed in service on January 2, 2003.

(4) Bad Debt: Represents the increase in the allowance for doubtful accounts based on an aging of accounts receivable. Actual bad debts written off were $7,000.

(5) Interest expense on

Mortgage loan	$10,000
Loan obtained to purchase municipal bonds	4,000
Line of credit loan	2,000

	Tax Return Amounts		
Situation		Deductibility	Research

Part a.

For **items 1 through 5,** determine the amount that should be reported on Kimberly Corporation's 2003 Federal income tax return.

Items to be answered

1. What amount of interest income is taxable from the US Treasury bonds?

2.   Determine the tax depreciation expense under the Modified Accelerated Cost Recovery System (MACRS), for the furniture and fixtures that were placed in service on January 2, 2003. Assume that no irrevocable depreciation election is made. Round the answer to the nearest thousand. Kimberly did not use the alternative depreciation system (ADS) or a straight-line method of depreciation. No election was made to expense part of the cost of the property, and no additional first-year depreciation was taken.

3.   Determine the amount of bad debt to be included as an expense item.

4.   Determine Kimberly's net long-term capital gain.

5.   What amount of interest expense is deductible?

Situation	Tax Return Amounts	Deductibility	Research

Part b.

For **items 6 through 10,** select whether the following expenses are fully deductible, partially deductible, or nondeductible, for regular tax purposes, on Kimberly's 2003 federal income tax return.

Selections

F.   Fully taxable for regular tax purposes on Kimberly Corp's 2003 federal income tax return.
P.   Partially taxable for regular tax purposes on Kimberly Corp's 2003 federal income tax return.
N.   Nontaxable for regular tax purposes on Kimberly Corp's 2003 federal income tax return.

	(F)	(P)	(N)
6. Organization expense incurred at corporate inception in 2000 to draft the corporate charter. No deduction was taken for the organization expense in 2000.	○	○	○
7. Life insurance premiums paid by the corporation for its executives as part of their compensation for services rendered. The corporation is neither the direct nor the indirect beneficiary of the policy and the amount of compensation is reasonable.	○	○	○
8. Vacation pay earned by employees which vested under a plan by December 31, 2003, and was paid February 1, 2004.	○	○	○
9. State franchise tax liability that has accrued during the year and was paid on March 15, 2004.	○	○	○
10. Entertainment expense to lease a luxury skybox during football season to entertain clients. A bona fide business discussion precedes each game. The cost of regular seats would have been one-half the amount paid.	○	○	○

Situation	Tax Return Amounts	Deductibility	Research

Part c.

Research the tax treatment of the dividend from the 30%-owned domestic corporation. Cut and paste the applicable Income Tax Code sections.

SOLUTION TO SIMULATION 2

Part a.

For **items 1 through 5,** candidates were required to determine the amount that should be reported on Kimberly Corp.'s 2003 Federal income tax return.

  1. **($26,000)** All $26,000 of interest income from US Treasury bonds is taxable.

  2. **($8,000)** The furniture and fixtures are classified as seven-year recovery property. Under MACRS, their cost of $56,000 will be recovered using the 200% declining balance method of depreciation and the half-year convention. Thus, the amount of depreciation for the year of acquisition would be $56,000 x 2/7 x 1/2 = $8,000.

  3. **($7,000)** The bad debt deduction consists of the $7,000 of bad debts actually written off during the year. The reserve method, using the increase in the allowance for doubtful accounts based on an aging of accounts receivable, cannot be used for tax purposes.

  4. **($25,000)** Since the unimproved lot was used in the business and held for more than one year, the $20,000 gain on its sale is classified as a Sec. 1231 gain. Since Kimberly had no previous nonrecaptured Sec. 1231 losses, the net Sec. 1231 gain is treated as a LTCG. Combining this $20,000 LTCG with the $5,000 LTCG from the sale of XYZ stock results in a net LTCG of $25,000.

  5. **($12,000)** Deductible interest expense consists of the $10,000 interest on the mortgage loan and the $2,000 interest on the line of credit loan. The $4,000 of interest expense on the loan obtained to purchase municipal bonds is not deductible because the municipal bonds produce tax-exempt income.

Part b.

For **items 6 through 10,** candidates were required to select whether the expenses are (F) fully deductible, (P) partially deductible, or (N) nondeductible, for regular tax purposes on Kimberly's 2003 federal income tax return.

  6. **(N)** Corporate organizational expenditures may be amortized over a period of sixty months or longer, beginning with the month that business begins, if a proper election statement is attached to the corporate return for the year that business begins. If no election is made, the expenditure must be capitalized and can only be deducted when the corporation is liquidated. Here, the problem indicates that Kimberly was formed and commenced operations during 2000, and further states that no deduction was taken for the organization expense in 2000. Although not specifically stated, this would indicate that no election was made to amortize the organization expense for 2000 and, as a result, no amortization deduction would be available for 2003.

  7. **(F)** The life insurance premiums are fully deductible because Kimberly is neither the direct nor indirect beneficiary of the policy. The life insurance premiums are deductible as part of the reasonable compensation paid to its executives.

  8. **(F)** An accrual method taxpayer can deduct vacation pay for employees **in the year earned** if (1) it is paid during the year, or (2) the vacation pay is vested and paid no later than 2 1/2 months after the end of the year. Here, the vacation pay was vested and paid on February 1, 2004.

  9. **(F)** Corporate franchise taxes are deductible as a business expense. An accrual method corporation can take a deduction for franchise taxes in the year it becomes legally liable to pay the tax regardless of the year that the tax is based on, or the year it is paid. The item indicates that the franchise tax liability accrued during the year (2003).

  10. **(P)** The cost to lease a skybox is disallowed as an entertainment expense to the extent that the amount paid exceeds the cost of the highest-priced nonluxury box seat tickets multiplied by the number of seats in the skybox. Since the item indicates that the cost of regular seats would have been one half the amount paid, only 50% of the cost of the skybox would qualify as an entertainment expense. Of this amount only 50% would be deductible for 2003.

Part c.

In researching the case, "corporate dividend exclusion" or "dividend exclusion" are appropriate keywords for the search. The appropriate excerpts from the IRC are presented below.

> *SEC. 243 Dividends Received by Corporations*
>
> > *243(a) General Rule—In the case of a corporation, there shall be allowed as a deduction an amount equal to the following percentages of the amount received as dividends from a domestic corporation which is subject to taxation under this chapter.*
> >
> > > *243(a)(1) 70 percent, in the case of dividends other than dividends described in paragraph (2) or (3);*
> > >
> > > *243(a)(2) 100 percent, in the case of dividends received by a small business investment company operating under the Small Business Investment Act of 1958 (15 U.S.C. 661 and following); and*
> > >
> > > *243(a)(3) 100 percent, in the case of qualifying dividends (as defined in subsection (b)(1)).*
> >
> > *243(b) Qualifying Dividends—*
> >
> > > *243(b)(1) In General—For purposes of this section, the term "qualifying dividend" means any dividend received by a corporation—*
> > >
> > > > *243(b)(1)(A) If at the close of the day on which such dividend is received, such corporation is a member of the same affiliated group as the corporation distributing such dividend, and*

243(b)(B) if—

243(b)(1)(B)(i) such dividend is distributed out of the earnings and profits of a taxable year of the distributing corporation which ends after December 31, 1963, for which an election under section 1562 was not in effect, and on each day of which the distributing corporation and the corporation receiving the dividend were members of such affiliated group, or

243(b)(1)(B)(ii) such dividends is paid by corporation with respect to which an election under section 936 is in effect for the taxable year in which such dividend is paid.

243(c) Retention of 80-Percent Dividends Received Deduction for Dividends from 20-Percent Owned Corporations.

243(c)(1) In General—In the case of any dividend received from a 20-percent owned corporation—

243(c)(1)(A) subsection (a)(1) of this section, and

243(c)(1)(B) subsections (a)(3) and (b)(2) of section 244, shall be applied by substituting "80 percent" for "70 percent."

1504(a)(4) Stock Not to Include Certain Preferred Stock—For purposes of this subsection, the term "stock" does not include any stock which—

1504(a)(4)(A) is not entitled to vote,

1504(a)(4)(B) is limited and preferred as to dividends and does not participate in corporate growth to any significant extent,

1504(a)(4)(C) has redemption and liquidation rights which do not exceed the issue price of such stock (except for a reasonable redemption or liquidation premium), and

1504(a)(4)(D) is not convertible into another class of stock.

SIMULATION 3   (25 to 30 minutes)

Topic—Individual Taxation

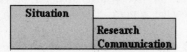

For 2003, Bill Marsh projects that he will pay interest expense of $40,000 on a loan that he used to purchase investment property. He further projects that for the year he will have investment interest income of $25,000, short-term capital gain from the sale of stock of $12,000, and will pay investment advisory fees of $2,000. Marsh is unmarried, projects his adjusted gross income to be $80,000, and plans to itemize deductions for 2003. He anticipates having no itemized deductions other than the investment advisory fees.

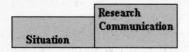

Marsh has contacted you to determine his projected 2003 deduction for investment interest expense. Use the Internal Revenue Code to research the amount of Marsh's deduction and prepare a memo for your firm's client files indicating the results of your research.

SOLUTION TO SIMULATION 3

Keywords you might have used include "interest paid," and "itemized deductions."

TO: Client Tax File

FROM: [*your name*]

DATE: [*today's date*]

Facts

For 2003, Bill Marsh projects that he will pay investment interest expense of $40,000, receive investment interest income of $25,000, recognize a short-term capital gain from the sale of stock of $12,000, and will pay investment advisory expenses of $2,000. Additionally, Marsh expects to have adjusted gross income of $80,000 and itemize deductions.

Issue

How much of the investment interest expense can be deducted by Marsh as an itemized deduction for 2003?

Conclusion

Marsh can deduct $36,600 of investment interest expense for 2003, and can carry forward the disallowed interest of $3,400 to 2004.

Support

Code Sec. 163(d)(1) provides that the amount allowed as a deduction for investment interest is limited to the taxpayer's net investment income. Sec. 163(d)(4)(A) provides that the term net investment income means the excess of investment income over investment expenses. Sec. 163(d)(2) provides that the amount of disallowed interest is carried forward and treated as investment interest in the succeeding year.

Sec. 163(d)(4)(B) indicates that the term investment income means (1) the gross income from property held for investment, plus (2) the net gain attributable to the disposition of property held for investment, reduced by the taxpayer's net capital gain. In this case Marsh has no net capital gain since Sec. 1222(11) provides that the term net capital gain means the excess of a taxpayer's net long-term capital gain over the taxpayer's net short-term capital loss. As a result, Marsh's investment income consists of his interest income of $25,000 plus his short-term capital gain of $12,000, a total of $37,000.

Sec. 163(d)(4)(C) provides that the term investment expenses means the deductions allowed that are directly connected with the production of income. Code Sec. 67 indicates that miscellaneous itemized deductions are allowed as a deduction only to the extent that they exceed 2 percent of adjusted gross income. In this case, Marsh's investment advisory fees of $2,000 will be allowed as a deduction to the extent that they exceed 2 percent of his $80,000 projected gross income (2% x $80,000 = $1,600), resulting in an itemized deduction of $400.

As a result, Marsh's projected $40,000 of investment interest will be deductible for 2003 to the extent of his net investment income which is projected to be $37,000 – $400 = $36,600. The disallowed interest of $3,400 will be carried forward to 2004.

Action to be Taken

Prepare letter and review results with client.

SIMULATION 4   (20 to 25 minutes)

Topic—Individual Taxation

Situation		
	Schedule A	Research

Fred (social security number 123-67-5489) and Laura Shaw provided you with the following tax return data. The amount from Form 1040, line 36 is $80,000.

Medical and dental expenses	
Medical insurance premiums	$3,600
Disability income insurance premiums	800
Prescription drugs	825
Nonprescription medicine	280
Dr. Jones – neurologist	2,250
Dentist	750
Dr. Smith – LASIK surgery	900
Insurance reimbursement for medical bills	2,000
Transportation to and from doctors	80

Taxes	
Balance of state income taxes due for 2001 paid on April 15, 2002	$ 225
State income taxes withheld for 2002	720
Real estate taxes on principal residence	7,000
Real estate taxes on summer residence	3,000
County personal property tax	410
Registration fee for automobiles	160
State sales taxes paid on purchase of new furniture (substantiated by receipts)	1,200

Interest	
Mortgage interest on principal residence	$5,500
Mortgage interest on summer residence	2,200
Interest paid on automobile loan	800
Interest paid on personal use credit cards	500

Contributions	
Cash donated to church	$2,500
Stock donated to church. (Shaws purchased it for $3,000 18 months ago)	4,000

Miscellaneous payments	
Legal fee for preparation of a will	$ 350
Rent for safety-deposit box containing stocks and bonds	120
Union dues	600
Subscriptions to investment publications	300
Life insurance premiums	2,800
Transportation to and from work	2,400
Fee paid for tax return preparation	400
Unreimbursed business travel away from home overnight	900
Contribution to a national political party	200
Repairs to principal residence	2,000

	Schedule A	
Situation		Research

Part a.

Complete the following 2002 Form 1040 Schedule for Fred and Laura.

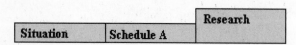

Part b.

For the 2003 income tax year the Shaws are considering donating to a state university a painting for display that they purchased three months ago for $90,000. The current market value of the painting is $92,000. Research the amount of the deductibility of the contribution and any limitations that might affect the deduction for 2003. Cut and paste applicable Internal Revenue Code sections.

SCHEDULES A&B
(Form 1040)

Department of the Treasury
Internal Revenue Service   (99)

Schedule A—Itemized Deductions

(Schedule B is on back)

▶ **Attach to Form 1040.** ▶ See Instructions for Schedules A and B (Form 1040).

OMB No. 1545-0074

2002

Attachment
Sequence No. **07**

Name(s) shown on Form 1040

Your social security number

Medical and Dental Expenses		**Caution.** Do not include expenses reimbursed or paid by others.		
	1	Medical and dental expenses (see page A-2) . . .	1	
	2	Enter amount from Form 1040, line 36 ⌊ 2 ⌋		
	3	Multiply line 2 by 7.5% (.075).	3	
	4	Subtract line 3 from line 1. If line 3 is more than line 1, enter -0-	4	
Taxes You Paid (See page A-2.)	5	State and local income taxes	5	
	6	Real estate taxes (see page A-2)	6	
	7	Personal property taxes	7	
	8	Other taxes. List type and amount ▶	8	
	9	Add lines 5 through 8	9	
Interest You Paid (See page A-3.)	10	Home mortgage interest and points reported to you on Form 1098	10	
	11	Home mortgage interest not reported to you on Form 1098. If paid to the person from whom you bought the home, see page A-3 and show that person's name, identifying no., and address ▶		
Note. Personal interest is not deductible.		....	11	
	12	Points not reported to you on Form 1098. See page A-3 for special rules . . .	12	
	13	Investment interest. Attach Form 4952 if required. (See page A-3.)	13	
	14	Add lines 10 through 13	14	
Gifts to Charity	15	Gifts by cash or check. If you made any gift of $250 or more, see page A-4	15	
If you made a gift and got a benefit for it, see page A-4.	16	Other than by cash or check. If any gift of $250 or more, see page A-4. You **must** attach Form 8283 if over $500	16	
	17	Carryover from prior year	17	
	18	Add lines 15 through 17	18	
Casualty and Theft Losses	19	Casualty or theft loss(es). Attach Form 4684. (See page A-5.)	19	
Job Expenses and Most Other Miscellaneous Deductions	20	Unreimbursed employee expenses—job travel, union dues, job education, etc. You **must** attach Form 2106 or 2106-EZ if required. (See page A-5.) ▶	20	
	21	Tax preparation fees.	21	
(See page A-5 for expenses to deduct here.)	22	Other expenses—investment, safe deposit box, etc. List type and amount ▶	22	
	23	Add lines 20 through 22	23	
	24	Enter amount from Form 1040, line 36 ⌊ 24 ⌋		
	25	Multiply line 24 by 2% (.02)	25	
	26	Subtract line 25 from line 23. If line 25 is more than line 23, enter -0-	26	
Other Miscellaneous Deductions	27	Other—from list on page A-6. List type and amount ▶		
			27	
Total Itemized Deductions	28	Is Form 1040, line 36, over $137,300 (over $68,650 if married filing separately)?		
		☐ **No.** Your deduction is not limited. Add the amounts in the far right column for lines 4 through 27. Also, enter this amount on Form 1040, line 38. ⎫ ⎬ ▶ ⎭	28	
		☐ **Yes.** Your deduction may be limited. See page A-6 for the amount to enter.		

For Paperwork Reduction Act Notice, see Form 1040 instructions.   Cat. No. 11330X   Schedule A (Form 1040) 2002

SOLUTION TO SIMULATION 4

Part a. (See Schedule A on the next page)

Medical and Dental Expenses

The disability income insurance premiums do not represent medical insurance and are not deductible. Similarly, although prescription drugs are deductible, nonprescription medicine is not deductible.

Taxes

Neither the automobile registration fees, nor the state sales taxes are deductible.

Interest

Only home mortgage interest and investment interest expense can be deducted as an itemized deduction. The interest on the automobile loan and the credit card interest are considered personal interest and are not deductible.

Contributions

The stock was appreciated and held for more than one year so it qualifies as capital gain property. As a result, the amount of contribution is the stock's fair market value of $4,000.

Miscellaneous

The legal fee for preparation of a will and life insurance premiums are nondeductible personal expenses. Similarly, no deduction is available for transportation to and from work (commuting), political contributions, and repairs to a principal residence.

Part b.

Appropriate keywords for the search include "section 170" or "charitable contributions." Because this is ordinary income property the deduction is limited to the fair market value of the gift reduced by the short-term capital gain that would have resulted from sale. The applicable IRC is shown below.

170(e) Certain Contributions of Ordinary Income and Capital Gain Property—

170(e)(1) General Rule—

> *The amount of any charitable contribution of property otherwise taken into account under this section shall be reduced by the sum of—*

> > *170(e)(1)(A) the amount of gain which would not have been long-term capital gain if the property contributed had been sold by the taxpayer at its fair market value (determined at the time of such contribution)*

The percentage limitation is 50% of the Shaws' adjusted gross income, computed without regard to any net operating loss carryback. The applicable IRC section is shown below.

170(b)(1) Individuals—

> *In the case if an individual, the deduction provided in subsection (a) shall be limited as provided in the succeeding subparagraphs.*

170(b)(1)(A) General Rule—

> *Any charitable contribution to—*

> > *170(b)(1)(A)(i) a church or a convention or association of churches,*

> > *170(b)(1)(A)(ii) an educational organization which normally maintains a regular faculty and curriculum and normally has a regularly enrolled body of pupils or students in attendance at the place where its educational activities are regularly carried on,*

> > *170(b)(A)(viii) an organization described in section 509(a)(2) or (3)*

> > > *Shall be allowed to the extent that the aggregate of such contributions does not exceed 50 percent of the taxpayer's contribution base for the taxable year.*

SCHEDULES A&B (Form 1040) Department of the Treasury Internal Revenue Service (99)	**Schedule A—Itemized Deductions** (Schedule B is on back) ▶ Attach to Form 1040. ▶ See Instructions for Schedules A and B (Form 1040).	OMB No. 1545-0074 20**02** Attachment Sequence No. **07**

Name(s) shown on Form 1040 FRED + LAURA SHAW   Your social security number 123 : 67 : 5489

Medical and Dental Expenses		**Caution.** Do not include expenses reimbursed or paid by others.			
	1	Medical and dental expenses (see page A-2)	1	6,405	
	2	Enter amount from Form 1040, line 36	2	80,000	
	3	Multiply line 2 by 7.5% (.075)	3	6,000	
	4	Subtract line 3 from line 1. If line 3 is more than line 1, enter -0-		4	405
Taxes You Paid (See page A-2.)	5	State and local income taxes	5	945	
	6	Real estate taxes (see page A-2)	6	10,000	
	7	Personal property taxes	7	410	
	8	Other taxes. List type and amount ▶ _____	8		
	9	Add lines 5 through 8		9	11,355
Interest You Paid (See page A-3.) **Note.** Personal interest is not deductible.	10	Home mortgage interest and points reported to you on Form 1098	10	7,700	
	11	Home mortgage interest not reported to you on Form 1098. If paid to the person from whom you bought the home, see page A-3 and show that person's name, identifying no., and address ▶	11		
	12	Points not reported to you on Form 1098. See page A-3 for special rules	12		
	13	Investment interest. Attach Form 4952 if required. (See page A-3.)	13		
	14	Add lines 10 through 13		14	7,700
Gifts to Charity If you made a gift and got a benefit for it, see page A-4.	15	Gifts by cash or check. If you made any gift of $250 or more, see page A-4	15	2,500	
	16	Other than by cash or check. If any gift of $250 or more, see page A-4. You **must** attach Form 8283 if over $500	16	4,000	
	17	Carryover from prior year	17		
	18	Add lines 15 through 17		18	6,500
Casualty and Theft Losses	19	Casualty or theft loss(es). Attach Form 4684. (See page A-5.)		19	
Job Expenses and Most Other Miscellaneous Deductions (See page A-5 for expenses to deduct here.)	20	Unreimbursed employee expenses—job travel, union dues, job education, etc. You **must** attach Form 2106 or 2106-EZ if required. (See page A-5.) ▶ UNION DUES #600 BUSINESS TRAVEL #900	20	1,500	
	21	Tax preparation fees	21	400	
	22	Other expenses—investment, safe deposit box, etc. List type and amount ▶ SAFE-DEPOSIT BOX #120 INVESTMENT PUBL. #300	22	420	
	23	Add lines 20 through 22	23	2,320	
	24	Enter amount from Form 1040, line 36	24	80,000	
	25	Multiply line 24 by 2% (.02)	25	1,600	
	26	Subtract line 25 from line 23. If line 25 is more than line 23, enter -0-		26	720
Other Miscellaneous Deductions	27	Other—from list on page A-6. List type and amount ▶ _____		27	
Total Itemized Deductions	28	Is Form 1040, line 36, over $137,300 (over $68,650 if married filing separately)? ☒ **No.** Your deduction is not limited. Add the amounts in the far right column for lines 4 through 27. Also, enter this amount on Form 1040, line 38. ☐ **Yes.** Your deduction may be limited. See page A-6 for the amount to enter. ▶		28	26,680

For Paperwork Reduction Act Notice, see Form 1040 instructions.   Cat. No. 11330X   Schedule A (Form 1040) 2002

SIMULATION 5   (40 to 45 minutes)

Topic—Partnership Taxation

Situation				
	Form 1065	**Schedule K**	**Schedule K-1**	**Research**

The Madison Restaurant (identification number 86-0806200) was formed last year as a cash method general partnership to operate the Madison Restaurant, which is located at 6001 Palm Trace Landing in Davie, Florida 33314. Bob Buron (social security number 347-54-1212) manages the restaurant and has a 60% capital and profits interest. His address is 1104 North 8th Court, Plantation, Florida 33324. Ray Hughes owns the remaining 40% partnership interest but is not active in the restaurant business. The partnership made cash distributions of $66,000 and $44,000 to Buron and Hughes respectively, on December 31 of the current year, but made no other property distributions. Madison's income statement for the year, ended December 31, 2002, is presented below.

Sales		$980,000
Cost of sales		460,000
Gross profit		520,000
Operating expenses		
Salaries and wages (excluding partners)	$190,000	
Guaranteed payment to Bob Buron	70,000	
Repairs and maintenance	10,000	
Rent expense	24,000	
Amortization of permanent liquor license	2,000	
Annual liquor license fee	1,000	
Depreciation	49,000	
Advertising	20,000	
Charitable contributions (cash)	8,000	
Total expenses		$374,000
Operating profit		$146,000
Other income and losses		
Gain on sale of ABE stock held 13 months	$12,000	
Loss on sale of TED stock held 7 months	(7,000)	
Sec. 1231 gain on sale of land	8,500	
Interest from US Treasury bills	3,000	
Dividends from ABE stock	1,500	
Interest from City of Ft. Lauderdale general obligation bonds	1,000	
Net other income		19,000
Net income		$165,000

Additional information

- Madison Restaurant began business on July 14, 2001, and its applicable business code number is 722110. It files its tax return with the Ogden, Utah IRS Service Center. The partnership had recourse liabilities at the end of the year of $25,000, and total assets of $282,000.
- The guaranteed payment to Bob Buron was for services rendered and was determined without regard to partnership profits. Buron's capital account at the beginning of 2002 totaled $135,000.
- The permanent liquor license was purchased for $10,000 from a café that had gone out of business. This license, which is renewable for an indefinite period, is being amortized per books over the five-year term of Madison's lease.
- The cost of depreciable personal property used in the restaurant operations was $200,000. Madison elected to expense the maximum allowable for these Sec. 179 assets, but elected not to take additional first-year depreciation. The $49,000 depreciation includes the Sec. 179 expense deduction.
- The gain on the sale of land resulted from the sale of a parking lot that the restaurant no longer needed.

	Form 1065			
Situation		**Schedule K**	**Schedule K-1**	**Research**

Part a.

Prepare Madison Restaurant's income and deductions on page 1 of Form 1065, Partnership Return.

		Schedule K		
Situation	Form 1065		Schedule K-1	Research

Part b.

Prepare Madison Restaurant's Schedule K, Partners' Shares of Income, Credits, Deduction, Etc.

Situation	Form 1065	Schedule K	Schedule K-1	Research

Part c.

Prepare Bob Buron's Schedule K-1, Partner's Share of Income, Credits, Deductions, Etc. (Do **not** prepare a Schedule K-1 for Ray Hughes.)

Situation	Form 1065	Schedule K	Schedule K-1	Research

Part d.

In 2003, Madison is considering distributing shares of stock in CDE Corporation to the partners. Research the applicable Internal Revenue Code sections to determine how the partners determine their basis in the stock distributed by the partnership.

Form **1065**	**U.S. Return of Partnership Income**	OMB No. 1545-0099
Department of the Treasury Internal Revenue Service	For calendar year 2002, or tax year beginning ...., 2002, and ending ...., 20..... . ▶ **See separate instructions.**	**2002**

A Principal business activity	Use the IRS label. Other- wise, print or type.	Name of partnership	**D** Employer identification number
B Principal product or service		Number, street, and room or suite no. If a P.O. box, see page 14 of the instructions.	**E** Date business started
C Business code number		City or town, state, and ZIP code	**F** Total assets (see page 14 of the instructions) $

G Check applicable boxes: **(1)** ☐ Initial return **(2)** ☐ Final return **(3)** ☐ Name change **(4)** ☐ Address change **(5)** ☐ Amended return
H Check accounting method: **(1)** ☐ Cash **(2)** ☐ Accrual **(3)** ☐ Other (specify) ▶ ....
I Number of Schedules K-1. Attach one for each person who was a partner at any time during the tax year ▶ ....

Caution: *Include **only** trade or business income and expenses on lines 1a through 22 below. See the instructions for more information.*

Income

1a	Gross receipts or sales	**1a**	
b	Less returns and allowances	**1b**	**1c**
2	Cost of goods sold (Schedule A, line 8)	**2**	
3	Gross profit. Subtract line 2 from line 1c	**3**	
4	Ordinary income (loss) from other partnerships, estates, and trusts *(attach schedule)* . . .	**4**	
5	Net farm profit (loss) *(attach Schedule F (Form 1040))*	**5**	
6	Net gain (loss) from Form 4797, Part II, line 18	**6**	
7	Other income (loss) *(attach schedule)*	**7**	
8	**Total income (loss).** Combine lines 3 through 7	**8**	

Deductions (see page 15 of the instructions for limitations)

9	Salaries and wages (other than to partners) (less employment credits) . . .	**9**	
10	Guaranteed payments to partners	**10**	
11	Repairs and maintenance	**11**	
12	Bad debts	**12**	
13	Rent	**13**	
14	Taxes and licenses	**14**	
15	Interest	**15**	
16a	Depreciation (if required, attach Form 4562) . . . **16a**		
b	Less depreciation reported on Schedule A and elsewhere on return **16b**		**16c**
17	Depletion **(Do not deduct oil and gas depletion.)**	**17**	
18	Retirement plans, etc.	**18**	
19	Employee benefit programs	**19**	
20	Other deductions *(attach schedule)*	**20**	
21	**Total deductions.** Add the amounts shown in the far right column for lines 9 through 20 .	**21**	
22	**Ordinary income (loss)** from trade or business activities. Subtract line 21 from line 8 . .	**22**	

Sign Here

Under penalties of perjury, I declare that I have examined this return, including accompanying schedules and statements, and to the best of my knowledge and belief, it is true, correct, and complete. Declaration of preparer (other than general partner or limited liability company member) is based on all information of which preparer has any knowledge.

May the IRS discuss this return with the preparer shown below (see instructions)? ☐ Yes ☐ No

▶ _____ ▶ _____
Signature of general partner or limited liability company member   Date

Paid Preparer's Use Only	Preparer's signature	Date	Check if self-employed ▶ ☐	Preparer's SSN or PTIN
	Firm's name (or yours if self-employed), address, and ZIP code ▶		EIN ▶	
			Phone no. ( )	

For Paperwork Reduction Act Notice, see separate instructions.   Cat. No. 11390Z   Form **1065** (2002)

Form 1065 (2002)

Schedule K	Partners' Shares of Income, Credits, Deductions, etc.			
	(a) Distributive share items		**(b) Total amount**	

Income (Loss)	**1** Ordinary income (loss) from trade or business activities (page 1, line 22)	**1**	
	2 Net income (loss) from rental real estate activities *(attach Form 8825)*	**2**	
	3a Gross income from other rental activities	**3a**	
	b Expenses from other rental activities *(attach schedule)*	**3b**	
	c Net income (loss) from other rental activities. Subtract line 3b from line 3a	**3c**	
	4 Portfolio income (loss): **a** Interest income	**4a**	
	b Ordinary dividends	**4b**	
	c Royalty income	**4c**	
	d Net short-term capital gain (loss) *(attach Schedule D (Form 1065))*	**4d**	
	e **(1)** Net long-term capital gain (loss) *(attach Schedule D (Form 1065))* ▶	**4e(1)**	
	(2) 28% rate gain (loss) ▶ .... **(3)** Qualified 5-year gain ▶		
	f Other portfolio income (loss) *(attach schedule)*	**4f**	
	5 Guaranteed payments to partners	**5**	
	6 Net section 1231 gain (loss) (other than due to casualty or theft) *(attach Form 4797)*	**6**	
	7 Other income (loss) *(attach schedule)*	**7**	
Deductions	**8** Charitable contributions *(attach schedule)*	**8**	
	9 Section 179 expense deduction *(attach Form 4562)* . . .	**9**	
	10 Deductions related to portfolio income (itemize) . . .	**10**	
	11 Other deductions *(attach schedule)*	**11**	
Credits	**12a** Low-income housing credit:		
	(1) From partnerships to which section 42(j)(5) applies . .	**12a(1)**	
	(2) Other than on line 12a(1)	**12a(2)**	
	b Qualified rehabilitation expenditures related to rental real estate activities *(attach Form 3468)*	**12b**	
	c Credits (other than credits shown on lines 12a and 12b) related to rental real estate activities	**12c**	
	d Credits related to other rental activities	**12d**	
	13 Other credits	**13**	
Invest-ment Interest	**14a** Interest expense on investment debts	**14a**	
	b **(1)** Investment income included on lines 4a, 4b, 4c, and 4f above	**14b(1)**	
	(2) Investment expenses included on line 10 above	**14b(2)**	
Self-Employ-ment	**15a** Net earnings (loss) from self-employment	**15a**	
	b Gross farming or fishing income	**15b**	
	c Gross nonfarm income	**15c**	
Adjustments and Tax Preference Items	**16a** Depreciation adjustment on property placed in service after 1986 . . .	**16a**	
	b Adjusted gain or loss	**16b**	
	c Depletion (other than oil and gas)	**16c**	
	d **(1)** Gross income from oil, gas, and geothermal properties . . .	**16d(1)**	
	(2) Deductions allocable to oil, gas, and geothermal properties . .	**16d(2)**	
	e Other adjustments and tax preference items *(attach schedule)*	**16e**	
Foreign Taxes	**17a** Name of foreign country or U.S. possession ▶		
	b Gross income from all sources	**17b**	
	c Gross income sourced at partner level	**17c**	
	d Foreign gross income sourced at partnership level:		
	(1) Passive ▶ .... **(2)** Listed categories *(attach schedule)* ▶ .... **(3)** General limitation ▶	**17d(3)**	
	e Deductions allocated and apportioned at partner level:		
	(1) Interest expense ▶ .... **(2)** Other . . . . . ▶	**17e(2)**	
	f Deductions allocated and apportioned at partnership level to foreign source income:		
	(1) Passive ▶ .... **(2)** Listed categories *(attach schedule)* ▶ .... **(3)** General limitation ▶	**17f(3)**	
	g Total foreign taxes (check one): ▶ Paid ☐ Accrued ☐	**17g**	
	h Reduction in taxes available for credit *(attach schedule)*	**17h**	
Other	**18** Section 59(e)(2) expenditures: **a** Type ▶ .... **b** Amount ▶	**18b**	
	19 Tax-exempt interest income	**19**	
	20 Other tax-exempt income	**20**	
	21 Nondeductible expenses	**21**	
	22 Distributions of money (cash and marketable securities) . . .	**22**	
	23 Distributions of property other than money	**23**	
	24 Other items and amounts required to be reported separately to partners *(attach schedule)*		

Form **1065** (2002)

| SCHEDULE K-1
(Form 1065)
Department of the Treasury
Internal Revenue Service | Partner's Share of Income, Credits, Deductions, etc.
► See separate instructions.
For calendar year 2002 or tax year beginning   , 2002, and ending   , 20 | OMB No. 1545-0099
2002 |

Partner's identifying number ► | **Partnership's identifying number ►**

Partner's name, address, and ZIP code | **Partnership's name, address, and ZIP code**

A This partner is a ☐ general partner ☐ limited partner
    ☐ limited liability company member
B What type of entity is this partner? ► ....
C Is this partner a ☐ domestic or a ☐ foreign partner?

	(i) Before change or termination	(ii) End of year

D Enter partner's percentage of:
    Profit sharing . . . . % .... %
    Loss sharing . . . . % .... %
    Ownership of capital . . . . % .... %
E IRS Center where partnership filed return:

F Partner's share of liabilities (see instructions):
    Nonrecourse . . . . $ ....
    Qualified nonrecourse financing . $ ....
    Other . . . . $ ....

G Tax shelter registration number . ► ....

H Check here if this partnership is a publicly traded
    partnership as defined in section 469(k)(2) . . . . . ☐

I Check applicable boxes: **(1)** ☐ Final K-1 **(2)** ☐ Amended K-1

J Analysis of partner's capital account:

(a) Capital account at beginning of year	(b) Capital contributed during year	(c) Partner's share of lines 3, 4, and 7, Form 1065, Schedule M-2	(d) Withdrawals and distributions	(e) Capital account at end of year (combine columns (a) through (d))
			( )	

	(a) Distributive share item		(b) Amount	(c) 1040 filers enter the amount in column (b) on:
Income (Loss)	**1** Ordinary income (loss) from trade or business activities . . .	**1**		See page 6 of Partner's Instructions for Schedule K-1 (Form 1065).
	2 Net income (loss) from rental real estate activities	**2**		
	3 Net income (loss) from other rental activities	**3**		
	4 Portfolio income (loss):			
	a Interest	**4a**		Sch. B, Part I, line 1
	b Ordinary dividends	**4b**		Sch. B, Part II, line 5
	c Royalties	**4c**		Sch. E, Part I, line 4
	d Net short-term capital gain (loss)	**4d**		Sch. D, line 5, col. (f)
	e (1) Net long-term capital gain (loss).	**4e(1)**		Sch. D, line 12, col. (f)
	(2) 28% rate gain (loss)	**4e(2)**		Sch. D, line 12, col. (g)
	(3) Qualified 5-year gain	**4e(3)**		Line 5 of worksheet for Sch. D, line 29
	f Other portfolio income (loss) (attach schedule)	**4f**		Enter on applicable line of your return.
	5 Guaranteed payments to partner	**5**		See page 6 of Partner's Instructions for Schedule K-1 (Form 1065).
	6 Net section 1231 gain (loss) (other than due to casualty or theft)	**6**		
	7 Other income (loss) (attach schedule)	**7**		Enter on applicable line of your return.
Deduc-tions	**8** Charitable contributions (see instructions) (attach schedule) . .	**8**		Sch. A, line 15 or 16
	9 Section 179 expense deduction	**9**		See pages 7 and 8 of Partner's Instructions for Schedule K-1 (Form 1065).
	10 Deductions related to portfolio income (attach schedule) . . .	**10**		
	11 Other deductions (attach schedule)	**11**		
Credits	**12a** Low-income housing credit:			
	(1) From section 42(j)(5) partnerships	**12a(1)**		Form 8586, line 5
	(2) Other than on line 12a(1)	**12a(2)**		
	b Qualified rehabilitation expenditures related to rental real estate activities	**12b**		
	c Credits (other than credits shown on lines 12a and 12b) related to rental real estate activities	**12c**		See page 8 of Partner's Instructions for Schedule K-1 (Form 1065).
	d Credits related to other rental activities	**12d**		
	13 Other credits	**13**		

For Paperwork Reduction Act Notice, see Instructions for Form 1065.   Cat. No. 11394R   **Schedule K-1 (Form 1065) 2002**

Schedule K-1 (Form 1065) 2002   Page **2**

	(a) Distributive share item		(b) Amount	(c) 1040 filers enter the amount in column (b) on:

Investment Interest

14a	Interest expense on investment debts	14a		Form 4952, line 1
b	(1) Investment income included on lines 4a, 4b, 4c, and 4f	14b(1)		} See page 9 of Partner's Instructions for Schedule K-1 (Form 1065).
	(2) Investment expenses included on line 10	14b(2)		

Self-employment

15a	Net earnings (loss) from self-employment	15a		Sch. SE, Section A or B
b	Gross farming or fishing income	15b		} See page 9 of Partner's Instructions for Schedule K-1 (Form 1065).
c	Gross nonfarm income	15c		

Adjustments and Tax Preference Items

16a	Depreciation adjustment on property placed in service after 1986	16a		
b	Adjusted gain or loss	16b		See page 9 of Partner's Instructions for Schedule K-1 (Form 1065) and Instructions for Form 6251.
c	Depletion (other than oil and gas)	16c		
d	(1) Gross income from oil, gas, and geothermal properties	16d(1)		
	(2) Deductions allocable to oil, gas, and geothermal properties	16d(2)		
e	Other adjustments and tax preference items (attach schedule)	16e		

Foreign Taxes

17a	Name of foreign country or U.S. possession ▶	17b		
b	Gross income from all sources	17b		
c	Gross income sourced at partner level	17c		
d	Foreign gross income sourced at partnership level:			
	(1) Passive	17d(1)		
	(2) Listed categories (attach schedule)	17d(2)		
	(3) General limitation	17d(3)		
e	Deductions allocated and apportioned at partner level:			Form 1116, Part I
	(1) Interest expense	17e(1)		
	(2) Other	17e(2)		
f	Deductions allocated and apportioned at partnership level to foreign source income:			
	(1) Passive	17f(1)		
	(2) Listed categories (attach schedule)	17f(2)		
	(3) General limitation	17f(3)		
g	Total foreign taxes (check one): ▶ ☐ Paid ☐ Accrued	17g		Form 1116, Part II
h	Reduction in taxes available for credit (attach schedule)	17h		Form 1116, line 12

Other

18	Section 59(e)(2) expenditures: **a** Type ▶			} See page 9 of Partner's Instructions for Schedule K-1 (Form 1065).
b	Amount	18b		
19	Tax-exempt interest income	19		Form 1040, line 8b
20	Other tax-exempt income	20		
21	Nondeductible expenses	21		See pages 9 and 10 of Partner's Instructions for Schedule K-1 (Form 1065).
22	Distributions of money (cash and marketable securities)	22		
23	Distributions of property other than money	23		
24	Recapture of low-income housing credit:			
a	From section 42(j)(5) partnerships	24a		} Form 8611, line 8
b	Other than on line 24a	24b		

Supplemental Information

25   Supplemental information required to be reported separately to each partner (attach additional schedules if more space is needed):

....

....

....

....

....

....

....

⊛   **Schedule K-1 (Form 1065) 2002**

SOLUTION TO SIMULATION 5

A partnership is a pass-through entity acting as a conduit to pass through items of income, deduction, and credit to be reported on the tax returns of its partners. Partnership items having special tax characteristics (e.g., passive activity losses, deductions subject to dollar or percentage limitations, etc.) must be separately listed and shown on Schedules K and K-1 so that their special characteristics are preserved when reported on partners' tax returns. In contrast, partnership ordinary income and deduction items having no special tax characteristics can be netted together in the computation of a partnership's ordinary income and deductions from trade or business activities on page 1 of Form 1065.

The solutions approach is to determine whether each item listed in the problem should be included in the computation of Madison's ordinary income and deductions on page 1 of Form 1065, or should be separately shown on Madison's Schedule K and Bob Buron's Schedule K-1 to retain any special tax characteristics that the item may have.

Schedule K is a summary schedule, listing the total of all partners' shares of income, deductions, and credits, including the net amount of a partnership's ordinary income (loss) from trade or business activities that is computed on page 1 of Form 1065. A Schedule K-1 is prepared for each partner listing only that particular partner's share of partnership income, deductions, credits, etc. Since Bob Buron has a 60% partnership interest, Buron's Schedule K-1 will generally reflect a 60% share of the amounts reported on Madison's Schedule K.

Specific Items

- Guaranteed payments made to a partner for services or for the use of capital are determined without regard to the income of the partnership. The $70,000 of guaranteed payments made to Bob Buron are deductible by the partnership in computing its ordinary income on page 1 of Form 1065, and must also be separately reported on line 5 of Schedules K and K-1 since the receipt of the guaranteed payments by Buron must be reported as ordinary income.

- No amortization of the permanent liquor license is allowed for tax purposes because the license is renewable for an indefinite period.

- The cost of qualifying property did not exceed $200,000 for 2002, so the maximum Sec. 179 expense deduction of $24,000 is available on Madison's return. Since this $24,000 limitation applies at both the partnership and partner levels, the Sec. 179 expense deduction must be separately reported on Schedules K and K-1. Since the depreciation deducted in the income statement includes the $24,000 of expense deduction, the income statement depreciation of $49,000 must be reduced by $24,000, which results in the $25,000 of depreciation that is deductible in computing Madison's ordinary income. The $24,000 Sec. 179 expense deduction must be separately shown on line 9 of Madison's Schedule K. $24,000 x 60% = $14,400 of Sec. 179 expense deduction reported on Bob Buron's Schedule K-1.

- The $8,000 of charitable contributions are not deductible in computing the partnership's ordinary income. Instead, charitable contributions are separately reported on line 8 of Madison's Schedule K and each partner's Schedule K-1 so the appropriate percentage limitation can be applied on partners' returns.

- The $12,000 of long-term capital gain, $7,000 of short-term capital loss, $3,000 of interest income from Treasury bills, and $1,500 of dividends are items of portfolio income and must be separately reported on line 4 of Madison's Schedule K, with 60% of each item reported on Buron's Schedule K-1. Similarly, the $8,500 of Sec. 1231 gain must be separately reported on Madison's Schedule K and partners' Schedules K-1 so that the Sec. 1231 netting process can take place at the partner level.

- The $1,000 of interest from City of Ft. Lauderdale bonds is tax-exempt and is reported on line 19 of Schedules K and K-1, while the $11,000 of cash distributions to partners is reported on line 22 of Schedules K and K-1.

- Partners are not employees but instead are treated as self-employed individuals. A partner's share of partnership's ordinary income plus any guaranteed payments received by the partner must be reported as self-employment income and is subject to self-employment tax. On Schedule K, the ordinary income from trade or business activities of $180,000 (line 1) is added to the $70,000 of guaranteed payments (line 5), with the total of $250,000 reported on lines 15a and 15c as net earnings from self-employment. On Schedule K-1, Buron's 60% share of the ordinary income ($180,000 x 60% = $108,000) is added to the $70,000 of guaranteed payments received by Buron with the total of $178,000 reported as Buron's net earnings from self-employment on lines 15a and 15c.

Form **1065**	**U.S. Return of Partnership Income**	OMB No. 1545-0099
Department of the Treasury Internal Revenue Service	For calendar year 2002, or tax year beginning ...., 2002, and ending ...., 20...... ▶ See separate instructions.	**2002**

A Principal business activity FOOD SERVICE	Use the IRS label. Other- wise, print or type.	Name of partnership MADISON RESTAURANT	**D** Employer identification number 86 : 0806200
B Principal product or service FOOD + DRINKS		Number, street, and room or suite no. If a P.O. box, see page 14 of the instructions. 6001 PALM TRACE LANDING	**E** Date business started 7-14-01
C Business code number 722110		City or town, state, and ZIP code DAVIE, FL 33314	**F** Total assets (see page 14 of the instructions) $ 282,000

G Check applicable boxes: (1) ☐ Initial return   (2) ☐ Final return   (3) ☐ Name change   (4) ☐ Address change   (5) ☐ Amended return

H Check accounting method: (1) ☒ Cash   (2) ☐ Accrual   (3) ☐ Other (specify) ▶ ....2....

I Number of Schedules K-1. Attach one for each person who was a partner at any time during the tax year ▶ ...2...

Caution: *Include **only** trade or business income and expenses on lines 1a through 22 below. See the instructions for more information.*

Income

1a	Gross receipts or sales	1a	980,000	
b	Less returns and allowances	1b		1c 980,000
2	Cost of goods sold (Schedule A, line 8)			2 460,000
3	Gross profit. Subtract line 2 from line 1c			3 520,000
4	Ordinary income (loss) from other partnerships, estates, and trusts *(attach schedule)*			4
5	Net farm profit (loss) *(attach Schedule F (Form 1040))*			5
6	Net gain (loss) from Form 4797, Part II, line 18			6
7	Other income (loss) *(attach schedule)*			7
8	**Total income (loss).** Combine lines 3 through 7			8 520,000

Deductions *(see page 15 of the instructions for limitations)*

9	Salaries and wages (other than to partners) (less employment credits)			9 190,000
10	Guaranteed payments to partners			10 70,000
11	Repairs and maintenance			11 10,000
12	Bad debts			12
13	Rent			13 24,000
14	Taxes and licenses			14 1,000
15	Interest			15
16a	Depreciation (if required, attach Form 4562)	16a	25,000	
b	Less depreciation reported on Schedule A and elsewhere on return	16b		16c 25,000
17	Depletion (**Do not deduct oil and gas depletion.**)			17
18	Retirement plans, etc.			18
19	Employee benefit programs			19
20	Other deductions *(attach schedule)* ADVERTISING			20 20,000
21	**Total deductions.** Add the amounts shown in the far right column for lines 9 through 20			21 340,000
22	**Ordinary income (loss)** from trade or business activities. Subtract line 21 from line 8			22 180,000

Sign Here

Under penalties of perjury, I declare that I have examined this return, including accompanying schedules and statements, and to the best of my knowledge and belief, it is true, correct, and complete. Declaration of preparer (other than general partner or limited liability company member) is based on all information of which preparer has any knowledge.

May the IRS discuss this return with the preparer shown below (see instructions)? ☐ Yes ☐ No

▶ _____   ▶ _____
Signature of general partner or limited liability company member   Date

Paid Preparer's Use Only	Preparer's signature		Date	Check if self-employed ▶ ☐	Preparer's SSN or PTIN
	Firm's name (or yours if self-employed), address, and ZIP code	▶		EIN ▶	
				Phone no. ( )	

For Paperwork Reduction Act Notice, see separate instructions.   Cat. No. 11390Z   Form **1065** (2002)

Form 1065 (2002)   Page **3**

Schedule K   **Partners' Shares of Income, Credits, Deductions, etc.**

	(a) Distributive share items		(b) Total amount
Income (Loss)	**1** Ordinary income (loss) from trade or business activities (page 1, line 22)	**1**	180,000
	2 Net income (loss) from rental real estate activities *(attach Form 8825)*	**2**	
	3a Gross income from other rental activities ⬚ **3a**		
	b Expenses from other rental activities *(attach schedule)* ⬚ **3b**		
	c Net income (loss) from other rental activities. Subtract line 3b from line 3a	**3c**	
	4 Portfolio income (loss): **a** Interest income	**4a**	3,000
	b Ordinary dividends	**4b**	1,500
	c Royalty income	**4c**	
	d Net short-term capital gain (loss) *(attach Schedule D (Form 1065))*	**4d**	(7,000)
	e **(1)** Net long-term capital gain (loss) *(attach Schedule D (Form 1065))*	**4e(1)**	12,000
	(2) 28% rate gain (loss) ▶ .... **(3)** Qualified 5-year gain ▶		
	f Other portfolio income (loss) *(attach schedule)*	**4f**	
	5 Guaranteed payments to partners	**5**	70,000
	6 Net section 1231 gain (loss) (other than due to casualty or theft) *(attach Form 4797)*	**6**	8,500
	7 Other income (loss) *(attach schedule)*	**7**	
Deductions	**8** Charitable contributions *(attach schedule)*	**8**	8,000
	9 Section 179 expense deduction *(attach Form 4562)*	**9**	24,000
	10 Deductions related to portfolio income (itemize)	**10**	
	11 Other deductions *(attach schedule)*	**11**	
Credits	**12a** Low-income housing credit:		
	(1) From partnerships to which section 42(j)(5) applies	**12a(1)**	
	(2) Other than on line 12a(1)	**12a(2)**	
	b Qualified rehabilitation expenditures related to rental real estate activities *(attach Form 3468)*	**12b**	
	c Credits (other than credits shown on lines 12a and 12b) related to rental real estate activities	**12c**	
	d Credits related to other rental activities	**12d**	
	13 Other credits	**13**	
Invest- ment Interest	**14a** Interest expense on investment debts	**14a**	
	b (1) Investment income included on lines 4a, 4b, 4c, and 4f above	**14b(1)**	
	(2) Investment expenses included on line 10 above	**14b(2)**	
Self- Employ- ment	**15a** Net earnings (loss) from self-employment	**15a**	250,000
	b Gross farming or fishing income	**15b**	
	c Gross nonfarm income	**15c**	250,000
Adjustments and Tax Preference Items	**16a** Depreciation adjustment on property placed in service after 1986	**16a**	
	b Adjusted gain or loss	**16b**	
	c Depletion (other than oil and gas)	**16c**	
	d (1) Gross income from oil, gas, and geothermal properties	**16d(1)**	
	(2) Deductions allocable to oil, gas, and geothermal properties	**16d(2)**	
	e Other adjustments and tax preference items *(attach schedule)*	**16e**	
Foreign Taxes	**17a** Name of foreign country or U.S. possession ▶		
	b Gross income from all sources	**17b**	
	c Gross income sourced at partner level	**17c**	
	d Foreign gross income sourced at partnership level:		
	(1) Passive ▶ .... **(2)** Listed categories *(attach schedule)* ▶ .... **(3)** General limitation ▶	**17d(3)**	
	e Deductions allocated and apportioned at partner level:		
	(1) Interest expense ▶ .... **(2)** Other	**17e(2)**	
	f Deductions allocated and apportioned at partnership level to foreign source income:		
	(1) Passive ▶ .... **(2)** Listed categories *(attach schedule)* ▶ .... **(3)** General limitation ▶	**17f(3)**	
	g Total foreign taxes (check one): ▶ Paid ☐ Accrued ☐	**17g**	
	h Reduction in taxes available for credit *(attach schedule)*	**17h**	
Other	**18** Section 59(e)(2) expenditures: **a** Type ▶ .... **b** Amount ▶	**18b**	
	19 Tax-exempt interest income	**19**	1,000
	20 Other tax-exempt income	**20**	
	21 Nondeductible expenses	**21**	
	22 Distributions of money (cash and marketable securities)	**22**	110,000
	23 Distributions of property other than money	**23**	
	24 Other items and amounts required to be reported separately to partners *(attach schedule)*		

Form **1065** (2002)

SCHEDULE K-1 (Form 1065) Department of the Treasury Internal Revenue Service	**Partner's Share of Income, Credits, Deductions, etc.** ▶ See separate instructions. For calendar year 2002 or tax year beginning , 2002, and ending , 20	OMB No. 1545-0099 **2002**

Partner's identifying number ▶	Partnership's identifying number ▶
Partner's name, address, and ZIP code BOB BURON 1104 NORTH 8th COURT PLANTATION, FL 33324	Partnership's name, address, and ZIP code MADISON RESTAURANT 6001 PALM TRACE LANDING DAVIE, FL 33314

A This partner is a ☒ general partner ☐ limited partner
☐ limited liability company member
B What type of entity is this partner? ▶ INDIVIDUAL
C Is this partner a ☒ domestic or a ☐ foreign partner?

F Partner's share of liabilities (see instructions):
Nonrecourse . . . . $ ....
Qualified nonrecourse financing . $ ....
Other . . . . $ ..15,000..

	(i) Before change or termination	(ii) End of year
D Enter partner's percentage of:		
Profit sharing . . . . %	.... %	60 %
Loss sharing . . . . %	.... %	60 %
Ownership of capital . . . . %	.... %	60 %

E IRS Center where partnership filed return: OGDEN, UT

G Tax shelter registration number . ▶ ....

H Check here if this partnership is a publicly traded partnership as defined in section 469(k)(2) . . . . . ☐

I Check applicable boxes: **(1)** ☐ Final K-1 **(2)** ☐ Amended K-1

J Analysis of partner's capital account:

(a) Capital account at beginning of year	(b) Capital contributed during year	(c) Partner's share of lines 3, 4, and 7, Form 1065, Schedule M-2	(d) Withdrawals and distributions	(e) Capital account at end of year (combine columns (a) through (d))
135,000	99,000	(66,000)		168,000

	(a) Distributive share item		(b) Amount	(c) 1040 filers enter the amount in column (b) on:
Income (Loss)	**1** Ordinary income (loss) from trade or business activities . . .	**1**	108,000	} See page 6 of Partner's Instructions for Schedule K-1 (Form 1065).
	2 Net income (loss) from rental real estate activities	**2**		
	3 Net income (loss) from other rental activities	**3**		
	4 Portfolio income (loss):			
	a Interest	**4a**	1,800	Sch. B, Part I, line 1
	b Ordinary dividends	**4b**	900	Sch. B, Part II, line 5
	c Royalties	**4c**		Sch. E, Part I, line 4
	d Net short-term capital gain (loss)	**4d**	(4,200)	Sch. D, line 5, col. (f)
	e (1) Net long-term capital gain (loss).	**4e(1)**	7,200	Sch. D, line 12, col. (f)
	(2) 28% rate gain (loss)	**4e(2)**		Sch. D, line 12, col. (g)
	(3) Qualified 5-year gain	**4e(3)**		Line 5 of worksheet for Sch. D, line 29
	f Other portfolio income (loss) (attach schedule)	**4f**		Enter on applicable line of your return.
	5 Guaranteed payments to partner	**5**	70,000	} See page 6 of Partner's Instructions for Schedule K-1 (Form 1065).
	6 Net section 1231 gain (loss) (other than due to casualty or theft)	**6**	5,100	
	7 Other income (loss) (attach schedule)	**7**		Enter on applicable line of your return.
Deductions	**8** Charitable contributions (see instructions) (attach schedule) . .	**8**	4,800	Sch. A, line 15 or 16
	9 Section 179 expense deduction	**9**	14,400	} See pages 7 and 8 of Partner's Instructions for Schedule K-1 (Form 1065).
	10 Deductions related to portfolio income (attach schedule) . . .	**10**		
	11 Other deductions (attach schedule)	**11**		
Credits	**12a** Low-income housing credit:			
	(1) From section 42(j)(5) partnerships	**12a(1)**		} Form 8586, line 5
	(2) Other than on line 12a(1)	**12a(2)**		
	b Qualified rehabilitation expenditures related to rental real estate activities	**12b**		
	c Credits (other than credits shown on lines 12a and 12b) related to rental real estate activities.	**12c**		See page 8 of Partner's Instructions for Schedule K-1 (Form 1065).
	d Credits related to other rental activities	**12d**		
	13 Other credits	**13**		

For Paperwork Reduction Act Notice, see Instructions for Form 1065.   Cat. No. 11394R   **Schedule K-1 (Form 1065) 2002**

Schedule K-1 (Form 1065) 2002   Page **2**

	(a) Distributive share item		(b) Amount	(c) 1040 filers enter the amount in column (b) on:
Investment Interest	**14a** Interest expense on investment debts	14a		Form 4952, line 1
	b (1) Investment income included on lines 4a, 4b, 4c, and 4f	14b(1)		See page 9 of Partner's Instructions for Schedule K-1 (Form 1065).
	(2) Investment expenses included on line 10	14b(2)		
Self-employment	**15a** Net earnings (loss) from self-employment	15a	178,000	Sch. SE, Section A or B
	b Gross farming or fishing income	15b		See page 9 of Partner's Instructions for Schedule K-1 (Form 1065).
	c Gross nonfarm income	15c	178,000	
Adjustments and Tax Preference Items	**16a** Depreciation adjustment on property placed in service after 1986	16a		
	b Adjusted gain or loss	16b		See page 9 of Partner's Instructions for Schedule K-1 (Form 1065) and Instructions for Form 6251.
	c Depletion (other than oil and gas)	16c		
	d (1) Gross income from oil, gas, and geothermal properties . .	16d(1)		
	(2) Deductions allocable to oil, gas, and geothermal properties	16d(2)		
	e Other adjustments and tax preference items *(attach schedule)*	16e		
Foreign Taxes	**17a** Name of foreign country or U.S. possession ▶			
	b Gross income from all sources	17b		
	c Gross income sourced at partner level	17c		
	d Foreign gross income sourced at partnership level:			
	(1) Passive	17d(1)		
	(2) Listed categories *(attach schedule)*	17d(2)		
	(3) General limitation	17d(3)		
	e Deductions allocated and apportioned at partner level:			Form 1116, Part I
	(1) Interest expense	17e(1)		
	(2) Other	17e(2)		
	f Deductions allocated and apportioned at partnership level to foreign source income:			
	(1) Passive	17f(1)		
	(2) Listed categories *(attach schedule)*	17f(2)		
	(3) General limitation	17f(3)		
	g Total foreign taxes (check one): ▶ ☐ Paid ☐ Accrued . .	17g		Form 1116, Part II
	h Reduction in taxes available for credit *(attach schedule)* . . .	17h		Form 1116, line 12
Other	**18** Section 59(e)(2) expenditures: **a** Type ▶			See page 9 of Partner's Instructions for Schedule K-1 (Form 1065).
	b Amount	18b		
	19 Tax-exempt interest income	19	600	Form 1040, line 8b
	20 Other tax-exempt income	20		
	21 Nondeductible expenses	21		See pages 9 and 10 of Partner's Instructions for Schedule K-1 (Form 1065).
	22 Distributions of money (cash and marketable securities) . . .	22	66,000	
	23 Distributions of property other than money	23		
	24 Recapture of low-income housing credit:			
	a From section 42(j)(5) partnerships	24a		Form 8611, line 8
	b Other than on line 24a	24b		
Supplemental Information	**25** Supplemental information required to be reported separately to each partner *(attach additional schedules if more space is needed)*:			

....

....

....

....

....

....

....

....

Schedule K-1 (Form 1065) 2002

Part d.

In researching this issue appropriate keywords include "basis of distributed property." The applicable IRS section is as follows:

SEC. 732. Basis of Distributed Property other than Money.

732(a) Distributions other than Liquidation of a Partner's Interest—

732(a)(1) General Rule—The basis of property (other than money) distributed by a partnership to a partner other than in liquidation of the partner's interest shall, except as provided in paragraph (2), be its adjusted basis to the partnership immediately before such distribution.

732(a)(2) Limitation—The basis to the distributee partner of property to which paragraph (1) is applicable shall not exceed the adjusted basis of such partner's interest in the partnership reduced by any money distributed in the same transaction.

REGULATION

TESTLET 1

1. Which of the following statements best describes the ethical standard of the profession pertaining to advertising and solicitation?
  - a. All forms of advertising and solicitation are prohibited.
  - b. There are **no** prohibitions regarding the manner in which CPAs may solicit new business.
  - c. A CPA may advertise in any manner that is **not** false, misleading, or deceptive.
  - d. A CPA may only solicit new clients through mass mailings.

2. Burrow & Co., CPAs, have provided annual audit and tax compliance services to Mare Corp. for several years. Mare has been unable to pay Burrow in full for services Burrow rendered nineteen months ago. Burrow is ready to begin fieldwork for the current year's audit. Under the ethical standards of the profession, which of the following arrangements will permit Burrow to begin the fieldwork on Mare's audit?
  - a. Mare sets up a two-year payment plan with Burrow to settle the unpaid fee balance.
  - b. Mare commits to pay the past due fee in full before the audit report is issued.
  - c. Mare gives Burrow an eighteen-month note payable for the full amount of the past due fees before Burrow begins the audit.
  - d. Mare engages another firm to perform the fieldwork, and Burrow is limited to reviewing the workpapers and issuing the audit report.

3. Which of the following is not a covered member for purposes of application of the independence requirements of the AICPA Code of Professional Conduct?
  - a. A staff person on the attest team.
  - b. A staff person that performs tax services for the attest client.
  - c. The partner in charge of the firm office that performs the attest engagement.
  - d. A partner that performs extensive consulting services for the attest client.

4. CPAs must be concerned with their responsibilities in the performance of professional services. In performing an audit, a CPA
  - a. Is strictly liable for failure to exercise due professional care.
  - b. Is strictly liable for failure to detect management fraud.
  - c. Is **not** liable unless the CPA is found to be grossly negligent.
  - d. Is strictly liable for failure to detect illegal acts.

5. The Apex Surety Company wrote a general fidelity bond covering defalcations by the employees of Watson, Inc. Thereafter, Grand, an employee of Watson, embezzled $18,900 of company funds. When his activities were discovered, Apex paid Watson the full amount in accordance with the terms of the fidelity bond, and then sought recovery against Watson's auditors, Kane & Dobbs, CPAs. Which of the following would be Kane & Dobbs' best defense?
  - a. Apex is not in privity of contract.

  - b. The shortages were the result of clever forgeries and collusive fraud that would not be detected by an examination made in accordance with generally accepted auditing standards.
  - c. Kane & Dobbs were not guilty either of gross negligence or fraud.
  - d. Kane & Dobbs were not aware of the Apex-Watson surety relationship.

6. If a stockholder sues a CPA for common law fraud based on false statements contained in the financial statements audited by the CPA, which of the following, if present, would be the CPA's best defense?
  - a. The stockholder lacks privity to sue.
  - b. The false statements were immaterial.
  - c. The CPA did **not** financially benefit from the alleged fraud.
  - d. The contributory negligence of the client.

7. Mathews is an agent for Sears with the express authority to solicit orders from customers in a geographic area assigned by Sears. Mathews has no authority to grant discounts nor to collect payment on orders solicited. Mathews secured an order from Davidson for $1,000 less a 10% discount if Davidson makes immediate payment. Davidson had previously done business with Sears through Mathews but this was the first time that a discount-payment offer had been made. Davidson gave Mathews a check for $900 and, thereafter, Mathews turned in both the check and the order to Sears. The order clearly indicated that a 10% discount had been given by Mathews. Sears shipped the order and cashed the check. Later, Sears attempted to collect $100 as the balance owed on the order from Davidson. Which of the following is correct?
  - a. Sears can collect the $100 from Davidson because Mathews contracted outside the scope of his express or implied authority.
  - b. Sears **cannot** collect the $100 from Davidson because Mathews, as an agent with express authority to solicit orders, had implied authority to give discounts and collect.
  - c. Sears **cannot** collect the $100 from Davidson as Sears has ratified the discount granted and made to Mathews.
  - d. Sears **cannot** collect the $100 from Davidson because, although Mathews had **no** express or implied authority to grant a discount and collect, Mathews had apparent authority to do so.

8. Which of the following regarding workers' compensation is correct?
  - a. A purpose of workers' compensation is for the employer to assume a definite liability in exchange for the employee giving up his common law rights.
  - b. It applies to workers engaged in or affecting interstate commerce only.
  - c. It is optional in most jurisdictions.
  - d. Once workers' compensation has been adopted by the employer, the amount of damages recoverable is based upon comparative negligence.

9. Regulation D of the Securities Act of 1933 is available to issuers without regard to the dollar amount of an offering only when the

    a.   Purchasers are all accredited investors.

    b.   Number of purchasers who are nonaccredited is thirty-five or less.

    c.   Issuer is **not** a reporting company under the Securities Exchange Act of 1934.

    d.   Issuer is **not** an investment company.

10. During an audit of Actee Corporation, you examine the following:

    (1) A check that is postdated and also says "Pay to Actee Corporation." You are concerned about these two issues but note that all other elements of negotiability are present in the check.

    (2) A note that is payable on demand and says "Pay to Actee Corporation" on its face. You see that all other issues about negotiability are satisfied.

You question whether or not the issues raised above destroy negotiability of these two instruments. Which of the instruments is(are) negotiable instruments?

	The check	*The note*
a.	Yes	Yes
b.	Yes	No
c.	No	Yes
d.	No	No

11. Nat purchased a typewriter from Rob. Rob is not in the business of selling typewriters. Rob tendered delivery of the typewriter after receiving payment in full from Nat. Nat informed Rob that he was unable to take possession of the typewriter at that time, but would return later that day. Before Nat returned, the typewriter was destroyed by a fire. The risk of loss

    a.   Passed to Nat upon Rob's tender of delivery.

    b.   Remained with Rob, since Nat had not yet received the typewriter.

    c.   Passed to Nat at the time the contract was formed and payment was made.

    d.   Remained with Rob, since title had **not** yet passed to Nat.

12. Marco Auto Inc. made many untrue statements in the course of inducing Rockford to purchase a used auto for $3,500. The car in question turned out to have some serious faults. Which of the following untrue statements made by Marco should Rockford use in seeking recovery from Marco for breach of warranty?

    a.   "I refused a $3,800 offer for this very same auto from another buyer last week."

    b.   "This auto is one of the best autos we have for sale."

    c.   "At this price the auto is a real steal."

    d.   "I can guarantee that you will never regret this purchase."

13. On April 14, 2003, Seeley Corp. entered into a written agreement to sell to Boone Corp. 1,200 cartons of certain goods at $.40 per carton, delivery within thirty days. The agreement contained no other terms. On April 15, 2003, Boone and Seeley orally agreed to modify their April 14 agreement so that the new quantity specified was 1,500 cartons, same price and delivery terms. What is the status of this modification?

    a.   Enforceable.

    b.   Unenforceable under the statute of frauds.

    c.   Unenforceable for lack of consideration.

    d.   Unenforceable because the change is substantial.

14. Purdy purchased real property from Hart and received a warranty deed with full covenants. Recordation of this deed is

    a.   Not necessary if the deed provides that recordation is not required.

    b.   Necessary to vest the purchaser's legal title to the property conveyed.

    c.   Required primarily for the purpose of providing the local taxing authorities with the information necessary to assess taxes.

    d.   Irrelevant if the subsequent party claiming superior title had actual notice of the unrecorded deed.

15. Peters defaulted on a purchase money mortgage held by Fairmont Realty. Fairmont's attempts to obtain payment have been futile and the mortgage payments are several months in arrears. Consequently, Fairmont decided to resort to its rights against the property. Fairmont foreclosed on the mortgage. Peters has all of the following rights **except**

    a.   To remain in possession as long as his equity in the property exceeds the amount of debt.

    b.   An equity of redemption.

    c.   To refinance the mortgage with another lender and repay the original mortgage.

    d.   A statutory right of redemption.

16. Richard Brown, who retired on May 31, 2003, receives a monthly pension benefit of $700 payable for life. His life expectancy at the date of retirement is ten years. The first pension check was received on June 15, 2003. During his years of employment, Brown contributed $12,000 to the cost of his company's pension plan. How much of the pension amounts received may Brown exclude from taxable income for the years 2003, 2004, and 2005?

	2003	*2004*	*2005*
a.	$0	$0	$0
b.	$4,900	$4,900	$4,900
c.	$ 700	$1,200	$1,200
d.	$4,900	$8,400	$8,400

17. Lee, an attorney, uses the cash receipts and disbursements method of reporting. In 2003, a client gave Lee 500 shares of a listed corporation's stock in full satisfaction of a $10,000 legal fee the client owed to Lee. This stock had a fair market value of $8,000 on the date it was given to Lee. The client's basis for this stock was $6,000. Lee sold the stock for cash in January 2004. In Lee's 2003 income tax return, what amount of income should be reported in connection with the receipt of the stock?

    a. $10,000

    b. $ 8,000

    c. $ 6,000

    d. $0

18. Don Wolf became a general partner in Gata Associates on January 1, 2003, with a 5% interest in Gata's profits, losses, and capital. Gata is a distributor of auto parts. Wolf does not materially participate in the partnership business. For the year ended December 31, 2003, Gata had an operating loss of $100,000. In addition, Gata earned interest of $20,000 on a temporary investment. Gata has kept the principal temporarily invested while awaiting delivery of equipment that is presently on order. The principal will be used to pay for this equipment. Wolf's passive loss for 2003 is

a. $0
b. $4,000
c. $5,000
d. $6,000

19. In 2003, Don Mills, a single taxpayer, had $70,000 in taxable income before personal exemptions. Mills had no tax preferences. His itemized deductions were as follows:

State and local income taxes	$5,000
Home mortgage interest on loan to acquire residence	6,000
Miscellaneous deductions that exceed 2% of adjusted gross income	2,000

What amount did Mills report as alternative minimum taxable income before the AMT exemption?

a. $72,000
b. $75,000
c. $77,000
d. $83,000

20. An accuracy-related penalty applies to the portion of tax underpayment attributable to

I. Negligence or a disregard of the tax rules or regulations.
II. Any substantial understatement of income tax.

a. I only.
b. II only.
c. Both I and II.
d. Neither I nor II.

21. Smith, an individual calendar-year taxpayer, purchased 100 shares of Core Co. common stock for $15,000 on December 15, 2003, and an additional 100 shares for $13,000 on December 30, 2003. On January 3, 2004, Smith sold the shares purchased on December 15, 2003, for $13,000. What amount of loss from the sale of Core's stock is deductible on Smith's 2003 and 2004 income tax returns?

	2003	2004
a.	$0	$0
b.	$0	$2,000
c.	$1,000	$1,000
d.	$2,000	$0

22. Strom acquired a 25% interest in Ace Partnership by contributing land having an adjusted basis of $16,000 and a fair market value of $50,000. The land was subject to a $24,000 mortgage, which was assumed by Ace. No other liabilities existed at the time of the contribution. What was Strom's basis in Ace?

a. $0
b. $16,000
c. $26,000
d. $32,000

Items 23 and 24 are based on the following data:

Mike Reed, a partner in Post Co., received the following distribution from Post:

	Post's basis	Fair market value
Cash	$11,000	$11,000
Land	5,000	12,500

Before this distribution, Reed's basis in Post was $25,000.

23. If this distribution were nonliquidating, Reed's recognized gain or loss on the distribution would be

a. $11,000 gain.
b. $ 9,000 loss.
c. $ 1,500 loss.
d. $0.

24. If this distribution were in complete liquidation of Reed's interest in Post, Reed's basis for the land would be

a. $14,000
b. $12,500
c. $ 5,000
d. $ 1,500

25. Finbury Corporation's taxable income for the year ended December 31, 2003, was $2,000,000 on which its tax liability was $680,000. In order for Finbury to escape the estimated tax underpayment penalty for the year ending December 31, 2004, Finbury's 2004 estimated tax payments must equal at least

a. 90% of the 2004 tax liability.
b. 93% of the 2004 tax liability.
c. 100% of the 2004 tax liability.
d. The 2003 tax liability of $680,000.

26. Barbaro Corporation's retained earnings at January 1, 2003, was $600,000. During 2003 Barbaro paid cash dividends of $150,000 and received a federal income tax refund of $26,000 as a result of an IRS audit of Barbaro's 2000 tax return. Barbaro's net income per books for the year ended December 31, 2003, was $274,900 after deducting federal income tax of $183,300. How much should be shown in the reconciliation Schedule M-2, of Form 1120, as Barbaro's retained earnings at December 31, 2003?

a. $443,600
b. $600,900
c. $626,900
d. $750,900

27. Brooke, Inc., an S corporation, was organized on January 2, 2003, with two equal stockholders who materially participate in the S corporation's business. Each stockholder invested $5,000 in Brooke's capital stock, and each loaned $15,000 to the corporation. Brooke then borrowed $60,000 from a bank for working capital. Brooke sustained an operating loss of $90,000 for the year ended December 31, 2003. How much of this loss can each stockholder claim on his 2003 income tax return?

a. $ 5,000
b. $20,000
c. $45,000
d. $50,000

28. When Jim and Nina became engaged in April 2003, Jim gave Nina a ring that had a fair market value of $50,000. After their wedding in July 2003, Jim gave Nina $75,000 in cash so that Nina could have her own bank account. Both Jim and Nina are US citizens. What was the amount of Jim's 2003 marital deduction?

a. $0
b. $ 75,000
c. $115,000
d. $125,000

29. Ross, a calendar-year, cash-basis taxpayer who died in June 2003, was entitled to receive a $10,000 accounting fee that had not been collected before the date of death. The executor of Ross' estate collected the full $10,000 in July 2003. This $10,000 should appear in

    a.   Only the decedent's final individual income tax return.

    b.   Only the estate's fiduciary income tax return.

    c.   Only the estate tax return.

    d.   Both the fiduciary income tax return and the estate tax return.

30. Kopel was engaged to prepare Raff's 2003 federal income tax return. During the tax preparation interview, Raff told Kopel that he paid $3,000 in property taxes in 2003. Actually, Raff's property taxes amounted to only $600. Based on Raff's word, Kopel deducted the $3,000 on Raff's return, resulting in an understatement of Raff's tax liability. Kopel had no reason to believe that the information was incorrect. Kopel did not request underlying documentation and was reasonably satisfied by Raff's representation that Raff had adequate records to support the deduction. Which of the following statements is correct?

    a.   To avoid the preparer penalty for willful understatement of tax liability, Kopel was obligated to examine the underlying documentation for the deduction.

    b.   To avoid the preparer penalty for willful understatement of tax liability, Kopel would be required to obtain Raff's representation in writing.

    c.   Kopel is **not** subject to the preparer penalty for willful understatement of tax liability because the deduction that was claimed was more than 25% of the actual amount that should have been deducted.

    d.   Kopel is **not** subject to the preparer penalty for willful understatement of tax liability because Kopel was justified in relying on Raff's representation.

REGULATION
ANSWERS TO TESTLET 1

1. c	**5.** b	**9.** b	**13.** b	**17.** b	**21.** a	**25.** c	**29.** d
2. b	**6.** b	**10.** b	**14.** d	**18.** c	**22.** a	**26.** d	**30.** d
3. b	**7.** c	**11.** a	**15.** a	**19.** c	**23.** d	**27.** b	
4. a	**8.** a	**12.** a	**16.** c	**20.** c	**24.** a	**28.** b	

Regulation Hints

1. Advertising must be appropriate.

2. Prior year past due fees impair independence.

3. Only managers or partners performing nonattest services for an attest client may become covered members.

4. Professionals must exercise due professional care.

5. Compliance with GAAS indicates due care.

6. Recall proof requirements.

7. The principal accepted the benefits of the unauthorized act.

8. Employee gives up rights but receives automatic payment.

9. Recall the requirements for a private placement.

10. A note, unlike a draft or a check, is a two-party instrument.

11. Rob is **not** a merchant.

12. An **explicit** declaration of fact forms an express warranty; sales talk and predictions do not.

13. After modification, contract is for >$500.

14. Notice can be constructive or actual.

15. Foreclosure ends the mortgagor's rights in the property.

16. Each payment is part income and part a return of Brown's investment.

17. The amount of compensation is determined from the value of the property received.

18. Interest is generally considered portfolio income.

19. Qualified residence interest in the form of acquisition indebtedness is deductible for AMT purposes.

20. The items listed are two components of the accuracy-related penalty.

21. The acquisition of substantially identical stock with a thirty-day period before or after the date of the loss results in a wash sale.

22. The 75% net reduction in liability is treated as a deemed cash distribution.

23. No loss can be recognized in a nonliquidating distribution.

24. No loss can be recognized in a liquidating distribution if property other than cash, receivables, or inventory is received.

25. Because of taxable income in excess of $1 million, Finbury cannot use its tax for the preceding year as a safe estimate.

26. Schedule M-2 provides a reconciliation of unappropriated retained earnings per books.

27. Shareholders do not receive basis for the corporation's debts to third parties.

28. The taxpayer must be married on the date of gift to qualify for the marital deduction.

29. The fee qualifies as income in respect of a decedent.

30. A preparer is not required to audit or examine a client's books and records.

REGULATION

TESTLET 2

1. Under the ethical standards of the profession, which of the following situations involving independent members of an auditor's family is most likely to impair the auditor's independence?
   a. A parent's immaterial investment in a client.
   b. A first cousin's loan from a client.
   c. A spouse's employment with a client.
   d. A sibling's loan to a director of a client.

2. What body has the responsibility for issuing auditing standards for auditors of public companies?
   a. The AICPA's Auditing Standards Board.
   b. The Chief Accountant of the Securities and Exchange Commission.
   c. The Public Company Accounting Oversight Board.
   d. The Financial Accounting Standards Board.

3. According to the ethical standards for the profession, which of the following would impair the independence of an auditor in providing an audit for First State Bank, a nonpublic financial institution?
   a. The accountant has an automobile loan with the bank collateralized by the automobile.
   b. The accountant has a credit card with the bank with an outstanding balance of $10,000.
   c. The accountant has a $20,000 loan at the bank collateralized by a certificate of deposit.
   d. The accountant has a demand deposit account of $25,000 with the bank.

4. Hart, CPA, is concerned about the type of fee arrangements that are permissible under the profession's ethical standards. Which of the following professional services may be performed for a contingent fee?
   a. A review of financial statements.
   b. An examination of prospective financial statements.
   c. Preparation of a tax return.
   d. Information technology consulting.

5. Rhodes Corp. desired to acquire the common stock of Harris Corp. and engaged Johnson & Co., CPAs, to audit the financial statements of Harris Corp. Johnson failed to discover a significant liability in performing the audit. In a common law action against Johnson, Rhodes at a minimum must prove
   a. Gross negligence on the part of Johnson.
   b. Negligence on the part of Johnson.
   c. Fraud on the part of Johnson.
   d. Johnson knew that the liability existed.

6. A debtor will be denied a discharge in bankruptcy if the debtor
   a. Failed to timely list a portion of his debts.
   b. Unjustifiably failed to preserve his books and records which could have been used to ascertain the debtor's financial condition.
   c. Has negligently made preferential transfers to favored creditors within ninety days of the filing of the bankruptcy petition.
   d. Has committed several willful and malicious acts that resulted in bodily injury to others.

7. Which of the following is a part of the social security law?
   a. A self-employed person must contribute an annual amount that is equal to the combined contributions of an employee and his or her employer.
   b. Upon the death of an employee prior to his retirement, his estate is entitled to receive the amount attributable to his contributions as a death benefit.
   c. Social security benefits must be fully funded and payments, current and future, must constitutionally come only from social security taxes.
   d. Social security benefits are taxable as income when they exceed the individual's total contributions.

8. Duval Manufacturing Industries, Inc. orally engaged Harris as one of its district sales managers for an eighteen-month period commencing April 1, 2003. Harris commenced work on that date and performed his duties in a highly competent manner for several months. On October 1, 2003, the company gave Harris a notice of termination as of November 1, 2003, citing a downturn in the market for its products. Harris sues seeking either specific performance or damages for breach of contract. Duval pleads the Statute of Frauds and/or a justified dismissal due to the economic situation. What is the probable outcome of the lawsuit?
   a. Harris will prevail because he has partially performed under the terms of the contract.
   b. Harris will lose because his termination was caused by economic factors beyond Duval's control.
   c. Harris will lose because such a contract must be in writing and signed by a proper agent of Duval.
   d. Harris will prevail because the Statute of Frauds does **not** apply to contracts such as his.

9. Harp Corp. is offering to issue $450,000 of its securities pursuant to Regulation D of the Securities Act of 1933. Harp is not required to deliver a disclosure document in the states where the offering is being conducted. The exemption for small issues of $500,000 or less (Rule 504) under Regulation D
   a. Requires that the issuer be subject to the reporting requirements of the Securities Exchange Act of 1934.
   b. Does **not** require that any specific information be furnished to investors.
   c. Permits the use of general solicitation.
   d. Requires that each investor be a sophisticated investor or be represented by a purchaser representative.

10. Which of the following will **not** constitute value in determining whether a person is a holder in due course?
   a. The taking of a negotiable instrument for a future consideration.
   b. The taking of a negotiable instrument as security for a loan.
   c. The giving of one's own negotiable instrument in connection with the purchase of another negotiable instrument.

d. The performance of services rendered the payee of a negotiable instrument who endorses it in payment for services.

11. Kent, a wholesale distributor of cameras, entered into a contract with Williams. Williams agreed to purchase 100 cameras with certain optional attachments. The contract was made on March 1, 2002, for delivery by March 15, 2002; terms: 2/10, net 30. Kent shipped the cameras on March 6, and they were delivered on March 10. The shipment did not conform to the contract, in that one of the attachments was not included. Williams immediately notified Kent that he was rejecting the goods. For maximum legal advantage Kent's most appropriate action is to

   a. Bring an action for the price less an allowance for the missing attachment.

   b. Notify Williams promptly of his intention to cure the defect and make a conforming delivery by March 15.

   c. Terminate his contract with Williams and recover for breach of contract.

   d. Sue Williams for specific performance.

12. If a seller repudiates his contract with a buyer for the sale of 100 radios, what recourse does the buyer have?

   a. He can "cover" (i.e., procure the goods elsewhere and recover the difference).

   b. He must await the seller's performance for a commercially reasonable time after repudiation.

   c. He can obtain specific performance by the seller.

   d. He can recover punitive damages.

13. Wilmont owned a tract of waterfront property on Big Lake. During Wilmont's ownership of the land, several frame bungalows were placed on the land by tenants who rented the land from Wilmont. In addition to paying rent, the tenants paid for the maintenance and insurance of the bungalows, repaired, altered and sold them, without permission or hindrance from Wilmont. The bungalows rested on surface cinderblock and were not bolted to the ground. The buildings could be removed without injury to either the buildings or the land. Wilmont sold the land to Marsh. The deed to Marsh recited that Wilmont sold the land, with buildings thereon, "subject to the rights of tenants, if any, ..." When the tenants attempted to remove the bungalows, Marsh claimed ownership of them. In deciding who owns the bungalows, which of the following is **least** significant?

   a. The leasehold agreement itself, to the extent it manifested the intent of the parties.

   b. The mode and degree of annexation of the buildings to the land.

   c. The degree to which removal would cause injury to the buildings or the land.

   d. The fact that the deed included a general clause relating to the buildings.

14. Smith purchased a tract of land. To protect himself, he ordered title insurance from Valor Title Insurance Company. The policy was the usual one issued by title companies. Accordingly

   a. Valor will not be permitted to take exceptions to its coverage if it agreed to insure and prepared the title abstract.

   b. The title policy is assignable in the event Smith subsequently sells the property.

   c. The title policy provides protection against defects in record title only.

   d. Valor will be liable for any title defect that arises, even though the defect could **not** have been discovered through the exercise of reasonable care.

15. Tremont Enterprises, Inc. needed some additional working capital to develop a new product line. It decided to obtain intermediate term financing by giving a second mortgage on its plant and warehouse. Which of the following is true with respect to the mortgages?

   a. If Tremont defaults on both mortgages and a bankruptcy proceeding is initiated, the second mortgagee has the status of general creditor.

   b. If the second mortgagee proceeds to foreclose on its mortgage, the first mortgagee must be satisfied completely before the second mortgagee is entitled to repayment.

   c. Default on payment to the second mortgagee will constitute default on the first mortgage.

   d. Tremont **cannot** prepay the second mortgage prior to its maturity without the consent of the first mortgagee.

16. Frank Lanier is a resident of a state that imposes a tax on income. The following information pertaining to Lanier's state income taxes is available:

Taxes withheld in 2003	$3,500
Refund received in 2003 of 2002 tax	400
Deficiency assessed and paid in 2003 for 2001:	
Tax	600
Interest	100

What amount should Lanier utilize as state and local income taxes in calculating itemized deductions for his 2003 federal tax return?

   a. $3,500

   b. $3,700

   c. $4,100

   d. $4,200

17. Ace Rentals, Inc., an accrual-basis taxpayer, reported rent receivable of $35,000 and $25,000 in its 2003 and 2002 balance sheets, respectively. During 2003, Ace received $50,000 in rent payments and $5,000 in nonrefundable rent deposits. In Ace's 2003 corporate income tax return, what amount should Ace include as rent revenue?

   a. $50,000

   b. $55,000

   c. $60,000

   d. $65,000

18. Sol and Julia Crane (both age 41) are married, and filed a joint return for 2003. Sol earned a salary of $80,000 in 2003 from his job at Troy Corp., where Sol is covered by his employer's pension plan. In addition, Sol and Julia earned interest of $3,000 in 2003 on their joint savings account. Julia is not employed, and the couple had no other income. On January 15, 2004, Sol contributed $3,000 to an IRA for himself, and $3,000 to an IRA for his spouse. The allowable IRA deduction in the Cranes' 2003 joint return is

   a. $0

   b. $1,500

   c. $3,000

   d. $6,000

19. Spencer, who itemizes deductions, had adjusted gross income of $60,000 in 2003. The following additional information is available for 2003:

Cash contribution to church	$4,000
Purchase of art object at church bazaar (with a fair market value of $800 on the date of purchase)	1,200
Donation of used clothing to Salvation Army (fair value evidenced by receipt received)	600

What is the maximum amount Spencer can claim as a deduction for charitable contributions in 2003?

- a. $5,400
- b. $5,200
- c. $5,000
- d. $4,400

20. The following information pertains to Wald Corp.'s operations for the year ended December 31, 2003:

Worldwide taxable income	$300,000
US source taxable income	180,000
US income tax before foreign tax credit	96,000
Foreign nonbusiness-related interest earned	30,000
Foreign income taxes paid on nonbusiness-related interest earned	12,000
Other foreign source taxable income	90,000
Foreign income taxes paid on other foreign source taxable income	27,000

What amount of foreign tax credit may Wald claim for 2003?

- a. $28,800
- b. $36,600
- c. $38,400
- d. $39,000

21. Platt owns land that is operated as a parking lot. A shed was erected on the lot for the related transactions with customers. With regard to capital assets and Section 1231 assets, how should these assets be classified?

	Land	Shed
a.	Capital	Capital
b.	Section 1231	Capital
c.	Capital	Section 1231
d.	Section 1231	Section 1231

22. At partnership inception, Black acquires a 50% interest in Decorators Partnership by contributing property with an adjusted basis of $80,000. Black recognizes a gain if

- I. The fair market value of the contributed property exceeds its adjusted basis.
- II. The property is encumbered by a mortgage with a balance of $100,000.

- a. I only.
- b. II only.
- c. Both I and II.
- d. Neither I nor II.

Items 23 and 24 are based on the following data:

The partnership of Hager, Mazer & Slagle had the following cash-basis balance sheet at December 31, 2003:

	Adjusted basis per books	Fair market value
Assets		
Cash	$51,000	$ 51,000
Accounts receivable	--	210,000
Totals	$51,000	$261,000

	Adjusted basis per books	Fair market value
Liabilities and Capital		
Note payable	$30,000	$ 30,000
Capital accounts:		
Hager	7,000	77,000
Mazer	7,000	77,000
Slagle	7,000	77,000
Totals	$51,000	$261,000

Slagle, an equal partner, sold his partnership interest to Burns, an outsider, for $77,000 cash on January 1, 2004. In addition, Burns assumed Slagle's share of partnership liabilities.

23. What was the total amount realized by Slagle on the sale of his partnership interest?

- a. $67,000
- b. $70,000
- c. $77,000
- d. $87,000

24. How much ordinary income should Slagle report in his 2004 income tax return on the sale of his partnership interest?

- a. $0
- b. $10,000
- c. $70,000
- d. $77,000

25. Eastern Corp., a calendar-year corporation, was formed in 2002. On January 2, 2003, it placed five-year property in service. The property was depreciated under the general MACRS system. Eastern did not elect to use the straight-line method. The following information pertains to Eastern:

Eastern's 2003 taxable income	$300,000
Adjustment for the accelerated depreciation taken on 2003 five-year property	1,000
2003 tax-exempt interest from specified private activity bonds issued in 1999	5,000

What was Eastern's 2003 alternative minimum taxable income before the adjusted current earnings (ACE) adjustment?

- a. $306,000
- b. $305,000
- c. $304,000
- d. $301,000

26. Bank Corp. owns 80% of Shore Corp.'s outstanding capital stock. Shore's capital stock consists of 50,000 shares of common stock issued and outstanding. Shore's 2003 net income was $140,000. During 2003, Shore declared and paid dividends of $60,000. In conformity with generally accepted accounting principles, Bank recorded the following entries in 2003:

	Debit	Credit
Investment in Shore Corp. common stock	$112,000	
Equity in earnings of subsidiary		$112,000
Cash	48,000	
Investment in Shore Corp. common stock		48,000

In its 2003 consolidated tax return, Bank should report dividend revenue of

- a. $48,000
- b. $14,400
- c. $ 9,600
- d. $0

27. Kari Corp., a manufacturing company, was organized on January 2, 2003. Its 2003 federal taxable income was $400,000 and its federal income tax was $100,000. What is the maximum amount of accumulated taxable income that may be subject to the accumulated earnings tax for 2003 if Kari takes only the minimum accumulated earnings credit?

    a. $300,000

    b. $150,000

    c. $ 50,000

    d. $0

28. On February 10, 2003, Ace Corp., a calendar-year corporation, elected S corporation status and all shareholders consented to the election. There was no change in shareholders in 2003. Ace met all eligibility requirements for S status during the preelection portion of the year. What is the earliest date on which Ace can be recognized as an S corporation?

    a.   February 10, 2003.

    b.   February 10, 2004.

    c.   January 1, 2003.

    d.   January 1, 2004.

29. Lyon, a cash-basis taxpayer, died on January 15, 2003. In 2003, the estate executor made the required periodic distribution of $9,000 from estate income to Lyon's sole heir. The following pertains to the estate's income and disbursements in 2003:

2003 Estate Income

$20,000	Taxable interest
10,000	Net long-term capital gains allocable to corpus

2003 Estate Disbursements

$5,000	Administrative expenses attributable to taxable income

For the 2003 calendar year, what was the estate's distributable net income (DNI)?

    a. $15,000

    b. $20,000

    c. $25,000

    d. $30,000

30. A tax return preparer may disclose or use tax return information without the taxpayer's consent to

    a.   Facilitate a supplier's or lender's credit evaluation of the taxpayer.

    b.   Accommodate the request of a financial institution that needs to determine the amount of taxpayer's debt to it, to be forgiven.

    c.   Be evaluated by a quality or peer review.

    d.   Solicit additional nontax business.

REGULATION
ANSWERS TO TESTLET 2

1. c	**5.** b	**9.** b	**13.** d	**17.** d	**21.** d	**25.** a	**29.** a
2. c	**6.** b	**10.** a	**14.** d	**18.** c	**22.** d	**26.** d	**30.** c
3. b	**7.** a	**11.** b	**15.** b	**19.** c	**23.** d	**27.** c	
4. d	**8.** c	**12.** a	**16.** c	**20.** b	**24.** c	**28.** c	

Regulation Hints

1. Which is a close relative?

2. What body was created by the Sarbanes-Oxley Act of 2002?

3. Which loan is unsecured?

4. Which services are performed only for the client?

5. Rhodes Corp. is the client, not Harris Corp.

6. Preferential transfers will simply be set aside.

7. There is no other party to split the payments with.

8. The agreement cannot be performed within one year.

9. It is a small issue of securities.

10. An executory promise is not value until performed.

11. Kent is subject to the perfect tender rule.

12. Specific performance is not allowed if the buyer can cover.

13. Recall factors determining whether item is a fixture.

14. Insurer is liable for all defects not disclosed by survey and physical inspection.

15. First mortgage has priority.

16. Include amounts withheld or actually paid during the year.

17. Try setting up a "T" account and analyzing the journal entries that would have been made.

18. The deduction is subject to a special phaseout since Sol (but not Julia) is a participant in a qualified employer retirement plan.

19. The amount of contribution includes the excess of the amount paid over the value of the object received.

20. A separate FTC limitation applies to non-business-related interest.

21. The definition of capital assets excludes property used in a trade or business.

22. Generally no gain is recognized when property is transferred in exchange for a partnership interest.

23. The amount realized includes the buyer's assumption of the seller's share of partnership liabilities.

24. Ordinary income must be reported to the extent of the seller's share of unrealized receivables and appreciated inventory.

25. The 150% declining balance method of depreciation must be used for AMT purposes.

26. Intercompany dividends from affiliated group members are eliminated in the consolidation process.

27. The minimum accumulated earnings credit is $250,000 for nonservice corporations.

28. An election is effective at the beginning of a corporation's tax year.

29. The computation of DNI excludes capital gains allocable to corpus.

30. Only one answer choice merits disclosure.

REGULATION

TESTLET 3

1. Under the ethical standards of the profession, which of the following investments in a client is not considered to be a direct financial interest?

    a.   An investment held through a nonclient regulated mutual fund.

    b.   An investment held through a nonclient investment club.

    c.   An investment held in a blind trust.

    d.   An investment held by the trustee of a trust.

2. Lott and Lott, CPAs, recently acquired a public company as an audit client. With respect to this client, the Sarbanes-Oxley Act of 2002 requires

    a.   Rotation of accounting firms every five years.

    b.   Joint audits by two auditing firms.

    c.   Rotation of the partner in charge of the audit every five years.

    d.   Joint management of the audit by two or more partners.

3. According to the ethical standards for the profession, which of the following fee arrangements is prohibited?

    a.   A fee for a review of financial statements that is based on time spent on the engagement.

    b.   A fee for a review of financial statements that is based on time spent and a premium for the risk involved.

    c.   A fee for a review engagement that is based on a fixed fee of $5,000.

    d.   A fee for a review engagement that varies depending on the amount of financing that the company may obtain.

4. According to the ethical standards for the profession, which of the following is **not** acceptable advertising content?

    a.   The fees for services.

    b.   The qualifications of professional staff.

    c.   Implications regarding the ability to influence regulatory bodies.

    d.   Implications regarding the value of the services.

5. The CPA firm of Knox & Knox has been subpoenaed to testify and produce its correspondence and working papers in connection with a lawsuit brought against Johnson, one of its clients. Regarding the attempted resort to the privileged communication rule in seeking to avoid admission of such evidence in the lawsuit, which of the following is correct?

    a.   Federal law recognizes such a privilege if the accountant is a Certified Public Accountant.

    b.   The privilege is available regarding the working papers since the accountant is deemed to own them.

    c.   The privilege is as widely available as the attorney-client privilege.

    d.   In the absence of a specific statutory provision, the law does not recognize the existence of the privileged communication rule between an accountant and his client.

6. Which of the following is(are) true under the Americans with Disabilities Act?

   I.   The Act requires companies to make reasonable accommodations for disabled persons unless this results in undue hardship on the operations of the company.

  II.   The Act requires that companies with 100 or more employees set up a plan to hire Americans with disabilities.

    a.   Both I and II.

    b.   Neither I nor II.

    c.   I only.

    d.   II only.

7. The partnership of Maxim & Rose, CPAs, has been engaged by their largest client, a limited partnership, to examine the financial statements in connection with the offering of 2,000 limited-partnership interests to the public at $5,000 per subscription. Under these circumstances, which of the following is true?

    a.   Maxim & Rose may disclaim any liability under the Federal Securities Acts by an unambiguous, boldfaced disclaimer of liability on its audit report.

    b.   Under the Securities Act of 1933, Maxim & Rose has responsibility only for the financial statements as of the close of the fiscal year in question.

    c.   The dollar amount in question is sufficiently small so as to provide an exemption from the Securities Act of 1933.

    d.   The Securities Act of 1933 requires a registration despite the fact that the client is not selling stock or another traditional "security."

8. One of the major purposes of federal security regulation is to

    a.   Establish the qualifications for accountants who are members of the profession.

    b.   Eliminate incompetent attorneys and accountants who participate in the registration of securities to be offered to the public.

    c.   Provide a set of uniform standards and tests for accountants, attorneys, and others who practice before the Securities and Exchange Commission.

    d.   Provide sufficient information to the investing public who purchases securities in the marketplace.

9. Which of the following statements is(are) true of the National Environment Policy Act?

   I.   The Act provides tax breaks for those companies that help accomplish national environmental policy.

  II.   Enforcement of the Act is primarily accomplished by litigation of persons who decide to challenge federal government decisions.

    a.   I only.

    b.   II only.

    c.   Both I and II.

    d.   Neither I nor II.

10. Your client has in its possession the following instrument:

$700.000	Provo, Utah	May 1, 2002
Thirty days after date I promise to pay to the order of		
_____Cash_____		
_____Seven hundred_____		Dollars
at	_____Boise, Idaho_____	
Value received with interest at the rate of 10% per annum.		
This instrument is secured by a conditional sales contract.		
No. 20	Due June 1, 2002	*Len Bowie*

This instrument is
- a. A negotiable time draft.
- b. A nonnegotiable note since it states that it is secured by a conditional sales contract.
- c. Not negotiable until June 1, 2002.
- d. A negotiable bearer note.

11. In which of the following situations would an oral agreement without any consideration be binding under the Uniform Commercial Code?
- a. A renunciation of a claim or right arising out of an alleged breach.
- b. A firm offer by a merchant to sell or buy goods which gives assurance that it will be held open.
- c. An agreement that is a requirements contract.
- d. An agreement that modifies an existing sales contract.

12. A dispute has arisen between two merchants over the question of who has the risk of loss in a given sales transaction. The contract does not specifically cover the point. The goods were shipped to the buyer who rightfully rejected them. Which of the following factors will be the most important factor in resolving their dispute?
- a. Who has title to the goods.
- b. The shipping terms.
- c. The credit terms.
- d. The fact that a breach has occurred.

13. Marcross and two business associates own real property as tenants in common that they have invested in as a speculation. The speculation proved to be highly successful, and the land is now worth substantially more than their investment. Which of the following is a correct legal incident of ownership of the property?
- a. Upon the death of any of the other tenants, the deceased's interest passes to the survivor(s) unless there is a will.
- b. Each of the cotenants owns an undivided interest in the whole.
- c. A cotenant cannot sell his interest in the property without the consent of the other tenants.
- d. Upon the death of a cotenant, his estate is entitled to the amount of the original investment, but not the appreciation.

14. Moch sold her farm to Watkins and took back a purchase money mortgage on the farm. Moch failed to record the mortgage. Moch's mortgage will be valid against all of the following parties **except**
- a. The heirs or estate of Watkins.

- b. A subsequent mortgagee who took a second mortgage since he had heard there was a prior mortgage.
- c. A subsequent bona fide purchaser from Watkins.
- d. A friend of Watkins to whom the farm was given as a gift and who took without knowledge of the mortgage.

15. Lake purchased a home from Walsh for $95,000. Lake obtained a $60,000 loan from Safe Bank to finance the purchase, executing a promissory note and mortgage. The recording of the mortgage by Safe
- a. Gives the world actual notice of Safe's interest.
- b. Protects Safe's interest against the claims of subsequent bona fide purchasers for value.
- c. Is necessary in order that Safe have rights against Lake under the promissory note.
- d. Is necessary in order to protect Safe's interest against the claim of a subsequent transferee who does **not** give value.

16. For the year ended December 31, 2003, Don Raff earned $1,000 interest at Ridge Savings Bank on a certificate of deposit scheduled to mature in 2004. In January 2004, before filing his 2003 income tax return, Raff incurred a forfeiture penalty of $500 for premature withdrawal of the funds. Raff should treat this $500 forfeiture penalty as a
- a. Reduction of interest earned in 2003, so that only $500 of such interest is taxable on Raff's 2003 return.
- b. Deduction from 2004 adjusted gross income, deductible only if Raff itemizes his deductions for 2004.
- c. Penalty **not** deductible for tax purposes.
- d. Deduction from gross income in arriving at 2004 adjusted gross income.

17. Axis Corp. is an accrual-basis calendar-year corporation. On December 13, 2003, the Board of Directors declared a 2% of profits bonus to all employees for services rendered during 2003 and notified them in writing. None of the employees own stock in Axis. The amount represents reasonable compensation for services rendered and was paid on March 13, 2004. Axis' bonus expense may
- a. Not be deducted on Axis' 2003 tax return because the per share employee amount **cannot** be determined with reasonable accuracy at the time of the declaration of the bonus.
- b. Be deducted on Axis' 2003 tax return.
- c. Be deducted on Axis' 2004 tax return.
- d. Not be deducted on Axis' tax return because payment is a disguised dividend.

18. On August 1, 2003, Graham purchased and placed into service an office building costing $264,000 including $30,000 for the land. What was Graham's MACRS deduction for the office building in 2003?
- a. $9,600
- b. $6,000
- c. $3,600
- d. $2,250

19. This item is based on the following selected 2003 information pertaining to Sam and Ann Hoyt, who filed a joint federal income tax return for the calendar year 2003. The Hoyts had adjusted gross income of $34,000 and itemized their deductions for 2003. Among the Hoyts' cash expenditures during 2003 were the following:

> $2,500 repairs in connection with 2003 fire damage to the Hoyt residence. This property has a basis of $50,000. Fair market value was $60,000 before the fire and $55,000 after the fire. Insurance on the property had lapsed in 2002 for nonpayment of premium.
>
> $800 appraisal fee to determine amount of fire loss.

What amount of fire loss were the Hoyts entitled to deduct as an itemized deduction on their 2003 return?

- a. $5,000
- b. $2,500
- c. $1,600
- d. $1,500

20. A calendar-year taxpayer files an individual tax return for 2002 on March 20, 2003. The taxpayer neither committed fraud nor omitted amounts in excess of 25% of gross income on the tax return. What is the latest date that the Internal Revenue Service can assess tax and assert a notice of deficiency?

- a. March 20, 2006.
- b. March 20, 2005.
- c. April 15, 2006.
- d. April 15, 2005.

21. On July 1, 2003, Riley exchanged investment real property, with an adjusted basis of $160,000 and subject to a mortgage of $70,000, and received from Wilson $30,000 cash and other investment real property having a fair market value of $250,000. Wilson assumed the mortgage. What is Riley's recognized gain in 2003 on the exchange?

- a. $ 30,000
- b. $ 70,000
- c. $ 90,000
- d. $100,000

22. In 2001, Martha received as a gift several shares of Good Corporation stock. The donor's basis of this stock was $2,800, and he paid gift tax of $50. On the date of the gift, the fair market value of the stock was $2,600. If Martha sells this stock in 2003 for $2,700, what amount and type of gain or loss should Martha report in her 2003 income tax return?

- a. $50 long-term capital gain.
- b. $100 long-term capital gain.
- c. $100 long-term capital loss.
- d. No gain or loss.

23. Hall and Haig are equal partners in the firm of Arosa Associates. On January 1, 2003, each partner's adjusted basis in Arosa was $40,000. During 2003 Arosa borrowed $60,000, for which Hall and Haig are personally liable. Arosa sustained an operating loss of $10,000 for the year ended December 31, 2003. The basis of each partner's interest in Arosa at December 31, 2003, was

- a. $35,000
- b. $40,000
- c. $65,000
- d. $70,000

24. Clark and Hunt organized Jet Corp, with authorized voting common stock of $400,000. Clark contributed $60,000 cash. Both Clark and Hunt transferred other property in exchange for Jet stock as follows:

| | Other property | | |
	Adjusted basis	*Fair market value*	*Percentage of Jet stock acquired*
Clark	$ 50,000	$100,000	40%
Hunt	120,000	240,000	60%

What was Clark's basis in Jet stock?

- a. $0
- b. $100,000
- c. $110,000
- d. $160,000

25. Roberta Warner and Sally Rogers formed the Acme Corporation on October 1, 2003. On the same date Warner paid $75,000 cash to Acme for 750 shares of its common stock. Simultaneously, Rogers received 100 shares of Acme's common stock for services rendered. How much should Rogers include as taxable income for 2003 and what will be the basis of her stock?

	Taxable income	*Basis of stock*
a.	$0	$0
b.	$0	$10,000
c.	$10,000	$0
d.	$10,000	$10,000

26. The following information pertains to Hull, Inc., a personal holding company, for the year ended December 31, 2003:

Undistributed personal holding company income	$100,000
Dividends paid during 2003	20,000
Consent dividends reported in the 2003 individual income tax returns of the holders of Hull's common stock, but **not** paid by Hull to its stockholders	10,000

In computing its 2003 personal holding company tax, what amount should Hull deduct for dividends paid?

- a. $0
- b. $10,000
- c. $20,000
- d. $30,000

27. Bern Corp., an S corporation, had an ordinary loss of $36,500 for the year ended December 31, 2003. At January 1, 2003, Meyer owned 50% of Bern's stock. Meyer held the stock for forty days in 2003 before selling the entire 50% interest to an unrelated third party. Meyer's basis for the stock was $10,000. Meyer was a full-time employee of Bern until the stock was sold. Meyer's share of Bern's 2003 loss was

- a. $0
- b. $ 2,000
- c. $10,000
- d. $18,300

28. On July 1, 2003, in connection with a recapitalization of Yorktown Corporation, Robert Moore exchanged 1,000 shares of stock that cost him $95,000 for 1,000 shares of new stock worth $108,000 and bonds in the principal amount of $10,000 with a fair market value of $10,500. What is the amount of Moore's recognized gain during 2003?

- a. $0
- b. $10,500
- c. $23,000
- d. $23,500

29. Steve and Kay Briar, US citizens, were married for the entire 2003 calendar year. In 2003, Steve gave a $30,000 cash gift to his sister. The Briars made no other gifts in 2003. They each signed a timely election to treat the $30,000 gift as made one-half by each spouse. Disregarding the unified credit and estate tax consequences, what amount of the 2003 gift is taxable to the Briars?

    a. $19,000
    b. $10,000
    c. $ 8,000
    d. $0

30. Following are the fair market values of Wald's assets at the date of death:

Personal effects and jewelry	$150,000
Land bought by Wald with Wald's funds five years prior to death and held with Wald's sister as joint tenants with right of survivorship	800,000

The executor of Wald's estate did not elect the alternate valuation date. The amount includible as Wald's gross estate in the federal estate tax return is

    a. $150,000
    b. $550,000
    c. $800,000
    d. $950,000

REGULATION

ANSWERS TO TESTLET 3

1. a	**5.** d	**9.** b	**13.** b	**17.** b	**21.** d	**25.** d	**29.** c
2. c	**6.** c	**10.** d	**14.** c	**18.** d	**22.** d	**26.** d	**30.** d
3. d	**7.** d	**11.** d	**15.** b	**19.** d	**23.** c	**27.** b	
4. c	**8.** d	**12.** d	**16.** d	**20.** c	**24.** c	**28.** b	

Regulation Hints

1. What is an indirect financial interest?
2. Partner rotation helps assure independence.
3. Which fee is contingent?
4. Which is false, misleading, or deceptive?
5. Accountant-client privilege does not exist in common law.
6. ADA applies to employers with at least fifteen employees; forbidding discrimination.
7. Must comply with **all** requirements of the 1933 Act.
8. The goal is to help investors avoid fraudulent offerings.
9. The EPA ensures compliance with environmental protection laws.
10. A note is a two-party instrument.
11. Review Module 24, Section A.2.d.
12. Risk of loss is independent of title under UCC.
13. Each owns the whole.
14. To prevail, subsequent party must give value and must not have notice.
15. Recording gives constructive notice.
16. The interest forfeiture results in a deduction.
17. The amount must be fixed by a predetermined formula.
18. Remember to use the midmonth averaging convention.
19. Remember to subtract a $100 floor and 10% of AGI.
20. A return filed early is treated as filed on its due date for statute of limitations purposes.
21. The assumption of Riley's mortgage is treated as boot received.
22. The basis for gain is $2,800, and the basis for loss is $2,600.
23. An increase in partnership liabilities is treated as a deemed cash contribution.
24. Clark's basis must reflect his nonrecognition of gain.
25. The shares received as compensation are worth $100 per share.
26. Consent dividends are included as part of the corporation's dividends paid deduction.
27. S corporation items are allocated per share, per day to shareholders.
28. The definition of boot (other property) includes the FMV of an excess principal amount of security received.
29. The gift is treated as made one-half by each spouse.
30. In the case of jointly held property by other than spouses, the property is included in the gross estate except to the extent that the surviving tenant contributed toward the purchase.

SIMULATION 1

Topic—Corporate Taxation (20 to 25 minutes)

Situation
Schedule M-1

Cada Corporation, a calendar-year, accrual-method taxpayer, is a manufacturer of spas and hot tubs. Cada provides the following information for 2003:

Net income per books (after tax)	$310,000
Federal income tax liability deducted per books	104,150
Retained earnings at January 1, 2003	425,000
Interest income from municipal general obligation bonds	20,000
Cash dividends paid to shareholders	60,000
Life insurance proceeds received on death of Cada's president (Cada was the owner and beneficiary of the policy)	100,000
Premiums paid on policy insuring Cada's president	5,000
Excess of capital losses over capital gains for 2003	7,000
Employee entertainment expenses reimbursed by Cada	6,000
Dividend income received from 5%-owned taxable domestic corporation	10,000
MACRS depreciation for 2003 in excess of straight-time depreciation deducted per books	9,000
Retained earnings at December 31, 2003	645,000

Schedule M-1
Situation

Prepare Schedule M-1, which will reconcile Cada's income reported per books with its income reported on its tax return Form 1120.

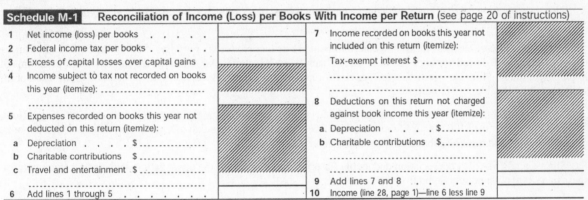

SOLUTION TO SIMULATION 1

Schedule M-1 of Form 1120 is used to reconcile a corporate taxpayer's income reported per books with income reported on the tax return. Generally, items of income or deduction whose book and tax treatment differ, result in Schedule M-1 items. However, since Schedule M-1 reconciles book income to taxable income before special deductions (line 28, page 1), the dividends received deduction and net operating loss deduction which are special deductions will never be reconciling items on Schedule M-1.

The beginning and ending balance of Retained Earnings and cash dividends paid to shareholders are neither deducted per books nor on the tax return and are not Schedule M-1 items. Instead they will be included on Schedule M-2 which provides an Analysis of Unappropriated Retained Earnings per books between the beginning and end of the year.

Schedule M-1	Reconciliation of Income (Loss) per Books With Income per Return (see page 20 of instructions)		
1 Net income (loss) per books	210,000	7 Income recorded on books this year not included on this return (itemize):	
2 Federal income tax per books	104,150	Tax-exempt interest $ 20,000	
3 Excess of capital losses over capital gains	7,000	Ins. proceeds 600,000	120,000
4 Income subject to tax not recorded on books this year (itemize):			
5 Expenses recorded on books this year not deducted on this return (itemize):		8 Deductions on this return not charged against book income this year (itemize):	
a Depreciation $		a Depreciation $ 9,000	
b Charitable contributions $		b Charitable contributions $	
c Travel and entertainment $ 3,000			9,000
Ins. premium 5,000		9 Add lines 7 and 8	129,000
6 Add lines 1 through 5		10 Income (line 28, page 1)—line 6 less line 9	300,150

Line 2. The federal income taxes of $104,150 deducted per books is not deductible for tax purposes and is added back to book income.

Line 3. Since a corporation is not allowed to deduct a net capital loss, the $7,000 net capital loss deducted per books must be added back to book income.

Line 5c. Since only 50% of business meals and entertainment are deductible for tax purposes, 50% of the $6,000 of business entertainment expense deducted per books must be added back to book income. Additionally, the life insurance premiums of $5,000 on the president's life that were deducted per books represent an expense incurred in the production of tax-exempt income and are not deductible for tax purposes.

Line 7. The $20,000 if interest income from municipal bonds included per books is tax-exempt and must be subtracted from book income. Similarly, the $100,000 of life insurance proceeds received on the death of Cada's president included in book income is not taxable and must be subtracted from book income.

Line 8a. Since Cada's MACRS depreciation deductible for tax purposes exceeds the depreciation deducted for book purposes, the excess of $9,000 must be subtracted from book income.

SIMULATION 2   (25 to 30 minutes)

Topic—Individual Taxation

Situation			
	Filing Status	Adjusted Gross Income	Tax Treatment

Mrs. Vick, a forty-year-old cash-basis taxpayer, earned $45,000 as a teacher and $5,000 as a part-time real estate agent in 2003. Mr. Vick, who died on July 1, 2003, had been permanently disabled on his job and collected state disability benefits until his death. For all of 2003 and 2004, the Vicks' residence was the principal home of both their eleven-year-old daughter Joan and Mrs. Vick's unmarried cousin, Fran Phillips, who had no income in either year. During 2003 Joan received $200 a month in survivor social security benefits that began on August 1, 2003, and will continue at least until her eighteenth birthday. In 2003 and 2004, Mrs. Vick provided over one-half the support for Joan and Fran, both of whom were US citizens. Mrs. Vick did not remarry. Mr. and Mrs. Vick received the following in 2003:

Earned income	$50,000
State disability benefits	1,500
Interest on:	
Refund from amended tax return	50
Savings account and certificates of deposit	350
Municipal bonds	100
Gift	3,000
Pension benefits	900
Jury duty pay	200
Gambling winnings	450
Life insurance proceeds	5,000

Additional information:

- Mrs. Vick received the $3,000 cash gift from her uncle.
- Mrs. Vick received the pension distributions from a qualified pension plan, paid for exclusively by her husband's employer.
- Mrs. Vick had $100 in gambling losses in 2003.
- Mrs. Vick was the beneficiary of the life insurance policy on her husband's life. She received a lump-sum distribution. The Vicks had paid $500 in premiums.
- Mrs. Vick received Mr. Vick's accrued vacation pay of $500 in 2004.

Situation	Filing Status	Adjusted Gross Income	Tax Treatment

Part a.

For **items 1 and 2,** determine and select from the choices below, **BOTH** the filing status and the number of exemptions for each item.

	Filing Status	*Exemptions*
S.	Single	1
M.	Married filing joint	2
H.	Head of household	3
Q.	Qualifying widow with dependent child	4

	Filing Status	*Exemptions*
	(S) (M) (H) (Q)	(1) (2) (3) (4)
1. Determine the filing status and the number of exemptions that Mrs. Vick can claim on the 2003 federal income tax return, to get the most favorable tax results.	○ ○ ○ ○	○ ○ ○ ○
2. Determine the filing status and the number of exemptions that Mrs. Vick can claim on the 2004 federal income tax return to get the most favorable tax results, if she solely maintains the costs of her home.	○ ○ ○ ○	○ ○ ○ ○

Situation	Filing Status	Adjusted Gross Income	Tax Treatment

Part b.

For **items 3 through 9,** determine the amount, if any, that is taxable and should be included in Adjusted Gross Income (AGI) on the 2003 federal income tax return filed by Mrs. Vick.

3. State disability benefits

4. Interest income

5. Pension benefits

6. Gift

7. Life insurance proceeds

8. Jury duty pay

9. Gambling winnings

Situation	Filing Status	Adjusted Gross Income	Tax Treatment

Part c.

During 2003 the following payments were made or losses were incurred. For **items 10 through 23,** select the appropriate tax treatment. A tax treatment may be selected once, more than once, or not at all.

Tax treatment

A. Not deductible.
B. Deductible in Schedule A—Itemized Deductions, subject to threshold of 7.5% of adjusted gross income.
C. Deductible in Schedule A—Itemized Deductions, subject to threshold of 2% of adjusted gross income.

D. Deductible on page 1 of Form 1040 to arrive at adjusted gross income.
E. Deductible in full in Schedule A—Itemized Deductions.
F. Deductible in Schedule A—Itemized Deductions, subject to maximum of 50% of adjusted gross income.

	(A)	(B)	(C)	(D)	(E)	(F)
10. Premiums on Mr. Vick's personal life insurance policy.	O	O	O	O	O	O
11. Penalty on Mrs. Vick's early withdrawal of funds from a certificate of deposit.	O	O	O	O	O	O
12. Mrs. Vick's substantiated cash donation to the American Red Cross.	O	O	O	O	O	O
13. Payment of estimated state income taxes.	O	O	O	O	O	O
14. Payment of real estate taxes on the Vick home.	O	O	O	O	O	O
15. Loss on the sale of the family car.	O	O	O	O	O	O
16. Cost in excess of the increase in value of residence, for the installation of a stairlift in January 2003, related directly to the medical care of Mr. Vick.	O	O	O	O	O	O
17. The Vicks' health insurance premiums for hospitalization coverage.	O	O	O	O	O	O
18. CPA fees to prepare the 2002 tax return.	O	O	O	O	O	O
19. Amortization over the life of the loan of points paid to refinance the mortgage at a lower rate on the Vick home.	O	O	O	O	O	O
20. One-half the self-employment tax paid by Mrs. Vick.	O	O	O	O	O	O
21. Mrs. Vick's $100 in gambling losses.	O	O	O	O	O	O
22. Mrs. Vick's union dues.	O	O	O	O	O	O
23. 2002 federal income tax paid with the Vicks' tax return on April 15, 2003.	O	O	O	O	O	O

SOLUTION TO SIMULATION 2

Part a.

For **items 1 and 2,** candidates were asked to determine the filing status and number of exemptions for Mrs. Vick.

1. **(M,4)** Since Mr. Vick died during the year, Mrs. Vick is considered married for the entire year for filing status purposes. There would be four exemptions on the Vicks' joint return—one each for Mr. and Mrs. Vick, one for their 11-year-old daughter Joan, and one for Mrs. Vick's unmarried cousin Fran Phillips. Although Fran is treated as unrelated to the Vicks for dependency exemption purposes, Fran qualifies as a dependency exemption because the Vicks' residence was Fran's principal home for 2003.

2. **(Q,3)** Mrs. Vick will file as a "qualifying widow with dependent child" which will entitle her to use the joint return rates for 2004. This filing status is available for the two years following the year of the spouse's death if (1) the surviving spouse was eligible to file a joint return in the year of the spouse's death, (2) does not remarry before the end of the taxable year, and (3) the surviving spouse pays over 50% of the cost of maintaining a household that is the principal home for the entire year of the surviving spouse's dependent child. There will be three exemptions on the return—one for Mrs. Vick, a dependency exemption for her daughter Joan, and a dependency exemption for her cousin Fran.

Part b.

For **items 3 through 9,** candidates were asked to determine the amount that is taxable and should be included in Adjusted Gross Income (AGI) on the 2003 federal income tax return filed by Mrs. Vick.

3. **($0)** State disability benefits are excluded from gross income.

4. **($400)** The $50 interest on the tax refund and $350 interest from a savings account and certificates of deposit are taxable; the $100 interest on municipal bonds is excluded from gross income.

5. **($900)** The pension benefits are fully taxable because it was paid for exclusively by Mr. Vick's employer.

6. **($0)** Property received as a gift is always excluded from gross income.

7. **($0)** The proceeds of life insurance paid because of Mr. Vick's death are excluded from gross income, without regard to the amount of premiums paid.

8. **($200)** Jury duty pay represents compensation for services and must be included in gross income.

9. **($450)** The $450 of gambling winnings must be included in gross income. Mrs. Vick's $100 of gambling losses are deductible only from AGI as a miscellaneous itemized deduction.

Part c.

For **items 10 through 23,** candidates were asked to select the appropriate tax treatment for the payments made or losses incurred by Mrs. Vick for 2003.

10. **(A)** Life insurance premiums are considered a personal expense and are not deductible.

11. **(D)** An interest forfeiture penalty for making an early withdrawal from a certificate of deposit is deductible on page 1 of Form 1040 to arrive at adjusted gross income.

12. **(F)** Charitable contributions are generally deductible as an itemized deduction up to a **maximum of 50% of AGI**.

13. **(E)** Estimated state income tax payments are deductible in full as an itemized deduction on Schedule A.

14. **(E)** Real estate taxes on a principal residence are deductible in full as an itemized deduction on Schedule A.

15. **(A)** A family car is a personal use asset and a loss from its sale is not deductible. The only type of loss that can be deducted on a personal use asset is a casualty or theft loss.

16. **(B)** A capital expenditure made for medical reasons that improves a residence is deductible as a medical expense to the extent that the expenditure exceeds the increase in value of the residence. As a medical expense, the excess expenditure is deductible as an itemized deduction on Schedule A subject to a 7.5% of AGI threshold.

17. **(B)** Health insurance premiums qualify as a medical expense and are deductible as an itemized deduction on Schedule A subject to a 7.5% of AGI threshold.

18. **(C)** Tax return preparation fees are deductible as an itemized deduction on Schedule A subject to a 2% of AGI threshold.

19. **(E)** Points paid to refinance a mortgage are deductible as interest expense over the term of the loan. Interest expense on a personal residence is deductible as an itemized deduction on Schedule A.

20. **(D)** One-half of a self-employed taxpayer's self-employment tax is deductible on page 1 of Form 1040 to arrive at AGI.

21. **(E)** Gambling losses are deductible as a miscellaneous itemized deduction on Schedule A to the extent that the taxpayer's gambling winnings are included in gross income. Since Mrs. Vick reported $450 of gambling winnings, her $100 of gambling losses are deductible.

22. **(C)** Unreimbursed employee expenses (including union dues) are generally deductible as miscellaneous itemized deductions on Schedule A subject to a 2% of AGI threshold.

23. **(A)** A payment of federal income tax is not deductible in computing a taxpayer's taxable income.

Meet Our Wiley CPA Examination Partners

The following live or video CPA Exam Review course operators use Wiley CPA Examination Review products as a core part of their curriculum.

If you are a course operator using Wiley CPA Examination Review products and are not on this list, please contact lkuet@wiley.com. If you are interested in using the Wiley CPA Examination Review in your course, please contact stesta@wiley.com

Yaeger CPA Review www.yaegerCPAreview.com	Washington DC	Phil Yaeger pyaeger801@aol.com 301/340-3344
KAIS Systems www.kais.co.kr Leading CPA Course Operator in Korea	Korea	Chang Ho Choi kais@kais.co.kr
US CPA Success www.uscpasuccess.com	USA, Canada, and many international locations.	Aubrey Glazman aubrey@uscpasuccess.com
Roger Philipp CPA Review www.rogercpareview.com	San Francisco, CA	Roger Philipp roger@rogercpareview.com
Arizona State University http://wpcarey.asu.edu/acct/CPAReview/index.cfm	Tempe, AZ	Julie Barnes juliebarnes@asu.edu 480/965-9268
Marquette University CPA Review www.busadm.mu.edu	Milwaukee, WI	Frank Probst 414/288-7344 (main) 414/288-6589 (Frank)
University of Arkansas http://waltoncollege.uark.edu/acct/exams.asp	Monticello, AR	Richard Wallace 870/460-1041 870/460-1784
East Carolina University www.business.ecu.edu/depts/ACCT/	Greenville, NC	Fredrick Nisewander niswander@mail.ecu.edu 252/328-6970
Cameron School of Business www.stthorn.edu/bschool/source/ungrad/acct.html	Wilmington, NC	John Marts 910/962-3071
University of Illinois—Urbana Champaign www.cba.uiuc.edu/accountancy/cpa/default.html	Champaign, IL	Jean Seibold 217/333-3688
Cayman CPA Review	Cayman Islands	Wayne McManus wayne_mcmanus@hotmail.com wayne_mcmanus@bpb.barclays.com